The Contemporary Management
Online Learning Center

www.mhhe.com/jonesgeorge4e

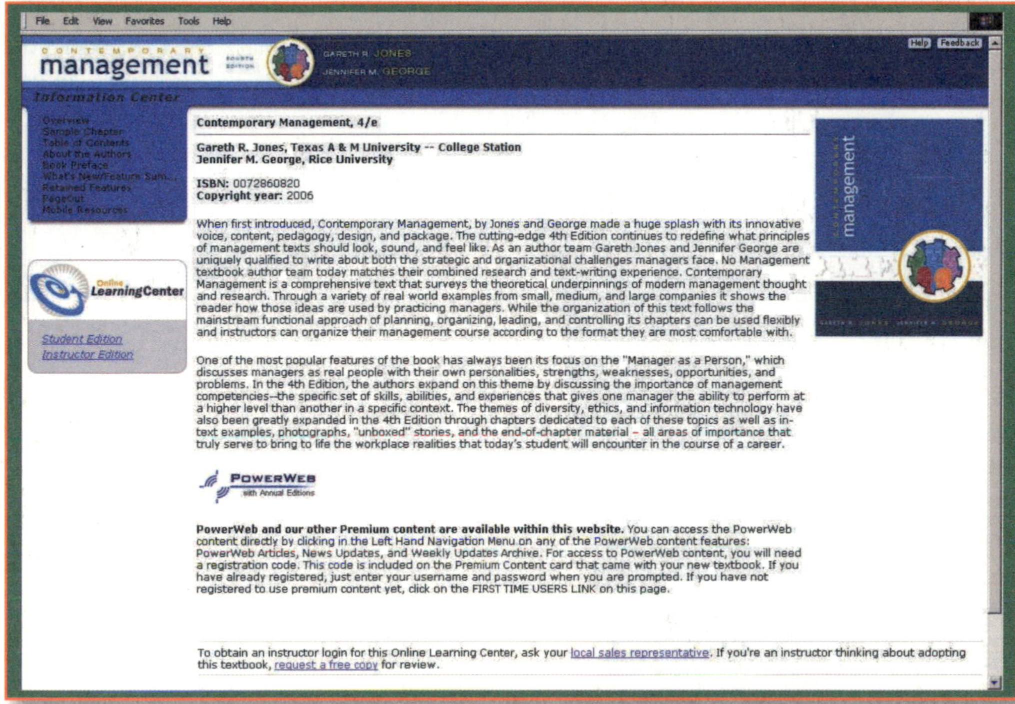

Access online study materials, articles, news feeds, and other Internet resources at the Contemporary Management Web site.

- Chapter Reviews–Review and apply text concepts with interactive practice quizzes, Flashcards, PowerPoint slides, World Wide Web exercises, and other materials.
- PowerWeb–Keep up-to-date with PowerWeb! This online resource provides up-to-date articles from leading periodicals and journals, current news, and weekly updates.

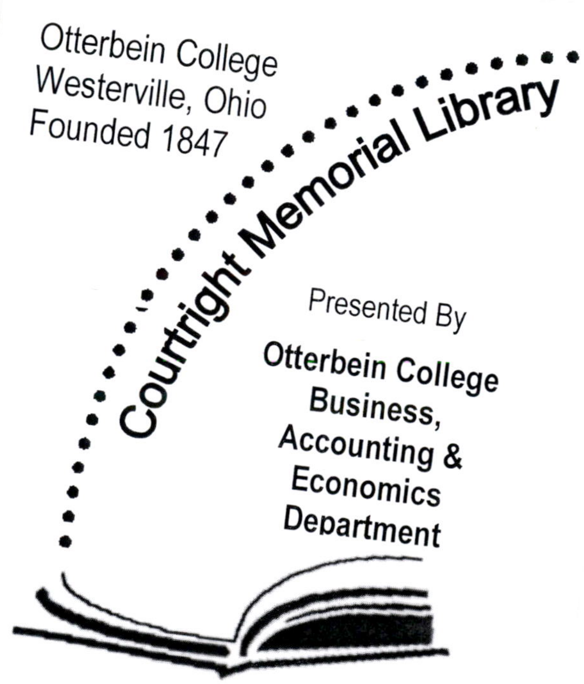

IMPORTANT

HERE IS YOUR REGISTRATION CODE TO ACCESS MCGRAW-HILL PREMIUM CONTENT AND MCGRAW-HILL ONLINE RESOURCES

For key premium online resources you need THIS CODE to gain access. Once the code is entered, you will be able to use the web resources for the length of your course.

Access is provided only if you have purchased a new book.

If the registration code is missing from this book, the registration screen on our website, and within your WebCT or Blackboard course will tell you how to obtain your new code. Your registration code can be used only once to establish access. It is not transferable

To gain access to these online resources

1. **USE** your web browser to go to: **www.mhhe.com/jonesgeorge4e**
2. **CLICK** on "First Time User"
3. **ENTER** the Registration Code printed on the tear-off bookmark on the right
4. After you have entered your registration code, click on "Register"
5. **FOLLOW** the instructions to setup your personal UserID and Password
6. **WRITE** your UserID and Password down for future reference. Keep it in a safe place.

If your course is using WebCT or Blackboard, you'll be able to use this code to access the McGraw-Hill content within your instructor's online course.

To gain access to the McGraw-Hill content in your instructor's WebCT or Blackboard course simply log into the course with the user ID and Password provided by your instructor. Enter the registration code exactly as it appears to the right when prompted by the system. You will only need to use this code the first time you click on McGraw-Hill content.

These instructions are specifically for student access. Instructors are not required to register via the above instructions.

Thank you, and welcome to your McGraw-Hill/Irwin Online Resources.

Jones/George
Contemporary Management, 4/E
0-07-304764-3

AFLZ-LIZS-JAGQ-D2PU-KIL3

REGISTRATION CODE

REGISTRATION CODE

The McGraw-Hill Companies

McGraw-Hill Irwin

Contemporary Management

Fourth Edition

Gareth R. Jones
Texas A&M University

Jennifer M. George
Rice University

Boston Burr Ridge, IL Dubuque, IA Madison, WI New York San Francisco St. Louis
Bangkok Bogotá Caracas Kuala Lumpur Lisbon London Madrid Mexico City
Milan Montreal New Delhi Santiago Seoul Singapore Sydney Taipei Toronto

For Nicholas and Julia

The McGraw·Hill Companies

CONTEMPORARY MANAGEMENT
Published by McGraw-Hill/Irwin, a business unit of The McGraw-Hill Companies, Inc., 1221 Avenue of the Americas, New York, NY 10020.

This book is printed on acid-free paper.

1 2 3 4 5 6 7 8 9 0 WCK/WCK 0 9 8 7 6 5 4

ISBN 0-07-286082-0

Editorial director: *John E. Biernat*
Senior sponsoring editor: *Kelly H. Lowery*
Managing developmental editor: *Laura Hurst Spell*
Editorial assistant: *Amy Luck*
Executive marketing manager: *Ellen Cleary*
Producer, Media technology: *Mark Molsky*
Lead project manager: *Mary Conzachi*
Senior production supervisor: *Sesha Bolisetty*
Coordinator freelance design: *Artemio Ortiz Jr.*
Photo research coordinator: *Lori Kramer*
Photo researcher: *Sarah Evertson*
Media project manager: *Betty Hadala*
Supplement producer: *Gina F. DiMartino*
Developer, Media technology: *Brian Nacik*
Cover and interior icon design: *Asylum Studios*
Interior design: *Artemio Ortiz Jr.*
Typeface: *10.25/12 Baskerville*
Compositor: *Precision Graphics*
Printer: *Quebecor World Versailles Inc.*

Library of Congress Cataloging-in-Publication Data

Jones, Gareth R.
Contemporary management / Gareth R. Jones, Jennifer M. George.-- 4th ed.
p. cm.
Includes index.
ISBN 0-07-286082-0 (alk. paper)
1. Management. I. George, Jennifer M. II. Title.
HD31.J597 2006
658--dc22

2004042322

http://www.mhhe.com

Brief Contents

Contents

Part One Management

Chapter One

Managers and Managing 2

A Manager's Challenge
Steve Jobs Transforms Apple Computer 3

Topics

Chapter Two

The Evolution of Management Thought 40

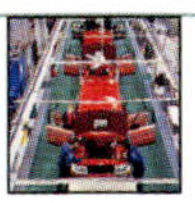

A Manager's Challenge
Finding Better Ways to Make Cars 41

Topics

Examples

Management in Action

Examples

Management in Action

Contents

Chapter Three

Chapter Four

Examples

Management in Action

Examples

Management in Action

Contents

Chapter Five

Managing Diverse Employees in a Multicultural Environment 146

A Manager's Challenge
Diversity in the Boardroom and on the Police Force 147

Topics

Chapter Six

Managing in the Global Environment 188

A Manager's Challenge
Nestlé's Global Food Empire 189

Topics

Examples

Management in Action

Examples

Management in Action

Contents

Part Three Decision Making, Planning, and Strategy

Chapter Seven

Chapter Eight

Examples

Management in Action

Examples

Management in Action

Contents

Chapter Nine

Value-Chain Management: Functional Strategies to Increase Quality, Efficiency, and Responsiveness to Customers 298

Chapter Ten

Managing Organizational Structure 332

Examples

Management in Action

Examples

Management in Action

Contents

Chapter Eleven Organizational Control and Change 374

A Manager's Challenge
Bob Nardelli's New Controls Change Home Depot 375

Topics

Chapter Twelve Human Resource Management 410

A Manager's Challenge
Democracy in Action at Semco 411

Topics

Contents

Part Five Managing Individuals and Groups

Examples

Management in Action

Examples

Management in Action

Contents

Chapter Fifteen

Effective Groups and Teams 528

Chapter Sixteen

Communication 566

Examples

Management in Action

Examples

Management in Action

Contents

Part Six Controlling Critical Organizational Processes

Chapter Seventeen Managing Organizational Conflict, Politics, and Negotiation 604

Topics

Chapter Eighteen Utilizing Advanced Information Technology 634

Topics

Examples

Management in Action

Examples

Management in Action

Contents

Examples

Management in Action

Preface

Many changes have taken place in the world of business in the three years since we last revised our book. Major companies such as Enron, Tyco, WorldCom, Arthur Andersen, and many mutual fund companies have been accused of acting either unethically or illegally. As a result, many of these companies have gone out of business or are close to bankruptcy, tens of thousands of employees have lost their jobs, and millions of ordinary investors have seen their savings plunge in value. At the same time, the dot-com bust and the growth in the outsourcing of information technology, services, and manufacturing jobs to countries overseas has led to further job losses. As a result of these developments, many people have begun to look closely at the way large global companies are managed and to closely scrutinize the behavior of their managers. The ethics of top managers and ethical concerns throughout organizations have come to the forefront of attention.

In addition, the fast-changing domestic and global environments increase the need for organizations and their managers to find new ways to respond in order to maintain and improve their performance. There are mounting pressures on managers to integrate new information technology into all aspects of an organization's operations to improve efficiency and customer responsiveness. The increasing diversity of the workforce has made it imperative for managers to understand how and why people differ so that they can effectively manage and reap the benefits of diversity. The continuing need to innovate and improve the quality of goods and services to allow an organization to compete effectively confronts managers on a daily basis. The tasks that managers must perform effectively have become more complex and challenging than ever before.

The fourth edition of *Contemporary Management* has been significantly revised to reflect and address these challenges to managers and their organizations. Encouraged by the favorable reception and increasing support for our book, and based on the reactions and suggestions of both users and reviewers, we have added new chapters and altered others to respond to the many changes that have been taking place.

Major Content Changes and Chapter Reorganization

To respond to the increasing need to expose students to the ethical implications of management decisions, the book now includes a complete chapter–Chapter 4, titled "Ethics and Social Responsibility"–which contains new and more detailed coverage of many important topics. For example, we examine the nature of ethical dilemmas and why they arise; we provide a new stakeholder approach to ethics; we discuss in depth the relationship between ethics and digital piracy (e.g., downloading of songs and movies); and we have increased our coverage of the nature of ethical principles and how to follow them. In addition, we have developed a new ethical exercise, found at the end of every chapter, which provides students with a hands-on ethics learning experience. Taken together, these additions provide an instructor with the materials and opportunity to make ethics a significant part of the course content, if so desired.

The creation of a separate chapter on ethics has also allowed us to expand our coverage of diversity, so we have a new chapter–Chapter 5, "Managing Diverse Employees in a Multicultural Environment"–that is devoted to diversity. Among the new issues we discuss are the effects of the population growth of Asians and Hispanics in the workplace, employee wage and position disparities and the advantages of ensuring fair treatment and representation, and the implications of disabilities and sexual orientation in the workplace. To address current issues, in an era when companies like Wal-Mart are facing diversity lawsuits involving hundreds of millions of dollars, we include new material on effectively managing diversity and eradicating sexual harassment.

Another major change has been the combination of the two separate chapters on the domestic and the global environments into one–Chapter 6, "Managing in the Global Environment." This change has resulted in a superior and more streamlined presentation of the material. Moreover, little has been lost, because material in the former two chapters has been incorporated into other chapters where it is better integrated. For example, the section on methods of expanding internationally has been incorporated into the discussion of global strategy in Chapter 8, "The Manager as a Planner and Strategist."

In another major change, we have rewritten the chapter on operations management to focus on issues in developing functional strategies for managing value-chain activities. In this edition, responding to our users' and reviewers' suggestions, we now have two sequential chapters on the strategy-making process: the revised Chapter 8 and a new Chapter 9, titled "Value-Chain Management: Functional Strategies to Increase Quality, Efficiency and Responsiveness to Customers." We are very pleased with this change for it has enabled us to link the different levels of strategy making while still maintaining a strong focus on managing operations and processes.

Finally, in reorganizing our chapters, we have moved our discussion of organizational change to Chapter 11, on organizational control, and begun our treatment of organizational culture in Chapter 3. Chapter 3, "The Manager as a Person: Values, Attitudes, Emotions, and Culture," now discusses the nature and significance of organizational culture. Chapter 11, "Organizational Control and Change," then discusses how culture is a powerful way of shaping behavior in organizations. In addition, the new Chapter 11 allows us to make clear the important link between an organization's ability to control its activities in order to be able to innovate and adapt to a changing environment.

We are very excited about the major changes we have made to the fourth edition of *Contemporary Management*. We feel they reflect, and challenge students to think beyond, the changes that are occurring in management and the workplace; we also feel they offer an account of management that will stimulate students.

Other Content Changes

In revising our book, we have kept at the forefront the fact that our users and reviewers are very supportive of our attempts to integrate contemporary management theories and issues into the analysis of management and organizations. As in previous editions, our goal has been to distill new and classic theorizing and research into a contemporary framework that is compatible with the traditional focus on management as planning, leading, organizing, and controlling but that transcends this traditional approach.

Users and reviewers report that students appreciate and enjoy our presentation of management, a presentation that makes its relevance obvious even to those who lack exposure to a real-life management context. Students like the book's content and the way we relate management theory to real-life examples to drive home the message that management matters both because it determines how well organizations perform and because managers and organizations affect the lives of people inside and outside the organization, such as customers and shareholders.

In keeping with this tradition, besides making the major content changes noted earlier, we've added many new and updated topics and issues throughout all of the chapters in the book. Some highlights are new coverage of the implications of global outsourcing; expanded coverage of information technology throughout the book, including the use of enterprise resource planning and B2B systems; inclusion of scales for measuring personality; new treatment of emotions and emotional intelligence, including a new scale that measures the latter; new treatment of dysfunctional cultures; new material on intuition and creativity; expanded focus on global strategy; new discussion of inert and adaptive cultures; expanded discussion of online recruiting, mentorship, and pay differentials; expanded coverage of gender, emotional intelligence, and leadership; discussion of the use of new communication systems to improve decisions making; and expanded coverage of the negotiating process.

Unique Emphasis on Contemporary, Applied Management

As these changes suggest, our contemporary approach has led us to discuss many concepts and issues that are not addressed in other management textbooks. Our contemporary approach also is illustrated by the way we have chosen to organize and discuss these management issues. We have gone to great lengths to bring the manager back into the subject matter of management. That is, we have written our chapters from the perspective of current or future managers to illustrate, in a hands-on way, the problems and opportunities they face and how they can effectively meet them. For example, in Chapter 3 we provide an integrated treatment of personality, attitudes, emotions, and culture; in Chapter 4, a focus on ethics from a student's and a manager's perspective; and in Chapter 5, an in-depth treatment of effectively managing diversity and eradicating sexual harassment. In Chapters 8 and 9, we provide an integrated treatment of strategy by highlighting the choices managers face as they go about performing their planning role.

This applied approach can also be clearly seen in the last three chapters of the book, which cover the topics of managing organizational conflict, politics, and negotiation; managing information technology; and promoting innovation, product development, and entrepreneurship. Our chapters provide a student-friendly, behavioral approach to understanding the management issues entailed in negotiations, information systems, and innovation and entrepreneurship. In fact, the management of information technology to create and sustain a competitive advantage has always been a major theme of our book.

Flexible Organization

Another factor of interest to instructors concerns the way we have designed the grouping of chapters to allow instructors to teach the chapter material in the order that best suits their needs. For example, the more micro-oriented instructor can follow Chapters 1 through 5 with Chapters 12 through 16 and then do the more macro chapters. The more macro-oriented professor can follow Chapters 1 and 2 with Chapters 6 through 11, jump to 17, 18, 19, and then do the micro chapters, 3 through 5 and 12 through 16. Our sequencing of parts and chapters gives instructors considerable freedom to design the course that best suits their needs. Instructors are not tied to the planning, organizing, leading, and controlling framework, even though our presentation remains consistent with this approach.

Acknowledgments

Finding a way to integrate and present the rapidly growing literature on contemporary management and make it interesting and meaningful for students is not an easy task. In writing and revising the various drafts of *Contemporary Management,* we have been fortunate to have the assistance of several people who have contributed greatly to the book's final form. First, we are grateful to Andy Winston, our sponsoring editor, for his ongoing support and commitment to our project and for always finding ways to provide the resources that we needed to continually improve and refine our book. Second, we are grateful to Laura Spell, our developmental editor, for so ably coordinating the book's progress and to her and Ellen Cleary, our marketing manager, for providing us with concise and timely feedback and information from professors and reviewers that have allowed us to shape the book to the needs of its intended market. We also thank Artemio Ortiz for executing an awe-inspiring design; Mary Conzachi for coordinating the production process; Alexander Ruiz, Denise Bear, and Kalin Fotev (Rice University) for their research assistance; and Elaine Morris (Rice University) and Patsy Hartmangruber (Texas A&M) for providing excellent word-processing and graphic support. We are also grateful to the many colleagues and reviewers who provided us with useful and detailed feedback and perceptive comments and valuable suggestions for improving the manuscript.

Producing any competitive work is a challenge. Producing a truly market-driven textbook requires tremendous effort beyond simply obtaining reviews of a draft manuscript. Our goal was simple with the development of *Contemporary Management:* to be the most customer-driven principles-of-management text and supplement package ever published! With the goal of exceeding the expectations of both faculty and students, we executed one of the most aggressive product development plans ever undertaken in textbook publishing. Hundreds of faculty have taken part in developmental activities ranging from regional focus groups to manuscript and supplement reviews and surveys. Consequently, we're confident in assuring you and your students, our customers, that every aspect of our text and support package reflects your advice and needs. As you review it, we're confident that your reaction will be, "They listened!"

We extend our special thanks to the faculty who gave us their feedback during the development of the fourth edition:

Gerald Baumgardner, *Pennsylvania College of Technology*
Barry Bunn, *Valencia Community College*
Gerald Calvasina, *Southern Utah University*
Bruce H. Charnov, *Hofstra University*
Jay Christensen-Szalanski, *University of Iowa*
Teresa A. Daniel, *Marshall University*
Sandra Edwards, *Northeastern State University*
Kim Hester, *Arkansas State University*
Gwendolyn Jones, *University of Akron*
Kathleen Jones, *University of North Dakota*
Joanne E. Kapp, *Siena College*
Nicholas Mathys, *DePaul University*
Douglas L. Micklich, *Illinois State University*
Clive Muir, *Stetson University*

Our thanks go also to the faculty who contributed greatly to previous editions of *Contemporary Management:*

Fred Anderson, *Indiana University of Pennsylvania*
Jacquelyn Appeldorn, *Dutchess Community College*
Barry Armandi, *SUNY–Old Westbury*
Dave Arnott, *Dallas Baptist University*
Douglas E. Ashby, *Lewis & Clark Community College*
Kenneth E. Aupperle, *University of Akron*
Barry S. Axe, *Florida Atlantic University*
Jeff Bailey, *University of Idaho*
Robert M. Ballinger, *Siena College*
Donita Whitney-Bammerlin, *Kansas State University*
Frank Barber, *Cuyahoga Community College*
Sandy Jeanquart Barone, *Murray State University*
Lorraine P. Bassette, *Prince George's Community College*
Gene Baten, *Central Connecticut State University*
Josephine Bazan, *Holyoke Community College*
Hrach Bedrosian, *New York University*
Ellen A. Benowitz, *Mercer County Community College*
Mary Jo Boehms, *Jackson State Community College*
Jack C. Blanton, *University of Kentucky*
David E. Blevins, *University of Arkansas at Little Rock*
Karen Boroff, *Seton Hall University*
Barbara Boyington, *Brookdale Community College*
Charles Braun, *Marshall University*
Gil Brookins, *Siena College*
Patricia M. Buhler, *Goldey-Beacom College*
David Cadden, *Quinnipiac College*
Thomas Campbell, *University of Texas–Austin*
Thomas Carey, *Western Michigan University*
Daniel P. Chamberlin, *Regents University–CRB*
Nicolette DeVille Christensen, *Guilford College*
Raul Chavez, *Eastern Mennonite University*
Anthony A. Cioffi, *Lorain County Community College*
Sharon F. Clark, *Lebanon Valley College*
Sharon Clinebell, *University of Northern Colorado*
Dianne Coleman, *Wichita State University*
Elizabeth Cooper, *University of Rhode Island*
Anne Cowden, *California State University–Sacramento*
Thomas D. Craven, *York College of Pennsylvania*
Kent Curran, *University of North Carolina*
Arthur L. Darrow, *Bowling Green State University*
Ron DiBattista, *Bryant College*
Thomas Duening, *University of Houston*
Charles P. Duffy, *Iona College*
Steve Dunphy, *University of Akron*
Subhash Durlabhji, *Northwestern State University*
Robert A. Eberle, *Iona College*
Karen Eboch, *Bowling Green State University*
Robert R. Edwards, *Arkansas Tech University*
William Eldridge, *Kean College*
Pat Ellsberg, *Lower Columbia College*
Stan Elsea, *Kansas State University*
Dale Finn, *University of New Haven*

Charles Flaherty, *University of Minnesota*
Robert Flemming, *Delta State University*
Jeanie M. Forray, *Eastern Connecticut State University*
Marilyn L. Fox, *Minnesota State University–Mankato*
Alisa Fleming, *University of Phoenix*
Ellen Frank, *Southern Connecticut State University*
Joseph A. Gemma, *Providence College*
Neal Gersony, *University of New Haven*
Donna H. Giertz, *Parkland College*
Leo Giglio, *Dowling College*
David Glew, *Texas A&M University*
Carol R. Graham, *Western Kentucky University*
Matthew Gross, *Moraine Valley Community College*
John Hall, *University of Florida*
Eric L. Hansen, *California State University–Long Beach*
Justin U. Harris, *Strayer College*
Allison Harrison, *Mississippi State University*
Brad D. Hays, *North Central State College*
Robert A. Herring, III, *Winston-Salem State University*
Eileen Hogan, *Kutztown University*
Eileen Bartels Hewitt, *University of Scranton*
Stephen R. Hiatt, *Catawba College*
Tammy Bunn Hiller, Bucknell University
Jerry Horgesheiner, *Southern Utah University*
Gordon K. Huddleston, *South Carolina State University*
John Hughes, *Texas Tech University*
Charleen Jaeb, *Cuyahoga Community College*
Richard E. Johe, *Salem College*
Velma Jesser, *Lane Community College*
Gwendolyn Jones, *University of Akron*
Jehan G. Kavoosi, *Clarion University of Pennsylvania*
Peggi Koenecke, *California State University–Sacramento*
Ken Lehmenn, *Forsyth Technical Community College*
Lianlian Lin, *California State Polytechnic University*
Grand Lindstrom, *University of Wyoming*
Mary Lou Lockerby, *College of DuPage*
Esther Long, *University of Florida*
George S. Lowry, *Randolph-Macon College*
Bryan Malcolm, *University of Wisconsin*
Z. A. Malik, *Governors State University*
Mary J. Mallott, *George Washington University*
Jennifer Martin, *York College of Pennsylvania*
Robert L. McKeage, *University of Scranton*
Reuben McDaniel, *University of Texas*
John A. Miller, *Bucknell University*
Richard R. J. Morin, *James Madison University*
Behnam Nakhai, *Millersville University of Pennsylvania*
Thomas C. Neil, *Clark Atlanta University*
Brian Niehoff, *Kansas State University*
Judy Nixon, *University of Tennessee*
Cliff Olson, *Southern Adventists University*
Ralph W. Parrish, *University of Central Oklahoma*
Dane Partridge, *University of Southern Indiana*
Sheila J. Pechinski, *University of Maine*
Fred Pierce, *Northwood University*
Mary Pisnar, *Baldwin Wallace College*
Laynie Pizzolatto, *Nicholls State University*
Eleanor Polster, *Florida International University*
Paul Preston, *University of Texas–San Antonio*
Samuel Rabinowitz, *Rutgers University–Camden*
Gerald Ramsey, *Indiana University Southeast*
Charles Rarick, *Transylvania University*
Robert A. Reber, *Western Kentucky University*
Bob Redick, *Lincoln Land Community College*
Tina L. Robbins, *Clemson University*
Kathleen Rust, *Elmhurst College*
Deborah Britt Roebuck, *Kennesaw State University*
Harvey Rothenberg, *Regis University*
George Ruggiero, *Community College of Rhode Island*
Cyndy Ruszkowski, *Illinois State University*
Michael Santoro, *Rutgers University*
Amit Shah, *Frostburg State University*
Richard Ray Shreve, *Indiana University Northwest*
Sidney Siegel, *Drexel University*
Raymond D. Smith, *Towson State University*
William Soukup, *University of San Diego*
H. T. Stanton, Jr., *Barton College*
Nestor St. Charles, *Dutchess Community College*
Lynda St. Clair, *Bryant College*
Gerald Schoenfeld, Jr., *James Madison University*
Don Schreiber, *Baylor University*
John L. Schmidt, Jr., *George Mason University*
Robert Schwartz, *University of Toledo*
Michael Shapiro, *Dowling College*
Roy L. Simerly, *East Carolina University*
Randi L. Sims, *Nova Southeastern University*
Raymond Shea, *Monroe Community College*
Sharon Sloan, *Northwood University*
William A. Sodeman, *University of Southern Indiana*
Carl J. Sonntag, *Pikes Peak Community College*

Robert W. Sosna, *Menlo College*
William A. Stoever, *Seton Hall University*
Charles I. Stubbart, *Southern Illinois University–Carbondale*
James K. Swenson, *Moorhead State University*
Karen Ann Tarnoff, *East Tennessee State University*
Jerry L. Thomas, *Arapahoe Community College*
Joe Thomas, *Middle Tennessee State University*
Kenneth Thompson, *DePaul University*
John Todd, *University of Arkansas*
Thomas Turk, *Chapman University*
Linn Van Dyne, *Michigan State University*
Jaen Vanhoegaerden, *Ashridge Management College*
Gloria Walker, *Florida Community College*
Stuart H. Warnock, *University of Southern Colorado*
Toomy Lee Waterson, *Northwood University*
Philip A. Weatherford, *Embry-Riddle Aeronautical University*
Ben Weeks, *St. Xavier University*
Emilia S. Westney, *Texas Tech University*
W. J. Williams, *Chicago State University*
Robert Williams, *University of North Alabama*
Shirley A. Wilson, *Bryant College*
Robert H. Woodhouse, *University of St. Thomas*
Michael A. Yahr, *Robert Morris College*
D. Kent Zimmerman, *James Madison University*

Finally we are grateful to two incredibly wonderful children, Nicholas and Julia, for being all that they are and the joy they bring to all who know them.

Gareth R. Jones
Lowry Mays College and Graduate School of Business
Texas A&M University

Jennifer M. George
Jesse H. Jones Graduate School of Management
Rice University

GUIDED TOUR

RICH AND RELEVANT EXAMPLES

An important feature of our book is the way we use real-world examples and stories about managers and companies to drive home the applied lessons to students. Our reviewers were unanimous in their praise of the sheer range and depth of the rich, interesting examples we use to illustrate the chapter material and make it come alive. Moreover, unlike boxed material in other books, our boxes are seamlessly integrated into the text; they are an integral part of the learning experience, and not tacked on or isolated from the text itself. This is central to our pedagogical approach.

Each chapter opens with "A Manager's Challenge," which poses a chapter-related challenge and then discusses how managers in one or more organizations responded to that challenge. "A Manager's Challenge" helps demonstrate the uncertainty and excitement surrounding the management process.

A Manager's Challenge

Steve Jobs Transforms Apple Computer

What is high-performance management?

In 1976, Steven P. Jobs sold his Volkswagen van, and his partner Steven Wozniak sold his two programmable calculators. They then invested the proceeds of $1,350 to build a computer circuit board in Jobs's garage. So popular was the circuit board, which was developed into the Apple II personal computer (PC), that in 1977 Jobs and Wozniak incorporated their new business as Apple Computer. By 1985 Apple's sales were almost $2 billion; nevertheless, in the same year Jobs was forced out of the company he founded. Jobs's approach to management was a big part of the reason he lost control of Apple.[1]

After Apple was founded, Steve Jobs saw his role as leading the development effort to create new and improved PCs, and he started many different project teams to develop new and different PC models. Although this was a good strategy, Jobs's management style was often arbitrary and overbearing and caused many problems. He often played favorites among various employees and teams, championing some (e.g., his personal project, the Lisa PC team), against others (the Macintosh team). His actions led to fierce competition among project teams, many misunderstandings, and a great deal of distrust among members of competing teams.[2]

Like many effective managers, Steve Jobs has learned from his mistakes.

Overt Discrimination

overt discrimination Knowingly and willingly denying diverse individuals access to opportunities and outcomes in an organization.

Focus on Diversity

Gender Disc

Information Technology Byte

Designing Global Information Systems

IMPORTING AND EXPORTING

exporting Making products at home and selling them abroad.

importing Selling at home products that are made abroad.

Managing Globally

Levi

Ethics in Action

Taking Responsibility for Exposing Wrongd

10 Chapter One

Manager as a Person

New CEOs Bring Change at Avon and Lucent

Additional in-depth examples appear in boxes throughout each chapter. "Management Insight" boxes illustrate the topics of the chapter, while the "Ethics in Action," "Managing Globally," "Focus on Diversity," and "Information Technology Byte" boxes examine the chapter topics from each of these perspectives.

These are not boxes in the traditional sense; that is, they're not disembodied from the chapter narrative. These thematic applications are fully integrated into the reading. Students will no longer be forced to decide whether to read boxed material. These features are interesting and engaging for students while bringing the chapter content to life.

NEW! "Manager as a Person" boxes focus on how real managers brought about change to their organizations. These examples within many chapters give students the opportunity to reflect on how individual managers dealt with real-life on-the-job challenges related to various chapter concepts.

EXPERIENTIAL LEARNING FEATURES

We have given considerable time and attention to developing state-of-the-art experiential end-of-chapter learning exercises that drive home the meaning of management to students. These exercises are grouped together at the end of each chapter in the section called Management in Action.

TOPICS FOR DISCUSSION AND ACTION A set of chapter-related questions and points for reflection, some of which ask students to research actual management issues and learn firsthand from practicing managers.

BUILDING MANAGEMENT SKILLS A self-development exercise that asks students to apply what they have learned to their own experience of organizations and managers or to the experiences of others.

***NEW!* MANAGING ETHICALLY** An exercise that presents students with an ethical scenario or dilemma and asks them, either individually or in a group, to think about the issue from an ethical perspective to understand the issues facing practicing managers.

SMALL GROUP BREAKOUT EXERCISE This unique exercise is designed to allow instructors in large classes to utilize interactive experiential exercises in groups of three to four students. The instructor calls on students to form into small groups simply by turning to people around them. All students participate in the exercise in class, and a mechanism is provided for the different groups to share what they have learned with one another.

EXPLORING THE WORLD WIDE WEB This is an Internet exercise designed to draw students into relevant material on the Web and give them the experience of judging its potential value while applying what they have learned.

Management in Action

Topics for Discussion and Action

Discussion

1. What is the relationship between ethics and the law?
2. Why do the claims and interests of stakeholders sometimes conflict?
3. Why should managers use ethical criteria to guide their decision making?
4. As an employee of a company, what are some of the most unethical business practices that you have encountered in its dealings with stakeholders?
5. What are the main determinants of business ethics?

Action

6. Find a manager and ask about the most important ethical rules that he or she uses to make the right decisions.
7. Find an example of (a) a company that has an obstructionist approach to social responsibility and (b) one that has an accommodative approach.

Building Management Skills

Dealing with Ethical Dilemmas

Use the chapter material to decide how you, as a manager, should respond to each of the following ethical dilemmas:

1. You are planning to leave your job to go work for a competitor; your boss invites you to an important meeting where you will learn about new products your company will be bringing out next year. Do you go to the meeting?
2. You're the manager of sales in an expensive sports-car dealership. A young executive who has just received a promotion comes in and wants to buy a car that you know is out of her price range. Do you encourage the executive to buy it so that you can receive a big commission on the sale?
3. You sign a contract to manage a young rock band, and that group agrees to let you produce their next seven records, for which they will receive royalties of 5 percent. Their first record is a smash hit and sells millions. Do you increase their royalty rate on their future records?

Managing Ethically

As the chapter discussed, Arthur Andersen's culture had become so strong that some of the company's partners and their subordinates acted unethically and pursued their own interests at the expense of other stakeholders. Many employees knew they were doing wrong but were afraid to refuse to follow orders. At Beech-Nut, the company's ethical values completely broke down; some managers joked about the harm being done to stakeholders.

1. Why is it that an organization's values and norms can become too strong and lead to unethical behavior?
2. What steps can a company take to prevent this problem—to stop its values and norms from becoming so inwardly focused that managers and employees lose sight of their responsibility to their stakeholders?

141

Small Group Breakout Exercise

Is Chewing Gum the "Right" Thing t

Read the paragraph below. Then break up into groups of three or four people and answ discussion questions.

In the United States the right to chew gum is taken for granted. Although it is often against the rules to chew gum in a high school classroom, church, and so on, it is legal to do so on the street. If you possess or chew gum on a street in Singapore, you can be arrested. Chewing gum has been made illegal in Singapore because those in power believe that it creates a disgusting mess on pavements and feel that people cannot be trusted to dispose of their gum properly and thus should have no right to use it.

1. What makes chewing gum acceptable in the United States and unacceptable in Singapore?
2. Why can you chew gu the street but not in a
3. How can you use ethi principles to decide w chewing is ethical or u and if and when it sho made illegal?

Exploring the World Wide Web

Go to Wal-Mart's Web site (www.walmart.com) and read the information there about the company's stance on the ethics of global outsourcing and the treatment of workers in countries abroad. Then search the Web for some recent stories about Wal-Mart's global purchasing practices and reports on the enforcement of its code of conduct.

1. What ethical principles Wal-Mart's approach t purchasing?
2. Does Wal-Mart appea doing a good job of en its global code of conc

Additional Activities on the Build Your Management Skills DVD

- **Test Your Knowledge:** Ethics
- **Self-Assessment:** Assessing Your Ethical Decision-Making Skills
- **Manager's Hot Seat:** Ethics: Let's Make a F Quarter Deal

Be the Manager

Creating an Ethical

You are an entrepreneur who has decided to go into business and open a steak and chicken restaurant. Your business plan requires that you hire at least 20 people as chefs, waiters, and so on. As the owner, you are drawing up a list of ethical principles that each of these people will receive and must agree to when he or she accepts a job offer. These principles outline your view of what is right or acceptable behavior and what will be expected both from you and from your employees.

Create a list of the five n cal rules or principles you w govern the way your busin ates. Be sure to spell out h principles relate to your st ers; for example, state the intend to follow in dealing employees and customers.

142

BusinessWeek **Cases in the News**

Can Boeing Get Out of Its "Ethical Cloud"?

The unexpected resignation of Boeing chairman and CEO Philip M. Condit on December 1, 2003, followed a year of turbulence at the world's largest aerospace company. The final straw for Condit, 62, may have been the previous week's ouster of two senior Boeing officials for an alleged ethics lapse.

Condit's resignation created several daunting challenges for his immediate successor—Harry C. Stonecipher, former Boeing president and chief operating officer. Stonecipher, 67, who retired last year and remained as a board member, immediately assumes the post of CEO and president of a company that has more than $54 billion in annual revenues.

In his first press conference as top gun, Stonecipher seemed to say all the right things by pledging to answer any and all questions, including those swirling around a highly criticized air-tanker deal with the federal government. The blunt-talking, no-nonsense leader will have to be true to his word and get Boeing soaring again.

Clearly, Stonecipher has his work cut out. Condit's resignation is tied to Boeing's persistent reluctance to disclose all the particulars of a controversial plan to lease Boeing 767 tankers to the Air Force. The plan was blasted for the secrecy in which the contract was negotiated and for the fact that leasing would be much more expensive for the federal government than an outright purchase (see BW, 7/7/03, "Inside Boeing's Sweet Deal").

Condit's departure came a week after Boeing CFO Michael Sears resigned. The company cited unethical conduct, saying he negotiated the hiring of an Air Force missile-defense expert while he was still working for the Pentagon and had direct influence over Boeing's bid to secure the tanker contract. Sears denied any wrongdoing.

"It's very surprising for a company such as Boeing to have not one but two apparent ethical breaches in less than six months," says Steven Ryan, a Washington (D.C.) attorney who represents contractors seeking work with the federal government. In July 2003 the Pentagon had punished Boeing for stealing trade secrets from rival Lockheed Martin to help win rocket-launch contracts. The punishment adds up to $1 billion in lost business, and the Pentagon has indefinitely banned Boeing from bidding on military satellite-launching contracts.

"Condit's resignation is a reflection of the seriousness of the problem," says Ryan. And the situation suggested that something wasn't right inside Boeing's culture—something that Stonecipher had helped change when he was president and was now responsible and accountable for coming clean.

"Everything the former leadership at Boeing did was surrounded by an ethical cloud of controversy and needed to be reviewed to ensure that it was in the best interest of the taxpayer and war-fighter," says Steve Ellis, vice president for Taxpayers for Common Sense. With Condit out, the board apparently chose the tough-talking Stonecipher because he's well regarded on Wall Street and because he knows the ways of the Pentagon. With the mandatory retirement set at 65 for Boeing execs, Stonecipher received a special exemption to return.

How Boeing got itself and its top execs tangled up in such a mess has yet to be fully explained. The stock, at just over $38, barely moved on the news of Condit's departure. And it has moved mostly higher last year from an all-time low of just over $24 hit back in March 2003. Still, analysts say, the stock should have been much higher, and Stonecipher had a long way to go to regain the trust of angry and skeptical investors, public-interest groups, and the U.S. government.

Questions

1. What kinds of unethical actions did Boeing's managers engage in?
2. What effect did this have on the company and how can its CEO prevent future unethical behavior?

Source: Stanley Holmes, "Can Boeing Get Out of Its Ethical Cloud?" *Business Week*, December 2003.

143

BUSINESSWEEK CASES IN THE NEWS Each chapter has two cases for analysis that are actual or shortened versions of *BusinessWeek* articles. The accompanying discussion questions encourage students to think about and analyze how real managers deal with real problems in the business world. These cases give instructors the opportunity to explore issues in more depth if they choose.

BE THE MANAGER This exercise presents a realistic scenario in which a manager/organization faces some kind of challenge, problem, or opportunity and the student plays the role of the focal manager figuring out how to address the challenge based on the chapter content. These exercises provide students with a real, hands-on way to take an action-oriented approach to solving "real" problems by applying what they've just learned in the chapter.

***NEW!* ADDITIONAL ACTIVITIES ON THE BUILD YOUR MANAGEMENT SKILLS DVD** Do you want to put your students' leadership skills to the test, assess their emotional intelligence, or see how they would handle an employee who is not meeting expectations? You'll have opportunities to do all of this and more with Test Your Knowledge, Self-Assessment, and Manager's Hot Seat exercises on the Build Your Management Skills DVD. A list of relevant exercises on the DVD is included at the end of each chapter.

CHOOSING EXERCISES Our idea in offering instructors such a wide array of exercises to promote the learning experience is that instructors can *choose and select* from these exercises and vary them over the semester so that students can learn the meaning of management through many different avenues. These exercises complement the chapter material and have been class tested to add to the overall learning experience. Students report that they enjoy and learn from them.

INTEGRATED LEARNING SYSTEM

Great care was used in the creation of the supplemental materials to accompany *Contemporary Management*. Whether you are a seasoned faculty member or a newly minted instructor, you'll find our support materials to be the most thorough and thoughtful ever created!

Instructor's Presentation Manager CD-ROM This presentation CD-ROM allows instructors to easily create their own custom presentations using resources on the CD, like the Instructor's Manual and PowerPoint. The computerized test bank is also included on this CD.

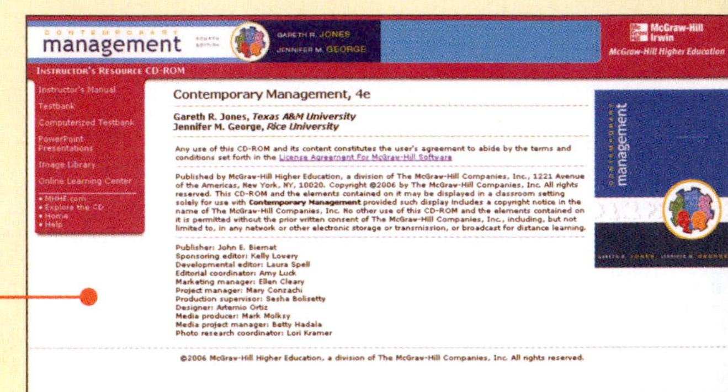

Instructor's Manual Prepared by Stephanie Bibb of Chicago State University, the IM contains a chapter overview; learning objectives; key terms; resources available; notes for opening case; a lecture outline; notes for Topics for Discussion and Action questions; notes for Building Management Skills exercises; notes for Small Group Breakout exercises; notes for Be the Manager exercises; notes for Exploring the World Wide Web exercises; notes for Test Your Knowledge, Self-Assessment, and Manager's Hot Seat DVD exercises; notes for *BusinessWeek* cases; lecture enhancers; and video case teaching notes.

PowerPoint® Presentation Approximately 400 slides feature reproductions of key tables and figures from the text as well as original content—prepared by Brad Cox of Midlands Tech. A new feature in the PowerPoint Presentation, "Movie Example" slides, will help you incorporate popular movies, such as *Office Space* and *Monty Python and the Holy Grail* into your management course. These slides appear at the end of each chapter presentation and include notes on how the movies can be used to generate discussion and to illustrate management concepts.

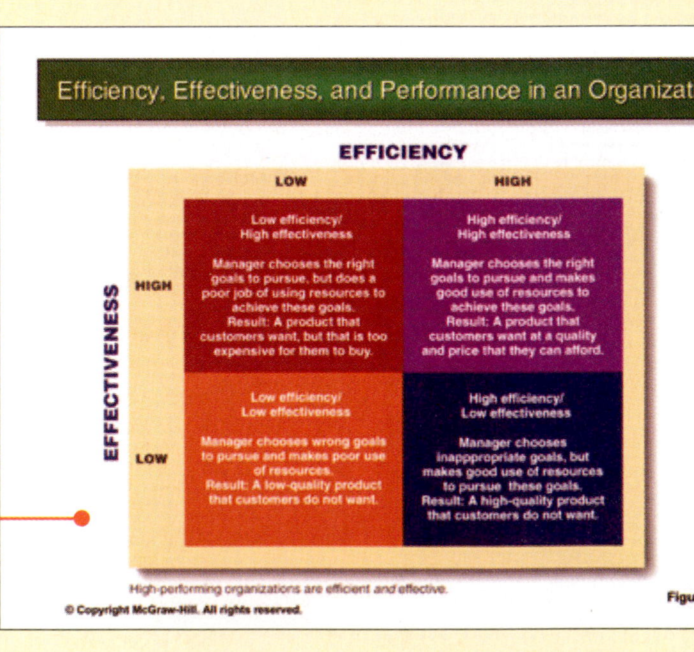

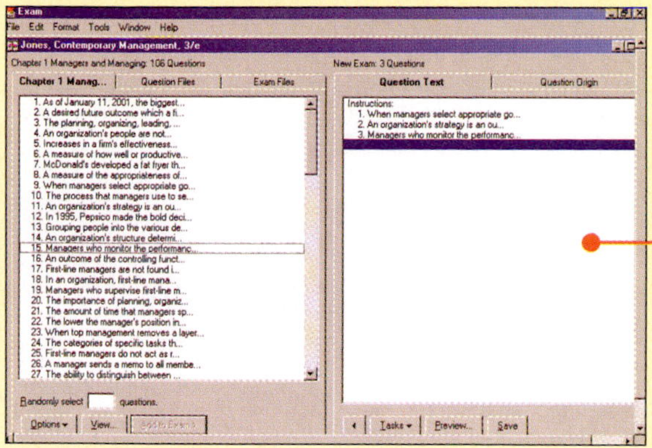

Test Bank and Computerized Test Bank The test bank has been thoroughly reviewed, revised, and improved, in response to customer feedback, by Eileen Hogan of Kutztown University. There are approximately 100 questions per chapter, including true-false, multiple-choice, and essay, each tagged with level of difficulty (corresponding to Bloom's taxonomy of educational objectives), correct answer, and page references to the text.

Video Cases

Chapter 1 Video Case: The Legacy of GE's Jack Welch

As General Electric's chairman, Jack Welch was one of the world's most powerful corporate leaders. He was also viewed as one of America's toughest executives and an icon to be admired. The now-retired Welch, his famous management style, and his accomplishments have been the subjects of books and university business classes.

Under Welch, from 1981 to 2001, GE became the world's most valuable company, with a market value of $406 billion. Welch spurred that dramatic growth by performing management functions his own way. He chose not to follow the traditional strategy of sticking with what a company knows but instead, accumulated diverse businesses. Originally a manufacturer of household appliances, lighting, and jet engines, GE bought NBC as well as companies offering medical products, financial services, and car leasing.

Welch restructured GE before restructuring became common among large corporations. Although his company was profitable, Welch sold some of GE's subsidiaries and reduced the payroll. Some 118,000 jobs—about one in four—were slashed. The deep cuts earned Welch the nickname "Neutron Jack," a moniker he is said to have detested. Welch endured the criticism and continued his practice of identifying, keeping, and rewarding high-performing employees at General Electric.

Welch is known for dismantling GE's large bureaucracy and opening up corporate communication. Some have said that Welch listened as much as he talked and that he always spoke in a straightforward manner. He excelled at personal interaction and motivation and as the top executive was highly visible in his company. Welch visited and taught at GE's famous Management Development Institute in Crotonville, New York. His leadership style centered on having strong employees and managers at all levels and empowering them to make decisions and engage in what he called "boundaryless thinking."[1]

Some people who worked with Welch have described the former chairman's interaction as more aggressive than egalitarian or cooperative. Others have said that Welch's often-used motivational technique was the fear factor: perform or hit the road. Welch determined in the early 1980s that to be at the top, GE could not fill management positions with deadwood—people who felt comfortable, secure, and protected from competition in their jobs within the depths of a large corporation. Welch thought it was better for individuals performing at the lowest levels to move on in other directions when they are young. During his tenure at GE, Welch selected the best people he could find and then trained and promoted them. Many who learned from him took their leadership skills to other large firms. Some of Welch's "lieutenants" head some of the world's major corporations, such as Home Depot, TRW, 3M, and others.

Widely publicized and lauded, Welch's leadership techniques also surface in noncorporate environments. The head of the Junior League of London, a nonprofit organization of volunteers offering social services, has employed Welch-style principles to motivate her group's 400 members.

Of course, Jack Welch's years at GE included not only stunning corporate accomplishments but also setbacks and controversies. A proposed merger with Honeywell was rejected by European Union regulators. The Environmental Protection Agency under the Bush administration ordered GE, at a cost of $500 million, to clean up 40 miles of Hudson River bottom polluted by PCBs before the substances were banned. After Welch's exit from GE in September 2001, critics attacked his substantial benefit package, including an arrangement that provided more than $2 million a year for an array of perks such as air transportation and personal services. Welch promptly agreed to give back $2 million.

Questions

1. In what ways did Jack Welch perform the leadership function effectively?
2. Identify the type of skills—conceptual, human, or technical—that was most likely Jack Welch's strong suit when he was GE's top executive. Explain.
3. Would you like to work for a leader like Jack Welch? What would be the advantages? What would be the disadvantages?

698

***NEW!* Case Videos** One video is provided for each of the 19 chapters, and each has a corresponding written Video Case included at the end of the book. These videos illustrate application of the relevant chapter concepts and feature timely and thought-provoking topics affecting the business environment, as well as profiles of successful businesses and managers. All videos are available in DVD or VHS format.

The videos and video cases will enliven the classroom through viewing and discussing interesting companies and people–such as Seattle's famous Pike Place Fish Market or Todd McFarlane, who founded a successful comic-book and toy company–or thought-provoking management topics and issues–such as the legacy of GE's Jack Welch; the federal government's investigation of Enron's bankruptcy, including the role played by whistle-blower Sherron Watkins; and *Supersize Me,* the documentary film that caused McDonald's to discontinue its supersize menu offerings. Each case provides a written overview of the video content as well as additional background information and discussion questions that encourage students to critically examine and apply chapter concepts to analyzing the case.

CD-ROM POWERPOINT®

FOR STUDENTS

Student Study Guide

Prepared by Thomas J. Quirk of Webster University, the Study Guide has been completely updated with the goal of helping students master course content. Each chapter includes learning objectives; a chapter outline; and matching, true-false, multiple-choice, and essay questions, with answer keys including page references to the text.

NEW! Student DVD—Build Your Management Skills

This DVD makes it easy to use the latest in technology to help students hone their personal management skills. Packaged free with every new copy of the text, the Student DVD features Manager's Hot Seat exercises such as "Ethics: Let's Make a Fourth Quarter Deal" and "Change: More Pain than Gain"; Test Your Knowledge exercises such as "Fiedler's Contingency Model of Leadership" and "Porter's Five Forces"; and Self-Assessments such as "Active Listening Skills Inventory" and "Do You Have What It Takes to Be a Leader?" An end-of-chapter section titled "Additional Activities on the Build Your Management Skills DVD" shows which exercises to use with a particular chapter. The DVD can also be ordered separately.

The Contemporary Management Online Learning Center

www.mhhe.com/jonesgeorge4e

The Online Learning Center (OLC) is a Web site that follows the text chapter by chapter. OLC content is designed to reinforce and build on the text content. As students read the book, they can go online to take self-grading quizzes, review material, or work through interactive exercises. OLCs can be delivered multiple ways–professors and students can access them directly through the textbook Web site, through PageOut, or within a course management system (i.e., WebCT, Blackboard, or eCollege). In addition, PowerWeb, which brings you up-to-date articles from leading periodicals and journals, as well as current news, is now fully integrated into the OLC and is available as premium content, requiring a passcode card that is bound into new texts for free. Premium-content passcode cards are also available separately.

BusinessWeek Edition

Students can subscribe to *BusinessWeek* for a specially priced rate of $8.25 in addition to the price of this text.

The Wall Street Journal Edition

Your students can subscribe to *The Wall Street Journal* for 15 weeks at a specially priced rate of $20 in addition to the price of the text. Students will receive the *How to Use the WSJ* handbook plus a subscription card shrink-wrapped with their new text. The subscription also gives students access to www.wsj.com.

FOR STUDENTS

Authors

Gareth Jones is a Professor of Management in the Lowry Mays College and Graduate School of Business at Texas A&M University. He received his B.A. in Economics/Psychology and his Ph.D. in Management from the University of Lancaster, U.K. He previously held teaching and research appointments at the University of Warwick, Michigan State University, and the University of Illinois at Urbana-Champaign. He is a frequent visitor and speaker at universities in both the United Kingdom and the United States.

He specializes in strategic management and organizational theory and is well known for his research that applies transaction cost analysis to explain many forms of strategic and organizational behavior. He is currently interested in strategy process, competitive advantage, and information technology issues. He is also investigating the relationships between ethics, trust, and organizational culture and studying the role of affect in the strategic decision-making process.

He has published many articles in leading journals of the field, and his recent work has appeared in the *Academy of Management Review,* the *Journal of International Business Studies,* and *Human Relations.* An article on the role of information technology in many aspects of organizational functioning was published in the *Journal of Management.* One of his articles won the *Academy of Management Journal*'s Best Paper Award, and he is one of the most prolific authors in the *Academy of Management Review.* He is or has served on the editorial boards of the *Academy of Management Review,* the *Journal of Management,* and *Management Inquiry.*

Gareth Jones has taken his academic knowledge and used it to craft leading textbooks in management and three other major areas in the management discipline: organizational behavior, organizational theory, and strategic management. His books are widely recognized for their innovative, contemporary content and for the clarity with which they communicate complex, real-world issues to students.

Jennifer George is the Mary Gibbs Jones Professor of Management and Professor of Psychology in the Jesse H. Jones Graduate School of Management at Rice University. She received her B.A. in Psychology/Sociology from Wesleyan University, her M.B.A. in Finance from New York University, and her Ph.D. in Management and Organizational Behavior from New York University. Prior to joining the faculty at Rice University, she was a Professor in the Department of Management at Texas A&M University.

Professor George specializes in organizational behavior and is well known for her research on mood and emotion in the workplace, their determinants, and their effects on various individual and group-level work outcomes. She is the author of many articles in leading peer-reviewed journals such as the *Academy of Management Journal,* the *Academy of Management Review,* the *Journal of Applied Psychology, Organizational Behavior and Human Decision Processes, Journal of Personality and Social Psychology,* and *Psychological Bulletin.* One of her papers won the Academy of Management's Organizational Behavior Division Outstanding Competitive Paper Award and another paper won the *Human Relations* Best Paper Award. She is, or has been, on the editorial review boards of the *Journal of Applied Psychology, Academy of Management Journal, Academy of Management Review, Journal of Management, Organizational Behavior and Human Decision Processes, International Journal of Selection and Assessment,* and *Journal of Managerial Issues,* was a consulting editor for the *Journal of Organizational Behavior,* and was a member of the SIOP *Organizational Frontiers Series* editorial board. She is a Fellow in the American Psychological Association, the American Psychological Society, and the Society for Industrial and Organizational Psychology and a member of the Society for Organizational Behavior. Professor George is currently an Associate Editor for the *Journal of Applied Psychology.* She also has co-authored a widely used textbook titled *Understanding and Managing Organizational Behavior.*

CHAPTER

1 Managers and Managing

Learning Objectives

After studying this chapter, you should be able to:

- Describe what management is, why management is important, what managers do, and how managers utilize organizational resources efficiently and effectively to achieve organizational goals.
- Distinguish among planning, organizing, leading, and controlling (the four principal managerial functions), and explain how managers' ability to handle each one can affect organizational performance.
- Differentiate among three levels of management, and understand the responsibilities of managers at different levels in the organizational hierarchy.
- Identify the roles managers perform, the skills they need to execute those roles effectively, and the way new information technology is affecting these roles and skills.
- Discuss the principal challenges managers face in today's increasingly competitive global environment.

A Manager's Challenge

Steve Jobs Transforms Apple Computer

What is high-performance management? In 1976, Steven P. Jobs sold his Volkswagen van, and his partner Steven Wozniak sold his two programmable calculators. They then invested the proceeds of $1,350 to build a computer circuit board in Jobs's garage. So popular was the circuit board, which was developed into the Apple II personal computer (PC), that in 1977 Jobs and Wozniak incorporated their new business as Apple Computer. By 1985 Apple's sales were almost $2 billion; nevertheless, in the same year Jobs was forced out of the company he founded. Jobs's approach to management was a big part of the reason he lost control of Apple.[1]

After Apple was founded, Steve Jobs saw his role as leading the development effort to create new and improved PCs, and he started many different project teams to develop new and different PC models. Although this was a good strategy, Jobs's management style was often arbitrary and overbearing and caused many problems. He often played favorites among various employees and teams, championing some (e.g., his personal project, the Lisa PC team), against others (the Macintosh team). His actions led to fierce competition among project teams, many misunderstandings, and a great deal of distrust among members of competing teams.[2]

Like many effective managers, Steve Jobs has learned from his mistakes.

Moreover, Jobs's abrasive management style brought him into conflict with other managers, particularly John Sculley, Apple's CEO. Employees became unsure whether Jobs (the chairman) or Sculley (the CEO) was leading the company, and both managers were so busy competing for control of Apple that neither had the time or energy to ensure that Apple's resources were being used efficiently. For example, little attention was paid to evaluating the performance of the project teams, and there was not even a budget in place to curb the teams' research and development spending. The result? Apple's costs started to soar and its performance and profits fell. Apple's board of directors became convinced that Jobs's management style was the heart of the problem and asked him to resign.

After leaving Apple, Jobs moved on to new ventures. He founded NEXT, which developed a powerful new PC, and Pixar, a computer animation company that become a major success story after it made movies such as *Toy Story* and *Finding Nemo.* In both these companies, Jobs developed a clear vision for managers to follow and built strong management teams. In the meantime, Apple was struggling to compete against Michael Dell's new, low-cost PCs and Microsoft's Windows software.

Apple's performance was declining rapidly, and in 1996 Jobs convinced Apple to buy NEXT for $400 million and use its powerful operating system in the next generation of Apple PCs. In 1997, Apple asked Jobs to take full control of the company and once again become its CEO.[3] Jobs agreed and quickly began to put the new management skills he had developed over time to good use. Understanding, more than he had ever before, that what a company needs is clear leadership and a guiding mission to energize and motivate employees, the charismatic Jobs strove to create a new vision for Apple.

Jobs decided that to survive, Apple had to introduce advanced PCs and related equipment. He instituted an across-the-board planning process, established clear company objectives, and created a team structure that allowed programmers and engineers to pool their skills to develop new PCs. He delegated considerable authority to the teams, but he also established strict timetables and challenging "stretch" goals, such as bringing new products to market as quickly as possible, for these groups to achieve. One result of these efforts was Apple's sleek new line of iMac PCs, which were quickly followed by a wide range of futuristic PC-related products. To profile the company's innovations, Jobs opened a nationwide chain of Apple stores.

Jobs's most recent attempt to revolutionize Apple and raise its performance came in 2003, when he announced that Apple was starting a new service called *iTunes.* Through iTunes, an online music store, people could legally download songs from the Internet by paying a dollar a song. At the same time, Apple introduced its iPod music player, which can store thousands of songs, and the player quickly became a runaway success. In 2004, Apple announced its new mini iPod, which was such a success that retailers could not keep it in stock. By then, Apple had 70 percent of the online music download business![4]

In 2004, it seemed that a new Apple was emerging. Analysts credit Apple's rising performance to the management skills Jobs was forced to develop after his ouster from the company he had founded. However, with Dell the acknowledged low-cost PC maker, will Apple's new venture into the music business be enough to guarantee its future success?

Overview

The history of Steve Jobs's ups and downs as both a founder and a manager at Apple Computer illustrates many of the challenges facing people who become managers: Managing a large company is a complex activity, and effective managers must possess many kinds of skills, knowledge, and abilities. Management is an unpredictable process. Making the right decision is difficult; even effective managers often make mistakes, but the most effective managers are the ones, like Jobs, who learn from their mistakes and continually strive to find ways to help their companies increase their competitive advantage and performance.

In this chapter, we look at what managers do and what skills and abilities they must develop if they are to manage their organizations successfully over time. We also identify the different kinds of managers that organizations need and the skills and abilities they must develop if they are to be successful. Finally, we identify some of the challenges that managers must address if their organizations are to grow and prosper.

What Is Management?

When you think of a manager, what kind of person comes to mind? Do you see someone who, like Steve Jobs, can determine the future prosperity of a large for-profit company? Or do you see the administrator of a not-for-profit organization, such as a school, library, or charity, or the person in charge of your local Wal-Mart store or McDonald's restaurant, or the person *you* answer to if you have a part-time job? What do all these managers have in common? First, they all work in organizations. *Organizations* are collections of people who work together and coordinate their actions to achieve a wide variety of *goals,* or desired future outcomes.[5] Second, as managers, they are the people responsible for supervising the use of an organization's human and other resources to achieve its goals. **Management,** then, is the planning, organizing, leading, and controlling of human and other resources to achieve organizational goals efficiently and effectively. An organization's *resources* include assets such as people and their skills, know-how, and knowledge; machinery; raw materials; computers and information technology; and financial capital.

management The planning, organizing, leading, and controlling of human and other resources to achieve organizational goals efficiently and effectively.

Achieving High Performance: A Manager's Goal

One of the most important goals that organizations and their members try to achieve is to provide some kind of good or service that customers desire. The principal goal of CEO Steve Jobs is to manage Apple so that a new stream of goods and services–such as more powerful PCs, new kinds of wafer-thin computer monitors, Internet music players, and the improved ability to download music from the Internet–are created that customers are willing to buy. The principal goal of doctors, nurses, and hospital administrators is to increase their hospital's ability to make sick people well. Likewise, the principal goal of each McDonald's restaurant manager is to produce burgers, fries, and shakes that people want to pay for and eat.

Organizational performance is a measure of how efficiently and effectively managers use resources to satisfy customers and achieve organizational goals. Organizational performance increases in direct proportion to increases in efficiency and effectiveness (see Figure 1.1, page 6).

organizational performance A measure of how efficiently and effectively a manager uses resources to satisfy customers and achieve organizational goals.

Efficiency is a measure of how well or how productively resources are used to achieve a goal.[6] Organizations are efficient when managers minimize the amount of input resources (such as labor, raw materials, and component parts) or the amount of time needed to produce a given output of goods or services. For example, McDonald's developed a more efficient fat fryer that not only reduces the amount of oil used in cooking by 30 percent but also speeds up the cooking of french fries. Steve Jobs instructed Apple's engineers to develop a

efficiency A measure of how well or how productively resources are used to achieve a goal.

Figure 1.1
Efficiency, Effectiveness, and Performance in an Organization

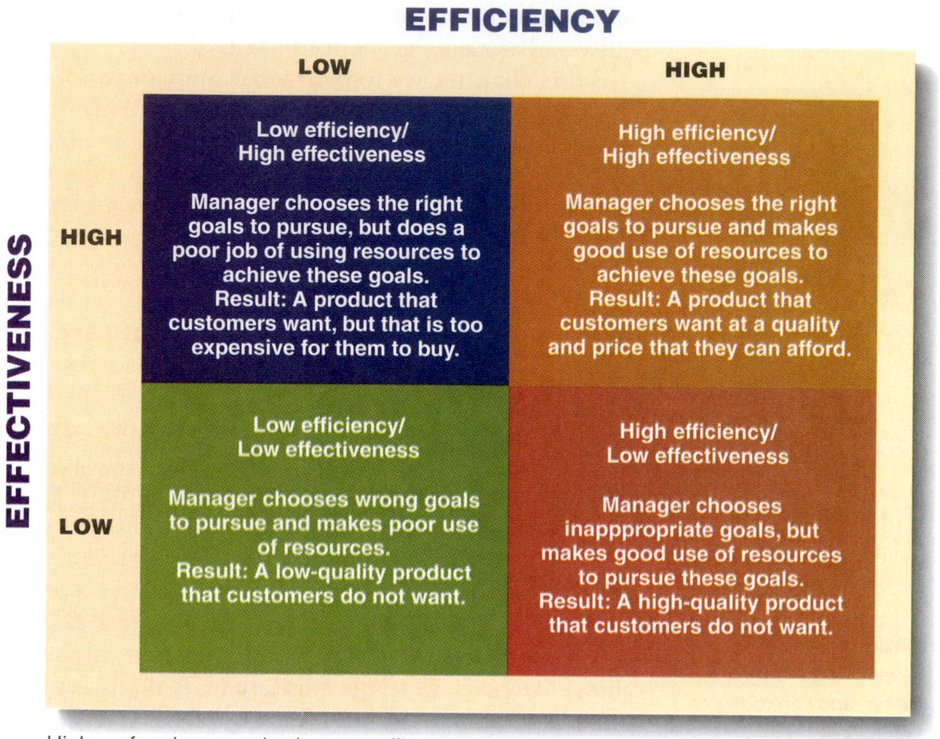

	EFFICIENCY: LOW	EFFICIENCY: HIGH
EFFECTIVENESS: HIGH	Low efficiency/ High effectiveness Manager chooses the right goals to pursue, but does a poor job of using resources to achieve these goals. Result: A product that customers want, but that is too expensive for them to buy.	High efficiency/ High effectiveness Manager chooses the right goals to pursue and makes good use of resources to achieve these goals. Result: A product that customers want at a quality and price that they can afford.
EFFECTIVENESS: LOW	Low efficiency/ Low effectiveness Manager chooses wrong goals to pursue and makes poor use of resources. Result: A low-quality product that customers do not want.	High efficiency/ Low effectiveness Manager chooses inapppropriate goals, but makes good use of resources to pursue these goals. Result: A high-quality product that customers do not want.

High-performing organizations are efficient *and* effective.

smaller, more compact version of its iPod player, which became a huge success, and he has undoubtedly told them to develop new kinds of music players. A manager's responsibility is to ensure that an organization and its members perform as efficiently as possible all the activities needed to provide goods and services to customers.

effectiveness A measure of the appropriateness of the goals an organization is pursuing and of the degree to which the organization achieves those goals.

Effectiveness is a measure of the appropriateness of the goals that managers have selected for the organization to pursue and of the degree to which the organization achieves those goals. Organizations are effective when managers choose appropriate goals and then achieve them. Some years ago, for example, managers at McDonald's decided on the goal of providing breakfast service to attract more customers. The choice of this goal has proved very smart, for sales of breakfast food now account for more than 30 percent of McDonald's revenues. Jobs's goal is to create a constant flow of innovative PC and digital entertainment products. High-performing organizations, such as Apple, McDonald's, Wal-Mart, Intel, Home Depot, Accenture, and the March of Dimes, are simultaneously efficient and effective, as shown in Figure 1.1. Effective managers are those who choose the right organizational goals to pursue and have the skills to utilize resources efficiently.

Why Study Management?

Today, more students are competing for places in business courses than ever before; the number of people wishing to pursue Master of Business Administration (MBA) degrees–today's passport to an advanced management position–

either on campus or from online universities is at an all-time high. Why is the study of management currently so popular?[7]

First, in any society or culture resources are valuable and scarce, so the more efficient and effective use that organizations can make of those resources, the greater the relative well-being and prosperity of people in that society. Because managers are the people who decide how to use many of a society's most valuable resources–its skilled employees, raw materials like oil and land, computers and information systems, and financial assets–they directly impact the well-being of a society and the people in it. Understanding what managers do and how they do it is of central importance to understanding how a society works and how it creates wealth.

Second, although most people are not managers, and many may never intend to become managers, almost all of us encounter managers because most people have jobs and bosses. Moreover, many people today are working in groups and teams and have to deal with co-workers. Studying management helps people to deal with their bosses and their co-workers. It reveals how to understand other people at work and make decisions and take actions that win the attention and support of the boss. Management also teaches people not yet in positions of authority how to lead co-workers, solve conflicts between them, and increase team performance.

Third, in any society, people are in competition for a very important resource–a well-paying job and an interesting and satisfying career–and understanding management is one important path toward obtaining such a position. In general, jobs become more interesting the more complex or responsible they are. Any person who desires a motivating job that changes over time might therefore do well to develop management skills and become promotable. A person who has been working for several years and then returns to school for an MBA can usually, after earning the degree, find a more interesting, satisfying job and one that pays significantly more than the previous job. Moreover, salaries increase rapidly as people move up the organizational hierarchy, whether it is a school system, a large for-profit business organization, or a not-for-profit charitable or medical institution.

Indeed, the salaries paid to top managers are enormous. For example, the CEOs and other top executives or managers of companies such as Apple, Dell, Walt Disney, GE, and McDonald's receive millions in actual salary each year. However, even more staggering is the fact that most top executives also receive stock or shares in the company they manage, as well as stock options that give them the right to sell these shares at a certain time in the future.[8] If the value of the stock goes up, then the managers keep the difference between the price they obtained the stock option for and what it is worth later. Michael Eisner, CEO of Walt Disney, for example, received stock options that were worth $1 *billion* when Disney's stock soared in the 1990s. When Steve Jobs again became CEO of Apple, he decided he would accept a salary of only $1 a year. However, Jobs was also awarded stock options that were worth over $100 million by 2004 and will be worth double or treble this amount if Apple continues to perform well and its stock price rises (he was also given the free use of a $90 million jet).[9] These incredible amounts of money provide some indication of both the responsibilities and the rewards that accompany the achievement of high management positions in major companies. What is it that managers actually do to receive such rewards?[10]

Managerial Functions

The job of management is to help an organization make the best use of its resources to achieve its goals. How do managers accomplish this objective? They do so by performing four essential managerial functions: *planning, organizing, leading,* and *controlling* (see Figure 1.2). The arrows linking these functions in Figure 1.2 suggest the sequence in which managers typically perform the functions. French manager Henri Fayol first outlined the nature of these managerial activities around the turn of the twentieth century in *General and Industrial Management,* a book that remains the classic statement of what managers must do to create a high-performing organization.[11]

Managers at all levels and in all departments–whether in small or large organizations, for-profit or not-for-profit organizations, or organizations that operate in one country or throughout the world–are responsible for performing these four functions, which we look at next. How well managers perform these functions determines how efficient and effective their organizations are.

Planning

planning Identifying and selecting appropriate goals; one of the four principal functions of management.

Planning is a process that managers use to identify and select appropriate goals and courses of action. Three steps in the planning process are (1) deciding which goals the organization will pursue, (2) deciding what courses of action to adopt to attain those goals, and (3) deciding how to allocate organizational resources to attain those goals. How well managers plan determines how effective and efficient the organization is–its performance level.[12]

As an example of planning in action, consider the situation confronting Michael Dell, CEO of Dell Computer, the most profitable PC maker and Apple's main competitor.[13] In 1984, the 19-year-old Dell saw an opportunity to enter the PC market by assembling PCs and then selling them directly to customers. Dell began to plan how to put his idea into practice. First, he decided that his goal was to sell an inexpensive PC, to undercut the prices of companies like Compaq and Apple. Second, he had to decide on a course of action to

Figure 1.2
Four Functions of Management

Planning
Choose appropriate organizational goals and courses of action to best achieve those goals
Organizing
Establish task and authority relationships that allow people to work together to achieve organization goals
Leading
Motivate, coordinate, and energize individuals and groups to work together to achieve organizational goals
Controlling
Establish accurate measuring and monitoring systems to evaluate how well the organization has achieved its goals

Michael Dell sits in the dorm room at the University of Texas, Austin where he launched his personal computer company as a college freshman. The room is now occupied by freshmen Russell Smith (left) and Jacob Frith, both from Plano, Texas.

achieve this goal. He decided to sell directly to customers by telephone and to bypass expensive computer stores that sold Compaq and Apple PCs. He also had to decide how to obtain low-cost components and how to tell potential customers about his products. Third, he had to decide how to allocate his limited funds (he only had $5,000) to buy labor and other resources. He chose to hire three people and work with them around a table to assemble his PCs.

Thus, to put his vision of making and selling PCs into practice, Dell had to plan, and as his organization grew, his plans changed and became progressively more complex. Dell and his managers are continually planning how to help the company maintain its position as the biggest and highest-performing PC maker. In 2003, Dell announced it would begin to sell printers and personal digital assistants (PDAs); this brought it into direct competition with Hewlett-Packard (HP) the leading printer maker, and Palm One, the maker of the Palm Pilot. In 2003, Dell also brought out its own Internet music player, the Digital Jukebox, to compete against Apple's iPod, and in 2004 it reduced the price of its player to compete more effectively against Apple. In April 2004, Dell's player was selling at $50 less that Apple's, and analysts were wondering what effect this would have on iPod sales and Apple's future performance.

strategy A cluster of decisions about what goals to pursue, what actions to take, and how to use resources to achieve goals.

As the battle between Dell and Apple suggests, the outcome of planning is a **strategy,** a cluster of decisions concerning what organizational goals to pursue, what actions to take, and how to use resources to achieve goals. The decisions that were the outcome of Michael Dell's planning formed a *low-cost strategy.* A low-cost strategy is a way of obtaining customers by making decisions that allow the organization to produce its goods or services cheaply so that prices can be kept low. Dell has been constantly refining this strategy and exploring new strategies to reduce costs. Dell has become the most profitable PC maker as a result of its low-cost strategy, and it is hoping to repeat its success in the music player business. By contrast, Apple's strategy has been to deliver new, exciting, and different computer and digital products, such as the iPod, to its customers–a strategy known as *differentiation.* The mini iPod was developed for people on the go, for example; it is as small as a (thick) credit card, has unique, easy-to-use controls, and comes in a variety of bright contemporary colors.[14]

Planning is a difficult activity because normally what goals an organization should pursue and how best to pursue them–which strategies to adopt–is not immediately clear. Managers take risks when they commit organizational resources to pursue a particular strategy. Either success or failure is a possible outcome of the planning process. Dell succeeded spectacularly, but many other PC makers either went out of business (such as Packard Bell and Digital) or lost huge sums of money (like IBM and AT&T) trying to compete in this industry. In Chapter 8 we focus on the planning process and on the strategies organizations can select to respond to opportunities or threats in an industry. The story of Patricia Russo's rise to power at Lucent illustrates well how important planning and strategy making are to a manager's career success.

Manager as a Person

New CEOs Bring Change at Avon and Lucent

Two global companies that have required a radical overhaul of their strategies in recent years are Avon, the well-known door-to-door selling cosmetics giant, and Lucent Technologies, the telecommunications company. In 2000, after several years of declining sales, Avon recognized the need for change and appointed Andrea Jung as its CEO, the first woman CEO in its history. Jung faced a tough task in trying to transform this tradition-laden company.[15] She began by searching for a new vision for the company.

Avon's main problem she decided was reaching beyond the typical 30-to-55-year-old woman who had always been its main customer. She decided to target the important 16-to-24-year-old segment and attract and build brand loyalty among young customers who will become its main customer base of the future. In 2003, a new Avon division called *Mark* began to distribute a new line of hip cometics designed specifically to meet the needs of this younger market segment. To meet the sales challenge of direct distribution to customers through a personal selling approach, Jung also decided to recruit a new generation of sales reps from the younger demographic groups. She hoped that with peers to serve their needs, its selling parties can be geared to the needs of this younger age group and its sales reps can be trained to respond to their unique needs.

The potential of this market is enormous for the 17 million women in this segment have a total purchasing power of almost $100 billion a year, and spend 20 percent of their income on beauty products. In 2001, Jung began to enthusiastically communicate her vision for Avon to 13,000 sales representatives who gathered in Las Vegas to preview Avon's new product lines, take in some shows, and listen to the new CEO. Jung let the sales representatives know that Avon's future success depended on their efforts and that they were at the heart of Avon.

Today, Avon has four million reps located around the world, and it plans to increase the number of its U.S. sales reps from 500,000 to 750,000 in the next few years.[16] In 2004 it reported record global profits on booming worldwide sales of its growing range of makeup, soaps, haircare, jewelry, and other products.

As Lucent's performance continued to plunge, because of shrinking sales due to the telecommunications bust in the early 2000s, it decided to bring back Patricia Russo (a former Lucent executive who had left to become the COO of Kodak) as its CEO. Russo faced a daunting task given that Lucent

Patricia Russo's industry knowledge and vision helped her establish a strategy that put Lucent's balance sheet back in the black.

lost over $16 billion in 2001.[17] How should she best position Lucent's different businesses to meet the needs of its global customers while continuing to find ways to reduce costs? Russo's answer was to refocus the company's activities on three main business areas: (1) enhancing telecommunications services, involving network design, management, and maintenance, to take advantage of the experience of Lucent's highly skilled engineers; (2) developing partnerships with other high-tech companies to jointly market their products; (3) boosting Lucent's ties with the federal government and offering a streamlined service to all areas of government from taxes to defense.[18] By 2004, the success of Russo's efforts was seen as Lucent finally broke even and returned to profit.[19]

Achieving such dramatic turnarounds at these companies was also the result of the way Jung and Russo changed the way their companies were organized. To quickly take advantage of the opportunities offered by the Internet and emerging information technology, both executives created a new organizing plan that focused on the need to develop and sell new products. At first, Avon's army of sales reps had viewed the Internet as a way of bypassing them and costing them their commissions. However, Jung worked hard to show reps that their company cared about them, and that customers who bought over the Internet would very likely prove to be good prospects for their personal selling approach once they had bought and tried Avon's products. Jung's predictions proved correct, Internet sales increased, not decreased, their commissions and its sales reps now actively embrace the new possibilities the Internet has opened up for their personal selling approach. In Lucent's case, utilizing the Internet meant streamlining services to customers such as large corporations and the federal government. In this way, Lucent could continuously monitor the performance of its customer's networks to prevent breakdowns in their operations.

Jung's flair and drive for making the most of Avon's resources is communicated clearly to reps in her leadership style. This is based on using her personality and charisma to convince sales reps that if they continue to work toward achieving her vision of making Avon the number one shopping place for women around the globe, the possibilities for them are endless. Russo, on her part noted that her return to Lucent was because "This was the only job I considered leaving for. It is in an industry I know, with customers and people I know." Her leadership approach is based on clearly communicating to her managers that her priorities are to improve relationships with customers and other companies to find new ways to create products and services they will value. For both CEOs, planning and organizing are vital functions that they insist must be continuously worked on by managers at all levels of the company.

Organizing

organizing Structuring working relationships in a way that allows organizational members to work together to achieve organizational goals; one of the four principal functions of management.

organizational structure A formal system of task and reporting relationships that coordinates and motivates organizational members so that they work together to achieve organizational goals.

Organizing is a process that managers use to establish a structure of working relationships that allow organizational members to interact and cooperate to achieve organizational goals. Organizing involves grouping people into departments according to the kinds of job-specific tasks they perform. In organizing, managers also lay out the lines of authority and responsibility between different individuals and groups, and they decide how best to coordinate organizational resources, particularly human resources.

The outcome of organizing is the creation of an **organizational structure,** a formal system of task and reporting relationships that coordinates and motivates members so that they work together to achieve organizational goals. Organizational structure determines how an organization's resources can be best used to create goods and services. As Dell Computer grew, for example, Michael Dell faced the issue of how to structure the organization. Early on he was hiring 100 new employees a week and deciding how to design his managerial hierarchy to best motivate and coordinate managers' activities. As his organization grew, he and his managers created progressively more complex kinds of organizational structures to help it achieve its goals. We examine the organizing process in detail in Chapters 9 through 11.

Leading

leading Articulating a clear vision and energizing and enabling organizational members so that they understand the part they play in achieving organizational goals; one of the four principal functions of management.

In **leading** managers not only articulate a clear vision for organizational members to follow but also energize and enable organizational members so that they understand the part they play in achieving organizational goals. Leadership depends on the use of power, influence, vision, persuasion, and communication skills to coordinate the behaviors of individuals and groups so that their activities and efforts are in harmony and to encourage employees to perform at a high level. The outcome of leadership is a high level of motivation and commitment among organizational members. Employees at Dell Computer, for example, responded well to Michael Dell's hands-on leadership style, which has resulted in a hardworking, committed workforce. Managers at Apple now appreciate Steve Jobs's new leadership style, a style based on his willingness to delegate authority and his ability to help managers resolve differences that could easily lead to bitter disputes and power struggles. We discuss the issues involved in managing and leading individuals and groups in Chapters 13 through 16.

Controlling

controlling Evaluating how well an organization is achieving its goals and taking action to maintain or improve performance; one of the four principal functions of management.

In **controlling,** managers evaluate how well an organization is achieving its goals and take action to maintain or improve performance. For example, managers monitor the performance of individuals, departments, and the organization as a whole to see whether they are meeting desired performance standards. Michael Dell learned early in his career how important this is; it took Steve Jobs longer. If standards are not being met, managers take action to improve performance.

The outcome of the control process is the ability to measure performance accurately and regulate organizational efficiency and effectiveness. To exercise control, managers must decide which goals to measure–perhaps goals pertaining to productivity, quality, or responsiveness to customers–and then they must design information and control systems that will provide the data they need to assess performance. The controlling function also allows managers to evaluate how well they themselves are performing the other three functions of management–planning, organizing, and leading–and to take corrective action.

Michael Dell had difficulty establishing effective control systems because his company was growing so rapidly and he lacked experienced managers. In 1988 Dell's costs soared because no controls were in place to monitor inventory, which had built up rapidly. In 1993 financial problems arose because of ill-advised foreign currency transactions. In 1994 Dell's new line of laptop computers crashed because poor quality control resulted in defective products, some of which caught fire. To solve these and other control problems, Dell hired experienced managers to put the right control systems in place. As a result, by 1998 Dell was able to make computers for about 10 percent less than its competitors, creating a major source of competitive advantage. By 2001 Dell had become so efficient it was driving its competitors out of the market because it had realized a 15 to 20 percent cost advantage over them.[20] By 2003 it was the biggest PC maker in the world. Controlling, like the other managerial functions, is an ongoing, fluid, always changing process that demands constant attention and action. We cover the most important aspects of the control function in Chapters 9, 11, 17, 18, and 19.

The four managerial functions–planning, organizing, leading, and controlling–are essential to a manager's job. At all levels in a managerial hierarchy, and across all departments in an organization, effective management means making decisions and managing these four activities successfully.

Types of Managers

To perform efficiently and effectively, organizations employ three types of managers–first-line managers, middle managers, and top managers–arranged in a hierarchy (see Figure 1.3, page 14). Typically, first-line managers report to middle managers, and middle managers report to top managers. Managers at each level have different but related responsibilities for utilizing organizational resources to increase efficiency and effectiveness. These three types of managers are grouped into departments (or *functions*) according to their specific job responsibilities. A **department,** such as manufacturing, accounting, or engineering, is a group of people who work together and possess similar skills or use the same kind of knowledge, tools, or techniques to perform their jobs. Within each department are all three levels of management. Next, we examine the reasons why organizations use a hierarchy of managers and group them into departments. We then examine some recent changes taking place in managerial hierarchies.

department A group of people who work together and possess similar skills or use the same knowledge, tools, or techniques to perform their jobs.

Levels of Management

As just discussed, organizations normally have three levels of management: first-line managers, middle managers, and top managers.

FIRST-LINE MANAGERS At the base of the managerial hierarchy are **first-line managers,** often called *supervisors*. They are responsible for the daily supervision of the nonmanagerial employees who perform many of the specific activities necessary to produce goods and services. First-line managers work in all departments or functions of an organization.

first-line manager A manager who is responsible for the daily supervision of nonmanagerial employees.

Figure 1.3
Types of Managers

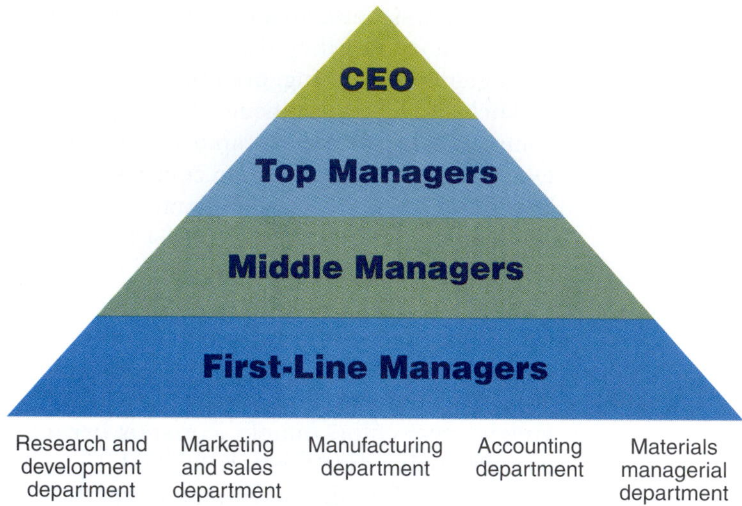

Examples of first-line managers include the supervisor of a work team in the manufacturing department of a car plant, the head nurse in the obstetrics department of a hospital, and the chief mechanic overseeing a crew of mechanics in the service function of a new-car dealership. At Dell Computer, first-line managers include the supervisors responsible for controlling the quality of Dell computers or the level of customer service provided by Dell's telephone salespeople. When Michael Dell started his company, he personally controlled the computer assembly process and thus performed as a first-line manager or supervisor.

middle manager A manager who supervises first-line managers and is responsible for finding the best way to use resources to achieve organizational goals.

MIDDLE MANAGERS Supervising the first-line managers are **middle managers,** responsible for finding the best way to organize human and other resources to achieve organizational goals. To increase efficiency, middle managers find ways to help first-line managers and nonmanagerial employees better utilize resources to reduce manufacturing costs or improve customer service. To increase effectiveness, middle managers evaluate whether the goals that the organization is pursuing are appropriate and suggest to top managers ways in which goals should be changed. Very often, the suggestions that middle managers make to top managers can dramatically increase organizational performance. A major part of the middle manager's job is developing and fine-tuning skills and know-how, such as manufacturing or marketing expertise, that allow the organization to be efficient and effective. Middle managers make thousands of specific decisions about the production of goods and services: Which first-line supervisors should be chosen for this particular project? Where can we find the highest-quality resources? How should employees be organized to allow them to make the best use of resources?

Behind a first-class sales force look for the middle managers responsible for training, motivating, and rewarding the salespeople. Behind a committed staff of high school teachers look for the principal who energizes them to find ways to obtain the resources they need to do outstanding and innovative jobs in the classroom.

TOP MANAGERS In contrast to middle managers, **top managers** are responsible for the performance of *all* departments.[21] They have *cross-departmental*

top manager A manager who establishes organizational goals, decides how departments should interact, and monitors the performance of middle managers.

responsibility. Top managers establish organizational goals, such as which goods and services the company should produce; they decide how the different departments should interact; and they monitor how well middle managers in each department utilize resources to achieve goals.[22] Top managers are ultimately responsible for the success or failure of an organization, and their performance (like that of Steve Jobs and Patricia Russo) is continually scrutinized by people inside and outside the organization, such as other employees and investors.[23]

The *chief executive officer (CEO)* is a company's most senior and important manager, the one to whom all other top managers report. Today, the term *chief operating officer (COO)* is often used to refer to the top manager who is being groomed to take over as CEO when the current CEO retires or leaves the company. Together, the CEO and COO are responsible for developing good working relationships among the top managers of various departments (manufacturing and marketing, for example); usually top managers have the title "vice president." A central concern of the CEO is the creation of a smoothly functioning **top-management team,** a group composed of the CEO, the COO, and the department heads most responsible for helping achieve organizational goals.[24]

top-management team A group composed of the CEO, the COO, and the heads of the most important departments.

The relative importance of planning, organizing, leading, and controlling–the four managerial functions–to any particular manager depends on the manager's position in the managerial hierarchy.[25] The amount of time that managers spend planning and organizing resources to maintain and improve organizational performance increases as they ascend the hierarchy (see Figure 1.4).[26] Top managers devote most of their time to planning and organizing, the functions so crucial to determining an organization's long-term performance. The lower that managers' positions are in the hierarchy, the more time the managers spend leading and controlling first-line managers or nonmanagerial employees.

Figure 1.4
Relative Amount of Time That Managers Spend on the Four Managerial Functions

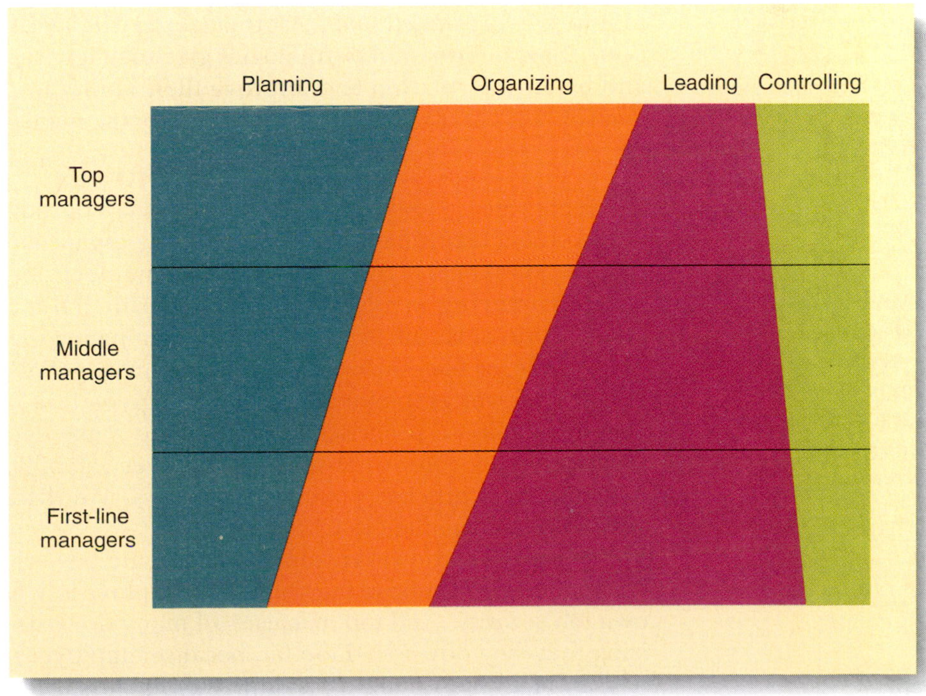

Areas of Managers

Because so much of a manager's responsibility is to acquire and develop critical resources, managers are typically members of specific departments.[27] Managers inside a department possess job-specific skills and are known as, for example, marketing managers or manufacturing managers. As Figure 1.3 indicates, first-line, middle, and top managers, who differ from one another by virtue of their job-specific responsibilities, are found in each of an organization's major departments. Inside each department, the managerial hierarchy also emerges.

At Dell Computer, for example, Michael Dell hired experts to take charge of the marketing, sales, and manufacturing departments and to develop work procedures to help first-line managers control the company's explosive sales growth. The head of manufacturing quickly found that he had no time to supervise computer assembly, so he recruited manufacturing middle managers from other companies to assume this responsibility.

Recent Changes in Managerial Hierarchies

The tasks and responsibilities of managers at different levels have been changing dramatically in recent years. Two major factors that have led to these changes are global competition and advances in new information technology (IT) and in e-commerce. Stiff competition for resources from organizations both at home and abroad has put increased pressure on all managers to improve efficiency, effectiveness, and organizational performance. Increasingly, top managers are encouraging lower-level managers to look beyond the goals of their own departments and take a cross-departmental view to find new opportunities to improve organizational performance, as Michael Dell and Steve Jobs have done. New information technologies give managers at all levels access to more and better information and improve their ability to plan, organize, lead, and control; this has also revolutionized the way the managerial hierarchy works.[28]

RESTRUCTURING AND OUTSOURCING To take advantage of IT and e-commerce and their ability to reduce operating costs, CEOs and top-management teams have been restructuring organizations and outsourcing specific organizational activities to reduce the number of employees on the payroll.

restructuring
Downsizing an organization by eliminating the jobs of large numbers of top, middle, and first-line managers and nonmanagerial employees.

Restructuring involves the use of information technology to downsize an organization or shrink its operations by eliminating the jobs of large numbers of top, middle, or first-line managers and nonmanagerial employees. For example, IT allows fewer employees to perform a given task because it increases each person's ability to process information and make decisions more quickly and accurately. U.S. companies are spending over $50 billion a year on advanced IT that improves efficiency and effectiveness. We discuss IT's many dramatic effects on management in Chapter 18.

Restructuring, however, can produce some powerful negative outcomes. IT can reduce the morale of the remaining employees, who are worried about their own job security. And top managers of many downsized organizations are realizing that they downsized too far, because employees complain they are overworked and because more customers complain about poor-quality service.[29]

outsourcing Contracting with another company, usually abroad, to have it perform an activity the organization previously performed itself.

Outsourcing involves contracting with another company, usually in a low-cost country abroad, to have it perform an activity the organization previously performed itself, such as manufacturing or marketing. Outsourcing promotes efficiency by reducing costs and by allowing an organization to make better use of its remaining resources. The need to respond to low-cost global competition has speeded outsourcing dramatically in the 2000s. Three million U.S. jobs in the manufacturing sector have been lost since 2000 as companies moved their operations to countries such as China, Taiwan, and Malaysia. Tens of thousands of high-paying jobs in IT have moved to countries like India and Russia, where programmers work for one-third the salary of those in the United States.

Large for-profit organizations today typically employ 10 to 20 percent fewer employees than they did 10 years ago because of restructuring and outsourcing. General Motors, IBM, AT&T, HP, Dell, and Du Pont are among the thousands of organizations that have streamlined their operations to increase efficiency and effectiveness. The argument is that the managers and employees who have lost their jobs will find employment in new and growing U.S. organizations where their skills and experience will be better utilized. For example, the millions of manufacturing jobs that have been lost overseas will soon be replaced by higher-paying U.S. jobs in the service sector that are made possible because of the growth in global trade.

empowerment The expansion of employees' knowledge, tasks, and responsibilities.

self-managed team A group of employees who supervises their own activities and monitor the quality of the goods and services they provide.

EMPOWERMENT AND SELF-MANAGED TEAMS Another major change in management has taken place at the level of first-line managers, who typically supervise the employees engaged in producing goods and services. By taking advantage of advanced IT, many companies have taken two steps to reduce costs and improve quality. One is the **empowerment** of their workforces by using powerful new software programs to expand employees' knowledge, tasks, and responsibilities. The other is the creation of **self-managed teams**–groups of employees given responsibility for supervising their own activities and for monitoring the quality of the goods and services they provide.[30]

Employees of 24/7 Customer in Bangalore provide phone support for United States and United Kingdom clients and must work through the night. It is estimated that up to 1.6 million U.S. jobs will shift offshore by 2010, however, the U.S. Bureau of Labor Statistics expects 22 million new jobs will be created by other industries.

Such teams input the results of their activities into computers, and through IT middle managers have immediate access to what is happening. As a result of IT, members of self-managed teams assume many of the responsibilities and duties previously performed by first-line managers.[31] What is the role of the first-line manager in this new IT work context? First-line managers act as coaches or mentors whose job is not to tell employees what to do but to provide advice and guidance and help teams find new ways to perform their tasks more efficiently.[32] Empire's use of IT to change the tasks and responsibilities of its sales force illustrates many important ways in which IT can affect the management process.

Information Technology Byte

Empire Insurance Uses CRM to Boost Sales

In 2001, Empire, the largest health insurance provider in New York, sold its health insurance policies through 1,800 sales agents who were responsible for collecting all the customer-specific information needed to determine the price of each customer's insurance policy. Once they had the necessary information, the agents phoned Empire's quotes department, where first-line managers drew up and approved price quotes. These quotes were then relayed to the agents, who in turn relayed them to the customers, who then often modified their requests to lower the cost of the insurance policy. For each modified request, the agent then had to phone the supervisor at Empire again to get a revised price quote. This often happened several times over, with the result that it frequently took over 20 days to close a sale and another 10 days for the customer to get his or her insurance card.

Recognizing that these delays were losing the company sales, Empire's managers decided to examine how a new type of software called *customer relationship management (CRM)* could help improve the sales process. CRM software creates a Web-based IT platform that monitors and controls each of the specific activities involved in selling and delivering products to customers, such as salespeople's selling activities, product pricing, and after-sales service. CRM software works to integrate all the activities necessary for salespeople in the field to make important decisions and make them quickly.[33]

CRM software improves sales performance by giving salespeople the tools they need to complete customer transactions on the spot.

To see if CRM would help improve performance, Empire's managers analyzed all the specific activities involved in their company's sales process. After doing so, they decided to implement a Web-based CRM system that would empower each agent to calculate the insurance quote and offer the customer a binding legal contract. Using the new software, agents themselves now enter all relevant customer data online, and Empire's CRM system generates the quote in a few seconds. Sitting face-to-face with a customer, an agent can continually modify a policy until its price suits the customer. The sales process that took over 20 days before can now be completed in a few hours using CRM, and customers receive their insurance cards in two to three days.

By promoting the flow of information within the sales function, CRM systems eliminate many problems, such as getting approval for a customer quote and offering a price discount. The role of the first-level manager in the new system is to watch how the now empowered sales agents close sales in order to detect ways to help all agents improve closings.[34] Having access to all salespeople's activities, managers, for example, can detect whether a certain selling approach works better than another, determine how much price discount should be offered, and identify changing customer needs so that they can better tailor the product to meet those needs. In essence, Empire's new CRM system not only empowers sales agents but also helps to pinpoint specific ways to improve best sales practices that can be shared across the entire sales force.

John Deere, the well-known manufacturer of tractors, also took steps to empower its employees to raise performance. Deere's managers realized that the employees who assemble its vehicles, with their detailed knowledge about how Deere products work, could become persuasive salespeople. So groups of these employees are now given training in sales techniques and sent to visit Deere customers to explain to them how to operate and service the organization's new products. While speaking with customers, these newly empowered "salespeople" are able to collect information that helps Deere develop new products that appeal to customers. The new sales jobs are temporary. Employees go on assignment but then return to the production line, where they use their new knowledge to find ways to improve efficiency and quality.

Its moves to empower employees have been so successful that Deere negotiated a new agreement with its workers designed to promote empowerment. The agreement specifies that pay increases will be based on workers' learning new skills and completing college courses in areas such as computer programming that will help the company increase efficiency and quality. And the satisfaction that workers feel as they use their new skills and develop new capabilities will increase their commitment to the company and thus help it succeed.

IT and Managerial Roles and Skills

As the example of Empire suggests, IT is having many important effects on the way managers perform their four functions. IT is also having major effects on the way managers perform their roles and on the skills they develop to perform those roles effectively. A **managerial role** is a set of specific tasks that a manager is expected to perform because of the position he or she holds in an organization. One well-known model of managerial roles was developed by Henry Mintzberg, who detailed 10 specific roles that effective managers undertake. Although Mintzberg's roles overlap with Fayol's model, they are useful because they focus on what managers do in a typical hour, day, or week in an organization as they go about the actual job of managing.[35] Below, we discuss these roles and the skills managers need to develop to perform effectively in a time when advanced IT and e-commerce are changing the way managers behave.

managerial role The set of specific tasks that a manager is expected to perform because of the position he or she holds in an organization.

Managerial Roles Identified by Mintzberg

Henry Mintzberg reduced to 10 roles the thousands of specific tasks that managers need to perform as they plan, organize, lead, and control organizational resources.[36] Managers assume each of these roles to influence the behavior of individuals and groups inside and outside the organization. People inside the organization include other managers and employees. People outside the organization include shareholders, customers, suppliers, the local community in which an organization is located, and any local or government agency that has an interest in the organization and what it does.[37] Mintzberg grouped the 10 roles into three broad categories: *decisional, informational,* and *interpersonal,* which are described in Table 1.1. Managers often perform many of these roles from minute to minute while engaged in the more general functions of planning, organizing, leading, and controlling. IT is changing how they do so.

DECISIONAL ROLES Decisional roles are closely associated with the methods managers use to plan strategy and utilize resources. IT helps a manager in the role of *entrepreneur* by providing more and better information to use in deciding which projects or programs to initiate and in investing resources to increase organizational performance. As a *disturbance handler,* a manager can get realtime information through IT to manage the unexpected event or crisis that threatens the organization and to implement solutions quickly. As a *resource allocator,* a manager using human resource software systems from companies such as Oracle and SAP has easy access to the detailed information needed to decide how best to use people and other resources to increase organizational performance. While engaged in that role, the manager must also be a *negotiator,* reaching agreements with other managers or groups claiming the first right to resources or with the organization and outside groups such as suppliers or customers. The emergence of electronic markets and business-to-business (B2B) networks that link organizations to thousands of suppliers is but one example of the many ways IT helps managers perform the negotiator role.

INFORMATIONAL ROLES Informational roles are closely associated with the tasks necessary to obtain and transmit information and so have obviously been dramatically impacted by IT. Acting as a *disseminator,* a manager can use IT to quickly and effectively transmit information to employees to influence their work attitudes and behavior. Wal-Mart, for example, has nationwide videoconferencing linking top managers to each individual store and uses the Internet to provide up-to-date training programs to its employees. IT also provides managers with much greater ability to act as a *spokesperson* and promote the organization so that people inside and outside the organization respond positively to it.

INTERPERSONAL ROLES Managers assume interpersonal roles to provide direction and supervision for both employees and the organization as a whole. IT can make managers much more visible throughout the organization. As a *figurehead,* the person who symbolizes an organization or a department, a CEO can use the Internet to inform employees and other interested parties, such as shareholders, about what the organization's mission is and what it is

Table 1.1
Managerial Roles Identified by Mintzberg

Type of Role	Specific Role	Examples of Role Activities
DECISIONAL	Entrepreneur	Commit organizational resources to develop innovative goods and services; decide to expand internationally to obtain new customers for the organization's products.
	Disturbance Handler	Move quickly to take corrective action to deal with unexpected problems facing the organization from the external environment, such as a crisis like an oil spill, or from the internal environment, such as producing faulty goods or services.
	Resource Allocator	Allocate organizational resources among different functions and departments of the organization; set budgets and salaries of middle and first-level managers.
	Negotiator	Work with suppliers, distributors, and labor unions to reach agreements about the quality and price of input, technical, and human resources; work with other organizations to establish agreements to pool resources to work on joint projects.
INTERPERSONAL	Figurehead	Outline future organizational goals to employees at company meetings; open a new corporate headquarters building; state the organization's ethical guidelines and the principles of behavior employees are to follow in their dealings with customers and suppliers.
	Leader	Provide an example for employees to follow; give direct commands and orders to subordinates; make decisions concerning the use of human and technical resources; mobilize employee support for specific organizational goals.
	Liaison	Coordinate the work of managers in different departments; establish alliances between different organizations to share resources to produce new goods and services.
INFORMATIONAL	Monitor	Evaluate the performance of managers in different functions and take corrective action to improve their performance; watch for changes occurring in the external and internal environments that may affect the organization in the future.
	Disseminator	Inform employees about changes taking place in the external and internal environments that will affect them and the organization; communicate to employees the organization's vision and purpose.
	Spokesperson	Launch a national advertising campaign to promote new goods and services; give a speech to inform the local community about the organization's future intentions.

seeking to achieve. At all levels managers can use email and the Internet to act as figureheads and role models who establish appropriate ways to behave in the organization. For example, anybody in Microsoft is allowed to directly email CEO Bill Gates if he or she thinks it necessary. For similar reasons IT allows managers to perform better as *leaders* because they have more and better-quality information available for training, counseling, and mentoring subordinates to

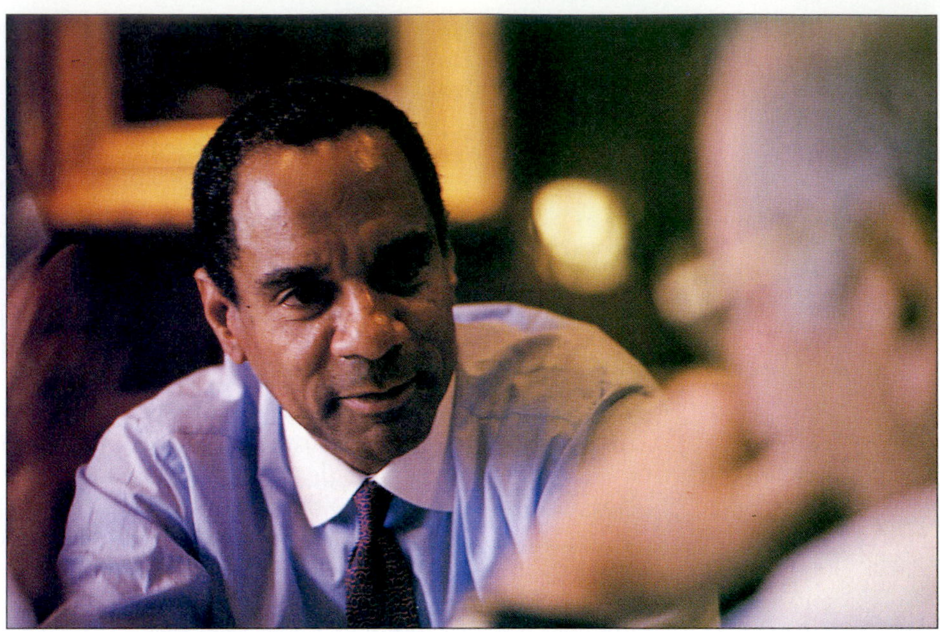

Ken Chenault, pictured here, is the President and CEO of American Express Company. Promoted in 1997, he climbed the ranks from their Travel Related Services Company, thanks to his "even temper and unrelenting drive." Respected by colleagues for his personality, most will say they can't remember him losing his temper or raising his voice. His open door policy for subordinates allows him to mentor AmEx mangers and encourages all to enter and "speak their minds."

help them reach their full potential. Finally, as a *liaison,* a manager can use IT to improve his or her ability to link and coordinate the activities of people and groups both inside and outside the organization.

Terri Patsos Stanley, the manager of a small short-term rental business, has used IT to help her better perform many of these roles. Patsos Stanley pioneered the concept of providing business travelers with high-quality apartments as an alternative to staying in more expensive and often less convenient hotels in the Boston area. Her company, Boston Short-Term Rentals, grew rapidly because of her drive to keep costs down and customers happy. To achieve these goals, Patsos Stanley had to learn all the different managerial roles.[38]

As the president of a rapidly growing company, Patsos Stanley is continually required to make decisions. In the role of *entrepreneur,* she searched for opportunities to increase revenues by increasing the number of apartments that she manages. One solution she adopted was to use the Internet and develop a strong presence on the World Wide Web to attract customers. As a *disturbance handler,* she deals with unexpected problems such as plumbing breakdowns in the middle of the night; therefore, all staff members are connected by electronic paging and personal messaging devices to speed response to customer problems. As a *resource allocator,* she decides how much money to spend to refurbish and upgrade the apartments to maintain their luxury appeal. She maintains close contact with the apartment owners through the Internet–she sends digital images of the apartments over the Web, for example. As a *negotiator,* she contracts with other organizations such as cleaning or painting services to obtain the most economical services her business requires–once again, the information available through the Internet makes this more efficient.

With more than 200 apartments to oversee, Boston Short-Term Rentals' information management is a vital activity, and Patsos Stanley's role as *monitor* is important. The sophisticated computer system she developed allows her to evaluate the performance of her business by occupancy rates, customer complaints, and other indicators of the quality of her service. The system facilitates her ability to respond quickly to problems as they arise. In her ongoing role as *disseminator,* she uses IT to update her staff with information about changes in visitor arrivals and departures, but as a *spokesperson* she is always on the phone to persuade visitors who may be somewhat hesitant about staying in an apartment that they know nothing about as opposed to staying with a hotel chain that has a well-recognized name.

In fact, Patsos Stanley learned the importance of an extremely hands-on approach to managing her company. She and her employees personally greet the new arrivals and perform the activities that porters, the concierge, and front-desk staff do in the typical hotel. In interpersonal terms, Patsos Stanley is the *figurehead* who provides the personal touch her guests expect; she is the person they can contact if problems arise. With her small staff of carpenters, electricians, interior decorators, and maintenance workers, she acts as a *leader,* energizing them to provide the quick service that guests expect. She is also a *liaison,* able to link her guests to organizations that provide services they may need, such as dry cleaning, catering, or hairdressing.

Patsos Stanley enjoys the variety of her work and relishes the pleasure of meeting the senior managers, actors, and overseas visitors who stay in the apartments.[39] The owner/manager of any small business such as Boston Short-Term Rentals continually performs all these managerial roles.

Being a Manager

Our discussion of managerial roles may seem to suggest that a manager's job is highly orchestrated and that management is a logical, orderly process in which managers rationally calculate the best way to use resources to achieve organizational goals. In reality, being a manager often involves acting emotionally and relying on gut feelings. Quick, immediate reactions to situations, rather than deliberate thought and reflection, are an important aspect of managerial action.[40] Often, managers are overloaded with responsibilities, do not have time to spend on analyzing every nuance of a situation, and therefore make decisions in uncertain conditions without being sure which outcomes will be best.[41] Moreover, for top managers in particular, the current situation is constantly changing, and a decision that seems right today may prove to be wrong tomorrow.

The range of problems that managers face is enormous (*high variety*). Managers frequently must deal with many problems simultaneously (*fragmentation*), often must make snap decisions (*brevity*), and many times must rely on experience gained throughout their careers to do their jobs to the best of their abilities.[42] It is no small wonder that many managers claim that they are performing their jobs well if they are right just half of the time, and it is understandable why many experienced managers accept failure by their subordinates as a normal part of the learning experience. Managers and their subordinates learn both from their successes and from their failures.

Managerial Skills

Both education and experience enable managers to recognize and develop the personal skills they need to put organizational resources to their best use. Michael Dell realized from the start that he lacked sufficient experience and technical expertise in marketing, finance, and planning to guide his company

Figure 1.5
Conceptual, Human, and Technical Skills Needed by Three Levels of Management

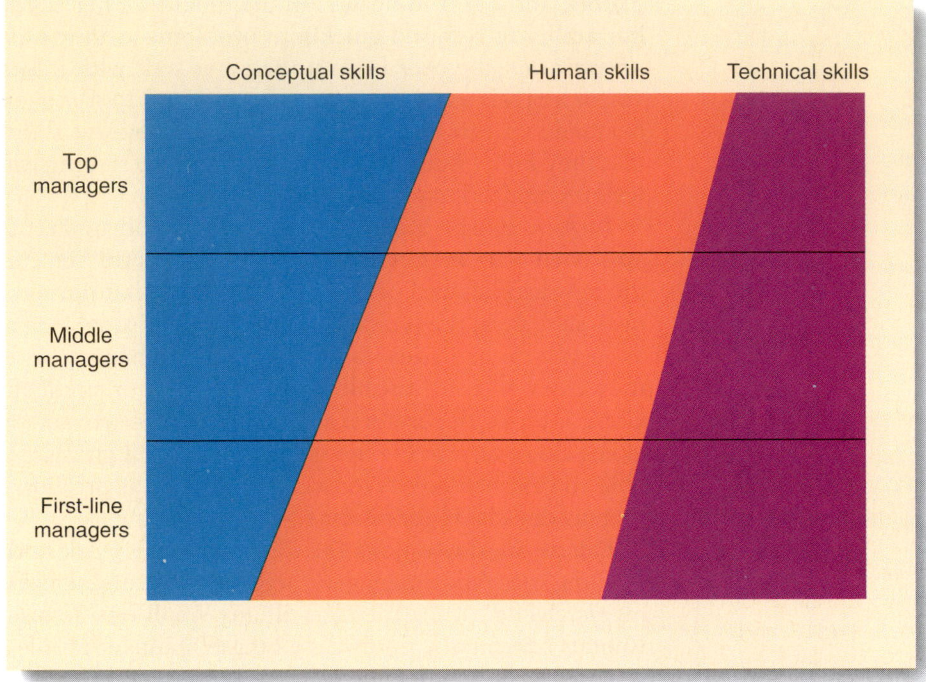

alone. Thus, he recruited experienced managers from other information technology companies, such as IBM and HP, to help him build his company. Research has shown that education and experience help managers acquire three principal types of skills: *conceptual, human,* and *technical*.[43] As you might expect, the level of these skills that managers need depends on their level in the managerial hierarchy. Typically planning and organizing require higher levels of conceptual skills, while leading and controlling require more human and technical skills (see Figure 1.5).

conceptual skills
The ability to analyze and diagnose a situation and to distinguish between cause and effect.

CONCEPTUAL SKILLS **Conceptual skills** are demonstrated in the ability to analyze and diagnose a situation and to distinguish between cause and effect. Top managers require the best conceptual skills because their primary responsibilities are planning and organizing.[44] By all accounts, Steve Jobs was reappointed as CEO of Apple because of his ability to identify new opportunities and mobilize managers and other resources to take advantage of those opportunities.

Formal education and training are very important in helping managers develop conceptual skills. Business training at the undergraduate and graduate (MBA) levels provides many of the conceptual tools (theories and techniques in marketing, finance, and other areas) that managers need to perform their roles effectively. The study of management helps develop the skills that allow managers to understand the big picture confronting an organization. The ability to focus on the big picture lets managers see beyond the situation immediately at hand and consider choices while keeping in mind the organization's long-term goals.

Today, continuing management education and training, including training in advanced IT, are an integral step in building managerial skills because new theories and techniques are constantly being developed to improve organizational effectiveness, such as B2B networks. A quick scan through a magazine such as

BusinessWeek or *Fortune* reveals a host of seminars on topics such as advanced marketing, finance, leadership, and human resources management that are offered to managers at many levels in the organization, from the most senior corporate executives to middle managers. Microsoft, IBM, Motorola, and many other organizations designate a portion of each manager's personal budget to be used at the manager's discretion to attend management development programs.

In addition, organizations may wish to develop a particular manager's abilities in a specific skill area–perhaps to learn an advanced component of departmental skills, such as international bond trading, or to learn the skills necessary to implement a new IT system. The organization thus pays for managers to attend specialized programs to develop these skills. Indeed, one signal that a manager is performing well is an organization's willingness to invest in that manager's skill development. Similarly, many nonmanagerial employees who are performing at a high level (because they have studied management) are often sent to intensive management training programs to develop their management skills and to prepare them for promotion to first-level management positions.

human skills The ability to understand, alter, lead, and control the behavior of other individuals and groups.

HUMAN SKILLS **Human skills** include the ability to understand, alter, lead, and control the behavior of other individuals and groups. The ability to communicate, to coordinate, and to motivate people, and to mold individuals into a cohesive team, distinguishes effective from ineffective managers. By all accounts, Steve Jobs, Michael Dell, Patricia Russo, and Terri Patsos Stanley all possess a high level of these human skills.

Like conceptual skills, human skills can be learned through education and training, as well as be developed through experience.[45] Organizations increasingly utilize advanced programs in leadership skills and team leadership as they seek to capitalize on the advantages of self-managed teams.[46] To manage personal interactions effectively, each person in an organization needs to learn how to empathize with other people–to understand their viewpoints and the problems they face. One way to help managers understand their personal strengths and weaknesses is to have their superiors, peers, and subordinates provide feedback about their performance in the roles identified by Mintzberg. Thorough and direct feedback allows managers to develop their human skills.

technical skills The job-specific knowledge and techniques required to perform an organizational role.

TECHNICAL SKILLS **Technical skills** are the job-specific knowledge and techniques required to perform an organizational role. Examples include a manager's specific manufacturing, accounting, marketing, and, increasingly, IT skills. Managers need a range of technical skills to be effective. The array of technical skills managers need depends on their positions in their organizations. The manager of a restaurant, for example, may need cooking skills to fill in for an absent cook, accounting and bookkeeping skills to keep track of receipts and costs and to administer the payroll, and aesthetic skills to keep the restaurant looking attractive for customers.

Effective managers need all three kinds of skills–conceptual, human, and technical. The absence of even one managerial skill can lead to failure. One of the biggest problems that people who start small businesses confront is their lack of appropriate conceptual and human skills. Someone who has the technical skills to start a new business does not necessarily know how to manage the venture successfully. Similarly, one of the biggest problems that scientists or engineers who switch careers from research to management confront is their lack of effective human skills. Management skills, roles, and functions are closely related, and wise managers or prospective managers are constantly in search of the latest educational contributions to help them develop the conceptual, human, and technical skills they need to function in today's changing and increasingly competitive global environment.

competencies The specific set of skills, abilities, and experiences that allows one manager to perform at a higher level than another manager in a particular setting.

Today, the term **competencies** is often used to refer to the specific set of skills, abilities, and experiences that gives one manager the ability to perform at a higher level than another manager in a particular organizational setting. Developing such competencies through education and training has become a major priority for both aspiring managers and the organizations they work for. As we discussed earlier, many people are enrolling in advanced management courses, but many companies, such as General Electric (GE) and IBM have established their own colleges to train and develop their employees and managers at all levels. Every year, for example, GE puts thousands of its employees through management programs designed to identify the employees who the company believes have superior competencies and whom it can develop to become its future top managers. In many organizations promotion is closely tied to a manager's ability to acquire the competencies that a particular company believes are important.[47] At 3M, for example, the ability to successfully lead a new product development team is viewed as a vital requirement for promotion; at IBM the ability to attract and retain clients is viewed as a vital competency its consultants must possess. We discuss specific kinds of managerial competencies in most of the chapters of this book.

Challenges For Management in a Global Environment

Because the world has been changing more rapidly than ever before, managers and other employees throughout an organization must perform at higher and higher levels.[48] In the last 20 years, competition between organizations competing domestically (in the same country) and globally (in countries abroad) has increased dramatically. The rise of **global organizations,** organizations that operate and compete in more than one country, has put severe pressure on many organizations to improve their performance and to identify better ways to use their resources. The successes of the German chemical companies Schering and Hoechst, Italian furniture manufacturer Natuzzi, Korean electronics companies Samsung and LG, Brazilian plane maker Embraer, and Europe's Airbus Industries are putting pressure on organizations in other countries to raise their level of performance to compete successfully with these global companies.

global organizations Organizations that operate and compete in more than one country.

Even in the not-for-profit sector, global competition is spurring change. Schools, universities, police forces, and government agencies are reexamining their operations because of looking at the way things are done in other countries. For example, many curriculum and teaching changes in the United States have resulted from the study of methods that Japanese and European school systems use. Similarly, European and Asian hospital systems have learned much from the U.S. system–which may be the most effective, though not the most efficient, in the world.

Today, managers who make no attempt to learn and adapt to changes in the global environment find themselves reacting rather than innovating, and their organizations often become uncompetitive and fail.[49] Four major challenges stand out for managers in today's world: building a competitive advantage, maintaining ethical standards, managing a diverse workforce, and utilizing new information systems and technologies.

Building Competitive Advantage

competitive advantage The ability of one organization to outperform other organizations because it produces desired goods or services more efficiently and effectively than they do.

What are the most important lessons for managers and organizations to learn if they are to reach and remain at the top of the competitive environment of business? The answer relates to the use of organizational resources to build a competitive advantage. **Competitive advantage** is the ability of one organization to outperform other organizations because it produces desired goods or services more efficiently and effectively than its competitors. The four building blocks of competitive advantage are superior *efficiency; quality; speed, flexibility,* and *innovation;* and *responsiveness to customers* (see Figure 1.6).

INCREASING EFFICIENCY Organizations increase their efficiency when they reduce the quantity of resources (such as people and raw materials) they use to produce goods or services. In today's competitive environment, organizations constantly are seeking new ways to use their resources to improve efficiency. Many organizations are training their workforces in the new skills and techniques needed to operate heavily computerized assembly plants. Similarly, cross-training gives employees the range of skills they need to perform many different tasks, and organizing employees in new ways, such as in self-managed teams, allows them to make good use of their skills. These are important steps in the effort to improve productivity. Japanese and German companies invest far more in training employees than do American or Italian companies.

Managers must improve efficiency if their organizations are to compete successfully with companies operating in Mexico, Malaysia, and other countries where employees are paid comparatively low wages. New methods must be

Figure 1.6
Building Blocks of Competitive Advantage

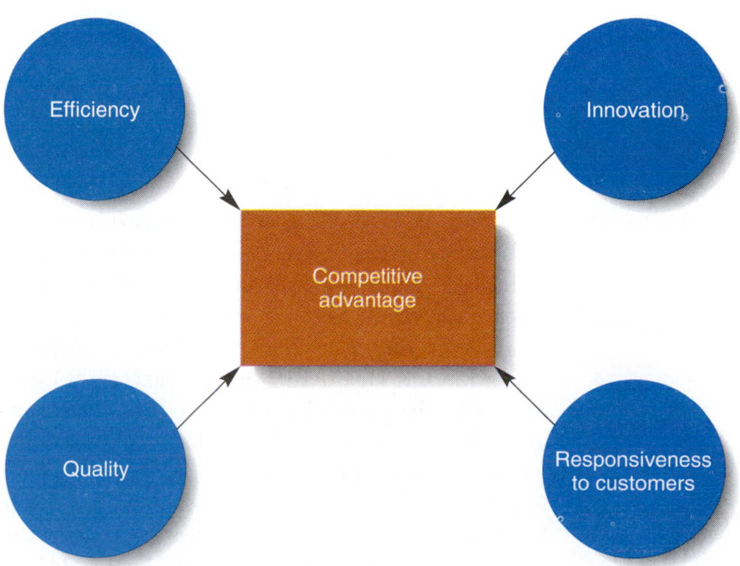

devised either to increase efficiency or to gain some other competitive advantage–higher-quality goods, for example–if outsourcing and the loss of jobs to low-cost countries are to be prevented.

INCREASING QUALITY The challenge from global organizations such as Korean electronics manufacturers, Mexican agricultural producers, and European marketing and financial firms also has increased pressure on companies to improve the skills and abilities of their workforces in order to improve the quality of their goods and services. One major thrust to improving quality has been to introduce the quality-enhancing techniques known as *total quality management (TQM)*. Employees involved in TQM are often organized into quality control teams and are responsible for continually finding new and better ways to perform their jobs; they also must monitor and evaluate the quality of the goods they produce. TQM is based on a significant new philosophy of managing behavior in organizations; we thoroughly discuss this approach and ways of managing TQM successfully in Chapter 9.

INCREASING SPEED, FLEXIBILITY, AND INNOVATION Today, companies can win or lose the competitive race depending on their speed–how fast they can bring new products to market–or their flexibility–how easily they can change or alter the way they perform their activities to respond to the actions of their competitors. Companies that have speed and flexibility are agile competitors: Their managers have superior planning and organizing abilities; they can think ahead, decide what to do, and then speedily mobilize their resources to respond to a changing environment. We examine how managers can build speed and flexibility in their organizations in later chapters. Steve Jobs's goal is to make Apple an agile company that can react to the continuous changes taking place in computing and digital entertainment so that it can build a competitive advantage.

Innovation, the process of creating new or improved goods and services that customers want or developing better ways to produce or provide goods and services, poses a special challenge. Managers must create an organizational setting in which people are encouraged to be innovative. Typically, innovation takes place in small groups or teams; management decentralizes control of work activities to team members and creates an organizational culture that rewards risk taking. Understanding and managing innovation and creating a work setting that encourages risk taking are among the most difficult managerial tasks. Innovation is discussed in depth in Chapter 19.

INCREASING RESPONSIVENESS TO CUSTOMERS Organizations compete for customers with their products and services, so training employees to be responsive to customers' needs is vital for all organizations, but particularly for service organizations. Retail stores, banks, and hospitals, for example, depend entirely on their employees to perform behaviors that result in high-quality service at a reasonable cost.[50] As many countries (the United States, Canada, and Great Britain are just a few) move toward a more service-based economy (in part because of the loss of manufacturing jobs to China, Malaysia, and other countries with low labor costs), managing behavior in service organizations is becoming increasingly important. Many organizations are empowering their customer service employees and giving them the authority to take the lead in providing high-quality customer service. As noted previously, the empowering of nonmanagerial employees changes the role of first-line managers and often leads to the more efficient use of organizational resources.

Achieving a competitive advantage requires that managers use all their skills and expertise to develop resources and improve efficiency, quality, innovation, and responsiveness to customers. We revisit this theme often as we examine the ways managers plan strategies, organize resources and activities, and lead and control people and groups to effectively use human and other resources to achieve organizational goals.

Maintaining Ethical and Socially Responsible Standards

While mobilizing organizational resources, managers at all levels are under considerable pressure to increase the level at which their organizations perform.[51] For example, top managers receive pressure from shareholders to increase the performance of the entire organization to boost the stock price, improve profits, or raise dividends. In turn, top managers may then pressure middle managers to find new ways to use organizational resources to increase efficiency or quality and thus attract new customers and earn more revenues.

Pressure to increase performance can be healthy for an organization because it causes managers to question the way the organization is working and it encourages them to find new and better ways to plan, organize, lead, and control. However, too much pressure to perform can be harmful.[52] It may induce managers to behave unethically in dealings with individuals and groups both inside and outside the organization.[53] For example, a purchasing manager for a large retail chain might buy inferior clothing as a cost-cutting measure; or to secure a large foreign contract, a sales manager in a large defense company might offer bribes to foreign officials. In 2004, the four top executives of Lucent's Korean division were fired after it was revealed they used bribery to obtain lucrative contracts for Lucent in that country.[54] The issue of social responsibility concerns the obligations that a company should have toward people and groups such as customers or the communities in which they operate. An example of companies that act in a socially irresponsible and unethical way is described in the following "Ethics in Action."

Ethics in Action

Diet Supplement Makers and the FDA

On April 12, 2004, it became illegal to make or sell the dietary supplement ephedra in the United States.[55] The Food and Drug Administration (FDA) had finally obtained information from users and from makers of ephedra pills, such as Yellow Jackets and Black Beauties, that revealed over 16,000 adverse-report events experienced by users of the drug. At least 36 deaths were directly related to the use of the drug, including the death of Baltimore Oriole pitcher Steven Bechler in 2003.

Ephedra has been widely available for a decade; why did it take the FDA so long to ban the use of the drug? Diet supplement makers, unlike major pharmaceutical companies, have been shielded by a 1994 law. The law does not require that the makers of dietary supplements report adverse incidents to the FDA, but it obligates the FDA to prove unreasonable public health risks.

To protect their businesses, ephedra makers like Metabolife and NVE Pharmaceuticals did not reveal complaints about their products–from thousands of customers–until forced to do so by lawsuits brought by people harmed by the drug. In 2003 Metabolife finally released over 16,000 customer reports about its ephedra products that listed nearly 2,000 adverse reactions, including 3 deaths, 20 heart attacks, 24 strokes, and 40 seizures.[56] Robert Occhifinto, a twice-convicted felon and the owner of NVE, with annual revenues of $80 million from sales of ephedra-based supplements, faces at least 30 product liability lawsuits.[57]

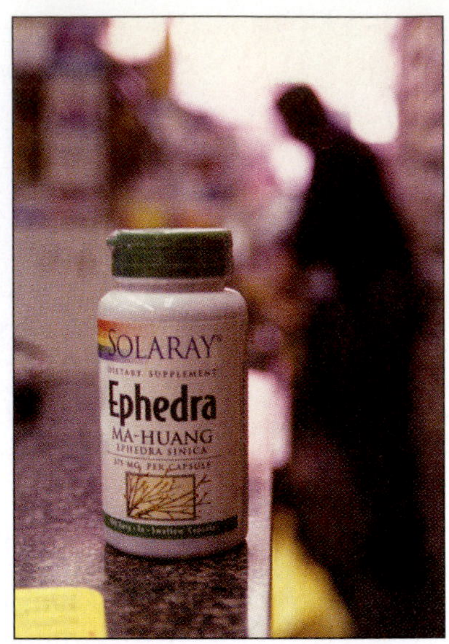

After being widely available for a decade, on April 12, 2004 it became illegal to make or sell Ephedra. Why did it take the FDA so long to ban the use of this dangerous drug?

In their attempts to protect the $18 billion-a-year dietary supplement business, makers of dangerous drugs like ephedra continue to behave in unethical and socially irresponsible ways. In particular, they have begun to use other chemical compounds that have ephedralike effects in new varieties of pills. In 2004, the FDA issued warnings on eight types of chemical compounds about which it is receiving many reports of adverse reactions and advised consumers not to use supplements containing these compounds.[58] In view of the fact that dietary supplement makers are making no attempts to ensure the safety of their products, the push is on for Congress to pass regulations that will subject these companies to the same kind of scrutiny and reporting requirements as those governing pharmaceutical companies.

Managing a Diverse Workforce

Another challenge for managers is to recognize the need to treat human resources in a fair and equitable manner. Today, the age, gender, race, ethnicity, religion, sexual preference, and socioeconomic makeup of the workforce present new challenges for managers. Managers must establish employment procedures and practices that are legal, are fair, and do not discriminate against any organizational members.[59]

In the past, white male employees dominated the ranks of management. Today increasing numbers of organizations are realizing that to motivate effectively and take advantage of the talents of a diverse workforce, they must make promotion opportunities available to all employees, including women and minorities.[60] Managers must also recognize the performance-enhancing possibilities of a diverse workforce, such as the ability to take advantage of the skills and experiences of different kinds of people.[61] The following "Focus on Diversity" feature looks at how one company took advantage of diversity to enhance its competitive advantage.

Focus on Diversity

How Diversity Can Promote Competitive Advantage

With assets of over $40 billion in 2004, Union Bank of California, based in San Francisco, is among the 30 largest banks in the United States.[62] It has enjoyed great success and growth throughout the last decade, in large part because of the approach it has developed to diversity–an approach that reflects the needs of its employees, customers, and environment. Indeed, from 1999 to 2004 the company has been listed among *Fortune* magazine's 50 best companies for minorities to work for, and its diversity practices have become a model for many other companies seeking to emulate its success.[63]

Union Bank operates in one of the most diverse states in the nation, California, where more than half the population is Asian, Black, Hispanic, or gay. Recognizing this fact, the bank always had a policy of hiring and recruiting diverse employees. However, not until 1996 did the bank realize that the diversity of its employees created a competitive advantage. In that year, George Ramirez, a vice president at Union Bank, suggested that the bank create a marketing group to develop a plan for attracting customers who were Hispanic, like himself. So successful was this venture that a group of African-American employees created a marketing group to develop a campaign aimed at attracting new African-American customers, and later Asian-American and gay and lesbian employees did the same. After these groups' considerable success in recruiting new customers, it was clear to Union Bank's managers that they should use employee diversity as a way of improving customer service. For example, when customers walk into a bank branch in a predominantly Latino neighborhood, they are now greeted by substantial numbers of Latino employees.[64]

The bank, like many other organizations, also discovered that diversity can lead to competitive advantage because diverse employees approach the same issue–for example, how to attract customers–in very different ways. The bank found that creating diverse teams of employees helped improve the quality of decision making inside the organization.[65] Furthermore, the bank's reputation of being a good place for minorities to work attracted highly skilled and motivated minority job candidates. As its former CEO Takahiro Moriguchi said when accepting a national diversity award for the company, "By searching for talent from among the disabled, both genders, veterans, all ethnic groups and all nationalities, we gain access to a pool of ideas, energy, and creativity as wide and varied as the human race itself. I expect diversity will become even more important as the world gradually becomes a truly global marketplace."[66]

Union Bank's customer service representatives, such as the employee pictured here, are well known for building relationships with their diverse customer groups to improve the level of customer service. The diverse nature of Union Bank's employees reflects the diverse customer groups the bank serves.

Managers who value their diverse employees not only invest in developing these employees' skills and capabilities but also link rewards to their performance. They are the managers who best succeed in promoting performance over the long run.[67] Today, more and more organizations are realizing that people are their most important resource and that developing and protecting human resources is an important challenge for management in a competitive global environment. We discuss the many issues surrounding the management of a diverse workforce in Chapter 5.

Utilizing IT and E-Commerce

As has already been discussed, another important challenge for managers is the efficient utilization of new information technology and e-commerce.[68] New technologies such as computer-controlled manufacturing and information systems that link and enable employees in new ways are continually being developed. In a setting that uses self-managed teams, for example, sophisticated computer information systems link the activities of team members so that each member knows what the others are doing. This coordination helps to improve quality and increase the pace of innovation. Microsoft, Hitachi, IBM, and other companies make extensive use of information systems such as email, the Internet, and videoconferencing, accessible by means of PCs, to build a competitive advantage. The importance of IT is discussed in detail in Chapters 16 and 18, and throughout the text you will find icons that alert you to examples of how IT is changing the way companies operate.

Summary and Review

WHAT IS MANAGEMENT? A manager is a person responsible for supervising the use of an organization's resources to meet its goals. An organization is a collection of people who work together and coordinate their actions to achieve a wide variety of goals. Management is the process of using organizational resources to achieve organizational goals effectively and efficiently through planning, organizing, leading, and controlling. An efficient organization makes the most productive use of its resources. An effective organization pursues appropriate goals and achieves these goals by using its resources to create the goods or services that customers want.

MANAGERIAL FUNCTIONS The four principal managerial functions are planning, organizing, leading, and controlling. Managers at all levels of the organization and in all departments perform these functions. Effective management means managing these activities successfully.

TYPES OF MANAGERS Organizations typically have three levels of management. First-line managers are responsible for the day-to-day supervision of nonmanagerial employees. Middle managers are responsible for developing and utilizing organizational resources efficiently and effectively. Top managers have cross-departmental responsibility. The top manager's job is to establish appropriate goals for the entire organization and to verify that department managers are utilizing resources to achieve those goals. To increase efficiency and effectiveness, some organizations have altered their managerial hierarchies by restructuring, empowering their workforces, utilizing self-managed teams, and utilizing new information technology.

IT AND MANAGERIAL ROLES AND SKILLS According to Mintzberg, managers play 10 different roles: figurehead, leader, liaison, monitor, disseminator, spokesperson, entrepreneur, disturbance handler, resource allocator, and negotiator. Three types of skills help managers perform these roles effectively: conceptual, human, and technical skills. IT is changing both the way managers perform their roles and the skills they need to perform these roles because it provides richer and more meaningful information.

CHALLENGES FOR MANAGEMENT IN A GLOBAL ENVIRONMENT Today's competitive global environment presents many interesting challenges to managers. One of the main challenges is building a competitive advantage by increasing efficiency; quality; speed, flexibility, and innovation; and customer responsiveness. Others are behaving ethically toward people inside and outside the organization; managing a diverse workforce; and utilizing new information systems and technologies.

Management in Action

Topics for Discussion and Action

Discussion

1. Describe the difference between efficiency and effectiveness, and identify real organizations that you think are, or are not, efficient and effective.
2. In what ways can managers at each of the three levels of management contribute to organizational efficiency and effectiveness?
3. Identify an organization that you believe is high-performing and one that you believe is low-performing. Give 10 reasons why you think the performance levels of the two organizations differ so much.
4. What are the building blocks of competitive advantage? Why is obtaining a competitive advantage important to managers?
5. In what ways do you think managers' jobs have changed the most over the last 10 years? Why have these changes occurred?

Action

6. Choose an organization such as a school or a bank; visit it; then list the different organizational resources it uses.
7. Visit an organization, and talk to first-line, middle, and top managers about their respective management roles in the organization and what they do to help the organization be efficient and effective.
8. Ask a middle or top manager, perhaps someone you already know, to give examples of how he or she performs the managerial functions of planning, organizing, leading, and controlling. How much time does he or she spend in performing each function?
9. Like Mintzberg, try to find a cooperative manager who will allow you to follow him or her around for a day. List the roles the manager plays, and indicate how much time he or she spends performing them.

Building Management Skills

Thinking About Managers and Management

Think of an organization that has provided you with work experience and of the manager to whom you reported (or talk to someone who has had extensive work experience); then answer these questions.

1. Think of your direct supervisor. Of what department is he or she a member, and at what level of management is this person?
2. How do you characterize your supervisor's approach to management? For example, which particular management functions and roles does this person perform most often? What kinds of management skills does this manager have?
3. Do you think the functions, roles, and skills of your supervisor are appropriate for the particular job he or she performs? How could this manager improve his or her task performance? How can IT affect this?
4. How did your supervisor's approach to management affect your attitudes and behavior? For example, how well did you perform as a subordinate, and how motivated were you?
5. Think of the organization and its resources. Do its managers utilize organizational resources effectively? Which resources contribute most to the organization's performance?
6. Describe the way the organization treats its human resources. How does this treatment affect the attitudes and behaviors of the workforce?

7. If you could give your manager one piece of advice or change one management practice in the organization, what would it be?

8. How attuned are the managers in the organization to the need to increase efficiency, quality, innovation, or responsiveness to customers? How well do you think the organization performs its prime goals of providing the goods or services that customers want or need the most?

Managing Ethically

Think about an example of unethical behavior that you observed in the past. The incident could be something you experienced as an employee or a customer or something you observed informally.

1. Either by yourself or in a group, give three reasons why you think the behavior was unethical. For example, what rules or norms were broken? Who benefited or was harmed by what took place? What was the outcome for the people involved?
2. What steps might you take to prevent such unethical behavior and encourage people to behave in an ethical way?

Small Group Breakout Exercise

Opening a New Restaurant

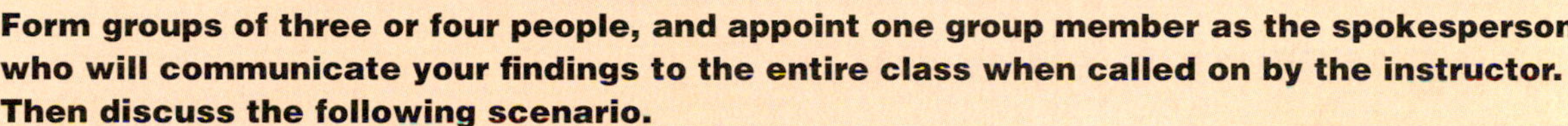

Form groups of three or four people, and appoint one group member as the spokesperson who will communicate your findings to the entire class when called on by the instructor. Then discuss the following scenario.

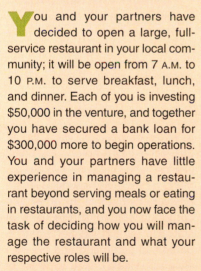

You and your partners have decided to open a large, full-service restaurant in your local community; it will be open from 7 A.M. to 10 P.M. to serve breakfast, lunch, and dinner. Each of you is investing $50,000 in the venture, and together you have secured a bank loan for $300,000 more to begin operations. You and your partners have little experience in managing a restaurant beyond serving meals or eating in restaurants, and you now face the task of deciding how you will manage the restaurant and what your respective roles will be.

1. Decide what each partner's managerial role in the restaurant will be. For example, who will be responsible for the necessary departments and specific activities? Describe your managerial hierarchy.
2. Which building blocks of competitive advantage do you need to establish to help your restaurant succeed? What criteria will you use to evaluate how successfully you are managing the restaurant?
3. Discuss the most important decisions that must be made about (a) planning, (b) organizing, (c) leading, and (d) controlling, to allow you and your partners to utilize organizational resources effectively and build a competitive advantage.
4. For each managerial function, list the issue that will contribute the most to your restaurant's success.

Exploring the World Wide Web

Go to the General Electric (GE) Web site at www.ge.com, click on "Our Company," then "company information," and then "Jeffrey Immelt," GE's CEO. You will see a list of recent articles that discuss his management style, click on the *Financial Times* article, for example, titled "Man of the Year 2003."

Search this article, or others, for information that describes Immelt's approach to planning, organizing, leading, and controlling GE. What is his approach to managing? What effects has this approach had on GE's performance?

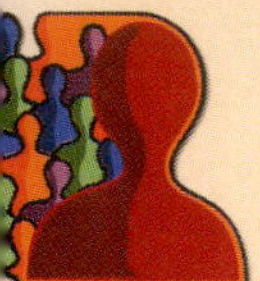

Be The Manager

Problems at Achieva

You have just been called in to help managers at Achieva, a fast-growing Internet software company that specializes in B2B network software. Your job is to help Achieva solve some management problems that have arisen because of its rapid growth.

Customer demand to license Achieva's software has boomed so much in just two years that more than 50 new software programmers have been added to help develop a new range of software products. Achieva's growth has been so swift that the company still operates informally, its organizational structure is loose and flexible, and programmers are encouraged to find solutions to problems as they go along. Although this structure worked well in the past, you have been told that problems are arising.

There have been increasing complaints from employees that good performance is not being recognized in the organization and that they do not feel equitably treated. Moreover, there have been complaints about getting managers to listen to their new ideas and to act on them. A bad atmosphere is developing in the company, and recently several talented employees have left. Your job is to help Achieva's managers solve these problems quickly and keep the company on the fast track.

Questions

1. What kinds of organizing and controlling problems is Achieva suffering from?
2. What kinds of management changes need to be made to solve them?

Additional Activities on the Build Your Management Skills DVD

- **Test Your Knowledge:** Managerial Functions
- **Self-Assessment:** Career Planning Based on Brain Dominance and Thinking Styles Inventory
- **Manager's Hot Seat:** Project Management: Steering the Committee

BusinessWeek Case in the News

The Hard Work in Leadership

W. James McNerney, Jr., has been running big outfits for a dozen years now, at General Electric (GE) and, since January 1, 2001, as chairman and chief executive of 3M. Success at these giants means more than drafting smart business plans, of course. It means getting tens of thousands of people to do what you want. But as the financial numbers at GE and 3M show, McNerney can do it.

His secret? Part of it is simply personality and upbringing: His father, Walter, instilled in him a sense of modesty and a drive to always do better, as well as passing along his own sharp intellect. Part of it is practice: McNerney has been a leader since his days at New Trier High School in Winnetka, Illinois, as president of the Tri-Ship boys club in 1966–67 and pitcher on the varsity baseball team. Another part of it is the tutelage he received during his 18 years at GE, working for now-retired Chairman and CEO Jack Welch.

Recently, McNerney sat down in his 14th-floor suite at 3M headquarters in St. Paul, Minnesota, with *BusinessWeek* Senior Correspondent Michael Arndt. The first outsider ever to become CEO at 3M, McNerney is notoriously press shy. Yet, when it comes to management, he's voluble, talking at length on everything from motivation and corporate culture to the uses of statistical gauges like Six Sigma in personnel screening and his own style as a boss. Edited excerpts of their conversation follow:

Q: I was here two years ago, when you were still pretty new, so I'd like to start by asking you how you think you've done since then.

A: The best measurement of progress is the engagement of the organization, the enthusiasm of the organization: Are we more one team focused on similar things, pulling together? And I feel pretty good about that.

The initiatives I talked about two years ago are exactly the same ones we have today. I believe in boring consistency of meaningful themes. Don't change the message. That's important when you're leading a big organization. Otherwise, people are waiting for the *initiative du jour.* The challenge for us is to keep refreshing them and making them meaningful.

Q: How do you achieve that team spirit?

A: My experience is that if people are convinced they're growing as they pursue company goals, that's when you get ignition. I'll use Six Sigma as an example. People are learning new ways to approach business problems, new ways to lead other people. They're achieving results that are better than what they had achieved before, so they feel they are becoming better managers.

I think when everybody does that, we become a better company. When people's growth lines up with corporate growth, that's when you get the motivation, the enthusiasm, the alignment that every CEO hopes for. The trick is to find these things.

Q: A lot of CEOs have these goals, but how do you actually get this accomplished?

A: It comes down to personal engagement. I spend a lot of time out with our people. Let me give you an example of this: leadership development. We need to get the middle of this company moving and growing and aspiring to be tomorrow's leaders. It's easy to make the speech about leadership and then disappear into a backroom grading everybody.

That's one approach. Another is what we try to do. We spent a year debating what leadership is. I made speeches on the subject and solicited input from everybody. So when we hammered it out, it was the company's leadership goals we were aspiring to—not the CEO's, not some consultant's, not what we read in a book last week. So now the organization is quite happy to be measured and to aspire to these things because they created them.

Now we could have done this Day One, but I learned over the years that to short-circuit that process is very risky for a guy running an organization. Most CEOs—and I don't want to preach here—are smart enough to figure out where to go with a company. The hard work is engaging everyone in doing it. That's the hard work in leadership.

Q: Looking at your typical workday, how do you spend your time? Is most of it spent on managing people? Or thinking up grand strategies? Or scrutinizing the company's numbers?

A: Designing business strategy is probably what I spend the least amount of time on. I rely on our business leadership to do a lot of that. I spend more time on people issues broadly defined: Who's in what job? How do we accelerate this career? What programs do we have in place to train people? How do we make people fit better? How do we pay them? How do you differentiate pay?

I also spend a lot of time on communication, broadly defined. I probably do 30 major events a year with 100 people or more, where I spend time debating things and pushing my ideas, telling them what I'm thinking that day and soliciting feedback. What is it we're doing? And why?

I want a lot of feedback on how to run this company. The trick for me is to create an environment where I get honest feedback. That's the hard part. The natural tendency for people is to say, Jim, what a great idea!

Q: Do you think you've got to the stage where you're getting honest feedback?

A: In some cases, but not always. It's hard for people to have self-confidence and say they disagree. 3M was a pretty hierarchical place with not a lot of free-form discussion. I think we've made a lot of progress there. But these changes don't happen overnight.

Q: You've been here since 2001. What surprised you in being difficult?

A: I think the whole issue of leadership development. I think we've made enormous progress, but I'm still impressed with how much farther we have to go. I wouldn't characterize it as a disappointment. I would say that where I'm going to be in two years, I wished I was there now.

3M is a business with a big brand and a big global stance and can be a bigger company. We have to keep growing big leaders. We've accelerated some careers. But we also have highly valued people who have been in jobs a while. You can't just throw people out. There's the balance between the young and energized and the experienced and effective. We're constantly wrestling with that.

Q: Let me ask you the corollary question: Are there things that you had expected to be real challenges when you came to 3M that turned out to be a snap?

A: The big surprise for me was how open 3M-ers were to change. I thought there would be more resistance to a new way of doing things, a new language, a new CEO. But I found a company who thought they weren't achieving all they could, and they were willing to team up with somebody to do more. That was a surprise.

Q: What skills and attributes that you developed at GE transferred easily here?

A: I think the thing that helped me the most was, at GE you run so many different businesses. I was changing jobs every two or three years, and each one of those businesses had very different cultures and different geographies and different values. So coming here and trying to force this alliance was something I had done three or four times before.

Q: It seems to me from what I'm hearing that you do a lot by encouraging people.

A: It's the balance between setting expectations and encouraging. I think the harder you push people, the more you have to encourage them.

Some people feel you either have a demanding, command-and-control management style or you have a nurturing, encouraging management style. I believe you have to have both. If you're only demanding, without encouraging, eventually that runs out of gas. And if you're only encouraging without setting high expectations, you're not getting as much out of people. It's not either/or. You can't have one without the other.

Questions

1. What is James McNerney's approach to managing?
2. What kind of skills and abilities does McNerney possess that led him to become 3M's CEO?

Source: Michael Arndt, "The Hard Work in Leadership." Reprinted from the April 12, 2004, issue of *BusinessWeek* by special permission. Copyright © by the McGraw-Hill Companies, Inc.

BusinessWeek Case in the News

Can A U.S.-Style Boss Rev Up Siemens?

It's safe to say Klaus Kleinfeld didn't have much trouble adjusting to life in America after Siemens made him chief operating officer of its U.S. unit in 2001. Kleinfeld soon won invitations to join the boards of a dozen prestigious organizations including the Metropolitan Opera and Alcoa Inc. He ran two New York marathons and frequented the city's jazz clubs. Under Kleinfeld, who was promoted to CEO of Siemens' U.S. unit in 2002, the company played a big role in building Houston's Reliant Stadium, scene in 2004 of that most American of events, the Super Bowl.

Now, Kleinfeld, 46, is set to become the latest German manager to parlay U.S. experience and attitude into a top job at a German corporate icon. On July 7, 2004, Siemens announced that, effective in January, Kleinfeld will succeed Heinrich von Pierer as CEO of the $89 billion Munich conglomerate, which makes everything from light bulbs and power plants to trains and mobile phones. The question is whether the energetic Kleinfeld will fare better than some other German bosses who tried to import U.S.-style management techniques, with their emphasis on speed and profit. "Kleinfeld stands for the modern approach in German industry, of trying to cope with globalization and move out of the old, well-trodden path," says Jens van Scherpenberg, head of the Americas Research Unit at the German Institute for International & Security Affairs, a Berlin think tank.

The Right Stuff?

The CEO-designate has already begun to make changes. His fingerprints were on Siemens' decision, also announced on July 7, 2004, to merge the mobile phone division with the land-line telecom unit. In the United States, Kleinfeld managed to get Siemens' disparate fiefdoms to cooperate more on marketing. One result was the contract to provide everything from telecom equipment to computer networks for Houston's $750 million Reliant Park convention and sporting complex.

In fact, Kleinfeld probably won the top job because he showed he could get Siemens divisions to work together to win big orders. The company has struggled for years to prove that synergies among branches justify the inherent unwieldiness of a far-flung conglomerate. He also got Siemens' legions of proud engineers to see things more from their customers' point of view. After a $553 million loss in 2001, Siemens reported an $810 million profit for its U.S. units in 2002 and a $561 million profit in 2003, after which Kleinfeld returned to Germany. "He was instrumental in getting it working," says Gerhard Schulmeyer, Kleinfeld's predecessor as CEO of Siemens in the U.S.

Back home, Kleinfeld will have to spend a lot of time smoothing out relations with politicians and unions. In the United States, where Siemens had sales of $16.6 billion in 2003, the company cut staff by 15,000 to 65,000, by selling or closing unprofitable units, but also by shifting work to lower-wage countries such as India. Von Pierer has reduced the German workforce by more than 50,000, to 167,000, since becoming CEO in 1992.

But by imposing cuts gradually, the diplomatic von Pierer managed to avoid serious confrontation with Germany's powerful labor unions and their allies in Parliament. That is becoming more difficult. Labor leaders are sore that they were forced recently to give in to demands that workers at a mobile phone factory put in extra hours without extra pay: Siemens threatened to shift the work to Hungary. "Siemens has damaged its image with that kind of action," says Wolfgang Müller, a worker on the supervisory board.

Kleinfeld will have to do a lot of creative thinking. But people who have worked with him say he's good at that. "He was exceptionally exact but not narrow-minded; on the contrary, very independent and creative," says Peter Fassheber, a retired professor at Georg-August University in Göttingen who supervised Kleinfeld's research in the early 1980s. Kleinfeld focused on the intersection of psychology and economics. If Kleinfeld can reconcile human nature with economic reality at Siemens, he might just succeed.

Questions

1. How would you describe Klaus Kleinfeld's approach to managing?
2. What skills and abilities helped him rise to become Seimen's CEO?

Source: Jack Ewing, "Can a U.S.-Style Boss Rev Up Siemen?" Reprinted from the July 26, 2004, issue of *Business Week* by special permission.

CHAPTER

2 The Evolution of Management Thought

Learning Objectives

After studying this chapter, you should be able to:

- Describe how the need to increase organizational efficiency and effectiveness has guided the evolution of management theory.
- Explain the principle of job specialization and division of labor, and tell why the study of person-task relationships is central to the pursuit of increased efficiency.
- Identify the principles of administration and organization that underlie effective organizations.
- Trace the changes in theories about how managers should behave to motivate and control employees.
- Explain the contributions of management science to the efficient use of organizational resources.
- Explain why the study of the external environment and its impact on an organization has become a central issue in management thought.

A Manager's Challenge

Finding Better Ways to Make Cars

What is the best way to use people's skills? Car production has changed dramatically over the years as managers have applied different principles of management to organize and control work activities. Prior to 1900, small groups of skilled workers cooperated to hand-build cars with parts that often had to be altered and modified to fit together. This system, a type of *small-batch production,* was very expensive; assembling just one car took considerable time and effort; and skilled workers could produce only a few cars in a day. Although these cars were of high quality, they were too expensive. Managers of early car companies needed better techniques to increase efficiency, reduce costs, and sell more cars.

Henry Ford revolutionized the car industry. In 1913, Ford opened the Highland Park car plant in Detroit to produce the Model T Ford, and his team of manufacturing managers pioneered the development of *mass-production manufacturing,* a system that made the small-batch system almost obsolete overnight. In mass production, moving conveyor belts bring the cars to the workers. Each worker performs a single assigned

(a) The photo on top, taken in 1904 inside a Daimler Motor Company factory, is an example of the use of small-batch production, a production system in which small groups of people work together and perform all the tasks needed to assemble a product. (b) In 1913, Henry Ford revolutionized the production process of a car by pioneering mass production manufacturing, a production system in which a conveyor belt brings each car to the workers, and each individual worker performs a single task along the production line. Even today cars are still built using this system, as evidenced in the photo of workers along a modern-day computerized automobile assembly line.

task along a production line, and the speed of the conveyor belt is the primary means of controlling workers' activities. Ford experimented to discover the most efficient way for each worker to perform an assigned task. The result was that each worker performed one narrow, specialized task, such as bolting on the door or attaching the door handle, and jobs in the Ford car plant became very repetitive. They required little use of a worker's skills.[1] Ford's management approach increased efficiency and reduced costs by so much that by 1920 he was able to reduce the price of a car by two-thirds and to sell more than 2 million cars a year.[2] Ford became the leading car company in the world, and competitors rushed to adopt the new mass-production techniques.

The next change in management thinking about car assembly occurred in Japan when Ohno Taiichi, a Toyota production engineer, pioneered the development of *lean manufacturing* in the 1960s after touring the U.S. plants of the Big Three car companies. The management philosophy behind lean manufacturing is to continuously find methods to improve the efficiency of the production process in order to reduce costs, increase quality, and reduce car assembly time. Lean production is based on the idea that if workers have input and can participate continually in the decision-making process, their skills and knowledge can be used to increase efficiency.

In lean manufacturing, workers work on a moving production line, but they are organized into small teams, each of which is responsible for a particular phase of car assembly, such as installing the car's transmission or electrical wiring system. Each team member is expected to learn the tasks of all members of that team, and each work group is responsible not only for assembling cars but also for continuously finding ways to increase quality and reduce costs. By 1970, Japanese managers had applied the new lean-production system so efficiently that they were producing higher-quality cars at lower prices than their U.S. counterparts. By 1980 Japanese companies dominated the global car market.

To compete with the Japanese, managers of U.S. carmakers visited Japan to learn the new management principles of lean production. As a result, companies such as General Motors (GM) established the Saturn plant to experiment with this new way of involving workers; GM also established a joint venture with Toyota called New United Motor Manufacturing Inc. (NUMMI) to learn how to achieve the benefits of lean production. Meanwhile, Ford and Chrysler began to change their work processes to take advantage of employees' skills and knowledge.

In the 1990s global car companies increased the number of robots used on the production line and began to use advanced IT to build and track the quality of cars being produced. Indeed, for a time it seemed that robots rather than employees would be building cars in the future. However, Toyota discovered something interesting at its fully roboticized car plant. When only robots build cars, efficiency does not continually increase because, unlike people, robots cannot provide input to improve the work process. The crucial thing is to find the right balance between using people, computers, and IT.

In the 2000s, global car companies are continuing to compete fiercely to improve and perfect better ways of making cars. Toyota is constantly pioneering new ways to manage its assembly lines to increase efficiency; however, other Japanese carmakers such as Nissan are catching up fast. U.S. carmakers are catching up too: Ford, which made major advances in the 1990s, has now been surpassed by both Chrysler and GM. Both announced in 2004 that their productivity was fast approaching that of Japanese companies and that they expected to match the leaders, Toyota and Nissan, within the next 10 years.

Overview

As this sketch of the evolution of management thinking in global car manufacturing suggests, changes in management practices occur as managers, theorists, researchers, and consultants seek new ways to increase organizational efficiency and effectiveness. The driving force

Figure 2.1
The Evolution of Management Theory

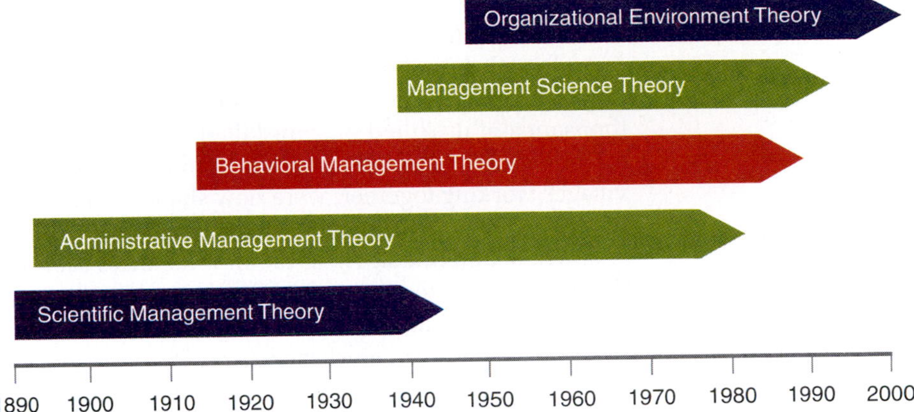

behind the evolution of management theory is the search for better ways to utilize organizational resources. Advances in management thought typically occur as managers and researchers find better ways to perform the principal management tasks: planning, organizing, leading, and controlling human and other organizational resources.

In this chapter, we examine how management thought has evolved in modern times and the central concerns that have guided ongoing advances in management theory. First, we examine the so-called classical management theories that emerged around the turn of the 20th century. These include scientific management, which focuses on matching people and tasks to maximize efficiency, and administrative management, which focuses on identifying the principles that will lead to the creation of the most efficient system of organization and management. Next, we consider behavioral management theories developed both before and after World War II; these focus on how managers should lead and control their workforces to increase performance. Then we discuss management science theory, which developed during World War II and has become increasingly important as researchers have developed rigorous analytical and quantitative techniques to help managers measure and control organizational performance. Finally, we discuss business in the 1960s and 1970s and focus on the theories developed to help explain how the external environment affects the way organizations and managers operate.

By the end of this chapter you will understand the ways in which management thought and theory have evolved over time. You will also understand how economic, political, and cultural forces have affected the development of these theories and the ways in which managers and their organizations behave. In Figure 2.1 we summarize the chronology of the management theories discussed in this chapter.

Scientific Management Theory

The evolution of modern management began in the closing decades of the 19th century, after the industrial revolution had swept through Europe and America. In the new economic climate, managers of all types of organizations—political, educational, and economic—were increasingly trying to find better ways to satisfy customers' needs. Many major economic, technical, and cultural changes were taking place at this time. The introduction of steam power and the development of sophisticated machinery and equipment changed the way goods were produced, particularly in the weaving and clothing industries. Small workshops run by skilled workers who produced hand-manufactured products (a system called *crafts production*) were being replaced by large factories in which sophisticated machines controlled by hundreds or even thousands of unskilled or semiskilled workers made products. For example, raw cotton and wool, which in the past had been spun into yarn by families or whole villages working together, were now shipped to factories where workers operated machines that spun and wove large quantities of yarn into cloth.

Owners and managers of the new factories found themselves unprepared for the challenges accompanying the change from small-scale crafts production to large-scale mechanized manufacturing. Moreover, many of the managers and supervisors in these workshops and factories were engineers who had only a technical orientation. They were unprepared for the social problems that occur when people work together in large groups in a factory or shop system. Managers began to search for new techniques to manage their organizations' resources, and soon they began to focus on ways to increase the efficiency of the worker-task mix.

Job Specialization and the Division of Labor

Initially, management theorists were interested in the subject of why the new machine shops and factory system were more efficient and produced greater quantities of goods and services than older, crafts-style production operations. Nearly 200 years before, Adam Smith had been one of the first writers to investigate the advantages associated with producing goods and services in factories. A famous economist, Smith journeyed around England in the 1700s studying the effects of the industrial revolution.[3] In a study of factories that produced various pins or nails, Smith identified two different manufacturing methods. The first was similar to crafts-style production, in which each worker was responsible for all of the 18 tasks involved in producing a pin. The other had each worker performing only 1 or a few of the 18 tasks that go into making a complete pin.

In a comparison of the relative performance of these different ways of organizing production, Smith found that the performance of the factories in which workers specialized in only one or a few tasks was much greater than the performance of the factory in which each worker performed all 18 pin-making tasks. In fact, Smith found that 10 workers specializing in a particular task could make 48,000 pins a day, whereas those workers who performed all the tasks could make only a few thousand at most.[4] Smith reasoned that this difference in performance was due to the fact that the workers who specialized became much more skilled at their specific tasks and as a group were thus able to produce a product faster than the group of workers who each performed many tasks. Smith concluded that increasing the level of **job specialization**—the process by which a division of labor occurs as different workers specialize in specific tasks over time—increases efficiency and leads to higher organizational performance.[5]

job specialization The process by which a division of labor occurs as different workers specialize in different tasks over time.

Armed with the insights gained from Adam Smith's observations, other managers and researchers began to investigate how to improve job specialization to increase performance. Management practitioners and theorists focused on how managers should organize and control the work process to maximize the advantages of job specialization and the division of labor.

Frederick W. Taylor, founder of Scientific Management, and one of the first people to study the behavior and performance of people at work.

F. W. Taylor and Scientific Management

Frederick W. Taylor (1856–1915) is best known for defining the techniques of **scientific management,** the systematic study of relationships between people and tasks for the purpose of redesigning the work process to increase efficiency. Taylor was a manufacturing manager who eventually became a consultant and taught other managers how to apply his scientific management techniques. Taylor believed that if the amount of time and effort that each worker expends to produce a unit of output (a finished good or service) can be reduced by increasing specialization and the division of labor, the production process will become more efficient. According to Taylor, the way to create the most efficient division of labor could best be determined by scientific management techniques, rather than intuitive or informal rule-of-thumb knowledge. Based on his experiments and observations as a manufacturing manager in a variety of settings, he developed four principles to increase efficiency in the workplace:

scientific management The systematic study of relationships between people and tasks for the purpose of redesigning the work process to increase efficiency.

- Principle 1: *Study the way workers perform their tasks, gather all the informal job knowledge that workers possess, and experiment with ways of improving how tasks are performed.*

  To discover the most efficient method of performing specific tasks, Taylor studied in great detail and measured the ways different workers went about performing their tasks. One of the main tools he used was a *time-and-motion study,* which involves the careful timing and recording of the actions taken to perform a particular task. Once Taylor understood the existing method of performing a task, he then experimented to increase specialization. He tried different methods of dividing and coordinating the various tasks necessary to produce a finished product. Usually this meant simplifying jobs and having each worker perform fewer, more routine tasks, as at the pin factory or on Ford's car assembly line. Taylor also sought to find ways to improve each worker's ability to perform a particular task–for example, by reducing the number of motions workers made to complete the task, by changing the layout of the work area or the type of tools workers used, or by experimenting with tools of different sizes.

- Principle 2: *Codify the new methods of performing tasks into written rules and standard operating procedures.*

  Once the best method of performing a particular task was determined, Taylor specified that it should be recorded so that this procedure could be taught to all workers performing the same task. These new methods further standardized and simplified jobs–essentially making jobs even more routine. In this way efficiency could be increased throughout an organization.

- Principle 3: *Carefully select workers who possess skills and abilities that match the needs of the task, and train them to perform the task according to the established rules and procedures.*

  To increase specialization, Taylor believed workers had to understand the tasks that were required and be thoroughly trained to perform the tasks at the required level. Workers who could not be trained to this level were to be transferred to a job where they were able to reach the minimum required level of proficiency.[6]

- Principle 4: *Establish a fair or acceptable level of performance for a task, and then develop a pay system that provides a reward for performance above the acceptable level.*

  To encourage workers to perform at a high level of efficiency, and to provide them with an incentive to reveal the most efficient techniques for performing a task, Taylor advocated that workers benefit from any gains in performance. They should be paid a bonus and receive some percentage of the performance gains achieved through the more efficient work process.[7]

By 1910 Taylor's system of scientific management had become nationally known and in many instances was faithfully and fully practiced.[8] However, managers in many organizations chose to implement the new principles of scientific management selectively. This decision ultimately resulted in problems. For example, some managers using scientific management obtained increases in performance, but rather than sharing performance gains with workers through bonuses as Taylor had advocated, they simply increased the amount of work that each worker was expected to do. Many workers experiencing the reorganized work system found that as their performance increased, managers required that they do more work for the same pay. Workers also learned that increases in performance often meant fewer jobs and a greater threat of layoffs because fewer workers were needed. In addition, the specialized, simplified jobs were often monotonous and repetitive, and many workers became dissatisfied with their jobs.

Scientific management brought many workers more hardship than gain and a distrust of managers who did not seem to care about workers' well-being.[9] These dissatisfied workers resisted attempts to use the new scientific management techniques and at times even withheld their job knowledge from managers to protect their jobs and pay. It is not difficult for workers to conceal the true potential efficiency of a work system to protect their interests. Experienced machine operators, for example, can slow their machines in undetectable ways by adjusting the tension in the belts or by misaligning the gears. Workers sometimes even develop informal work rules that discourage high performance and encourage shirking as work groups attempt to identify an acceptable or fair performance level (a tactic discussed in the next section).

Unable to inspire workers to accept the new scientific management techniques for performing tasks, some organizations increased the mechanization of the work process. For example, one reason why Henry Ford introduced moving conveyor belts in his factory was the realization that when a conveyor belt controls the pace of work (instead of workers setting their own pace), workers can be pushed to perform at higher levels–levels that they may have thought were beyond their reach. Charlie Chaplin captured this aspect of mass production in one of the opening scenes of his famous movie *Modern Times* (1936). In the film, Chaplin caricatured a new factory employee fighting to work at the machine-imposed pace but losing the battle to the machine. Henry Ford also used the principles of scientific management to identify the tasks that each worker should perform on the production line and thus to determine the most effective way to create a division of labor to suit the needs of a mechanized production system.

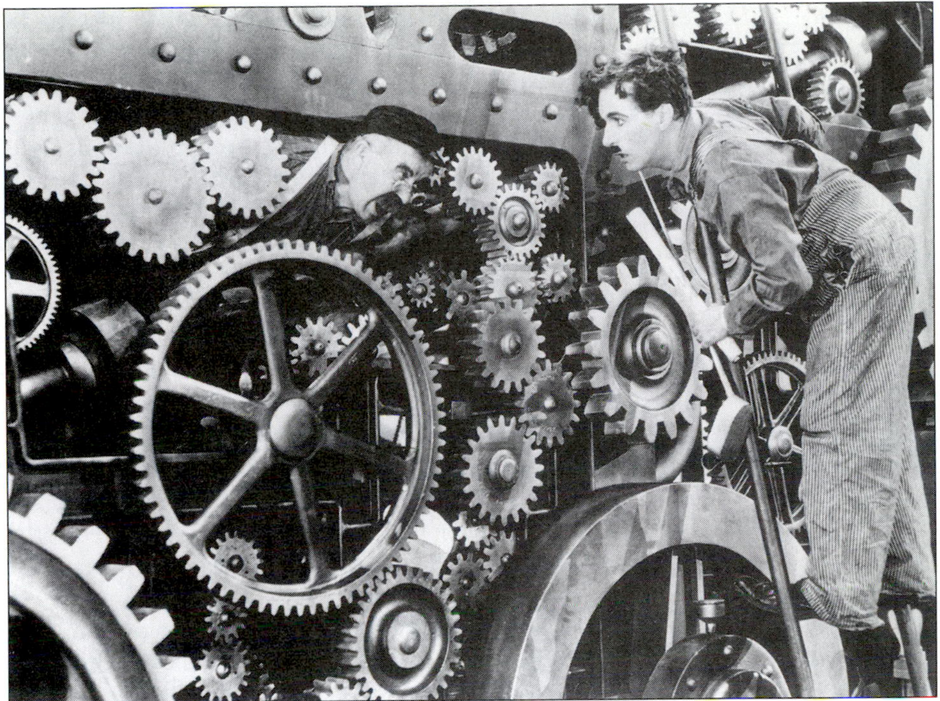

Charlie Chaplin tries to extricate a fellow employee from the machinery of mass production in this scene from *Modern Times*. The complex machinery is meant to represent the power that machinery has over the worker in the new work system.

From a performance perspective, the combination of the two management practices–(1) achieving the right mix of worker-task specialization and (2) linking people and tasks by the speed of the production line–makes sense. It produces the huge savings in cost and huge increases in output that occur in large, organized work settings. For example, in 1908 managers at the Franklin Motor Company using scientific management principles redesigned the work process, and the output of cars increased from 100 cars a *month* to 45 cars a *day;* workers' wages, however, increased by only 90 percent.[10] From other perspectives, however, scientific management practices raise many concerns. The definition of workers' rights, not by the workers themselves, but by the owners or managers as a result of the introduction of the new management practices, raised an ethical issue, which we examine in the following "Ethics in Action."

Ethics in Action

Fordism in Practice

From 1908 to 1914, through trial and error, Henry Ford's talented team of production managers pioneered the development of the moving conveyor belt and thus changed manufacturing practices forever. Although the technical aspects of the move to mass production were a dramatic financial success for Ford and for the millions of Americans who could now afford cars, for the workers who actually produced the cars many human and social problems resulted.

With simplification of the work process, workers grew to hate the monotony of the moving conveyor belt. By 1914 Ford's car plants were experiencing huge employee turnover–often reaching levels as high as 300 or 400 percent per year as workers left because they could not handle the work-induced stress.[11] Henry Ford recognized these problems and made an announcement:

From that point on, to motivate his workforce, he would reduce the length of the workday from nine hours to eight hours, and the company would *double* the basic wage from $2.50 to $5.00 per day. This was a dramatic increase, similar to an announcement today of an overnight doubling of the minimum wage. Ford became an internationally famous figure, and the word *Fordism* was coined for his new approach.[12]

Ford's apparent generosity, however, was matched by an intense effort to control the resources–both human and material–with which his empire was built. He employed hundreds of inspectors to check up on employees, both inside and outside his factories. In the factory supervision was close and confining. Employees were not allowed to leave their places at the production line, and they were not permitted to talk to one another. Their job was to concentrate fully on the task at hand. Few employees could adapt to this system, and they developed ways of talking out of the sides of their mouths, like ventriloquists, and invented a form of speech that became known as the "Ford Lisp."[13] Ford's obsession with control brought him into greater and greater conflict with managers, who often were fired when they disagreed with him. As a result, many talented people left Ford to join a growing number of rival car companies.

Outside the workplace, Ford went so far as to establish what he called the "Sociological Department" to check up on how his employees lived and the ways they spent their time. Inspectors from this department visited the homes of employees and investigated their habits and problems. Employees who exhibited behaviors contrary to Ford's standards (for instance, if they drank too much or were always in debt) were likely to be fired. Clearly, Ford's efforts to control his employees led him and his managers to behave in ways that today would be considered unacceptable and unethical and in the long run would impair an organization's ability to prosper.

Despite the problems of worker turnover, absenteeism, and discontent at Ford Motor Company, managers of the other car companies watched Ford reap huge gains in efficiency from the application of the new management principles. They believed that their companies would have to imitate Ford if they were to survive. They followed Taylor and used many of his followers as consultants to teach them how to adopt the techniques of scientific management. In addition, Taylor elaborated his principles in several books, including *Shop Management* (1903) and *The Principles of Scientific Management* (1911), which explain in detail how to apply the principles of scientific management to reorganize the work system.[14]

Taylor's work has had an enduring effect on the management of production systems. Managers in every organization, whether it produces goods or services, now carefully analyze the basic tasks that must be performed and try to devise the work systems that allow their organizations to operate most efficiently.

The Gilbreths

Two prominent followers of Taylor were Frank Gilbreth (1868–1924) and Lillian Gilbreth (1878–1972), who refined Taylor's analysis of work movements and made many contributions to time-and-motion study.[15] Their aims were to (1) break up and analyze every individual action necessary to perform a partic-

This scene from *Cheaper by the Dozen* illustrates how "efficient families," such as the Gilbreths, use formal family courts to solve problems of assigning chores to different family members and to solve disputes when they arise.

ular task into each of its component actions, (2) find better ways to perform each component action, and (3) reorganize each of the component actions so that the action as a whole could be performed more efficiently–at less cost in time and effort.

The Gilbreths often filmed a worker performing a particular task and then separated the task actions, frame by frame, into their component movements. Their goal was to maximize the efficiency with which each individual task was performed so that gains across tasks would add up to enormous savings of time and effort. Their attempts to develop improved management principles were captured–at times quite humorously–in the movie *Cheaper by the Dozen,* a new version of which appeared in 2004, which depicts how the Gilbreths (with their 12 children) tried to live their own lives according to these efficiency principles and apply them to daily actions such as shaving, cooking, and even raising a family.[16]

Eventually, the Gilbreths became increasingly interested in the study of fatigue. They studied how the physical characteristics of the workplace contribute to job stress that often leads to fatigue and thus poor performance. They isolated factors that result in worker fatigue, such as lighting, heating, the color of walls, and the design of tools and machines. Their pioneering studies paved the way for new advances in management theory.

In workshops and factories, the work of the Gilbreths, Taylor, and many others had a major effect on the practice of management. In comparison with the old crafts system, jobs in the new system were more repetitive, boring, and monotonous as a result of the application of scientific management principles, and workers became increasingly dissatisfied. Frequently, the management of work settings became a game between workers and managers: Managers tried to initiate work practices to increase performance, and workers tried to hide the true potential efficiency of the work setting to protect their own well-being.[17]

Administrative Management Theory

administrative management The study of how to create an organizational structure that leads to high efficiency and effectiveness.

Side by side with scientific managers studying the person-task mix to increase efficiency, other researchers were focusing on **administrative management,** the study of how to create an organizational structure that leads to high efficiency and effectiveness. *Organizational structure* is the system of task and authority relationships that control how employees use resources to achieve the organization's goals. Two of the most influential views regarding the creation of efficient systems of organizational administration were developed in Europe: Max Weber, a

German professor of sociology, developed one theory; Henri Fayol, the French manager who developed the model of management introduced in Chapter 1, developed the other.

The Theory of Bureaucracy

bureaucracy A formal system of organization and administration designed to ensure efficiency and effectiveness.

authority The power to hold people accountable for their actions and to make decisions concerning the use of organizational resources.

Max Weber (1864–1920), wrote at the turn of the 20th century, when Germany was undergoing its industrial revolution.[18] To help Germany manage its growing industrial enterprises at a time when it was striving to become a world power, Weber developed the principles of **bureaucracy**–a formal system of organization and administration designed to ensure efficiency and effectiveness. A bureaucratic system of administration is based on the five principles summarized in Figure 2.2.

- Principle 1: *In a bureaucracy, a manager's formal authority derives from the position he or she holds in the organization.*

  Authority is the power to hold people accountable for their actions and to make decisions concerning the use of organizational resources. Authority gives managers the right to direct and control their subordinates' behavior to achieve organizational goals. In a bureaucratic system of administration, obedience is owed to a manager, not because of any personal qualities–such as personality, wealth, or social status–but because the manager occupies a position that is associated with a certain level of authority and responsibility.[19]

- Principle 2: *In a bureaucracy, people should occupy positions because of their performance, not because of their social standing or personal contacts.*

  This principle was not always followed in Weber's time and is often ignored today. Some organizations and industries are still affected by social networks in which personal contacts and relations, not job-related skills, influence hiring and promotional decisions.

- Principle 3: *The extent of each position's formal authority and task responsibilities, and its relationship to other positions in an organization, should be clearly specified.*

  When the tasks and authority associated with various positions in the organization are clearly specified, managers and workers know what is expected of them and what to expect from each other. Moreover, an organization can hold all its employees strictly accountable for their actions when they know their exact responsibilities.

- Principle 4: *Authority can be exercised effectively in an organization when positions are arranged hierarchically, so employees know whom to report to and who reports to them.*[20]

  Managers must create an organizational hierarchy of authority that makes it clear who reports to whom and to whom managers and workers should go if conflicts or problems arise. This principle is especially important in the armed forces, FBI, CIA, and other organizations that deal with sensitive issues involving possible major repercussions. It is vital that managers at high levels of the hierarchy be able to hold subordinates accountable for their actions.

- Principle 5: *Managers must create a well-defined system of rules, standard operating procedures, and norms so that they can effectively control behavior within an organization.*

Figure 2.2
Weber's Principles of Bureaucracy

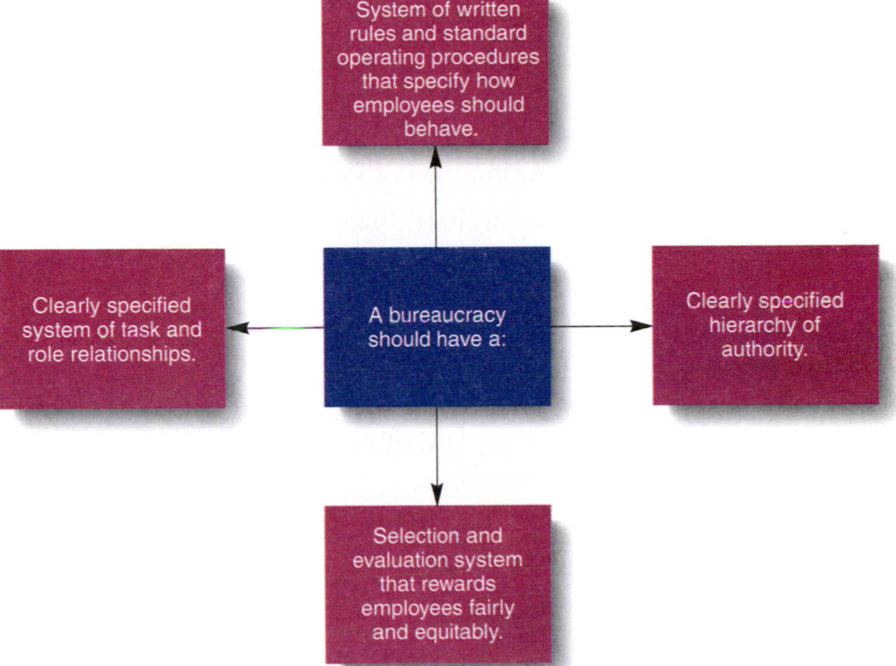
System of written rules and standard operating procedures that specify how employees should behave.
Clearly specified system of task and role relationships.
A bureaucracy should have a:
Clearly specified hierarchy of authority.
Selection and evaluation system that rewards employees fairly and equitably.

rules Formal written instructions that specify actions to be taken under different circumstances to achieve specific goals.

standard operating procedures (SOPs) Specific sets of written instructions about how to perform a certain aspect of a task.

norms Unwritten, informal codes of conduct that prescribe how people should act in particular situations.

Rules are formal written instructions that specify actions to be taken under different circumstances to achieve specific goals (for example, if A happens, do B). **Standard operating procedures (SOPs)** are specific sets of written instructions about how to perform a certain aspect of a task. A rule might state that at the end of the workday employees are to leave their machines in good order, and a set of SOPs would specify exactly how they should do so, itemizing which machine parts must be oiled or replaced. **Norms** are unwritten, informal codes of conduct that prescribe how people should act in particular situations. For example, an organizational norm in a restaurant might be that waiters should help each other if time permits.

Rules, SOPs, and norms provide behavioral guidelines that increase the performance of a bureaucratic system because they specify the best ways to accomplish organizational tasks. Companies such as McDonald's and Wal-Mart have developed extensive rules and procedures to specify the behaviors required of their employees, such as "Always greet the customer with a smile."

Weber believed that organizations that implement all five principles establish a bureaucratic system that improves organizational performance. The specification of positions and the use of rules and SOPs to regulate how tasks are performed make it easier for managers to organize and control the work of subordinates. Similarly, fair and equitable selection and promotion systems improve managers' feelings of security, reduce stress, and encourage organizational members to act ethically and further promote the interests of the organization.[21]

If bureaucracies are not managed well, however, many problems can result. Sometimes, managers allow rules and SOPs, "bureaucratic red tape," to become so cumbersome that decision making is slow and inefficient and organizations are unable to change. When managers rely too much on rules to solve problems and not enough on their own skills and judgment, their behavior becomes inflexible. A key challenge for managers is to use bureaucratic principles to benefit, rather than harm, an organization.

Fayol's Principles of Management

Henri Fayol (1841–1925), was the CEO of Comambault Mining. Working at the same time as, but independently from, Weber, Fayol identified 14 principles (summarized in Table 2.1) that he believed essential to increase the efficiency of the management process.[22] We discuss these principles in detail here because, although they were developed at the turn of the 20th century, they remain the bedrock on which much of recent management theory and research is based. In fact, as the "Management Insight" following this discussion suggests, modern writers such as well-known management guru Tom Peters continue to extol these principles.

DIVISION OF LABOR A champion of job specialization and the division of labor for reasons already mentioned, Fayol was nevertheless among the first to point out the downside of too much specialization: boredom–a state of mind likely to cause a fall in product quality, worker initiative, and flexibility. As a result, Fayol advocated that workers be given more job duties to perform or be encouraged to assume more responsibility for work outcomes, a principle increasingly applied today in organizations that empower their workers.

AUTHORITY AND RESPONSIBILITY Like Weber, Fayol emphasized the importance of authority and responsibility. Fayol, however, went beyond Weber's formal authority, which derives from a manager's position in the hierarchy, to recognize the *informal* authority that derives from personal expertise, technical knowledge, moral worth, and the ability to lead and to generate commitment from subordinates. (The study of authority is the subject of recent research into leadership, discussed in Chapter 12.)

unity of command A reporting relationship in which an employee receives orders from, and reports to, only one superior.

UNITY OF COMMAND The principle of **unity of command** specifies that an employee should receive orders from, and report to, only one superior. Fayol believed that *dual command,* the reporting relationship that exists when two supervisors give orders to the same subordinate, should be avoided except in exceptional circumstances. Dual command confuses subordinates, undermines order and discipline, and creates havoc within the formal hierarchy of authority. Assessing any manager's authority and responsibility in a system of dual command is difficult, and the manager who is bypassed feels slighted and angry and may be uncooperative in the future.

line of authority The chain of command extending from the top to the bottom of an organization.

LINE OF AUTHORITY The **line of authority** is the chain of command extending from the top to the bottom of an organization. Fayol was one of the first management theorists to point out the importance of limiting the length of the chain of command by controlling the number of levels in the managerial hierarchy. The greater the number of levels in the hierarchy, the longer communication between managers at the top and bottom takes and the slower the pace of planning and organizing. Restricting the number of hierarchical levels to lessen these communication problems enables an organization to act quickly and flexibly; this is one reason for the recent trend toward restructuring (discussed in Chapter 1).

Table 2.1
Fayol's 14 Principles of Management

Division of Labor Job specialization and the division of labor should increase efficiency, especially if managers take steps to lessen workers' boredom.
Authority and Responsibility Managers have the right to give orders and the power to exhort subordinates for obedience.
Unity of Command An employee should receive orders from only one superior.
Line of Authority The length of the chain of command that extends from the top to the bottom of an organization should be limited.
Centralization Authority should not be concentrated at the top of the chain of command.
Unity of Direction The organization should have a single plan of action to guide managers and workers.
Equity All organizational members are entitled to be treated with justice and respect.
Order The arrangement of organizational positions should maximize organizational efficiency and provide employees with satisfying career opportunities.
Initiative Managers should allow employees to be innovative and creative.
Discipline Managers need to create a workforce that strives to achieve organizational goals.
Remuneration of Personnel The system that managers use to reward employees should be equitable for both employees and the organization.
Stability of Tenure of Personnel Long-term employees develop skills that can improve organizational efficiency.
Subordination of Individual Interests to the Common Interest Employees should understand how their performance affects the performance of the whole organization.
Esprit de Corps Managers should encourage the development of shared feelings of comradeship, enthusiasm, or devotion to a common cause.

Fayol also pointed out that when organizations are split into different departments or functions, each with its own hierarchy, it is important to allow middle and first-line managers in each department to interact with managers at similar levels in other departments. This interaction helps to speed decision making, because managers know each other and know whom to go to when problems arise. For cross-departmental integration to work, Fayol noted the importance of keeping one's superiors informed about what is taking place so that lower-level decisions do not harm activities taking place in other parts of the organization. One alternative to cross-departmental integration is to create cross-departmental teams controlled by a team leader (see Chapter 1).

centralization The concentration of authority at the top of the managerial hierarchy.

CENTRALIZATION Fayol also was one of the first management writers to focus on **centralization,** the concentration of authority at the top of the managerial hierarchy. Fayol believed that authority should not be concentrated at the top of the chain of command. One of the most significant issues that top managers face is how much authority to centralize at the top of the organization and what authority to decentralize to managers and workers at lower hierarchical levels. This is an important issue because it affects the behavior of people at all levels in the organization.

If authority is very centralized, only managers at the top make important decisions, and subordinates simply follow orders. This arrangement gives top managers great control over organizational activities and helps ensure that the organization is pursuing its strategy, but it makes it difficult for the people who are closest to problems and issues to respond to them in a timely manner. It also can lower the motivation of middle and first-line managers and make them less flexible and adaptable because they become reluctant to make decisions on their own, even when doing so is necessary. They get used to passing the buck. As we saw in Chapter 1, the pendulum is now swinging toward decentralization, as organizations seek to empower middle managers and create self-managed teams that monitor and control their own activities both to increase organizational flexibility and to reduce operating costs and increase efficiency.

unity of direction The singleness of purpose that makes possible the creation of one plan of action to guide managers and workers as they use organizational resources.

UNITY OF DIRECTION Just as there is a need for unity of command, there is also a need for **unity of direction,** the singleness of purpose that makes possible the creation of one plan of action to guide managers and workers as they use organizational resources. An organization without a single guiding plan becomes inefficient and ineffective; its activities become unfocused, and individuals and groups work at cross-purposes. Successful planning starts with top managers working as a team to craft the organization's strategy, which they communicate to middle managers, who decide how to use organizational resources to implement the strategy.

equity The justice, impartiality, and fairness to which all organizational members are entitled.

EQUITY As Fayol wrote, "For personnel to be encouraged to carry out their duties with all the devotion and loyalty of which they are capable, they must be treated with respect for their own sense of integrity, and equity results from the combination of respect and justice."[23] **Equity**–the justice, impartiality, and fairness to which all organizational members are entitled–is receiving much attention today; the desire to treat employees fairly is a primary concern for many managers. (Equity theory is discussed in Chapter 12).

order The methodical arrangement of positions to provide the organization with the greatest benefit and to provide employees with career opportunities.

ORDER Like Taylor and the Gilbreths, Fayol was interested in analyzing jobs, positions, and individuals to ensure that the organization was using resources as efficiently as possible. To Fayol, **order** meant the methodical arrangement of positions to provide the organization with the greatest benefit and to provide employees with career opportunities that satisfy their needs. Thus, Fayol recommended the use of organizational charts to show the position and duties of each employee and to indicate which positions an employee might move to or be promoted into in the future. He also advocated that managers engage in extensive career planning to help ensure orderly career paths. Career planning is of primary interest today as organizations increase the resources they are willing to devote to training and developing their workforces.

initiative The ability to act on one's own, without direction from a superior.

INITIATIVE Although order and equity are important means to fostering commitment and loyalty among employees, Fayol believed that managers must also encourage employees to exercise **initiative,** the ability to act on their own, without direction from a superior. Used properly, initiative can be a major source of strength for an organization because it leads to creativity and innovation. Managers need skill and tact to achieve the difficult balance between the organization's need for order and employees' desire for initiative.

Fayol believed that the ability to strike this balance was a key indicator of a superior manager.

discipline Obedience, energy, application, and other outward marks of respect for a superior's authority.

DISCIPLINE In focusing on the importance of **discipline**–obedience, energy, application, and other outward marks of respect for a superior's authority–Fayol was addressing the concern of many early managers: How to create a workforce that was reliable and hardworking and would strive to achieve organizational goals. According to Fayol, discipline results in respectful relations between organizational members and reflects the quality of an organization's leadership and a manager's ability to act fairly and equitably.

REMUNERATION OF PERSONNEL Fayol proposed reward systems including bonuses and profit-sharing plans, which are increasingly utilized today as organizations seek improved ways to motivate employees. Convinced from his own experience that an organization's payment system has important implications for organizational success, Fayol believed that effective reward systems should be equitable for both employees and the organization, encourage productivity by rewarding well-directed effort, not be subject to abuse, and be uniformly applied to employees.

STABILITY OF TENURE OF PERSONNEL Fayol also recognized the importance of long-term employment, and the idea has been echoed by contemporary management gurus such as Tom Peters, Jeff Pfeffer, and William Ouchi. When employees stay with an organization for extended periods of time, they develop skills that improve the organization's ability to utilize its resources.

SUBORDINATION OF INDIVIDUAL INTERESTS TO THE COMMON INTEREST The interests of the organization as a whole must take precedence over the interests of any one individual or group if the organization is to survive. Equitable agreements must be established between the organization and its members to ensure that employees are treated fairly and rewarded for their performance and to maintain the disciplined organizational relationships so vital to an efficient system of administration.

esprit de corps Shared feelings of comradeship, enthusiasm, or devotion to a common cause among members of a group.

ESPRIT DE CORPS As this discussion of Fayol's ideas suggests, the appropriate design of an organization's hierarchy of authority and the right mix of order and discipline foster cooperation and commitment. Likewise, a key element in a successful organization is the development of **esprit de corps,** a French expression that refers to shared feelings of comradeship, enthusiasm, or devotion to a common cause among members of a group. Esprit de corps can result when managers encourage personal, verbal contact between managers and workers and encourage communication to solve problems and implement solutions. (Today, the term *organizational culture* is used to refer to these shared feelings; this concept is discussed at length in Chapter 3.)

Some of the principles that Fayol outlined have faded from contemporary management practices, but most have endured. The characteristics of organizations that Tom Peters and Robert Waterman identified as being "excellently managed" in their best-selling book *In Search of Excellence* (1982) are discussed in the following "Management Insight."[24]

Management Insight

Peters and Waterman's Excellent Companies

In the early 1980s, Tom Peters and Robert Waterman identified 62 organizations that they considered to be the best-performing organizations in the United States. They asked the question: Why do these companies perform better than their rivals? and discovered that successful organizations have managers who manage according to three sets of related principles. Those principles have a great deal in common with Fayol's principles.

First, Peters and Waterman argued, top managers of successful companies create principles and guidelines that emphasize managerial autonomy and entrepreneurship and encourage risk taking and *initiative.* For example, they allow middle managers to develop new products, even though there is no assurance that these products will be winners. In high-performing organizations, top managers are closely involved in the day-to-day operations of the company, provide *unity of command* and *unity of direction,* and do not simply make decisions in an isolated ivory tower. Top managers *decentralize authority* to lower-level managers and nonmanagerial employees and give them the freedom to get involved and the motivation to get things done.

The second approach that managers of excellent organizations use to increase performance is to create one central plan that puts organizational goals at center stage. In high-performing organizations, managers focus attention on what the organization does best, and the emphasis is on continuously improving the goods and services the organization provides to its customers. Managers of top-performing companies resist the temptation to get sidetracked into pursuing ventures outside their area of expertise just because they seem to promise a quick return. These managers also focus on customers and establish close relationships with them to learn their needs, for responsiveness to customers increases competitive advantage.

The third set of management principles pertains to organizing and controlling the organization. Excellent companies establish a *division of work* and a *division of authority and responsibility* that will motivate employees to *subordinate their individual interests to the common interest.* Inherent in this approach is the belief that high performance derives from individual skills and abilities and that *equity, order, initiative,* and other indications of respect for the individual create the *esprit de corps* that fosters productive behavior. An emphasis on entrepreneurship and respect for every employee leads the best managers to create a structure that gives employees room to exercise *initiative* and motivates them to succeed. Because a simple, streamlined managerial hierarchy is best suited to achieve this outcome, top managers keep the *line of authority* as short as possible. They also decentralize authority to permit employee participation, but they keep enough control to maintain *unity of direction.*

As this insight into contemporary management suggests, the basic concerns that motivated Fayol continue to motivate management theorists.[25] The principles that Fayol and Weber set forth still provide a clear and appropriate set of guidelines that managers can use to create a work setting that makes efficient and effective use of organizational resources. These principles remain the bedrock of modern management theory; recent researchers have refined or developed them to suit modern conditions. For example, Weber's and Fayol's concerns for equity and for establishing appropriate links between performance and reward are central themes in contemporary theories of motivation and leadership.

Behavioral Management Theory

Because the writings of Weber and Fayol were not translated into English and published in the United States until the late 1940s, American management theorists in the first half of the 20th century were unaware of the contributions of these European pioneers. American management theorists began where Taylor and his followers left off. Although their writings were all very different, these theorists all espoused a theme that focused on **behavioral management,** the study of how managers should personally behave to motivate employees and encourage them to perform at high levels and be committed to achieving organizational goals.

behavioral management The study of how managers should behave to motivate employees and encourage them to perform at high levels and be committed to the achievement of organizational goals.

The Work of Mary Parker Follett

If F. W. Taylor is considered the father of management thought, Mary Parker Follett (1868–1933) serves as its mother.[26] Much of her writing about management and about the way managers should behave toward workers was a response to her concern that Taylor was ignoring the human side of the organization. She pointed out that management often overlooks the multitude of ways in which employees can contribute to the organization when managers allow them to participate and exercise initiative in their everyday work lives.[27] Taylor, for example, never proposed that managers should involve workers in analyzing their jobs to identify better ways to perform tasks or should even ask workers how they felt about their jobs. Instead, he used time-and-motion experts to analyze workers' jobs for them. Follett, in contrast, argued that because workers know the most about their jobs, they should be involved in job analysis and managers should allow them to participate in the work development process.

Mary Parker Follett, an early management thinker who advocated that "Authority should go with knowledge . . . whether it is up the line or down."

Follett proposed that "authority should go with knowledge . . . whether it is up the line or down." In other words, if workers have the relevant knowledge, then workers, rather than managers, should be in control of the work process itself, and managers should behave as coaches and facilitators–not as monitors and supervisors. In making this statement, Follett anticipated the current interest in self-managed teams and empowerment. She also recognized the importance of having managers in different departments communicate directly with each other to speed decision making. She advocated what she called "cross-functioning": members of different departments working together in cross-departmental teams to accomplish projects–an approach that is increasingly utilized today.[28]

Fayol also mentioned expertise and knowledge as important sources of managers' authority, but Follett went further. She proposed that knowledge and expertise, and not managers' formal authority deriving from their position in the hierarchy, should decide who will lead at any particular moment. She believed, as do many management theorists today, that power is fluid and should flow to the person who can best help the organization achieve its goals. Follett took a horizontal view of power and authority, in contrast to Fayol, who saw the formal line of authority and vertical chain of command as being most essential to effective management. Follett's behavioral approach to management was very radical for its time.

The Hawthorne Studies and Human Relations

Probably because of its radical nature, Follett's work was unappreciated by managers and researchers until quite recently. Most continued to follow in the footsteps of Taylor and the Gilbreths. To increase efficiency, they studied ways to improve various characteristics of the work setting, such as job specialization or the kinds of tools workers used. One series of studies was conducted from 1924 to 1932 at the Hawthorne Works of the Western Electric Company.[29] This research, now known as the *Hawthorne studies,* began as an attempt to investigate how characteristics of the work setting–specifically the level of lighting or illumination–affect worker fatigue and performance. The researchers conducted an experiment in which they systematically measured worker productivity at various levels of illumination.

The experiment produced some unexpected results. The researchers found that regardless of whether they raised or lowered the level of illumination, productivity increased. In fact, productivity began to fall only when the level of illumination dropped to the level of moonlight, a level at which, presumably, workers could no longer see well enough to do their work efficiently.

The researchers found these results puzzling and invited a noted Harvard psychologist, Elton Mayo, to help them. Mayo proposed another series of experiments to solve the mystery. These experiments, known as the *relay assembly test experiments,* were designed to investigate the effects of other aspects of the work context on job performance, such as the effect of the number and length of rest periods and hours of work on fatigue and monotony.[30] The goal was to raise productivity.

Workers in a telephone manufacturing plant, in 1931. Around this time, researchers at the Hawthorne Works of the Western Electric Company began to study the effects of work setting characteristics—such as lighting and rest periods—on productivity. To their surprise, they discovered that workers' productivity was affected more by the attention they received from researchers than by the characteristics of the work setting—a phenomenon that became known as the Hawthorne Effect.

During a two-year study of a small group of female workers, the researchers again observed that productivity increased over time, but the increases could not be solely attributed to the effects of changes in the work setting. Gradually, the researchers discovered that, to some degree, the results they were obtaining were influenced by the fact that the researchers themselves had become part of the experiment. In other words, the presence of the researchers was affecting the results because the workers enjoyed receiving attention and being the subject of study and were willing to cooperate with the researchers to produce the results they believed the researchers desired.

Subsequently, it was found that many other factors also influence worker behavior, and it was not clear what was actually influencing the Hawthorne workers' behavior. However, this particular effect–which became known as the **Hawthorne effect**–seemed to suggest that workers' attitudes toward their managers affect the level of workers' performance. In particular, the significant finding was that each manager's personal behavior or leadership approach can affect performance. This finding led many researchers to turn their attention to managerial behavior and leadership. If supervisors could be trained to behave in ways that would elicit cooperative behavior from their subordinates, then productivity could be increased. From this view emerged the **human relations movement,** which advocates that supervisors be behaviorally trained to manage subordinates in ways that elicit their cooperation and increase their productivity.

Hawthorne effect The finding that a manager's behavior or leadership approach can affect workers' level of performance.

human relations movement A management approach that advocates the idea that supervisors should receive behavioral training to manage subordinates in ways that elicit their cooperation and increase their productivity.

The importance of behavioral or human relations training became even clearer to its supporters after another series of experiments–the *bank wiring room experiments.* In a study of workers making telephone switching equipment, researchers Elton Mayo and F. J. Roethlisberger discovered that the workers, as a group, had deliberately adopted a norm of output restriction to protect their jobs. Workers who violated this informal production norm were subjected to sanctions by other group members. Those who violated group performance norms and performed above the norm were called "ratebusters"; those who performed below the norm were called "chiselers."

The experimenters concluded that both types of workers threatened the group as a whole. Ratebusters threatened group members because they revealed to managers how fast the work could be done. Chiselers were looked down on because they were not doing their share of the work. Work-group members disciplined both ratebusters and chiselers to create a pace of work that the workers (not the managers) thought was fair. Thus, a work group's influence over output can be as great as the supervisors' influence. Since the work group can influence the behavior of its members, some management theorists argue that supervisors should be trained to behave in ways that gain the goodwill and cooperation of workers so that supervisors, not workers, control the level of work-group performance.

One of the main implications of the Hawthorne studies was that the behavior of managers and workers in the work setting is as important in explaining the level of performance as the technical aspects of the task. Managers must understand the workings of the **informal organization,** the system of behavioral rules and norms that emerge in a group, when they try to manage or change behavior in organizations. Many studies have found that, as time passes, groups often develop elaborate procedures and norms that bond members together, allowing unified action either to cooperate with management to raise performance or to restrict output and thwart the attainment of organizational goals.[31] The Hawthorne studies demonstrated the importance of understanding how the feelings, thoughts, and behavior of work-group members and managers affect performance. It was becoming increasingly clear to researchers that understanding behavior in organizations is a complex process that is critical to increasing performance.[32] Indeed, the increasing interest in the area of management known as **organizational behavior,** the study of the factors that have an impact on how individuals and groups respond to and act in organizations, dates from these early studies.

informal organization The system of behavioral rules and norms that emerge in a group.

organizational behavior The study of the factors that have an impact on how individuals and groups respond to and act in organizations.

Theory X and Theory Y

Several studies after World War II revealed how assumptions about workers' attitudes and behavior affect managers' behavior. Perhaps the most influential approach was developed by Douglas McGregor. He proposed two sets of assumptions about how work attitudes and behaviors not only dominate the way managers think but also affect how they behave in organizations. McGregor named these two contrasting sets of assumptions *Theory X* and *Theory Y* (see Figure 2.3).[33]

Theory X A set of negative assumptions about workers that lead to the conclusion that a manager's task is to supervise workers closely and control their behavior.

THEORY X According to the assumptions of **Theory X,** the average worker is lazy, dislikes work, and will try to do as little as possible. Moreover, workers have little ambition and wish to avoid responsibility. Thus, the manager's task is to counteract workers' natural tendencies to avoid work. To keep workers' performance at a high level, the manager must supervise workers closely and control their behavior by means of "the carrot and stick"–rewards and punishments.

Managers who accept the assumptions of Theory X design and shape the work setting to maximize their control over workers' behaviors and minimize workers' control over the pace of work. These managers believe that workers must be made to do what is necessary for the success of the organization, and they focus on developing rules, SOPs, and a well-defined system of rewards and punishments to control behavior. They see little point in giving workers autonomy to solve their own problems because they think that the workforce neither expects nor desires cooperation. Theory X managers see their role as closely monitoring workers to ensure that they contribute to the production process and do not threaten product quality. Henry Ford, who closely supervised and managed his workforce, fits McGregor's description of a manager who holds Theory X assumptions.

Theory Y A set of positive assumptions about workers that lead to the conclusion that a manager's task is to create a work setting that encourages commitment to organizational goals and provides opportunities for workers to be imaginative and to exercise initiative and self-direction.

THEORY Y In contrast, **Theory Y** assumes that workers are not inherently lazy, do not naturally dislike work, and, if given the opportunity, will do what is good for the organization. According to Theory Y, the characteristics of the work setting determine whether workers consider work to be a source of satisfaction or punishment, and managers do not need to closely control workers' behavior to make them perform at a high level because workers exercise self-control when they are committed to organizational goals. The implication of Theory Y, according to McGregor, is that "the limits of collaboration in the

Figure 2.3
Theory X versus Theory Y
Source: D. McGregor, *The Human Side of Enterprise,* 1960, McGraw-Hill, reproduced with permission of the McGraw-Hill Companies, Inc.

THEORY X	THEORY Y
The average employee is lazy, dislikes work, and will try to do as little as possible.	Employees are not inherently lazy. Given the chance, employees will do what is good for the organization.
To ensure that employees work hard, managers should closely supervise employees.	To allow employees to work in the organization's interest, managers must create a work setting that provides opportunities for workers to exercise initiative and self-direction.
Managers should create strict work rules and implement a well-defined system of rewards and punishments to control employees.	Managers should decentralize authority to employees and make sure employees have the resources necessary to achieve organizational goals.

organizational setting are not limits of human nature but of management's ingenuity in discovering how to realize the potential represented by its human resources."[34] It is the manager's task to create a work setting that encourages commitment to organizational goals and provides opportunities for workers to be imaginative and to exercise initiative and self-direction.

When managers design the organizational setting to reflect the assumptions about attitudes and behavior suggested by Theory Y, the characteristics of the organization are quite different from those of an organizational setting based on Theory X. Managers who believe that workers are motivated to help the organization reach its goals can decentralize authority and give more control over the job to workers, both as individuals and in groups. In this setting, individuals and groups are still accountable for their activities, but the manager's role is not to control employees but to provide support and advice, to make sure employees have the resources they need to perform their jobs, and to evaluate them on their ability to help the organization meet its goals. Henri Fayol's approach to administration more closely reflects the assumptions of Theory Y, rather than Theory X. One company that has always operated with the type of management philosophy inherent in Theory Y is Hewlett-Packard, the subject of the next "Manager as a Person."

Manager as a Person

The Hewlett-Packard Way

Managers at the electronics company Hewlett-Packard (HP) consistently put into practice principles derived from Theory Y. (Go to the company's Web site at www.hp.com for additional information.) Founders William Hewlett and David Packard–Bill and Dave, as they are still known throughout the organization–established a philosophy of management known as the "HP Way" that is people-oriented, stresses the importance of treating every person with consideration and respect, and offers recognition for achievements.[35]

Faced with questions about the company's survival, HP CEO Carly Fiorina was forced break with the tradition of "long-term employment" and lay off over 40 percent of the workforce.

HP's philosophy rests on a few guiding principles. One is a policy of long-term employment. HP goes to great lengths not to lay off workers. At times when fewer people were needed, rather than lay off workers management cut pay and shortened the workday until demand for HP products picked up. This policy strengthened employees' loyalty to the organization.

The HP Way is based on several golden rules about how to treat members of the organization so that they feel free to be innovative and creative. HP managers believe that every employee of the company is a member of the HP team. They emphasize the need to increase the level of communication among employees, believing that horizontal communication between peers, not just vertical communication up and down the hierarchy, is essential for creating a positive climate for innovation.

To promote communication and cooperation between employees at different levels of the hierarchy, HP encourages informality. Managers and workers are on a first-name basis with each other and with the founders, Bill and Dave. In addition, Bill and Dave pioneered the technique known as "managing by wandering around." People are expected to wander around learning what others are doing so that they can tap into opportunities to develop new products or find new avenues for cooperation. Bill and Dave also pioneered the principle that employees should spend 15 percent of their time working on projects of their own choosing, and they encouraged employees to take equipment and supplies home to experiment with them on their own time. HP's product design engineers leave their current work out in the open on their desks so that anybody can see what they are doing, can learn from it, or can suggest ways to improve it. Managers are selected and promoted because of their ability to engender excitement and enthusiasm for innovation in their subordinates. HP's offices have low walls and shared laboratories to facilitate communication and cooperation between managers and workers. In all these ways, HP managers seek to promote each employee's desire to be innovative and also to create a team and family atmosphere based on cooperation.[36]

The results of HP's practices helped it become one of the leading electronics companies in the world. In 2001, however, HP, like most other high-tech companies, was experiencing major problems because of the collapse of the telecommunications industry, and the company announced that it was searching for ways to reduce costs. At first, its current CEO, Carly Fiorino, in keeping with the management philosophy and values of the company's founders, announced that HP would not lay off employees but asked them to accept lower salaries and unpaid leave to help the company through this rough spot.[37] It soon became clear, however, that HP's very survival was at stake as it battled with efficient global competitors such as Dell and Canon. To fight back, HP merged with Compaq, but by 2004 it had been forced to lay off over 40 percent of its employees and outsource thousands of jobs abroad in order to remain competitive. Fiorino still believes, however, that HP's values will survive its crisis and help it become the global leader in the next decade.[38]

Management Science Theory

Management science theory is a contemporary approach to management that focuses on the use of rigorous quantitative techniques to help managers make maximum use of organizational resources to produce goods and services. In essence, management science theory is a contemporary extension of scientific management, which, as developed by Taylor, also took a quantitative approach to measuring the worker-task mix to raise efficiency. There are many branches of management science, and once again, IT, which is having a significant impact on all kinds of management practices, is affecting the tools managers use to make decisions.[39] Each branch of management science deals with a specific set of concerns:

management science theory An approach to management that uses rigorous quantitative techniques to help managers make maximum use of organizational resources.

- *Quantitative management* utilizes mathematical techniques–such as linear and nonlinear programming, modeling, simulation, queuing theory, and chaos theory–to help managers decide, for example, how much inventory to hold at different times of the year, where to locate a new factory, and how best to invest an organization's financial capital. IT offers managers new and improved ways of handling information so that they can make more accurate assessments of the situation and better decisions.

- *Operations management* provides managers with a set of techniques that they can use to analyze any aspect of an organization's production system to increase efficiency. IT, through the Internet and through growing B2B networks, is transforming the way managers handle the acquisition of inputs and the disposal of finished products.
- *Total quality management (TQM)* focuses on analyzing an organization's input, conversion, and output activities to increase product quality.[40] Once again, through sophisticated software packages and computer-controlled production, IT is changing the way managers and employees think about the work process and ways of improving it.
- *Management information systems (MISs)* help managers design systems that provide information about events occurring inside the organization as well as in its external environment–information that is vital for effective decision making. Once again, IT gives managers access to more and better information and allows more managers at all levels to participate in the decision-making process.

All these subfields of management science, enhanced by sophisticated IT, provide tools and techniques that managers can use to help improve the quality of their decision making and increase efficiency and effectiveness. We discuss many of the important developments in management science theory thoroughly in Part 6 of this book. In particular, Chapter 17, "Managing Information Systems and Technologies," describes the management of information systems and technologies, and Chapter 18, "Operations Management: Managing Quality, Efficiency, and Responsiveness to Customers," focuses on IT, operations management, and TQM.

Organizational Environment Theory

An important milestone in the history of management thought occurred when researchers went beyond the study of how managers can influence behavior within organizations to consider how managers control the organization's relationship with its external environment, or **organizational environment**–the set of forces and conditions that operate beyond an organization's boundaries but affect a manager's ability to acquire and utilize resources. Resources in the organizational environment include the raw materials and skilled people that an organization requires to produce goods and services, as well as the support of groups, including customers who buy these goods and services and provide the organization with financial resources. One way of determining the relative success of an organization is to consider how effective its managers are at obtaining scarce and valuable resources.[41] The importance of studying the environment became clear after the development of open-systems theory and contingency theory during the 1960s.

organizational environment The set of forces and conditions that operate beyond an organization's boundaries but affect a manager's ability to acquire and utilize resources.

The Open-Systems View

One of the most influential views of how an organization is affected by its external environment was developed by Daniel Katz, Robert Kahn, and James Thompson in the 1960s.[42] These theorists viewed the organization as an

Figure 2.4
The Organization as an Open System

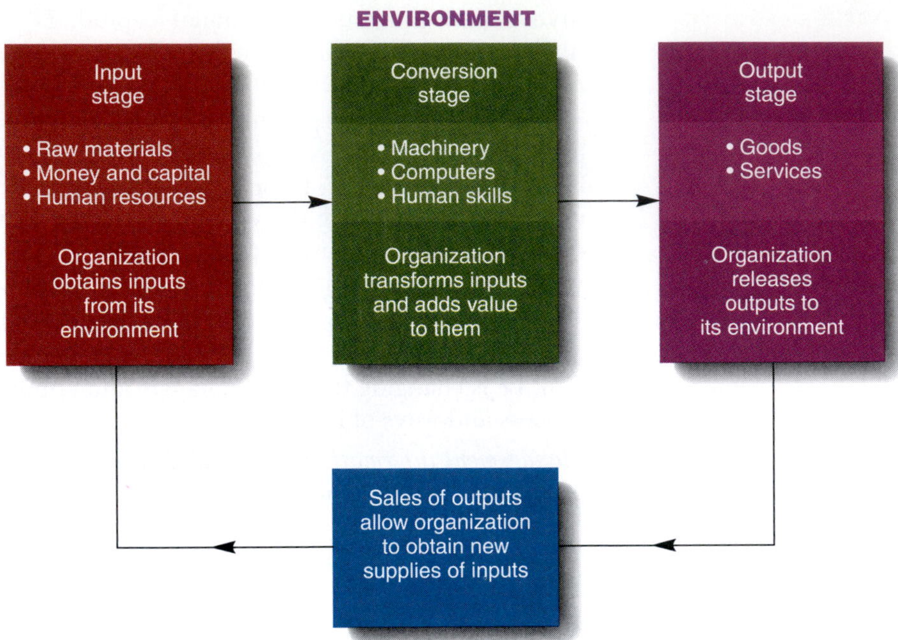
ENVIRONMENT
Input stage
• Raw materials
• Money and capital
• Human resources
Organization obtains inputs from its environment
Conversion stage
• Machinery
• Computers
• Human skills
Organization transforms inputs and adds value to them
Output stage
• Goods
• Services
Organization releases outputs to its environment
Sales of outputs allow organization to obtain new supplies of inputs

open system A system that takes in resources from its external environment and converts them into goods and services that are then sent back to that environment for purchase by customers.

open system—a system that takes in resources from its external environment and converts or transforms them into goods and services that are sent back to that environment, where they are bought by customers (see Figure 2.4).

At the *input stage* an organization acquires resources such as raw materials, money, and skilled workers to produce goods and services. Once the organization has gathered the necessary resources, conversion begins. At the *conversion stage* the organization's workforce, using appropriate tools, techniques, and machinery, transforms the inputs into outputs of finished goods and services such as cars, hamburgers, or flights to Hawaii. At the *output stage* the organization releases finished goods and services to its external environment, where customers purchase and use them to satisfy their needs. The money the organization obtains from the sales of its outputs allows the organization to acquire more resources so that the cycle can begin again.

closed system A system that is self-contained and thus not affected by changes occurring in its external environment.

entropy The tendency of a closed system to lose its ability to control itself and thus to dissolve and disintegrate.

The system just described is said to be open because the organization draws from and interacts with the external environment in order to survive; in other words, the organization is open to its environment. A **closed system,** in contrast, is a self-contained system that is not affected by changes in its external environment. Organizations that operate as closed systems, that ignore the external environment, and that fail to acquire inputs are likely to experience **entropy,** the tendency of a closed system to lose its ability to control itself and thus to dissolve and disintegrate.

Management theorists can model the activities of most organizations by using the open-systems view. Manufacturing companies like Ford and General Electric, for example, buy inputs such as component parts, skilled and semiskilled labor, and robots and computer-controlled manufacturing equipment; then at the conversion stage they use their manufacturing skills to assemble inputs into outputs of cars and appliances. As we discuss in later chapters, competition between organizations for resources is one of several major challenges to managing the organizational environment.

Figure 2.5
Contingency Theory of Organizational Design

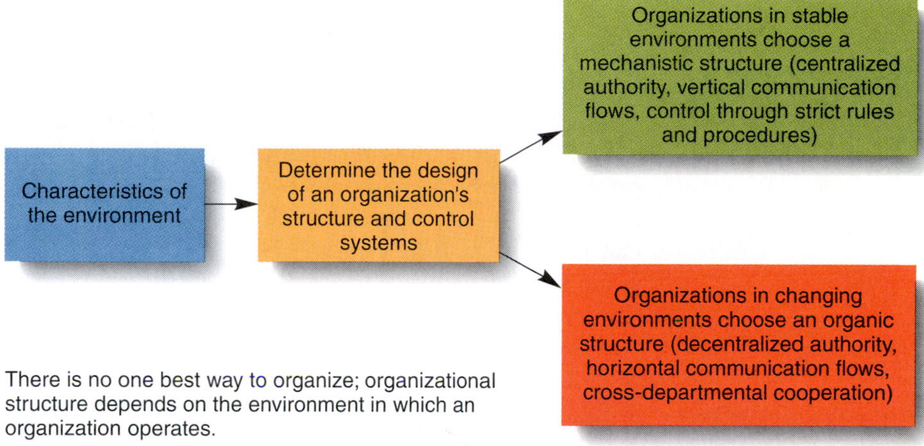

There is no one best way to organize; organizational structure depends on the environment in which an organization operates.

synergy Performance gains that result when individuals and departments coordinate their actions.

Researchers using the open-systems view are also interested in how the various parts of a system work together to promote efficiency and effectiveness. Systems theorists like to argue that the whole is greater than the sum of its parts; they mean that an organization performs at a higher level when its departments work together rather than separately. **Synergy,** the performance gains that result from the *combined* actions of individuals and departments, is possible only in an organized system. The recent interest in using teams combined or composed of people from different departments reflects systems theorists' interest in designing organizational systems to create synergy and thus increase efficiency and effectiveness.

Contingency Theory

contingency theory The idea that the organizational structures and control systems managers choose depend on—are contingent on—characteristics of the external environment in which the organization operates.

Another milestone in management theory was the development of **contingency theory** in the 1960s by Tom Burns and G. M. Stalker in Britain and Paul Lawrence and Jay Lorsch in the United States.[43] The crucial message of contingency theory is that *there is no one best way to organize:* The organizational structures and the control systems that managers choose depend on–are contingent on–characteristics of the external environment in which the organization operates. According to contingency theory, the characteristics of the environment affect an organization's ability to obtain resources; and to maximize the likelihood of gaining access to resources, managers must allow an organization's departments to organize and control their activities in ways most likely to allow them to obtain resources, given the constraints of the particular environment they face. In other words, how managers design the organizational hierarchy, choose a control system, and lead and motivate their employees is contingent on the characteristics of the organizational environment (see Figure 2.5).

An important characteristic of the external environment that affects an organization's ability to obtain resources is the degree to which the environment is changing. Changes in the organizational environment include changes in technology, which can lead to the creation of new products (such as compact discs) and result in the obsolescence of existing products (eight-track tapes); the entry of new competitors (such as foreign organizations that compete for available resources); and unstable economic conditions. In general, the more quickly the organizational environment is changing, the greater are the problems associated with gaining access to resources and the greater is managers' need to find ways to coordinate the activities of people in different departments to respond to the environment quickly and effectively.

MECHANISTIC AND ORGANIC STRUCTURES Drawing on Weber's and Fayol's principles of organization and management, Burns and Stalker proposed two basic ways in which managers can organize and control an organization's activities to respond to characteristics of its external environment: They can use a *mechanistic structure* or an *organic structure*.[44] As you will see, a mechanistic structure typically rests on Theory X assumptions, and an organic structure typically rests on Theory Y assumptions.

mechanistic structure An organizational structure in which authority is centralized, tasks and rules are clearly specified, and employees are closely supervised.

When the environment surrounding an organization is stable, managers tend to choose a mechanistic structure to organize and control activities and make employee behavior predictable. In a **mechanistic structure,** authority is centralized at the top of the managerial hierarchy, and the vertical hierarchy of authority is the main means used to control subordinates' behavior. Tasks and roles are clearly specified, subordinates are closely supervised, and the emphasis is on strict discipline and order. Everyone knows his or her place, and there is a place for everyone. A mechanistic structure provides the most efficient way to operate in a stable environment because it allows managers to obtain inputs at the lowest cost, giving an organization the most control over its conversion processes and enabling the most efficient production of goods and services with the smallest expenditure of resources. McDonald's restaurants operate with a mechanistic structure. Supervisors make all important decisions; employees are closely supervised and follow well-defined rules and standard operating procedures.

organic structure An organizational structure in which authority is decentralized to middle and first-line managers and tasks and roles are left ambiguous to encourage employees to cooperate and respond quickly to the unexpected.

In contrast, when the environment is changing rapidly, it is difficult to obtain access to resources, and managers need to organize their activities in a way that allows them to cooperate, to act quickly to acquire resources (such as new types of inputs to produce new kinds of products), and to respond effectively to the unexpected. In an **organic structure,** authority is decentralized to middle and first-line managers to encourage them to take responsibility and act quickly to pursue scarce resources. Departments are encouraged to take a cross-departmental or functional perspective, and, as in Mary Parker Follett's model, authority rests with the individuals and departments best positioned to control the current problems the organization is facing. In an organic structure, control is much looser than it is in a mechanistic structure, and reliance on shared norms to guide organizational activities is greater. Managers in an organic structure can react more quickly to a changing environment than can managers in a mechanistic structure. However, an organic structure is generally more expensive to operate because it requires that more managerial time, money, and effort be spent on coordination. So it is used only when needed–when the organizational environment is unstable and rapidly changing.

Summary and Review

In this chapter we examined the evolution of management theory and research over the last century. Much of the material in the rest of this book stems from developments and refinements of this work.

SCIENTIFIC MANAGEMENT THEORY The search for efficiency started with the study of how managers could improve person-task relationships to increase efficiency. The concept of job specialization and division of labor remains the basis for the design of work settings in modern organizations. New developments such as lean production and total quality management are often viewed as advances on the early scientific management principles developed by Taylor and the Gilbreths.

ADMINISTRATIVE MANAGEMENT THEORY Max Weber and Henri Fayol outlined principles of bureaucracy and administration that are as relevant to managers today as they were when developed at the turn of the 20th century. Much of modern management research refines these principles to suit contemporary conditions. For example, the increasing interest in the use of cross-departmental teams and the empowerment of workers are issues that managers also faced a century ago.

BEHAVIORAL MANAGEMENT THEORY Researchers have described many different approaches to managerial behavior, including Theories X and Y. Often, the managerial behavior that researchers suggest reflects the context of their own historical era and culture. Mary Parker Follett advocated managerial behaviors that did not reflect accepted modes of managerial behavior at the time, and her work was largely ignored until conditions changed.

MANAGEMENT SCIENCE THEORY The various branches of management science theory provide rigorous quantitative techniques that give managers more control over each organization's use of resources to produce goods and services.

ORGANIZATIONAL ENVIRONMENT THEORY The importance of studying the organization's external environment became clear after the development of open-systems theory and contingency theory during the 1960s. A main focus of contemporary management research is to find methods to help managers improve the ways they utilize organizational resources and compete successfully in the global environment. Strategic management and total quality management are two important approaches intended to help managers make better use of organizational resources.

Management in Action

Topics for Discussion and Action

Discussion

1. Choose a fast-food restaurant, a department store, or some other organization with which you are familiar, and describe the division of labor and job specialization it uses to produce goods and services. How might this division of labor be improved?
2. Apply Taylor's principles of scientific management to improve the performance of the organization you chose in item 1.
3. In what ways are Weber's and Fayol's ideas about bureaucracy and administration similar? In what ways do they differ?
4. Which of Weber's and Fayol's principles seem most relevant to the creation of an ethical organization?
5. Why was the work of Mary Parker Follett ahead of its time? To what degree do you think it is appropriate today?
6. What is contingency theory? What kinds of organizations familiar to you have been successful or unsuccessful in dealing with contingencies from the external environment?
7. Why are mechanistic and organic structures suited to different organizational environments?

Action

8. Question a manager about his or her views of the relative importance of Fayol's 14 principles of management.
9. Visit at least two organizations in your community, and identify those that seem to operate with a Theory X or a Theory Y approach to management.

Building Management Skills

Managing Your Own Business

Now that you understand the concerns addressed by management thinkers over the last century, use this exercise to apply your knowledge to developing your management skills.

Imagine that you are the founding entrepreneur of a software company that specializes in developing games for home computers. Customer demand for your games has increased so much that over the last year your company has grown from a busy 1-person operation to one with 16 employees. In addition to yourself, you employ six software developers to produce the software, three graphic artists, two computer technicians, two marketing and sales personnel, and two secretaries. In the next year you expect to hire 30 new employees, and you are wondering how best to manage your growing company.

1. Use the principles of Weber and Fayol to decide on the system of organization and management that you think will be most effective for your growing organization. How many levels will the managerial hierarchy of your organization have? How much authority will you decentralize to your subordinates? How will you establish the division of labor between subordinates? Will your subordinates work alone and report to you or work in teams?
2. Which management approach (for example, Theory X or Y) do you propose to use to run your organization? In 50 words or less write a statement describing the management approach you believe will motivate and coordinate your subordinates, and tell why you think this style will be best.

Managing Ethically

Mr. Edens Profits from Watching His Workers' Every Move

Read the case below, "Mr. Edens Profits from Watching His Workers' Every Move," and think about the following issues.

Control is one of Ron Edens's favorite words. "This is a controlled environment," he says of the blank brick building that houses his company, Electronic Banking System Inc.

Inside, long lines of women sit at spartan desks, slitting envelopes, sorting contents and filling out "control cards" that record how many letters they have opened and how long it has taken them. Workers here, in "the cage," must process three envelopes a minute. Nearby, other women tap keyboards, keeping pace with a quota that demands 8,500 strokes an hour.

The room is silent. Talking is forbidden. The windows are covered. Coffee mugs, religious pictures and other adornments are barred from workers' desks.

In his office upstairs, Mr. Edens sits before a TV monitor that flashes images from eight cameras posted through the plant. "There's a little bit of Sneaky Pete to it," he says, using a remote control to zoom in on a document atop a worker's desk. "I can basically read that and figure out how someone's day is going."

This day, like most others, is going smoothly, and Mr. Edens's business has boomed as a result. "We maintain a lot of control," he says. "Order and control are everything in this business."

Mr. Edens's business belongs to a small but expanding financial service known as "lockbox processing." Many companies and charities that once did their paperwork in-house now "out-source" clerical tasks to firms like EBS, which processes donations to groups such as Mothers Against Drunk Driving, the Doris Day Animal League, Greenpeace and the National Organization for Women.

More broadly, EBS reflects the explosive growth of jobs in which workers perform low-wage and limited tasks in white-collar settings. This has transformed towns like Hagerstown—a blue-collar community hit hard by industrial layoffs in the 1970s—into sites for thousands of jobs in factory-sized offices.

Many of these jobs, though, are part time and most pay far less than the manufacturing occupations they replaced. Some workers at EBS start at the minimum wage of $4.25 an hour and most earn about $6 an hour. The growth of such jobs—which often cluster outside major cities—also completes a curious historic circle. During the Industrial Revolution, farmers' daughters went to work in textile towns like Lowell, Mass. In post-industrial America, many women of modest means and skills are entering clerical mills where they process paper instead of cloth (coincidentally, EBS occupies a former garment factory).

"The office of the future can look a lot like the factory of the past," says Barbara Garson, author of *The Electronic Sweatshop* and other books on the modern workplace. "Modern tools are being used to bring 19th-century working conditions into the white-collar world."

The time-motion philosophies of Frederick Taylor, for instance, have found a 1990s correlate in the phone, computer and camera, which can be used to monitor workers more closely than a foreman with a stopwatch ever could. Also, the nature of the work often justifies a vigilant eye. In EBS workers handle thousands of dollars in checks and cash, and Mr. Edens says cameras help deter would-be thieves. Tight security also reassures visiting clients. "If you're disorderly, they'll think we're out of control and that things could get lost," says Mr. Edens, who worked as a financial controller for the National Rifle Association before founding EBS in 1983.

But tight observation also helps EBS monitor productivity and weed out workers who don't keep up. "There's multiple uses," Mr. Edens says of surveillance. His desk is covered with computer printouts recording the precise toll of keystrokes tapped by each data-entry worker. He also keeps a day-to-day tally of errors. The work floor itself resembles an enormous classroom in the throes of exam period. Desks point toward the front, where a manager keeps watch from a raised platform that workers call "the pedestal" or "the birdhouse." Other supervisors are positioned toward the back of the room. "If you want to watch someone," Mr. Edens explains, "it's easier from behind because they don't know you're watching." There also is a black globe hanging from the ceiling, in which cameras are positioned.

Mr. Edens sees nothing Orwellian about this omniscience. "It's not a Big Brother attitude," he says. "It's more of a calming attitude."

But studies of workplace monitoring suggest otherwise. Experts say that surveillance can create a hostile environment in which workers feel pressured, paranoid and prone to stress-related illness. Surveillance also can be used punitively, to intimidate workers or to justify their firing.

Following a failed union drive at EBS, the National Labor Relations Board filed a series of complaints against the company, including charges that EBS threatened, interrogated, and spied on workers. As part of an out-of-court settlement, EBS reinstated a fired worker and posted a notice that it would refrain from illegal practices during a second union vote, which also failed.

"It's all noise," Mr. Edens says of the unfair labor charges. As to the pressure that surveillance creates, Mr. Edens sees that simply as "the nature of the beast." He adds: "It's got to add stress when everyone knows their production is being monitored. I don't apologize for that."

Mr. Edens also is unapologetic about the Draconian work rules he maintains, including one that forbids all talk unrelated to the completion of each task. "I'm not paying people to chat. I'm paying them to open envelopes," he says. Of the blocked windows. Mr. Edens adds: "I don't want them looking out—it's distracting. They'll make mistakes."

This total focus boosts productivity but it makes many workers feel lonely and trapped. Some try to circumvent the silence rule, like kids in a school library. "If you don't turn your head and sort of mumble out of the side of your mouth, supervisors won't hear you most of the time," Cindy Kesselring explains during her lunch break. Even so, she feels isolated and often longs for her former job as a waitress. "Work is your social life, particularly if you've got kids," says the 27-year-old mother. "Here it's hard to get to know people because you can't talk."

During lunch, workers crowd in the parking lot outside, chatting nonstop. "Some of us don't eat much because the more you chew the less you can talk," Ms. Kesselring says. There aren't other breaks and workers aren't allowed to sip coffee or eat at their desks during the long stretches before and after lunch. Hard candy is the only permitted desk snack.

New technology, and the breaking down of labor into discrete, repetitive tasks, also have effectively stripped jobs such as those at EBS of whatever variety and skills clerical work once possessed. Workers in the cage (an antiquated banking term for a money-handling area) only open envelopes and sort contents; those in the audit department compute figures; and data-entry clerks punch in the information that the others have collected. If they make a mistake, the computer buzzes and a message such as "check digit error" flashes on the screen.

"We don't ask these people to think—the machines think for them," Mr. Edens says. "They don't have to make any decisions." This makes the work simpler but also deepens its monotony. In the cage, Carol Smith says she looks forward to envelopes that contain anything out of the ordinary, such as letters reporting that the donor is deceased. Or she plays mental games. "I think to myself, A goes in this pile, B goes here and C goes there—sort of like Bingo." She says she sometimes feels "like a machine," particularly when she fills out the "control card" on which she lists "time in" and "time out" for each tray of envelopes. In a slot marked "cage operator" Ms. Smith writes her code number, 3173. "That's me," she says.

Barbara Ann Wiles, a keyboard operator, also plays mind games to break up the boredom. Tapping in the names and addresses of new donors, she tries to imagine the faces behind the names, particularly the odd ones. "Like this one, Mrs. Fittizzi," she chuckles. "I can picture her as a very stout lady with a strong accent, hollering on a street corner." She picks out another: "Doris Angelroth—she's very sophisticated, a monocle maybe, drinking tea on an overstuffed mohair couch."

It is a world remote from the one Ms. Wiles inhabits. Like most EBS employees, she must juggle her low-paying job with child care. On this Friday, for instance, Ms. Wiles will finish her eight-hour shift at about 4 P.M., go home for a few hours, then return for a second shift from midnight to 8 A.M. Otherwise, she would have to come in on Saturday to finish the week's work.

This way I can be home on the weekend to look after my kids," she says.

Others find the work harder to leave behind at the end of the day. In the cage, Ms. Smith says her husband used to complain because she often woke him in the middle of the night. "I'd be shuffling my hands in my sleep," she says, mimicking the motion of opening envelopes.

Her cage colleague, Ms. Kesselring, says her fiancé has a different gripe. "He dodges me for a couple of hours after work because I don't shut up—I need to talk, talk, talk," she says. And there is one household task she can no longer abide.

"I won't pay bills because I can't stand to open another envelope," she says. "I'll leave letters sitting in the mailbox for days."

Questions

1. Which of the management theories described in the chapter does Ron Edens make most use of?
2. What do you think are the effects of this approach on (a) workers and (b) supervisors?
3. Do you regard Ron Eden's approach to management as ethical and acceptable or unethical and unacceptable in the 2000s? Why?

Source: Tony Horwitz, "Mr. Edens Profits from Watching His Workers' Every Move," *The Wall Street Journal,* December 1, 1994.

Small Group Breakout Exercise

Modeling an Open System

Form groups of three to five people, and appoint one group member as the spokesperson who will communicate your findings to the class when called on by the instructor. Then discuss the following scenario.

Think of an organization with which you are all familiar, such as a local restaurant, store, or bank. After choosing an organization, model it from an open-systems perspective. Identify its input, conversion, and output processes; and identify forces in the external environment that help or hurt the organization's ability to obtain resources and dispose of its goods or services.

Exploring the World Wide Web

Research Ford's Web site (www.ford.com), and locate and read the material on Ford's history and evolution over time. What have been the significant stages in the company's development? What problems and issues confronted managers at these stages? What are the challenges facing Ford's managers now?

Be the Manager

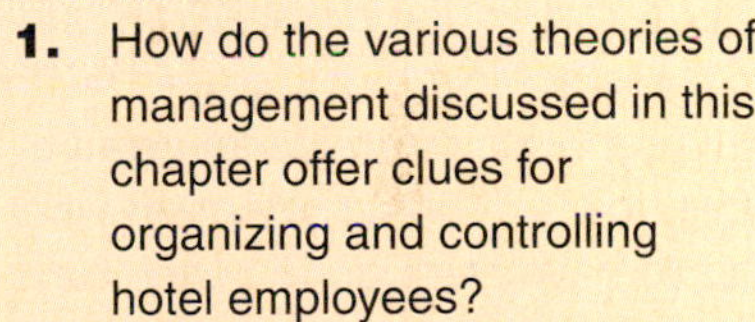

How to Manage a Hotel

You have been called in to advise the owners of an exclusive new luxury hotel. For the venture to succeed, hotel employees must focus on providing customers with the highest-quality customer service possible. The challenge is to devise a way of organizing and controlling employees that will promote high-quality service, that will encourage employees to be committed to the hotel, and that will reduce the level of employee turnover and absenteeism—which are typically high in the hotel business.

Questions

1. How do the various theories of management discussed in this chapter offer clues for organizing and controlling hotel employees?
2. Which parts would be the most important for an effective system to organize and control employees?

Additional Activities on the Build Your Management Skills DVD

- **Test Your Knowledge:** Management's Historical Figures

What You Don't Know About Dell

Dell is the master at selling direct, bypassing middlemen to deliver PCs cheaper than any of its rivals. And few would quarrel that it's the model of efficiency, with a far-flung supply chain knitted together so tightly that it's like one electrical wire, humming 24/7. Yet all this has been true for more than a decade. And although the entire computer industry has tried to replicate Dell's tactics, none can hold a candle to the company's results.

As it turns out, it's how Michael Dell manages the company that has elevated it far above its sell-direct business model. What's Dell's secret? At its heart is his belief that the status quo is never good enough, even if it means painful changes for the man with his name on the door. When success is achieved, it's greeted with five seconds of praise followed by five hours of postmortem on what could have been done better. Says Michael Dell: "Celebrate for a nanosecond. Then move on." After the outfit opened its first Asian factory, in Malaysia, the CEO sent the manager heading the job one of his old running shoes to congratulate him. The message: This is only the first step in a marathon.

Just as crucial is Michael Dell's belief that once a problem is uncovered, it should be dealt with quickly and directly, without excuses. "There's no 'The dog ate my homework' here," says Dell. No, indeedy. After Randall D. Groves, then head of the server business, delivered 16 percent higher sales last year, he was demoted. Never mind that none of its rivals came close to that. It could have been better, say two former Dell executives. Groves referred calls to a Dell spokesman, who says Groves's job change was part of a broader reorganization.

Above all, Michael Dell expects everyone to watch each dime—and turn it into at least a quarter. Unlike most tech bosses, Dell believes every product should be profitable from Day One. To ensure that, he expects his managers to be walking databases, able to cough up information on everything from top-line growth to the average number of times a part has to be replaced in the first 30 days after a computer is sold.

But there's one number he cares about most: operating margin. To Dell, it's not enough to rack up profits or grow fast. Execs must do both to maximize long-term profitability. That means products need to be priced low enough to induce shoppers to buy, but not so low that they cut unnecessarily into profits. When Dell's top managers in Europe lost out on profits in 1999 because they hadn't cut costs far enough, they were replaced. "There are some organizations where people think they're a hero if they invent a new thing," says Rollins. "Being a hero at Dell means saving money."

It's this combination—reaching for the heights of perfection while burrowing down into every last data point—that no rival has been able to imitate. "It's like watching Michael Jordan stuff the basketball," says Merrill Lynch & Co. technology strategist Steven Milunovich. "I see it. I understand it. But I can't do it."

How did this Mike come by his management philosophy? It started 19 years ago, when he was ditching classes to sell homemade PCs out of his University of Texas dorm room. Dell was the scrappy underdog, fighting for his company's life against the likes of IBM and Compaq Computer Corp. with a direct-sales model that people thought was plain nuts. Now, Michael Dell is worth $17 billion, while his 40,000-employee company is about to top $40 billion in sales. Yet he continues to manage Dell with the urgency and determination of a college kid with his back to the wall. "I still think of us as a challenger," he says. "I still think of us attacking."

All this has kept Dell on track as rivals have gone off the rails. Since 2000, the company has been adding market share at a faster pace than at any time in its history—nearly three percentage points in 2002. A renewed effort to control costs sliced overhead expenses to just 9.6 percent of revenue in the most recent quarter and boosted productivity to nearly $1 million in revenue per employee. That's three times the revenue per employee at IBM and almost twice Hewlett-Packard Co.'s rate.

Still, for the restless Michael Dell, that's not nearly enough. He wants to make sure the company he has spent half his life building can endure after he's gone. So he and Rollins have sketched out an ambitious financial target: $60 billion in revenues by 2006. That's twice what the company did in 2001 and enough to put it in league with the largest, most powerful companies in the world. Getting there will require the same kind of success that the company achieved in PCs—but in altogether new markets. Already, Michael Dell is moving the company into printers, networking, handheld computers, and tech services. His latest foray: Dell is entering the cutthroat $95 billion consumer-electronics market with a portable digital-music player, an online music store, and a flat-panel television set slated to go on sale in October 2004.

Dell also faces an innovation dilemma. Its penny-pinching ways leave little room for investments in product development and future technologies, especially compared with rivals. Even in the midst of the recession, IBM spent $4.75 billion or 5.9 percent of its revenues, on research and development in 2002, while HP ponied up $3.3 billion, or 4.8 percent of revenues. And Dell? Just a paltry $455 million, or 1.3 percent. Rivals say that handicaps Dell's ability to move much beyond PCs, particularly in such promising markets as digital imaging and utility computing. "Dell is a great company, but they are a one-trick pony," says HP CEO Carleton S. Fiorina. What's more, Dell has shown little patience for the costs of entering new markets, killing off products—like its high-end server—when they didn't produce quick profits, rather than staying committed to a long-term investment. "They're the best in the world at what they do," says IBM server chief William M. Zeitler. "The question is, will they be best at the Next Big Thing?"

Dell's track record suggests the CEO will meet his $60 billion revenue goal by 2006. Already, Dell has grabbed large chunks of the markets for inexpensive servers and data-storage gear. After just two quarters, its first handheld computer has captured 37 percent of the U.S. market for such devices. And Rollins says initial sales of Dell printers are double its internal targets. With the potential growth in PCs and new markets, few analysts doubt that Dell can generate the 15 percent annual growth needed to reach the mark.

Questions

1. What are the main principles behind Michael Dell's approach to managing?
2. List these principles then compare them to those developed by Henry Fayol. In what ways are they similar or different?

Source: Andrew Park and Peter Burrows, "What You Don't Know About Dell." Reprinted from the November 3, 2003, issue of BusinessWeek Online by special permission.

CHAPTER 3

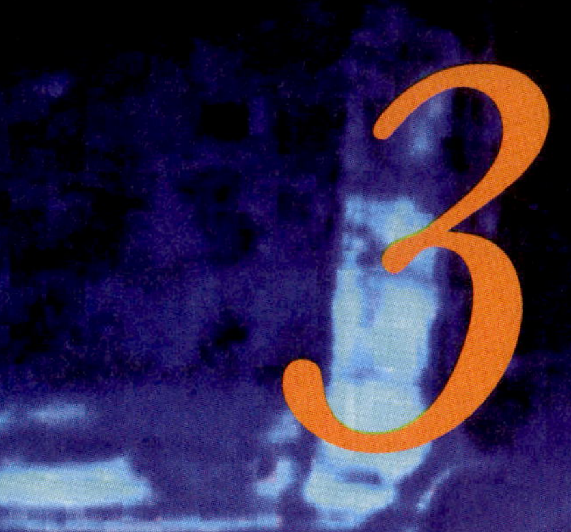

The Manager as a Person: Values, Attitudes, Emotions, and Culture

Learning Objectives

After studying this chapter, you should be able to:

- Describe the various personality traits that affect how managers think, feel, and behave.
- Explain what values and attitudes are and describe their impact on managerial action.
- Appreciate how moods and emotions influence all members of an organization.
- Describe the nature of emotional intelligence and its role in management.
- Define organizational culture and explain how managers both create and are influenced by organizational culture.

A Manager's Challenge

Employees Come First at PAETEC

How can managers in troubled industries promote organizational growth and effectiveness?

PAETEC Communications is a privately owned broadband telecommunications company that provides local, long distance, data, and Internet services in 27 markets across the United States.[1] When PAETEC was founded in 1998, it had less than 20 employees and revenues of only $150,000; by 2004, it had 1,000 employees and $360 million in revenues.[2] Moreover, this phenomenal rate of growth occurred during a period when the telecommunications industry lost over 500,000 jobs.[3] PAETEC's amazing growth trajectory has not gone without notice; the company recently was ranked second in Deloitte Technology's Fast 500 list, which ranks the technology industry's top 500 fastest-growing companies in North America. Firms like Yahoo and eBay debuted on this list in their early days.[4]

PAETEC's growth and ongoing success are a tribute to the values of its five founders and the culture they created. In particular, Arunas Chesonis, one of the founders and its current CEO, ensures that PAETEC's values are upheld by using them to guide the way he manages on a day-to-day basis. The result is a satisfied, motivated, and loyal workforce whose members have developed a unique and distinct approach to the way they perform their jobs.[5]

PAETEC founder and current CEO Arunas Chesonis believes that when a company takes good care of its employees, they will take good care of their customers.

An overarching principle at PAETEC is "Employees come first."[6] This does not mean that PAETEC doesn't care about customers; nothing could be further from the truth. Chesonis believes that when a company takes good care of its employees, they will take good care of their customers. For Chesonis, putting employees first means helping them attain a well-balanced and prosperous work and family life, providing them with deserved recognition and admiration, and fostering open communication and helping behavior.[7] Chesonis also believes that all employees should be treated with respect and as equals.

Managers at PAETEC do not receive special perks, and pay differentials between managers and nonmanagers are deliberately kept relatively low.

Chesonis takes daily walks around PAETEC's headquarters in Rochester, New York, talking with employees, answering questions, and recognizing accomplishments. Accomplishments are also recognized through two kinds of special awards, Maestro Awards and Chairman Awards. Maestro Awards of stock options are given to recognize outstanding employee accomplishments. Employees who have sustained levels of exceptional performance receive the Chairman Award, a $5,000 award that might include a Rolex watch or a luxury vacation. The contributions of all employees are recognized with an annual 10 percent bonus;[8] PAETEC pays out around $3.5 million in bonuses each year.[9]

Chesonis also nurtures a culture of cooperation and open communication in which every employee voluntarily offers help when it is needed. Employees are expected to share their knowledge, and Chesonis strives to eliminate boundaries between departments and units. True to this culture, Chesonis has a companywide conference call every two weeks in which he shares up-to-date information with employees and solicits and answers their questions. More often than not, the information he conveys is the kind that managers in other companies rarely, if ever, would share with their employees.[10]

He also recognizes that employees at the front line are often in the best position to make suggestions for improvements and develop new services and ways to deliver them. For example, Mike Meath, an employee in the Network Operations Center, came up with the idea of a managed router service whereby companies (i.e., PAETEC's customers) could remotely maintain their customers' voice and data services. Meath presented his idea to his team, the team implemented the idea, and the new service increased revenues by $50,000 in its first six months. Meath's contribution to PAETEC was recognized with a Maestro Award.[11]

While Chesonis is driven to succeed and motivates those around him to have equally high aspirations, he also values family life and the need for "play." Chesonis has been described as a "fanatical family man," and he named the company with the initials of his wife and children (*P* for his wife Pam; *A, E, T,* and *E* for his children, Adam, Erik, Tessa, and Emma; and *C* for Chesonis). Employees are able to take as much time off as they need, with pay, to deal with family emergencies and illnesses.[12] PAETEC also celebrates holidays with parties that include employees, their families, and customers. For example, employees dress up for Halloween, and their children trick-or-treat from office to office. Outings are planned, such as a scavenger hunt around Rochester culminating in dinner and an open bar, so that employees can spend a day socializing with one another.[13]

Chesonis's values and PAETEC's culture emphasize putting employees first; this employee-centered approach makes good business sense. Employees at PAETEC really want the company to continue to grow and succeed; they are highly motivated and committed to providing the best service they can to their customers.[14]

Overview

Like people everywhere, Arunas Chesonis has his own distinctive personality, values, ways of viewing things, and personal challenges and disappointments. In this chapter, we focus on the manager as a feeling, thinking human being. We start by describing enduring characteristics that influence how managers "manage," as well as how they view other people, their organizations, and the world around them. We discuss as well how managers' values, attitudes, and moods play out in organizations, shaping organizational culture. By the end of this chapter, you will have a good appreciation of how the personal characteristics of managers influence the process of management in general and organizational culture in particular.

Enduring Characteristics: Personality Traits

All people, including managers, have certain enduring characteristics that influence how they think, feel, and behave both on and off the job. These characteristics are **personality traits,** particular tendencies to feel, think, and act in certain ways that can be used to describe the personality of every individual. It is important to understand the personalities of managers because their personalities influence their behavior and their approach to managing people and resources.

personality traits
Enduring tendencies to feel, think, and act in certain ways.

Some managers, like Procter & Gamble's former chairman Edwin Artzt, are demanding, difficult to get along with, and highly critical of other people.[15] Other managers, like Southwest Airlines' former CEO Herb Kelleher, may be as concerned about effectiveness and efficiency as highly critical managers but are easier to get along with, are likable, and frequently praise the people around them. Both styles of management may produce excellent results, but their effects on employees are quite different. Do managers deliberately decide to adopt one or the other of these approaches to management? Although they may do so part of the time, in all likelihood their personalities also account for their different approaches. Indeed, research suggests that the way people react to different conditions depends, in part, on their personalities.[16]

The Big Five Personality Traits

We can think of an individual's personality as being composed of five general traits or characteristics: extraversion, negative affectivity, agreeableness, conscientiousness, and openness to experience.[17] Researchers often consider these the Big Five personality traits.[18] Each of them can be viewed as a continuum along which every individual or, more specifically, every manager falls (see Figure 3.1).

Figure 3.1
The Big Five Personality Traits

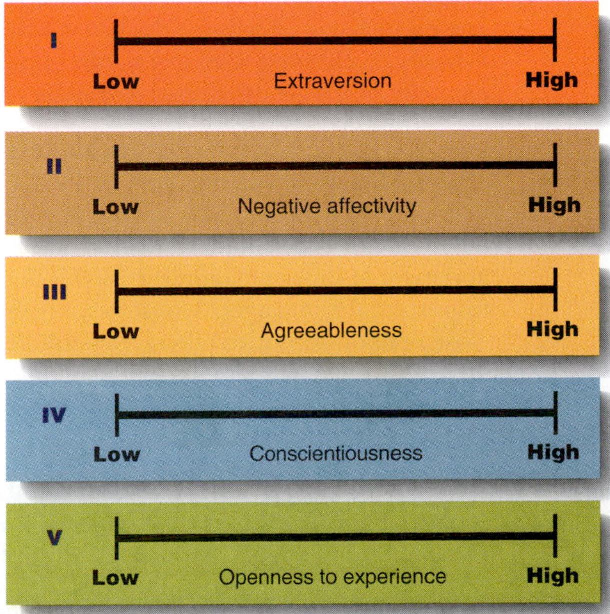

Some managers may be at the high end of one trait continuum, others at the low end, and still others somewhere in between. An easy way to understand how these traits can affect a person's approach to management is to describe what people are like at the high and low ends of each trait continuum. As will become evident as you read about each trait, no single trait is right or wrong for being an effective manager. Rather, effectiveness is determined by a complex interaction between the characteristics of managers (including personality traits) and the nature of the job and organization in which they are working. Moreover, personality traits that enhance managerial effectiveness in one situation may actually impair it in another situation.

extraversion The tendency to experience positive emotions and moods and to feel good about oneself and the rest of the world.

EXTRAVERSION **Extraversion** is the tendency to experience positive emotions and moods and feel good about oneself and the rest of the world. Managers who are high on extraversion (often called *extraverts*) tend to be sociable, affectionate, outgoing, and friendly. Managers who are low on extraversion (often called *introverts*) tend to be less inclined toward social interactions and to have a less positive outlook. Being high on extraversion may be an asset for managers whose jobs entail especially high levels of social interaction. Managers who are low on extraversion may nevertheless be highly effective and efficient, especially when their jobs do not require excessive social interaction. Their more "quiet" approach may enable them to accomplish quite a bit of work in limited time. See Figure 3.2 for an example of a scale that can be used to measure a person's level of extraversion.

negative affectivity The tendency to experience negative emotions and moods, to feel distressed, and to be critical of oneself and others.

NEGATIVE AFFECTIVITY **Negative affectivity** is the tendency to experience negative emotions and moods, feel distressed, and be critical of oneself and others. Managers high on this trait may often feel angry and dissatisfied and complain about their own and others' lack of progress. Managers who are low on negative affectivity do not tend to experience many negative emotions and moods and are less pessimistic and critical of themselves and others. On the plus side, the critical approach of a manager high on negative affectivity may sometimes be effective if it spurs both the manager and others to improve their performance. Nevertheless, it is probably more pleasant to work with a manager who is low on negative affectivity; the better working relationships that such a manager is likely to cultivate also can be an important asset. Figure 3.3 (page 80) is an example of a scale developed to measure a person's level of negative affectivity.

agreeableness The tendency to get along well with other people.

AGREEABLENESS **Agreeableness** is the tendency to get along well with others. Managers who are high on the agreeableness continuum are likable, tend to be affectionate, and care about other people. Managers who are low on agreeableness may be somewhat distrustful of others, unsympathetic, uncooperative, and even at times antagonistic. Being high on agreeableness may be especially important for managers whose responsibilities require that they develop good, close relationships with others. Nevertheless, a low level of agreeableness may be an asset in managerial jobs that actually require that managers be antagonistic, such as drill sergeants, and some other kinds of military managers. See Figure 3.2 for an example of a scale that measures a person's level of agreeableness.

conscientiousness The tendency to be careful, scrupulous, and persevering.

CONSCIENTIOUSNESS **Conscientiousness** is the tendency to be careful, scrupulous, and persevering.[19] Managers who are high on the conscientiousness continuum are organized and self-disciplined; those who are low on this trait might sometimes appear to lack direction and self-discipline. Conscientiousness has been found to be a good predictor of performance in many kinds of jobs,

Figure 3.2
Measures of Extraversion, Agreeableness, Conscientiousness, and Openness to Experience

Source: Lewis R. Goldberg, Oregon Research Institute, http://ipip.ori.org/ipip/.

Listed below are phrases describing people's behaviors. Please use the rating scale below to describe how accurately each statement describes *you*. Describe yourself as you generally are now, not as you wish to be in the future. Describe yourself as you honestly see yourself, in relation to other people you know of the same sex as you are and roughly your same age.

1	2	3	4	5
Very inaccurate	Moderately inaccurate	Neither inaccurate nor accurate	Moderately accurate	Very accurate

____ **1.** Am interested in people.
____ **2.** Have a rich vocabulary.
____ **3.** Am always prepared.
____ **4.** Am not really interested in others.*
____ **5.** Leave my belongings around.*
____ **6.** Am the life of the party.
____ **7.** Have difficulty understanding abstract ideas.*
____ **8.** Sympathize with others' feelings.
____ **9.** Don't talk a lot.*
____ **10.** Pay attention to details.
____ **11.** Have a vivid imagination.
____ **12.** Insult people.*
____ **13.** Make a mess of things.*
____ **14.** Feel comfortable around people.
____ **15.** Am not interested in abstract ideas.*
____ **16.** Have a soft heart.
____ **17.** Get chores done right away.
____ **18.** Keep in the background.*
____ **19.** Have excellent ideas.
____ **20.** Start conversations.
____ **21.** Am not interested in other people's problems.*
____ **22.** Often forget to put things back in their proper place.*
____ **23.** Have little to say.*
____ **24.** Do not have a good imagination.*
____ **25.** Take time out for others.
____ **26.** Like order.
____ **27.** Talk to a lot of different people at parties.
____ **28.** Am quick to understand things.
____ **29.** Feel little concern for others.*
____ **30.** Shirk my duties.*
____ **31.** Don't like to draw attention to myself.*
____ **32.** Use difficult words.
____ **33.** Feel others' emotions.
____ **34.** Follow a schedule.
____ **35.** Spend time reflecting on things.
____ **36.** Don't mind being the center of attention.
____ **37.** Make people feel at ease.
____ **38.** Am exacting in my work.
____ **39.** Am quiet around strangers.*
____ **40.** Am full of ideas.

* Item is reverse-scored: 1 = 5, 2 = 4, 4 = 2, 5 = 1
Scoring: Sum responses to items for an overall scale.
Extraversion = sum of items 6, 9, 14, 18, 20, 23, 27, 31, 36, 39
Agreeableness = sum of items 1, 4, 8, 12, 16, 21, 25, 29, 33, 37
Conscientiousness = sum of items 3, 5, 10, 13, 17, 22, 26, 30, 34, 38
Openness to experience = sum of items 2, 7, 11, 15, 19, 24, 28, 32, 35, 40

including managerial jobs in a variety of organizations.[20] CEOs of major companies, such as Carly Fiorino of Hewlett-Packard and Samuel J. Palmisano of IBM. often show signs of being high on conscientiousness–the long hours they work, their attention to detail, and their ability to handle their multiple responsibilities in an organized manner. Figure 3.2 provides an example of a scale that measures conscientiousness.

openness to experience The tendency to be original, have broad interests, be open to a wide range of stimuli, be daring, and take risks.

OPENNESS TO EXPERIENCE **Openness to experience** is the tendency to be original, have broad interests, be open to a wide range of stimuli, be daring, and take risks.[21] Managers who are high on this trait continuum may be

Figure 3.3
A Measure of Negative Affectivity

Source: Auke Tellegen, *Brief Manual for the Differential Personality Questionnaire.* Copyright © 1982. Reproduced by permission.

Instructions: Listed below are a series of statements a person might use to describe her/his attitudes, opinions, interests, and other characteristics. If a statement is true or largely true, put a "T" in the space next to the item. Or if the statement is false or largely false, mark an "F" in the space.

Please answer every statement, even if you are not completely sure of the answer. Read each statement carefully, but don't spend too much time deciding on the answer.

____ **1.** I often find myself worrying about something.

____ **2.** My feelings are hurt rather easily.

____ **3.** Often I get irritated at little annoyances.

____ **4.** I suffer from nervousness.

____ **5.** My mood often goes up and down.

____ **6.** I sometimes feel "just miserable" for no good reason.

____ **7.** Often I experience strong emotions—anxiety, anger—without really knowing what causes them.

____ **8.** I am easily startled by things that happen unexpectedly.

____ **9.** I sometimes get myself into a state of tension and turmoil as I think of the day's events.

____ **10.** Minor setbacks sometimes irritate me too much.

____ **11.** I often lose sleep over my worries.

____ **12.** There are days when I'm "on edge" all of the time.

____ **13.** I am too sensitive for my own good.

____ **14.** I sometimes change from happy to sad, or vice versa, without good reason.

Scoring: Level of negative affectivity is equal to the number of items answered "True."

especially likely to take risks and be innovative in their planning and decision making. Entrepreneurs who start their own businesses–like Bill Gates of Microsoft, Jeff Bezos of Amazon.com, and Anita Roddick of The Body Shop–are, in all likelihood, high on openness to experience, which has contributed to their success as entrepreneurs and managers. Arunas Chesonis, discussed in this chapter's "A Manager's Challenge," founded his own company and continues to explore new ways for it to grow–a testament to his high level of openness to experience. Managers who are low on openness to experience may be less prone to take risks and more conservative in their planning and decision making. In certain organizations and positions, this tendency might be an asset. The manager of the fiscal office in a public university, for example, must ensure that all university departments and units follow the university's rules and regulations pertaining to budgets, spending accounts, and reimbursements of expenses. Figure 3.2 provides an example of a measure of openness to experience.

Managers who initiate major changes in their organizations often are high on openness to experience, as is true of IBM CEO and chairman Samuel Palmisano, profiled in the "Information Technology Byte" on page 81.

Information Technology Byte

Sam Palmisano Reinvents IBM

Samuel Palmisano started his career at IBM over 30 years ago as a sales representative. He went on to head many of IBM's major divisions before becoming CEO in 2002 and chairman of the board in 2004.[22] Palmisano is spearheading a major redirection of IBM that changes the company's focus and activities in fundamental ways. Essentially, he is transforming IBM from being a hardware and software provider to being a business solution provider to corporate customers.[23] Thus, IBM is focusing on developing close, long-term relationships with customers that will enable it to help them with their pressing business problems, problems ranging from purchasing and marketing to production and customer service. In becoming close to its customers and helping them meet their business needs, IBM will also be providing them with its mainstay hardware and software. But the latter is part of a bigger package oriented around being a total-solution provider to meet customers' business needs.[24]

To accomplish this aim, Palmisano has taken many bold steps. For example, IBM acquired Pricewaterhouse Coopers and Rational Software in 2002 at a cost of over $5.5 billion. These acquisitions will help IBM provide more high-level, all-encompassing consulting-type services to its customers. Realizing that these changes will require changes in the mindsets and skills of employees, Palmisano spent $800 million on employee education in 2004.[25]

Palmisano is encouraging IBM managers to go out and talk to customers, learn about their business needs, and develop comprehensive solutions to meet them. The solutions should be the kind that address a fundamental problem organizations in a particular industry face and, thus, can be sold to other companies in that industry. As Palmisano puts it, "If they got out there and actually solved the problem with the client . . . they would understand what they needed to do." For example, while IBM has sold hardware and data center services to FinnAir for years, now it has begun using mathematical modeling to help FinnAir improve customer loyalty while reducing marketing costs–a major pressing concern for FinnAir today.[26]

Sam Palmisano spent over 30 years as a sales representative for IBM. Now, as CEO, he is encouraging IBM managers go out and talk to customers to learn about their needs.

Interestingly enough, Palmisano's personality and management style are very different from those of his highly successful predecessor, former CEO Lou Gerstner. While Gerstner was formal and direct, Palmisano is more relaxed and understated. Industry watchers suggest that Palmisano's bold changes are right on track with where the hardware and software industry needs to be headed, and competitors like Hewlett-Packard and Microsoft seem to be copying some of his initiatives. While time will tell if Palmisano's vision for the new IBM will deliver on its promises, his openness to experience contributes to his confidence that "we are on the verge of the next great opportunity for our company, and for the entire information technology industry."[27]

By now it should be clear that successful managers like Palmisano and Gerstner occupy a variety of positions on the Big Five personality-trait continua. One highly effective manager may be high on extraversion and negative affectivity, another equally effective manager may be low on both these traits, and still another may be somewhere in between. Members of an organization must understand these differences among managers because they can shed light on how managers behave and on their approach to planning, leading, organizing, or controlling. If subordinates realize, for example, that their manager is low on extraversion, they will not feel slighted when their manager seems to be aloof because they will realize that by nature he or she is simply not outgoing.

Managers themselves also need to be aware of their own personality traits and the traits of others, including their subordinates and fellow managers. A manager who knows that he has a tendency to be highly critical of other people might try to tone down his negative approach. Similarly, a manager who realizes that her chronically complaining subordinate tends to be so negative because of his personality may take all his complaints with a grain of salt and realize that things probably are not as bad as this subordinate says they are.

In order for all members of an organization to work well together and with people outside the organization, such as customers and suppliers, they must understand each other. Such understanding comes, in part, from an appreciation of some of the fundamental ways in which people differ from one another–that is, an appreciation of personality traits.

Other Personality Traits That Affect Managerial Behavior

Many other specific traits in addition to the Big Five describe people's personalities. Here we look at traits that are particularly important for understanding managerial effectiveness: locus of control; self-esteem; and the needs for achievement, affiliation, and power.

internal locus of control The tendency to locate responsibility for one's fate within oneself.

LOCUS OF CONTROL People differ in their views about how much control they have over what happens to and around them. The locus-of-control trait captures these beliefs.[28] People with an **internal locus of control** believe that they themselves are responsible for their own fate; they see their own actions and behaviors as being major and decisive determinants of important outcomes such as attaining levels of job performance, being promoted, or being turned down for a choice job assignment. Some managers with an internal locus of control see the success of a whole organization resting on their shoulders. One example is Arunas Chesonis in "A Manager's Challenge." An internal locus of control also helps to ensure ethical behavior and decision making in an organization because people feel accountable and responsible for their own actions. Managers with an internal locus may also feel obligated to expose wrongdoing in an organization, even if they are personally not responsible for it, as indicated in the following "Ethics in Action."

Ethics in Action

Taking Responsibility for Exposing Wrongdoing

Noreen Harrington, a former fund manager at the Hartz Group investment firm based in Secaucus, New Jersey, became aware of illegal activity in the firm by overhearing traders discussing after-hours trades. These traders managed hedge funds–investment funds that hold a variety of types of financial assets to offset risks and provide a consistent return to shareholders.[29] Harrington was not involved in these hedge funds herself but could not help overhearing the traders. From their conversation, she learned that some mutual fund managers were allowing the traders to buy and sell their shares in the fund after the market had closed.[30] This is illegal and unethical and gave the traders an unfair advantage over other investors in the mutual funds, who were able to trade only when the market was open.

Harrington told Edward J. Stern, a member of the Stern family that owns the Hartz Group, what she had overheard but this changed nothing–the illegal trading carried on. Harrington resigned but kept an eye on the news, hoping that security regulators would uncover what she had witnessed.[31]

New York State Attorney General Eliot Spitzer called Noreen Harrington's decision to report her knowledge of insider trading a "gutsy move."

After a year of waiting, Harrington felt a responsibility to report the illegal trading, as it was most likely still going on and hurting ordinary investors. She relayed what she had observed as a Hartz manager to Eliot Spitzer, the New York State attorney general. Spitzer's investigation of her claim led the Stern family to settle the case for $40 million, although they admitted no wrongdoing. In taking responsibility for exposing what she knew was wrong, Harrington set events in motion that ultimately had a major impact on the mutual fund industry as a whole: Other funds were scrutinized and additional instances of after-hours trading were uncovered.[32] As Spitzer puts it, "Because of her gutsy move, there will be dramatic reform in a sector that has the life savings of 95 million Americans."[33]

external locus of control The tendency to locate responsibility for one's fate in outside forces and to believe that one's own behavior has little impact on outcomes.

People with an **external locus of control** believe that outside forces are responsible for what happens to and around them; they do not think that their own actions make much of a difference. As such, they tend not to intervene to try to change a situation or solve a problem, leaving it to someone else.

Managers need to have an internal locus of control because they are responsible for what happens in organizations; they need to believe that they can and do make a difference, as does Arunas Chesonis at PAETEC Communications. Moreover, managers are responsible for ensuring that organizations and their members behave in an ethical fashion, and for this as well they need to have an internal locus of control–they need to know and feel they can make a difference.

self-esteem The degree to which individuals feel good about themselves and their capabilities.

SELF-ESTEEM **Self-esteem** is the degree to which individuals feel good about themselves and their capabilities. People with high self-esteem believe that they are competent, deserving, and capable of handling most situations, as does Arunas Chesonis. People with low self-esteem have poor opinions of themselves, are unsure about their capabilities, and question their ability to succeed at different endeavors.[34] Research suggests that people tend to choose activities and goals consistent with their levels of self-esteem. High self-esteem is desirable for managers because it facilitates their setting and keeping high standards for themselves, pushes them ahead on difficult projects, and gives them the confidence they need to make and carry out important decisions.

need for achievement The extent to which an individual has a strong desire to perform challenging tasks well and to meet personal standards for excellence.

need for affiliation The extent to which an individual is concerned about establishing and maintaining good interpersonal relations, being liked, and having other people get along.

need for power The extent to which an individual desires to control or influence others.

NEEDS FOR ACHIEVEMENT, AFFILIATION, AND POWER Psychologist David McClelland has extensively researched the needs for achievement, affiliation, and power.[35] The **need for achievement** is the extent to which an individual has a strong desire to perform challenging tasks well and to meet personal standards for excellence. People with a high need for achievement often set clear goals for themselves and like to receive performance feedback. The **need for affiliation** is the extent to which an individual is concerned about establishing and maintaining good interpersonal relations, being liked, and having the people around him or her get along with one another. The **need for power** is the extent to which an individual desires to control or influence others.[36]

Research suggests that high needs for achievement and for power are assets for first-line and middle managers, and that a high need for power is especially important for upper-level managers.[37] One study found that U.S. presidents with a relatively high need for power tended to be especially effective during their terms of office.[38] A high need for affiliation may not always be desirable in managers because it might lead them to try too hard to be liked by others (including subordinates) rather than doing all they can to ensure that performance is as high as it can and should be. Although most research on these needs has been done in the United States, some studies suggest that these findings may also be applicable to people in other countries such as India and New Zealand.[39]

Taken together, these desirable personality traits for managers–an internal locus of control, high self-esteem, and high needs for achievement and power–suggest that managers need to be take-charge people who not only believe that their own actions are decisive in determining their own and their organizations' fates but also believe in their own capabilities. Such managers have a personal desire for accomplishment and influence over others.

Values, Attitudes, and Moods and Emotions

What are managers striving to achieve? How do they think they should behave? What do they think about their jobs and organizations? And how do they actually feel at work? Some answers to these questions can be found by exploring managers' values, attitudes, and moods.

Values, attitudes, and moods and emotions capture how managers experience their jobs as individuals. *Values* describe what managers are trying to achieve through work and how they think they should behave. *Attitudes* capture their thoughts and feelings about their specific jobs and organizations. *Moods and emotions* encompass how managers actually feel when they are managing. Although these three aspects of managers' work experience are highly personal, they also have important implications for understanding how managers behave, how they treat and respond to others, and how, through their efforts, they help contribute to organizational effectiveness through planning, leading, organizing, and controlling.

terminal value A lifelong goal or objective that an individual seeks to achieve.

instrumental value A mode of conduct that an individual seeks to follow.

norms Informal rules of conduct for behaviors considered important by most members of a group or organization.

value system The terminal and instrumental values that are guiding principles in an individual's life.

Values: Terminal and Instrumental

The two kinds of personal values are *terminal* and *instrumental.* A **terminal value** is a personal conviction about lifelong goals or objectives; an **instrumental value** is a personal conviction about desired modes of conduct or ways of behaving.[40] Terminal values often lead to the formation of **norms,** or informal rules of conduct, for behaviors considered important by most members of a group or organization, such as behaving honestly or courteously.

Milton Rokeach, one of the leading researchers in the area of human values, identified 18 terminal values and 18 instrumental values that describe each person's value system (see Figure 3.4).[41] By rank ordering the terminal values from 1 (most important as a guiding principle in one's life) to 18 (least important as a guiding principle in one's life) and then rank ordering the instrumental values from 1 to 18, people can give good pictures of their **value systems**—what they are striving to achieve in life and how they want to behave.[42] (You can gain a good understanding of your own values by rank ordering first the terminal values and then the instrumental values listed in Figure 3.4).

Figure 3.4
Terminal and Instrumental Values

Source: Reprinted with permission of The Free Press, a Division of Simon & Schuster Adult Publishing Group, from *The Nature of Human Values* by Milton Rokeach. Copyright © 1973 by The Free Press. All rights reserved.

Terminal Values	Instrumental Values
A comfortable life (a prosperous life)	Ambitious (hard-working, aspiring)
An exciting life (a stimulating, active life)	Broad-minded (open-minded)
A sense of accomplishment (lasting contribution)	Capable (competent, effective)
A world at peace (free of war and conflict)	Cheerful (lighthearted, joyful)
A world of beauty (beauty of nature and the arts)	Clean (neat, tidy)
Equality (brotherhood, equal opportunity for all)	Courageous (standing up for your beliefs)
Family security (taking care of loved ones)	Forgiving (willlng to pardon others)
Freedom (independence, free choice)	Helpful (working for the welfare of others)
Happiness (contentedness)	Honest (sincere, truthful)
Inner harmony (freedom from inner conflict)	Imaginative (daring, creative)
Mature love (sexual and spiritual intimacy)	Independent (self-reliant, self-sufficient)
National security (protection from attack)	Intellectual (intelligent, reflective)
Pleasure (an enjoyable, leisurely life)	Logical (consistent, rational)
Salvation (saved, eternal life)	Loving (affectionate, tender)
Self-respect (self-esteem)	Obedient (dutiful, respectful)
Social recognition (respect, admiration)	Polite (courteous, well-mannered)
True friendship (close companionship)	Responsible (dependable, reliable)
Wisdom (a mature understanding of life)	Self-controlled (restrained, self-disciplined)

Several of the terminal values listed in Figure 3.4 seem to be especially important for managers–such as *a sense of accomplishment (a lasting contribution), equality (brotherhood, equal opportunity for all), and self-respect (self-esteem).* A manager who thinks a sense of accomplishment is of paramount importance might focus on making a lasting contribution to an organization by developing a new product that can save or prolong lives, as is true of managers at Medtronic (a company that makes medical devices such as cardiac pacemakers), or by opening a new foreign subsidiary. A manager who places equality at the top of his or her list of terminal values may be at the forefront of an organization's efforts to support, provide equal opportunities to, and capitalize on the many talents of an increasingly diverse workforce.

Other values are likely to be considered important by many managers, such as *a comfortable life (a prosperous life), an exciting life (a stimulating, active life), freedom (independence, free choice),* and *social recognition (respect, admiration).* The relative importance that managers place on each terminal value helps explain what they are striving to achieve in their organizations and what they will focus their efforts on.

Several of the instrumental values listed in Figure 3.3 seem to be important modes of conduct for managers, such as being *ambitious (hardworking, aspiring), broad-minded (open-minded), capable (competent, effective), responsible (dependable, reliable),* and *self-controlled (restrained, self-disciplined).* Moreover, the relative importance a manager places on these and other instrumental values may be a significant determinant of actual behaviors on the job. A manager who considers being *imaginative (daring, creative)* to be highly important, for example, is more likely to be innovative and take risks than is a manager who considers this to be less important (all else being equal). A manager who considers being *honest (sincere, truthful)* to be of paramount importance may be a driving force for taking steps to ensure that all members of a unit or organization behave ethically. As indicated in the following "Ethics in Action," taking ethical action sometimes requires that managers be courageous in addition to being honest.

Ethics in Action

The Courage to Be Honest

Peter Scannell was a manager at a Boston-area call center of Putnam Investments when he observed something troubling: Putnam managers were allowing some retirement mutual fund investors to make illegal quick buy and sell trades to take advantage of short-term fluctuations in fund prices. In fact, some of these investors were regularly engaging in short-term trades even though this kind of trading was prohibited by Putnam's own policies.[43]

A few days after Scannell told his supervisor of his concerns, he was taken from his car and beaten up; the assailant was allegedly an investor engaged in the activity Scannell had reported to his supervisor. Scannell says that a manager at Putnam was dismayed by his concern over the trading abuses and seemed to threaten him. Even when Scannell approached regulators in the Boston office of the Securities and Exchange Commission (SEC), he felt that his efforts to uphold ethical standards were being resisted.[44]

Scannell discussed his concerns about the SEC with his lawyer, and eventually Scannell met with the SEC. Scannell later testified to the Governmental Affairs subcommittee of the U.S. Senate about the reactions of Putnam managers to his allegations of unethical behavior and the initial unresponsiveness of the SEC.[45]

Scannell and others who have exposed instances of illegal activity and trading abuses regarding mutual funds recognize that these unethical actions end up hurting millions of honest people who invest in mutual funds. Senator Peter Fitzgerald of Illinois, head of the Senate subcommittee, suggests that mutual fund trading abuses represent "the world's largest skimming operation . . . a trough from which fund managers, brokers and other insiders are steadily siphoning off an excessive slice of the nation's household, college and retirement savings."[46] In Scannell's case, his persistent efforts to halt the unethical trading at Putnam hinged not only on his honesty but also on his courage to stand up for what he believed to be right, no matter what the consequences would be for him personally.

All in all, managers' value systems signify what managers as individuals are trying to accomplish and become in their personal lives and at work. Thus, managers' value systems are fundamental guides to their behavior and efforts at planning, leading, organizing, and controlling.

Attitudes

attitude A collection of feelings and beliefs.

An **attitude** is a collection of feelings and beliefs. Like everyone else, managers have attitudes about their jobs and organizations, and these attitudes affect how they approach their jobs. Two of the most important attitudes in this context are job satisfaction and organizational commitment.

job satisfaction The collection of feelings and beliefs that managers have about their current jobs.

JOB SATISFACTION **Job satisfaction** is the collection of feelings and beliefs that managers have about their current jobs.[47] Managers who have high levels of job satisfaction generally like their jobs, feel that they are being fairly treated, and believe that their jobs have many desirable features or characteristics (such as interesting work, good pay and job security, autonomy, or nice co-workers). Figure 3.5 (page 89) shows sample items from two scales that managers can use to measure job satisfaction. Levels of job satisfaction tend to increase as one moves up the hierarchy in an organization. Upper managers, in general, tend to be more satisfied with their jobs than entry-level employees. Managers' levels of job satisfaction can range from very low to very high and anywhere in between.

Focus on Diversity

Changing Attitudes

An interesting trend in job attitudes has been observed among some managers in their 20s and 30s. For example, after Sandi Garcia graduated from the University of Wyoming with a degree in marketing, she landed a good job in Florida and was soon promoted into the managerial ranks. By all counts, Garcia should have been satisfied with her job–she was advancing in the company, making good money, and doing the kind of work she had hoped to do. Ironically, Garcia found herself becoming increasingly dissatisfied with her job. Putting in 12-hour workdays was not unusual for Garcia, nor was it unusual for her to work during the weekends. Living a hectic, fast-paced life revolving around work soon made Garcia dream of a simpler life where she would have time to do things she enjoyed such as skiing, being with family and friends, and doing volunteer work. Garcia acted on her dream: She moved back to Wyoming, and is now more satisfied with a less demanding job at the Wyoming Business Council.[48]

Gregg Steiner was a high-tech manager on the West Coast who seemed to have everything, including a Malibu beach house. However, he was dissatisfied with a job that left him no free time to enjoy the beach or much else. Steiner quit the high-tech world and works at his now more modest home, handling customer service for his family's diaper rash ointment business (Pinxav).[49]

Young managers like Garcia and Steiner are not lazy, nor do they lack ambition. Rather, they have lived through changes in the corporate landscape that cause them to question what work should be and should mean to them. Some of these young managers have seen their parents slaving away at their jobs in corporate America year after year, only to be laid off in tough times. While their parents might never have questioned their commitment to their organizations, the need to work long hours, and the lack of time for much else other than work and raising a family, Garcia and Steiner desire the flexibility and time to live lives that are simpler but also richer in terms of meaningful activities. And they want to be in charge of their own lives rather than having their lives dictated by persons higher up the corporate hierarchy.[50]

Of course, for every young manager like Garcia and Steiner who voluntarily leaves the fast track for a more balanced life, there are other young prospective managers eager to take their place in the corporate world. And a job that is dissatisfying for one manager might be satisfying for another. In any case, in an era when trust in corporations has come under question (e.g., due to ethical lapses and fraud at companies like Enron), some young managers are seeking to invest themselves in things they can really trust.[51]

organizational citizenship behaviors (OCBs) Behaviors that are not required of organizational members but that contribute to and are necessary for organizational efficiency, effectiveness, and gaining a competitive advantage.

In general, it is desirable for managers to be satisfied with their jobs, for at least two reasons. First, satisfied managers may be more likely to go the extra mile for their organization or perform **organizational citizenship behaviors (OCBs),** behaviors that are not required of organizational members but that contribute to and are necessary for organizational efficiency, effectiveness, and gaining a competitive advantage.[52] Managers who are satisfied with their jobs are more likely to perform these "above and beyond the call of duty" behaviors, which can range from putting in extra-long hours when needed to coming up with truly creative ideas and overcoming obstacles to implement them (even when doing so is not part of the manager's job) or to going out of his or her way to help a co-worker, subordinate, or superior (even when doing so entails considerable personal sacrifice).[53]

A second reason why it is desirable for managers to be satisfied with their jobs is that satisfied managers may be less likely to quit.[54] A manager who is highly satisfied may never even think about looking for another position; a dissatisfied manager may always be on the lookout for new opportunities. Turnover can hurt an organization because it results in the loss of the experience and knowledge that managers have gained about the company, industry, and business environment.

A growing source of dissatisfaction for many lower- and middle-level managers, as well as for nonmanagerial employees, is the threat of unemployment and increased workloads from organizational downsizings. A recent study of 4,300 workers conducted by Wyatt Co. found that 76 percent of the employees of

Figure 3.5
Sample Items from Two Measures of Job Satisfaction

Source: Copyright © 1975 by the American Psychological Association. Reprinted with permission. Reprinted by permission of Randall B. Dunham and J. B. Brett.

Sample items from the Minnesota Satisfaction Questionnaire:
People respond to each of the items in the scale by checking whether they are:

[ ] Very dissatisfied
[ ] Dissatisfied
[ ] Can't decide whether satisfied or not
[ ] Satisfied
[ ] Very satisfied

On my present job, this is how I feel about . . .

____ **1.** Being able to do things that don't go against my conscience.

____ **2.** The way my job provides for steady employment.

____ **3.** The chance to do things for other people.

____ **4.** The chance to do something that makes use of my abilities.

____ **5.** The way company policies are put into practice.

____ **6.** My pay and the amount of work I do.

____ **7.** The chances for advancement on this job.

____ **8.** The freedom to use my own judgment.

____ **9.** The working conditions.

____ **10.** The way my co-workers get along with each other.

____ **11.** The praise I get for doing a good job.

____ **12.** The feeling of accomplishment I get from the job.

The Faces Scale
Workers select the face which best expresses how they feel about their job in general.

11 10 9 8 7 6 5 4 3 2 1

expanding companies are satisfied with their jobs but only 57 percent of the employees of companies that have downsized are satisfied.[55] Organizations that try to improve their efficiency through restructuring often eliminate a sizable number of first-line and middle management positions. This decision obviously hurts the managers who are laid off, and it also can reduce the job satisfaction levels of managers who remain. They might fear that they may be the next to be let go. In addition, the workloads of remaining managers often are dramatically increased as a result of restructuring, and this also can contribute to dissatisfaction.

organizational commitment The collection of feelings and beliefs that managers have about their organization as a whole.

ORGANIZATIONAL COMMITMENT **Organizational commitment** is the collection of feelings and beliefs that managers have about their organization as a whole. Managers who are committed to their organizations believe in what their organizations are doing, are proud of what these organizations stand for, and feel a high degree of loyalty toward their organizations. Committed managers are more likely to go above and beyond the call of duty to help their company and are less likely to quit.[56] Organizational commitment can be especially strong when employees and managers truly believe in organizational values; it also leads to a strong organizational culture, as found in PAETEC.

Organizational commitment is likely to help managers perform some of their figurehead and spokesperson roles (see Chapter 1). It is much easier for a manager to persuade others both inside and outside the organization of the merits of what the organization has done and is seeking to accomplish if the manager truly believes in and is committed to the organization. Figure 3.6 is an example of a scale that managers can use to measure a person's level of organizational commitment.

Do managers in different countries have similar or different attitudes? Differences in the levels of job satisfaction and organizational commitment among managers in different countries are likely because these managers have different kinds of opportunities and rewards and because they face different economic, political,

Figure 3.6

A Measure of Organizational Commitment

Source: L. W. Porter and F. J. Smith, "Organizational Commitment Questionnaire," in J. D. Cook, S. J. Hepworth, T. D. Wall, and P. B. Warr, eds., *The Experience of Work: A Compendium and Review of 249 Measures and Their Use* (New York: Academic Press, 1981), 84–86.

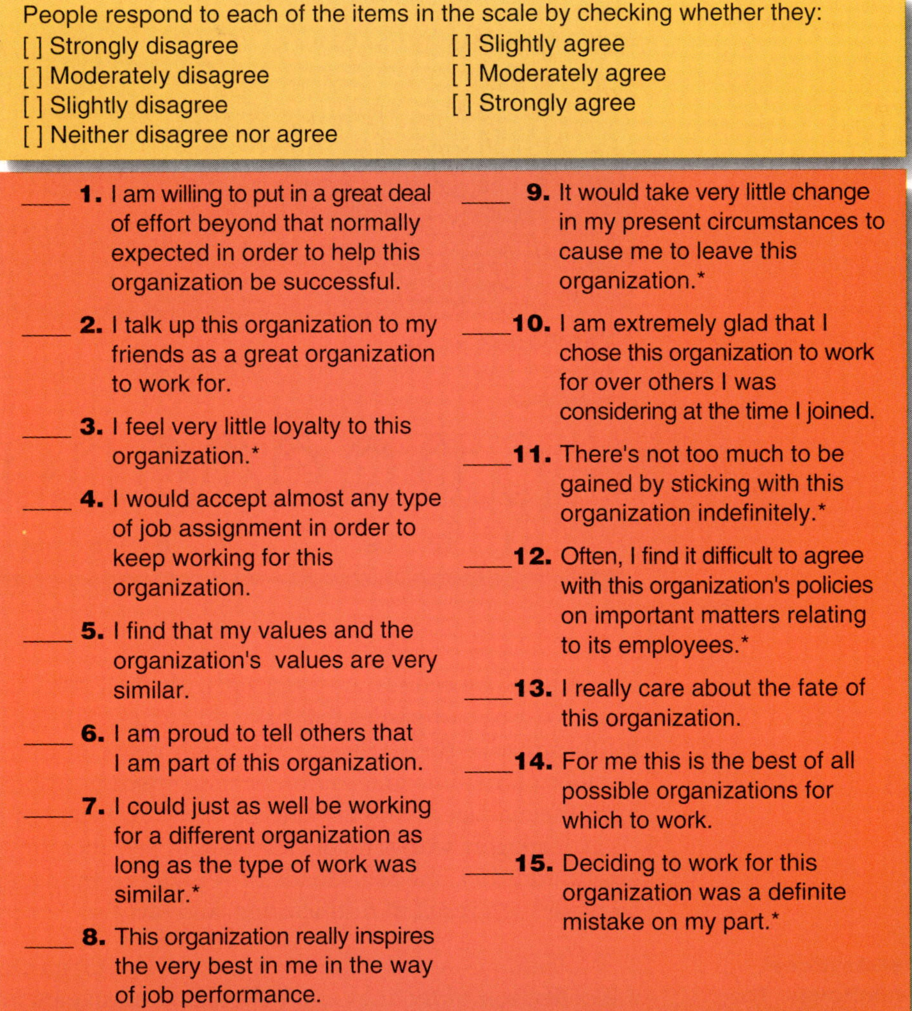

People respond to each of the items in the scale by checking whether they:

[ ] Strongly disagree
[ ] Moderately disagree
[ ] Slightly disagree
[ ] Neither disagree nor agree
[ ] Slightly agree
[ ] Moderately agree
[ ] Strongly agree

____ **1.** I am willing to put in a great deal of effort beyond that normally expected in order to help this organization be successful.

____ **2.** I talk up this organization to my friends as a great organization to work for.

____ **3.** I feel very little loyalty to this organization.*

____ **4.** I would accept almost any type of job assignment in order to keep working for this organization.

____ **5.** I find that my values and the organization's values are very similar.

____ **6.** I am proud to tell others that I am part of this organization.

____ **7.** I could just as well be working for a different organization as long as the type of work was similar.*

____ **8.** This organization really inspires the very best in me in the way of job performance.

____ **9.** It would take very little change in my present circumstances to cause me to leave this organization.*

____ **10.** I am extremely glad that I chose this organization to work for over others I was considering at the time I joined.

____ **11.** There's not too much to be gained by sticking with this organization indefinitely.*

____ **12.** Often, I find it difficult to agree with this organization's policies on important matters relating to its employees.*

____ **13.** I really care about the fate of this organization.

____ **14.** For me this is the best of all possible organizations for which to work.

____ **15.** Deciding to work for this organization was a definite mistake on my part.*

Scoring: Responses to items 1, 2, 4, 5, 6, 8, 10, 13, and 14 are scored such that 1 = strongly disagree; 2 = moderately disagree; 3 = slightly disagree; 4 = neither disagree nor agree; 5 = slightly agree; 6 = moderately agree; and 7 = strongly agree. Responses to "*" items 3, 7, 9, 11, 12, and 15 are scored 7 = strongly disagree; 6 = moderately disagree; 5 = slightly disagree; 4 = neither disagree nor agree; 3 = slightly agree; 2 = moderately agree; and 1 = strongly agree. Responses to the 15 items are averaged for an overall score from 1 to 7; the higher the score, the higher the level of organizational commitment.

To what extent does organizational commitment vary from country to country? Compared to the U.S., many French managers, like the one pictured here, have more job security and tend to be less geographically mobile, which may translate into higher levels of organizational commitment.

or sociocultural forces in their organizations' general environments. In countries with relatively high unemployment rates, such as France, levels of job satisfaction may be higher among employed managers because they may be happy simply to have a job.

Levels of organizational commitment from one country to another may depend on the extent to which countries have legislation affecting firings and layoffs and the extent to which citizens of a country are geographically mobile. In both France and Germany legislation protects workers (including managers) from being fired or laid off. U.S. workers, in contrast, have very little protection. In addition, managers in the United States are more willing to relocate than managers in France and Germany. In France citizens have relatively strong family and community ties; and in Germany housing is expensive and difficult to find. For those reasons citizens in both countries tend to be less geographically mobile than Americans.[57] Managers who know that their jobs are secure and who are reluctant to relocate (such as those in Germany and France) may be more committed to their organizations than managers who know that their organizations could lay them off any day and who would not mind geographic relocations.

Moods and Emotions

mood A feeling or state of mind.

Just as you sometimes are in a bad mood and at other times are in a good mood, so too are managers. A **mood** is a feeling or state of mind. When people are in a positive mood, they feel excited, enthusiastic, active, or elated.[58] When people are in a negative mood, they feel distressed, fearful, scornful, hostile, jittery, or nervous.[59] People who are high on extraversion are especially likely to experience positive moods; people who are high on negative affectivity are especially likely to experience negative moods. People's situations or circumstances also determine their moods; however, receiving a raise is likely to put most people in a good mood regardless of their personality traits. People who are high on negative affectivity are not always in a bad mood, and people who are low on extraversion still experience positive moods.[60]

emotions Intense, relatively short-lived feelings.

Emotions are more intense feelings than moods, are often directly linked to whatever caused the emotion, and are more short-lived. However, once whatever has triggered the emotion has been dealt with, the feelings may linger in the form of a less intense mood.[61] For example, a manager who gets very angry when one of his subordinates has engaged in an unethical behavior may find his anger decreasing in intensity once he has decided how to address the problem. Yet he continues to be in a bad mood the rest of the day, even though he is not directly thinking about the unfortunate incident.[62]

Research has found that moods and emotions affect the behavior of managers and all members of an organization. For example, research suggests that the subordinates of managers who experience positive moods at work may perform at somewhat higher levels and be less likely to resign and leave the organization than the subordinates of managers who do not tend to be in a positive mood at work.[63] Other research suggests that under certain conditions creativity might be enhanced by positive moods, whereas under other conditions negative moods might push people to work harder to come up with truly creative ideas.[64]

Other research suggests that moods and emotions (which are more intense and short-lived feelings that are triggered by something specific) may play an important role in ethical decision making. For example, researchers at Princeton University found that when people are trying to solve difficult personal moral dilemmas, the parts of their brains that are responsible for emotions and moods are especially active.[65]

Recognizing the benefits of positive moods, the Northbrook, Illinois, accounting firm of Lipschultz, Levin, & Gray has gone to great lengths to promote positive feelings among its employees. Chief executive Steven Siegel claims that positive feelings promote relaxation and alleviate stress, increase revenues and attract clients, and reduce turnover. Positive moods are promoted in a variety of ways at Lipschultz, Levin, & Gray. Siegel has been known to put on a gorilla mask at especially busy times; clerks sometimes don chicken costumes; a foghorn announces the signing of a new client; employees can take a break and play miniature golf in the office, play darts, or exercise with a hula-hoop (even during tax time). A casual dress code also lightens things up at the firm. By all counts, positive moods seem to be paying off for this group of accountants, whose good feelings seem to be attracting new clients.

Patrick Corboy, president and chief executive of Austin Chemical, switched his account from a bigger firm to Lipschultz, Levin, & Gray because he found the people at the bigger firm to be "too stuffy and dour for us." Of the accountant William Finestone, who now manages the Austin Chemical account, Corboy says the following: "[He] is a barrel of laughs . . . Bill not only solves our problems more quickly but he puts us at ease, too."[66]

Nevertheless, sometimes negative moods can have their advantages. Some studies suggest that critical thinking and devil's advocacy may be promoted by a negative mood, and sometimes especially accurate judgments may be made by managers in negative moods.[67]

Managers and other members of an organization need to realize that how they feel affects how they treat others and how others respond to them, including their subordinates. For example, a subordinate may be more likely to approach a manager with a somewhat far-out but potentially useful idea if the subordinate thinks the manager is in a good mood. Likewise, when managers are in very bad moods, their subordinates might try to avoid them at all costs. Figure 3.7 is an example of a scale that managers can use to measure the extent to which a person experiences positive and negative moods at work.

Emotional Intelligence

emotional intelligence The ability to understand and manage one's own moods and emotions and the moods and emotions of other people.

In understanding the effects of managers' and all employees' moods and emotions, it is important to take into account their levels of emotional intelligence. **Emotional intelligence** is the ability to understand and manage one's own moods and emotions and the moods and emotions of other people.[68] Managers with a high level of emotional intelligence are more likely to understand how they are feeling and why, and they are more able to effectively manage their feelings.

Figure 3.7
A Measure of Positive and Negative Mood at Work

Source: A. P. Brief, M. J. Burke, J. M. George, B. Robinson, and J. Webster, "Should Negative Affectivity Remain an Unmeasured Variable in the Study of Job Stress?" *Journal of Applied Psychology* 73 (1988), 193–98; M. J. Burke, A. P. Brief, J. M. George, L. Roberson, and J. Webster, "Measuring Affect at Work: Confirmatory Analyses of Competing Mood Structures with Conceptual Linkage in Cortical Regulatory Systems," *Journal of Personality and Social Psychology* 57 (1989), 1901–1102.

People respond to each item by indicating the extent to which the item descibes how they felt at work during the past week on the following scale:

1 = Very slightly or not at all
2 = A little
3 = Moderately
4 = Quite a bit
5 = Very much

____ **1.** Active
____ **2.** Distressed
____ **3.** Strong
____ **4.** Excited
____ **5.** Scornful
____ **6.** Hostile
____ **7.** Enthusiastic
____ **8.** Fearful
____ **9.** Peppy
____ **10.** Nervous
____ **11.** Elated
____ **12.** Jittery

Scoring: Responses to items 1, 3, 4, 7, 9, and 11 are summed for a positive mood score; the higher the score, the more positive mood is experienced at work. Responses to items 2, 5, 6, 8, 10, and 12 are summed for a negative mood score; the higher the score, the more negative mood is experienced at work.

When managers are experiencing stressful feelings and emotions such as fear or anxiety, emotional intelligence enables them to understand why and manage these feelings so that they do not get in the way of effective decision making.[69]

Emotional intelligence also can help managers perform their important roles such as their interpersonal roles (figurehead, leader, and liaison).[70] Understanding how your subordinates feel, why they feel that way, and how to manage these feelings is central to developing strong interpersonal bonds with them.[71] Moreover, emotional intelligence has the potential to contribute to effective leadership in multiple ways[72] and can help managers make lasting contributions to society, as profiled in the following "Manager as a Person."

Manager as a Person

Bernie Goldhirsh's Legacy

Bernard (Bernie) Goldhirsh founded *INC.* magazine back in 1979, when entrepreneurs received more notoriety than respect, if they were paid attention to at all.[73] Goldhirsh was an entrepreneur himself at the time, with his own publishing company. He recognized the vast contributions entrepreneurs could make to society, creating something out of nothing, and also realized firsthand what a tough task entrepreneurs faced.[74] His emotional intelligence helped him to understand the challenges and frustrations entrepreneurs like himself faced and their need for support.

When Goldhirsh founded *INC.*, entrepreneurs had little they could turn to for advice, guidance, and solutions to management problems. *INC.* was born to fill this gap and provide entrepreneurs with information and support by profiling successful and unsuccessful entrepreneurial ventures, highlighting management techniques that work, and providing readers with firsthand accounts of how successful entrepreneurs developed and managed their businesses.[75]

Goldhirsh had an inquisitive mind and liked to go where his thoughts and conversations took him. Although he founded *INC.* magazine and inspired his staff, he let his writers and editors have free reign with the magazine's content. They were the experts he chose to write and edit the magazine, and he realized it was not his place to interfere with editorial matters. What he did do, and do very well, was inspire his staff to be enthusiastic about the mission of *INC.* and the role of the entrepreneur as a self-reliant explorer, going off into the unknown. As Goldhirsh put it, entrepreneurs create new businesses "from nothing, just blank canvas. . . . It's amazing. Somebody goes into a garage, has nothing but an idea, and out of the garage comes a company, a living company. It's so special what they do. They are a treasure."[76]

Goldhirsh's emotional intelligence helped him recognize the many barriers entrepreneurs face and the emotional roller coaster of staking all one has on an idea that may or may not work. Goldhirsh believed that helping society understand the entrepreneurial process through *INC.* magazine not only helped entrepreneurs but also enlightened bankers, lawmakers, and the public at large about the role these visionaries play, the challenges they face, and the support their ventures depend on.[77]

When Goldhirsh was diagnosed with brain cancer at age 60, he sold *INC.* magazine at the urging of his doctors. From the proceeds of the sale, he distributed $20 million to *INC.*'s employees, and he dedicated $50 million to a foundation supporting brain cancer research. Goldhirsh inspired *INC.*'s employees to recognize that the magazine had only gotten started and had an important and growing future ahead, and this has certainly been the case.[78] It was a sad day at *INC.* when Goldhirsh passed away but also an opportunity to reflect on the ongoing contributions of a man who saw the ultimate good in entrepreneurship and whose efforts to support it live on today through the magazine he founded.[79]

Emotional intelligence helps managers understand and relate well to other people.[80] It also helps managers maintain their enthusiasm and confidence and energize subordinates to help the organization attain its goals.[81] Recent theorizing and research suggest that emotional intelligence may be especially important in awakening employee creativity.[82] Managers themselves are increasingly recognizing the importance of emotional intelligence. As Andrea Jung, CEO of Avon Products, indicates, "Emotional intelligence is in our DNA here at Avon because relationships are critical at every stage of our business."[83] An example of a scale that measures emotional intelligence is provided in Figure 3.8.

Organizational Culture

Personality is a way of understanding why all managers and employees, as individuals, characteristically think and behave in different ways. However, when people belong to the same organization, they often tend to share certain beliefs and values that lead them to act in similar ways.[84] **Organizational culture** comprises the shared set of beliefs, expectations, values, norms, and work routines that influence how members of an organization relate to one another and work together to achieve organizational goals. In

Figure 3.8
A Measure of Emotional Intelligence
Source: K. Law, C. Wong, and L. Song, "The Construct and Criterion Validity of Emotional Intelligence and Its Potential Utility for Management Studies," *Journal of Applied Psychology* 89, no. 3 (2004), 496; C. S. Wong and K. S. Law, "The Effects of Leader and Follower Emotional Intelligence on Performance and Attitude: An Exploratory Study," *Leadership Quarterly* 13 (2002), 243–74.

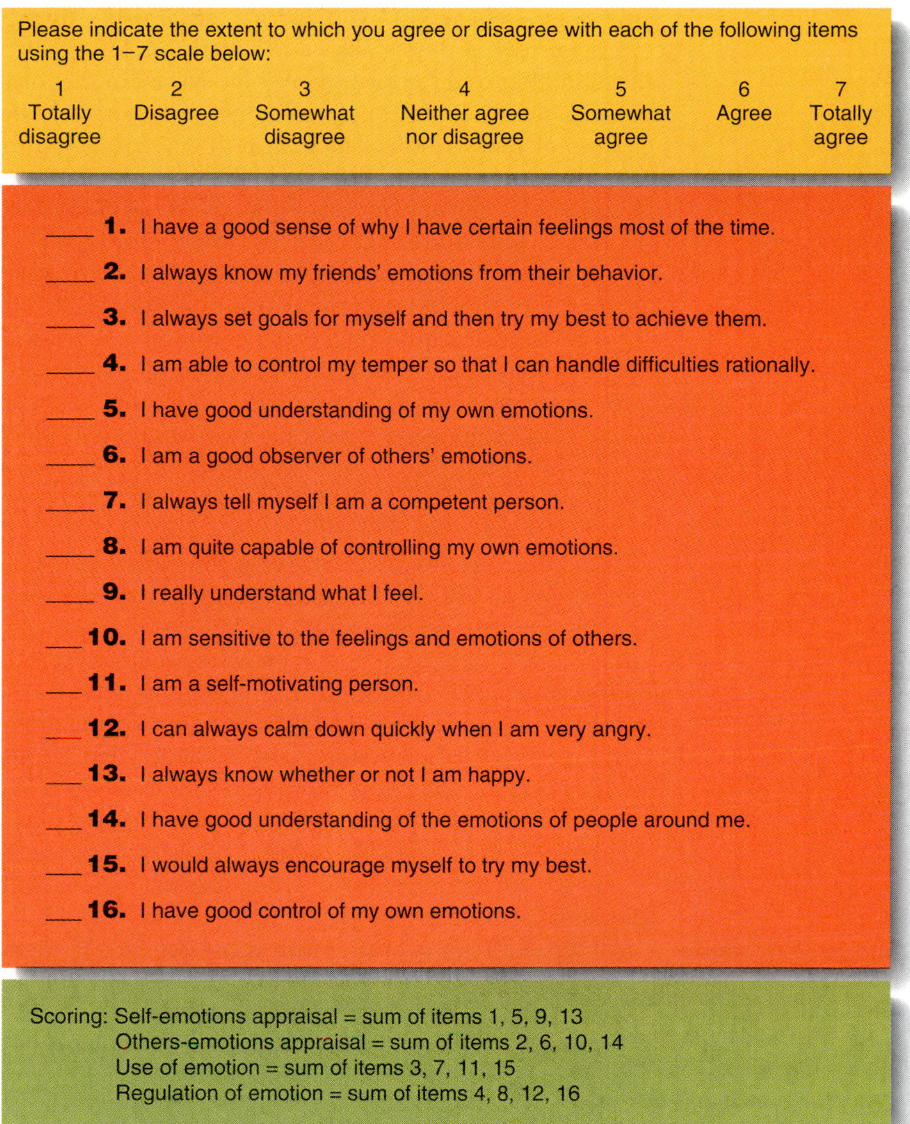

Please indicate the extent to which you agree or disagree with each of the following items using the 1–7 scale below:

1	2	3	4	5	6	7
Totally disagree	Disagree	Somewhat disagree	Neither agree nor disagree	Somewhat agree	Agree	Totally agree

____ **1.** I have a good sense of why I have certain feelings most of the time.
____ **2.** I always know my friends' emotions from their behavior.
____ **3.** I always set goals for myself and then try my best to achieve them.
____ **4.** I am able to control my temper so that I can handle difficulties rationally.
____ **5.** I have good understanding of my own emotions.
____ **6.** I am a good observer of others' emotions.
____ **7.** I always tell myself I am a competent person.
____ **8.** I am quite capable of controlling my own emotions.
____ **9.** I really understand what I feel.
____ **10.** I am sensitive to the feelings and emotions of others.
____ **11.** I am a self-motivating person.
____ **12.** I can always calm down quickly when I am very angry.
____ **13.** I always know whether or not I am happy.
____ **14.** I have good understanding of the emotions of people around me.
____ **15.** I would always encourage myself to try my best.
____ **16.** I have good control of my own emotions.

Scoring: Self-emotions appraisal = sum of items 1, 5, 9, 13
Others-emotions appraisal = sum of items 2, 6, 10, 14
Use of emotion = sum of items 3, 7, 11, 15
Regulation of emotion = sum of items 4, 8, 12, 16

organizational culture The shared set of beliefs, expectations, values, norms, and work routines that influence the ways in which individuals, groups, and teams interact with one another and cooperate to achieve organizational goals.

essence, organizational culture reflects the distinctive ways organizational members go about performing their jobs and relating to others inside and outside the organization. It may, for example, be a distinctive way in which customers in a particular hotel chain are treated from the time they are greeted at check-in until their stay is completed; or it may be the shared work routines that research teams use to guide new product development. When organizational members share an intense commitment to cultural values, beliefs, and routines and use them to achieve their goals, a *strong* organizational culture exists. When organizational members are not strongly committed to a shared system of values, beliefs, and routines, organizational culture is weak.

The stronger the culture of an organization, the more one can think about it as being the "personality" of an organization because it influences the way its members behave.[85] Organizations that possess strong cultures may differ on a wide variety of dimensions that determine how their members behave toward one another and perform their jobs. For example, organizations differ in terms of how members relate to each other (e.g., formally or informally), how important decisions are made (e.g., top-down or bottom-up), willingness to change (e.g., flexible or unyielding), innovation (e.g., creative or predictable), and playfulness (e.g., serious or serendipitous). In an innovative design firm like IDEO Product Development in Silicon Valley, employees are encouraged to adopt a playful attitude to their work, look outside the organization to find inspiration, and adopt a flexible approach toward product design that uses multiple perspectives.[86] IDEO's culture is vastly different from that of companies such as Citibank and ExxonMobil, in which employees treat each other in a more formal or deferential way, employees are expected to adopt a serious approach to their work, and decision making is constrained by the hierarchy of authority.

Managers and Organizational Culture

While all members of an organization can contribute to the development and maintenance of organizational culture, managers play a particularly important part in influencing organizational culture,[87] given their multiple and important roles (see Chapter 1). How managers create culture is most vividly evident in start-ups of new companies. Entrepreneurs who start their own companies are typically also the start-ups' top managers until the companies grow and/or become profitable. Often referred to as the firms' founders, these managers literally create their organizations' cultures.

Often, the founders' personal characteristics play an important role in the creation of organizational culture. Benjamin Schneider, a well-known management researcher, developed a model that helps to explain the role that founders' personal characteristics play in determining organizational culture.[88] His model, called the **attraction-selection-attrition (ASA) framework,** posits that when founders hire employees for their new ventures, they tend to be attracted to and choose employees whose personalities are similar to their own.[89] These similar employees are more likely to stay with the organization. While employees who are dissimilar in personality might be hired, they are more likely to leave the organization over time.[90] As a result of these attraction, selection, and attrition processes, people in the organization tend to have similar personalities, and the typical or dominant personality profile of organizational members determines and shapes organizational culture.[91]

attraction-selection-attrition (ASA) framework A model that explains how personality may influence organizational culture.

For example, when David Kelley became interested in engineering and product design challenges in the late 1970s, he realized that who he was as a person meant that he would not be happy working in the typical corporate environment. Kelley is high on openness to experience, driven to go where his interests take him, and not content to follow others' directives. Kelley recognized that he needed to start his own business and, with the help of other Stanford-schooled engineers and design experts, IDEO was born.[92]

From the start, IDEO's culture has embodied Kelley's spirited, freewheeling approach to work and design—from colorful and informal work spaces to an emphasis on networking and communicating with as many people as possible to understand a design problem. No project or problem is too big or too small for IDEO: The company designed the Apple Lisa computer and mouse (the

An IDEO team works on a project. IDEO designed many products we take for granted, such as the first Apple mouse and stand-up toothpaste containers. IDEO's "playful" culture goes hand-in-hand with the creative nature of its products and services.

precursor of the Mac) and the Palm as well as the Crest Neat Squeeze toothpaste dispenser and the Racer's Edge water bottle. Kelley hates rules, job titles, big corner offices, and all the other trappings of large traditional organizations that stifle creativity. Employees who are attracted to, selected by, and remain with IDEO value creativity and innovation and embrace one of IDEO's mottos: "Fail often to succeed sooner."[93]

While ASA processes are most evident in small firms such as IDEO, they also can operate in large companies.[94] According to the ASA model, this is a naturally occurring phenomenon to the extent that managers and new hires are free to make the kinds of choices the model specifies. While people tend to get along well with others who are similar to themselves, too much similarity in an organization can actually impair organizational effectiveness. That is, similar people tend to view conditions and events in similar ways and thus can be resistant to change. Moreover, organizations benefit from a diversity of perspectives rather than similarity in perspectives (see Chapter 4). At IDEO, Kelley recognized early on how important it is to take advantage of the diverse talents and perspectives that people with different personalities, backgrounds, experiences, and education can bring to a design team. Hence, IDEO's design teams include not only engineers but others who might have a unique insight into a problem, such as anthropologists, communications experts, doctors, and users of a product. When new employees are hired at IDEO, they meet with many employees who have different backgrounds and characteristics–the focus is not on hiring someone who will "fit in" but, rather, on hiring someone who has something to offer and can "wow" different kinds of people with his or her insights.[95]

In addition to personality, other personal characteristics of managers shape organizational culture; these include managers' values, attitudes, moods and emotions, and emotional intelligence.[96] For example, both terminal and instrumental values of managers play a role in determining organizational culture. Managers who highly value freedom and equality, for example, might be more likely to stress the importance of autonomy and empowerment in their organizations, as well as fair treatment for all. As another example, managers who highly value being helpful and forgiving may not only be tolerant of mistakes but also be prone to emphasize the importance of organizational members' being kind and helpful to one another.

Managers who are satisfied with their jobs, are committed to their organizations, and experience positive moods and emotions might also encourage these attitudes and feelings in others. The result would be an organizational culture emphasizing positive attitudes and feelings. Research suggests that attitudes like job satisfaction and organizational commitment can be affected by the influence of others. Managers are in a particularly strong position to engage in social influence given their multiple roles. Moreover, research suggests that moods and emotions can be "contagious" and that spending time with people who are excited and enthusiastic can increase one's own levels of excitement and enthusiasm.

The Role of Values and Norms in Organizational Culture

Shared terminal and instrumental values play a particularly important role in organizational culture. *Terminal values* signify what an organization and its employees are trying to accomplish, and *instrumental values* guide the ways in which the organization and its members achieve organizational goals. In addition to values, shared norms also are a key aspect of organizational culture. Recall that norms are unwritten, informal rules or guidelines that prescribe appropriate behavior in particular situations. For example, norms at IDEO include not being critical of others' ideas, coming up with multiple ideas before settling on one, and developing prototypes of new products.[97]

Managers determine and shape organizational culture through the kinds of values and norms they promote in an organization. Some managers, like David Kelley of IDEO, cultivate values and norms that encourage risk taking, creative responses to problems and opportunities, experimentation, tolerance of failure in order to succeed, and autonomy.[98] Top managers at organizations such as Intel, Microsoft, and Sun Microsystems encourage employees to adopt such values to support their commitment to innovation as a source of competitive advantage.

Other managers, however, might cultivate values and norms that indicate to employees that they should always be conservative and cautious in their dealings with others and should try to consult with their superiors before making important decisions or any changes to the status quo. Accountability for actions and decisions is stressed, and detailed records are kept to ensure that policies and procedures are followed. In settings where caution is needed–nuclear power stations, large oil refineries, chemical plants, financial institutions, insurance companies–a conservative, cautious approach to making decisions might be highly appropriate.[99] In a nuclear power plant, for example, the catastrophic consequences of a mistake make a high level of supervision vital. Similarly, in a bank or mutual fund company, the risk of losing investors' money makes a cautious approach to investing highly appropriate.

Managers of different kinds of organizations deliberately cultivate and develop the organizational values and norms that are best suited to their task and general environments, strategy, or technology. Organizational culture is maintained and transmitted to organizational members through the values of the founder, the process of socialization, ceremonies and rites, and stories and language (see Figure 3.9).

Figure 3.9
Factors That Maintain and Transmit Organizational Culture

VALUES OF THE FOUNDER From the ASA model discussed above, it is clear that founders of an organization can have profound and long-lasting effects on organizational culture. Founders' values inspire the founders to start their own companies and, in turn, drive the nature of these new companies and their defining characteristics. Thus, an organization's founder and his or her terminal and instrumental values have a substantial influence on the values, norms, and standards of behavior that develop over time within the organization.[100] Founders set the scene for the way cultural values and norms develop because their own values guide the building of the company and they hire other managers and employees who they believe will share these values and help the organization to attain them. Moreover, new managers quickly learn from the founder what values and norms are appropriate in the organization and thus what is desired of them. Subordinates imitate the style of the founder and, in turn, transmit their values and norms to their subordinates. Gradually, over time, the founder's values and norms permeate the organization.[101]

A founder who requires a great display of respect from subordinates and insists on proprieties such as formal job titles and formal modes of dress encourages subordinates to act in this way toward their subordinates. Often, a founder's personal values affect an organization's competitive advantage. For example, McDonald's founder Ray Kroc insisted from the beginning on high standards of customer service and cleanliness at McDonald's restaurants; these became core sources of McDonald's competitive advantage. Similarly, Bill Gates, the founder of Microsoft, pioneered certain cultural values in Microsoft. Employees are expected to be creative and to work hard, but they are encouraged to dress informally and to personalize their offices. Gates also established a host of company events such as cookouts, picnics, and sports events to emphasize to employees the importance of being both an individual and a team player.

SOCIALIZATION Over time, organizational members learn from each other which values are important in an organization and the norms that specify appropriate and inappropriate behaviors. Eventually, organizational members behave in accordance with the organization's values and norms–often without realizing they are doing so. **Organizational socialization** is the process by which newcomers learn an organization's values and norms and acquire the work behaviors necessary to perform jobs effectively.[102] As a result of their socialization experiences, organizational members internalize an organization's values and norms and behave in accordance with them not only because they think they have to but because they think that these values and norms describe the right and proper way to behave.[103]

organizational socialization The process by which newcomers learn an organization's values and norms and acquire the work behaviors necessary to perform jobs effectively.

At Texas A&M University, for example, all new students are encouraged to go to "Fish Camp" to learn how to be an "Aggie" (the traditional nickname of students at the university). They learn about the ceremonies that have developed over time to commemorate significant events or people in A&M's history. In addition, they learn how to behave at football games and in class and what it means to be an Aggie. As a result of this highly organized socialization program, by the time new students arrive on campus and start their first semester, they have been socialized into what a Texas A&M student is supposed to do, and they have relatively few problems adjusting to the college environment.

Most organizations have some kind of socialization program to help new employees learn the ropes–the values, norms, and culture of the organization. The military, for example, is well known for the rigorous socialization process it uses to

Texas A&M's Fish Camp is an annual orientation program designed to help freshmen (or Fish) make the transition from high school to college life. Texas A&M's Fish Camp runs for four days and is attended by over 4,500 freshmen each year.

turn raw recruits into trained soldiers. Organizations such as the Walt Disney Company also put new recruits through a rigorous training program to provide them with the knowledge they need not only to perform well in their jobs but also to ensure that each employee plays his or her part in helping visitors to Disneyland have fun in a wholesome theme park. New recruits at Disney are called "cast members" and attend Disney University to learn the Disney culture and their part in it. Disney's culture emphasizes the values of safety, courtesy, entertainment, and efficiency, and these values are brought to life for newcomers at Disney University. Newcomers also learn about the attraction area they will be joining (e.g., Adventureland or Fantasyland) at Disney University and then receive on-the-job socialization in the area itself from experienced cast members.[104] Through organizational socialization, founders and managers of an organization transmit to employees the cultural values and norms that shape the behavior of organizational members. Thus, the values and norms of founder Walt Disney live on today at Disneyland as newcomers are socialized into the Disney way.

CEREMONIES AND RITES Another way in which managers can create or influence organizational culture is by developing organizational *ceremonies and rites*–formal events that recognize incidents of importance to the organization as a whole and to specific employees.[105] The most common rites that organizations use to transmit cultural norms and values to their members are rites of passage, of integration, and of enhancement (see Table 3.1).[106]

Rites of passage determine how individuals enter, advance within, or leave the organization. The socialization programs developed by military organizations (such as the U.S. Army) or by large accountancy and law firms are rites of passage. Likewise, the ways in which an organization prepares people for promotion or retirement are rites of passage.

Rites of integration, such as shared announcements of organizational successes, office parties, and company cookouts, build and reinforce common bonds

Table 3.1
Organizational Rites

Type of Rite	Example of Rite	Purpose of Rite
Rite of passage	Induction and basic training	Learn and internalize norms and values
Rite of integration	Office Christmas party	Build common norms and values
Rite of enhancement	Presentation of annual award	Motivate commitment to norms and values

among organizational members. IDEO uses many rites of integration to make its employees feel connected to one another and special. In addition to having wild "end-of-year" celebratory bashes, groups of IDEO employees periodically take time off to go to a sporting event, movie, or meal or, sometimes, on a long bike ride or sail. These kinds of shared activities not only reinforce IDEO's culture but also can be a source of inspiration on the job (e.g., IDEO has been involved in the making of movies such as *The Abyss* and *Free Willy*). One 35-member design studio at IDEO led by Dennis Boyle has bimonthly lunch fests with no set agenda–anything goes. While enjoying great food, jokes, and camaraderie, studio members often end up sharing ideas for their latest great products, and the freely flowing conversation that results often leads to creative insights.[107]

A company's annual meeting also may be used as a ritual of integration, offering an opportunity to communicate organizational values to managers, other employees, and shareholders. Wal-Mart, for example, makes its annual stockholders' meeting an extravagant ceremony that celebrates the company's success. The company often flies thousands of its highest-performing employees to its annual meeting at its Bentonville, Arkansas, headquarters for a huge weekend entertainment festival complete with performances by country and western stars. Wal-Mart believes that rewarding its supporters with entertainment reinforces the company's high-performance values and culture. The proceedings are shown live over closed-circuit television in all Wal-Mart stores so that all employees can join in the rites celebrating the company's achievements.[108]

Wal-Mart managers attending an annual meeting in Kansas City, Missouri. Wal-Mart believes that entertainment reinforces its high-performance culture and values. These events, or "rites of integration," reinforce common bonds among members of an organization.

Rites of enhancement, such as awards dinners, newspaper releases, and employee promotions, let organizations publicly recognize and reward employees' contributions and thus strengthen their commitment to organizational values. By bonding members within the organization, rites of enhancement reinforce an organization's values and norms.

Stories and language also communicate organizational culture. Stories (whether fact or fiction) about organizational heroes and villains and their actions provide important clues about values and norms. Such stories can reveal the kinds of behaviors that are valued by the organization and the kinds of practices that are frowned on.[109] At the heart of McDonald's rich culture are hundreds of stories that organizational members tell about founder Ray Kroc. Most of these stories focus on how Kroc established the strict operating values and norms that are at the heart of McDonald's culture. Kroc was dedicated to achieving perfection in McDonald's quality, service, cleanliness, and value for money (QSC&V), and these four central values permeate McDonald's culture. For example, an often retold story describes what happened when Kroc and a group of managers from the Houston region were touring various restaurants. One of the restaurants was having a bad day operationally. Kroc was incensed about the long lines of customers, and he was furious when he realized that the product customers were receiving that day was not up to his high standards. To address the problem, he jumped up and stood on the front counter and got the attention of all customers and operating crew personnel. He introduced himself, apologized for the long wait and cold food, and told the customers that they could have freshly cooked food or their money back–whichever they wanted. As a result, the customers left happy, and when Kroc checked on the restaurant later, he found that his message had gotten through to its managers and crew–performance had improved. Other stories describe Kroc scrubbing dirty toilets and picking up litter inside or outside a restaurant. These and similar stories are spread around the organization by McDonald's employees. They are the stories that have helped establish Kroc as McDonald's "hero."

Because spoken language is a principal medium of communication in organizations, the characteristic slang or jargon–that is, organization-specific words or phrases–that people use to frame and describe events provides important clues about norms and values. "McLanguage," for example, is prevalent at all levels of McDonald's. A McDonald's employee described as having "ketchup in his (or her) blood" is someone who is truly dedicated to the McDonald's way–someone who has been completely socialized to its culture. McDonald's has an extensive training program that teaches new employees "McDonald's speak," and new employees are welcomed into the family with a formal orientation that illustrates Kroc's dedication to QSC&V.

The concept of organizational language encompasses not only spoken language but how people dress, the offices they occupy, the cars they drive, and the degree of formality they use when they address one another. Casual dress reflects and reinforces Microsoft's entrepreneurial culture and values. Formal business attire supports the conservative culture found in many banks, which emphasize the importance of conforming to organizational norms such as respect for authority and staying within one's prescribed role. Traders in the Chicago futures and options trading pits frequently wear garish and flamboyant ties and jackets to make their presence known in a sea of faces. The demand for magenta, lime green, and silver lamé jackets featuring bold images such as the Power Rangers–anything that helps the traders stand out and attract customers–is enormous.[110] When employees speak and understand the language of their organization's culture, they know how to behave in the organization and what is expected of them.

At IDEO, language, dress, the physical work environment, and extreme informality all underscore a culture that is adventuresome, playful, risk taking, egalitarian, and innovative. For example, at IDEO, employees refer to taking the consumers' perspective when designing products as "being left-handed." Employees dress in T-shirts and jeans, the physical work environment is continually evolving and changing depending upon how employees wish to personalize their workspace, no one "owns" a fancy office with a window, and rules are nonexistent.[111]

Culture and Managerial Action

While founders and managers play a critical role in the development, maintenance, and communication of organizational culture, this same culture shapes and controls the behavior of all employees, including managers themselves. For example, culture influences the way managers perform their four main functions: planning, organizing, leading, and controlling. As we consider these functions, we continue to distinguish between top managers who create organizational values and norms that encourage creative, innovative behavior and top managers who encourage a conservative, cautious approach by their subordinates. We noted earlier that both kinds of values and norms can be appropriate depending upon the situation and type of organization.

PLANNING Top managers in an organization with an innovative culture are likely to encourage lower-level managers to participate in the planning process and develop a flexible approach to planning. They are likely to be willing to listen to new ideas and to take risks involving the development of new products. In contrast, top managers in an organization with conservative values are likely to emphasize formal top-down planning. Suggestions from lower-level managers are likely to be subjected to a formal review process, which can significantly slow decision making. Although this deliberate approach may improve the quality of decision making in a nuclear power plant, it can have unintended consequences. In the past, at conservative IBM, the planning process became so formalized that managers spent most of their time assembling complex slide shows and overheads to defend their current positions rather than thinking about what they should be doing to keep IBM abreast of the changes taking place in the computer industry. When former CEO Lou Gerstner took over, he used every means at his disposal to abolish this culture, even building a brand-new campus-style headquarters to change managers' mind-sets. As indicated in the earlier IT Byte, IBM's culture is undergoing further changes initiated by its new CEO, Samuel Palmisano.

ORGANIZING What kinds of organizing will managers in innovative and in conservative cultures encourage? Valuing creativity, managers in innovative cultures are likely to try to create an organic structure, one that is flat, with few levels in the hierarchy, and one in which authority is decentralized so that employees are encouraged to work together to find solutions to ongoing problems. A product team structure may be very suitable for an organization with an innovative culture. In contrast, managers in a conservative culture are likely to create a well-defined hierarchy of authority and establish clear reporting relationships so that employees know exactly whom to report to and how to react to any problems that arise.

LEADING In an innovative culture, managers are likely to lead by example, encouraging employees to take risks and experiment. They are supportive regardless of whether employees succeed or fail. In contrast, managers in a conservative culture are likely to use management by objectives and to constantly monitor subordinates' progress toward goals, overseeing their every move. We examine leadership in detail in Chapter 13 when we consider the leadership styles that managers can adopt to influence and shape employee behavior.

CONTROLLING The ways in which managers evaluate, and take actions to improve, performance differ depending upon whether the organizational culture emphasizes formality and caution or innovation and change. Managers who want to encourage risk taking, creativity, and innovation recognize that there are multiple potential paths to success and that failure must be accepted in order for creativity to thrive. Thus, they are less concerned about employees' performing their jobs in a specific, predetermined manner and in strict adherence to preset goals and more concerned about employees' being flexible and taking the initiative to come up with ideas for improving performance. Managers in innovative cultures are also more concerned about long-run performance than short-term targets because they recognize that real innovation entails much uncertainty that necessitates flexibility. In contrast, managers in cultures that emphasize caution and maintenance of the status quo often set specific, difficult goals for employees, frequently monitor progress toward these goals, and develop a clear set of rules that employees are expected to adhere to.

The values and norms of an organization's culture strongly affect the way managers perform their management functions. The extent to which managers buy into the values and norms of their organization shapes their view of the world and their actions and decisions in particular circumstances.[112] In turn, the actions that managers take can have an impact on the performance of the organization. Thus, organizational culture, managerial action, and organizational performance are all linked together.

This linkage is apparent at Hewlett-Packard (HP), a leader in the electronic instrumentation and computer industries. Established in the 1940s, HP developed a culture that is an outgrowth of the strong personal beliefs of the company's founders, William Hewlett and David Packard. Bill and Dave, as they are known within the company, formalized HP's culture in 1957 in a statement of corporate objectives known as the "HP Way." The basic values informing the HP Way stress serving everyone who has a stake in the company with integrity and fairness, including customers, suppliers, employees, stockholders, and society in general. Bill and Dave helped build this culture within HP by hiring like-minded people and by letting the HP Way guide their own actions as managers.

Although the Hewlett-Packard example and our earlier example of IDEO illustrate how organizational culture can give rise to managerial actions that ultimately benefit the organization, this is not always the case. The cultures of some organizations become dysfunctional, encouraging managerial actions that harm the organization and discouraging actions that might lead to an improvement in performance.[113] Recent corporate scandals at large companies like Enron, Tyco, and WorldCom show how damaging a dysfunctional culture can be to an organization and its members. For example, Enron's arrogant, "success-at-all costs" culture led to fraudulent behavior on the part of its top managers.[114] Unfortunately, hundreds of Enron employees have paid a heavy price for the unethical behavior of these top managers and the dysfunctional organizational culture. Not only have these employees lost their jobs, but many also have lost their life savings in Enron stock and pension funds, which became worth just a fraction of their former value before the wrongdoing at Enron came to light. We discuss ethics and ethical cultures in depth in the next chapter.

Summary and Review

ENDURING CHARACTERISTICS: PERSONALITY TRAITS Personality traits are enduring tendencies to feel, think, and act in certain ways. The Big Five general traits are extraversion, negative affectivity, agreeableness, conscientiousness, and openness to experience. Other personality traits that affect managerial behavior are locus of control, self-esteem, and the needs for achievement, affiliation, and power.

VALUES, ATTITUDES, AND MOODS AND EMOTIONS A terminal value is a personal conviction about lifelong goals or objectives; an instrumental value is a personal conviction about modes of conduct. Terminal and instrumental values have an impact on what managers try to achieve in their organizations and the kinds of behaviors they engage in. An attitude is a collection of feelings and beliefs. Two attitudes important for understanding managerial behaviors include job satisfaction (the collection of feelings and beliefs that managers have about their jobs) and organizational commitment (the collection of feelings and beliefs that managers have about their organizations). A mood is a feeling or state of mind; emotions are intense feelings that are short-lived and directly linked to their causes. Managers' moods and emotions, or how they feel at work on a day-to-day basis, have the potential to impact not only their own behavior and effectiveness but also those of their subordinates. Emotional intelligence is the ability to understand and manage one's own and other people's moods and emotions.

ORGANIZATIONAL CULTURE Organizational culture is the shared set of beliefs, expectations, values, norms, and work routines that influence how members of an organization relate to one another and work together to achieve organizational goals. Founders of new organizations and managers play an important role in creating and maintaining organizational culture. Organizational socialization is the process by which newcomers learn an organization's values and norms and acquire the work behaviors necessary to perform jobs effectively.

Management in Action

Topics for Discussion and Action

Discussion

1. Discuss why managers who have different types of personalities can be equally effective and successful.
2. Can managers be too satisfied with their jobs? Can they be too committed to their organizations? Why or why not?
3. Assume that you are a manager of a restaurant. Describe what it is like to work for you when you are in a negative mood.
4. Why might managers be disadvantaged by low levels of emotional intelligence?

Action

5. Interview a manager in a local organization. Ask the manager to describe situations in which he or she is especially likely to act in accordance with his or her values. Ask the manager to describe situations in which he or she is less likely to act in accordance with his or her values.
6. Watch a popular television show, and as you watch it, try to determine the emotional intelligence levels of the characters the actors in the show portray. Rank the characters from highest to lowest in terms of emotional intelligence. As you watched the show, what factors influenced your assessments of emotional intelligence levels.
7. Go to an upscale clothing store in your neighborhood, and go to a clothing store that is definitely not upscale. Observe the behavior of employees in each store as well as the store's environment. In what ways are the organizational cultures in each store similar? In what ways are they different?

Building Management Skills

Diagnosing Culture

Think about the culture of the last organization you worked for, your current university, or another organization or club to which you belong. Then, answer the following questions:

1. What values are emphasized in this culture?
2. What norms do members of this organization follow?
3. Who seems to have played an important role in creating the culture?
4. In what ways is the organizational culture communicated to organizational members.

Managing Ethically

Some organizations rely on personality and interest inventories to screen potential employees. Other organizations attempt to screen employees by using paper-and-pencil honesty tests.

Questions

1. Either individually or in a group, think about the ethical implications of using personality and interest inventories to screen potential employees. How might this practice be unfair to potential applicants? How might organizational members who are in charge of hiring misuse it?
2. Because of measurement error and validity problems, some relatively trustworthy people may "fail" an honesty test given by an employer. What are the ethical implications of trustworthy people "failing" honesty tests, and what obligations do you think employers should have when relying on honesty tests for screening purposes?

Small Group Breakout Exercise

Making Difficult Decisions in Hard Times

Form groups of three or four people, and appoint one member as the spokesperson who will communicate your findings to the whole class when called on by the instructor. Then discuss the following scenario.

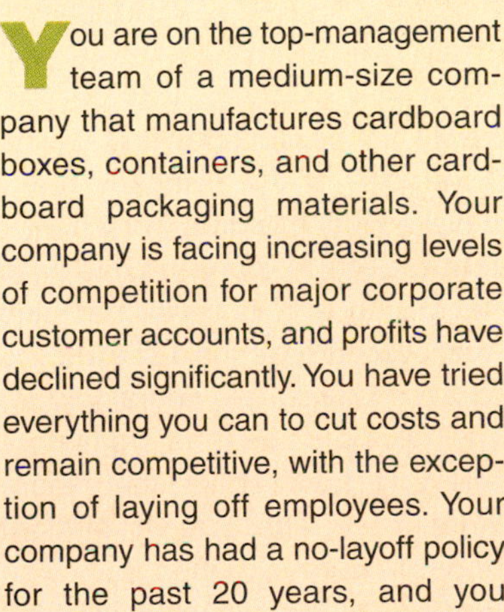

You are on the top-management team of a medium-size company that manufactures cardboard boxes, containers, and other cardboard packaging materials. Your company is facing increasing levels of competition for major corporate customer accounts, and profits have declined significantly. You have tried everything you can to cut costs and remain competitive, with the exception of laying off employees. Your company has had a no-layoff policy for the past 20 years, and you believe it is an important part of the organization's culture. However, you are experiencing mounting pressure to increase your firm's performance, and your no-layoff policy has been questioned by shareholders. Even though you haven't decided whether to lay off employees and thus break with a 20-year tradition for your company, rumors are rampant in your organization that something is afoot, and employees are worried. You are meeting today to address this problem.

1. Develop a list of options and potential courses of action to address the heightened competition and decline in profitability that your company has been experiencing.
2. Choose your preferred course of action, and justify why you will take this route.
3. Describe how you will communicate your decision to employees.
4. If your preferred option involves a layoff, justify why. If it doesn't involve a layoff, explain why.

Exploring the World Wide Web

Go to IDEO's Web site (www.ideo.com) and read about this company. Try to find indicators of IDEO's culture that are provided on the Web site. How does the design of the Web site itself, and the pictures and words it contains, communicate the nature of IDEO's organizational culture? What kinds of people do you think would be attracted to IDEO? What kinds of people do you think would be likely to be dissatisfied with a job at IDEO?

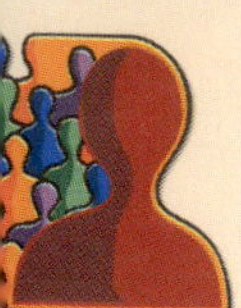

Be the Manager

You have recently been hired as the vice president for human resources in an advertising agency. One of the problems that has been brought to your attention is the fact that in the creative departments at the agency, there are dysfunctionally high levels of conflict. You have spoken with members of each of these departments, and in each one it seems that there are a few members of the department who are creating all the problems. All of these individuals are valued contributors who have many creative ad campaigns to their credit. The very high levels of conflict are creating problems in the departments, and negative moods and emotions are much more prevalent than positive feelings. What are you going to do to both retain valued employees and alleviate the excessive conflict and negative feelings in these departments?

Additional Activities on the Build Your Management Skills DVD

- **Test Your Knowledge:** (1) Types, Causes, and Management of Stress; (2) Corporate Cultures Preferences Scale; (3) Type "A" Scale; and (4) What Is Your Level of Self-Esteem?
- **Self-Assessment:** Assessing Your Emotional Intelligence
- **Manager's Hot Seat:** Personal Disclosure: Confession Coincidence

BusinessWeek Case in the News

The Odyssey of a Cancer Drug

Harlan W. Waksal had just landed in Telluride, Colo., for a ski vacation with his family when he got a call on his cell phone that he can only describe as "bittersweet." Erbitux, the cancer drug that Dr. Waksal spent the past decade developing as a co-founder of ImClone Systems Inc., had finally won approval from the Food & Drug Administration on Feb. 12.

But Waksal couldn't celebrate with his ImClone colleagues; he had resigned last July. Nor could he share his joy with his brother and ImClone co-founder Samuel D. Waksal. Sam is currently serving seven years in a federal prison for insider trading, and Harlan's cell phone is not one of the phone numbers he is allowed to call.

Still, says Harlan, "I fell vindicated. I an elated that we were able to bring a new cancer drug to patients. I'm disappointed about the fact that it took so long. And I'm sad that I wasn't at the company that has been such an important part of my life for 20 years."

A similar stew of emotions has gripped virtually everyone connected with Erbitux, a drug that has gained more fame for its role in a series of corporate scandals than for its efficacy against cancer. Ever since the FDA refused to consider ImClone's first application on Dec. 28, 2001, the company has staggered through insider trading and tax scandals, ricocheting share prices, congressional hearings, management changes, and constant questions about whether the drug really works. The final indignity: Erbitux played a leading role in Martha Stewart's trial for obstruction of justice, related to her sale of ImClone stock on Dec. 27, 2001.

True Believers

ImClone survived all the turmoil for only one reason, according to newly named CEO Daniel S. Lynch: "Everyone at the company really believed that this drug worked." For that reason ImClone managed to hang on to all of its senior staff, and employee turnover held at a low 2% to 3% the past two years. Lily W. Lee, vice-president for regulatory affairs, acknowledges that "there were times when we all thought about leaving, or when our close friends would say, 'Don't you think you should get out?'" But, she says, "everyone was focused on getting the drug to the patients. All the rest was just noise."

It wasn't supposed to be so hard. In 2001, Erbitux, an antibody that blocks cancer cell growth, was a biotech star. A clinical trial found that Erbitux shrank or stabilized tumors in 22.5% of patients with advanced colon cancer, a strong result for a cancer drug. That September, Bristol-Myers Squibb Co. paid $2 billion for a 20% stake in ImClone and a share of the U.S. marketing rights.

ImClone filed its application for approval a month later.

But by early December, the FDA was losing enthusiasm. Sources close to the application process say there was a split at the agency, which at that time had no director. Some staffers disagreed with the design of ImClone's clinical trial because it tested Erbitux only in combination with standard chemotherapy. There was no "control arm" that tested the drug alone.

When the FDA rejected the application on Dec. 28, Lee says the ImClone team was stunned by the number of objections. Most letters refusing a filing run a page or two and are never made public. "A nine-page refusal-to-file letter is pretty daunting," says Lee. On top of that, the letter was leaked to the press in January. "That letter rewrote the history of our interactions with the FDA, and when it became public it made it seem as though the company had been dishonest," says Harlan.

The appearance of dishonesty was only heightened in the spring when it came out that Sam Waksal had tried to dump all his ImClone stock on Dec. 27, after an FDA staffer leaked that the application would be refused. Even before his panic became public, Bristol-Myers was not sure it wanted any part of the mess. Lynch, who had arrived at ImClone as chief financial officer in April, 2001, had been a key negotiator in the original deal with Bristol. In January, 2002, he had to head off Bristol's efforts to renege. His attitude: "The deal was a deal." ImClone agreed to accept slightly lower payments from Bristol, but that was it.

"Hail Mary Pass"

After a meeting with the FDA in February, 2002, Bristol decided it was worth its while to embrace Erbitux. "There was a lot of discussion about where to go from there, but all of our attention was focused on the fact that the refusal-to-file letter never questioned whether the drug was effective," says Dr. Andrew G. Bodnar, Bristol's senior vice-president for strategy.

The relationship between the two partners remained chilly for some time, however. ImClone stayed firmly in charge of the application process, and an ImClone source says Bristol "mocked the approach we were taking. They called it our 'Hail Mary pass.'" That approach was to base a new filing on a 329-patient trial of Erbitux in Europe, run by Merck KGaA of Germany. Merck was testing Erbitux alone in half the patients and in combination with chemo in the other half, giving the FDA the control arm it wanted. "It's hard to say whether Bristol was in agreement with the Merck study," says Lee, "but the FDA was."

Publicly, ImClone was getting raked over many different coals. Sam Waksal resigned as CEO in April, 2002, and was succeeded by Harlan. In June, Sam was arrested for insider trading, and he pleaded guilty in October. "Everyone was under incredible stress, but I was extremely impressed with the ability of the ImClone people to compartmentalize," says Dr. John Mendelsohn, a co-discoverer of Erbitux and president of M.D. Anderson Cancer Center in Houston. At Bristol, according to Bodnar, "we just kept saying, 'It's the drug, stupid.'"

Harlan, who headed up the approval process, says he met every week with ImClone staffers in an effort to bolster morale. "I encouraged them to ask any questions they wanted." ImClone also set up a system that allowed employees to ask questions anonymously.

Bolstering investor confidence was a lot harder. By September, 2002, ImClone's stock had sunk to $5.24, from more than $70 a share a year earlier. But the situation started improving in November, when the FDA, which had been leaderless for almost two years, finally got a commissioner. Dr. Mark B. McClellan made it clear that he wanted to streamline drug approvals, which had slowed to a trickle since 2000, and Wall Street's confidence in the entire biotech industry rose. "Whether the application would have gone differently without Commissioner McClellan, I can't say," says Bodnar. "But his presence certainly didn't retard the process."

ImClone soon went through its own leadership change. Harlan was asked to step down as CEO in April, 2003, in the wake of a federal probe into taxes the company failed to pay on Sam's stock options. In July, Harlan decided to resign altogether. Lynch became the first person not named Waksal to run ImClone.

Lynch's job quickly got a lot easier. By spring of 2003, preliminary results from the Merck trial were in, and the German company reported a 22.9% response rate, slightly better than ImClone had gotten in its earlier trial. On June 5, 2003, Bristol and ImClone officials met with FDA staffers. "They told us, 'submit the results,'" says Bodnar, a sure sign that the agency was happy with the new Erbitux data.

On Aug. 14, ImClone refiled its application and this time the drug breezed through. Erbituz won approval exactly six months later, and went on sale Feb. 24, at a cost of $2,500 per dose.

There are still some potential blocks. ImClone must win FDA certification of its own manufacturing plant for Erbitux; production is currently contracted out. The company also needs to win approvals for other cancers if it wants to maximize sales. Erbitux is now being tested in ovarian, head and neck, and lung cancers.

As for the two founders, Sam has six years of his sentence left to serve, and Harlan is mulling over what to do next. Mendelsohn refuses to cast stones at the only two men willing to take a chance on his drug in the early 1990s. Whatever else one might say of the man, "Sam was very much a visionary," says Mendelsohn. And Harlan notes that unlike so many other companies caught up in recent scancals, ImClone—and patients—ended up with a product.

Questions

1. What values and norms are emphasized in ImClone's culture?
2. Why did employees stay with the company through all of the scandals and hard times?
3. How would you characterize the attitudes and values of ImClone's employees?
4. How might emotional intelligence help explain ImClone's success in bringing Erbitux to market?

Source: Reprinted from March 8, 2004, issue of *BusinessWeek* by special permission.

BusinessWeek Case in the News

I'm a Bad Boss? Blame My Dad

For Peter Tilton, the office revelation came last February. He was sitting in a conference room at company headquarters, meeting with the group he managed, when an "incompetent" colleague began needling him about his own progress on a project. Tilton felt the trip wire go off, the raw rush that made him feel as if he were slipping into a state of adolescent siege.

Within seconds, he was banging his fist on the whiteboard and "yelling his face off." Even at a place like Microsoft Corp., where Tilton says co-workers routinely blast each others' ideas as "stupid," this wasn't exactly behavior becoming a director-level executive. The emotional outburst, Tilton now realizes, was eerily similar to one he had back in seventh grade, when his parents—"chronic misunderstanders"—forbade him to wear his jeans with the holey knees to school. It was 1967, and he was heavy into his hippie protest phase. "And they wanted me to wear slacks," Tilton says.

For Bert Whitehead, CEO of Cambridge Connection, a financial-planning company in Franklin Village, Mich., the epiphany came when, after announcing he would be away on a business trip, he noticed a stealthy rejoicing rippling through his offices. Today, he knows Why. "Nobody was ever quite good enough," says Whitehead, who refers to himself as a moody stress-generator. "I had a mother I could never get approval from, and I had unknowingly really adopted that into my management style."

That these highly rational, utterly left-brained executives are delving into their pasts illustrates a new strain of organizational therapy coursing through the inner sanctums of corporate power. The basic concept: that people tend to recreate their family dynamics at the office. The idea is being fanned by organizational experts, who say that corporate strivers can at times behave a bit like thumb-suckers in knee pants, yearning for pats on the back from boss "daddies and mommies" and wishing those scene-stealing co-worker "siblings" would, well, die. Boardroom arguments can parallel spats at the family dinner table. Office politics can take on the dimensions of Icarus blowing off his Dad—or Hamlet offing Uncle Claudius.

Buttressed by new research in workplace dynamics, more high-profile coaches and consultants are applying family-systems therapy to business organizations, to grapple with what has come to be seen as a new frontier in productivity; emotional inefficiency, which includes all that bickering, back-stabbing, and ridiculous playing for approval that are a mark of the modern workplace. A two-year study by Seattle psychologist Brian DesRoches found that such dramas routinely waste 20% to 50% of workers' time. The theory is also gaining more resonance as corporations become ever more cognizant that talented employees quit bosses, not companies, and that CEOs often get hired for their skills—and fired for their personalities.

Looking backward to move forward makes sense, say group dynamic researchers, considering that the first organization people ever belong to is their families, with parents the first bosses and siblings the first colleagues. "Our original notions of an institution, of an authority structure, of power and influence are all forged in the family," says Warren Bennis, management guru and professor of business at the University of Southern California. Adds Dr. Scott C. Stacy, clinical program director of the Professional Renewal Center in

Lawrence, Kan.: "This is a huge piece of understanding how businesses everywhere work."

Hero, Scapegoat, Martyr

This may seem like so much EST-era drivel, but by performing psychological X-rays on clients' pasts, coaches have helped executives at companies as diverse as the *Los Angeles Times,* State Farm Insurance, and American Express understand this own and others' dysfunctional behavior. They learn how to recognize the shadowy emotional subtext that drives many encounters, deconstructing how they may be subconsciously sabotaging themselves, shying from authority figures, or engaging in hypercritical judgments of subordinates. Or why they may unwittingly play the role of the hero, scapegoat, or martyr. "I'm not suggesting that our employees are our kids," says Kenneth Sole, a consulting social psychologist who has worked with Apple Computer Inc. and the U.N. "But the psychology is parallel."

Indeed, brain research over the past decade has shown that during stress—when people's need to feel included, competent, and liked is thwarted—their minds are hardwired to default to defensive family scripts. "We project onto others the conflicts we experienced growing up," says Robert Pasick, president of LeadersConnect in Ann Arbor, Mich. He teaches a course at the University of Michigan Business School on how family dynamics affect teams.

Such corporate head-shrinking is gaining more ground in part because of how much interdependence companies face on the global stage. In the manual economy, work was a regimented, militaristic affair in which it was easier to subsume personality differences. Today, success hinges on teams performing as seamlessly as the flawless machinery in a showcase Six Sigma plant. And corporations hire workers whose families are more likely to resemble The Osbournes than Ozzie and Harriet. Personalities, emotions, behavioral tics—all have started to take on a bigger dimension in an era in which businesses increasingly sell the ideas that come from employees' heads, not just the products from their machines.

Moreover, as scandals have heightened the need for transparency, disclosure, and ethics, many execs have begun to see the importance of matching the corporate culture with employees' personal cultures, given that most people get their ethical foundations from their families. That's why a number of financial, utility, and manufacturing clients are lobbing interview questions about families at job candidates in the hope of yielding unvarnished responses, says Neil Lebovits, president of Ajilon Finance in Saddle Brook, N.J. Anything to avoid hiring the next Jeffrey K. Skilling.

Of course, plenty of leaders and their consultants object to therapy invading the office. "The workplace is not the place to explore psychological foibles," says Richard A. Chaifetz, CEO of ComPsych Corp., a Chicago employee-assistance firm. "It can open up a can of worms." Chaifetz approves of this kind of inquiry only if it's done off-site, one-on-one, and with a trained professional. And many work dynamics can't be analyzed solely through a family filter. More likely, say critics, work teams carry traits that are characteristic of all group dynamics. Pairing off, for example, usually happens any time people gather. So does complaining.

Historic Hysterics

Still, someone's familial past can certainly seep into the office scene. It's most recognizable, say experts, when a co-worker or supervisor has highly emotional, intense reactions: When it's hysterical, it's historical. Other symptoms—an inability to maintain a reflective distance, repeated outbursts of anger, and having the same battles with the same people over and over.

In Tilton's case, the Microsoft exec had disdained therapy "ever since my parents tried to send me to a pipe-smoking guy in seventh grade." But in the months he has been working with an executive coach, he only wishes he could have cracked through his denial sooner. Like many, he realizes that being analytically savvy isn't enough. Being emotionally competent is now part of the job, too.

Questions

1. In what ways do managers' personalities and experiences as they were growing up play out in the workplace?
2. Why might personality be becoming a more important factor in understanding managerial effectiveness?
3. Why aren't technical and analytical skills alone sufficient for being an effective manager?
4. What roles does emotional intelligence play in managerial effectiveness?

Source: Reprinted from May 10, 2004, issue of *BusinessWeek* by special permission.

CHAPTER

4 Ethics and Social Responsibility

Learning Objectives

After studying this chapter, you should be able to:

- Understand the relationship between ethics and the law.
- Appreciate why it is important to behave ethically.
- Differentiate between the claims of the different stakeholder groups that are affected by managers and their companies' actions.
- Describe four rules that can be used to help companies and their managers act in ethical ways.
- Identify the four main sources of managerial ethics.
- Distinguish between the four main approaches toward social responsibility that a company can take.

A Manager's Challenge

Digital Piracy, Ethics, and Napster

What is the right or ethical thing to do? Today, almost all written text, music, movies, and software are recorded in digital form and can be easily copied electronically and sent between personal computers through the Internet. Many sites on the Internet contain illegal copies of music, movies, and so on, that can be easily accessed and downloaded. Millions of people and companies have taken advantage of this to make illegal copies of music CDs, software programs, and DVDs. As a result, it has been estimated that by 2003 over one-third of all CDs and cassettes recorded around the world were illegally produced and sold.[1] Because so many people now make copies of music they like rather than buying the CDs, the music industry has lost over $10 billion in sales revenues.

As you can imagine, the managers of movie and music companies have been doing all they can to reduce the problem of illegal recording because it decreases their sales and profits. One enterprise that music company CEOs went after with a vengeance was Napster.[2] Shawn Fanning created Napster while he was an undergraduate student at Northeastern University. His roommate had the habit of downloading music from Internet sites using the MP3 format, which compresses digital files, making them faster to transit and easier to store. Fanning watched his roommate search the Internet for new material, and he realized that there was an opportunity to create a software platform that would allow people to more easily locate and download digital music files stored in any PC that was logged into this platform. Fanning created the software needed to do this, and word of mouth about the ease of using Napster's system, and the enormous volume of music that was soon available for the taking, made Napster a phenomenon. Soon, hundreds of thousands of people were swapping and downloading music. At many colleges, demand to access

Customers search for their favorite music CDs. Meanwhile, the illegal copying of digital material is on the rise.

and download files from Napster overwhelmed their computing resources.[3]

Obviously, managers in the music industry became desperate to stop this practice. The value of their companies' copyrights to songs and contracts with artists was being destroyed by this new technology that allowed pirating of their products. They sought legal injunctions against Napster to shut the company down. Since it was clear that Napster was violating copyright laws, the courts stopped Napster from providing this free service. However, many other Internet sites have sprung up from which people can still download music and other digital media.

Today, the copying of digital material is increasing. This copying is illegal because it infringes on copyright laws that protect the rights of artists, authors, composers, and the companies that produce and distribute their work. Is this copying unethical? Is it an unacceptable or acceptable way to behave? Why are so many people doing it if it is illegal? The obvious answer is that people are doing it to pursue their own self-interest. Paying nothing for valuable digital media is attractive, and who, goes the argument, suffers anyway? Music companies have been making billions of dollars of profit out of music sales for decades. Songs may be the property of music stars like the Rolling Stones and Eminem, but these people are fabulously wealthy. Why shouldn't the average person benefit from the new technology? After all, the pleasure gained by hundreds of millions of people is more important than the harm done to only a few thousand musicians and a handful of music companies, so copying is not "really" unethical. It may be illegal, but it's not actually such a bad thing to do, is it?

Arguments like these may make people feel that their copying is doing no real harm to others. But what about the rights of artists and companies to profit from their property—the songs, books, and movies that result from their creative endeavors? The average person would not like it if a "poorer" person came along and said, "You don't need all those appliances, cars, and jewelry? I'll just help myself; you'll never miss it." Those who steal digital media not only are weakening the rights of musicians and writers to own property but also are weakening *their* rights to own property. Digital piracy is not a fair or equitable practice. And, although each person may argue that engaging in it doesn't have much of an affect since he or she is "only one person," if many people do it a major problem emerges.

To illustrate the problem, suppose that by 2008 about 75 percent of all music and movies are illegally copied rather than bought. What will musicians and music companies and movie stars and movie studios do? If these people and companies cannot protect their property and profit from it, then they are not going to make or sell digital products. Over time, music and movie companies will cease to operate. Creative people will find new ways to make money, or musicians will make music only for their own pleasure or in live concerts (where recording devices are not permitted!). The result will be a loss to everyone because no new music or movies will be made and the world will become a less interesting place to live in.

Overview

As the story of Napster and digital piracy suggests, an important ethical dimension is present in most kinds of decision making. In business, every party seeks to profit from the exchange, but it is no easy matter to determine what is a fair or equitable division of profit in a particular business activity or relationship. Music companies have no desire to see their revenues fall because potential customers are "profiting" from their ability to make illegal copies of CDs. Music companies have a responsibility to make profits so that they can reward their stockholders, pay the musicians who receive royalties on their record sales, and pay their employees salaries. Of course, they also have a responsibility toward customers–they should charge only a fair price for their CDs.

In this chapter, we examine the nature of the obligations and responsibilities of managers and the companies they work for toward the people and society that are affected by their actions. First, we examine the nature of ethics and the sources of ethical problems. Second, we discuss the major groups of people, called *stakeholders,* who are affected by the way companies operate. Third, we look at four rules or guidelines that managers can use to decide whether a specific business decision is ethical or unethical. Finally, we consider the sources of managerial ethics and the reasons why it is important for a company to behave in a socially responsible manner. By the end of this chapter you will understand the central role that ethics plays in shaping the practice of business and the life of a people, society, and nation.

The Nature of Ethics

Suppose you see a person being mugged in the street. How will you behave? Will you act in some way to help, even though you risk being hurt? Will you walk away? Perhaps you might adopt a "middle way" and not intervene but call the police? Does the way you act depend on whether the person being mugged is a fit male, an elderly person, or even a street person? Does it depend on whether there are other people around, so you can tell yourself, "Oh well, someone else will help or call the police, I don't need to"?

Ethical Dilemmas

ethical dilemma The quandary people find themselves in when they have to decide if they should act in a way that might help another person or group even though doing so might go against their own self-interest.

ethics The inner-guiding moral principles, values, and beliefs that people use to analyze or interpret a situation and then decide what is the "right" or appropriate way to behave.

The situation described above is an example of an **ethical dilemma,** the quandary people find themselves in when they have to decide if they should act in a way that might help another person or group, and is the "right" thing to do, even though doing so might go against their own self-interest.[4] A dilemma may also arise when a person has to decide between two different courses of action, knowing that whichever course he or she chooses will result in harm to one person or group even while it may benefit another. The ethical dilemma here is to decide which course of action is the "lesser of two evils."

People often know they are confronting an ethical dilemma when their moral scruples come into play and cause them to hesitate, debate, and reflect upon the "rightness" or "goodness" of a course of action. Moral scruples are thoughts and feelings that tell a person what is right or wrong; they are a part of a person's ethics. **Ethics** are the inner-guiding moral principles, values, and beliefs that people use to analyze or interpret a situation and then decide what is the "right" or appropriate way to behave. At the same time, ethics also indicate what is inappropriate behavior and how a person should behave to avoid doing harm to another person.

The essential problem in dealing with ethical issues, and thus solving moral dilemmas, is that there are no absolute or indisputable rules or principles that can be developed to decide if an action is ethical or unethical. Put simply, different people or groups may dispute which actions are ethical or unethical depending on their own personal self-interest and specific attitudes, beliefs, and values–concepts we discussed in Chapter 3. How, therefore, are we and companies and their managers and employees to decide what is ethical and so act appropriately toward other people and groups?

Ethics and the Law

The first answer to this question is that society as a whole, using the political and legal process, can lobby for and pass laws that specify what people can and cannot do. Many different kinds of laws exist to govern business, for example, laws against fraud and deception and laws governing how companies can treat their employees and customers. Laws also specify what sanctions or punishments will follow if those laws are broken. Different groups in society lobby for which laws should be passed based on their own personal interests and beliefs with regard to what is right or wrong. The group that can summon most support is able to pass the laws that most closely align with its interests and beliefs. Once a law is passed, a decision about what the appropriate behavior is with regard to a person or situation is taken from the personally determined ethical realm to the societally determined legal realm. If you do not conform to the law, you can be prosecuted; and if you are found guilty of breaking the law, you can be punished. You have little say in the matter; your fate is in the hands of the court and its lawyers.

In studying the relationship between ethics and law, it is important to understand that *neither laws nor ethics are fixed principles,* cast in stone, which do not change over time. Ethical beliefs alter and change as time passes, and as they do so, laws change to reflect the changing ethical beliefs of a society. It was seen as ethical, and it was legal, for example, to acquire and possess slaves in ancient Rome and Greece and in the United States until the 19th century. Ethical views regarding whether slavery was morally right or appropriate changed, however. Slavery was made illegal in the United States when those in power decided that slavery degraded the very meaning of being human. Slavery is a statement about the value or worth of human beings and about their right to life, liberty, and the pursuit of happiness. And if I deny these rights to other people, how then can I claim to have any natural or "god-given" rights to these things myself?

Moreover, what is to stop any person or group that becomes powerful enough to take control of the political and legal process from enslaving me and denying me the right to be free and to own property? In denying freedom to others, one risks losing it oneself, just as stealing from others opens the door for them to steal from me in return. "Do unto others as you would have them do unto you" is a commonly used ethical or moral rule that people apply in such situations to decide what is the right thing to do. This moral rule is discussed in detail below.

Changes in Ethics over Time

There are many types of behavior–such as murder, theft, slavery, rape, driving while intoxicated–that most, if not all, people currently believe are totally unacceptable and unethical and should therefore be illegal. There are also, however, many other kinds of actions and behaviors whose ethical nature is open to dispute. Some people might believe that a particular behavior–for example, smoking tobacco or possessing guns–is unethical and so should be made illegal. Others might argue that it is up to the individual or a group to decide if such behaviors are ethical or not and thus whether a particular behavior should remain legal.

As ethical beliefs change over time, some people may begin to question whether existing laws that make specific behaviors illegal are still appropriate today. They might argue that although a specific behavior is deemed illegal, this does not make it unethical and thus the law should be changed. In the United States, for example, it is illegal to possess or use marijuana (cannabis). To justify this law, it is commonly argued that smoking marijuana leads people to try more dangerous drugs. Once the habit of taking drugs has been acquired, people can get hooked on them. More powerful drugs such as the murderous heroin are fearfully addictive, and most people cannot stop using them without help from others. Thus, the use of marijuana, because it might lead to further harm, is an unethical practice.

It has been documented medically, however, that the use of marijuana has many medical benefits for people with certain illnesses. For example, for cancer sufferers who are undergoing chemotherapy and for those with AIDS who are on potent medications, marijuana offers relief from many of the treatment's side effects, such as nausea and lack of appetite. Yet, in the United States, it is illegal in many states for doctors to prescribe marijuana for these patients, so their suffering goes on. Since 1996, however, 35 states have made it legal to prescribe marijuana for medical purposes; nevertheless, the federal government has sought to stop such state legislaton. People in many states are currently lobbying for a relaxation of the law against the use of marijuana for medical purposes, and in June 2004 the U.S. Supreme Court agreed to hear the case on the medical use of the drug.[5] In Canada there has been a widespread movement to decriminalize marijuana. While not making the drug legal, decriminalization removes the threat of prosecution even for uses that are not medically related. A major ethical debate is currently raging over this issue in many countries.

The important point to note is that while ethical beliefs lead to the development of laws and regulations to prevent certain behaviors or encourage others, laws themselves can and do change or even disappear as ethical beliefs change. In Britain in 1830 there were over 350 different crimes for which a person could be executed, including sheep stealing. Today there are none; capital punishment and the death penalty are no longer legal. Thus, both ethical and legal rules are relative: No absolute or unvarying standards exist to determine how we should behave, and people are caught up in moral dilemmas all the time. Because of this we have to make ethical choices.

Coldbath Fields Prison, London, circa 1810. The British criminal justice system around this time was quite severe: There were over 350 different crimes for which a person could be executed, including sheep stealing. Thankfully in this case, as ethical beliefs change over time, so do laws.

The discussion above highlights an important issue in understanding the relationship between ethics, law, and business. In the early 2000s, many scandals plagued major companies such as Enron, Arthur Andersen, WorldCom, Tyco, and others. Managers in some of these companies clearly broke the law and used illegal means to defraud investors. At Enron, former chief financial officer Andrew Fastow, and his wife, pleaded guilty to falsifying the company's books so that they could siphon off tens of millions of dollars of Enron's money for their own use.

In other cases, some managers took advantage of loopholes in the law to divert hundreds of millions of dollars of company capital into their own personal fortunes. At WorldCom, for example, former CEO Bernie Ebbers used his position to place six personal, long-time friends on its 13-member board of directors. While this is not illegal, obviously these people would vote in his favor at board meetings. As a result of their support Ebbers received huge stock options and a personal loan of over $150 million from WorldCom. In return, his supporters were well rewarded for being directors; for example, Ebbers allowed them to use WorldCom's corporate jets for a minimal cost–something that saved them hundreds of thousands of dollars a year.[6]

In the light of these events some people said, "Well, what these people did was not illegal," implying that because such behavior was not illegal it was also not unethical. However, not being illegal does *not* make it ethical; such behavior is clearly unethical.[7] In many cases laws are passed *later* to close the loopholes and prevent unethical people, such as Fastow and Ebbers, from taking advantage of them to pursue their own self-interest at the expense of others. Like ordinary people, managers must confront the need to decide what is appropriate and inappropriate as they use a company's resources to produce goods and services for customers.[8]

Stakeholders and Ethics

Just as people have to work out the right and wrong ways to act, so do companies. When the law does not specify how companies should behave, their managers must decide what is the right or ethical way to behave toward the people and groups affected by their actions. Who are the people or groups that are affected by a company's business decisions? If a company behaves in an ethical way how does this benefit people and society? Conversely, how are people harmed by a company's unethical actions?

stakeholders The people and groups that supply a company with its productive resources and so have a claim on and stake in the company.

The people and groups affected by the way a company and its managers behave are called its stakeholders. **Stakeholders** supply a company with its productive resources; as a result, they have a claim on and stake in the company.[9] Since stakeholders can directly benefit or be harmed by its actions, the ethics of a company and its managers are important to them. Who are a company's major stakeholders? What do they contribute to a company, and what do they claim in return? Below we examine the claims of these stakeholders–stockholders, managers, employees, suppliers and distributors, customers, and community, society, and nation-state (Figure 4.1).

Figure 4.1 Types of Company Stakeholders

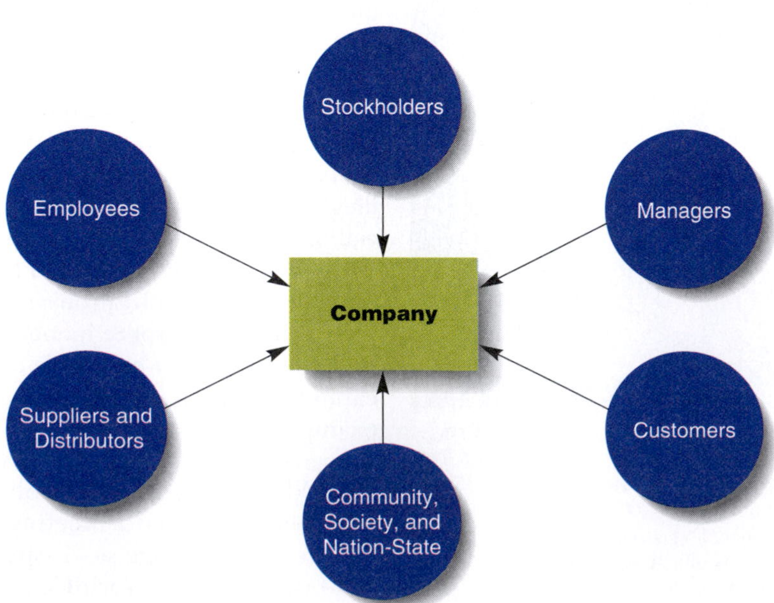

Stockholders

Stockholders have a claim on a company because when they buy its stock or shares they become its owners. Whenever the founder of a company decides to publicly incorporate the business to raise capital, shares of the stock of that company are issued. This stock grants its buyers ownership of a certain percentage of the company and the right to receive any future stock dividends. For example, in 2003 Microsoft had over $46 billion in cash, money it retained in the company to fund its future operations. After pressure from shareholders it declared a dividend of 31 cents per share for the owners of its 5 billion shares; Bill Gates received $100 million in dividends based on his stockholding.

Stockholders are interested in the way a company operates because they want to maximize the return on their investment. Thus, they watch the company and its managers closely to ensure that management is working diligently to increase the company's profitability.[10] Stockholders also want to ensure that managers are behaving ethically and not risking investors' capital by engaging in actions that could hurt the company's reputation. The fall of Enron from being one of the biggest and most profitable companies in the United States to declaring bankruptcy took less than one year after the illegal and unethical actions of its top managers came to light. The Enron tragedy was brought about by a handful of greedy top managers who abused their positions of trust. It has been estimated that Enron's collapse, by precipitating the crash of the stock market, caused the average U.S. household to lose over $66,000 of its hard-earned savings as trillions of dollars were wiped off the value of the stock of publicly traded U.S. companies.

Managers

Managers are a vital stakeholder group because they are responsible for using a company's financial capital and human resources to increase its performance and thus its stock price.[11] Managers have a claim on an organization because they bring to it their skills, expertise, and experience. They have the right to expect a good return or reward by investing their human capital to improve a company's performance. Such rewards include good salaries and benefits, the prospect of promotion and a career, and stock options and bonuses tied to company performance.

Managers are the stakeholder group with the responsibility of deciding which goals an organization should pursue to most benefit stakeholders and how to make the most efficient use of resources to achieve those goals. In making such decisions, managers are frequently in the position of having to juggle the interests of different stakeholders, including themselves.[12] These decisions are sometimes very difficult and challenge managers to uphold ethical values because in some cases decisions that benefit some stakeholder groups (managers and stockholders) harm other groups (individual workers and local communities). For example, in economic downturns or when a company experiences performance shortfalls, layoffs may help to cut costs (thus benefiting shareholders) at the expense of the employees laid off. Many U.S. managers have recently been faced with this very difficult decision–over 700,000 layoffs were announced in the first six months of 2001 according to Challenger, Gray, and Christmas (a firm specializing in outplacement services).[13] Layoff decisions are always difficult, as they not only take a heavy toll on workers, their families, and local communities but also mean the loss of the contributions of valued employees to an organization. Whenever decisions such as these are made–benefiting some groups at the expense of others–ethics come into play.

As we discussed in Chapter 1, managers must be motivated and given incentives to work hard in the interests of stockholders. Their behavior must also be scrutinized to ensure they do not behave illegally or unethically, pursuing goals that threaten stockholders and the company's interests.[14] Unfortunately, we have seen in the 2000s how easy it is for top managers to find ways to ruthlessly pursue their self-interest at the expense of stockholders and employees because laws and regulations were not strong enough to force them to behave ethically.

In a nutshell, the problem has been that in many companies corrupt managers focus not on building the company's capital and stockholders' wealth but on maximizing their own *personal capital and wealth.* In an effort to prevent future scandals the Securities and Exchange Commission (SEC), the government's top business watchdog, began in 2003 to rework the rules governing a company's relationship with its auditor, as well as regulations concerning stock options, and to increase the power of outside directors to scrutinize a CEO. The SEC's goal is to turn many acts that were only unethical behavior in 2003 into illegal behavior in the near future. Managers could then be prosecuted if they engage in these acts.

Many experts are also arguing that the rewards given to top managers, particularly the CEO and COO, have grown out of control in the 1990s. Top managers are the new "aristocrats" today; through their ability to influence the board of directors and raise their own pay, they have amassed personal fortunes worth hundreds of millions of dollars. For example, while in 1982 a typical CEO earned about 18 times as much as the average worker, by 2002 that number had risen to 2,600 times as much–a staggering increase. Michael Eisner, CEO of Disney, has received over $800 million in Disney stock options. Jack Welch, the former CEO of General Electric and one of the most admired managers in the United States, received more than $500 million in GE stock options as a reward for his services. On his retirement he was also awarded $2.5 million in annual perks ranging from round-the-clock access to a corporate jet to free dry cleaning. When this information was revealed to the press, Welch quickly agreed to pay GE $2 million for these services.

Is it ethical for top managers to receive such vast amounts of money from their companies? Do they really earn it? Remember, this money could have gone to shareholders in the form of dividends. It could also have gone to reduce the huge salary gap between those at the top and those at the bottom of the hierarchy. Many people argue that the growing disparity between the rewards given to CEOs and to other employees is unethical and should be regulated. CEO pay has become too high because CEOs are the people who set and control one another's salaries and bonuses! They can do this because they sit on the boards of other companies, as outside directors, and thus can control the salaries and stock options paid to other CEOs. As the example of Bernie Ebbers at WorldCom, discussed earlier, suggests, when a CEO can control and select many of the outside directors, the CEO can abuse his or her power.

Others argue that because top managers play an important role in building a company's capital and wealth, they deserve a significant share of its profits. Jack Welch, for example, deserved his $500 million because he created hundreds of billions of dollars in stockholder wealth. The debate over how much money CEOs and other top managers should be paid is currently raging. Some changes at Walt Disney illustrate many of these issues, as discussed in the following "Manager as a Person."

Manager as a Person

Walt Disney's New Board of Directors

In the last few years, the performance of the Walt Disney Company has fallen precipitously. In 2004 many analysts were wondering if Michael Eisner, who has been its CEO for the last 18 years, is still the right person to run the company. Eisner has always had a hands-on approach to running the business: He wants to be involved in every major business decision, and he keeps a tight reign on his managers. In recent years he has been criticized because, although over 60 and due to retire in less than five years, he has not laid out a succession plan indicating which managers will assume the top roles in Disney after he steps down. Such a plan is important because many companies flounder if a new CEO has not been groomed to take over the top job.

In addition, Eisner has been criticized for creating a weak, or captive, board of directors that has been unable or unwilling to scrutinize and question his business decisions, some of which seem to have been major errors. Over the years, Eisner created a 16-member board of directors in the company, at least 8 of whom had personal ties to him. This weak board allowed him to make all the important decisions, and it did not serve Disney's stockholders well because Eisner's decisions not only did not increase company performance but sometimes reduced it. For example, Eisner pushed through the merger of Disney with Capital/ABC. Since then the ABC television network has been a poor performer, dragging down Disney's stock price. In the meantime, over the past 18 years Eisner has received more than $800 million in stock options from the company and enjoys all the lavish perks–corporate jets, penthouse suites, and all-expenses-paid business trips–that most CEOs of large companies receive today.

With its performance falling, Eisner came under increasing criticism for his autocratic management style, his lack of a succession plan for the company, and his creation of a weak board of directors, as well as the fact that he is still paid vast sums of money despite his company's poor performance. So in 2003 the company began to reorganize its board of directors. Two new special outside directors were appointed, one of whom will chair two board meetings a year that Eisner–who normally chairs these meetings–will not be permitted to attend. The board will now have more freedom to assess Eisner's performance. Eisner, under pressure from the board, has also chosen his successor.

Mickey has stood by Disney CEO Michael Eisner's side through thick and thin.

Some analysts say these changes are not enough. Eisner still has the backing of the majority of the board, who are beholden to him. He is still in control of all Disney's important committees. The question is what will the board of directors do if Disney's performance continues to deteriorate. Will it continue to let Eisner make all the important decisions, or will it demand fresh leadership at the top and force Eisner to step down as CEO? Only time will tell, but Eisner is still in the driver's seat and, like most CEOs, will do all he can to retain his privileged position.

Employees

A company's employees are the hundreds of thousands of people who work in its various departments and functions, such as research, sales, and manufacturing. Employees expect that they will receive rewards consistent with their performance. One principle way that a company can act ethically toward employees and meet their expectations is by creating an occupational structure that fairly and equitably rewards employees for their contributions. Companies, for example, need to develop recruitment, training, performance appraisal, and reward systems that do not discriminate between employees and that employees believe are fair.

Suppliers and Distributors

No company operates alone. Every company is in a network of relationships with other companies that supply it with the inputs (e.g., raw materials, component parts, contract labor, and clients) that it needs to operate. It also depends on intermediaries such as wholesalers and retailers to distribute its products to the final customer. Suppliers expect to be paid fairly and promptly for their inputs; distributors expect to receive quality products at agreed-upon prices.

Once again, many ethical issues arise in the way companies contract and interact with their suppliers and distributors. Important issues concerning how and when payments are to be made or product quality specifications are governed by the terms of the legal contracts a company signs with its suppliers and distributors. Many other issues are dependent on business ethics. For example, numerous products sold in U.S. stores have been outsourced to countries that do not have U.S.-style regulations and laws to protect the workers who make these products. All companies must take an ethical position on the way they obtain and make the products they sell. Commonly this stance is published on the company's Web site. Table 4.1 presents part of the The Gap's statement on its approach to global ethics (www.thegap.com).

Customers

Customers are often regarded as the most critical stakeholder group since if a company cannot attract them to buy its products, it cannot stay in business. Thus, managers and employees must work to increase efficiency and effectiveness in order to create loyal customers and attract new ones. They do so by selling customers quality products at a fair price and providing good after-sales service. They can also strive to improve their products over time.

Many laws exist that protect customers from companies that attempt to provide dangerous or shoddy products. Laws exist that allow customers to sue a company whose product causes them injury or harm, such as a defective tire or vehicle. Other laws force companies to clearly disclose the interest rates they charge on purchases–an important hidden cost that customers frequently do not factor into their purchase decisions. Every year thousands of companies are prosecuted for breaking these laws, so "buyer beware" is an important rule customers must follow when buying goods and services.

Table 4.1
Some Principles from the Gap's Code of Vendor Conduct

As a condition of doing business with Gap Inc., each and every factory must comply with this Code of Vendor Conduct. Gap Inc. will continue to develop monitoring systems to assess and ensure compliance. If Gap Inc. determines that any factory has violated this Code, Gap Inc. may either terminate its business relationship or require the factory to implement a corrective action plan. If corrective action is advised but not taken, Gap Inc. will suspend placement of future orders and may terminate current production.

I. General Principles
Factories that produce goods for Gap Inc. shall operate in full compliance with the laws of their respective countries and with all other applicable laws, rules and regulations.

II. Environment
Factories must comply with all applicable environmental laws and regulations. Where such requirements are less stringent than Gap Inc.'s own, factories are encouraged to meet the standards outlined in Gap Inc.'s statement of environmental principles.

III. Discrimination
Factories shall employ workers on the basis of their ability to do the job, without regard to race, color, gender, nationality, religion, age, maternity or marital status.

IV. Forced Labor
Factories shall not use any prison, indentured or forced labor.

V. Child Labor
Factories shall employ only workers who meet the applicable minimum legal age requirement or are at least 14 years of age, whichever is greater. Factories must also comply with all other applicable child labor laws. Factories are encouraged to develop lawful workplace apprenticeship programs for the educational benefit of their workers, provided that all participants meet both Gap Inc.'s minimum age standard of 14 and the minimum legal age requirement.

VI. Wages & Hours
Factories shall set working hours, wages and overtime pay in compliance with all applicable laws. Workers shall be paid at least the minimum legal wage or a wage that meets local industry standards, whichever is greater. While it is understood that overtime is often required in garment production, factories shall carry out operations in ways that limit overtime to a level that ensures humane and productive working conditions.

Community, Society, and Nation

The effects of the decisions made by companies and their managers permeate all aspects of the communities, societies, and nations in which they operate. *Community* refers to physical locations like towns or cities or to social milieus like ethnic neighborhoods in which companies are located. A community provides a company with the physical and social infrastructure that allows it to operate; its utilities and labor force; the homes in which its managers and employees live; the schools, colleges, and hospitals that service their needs; and so on.

Through the salaries, wages, and taxes it pays, a company contributes to the economy of the town or region and often determines whether the community prospers or declines. Similarly, a company affects the prosperity of a society and a nation and, to the degree that a company is involved in global trade, all the countries it operates in and thus the prosperity of the global economy. We have already discussed the many issues surrounding global outsourcing and the loss of jobs in the United States, for example.

In 2001 McDonald's announced new standards that would require egg suppliers to improve the conditions under which chickens are housed and treated. Since McDonald's is an important customer, suppliers are likely to follow these new standards.

Although the individual effects of the way each McDonald's restaurant operates might be small, for instance, the combined effects of the way all McDonald's and other fast-food companies do business are enormous. In the United States alone, over 500,000 people work in the fast-food industry, and many thousands of suppliers like farmers, paper cup manufacturers, builders, and so on, depend on it for their livelihood. Small wonder then that the ethics of the fast-food business are scrutinized closely. The industry is the major lobbyer against attempts to raise the national minimum wage, which was $5.15 in 2004, for example, because a higher minimum wage would substantially increase its operating costs. However, responding to protests about chickens raised in cages where they cannot move their wings, McDonald's–the largest egg buyer in the United States–issued new ethical guidelines concerning cage size and related matters that its egg suppliers must abide by if they are to retain its business. What ethical rules does McDonald's use to decide its stance toward minimum pay or minimum cage size?

Business ethics are also important because the failure of companies can have catastrophic effects on a community; a general decline in business activity affects a whole nation. The decision of a large company to pull out of a community, for example, can seriously threaten the community's future. Some companies may attempt to improve their profits by engaging in actions that, although not illegal, can hurt communities and nations. One of these actions is pollution. For example, many U.S. companies reduce costs by trucking their waste to Mexico where it is legal to dump waste in the Rio Grande. The dumping pollutes the river from the Mexican side, and the effects are increasingly being felt on the U.S. side too.

Rules for Ethical Decision Making

When a stakeholder perspective is taken, questions on company ethics abound.[15] What is the appropriate way to manage the claims of all stakeholders? Company decisions that favor one group of stakeholders, for example, are likely to harm the interests of others.[16] High prices to customers may lead to high returns to shareholders and high salaries for managers in the short run. If in the long run customers turn to companies that offer lower-cost products, however, the result may be declining sales, laid-off employees, and the decline of the communities that support the high-price company's business activity.

When companies act ethically, their stakeholders support them. For example, banks are willing to supply them with new capital, they attract highly qualified job applicants, and new customers are drawn to their products. Thus ethical companies grow and expand over time, and all their stakeholders benefit. The result of unethical behavior is the loss of reputation and resources, shareholders who sell their shares, skilled managers and employees who leave the company, and customers who turn to the products of more reputable companies.

When making business decisions, managers must take the claims of all stakeholders into consideration.[17] To help themselves and employees make ethical decisions and behave in ways that benefit their stakeholders, managers can use

Figure 4.2
Four Ethical Rules

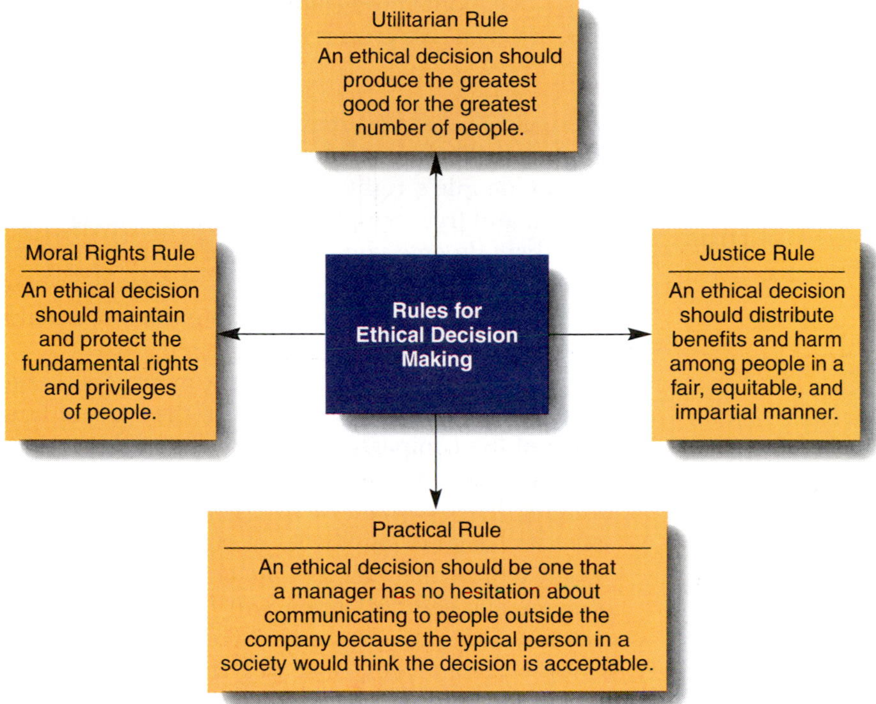

four ethical rules or principles to analyze the effects of their business decisions on stakeholders: the *utilitarian, moral rights, justice,* and *practical* rules (Figure 4.2).[18] These rules are useful guidelines that help managers decide on the appropriate way to behave in situations where it is necessary to balance a company's self-interest against the interests of its stakeholders. Remember, the right choices will lead resources to be used where they can create the most value. If all companies make the right choices, all stakeholders will benefit in the long run.[19]

utilitarian rule An ethical decision is a decision that produces the greatest good for the greatest number of people.

UTILITARIAN RULE The **utilitarian rule** is that an ethical decision is a decision that produces the greatest good for the greatest number of people. To decide which is the most ethical course of business action, managers should first consider how different possible courses of business action would benefit or harm different stakeholders. They should then choose the course of action that provides the most benefits, or conversely the one that does the least harm, to stakeholders.[20]

The ethical dilemma for managers is, How do you measure the benefits and harms that will be done to each stakeholder group? Moreover, how do you evaluate the rights of different stakeholder groups, and the relative importance of each group, in coming to a decision? Since stockholders are the owners of the company, shouldn't their claims be held above those of employees? For example, managers might be faced with a choice of using global outsourcing to reduce costs and lower prices to customers or continuing with high-cost production at home. A decision to use global outsourcing benefits shareholders and customers but will result in major layoffs that will harm employees and the communities in which they live. Typically, in a capitalist society, like the United States, the interests of shareholders are put above those of employees, so production will move abroad. This is commonly regarded as being an ethical choice because in the long run the alternative, home production, might cause the business to collapse and go bankrupt, in which case greater harm will be done to all stakeholders.

moral rights rule An ethical decision is one that best maintains and protects the fundamental or inalienable rights and privileges of the people affected by it.

MORAL RIGHTS RULE Under the **moral rights rule,** an ethical decision is a decision that best maintains and protects the fundamental or inalienable rights and privileges of the people affected by it. For example, ethical decisions protect people's rights to freedom, life and safety, property, privacy, free speech, and freedom of conscience. The adage "Do unto others as you would have them do unto you," is a moral rights principle that managers should use to decide which rights to uphold. As the Napster case suggests, customers must also consider the rights of the companies and people who create the products they wish to consume.

From a moral rights perspective, managers should compare and contrast different courses of business action on the basis of how each course will affect the rights of the company's different stakeholders. Managers should then choose the course of action that best protects and upholds the rights of *all* the stakeholders. For example, decisions that might result in significant harm to the safety or health of employees or customers would clearly be unethical choices.

The ethical dilemma for managers is that decisions that will protect the rights of some stakeholders often will hurt the rights of others. How should they choose which group to protect? For example, in deciding whether it is ethical to snoop on employees, or search them when they leave work to prevent theft, does an employee's right to privacy outweigh an organization's right to protect its property? Suppose a co-worker is having personal problems and is coming in late and leaving early, placing you in the position of being forced to pick up the person's workload. Do you tell your boss even though you know this will probably get that person fired?

justice rule An ethical decision is a decision that distributes benefits and harms among people and groups in a fair, equitable, or impartial way.

JUSTICE RULE The **justice rule** is that an ethical decision is a decision that distributes benefits and harms among people and groups in a fair, equitable, or impartial way. Managers should compare and contrast alternative courses of action based on the degree to which they will result in a fair or equitable distribution of outcomes for stakeholders. For example, employees who are similar in their level of skill, performance, or responsibility should receive the same kind of pay. The allocation of outcomes should not be based on differences such as gender, race, or religion.

The ethical dilemma for managers is to determine the fair rules and procedures for distributing outcomes to stakeholders. Managers must not give people they like bigger raises than they give to people they do not like, for example, or bend the rules to help their favorites. On the other hand, if employees want managers to act fairly toward them, then employees need to act fairly toward their companies and work hard and be loyal. Similarly, customers need to act fairly toward a company if they expect it to be fair to them–something people who illegally copy digital media should consider.

practical rule An ethical decision is one that a manager has no reluctance about communicating to people outside the company because the typical person in a society would think it is acceptable.

PRACTICAL RULE Each of the above rules offers a different and complementary way of determining whether a decision or behavior is ethical, and all three rules should be used to sort out the ethics of a particular course of action. Ethical issues, as we just discussed, are seldom clear-cut, however, because the rights, interests, goals, and incentives of different stakeholders often conflict. For this reason many experts on ethics add a fourth rule to determine whether a business decision is ethical: The **practical rule** is that an ethical decision is one that a manager has no hesitation or reluctance about communicating to people outside the company because the typical person in a society would think it is acceptable. A business decision is probably acceptable on ethical grounds if a manager can answer yes to each of these questions:

1. Does my decision fall within the accepted *values* or *standards* that typically apply in business activity today?
2. Am I willing to see the decision *communicated* to all people and groups *affected* by it–for example, by having it reported in newspapers or on television?
3. Would the people with whom I have a *significant* personal relationship, such as family members, friends, or even managers in other organizations, *approve* of the decision?

Applying the practical rule to analyze a business decision ensures that managers are taking into account the interests of all stakeholders.[21] After applying this rule managers can judge if they have chosen to act in an ethical or unethical way and they must abide by the consequences.

Why Should Managers Behave Ethically?

Why is it so important that managers, and people in general, should act ethically and temper their pursuit of self-interest by considering the effects of their actions on others? The answer is that the relentless pursuit of self-interest can lead to a collective disaster when one or more people start to profit from being unethical because this encourages other people to act in the same way.[22] Quickly, more and more people jump onto the bandwagon, and soon everybody is trying to manipulate the situation in the way that best serves his or her personal ends with no regard for the effects of the action on others. The situation brought about by Napster is an example of how what is called the "tragedy of the commons" works.

Suppose that in an agricultural community there is common land that everybody has an equal right to use. Pursuing self-interest, each farmer acts to make the maximum use of the free resource by grazing his or her own cattle and sheep. Collectively, all the farmers overgraze the land, which quickly becomes worn out. Then a strong wind blows away the exposed topsoil, so the common land is destroyed. The pursuit of individual self-interest with no consideration for societal interests leads to disaster for each individual and for the whole society because scarce resources are destroyed.[23] In the Napster case the tragedy that would result if all people were to steal digital media would be the disappearance of music, movie, and book companies as creative people decided there was no point in their working hard to produce original songs, stories, and so on.

We can look at the effects of unethical behavior on business commerce and activity in another way. Suppose companies and their managers operate in an unethical society, meaning one in which stakeholders routinely try to cheat and defraud one another. If stakeholders expect each other to cheat, how long will it take them to negotiate the purchase and shipment of products? When they do not trust each other, stakeholders will probably spend hours bargaining over fair prices, and this is a largely unproductive activity that reduces efficiency and effectiveness.[24] All the time and effort that could be spent improving product quality or customer service is being lost because it is spent on negotiating and bargaining. Thus, unethical behavior ruins business commerce, and society has a lower standard of living because fewer goods and services are produced, as Figure 4.3 (page 128) illustrates.

Figure 4.3
Some Effects of Ethical and Unethical Behavior

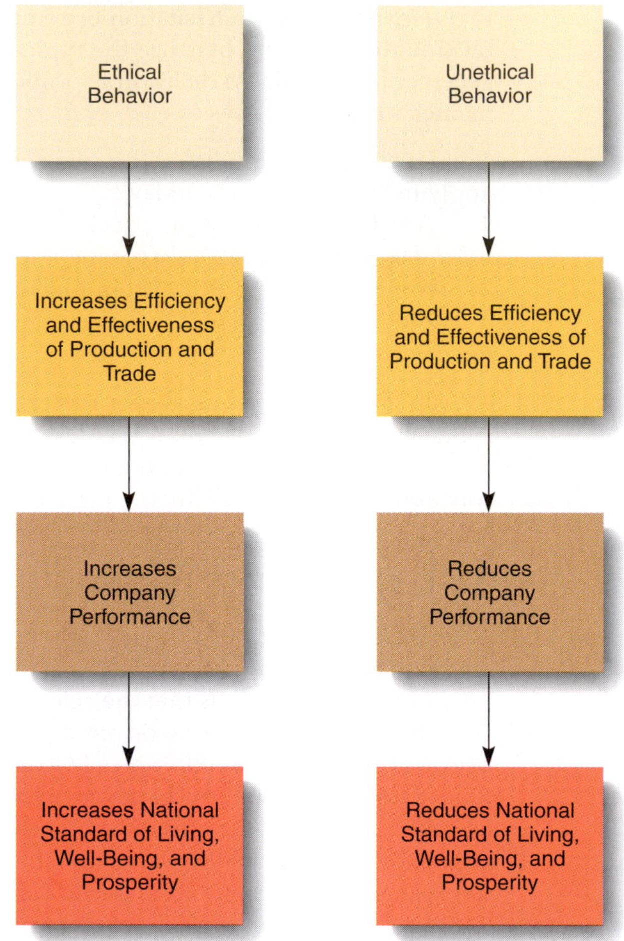

trust A person's confidence and faith in another person's goodwill.

On the other hand, suppose companies and their managers operate in an ethical society, meaning that stakeholders believe they are dealing with others who are basically moral and honest. In this society stakeholders have a greater reason to **trust** others, which means they have more confidence and faith in the other person's goodwill. When trust exists, stakeholders are more likely to signal their good intentions by cooperating and providing information that makes it easier to trade and price goods and services. When one party does so, this encourages others to act in the same way. Over time greater trust between stakeholders allows them to work together more efficiently and effectively, and this raises company performance (see Figure 4.3). As people see the positive results of acting in an honest way, ethical behavior becomes a valued social norm and society in general becomes increasingly ethical.

As noted in Chapter 1, one of the major tasks of managers is to protect and nurture the resources under their control. Any organizational stakeholders–managers, workers, stockholders, suppliers–who advance their own interests by behaving unethically toward other stakeholders, either by taking resources or by denying resources to others, waste collective resources. If other individuals or groups copy the behavior of the unethical stakeholder ("If he can do it, we can do it, too"), the rate at which collective resources are misused increases, and eventually there are few resources for producing goods and services. Unethical behavior that goes unpunished creates incentives for people to put their unbridled self-interests above the rights of others.[25] When this happens, the benefits that people reap from joining together in organizations disappear very quickly.

reputation The esteem or high repute that individuals or organizations gain when they behave ethically.

An important safeguard against unethical behavior is the potential for loss of reputation.[26] **Reputation,** the esteem or high repute that individuals or organizations gain when they behave ethically, is an important asset. Stakeholders have valuable reputations that they must protect because their ability to earn a living and obtain resources in the long run depends on the way they behave on a day-to-day, week-to-week, and month-to-month basis.

If a manager misuses resources and other parties regard that behavior as being at odds with acceptable standards, the manager's reputation will suffer. Behaving unethically in the short run can have serious long-term consequences. A manager who has a poor reputation will have difficulty finding employment with other companies. Stockholders who see managers behaving unethically may refuse to invest in their companies, and this will decrease the stock price, undermine the companies' reputations, and ultimately put the managers' jobs at risk.[27]

All stakeholders have reputations to lose. Suppliers who provide shoddy inputs find that organizations learn over time not to deal with them, and eventually they go out of business. Powerful customers who demand ridiculously low prices find that their suppliers become less willing to deal with them, and resources ultimately become harder for them to obtain. Workers who shirk responsibilities on the job find it hard to get new jobs when they are fired. In general, if a manager or company is known for being unethical, other stakeholders are likely to view that individual or organization with suspicion and hostility, and the reputation of each will be poor. But if a manager or company is known for ethical business practices, each will develop a good reputation.[28]

In summary, in a complex, diverse society, stakeholders, and people in general, need to recognize they are all part of a larger social group. The way in which they make decisions and act not only affects them personally but also affects the lives of many other people. The problem is that for some people their daily struggle to survive and succeed or their total disregard for the rights of others can lead them to lose that "bigger" connection to other people. We can see our relationships to our families and friends, to our school, church, and so on. But, we need always to go further and keep in mind the effects of our actions on other people–people who will be judging our actions and whom we might harm by acting unethically. Our moral scruples are like that "other person" but are inside our heads.

Ethics and Social Responsibility

Some companies, like Merck, Johnson & Johnson, Prudential Insurance, Fannie May, and Blue Cross–Blue Shield, are well known for their ethical business practices. Other companies, such as Arthur Andersen and Enron, which are now out of business, or phone companies WorldCom and Qwest, which were struggling to survive in 2004, repeatedly engaged in unethical and illegal business activities. What explains such differences between the ethics of these companies and their managers?

There are four main determinants of differences in ethics between people, employees, companies, and countries: *societal* ethics, *occupational* ethics, *individual* ethics, and *organizational* ethics, especially the ethics of a company's top managers.[29] (See Figure 4.4, page 130.)

Figure 4.4
Sources of Ethics

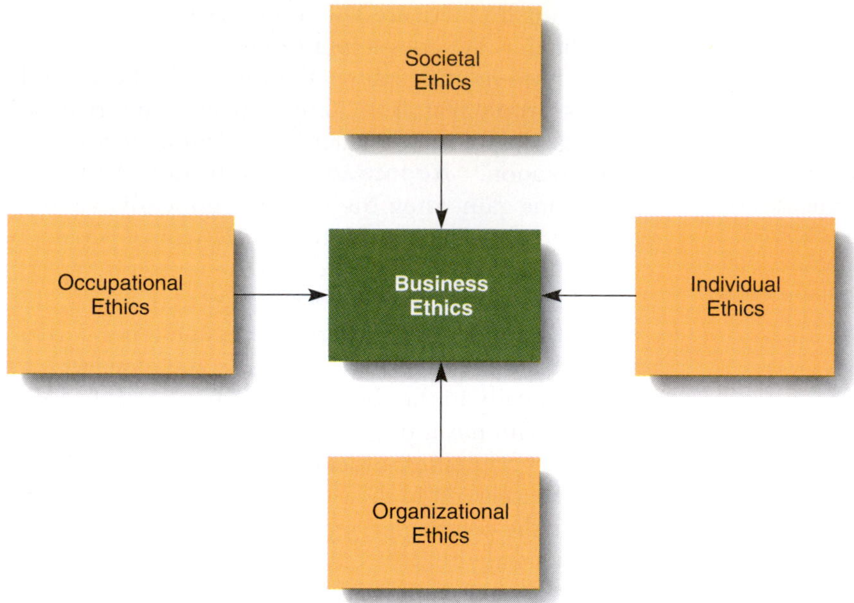

Societal Ethics

societal ethics
Standards that govern how members of a society should deal with one another in matters involving issues such as fairness, justice, poverty, and the rights of the individual.

Societal ethics are standards that govern how members of a society should deal with one another in matters involving issues such as fairness, justice, poverty, and the rights of the individual. Societal ethics emanate from a society's laws, customs and practices and from the unwritten values and norms that influence how people interact with each other. People in a particular country may automatically behave ethically because they have *internalized* (i.e., made a part of their morals) certain values, beliefs, and norms that specify how they should behave when confronted with an ethical dilemma.

Societal ethics vary among societies. Countries like Germany, Japan, Sweden, and Switzerland are well known as being some of the most ethical countries in the world, with strong values about social order and the need to create a society that protects the welfare of all groups of their citizens. In other countries the situation is very different. In many economically poor countries bribery is standard practice to get things done–such as getting a telephone installed or a contract awarded. In the United States and other economically advanced countries, bribery is considered unethical and has been made illegal.

IBM experienced the problem of differences in ethical standards in its Argentinean division. Managers there became involved in an unethical scheme to secure a $250 million contract for IBM to provide and service the computers of one of Argentina's largest state-owned banks. After $6 million was paid to bribe the bank executives who agreed to give IBM the contract, IBM announced that it had fired the three top managers of its Argentine division. According to IBM, transactions like this, though unethical by IBM's standards, are not necessarily illegal under Argentine law. The Argentine managers were fired, however, for failing to follow IBM's organizational rules, which preclude the payment of bribes to obtain contracts in foreign countries. Moreover, the payment of bribes violates the U.S. *Foreign Corrupt Practices Act,* which forbids payment of bribes by U.S. companies to secure contracts abroad, makes companies liable for the actions of their foreign managers, and allows companies found in violation to be prosecuted in the United States. By firing the managers, IBM signaled that it would not tolerate unethical behavior by any of its employees, and it continues today to take a rigorous stance toward ethical issues.

Countries also differ widely in their beliefs about appropriate treatment for their employees. In general, the poorer a country is, the more likely employees are to be treated with little regard. One issue of particular concern on a global level is whether it is ethical to use child labor, as discussed in the following "Ethics in Action."

Ethics in Action

Is It Right to Use Child Labor?

In recent years, the number of U.S. companies that buy their products from low-cost foreign suppliers has been growing, and concern about the ethics associated with employing young children in factories has been increasing. In Pakistan, children as young as age six work long hours in deplorable conditions to make rugs and carpets for export to Western countries. Children in poor countries throughout Africa, Asia, and South America work in similar conditions. Is it ethical to employ children in factories, and should U.S. companies buy and sell products made by these children?

Opinions about the ethics of child labor vary widely. Robert Reich, an economist and secretary of labor in the first Clinton administration, believes that the practice is totally reprehensible and should be outlawed on a global level. Another view, championed by *The Economist* magazine, is that, while nobody wants to see children employed in factories, citizens of rich countries need to recognize that in poor countries children are often a family's only breadwinners. Thus, denying children employment would cause whole families to suffer, and one wrong (child labor) might produce a greater wrong (poverty). Instead, *The Economist* favors regulating the conditions under which children are employed and hopes that over time, as poor countries become richer, the need for child employment will disappear.

Many U.S. retailers typically buy their clothing from low-cost foreign suppliers, and managers in these companies have had to take their own ethical stance on child labor. Managers in Wal-Mart, Target, JCPenney, and The Gap (see Table 4.1) have followed U.S. standards and rules and have policies dictating that their foreign suppliers not employ child labor. They also vow to sever ties with any foreign supplier found to be in violation of this standard.

Afghan boys weave a rug in April, 2003, while their father stands nearby inside their home in Kabul, Afghanistan. Afghan rug makers contract children to make rugs, paying their families roughly 8 U.S. dollars a yard. To make one 18-foot rug takes approximately one month, and the children often work in shifts around their schooling or other household duties.

Apparently, however, retailers differ widely in the way they choose to enforce such policies. It has been estimated that more than 300,000 children under age 14 are being employed in garment factories in Guatemala, a popular low-cost location for clothing manufacturers that supply the U.S. market. These children frequently work more than 60 hours a week and often are paid less than $3 a day, close to the minimum wage in Guatemala. Many U.S. retailers do not check up on their foreign suppliers. Clearly, if U.S. retailers are to be true to their ethical stance on this troubling issue, they cannot ignore the fact that they are buying clothing made by children and they must do more to regulate the conditions under which these children work.

Occupational Ethics

occupational ethics Standards that govern how members of a profession, trade, or craft should conduct themselves when performing work-related activities.

Occupational ethics are standards that govern how members of a profession, trade, or craft should conduct themselves when performing work-related activities.[30] For example, medical ethics govern the way doctors and nurses should treat their patients. Doctors are expected to perform only necessary medical procedures and to act in the patient's interest and not in their own. The ethics of scientific research require that scientists conduct their experiments and present their findings in ways that ensure the validity of their conclusions. Like society at large, most professional groups can impose punishments for violations of ethical standards.[31] Doctors and lawyers can be prevented from practicing their professions if they disregard professional ethics and put their own interests first.

Within an organization, occupational rules and norms often govern how employees such as lawyers, researchers, and accountants should make decisions to further stakeholder interests. Employees internalize the rules and norms of their occupational group (just as they do those of society) and often follow them automatically when deciding how to behave. Because most people tend to follow established rules of behavior, people often take ethics for granted. However, when occupational ethics are violated, such as when scientists fabricate data to disguise the harmful effects of products, ethical issues come to the forefront of attention.

Individual Ethics

individual ethics Personal standards and values that determine how people view their responsibilities to others and how they should act in situations when their own self-interest is at stake.

Individual ethics are personal standards and values that determine how people view their responsibilities to other people and groups and thus how they should act in situations when their own self-interests are at stake.[32] Sources of individual ethics include the influence of one's family, peers, and upbringing in general. The experiences gained over a lifetime–through membership in social institutions such as schools and religions, for example–also contribute to the development of the personal standards and values that a person applies to decide what is right or wrong and whether to perform certain actions or make certain decisions.

Many decisions or behaviors that one person finds unethical, such as using animals for cosmetics testing, may be acceptable to another person. If decisions or behaviors are not illegal, individuals may agree to disagree about their ethical beliefs, or they may try to impose their own beliefs on other people and make those ethical beliefs the law. In all cases, however, people should develop and follow the ethical criteria described earlier to balance their self-interests against those of others when determining how they should behave in a particular situation.

Organizational Ethics

organizational ethics The guiding practices and beliefs through which a particular company and its managers view their responsibility toward their stakeholders.

Organizational ethics are the guiding practices and beliefs through which a particular company and its managers view their responsibility toward their stakeholders. The individual ethics of a company's founders and top managers are especially important in shaping the organization's code of ethics. Organizations whose founders had a vital role in creating a highly ethical code of organizational behavior include Merck, Hewlett-Packard, Johnson & Johnson, and the Prudential Insurance Company. Johnson & Johnson's code of ethics–its credo–reflects a well-developed concern for its stakeholders (see Table 4.2). Company credos, such as that of Johnson & Johnson, are meant to deter self-interested, unethical

Table 4.2
Forms of Socially Responsible Behavior

Managers are being socially responsible and showing their support for their stakeholders when they:

- Provide severance payments to help laid-off workers make ends meet until they can find another job.
- Provide workers with opportunities to enhance their skills and acquire additional education so that they can remain productive and do not become obsolete because of changes in technology.
- Allow employees to take time off when they need to and provide health care and pension benefits for employees.
- Contribute to charities or support various civic-minded activities in the cities or towns in which they are located. (Target and Levi Strauss both contribute 5 percent of their profits to support schools, charities, the arts, and other good works.)
- Decide to keep open a factory whose closure would devastate the local community.
- Decide to keep a company's operations in the United States to protect the jobs of American workers rather than move abroad.
- Decide to spend money to improve a new factory so that it will not pollute the environment.
- Decline to invest in countries that have poor human rights records.
- Choose to help poor countries develop an economic base to improve living standards.

behavior; to demonstrate to managers and employees that a company will not tolerate people who, because of their own poor ethics, put their personal interests above the interests of other organizational stakeholders and ignore the harm that they are inflicting on others; and to demonstrate that those who act unethically will be punished.

Managers or workers may behave unethically if they feel pressured to do so by the situation they are in and by unethical top managers. Once again, if a company's top managers consistently endorse the ethical principles in its corporate credo, they can prevent this perception from occurring. Employees are much more likely to act unethically when a credo does not exist or is disregarded. Arthur Andersen, for example, did not follow its credo at all; its unscrupulous partners ordered middle managers to shred records that showed evidence of their wrongdoing. Although middle managers knew this was wrong, they followed the orders because they responded to the personal power and status of the partners and not the company's code of ethics. They were afraid they would lose their jobs if they did not behave unethically, but their actions still cost them their jobs.

Top managers play a crucial role in determining a company's ethics. It is clearly important, then, that when making appointment decisions the board of directors should scrutinize the reputations and ethical records of top managers. It is the responsibility of the board to decide if a prospective CEO has the maturity, experience, and integrity needed to head a company and be entrusted with the capital and wealth of the organization, on which the fate of all its stakeholders depends. In 2003, the former CEO of Kmart, who had led the company into bankruptcy, was being scrutinized for poor managerial decision making; in 2004, Martha Stewart, the largest shareholder of her company, left its board after she was found guilty of insider trading.

A track record of success is not enough to decide this issue, for a manager might have achieved this success through unethical or illegal means. It is important to investigate prospective top managers and examine their credentials. In the early 2000s it was disclosed that the top managers of several major companies did not have the kinds of degrees or experience they had claimed on their résumés and that they had acted unethically to get their current jobs! Often, the best predictor of future behavior is past behavior, but the board of directors needs to be on guard against unethical people who use unethical means to rise to the top of the organizational hierarchy.

Approaches to Social Responsibility

A company's ethics are the result of differences in societal, organizational, occupational, and individual ethics. In turn, a company's ethics determine its stance or position on social responsibility. A company's stance on **social responsibility** is the way its managers and employees view their duty or obligation to make decisions that protect, enhance, and promote the welfare and well-being of stakeholders and society as a whole.[33] As we noted earlier, when no laws exist that specify how a company should act toward stakeholders, managers must decide what the right, ethical, and socially responsible thing to do is. Differences in business ethics can lead companies to take very different positions or views on what their responsibility is toward their stakeholders.

social responsibility The way a company's managers and employees view their duty or obligation to make decisions that protect, enhance, and promote the welfare and well-being of stakeholders and society as a whole.

Many kinds of decisions signal a company's beliefs about its obligations to make socially responsible business decisions. (See Table 4.2.) The decision to spend money on training and educating employees–investing in them–is one such decision; so is the decision to minimize or avoid layoffs whenever possible. The decision to act promptly and warn customers when a batch of defective merchandise has been accidentally sold is another one. Companies that try to hide such problems show little regard for social responsibility. In the 1990s, both GM and Ford tried to hide the fact that several of their vehicles had defects that rendered them dangerous to drive; the companies were penalized with hundreds of millions of dollars in damages for their unethical behavior. On the other hand, in 2002, when Campbell Soup discovered that thousands of cans of soup labeled as cream of mushroom actually contained clam chowder, it quickly announced the problem publicly. Since the mislabeling could cause severe problems to customers with allergies to shellfish, informing the public was the right thing to do.[34] The way a company announces business problems or admits its mistakes provides strong clues about its stance on social responsibility.

Four Different Approaches

obstructionist approach Companies and their managers choose *not* to behave in a socially responsible way and behave unethically and illegally.

The strength of companies' commitment to social responsibility can range from low to high (see Figure 4.5). At the low end of the range is an **obstructionist approach,** in which companies and their managers choose *not* to behave in a

Figure 4.5
Four Approaches to Social Responsibility

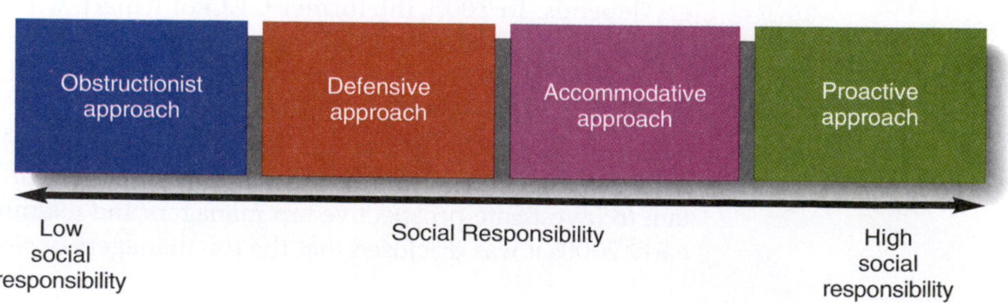

socially responsible way. Instead, they behave unethically and illegally and do all they can to prevent knowledge of their behavior from reaching other organizational stakeholders and society at large. Managers at the Mansville Corporation adopted this approach when they sought to hide evidence that asbestos causes lung damage; so too did tobacco companies when they sought to hide evidence that cigarette smoking causes lung cancer.

Top managers at Enron also acted in an obstructionist way when they prevented employees from selling Enron shares in their pension funds even before employees knew the company was in trouble. At the same time, top managers sold hundreds of millions of dollars' worth of their own Enron stock. Senior partners at Arthur Andersen who instructed their subordinates to shred files chose, like the managers of all these organizations, an obstructionist approach. The result was not only a loss of reputation but devastation for the organization and for all stakeholders involved. All these companies are no longer in business. The unethical behavior characteristic of the obstructionist approach is exemplified in the way Beech-Nut's management team in the 1980s put personal interests before customers' health and above the law.

Ethics in Action

Apple Juice or Sugar Water?

In the early 1980s Beech-Nut, a maker of baby foods, was in grave financial trouble as it strove to compete with Gerber Products, the market leader. Threatened with the bankruptcy of the company if it could not lower its operating costs, Beech-Nut entered into an agreement with a low-cost supplier of apple juice concentrate. The agreement would save the company over $250,000 annually at a time when every dollar counted. Soon, one of Beech-Nut's food scientists became concerned about the quality of the concentrate. He believed that it was not made from apples alone but contained large quantities of corn syrup and cane sugar. He brought this information to the attention of top managers at Beech-Nut, but they were obsessed with the need to keep costs down and chose to ignore his concerns. The company continued to produce and sell its product as pure apple juice.[35]

Eventually investigators from the U.S. Food and Drug Administration (FDA) confronted Beech-Nut with evidence that the concentrate was adulterated. The top managers issued denials and quickly shipped the remaining stock of apple juice to the market before their inventory could be seized. The scientist who had questioned the purity of the apple juice had resigned from Beech-Nut, but he decided to blow the whistle on the company. He told the FDA that Beech-Nut's top management had known of the problem with the concentrate and had acted to maximize company profits rather than to inform customers about the additives in the apple juice. In 1987, the company pleaded guilty to charges that it had deliberately sold adulterated juice and was fined over $2 million. Its top managers were also found guilty and were sentenced to prison terms.

Consumer trust in Beech-Nut products plummeted, as did the value of Beech-Nut stock. The company's reputation was ruined, and it was eventually sold to Ralston Purina, now owned by Nestlé, which installed a new management team and a new ethical code of values to guide future business decisions.

defensive approach Companies and their managers behave ethically to the degree that they stay within the law and abide strictly with legal requirements.

A **defensive approach** indicates at least a commitment to ethical behavior.[36] Defensive companies and managers stay within the law and abide strictly with legal requirements but make no attempt to exercise social responsibility beyond what the law dictates–thus they can and often do act unethically. These are the kinds of companies, like Computer Associates and WorldCom, that give their managers large stock options and bonuses even when company performance is declining. The managers are the kind who sell their stock in advance of other stockholders because they know that their company's performance is about to fall. Although acting on inside information is illegal, it is often very hard to prove since top managers have the right to sell their shares whenever they choose. The founders of most dot-com companies took advantage of this legal loophole to sell hundreds of millions of dollars of their dot-com shares before their stock prices collapsed. When making ethical decisions, such managers put their own interests first and commonly harm other stakeholders.

accommodative approach Companies and their managers behave legally and ethically and try to balance the interests of different stakeholders as the need arises.

An **accommodative approach** is an acknowledgment of the need to support social responsibility. Accommodative companies and managers agree that organizational members ought to behave legally and ethically, and they try to balance the interests of different stakeholders against one another so that the claims of stockholders are seen in relation to the claims of other stakeholders. Managers adopting this approach want to make choices that are reasonable in the eyes of society and want to do the right thing when called on to do so.

This approach is the one taken by the typical large U.S. company, which has the most to lose from unethical or illegal behavior. Generally, the older and more reputable a company, the more likely are its managers to curb attempts by their subordinates to act unethically. Large companies like GM, Intel, Du Pont, and Dell seek every way to build their companies' competitive advantages. Nevertheless, they reign in attempts by their managers to behave unethically or illegally, knowing the grave consequences such behavior can have on future profitability.

proactive approach Companies and their managers actively embrace socially responsible behavior, going out of their way to learn about the needs of different stakeholder groups and utilizing organizational resources to promote the interests of all stakeholders.

Companies and managers taking a **proactive approach** actively embrace the need to behave in socially responsible ways. They go out of their way to learn about the needs of different stakeholder groups and are willing to utilize organizational resources to promote the interests not only of stockholders but also of the other stakeholders. Such companies are at the forefront of campaigns for causes such as a pollution-free environment, recycling and conservation of resources, the minimization or elimination of the use of animals in drug and cosmetics testing, and the reduction of crime, illiteracy, and poverty. For example, companies like McDonald's, Green Mountain Coffee, Ben and Jerry's, and

You can feel good about indulging in a pint of Ben & Jerry's Primary Berry Graham. The company has a long history of taking a proactive approach to social responsibility by donating profits to charity, providing economic opportunities, and protecting the environment. For example, in 2003 the company launched sustainable dairy farming projects in the U.S. and in Hellendorn, Holland. Meanwhile, the company's employee-led Packaging Innovation Group achieved a major plastic packaging reduction goal—instead of receiving bulk ingredients (cherries, specifically) in "bazillions" of 5-gallon plastic pails, they're now receiving these ingredients in 2,300 lb. "totes."

Target all have a reputation for being proactive in the support of stakeholders such as their suppliers or the community in which they operate.

Why Be Socially Responsible?

Several advantages result when companies and their managers behave in a socially responsible manner. First, demonstrating its social responsibility helps a company build a good reputation. Reputation is the trust, goodwill, and confidence others have in a company that leads them to want to do business with it. The reward for a good company reputation is increased trade and improved ability to obtain resources from stakeholders. Reputation thus can enhance profitability and build stockholder wealth. Therefore, behaving socially responsibly is the economically right thing to do because companies that do so benefit from increasing business and rising profits.

A second major reason for companies to act socially responsibly toward employees, customers, and society is that in a capitalist system companies, as well as the government, have to bear the costs of protecting their stakeholders, providing health care and income, paying taxes, and so on. So if all companies in a society act socially responsibly, the quality of life as a whole increases.

Moreover, the way companies behave toward their employees determines many of a society's values and norms and the ethics of its citizens, as noted above. It has been suggested that if all organizations adopted a caring approach and agreed that their responsibility is to promote the interests of their employees, a climate of caring would pervade the wider society. Experts point to Japan, Sweden, Germany, the Netherlands, and Switzerland as countries where organizations are highly socially responsible and where, as a result, crime, poverty, and unemployment rates are relatively low, literacy rates are relatively high, and sociocultural values promote harmony between different groups of people. Business activity affects all aspects of people's lives, so the way business behaves toward stakeholders affects how stakeholders will behave toward business. You "reap what you sow," as the adage goes.

The Role of Organizational Culture

While an organization's code of ethics guides decision making when ethical questions arise, managers can go one step further by ensuring that important ethical values and norms are key features of an organization's culture. For example, Herb Kelleher and Southwest Airlines' culture value employee well-being; this translates into norms dictating that layoffs should be avoided.[37] When ethical values and norms such as these are part of an organization's culture, they help organizational members resist self-interested action and recognize that they are part of something bigger than themselves.[38]

Managers' roles in developing ethical values and standards in other employees is very important. Employees naturally look to those in authority to provide leadership, and managers become ethical role models whose behavior is scrutinized by their subordinates. If top managers are not ethical, their subordinates are not likely to behave in an ethical manner. Employees may think that if it's all right for a top manager to engage in dubious behavior, it's all right for them too. The actions of top managers such as CEOs and the president of the United States are scrutinized so closely for ethical improprieties because their actions represent the values of their organizations and, in the case of the president, the values of the nation.

ethics ombudsman A manager responsible for communicating and teaching ethical standards to all employees and monitoring their conformity to those standards.

Managers can also provide a visible means of support to develop an ethical culture. Increasingly, organizations are creating the role of ethics officer, or **ethics ombudsman,** to monitor their ethical practices and procedures. The ethics ombudsman is responsible for communicating ethical standards to all employees, for designing systems to monitor employees' conformity to those standards, and for teaching managers and employees at all levels of the organization how to respond to ethical dilemmas appropriately.[39] Because the ethics ombudsman has organizationwide authority, organizational members in any department can communicate instances of unethical behavior by their managers or co-workers without fear of retribution. This arrangement makes it easier for

Figure 4.6
Johnson & Johnson's Credo

Our Credo

We believe our first responsibility is to the doctors, nurses and patients,
to mothers and fathers and all others who use our products and services.
In meeting their needs everything we do must be of high quality.
We must constantly strive to reduce our costs
in order to maintain reasonable prices.
Customers' orders must be serviced promptly and accurately.
Our suppliers and distributors must have an opportunity
to make a fair profit.

We are responsible to our employees,
the men and women who work with us throughout the world.
Everyone must be considered as an individual.
We must respect their dignity and recognize their merit.
They must have a sense of security in their jobs.
Compensation must be fair and adequate,
and working conditions clean, orderly and safe.
We must be mindful of ways to help our employees fulfill
their family responsibilities.
Employees must feel free to make suggestions and complaints.
There must be equal opportunity for employment, development
and advancement for those qualified.
We must provide competent management,
and their actions must be just and ethical.

We are responsible to the communities in which we live and work
and to the world community as well.
We must be good citizens—support good works and charities
and bear our fair share of taxes.
We must encourage civic improvements and better health and education.
We must maintain in good order
the property we are privileged to use,
protecting the environment and natural resources.

Our final responsibility is to our stockholders.
Business must make a sound profit.
We must experiment wlth new ideas.
Research must be carried on, innovative programs developed
and mistakes paid for.
New equipment must be purchased, new facilities provided
and new products launched.
Reserves must be created to provide for adverse times.
When we operate according to these principles,
the stock holders should realize a fair return.

Johnson & Johnson

Source: © Johnson & Johnson. Used with permission.

everyone to behave ethically. In addition, ethics ombudsmen can provide guidance when organizational members are uncertain about whether an action is ethical. Some organizations have an organizationwide ethics committee to provide guidance on ethical issues and help write and update the company code of ethics.

Ethical organizational cultures encourage organizational members to behave in a socially responsible manner. In fact, managers at Johnson & Johnson take social responsibility so seriously that their organization is often held up as an example of a socially responsible firm. The Johnson & Johnson Credo (see Figure 4.6) is one of the many ways in which social responsibility is emphasized at the company. As discussed in the "Ethics in Action" below, Johnson & Johnson's ethical organizational culture provides the company and its various stakeholder groups with numerous benefits.

Ethics in Action

Johnson & Johnson's Ethical Culture

Johnson & Johnson is so well known for its ethical culture that it has been judged as having the best corporate reputation for two years in a row based on a survey of over 26,000 consumers conducted by Harris Interactive and the Reputation Institute at New York University.[40] Johnson & Johnson grew from a family business led by General Robert Wood Johnson in the 1930s to a major maker of pharmaceutical and medical products. Attesting to the role of managers in creating ethical organizational cultures, Johnson emphasized the importance of ethics and responsibility to stakeholders and wrote the first Johnson & Johnson Credo in 1943.[41]

The credo continues to guide employees at Johnson & Johnson today and outlines the company's commitments to its different stakeholder groups. It emphasizes that the organization's first responsibility is to doctors, nurses, patients, and consumers. Following this group are suppliers and distributors, employees, communities, and, lastly, stockholders.[42] This credo has served managers and employees at Johnson & Johnson well and guided some difficult decision making, such as the decision to recall all Tylenol capsules in the U.S. market after cyanide-laced capsules were responsible for seven deaths in Chicago.

True to its ethical culture and outstanding reputation, consumer well-being always comes before profit considerations at Johnson & Johnson. For example, around 20 years ago, Johnson & Johnson's baby oil was used as a tanning product at a time when the harmful effects of sun exposure were not well known by the public.[43] The product manager for baby oil at the time, Carl Spalding, was making a presentation to top management about marketing plans when the company's president, David Clare, mentioned that tanning might not be healthy.[44] Before launching his planned marketing campaign, Spalding looked into the health-related concerns connected with tanning and discovered some evidence suggesting that health problems could arise from too much exposure to the sun. Even though the evidence was not definitive, Spalding recommended that baby oil no longer be marketed as a tanning aid, a decision that resulted in a 50 percent decrease in sales of baby oil, to the tune of $5 million.[45]

The ethical values and norms in Johnson & Johnson's culture, along with its credo, guide managers such as Spalding to make the right decision in difficult situations. Hence, it is understandable why Johnson & Johnson is renowned for its corporate reputation. An ethical culture and outstanding reputation have other benefits in addition to helping employees make the right decisions in questionable situations. Jeanne Hamway, vice president for recruiting, finds that Johnson & Johnson's reputation helps the company recruit and attract a diverse workforce.[46] Moreover, when organizations develop an outstanding reputation, their employees often are less tempted to act in a self-interested or unethical manner. For example, managers at Johnson & Johnson suggest that since employees in the company never accept bribes, the company is known as one in which bribes should not be offered in the first place.[47] All in all, ethical cultures such as Johnson & Johnson's benefit various stakeholder groups in multiple ways.

Summary and Review

THE NATURE OF ETHICS Ethical issues are central to the way companies and their managers make decisions, and they affect not only the efficiency and effectiveness of the way companies operate but also the prosperity of a nation. The result of ethical behavior is a general increase in company performance and in a nation's standard of living, well being, and wealth.

An ethical dilemma is the quandary people find themselves in when they have to decide if they should act in a way that might help another person or group, and is the "right" thing to do, even though it might go against their own self-interest. Ethics are the inner-guiding moral principles, values, and beliefs that people use to analyze or interpret a situation and then decide what is the "right" or appropriate way to behave.

Ethical beliefs alter and change as time passes, and as they do so laws change to reflect the changing ethical beliefs of a society.

STAKEHOLDERS AND ETHICS Stakeholders are people and groups who have a claim on and a stake in a company. The main stakeholder groups are stockholders, managers, employees, suppliers and distributors, customers, and a community, society, and nation. Companies and their managers need to make ethical business decisions that promote the well being of their stakeholders and avoid doing them harm.

To determine if a business decision is ethical, managers can use four ethical rules to analyze it: the utilitarian, moral rights, justice, and practical rules. Managers should behave ethically because this avoids the tragedy of the commons and results in a general increase in efficiency, effectiveness, and company performance. The main determinants of differences in a manager's, company's, and country's business ethics are societal, occupational, individual, and organizational.

ETHICS AND SOCIAL RESPONSIBILITY A company's stance on social responsibility is the way its managers and employees view their duty or obligation to make decisions that protect, enhance, and promote the welfare and well-being of stakeholders and society as a whole.

APPROACHES TO SOCIAL RESPONSIBILITY There are four main approaches to social responsibility: obstructionist, defensive, accommodative, and proactive. The rewards from behaving in a socially responsible way are a good reputation, the support of all organizational stakeholders, and thus superior company performance.

Management in Action

Topics for Discussion and Action

Discussion

1. What is the relationship between ethics and the law?
2. Why do the claims and interests of stakeholders sometimes conflict?
3. Why should managers use ethical criteria to guide their decision making?
4. As an employee of a company, what are some of the most unethical business practices that you have encountered in its dealings with stakeholders?
5. What are the main determinants of business ethics?

Action

6. Find a manager and ask about the most important ethical rules that he or she uses to make the right decisions.
7. Find an example of (a) a company that has an obstructionist approach to social responsibility and (b) one that has an accommodative approach.

Building Management Skills

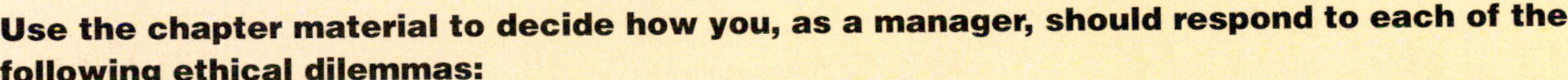

Dealing with Ethical Dilemmas

Use the chapter material to decide how you, as a manager, should respond to each of the following ethical dilemmas:

1. You are planning to leave your job to go work for a competitor; your boss invites you to an important meeting where you will learn about new products your company will be bringing out next year. Do you go to the meeting?
2. You're the manager of sales in an expensive sports-car dealership. A young executive who has just received a promotion comes in and wants to buy a car that you know is out of her price range. Do you encourage the executive to buy it so that you can receive a big commission on the sale?
3. You sign a contract to manage a young rock band, and that group agrees to let you produce their next seven records, for which they will receive royalties of 5 percent. Their first record is a smash hit and sells millions. Do you increase their royalty rate on their future records?

Managing Ethically

As the chapter discussed, Arthur Andersen's culture had become so strong that some of the company's partners and their subordinates acted unethically and pursued their own interests at the expense of other stakeholders. Many employees knew they were doing wrong but were afraid to refuse to follow orders. At Beech-Nut, the company's ethical values completely broke down; some managers joked about the harm being done to stakeholders.

Questions

1. Why is it that an organization's values and norms can become too strong and lead to unethical behavior?
2. What steps can a company take to prevent this problem—to stop its values and norms from becoming so inwardly focused that managers and employees lose sight of their responsibility to their stakeholders?

Small Group Breakout Exercise

Is Chewing Gum the "Right" Thing to Do?

Read the paragraph below. Then break up into groups of three or four people and answer the discussion questions.

In the United States the right to chew gum is taken for granted. Although it is often against the rules to chew gum in a high school classroom, church, and so on, it is legal to do so on the street. If you possess or chew gum on a street in Singapore, you can be arrested. Chewing gum has been made illegal in Singapore because those in power believe that it creates a disgusting mess on pavements and feel that people cannot be trusted to dispose of their gum properly and thus should have no right to use it.

1. What makes chewing gum acceptable in the United States and unacceptable in Singapore?
2. Why can you chew gum on the street but not in a church?
3. How can you use ethical principles to decide when gum chewing is ethical or unethical and if and when it should be made illegal?

Exploring the World Wide Web

Go to Wal-Mart's Web site (www.walmart.com) and read the information there about the company's stance on the ethics of global outsourcing and the treatment of workers in countries abroad. Then search the Web for some recent stories about Wal-Mart's global purchasing practices and reports on the enforcement of its code of conduct.

1. What ethical principles guide Wal-Mart's approach to global purchasing?
2. Does Wal-Mart appear to be doing a good job of enforcing its global code of conduct?

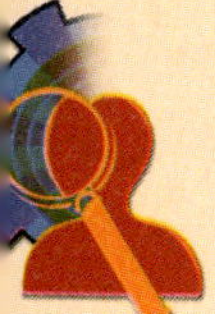

Additional Activities on the Build Your Management Skills DVD

- **Test Your Knowledge:** Ethics
- **Self-Assessment:** Assessing Your Ethical Decision-Making Skills
- **Manager's Hot Seat:** Ethics: Let's Make a Fourth Quarter Deal

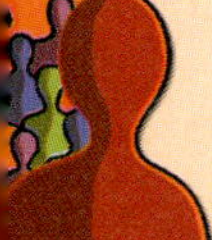

Be the Manager

Creating an Ethical Code

You are an entrepreneur who has decided to go into business and open a steak and chicken restaurant. Your business plan requires that you hire at least 20 people as chefs, waiters, and so on. As the owner, you are drawing up a list of ethical principles that each of these people will receive and must agree to when he or she accepts a job offer. These principles outline your view of what is right or acceptable behavior and what will be expected both from you and from your employees.

Create a list of the five main ethical rules or principles you will use to govern the way your business operates. Be sure to spell out how these principles relate to your stakeholders; for example, state the rules you intend to follow in dealing with your employees and customers.

BusinessWeek **Case in the News**

Can Boeing Get Out of Its "Ethical Cloud"?

The unexpected resignation of Boeing chairman and CEO Philip M. Condit on December 1, 2003, followed a year of turbulence at the world's largest aerospace company. The final straw for Condit, 62, may have been the previous week's ouster of two senior Boeing officials for an alleged ethics lapse.

Condit's resignation created several daunting challenges for his immediate successor—Harry C. Stonecipher, former Boeing president and chief operating officer. Stonecipher, 67, who retired last year and remained as a board member, immediately assumed the post of CEO and president of a company that has more than $54 billion in annual revenues.

In his first press conference as top gun, Stonecipher seemed to say all the right things by pledging to answer any and all questions, including those swirling around a highly criticized air-tanker deal with the federal government. The blunt-talking, no-nonsense leader will have to be true to his word and get Boeing soaring again.

Clearly, Stonecipher has his work cut out. Condit's resignation is tied to Boeing's persistent reluctance to disclose all the particulars of a controversial plan to lease Boeing 767 tankers to the Air Force. The plan was blasted for the secrecy in which the contract was negotiated and for the fact that leasing would be much more expensive for the federal government than an outright purchase (see BW, 7/7/03, "Inside Boeing's Sweet Deal").

Condit's departure came a week after Boeing CFO Michael Sears resigned. The company cited unethical conduct, saying he negotiated the hiring of an Air Force missile-defense expert while she was still working for the Pentagon and had direct influence over Boeing's bid to secure the tanker contract. Sears denied any wrongdoing.

"It's very surprising for a company such as Boeing to have not one but two apparent ethical breaches in less than six months," said Steven Ryan, a Washington (D.C.) attorney who represents contractors seeking work with the federal government. In July 2003 the Pentagon had punished Boeing for stealing trade secrets from rival Lockheed Martin to help win rocket-launch contracts. The punishment added up to $1 billion in lost business, and the Pentagon had indefinitely banned Boeing from bidding on military satellite-launching contracts.

"Condit's resignation is a reflection of the seriousness of the problem," said Ryan. And the situation suggested that something wasn't right inside Boeing's culture—something that Stonecipher had helped change when he was president and was now responsible and accountable for coming clean.

"Everything the former leadership at Boeing did was surrounded by an ethical cloud of controversy and needed to be reviewed to ensure that it was in the best interest of the taxpayer and war-fighter," said Steve Ellis, vice president for Taxpayers for Common Sense. With Condit out, the board apparently chose the tough-talking Stonecipher because he's well regarded on Wall Street and because he knows the ways of the Pentagon. With the mandatory retirement set at 65 for Boeing execs, Stonecipher received a special exemption to return.

How Boeing got itself and its top execs tangled up in such a mess has yet to be fully explained. The stock, at just over $38, barely moved on the news of Condit's departure. And it had moved mostly higher last year from an all-time low of just over $24 hit back in March 2003. Still, analysts say, the stock should have been much higher, and Stonecipher had a long way to go to regain the trust of angry and skeptical investors, public-interest groups, and the U.S. government.

Questions

1. What kinds of unethical actions did Boeing's managers engage in?
2. What effect did this have on the company and how can its CEO prevent future unethical behavior?

Source: Stanley Holmes, "Can Boeing Get Out of Its 'Ethical Cloud'?" Reprinted from the December 1, 2003, issue of *BusinessWeek* Online by special permission.

Can This Man Save Putnam?

Charles E. "Ed" Haldeman manages money the way he plays tennis. Putnam Investments' lanky new chief executive doesn't hit hard, keeps the ball in play, avoids mistakes, and wears down opponents by staying on court a long time.

That's just as well. With the Boston mutual-fund giant still hemorrhaging $3 billion of assets a month in the wake of trading scandals, he's in a game of survival. Haldeman is grappling with the worst crisis in the old-line firm's 67-year history. Investors have rushed to pull out more than $70 billion of their money. That's a massive 26 percent of the assets Putnam had on September 30, 2003, just before two managers were implicated in the rapid buying and selling of their own funds to the detriment of shareholders. Putnam is also in a knock-down-drag-out row with the Securities & Exchange Commission over potential fines of $138 million as well as an undetermined amount of restitution to shareholders.

How Haldeman handles the crisis will have a major impact on the $7.5 trillion mutual-fund industry. Enforcers seem intent on using the Putnam case as a lever to make big changes in the way mutual funds are run in the future. In a partial settlement announced on November 13, 2003, the SEC imposed on Putnam rules that the industry has fought for years.

The SEC ordered Putnam to ensure that 75 percent of fund directors are independent and re-elected every five years. Also it set strict limits on employee trading—and ruled that any illicit trading in the future must be reported directly to fund boards. Other controversial measures may be part of a final settlement, insiders say, including controls on so-called soft dollars—rebates of brokerage commissions to fund companies, with which they buy research or equipment such as computers—and incentive payments to intermediaries who sell mutual funds. Unless Putnam and the SEC reach a settlement by April 19, an administrative law judge will fix the penalties. Says Jeff Keil, vice president for global fiduciary review at fund rater Lipper Inc.: "The SEC seems to be pulling out all the stops to make an example of Putnam."

The cleanup could transform the industry. Fees of all sorts will be a lot more transparent. Haldeman, for example, is now telling investors exactly how much they're paying in dollars and cents for fees and services. Fund expenses may head lower, though an end to soft-dollar rebates could limit the fall. And fund directors will come under pressure to do a better job in protecting fund shareholders' interests. Putnam directors say they were never told there was a problem—an excuse that won't fly in the future.

Can Haldeman save Putnam? If personal probity were the sole determining factor, the answer would be a resounding yes. Haldeman, 55, an investment manager for 30 years, is widely admired in the industry for his commitment to investors and high ethical standards. Says Philadelphia-based fund consultant Burton J. Greenwald: "He's an absolutely straight arrow. There's no question about his integrity and character." Adds Vanguard Group founder and Haldeman friend John C. Bogle: "If anyone can [fix Putnam], he's the one. But it's not going to be easy."

Probably Haldeman's biggest challenge is to root out the cowboy culture that ran amok during the autocratic Lasser's 18-year reign. The three top goals were: sell, sell, sell. Says Bedda Emous, a certified financial planner with Fiduciary Solutions in Andover, Massachusetts, who hasn't recommended a Putnam fund since 1998: "It was patently obvious that Putnam was a marketing company and not a money management company." Former Putnam salespeople concluded that winning new accounts mattered more than good investment returns. Lasser encouraged a "gotcha" culture. When portfolio managers' returns started to lag, he would send "Lassergrams"—terse letters on gray paper—that bred paranoia and resentment. Worse, it encouraged some managers to gamble by taking big risks in the hope of making big returns.

Now, instead of swinging for the fences as Putnam's leadership did in the go-go days of the 1990s, Haldeman has ordered managers to aim for reliable returns over the long haul. Haldeman wants each of Putnam's 54 funds to rank in the top half of its category every year. (On an asset-weighted basis fewer than half the equity funds did in the year through March 31.) In the future, managers will earn bonuses by achieving just that—and not get a penny more for edging their funds into the top 10 percent, as they once did. To ram his message home, Haldeman wrote up his "guiding beliefs" on laminated cards that now hang on the walls of managers' offices.

At the same time, Haldeman has been putting his own stamp on the firm with a thorough housecleaning of its top echelons. On

April 5, Haldeman hired Francis J. McNamara III from the rival Boston fund firm State Street Research & Management Co. as general counsel, reporting directly to himself. All told, 10 of Putnam's 20 highest-ranking managers have left in the past year. Haldeman let many of them go, including fund managers Justin M. Scott and Omid Kamshad, who were implicated by enforcers in illicit trading. Lawyers for Scott and Kamshad declined to comment. Others chose to go. In addition, Putnam has shed 13 employees for alleged abusive trading. Says Haldeman: "Several of our senior people had violated a fiduciary trust, and they needed to leave."

Fixing lax internal governance was high on Haldeman's agenda. On becoming CEO, he ordered a review of the trading records of the 12,700 people who had worked at Putnam since 1998. And because most of the abuses arose from the fast buying and selling of Putnam's funds, Haldeman immediately banned employees from selling any fund within 90 days of buying, and a year for funds on which they work. In January, he promised to publish the size of holdings that managers and directors have in Putnam funds.

That same month, he promoted Tony Ruys de Perez to be chief compliance officer, responsible for making sure that employees and clients follow securities laws. The new appointee will report directly to Haldeman and have an office near him in Putnam's downtown Boston headquarters.

Questions

1. What unethical and illegal acts did Putnam's fund managers commit?
2. How has its new CEO been working to prevent future ethical lapses?

Source: Faith Arner and Lauren Young, "Can This Man Save Putnam?" Reprinted from the April 19, 2004, issue of *BusinessWeek* Online by special permission. Copyright © 2004 by the McGraw-Hill Companies.

CHAPTER

5 Managing Diverse Employees in a Multicultural Environment

Learning Objectives

After studying this chapter, you should be able to:

- Appreciate the increasing diversity of the workforce and of the organizational environment.
- Grasp the central role that managers play in the effective management of diversity.
- Understand why the effective management of diversity is both an ethical and a business imperative.
- Appreciate how perception and the use of schemas can result in unfair treatment.
- Appreciate the steps managers can take to effectively manage diversity.
- Understand the two major forms of sexual harassment and how they can be eliminated.

A Manager's Challenge

Diversity in the Boardroom and on the Police Force

How can managers diversify nontraditional work groups and organizations? For any demographic group such as women, Hispanics, and African-Americans, nontraditional work groups and organizations are work settings in which the demographic group in question is very underrepresented. For example, given that women make up about half of the population, a nontraditional organization for women is one in which less than 25 percent of employees are women.[1] Recognizing that diversity on multiple dimensions makes good business sense, managers are increasingly seeking to diversify jobs and work groups that traditionally have comprised very few women or minorities. In the United States and other countries such as Norway and Sweden, efforts to diversify nontraditional work settings are occurring at every organizational level.[2] The need for diversification at the very top of organizations is reflected in the composition of boards of directors. Women make up only about 10 percent of the boards of the S&P 1500 (which comprises about 87 percent of public companies in the United States and represents 7,500 board positions); minorities make up only about 8.8 percent of these boards.[3]

Boston Mayor Menino says he chose Kathleen O'Toole, pictured here, to be the city's Chief of Police because she was the best person for the job.

Leonard Schaeffer, chairman and CEO of Wellpoint Health Networks in Thousand Oaks, California, suggests that managers can diversify boards of directors if they try. Moreover, Schaeffer believes that boards should reflect the diversity in the population for business reasons. Having different experiences, backgrounds, and perspectives represented on a board can help ensure that the organization appeals to diverse markets for its goods and services and makes well-informed decisions that take into account all relevant information. Wellpoint's nine-member board includes four women and one minority-group member. As Schaeffer puts it, "Women make most health-care decisions in American families, so if we are going to reach out to our customers, we need gender diversity."[4] Consistent with Wellpoint's experience, when Jill Kerr Conway was on Nike's board of directors in the early 1990s, her valuable input led Nike to launch its successful women's sports apparel division.[5]

At lower levels in organizations, more managers and employees alike are beginning to question why certain jobs, such as those in construction, tend to be dominated by men. Linda Simpson created her own handywoman-referral service in Denver, Colorado, to help customers and handywomen connect for their mutual benefit.[6] Often, in certain nontraditional jobs, people think that women are underrepresented because of size and strength issues. However, petite women such as Jeannette Patane of Fairbanks, Alaska, have successful careers as handywomen. And for many positions such as painter and electrician, physical differences between men and women really don't enter the picture even though many people assume they do. Ask Joi Beard, who has been an electrician for 24 years and owns Derby Electric Inc. in New York.[7]

In the health care arena, Dr. Harry R. Gibbs, a cardiologist and vice president of Institutional Diversity at the M. D. Anderson Cancer Center in Houston, Texas, believes that the effective management of diversity is important in all aspects of health care research and delivery and that a proactive approach to managing diversity is a necessity.[8] Whether it is scientific research, disease detection, participation in drug trials, laboratory testing, or marketing to patients, diversity enters into the equation. And in all of these venues, good communication is a necessity, as is mutual understanding and the ability to converse in the same language, whether it be English, Spanish, or Chinese.[9]

What about law enforcement? Women currently make up less than 15 percent of the 880,000 members of the police forces in the United States.[10] Traditionally, even if a woman became a law enforcement officer, it was very unlikely that she would ever rise to the top and assume a leadership position. Often, the reasoning revolved around issues of physical strength. However, this situation is changing as women are currently assuming high level leadership positions in law enforcement. For example, Kathleen O'Toole recently became chief of police for the Boston Police Department, and both the San Francisco and Detroit police departments have female chiefs of police. Boston Mayor Menino, who chose O'Toole for the top spot, indicates that he did so because she was the best person for the job and that gender was not a factor in the decision.[11] As decision makers like Menino increasingly recognize that leaders in law enforcement need many of the same leadership qualities that are important in other kinds of organizations—intelligence, interpersonal skills, education, experience, and the ability and desire to make difficult decisions—excluding women from serious consideration for such positions for irrelevant reasons will hopefully decline.

Overview

The effective management of diversity means much more than hiring diverse employees. It means learning to appreciate and respond appropriately to the needs, attitudes, beliefs, and values that diverse people bring to an organization. It also means correcting misconceptions about why and how different kinds of employee groups are different from one another and finding the most effective way to utilize the skills and talents of diverse employees.

In this chapter, we focus on the effective management of diversity in an environment that is becoming increasingly diverse in all respects. Not only is the diversity of the global workforce increasing, but suppliers and customers are also becoming increasingly diverse. Managers need to proactively manage diversity to be able to attract and retain the best employees and effectively compete in a diverse global environment. For example, managers at the audit and consulting firm Deloitte & Touche have instituted a program to encourage minority suppliers to compete for its business, and the firm sponsors schools and colleges that supply a stream of well-trained recruits.[12]

Sometimes well-intentioned managers inadvertently treat one group of employees differently from another group, even though there are no performance-based differences between the two groups. As illustrated in the opening case, women were traditionally excluded from top-management positions in law enforcement for reasons that were irrelevant to performance in leadership roles. This chapter explores why differential treatment occurs and the steps managers and organizations can take to ensure that diversity, in all respects, is effectively managed for the good of all organizational stakeholders.

The Increasing Diversity of the Workforce and the Environment

One of the most important management issues to emerge over the last 30 years has been the increasing diversity of the workforce. **Diversity** is dissimilarities–differences–among people due to age, gender, race, ethnicity, religion, sexual orientation, socioeconomic background, education, experience, physical appearance, capabilities/disabilities, and any other characteristic that is used to distinguish between people (see Figure 5.1, page 150).

diversity Differences among people in age, gender, race, ethnicity, religion, sexual orientation, socioeconomic background, and capabilities/disabilities.

Diversity raises important ethical issues and social responsibility issues (see Chapter 4). It is also a critical issue for organizations, one that if not handled well can bring an organization to its knees, especially in our increasingly global environment. There are several reasons why diversity is such a pressing concern and issue both in the popular press and for managers and organizations:

- There is a strong ethical imperative in many societies that diverse people receive equal opportunities and be treated fairly and justly. Unfair treatment is also illegal.
- Effectively managing diversity can improve organizational effectiveness.[13] When managers effectively manage diversity, they not only encourage other managers to treat diverse members of an organization fairly and justly but also realize that diversity is an important organizational resource that can help an organization gain a competitive advantage.
- There is substantial evidence that diverse individuals continue to experience unfair treatment in the workplace as a result of biases, stereotypes, and overt discrimination.[14] In one study, résumés of equally qualified men and women were sent to high-priced Philadelphia restaurants (where potential earnings are high). Though equally qualified, men were more than twice as likely as women to be called for a job interview and more than five times as likely to receive a job offer.[15] Findings from another study suggest that both women and men tend to believe that women will accept lower pay than men; this is a possible explanation for the continuing gap in pay between men and women.[16]

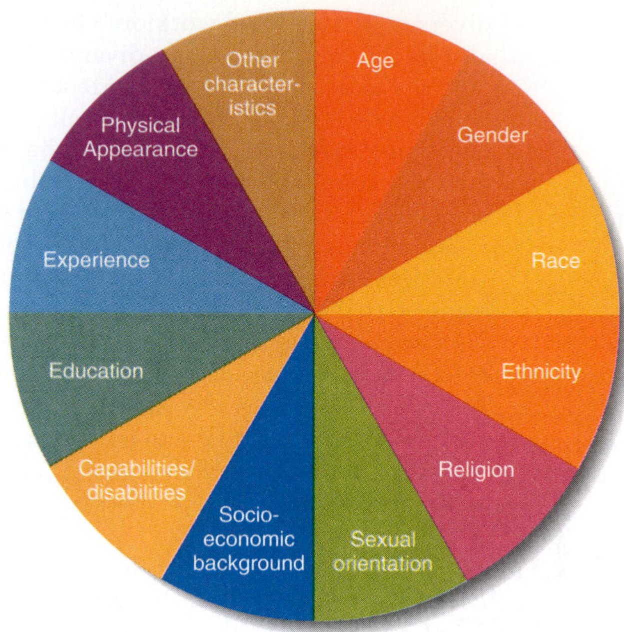

Figure 5.1 Sources of Diversity in the Workplace

Other kinds of diverse employees may face even greater barriers. For example, the federal Glass Ceiling Commission Report indicated that African-Americans have the hardest time being promoted and climbing the corporate ladder, that Asians are often stereotyped into technical jobs, and that Hispanics are assumed to be less well educated than other minority groups.[17] (The term **glass ceiling** alludes to the invisible barriers that prevent minorities and women from being promoted to top corporate positions.)[18]

glass ceiling
A metaphor alluding to the invisible barriers that prevent minorities and women from being promoted to top corporate positions.

Before we can discuss the multitude of issues surrounding the effective management of diversity, we must document just how diverse the U.S. workforce is becoming.

Age

According to the latest data from the U.S. Census Bureau, the median age of a person in the United States is the highest it has ever been, 35.3 years.[19] Moreover, by 2030, it is projected that 20 percent of the population will be over 65.[20] Title VII of the Civil Rights Act of 1964 and the Age Discrimination in Employment Act of 1967 are the major federal laws prohibiting age discrimination.[21] While we discuss federal employment legislation in more depth in Chapter 12, major equal employment opportunity legislation that prohibits discrimination among diverse groups is summarized in Table 5.1.

The aging of the population suggests managers need to be vigilant that employees are not discriminated against because of age. Moreover, managers need to ensure that the policies and procedures they have in place treat all workers fairly, regardless of their ages.

Gender

Women and men are almost equally represented in the U.S. workforce (approximately 53.5 percent of the U.S. workforce is male and 46.5 percent female),[22] yet

Table 5.1
Major Equal Employment Opportunity Laws Affecting Human Resources Management

Year	Law	Description
1963	Equal Pay Act	Requires that men and women be paid equally if they are performing equal work
1964	Title VII of the Civil Rights Act	Prohibits discrimination in employment decisions on the basis of race, religion, sex, color, or national origin; covers a wide range of employment decisions, including hiring, firing, pay, promotion, and working conditions
1967	Age Discrimination in Employment Act	Prohibits discrimination against workers over the age of 40 and restricts mandatory retirement
1978	Pregnancy Discrimination Act	Prohibits discrimination against women in employment decisions on the basis of pregnancy, childbirth, and related medical decisions
1990	Americans with Disabilities Act	Prohibits discrimination against disabled individuals in employment decisions and requires that employers make accommodations for disabled workers to enable them to perform their jobs
1991	Civil Rights Act	Prohibits discrimination (as does Title VII) and allows for the awarding of punitive and compensatory damages, in addition to back pay, in cases of intentional discrimination
1993	Family and Medical Leave Act	Requires that employers provide 12 weeks of unpaid leave for medical and family reasons, including paternity and illness of a family member

women's median weekly earnings are estimated to be $572 compared to $714 for men.[23] Thus, the gender pay gap appears to be as alive and well as the glass ceiling. According to the nonprofit organization Catalyst, which studies women in business, while women comprise about 50.5 percent of the employees in managerial and professional positions, only around 15.7 percent of corporate officers in the 500 largest U.S. companies (i.e., Fortune 500) are women, only 5.2 percent of the top earners are women, only 7.9 percent of those with the highest-ranking titles in corporate America are women (e.g., CEO or executive vice president), and only eight Fortune 500 companies have women as CEOs.[24] These women, such as Andrea Jung, CEO of Avon Products, and Carly S. Fiorina, CEO of Hewlett-Packard, stand out among their male peers and often receive a disparate amount of attention in the media. (We address this issue later, when we discuss the effects of being salient.) Women are also very underrepresented on boards of directors–they currently hold 13.6 percent of the board seats of Fortune 500 companies.[25] However, as Sheila Wellington, president of Catalyst, indicates, "Women either control or influence nearly all consumer purchases, so it's important to have their perspective represented on boards."[26]

Additionally, research conducted by consulting firms suggests that female executives outperform their male colleagues on skills such as motivating others, promoting good communication, turning out high-quality work, and being a good listener.[27] For example, the Hagberg Group performed in-depth evaluations of 425 top executives in a variety of industries, with each executive rated by approximately 25 people. Of the 52 skills assessed, women received higher ratings than men on 42 skills, although at times the differences were small.[28] Results of a recent study conducted by Catalyst found that organizations with higher proportions of women in top-management positions had significantly better financial performance than organizations with lower proportions of female top managers.[29] All in all, studies such as these make one wonder why the glass ceiling continues to hamper the progress of women in business (a topic we address later in the chapter).

Race and Ethnicity

The U.S. Census Bureau typically distinguishes between the following races: American Indian or Alaska Native (native Americans of origins in North, Central, or South America), Asian (origins in the Far East, Southeast Asia, or India), African-American (origins in Africa), Native Hawaiian or Pacific Islander (origins in the Pacific Islands such as Hawaii, Guam, and Somoa), and white (origins in Europe, the Middle East, or North Africa). While ethnicity refers to a grouping of people based on some shared characteristics such as national origin, language, or culture, the U.S. Census Bureau treats ethnicity in terms of whether a person is Hispanic or not Hispanic. Hispanics, also referred to as Latinos, are people whose origins are in Spanish cultures such as those of Cuba, Mexico, Puerto Rico, and South and Central America. Hispanics can be of different races.[30] According to a recent poll, most Hispanics prefer to be identified by their country of origin (e.g., Mexican, Cuban, or Salvadoran) rather than by the overarching term *Hispanic*.[31]

The racial and ethnic diversity of the U.S. population is increasing at an exponential rate, as is the composition of the workforce.[32] According to the U.S. Census in 2000, 75.1 percent of the population was white, 12.9 percent was African-American, 12.5 percent was Hispanic, and 3.6 percent was Asian.[33] Mexican-Americans are estimated to constitute over 60 percent of the U.S. Hispanic population, with the remainder of Hispanics having diverse countries of origin. As indicated in the following "Managing Globally," the diversity of the U.S. population based on race and ethnicity will increase dramatically over the next few decades.

Managing Globally

Asians and Hispanics Projected to Be Fastest-Growing Group

According to projections released by the U.S. Census Bureau in the spring of 2004, the composition of the U.S. population in 2050 will be quite different from its composition in 2000. It is estimated that the Hispanic and Asian populations will triple during this 50-year period.[34] While the overall population in the United States is projected to grow from 282 billion in 2000 to 419 billion in 2050 (a 49 percent increase), estimated percentage growth rates for different ethnic and racial groups show that racial and ethnic diversity will definitely be on the rise.[35] Interestingly, while the U.S. population will increase by almost 50 percent in this next half-century, populations in many European countries are actually expected to decline.[36]

Percentage growth rates for African-Americans, Asians, Hispanics (of any race), and other races are well above the overall population growth estimate,

Puerto Rican Day Parade in New York City. It is estimated that the U.S. Hispanic and Asian populations will triple by 2050.

while the percentage growth rate for non-Hispanic whites is far below this figure.[37] More specifically, from 2000 to 2050, African-Americans, Asians, Hispanics (of any race), other races, and non-Hispanic whites have estimated growth rates of 71.3 percent, 212.9 percent, 187.9 percent, 217.1 percent, and 7.4 percent, respectively.[38]

In addition to experiencing increased racial and ethnic diversity, the U.S. population is also projected to get older. While the overall population growth rate is an estimated 48.8 percent, the segments of the population in the age groups of 45–64, 65–84, and 85 and over are expected to grow by 49.1 percent, 113.8 percent, and 388.9 percent, respectively.[39] The U.S. Census Bureau made these projections based on Census 2000 data and assumptions regarding immigration patterns, mortality rates, and birth rates during the 2000–2050 period. For example, assumptions regarding immigration from China and India to the United States in the next several decades contribute to the projected high rate of growth in the Asian segment of the population.[40] All in all, these projections underscore the fact that the effective management of diversity in the workplace will only increase in importance in the years ahead.

The increasing racial and ethnic diversity of the workforce and the population as a whole underscores the importance of effectively managing diversity. Statistics compiled by the National Urban League suggest that much needs to be done in terms of ensuring that diverse employees are provided with equal opportunities. For example, African-Americans' earnings are approximately 73 percent of the earnings of whites,[41] and of 10,092 corporate officers in Fortune 500 companies, only 106 are African-American women.[42] In the remainder of this chapter, we focus on the fair treatment of diverse employees and explore why this is such an important challenge and what managers can do to meet it. We begin by taking a broader perspective and considering how increasing racial and ethnic diversity in an organization's environment (e.g., customers and suppliers) affects decision making and organizational effectiveness.

At a general level, managers and organizations are increasingly being reminded that stakeholders in the environment are diverse and expect organizational decisions and actions to reflect this diversity. For example, the NAACP (National Association for the Advancement of Colored People) and Children Now (an advocacy group) have lobbied the entertainment industry to increase the diversity in television programming, writing, and producing.[43] The need for such increased diversity is more than apparent. For example, while Hispanics make up 12.5 percent of the U.S. population (or 35 million potential TV viewers), only about 2 percent of the characters in prime-time TV shows are Hispanics (i.e., of the 2,251 characters in prime-time shows, only 47 are Hispanic), according to a study conducted by Children Now.[44] Moreover, only about 1.3 percent of the evening network TV news stories are reported by Hispanic correspondents, according to the Center for Media and Public Affairs.[45]

Pressure is mounting on networks to increase diversity for a variety of reasons revolving around the diversity of the population as a whole, TV viewers, and consumers. For example, home and automobile buyers are increasingly diverse, reflecting the increasing diversity of the population as a whole.[46] Moreover, managers have to be especially sensitive to avoid stereotyping different groups when they communicate with potential customers. For example, Toyota Motor Sales USA made a public apology to the Reverend Jesse Jackson and his Rainbow Coalition for using a print advertisement depicting an African-American man with a Toyota RAV4 sport utility image embossed on his gold front tooth.[47]

Religion

Title VII of the Civil Rights Act prohibits discrimination based on religion (as well as based on race/ethnicity, country of origin, and sex; see Table 5.1 and Chapter 12). In addition to enacting Title VII, in 1997 the federal government issued "The White House Guidelines on Religious Exercise and Expression in the Federal Workplace."[48] These guidelines, while technically only applicable in federal offices, also are frequently relied on by large corporations. The guidelines require that employers make reasonable accommodations for religious practices such as observances of holidays as long as doing so does not entail major costs or hardships.[49]

A key issue for managers when it comes to religious diversity is recognizing and being aware of different religions and their beliefs, with particular attention being paid to when religious holidays fall. For example, critical meetings should not be scheduled during a holy day for members of a certain faith, and managers should be flexible in allowing people to have time off for religious observances. According to Lobna Ismail, director of a diversity training company in Silver Spring, Maryland, when managers acknowledge, respect, and make even small accommodations for religious diversity, employee loyalty is often enhanced. For example, allowing employees to leave work early on certain days instead of taking a lunch break or posting holidays for different religions on the company calendar can go a long way toward making individuals of diverse religions feel respected and valued as well as enable them to practice their faith.[50]

Capabilities/Disabilities

The Americans with Disabilities Act (ADA) of 1990 prohibits discrimination against persons with disabilities and also requires that employers make reasonable accommodations to enable these people to effectively perform their jobs. In force for more than a decade, the ADA is not uncontroversial. On the surface, few would argue with the intent of this legislation. However, as managers attempt to implement policies and procedures to comply with the ADA, they face a number of interpretation and fairness challenges.

On the one hand, some people with real disabilities warranting workplace accommodations are hesitant to reveal their disabilities to their employers and claim the accommodations they deserve.[51] On the other hand, some employees abuse the ADA by seeking unnecessary accommodations for disabilities that may or may not exist.[52] Thus, it is perhaps not surprising that the passage of the ADA does not appear to have increased employment rates significantly for those with disabilities.[53] A key challenge for managers is to promote an environment in which employees needing accommodations feel comfortable disclosing their need and, at the same time, to ensure that the accommodations not only enable those with disabilities to effectively perform their jobs but also are perceived to be fair by those not disabled.[54] In addressing this challenge, often managers must educate both themselves and their employees about the disabilities, as well as the very real capabilities, of those who are disabled. For example, during Disability Awareness Week 2004, administrators at the University of Notre Dame sought to increase the public's knowledge of disabilities while also heightening awareness of the abilities of persons who are disabled.[55] The University of Houston conducted a similar program called "Think Ability."[56] According to Cheryl Amoruso, director of the University of Houston's Center for Students with Disabilities, many people are unaware of the prevalence of disabilities as well as misinformed about their consequences. She suggests, for example, that although students may not be able to see, they can still excel in their coursework and have very successful careers.[57] Accommodations enabling such students to perform up to their capabilities are covered under the ADA.

The ADA also protects employees with acquired immune deficiency syndrome (AIDS) from being discriminated against in the workplace. AIDS is caused by the human immunodeficiency virus (HIV) and is transmitted through sexual contact, infected needles, and contaminated blood products. HIV is not spread through casual, nonsexual contact. Yet, out of ignorance, fear, or prejudice, some people wish to avoid all contact with anyone infected with HIV. Infected individuals may not necessarily develop AIDS, and some individuals with HIV are able to remain effective performers of their jobs, while not putting others at risk.[58]

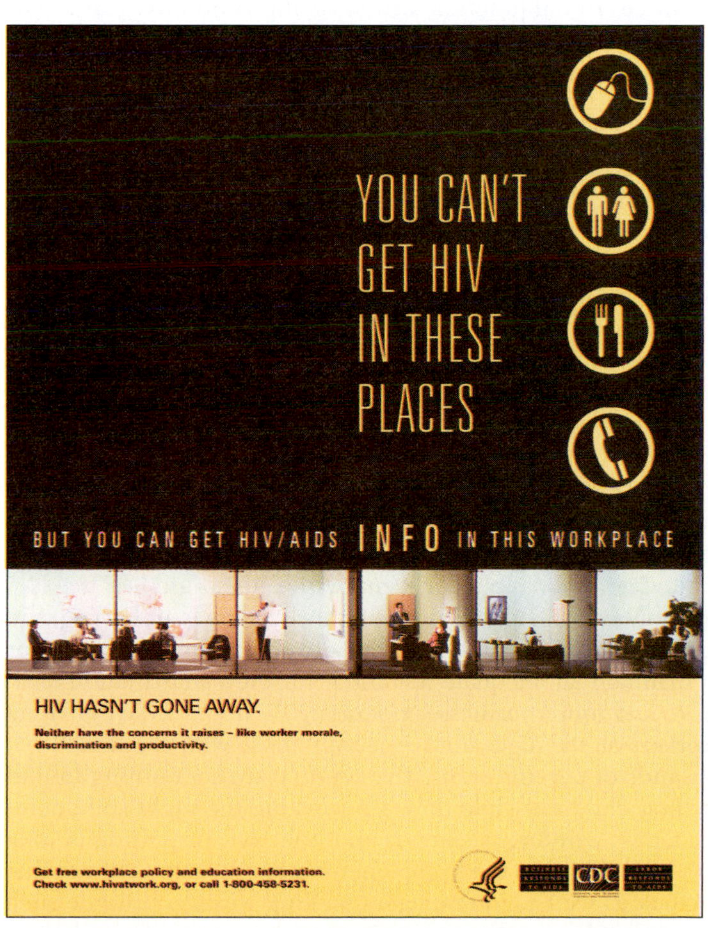

One way managers can educate employees about HIV and AIDS is by hanging AIDS awareness posters in the workplace, such as the one depicted here.

AIDS awareness training can help people overcome their fears and also provide managers with a tool to prevent illegal discrimination against HIV-infected employees. Such training focuses on educating employees about HIV and AIDS, dispelling myths, communicating relevant organizational policies, and emphasizing the rights of HIV-positive employees to privacy and an environment that allows them to be productive.[59] The need for AIDS awareness training is underscored by some of the problems HIV-positive employees experience once others in their workplace become aware of their condition.[60] Moreover, organizations are required to make reasonable accommodations to enable people with AIDS to effectively perform their jobs.

Thus, managers have an obligation to educate employees about HIV and AIDS, dispel myths and the stigma of AIDS, and ensure that HIV-related discrimination is not occurring in the workplace. For example, Home Depot has provided HIV training and education to its store managers; such training was sorely needed given that over half of the managers indicated it was the first time they had the opportunity to talk about AIDS.[61] Moreover, advances in medication and treatment mean that more infected individuals are able to continue working or are able to return to work after their condition improves.[62] Thus, managers need to ensure that these employees are fairly treated by all members of their organizations. And managers and organizations that do not treat HIV-positive employees in a fair manner, as well as provide reasonable accommodations (e.g., allowing time off for doctor visits or to take medicine), risk costly lawsuits.

Socioeconomic Background

The term *socioeconomic background* typically refers to a combination of social class and income-related factors. From a management perspective, socioeconomic diversity (and, in particular, diversity in income levels) requires that managers be sensitive and responsive to the needs and concerns of individuals who might not be as well off as others. U.S. welfare reform in the mid- to late 1990s emphasized the need for single mothers and others receiving public assistance to join or return to the workforce. In conjunction with a strong economy, this led to record declines in the number of families, households, and children living below the poverty level, according to the 2000 U.S. census.[63] However, the economic downturn in the early 2000s, along with increased terrorism and the tragic collapse of the World Trade Center in New York City, resulted in domestic and international repercussions. These suggest that some past gains, which lifted families out of poverty, have been reversed. In a very strong economy, it is much easier for poor people with few skills to find jobs; in a weak economy, when companies lay off employees in hard times, people who need their incomes the most are unfortunately often the first to lose their jobs.[64]

Even with all the gains from the 1990s, the U.S. Census Bureau estimates that 6,825,399 families had incomes below the poverty level in 2000, with 3,581,475 of these families being headed by single women.[65] The Census Bureau relies on predetermined threshold income figures, based on family size and composition, adjusted annually for inflation, to determine the poverty level. Families whose income falls below the threshold level are considered poor.[66] For example, in 2000 a family of four with two children under 18 was considered poor if their annual income fell below $17,463.[67] When workers earn less than $10 or $15 per hour, it is often difficult, if not impossible, for them to meet their families' needs.[68] Moreover, increasing numbers of families are facing the challenge of finding suitable child care arrangements that enable the adults to work long hours and/or through the night to maintain an adequate income level. New information technology has led to more and more businesses operating 24 hours a day, creating real challenges for workers on the night shift, especially those with children.[69]

Hundreds of thousands of parents across the country are scrambling to find someone to care for their children while they are working the night shift, commuting several hours a day, working weekends and holidays, or putting in long hours on one or more jobs. This has led to the opening of day care facilities that operate around the clock as well as to managers seeking ways to provide such care for children of their employees. For example, the Children's Choice Learning Center in Las Vegas, Nevada, operates around the clock to accommodate employees working nights in neighboring casinos as cashiers and dealers as well as nurses, hospital workers, and call-center operators on the night shift. Randy Donahue, a security guard who works until midnight, picks his children up from the center when he gets off work; his wife is a nurse on the night shift. There currently are five Children's Choice Learning Centers in the United States operating 24 hours a day, and plans are under way to add seven more.[70]

Judy Harden, who focuses on families and child care issues for the United Workers Union, indicates that the demands families are facing necessitate around-the-clock and odd-hour child care options. Many parents simply do not have the choice of working at hours that allow them to take care of their children at night and/or on weekends, never mind when the children are sick.[71] In 1993, Ford Motor Company built an around-the-clock child care facility for 175 children of employees in Livonia, Michigan. However, a recent survey of child care needs indicates that many employees in other locations, such as Detroit and Kansas City, require such a facility. Some parents and psychologists feel uneasy having children separated from their families for so much time and particularly at night. Most agree that unfortunately for many families this is not a choice but a necessity.[72]

Socioeconomic diversity suggests that managers need to be sensitive and responsive to the needs and concerns of workers who may be less fortunate than themselves in terms of income and financial resources, child care and elder care options, housing opportunities, and existence of sources of social and family support. Moreover–and equally important–managers should try to provide such individuals with opportunities to learn, advance, and make meaningful contributions to their organizations while improving their economic well-being.

Sexual Orientation

Approximately 2 to 6 percent of the U.S. population is gay or lesbian.[73] While no federal law prohibits discrimination based on sexual orientation, 14 states have such laws, and a 1998 executive order prohibits sexual orientation discrimination in civilian federal offices. Moreover, an increasing number of organizations recognize the minority status of gay and lesbian employees, affirm their rights to fair and equal treatment, and provide benefits to same-sex partners of gay and lesbian employees. For example, 95 percent of Fortune 500 companies prohibit discrimination based on sexual orientation, and 70 percent of the Fortune 500 companies provide domestic-partner benefits.[74] As indicated in the following "Focus on Diversity," there are many steps that managers can take to ensure that sexual orientation is not used to unfairly discriminate among employees.

Focus on Diversity

Gays and Lesbians in the Workplace

While gays and lesbians have made great strides in terms of attaining fair treatment in the workplace, much more needs to be done. In a recent study conducted by Harris Interactive Inc. (a research firm) and Witeck Communications Inc. (a marketing firm), over 40 percent of gay and lesbian employees indicated that they had been unfairly treated, denied a promotion, or pushed to quit their jobs because of their sexual orientation.[75] Given continued harassment and discrimination despite the progress that has been made,[76] many gay and lesbian employees fear disclosing their sexual orientation in the workplace and thus live a life of secrecy. While there are a few openly gay top managers, such as David Geffen, cofounder of DreamWorks SKG and Allan Gilmour, vice chairman of Ford, many others choose not to disclose or discuss their personal lives, including long-term partners.[77]

Thus, it is not surprising that many managers are taking active steps to educate and train their employees in regard to issues of sexual orientation. S. C. Johnson & Sons, Inc., maker of Raid insecticide and Glade air fresheners in Racine, Wisconsin, provides mandatory training to its plant managers to overturn stereotypes, as does Eastman Kodak. Other organizations such as Lucent Technologies, Microsoft, and Southern California Edison send employees to seminars conducted at prominent business schools such as the Anderson School of Management at the University of California, Los Angeles. Companies like Raytheon, IBM, Eastman Kodak, and Lockheed Martin provide assistance to their gay and lesbian employees through gay and lesbian support groups.[78]

More generally, the presence of a gay, lesbian, bisexual, and transgender (GLBT) rights movement in the workplace is steadily increasing. From an individual employee perspective, sometimes these rights boil down to receiving the same kind of treatment as one's heterosexual co-workers. For example, when Daniel Kline applied to use United Parcel Service's Management Initiated Transfer to follow his partner of 27 years to another state, he was initially denied. This program allows employees to transfer to UPS offices in other states and retain their seniority when the employee's spouse accepts a job in another state. Kline's partner was transferred from United Airlines' office in San Francisco to its office in Chicago, and Kline was hoping to remain with UPS when he, too, moved to Chicago. After Kline took his case to the Lambda Legal Defense and Education Fund, a GLBT advocacy organization, and threatened legal action based on California's antidiscrimination laws, UPS reversed its position and allowed the transfer.[79]

Clearly, many highly qualified potential and current employees might happen to be gay or lesbian. An organization that does not welcome and support such employees not only is unfairly discriminating against this group but also is losing the contributions of valued potential employees. Additionally, an organization that discriminates against this group risks alienating customers. Fifteen million consumers are in the GLBT group in the United States, and according to research conducted by MarketResearch.com, their purchasing power is around $485 billion.[80]

Other Kinds of Diversity

There are other kinds of diversity that are important in organizations, critical for managers to deal with effectively, and also potential sources of unfair treatment. For example, organizations and teams need members with diverse backgrounds and experiences. This is clearly illustrated by the prevalence of cross-functional teams in organizations whose members might come from various departments such as marketing, production, finance, and sales (teams are covered in depth in Chapter 15). A team responsible for developing and introducing a new product, for example, often will need the expertise of employees not only from R&D and engineering but also from marketing, sales, production, and finance.

Other types of diversity can also affect how employees are treated in the workplace. For example, employees differ from each other in how attractive they are [based on the standards of the culture(s) in which an organization operates] and in terms of body weight. Whether individuals are attractive or thin or unattractive or overweight, in most cases, has no bearing on their job performance unless they have jobs in which physical appearance plays a role, such as modeling. Yet sometimes these physical sources of diversity end up influencing advancement rates and salaries. For example, a recent study published in the *American Journal of Public Health* found that highly educated obese women earned approximately 30 percent less per year than women who were not obese and men (regardless of whether or not the men were obese).[81] Clearly, managers need to ensure that all employees are treated fairly, regardless of their physical appearance.

Managers and the Effective Management of Diversity

The increasing diversity of the environment–which, in turn, increases the diversity of an organization's workforce–increases the challenges managers face in effectively managing diversity. Each of the eight kinds of diversity discussed above presents managers with a particular set of issues they need to appreciate before they can respond to them effectively. Understanding these issues is not always a simple matter, as many informed managers have discovered. Research on how different groups are currently treated and the unconscious biases that might adversely affect them is critical because it helps managers become aware of the many subtle and unobtrusive ways in which diverse employee groups can come to be treated unfairly over time. There are many more steps managers can take to become sensitive to the ongoing effects of diversity in their organizations, take advantage of all the contributions diverse employees can make, and prevent diverse employees from being unfairly treated.

Critical Managerial Roles

In each of their managerial roles (see Chapter 1), managers can either promote the effective management of diversity or derail such efforts; thus, they are critical to this process. For example, in their interpersonal roles, managers can convey that the effective management of diversity is a valued goal and objective (figurehead role), can serve as a role model and institute policies and procedures to ensure that diverse organizational members are treated fairly (leader role), and can enable diverse individuals and groups to coordinate their efforts and cooperate with each other both inside the organization and at the organization's boundaries (liaison role). In Table 5.2 (page 160) we summarize some of the ways in which managers can ensure that diversity is effectively managed as they perform their different roles.

Given the formal authority that managers have in organizations, they typically have more influence than rank-and-file employees. When managers commit to supporting diversity, as was true of Leonard Schaeffer and Mayor Menino in "A Manager's Challenge," their authority and positions of power and status influence other members of an organization to make a similar commitment.[82] Research on social influence supports such a link, as people are more likely to be influenced and persuaded by others who have high status.[83]

Table 5.2
Managerial Roles and the Effective Management of Diversity

Type of Role	Specific Role	Example
Interpersonal	Figurehead	Convey that the effective management of diversity is a valued goal and objective.
	Leader	Serve as a role model and institute policies and procedures to ensure that diverse members are treated fairly.
	Liaison	Enable diverse individuals to coordinate their efforts and cooperate with one another.
Informational	Monitor	Evaluate the extent to which diverse employees are being treated fairly.
	Disseminator	Inform employees about diversity policies and initiatives and the intolerance of discrimination.
	Spokesperson	Support diversity initiatives in the wider community and speak to diverse groups to interest them in career opportunities.
Decisional	Entrepreneur	Commit resources to develop new ways to effectively manage diversity and eliminate biases and discrimination.
	Disturbance handler	Take quick action to correct inequalities and curtail discriminatory behavior.
	Resource allocator	Allocate resources to support and encourage the effective management of diversity.
	Negotiator	Work with organizations (e.g., suppliers) and groups (e.g., labor unions) to support and encourage the effective management of diversity.

Moreover, when managers commit to diversity, their commitment legitimizes the diversity management efforts of others.[84] In addition, resources are devoted to such efforts and all members of an organization believe that their diversity-related efforts are supported and valued. Consistent with this reasoning, top-management commitment and rewards for the support of diversity are often cited as critical ingredients for the success of diversity management initiatives.[85] Additionally, seeing managers express confidence in the abilities and talents of diverse employees causes other organizational members to be similarly confident and helps to reduce any misconceived misgivings they may have as a result of ignorance or stereotypes.[86]

Another important reason that managers are so central to the effective management of diversity hinges on two factors. The first factor is that women, African-Americans, Hispanics, and other minorities often start out at a slight disadvantage due to the ways in which they are perceived by others in organizations, particularly in work settings where they are a numerical minority. As Virginia Valian, a psychologist at Hunter College who studies gender, indicates, "In most organizations women begin at a slight disadvantage. A woman does not walk into the room with the same status as an equivalent man, because she is less likely than a man to be viewed as a serious professional."[87]

The second factor is that research suggests slight differences in treatment can cumulate and result in major disparities over time. Even small differences–such as a very slight favorable bias toward men for promotions–can lead to major differences in the number of male and female managers over time.[88] Thus, while women and other minorities are sometimes advised not to make "a mountain out of a molehill" when they perceive they have been unfairly treated, research conducted by Valian and others suggests that molehills (i.e., slight differences in treatment based on irrelevant distinctions such as race, gender, or ethnicity) can turn into mountains over time (i.e., major disparities in important outcomes such as promotions) if they are ignored.[89] Once again, managers play a crucial role in ensuring that neither large nor small disparities in treatment and outcomes due to irrelevant distinctions such as race or ethnicity occur in organizations. Moreover, managers have the obligation, from both an ethical and a business perspective, to ensure that such disparities do not occur and are not tolerated in organizations.

The Ethical Imperative to Manage Diversity Effectively

Effectively managing diversity not only makes good business sense (which is discussed in the next section) but also is an ethical imperative in U.S. society. Two moral principles provide managers with guidance in their efforts to meet this imperative: distributive justice and procedural justice.

distributive justice
A moral principle calling for the distribution of pay raises, promotions, and other organizational resources to be based on meaningful contributions that individuals have made and not on personal characteristics over which they have no control.

DISTRIBUTIVE JUSTICE The principle of **distributive justice** dictates that the distribution of pay raises, promotions, job titles, interesting job assignments, office space, and other organizational resources among members of an organization should be fair. The distribution of these outcomes should be based on the meaningful contributions that individuals have made to the organization (such as time, effort, education, skills, abilities, and performance levels) and not on irrelevant personal characteristics over which individuals have no control (such as gender, race, or age).[90] Managers have an obligation to ensure that distributive justice exists in their organizations. This does not mean that all members of an organization receive identical or similar outcomes; rather, it means that members who receive more outcomes than others have made substantially higher or more significant contributions to the organization.

Is distributive justice common in organizations in corporate America? Probably the best way to answer this question is by saying that things are getting better. Fifty years ago, overt discrimination against women and minorities was not uncommon; today, organizations are inching closer toward the ideal of distributive justice. Statistics comparing the treatment of women and minorities with the treatment of other employees suggest that most managers would need to take a proactive approach to achieve distributive justice in their organizations.[91] For example, across occupations, women consistently earn less than men (see Table 5.3, page 162) according to data collected by the U.S. Bureau of Labor Statistics.[92] Even in occupations dominated by women, such as teacher assistants and elementary and secondary school teachers, men tend to earn more than women.[93]

In many countries, managers have not only an ethical obligation to strive to achieve distributive justice in their organizations but also a legal obligation to treat

Table 5.3
Weekly Salaries by Sex and Occupation

Occupation	Median Weekly Salaries: Men	Median Weekly Salaries: Women	Women's Salaries as a Percentage of Men's
Management	$1,172	$849	72
Business and finance	1,014	744	73
Computer and mathematics	1,130	906	80
Architecture and engineering	1,094	827	76
Life, physical, and social science	970	773	80
Community and social service	746	655	88
Law	1,480	796	54
Education, training, library	904	708	78
Art, entertainment, sports, media	837	648	77
Health care	1,002	770	77
Service	463	366	79
Sales and office work	658	502	76
Resources and construction	613	449	73
Production and transportation	570	407	71

Source: "Median Weekly Earnings of Full-Time Wage and Salary Workers by Selected Characteristics," www.bls.gov, May 1, 2004.

all employees fairly. They risk being sued by employees who believe that they are not being fairly treated. That is precisely what six African-American employees at Texaco did when they experienced racial bias and discrimination.[94]

procedural justice A moral principle calling for the use of fair procedures to determine how to distribute outcomes to organizational members.

PROCEDURAL JUSTICE The principle of **procedural justice** requires that managers use fair procedures to determine how to distribute outcomes to organizational members.[95] This principle applies to typical procedures such as appraising subordinates' performance, deciding who should receive a raise or a promotion, and deciding whom to lay off when an organization is forced to downsize. Procedural justice exists, for example, when managers (1) carefully appraise a subordinate's performance, (2) take into account any environmental obstacles to high performance beyond the subordinate's control, such as lack of supplies, machine breakdowns, or dwindling customer demand for a product, and (3) ignore irrelevant personal characteristics such as the subordinate's age or ethnicity. Like distributive justice, procedural justice is necessary not only to ensure ethical conduct but also to avoid costly lawsuits.

Effectively Managing Diversity Makes Good Business Sense

The diversity of organizational members can be a source of competitive advantage, helping an organization provide customers with better goods and services.[96] The variety of points of view and approaches to problems and opportunities that diverse employees provide can improve managerial decision making. Suppose the Budget Gourmet frozen-food company is trying to come up with some creative ideas for new frozen meals that will appeal to health-conscious, time-conscious customers tired of the same old frozen-food fare. Which group do you think is likely to come up with the most creative ideas: a group of white women with master's degrees in marketing from Yale University who grew up in upper-middle-class families in the Northeast or a racially mixed group of men and women who grew up in families with varying income levels in different parts of the country and attended a mix of business schools (New York University, Oklahoma State, University of Michigan, UCLA, Cornell University, Texas A&M University, and Iowa State)? Most people would agree that the diverse group is likely to come up with a wider range of creative ideas. Although this example is simplistic, it underscores one way in which diversity can lead to a competitive advantage.

Just as the workforce is becoming increasingly diverse, so too are the customers who buy an organization's goods or services. In an attempt to suit local customers' needs and tastes, managers of Target's chain of 623 discount stores vary the selection of products available in stores in different cities and regions. For example, the Target store in Phoenix, Arizona, stocks religious candles and Spanish-language diskettes and Disney videos to appeal to local Hispanic Catholics; the Target store in Scottsdale, Arizona, stocks in-line skates and bicycle baby trailers that appeal to well-to-do yuppies.[97] In some large cities such as Houston, Texas, Hispanic immigrants have created communities of businesses that cater to diverse customers, as highlighted in the following "Manager as a Person."

Manager as a Person

Creating a Business Through Sheer Determination

In Houston, Texas, there are over 500 businesses that have been founded by immigrants to serve diverse customers and clients.[98] Often, these immigrants arrived in the city with little else but their will and determination. Take the case of Jose Camarena, who started working at the age of 10 in Mexico City, came to the United States in 1978 with his wife. After working in restaurants in Chicago for a few years, Camarena decided in the early 1980s to move to Houston and open a restaurant.[99] Camarena realized there were actually few Mexican fast-food restaurants in the city, and that became the niche of his restaurant, Taqueria Arandas.[100] The restaurant was so popular that Camarena was able to open seven more restaurants within 10 years and now sells Taqueria Arandas franchises. Taqueria Arandas now has 27 franchised Taquerias as well as 2 seafood restaurants and 4 Arandas bakeries. As with Rodriguez, Camarena's belief in the value of hard work and his determination to succeed underlie the growth of his business. With a successful company earning $36 million in annual revenues and 900 employees, Camarena has not slowed down and continues to put in a full day's work. As he puts it, "I love to work . . . Lazy people, it doesn't go well for them."[101]

Similar success stories are found among other entrepreneurs in Houston who started businesses from scratch in Hispanic communities. Cesar Rodriguez, who arrived in Houston with his mother and brothers in 1973,

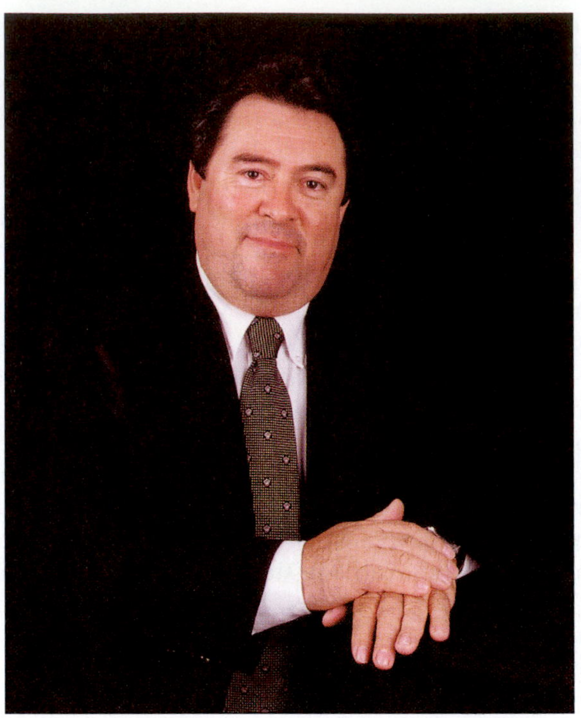

Jose Camarena's determination helped him create his successful Mexican fast-food restaurant, Taquerias Arandas.

lived in a run-down boarding house, and took whatever odd jobs he could find, ranging from cleaning offices to busing restaurant tables to help out his family.[102]

After a year of working at these jobs, Rodriguez received an income tax refund from the IRS for $600. Even though he didn't own a car or a home, he decided to use his tax refund to open a restaurant serving tacos, shrimp cocktails, margaritas, and other delicacies that appealed to his then mainly Hispanic customers. Doneraki, as the restaurant was called, grossed $1 million in sales its first year. Today, Doneraki operates four successful restaurants with combined revenues of about $12 million and 300 employees.[103] Moreover, its restaurants appeal to all kinds of customers in diverse neighborhoods. Rodriguez's success story illustrates how entrepreneurs and managers who are driven to succeed can overcome what might seem to others to be insurmountable odds.

Diverse members of an organization are likely to be attuned to what goods and services diverse segments of the market want and do not want. Major car companies, for example, are increasingly assigning women to their design teams to ensure that the needs and desires of female customers (a growing segment of the market) are taken into account in new car design.

For Darden Restaurants, the business case for diversity rests on market share and growth. Darden seeks to satisfy the needs and tastes of diverse customers by providing menus in Spanish in communities with large Hispanic populations.[104] Similarly, market share and growth and the identification of niche markets led Tracey Campbell to cater to travelers with disabilities.[105] She heads InnSeekers, a telephone and online listing resource for bed and breakfasts. Nikki Daruwala works for the Calvert Group in Bethesda, Maryland, a mutual fund that emphasizes social responsibility and diversity. She indicates that profit alone is more than enough of an incentive to effectively manage diversity. As she puts it, "You can look at an automaker. There are more women making decisions about car buying or home buying . . . $3.72 trillion per year are spent by women."[106]

Another way in which the effective management of diversity can positively affect profitability is that it increases retention of valued employees, which decreases the costs of hiring replacements for those who quit as well as ensures that all employees are highly motivated. In terms of retention, given the current legal environment, more and more organizations are attuned to the need to emphasize the importance of diversity in hiring. Once hired, if diverse employees think they are being unfairly treated, however, they will be likely to seek opportunities elsewhere. Thus, the recruiting of diverse employees has to be followed up by the ongoing effective management of diversity to retain these valued organizational members.

If diversity is not effectively managed and results in turnover rates being higher for members of certain groups who are not treated fairly, profitability will suffer on several counts. Not only are the future contributions of diverse employees lost when they quit, but the organization also has to bear the costs of hiring replacement workers. According to the Employment Management Association, on average it costs more than $10,000 to hire a new employee; other estimates are significantly higher. For example, Ernst & Young estimates it costs about $1,200,000 to replace 10 professionals, and the diversity consulting firm Hubbard & Hubbard estimates replacement costs average one-and-a-half times an employee's annual salary.[107] Moreover, additional costs from failing to effectively manage diversity stem from time lost due to the barriers diverse members of an organization perceive as thwarting their progress and advancement.[108]

Effectively managing diversity makes good business sense for another reason. More and more, managers and organizations concerned about diversity are insisting that their suppliers also support diversity. Managers of American Airlines, for example, recently announced that all the law firms they hire must submit quarterly reports indicating the extent to which diverse employees worked on the airline's account. Similarly, managers at Chrysler, Aetna Life & Casualty, and General Motors all consider information about the extent to which law firms support diversity when they are deciding which law firms will represent them.[109] Managers in the Teachers Insurance and Annuity Association–College Retirement Equities Fund (TIAA–CREF) are putting pressure on Nucor Corporation to add women and minorities to its board of directors, which currently consists entirely of white men. TIAA–CREF owns 912,900 shares in Nucor, and its managers believe that their heavy investment in Nucor gives them enough clout to bring diversity to the board of directors.[110]

Finally, from both a business and an ethical perspective, the effective management of diversity is necessary to avoid costly lawsuits such as those settled by Advantica (owner of the Denny's chain) and the Coca-Cola Company. Recently Coca-Cola settled a class-action suit brought by African-American employees, at a cost of $192 million. The damage such lawsuits cause goes beyond the monetary awards to the injured parties; it can tarnish a company's image. One positive outcome of Coca-Cola's recent settlement is the company's recognition of the need to commit additional resources to diversity management initiatives. In this regard, Coca-Cola is increasing its use of minority suppliers, instituting a formal mentoring program, and instituting days to celebrate diversity with its workforce.[111]

By now, it should be clear that effectively managing diversity is a necessity on both ethical and business grounds. This brings us to the question of why diversity presents managers and all of us with so many challenges–a question we address in the next section, on perception.

Perception

Most people tend to think that the decisions managers make in organizations and the actions they take are the result of some objective determination of the issues involved and the surrounding situation. However, each manager's interpretation of a situation or even of another person is precisely that–an interpretation. Nowhere are the effects of perception more likely to lead to different interpretations than in the area of diversity. This is because each person's interpretation of a situation, and subsequent response to it, is affected by his or her own age, race, gender, religion, socioeconomic status, capabilities, and sexual orientation. For example, different managers may see the same 21-year-old, black, male, gay, gifted and talented subordinate in different ways: One may see a creative maverick with a great future in the organization, while another may see a potential troublemaker who needs to be watched closely.

perception The process through which people select, organize, and interpret what they see, hear, touch, smell, and taste to give meaning and order to the world around them.

Perception is the process through which people select, organize, and interpret sensory input–what they see, hear, touch, smell, and taste–to give meaning and order to the world around them.[112] All decisions and actions that managers take are based on their subjective perceptions. When these perceptions are relatively accurate–close to the true nature of what is actually being perceived–good decisions are likely to be made and appropriate actions taken. Managers of fast-food restaurant chains such as McDonald's, Pizza Hut, and Wendy's accurately perceived that their customers were becoming more health-conscious in the 1980s and 1990s and added salad bars and low-fat entries to their menus. Managers at Kentucky Fried Chicken, Jack-in-the-Box, and Burger King took much longer to perceive this change in what customers wanted.

One reason why McDonald's is so successful is that its managers go to great lengths to make sure that their perceptions of what customers want are accurate. McDonald's has 4,700 restaurants outside the United States (including 1,070 in Japan, 694 in Canada, 550 in Britain, 535 in Germany, 411 in Australia, 314 in France, 23 in China, and 3 in Russia) that generate approximately $3.4 billion in annual revenues. Key to McDonald's success in these diverse markets are managers' efforts to perceive accurately a country's culture and taste in food and then to act on these perceptions. For instance, McDonald's serves veggie burgers in Holland and black currant shakes in Poland.[113]

From Poland's black currant shakes to Japan's new "Fish McDippers"—6 pieces of fried whitefish served w/ sweet chili sauce or tartar sauce—McDonald's managers have diversified the menu to suit international customer's varied tastes.

When managers' perceptions are relatively inaccurate, managers are likely to make bad decisions and take inappropriate actions, which hurt organizational effectiveness. Bad decisions concerning diversity for reasons of age, ethnicity, or sexual orientation include (1) not hiring qualified people, (2) failing to promote top-performing subordinates, who subsequently decide to take their skills to competing organizations, and (3) promoting poorly performing managers because they have the same "diversity profile" as the manager or managers making the decision.

Factors That Influence Managerial Perception

Several managers' perceptions of the same person, event, or situation are likely to differ because managers differ in personality, values, attitudes, and moods (see Chapter 3). Each of these factors can influence the way someone perceives a person or situation. An older middle manager who is high on openness to experience is likely to perceive the recruitment of able young managers as a positive learning opportunity; a similar middle manager who is low on openness to experience may perceive able younger subordinates as a threat. A manager who has high levels of job satisfaction and organizational commitment may perceive a job transfer to another department or geographic location that has very different employees (age, ethnicity, and so on) as an opportunity to learn and develop new skills. A dissatisfied, uncommitted manager may perceive the same transfer as a demotion.

schema An abstract knowledge structure that is stored in memory and makes possible the interpretation and organization of information about a person, event, or situation.

Managers' and all organizational members' perceptions about one another also are affected by their past experience and acquired knowledge about people, events, and situations–information that is organized into preexisting schemas. **Schemas** are abstract knowledge structures stored in memory that allow people to organize and interpret information about a person, an event, or a situation.[114] Once a person develops a schema for a kind of person or event, any newly encountered person or situation that is related to the schema activates it and information is processed in ways consistent with the information stored in the schema. Thus, people tend to perceive others by using the expectations or preconceived notions contained in their schemas.[115] Once again, these expectations are derived from past experience and knowledge.

People tend to pay attention to information that is consistent with their schemas and to ignore or discount inconsistent information. Thus, schemas tend to be reinforced and strengthened over time because the information attended to is seen as confirming the schemas. This also results in schemas being resistant to change.[116] This does not mean that schemas never change; if that were the case, people could never adapt to changing conditions and learn from their mistakes. Rather, it suggests that schemas are slow to change and that a considerable amount of contradictory information needs to be encountered for people to change their schemas.

Schemas, when they are relatively accurate depictions of the true nature of a person or situation, are functional because they help people make sense of the world around them. People are typically confronted with so much information that it is not possible to make sense of it without relying on schemas.

Schemas are dysfunctional when they are inaccurate because they cause managers and all members of an organization to perceive people and situations inaccurately and assume certain things that are not necessarily true. Recall from the opening case how some managers in law enforcement were guided by inaccurate schemas that led them to believe that women should not be promoted to top-management positions because of physical strength differences between men and women.

gender schemas Preconceived beliefs or ideas about the nature of men and women, their traits, attitudes, behaviors, and preferences.

Psychologist Virginia Valian refers to such inaccurate preconceived notions of men and women as gender schemas. **Gender schemas** are a person's preconceived notions about the nature of men and women, their traits, attitudes, behaviors, and preferences.[117] Research suggests that among white, middle-class Americans, the following gender schemas are prevalent: Men are action-oriented, assertive, independent, and task-focused; women are expressive, nurturing, and oriented toward and caring of other people.[118] Any schemas such as these–which assume a single visible characteristic such as one's sex causes a person to possess specific traits and tendencies–are bound to be inaccurate. For example, not all women are alike and not all men are alike, and there are many women who are more independent and task-focused than men. Gender schemas can be learned in childhood and are reinforced in a number of ways in society. For instance, while young girls may be encouraged by their parents to play with toy trucks and tools (stereotypically masculine toys), boys generally are not encouraged, and sometimes are actively discouraged, from playing with dolls (stereotypically feminine toys).[119] As children grow up, they learn that occupations dominated by men have higher status than occupations dominated by women.

Perception as a Determinant of Unfair Treatment

Even though most people would agree that distributive justice and procedural justice are desirable goals, diverse organizational members are sometimes treated unfairly, as previous examples illustrate. Why is this problem occurring? One important overarching reason is inaccurate perceptions. To the extent that managers and other members of an organization rely on inaccurate schemas such as gender schemas to guide their perceptions of each other, unfair treatment is likely to occur.

stereotype Simplistic and often inaccurate beliefs about the typical characteristics of particular groups of people.

Gender schemas are a kind of **stereotype,** simplistic and often inaccurate beliefs about the typical characteristics of particular groups of people. Stereotypes are usually based on a highly visible characteristic such as a person's age, gender, or race.[120] Managers who allow stereotypes to influence their perceptions assume erroneously that a person possesses a whole host of characteristics simply because the person happens to be an Asian woman, a white man, or a lesbian, for example. African-American men are often stereotyped as good athletes, Hispanic women as subservient.[121] Obviously, there is no reason to assume that every African-American man is a good athlete or that every Hispanic woman is subservient. Stereotypes, however, lead people to make such erroneous assumptions. A manager who accepts stereotypes might, for example, decide not to promote a highly capable Hispanic woman into a management position because the manager is certain that she will not be assertive enough to supervise others.

bias The systematic tendency to use information about others in ways that result in inaccurate perceptions.

Inaccurate perceptions leading to unfair treatment of diverse members of an organization also can be due to biases. **Biases** are systematic tendencies to use information about others in ways that result in inaccurate perceptions. Because of the way biases operate, people often are unaware that their perceptions of others are inaccurate. There are several types of biases.

The *similar-to-me effect* is the tendency to perceive others who are similar to ourselves more positively than we perceive people who are different.[122] The similar-to-me effect is summed up by the saying, "Birds of a feather flock together." It can lead to unfair treatment of diverse employees simply because they are different from the managers who are perceiving them, evaluating them, and making decisions that affect their future in the organization.

Managers (particularly top managers) are likely to be white men. Although these managers may endorse the principles of distributive and procedural justice, they may unintentionally fall into the trap of perceiving other white men more positively than they perceive women and minorities. This is the similar-to-me effect. Being aware of this bias as well as using objective information about employees' capabilities and performance as much as possible in decision making about job assignments, pay raises, promotions, and other outcomes can help managers avoid the similar-to-me effect.

Social status, a person's real or perceived position in a society or an organization, can be the source of another bias. The *social status effect* is the tendency to perceive individuals with high social status more positively than we perceive those with low social status. A high-status person may be perceived as smarter and more believable, capable, knowledgeable, and responsible than a low-status person, even in the absence of objective information about either person.

Imagine being introduced to two people at a company Christmas party. Both are white men in their late 30s, and you learn that one is a member of the company's top-management team and the other is a supervisor in the mailroom. From this information alone, you are likely to assume that the top manager is smarter, more capable, more responsible, and even more interesting than the mailroom supervisor. Because women and minorities have traditionally had lower social status than white men, the social status effect may lead some people to perceive women and minorities less positively than they perceive white men.

Have you ever stood out in a crowd? Maybe you were the only man in a group of women; or maybe you were dressed formally for a social gathering, and everyone else was in jeans. Salience (i.e., conspicuousness) is another source of bias. The *salience effect* is the tendency to focus attention on individuals who are conspicuously different from us. When people are salient, they often feel as though all eyes are watching them, and this perception is not too far off the mark. Salient individuals are more often the object of attention than are other members of a work group, for example. A manager who has six white subordinates and one Hispanic subordinate reporting to her may inadvertently pay more attention to the Hispanic in group meetings because of the salience effect.

Individuals who are salient are often perceived to be primarily responsible for outcomes and operations and are evaluated more extremely, in either a positive or a negative direction.[123] Thus, when the Hispanic subordinate does a good job on a project, she receives excessive praise, and when she misses a deadline, she is excessively chastised.

Overt Discrimination

overt discrimination Knowingly and willingly denying diverse individuals access to opportunities and outcomes in an organization.

Inaccurate schemas and perceptual biases can lead well-meaning managers and organizational members to unintentionally discriminate against others due to their inaccurate perceptions. On the other hand, **overt discrimination,** or knowingly and willingly denying diverse individuals access to opportunities and outcomes in an organization, is intentional and deliberate. Overt discrimination is not only unethical but also illegal. Unfortunately, just as some managers steal from their organizations, others engage in overt discrimination.

Overt discrimination is a clear violation of the principles of distributive and procedural justice. Moreover, when managers are charged with overt discrimination, costly lawsuits can ensue, as indicated in the following "Focus on Diversity."

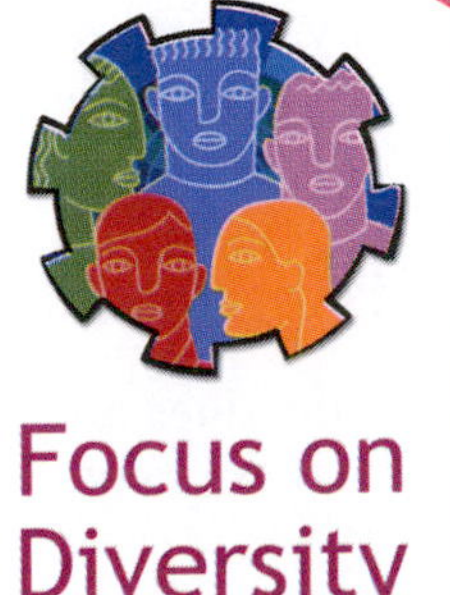

Focus on Diversity

Gender Discrimination at Wal-Mart

In June 2001, six Wal-Mart employees filed a class-action lawsuit against the retailer alleging widespread discrimination against women. In September 2002, additional female employees of Wal-Mart were added as plaintiffs in the case.[124] Potentially the largest discrimination lawsuit targeting a private employer, the suit claims that women are assigned to the lowest-level positions in Wal-Mart and have little chance of advancement.[125] In April 2004, the case advanced when the California Supreme Court denied a requested reconsideration of the class-action status of the case filed by an Alameda county judge.[126] The number of employees represented in the California case could be over 200,000. A case currently pending could potentially involve over 1 million former and current female Wal-Mart employees alleging sex discrimination in promotions and raises.[127]

While 72 percent of Wal-Mart employees are women, only about 33 percent of the managers at Wal-Mart are women. At Wal-Mart's main competitors, 56 percent of managers, on average, are women.[128] Kim Miller, a Wal-Mart sales associate and a party to the lawsuit, indicates that her performance was appraised positively; she received compliments from customers and was honored with the Employee of the Year Award. Yet she repeatedly was passed over for promotions during a nine-year period, and sometimes less qualified men received the promotions. Miller's complaints to managers fell on deaf ears, and she believes she was even retaliated against for complaining in the first place.[129] Edith Arana, another plaintiff in the case, witnessed her store manager refusing to interview women for department manager positions repeatedly for six years, voiced her concerns to Wal-Mart's complaint hotline, and then was retaliated against with a transfer to a less desirable job in the store.[130]

Stephanie Odle, another party to the lawsuit, commented, "I guess you could say I was Wal-Martized. . . . I gave up my nights, my days, my weekends, my holidays. Time and again the jobs I should have had were given to men."[131] According to Christine Kwapnoski, employed by Sam's Clubs since 1986, she was denied promotions to better positions in favor of less qualified men whom she then trained to be her own boss.[132] While specific women are listed in the lawsuit, they are seeking class-action status on behalf of hundreds of thousands of former and current female Wal-Mart employees; this would allow the plaintiffs to collect damages on their co-workers' behalf.[133] Joe Sellers, one of the lawyers for the women named in the suit, puts it this way, "Wal-Mart has operated the largest glass ceiling for its women employees in the country and we want to shatter it. . . . We want to dismantle the procedures and practices by which Wal-Mart has kept its female employees from getting promoted."[134] Wal-Mart has denied the charges, and it will be up to the courts to decide the ultimate outcome of this case.

How to Manage Diversity Effectively

Various kinds of barriers arise to managing diversity effectively in organizations. Some barriers have their origins in the person doing the perceiving; some, in the information and schemas that have built up over time concerning the person being perceived. To overcome these barriers and effectively manage diversity, managers (and other organizational members) must possess or develop certain attitudes and values and the skills needed to change other people's attitudes and values.

Steps in Managing Diversity Effectively

Managers can take a number of steps to change attitudes and values and promote the effective management of diversity. Here, we describe these steps, some of which we have referred to previously (see Table 5.4).

Table 5.4
Promoting the Effective Management of Diversity

- Secure top management commitment.
- Increase the accuracy of perceptions.
- Increase diversity awareness.
- Increase diversity skills.
- Encourage flexibility.
- Pay close attention to how employees are evaluated.
- Consider the numbers.
- Empower employees to challenge discriminatory behaviors, actions, and remarks.
- Reward employees for effectively managing diversity.
- Provide training utilizing a multipronged, ongoing approach.
- Encourage mentoring of diverse employees.

SECURE TOP-MANAGEMENT COMMITMENT As we mentioned earlier in the chapter, top management's commitment to diversity is crucial for the success of any diversity-related initiatives. Top managers need to develop the correct ethical values and performance or business-oriented attitudes that allow them to make appropriate use of their human resources.

STRIVE TO INCREASE THE ACCURACY OF PERCEPTIONS One aspect of developing the appropriate values and attitudes is to take steps to increase the accuracy of perceptions. Managers should consciously attempt to be open to other points of view and perspectives, seek them out, and encourage their subordinates to do the same.[135] Organizational members who are open to other perspectives put their own beliefs and knowledge to an important reality test and will be more inclined to modify or change them when necessary. Managers should not be afraid to change their views about a person, issue, or event; moreover, they should encourage their subordinates to be open to changing their views in the light of disconfirming evidence. Additionally, managers and all members of an organization should strive to avoid making snap judgments about people; rather, judgments should be made only when sufficient and relevant information has been gathered.[136]

INCREASE DIVERSITY AWARENESS It is natural for managers and other members of an organization to view other people from their own perspective, because their own feelings, thoughts, attitudes, and experiences guide their perceptions and interactions. The ability to appreciate diversity, however, requires that people become aware of other perspectives and the various attitudes and experiences of others. Many diversity awareness programs in organizations strive to increase managers' and workers' awareness of (1) their own attitudes, biases, and stereotypes and (2) the differing perspectives of diverse managers, subordinates, co-workers, and customers. Diversity awareness programs often have these goals:[137]

- Providing organizational members with accurate information about diversity.
- Uncovering personal biases and stereotypes.

- Assessing personal beliefs, attitudes, and values and learning about other points of view.
- Overturning inaccurate stereotypes and beliefs about different groups.
- Developing an atmosphere in which people feel free to share their differing perspectives and points of view.
- Improving understanding of others who are different from oneself.

Sometimes, simply taking the time to interact with someone who is different on some dimension can help to increase awareness. When employees and managers are at social functions or just having lunch with a co-worker, often the people they interact with are those they feel most comfortable with. If all members of an organization make an effort to interact with people they ordinarily would not, mutual understanding is likely to be enhanced.[138]

INCREASE DIVERSITY SKILLS Efforts to increase diversity skills focus on improving the way managers and their subordinates interact with each other and on improving their ability to work with different kinds of people.[139] An important issue here is being able to communicate with diverse employees. Diverse organizational members may have different styles of communication, may differ in their language fluency, may use words differently, may differ in the nonverbal signals they send through facial expression and body language, and may differ in the way they perceive and interpret information. Managers and their subordinates must learn to communicate effectively with one another if an organization is to take advantage of the skills and abilities of its diverse workforce. Educating organizational members about differences in ways of communicating is often a good starting point.

Organizational members should also feel comfortable enough to "clear the air" and solve communication difficulties and misunderstandings as they occur rather than letting problems grow and fester without acknowledgment.

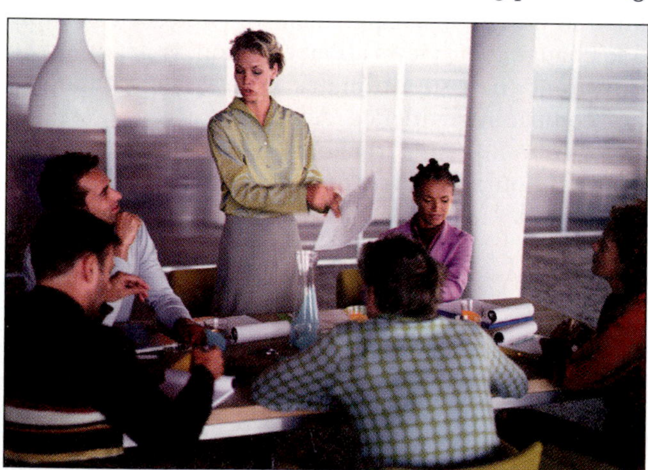

Managers and employees all have different communication styles. If an organization is to take advantage of the skills and abilities of a diverse workforce, organizational members must learn to communicate effectively with one another. Diversity education is a good place to start because it helps people gain a better understanding of how others may interpret certain kinds of comments.

Diversity education can help managers and subordinates gain a better understanding of how people may interpret certain kinds of comments. Diversity education also can help employees learn how to resolve misunderstandings.

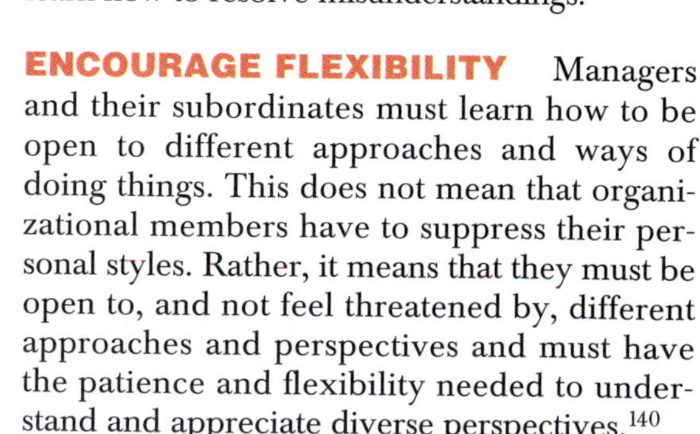

ENCOURAGE FLEXIBILITY Managers and their subordinates must learn how to be open to different approaches and ways of doing things. This does not mean that organizational members have to suppress their personal styles. Rather, it means that they must be open to, and not feel threatened by, different approaches and perspectives and must have the patience and flexibility needed to understand and appreciate diverse perspectives.[140]

To the extent it is feasible, managers should also be flexible enough to incorporate the differing needs of diverse employees. Earlier we mentioned that religious diversity suggests that people of certain religions might need time off for holidays that are traditionally workdays in the United States; managers need to anticipate and respond to such needs with flexibility (e.g., letting people skip the lunch hour so that they can leave work early). Moreover, flexible work hours, having the option to work from home, and cafeteria-style benefit plans (see Chapter 11) are just a few of the many ways in which managers can be responsive to the differing needs of diverse employees while enabling those employees to be effective contributors to an organization.

PAY CLOSE ATTENTION TO HOW ORGANIZATIONAL MEMBERS ARE EVALUATED Whenever feasible, it is desirable to rely on objective performance indicators (see Chapter 11) as they are less subject to bias. When objective indicators are not available or are inappropriate, managers should ensure that adequate time and attention are focused on the evaluation of employees' performance and that evaluators are held accountable for their evaluations.[141] Vague performance standards should be avoided.[142]

CONSIDER THE NUMBERS Looking at the numbers of members of different minority groups and women in various positions, at various levels in the hierarchy, in locations that differ in their desirability, and in any other relevant categorizations in an organization can provide managers with important information about potential problems and ways to rectify them, as it has done for many organizations such as Deloitte & Touche.[143] If members of certain groups are very under-represented in particular kinds of jobs or units, managers need to understand why this is the case and resolve any problems they might uncover.

EMPOWER EMPLOYEES TO CHALLENGE DISCRIMINATORY BEHAVIORS, ACTIONS, AND REMARKS When managers or employees witness another organizational member being unfairly treated, they should be encouraged to speak up and rectify the situation. Top managers can make this happen by creating an organizational culture (see Chapter 3) that has zero tolerance for discrimination. As part of such a culture, organizational members should feel empowered to challenge discriminatory behavior, whether the behavior is directed at them or they witness it being directed at another employee.[144]

REWARD EMPLOYEES FOR EFFECTIVELY MANAGING DIVERSITY If the effective management of diversity is a valued organizational objective, then employees should be rewarded for their contributions to this objective.[145] For example, after settling a major race discrimination lawsuit, Coca-Cola Company now ties managers' pay to their achievement of diversity goals. Other examples of organizations that link executive pay to achievement of diversity goals include American Express and Bayer Corporation.[146]

PROVIDE TRAINING UTILIZING A MULTIPRONGED, ONGOING APPROACH Many managers use a multipronged approach to increase diversity awareness and skills in their organizations; they use films and printed materials supplemented by experiential exercises to uncover hidden biases and stereotypes. Sometimes simply providing a forum for people to learn about and discuss their differing attitudes, values, and experiences can be a powerful means for increasing awareness. Also useful are role-plays that enact problems resulting from lack of awareness and indicate the increased understanding that comes from appreciating others' viewpoints. Accurate information and training experiences can debunk stereotypes. Group exercises, role-plays, and diversity-related experiences can help organizational members develop the skills they need to work effectively with a variety of people. Many organizations hire outside consultants to provide diversity training, in addition to utilizing their own in-house diversity experts.[147]

United Parcel Service (UPS), a package delivery company, developed an innovative community internship program to increase the diversity awareness and skills of its managers and, at the same time, benefit the wider community. Upper and middle managers participating in the program take one month off the job to be community interns. They work in community organizations helping people who in many instances are very different from themselves–such organizations include a detention center in McAllen, Texas, for Mexican immigrants; homeless shelters; AIDS centers; Head Start programs; migrant-farm-worker assistance groups; and groups aiming to halt the spread of drug abuse in inner cities. Approximately 40 managers a year are community interns at an annual cost to UPS of $400,000.

Since the program began in 1968, 800 managers have been community interns. Interacting with and helping diverse people enhances the interns' awareness of diversity because they experience it firsthand. Bill Cox, a UPS division manager who spent a month in the McAllen detention center, summed up his experience of diversity: "You've got these [thousands of] migrant workers down in McAllen . . . and they don't want what you have. All they want is an opportunity to earn what you have. That's a fundamental change in understanding that only comes from spending time with these people."[148]

Many managers who complete the UPS community internship program have superior diversity skills as a result of their experiences. During their internships, they learn about different cultures and approaches to work and life; they learn to interact effectively with people with whom they ordinarily do not come into contact; and they are forced to learn flexibility because of the dramatic difference between their role at the internship sites and their role as managers at UPS.

ENCOURAGE MENTORING OF DIVERSE EMPLOYEES Unfortunately, African-Americans and other minorities continue to be less likely to attain high-level positions in their organizations, and for those who do, the climb up the corporate ladder typically takes longer than it does for white men. David Thomas, a professor at the Harvard Business School, has studied the careers of minorities in corporate America. One of his major conclusions is that mentoring is very important for minorities, most of whom have reached high levels in their organizations by having a solid network of mentors and contacts.[149] **Mentoring** is a process by which an experienced member of an organization (the mentor) provides advice and guidance to a less experienced member (the protégé) and helps the less experienced member learn how to advance in the organization and in his or her career.

mentoring A process by which an experienced member of an organization (the mentor) provides advice and guidance to a less experienced member (the protégé) and helps the less experienced member learn how to advance in the organization and in his or her career.

According to Thomas, effective mentoring is more than providing instruction, offering advice, helping build skills, and sharing technical expertise. Of course, these aspects of mentoring are important and necessary. However, equally important is developing a high-quality, close, and supportive relationship with the protégé. Emotional bonds between a mentor and a protégé can enable a protégé, for example, to express fears and concerns, and sometimes even reluctance to follow a mentor's advice. The mentor can then help the protégé build his or her confidence and feel comfortable engaging in unfamiliar work behaviors.[150]

Pat Carmichael, a senior vice president at JP Morgan Chase who happens to be an African-American woman, has mentored hundreds of protégés throughout her career and exemplifies effective mentoring.[151] She encourages her protégés to seek out difficult assignments and feedback from their supervisors. She also helps her protégés build networks of contacts and has a very extensive network herself. She serves as both a coach and a counselor to her protégés and encourages them to seek out opportunities to address their weaknesses and broaden their horizons.[152]

Sexual Harassment

Sexual harassment seriously damages both the people who are harassed and the reputation of the organization in which it occurs. It also can cost organizations large amounts of money. In 1995, for example, Chevron Corporation agreed to pay $2.2 million to settle a sexual harassment lawsuit filed by four women who worked at the Chevron Information Technology Company in San Ramon, California. One woman involved in the suit said that she had received violent pornographic material through the company mail. Another, an electrical engineer, said that she had been asked to bring pornographic videos to Chevron workers at an Alaska drill site.[153] More recently, TWA settled a lawsuit to the tune of $2.6 million that alleged that female employees were sexually harassed at JFK International Airport in New York. According to the EEOC, not only was sexual harassment tolerated at TWA, but also company officials did little to curtail it when it was brought to their attention.[154]

Unfortunately, the events at Chevron and TWA are not isolated incidents.[155] Sixty percent of the 607 women surveyed by the National Association for Female Executives indicated that they had experienced some form of sexual harassment.[156] Sexual harassment victims can be women or men, and their harassers do not necessarily have to be of the opposite sex.[157] However, women are the most frequent victims of sexual harassment, particularly those in male-dominated occupations or those who occupy positions stereotypically associated with certain gender relationships, such as a female secretary reporting to a male boss. Though it occurs less frequently, men can also be victims of sexual harassment. For instance, several male employees at Jenny Craig filed a lawsuit claiming that they were subject to lewd and inappropriate comments from female co-workers and managers.[158] Sexual harassment is not only unethical; it is also illegal. Managers have an ethical obligation to ensure that they, their co-workers, and their subordinates never engage in sexual harassment, even unintentionally.

quid pro quo sexual harassment Asking for or forcing an employee to perform sexual favors in exchange for some reward or to avoid negative consequences.

hostile work environment sexual harassment Telling lewd jokes, displaying pornography, making sexually oriented remarks about someone's personal appearance, and other sex-related actions that make the work environment unpleasant.

Forms of Sexual Harassment

There are two basic forms of sexual harassment: quid pro quo sexual harassment and hostile work environment sexual harassment. **Quid pro quo sexual harassment** occurs when a harasser asks or forces an employee to perform sexual favors to keep a job, receive a promotion, receive a raise, obtain some other work-related opportunity, or avoid receiving negative consequences such as demotion or dismissal.[159] This "Sleep with me, honey, or you're fired" form of harassment is the more extreme type and leaves no doubt in anyone's mind that sexual harassment has taken place.[160]

Hostile work environment sexual harassment is more subtle. It occurs when organizational members are faced with an intimidating, hostile, or offensive work environment because of their sex.[161] Lewd jokes, sexually oriented comments or innuendos, vulgar language, displays of pornography, displays or distribution of sexually oriented objects, and sexually oriented remarks about one's physical appearance are examples of hostile work environment sexual harassment.[162] A hostile work environment interferes with organizational members' ability to perform their jobs effectively and has been deemed illegal by the courts. Managers who engage in hostile work environment harassment or allow others to do so risk costly lawsuits for their organizations, as indicated in the following "Ethics in Action."

Ethics in Action

Sexual Harassment at FedEx and DaimlerChrysler

In February 2004, a federal jury awarded Marion Schwab $3.24 million after deliberating on her sexual harassment case against Federal Express.[163] Schwab was the only female tractor-trailer driver at the FedEx serving the Harrisburg International Airport vicinity in Middletown, Pennsylvania, from 1997 to 2000. During that period, she was the target of sexual innuendos, was given inferior work assignments, and was the brunt of derogatory comments about her appearance and the role of women in society. On five occasions, the brakes on her truck were tampered with. The federal EEOC sued FedEx, and Schwab was part of the suit. FedEx plans to appeal the decision.[164]

FedEx is not alone in facing sexual harassment awards in the millions of dollars. In 1999, a Wayne County circuit court jury in Detroit, Michigan, awarded a DaimlerChrysler employee, Linda Gilbert, $21 million after hearing her sexual harassment case.[165] Gilbert, the first female millwright at the Jefferson North Plant in Michigan when she was hired in 1992, testified that she was subject to abusive comments, called names, had her work sabotaged, and had pornographic drawings and cartoons of her displayed in the workplace, sometimes even in the presence of her supervisors. Gilbert endured sexual harassment of this sort on almost a daily basis over a period of years. Once, a co-worker urinated on a chair she had used. She complained to managers on several occasions, but the harassment continued.[166]

DaimlerChrysler appealed the $21 million judgment for Gilbert. In 2002, a Michigan Court of Appeals upheld the verdict and judgment against DaimlerChrysler. In 2004, the Michigan Supreme Court was considering the case. If the judgment is upheld, it will be among the largest sexual harassment settlements. Gilbert still works at the plant, and hopefully her efforts have made the plant a less stressful workplace for female employees.[167]

Steps Managers Can Take to Eradicate Sexual Harassment

Managers have an ethical obligation to eradicate sexual harassment in their organizations. There are many ways to accomplish this objective. Here are four initial steps that managers can take to deal with the problem.[168]

- *Develop and clearly communicate a sexual harassment policy endorsed by top management.* This policy should include prohibitions against both quid pro quo and hostile work environment sexual harassment. It should contain (1) examples of types of behavior that are unacceptable, (2) a procedure for employees to use to report instances of harassment, (3) a discussion of the disciplinary actions that will be taken when harassment has taken place, and (4) a commitment to educate and train organizational members about sexual harassment.
- *Use a fair complaint procedure to investigate charges of sexual harassment.* Such a procedure should (1) be managed by a neutral third party, (2) ensure that complaints are dealt with promptly and thoroughly, (3) protect and fairly treat victims, and (4) ensure that alleged harassers are fairly treated.
- *When it has been determined that sexual harassment has taken place, take corrective actions as soon as possible.* These actions can vary depending on the severity of the harassment. When harassment is extensive, prolonged over a period of time, of a quid pro quo nature, or severely objectionable in some other manner, corrective action may include firing the harasser.
- *Provide sexual harassment education and training to all organizational members, including managers.* The majority of Fortune 500 firms currently provide this education and training for their employees. Managers at Du Pont, for example, developed Du Pont's "A Matter of Respect" program to help educate employees about sexual harassment and eliminate its occurrence. The program includes a four-hour workshop in which participants are given information that defines sexual harassment, sets forth the company's policy against it, and explains how to report complaints and access a 24-hour hotline. Participants watch video clips showing actual instances of harassment. One clip shows a saleswoman having dinner with a male client who, after much negotiating, seems about to give her company his business when he suddenly suggests that they continue their conversation in his hotel room. The saleswoman is confused about what to do. Will she be reprimanded if she says no and the deal is lost? After watching a video, participants discuss what they have seen, why the behavior is inappropriate, and what organizations can do to alleviate the problem.[169] Throughout the program, managers stress to employees that they do not have to tolerate sexual harassment or get involved in situations in which harassment is likely to occur.

Barry S. Roberts and Richard A. Mann, experts on business law and authors of several books on the topic, suggest a number of additional factors that managers and all members of an organization need to keep in mind about sexual harassment:[170]

- Every sexual harassment charge should be taken very seriously.
- Employees who go along with unwanted sexual attention in the workplace can be sexual harassment victims.
- Employees sometimes wait before they file complaints of sexual harassment.
- An organization's sexual harassment policy should be communicated to each new employee and reviewed with current employees on a periodic basis.
- Suppliers and customers need to be familiar with an organization's sexual harassment policy.

- Managers should provide employees with alternative ways to report incidents of sexual harassment.
- Employees who report sexual harassment must have their rights protected; this includes being protected from any potential retaliation.
- Allegations of sexual harassment should be kept confidential; those accused of harassment should have their rights protected.
- Investigations of harassment charges and any resultant disciplinary actions need to proceed in a very timely manner.
- Managers must protect employees from sexual harassment from any third-party employees they may interact with in the course of performing their jobs, such as suppliers or customers.[171]

Summary and Review

THE INCREASING DIVERSITY OF THE WORKFORCE AND THE ENVIRONMENT Diversity is dissimilarity or differences among people. Diversity is a pressing concern for managers and organizations for business and ethical reasons. There are multiple forms of diversity such as age, gender, race and ethnicity, religion, capabilities/disabilities, socioeconomic background, sexual orientation, and physical appearance.

MANAGERS AND THE EFFECTIVE MANAGEMENT OF DIVERSITY Both the workforce and the organizational environment are increasingly diverse, and effectively managing this diversity is an essential component of management. In each of their managerial roles, managers can encourage the effective management of diversity, which is both an ethical and a business imperative.

PERCEPTION Perception is the process through which people select, organize, and interpret sensory input to give meaning and order to the world around them. It is inherently subjective. Schemas guide perception; when schemas are based on a single visible characteristic such as race or gender, they are stereotypes and highly inaccurate, leading to unfair treatment. Unfair treatment also can result from biases and overt discrimination.

HOW TO MANAGE DIVERSITY EFFECTIVELY There are a number of steps that managers can take to effectively manage diversity. The effective management of diversity is an ongoing process that requires frequent monitoring.

SEXUAL HARASSMENT Two forms of sexual harassment are quid pro quo sexual harassment and hostile work environment sexual harassment. Steps that managers can take to eradicate sexual harassment include development and communication of a sexual harassment policy endorsed by top management, use of fair complaint procedures, prompt corrective action when harassment occurs, and sexual harassment training and education.

Management in Action

Topics for Discussion and Action

Discussion

1. Discuss why violations of the principles of distributive and procedural justice continue to occur in modern organizations. What can managers do to uphold these principles in their organizations?
2. Why do workers who test positive for HIV sometimes get discriminated against?
3. Why would some employees resent accommodations made for employees with disabilities that are dictated by the Americans with Disabilities Act?
4. Discuss the ways in which schemas can be functional and dysfunctional.
5. Discuss an occasion when you may have been treated unfairly because of stereotypical thinking. What stereotypes were applied to you? How did they result in your being treated unfairly?
6. How does the similar-to-me effect influence your own behavior and decisions?
7. Why is mentoring particularly important for minorities?
8. Why is it important to consider the numbers of different groups of employees at various levels in an organization's hierarchy?
9. Think about a situation in which you would have benefited from mentoring but a mentor was not available. What could you have done to try to get the help of a mentor in this situation?

Action

10. Choose a Fortune 500 company not mentioned in the chapter. Conduct research to determine what steps this organization has taken to effectively manage diversity and eliminate sexual harassment.

Building Management Skills

Solving Diversity-Related Problems

Think about the last time that you (1) were treated unfairly because you differed from a decision maker on a particular dimension of diversity or (2) observed someone else being treated unfairly because that person differed from a decision maker on a particular dimension of diversity. Then answer these questions:

1. Why do you think the decision maker acted unfairly in this situation?
2. In what ways, if any, were biases, stereotypes, or overt discrimination involved in this situation?
3. Was the decision maker aware that he or she was acting unfairly?
4. What could you or the person who was treated unfairly have done to improve matters and rectify the injustice on the spot?
5. Was any sexual harassment involved in this situation? If so, what kind was it?
6. If you had authority over the decision maker (e.g., if you were his or her manager or supervisor), what steps would you take to ensure that the decision maker no longer treated diverse individuals unfairly?

Managing Ethically

Some companies require that their employees work very long hours and travel extensively. Employees with young children, employees taking care of elderly relatives, and employees who have interests outside the workplace sometimes find that their careers are jeopardized if they try to work more reasonable hours or limit their work-related travel. Some of these employees feel that it is unethical for their manager to expect so much of them in the workplace and not understand their needs as parents and caregivers.

Questions

1. Either individually or in a group, think about the ethical implications of requiring long hours and extensive amounts of travel for some jobs.
2. What obligations do you think managers and companies have to enable employees to have a balanced life and meet nonwork needs and demands?

Small Group Breakout Exercise

Determining if a Problem Exists

Form groups of three or four people, and appoint one member as the spokesperson who will communicate your findings to the whole class when called on by the instructor. Then discuss the following scenario.

You and your partners own and manage a local chain of restaurants, with moderate to expensive prices, that are open for lunch and dinner during the week and for dinner on weekends. Your staff is diverse, and you believe that you are effectively managing diversity. Yet on visits to the different restaurants you have noticed that your African-American employees tend to congregate together and communicate mainly with each other. The same is true for your Hispanic employees and your white employees. You are meeting with your partners today to discuss this observation.

1. Discuss why the patterns of communication that you observed might be occurring in your restaurants.
2. Discuss whether your observation reflects an underlying problem. If so, why? If not, why not?
3. Discuss whether you should address this issue with your staff and in your restaurants. If so, how and why? If not, why not?

Exploring the World Wide Web

Go to the U.S. government Web sites that deal with employment issues, diversity, and sexual harassment, such as the Web sites of the Equal Employment Opportunity Commission (EEOC) and the Bureau of Labor Statistics. After reviewing these Web sites, develop a list of tips to help managers effectively manage diversity and avoid costly lawsuits.

Be the Manager

You are Maria Herrera and have been recently promoted to the position of director of financial analysis for a medium-size consumer goods firm. During your first few weeks on the job, you took the time to have lunch with each of your subordinates to try to get to know them better. You have 12 direct reports who are junior and senior financial analysts who support different product lines. Susan Epstein, one of the female financial analysts you had lunch with, made the following statement, "I'm so glad we finally have a woman in charge. Now, hopefully things will get better around here." You pressed Epstein to elaborate, but she clammed up. She indicated that she didn't want to unnecessarily bias you and that the problems were pretty self-evident. In fact, Epstein was surprised that you didn't know what she was talking about and jokingly mentioned that perhaps you should spend some time undercover, observing her group and their interactions with others.

You spoke with your supervisor and the former director who had been promoted and had volunteered to be on call if you had any questions. Neither man knew of any diversity-related issues in your group. In fact, your supervisor's response was, "We've got a lot of problems, but fortunately that's not one of them." What are you going to do to address this issue?

Additional Activities on the Build Your Management Skills DVD

- **Test Your Knowledge:** (1) Comparing Affirmative Action, Valuing Diversity, and Managing Diversity; (2) Mentoring; and (3) International Cultural Diversity
- **Self-Assessment:** Appreciating and Valuing Diversity
- **Manager's Hot Seat:** Office Romance: Groping for Answers

BusinessWeek Case in the News

Hispanic Nation

Maria Velazquez was born in a dingy hospital on the U.S.-Mexican border and has been straddling the two nations ever since. The 36-year-old daughter of a bracero, a Mexican migrant who tended California strawberry and lettuce fields in the 1960s, she spent her first nine years like a nomad, crossing the border with her family each summer to follow her father to work. Then her parents and their six children settled down in a Chicago barrio, where Maria learned English in the local public school and met Carlos Velazquez, who had immigrated from Mexico as a teenager. The two married in 1984, when Maria was 17, and relocated to nearby Cicero, Ill. Her parents returned to their homeland the next year with five younger kids.

The Velazquezes speak fluent English and cherish their middle-class foothold in America. Maria and Carlos each earn about $20,000 a year as a school administrator and a graveyard foreman, respectively, and they own a simple three-bedroom home. But they remain wedded to their native language and culture. Spanish is the language at home, even for their five boys ages 6 to 18. The kids speak to each other and their friends in English flecked with "dude" and "man," but in Cicero, where 77% of the 86,000 residents are Hispanic, Spanish dominates.

The older boys snack at local *taquerias* when they don't eat at home, where Maria's cooking runs to dishes like chicken mole and enchiladas. The family reads and watches TV in Spanish and English. The eldest, Jesse, is a freshman at nearby Morton College and dreams of becoming a state trooper; his girlfriend is also Mexican-American. "It's important that they know where they're from, that they're connected to their roots," says Maria, who bounced between Spanish and English while speaking to *BusinessWeek.* She tries to take the kids to visit her parents in the tiny Mexican town of Valle de Guadalupe at least once a year. "It gives them a good base to start from."

The Velazquezes, with their mixed cultural loyalties, are at the center of America's new demographic bulge. Baby boomers, move over—the *bebé* boomers are coming. They are 30 million strong, including some 8 million illegal immigrants—bilingual, bicultural, mostly younger Hispanics who will drive growth in the U.S. population and workforce as far out as statisticians can project (charts). Coming from across Latin America, but predominantly Mexico, and with high birth rates, these immigrants are creating what experts are calling a "tamale in the snake," a huge cohort of kindergarten to thirtysomething Hispanics created by the sheer velocity of their population growth—3% a year, vs. 0.8% for everyone else.

It's not just that Latinos, as many prefer to be called, officially passed African Americans last year to become the nation's largest minority. Their numbers are so great that, like the post-war baby boomers before them, the Latino Generation is becoming a driving force in the economy, politics, and culture.

Cultural Clout

It amounts to no less than a shift in the nation's center of gravity. Hispanics made up half of all new workers in the past decade, a trend that will lift them from roughly 12% of the workforce today to nearly 25% two generations from now. Despite low family incomes, which at $33,000 a year lag the national average of $42,000, Hispanics' soaring buying power increasingly influences the food Americans eat, the clothes they buy, and the cars they drive. Companies are scrambling to revamp products and marketing to reach the fastest-growing consumer group. Latino flavors are seeping into mainstream culture, too. With Hispanic youth a majority of the under-18 set, or close to it, in cities such as Los Angeles, Miami, and San Antonio, what's hip there is spreading into suburbia, much the way rap exploded out of black neighborhoods in the late 1980s. . . .

The U.S. has never faced demographic change quite like this before. Certainly, the Latino boom brings a welcome charge to the economy at a time when others' population growth has slowed to a crawl. Without a steady supply of new workers and consumers, a graying U.S. might see a long-term slowdown along the lines of aging Japan, says former Housing and Urban Development chief Henry Cisneros, who now builds homes in Hispanic-rich markets such as San Antonio. "Here we have this younger, hard-working Latino population whose best working years are still ahead," he says.

Already, Latinos are a key catalyst of economic growth. Their disposable income has jumped 29% since 2001, to $652 billion last year, double the pace of the rest of the population according to the Selig Center for Economic Growth at the University of Georgia. Similarly, the ranks of Latino entrepreneurs has jumped by 30% since 1998, calculates the Internal Revenue Service. "The impact of Hispanics is huge, especially since they're the fastest-growing demographic," says Merrill Lynch & Co. Vice-President Carlos Vaquero, himself a Mexican immigrant based in Houston. Vaquero oversees part of the company's 350-person Hispanic unit, which is hiring 100 mostly bilingual financial advisers this year and which generated $1 billion worth of new business nationwide last year, double its goal.

Yet the rise of a minority group this distinct requires major adjustments, as well. Already, Hispanics are spurring U.S. institutions to accommodate a second linguistic group. The Labor Dept. and Social Security Administration are hiring more Spanish-language administrators to cope with the surge in Spanish speakers in the workforce. Politicians, too, increasingly reach out to Hispanics in their own language.

What's not yet clear is whether Hispanic social cohesion will be so strong as to actually challenge the idea of the American melting pot. At the extreme, ardent assimilationists worry that the spread of Spanish eventually could prompt Congress to recognize it as an official second language, much as French is in Canada today. Some even predict a Quebec-style Latino dominance in states such as Texas and California that will encourage separatism, a view expressed in a recent book called *Mexifornia: A State of Becoming* by Victor Davis Hanson, a history professor at California State University at Fresno. These views have recently been echoed by Harvard University political scientist Samuel P. Huntington in a forthcoming book, *Who Are We.*

These critics argue that legions of poorly educated non-English speakers undermine the U.S. economy. Although the steady influx of low-skilled workers helps keep America's gardens tended and floors cleaned, those workers also exert downward pressure on wages across the lower end of the pay structure. Already, this is causing friction with African Americans, who see their jobs and pay being hit. "How are we going to compete in a global market when 50% of our fastest-growing group doesn't graduate from high school?" demands former Colorado Governor Richard D. Lamm, who now co-directs a public policy center at the University of Denver.

Still, many experts think it's more likely that the U.S. will find a new model, more salad bowl than melting pot, that accommodates a Latino subgroup without major upheaval. "America has to learn to live with diversity—the change in population, in [Spanish-language] media, in immigration," says Andrew Erlich, the founder of Erlich Transcultural Consultants Inc. in North Hollywood, Calif. Hispanics aren't so much assimilating as acculturating—acquiring a new culture while retaining their original one—says Felipe Korzenny, a professor of Hispanic marketing at Florida State University.

It boils down to this: How much will Hispanics change America, and how much will America change them? Throughout the country's history, successive waves of immigrants eventually surrendered their native languages and cultures and melted into the middle class. It didn't always happen right away. During the great European migrations of the 1800s, Germans settled in an area stretching from Pennsylvania to Minnesota. They had their own schools, newspapers, and businesses, and spoke German, says Demetrios G. Papademetriou, co-founder of the Migration Policy Institute in Washington. But in a few generations, their kids spoke only English and embraced American aspirations and habits.

Hispanics may be different, and not just because many are nonwhites. True, Maria Velazquez worries that her boys may lose their Spanish and urges them to speak it more. Even so, Hispanics today may have more choice than other immigrant groups to remain within their culture. With national TV networks such as Univision Communications Inc. and hundreds of mostly Spanish-speaking enclaves like Cicero, Hispanics may find it practical to remain bilingual. Today, 78% of U.S. Latinos speak Spanish, even if they also know English, according to the Census Bureau.

Back and Forth

The 21 million Mexicans among them also have something else no other immigrant group has had: They're a car ride away from their home country. Many routinely journey back and forth, allowing them to maintain ties that Europeans never could. The dual identities are reinforced by the constant influx of new Latino immigrants—roughly 400,000 a year, the highest flow in U.S. history. The steady stream of newcomers will likely keep the foreign-born, who typically speak mostly or only Spanish at one-third of the U.S. Hispanic population for several decades. Their presence means that "Spanish is constantly refreshed, which is one of the key contrasts with what people think of as the melting pot," says Roberto Suro, director of the Pew Hispanic Center, a Latino research group in Washington.

A slow pace of assimilation is likely to hurt Hispanics themselves the most, especially poor immigrants who show up with no English and few skills. Latinos have long lagged in U.S. schools, in part because many families remain cloistered in Spanish-speaking neighborhoods. Their strong work ethics can compound the problem by propelling many young Latinos into the workforce before they finish high school. So while the Hispanic high-school-graduation rate has climbed 12 percentage points since 1980, to 57%, that's still woefully short of the 88% for non-Hispanic whites and 80% for African Americans.

Meld into the Mainstream

The failure to develop skills leaves many Hispanics trapped in low-wage service jobs that offer few avenues for advancement. Incomes may not catch up anytime soon, either, certainly not for the millions of undocumented Hispanics. Most of these, from Mexican street-corner day laborers in Los Angeles to Guatemalan poultry-plant workers in North Carolina, toil in the underbelly of the U.S. economy. Many low-wage Hispanics would fare better economically if they moved out of the barrios and assimilated into U.S. society. Most probably face less racism than African Americans, since Latinos are a diverse ethnic and linguistic group comprising every nationality from Argentinians, who have a strong European heritage, to Dominicans, with their large black population. Even so, the pull of a common language may keep many in a country apart.

Certainly immigrants often head for a place where they can get support from fellow citizens, or even former neighbors. Some 90% of immigrants from Tonatico, a small town 100 miles south of Mexico City, head for Waukegan, Ill., joining 5,000 Tonaticans already there. In Miami, of course, Cubans dominate. "Miami has Hispanic banks, Hispanic law firms, Hispanic hospitals, so you can more or less conduct your entire life in Spanish here," says Leopoldo E. Guzman, 57. He came to the U.S. from Cuba at 15 and turned a Columbia University degree into a job at Lazard Frères & Co. before founding investmant bank Guzman & Co. . . .

It's still possible that Cicero's Latino children will follow the path of so many other immigrants and move out into non-Hispanic neighborhoods. If they do, they, or at least their children, will likely all but abandon Spanish, gradually marry non-Hispanics, and meld into the mainstream.

But many researchers and academics say that's not likely for many

Hispanics. In fact, a study of assimilation and other factors shows that while the number of Hispanics who prefer to speak mostly Spanish has dipped in recent years as the children of immigrants grow up with English, there has been no increase in those who prefer only English. Instead, the HispanTelligence study found that the group speaking both languages has climbed six percentage points since 1995, to 63%, and is likely to jump to 67% in 2010.

The trend to acculturate rather than assimilate is even more stark among Latino youth. Today, 97% of Mexican kids whose parents are immigrants and 76% of other Hispanic immigrant children know Spanish, even as nearly 90% also speak English very well, according to a decade-long study by University of California at Irvine sociologist Rubén G. Rumbaut. More striking, those Latino kids keep their native language at four times the rate of Filipino, Vietnamese, or Chinese children of immigrants. "Before, immigrants tried to become Americans as soon as possible," says Sergio Bendixen, founder of Bendixen & Associates, a polling firm in Coral Gables, Fla., that specializes in Hispanics. "Now, it's the opposite."

Selling in Spanish

In its eagerness to tap the exploding Hispanic market, Corporate America itself is helping to reinforce Hispanics' bicultural preferences. Last year, Procter & Gamble Co. spent $90 million on advertising directed at Latinos for 12 products such as Crest and Tide—10% of its ad budget for those brands and a 28% hike in just a year. Sure, P&G has been marketing to Hispanics for decades, but spending took off after 2000, when the company set up a 65-person bilingual team to target Hispanics. Now, P&G tailors everything from detergent to toothpaste to Latino tastes. Last year, it added a third scent to Gain detergent called "white-water fresh" after finding that 57% of Hispanics like to smell their purchases. Now, Gain's sales growth is double-digit in the Hispanic market, outpacing general U.S. sales. "Hispanics are a cornerstone of our growth in North America," says Graciela Eleta, vice-president of P&G's multicultural team in Puerto Rico.

Other companies are making similar assumptions. In 2002, Cypress (Calif.)-based PacifiCare Health Systems Inc. hired Russell A. Bennett, a longtime Mexico City resident, to help target Hispanics. He soon found that they were already 20% of PacifiCare's 3 million policyholders. So Bennett's new unit, Latino Health Solutions, began marketing health insurance in Spanish, directing Hispanics to Spanish-speaking doctors, and translating documents into Spanish for Hispanic workers. "We knew we had to remake the entire company, linguistically and culturally, to deal with this market," says Bennett.

A few companies are even going all-Spanish. After local Hispanic merchants stole much of its business in a Houston neighborhood that became 85% Latino, Kroger Co., the nation's No. 1 grocery chain, spent $1.8 million last year to convert the 59,000-sq.ft. store into an all-Hispanic *supermercados.* Now, Spanish-language signs welcome customers, and catfish and banana leaves line the aisles. Across the country, Kroger has expanded its private-label Buena Comida line from the standard rice and beans to 105 different items.

As the ranks of Spanish speakers swell, Spanish-language media are transforming from a niche market into a stand-alone industry. Ad revenues on Spanish-language TV should climb by 16% this year, more than other media segments, according to TNS Media Intelligence/CMR. The audience of Univision, the No. 1 Spanish-language media conglomerate in the U.S., has soared by 44% since 2001, and by 146% in the 18- to 34-year-old group. Many viewers have come from English-language networks, whose audiences have declined in that period.

In fact, Univision tried to reach out to assimilated Hispanics a few years ago by putting English-language programs on its cable channel Galavision. They bombed, says Univision President Ray Rodriguez, so he switched back to Spanish-only in 2002—and 18- to 34-year-old viewership shot up by 95% that year. "We do what the networks don't, and that's devote a lot of our show to what interests the Latino community," says Univision news anchor Jorge Ramos. . . .

For more than 200 years, the nation has succeeded in weaving the foreign-born into the fabric of U.S. society, incorporating strands of new cultures along the way. With their huge numbers, Hispanics are adding all kinds of new influences. Cinco de Mayo has joined St. Patrick's Day as a public celebration in some neighborhoods, and burritos are everyday fare. More and more, Americans hablan Español. Will Hispanics be absorbed just as other waves of immigrants were? It's possible, but more likely they will continue to straddle two worlds, figuring out ways to remain Hispanic even as they become Americans.

—With Ronald Grover, Arlene Weintraub, and Christopher Palmeri in Los Angeles, Mara Der Hovanesian in New York, Michael Eidam in Atlanta, and bureau reports

Questions

1. What are the implications of the influx of Hispanics for diversity in the United States?
2. What are the costs and benefits for Hispanics of trying to retain their own cultures while assimilating into the U.S. culture?
3. Is the notion of the United States as a "melting pot" outdated? Why or why not?
4. To what extent does increasing globalization mean more multiculturalism and more multilingual citizens in a variety of countries, including the United States?

BusinessWeek Case in the News

Shifting Work Offshore? Outsourcer Beware

Like a lot of companies, Intentia International, a $430 million business-software maker with operations in Stockholm and Palo Alto, Calif., was looking for ways to cut costs. So two years ago, it farmed out a software-programming project to a small outfit in India, expecting to cut expenses by 40%. But the savings never materialized. The main reason: The code the Indians delivered was riddled with errors. Intentia's own engineers had to redo it from scratch. "Indian companies are very aggressive," says Linus Parker, president of U.S. subsidiary Intentia America Inc. However, leaders of this Indian company, which he would not name, "overstated their technical skills."

These days, it's all the rage among corporations to shift a wide array of computer-programming and customer-service operations to low-cost countries. They expect to cut their labor costs 25% to 75% by using workers in India, China, and the Philippines. But as Intentia's experience shows, these shifts overseas carry risks that need to be considered along with the potential rewards. Shoddy quality, security snafus, and poor customer service often wipe out any benefits.

Until recently, the downside of "offshoring" wasn't clear. But recently published studies by Forrester Research Inc. and Gartner Inc. suggest that the practice shouldn't be undertaken lightly. Gartner says that based on a survey of 219 clients who outsource projects offshore and domestically, it expects half of such projects undertaken in 2003 to fail to deliver anticipated savings. The main cause of problems, according to analysis, is poor project management by the companies shipping work overseas. "It's all about how you monitor," says Dale L. Fuller, CEO of Borland Software Corp. in Scotts Valley, Calif.

There are still plenty of good reasons to shift some tasks offshore. In addition to low labor costs, companies can tap into a skilled workforce that in many cases is just as effective if not more so than in-house staff. Indian programming, for instance, is fast reaching U.S. levels. A June, 2003, survey of 104 software projects by the Center for eBusiness at Massachusetts Institute of Technology found that the median Indian project had just 10% more bugs than comparable U.S. projects. So it's not a matter of whether to send work offshore but rather under what circumstances and how to minimize risks.

Choose Carefully

Figuring out what tasks to move overseas is a critical first step. Jobs that involve repetition and are predictable work best. Any job that requires strong English-language skills, deep knowledge of U.S. accounting rules or law, or think-on-your-feet decision-making, probably won't fly. Nemo Azamian, senior vice-president for customer service at Gateway Inc., says Gateway does not send business customers to its Indian call center because they require a more nuanced level of communication than many offshore companies may be able to provide. "No matter how hard you try to Americanize a non-American, it's just not the same as talking to someone in Salt Lake City," he says.

Once you've decided to send work offshore, picking a reliable partner is the next key step. Most analysts say the largest providers, such as India's Infosys Technologies Ltd., generally do quality work. But smaller companies that have jumped into the business recently may be riskier. Sunil Mehta, vice-president of NASSCOM, the leading Indian technology trade group, concedes there are differences in the quality of Indian tech shops. "You have to do due diligence on the vendor," he says. That means checking the company's customer references, financial health, and software-certification levels.

Companies that have done extensive offshoring say it's best to start with a small project. That cautious approach saved Brookfield (Conn.) Web-hosting company Web.com when it ran into trouble after farming out some of its customer service to 24/7 Customer, based in Bangalore, India. Hundreds of customers began leaving, complaining that service reps didn't understand the technology. It could have been worse. Web.com had handed over only night and weekend service calls. When Web.com pulled the plug last summer, it took just eight weeks to hire and train U.S. staff. 24/7 Customer blames Web.com for the problems. "It's a very small company," says CEO P. V. Kannan. "they did not have well-defined processes."

Security is also a thorny issue. It's simply harder to safeguard projects handled by other companies thousands of miles away. One reason is differing legal systems and values. India, for instance, has the world's 16th-highest piracy rate. Outright theft can also be a problem. Last year, after SolidWorks Corp., a software maker in Concord, Mass., outsourced programming to India-based Geometric Software Solutions Co., a Geometric employee allegedly stole SolidWorks' intellectual property and tried to sell it to the company's rivals. The FBI helped Indian authorities make an arrest, and the programmer is awaiting trial.

Despite the theft, Solidworks continues to send work offshore. It even stuck with Geometric, which beefed up security and says it wants to make amends. "The efficiencies are so compelling that we're not willing to give [offshoring] up," says SolidWorks counsel Holly Stratford. For SolidWorks and other American companies under pressure to cut costs, the trick is learning to manage the shift overseas closely. If they don't, they'd better brace themselves for some nasty—and costly—surprises.

Questions

1. What are the advantages and disadvantages of outsourcing work offshore?
2. What kinds of tasks might be appropriate to outsource offshore? What kinds of tasks might be inappropriate to outsource? Why?
3. When considering outsourcing, what factors do managers need to take into account?
4. Do you think outsourcing work offshore will increase in popularity or decrease? Why?

Source: S. E. Ante, "Shifting Work Offshore? Outsourcer Beware." Reprinted from the January 12, 2004, issue of *BusinessWeek* by special permission.

CHAPTER

6 Managing in the Global Environment

Learning Objectives

After studying this chapter, you should be able to:

- Explain why the ability to perceive, interpret, and respond appropriately to the organizational environment is crucial for managerial success.
- Identify the main forces in a global organization's task and general environments, and describe the challenges that each force presents to managers.
- Explain why the global environment is becoming more open and competitive and why barriers to the global transfer of goods and services are falling, increasing the opportunities, complexities, challenges, and threats that managers face.

A Manager's Challenge

Nestlé's Global Food Empire

Why is managing the global environment so complex today?

Nestle's Web site invites visitors to browse its extensive product line.

Nestlé is the world's largest food company, with over $50 billion in annual sales, 224,000 employees, and 500 factories in 80 countries. In 2004, it made and sold over 8,000 food products, including such popular brands as Kit-Kat chocolate bars, Taster's Choice coffee, Carnation Instant milk, and Stouffer's Foods. At its corporate headquarters in Vevey, Switzerland, CEO Peter Brabeck-Latmathe, who has been in charge since 1997, is responsible for boosting Nestlé's global performance. He has faced many challenges.[1]

Brabeck has been working to increase Nestlé's revenues and profits by entering attractive markets in both developed and emerging nations. He is continuing the global expansion that Nestlé began in the 1990s, when, for example, it bought the U.S. food companies Carnation and Buitoni Pasta, the British chocolate maker Rowntree, the French bottled-water company Perrier, and the Mexican food maker Ortega. Under Brabeck, Nestlé has spent $18 billion to acquire U.S. companies Ralston Purina, Dreyer's Ice-cream, and Chef America. Brabeck intends not only to develop these food brands in the United States but also to modify their products to suit the tastes of customers in countries around the world. He is particularly anxious to enter emerging markets such as those in eastern Europe and Asia to take advantage of the enormous numbers of potential new customers in these regions. In this way Nestlé can leverage its well-known products and brand image around the world to drive up its performance.

Increasing global revenues from increased product sales is only the first leg of Brabeck's global business model, however. He is also anxious to increase Nestlé's operating efficiency and reduce the cost of managing its global operations. As you can imagine, with 224,000 employees and 500 factories the costs of organizing Nestlé's global activities are enormous. Brabeck benchmarked its operating costs to those of competitors such as Kraft Foods and Unilever and found Nestlé's costs were significantly higher than theirs. Brabeck has cut the workforce by 15 percent, closed 114 factories, and reduced operating costs by over 10 percent. He plans to make more sizable cuts in the next five years.

As another way to reduce global operating costs, Nestlé is investing $1.8 billion to install a companywide global information system to link all its companies to the corporate headquarters in Vevey and to their global suppliers. Brabeck's goal is to automate and integrate all of Nestlé's operations from purchasing through manufacturing, distribution, and marketing. Nestlé began its overhaul by signing a $200 million contract with SAP, the world's leading enterprise management software supplier. It will use the SAP software to monitor its purchasing activities around the globe to ensure it is getting the lowest-priced and highest-quality inputs possible. Nestlé is also using the IT both to reduce the number of its global suppliers and to negotiate more favorable supply contracts with them—moves that should result in a significant drop in purchasing costs. To improve the efficiency of its purchasing and retailing functions, Nestlé has developed e-business Web sites where it lists the detailed specifications of the inputs it requires from suppliers.

Brabeck hopes that the new IT system will result in an increased flow of information that will allow Nestlé to capitalize on what has always been its main source of competitive advantage: superior innovation. In 1886 Henri Nestlé, a pharmacist living in Vevey, invented an infant formula made from cow's milk and wheat flour that could be used as a substitute for mother's milk. Since then the company he founded has been a pioneer in food product innovation. One of his company's later innovations was Nescafe instant coffee, introduced in 1938 and still the best-selling brand in the world today. Brabeck's goal is to use Nestlé's new IT system to share information between its global food divisions and thus enhance their ability to innovate a flow of new and improved products for markets around the world.

Brabeck's global vision for Nestlé is therefore driven by three main goals: (1) expand Nestlé's range of products and offer them to new and existing customers in countries throughout the world; (2) find lower-cost ways to make and sell these products; and (3) speed up Nestlé's product innovation by leveraging its expertise across its food businesses to create more attractive food products that will increase its global market share. If his plan works, then Brabeck will be well on the way to making Nestlé not only the largest but also the most profitable global food company.

Overview

Top managers of a global company like Nestlé are always operating in an environment where they are competing with other companies for scarce and valuable resources. Managers of companies large and small have concluded that in order to survive in the 21st century most organizations must become **global organizations,** organizations that operate and compete not only domestically, at home, but also globally, in countries around the world. Operating in a global environment is uncertain and unpredictable because it is complex and constantly changing.

global organization An organization that operates and competes in more than one country.

If organizations are to adapt to this changing environment, their managers must learn to understand the forces that operate in it and how these forces give rise to opportunities and threats. In this chapter, we examine why the environment, both domestically and globally, has become more open, vibrant, and competitive. We examine how forces in the task and general environments affect global organizations and their managers. By the end of this chapter, you will appreciate the changes that have been taking place in the environment and understand why it is important for managers to develop a global perspective as they strive to increase organizational efficiency and effectiveness.

What Is the Organizational Environment?

organizational environment The set of forces and conditions that operate beyond an organization's boundaries but affect a manager's ability to acquire and utilize resources.

The **organizational environment** is a set of forces and conditions outside the organization's boundaries that have the potential to affect the way the organization operates.[2] These forces change over time and thus present managers with *opportunities* and *threats*. Changes in the environment, such as the introduction of new technology or the opening of global markets, create opportunities for managers to obtain resources or enter new markets and thereby strengthen their organizations. In contrast, the rise of new competitors, a global economic recession, or an oil shortage poses threats that can devastate an organization if managers are unable to obtain resources or sell the organization's goods and services. The quality of managers' understanding of organizational environment forces and their ability to respond appropriately to those forces, such as Brabeck's plan for Nestlé, are critical factors affecting organizational performance.

In this chapter we explore the nature of these forces and consider how managers can respond to them. To identify opportunities and threats caused by forces in the organizational environment, it is helpful for managers to distinguish between the *task environment* and the more encompassing *general environment* (see Figure 6.1, page 192).

task environment The set of forces and conditions that originate with suppliers, distributors, customers, and competitors and affect an organization's ability to obtain inputs and dispose of its outputs because they influence managers on a daily basis.

general environment The wide-ranging economic, technological, sociocultural, demographic, political and legal, and global forces that affect an organization and its task environment.

The **task environment** is the set of forces and conditions that originate with suppliers, distributors, customers, and competitors; these forces and conditions affect an organization's ability to obtain inputs and dispose of its outputs. The task environment contains the forces that have the most *immediate* and *direct* effect on managers because they pressure and influence managers on a daily basis. When managers turn on the radio or television, arrive at their offices in the morning, open their mail, or look at their computer screens, they are likely to learn about problems facing them because of changing conditions in their organization's task environment.

The **general environment** includes the wide-ranging economic, technological, sociocultural, demographic, political and legal, and global forces that affect the organization and its task environment. For the individual manager, opportunities and threats resulting from changes in the general environment are often more difficult to identify and respond to than are events in the task environment. However, changes in these forces can have major impacts on managers and their organizations.

The Task Environment

Forces in the task environment result from the actions of suppliers, distributors, customers, and competitors (see Figure 6.1). These four groups affect a manager's ability to obtain resources and dispose of outputs on a daily, weekly, and monthly basis and thus have a significant impact on short-term decision making.

Suppliers

suppliers Individuals and organizations that provide an organization with the input resources that it needs to produce goods and services.

Suppliers are the individuals and companies that provide an organization with the input resources (such as raw materials, component parts, or employees) that it needs to produce goods and services. In return, the supplier receives compensation for those goods and services. An important aspect of a manager's job is to ensure a reliable supply of input resources.

Figure 6.1
Forces in the Organizational Environment

Take Dell Computer, for example, the company we focused on in Chapter 1. Dell has many suppliers of component parts such as microprocessors (Intel and AMD) and disk drives (Quantum and Seagate Technologies). It also has suppliers of preinstalled software, including the operating system (Microsoft) and specific applications software (IBM, Oracle, and America Online). Dell's providers of capital, such as banks and financial institutions, are also important suppliers. Cisco Systems and Oracle are important providers of Internet hardware and software for dot-coms.

Dell has several suppliers of labor. One source is the educational institutions that train future Dell employees and therefore provide the company with skilled workers. Another is trade unions, organizations that represent employee interests and can control the supply of labor by exercising the right of unionized workers to strike. Unions also can influence the terms and conditions under which labor is employed. Dell's workers are not unionized; when layoffs became necessary due to an economic slowdown in the early 2000s, Dell had few problems in laying off workers to reduce costs. In organizations and industries where unions are very strong, however, an important part of a manager's job is negotiating and administering agreements with unions and their representatives.

Changes in the nature, numbers, or types of any supplier result in forces that produce opportunities and threats to which managers must respond if their organizations are to prosper. For example, a major supplier-related threat that confronts managers arises when suppliers' bargaining position is so strong that they can raise the prices of the inputs they supply to the organization. A supplier's bargaining position is especially strong when (1) the supplier is the sole source of an input and (2) the input is vital to the organization.[3] For example, for 17 years G. D. Searle was the sole supplier of NutraSweet, the artificial sweetener used in most diet soft drinks. Not only was NutraSweet an important ingredient in diet soft drinks, but it also was one for which there was no acceptable substitute (saccharin and other artificial sweeteners raised health concerns). Searle earned its privileged position because it invented and held the patent for NutraSweet. Patents prohibit other organizations from introducing competing products for 17 years. In 1992, Searle's patent expired, and many companies began to produce products similar to NutraSweet. Prior to 1992, Searle was able to demand a high price for NutraSweet, charging twice as much as the price of an equivalent amount of sugar. Paying that price raised the costs of soft-drink manufacturers, including Coca-Cola and PepsiCo, which had no alternative but to buy the product.[4] Today, NutraSweet is still the artificial sweetener of choice, but soft-drink companies pay much less for it.

In contrast, when an organization has many suppliers for a particular input, it is in a relatively strong bargaining position with those suppliers and can demand low-cost, high-quality inputs from them. Often, an organization can use its power with suppliers to force them to reduce their prices, as Dell frequently does.

Dell, for example, is constantly searching for global low-cost suppliers to keep its PC prices competitive. At a global level, managers have the opportunity to buy products from foreign suppliers or to become their own suppliers and manufacture their own products abroad. It is important that managers recognize the opportunities and threats associated with managing the global supply chain. On the one hand, gaining access to low-cost products made abroad represents an opportunity for U.S companies to lower their input costs. On the other hand, managers who fail to utilize low-cost foreign suppliers create a threat and put their organizations at a competitive disadvantage.[5] Levi Strauss, for example, was slow to realize that it could not compete with the low-priced jeans sold by Wal-Mart and other retailers, and it was eventually forced to close almost all of its U.S. jean factories and utilize low-cost foreign suppliers to keep the price of its jeans competitive. Now it sells its low-priced jeans in Wal-Mart! The downside to global outsourcing is, of course, the loss of millions of U.S. jobs, an issue we have discussed in previous chapters.

A common problem facing managers of large global companies such as Ford, Procter & Gamble, and IBM is managing the development of a global network of suppliers that will allow their companies to keep costs down and quality high. For example, the building of Boeing's newest jet airliner, the 777, required 132,500 engineered parts produced around the world by 545 suppliers.[6] While Boeing makes the majority of these parts, eight Japanese suppliers make parts for the 777's fuselage, doors, and wings; a Singapore supplier makes the doors for the plane's forward landing gear; and three Italian suppliers manufacture wing flaps. Boeing's rationale for buying so many inputs from foreign suppliers is that these suppliers are the best in the world at performing their particular activity and doing business with them helps Boeing to produce a high-quality final product, a vital requirement given the need for aircraft safety and reliability.[7]

The purchasing activities of global companies have become increasingly complicated as a result of the development of a whole range of skills and competences in different countries around the world. It is clearly in their interests to search out the lowest-cost, best-quality suppliers no matter where they may be. Also, the Internet makes it possible for companies to coordinate complicated, arm's-length exchanges involving the purchasing of inputs and the disposal of outputs.

global outsourcing The purchase of inputs from foreign suppliers or the production of inputs abroad to lower production costs and improve product quality or design.

Global outsourcing is the process by which organizations purchase inputs from other companies or produce inputs themselves throughout the world to lower their production costs and improve the quality or design of their products.[8] To take advantage of national differences in the cost and quality of resources such as labor or raw materials, GM might build its own engines in one country, transmissions in another, and brakes in a third and buy other components from hundreds of global suppliers. Trade expert Robert Reich once calculated that of the $20,000 that customers pay GM for a Pontiac Le Mans, about $6,000 goes to South Korea, where the Le Mans is assembled; $3,500, to Japan for advanced components such as engines, transaxles, and electronics; $1,500, to Germany, where the Le Mans was designed; $800, to Taiwan, Singapore, and Japan for small components; $500, to Britain for advertising and marketing services; and about $100, to Ireland for data-processing services. The remaining $7,000 goes to GM–and to the lawyers, bankers, and insurance agents that GM retains in the United States.[9]

Is the Le Mans a U.S. product? Yes, but it is also a Korean product, a Japanese product, and a German product. Today, such global exchanges are becoming so complex that specialized organizations are emerging to help manage global organizations' supply chains, that is, the flow of inputs necessary to produce a product. One example is Li & Fung, profiled below in "Managing Globally."

Managing Globally

Global Supply Chain Management

Finding the foreign suppliers that offer the lowest-priced and highest-quality products is an important task facing the managers of global organizations. Since these suppliers are located in thousands of cities in many countries around the world finding them is a difficult business. Often, global companies use the services of foreign intermediaries or brokers, located near these suppliers, to find the one that best meets their input requirements. Li & Fung, now run by brothers Victor and William Fung, is one of the brokers that has helped hundreds of global companies to locate suitable foreign suppliers, especially suppliers in mainland China.[10]

In the 2000s, however, managing global companies' supply chains became a more complicated task. To reduce costs, foreign suppliers were increasingly *specializing* in just one part of the task of producing a product. For example, in the past, a company such as Target might have negotiated with a foreign supplier to manufacture 1 million units of some particular shirt at a certain cost per unit. But with specialization, Target might find it can reduce the costs of producing the shirt even further by splitting apart the operations involved in its production and having *different* foreign suppliers, often in *different* countries, perform each operation. For example, to get the lowest cost per unit, rather than negotiating with a single foreign supplier over the price of making a particular shirt, Target might first negotiate with a yarn manufacturer in Vietnam to make the yarn; then ship the yarn to a Chinese supplier to weave it into cloth; and then ship the cloth to several different factories in Malaysia and the Philippines to cut the fabric and sew the shirts. Then, another foreign company might take responsibility for packaging and shipping the shirts to wherever in the world they are required. Because

Clothing companies like Target keep their prices low by locating in countries abroad where labor costs are low.

a company such as Target has thousands of different clothing products under production, and they change all the time, the problems of managing such a supply chain to get the full cost savings from global expansion are clearly difficult and costly.

Li & Fung capitalized on this opportunity. Realizing that many global companies do not have the time or expertise to find such specialized low-price suppliers, its founders moved quickly to provide such a service. Li & Fung employs 3,600 agents who travel across 37 countries to locate new suppliers and inspect existing suppliers to find new ways to help its global clients get lower prices or higher-quality products. Global companies are happy to outsource their supply chain management to Li & Fung because they realize significant cost savings. Even though they pay a hefty fee to Li & Fung, they avoid the costs of employing their own agents. As the complexity of supply chain management continues to increase, more and more companies like Li & Fung are appearing.

Distributors

distributors Organizations that help other organizations sell their goods or services to customers.

Distributors are organizations that help other organizations sell their goods or services to customers. The decisions that managers make about how to distribute products to customers can have important effects on organizational performance. For example, package delivery companies such as Federal Express, UPS, and the U.S. Postal Service became vital distributors for the millions of items bought online and shipped to customers by dot-com companies.

The changing nature of distributors and distribution methods can bring opportunities and threats for managers. If distributors become so large and powerful that they can control customers' access to a particular organization's goods and services, they can threaten the organization by demanding that it reduce the prices of its goods and services.[11] For example, the huge retail distributor Wal-Mart controls its suppliers' access to a great number of customers and thus often demands that its suppliers reduce their prices. If an organization such as Procter & Gamble refuses to reduce its prices, Wal-Mart might respond by buying products only from Procter & Gamble's competitors–companies such as Unilever and Dial. In 2004, Wal-Mart announced that by 2006 all its suppliers must adopt a new wireless scanning technology that will reduce its cost of distributing products to its stores or it will stop doing business with them.[12]

In contrast, the power of a distributor may be weakened if there are many options. This has been the experience of the three broadcast television networks–ABC, NBC, and CBS. Their ability to demand lower prices from the producers of television programs has been weakened. The presence of hundreds of new cable television channels has reduced the three networks' clout by decreasing their share of the viewing audience to less than 40 percent in 2004, down from more than 90 percent a decade ago. Similarly, because there are many package delivery companies, the dot-coms would not really be threatened if one delivery firm tried to increase its prices; they could simply switch delivery companies.

Another force that creates opportunities and threats for global managers is the nature of a country's distribution system. For example, consider how Japan's systems of distributing Japanese-made products caused problems for Toys 'R' Us managers when they were seeking to establish a chain of stores in Japan. Traditionally, Japanese manufacturers sold their products only by means of wholesalers with which they had developed long-term business relationships. Because the wholesalers added their own price markup, the price Toys 'R' Us had to pay for Japanese toys increased, and this thwarted the U.S. company's attempt to establish a competitive advantage in Japan based on price discounting. To keep its costs low, Toys 'R' Us insisted on buying directly from Japanese manufacturers, but the manufacturers refused.

This standoff was finally broken by Japan's deep recession in the early 1990s. Faced with slumping orders, computer-game maker Nintendo reversed its earlier decision and agreed to sell merchandise directly to Toys 'R' Us. Soon a host of other Japanese toy companies followed Nintendo's lead. With these major problems solved, average sales in Toys 'R' Us's Japanese stores were between $15 million and $20 million a year, roughly double the sales per store in the United States. As Toys 'R' Us discovered in Japan, the traditional means by which goods and services are distributed and sold to customers can present challenges to managers of organizations pursuing international expansion. Managers must identify the hidden problems surrounding the distribution and sale of goods and services–such as anticompetitive government regulations, discussed later–in order to discover hidden threats early and find ways to overcome them before significant resources are invested.

Customers

customers Individuals and groups that buy the goods and services that an organization produces.

Customers are the individuals and groups that buy the goods and services that an organization produces. For example, Dell's customers can be segmented into several distinct groups: (1) individuals who purchase PCs for home use, (2) small companies, (3) large companies, (4) government agencies, and (5) educational institutions. Changes in the number and types of customers or changes in customers' tastes and needs result in opportunities and threats. An organization's success depends on its response to customers. In the PC industry, customers are demanding lower prices and increased multimedia capability, and PC companies must respond to the changing types and needs of customers.[13] A school, too, must adapt to the changing needs of its customers. For example, if more Spanish-speaking students enroll, additional classes in English as a second language may need to be scheduled. A manager's ability to identify an organization's main customers and produce the goods and services they want is a crucial factor affecting organizational and managerial success.

The most obvious opportunity associated with expanding into the global environment is the prospect of selling goods and services to new customers, as Amazon.com's CEO Jeff Bezos discovered when he began to start operating in many countries abroad. Similarly, Accenture and Cap Gemini, two large consulting companies, have established operations throughout the world and recruit and train thousands of foreign consultants to serve the needs of customers in a wide variety of countries.

Today, once-distinct national markets are merging into one huge global marketplace where the same basic product can be sold to customers worldwide. This consolidation is occurring both for consumer goods and for business products and has created enormous opportunities for managers. The global acceptance of Coca-Cola, Sony Walkmans, McDonald's hamburgers, Doc Martin boots, and Nokia cell phones is a sign that the tastes and preferences of consumers in different countries are beginning to become more similar.[14] Likewise, large global markets currently exist for business products such as telecommunications equipment, electronic components, computer services, and financial services. Thus, Motorola sells its telecommunications equipment, Intel its microprocessors, and SAP its business systems management software to customers throughout the world.

Nevertheless, despite evidence that the same goods and services are receiving acceptance from customers worldwide, it is important not to place too much emphasis on this development. Because national cultures differ in many ways, significant differences between countries in consumer tastes and preferences still remain. These differences often require that managers customize goods and services to suit the preferences of local consumers. For example, despite McDonald's position as a leading global organization, its management has recognized a need for local customization. In Brazil, McDonald's sells a soft drink made from the guarana, an exotic berry that grows along the Amazon River. In Malaysia, McDonald's sells milk shakes flavored with durian, a strong-smelling fruit that local people consider an aphrodisiac.[15] Similarly, when Mattel decided to begin selling Barbie dolls in Japan, it had to redesign the doll's appearance (color of hair, facial features, and so on) to suit the tastes of its prospective customers. Companies also have to be careful to design and select the right kind of information systems and Web sites to enable customers to buy their products.

Information Technology Byte

Designing Global Information Systems

As more and more customers buy products online, the importance of a company's Web site is increasing. Good design is essential for attracting not only domestic customers but also those overseas. Domestically, the problems involved in designing a good Web site caused even information technology expert Wal-Mart to close down its Web site for two weeks in 2000 while it reworked its search and ordering system.[16] Dell Computer, however, has one of the easiest-to-use and most popular Web sites of a U.S. company, so imagine its surprise when, after creating a Japanese Web site, it found that Japanese customers were not attracted to it at all.

The reason? Dell's designers decided to give the Web site a thick black border around the outside of the screen, and in Japan black is a symbol of negative feelings and emotions.[17] Dell's designers moved quickly to solve this problem, and now, whenever they create a Web site in a foreign country, they are careful to work with local managers to make sure that their screen colors or icons do not offend local tastes or customs. Another common problem is linguistic errors. To avoid embarrassing mistakes, companies must ensure that designers are correctly using the country's language. This is particularly important in

Asia, where local scripts are easy to misinterpret. Also, companies must take into consideration how customers like to pay for their online products. Unlike U.S. consumers, who make constant use of credit cards, consumers in Germany and Japan like to avoid debt and pay by cash or debit card.

To respond to these problems, companies such as Yahoo, Dell, and SAP are increasingly developing local management teams based in each country in which they operate to oversee their businesses.[18] Often, this can involve giving domestic managers foreign assignments to help develop their global expertise. For example, managers can learn about each country's different regulatory environment; they can also help develop a strategy to customize products to suit local tastes. In this way, a company's global knowledge increases.

Beyond having Web sites directed at customers, companies also have to be sure they are developing information systems and intranets that are understandable and usable not only by domestic and foreign managers but also by their suppliers worldwide. For example, Wal-Mart's push to become a global company has led it to develop a global knowledge management system that tells foreign suppliers what kinds of products Wal-Mart requires and what it is willing to pay for them.[19] Foreign suppliers can then bid for Wal-Mart's business; in this way, Wal-Mart makes sure it is securing the lowest prices. Its global knowledge system is also used to share merchandising information from country to country so that Wal-Mart can quickly take advantage of changing trends and ideas.

Competitors

competitors Organizations that produce goods and services that are similar to a particular organization's goods and services.

One of the most important forces that an organization confronts in its task environment is competitors. **Competitors** are organizations that produce goods and services similar to a particular organization's goods and services. In other words, competitors are organizations vying for the same customers. Dell's competitors include other domestic manufacturers of PCs (such as Apple, Compaq, and Gateway) as well as foreign competitors (such as Sony and Toshiba in Japan and Group Bull in France). Dot-com stockbroker E*Trade has other dot-com competitors, like Ameritrade and TD Waterhouse, as well as bricks-and-clicks competitors, such as Merrill Lynch and Charles Schwab.

Rivalry between competitors is potentially the most threatening force that managers must deal with. A high level of rivalry often results in price competition, and falling prices reduce access to resources and lower profits. In the 2000s, competition in the personal computer industry became intense not only because of an economic slowdown but also because Dell was aggressively cutting costs and prices to try to increase its market share. Michael Dell announced that he wanted to increase Dell's market share from 13 to 40 percent–and Dell was already the global leader.[20] By 2004 Dell had increased its global market share to 35 percent.[21] Unable to compete, IBM announced it was exiting the PC business because it was losing millions in its battle against low-cost rivals such as Dell and Gateway.

potential competitors Organizations that presently are not in a task environment but could enter if they so choose.

Although the rivalry between existing competitors is a major threat, so is the potential for new competitors to enter the task environment. **Potential competitors** are organizations that are not presently in a task environment but could enter if they so choose. Amazon.com, for example, is not currently in the retail furniture or appliance business, but it could enter these businesses if its managers decided it could profitably sell such products. When new competitors enter an industry, competition increases and prices decrease.

barriers to entry Factors that make it difficult and costly for an organization to enter a particular task environment or industry.

In general, the potential for new competitors to enter a task environment (and thus boost the level of competition) is a function of barriers to entry.[22] **Barriers to entry** are factors that make it difficult and costly for an organization to enter a particular task environment or industry.[23] In other words, the more difficult and costly it is to enter the task environment, the higher are the barriers to entry. The higher the barriers to entry, the fewer the competitors in an organization's task environment and thus the lower the threat of competition. With fewer competitors, it is easier to obtain customers and keep prices high.

economies of scale Cost advantages associated with large operations.

Barriers to entry result from three main sources: economies of scale, brand loyalty, and government regulations that impede entry (see Figure 6.2). **Economies of scale** are the cost advantages associated with large operations. Economies of scale result from factors such as manufacturing products in very large quantities, buying inputs in bulk, or making more effective use of organizational resources than do competitors by fully utilizing employees' skills and knowledge. If organizations already in the task environment are large and enjoy significant economies of scale, then their costs are lower than the costs of potential entrants will be, and newcomers will find it very expensive to enter the industry. Amazon.com, for example, enjoys significant economies of scale relative to most other dot-com companies.[24]

brand loyalty Customers' preference for the products of organizations currently existing in the task environment.

Brand loyalty is customers' preference for the products of organizations currently existing in the task environment. If established organizations enjoy significant brand loyalty, then a new entrant will find it extremely difficult and costly to obtain a share of the market. Newcomers must bear huge advertising costs to build customer awareness of the goods or services they intend to provide.[25] Both Amazon.com and Yahoo, for example, two of the first dot-coms to go online, enjoy a high level of brand loyalty and have some of the highest Web-site hit rates of all dot-coms (the latter also allows them to increase their advertising revenues).

In some cases, *government regulations* function as a barrier to entry at both the industry and the country levels. Many industries that were deregulated, such as air transport, trucking, utilities, and telecommunications, experienced a high level of new entry after deregulation; this forced existing companies in those industries to operate more efficiently or risk being put out of business.

At the national and global level, administrative barriers are government policies that create a barrier to entry and limit imports of goods by foreign companies. Japan is well known for the many ways in which it attempts to restrict the entry of foreign competitors or lessen their impact on Japanese firms. For example, why do Dutch companies export tulip bulbs to almost every country in the

Figure 6.2
Barriers to Entry and Competition

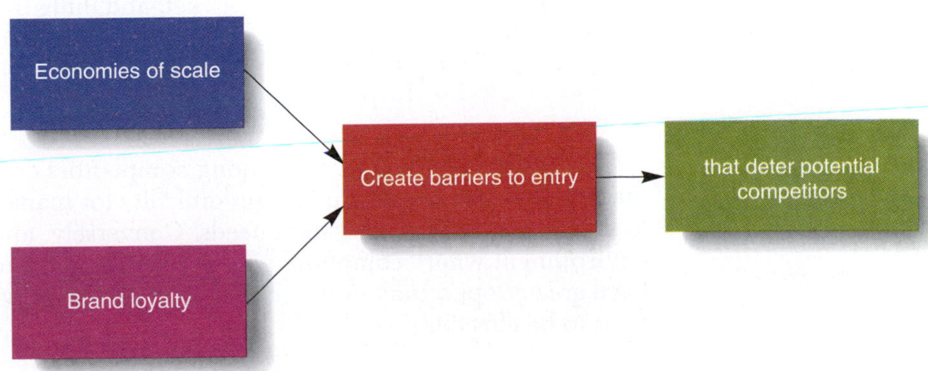

world except Japan? Japanese customs inspectors insist on checking every tulip bulb by cutting the stems vertically down the middle, and even Japanese ingenuity cannot put them back together.[26] Japan has come under intense pressure to relax and abolish such regulations, as the following suggests.

Managing Globally

American Rice Invades Japan

The Japanese rice market, similar to many other Japanese markets, was closed to foreign competitors until 1993 to protect Japan's thousands of high-cost, low-output rice farmers. Rice cultivation is expensive in Japan because of the country's mountainous terrain, so Japanese consumers have always paid high prices for rice. Under foreign pressure, the Japanese government opened the market, and foreign competitors are now allowed to export to Japan 8 percent of its annual rice consumption. Despite the still-present hefty foreign tariff on rice–$2.33 per 2.2 pounds–U.S. rice sells for $14 dollars per pound bag while Japanese rice sells for about $19. With the recession affecting Japan, price-conscious consumers are turning to foreign rice, which has hurt domestic farmers.

In 2001, however, an alliance between organic rice grower Lundberg Family Farms of California and the Nippon Restaurant Enterprise Co. found a new way to break into the Japanese rice market. Because there is no tariff on rice used in processed foods, Nippon takes the U.S. organic rice and converts it into "O-bento," an organic hot boxed lunch packed with rice, vegetables, chicken, beef, and salmon, all imported from the United States. The new lunches, which cost about $4 compared to a Japanese rice bento that costs about $9, are sold at railway stations and other outlets throughout Japan.[27] They are proving to be very popular and are creating a storm of protest from Japanese rice farmers, who already have been forced to leave 37 percent of their rice fields idle and grow less-profitable crops because of the entry of U.S. rice growers. Japanese and foreign companies are increasingly forming alliances to find new ways to break into the high-price Japanese market, and, little by little, Japan's restrictive trade practices are being whittled away.

A Japanese businessman receives a lunch box at a Nippon restaurant shop at the Tokyo Railway Station. Nippon began selling lunch boxes prepared from U.S. rice, frozen and imported from the United States, in 2001, drawing harsh protests from Japanese rice farmers.

In summary, intense rivalry among competitors creates a task environment that is highly threatening and causes difficulty for managers trying to gain access to the resources an organization needs. Conversely, low rivalry results in a task environment where competitive pressures are more moderate and managers have greater opportunities to acquire the resources they need for their organizations to be effective.

The General Environment

Economic, technological, sociocultural, demographic, political and legal, and global forces in an organization's general environment can have profound effects on the organization's task environment, effects that may not be evident to managers. For example, the sudden, dramatic upheavals in the Internet and dot-com industry environment were brought about by a combination of changing Internet technology, the softening U.S. stock market and economy, and increasing fears about the health of the global economy. These changes triggered intense competition between dot-com companies that further worsened the industry situation.

The implication is clear: Managers must constantly analyze forces in the general environment because these forces affect ongoing decision making and planning. Next, we discuss the major forces in the general environment, and examine their impacts on an organization's task environment.

Economic Forces

economic forces Interest rates, inflation, unemployment, economic growth, and other factors that affect the general health and well-being of a nation or the regional economy of an organization.

Economic forces affect the general health and well-being of a country or world region. They include interest rates, inflation, unemployment, and economic growth. Economic forces produce many opportunities and threats for managers. Low levels of unemployment and falling interest rates mean a change in the customer base: More people have more money to spend, and as a result organizations have an opportunity to sell more goods and services. Good economic times affect supplies: Resources become easier to acquire, and organizations have an opportunity to flourish, as high-tech companies did throughout the 1990s. The high-techs made record profits as the economy boomed in large part because of advances in information technology and growing global trade.

In contrast, worsening macroeconomic conditions, as in the early 2000s, pose a major threat because they limit managers' ability to gain access to the resources their organizations need. Profit-oriented organizations such as retail stores and hotels have fewer customers for their goods and services during economic downturns. Not-for-profit organizations such as charities and colleges receive fewer donations during economic downturns. Even a moderate deterioration in national or regional economic conditions can seriously affect performance. A relatively mild recession was a major factor in the staggering collapse of dot-com companies in the early 2000s.

Poor economic conditions make the environment more complex and managers' jobs more difficult and demanding. Managers may need to reduce the number of individuals in their departments and increase the motivation of remaining employees, and managers and workers alike may need to identify ways to acquire and utilize resources more efficiently. Successful managers realize the important effects that economic forces have on their organizations, and they pay close attention to what is occurring in the national and regional economies to respond appropriately.

technology The combination of skills and equipment that managers use in the design, production, and distribution of goods and services.

technological forces Outcomes of changes in the technology that managers use to design, produce, or distribute goods and services.

Technological Forces

Technology is the combination of tools, machines, computers, skills, information, and knowledge that managers use in the design, production, and distribution of goods and services. **Technological forces** are outcomes of changes in the technology that managers use to design, produce, or distribute goods and services. The overall pace of technological change has accelerated greatly in the last decade because of advances in microprocessors and computer hardware and software, and technological forces have increased in magnitude.[28]

Technological forces can have profound implications for managers and organizations. Technological change can make established products obsolete—for example, typewriters, black-and-white televisions, bound sets of encyclopedias—forcing managers to find new ways to satisfy customer needs. Although technological change can threaten an organization, it also can create a host of new opportunities for designing, making, or distributing new and better kinds of goods and services. More powerful microprocessors, primarily developed by Intel, caused a revolution in information technology that spurred demand for PCs, contributed to the success of companies such as Dell and Compaq, and led to the decline of others such as IBM.[29] IBM and other producers of mainframe computers have seen demand for their products decrease as organizationwide networks of PCs have replaced mainframes in many computing applications.[30] However, IBM has responded in the last decade by changing its emphasis from providing computer hardware to providing computer services and consulting and is once again in a strong global position. Managers must move quickly to respond to such changes if their organizations are to survive and prosper.

sociocultural forces Pressures emanating from the social structure of a country or society or from the national culture.

social structure The arrangement of relationships between individuals and groups in a society.

Changes in information technology are altering the very nature of work itself within organizations, including that of the manager's job. Telecommuting along the information superhighway and videoconferencing are now everyday activities that provide opportunities for managers to supervise and coordinate geographically dispersed employees. Salespeople in many companies work from home offices and commute electronically to work. They communicate with other employees through companywide electronic mail networks and use video cameras attached to PCs for "face-to-face" meetings with co-workers who may be across the country.

In today's wired world, many employees have the option of working from home offices and commuting electronically to work. What do you think some of the challenges might be in supervising and coordinating a group of geographically dispersed employees?

Sociocultural Forces

Sociocultural forces are pressures emanating from the social structure of a country or society or from the national culture, pressures that were discussed at length in the previous chapter. Pressures from both sources can either constrain or facilitate the way organizations operate and managers behave. **Social structure** is the arrangement of relationships between individuals and groups in a society. Societies differ substantially in social structure. In societies that have a high degree of social stratification, there are many distinctions among individuals and groups. Caste systems in India and Tibet and the recognition of numerous social classes in Great Britain and

France produce a multilayered social structure in each of those countries. In contrast, social stratification is lower in relatively egalitarian New Zealand and in the United States, where the social structure reveals few distinctions among people. Most top managers in France come from the upper classes of French society, but top managers in the United States come from all strata of American society.

Societies also differ in the extent to which they emphasize the individual over the group. For example, the United States emphasizes the primacy of the individual, and Japan emphasizes the primacy of the group. This difference may dictate the methods managers need to use to motivate and lead employees. **National culture** is the set of values that a society considers important and the norms of behavior that are approved or sanctioned in that society. Societies differ substantially in the values and norms that they emphasize. For example, in the United States individualism is highly valued, and in Korea and Japan individuals are expected to conform to group expectations.[31] National culture, discussed at length later in this chapter, also affects the way managers motivate and coordinate employees and the way organizations do business. Ethics, an important aspect of national culture, was discussed in detail in Chapter 4.

national culture The set of values that a society considers important and the norms of behavior that are approved or sanctioned in that society.

Social structure and national culture not only differ across societies but also change within societies over time. In the United States, attitudes toward the roles of women, love, sex, and marriage changed in each past decade. Many people in Asian countries such as Hong Kong, Singapore, Korea, and Japan think that the younger generation is far more individualistic and "American-like" than previous generations. Currently, throughout much of eastern Europe, new values that emphasize individualism and entrepreneurship are replacing communist values based on collectivism and obedience to the state. The pace of change is accelerating.

Individual managers and organizations must be responsive to changes in, and differences among, the social structures and national cultures of all the countries in which they operate. In today's increasingly integrated global economy, managers are likely to interact with people from several countries, and many managers live and work abroad. Effective managers are sensitive to differences between societies and adjust their behaviors accordingly.

Managers and organizations also must respond to social changes within a society. In the last few decades, for example, Americans have become increasingly interested in their personal health and fitness. Managers who recognized this trend early and exploited the opportunities that resulted from it were able to reap significant gains for their organizations. PepsiCo used the opportunity presented by the fitness trend and took market share from archrival Coca-Cola by being the first to introduce diet colas and fruit-based soft drinks. Quaker Oats made Gatorade the most popular sports drink and brought out a whole host of low-fat food products. The health trend, however, did not offer opportunities to all companies; to some it posed a threat. Tobacco companies came under intense pressure due to consumers' greater awareness of negative health impacts from smoking. Hershey Foods and other manufacturers of candy bars have been threatened by customers' desires for low-fat, healthy foods. The

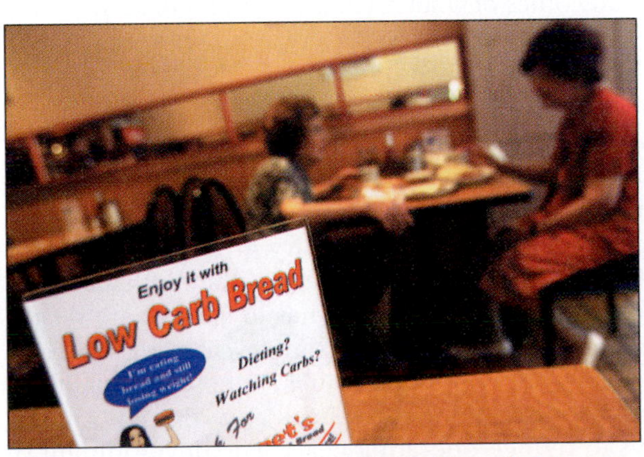

Managers and organizations must respond to social changes within a society. One example is the rage for "low-carb" foods, which affected not only large businesses like Krispy Kreme but also smaller ones such as this local diner.

rage for "low-carb" foods in 2004 led to a huge increase in demand for meat and hurt bread and doughnut companies such as Kraft and Krispy Kreme.

Demographic Forces

demographic forces Outcomes of changes in, or changing attitudes toward, the characteristics of a population, such as age, gender, ethnic origin, race, sexual orientation, and social class.

Demographic forces are outcomes of changes in, or changing attitudes toward, the characteristics of a population, such as age, gender, ethnic origin, race, sexual orientation, and social class. Like the other forces in the general environment, demographic forces present managers with opportunities and threats and can have major implications for organizations. We examined the nature of these challenges in depth in our discussion of diversity in Chapter 5, so we will not discuss these forces again here.

We will just note one important change occurring today: Most industrialized nations are experiencing the aging of their populations as a consequence of falling birth and death rates and the aging of the baby-boom generation. In Germany, for example, the percentage of the population over age 65 is expected to rise to 20.7 percent by 2010 from 15.4 percent in 1990. Comparable figures for Canada are 14.4 and 11.4 percent; for Japan, 19.5 and 11.7 percent; and for the United States, 13.5 and 12.6 percent.[32] In the United States the percentage increase is far smaller because of the huge wave of immigration during the 1990s and the large families that new immigrants typically have. However, the absolute number of older people has increased substantially and is increasing opportunities for organizations that cater to older people; the home health care and recreation industries, for example, are seeing an upswing in demand for their services.

The aging of the population also has several implications for the workplace. Most significant are a relative decline in the young people joining the workforce and an increase in the number of active employees willing to postpone retirement past the traditional retirement age of 65. These changes suggest that organizations need to find ways to motivate and utilize the skills and knowledge of older employees, an issue that many Western societies have yet to tackle.

Political and Legal Forces

political and legal forces Outcomes of changes in laws and regulations, such as the deregulation of industries, the privatization of organizations, and the increased emphasis on environmental protection.

Political and legal forces are outcomes of changes in laws and regulations. They result from political and legal developments within society and significantly affect managers and organizations. Political processes shape a society's laws. Laws constrain the operations of organizations and managers, and thus create both opportunities and threats.[33] For example, throughout much of the industrialized world there has been a strong trend toward deregulation of industries previously controlled by the state and privatization of organizations once owned by the state.

In the United States, deregulation of the airline industry in 1978 ushered into the task environment of commercial airlines major changes that are still working themselves out. Deregulation allowed 29 new airlines to enter the industry between 1978 and 1993. The increase in airline-passenger carrying capacity after deregulation led to excess capacity on many routes, intense competition, and fare wars. To respond to this more competitive task environment, in the 1980s airlines looked for ways to reduce operating costs. The development of hub-and-spoke systems, the rise of nonunion airlines, and the introduction of no-frills discount service are all responses to increased competition in the airlines' task environment. By the 1990s, once again in control of their environments, airlines were making record profits. However, soaring oil prices in the

2000s wiped out these profits, and airlines found themselves once again under pressure. In 2004, for example, both United Airlines and Delta announced that they were close to bankruptcy, and their futures were uncertain.[34]

Deregulation and privatization are just two examples of political and legal forces that can challenge organizations and managers. Others include increased emphasis on environmental protection and the preservation of endangered species, increased emphasis on safety in the workplace, and legal constraints against discrimination on the basis of race, gender, or age. Managers who want to take advantage of the opportunities created by changing global political and legal and economic forces face a major challenge, and nowhere has this been seen more clearly than in the global car industry.

Managing Globally

Car Manufacturing Is Changing Around the World

In the last decade, a huge wave of mergers and alliances between global car manufacturers resulted from changing economic and political conditions. Ford, for example, bought Jaguar and Volvo and owns the majority share in Mazda.[35] GM owns Germany's Opel, Sweden's Saab, and Japan's Isuzu; Chrysler and Daimler-Benz merged and bought Mitsubishi in 2000; and Renault bought Nissan in 2000.[36]

These global mergers occurred because car makers realize that they need to have a strong presence in every region of the world if they are to obtain the full benefits from globalization. Car companies have been merging rapidly to achieve global economies of scale.[37] The goal of these companies is to design and produce cars that can be sold throughout the world, making it easier to recoup the huge costs of developing a new vehicle. Also, global car companies can enjoy the low costs that can be obtained from having global supply chains, as discussed earlier. Moreover, they can obtain and share valuable design or car-making skills that may be present in one car company but not in another, such as Mercedes-Benz's safety features or Mitsubishi's low-cost, small-car design skills.

Some of these mergers have been successful. The merger between Renault and Nissan has paid off handsomely as Nissan introduced new global models of cars and SUVs in the 2000s that proved popular around the world; similarly, Ford's merger with Mazda has worked out well.[38] Others have been less successful. The DaimlerChrysler and Mitsubishi merger led to no cost savings and proved a disaster; it was announced that the German company was essentially abandoning its links with the Japanese company in 2004. Until 2004, many analysts felt the merger between Daimler-Benz and Chrysler had also been a mistake, as costs rose and the company made record losses. In 2004, however, Chrysler began to introduce many innovative vehicles, so the merger might have a bright future after all. Nevertheless, to date DaimlerChrysler has lost billions from its takeover of Chrysler, as has GM from its investments in Saab and Isuzu.[39]

Despite their short-term economic problems, however, these mergers are expected to pay off during the next decades as car companies jockey for position as world leaders. Indeed, politically, as the world divides into economic regions, only a global presence will allow a car company to play in the world league. Also, to enter new, largely untapped markets such as eastern Europe and China, car companies have to be able to respond to the different political and cultural forces that characterize business in different countries–hence, the need for operations on a truly global level. Indeed, the takeover of Japanese car companies has been due to the combination of a severe recession in Japan and an increasing political willingness by the Japanese government to allow foreign firms to control Japanese companies.[40] The same situation is occurring in Korea, where U.S. car companies are targeting bankrupt Korean car companies.

Global Forces

global forces Outcomes of changes in international relationships, changes in nations' economic, political, and legal systems, and changes in technology, such as falling trade barriers, the growth of representative democracies, and reliable and instantaneous communication.

Global forces are outcomes of changes in international relationships, changes in nations' economic, political, and legal systems, and changes in technology. Perhaps the most important global force affecting managers and organizations is the increasing economic integration of countries around the world that has been taking place during the past decades.[41] Free trade agreements such as the General Agreement on Tariffs and Trade (GATT), the North American Free Trade Agreement (NAFTA), and the growth of the European Union (EU) have led to a lowering of barriers to the free flow of goods and services between nations.[42]

Falling trade barriers have created enormous opportunities for companies in one country to sell goods and services in other countries. By allowing companies from other countries to compete for domestic customers, however, falling trade barriers also pose a serious threat because they increase competition in the task environment. Between 1973 and 2004, for example, U.S. carmakers saw Japanese competitors increase their share of the U.S. car market from 3 to 30 percent.[43] This growth would not have been possible without relatively low trade barriers, which allowed producers in Japan to export cars to the United States.

Competition from Toyota, Honda, and other Japanese companies forced managers of the U.S. car companies to find ways to improve their operations. To remain competitive, they had to transform the way their organizations designed and manufactured cars. As a result of these changes, U.S. companies gained ground against their foreign competitors; if they had not, the percentage of foreign cars sold in 2004 in the United States would have been far higher. However, if global forces had not increased the intensity of competition in the task environment of U.S. car companies, U.S. managers might have been slow to make such changes. The U.S. car industry used to be very conservative and slow-moving, but this is no longer the case; it has learned new global values and norms, such as product quality and reliability, for reasons discussed in the next section.

The Changing Global Environment

In the 21st century, any idea that the world is composed of a set of distinct national countries and markets that are separated physically, economically, and culturally from one another has vanished. Managers now recognize that companies exist and compete in a truly global market. Today, managers regard the global environment as a source of important opportunities and threats that they must respond to. Managers constantly confront the challenges of global competition–establishing operations in a country abroad or obtaining inputs from suppliers abroad–or the challenges of managing in a different national culture.[44] (See Figure 6.3.)

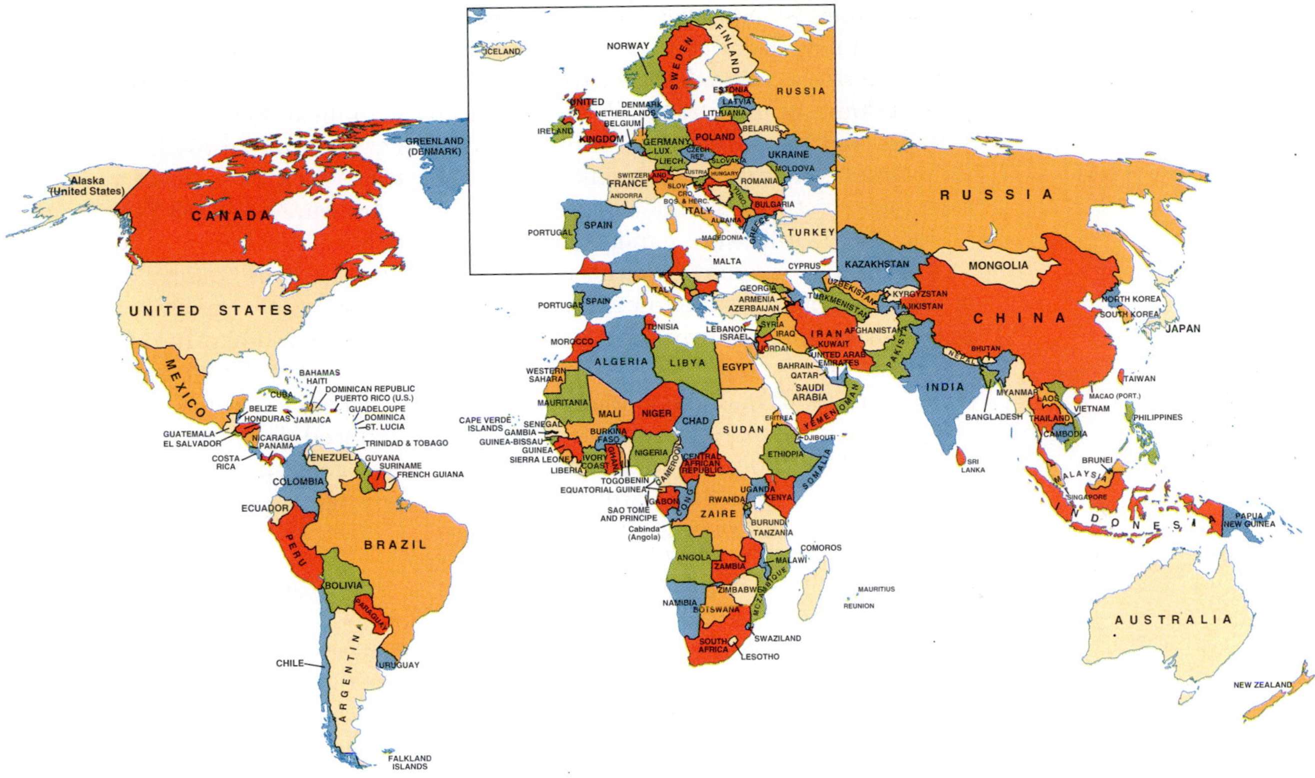

Figure 6.3
The Global Environment

In essence, managers view the global environment as open, that is, as an environment in which they and their organizations are free to buy goods and services from, and sell goods and services to, whichever countries they choose. An open environment is also one in which global organizations are free not only to compete against each other to attract customers but also to establish operations or subsidiaries abroad to become the strongest competitors throughout the world. Coca-Cola and PepsiCo, for example, have competed aggressively for 20 years to develop the strongest global soft-drink empire.

In this section, we explain why the global environment has become more open and competitive and why this development is so significant for managers today. We examine how economic changes such as the lowering of barriers to trade and investment have led to greater interaction and exchanges between organizations and countries. We discuss how declines in barriers of distance and culture have increased the interdependencies between organizations and countries. And we consider the specific implications of these changes for managers and organizations.

Declining Barriers to Trade and Investment

During the 1920s and 1930s, many countries erected formidable barriers to international trade and investment in the belief that this was the best way to promote their economic well-being. Many of these barriers were high tariffs on imports of manufactured goods. A **tariff** is a tax that a government imposes on imported or, occasionally, on exported goods. The aim of import tariffs is to protect domestic industries and jobs, such as those in the auto or steel industry, from foreign competition by raising the price of goods from abroad. In 2001, for example, the U.S. government increased the tariffs on the import of foreign steel to protect U.S. steelmakers; however, under pressure from the European Union, these tariffs were significantly reduced in 2003.

tariff A tax that a government imposes on imported or, occasionally, exported goods.

The reason for removing tariffs is that, very often, when one country imposes an import tariff, others follow suit and the result is a series of retaliatory moves as countries progressively raise tariff barriers against each other. In the 1920s this behavior depressed world demand and helped usher in the Great Depression of the 1930s and massive unemployment. It was to avoid tariffs on U.S. goods entering Europe that the steel tariffs were reduced. In short, rather than protecting jobs and promoting economic well-being, governments of countries that resort to raising high tariff barriers ultimately reduce employment and undermine economic growth.[45]

GATT AND THE RISE OF FREE TRADE After World War II, advanced Western industrial countries, having learned from the Great Depression, committed themselves to the goal of removing barriers to the free flow of resources between countries. This commitment was reinforced by acceptance of the principle that free trade, rather than tariff barriers, was the best way to foster a healthy domestic economy and low unemployment.[46]

free-trade doctrine The idea that if each country specializes in the production of the goods and services that it can produce most efficiently, this will make the best use of global resources.

The **free-trade doctrine** predicts that if each country agrees to specialize in the production of the goods and services that it can produce most efficiently, this will make the best use of global resources and will result in lower prices.[47] For example, if Indian companies are highly efficient in the production of textiles and U.S. companies are highly efficient in the production of computer software, then under a free-trade agreement production of textiles would shift to India and that of computer software to the United States. Consequently, prices of both textiles and software should fall because each good is being produced in the location where it can be made at the lowest cost, benefiting consumers and making the best use of scarce resources. This doctrine is, of course, responsible for the increase in global outsourcing and the loss of millions of U.S. jobs in textiles and manufacturing. However, millions of jobs have been created in high-tech, in IT, and in the service sector that in theory should more than offset these job losses in the long run.

Historically, countries that accepted this free-trade doctrine set as their goal the removal of barriers to the free flow of goods between countries. They attempted to achieve this through an international treaty known as the General Agreement on Tariffs and Trade (GATT). In the half-century since World War II, there have been eight rounds of GATT negotiations aimed at lowering tariff barriers. The last round, the Uruguay Round, involved 117 countries and was completed in December 1993. This round succeeded in lowering tariffs by over 30 percent from the previous level. It also led to the dissolving of GATT and its replacement by the World Trade Organization (WTO), which today, in 2005, continues the struggle to reduce tariffs, and has more power to sanction countries that break global agreements.[48] On average, the tariff barriers among the governments of developed countries declined from over 40 percent in 1948 to about 3 percent in 2000, causing a dramatic increase in world trade.[49]

Declining Barriers of Distance and Culture

Barriers of distance and culture also closed the global environment and kept managers looking inward. The management problems Unilever, the huge British-based, global soap and detergent maker, experienced at the turn of the 20th century illustrate the effect of these barriers.

Founded in London during the 1880s by William Lever, a quaker, Unilever had a worldwide reach by the early 1900s and operated subsidiaries in most major countries of the British Empire, including India, Canada, and Australia. Lever had a very hands-on, autocratic management style and found his far-flung business empire difficult to control. The reason for Lever's control problems was that communication over great distances was difficult. It took six weeks to reach India by ship from England, and international telephone and telegraph services were very unreliable.

Another problem that Unilever encountered was the difficulty of doing business in societies that were separated from Britain by barriers of language and culture. Different countries have different sets of national beliefs, values, and norms, and Lever found that a management approach that worked in Britain did not necessarily work in India or Persia (now Iran). As a result, management practices had to be tailored to suit each unique national culture. After Lever's death in 1925, top management at Unilever lowered or *decentralized* (see Chapter 10) decision-making authority to the managers of the various national subsidiaries so that they could develop a management approach that suited the country in which they were operating. One result of this strategy was that the subsidiaries grew distant and remote from one another–something that reduced Unilever's performance.[50]

Since the end of World War II, major advances in communications and transportation technology have been reducing the barriers of distance and culture that affected Unilever and other global organizations. Over the last 30 years, global communications have been revolutionized by developments in satellites, digital switching, and optical-fiber telephone lines–and, most recently, by the exploding growth of the Internet and global computer networks. Satellites and optical fibers can carry hundreds of thousands of messages simultaneously, making possible global video teleconferencing and allowing companies to develop global intranets that are company-specific information and decision making systems.[51]

As a result of such developments, reliable, secure, and instantaneous communication is now possible with nearly any location in the world.[52] Fax machines in Sri Lanka, cellular phones in the Brazilian rain forest, satellite dishes in Russia, video phones in Manhattan, and videoconferencing facilities in Japan are all part of the communications revolution that is changing the way the world works. This revolution has made it possible for a global organization–a tiny garment factory in Li & Fung's network or a huge company such as Nestlé or Unilever–to do business anywhere, anytime, and to search for customers and suppliers around the world. The way in which U.S. retailers have used the possibilities of e-commerce to expand globally is very instructive.

Managing Globally

E-Commerce and Global Customer Responsiveness

The top managers of U.S. dot-com companies such as Amazon.com and eBay were quick to understand the potential of the Internet as a new way to reach customers and create a competitive advantage. These companies' managers quickly built their virtual storefronts and began to offer their products to U.S. customers. Amazon.com, for example, is the acknowledged leader in designing an online storefront that offers its customers an easy-to use, personalized shopping experience. Its ability to offer customers every book in publication, and at a low price, wiped out thousands of small bookstores throughout the United States. Similarly, eBay's ability to connect buyers and sellers and create a market in which fair prices could be determined revolutionized the auction business.

Given their companies' appeal in the United States, it seemed natural to dot-com managers that they should expand their operations globally to take advantage of the huge number of potential customers worldwide. They also believed they could develop a global business model quite inexpensively. With the U.S. storefront up and running, all they would need to do was transfer it to an overseas market. There, it could be easily customized to the needs of consumers in a particular country. Amazon.com was particularly aggressive in its expansions plans. In 1996 it established an online bookstore in the United Kingdom; in 1998 it entered the German market; and since then it has entered countries such as Japan and France. Similarly, E*Trade, the stock brokerage and banking company, entered the Japanese market and expanded into Europe.

Given Amazon's appeal in the United States, it seemed natural to expand operations globally. But dot-com managers discovered that developing a successful global business model takes a great deal of time and money. Creating a virtual storefront such as Amazon's Web site for the Japanese market is only one component of the expansion process. To support this storefront, the company must also build a sophisticated purchasing and distribution network.

Developing a successful global business model, however, was much more difficult and expensive than dot-com managers had anticipated. As Amazon.com discovered in the United States, having a successful virtual store is only one of the many pieces of a viable global business model. Creating a sophisticated purchasing and distribution network to get the product to the customer is also vital, and globally this is an expensive proposition. Indeed, because of the enormous investment needed to establish its overseas operations, Amazon.com could not declare its second quarterly profit until the spring of 2003. Similarly, E*Trade found that customizing its brokerage and banking services to the legal and tax regulations that differ from country to country was much more time-consuming and costly than it expected.

In turned out that the dot-coms that performed the best on a global level were those like Lands' End and Avon that had been catalog sellers. These companies had well-managed overseas sales and distribution networks and were in a strong position to profit from their global networks when they took their catalogs online. Other companies that also performed well were those whose products did not require a high investment in a physical business infrastructure. eBay, for example, provides an electronic platform that links buyers and sellers and allows them to trade. All the actual time and cost involved in shipping products globally is borne by the buyers and sellers, so eBay needed to invest far less in building operations overseas. The job of its managers was to tailor its operating system to the local national culture. Similarly, today most stocks are sold electronically. So companies like E*Trade, which have also created storefronts that match the needs of customers in a particular national culture, seem likely to fare particularly well in the future.

One of the most important innovations in transportation technology that has made the global environment more open has been the growth of commercial jet travel, which reduced the time it takes to get from one location to another. Because of jet travel, New York is now closer to Tokyo than it was to Philadelphia in the days of the 13 colonies–a fact that makes control of far-flung international businesses much easier today than in William Lever's era.

In addition to making travel faster, modern communications and transportation technologies have also helped reduce the cultural distance between countries. The Internet and its millions of Web sites facilitate the development of global communications networks and media that are helping to create a worldwide culture above and beyond unique national cultures. Moreover, television networks such as CNN, MTV, ESPN, BBC, and HBO can now be received in many countries, and Hollywood films are shown throughout the world.

Effects of Free Trade on Managers

The lowering of barriers to trade and investment and the decline of distance and culture barriers have created enormous opportunities for companies to expand the market for their goods and services through exports and investments in foreign countries. Although managers at some organizations, like Barnes & Noble, have shied away from trying to sell their goods and services overseas, the situation of Wal-Mart and Lands' End, which have developed profitable global operations, is more typical. The shift toward a more open global economy has created not only more opportunities to sell goods and services in markets abroad but also the opportunity to buy more from other countries. Indeed, the success in the United States of Lands' End has been based in part on its managers' willingness to import low-cost clothes and bedding from foreign manufacturers. Lands' End purchases clothing from manufacturers in Hong Kong, Malaysia, Taiwan, and China because U.S. textile makers often do not offer the same quality, styling, flexibility, or price.[53] Indeed, most clothing companies such as Levi Strauss, Wal-Mart, and Target are major players in the global environment by virtue of their purchasing activities, even if like Target or Dillard's they sell only in the United States.

The manager's job is more challenging in a dynamic global environment because of the increased intensity of competition that goes hand in hand with the lowering of barriers to trade and investment. Thus, as discussed above, the job of the average manager in a U.S. car company became a lot harder from the mid-1970s on as a result of the penetration of the U.S. market by efficient Japanese competitors. Recall that Levi Strauss closed its last U.S. clothing factory in 2001 because it could not match the prices of low-cost foreign jeans manufacturers that compete with Levi's to sell to clothing chains such as Wal-Mart, Dillard's, and Target.

NAFTA The growth of regional trade agreements such as the North American Free Trade Agreement (NAFTA) also presents opportunities and threats for managers and their organizations. NAFTA, which became effective on January 1, 1994, had the aim of abolishing the tariffs on 99 percent of the goods traded between Mexico, Canada, and the United States by 2004. Although it has not achieved this lofty goal, NAFTA has removed most barriers on the cross-border flow of resources, giving, for example, financial institutions and retail businesses in Canada and the United States unrestricted access to the Mexican marketplace. After NAFTA was signed, there was a flood of investment into Mexico from the United States, as well as many other countries such as Japan. Wal-Mart, Costco, Radio Shack, and other major U.S. retail chains plan to expand their operations in Mexico.

The establishment of free-trade areas creates an opportunity for manufacturing organizations because it allows them to reduce their costs. They can do this either by shifting production to the lowest-cost location within the free-trade area (for example, U.S. auto and textile companies shifting production to Mexico) or by serving the whole region from one location, rather than establishing separate operations in each country.

Some managers, however, might see regional free-trade agreements as a threat because the agreements expose a company based in one member country to increased competition from companies based in the other member countries. Managers in Mexico, the United States, and Canada are experiencing this now through NAFTA. For the first time, Mexican managers find themselves facing a threat: head-to-head competition in some industries against efficient U.S. and Canadian organizations. But the opposite is true as well: U.S. and Canadian managers are experiencing threats in labor-intensive industries, such as the flooring tile and textile industries, where Mexican businesses have a cost advantage.

The three current NAFTA members have announced that they hope to expand the treaty in the future to include countries in Central and South America and thus increase economic prosperity throughout the Americas. Chile is a possible future member, as are Brazil and Argentina. However, the recent currency and economic problems that these countries have been experiencing have slowed down the attempt to expand NAFTA, as has political resistance within the United States because of jobs lost to Mexico and Canada.

In essence, the shift toward a more open, competitive global environment has increased both the opportunities that managers can take advantage of and the threats they must respond to in performing their jobs effectively.

The Role of National Culture

Despite evidence that countries are becoming more similar to one another and that the world is on the verge of becoming a global village, the cultures of different countries still vary widely because of critical differences in their values, norms, and attitudes. As noted earlier, national culture includes the values, norms, knowledge, beliefs, moral principles, laws, customs, and other practices that unite the citizens of a country.[54] National culture shapes individual behavior by specifying appropriate and inappropriate behavior and interaction with others. People learn national culture in their everyday lives by interacting with those around them. This learning starts at an early age and continues throughout their lives.

values Ideas about what a society believes to be good, right, desirable, or beautiful.

VALUES AND NORMS The basic building blocks of national culture are values and norms. **Values** are ideas about what a society believes to be good, right, desirable, or beautiful. They provide the basic underpinnings for notions of individual freedom, democracy, truth, justice, honesty, loyalty, social obligation, collective responsibility, the appropriate roles for men and women, love, sex, marriage, and so on. Values are more than merely abstract concepts; they are invested with considerable emotional significance. People argue, fight, and even die over values such as freedom.

Although deeply embedded in society, values are not static; however, change in a country's values is likely to be slow and painful. For example, the value systems of many formerly communist states, such as Russia, are undergoing significant changes as those countries move away from a value system that emphasizes the state and toward one that emphasizes individual freedom. Social turmoil often results when countries undergo major changes in their values.

norms Unwritten rules and codes of conduct that prescribe how people should act in particular situations.

folkways The routine social conventions of everyday life.

Norms are unwritten rules and codes of conduct that prescribe appropriate behavior in particular situations and shape the behavior of people toward one another. Two types of norms play a major role in national culture: folkways and mores. **Folkways** are the routine social conventions of everyday life. They concern customs and practices such as dressing appropriately for particular situations, good social manners, eating with the correct utensils, and neighborly behavior. Although folkways define the way people are expected to behave, violation of folkways is not a serious or moral matter. People who violate folkways are often thought to be eccentric or ill-mannered, but they are not usually considered to be evil or bad. In many countries, initially foreigners may be excused for violating folkways because they are unaccustomed to local behavior, but repeated violations are not excused because foreigners are expected to learn appropriate behavior.

mores Norms that are considered to be central to the functioning of society and to social life.

Mores are norms that are considered to be central to the functioning of society and to social life. They have much greater significance than folkways. Accordingly, the violation of mores can be expected to bring serious retribution. Mores include proscriptions against theft, adultery, and incest. In many societies mores have been enacted into law. Thus, all advanced societies have laws against theft and incest.

Young Saudi men eat in a fast-food restaurant in Jiddah, Saudi Arabia, March 29, 2002. Saudi Arabia's strict and ascetic interpretation of Islam means movie theaters, nightclubs and dating are banned. Young Saudi's now hang out on the streets, in coffee shops and fast food restaurants. Teen-agers flash their phone numbers on pieces of cardboard or leave them on bits of paper stuck to car windows, in the hopes of getting a date, even if it is confined to the phone.

However, there are many differences in mores from one society to another.[55] In the United States, for example, drinking alcohol is widely accepted; but in Saudi Arabia, the consumption of alcohol is viewed as a violation of social norms and is punishable by imprisonment (as many U.S. citizens working in Saudi Arabia have discovered).

Hofstede's Model of National Culture

Researchers have spent considerable time and effort identifying similarities and differences in the values and norms of different countries. One model of national culture was developed by Geert Hofstede.[56] As a psychologist for IBM, Hofstede collected data on employee values and norms from more than 100,000 IBM employees in 64 countries. Based on his research, Hofstede developed five dimensions along which national cultures can be placed (see Figure 6.4).[57]

individualism A worldview that values individual freedom and self-expression and adherence to the principle that people should be judged by their individual achievements rather than by their social background.

INDIVIDUALISM VERSUS COLLECTIVISM The first dimension, which Hofstede labeled "individualism versus collectivism," has a long history in human thought. **Individualism** is a worldview that values individual freedom and self-expression and adherence to the principle that people should be judged by their individual achievements rather than by their social background. In Western countries, individualism usually includes admiration for personal success, a strong belief in individual rights, and high regard for individual entrepreneurs.[58]

In contrast, **collectivism** is a worldview that values subordination of the individual to the goals of the group and adherence to the principle that people should be judged by their contribution to the group. Collectivism was widespread in communist countries but has become less prevalent since the collapse of communism in most of those countries. Japan is a noncommunist country where collectivism is highly valued.

Figure 6.4
Hofstede's Model of National Culture

Source: Administrative Science Quarterly, Geert Hofstede, Bram Nevijen, Denise Daval Ohayv, and Geert Sanders, *Measuring Organizational Cultures: A Qualitative and Quantitative Study Across Twenty Cases,* Volume 35, Number 2 (June 1990), pp. 286–316. Approval of Request for Permission to Reprint. © Johnson Graduate School of Management, Cornell University.

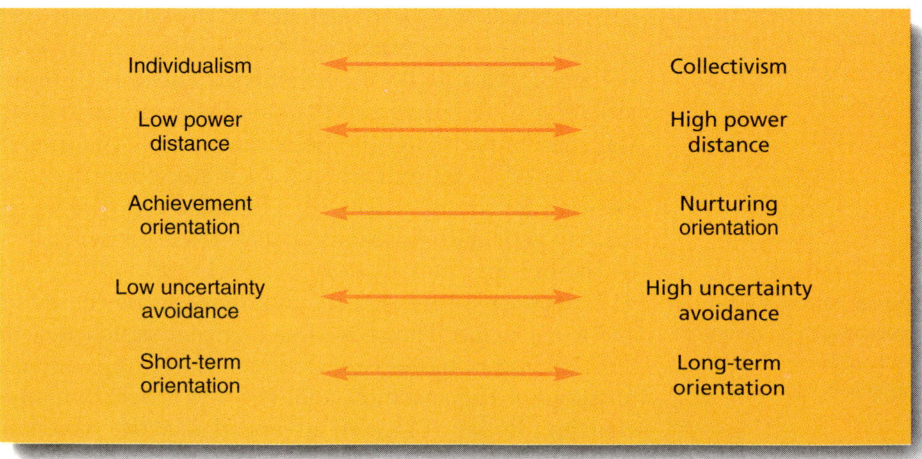

collectivism A worldview that values subordination of the individual to the goals of the group and adherence to the principle that people should be judged by their contribution to the group.

Collectivism in Japan traces its roots to the fusion of Confucian, Buddhist, and Shinto thought that occurred during the Tokugawa period in Japanese history (1600–1870s).[59] One of the central values that emerged during this period was strong attachment to the group–whether a village, a work group, or a company. Strong identification with the group is said to create pressures for collective action in Japan, as well as strong pressure for conformity to group norms and a relative lack of individualism.[60]

Managers must realize that organizations and organizational members reflect their national culture's emphasis on individualism or collectivism. Indeed, one of the major reasons why Japanese and American management practices differ is that Japanese culture values collectivism and U.S. culture values individualism.[61]

power distance The degree to which societies accept the idea that inequalities in the power and well-being of their citizens are due to differences in individuals' physical and intellectual capabilities and heritage.

POWER DISTANCE By **power distance** Hofstede meant the degree to which societies accept the idea that inequalities in the power and well-being of their citizens are due to differences in individuals' physical and intellectual capabilities and heritage. This concept also encompasses the degree to which societies accept the economic and social differences in wealth, status, and well-being that result from differences in individual capabilities.

Societies in which inequalities are allowed to persist or grow over time have *high power distance.* In high-power-distance societies, workers who are professionally successful amass wealth and pass it on to their children, and, as a result, inequalities may grow over time. In such societies, the gap between rich and poor, with all the attendant political and social consequences, grows very large. In contrast, in societies with *low power distance,* large inequalities between citizens are not allowed to develop. In low-power-distance countries, the government uses taxation and social welfare programs to reduce inequality and improve the welfare of the least fortunate. These societies are more attuned to preventing a large gap between rich and poor and minimizing discord between different classes of citizens.

Advanced Western countries such as the United States, Germany, the Netherlands, and the United Kingdom have relatively low power distance and high individualism. Economically poor Latin American countries such as Guatemala and Panama, and Asian countries such as Malaysia and the Philippines, have high power distance and low individualism.[62] These findings suggest that the cultural values of richer countries emphasize protecting the rights of individuals and, at the same time, provide a fair chance of success to every member of society.

achievement orientation A worldview that values assertiveness, performance, success, and competition.

nurturing orientation A worldview that values the quality of life, warm personal friendships, and services and care for the weak.

uncertainty avoidance The degree to which societies are willing to tolerate uncertainty and risk.

ACHIEVEMENT VERSUS NURTURING ORIENTATION Societies that have an **achievement orientation** value assertiveness, performance, success, competition, and results. Societies that have a **nurturing orientation** value the quality of life, warm personal relationships, and services and care for the weak. Japan and the United States tend to be achievement-oriented; the Netherlands, Sweden, and Denmark are more nurturing-oriented.

UNCERTAINTY AVOIDANCE Societies as well as individuals differ in their tolerance for uncertainty and risk. Societies low on **uncertainty avoidance** (such as the United States and Hong Kong) are easygoing, value diversity, and tolerate differences in personal beliefs and actions. Societies high on uncertainty avoidance (such as Japan and France) are more rigid and skeptical about people whose behaviors or beliefs differ from the norm. In these societies, conformity to the values of the social and work groups to which a person belongs is the norm, and structured situations are preferred because they provide a sense of security.

long-term orientation A worldview that values thrift and persistence in achieving goals.

short-term orientation A worldview that values personal stability or happiness and living for the present.

LONG-TERM VERSUS SHORT-TERM ORIENTATION The last dimension that Hofstede described is orientation toward life and work.[63] A national culture with a **long-term orientation** rests on values such as thrift (saving) and persistence in achieving goals. A national culture with a **short-term orientation** is concerned with maintaining personal stability or happiness and living for the present. Societies with a long-term orientation include Taiwan and Hong Kong, well known for their high rate of per capita savings. The United States and France have a short-term orientation, and their citizens tend to spend more and save less.

National Culture and Global Management

Differences among national cultures have important implications for managers. First, because of cultural differences, management practices that are effective in one country might be troublesome in another. General Electric's managers learned this while trying to manage Tungsram, a Hungarian lighting products company it acquired for $150 million. GE was attracted to Tungsram, widely regarded as one of Hungary's best companies, because of Hungary's low wage rates and the possibility of using the company as a base from which to export lighting products to western Europe. GE transferred some of its best managers to Tungsram and hoped it would soon become a leader in Europe. Unfortunately, many problems arose.

One of the problems resulted from major misunderstandings between the American managers and the Hungarian workers. The Americans complained that the Hungarians were lazy; the Hungarians thought the Americans were pushy. The Americans wanted strong sales and marketing functions that would pamper customers. In the prior command economy, sales and marketing activities were unnecessary. In addition, Hungarians expected GE to deliver Western-style wages, but GE came to Hungary to take advantage of the country's low-wage structure.[64] As Tungsram's losses mounted, GE managers had to admit that, because of differences in basic attitudes between countries, they had underestimated the difficulties they would face in turning Tungsram around. Nevertheless, by 2001, these problems had been solved, and the increased efficiency of GE's Hungarian operations made General Electric a major player in the European lighting market, causing it to invest another $1 billion.[65]

Often, management practices must be tailored to suit the cultural contexts within which an organization operates. An approach effective in the United States might not work in Japan, Hungary, or Mexico because of differences in national culture. For example, U.S.-style pay-for-performance systems that emphasize the performance of individuals alone might not work well in Japan, where individual performance in pursuit of group goals is the value that receives emphasis.

Managers doing business with individuals from another country must be sensitive to the value systems and norms of that country and behave accordingly. For example, Friday is the Islamic Sabbath. Thus, it would be impolite and inappropriate for a U.S. manager to schedule a busy day of activities for Saudi Arabian managers visiting on a Friday.

A culturally diverse management team can be a source of strength for an organization participating in the global marketplace. Organizations that employ managers from a variety of cultures appreciate better than do organizations with culturally homogeneous management teams how national cultures differ, and they tailor their management systems and behaviors to the differences. Indeed, one of the advantages that many Western companies have over their Japanese competitors is greater willingness to build an international team of senior managers.[66]

Summary and Review

WHAT IS THE ORGANIZATIONAL ENVIRONMENT? The organizational environment is the set of forces and conditions that operate beyond an organization's boundaries but affect a manager's ability to acquire and utilize resources. The organizational environment has two components, the task environment and the general environment.

THE TASK ENVIRONMENT The task environment is the set of forces and conditions that originate with suppliers, distributors, customers, and competitors that influence managers on a daily basis. The opportunities and threats associated with forces in the task environment become more complex as a company begins to operate in more than one country and expands globally.

THE GENERAL ENVIRONMENT The general environment is wider-ranging economic, technological, sociocultural, demographic, political and legal, and global forces that affect an organization and its task environment.

THE CHANGING GLOBAL ENVIRONMENT In recent years there has been a marked shift away from a closed global environment, in which countries are cut off from one another by barriers to international trade and investment and by barriers of distance and culture, and toward a more open global environment. The emergence of an open global environment and the reduction of barriers to the free flow of goods, services, and investment owe much to the rise of global trade agreements such as GATT, to the growing global acceptance of a free-market philosophy, and to the poor performance of countries that protected their markets from international trade and investment.

Management in Action

Topics for Discussion and Action

Discussion

1. Why is it important for managers to understand the nature of the environmental forces that are acting on them and their organization?
2. Which organization is likely to face the most complex task environment, a biotechnology company trying to develop a new cure for cancer or a large retailer like The Gap or Macy's? Why?
3. The population is aging because of declining birth rates, declining death rates, and the aging of the baby-boom generation. What might some of the implications of this demographic trend be for (a) a pharmaceutical company, (b) the home construction industry?
4. How do political, legal, and economic forces shape national culture? What characteristics of national culture do you think have the most important effect on how successful a country is in doing business abroad?
5. After the passage of the North American Free Trade Agreement, many U.S. companies shifted production operations to Mexico to take advantage of lower labor costs and lower standards for environmental and worker protection. As a result, they cut their costs and were better able to survive in an increasingly competitive global environment. Was their behavior ethical—that is, did the ends justify the means?

Action

6. Choose an organization, and ask a manager in that organization to list the number and strengths of forces in the organization's task environment. Ask the manager to pay particular attention to identifying opportunities and threats that result from pressures and changes in customers, competitors, and suppliers.

Building Management Skills

Analyzing an Organization's Task and General Environments

Pick an organization with which you are familiar. It can be an organization in which you have worked or currently work or one that you interact with regularly as a customer (such as the college that you are currently attending). For this organization do the following:

1. Describe the main forces in the task environment that are affecting the organization.
2. Describe the main forces in the general environment that are affecting the organization.
3. Describe the main global forces that are affecting the organization.
4. Explain how environmental forces affect the job of an individual manager within this organization. How do they determine the opportunities and threats that its managers must confront?

Managing Ethically

In recent years, the number of U.S. companies that buy their inputs from low-cost foreign suppliers has been growing, and concern about the ethics associated with employing young children in factories has been increasing. In Pakistan and India, children as young as six years old work long hours to make rugs and carpets for export to Western countries or clay bricks for local use. In countries like

Malaysia and in Central America, children and teenagers routinely work long hours in factories and sweat shops to produce the clothing that is found in most U.S. discount and department stores.

Questions

1. Either by yourself or in a group, discuss whether it is ethical to employ children in factories and whether U.S. companies should buy and sell products made by these children? What are some arguments for and against child labor?
2. If child labor is an economic necessity, what ways could be employed to make it as ethical a practice as possible? Or is it simply unethical?

Small Group Breakout Exercise

How to Enter the Copying Business

Form groups of three to five people, and appoint one group member as the spokesperson who will communicate your findings to the whole class when called on by the instructor. Then discuss the following scenario.

You and your partners have decided to open a small printing and copying business in a college town of 100,000 people. Your business will compete with companies like Kinko's. You know that over 50 percent of small businesses fail in their first year, so to increase your chances of success, you have decided to do a detailed analysis of the task environment of the copying business to discover what opportunities and threats you will encounter. As a group:

1. Decide what you must know about (a) your future customers, (b) your future competitors, and (c) other critical forces in the task environment if you are to be successful.
2. Evaluate the main barriers to entry into the copying business.
3. Based on this analysis, list some of the steps you would take to help your new copying business succeed.

Exploring the World Wide Web

Go to Fuji Films' Web site (home.fujifilm.com),and then click on "corporate," "profile," and "global operations" and read about Fuji's global activities.

1. How would you characterize the way Fuji manages the global environment? For example, how has Fuji responded to the needs of customers in different countries?
2. How have increasing global competition and declining barriers of distance and culture been affecting Fuji's operations?

Be the Manager

The Changing Environment of Retailing

You are the new manager of a major clothing store that is facing a crisis. This clothing store has been the leader in its market for the last 15 years. In the last three years, however, two other major clothing store chains have opened up, and they have steadily been attracting customers away from your store—your sales are down 30 percent. To find out why, your store surveyed former customers and learned that they perceive the store as not keeping up with changing fashion trends and new forms of customer service. In examining the way the store operates, you found out that the 10 purchasing managers who buy the clothing and accessories for the store have been buying increasingly from the same clothing suppliers and have become reluctant to try new ones. Moreover, salespeople rarely, if ever, make suggestions for changing the way the store operates, they don't respond to customer requests, and the culture of the store has become conservative and risk-averse.

Questions

1. Analyze the major forces in the task environment of a retail clothing store.
2. Devise a program that will help other managers and employees to better understand and respond to their store's task environment.

Additional Activities on the Build Your Management Skills DVD

- **Test Your Knowledge:** (1) Macroenvironmental Forces and (2) Hofstede's Model of National Culture
- **Manager's Hot Seat:** Cultural Differences: Let's Break a Deal

BusinessWeek Case in the News

The Vanishing Mass Market

To most of us, Tide is as familiar as home. Last year, Americans bought some $2 billion worth of Tide, which has ranked as the country's biggest-selling laundry detergent ever since Procter & Gamble Co. took it national in 1949. If ever a brand epitomized the great, one-size-fits-all mass market, it is Tide, right? Wrong. Or so says Procter & Gamble itself. James R. Stengel, P&G's global marketing officer, insists that his company's bulging portfolio of big brands contains "not one mass-market brand, whether it's Tide or Old Spice"—or Crest or Pampers or Ivory. "Every one of our brands is targeted."

In the boom decades after World War II, it was P&G more than any other company that put the mass in marketing, relying on TV commercials and print ads to flog its standardized wares from coast to coast. Along with Coca-Cola, McDonald's, General Motors, Unilever Group, American Express, and many other consumer-products giants, P&G now is standing mass marketing on its head by shifting emphasis from selling to the vast, anonymous crowd to selling to millions of particular consumers. "You find the people. You are very focused on them," Stengel says. "You become relevant to them."

For marketers, the evolution from mass to micromarketing is a fundamental change driven as much by necessity as opportunity. America today is a far more diverse and commercially self-indulgent society than it was in the heyday of the mass market. The country has atomized into countless market segments defined not only by demography, but by increasingly nuanced and insistent product preferences. "All the research we're doing tells us that the driver of demand going forward is all about products that are 'right for me'," says David Martin, president of Interbrand Corp. "And that's ultimately about offering a degree of customization for all."

At the same time, the almost-universal audience assembled long ago by network television and augmented by the other mass media is fragmenting at an accelerating rate. The mass media's decline is an old story in many respects; prime-time network ratings and newspaper circulation have been sliding since the 1970s. What's new is that the proliferation of digital and wireless communication channels is spreading the mass audience of yore ever-thinner across hundreds of narrowcast cable-TV and radio channels, thousands of specialized magazines, and millions of computer terminals, video-game consoles, personal digital assistants, and cell-phone screens.

In the 1960s, an advertiser could reach 80 percent of U.S. women with a spot aired simultaneously on CBS, NBC, and ABC. Today, an ad would have to run on 100 TV channels to have a prayer of duplicating this feat. Adding a few Web sites would help, but not even the biggest new media conduits—not Home Box Office, not Yahoo, not AOL Instant Messenger, not even X-Box—is likely to ever match the ubiquity of the Big Three networks in their prime.

Questions

1. How do changes in the mass market affect the task environment facing organizations?
2. How can companies respond to the changes taking place?

Source: Anthony Bianco, Tom Lowry, Robert Berner, Michael Arndt, and Ronald Grover, "The Vanishing Mass Market." Reprinted from the July 12, 2004, issue of *BusinessWeek* by special permission.

BusinessWeek **Case in the News**

Posco: One Sharp Steelmaker

Korea these days enjoys a well-deserved reputation for its digital prowess: A land where lab-coated engineers and scientists work with delicate wafer chips, while pink-haired youths write software for the latest cell phone. But you don't have to dig too deep to find another Korea, one where hard-bodied workers labor in factories to produce the stuff that makes the physical world go. To get an idea of the vibrancy of this part of the economy, visit the Posco steelworks in Pohang, on the peninsula's east coast. Here, in sweltering heat, sparks fly as molten iron is ladled into vast bins, and ribbons of fiery metal roll through milling machines.

Old Economy? Sure. But Posco is no rust-belt relic. True, with $12 billion in sales, it isn't the biggest steelmaker on earth. That title belongs to Luxembourg-based Arcelor, more than double Posco's size. But where it really counts, Posco is in a class all its own. The company enjoys the biggest profits in the global steel industry, raking in enough cash to make many a high-tech outfit envious. Thanks to robust demand at home and in China, net earnings from Posco's array of steel products—used in everything from screws to skyscrapers—last year shot up 80 percent, to $1.66 billion. And Daewoo Securities Co. is forecasting a 61 percent jump in profits, to $2.7 billion, on $15.6 billion in sales this year. "As far as efficiency is concerned, Posco stands taller than any other steelmaker in the world," says Daewoo analyst Yang Ki In.

In fact, Posco isn't as different from South Korea's New Economy innovators as all the sweat and sparks might lead you to believe. The company is considered one of the industry's high-tech paladins. In August 2004, Posco enhanced that reputation when it broke ground on a $1.1 billion mill that could boost productivity even higher. The mill will use a new technology, called Finex, that will help cut costs by nearly a fifth and harmful emissions by more than 90 percent, says Chairman and CEO Lee Ku Taek. For decades, steelmakers have used highly polluting ovens to turn powdery coal and iron ore into chunks called coke and sinter, which are melted with superheated air to make iron. With Finex, coal and ore are turned into iron without coking and sintering. After the plant opens, in about two years, Posco plans to roll out the technology in other mills. "I want to be remembered as the CEO who started another leap forward," says Lee, a 35-year Posco veteran who has become the project's champion since taking over the top job a year ago.

Posco has put plenty of slick information technology to work, too. The company has invested $179 million to network its 80 Korean plants so that it can take orders online and coordinate production and deliveries. So, as molten steel slabs wend their way through the mills at Posco's two major steelworks—in Pohang and at Gwangyang, on the southern coast—each is pressed to a specified weight and width depending on a particular customer's needs. This mill-level customization helps push steel out the door faster, which has enabled Posco to halve delivery times and slash inventories by 60 percent.

Like the rest of Korea Inc., Posco believes its future lies across the Yellow Sea in China. The country has become the world's biggest steel market as well as the biggest producer, with more than 1,000 mills, from giants such as Shanghai BaoSteel Group and Wuhan Iron & Steel Group to tiny operations in outlying provinces. To cash in on this vast opportunity, Posco has invested $800 million in China, its biggest export market. One joint venture, with Benxi Iron & Steel (Group) Co., near Shenyang, will churn out 1.8 million tons of cold-rolled sheets annually for autos and home appliances when it opens in 2006. Another, with Jiangsu Shagang Group, already produces 280,000 tons of stainless cold-rolled coils and some 100,000 tons of galvanized steel every year. In all, Posco has 14 joint ventures in China. By 2006, Posco plans some $1.4 billion in fresh investment on the mainland, especially in galvanized and stainless steel to supply global auto and appliance makers that have opened plants there.

Questions

1. In what ways is Posco responding to the changing forces in its task environment?
2. In what ways is Posco responding to the changing forces in its general environment?

Source: Brian Bremmer, Moon Ihlwan and Dexter Roberts, "Posco: One Sharp Steelmaker." Reprinted from the August 30, 2004, issue of *BusinessWeek* by special permission.

CHAPTER

7 The Manager as a Decision Maker

Learning Objectives

After studying this chapter, you should be able to:

- Differentiate between programmed and nonprogrammed decisions, and explain why nonprogrammed decision making is a complex, uncertain process.
- Describe the six steps that managers should take to make the best decisions.
- Explain how cognitive biases can affect decision making and lead managers to make poor decisions.
- Identify the advantages and disadvantages of group decision making, and describe techniques that can improve it.
- Explain the role that organizational learning and creativity play in helping managers to improve their decisions.

A Manager's Challenge

Yamada Transforms GlaxoSmithKline

How can top managers in large corporations encourage effective decision making, creativity, and entrepreneurship?

By all counts, Tadataka (Tachi) Yamada faced a challenging task. Yamada was a top manager at SmithKline Beecham, one of the world's largest pharmaceutical companies, when things couldn't seem more dismal.[1] Not enough potential drugs were in the pipeline, patents on top-selling drugs like Paxil were nearing their expiration dates, and SmithKline Beecham was in the process of merging with Glaxo Wellcome, a pharmaceutical company with similar challenges.[2] Yamada's task was no less than daunting—reinvent the 15,000-people-strong R&D function of the merged company, GlaxoSmithKline, to fill the company's pipeline with promising new drugs. As Jean-Pierre Garnier, the new CEO of the just merged company, put it, "We can't keep doing what we're doing. . . . So start thinking about something radical."[3]

Yamada was up for the challenge and made bold decisions to reinvent R&D at GlaxoSmithKline (Glaxo). Interestingly, his efforts focused on changing the way decisions were traditionally made in the company. This was not an easy process—it took three years, the support and commitment of Garnier, and the courage of Yamada. It was rough going during much of this period, but by 2004 Yamada's reorientation of decision making started paying off. While only a few new drugs were under development in 2001, by 2004 Glaxo had over 40 drugs in phases 2 and 3 of clinical trials.[4]

Tachi Yamada faced some tough decisions in taking on the task of reinventing the 15,000-people-strong R&D function at the newly merged company, GlaxoSmithKline.

What did Yamada decide that changed the fate of Glaxo? Taking a bold step, he decided not to do what typically is done after such a mega-merger—consolidate R&D across the newly merged companies, lay off employees, and focus on cutting costs. Rather, Yamada went back to his research roots (he has an MD degree and was formerly the chairman of the Internal

Medicine Department at the University of Michigan Medical School).[5] He decided that to develop new drugs, R&D employees need to think and act like entrepreneurs—making decisions that they believe in and being highly motivated to follow through to make them a success.[6]

Yamada restructured R&D at Glaxo by forming autonomous, entrepreneurial start-up labs to develop new drugs. Rather than consolidating decision making at the top, which usually happens after a merger, he empowered researchers in the labs to make the decisions that would hopefully revive Glaxo or seal its fate. Yamada's bold experiment was a testament to his belief that the research scientists responsible for discovering and developing new drugs should be making the key decisions—not top executives, who are a step removed from the research process on a day-to-day basis. Given the huge investments and lengthy time horizons involved—developing a new drug and getting it approved by the U.S. Food and Drug Administration (FDA) typically takes about 10 years and costs about $800 million—giving research scientists the final say on what new drugs to pursue was a dramatic departure from the tradition of having top managers make such decisions.[7]

Yamada divided R&D at Glaxo into six small, semiautonomous labs, each with a primary research focus, such as cardiovascular disease or cancer. Rather than operating as R&D typically does in a large company, these labs resemble biotech start-ups: Each has its own top managers, budget, and staff (kept deliberately small, at no more than 400 employees). Not only do the labs decide what drugs to pursue, but they also follow through with their decisions into the clinical testing phase. Previously, as is typical in large pharmaceutical companies, once R&D discovered new drugs, it passed them on to other units responsible for getting the drugs into clinical testing. Yamada wanted the researchers who were closest to the new discoveries to take ownership of them, make key decisions on how to proceed, and be responsible for their success (or failure). Importantly, researchers are rewarded for their expanded role in drug development; those who succeed at discovering a new drug and moving it into clinical testing are rewarded with bonuses and royalties.[8]

This restructuring of R&D was a major change from the status quo at Glaxo, a change that during the first two years seemed doomed to failure. Setting up the new lab structure, redesigning jobs, dismantling the decision-making hierarchy, and empowering scientists to make key decisions resulted in turf battles, chaos, and high levels of uncertainty and stress. Many R&D scientists and executives fled the chaos to work for other companies, and the price of Glaxo shares declined by almost 20 percent.[9]

Garnier and Yamada believed in what they were doing and were willing to carry on making tough decisions to make it a success. While the ultimate outcome of their bold decisions will take years to crystallize in terms of FDA-approved, effective new drugs for treating diseases, things are now looking bright at Glaxo. In 2003, Glaxo approximately doubled over 2001 the number of new drugs it was advancing into Phase I and II trials, and accelerated earlier-stage discovery efforts with new automated drug-screening facilities.[10] Yamada's willingness to take risks to enhance long-term viability, innovation, and success seems to be paying off at Glaxo. It has convinced many, including Allen Oliff, a top research executive recruited from Merck to head a new cancer lab,[11] that Yamada has successfully reinvented R&D at Glaxo. The wisdom of his efforts has not gone unnoticed at the very highest levels of the company. In 2004, the 58-year-old Yamada was named executive director/chairman of research and development and became a member of Glaxo's board of directors.[12]

Overview

"A Manager's Challenge" describes how the ways in which decisions are made in an organization, and who makes them, can have a profound influence on organizational effectiveness and innovation. Glaxo was floundering, and the bold decisions Yamada made to reinvent R&D and push decision-making authority down the hierarchy to the research labs has paid off in terms of a rich pipeline of promising new drugs. In contrast, Merck, another large pharmaceutical company, is currently suffering the consequences of a series of poor decisions such as halting the development of promising new drugs.[13] The decisions managers make, managers like Glaxo's Yamada and Garnier and Merck's CEO Ray Gilmartin, and the effects that these decisions have on the decision-making process throughout an organization, profoundly influence organizational effectiveness.[14] Yet such decisions can be very difficult to make because they are fraught with uncertainty.

In this chapter, we examine how managers make decisions and explore how individual, group, and organizational factors affect the quality of the decisions they make and ultimately determine organizational performance. We discuss the nature of managerial decision making and examine some models of the decision-making process that help reveal the complexities of successful decision making. Then we outline the main steps of the decision-making process; in addition, we explore the biases that may cause capable managers to make poor decisions both as individuals and as members of a group. Finally, we examine how managers can promote organizational learning and creativity and improve the quality of decision making throughout an organization. By the end of this chapter, you will appreciate the critical role decision making plays in creating a high-performing organization.

The Nature of Managerial Decision Making

Every time managers act to plan, organize, direct, or control organizational activities, they make a stream of decisions. In opening a new restaurant, for example, managers have to decide where to locate it, what kinds of food to provide to customers, which people to employ, and so on. Decision making is a basic part of every task managers perform. In this chapter we study how these decisions are made.

As we discussed in the last three chapters, one of the main tasks facing a manager is to manage the organizational environment. Forces in the external environment give rise to many opportunities and threats for managers and their organizations. In addition, inside an organization managers must address many opportunities and threats that may arise during the course of utilizing organizational resources. To deal with these opportunities and threats, managers must make decisions–that is, they must select one solution from a set of alternatives. **Decision making** is the process by which managers respond to the opportunities and threats that confront them by analyzing the options and making determinations, or *decisions,* about specific organizational goals and courses of action. Good decisions result in the selection of appropriate goals and courses of action that increase organizational performance; bad decisions result in lower performance.

decision making The process by which managers respond to opportunities and threats by analyzing options and making determinations about specific organizational goals and courses of action.

Decision making in response to opportunities occurs when managers search for ways to improve organizational performance to benefit customers, employees, and other stakeholder groups. In "A Manager's Challenge," Tachi Yamada saw an opportunity to fill Glaxo's pipeline with promising new drugs by restructuring R&D into entrepreneurial biotech labs. *Decision making in response to threats* occurs when events inside or outside the organization are adversely affecting organizational performance and managers are searching for ways to increase performance.[15] At Glaxo, Yamada realized that being the world's second-largest pharmaceutical company in what CEO Garnier refers to as a "brutal industry" was proving to be a liability for R&D. Pharmaceuticals like Glaxo must have a pipeline of new drugs to remain competitive because even when they develop blockbusters like Paxil and Wellbutrin, once their patent protection expires, revenues plummet as generic forms of the drugs hit the market. As Yamada puts it, "The answer to the pipeline problem is to be big and small at the same time. . . . You need people who think like entrepreneurs and play the hunches. That's what the industry lost when it got too big."[16] Decision making is central to being a manager, and whenever managers engage in planning, organizing, leading, and controlling–their four principal functions–they are constantly making decisions.

Managers are always searching for ways to make better decisions to improve organizational performance. At the same time, they do their best to avoid costly mistakes that will hurt organizational performance. Examples of spectacularly good decisions include Liz Claiborne's decision in the 1980s to focus on producing clothes for the growing number of women entering the workforce–a decision that contributed to making her company one of the largest clothing manufacturers. Also, Bill Gates's decision to buy a computer operating system for $50,000 from a small company in Seattle and sell it to IBM for the new IBM personal computer turned Gates and Microsoft, respectively, into the richest man and richest software company in the United States. Examples of spectacularly bad decisions include the decision by managers at NASA and Morton Thiokol to launch the *Challenger* space shuttle–a decision that resulted in the deaths of six astronauts in 1986. Also, the decision of Ken Olsen, founder of Digital Equipment Corporation, to stay with mainframe computers in the 1980s and not allow his engineers to spend the company's resources on creating new kinds of personal computers because of his belief that "personal computers are just toys" was a decision that cost Olsen his job as CEO and almost ruined his company.

Programmed and Nonprogrammed Decision Making

Regardless of the specific decisions that a manager makes, the decision-making process is either programmed or nonprogrammed.[17]

programmed decision making Routine, virtually automatic decision making that follows established rules or guidelines.

PROGRAMMED DECISION MAKING

Programmed decision making is a *routine,* virtually automatic process. Programmed decisions are decisions that have been made so many times in the past that managers have developed rules or guidelines to be applied when certain situations inevitably occur. Programmed decision making takes place when a school principal asks the school board to hire a new teacher whenever student enrollment increases by 40 students; when a manufacturing supervisor hires new workers whenever existing workers' overtime increases by more than 10 percent; and when an office manager orders basic office supplies, such as paper and pens, whenever the inventory of supplies on hand drops below a certain level. Furthermore, in the last example, the office manager probably orders the same amount of supplies each time.

This decision making is called *programmed* because office managers, for example, do not need to repeatedly make new judgments about what should be done. They can rely on long-established decision rules such as these:

- *Rule 1:* When the storage shelves are three-quarters empty, order more copy paper.
- *Rule 2:* When ordering paper, order enough to fill the shelves.

Managers can develop rules and guidelines to regulate all routine organizational activities. For example, rules can specify how a worker should perform a certain task, and rules can specify the quality standards that raw materials must meet to be acceptable. Most decision making that relates to the day-to-day running of an organization is programmed decision making. Examples include decision making about how much inventory to hold, when to pay bills, when to bill customers, and when to order materials and supplies. Programmed decision making occurs when managers have the information they need to create rules that will guide decision making. There is little ambiguity involved in assessing when the stockroom is empty or counting the number of new students in class.

NONPROGRAMMED DECISION MAKING Suppose, however, managers are not at all certain that a course of action will lead to a desired outcome. Or, in even more ambiguous terms, suppose managers are not even clear about what they are really trying to achieve. Obviously, rules cannot be developed to predict uncertain events. **Nonprogrammed decision making** is required for these nonroutine decisions. Nonprogrammed decisions are made in response to unusual or novel opportunities and threats. Nonprogrammed decision making occurs when there are no ready-made decision rules that managers can apply to a situation. Rules do not exist because the situation is unexpected or uncertain and managers lack the information they would need to develop rules to cover it. Examples of nonprogrammed decision making include decisions to invest in a new kind of technology, develop a new kind of product, launch a new promotional campaign, enter a new market, expand internationally, or restructure an organization or function as did Yamada in "A Manager's Challenge."

nonprogrammed decision making Nonroutine decision making that occurs in response to unusual, unpredictable opportunities and threats.

How do managers make decisions in the absence of decision rules? They may rely on their **intuition**–feelings, beliefs, and hunches that come readily to mind, require little effort and information gathering, and result in on-the-spot decisions.[18] Or they may make **reasoned judgments**–decisions that take time and effort to make and result from careful information gathering, generation of alternatives, and evaluation of alternatives. "Exercising" one's judgment is a more rational process than "going with" one's intuition. For reasons that we examine later in this chapter, both intuition and judgment often are flawed and can result in poor decision making. Thus, the likelihood of error is much greater in nonprogrammed decision making than in programmed decision making.[19] In the remainder of this chapter, when we talk about decision making, we are referring to *nonprogrammed* decision making because it causes the most problems for managers and is inherently challenging.

intuition Feelings, beliefs, and hunches that come readily to mind, require little effort and information gathering, and result in on-the-spot decisions.

reasoned judgment A decision that takes time and effort to make and results from careful information gathering, generation of alternatives, and evaluation of alternatives.

Sometimes managers have to make rapid decisions and don't have the time for careful consideration of the issues involved. They must rely on their intuition

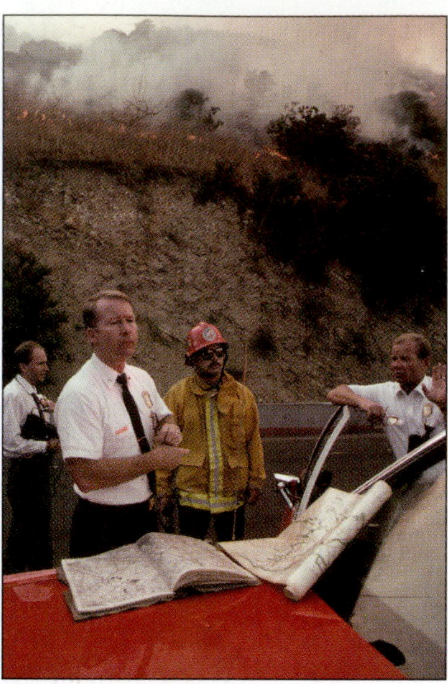

Fire chiefs and firefighters gather to plan strategy at the scene of a brush fire in Los Angeles' Griffith Park. In a crisis like this, managers don't have much time for decision making and, therefore, must rely on their expert intuition.

to quickly respond to a pressing concern. For example, when fire chiefs, captains, and lieutenants manage firefighters battling dangerous, out-of-control fires, they often need to rely on their expert intuition to make on-the-spot decisions that will protect the lives of the firefighters and save the lives of others, contain the fires, and preserve property–decisions made in emergency situations entailing high uncertainty, high risk, and rapidly changing conditions.[20] Other times, managers do have the time available to make reasoned judgments but there are no established rules to guide their decisions, such as when deciding whether or not to proceed with a proposed merger. Regardless of the circumstances, making nonprogrammed decisions can result in effective or ineffective decision making. As indicated in the following "Manager as a Person," managers have to be on their guard to avoid being overconfident in decisions that result from their intuition and reasoned judgment.

Manager as a Person

Curbing Overconfidence

Should managers be confident in their intuition and reasoned judgments?[21] Decades of research by Nobel Prize winner Daniel Kahneman, his long-time collaborator the late Amos Tversy, and other researchers suggests that, if anything, managers (like all people) tend to be overconfident in the decisions they make (whether based on intuition or reasoned judgments). And with overconfidence comes the failure to evaluate and rethink the wisdom of the decisions one makes and to learn from mistakes.[22]

Kahneman distinguishes between the intuitions of managers who are truly expert in the content domain of a decision and the intuition of managers who have some knowledge and experience but are not true experts.[23] While the intuition of both types can be faulty, that of experts is less likely to be flawed. This is why fire captains can make good decisions and why expert chess players can make good moves, in both cases without spending much time, and deliberate carefully on what, for nonexperts, is a very complicated set of circumstances. What distinguishes expert managers from those with "some" expertise is that the experts have extensive experience under conditions in which they receive quick and clear feedback about the outcomes of their decisions.[24]

Unfortunately, managers who have some experience in a content area but are not true experts tend to be overly confident in their intuition and their judgments.[25] As Kahneman puts it, "People jump to statistical conclusions on the basis of very weak evidence. We form powerful intuitions about trends and about the replicability of results on the basis of information that is truly inadequate."[26] Not only do managers, and all people, tend to be overconfident about their intuitions and judgments, but they also tend not to learn from mistakes. Compounding this undue optimism is a very human tendency to be overconfident in one's own abilities and influence over unpredictable events. Surveys have found that the majority of people think they are above average, make better decisions, and are less prone to making bad decisions than others (of course, it is impossible for most people to be above average on any dimension).[27]

A recent example of managerial overconfidence is particularly telling. Research has consistently found that mergers tend to turn out poorly–post-merger profitability declines, stock prices decline, and so forth. (For example, Chrysler had the biggest profits of the three largest automobile makers in the United States when it merged with Daimler; the merger has not worked out well and Chrysler would have been better off if it never had happened.) So one would imagine that top executives and boards of directors would learn from this research and from articles in the business press about the woes of merged companies (e.g., the AOL–Time Warner merger). Evidently not. According to a recent study by Hewitt Associates, top executives and board members are, if anything, planning on increasing their involvement in mergers over the next few years. These top managers evidently overconfidently believe that they can succeed where others have failed.[28]

Jeffrey Pfeffer, a professor at Stanford University's Graduate School of Business, suggests that managers can avoid the perils of overconfidence by critically evaluating the decisions they have made and the outcomes of those decisions. They should admit to themselves when they have made a mistake and really learn from their mistakes (rather than dismissing them as flukes or situations out of their control). In addition, managers should be leery of too much agreement at the top. As Pfeffer puts it, "If two people agree all the time, one of them is redundant").[29]

The classical and the administrative decision-making models reveal many of the assumptions, complexities, and pitfalls that affect decision making. These models help reveal the factors that managers and other decision makers must be aware of to improve the quality of their decision making. Keep in mind, however, that the classical and administrative models are just guides that can help managers understand the decision-making process. In real life, the process is typically not cut-and-dried, but these models can help guide a manager through it.

classical decision-making model A prescriptive approach to decision making based on the assumption that the decision maker can identify and evaluate all possible alternatives and their consequences and rationally choose the most appropriate course of action.

The Classical Model

One of the earliest models of decision making, the **classical model,** is *prescriptive,* which means that it specifies how decisions *should* be made. Managers using the classical model make a series of simplifying assumptions about the nature of the decision-making process (see Figure 7.1, page 230). The premise of the classical model is that once managers recognize the need to make a decision, they should be able to generate a complete list of all alternatives and consequences and make the best choice. In other words, the classical model assumes that managers have

Figure 7.1
The Classical Model of Decision Making

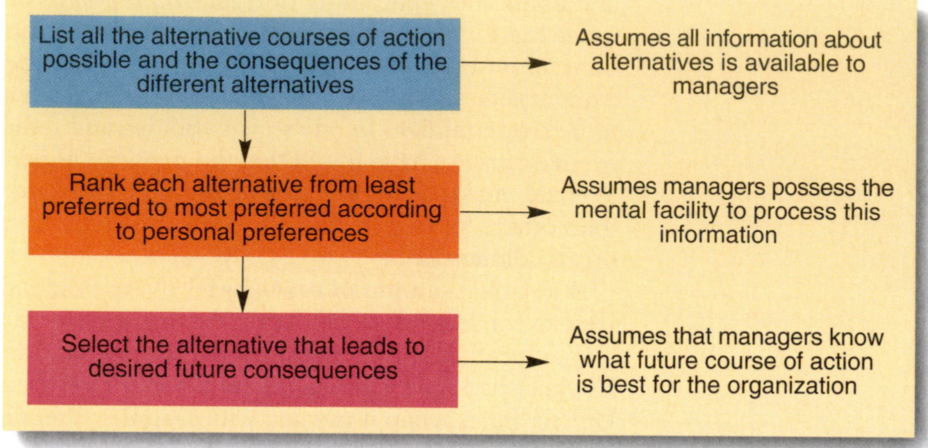

optimum decision The most appropriate decision in light of what managers believe to be the most desirable future consequences for the organization.

access to *all* the information they need to make the **optimum decision,** which is the most appropriate decision possible in light of what they believe to be the most desirable future consequences for the organization. Furthermore, the classical model assumes that managers can easily list their own preferences for each alternative and rank them from least to most preferred to make the optimum decision.

The Administrative Model

administrative model An approach to decision making that explains why decision making is inherently uncertain and risky and why managers usually make satisfactory rather than optimum decisions.

James March and Herbert Simon disagreed with the underlying assumptions of the classical model of decision making. In contrast, they proposed that managers in the real world do *not* have access to all the information they need to make a decision. Moreover, they pointed out that even if all information were readily available, many managers would lack the mental or psychological ability to absorb and evaluate it correctly. As a result, March and Simon developed the **administrative model** of decision making to explain why decision making is always an inherently uncertain and risky process–and why managers can rarely make decisions in the manner prescribed by the classical model. The administrative model is based on three important concepts: bounded rationality, incomplete information, and satisficing.

bounded rationality Cognitive limitations that constrain one's ability to interpret, process, and act on information.

BOUNDED RATIONALITY March and Simon pointed out that human decision-making capabilities are bounded by people's cognitive limitations–that is, limitations in their ability to interpret, process, and act on information.[30] They argued that the limitations of human intelligence constrain the ability of decision makers to determine the optimum decision. March and Simon coined the term **bounded rationality** to describe the situation in which the number of alternatives a manager must identify is so great and the amount of information so vast that it is difficult for the manager to even come close to evaluating it all before making a decision.[31]

INCOMPLETE INFORMATION Even if managers did have an unlimited ability to evaluate information, they still would not be able to arrive at the optimum decision because they would have incomplete information. Information is

Figure 7.2
Why Information is Incomplete

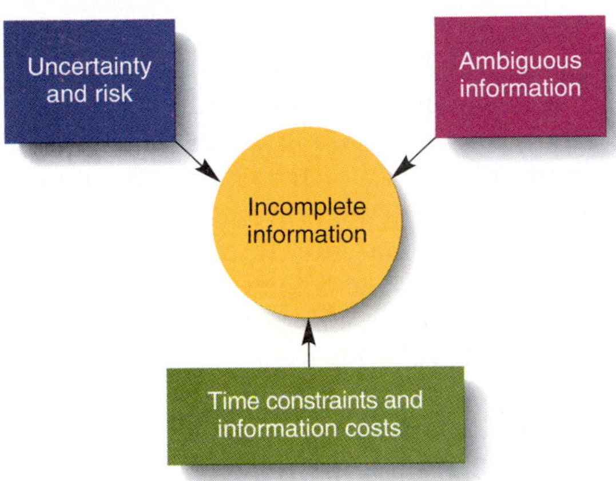

incomplete because the full range of decision-making alternatives is unknowable in most situations and the consequences associated with known alternatives are uncertain, as is true at GlaxoSmithKline in "A Manager's Challenge."[32] In other words, information is incomplete because of risk and uncertainty, ambiguity, and time constraints (see Figure 7.2).

RISK AND UNCERTAINTY As we saw in Chapter 6, forces in the organizational environment are constantly changing. **Risk** is present when managers know the possible outcomes of a particular course of action and can assign probabilities to them. For example, managers in the biotechnology industry know that new drugs have a 10 percent probability of successfully passing advanced clinical trials and a 90 percent probability of failing. These probabilities reflect the experiences of thousands of drugs that have gone through advanced clinical trials. Thus, when managers in the biotechnology industry decide to submit a drug for testing, they know that there is only a 10 percent chance that the drug will succeed, but at least they have some information on which to base their decision.

risk The degree of probability that the possible outcomes of a particular course of action will occur.

uncertainty Unpredictability.

When **uncertainty** exists, the probabilities of alternative outcomes *cannot* be determined and future outcomes are *unknown*. Managers are working blind. Since the probability of a given outcome occurring is *not* known, managers have little information to use in making a decision. For example, in 1993, when Apple Computer introduced the Newton, its personal digital assistant (PDA), managers had no idea what the probability of a successful product launch for a PDA might be. Because Apple was the first to market this totally new product, there was no body of well-known data that Apple's managers could draw on to calculate the probability of a successful launch. Uncertainty plagues most managerial decision making.[33] Although Apple's initial launch of its PDA was a disaster due to technical problems, an improved version was more successful. In fact, Apple created the PDA market that has boomed during the 2000s as new and different wireless products have been introduced.

When Apple introduced the Newton, shown here, managers were working under conditions of extreme uncertainty. Because Apple was the first to market this type of product, there was no body of well-known data that managers could draw on to calculate the probability of a successful product launch.

As indicated in the following "Information Technology Byte," a major source of uncertainty for top managers revolves around being unable to accurately predict or forecast future demand for products and services.

Information Technology Byte

Revising Plans Never Ends for Craig Knouf

Having a good business plan is essential for entrepreneurs to obtain funding from banks, venture capitalists, and other sources of funds. Once entrepreneurs have secured funding and their businesses are up and running, their business plans are typically reviewed only once a year as part of an annual planning process, unless, of course, the entrepreneurs are seeking to obtain additional funds. These business plans are inherently fraught with uncertainty, as is starting a new business and having it actually succeed. However, viewing a business plan as a work in progress that should be evolving on an almost continuous basis has turned out to be a blessing for Craig Knouf, founder, CEO, and majority owner of Associated Business Systems (ABS), a Portland, Oregon, supplier of office equipment.[34]

Knouf estimates that he has revised his business plan over 120 times since founding ABS in 1997; he makes a point of reviewing and, if necessary, revising ABS's business plan on a monthly basis after consulting with the firm's seven vice presidents. As Knouf puts it, "If you only looked at the plan every quarter, by the time you realize the mistake, you're five months off. . . . You're done. You're not going to get back on track."[35] Of course, the reason why managers like Knouf have to continually rethink their decisions is the inherent uncertainty in all that they do. As a case in point, in the early years Knouf never anticipated that scanners would be a significant part of his business. But during his monthly reviews of the business, he noticed that sales of office equipment with scanning capabilities were steadily increasing. Acting on what his sales data were telling him, Knouf quickly added products with scanning capabilities to his company's offerings, and by 2004 sales of these products were over $3 million.[36]

Knouf's ability to appreciate the inherent uncertainty of the best-made plans and decisions, and the benefit of frequently changing courses of action in response to feedback from customers and the market, has certainly paid off handsomely for his company. Since its founding in 1997, ABS's revenues have grown from $880,000 to over $20 million.[37] ABS appeared on *Inc.* magazine's list of fastest-growing private companies in 2002 and 2003 and was on the *Portland Business Journal*'s list of fastest-growing companies in Oregon from 1999 to 2003.[38] Even suppliers have taken notice of ABS's ability to stay in touch with the market, provide excellent, timely service to customers, and actively respond to changing market conditions.[39] For example, ABS was one of only eight distributors across the United States selected by Hewlett-Packard to launch a new line of high-speed copiers with multiple functions such as printing and scanning.[40] Management experts agree that Knouf's approach to planning makes good business sense. As Eric Siegel, Wharton Business School lecturer and president of Siegel Management Consultants, puts it, "The world turns; things change. . . . What you commit to a document on Dec. 19 is not necessarily appropriate on Jan. 19."[41]

ambiguous information
Information that can be interpreted in multiple and often conflicting ways.

AMBIGUOUS INFORMATION A second reason why information is incomplete is that much of the information managers have at their disposal is **ambiguous information.** Its meaning is not clear–it can be interpreted in

Figure 7.3
Ambiguous Information: Young Woman or Old Woman?

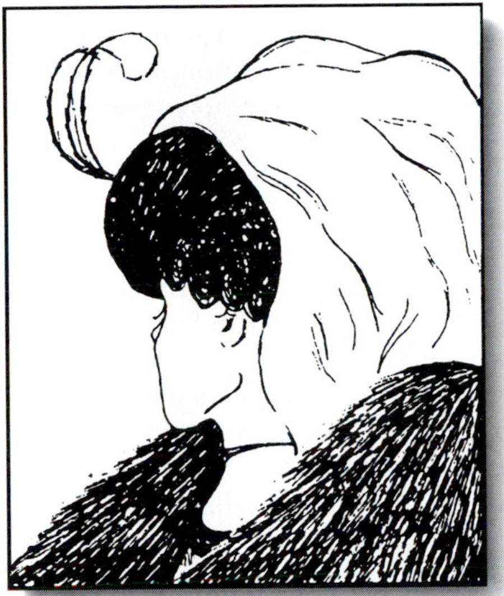

multiple and often conflicting ways.[42] Take a look at Figure 7.3. Do you see a young woman or an old woman? In a similar fashion, managers often interpret the same piece of information differently and make decisions based on their own interpretations. Recall from "A Manager's Challenge" that Yamada perceived Glaxo's problems in 2001 in terms of too much top-down decision making and an R&D function that needed to be much more entrepreneurial. Merck is currently facing similar problems, but its CEO, Ray Gilmartin, seems to perceive Merck's troubles in terms of the need to cut costs–in November 2003, Gilmartin made the decision to lay off 4,400 Merck employees–7 percent of the workforce–the largest layoff Merck has had in over 100 years.[43]

TIME CONSTRAINTS AND INFORMATION COSTS The third reason why information is incomplete is that managers have neither the time nor the money to search for all possible alternative solutions and evaluate all the potential consequences of those alternatives. Consider the situation confronting a Ford Motor Company purchasing manager who has one month to choose a supplier for a small engine part. Of the thousands of potential suppliers for this part, there are 20,000 in the United States alone. Given the time available, the purchasing manager cannot contact all potential suppliers and ask each for its terms (price, delivery schedules, and so on). Moreover, even if the time were available, the costs of obtaining the information, including the manager's own time, would be prohibitive.

SATISFICING March and Simon argue that managers do not attempt to discover every alternative when faced with bounded rationality, an uncertain future, unquantifiable risks, considerable ambiguity, time constraints, and high information costs. Rather, they use a strategy known as **satisficing,** exploring a limited sample of all potential alternatives.[44] When managers satisfice, they search for and choose acceptable, or satisfactory, ways to respond to problems and opportunities rather than trying to make the optimal decision.[45] In the case of the Ford purchasing manager's search, for example, satisficing may involve asking a limited number of suppliers for their terms, trusting that they are representative of suppliers in general, and making a choice from that set. Although this course of action is reasonable from the perspective of the purchasing manager, it may mean that a potentially superior supplier is overlooked.

satisficing Searching for and choosing an acceptable, or satisfactory, response to problems and opportunities, rather than trying to make the best decision.

March and Simon pointed out that managerial decision making is often more art than science. In the real world, managers must rely on their intuition and judgment to make what seems to them to be the best decision in the face of uncertainty and ambiguity.[46]

Moreover, managerial decision making is often fast-paced, as managers use their experience and judgment to make crucial decisions under conditions of incomplete information. Although there is nothing wrong with this approach, decision makers should be aware that human judgment is often flawed. As a result, even the best managers sometimes end up making very poor decisions.[47]

Steps in the Decision-Making Process

Using the work of March and Simon as a basis, researchers have developed a step-by-step model of the decision-making process and the issues and problems that managers confront at each step. Perhaps the best way to introduce this model is to examine the real-world nonprogrammed decision making that Scott McNealy had to engage in at a crucial point in Sun Microsystems' history.

In early August 1985, Scott McNealy, CEO of Sun Microsystems[48] (a hardware and software computer workstation manufacturer focused on network solutions), had to decide whether to go ahead with the launch of the new Carrera workstation computer, scheduled for September 10. Sun's managers had chosen the date nine months earlier when the development plan for the Carrera was first proposed. McNealy knew that it would take at least a month to prepare for the September 10 launch and that the decision could not be put off.

Customers were waiting for the new machine, and McNealy wanted to be the first to provide a workstation that took advantage of Motorola's powerful 16-megahertz 68020 microprocessor. Capitalizing on this opportunity would give Sun a significant edge over Apollo, its main competitor in the workstation market. McNealy knew, however, that committing to the September 10 launch date was risky. Motorola was having production problems with the 16-megahertz 68020 microprocessor and could not guarantee Sun a steady supply of these chips. Moreover, the operating system software was not completely free of bugs.

If Sun launched the Carrera on September 10, the company might have to ship some machines with software that was not fully operational, was prone to crash the system, and utilized Motorola's less-powerful 12-megahertz 68020 microprocessor instead of the 16-megahertz version.[49] Of course, Sun could later upgrade the microprocessor and operating system software in any machines purchased by early customers, but the company's reputation would suffer as a result. If Sun did not go ahead with the September launch, the company would miss an important opportunity.[50] Rumors were circulating in the industry that Apollo would be launching a new machine of its own in December. McNealy wondered what he should do. The microprocessor and operating system problems might be resolved by September 10, but then again they might not be.

Scott McNealy clearly had a difficult decision to make. He had to decide quickly whether to launch the Carrera, but he was not in possession of all the facts. He did not know, for example, whether the microprocessor or operating system problems could be resolved by September 10; nor did he know whether Apollo was going to launch a competing machine in December. But he could not wait to find these things out–he had to make a decision. We'll see what he decided later in the chapter.

Many managers who must make important decisions with incomplete information face dilemmas similar to McNealy's. There are six steps that managers should consciously follow to make a good decision (see Figure 7.4).[51] We review them in the remainder of this section.

Recognize the Need for a Decision

The first step in the decision-making process is to recognize the need for a decision. Scott McNealy recognized this need, and he realized that a decision had to be made quickly because it would take a month to get ready for the September

Figure 7.4
Six Steps in Decision Making

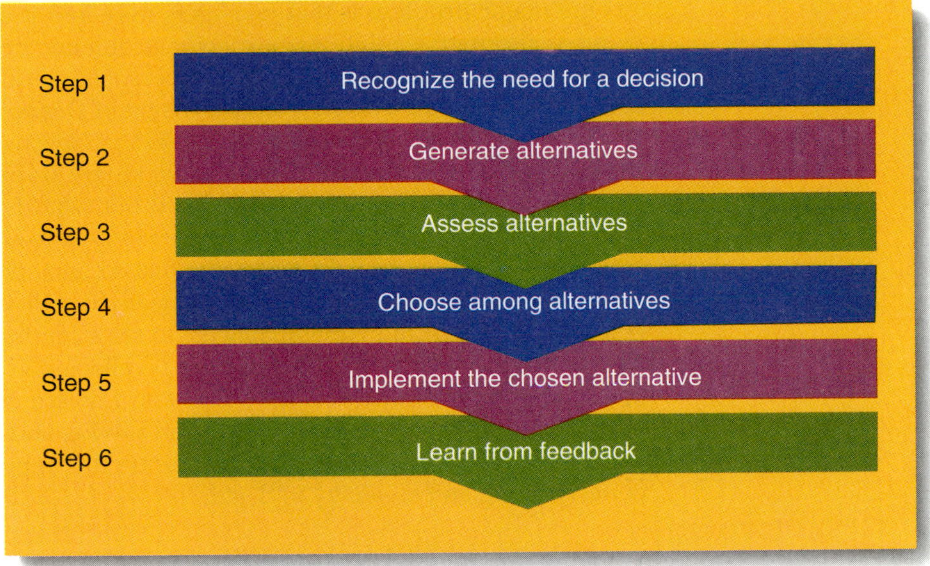
Step 1
Recognize the need for a decision
Step 2
Generate alternatives
Step 3
Assess alternatives
Step 4
Choose among alternatives
Step 5
Implement the chosen alternative
Step 6
Learn from feedback

10 launch. McNealy also knew that the September 10 launch was a critical goal because Sun needed to beat Apollo to the market with a new machine to gain a competitive advantage over this strong challenger.

Some stimuli usually spark the realization that there is a need to make a decision. These stimuli often become apparent because changes in the organizational environment result in new kinds of opportunities and threats. This happened at Sun Microsystems. The September 10 launch date had been set when it seemed that Motorola chips would be readily available. Later, with the supply of chips in doubt and bugs remaining in the system software, Sun was in danger of failing to meet its launch date.

The stimuli that spark decision making are as likely to result from the actions of managers inside an organization as they are from changes in the external environment.[52] An organization possesses a set of skills, competencies, and resources in its employees and in departments such as marketing, manufacturing, and research and development. Managers who actively pursue opportunities to use these competencies create the need to make decisions. Managers thus can be proactive or reactive in recognizing the need to make a decision, but the important issue is that they must recognize this need and respond in a timely and appropriate way.[53]

Generate Alternatives

Having recognized the need to make a decision, a manager must generate a set of feasible alternative courses of action to take in response to the opportunity or threat. Management experts cite failure to properly generate and consider different alternatives as one reason why managers sometimes make bad decisions.[54] In the Sun Microsystems decision, the alternatives seem clear: to go ahead with the September 10 launch or to delay the launch until the Carrera was 100 percent ready for market introduction. Often, however, the alternatives are not so obvious or so clearly specified.

One major problem is that managers may find it difficult to come up with creative alternative solutions to specific problems. Perhaps some of them are used to seeing the world from a single perspective–they have a certain "managerial mind-set." In a manner similar to that of Digital's Olsen, many managers find it difficult to view problems from a fresh perspective. According to best-selling management author Peter Senge, we all are trapped within our personal mental models of the world–our ideas about what is important and how the world works.[55] Generating creative alternatives to solve problems and take advantage of opportunities may require that we abandon our existing mind-sets and develop new ones–something that usually is difficult to do.

The importance of getting managers to set aside their mental models of the world and generate creative alternatives is reflected in the growth of interest in the work of authors such as Peter Senge and Edward de Bono, who have popularized techniques for stimulating problem solving and creative thinking among managers.[56] Later in this chapter, we discuss the important issues of organizational learning and creativity in detail.

Evaluate Alternatives

Once managers have generated a set of alternatives, they must evaluate the advantages and disadvantages of each one.[57] The key to a good assessment of the alternatives is to define the opportunity or threat exactly and then specify the criteria that should influence the selection of alternatives for responding to the problem or opportunity. One reason for bad decisions is that managers often fail to specify the criteria that are important in reaching a decision.[58] In general, successful managers use four criteria to evaluate the pros and cons of alternative courses of action (see Figure 7.5):

1. *Legality.* Managers must ensure that a possible course of action is legal and will not violate any domestic and international laws or government regulations.
2. *Ethicalness.* Managers must ensure that a possible course of action is ethical and will not unnecessarily harm any stakeholder group. Many of the decisions that managers make may help some organizational stakeholders and harm others (see Chapter 3). When examining alternative courses of action, managers need to be very clear about the potential effects of their decisions.
3. *Economic feasibility.* Managers must decide whether the alternatives are economically feasible–that is, whether they can be accomplished given the organization's performance goals. Typically, managers perform a cost-benefit analysis of the various alternatives to determine which one will have the best net financial payoff.
4. *Practicality.* Managers must decide whether they have the capabilities and resources required to implement the alternative, and they must be sure that the alternative will not threaten the attainment of other organizational goals. At first glance, an alternative might seem to be economically superior to other alternatives, but if managers realize that it is likely to threaten other important projects, they might decide that it is not practical after all.

Very often, a manager must consider these four criteria simultaneously. Scott McNealy framed the problem at hand at Sun Microsystems quite well. The key question was whether to go ahead with the September 10 launch date. Two main criteria were influencing McNealy's choice: the need to ship a machine that was as "complete" as possible (the *practicality* criterion) and the need to beat Apollo to

Figure 7.5
General Criteria for Evaluating Possible Courses of Action

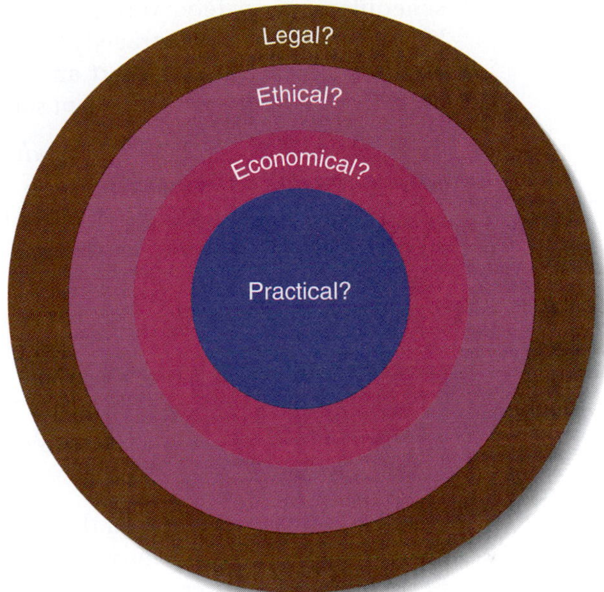
Is the possible course of action:
Legal?
Ethical?
Economical?
Practical?

market with a new workstation (the *economic feasibility* criterion). These two criteria conflicted. The first suggested that the launch should be delayed; the second, that the launch should go ahead. McNealy's actual choice was based on the relative importance that he assigned to these two criteria. In fact, Sun Microsystems went ahead with the September 10 launch, which suggests that McNealy thought the need to beat Apollo to market was the more important criterion.

Some of the worst managerial decisions can be traced to poor assessment of the alternatives, such as the decision to launch the *Challenger* space shuttle, mentioned earlier. In that case, the desire of NASA and Morton Thiokol managers to demonstrate to the public the success of the U.S. space program in order to ensure future funding *(economic feasibility)* conflicted with the need to ensure the safety of the astronauts *(ethicalness)*. Managers deemed the economic criterion more important and decided to launch the space shuttle even though there were unanswered questions about safety. Tragically, some of the same decision-making problems that resulted in the *Challenger* tragedy led to the demise of the *Columbia* space shuttle in 2003, 17 years later, killing all seven astronauts on board.[59]

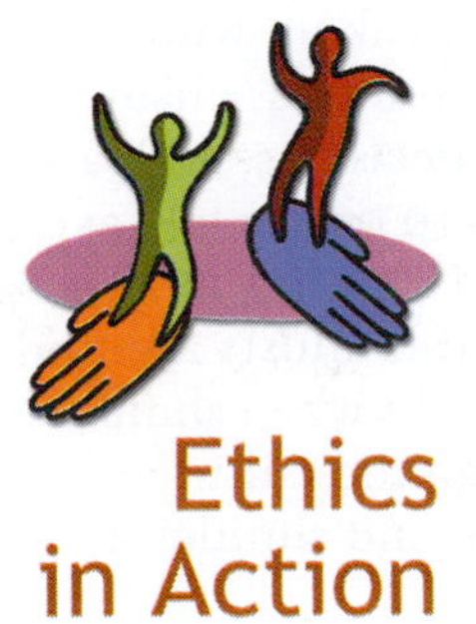

Ethics in Action

NASA's Flawed Culture

Seventeen years after the *Challenger* disaster, history repeated itself on February 1, 2003, when *Columbia* broke up over Texas on the final day of its mission, killing all seven astronauts on board.[60] While different specific causes resulted in each of these tragedies, they were both at least partially the result of a deeper, more widespread problem: a flawed safety culture at NASA where concerns with budgets and schedules were emphasized at the expense of safety.[61]

Both the Columbia Accident Investigation Board (CAIB) and a NASA team headed by Al Diaz, director of the Goddard Space Flight Center, concluded–after intensive investigations involving employees at all ranks, outside contractors, and engineering and scientific data–that NASA's flawed, can-do culture, emphasizing budgets and schedules over safety, was partially to blame for the *Columbia* tragedy.[62] Commenting on the CAIB report and their own investigations, the Diaz team stated:

> *Had the fate of STS-107 been the result of a small number of well-defined problems in a single program, finding solutions would be a relatively straightforward matter. But the CAIB determined that such is not the case. . . . It was their conclusion that the mistakes made on STS-107 were not isolated failures but rather were indicative of systemic flaws that existed prior to the accident. The Diaz Team believes that some of these systemic flaws exist beyond the shuttle program.*[63]

The Columbia crew wave to onlookers on their way to the launch pad for liftoff. Leading the way are Pilot William "Willie" McCool (left) and Commander Rick Husband. Following in the second row are Mission Specialists Kalpana Chawla (left) and Laurel Clark; in the rear are Payload Specialist Ilan Ramon (left), Payload Commander Michael Anderson, and Mission Specialist David Brown. Ramon was the first astronaut from Israel to fly on a shuttle.

In both the *Challenger* and the *Columbia* disasters, safety questions were raised before the shuttles were launched; safety concerns took second place to budgets, economic feasibility, and schedules; top decision makers seemed to ignore or downplay the inputs of those with relevant technical expertise; and speaking up was discouraged.[64] Rather than making safety a top priority, decision makers seemed overly concerned with keeping on schedule and within budget.[65] The day before *Columbia* lifted off, mission managers were presented with data indicating that a ring that linked the rocket boosters to the external tank failed to meet strength requirements. Rather than postponing the launch to address this problem, a shuttle manager temporarily waived the requirements based on what later turned out to be faulty data.[66] After foam had broken loose the next day during liftoff (a recurring problem) and struck the left wing, NASA engineers repeatedly and doggedly requested that images of the area in which the foam had struck be obtained to assess the extent of the damage and perhaps plan a rescue mission. Mission managers actively opposed their requests and no images were obtained.[67]

Bill Parsons, who now heads the troubled shuttle program, is committed to changing the organization's culture.[68] Among other things, he is trying to improve communication, encourage all employees to speak up without fear of retribution, make sure that all employees' inputs are heard, ensure that technical expertise is taken into account when making decisions, and, above all, emphasize safety.[69] Currently, NASA engineers are trying to develop fillers and wrappings that astronauts can use to repair unexpected cracks, gashes, and holes on shuttles during space flights.[70] And efforts are under way to prevent foam insulation from breaking off fuel tanks when shuttles are launched.[71] Above all else, Parsons is trying to change the culture so that safety is a top priority, technical expertise is respected, and shuttles are not launched until all known problems are addressed.[72]

Choose Among Alternatives

Once the set of alternative solutions has been carefully evaluated, the next task is to rank the various alternatives (using the criteria discussed in the previous section) and make a decision. When ranking alternatives, managers must be sure *all* the information available is brought to bear on the problem or issue at hand. As the Sun Microsystems case indicates, however, identifying all *relevant* information for a decision does not mean that the manager has *complete* information; in most instances, information is incomplete.

Perhaps more serious than the existence of incomplete information is the often-documented tendency of managers to ignore critical information, even when it is available. We discuss this tendency in detail below when we examine the operation of cognitive biases and groupthink.

Implement the Chosen Alternative

Once a decision has been made and an alternative has been selected, it must be implemented, and many subsequent and related decisions must be made. After a course of action has been decided–say, to develop a new line of women's clothing–thousands of subsequent decisions are necessary to implement it. These decisions would involve recruiting dress designers, obtaining fabrics, finding high-quality manufacturers, and signing contracts with clothing stores to sell the new line.

Although the need to make subsequent decisions to implement the chosen course of action may seem obvious, many managers make a decision and then fail to act on it. This is the same as not making a decision at all. To ensure that a decision is implemented, top managers must assign to middle managers the responsibility for making the follow-up decisions necessary to achieve the goal. They must give middle managers sufficient resources to achieve the goal, and they must hold the middle managers accountable for their performance. If the middle managers are successful at implementing the decision, they should be rewarded; if they fail, they should be subject to sanctions.

Learn from Feedback

The final step in the decision-making process is learning from feedback. Effective managers always conduct a retrospective analysis to see what they can learn from past successes or failures. Managers who do not evaluate the results of their decisions do not learn from experience; instead, they stagnate and are likely to make the same mistakes again and again.[73] To avoid this problem, managers must establish a formal procedure with which they can learn from the results of past decisions. The procedure should include these steps:

1. Compare what actually happened to what was expected to happen as a result of the decision.
2. Explore why any expectations for the decision were not met.
3. Derive guidelines that will help in future decision making.

Managers who always strive to learn from past mistakes and successes are likely to continuously improve the decisions they make. A significant amount of learning can take place when the outcomes of decisions are evaluated, and this assessment can produce enormous benefits.

Cognitive Biases and Decision Making

In the 1970s psychologists Daniel Kahneman and Amos Tversky suggested that because all decision makers are subject to bounded rationality, they tend to use **heuristics,** rules of thumb that simplify the process of making decisions.[74] Kahneman and Tversky argued that rules of thumb are often useful because they help decision makers make sense of complex, uncertain, and ambiguous information. Sometimes, however, the use of heuristics can lead to systematic errors in the way decision makers process information about alternatives and make decisions. **Systematic errors** are errors that people make over and over and that result in poor decision making. Because of cognitive biases, which are caused by systematic errors, otherwise-capable managers may end up making bad decisions.[75] Four sources of bias that can adversely affect the way managers make decisions are prior hypotheses, representativeness, the illusion of control, and escalating commitment (see Figure 7.6).

heuristics Rules of thumb that simplify decision making.

systematic errors Errors that people make over and over and that result in poor decision making.

Prior-Hypothesis Bias

Decision makers who have strong prior beliefs about the relationship between two variables tend to make decisions based on those beliefs *even when presented with evidence that their beliefs are wrong*. In doing so, they are falling victim to **prior-hypothesis bias.** Moreover, decision makers tend to seek and use information that is consistent with their prior beliefs and to ignore information that contradicts those beliefs.

prior-hypothesis bias A cognitive bias resulting from the tendency to base decisions on strong prior beliefs even if evidence shows that those beliefs are wrong.

Representativeness Bias

Many decision makers inappropriately generalize from a small sample or even from a single vivid case or episode. An interesting example of the **representativeness bias** occurred after World War II, when Seawell Avery, the CEO of Montgomery Ward, shelved plans for national expansion to meet competition from Sears because he believed there would be a depression after the war. The basis for Avery's belief was the occurrence of the Great Depression after World War I. However, there was no second Great Depression, and Avery's poor decision allowed Sears to establish itself as the number-one nationwide retailer. Avery's mistake was generalizing from the post-World War I experience and assuming that "depressions always follow wars."

representativeness bias A cognitive bias resulting from the tendency to generalize inappropriately from a small sample or from a single vivid event or episode.

Illusion of Control

Other errors in decision making result from the **illusion of control,** the tendency of decision makers to overestimate their ability to control activities and events. Top-level managers seem to be particularly prone to this bias. Having

illusion of control A source of cognitive bias resulting from the tendency to overestimate one's own ability to control activities and events.

Figure 7.6
Sources of Cognitive Bias at the Individual and Group Levels

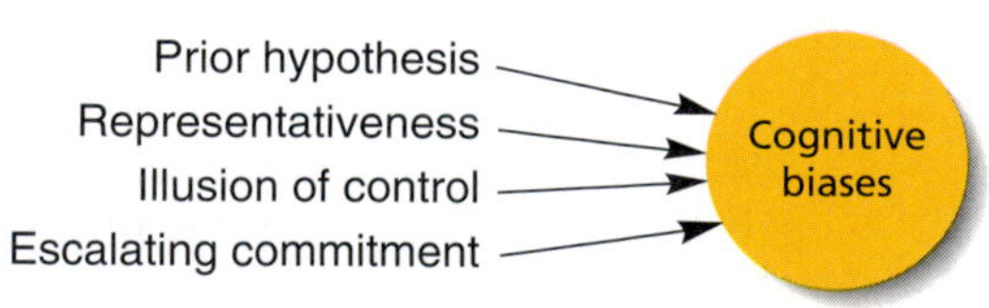

worked their way to the top of an organization, they tend to have an exaggerated sense of their own worth and are overconfident about their ability to succeed and to control events.[76] The illusion of control causes managers to overestimate the odds of a favorable outcome and, consequently, to make inappropriate decisions. For example, Nissan used to be controlled by Katsuji Kawamata, an autocratic CEO who thought he had the ability to run the car company single-handedly. He made all the decisions, some of which resulted in a series of spectacular mistakes, including changing the company's name from Datsun to Nissan.

Escalating Commitment

escalating commitment A source of cognitive bias resulting from the tendency to commit additional resources to a project even if evidence shows that the project is failing.

Having already committed significant resources to a course of action, some managers commit more resources to the project *even if they receive feedback that the project is failing.*[77] Feelings of personal responsibility for a project apparently bias the analysis of decision makers and lead to this **escalating commitment.** The managers decide to increase their investment of time and money in a course of action and ignore evidence that it is illegal, unethical, uneconomical, or impractical (see Figure 7.5). Often, the more appropriate decision would be to cut their losses and run.

A tragic example of where escalating commitment can lead is the *Challenger* disaster. Apparently, managers at both NASA and Morton Thiokol were so anxious to keep the shuttle program on schedule that they ignored or discounted any evidence that would slow the program down. Thus, the information offered by two Thiokol engineers, who warned about O-ring failure in cold weather, was discounted, and the shuttle was launched on a chilly day in January 1986.

Another example of escalating commitment occurred during the 1960s and 1970s when large U.S. steelmakers responded to low-cost competition from minimills and foreign steelmakers by increasing their investments in the technologically obsolete steelmaking facilities they already possessed, rather than investing in new, cutting-edge technology.[78] This decision was irrational because investment in obsolete technology would never enable them to lower their costs and compete successfully. Similarly, overly optimistic top managers at Lucent Technologies escalated their commitment to growth, engaging in practices like discounting and vendor loans that ultimately may have hurt organizational performance.[79]

Be Aware of Your Biases

How can managers avoid the negative effects of cognitive biases and improve their decision-making and problem-solving abilities? Managers must become aware of biases and their effects, and they must identify their own personal style of making decisions.[80] One useful way for managers to analyze their decision-making style is to review two decisions that they made recently–one decision that turned out well and one that turned out poorly. Problem-solving experts recommend that managers start by determining how much time to spend on each of the decision-making steps, such as gathering information to identify the pros and cons of alternatives or ranking the alternatives, to make sure that they spend sufficient time on each step.[81]

Another recommended technique for examining decision-making style is for managers to list the criteria they typically use to assess and evaluate alternatives—the heuristics (rules of thumb) they typically employ, their personal biases, and so on—and then critically evaluate the appropriateness of these different factors.

Many individual managers are likely to have difficulty identifying their own biases, so it is often advisable for managers to scrutinize their own assumptions by working with other managers to help expose weaknesses in their decision-making style. In this context, the issue of group decision making becomes important.

Group Decision Making

Many, perhaps most, important organizational decisions are made by groups or teams of managers rather than by individuals. Group decision making is superior to individual decision making in several respects. When managers work as a team to make decisions and solve problems, their choices of alternatives are less likely to fall victim to the biases and errors discussed previously. They are able to draw on the combined skills, competencies, and accumulated knowledge of group members and thereby improve their ability to generate feasible alternatives and make good decisions. Group decision making also allows managers to process more information and to correct one another's errors. And in the implementation phase, all managers affected by the decisions agree to cooperate. When a group of managers makes a decision (as opposed to one top manager making a decision and imposing it on subordinate managers), the probability that the decision will be implemented successfully increases. (We discuss how to encourage employee participation in decision making in Chapter 13.) Advances in information technology can facilitate the group decision-making process, as indicated in the following "Information Technology Byte."

Information Technology Byte

Improving Medical Decision Making

Physicians and medical professionals are often skeptical about the ability of advances in information technology to improve medical decision making. Dr. John Halamka is on a mission to change this.[82] In 1998, Halamka became chief information officer (CIO) for CareGroup, a company that owns hospitals in the Boston area.[83] Two of the hospitals owned by CareGroup had merged a few years earlier to form Beth Israel Deaconess Hospital, and the merger was proving to be a financial drain. The two hospitals had different computer systems, a patient who had been to each of the hospitals would have two different ID numbers, many records were handwritten, and files often had to be walked from one hospital to the other.[84] The inability to access and share information across and within the hospitals hampered decision making.

When Halamka, an emergency room physician, became CIO he decided to develop an integrated IT system to improve decision making and reduce medical errors at Beth Israel Deaconess. Given CareGroup's financial woes, funds were tight, so Halamka and a team of three developers designed and wrote the code for the system themselves.[85] Implementing the system was a real challenge, as physicians tend to resist using computers in their medical practices for a variety of reasons. Originally, the IT system focused on medical records, and later it was expanded to computerize doctors' orders. The system saved CareGroup money and also reduced medical errors.[86] For example, doctors' orders and dosages could be checked against patient records to ensure they were correct and there were no incompatibilities; doctors, nurses, and pharmacies could easily share information; and all patient records could be accessed by any member of a health care team as needed via computer.[87]

Integrated IT systems can save medical providers money and, more importantly, reduce medical errors.

For Joe S., who recently made a trip to Beth Israel's emergency room at the urging of his wife, the IT system was a life saver. Joe felt dizzy and was having a bit of trouble breathing but otherwise felt fine. Using the IT system, emergency room doctors were able to access Joe's medical history, including an EKG from a year earlier, which they compared with a current EKG. Being able to make this instant comparison (and not having to wait to retrieve and compare actual films) saved Joe's life: Based on the EKG comparisons, his doctors correctly determined that Joe was having a heart attack and were able to immediately race him to the cardiac unit, where he was administered anticoagulants and a blocked artery was opened through angioplasty.

Unfortunately, many hospitals do not have the kind of IT system that enables doctors to view a patient's medical records on the spot. Halamka is on a mission to change that. As he puts it, "IT saves money, and that's very important. . . . But in the end, the lives that it saves is why every single hospital system has to embrace this stuff."[88]

There are some potential disadvantages associated with group decision making. Groups often take much longer than individuals to make decisions. Getting two or more managers to agree to the same solution can be difficult because managers' interests and preferences are often different. In addition, just like decision making by individual managers, group decision making can be undermined by biases. A major source of group bias is *groupthink.*

The Perils of Groupthink

groupthink A pattern of faulty and biased decision making that occurs in groups whose members strive for agreement among themselves at the expense of accurately assessing information relevant to a decision.

Groupthink is a pattern of faulty and biased decision making that occurs in groups whose members strive for agreement among themselves at the expense of accurately assessing information relevant to a decision.[89] When managers are subject to groupthink, they collectively embark on a course of action without developing appropriate criteria to evaluate alternatives. Typically, a group rallies around one central manager, such as the CEO, and the course of action that manager supports. Group members become blindly committed to that course of action without evaluating its merits. Commitment is often based on an emotional, rather than an objective, assessment of the optimal course of action.

The decision President Kennedy and his advisers made to launch the unfortunate Bay of Pigs invasion in Cuba in 1962, the decisions made by President Johnson and his advisers from 1964 to 1967 to escalate the war in Vietnam, the decision made by President Nixon and his advisers in 1972 to cover up the Watergate break-in, and the decision made by NASA and Morton Thiokol in 1986 to launch the ill-fated *Challenger* shuttle, which exploded after takeoff–all were likely influenced by groupthink. After the fact, decision makers such as these who may fall victim to groupthink are often surprised that their decision-making process and outcomes were so flawed.

When groupthink occurs, pressures for agreement and harmony within a group have the unintended effect of discouraging individuals from raising issues that run counter to majority opinion. For example, when managers at NASA and Morton Thiokol fell victim to groupthink, they convinced each other that all was well and that there was no need to delay the launch of the *Challenger* space shuttle.

Devil's Advocacy and Dialectical Inquiry

The existence of cognitive biases and groupthink raises the question of how to improve the quality of group and individual decision making so that managers make decisions that are realistic and are based on a thorough evaluation of alternatives. Two techniques known to counteract groupthink and cognitive biases are devil's advocacy and dialectic inquiry (see Figure 7.7).[90]

devil's advocacy Critical analysis of a preferred alternative, made in response to challenges raised by a group member who, playing the role of devil's advocate, defends unpopular or opposing alternatives for the sake of argument.

dialectical inquiry Critical analysis of two preferred alternatives in order to find an even better alternative for the organization to adopt.

Devil's advocacy is a critical analysis of a preferred alternative to ascertain its strengths and weaknesses before it is implemented.[91] Typically, one member of the decision-making group plays the role of devil's advocate. The devil's advocate critiques and challenges the way the group evaluated alternatives and chose one over the others. The purpose of devil's advocacy is to identify all the reasons that might make the preferred alternative unacceptable after all. In this way, decision makers can be made aware of the possible perils of recommended courses of action.

Dialectical inquiry goes one step further. Two groups of managers are assigned to a problem, and each group is responsible for evaluating alternatives and selecting one of them.[92] Top managers hear each group present its preferred alternative, and then each group critiques the other's position. During this

Figure 7.7
Devil's Advocacy and Dialectical Inquiry

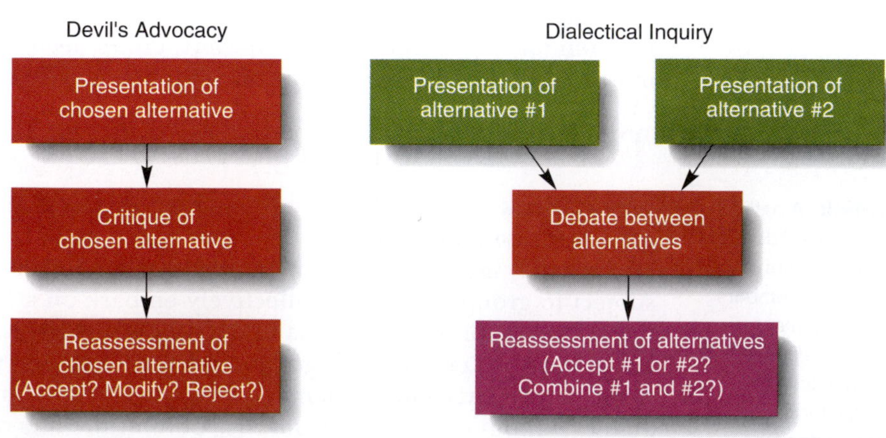

debate, top managers challenge both groups' positions to uncover potential problems and perils associated with their solutions. The goal is to find an even better alternative course of action for the organization to adopt.

Both devil's advocacy and dialectical inquiry can help counter the effects of cognitive biases and groupthink.[93] In practice, devil's advocacy is probably the easier method to implement because it involves less commitment in managerial time and effort than does dialectical inquiry.

Diversity Among Decision Makers

Another way to improve group decision making is to promote diversity in decision-making groups (see Chapter 4).[94] Bringing together managers of both genders from various ethnic, national, and functional backgrounds broadens the range of life experiences and opinions that group members can draw on as they generate, assess, and choose among alternatives. Moreover, diverse groups are sometimes less prone to groupthink because group members already differ from each other and thus are less subject to pressures for uniformity.

Organizational Learning and Creativity

The quality of managerial decision making ultimately depends on innovative responses to opportunities and threats. How can managers increase their ability to make nonprogrammed decisions, decisions that will allow them to adapt to, modify, and even drastically alter their task environments so that they can continually increase organizational performance? The answer is by encouraging organizational learning.[95]

organizational learning The process through which managers seek to improve employees' desire and ability to understand and manage the organization and its task environment.

learning organization An organization in which managers try to maximize the ability of individuals and groups to think and behave creatively and thus maximize the potential for organizational learning to take place.

creativity A decision maker's ability to discover original and novel ideas that lead to feasible alternative courses of action.

Organizational learning is the process through which managers seek to improve employees' desire and ability to understand and manage the organization and its task environment so that employees can make decisions that continuously raise organizational effectiveness.[96] A **learning organization** is one in which managers do everything possible to maximize the ability of individuals and groups to think and behave creatively and thus maximize the potential for organizational learning to take place. At the heart of organizational learning is **creativity,** the ability of a decision maker to discover original and novel ideas that lead to feasible alternative courses of action. Encouraging creativity among managers is such a pressing organizational concern that many organizations hire outside experts to help them develop programs to train their managers in the art of creative thinking and problem solving.

Creating a Learning Organization

How do managers go about creating a learning organization? Learning theorist Peter Senge identified five principles for creating a learning organization (see Figure 7.8, page 246).[97]

1. For organizational learning to occur, top managers must allow every person in the organization to develop a sense of personal mastery. Managers must empower employees and allow them to experiment and create and explore what they want.

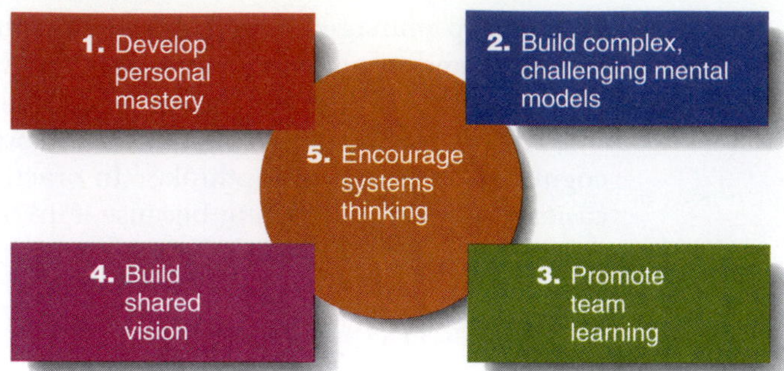

Figure 7.8
Senge's Principles for Creating a Learning Organization

2. As part of attaining personal mastery, organizations need to encourage employees to develop and use *complex mental models*–sophisticated ways of thinking that challenge them to find new or better ways of performing a task–to deepen their understanding of what is involved in a particular activity. Here Senge is arguing that managers must encourage employees to develop a taste for experimenting and risk taking.[98]

3. Managers must do everything they can to promote group creativity. Senge thinks that *team learning* (learning that takes place in a group or team) is more important than individual learning in increasing organizational learning. He points out that most important decisions are made in subunits such as groups, functions, and divisions.

4. Managers must emphasize the importance of *building a shared vision*–a common mental model that all organizational members use to frame problems or opportunities.

5. Managers must encourage *systems thinking* (a concept drawn from systems theory, discussed in Chapter 2). Senge emphasizes that to create a learning organization, managers must recognize the effects of one level of learning on another. Thus, for example, there is little point in creating teams to facilitate team learning if managers do not also take steps to give employees the freedom to develop a sense of personal mastery.

Building a learning organization requires that managers change their management assumptions radically. Developing a learning organization is neither a quick nor an easy process. Senge has been working with Ford Motor Company to help managers make Ford a learning organization. Why does Ford want this? Top management believes that to compete successfully, Ford must improve its members' ability to be creative and make the right decisions.

Increasingly, managers are being called on to promote global organizational learning. For example, managers at Wal-Mart use the lessons derived from its failures and successes in one country to promote global organizational learning across the many countries in which it now operates. For instance, when Wal-Mart entered Malaysia, it was convinced customers there would respond to its one-stop shopping format. It found, however, that Malaysians enjoy the social experience of shopping in a lively market or bazaar and thus did not like the impersonal efficiency of the typical Wal-Mart store. As a result, Wal-Mart has learned the importance of designing store layouts to appeal specifically to the customers of each country in which it operates.

When purchasing and operating a chain of stores in another country, such as the British ASDA chain, Wal-Mart now strives to retain what customers value in the local market while taking advantage of all of its own accumulated organizational learning. For example, Wal-Mart improved ASDA's information technology used for inventory and sales tracking in stores and enrolled ASDA in Wal-Mart's global purchasing operations, which has enabled the chain to pay less for certain products, sell them for less, and, overall, significantly increase sales. At the same time, Wal-Mart empowered local ASDA managers to run the stores; as the president of ASDA indicates, "This is still essentially a British business in the way it's run day to day."[99] Clearly, global organizational learning is essential for companies such as Wal-Mart that have significant operations in multiple countries.

Promoting Individual Creativity

Research suggests that when certain conditions are met, managers are more likely to be creative. As just discussed, people must be given the opportunity and freedom to generate new ideas. Creativity declines when managers look over the shoulders of talented employees and try to "hurry up" a creative solution. How would you feel if your boss said you had one week to come up with a new product idea to beat the competition? Creativity results when employees have an opportunity to experiment, to take risks, and to make mistakes and learn from them. And employees must not fear that they will be looked down on or penalized for ideas that might at first seem outlandish, as it is sometimes the ideas that initially seem outlandish that yield truly innovative products and services, as indicated in the following "Focus on Diversity."

Focus on Diversity

Asking Different Questions and Providing Different Answers

Ideas for truly creative goods, products, and services sometimes come from asking different kinds of questions and seeking different kinds of answers. When George Ohr discovered the wonders of making clay pots at a potter's wheel in the late 1800s, he learned as much as he could about pots and then proceeded to question everything that people at the time thought pots should look like and provided answers in his own unique form of pottery art.[100]

Disdained at the time, Ohr's pottery is now so revered for its creativity and beauty that his pots command five-digit prices and famed architect Frank Gehry is designing a museum (opening in 2006) in Ohr's hometown of Biloxi, Mississippi, to display Ohr's work.[101] Ohr turned pot making on its head. Each of his pots was unique: He would form perfect shapes and then crumple them like newspaper; he would make delicate, paper-thin pots; he carved writings into his pots; and he used bright, bold colors–all unheard of at the time and hailed as innovations decades later. It was only after Ohr's death that the art world recognized the genius and beauty in his work, which came from Ohr's unique answers to the question of pottery as an art form.[102]

Asking the right questions and providing different kinds of answers can lead to creativity in other arenas as well.[103] Dr. William Hunter learned this from one of his professors in graduate school and has worked by it ever since.[104] Now, as CEO of Angiotech Pharmaceuticals in Vancouver, California, he encourages his employees to ask different kinds of questions and seek different answers. As a physician, he wondered whether drugs that were administered in massive doses to combat diseases like cancer could be used to cure or prevent other kinds of ailments when used in more moderate doses. And he also asked why medical implants like catheters and stents rarely included administrations of drugs. After extensive research, the answers to these questions led to the development of paclitaxel-coated coronary stents, a successful public offering of stock in Angiotech, and more questions for future research.[105]

Creativity can sometimes seem initially outlandish. George Ohr turned pot making on its head in the early 1800s by questioning every pot-making norm of the time. Now his techniques are hailed as innovations.

Hunter learned that stents were not coated with drugs because of the questions stent manufacturers asked physicians. Typically, they would ask surgeons for advice on how to make better stents. Hunter, on the other hand, asked surgeons why stents sometimes fail and cause problems for about 20 percent of patients receiving them. The answer to this question is that stents used to open arteries can cause scar tissue to form around the stent, ultimately clogging the artery once again for certain patients. So why aren't stents coated with drugs that might help prevent the problem? Well, pharmaceutical companies have very long time horizons and spend large amounts of money on developing and testing new drugs. Medical equipment makers that develop and manufacture stents typically have much shorter time horizons. Hunter reasoned that paclitaxel, used in large dosages to stop the growth of cancer tumors, might prevent the growth of scar tissue when coated on stents in much smaller dosages.

After years of testing, Angiotech has a successful new product in paclitaxel-coated stents with only a 3 percent failure rate.[106] However, Hunter is the first to acknowledge that creative success and failure go hand in hand. For example, Angiotech unsuccessfully tried to develop a form of paclitaxel to treat multiple sclerosis. As Hunter puts it, "You have to celebrate the failures. . . . If you send the message that the only road to career success is experiments that work, people won't ask risky questions, or get any dramatically new answers."[107] If he were alive today, George Ohr would likely concur.

Highly innovative companies like 3M are well known for the wide degree of freedom they give their managers and employees to ask different questions and seek their answers. For example, at 3M employees are expected to spend a certain percentage of their time on projects of their own choosing, a policy that fosters creativity.

Once managers have generated alternatives, creativity can be fostered by providing them with constructive feedback so that they know how well they are doing. Ideas that seem to be going nowhere can be eliminated and creative energies refocused in other directions. Ideas that seem promising can be promoted, and help from other managers can be obtained as well.[108]

Top managers must also stress the importance of looking for alternative solutions and should visibly reward employees who come up with creative ideas. Being creative can be demanding and stressful. Employees who believe that they are working on important, vital issues are motivated to put forth the high levels of effort that creativity demands. Creative people like to receive the acclaim of others, and innovative organizations have many kinds of ceremonies and rewards to recognize creative employees. For example, 3M established the Carlton Hall of Fame to recognize successful innovators. These employees not only become members of the hall of fame but also receive financial rewards through the Golden Step program.

Promoting Group Creativity

To encourage creativity at the group level, organizations can make use of group problem-solving techniques that promote creative ideas and innovative solutions. These techniques can also be used to prevent groupthink and to help managers uncover biases. Here, we look at three group decision-making techniques: brainstorming, the nominal group technique, and the Delphi technique.

BRAINSTORMING *Brainstorming* is a group problem-solving technique in which managers meet face-to-face to generate and debate a wide variety of alternatives from which to make a decision.[109] Generally, from 5 to 15 managers meet in a closed-door session and proceed like this:

- One manager describes in broad outline the problem the group is to address.
- Group members then share their ideas and generate alternative courses of action.
- As each alternative is described, group members are not allowed to criticize it; everyone withholds judgment until all alternatives have been heard. One member of the group records the alternatives on a flip chart.
- Group members are encouraged to be as innovative and radical as possible. Anything goes; and the greater the number of ideas put forth, the better. Moreover, group members are encouraged to "piggyback" or build on each other's suggestions.
- When all alternatives have been generated, group members debate the pros and cons of each and develop a short list of the best alternatives.

production blocking A loss of productivity in brainstorming sessions due to the unstructured nature of brainstorming.

nominal group technique A decision-making technique in which group members write down ideas and solutions, read their suggestions to the whole group, and discuss and then rank the alternatives.

Brainstorming is very useful in some problem-solving situations–for example, when managers are trying to find a new name for a perfume or for a model of car. But sometimes individuals working alone can generate more alternatives. The main reason for the loss of productivity in brainstorming appears to be **production blocking** which occurs because group members cannot always simultaneously make sense of all the alternatives being generated, think up additional alternatives, and remember what they were thinking.[110]

NOMINAL GROUP TECHNIQUE To avoid production blocking, the **nominal group technique** is often used. It provides a more structured way of generating alternatives in writing and gives each manager more time and opportunity to come up with potential solutions. The nominal group technique is especially useful when an issue is controversial and when different managers might be expected to champion different courses of action. Generally, a small group of managers meet in a closed-door session and adopt the following procedures:

- One manager outlines the problem to be addressed, and 30 or 40 minutes are allocated for group members working individually, to write down their ideas and solutions. Group members are encouraged to be innovative.
- Managers take turns reading their suggestions to the group. One manager writes all the alternatives on a flip chart. No criticism or evaluation of alternatives is allowed until all alternatives have been read.
- The alternatives are then discussed, one by one, in the sequence in which they were first proposed. Group members can ask for clarifying information and critique each alternative to identify its pros and cons.
- When all alternatives have been discussed, each group member ranks all the alternatives from most preferred to least preferred, and the alternative that receives the highest ranking is chosen.[111]

delphi technique A decision-making technique in which group members do not meet face-to-face but respond in writing to questions posed by the group leader.

DELPHI TECHNIQUE Both the nominal group technique and brainstorming require that managers meet together to generate creative ideas and engage in joint problem solving. What happens if managers are in different cities or in different parts of the world and cannot meet face-to-face? Videoconferencing is one way to bring distant managers together to brainstorm. Another way is to use the **Delphi technique,** a written approach to creative problem solving.[112] The Delphi technique works like this:

- The group leader writes a statement of the problem and a series of questions to which participating managers are to respond.
- The questionnaire is sent to the managers and departmental experts who are most knowledgeable about the problem. They are asked to generate solutions and mail the questionnaire back to the group leader.
- A team of top managers records and summarizes the responses. The results are then sent back to the participants, with additional questions to be answered before a decision can be made.
- The process is repeated until a consensus is reached and the most suitable course of action is apparent.

Promoting Creativity at the Global Level

The Delphi technique is particularly useful when barriers of time and distance, a situation that is common in the global environment, separate managers. Today, organizations are under increasing pressure to reduce costs and develop global products. To do so, they typically centralize their research and development expertise by bringing R&D managers together at one location. Encouraging creativity among teams of R&D experts from different countries poses special problems, however. First, R&D experts often have difficulty communicating their ideas to one another because of language problems and because of cultural differences in their approaches to problem solving. Second, the decision-making process differs from country to country. In Japan, for example, decisions tend to be made in a very participative manner, and the group as a whole must agree on a course of action before a decision is made. In contrast, decision making is very centralized in Mexico; top managers decide what to do, with little input from subordinates.

Managers must take special steps to encourage creativity among people from different countries who are supposed to be working together. They must develop training programs that promote awareness and understanding so that diverse individuals can cooperate and brainstorm new ideas and approaches to problems, opportunities, and threats.

Summary and Review

THE NATURE OF MANAGERIAL DECISION MAKING Programmed decisions are routine decisions made so often that managers have developed decision rules to be followed automatically. Nonprogrammed decisions are made in response to situations that are unusual or novel; they are nonroutine decisions. The classical model of decision making assumes that decision makers have complete information; are able to process that information in an objective, rational manner; and make optimum decisions. March and Simon argue that managers are boundedly rational, rarely have access to all the information they need to make optimum decisions, and consequently satisfice and rely on their intuition and judgment when making decisions.

STEPS IN THE DECISION-MAKING PROCESS When making decisions, managers should take these six steps: Recognize the need for a decision, generate alternatives, assess alternatives, choose among alternatives, implement the chosen alternative, and learn from feedback.

COGNITIVE BIASES AND DECISION MAKING Most of the time, managers are fairly good decision makers. On occasion, however, problems can result because human judgment can be adversely affected by the operation of cognitive biases that result in poor decisions. Cognitive biases are caused by systematic errors in the way decision makers process information and make decisions. Sources of these errors include prior hypotheses, representativeness, the illusion of control, and escalating commitment. Managers should undertake a personal decision audit to become aware of their biases and thus improve their decision making.

GROUP DECISION MAKING Many advantages are associated with group decision making, but there are also several disadvantages. One major source of poor decision making is groupthink. Afflicted decision makers collectively embark on a dubious course of action without questioning the assumptions that underlie their decision. Managers can improve the quality of group decision making by using techniques such as devil's advocacy and dialectical inquiry and by increasing diversity in the decision-making group.

ORGANIZATIONAL LEARNING AND CREATIVITY Organizational learning is the process through which managers seek to improve employees' desire and ability to understand and manage the organization and its task environment so that employees can make decisions that continuously raise organizational effectiveness. Managers must take steps to promote organizational learning and creativity at the individual and group levels to improve the quality of decision making.

Management in Action

Topics for Discussion and Action

Discussion

1. What are the main differences between programmed decision making and nonprogrammed decision making?
2. In what ways do the classical and administrative models of decision making help managers appreciate the complexities of real-world decision making?
3. Why do capable managers sometimes make bad decisions? What can individual managers do to improve their decision-making skills?
4. In what kinds of groups is groupthink most likely to be a problem? When is it least likely to be a problem? What steps can group members take to ward off groupthink?
5. What is organizational learning, and how can managers promote it?

Action

6. Ask a manager to recall the best and the worst decisions he or she ever made. Try to determine why these decisions were so good or so bad.
7. Think about an organization in your local community, your university, or an organization that you are familiar with that is doing poorly. Now come up with questions managers in this organization should ask stakeholders to elicit creative ideas for turning around the organization's fortunes.

Building Management Skills

How Do You Make Decisions?

Pick a decision that you made recently and that has had important consequences for you. It may be your decision about which college to attend, which major to select, whether to take a part-time job, or which part-time job to take. Using the material in this chapter, analyze the way in which you made the decision—in particular:

1. Identify the criteria you used, either consciously or unconsciously, to guide your decision making.
2. List the alternatives you considered. Were they all possible alternatives? Did you unconsciously (or consciously) ignore some important alternatives?
3. How much information did you have about each alternative? Were you making the decision on the basis of complete or incomplete information?
4. Try to remember how you reached the decision. Did you sit down and consciously think through the implications of each alternative, or did you make the decision on the basis of intuition? Did you use any rules of thumb to help you make the decision?
5. In retrospect, do you think that your choice or alternative was shaped by any of the cognitive biases discussed in this chapter?
6. Having answered the previous five questions, do you think in retrospect that you made a reasonable decision? What, if anything, might you do to improve your ability to make good decisions in the future?

Managing Ethically

Sometimes groups make extreme decisions—decisions that are either more risky or more conservative than they would have been if individuals acting alone had made them. One explanation for the tendency of groups to make extreme decisions is diffusion of responsibility. In a group, responsibility for the outcomes of a decision is spread among group members, so each person feels less than fully accountable. The group's decision is extreme because no individual has taken full responsibility for it.

Questions

1. Either alone or in a group, think about the ethical implications of extreme decision making by groups.
2. When group decision making takes place, should members of the group each feel fully accountable for outcomes of the decision? Why or why not?

Small Group Breakout Exercise

Brainstorming

Form groups of three or four people, and appoint one member as the spokesperson who will communicate your findings to the whole class when called on by the instructor. Then discuss the following scenario.

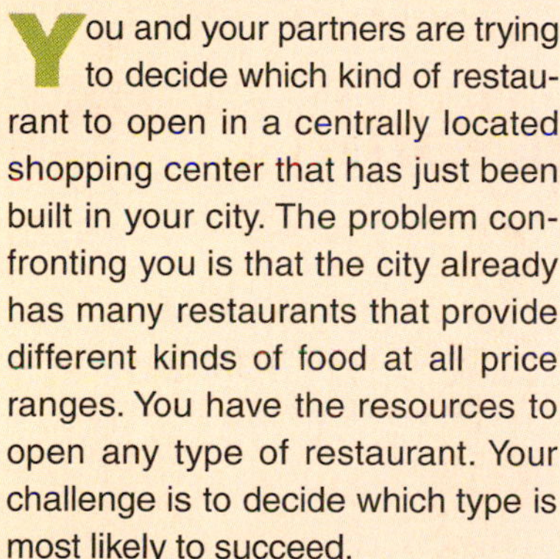

You and your partners are trying to decide which kind of restaurant to open in a centrally located shopping center that has just been built in your city. The problem confronting you is that the city already has many restaurants that provide different kinds of food at all price ranges. You have the resources to open any type of restaurant. Your challenge is to decide which type is most likely to succeed.

Use the brainstorming technique to decide which type of restaurant to open. Follow these steps:

1. As a group, spend 5 or 10 minutes generating ideas about the alternative restaurants that the members think will be most likely to succeed. Each group member should be as innovative and creative as possible, and no suggestions should be criticized.
2. Appoint one group member to write down the alternatives as they are identified.
3. Spend the next 10 or 15 minutes debating the pros and cons of the alternatives. As a group, try to reach a consensus on which alternative is most likely to succeed.

After making your decision, discuss the pros and cons of the brainstorming method, and decide whether any production blocking occurred.

When called on by the instructor, the spokesperson should be prepared to share your group's decision with the class, as well as the reasons the group made its decision.

Exploring the World Wide Web

Go to www.brainstorming.co.uk. This website contains "Training on Creativity Techniques" and "Creativity Puzzles." Spend at least 30 minutes on the training and/or puzzles. Think about what you have learned. Come up with specific ways in which you can be more creative in your thinking and decision making based on what you have learned.

Be the Manager

You are a top manager who was recently hired by an oil field services company in Oklahoma to help it respond more quickly and proactively to potential opportunities in its market. You report to the chief operating officer (COO), who reports to the CEO, and you have been on the job for eight months. Thus far, you have come up with three initiatives you carefully studied, thought were noteworthy, and proposed and justified to the COO. The COO seemed cautiously interested when you presented the proposals, and each time he indicated he would think about them and discuss them with the CEO as considerable resources were involved. Each time, you never heard back from the COO, and after a few weeks elapsed, you casually asked the COO if there was any news on the proposal in question. For the first proposal, the COO said, "We think it's a good idea but the timing is off. Let's shelve it for the time being and reconsider it next year." For the second proposal, the COO said, "Mike [the CEO] reminded me that we tried that two years ago and it wasn't well received in the market. I am surprised I didn't remember it myself when you first described the proposal, but it came right back to me once Mike mentioned it." For the third proposal, the COO simply said, "We're not convinced it will work."

You believe that your three proposed initiatives are viable ways to seize opportunities in the marketplace, yet you cannot proceed with any of them. Moreover, for each proposal, you invested considerable amounts of time and even worked to bring others on board to support the proposal, only to have it shot down by the CEO. When you interviewed for the position, both the COO and the CEO claimed they wanted "an outsider to help them step out of the box and innovate." Yet your experience to date has been just the opposite. What are you going to do?

Additional Activities on the Build Your Management Skills DVD

- **Test Your Knowledge:** The Vroom/Yetton/Jago Decision Model
- **Self-Assessment:** (1) Your Preferred Decision-Making Style and (2) Assessing Your Creativity Quotient
- **Manager's Hot Seat:** (2) Whistleblowing: Code Red or Red Ink

BusinessWeek Case in the News

The Brains Behind BlackBerry

They are the odd couple of the wireless world. One is a Turkish-born whiz kid who grew up across the border from Detroit and later dropped out of college to build an industrial display network for General Motors Corp.; the other, an ambitious tradesman's son from rural Ontario who glided through one of Canada's top colleges and Harvard Business School before settling into corporate life. But as co-chief executives of Research in Motion Ltd. (RIM), Mike Lazaridis and Jim Balsillie, both 43, are the quiet men behind the hottest wireless e-mail gadget around: the BlackBerry. Among the million-plus subscribers are such reported fans as Jeb Bush, Bill Gates, Sarah Jessica Parker, and Jack Welch. From the near-constant clicking in the halls of Congress to its spot on Oprah Winfrey's "favorite things of 2003" list, the BlackBerry has become almost shorthand for wireless e-mail itself.

The addictive little devices, introduced in early 1999, defy many of the stereotypes of high tech. They were spawned far from Silicon Valley in Waterloo, Ont., a quiet university town of 99,000 about an hour's drive west of Toronto. And RIM is no glitzy startup; Lazaridis founded it two decades ago to consult and develop technologies like the film bar-code readers that would eventually win him a technical Emmy and an Oscar.

Still, nothing has ever rocked RIM and its hometown like the

BlackBerry. The brand has become the industry standard, far better known than its cryptically named parent, and a cultural icon to boot. Every major carrier wants to offer it to its customers. Everyone wants to work there. And that stock price! It has roared from $12.75 to $108 over the past year, and on April 7 the company announced a two-for-one split. Lazaridis' stake is worth $782 million, while Balsillie's comes to $674 million. Even so, Balsillie has banned staff from checking the price at the office.

Instead, the co-CEOs have obsessed over the core product: e-mail that is automatically pushed to the BlackBerry as it's going to the desktop and can be instantly answered with an intuitive, thumb-operated keyboard. Notes Andy Brown, chief technology architect at Merrill Lynch & Co.: "People don't want wireless e-mail. They want a BlackBerry." But that may not always be so. The duo have forged deals with companies ranging from Microsoft Corp. to Palm-Source Inc. to license BlackBerry software. Think "Intel Inside." And they recently signed a deal with Sun Microsystems Inc. to extend wireless Web services to Black-Berry customers. The goal, says Balsillie, is "to enable wireless e-mail whenever and on whatever device people want."

But RIM's quirky duo are hardly alone in their passion for wireless e-mail. They face competition ranging from pocket PC devices to similar handhelds put out by Good Technology Inc., which just settled a patent lawsuit with RIM and agreed to pay royalties for using its technology. And they have their own legal battles with Virginia's NTP Inc., which alleges RIM and numerous other wireless e-mail operators infringed its 1990 patents. RIM lost the first round in court; the case is on appeal.

"Science is the Core"

Still, the company's main challenge at the moment may be gearing up for explosive growth. With added features like voice, color screens, and international roaming, analysts predict that the number of customers could easily double this year, to 2 million. On April 7, RIM said its subscriber base increased by 24 percent, to almost 1.1 million, in the fourth quarter ended February 28. It also reported sales of $210.6 million, up 37 percent from the previous quarter, while profits rose 255 percent, to $41.5 million.

Those who know RIM attribute much of its success to the complementary relationship of its co-CEOs. Without Lazaridis, the silver-haired science buff who once won a special award from his public school for checking every science and math book out of the library, RIM would have no technology. "Science is the core of everything, yet we take it for granted," he says. And without Balsillie, the business maven who as a young father mortgaged his house and poured much of his net worth into Lazaridis' fledgling operation in 1992, it would have far less commercial success. As he puts it; "People capitalize on opportunities. They don't create them." He is the corporate strategist, the financial wizard, the negotiator, and the face of the company on Wall Street. Lazaridis is the science mastermind, the production guru, the dreamer, and the one who solves customers' problems. He likes to frequent physics lectures and read books like *Sojourner: An Insider's View of the Mars Pathfinder Mission.* But his real hobby is, well, thinking about RIM. Balsillie coaches his son's basketball team, races into Toronto for Maple Leafs hockey games, and cherishes time in his cottage on Georgian Bay.

Despite such obvious differences, though, the two men share some important similarities. First is their conviction, stretching back a decade, that people would one day want constant access to e-mail through a device they could hook on their belts. Balsillie, who joined the then-tiny outfit when Lazaridis wooed him from a customer to manage the business in 1992, calls e-mail "one of the most profound medium shifts we'll ever see." Lazaridis never doubted it for a minute. Even now, he gets visibly exasperated when RIM is treated like some kind of here-today-gone-tomorrow dot-com. "We've passed all the initiation by fire to get to 20 years old," he says, noting that RIM went public five years ago and now has a market capitalization of almost $10 billion.

They are equally relentless about pushing the BlackBerry. In 1999, they were so sure that it would just take a few days with one to get hooked that they hired "evangelists" to lend the devices out to executives on Wall Street. That helped the no-name Canadian company win contracts with a number of big firms. "You immediately saw everyone get it," recalls Leonard G. Rosen, a technology banker and managing director at Lehman Brothers Inc., which works with RIM. Soon, the company decided to let the network carriers offer BlackBerries to their customers. The payoff for RIM is clear: 65 percent plus margins on the service and 35 percent plus margins on the hardware, according to analyst Deepak Chopra of National Bank Financial.

Both men are building a legacy beyond the BlackBerry. Lazardis donated about $100 million (Canadian) in stock to start Waterloo's Perimeter Institute for Theoretical Physics in 2000, while Balsillie gave $30 million to start the Centre for International Governance Innovation two years later. But they're nowhere near retirement. Defending RIM's niche will take all of Balsillie's strategic smarts. This odd couple is smack in the middle of the hot zone.

Questions

1. What factors are responsible for the success of BlackBerry?
2. What are Lazaridis's and Balsillie's distinctive qualities as top managers and decision makers?
3. Up to this point, these two top managers at RIM have seemed to make good decisions. Why do you think they have been successful?
4. Looking to the future, what challenges will RIM, BlackBerry, and Lazaridis and Balsillie face? Do you think these co-CEOs are up for the challenge and will continue to make decisions that contribute to the success of RIM and BlackBerry? Why or why not?

Source: D. Brady, "The Brains Behind BlackBerry." Reprinted from the April 19, 2004, issue of *BusinessWeek* by special permission.

BusinessWeek Case in the News

Detroit Tries It the Japanese Way

Not So Nimble

By some calculations, the Japanese today are where GM hopes to be in 2005. Honda currently builds four very different vehicles on the Civic platform that it redesigned in 2001. In addition to the Civic compact, it makes the CR-V "cute ute," the boxy Element SUV, and the Acura RSX sports coupe. All four were brought to market in the three years following the redesign, with combined sales hitting 535,000 last year. Toyota can work nearly the same magic. It developed its Sienna minivan, the Lexus RX 330, and the Highlander crossover SUV using a modified version of the Camry sedan platform. GM, on the other hand, only recently unveiled plans to build multiple vehicles on its Chevy Cobalt compact platform. "The Big Three still are not pushing the envelope," says Joseph Phillippi, president of consultant AutoSource.

They are learning, however. Motown's top brass used to boast that nearly every part in an overhauled model was different from its predecessor—never mind that all those changes drove up costs and took time to engineer. In past decades, only a small percentage of parts were reused from one generation to the next. Now, Lutz wants to raise that to 40 percent to 60 percent—about on par with the Japanese. As GM develops the next-generation Chevy Silverado and GMC Sierra pickups for 2008, for example, it aims to reuse much of the existing platform. That should cut development costs in half, to nearly $3 billion.

For Detroit, such plans carry built-in frustrations: Even as GM saves money by carrying over some parts on its next-generation Silverado, its frame and the truck plants aren't flexible enough to make all the adjustments the designers want. At last year's Detroit auto show, the Chevrolet Cheyenne pickup concept was voted best truck by a panel of designers. The truck looked macho, with high window sills and a tall bed. And the windshield was pushed forward, pulling up the dashboard and leaving lots of room in the cabin. GM tried to make the bold styling and advanced proportions work. But its underlying pickup-truck platform wasn't flexible enough to handle the design changes. Lutz now concedes that "there's a limit on how far you can change the manufacturing process."

On the bright side, GM is putting its global resources behind its platforms, mining its European and Asian affiliates for vehicles, engines, and architectures that can deliver new cars to North America. A few years ago, Lutz happened to drive the Subaru WRX—one of the best low-price sports sedans on the market—and loved its precise handling and fast engine. GM owns 20 percent of Subaru, so Lutz was able to order up WRX parts quickly for a car on the drawing board at its Swedish Saab unit, the sporty 9-2X.

Slow Progress

Ford is on the same page regarding the consolidation of platforms. Martens learned about the approach while working at Ford's Mazda Motor Corp. affiliate from 1999 to 2002. Since returning to Ford's Dearborn (Mich.) headquarters, he has been on a mission to limit needless reengineering of parts. Ford engineers now choose from among just 4 steering wheels instead of contemplating 14, as they did in the past. And Martens has merged six separate vehicle-development groups into a single team, speeding decision-making and encouraging parts sharing. That has helped shave Ford's vehicle-development time—a measure that is independent of the vehicle life cycle—to 21 months, down from 29.

The idea, says Ford Chief Operating Officer Nicholas V. Scheele: "Engineer it once, use it often." And that goes for whole car architectures. Over the next eight years, Ford plans to use the Mazda 6 sedan platform as the base for 10 new vehicles. This base will spawn the Ford Futura family sedan and different versions for its Lincoln and Mercury divisions, as well as some future SUVs and minivans.

That strategy will take years to play out, however. At the moment, Ford still makes its Taurus sedan, Freestar minivan, and crossover SUVs on different platforms. Honda, in contrast, builds its Odyssey minivan and Pilot and Acura MDX SUVs on the same platform, and it will soon add a pickup truck. And all of these share many parts with the Accord sedan.

Chrysler is in this game, too. Three years ago, almost every one of its vehicles had its own platform. Even when the company decided to build the PT Cruiser on the Neon chassis in 2000, Chrysler couldn't reap the full benefits: Unable to assemble the cars in the same factory without making a huge investment, the company had to build the Cruiser in Mexico and the Neon in Illinois. Now, Chrysler Group CEO Dieter Zetsche wants to base the company's entire fleet of cars, trucks, and SUVs on just four platforms, down from 13. The consolidation will help Chrysler cut its five-year vehicle-development budget from $42 billion to $30 billion, he says.

Can Detroit catch up with Japan on versatile platforms? With cars like the Solstice, GM has shown that it can create attractive models on a budget and spin them into families. But matching Japan on speed and efficiency is still far down the road.

Questions

1. How would you characterize decision making at General Motors?
2. Compare and contrast decision making by Japanese automakers and that of their counterparts in Detroit.
3. To what extent is organizational learning taking place at General Motors and other U.S. automakers? Is enough learning taking place? Why or why not?
4. What role does creativity play in decision making at U.S. automakers? What role do you think it should play?

Source: D. Welch and K. Kerwin, "Detroit Tries It the Japanese Way." Reprinted from the January 26, 2004, issue of *BusinessWeek* by special permission.

CHAPTER

8 The Manager as a Planner and Strategist

Learning Objectives

After studying this chapter, you should be able to:

- Describe the three steps of the planning process and the relationship between planning and strategy.
- Explain the role of planning in predicting the future and in mobilizing organizational resources to meet future contingencies.
- Outline the main steps in SWOT analysis.
- Differentiate among corporate-, business-, and functional-level strategies.
- Describe the vital role played by strategy implementation in determining managers' ability to achieve an organization's mission and goals.

A Manager's Challenge

How to Compete in the Soft-Drink Business

What is the best way to compete in an industry?

Coca-Cola and Pepsi-Cola are household names worldwide. Together they control over 70 percent of the global soft-drink market and over 75 percent of the U.S. soft-drink market. Their success can be attributed in part to the overall strategy that Coca-Cola and PepsiCo developed to produce and promote their products. Both companies decided to build global brands by manufacturing the soft-drink concentrate that gives cola its flavor and then selling the concentrate in a syrup form to bottlers throughout the world. Coca-Cola and PepsiCo charge the bottlers a premium price for the syrup; they then invest part of the proceeds in advertising to build and maintain brand awareness. The bottlers are responsible for producing and distributing the actual cola. They add carbonated water to the syrup, package the resulting drink, and distribute it to vending machines, supermarkets, restaurants, and other retail outlets.

Cott Corporation's "house-brand" soft drinks have recently caused quite a stir in the soft-drink market.

The bottlers leave all the advertising to Coca-Cola and PepsiCo. In addition, the bottlers must sign an exclusive agreement that prohibits them from distributing competing cola brands. A Coke or Pepsi bottler cannot bottle any other cola drink. This strategy has two major advantages for Coca-Cola and PepsiCo. First, it forces bottlers to enter into exclusive agreements, which create a high barrier to entry into the industry; any potential competitors that might want to produce and distribute a new cola product must create their own distribution network rather than use the existing network. Second, the large amount of money spent on advertising (in 2003 both companies spent over $500 million each) to develop a global brand name has helped Coca-Cola and PepsiCo differentiate their products so that consumers are more likely to buy a Coke or a Pepsi rather than a lesser-known cola. Moreover, brand loyalty allows both companies to charge a premium or comparatively high price for what is, after all, merely colored water and flavoring. This differentiation strategy has made Coca-Cola and PepsiCo two of the most profitable companies in the world.

In the last decade the global soft-drink environment has undergone a major change, however, because of Gerald Pencer, a Canadian entrepreneur, who in the early 1990s came up with a new plan for competing in the cola market and created a new strategy to attract customers. Pencer's strategy was to produce a high-quality, low-priced cola, manufactured and bottled by the Cott Corporation, of which he was CEO at the time, and sell directly to major retail establishments (such as supermarket chains) as a private-label "house brand," thus bypassing the bottlers. He implemented this plan first in Canada and then quickly expanded into the United States because of interest in his product. Retailers were attracted to Cott's cola and other soft drink flavors because its low cost allows them to make more profit than they receive from selling Coke or Pepsi while building their store brand image.

To implement his strategy, Pencer decided to spend no money on advertising (so that he could charge a lower price for its soft drinks) and to take advantage of efficient national distribution systems that giant retailers such as Wal-Mart have created in recent years. This *low-cost strategy* enables Cott to circumvent the barrier to entry created by the exclusive distribution agreements that Coca-Cola and PepsiCo have signed with their bottlers.

Pencer went on to supply an international market by offering to sell soft drinks concentrate at prices lower than Coca-Cola and PepsiCo charge. In April 1994, for example, Cott launched a cola product in Britain for Sainsbury's, Britain's biggest food retailer. The product was sold as "Sainsbury's Classic Cola" and was priced 30 percent below Coke and Pepsi.

In 2004, Cott was the world's largest supplier of retailer-branded carbonated soft drinks.[1] It has 19 manufacturing facilities in Canada, the United States, and the United Kingdom and a syrup concentrate production plant in Columbus, Georgia, that supply most of the private-label grocery store, drugstore, mass-merchandising, and convenience store chains in these countries. In successfully capturing the retailer brands, Cott has created a leadership position in the international soft drinks market by providing high quality retailer brand beverages to the benefit of discerning customers.

Overview

As the opening case suggests, there is more than one way to compete in an industry, and to find a viable way to enter and compete in an industry, managers must study the way other organizations behave and identify their strategies. By studying the strategies of Coca-Cola and PepsiCo, Gerald Pencer was able to devise a strategy that allowed him to enter the cola industry and take on these global giants; so far, Cott has had considerable success.

In an uncertain competitive environment, managers must engage in thorough planning to find a strategy that will allow them to compete effectively. This chapter explores the manager's role both as planner and as strategist. We discuss the different elements involved in the planning process, including its three major steps: (1) determining an organization's mission and major goals, (2) choosing strategies to realize the mission and goals, and (3) selecting the appropriate way of organizing resources to implement the strategies. We also discuss scenario planning and SWOT analysis, important techniques that managers use to analyze their current situation. By the end of this chapter, you will understand the role managers play in the planning and strategy-making process to create high-performing organizations.

The Nature of the Planning Process

Planning, as we noted in Chapter 1, is a process that managers use to identify and select appropriate goals and courses of action for an organization.[2] The organizational plan that results from the planning process details the goals of the organization and specifies how managers intend to attain those goals. The cluster of decisions and actions that managers take to help an organization attain its goals is its **strategy.** Thus, planning is both a goal-making and a strategy-making process.

planning Identifying and selecting appropriate goals and courses of action; one of the four principal functions of management.

strategy A cluster of decisions about what goals to pursue, what actions to take, and how to use resources to achieve goals.

mission statement A broad declaration of an organization's purpose that identifies the organization's products and customers and distinguishes the organization from its competitors.

In most organizations, planning is a three-step activity (see Figure 8.1). The first step is determining the organization's mission and goals. A **mission statement** is a broad declaration of an organization's overriding purpose; this statement is intended to identify an organization's products and customers as well as to distinguish the organization in some way from its competitors. The second step is formulating strategy. Managers analyze the organization's current situation and then conceive and develop the strategies necessary to attain the organization's mission and goals. The third step is implementing strategy. Managers decide how to allocate the resources and responsibilities required to implement the strategies between people and groups within the organization.[3] In subsequent sections of this chapter we look in detail at the specifics of each of these steps. But first we examine the general nature and purpose of planning, one of the four managerial functions identified by Henri Fayol.

Figure 8.1
Three Steps in Planning

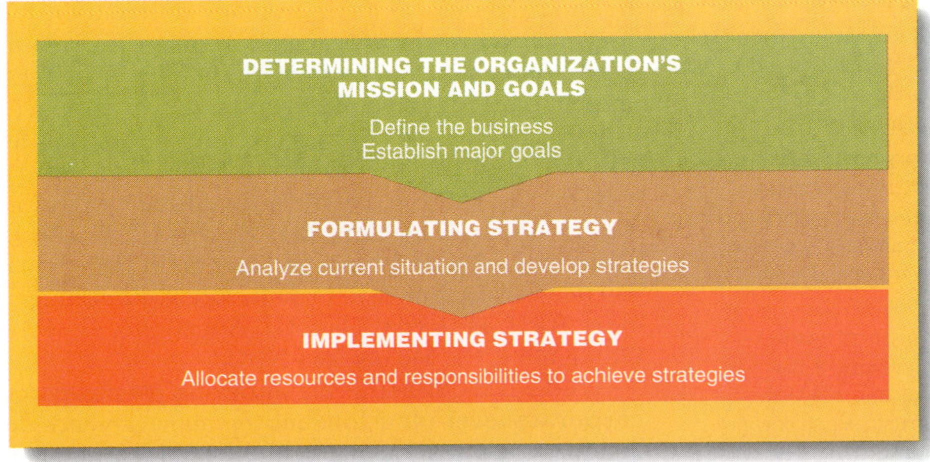

DETERMINING THE ORGANIZATION'S MISSION AND GOALS
Define the business
Establish major goals
FORMULATING STRATEGY
Analyze current situation and develop strategies
IMPLEMENTING STRATEGY
Allocate resources and responsibilities to achieve strategies

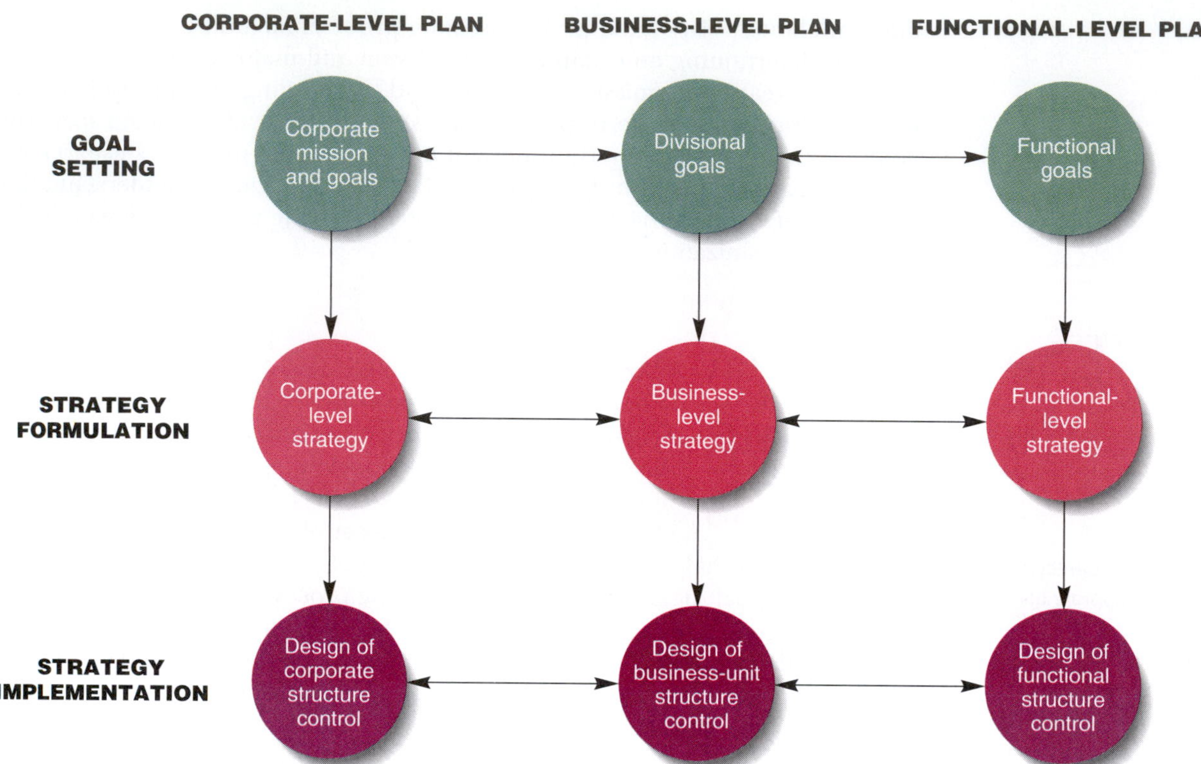

Figure 8.2
Levels and Types of Planning

Levels of Planning

division A business unit that has its own set of managers and functions or departments and competes in a distinct industry.

divisional managers Managers who control the various divisions of an organization.

corporate-level plan Top management's decisions pertaining to the organization's mission, overall strategy, and structure.

corporate-level strategy A plan that indicates in which industries and national markets an organization intends to compete.

In large organizations planning usually takes place at three levels of management: corporate, business or division, and department or functional. Figure 8.2 shows the link between the three steps in the planning process and these three levels. To understand this model, consider how General Electric (GE), a large organization that competes in many different businesses, operates.[4] GE has three main levels of management: corporate level, business level, and functional level (see Figure 8.3). At the corporate level are CEO and Chairman Jeffrey Immelt, three other top managers, and their corporate support staff. Below the corporate level is the business level. At the business level are the different divisions of the company. A **division** is a business unit that competes in a distinct industry; GE has over 150 divisions, including GE Aircraft Engines, GE Financial Services, GE Lighting, GE Motors, GE Plastics, and NBC. Each division has its own set of **divisional managers.** In turn, each division has its own set of functions or departments–manufacturing, marketing, human resource management, R&D, and so on. Thus, GE Aircraft has its own marketing function, as do GE Lighting, GE Motors, and NBC.

At GE, as at other large organizations, planning takes place at each level. The **corporate-level plan** contains top management's decisions pertaining to the organization's mission and goals, overall (corporate-level) strategy, and structure (see Figure 8.2). **Corporate-level strategy** indicates in which industries

Figure 8.3
Levels of Planning at General Electric

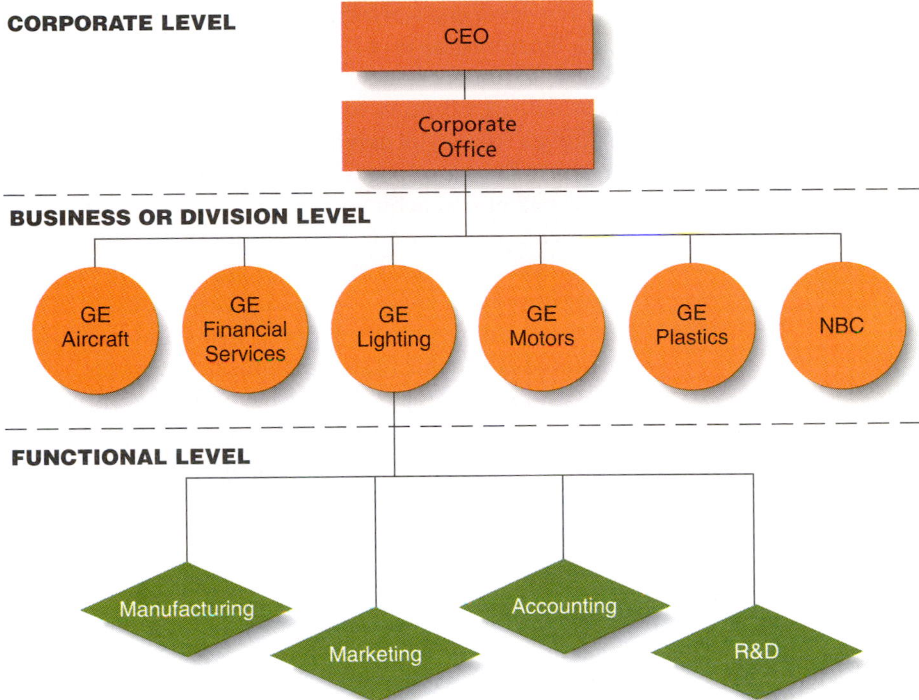

business-level plan Divisional managers' decisions pertaining to divisions' long-term goals, overall strategy, and structure.

business-level strategy A plan that indicates how a division intends to compete against its rivals in an industry.

function A unit or department in which people have the same skills or use the same resources to perform their jobs.

functional managers Managers who supervise the various functions, such as manufacturing, accounting, and sales, within a division.

functional-level plan Functional managers' decisions pertaining to the goals that they propose to pursue to help the division attain its business-level goals.

and national markets an organization intends to compete. One of the goals stated in GE's corporate-level plan is that GE should be first or second in market share in every industry in which it competes. A division that cannot attain this goal may be sold to another company. GE Medical Systems was sold to Thompson of France for this reason. Another GE goal is the acquisition of other companies to help build market share. Over the last decade, GE has acquired several financial services companies and has transformed the GE Financial Services Division into one of the largest financial services operations in the world.

The corporate-level plan provides the framework within which divisional managers create their business-level plans. At the business level, the managers of each division create a **business-level plan** that details (1) long-term goals that will allow the division to meet corporate goals and (2) the division's business-level strategy and structure. **Business-level strategy** states the methods a division or business intends to use to compete against its rivals in an industry. Managers at GE Lighting (currently number two in the global lighting industry, behind the Dutch company Philips NV) develop strategies designed to help the division take over the number-one spot and better contribute to GE's corporate goals. The lighting division's competitive strategy might emphasize, for example, trying to reduce costs in all departments in order to lower prices and gain market share from Philips. GE is currently planning to expand its European lighting operations, which, as we discussed in Chapter 6, is based in Hungary.[5]

A **function** is a unit or department in which people have the same skills or use the same resources to perform their jobs. Examples include manufacturing, accounting, and sales. The business-level plan provides the framework within which **functional managers** devise their plans. A **functional-level plan** states the goals that functional managers propose to pursue to help the division attain its business-level goals, which, in turn, allow the organization to achieve its corporate goals. **Functional-level strategy** sets forth the actions that managers intend to take at the level of departments such as manufacturing, marketing, and R&D to allow the organization to attain its goals. Thus, for example, consistent with GE Lighting's strategy of driving down costs, the manufacturing function might adopt the goal "To reduce production costs by 20 percent over three years," and its functional strategy to achieve this goal might include (1) investing in state-of-the-art European production facilities, and (2) developing an electronic global business-to-business network to reduce the costs of inputs and inventory holding.

functional-level strategy A plan that indicates how a function intends to achieve its goals.

An important issue in planning is ensuring consistency in planning across the three different levels. Functional goals and strategies should be consistent with divisional goals and strategies, which in turn should be consistent with corporate goals and strategies, and vice versa. Once complete, each function's plan is normally linked to its division's business-level plan, which, in turn, is linked to the corporate plan. Although few organizations are as large and complex as GE, most plan as GE does and have written plans to guide managerial decision making.

Who Plans?

In general, corporate-level planning is the primary responsibility of top managers.[6] At General Electric, the corporate-level goal that GE be first or second in every industry in which it competes was first articulated by former CEO Jack Welch, who stepped down in September 2001. Now, Welch's hand-selected successor, Jeffrey Immelt, and his top-management team decide which industries GE should compete in. Corporate-level managers are responsible for approving business- and functional-level plans to ensure that they are consistent with the corporate plan.

Corporate planning decisions are not made in a vacuum. Other managers do have input to corporate-level planning. At General Electric and many other companies, divisional and functional managers are encouraged to submit proposals for new business ventures to the CEO and top managers, who evaluate the proposals and decide whether to fund them.[7] Thus, even though corporate-level planning is the responsibility of top managers, lower-level managers can and usually are given the opportunity to become involved in the process.

This approach is common not only at the corporate level but also at the business and functional levels. At the business level, planning is the responsibility of divisional managers, who also review functional plans. Functional managers also typically participate in business-level planning. Similarly, although the functional managers bear primary responsibility for functional-level planning, they can and do involve their subordinates in this process. Thus, although ultimate responsibility for planning may lie with certain select managers within an organization, all managers and many nonmanagerial employees typically participate in the planning process.

Time Horizons of Plans

time horizon The intended duration of a plan.

Plans differ in their **time horizons,** or intended durations. Managers usually distinguish among *long-term plans,* with a horizon of five years or more; intermediate-term plans, with a horizon between one and five years; and *short-term plans,* with a horizon of one year or less.[8] Typically, corporate- and business-level goals and strategies require long- and intermediate-term plans, and functional-level goals and strategies require intermediate- and short-term plans.

Although most organizations operate with planning horizons of five years or more, it would be inaccurate to infer from this that they undertake major planning exercises only once every five years and then "lock in" a specific set of goals and strategies for that time period. Most organizations have an annual planning cycle, which is usually linked to the annual financial budget (although a major planning effort may be undertaken only every few years).

Although a corporate- or business-level plan may extend over five years or more, it is typically treated as a *rolling plan,* a plan that is updated and amended every year to take account of changing conditions in the external environment. Thus, the time horizon for an organization's 2002 corporate-level plan might be 2007; for the 2003 plan it might be 2008; and so on. The use of rolling plans is essential because of the high rate of change in the environment and the difficulty of predicting competitive conditions five years in the future. Rolling plans allow managers to make midcourse corrections if environmental changes warrant or to change the thrust of the plan altogether if it no longer seems appropriate. The use of rolling plans allows managers to plan flexibly, without losing sight of the need to plan for the long term.

Standing Plans and Single-Use Plans

Another distinction often made between plans is whether they are standing plans or single-use plans. Managers create standing and single-use plans to help achieve an organization's specific goals. *Standing plans* are used in situations in which programmed decision making is appropriate. When the same situations occur repeatedly, managers develop policies, rules, and standard operating procedures (SOPs) to control the way employees perform their tasks. A *policy* is a general guide to action; a *rule* is a formal, written guide to action; and a *standing operating procedure* is a written instruction describing the exact series of actions that should be followed in a specific situation. For example, an organization may have a standing plan about ethical behavior by employees. This plan includes a policy that all employees are expected to behave ethically in their dealings with suppliers and customers; a rule that requires any employee who receives from a supplier or customer a gift worth more than $10 to report the gift; and an SOP that obliges the recipient of the gift to make the disclosure in writing within 30 days.

In contrast, *single-use plans* are developed to handle nonprogrammed decision making in unusual or one-of-a-kind situations. Examples of single-use plans include *programs,* which are integrated sets of plans for achieving certain goals, and *projects,* which are specific action plans created to complete various aspects of a program. One of NASA's major programs was to reach the moon, and one project in this program was to develop a lunar module capable of landing on the moon and returning to the earth.

Why Planning Is Important

Essentially, planning is ascertaining where an organization is at the present time and deciding where it should be in the future and how to move it forward. When managers plan, they must consider the future and forecast what may happen in order to take actions in the present and mobilize organizational resources to deal with future opportunities and threats. As we have discussed in previous chapters, however, the external environment is uncertain and complex, and managers typically must deal with incomplete information and bounded rationality. This is one reason why planning is so complex and difficult.

Almost all managers engage in planning, and all should participate because they must try to predict future opportunities and threats. The absence of a plan often results in hesitations, false steps, and mistaken changes of direction that can hurt an organization or even lead to disaster. Planning is important for four main reasons:

1. Planning is a useful way of getting managers to participate in decision making about the appropriate goals and strategies for an organization. Effective planning gives all managers the opportunity to participate in decision making. At Intel, for example, top managers, as part of their annual planning process, regularly request input from lower-level managers to determine what the organization's goals and strategies should be.

2. Planning is necessary to give the organization a sense of direction and purpose.[9] A plan states what goals an organization is trying to achieve and what strategies it intends to use to achieve them. Without the sense of direction and purpose that a formal plan provides, managers may interpret their own tasks and roles in ways that best suit themselves. The result will be an organization that is pursuing multiple and often conflicting goals and a set of managers who do not cooperate and work well together. By stating which organizational goals and strategies are important, a plan keeps managers on track so that they use the resources under their control effectively.

3. A plan helps coordinate managers of the different functions and divisions of an organization to ensure that they all pull in the same direction. Without a good plan, it is possible that the members of the manufacturing function will produce more products than the members of the sales function can sell, resulting in a mass of unsold inventory. Implausible as this might seem, it happened to the high-flying Internet router supplier Cisco Systems in the early 2000s when manufacturing, which had been able to sell all the routers that it produced, found it had over $2 billion of unsold inventory because of the combination of an economic recession and customers' demands for new kinds of optical routers that Cisco did not have in stock.

4. A plan can be used as a device for controlling managers within an organization. A good plan specifies not only which goals and strategies the organization is committed to but also who is responsible for putting the strategies into action to attain the goals. When managers know that they will be held accountable for attaining a goal, they are motivated to do their best to make sure the goal is achieved.

Henri Fayol, the originator of the model of management we discussed in Chapter 1, said that effective plans should have four qualities: unity, continuity, accuracy, and flexibility.[10] *Unity* means that at any one time only one central, guiding plan is put into operation to achieve an organizational goal; more than one plan to achieve a goal would cause confusion and disorder. *Continuity* means that planning is an ongoing process in which managers build and refine previous plans and continually modify plans at all levels–corporate, business, and functional–so that they fit together into one broad framework. *Accuracy* means that managers need to make every attempt to collect and utilize all available information at their disposal in the planning process. Of course, managers must recognize the fact that uncertainty exists and that information is almost always incomplete (for reasons we discussed in Chapter 7). Despite the need for continuity and accuracy, however, Fayol emphasized that the planning process should be *flexible* enough so that plans can be altered and changed if the situation changes; managers must not be bound to a static plan.

Scenario Planning

scenario planning The generation of multiple forecasts of future conditions followed by an analysis of how to respond effectively to each of those conditions; also called *contingency planning*.

One way in which managers can try to create plans that have the four qualities that Fayol described is by utilizing scenario planning, one of the most widely used planning techniques. **Scenario planning** (also known as *contingency planning*) is the generation of multiple forecasts of future conditions followed by an analysis of how to respond effectively to each of those conditions.

As noted previously, planning is about trying to forecast and predict the future in order to be able to anticipate future opportunities and threats. The future, however, is inherently unpredictable. How can managers best deal with this unpredictability? This question preoccupied managers at Royal Dutch Shell, the third-largest global oil company in the 1980s. In 1984, oil was $30 a barrel, and most analysts and managers, including Shell's, believed that it would hit $50 per barrel by 1990. Nevertheless, Shell conducted a scenario-planning exercise for its managers. Shell's managers were asked to use scenario planning to generate different future scenarios of conditions in the oil market and then to develop a set of plans that detailed how they would respond to these opportunities and threats if any such scenario occurred.

One scenario used the assumption that oil prices would fall to $15 per barrel, and managers had to decide what they should do in such a case. Managers went to work with the goal of creating a plan consisting of a series of recommendations. The final plan included proposals to cut oil exploration costs by investing in new technologies, to accelerate investments in cost-efficient oil-refining facilities, and to weed out unprofitable gas stations.[11] In reviewing these proposals, top management came to the conclusion that even if oil prices continued to rise, all of these actions would benefit Shell by widening the company's profit margin. They decided to put the plan into action. As it happened, in the mid-1980s oil prices did collapse to $15 a barrel, but Shell, unlike its competitors, had already taken steps to be profitable in a low-oil-price world. Consequently, by 1990, the company was twice as profitable as its major competitors.

Because the future is unpredictable, the only reasonable approach to planning is first to generate "multiple futures"–or scenarios of the future–based on different assumptions about conditions that *might prevail* in the future and then to develop different plans that detail what a company *should do* in the event that one of these scenarios actually occurs. Scenario planning is a learning tool that raises the quality of the planning process and can bring real benefits to an organization.[12] Shell's success with scenario planning influenced many other companies to adopt similar systems. By 1990, more than 50 percent of Fortune 500 companies were using some version of scenario planning, and the number has increased since then.[13] The great strength of scenario planning is its ability not only to anticipate the challenges of an uncertain future but also to educate managers to think about the future–*to think strategically*.[14]

Determining the Organization's Mission and Goals

Determining the organization's mission and goals is the first step of the planning process. Once the mission and goals are agreed upon and formally stated in the corporate plan, they guide the next steps by defining which strategies are appropriate and which are inappropriate.[15]

Defining the Business

To determine an organization's mission, managers must first define its business so that they can identify what kind of value they will provide to customers. To define the business, managers must ask three questions: (1) Who are our customers? (2) What customer needs are being satisfied? (3) How are we satisfying customer needs?[16] They ask these questions to identify the customer needs that the organization satisfies and the way the organization satisfies those needs. Answering these questions helps managers to identify not only the customer needs they are satisfying now but the needs they should try to satisfy in the future and who their true competitors are. All of this information helps managers plan and establish appropriate goals. The case of Mattel shows the important role that defining the business has in the planning process.

Management Insight

Ups and Downs at Mattel

In the 1990s, Mattel Inc., the well-known maker of such classic toys as Barbie dolls and Hot Wheels, believed that the toy market and customer preferences for toys were changing rapidly. This was because of the growing popularity of electronic toys and computer games. Sales of computer games had increased dramatically as more and more parents saw the educational opportunities offered by games that children would enjoy playing. Moreover, many kinds of computer games could be played with other people over the Internet, so it seemed that in the future the magic of electronics and information technology would turn the toy world upside down. Mattel's managers feared that core products, such as its range of Barbie dolls, might lose their appeal and become passé given the future possibilities opened up by chips, computers, and the Internet. Mattel's managers believed that its customers' needs were changing and that the company needed to find new ways to satisfy those needs if it was to remain the biggest toy seller in the United States. Fearing they would lose their customers to the new computer game companies, Mattel's managers decided that the quickest and easiest way to redefine its business and become a major player in the computer game market would be to acquire one of these companies. So in 1998 Mattel paid $3.5 billion for The Learning Company, the maker of such popular games as "Thinking Things." Its goal was to use this company's expertise and knowledge both to build an array of new computer games and to take Mattel toys such as Barbie and create new games around them. In this way Mattel hoped to better meet the needs of its existing customers and cater to the needs of the new computer game customers.[17]

In addition, while some classic toys like Barbie have the potential to satisfy customers' needs for generations, the popularity of many toys is temporary

One of the new Harry Potter products: a life-sized replica of "Fluffy" the three-headed dog that guards the Sorcerer's Stone in the popular book series. Mattel has a license to manufacture and sell a whole range of Harry Potter products.

and is often linked to the introduction of a new movie from Disney, Pixar, or Dreamworks. To ensure that it could meet the changing needs of customers for these kinds of toys, Mattel contracted with the three film companies to become the supplier of the toys linked to their movies. For example, in 2001 it agreed to pay Warner Brothers 15 percent of the gross revenues, and a guaranteed $20 million, for the rights to produce toys linked to the Harry Potter movie, based on the books of the same name. It launched a line of toys, filled with electronics, that allow them to move and make sounds and also created Harry Potter computer games that satisfied its customers' needs.[18]

While Mattel's managers correctly sensed that customers' needs were changing, the way in which it decided to satisfy customers new needs–namely, by buying The Learning Company–was not the right decision. It turned out that the skills required to rapidly develop new games linked to Mattel's products were not present in The Learning Company and few popular games were forthcoming. Moreover, Mattel had underestimated the need to promote and update its core toys, and the $3.5 billion could have been much better spent boosting and developing these toys. In 2001, CEO Bob Eckert sold The Learning Company and decided that henceforth Mattel would hire independent specialist companies to develop new electronic toys and computer games, including many related to its well-known products.

In the fast-paced toy market where customers' needs change and evolve, and where new groups of customers emerge as new technologies result in new kinds of toys, toy companies like Mattel must learn to define and redefine their businesses to satisfy those needs. By 2001, Mattel had begun to turn out whole new ranges of electronic products linked to Barbie, a new Diva Starz doll line, and new electronic games, and its profits started to recover in the early 2000s.

In 2004, however, sales of Barbie products faltered; international Barbie sales dipped by 11 percent and domestic sales by 15 percent. In July 2004 Eckert announced, "Our biggest challenge ahead is reinvigorating the fashion (doll) business. We're directing tremendous time, energy and resources to regain our momentum in the fashion doll category."[19] Mattel is continuing to revamp the Barbie product line, incorporating themes and story lines into the brand in hopes it will widen the dolls' appeal, particularly with 8- to 10-year-old girls. As Mattel's experience suggests, companies have to listen closely to their customers and decide how best to meet their changing needs and preferences.

Establishing Major Goals

Once the business is defined, managers must establish a set of primary goals to which the organization is committed. Developing these goals gives the organization a sense of direction or purpose. In most organizations, articulating major goals is the job of the CEO, although other managers have input into the process. Thus, at Mattel, CEO Eckert operates with the primary goal of being the leader in every segment of the toy market in which the company competes.

The best statements of organizational goals are ambitious–that is, they stretch the organization and require that managers improve its performance capabilities.[20] For example, in 2001 Cisco Systems CEO John Chambers outlined a very challenging goal. This Internet hardware company had been the success story of the 1990s. Cisco had enjoyed yearly growth of 30 to 50 percent in sales revenue, but it was hit in 2000 with over $2.2 billion in excess inventory it could not sell as many of the dot-com companies went belly up and its sales plummeted.[21] Nevertheless, Chambers announced that the company intended to return to its 30 to 50 percent growth rate within three years and was taking the appropriate steps to get there–steps that included the firing of thousands of employees, a big push to increase global sales, and the investment of billions in research to produce new generations of optical networking equipment. This goal represented a significant challenge for Cisco because by the top-management team's own admission, many of its largest customers were cutting back on Internet expenditures and the dot-com boom was over. In fact, Cisco did not achieve its ambitious growth rate because of the recession of the early 2000s; however, its financial performance did improve dramatically, and it maintained its competitive advantage over its industry rivals because of its new strategies. Cisco's managers' vision of the mission and goals of their company, along with the managerial visions at AT&T and Wal-Mart, is presented in Figure 8.4.

Although goals should be challenging, they should also be realistic. Challenging goals give managers an incentive to look for ways to improve an organization's operation, but a goal that is unrealistic and impossible to attain may prompt managers to give up.[22] For example, Cisco set the challenging, realistic goal of reducing its costs by $1 billion a year, and managers were able to improve the efficiency of Cisco's operations and achieve this goal.[23]

The time period in which a goal is expected to be achieved should be stated. Cisco's managers committed themselves to achieving the sales increases by 2004, but conditions in the global environment prevented this and now their goal is 2006. Time constraints are important because they emphasize that a goal must be attained within a reasonable period; they inject a sense of urgency into goal attainment and act as a motivator.

Figure 8.4
Three Mission Statements

COMPANY	MISSION STATEMENT
Cisco	Cisco solutions provide competitive advantage to our customers through more efficient and timely exchange of information, which in turn leads to cost savings, process efficiencies, and closer relationships with our customers, prospects, business partners, suppliers, and employees.
Wal-Mart	We work for you. We think of ourselves as buyers for our customers, and we apply our considerable strengths to get the best value for you. We've built Wal-Mart by acting on behalf of our customers, and that concept continues to propel us. We're working hard to make our customers' shopping easy.
AT&T	We are dedicated to being the world's best at bringing people together–giving them easy access to each other and to the information and services they want and need–anytime, anywhere.

Formulating Strategy

strategy formulation Analysis of an organization's current situation followed by the development of strategies to accomplish its mission and achieve its goals.

In **strategy formulation** managers analyze an organization's current situation and then develop strategies to accomplish its mission and achieve its goals.[24] Strategy formulation begins with managers' analyzing the factors within an organization and outside, in the global environment, that affect or may affect the organization's ability to meet its goals now and in the future. SWOT analysis and the five forces model are two useful techniques managers use to analyze these factors.

SWOT Analysis

SWOT analysis A planning exercise in which managers identify organizational strengths (S), weaknesses (W), environmental opportunities (O), and threats (T).

SWOT analysis is a planning exercise in which managers identify organizational strengths (S), weaknesses (W), environmental opportunities (O), and threats (T). Based on a SWOT analysis, managers at the different levels of the organization select the corporate-, business-, and functional-level strategies to best position the organization to achieve its mission and goals (see Figure 8.5). Because SWOT analysis is the first step in strategy formulation at any level, we consider it first, before turning specifically to corporate-, business-, and functional-level strategies.

In Chapter 6 we discussed forces in the task and general environments that have the potential to affect an organization. We noted that changes in these forces can produce opportunities that an organization might take advantage of and threats that may harm its current situation. The first step in SWOT analysis is to identify an organization's strengths and weaknesses. Table 8.1 (page 272) lists many important strengths (such as high-quality skills in marketing and in research and development) and weaknesses (such as rising manufacturing costs and outdated technology). The task facing managers is to identify the strengths and weaknesses that characterize the present state of their organization.

The second step in SWOT analysis begins when managers embark on a full-scale SWOT planning exercise to identify potential opportunities and threats in the environment that affect the organization at the present or may affect it in the

Figure 8.5 Planning and Strategy Formulation

Table 8.1
Questions for SWOT Analysis

Potential Strengths	Potential Opportunities	Potential Weaknesses	Potential Threats
Well-developed strategy?	Expand core business(es)?	Poorly developed strategy?	Attacks on core business(es)?
Strong product lines?	Exploit new market segments?	Obsolete, narrow product lines?	Increase in domestic competition?
Broad market coverage?	Widen product range?	Rising manufacturing costs?	Increase in foreign competition?
Manufacturing competence?	Extend cost or differentiation advantage?	Decline in R&D innovations?	Change in consumer tastes?
Good marketing skills?	Diversify into new growth businesses?	Poor marketing plan?	Fall in barriers to entry?
Good materials management systems?	Expand into foreign markets?	Poor materials management systems?	Rise in new or substitute products?
R&D skills and leadership?	Apply R&D skills in new areas?	Loss of customer goodwill?	Increase in industry rivalry?
Human resource competencies?	Enter new related businesses?	Inadequate human resources?	New forms of industry competition?
Brand-name reputation?	Vertically integrate forward?	Loss of brand name?	Potential for takeover?
Cost of differentiation advantage?	Vertically integrate backward?	Growth without direction?	Changes in demographic factors?
Appropriate management style?	Overcome barriers to entry?	Loss of corporate direction?	Changes in economic factors?
Appropriate organizational structure?	Reduce rivalry among competitors?	Infighting among divisions?	Downturn in economy?
Appropriate control systems?	Apply brand-name capital in new areas?	Loss of corporate control?	Rising labor costs?
Ability to manage strategic change?	Seek fast market growth?	Inappropriate organizational structure and control systems?	Slower market growth?
Others?	Others?	High conflict and politics?	Others?
		Others?	

future. Examples of possible opportunities and threats that must be anticipated (many of which were discussed in Chapter 5) are listed in Table 8.1.

With the SWOT analysis completed, and strengths, weaknesses, opportunities, and threats identified, managers can begin the planning process and determine strategies for achieving the organization's mission and goals. The resulting strategies should enable the organization to attain its goals by taking advantage of opportunities, countering threats, building strengths, and correcting organizational weaknesses. To appreciate how managers use SWOT analysis to formulate strategy, consider how Douglas Conant, CEO of Campbell Soup, has used it to try to find strategies to turn around the troubled food products maker.

Manager as a Person

Douglas Conant Is in the Soup

As part of an attempt to turn around its ailing condensed soup business, Campbell's used some innovative marketing ploys. Here Steve Solomon puts the finishing touches on a 10-foot tall Campbell's Tomato Soup can displaying the company's newly designed soup label. It was unveiled at the Andy Warhol Museum in Pittsburgh, the home of many of Warhol's pop art Campbell's Soup pictures.

Campbell Soup Co. is one of the oldest and best-known companies in the world. However, in recent years Campbell has seen demand for its major products like condensed soup plummet as customers have switched from high-salt, processed soups to healthier low-fat, low-salt varieties. Indeed, its condensed soup business fell by 30 percent between 1998 and 2004. By the early 2000s Campbell's market share and profits were falling, and its new CEO Douglas Conant decided it was necessary to devise a three-year turnaround plan to help the company maintain its market position.

One of Conant's first actions was to initiate a thorough SWOT planning exercise. An analysis of the environment identified the growth of the organic- and health-food segment of the food market and the increasing number of other kinds of convenience foods as a threat to Campbell's core soup business. The analysis of the environment also revealed three growth opportunities: (1) the growing market for health and sports drinks, in which Campbell already was a competitor with its V8 juice, (2) the growing market for salsas, in which Campbell competed with its Pace salsa, and (3) chocolate products, where Campbell's Godiva brand had enjoyed increasing sales throughout the 1990s.

With the analysis of the environment complete, Conant turned his attention to his organization's resources and capabilities. His internal analysis of Campbell identified a number of major weaknesses. These included staffing levels that were too high relative to its competitors and high costs associated with manufacturing its soups because of the use of outdated machinery. Also, Conant noted that Campbell had a very conservative culture in which people seemed to be afraid to take risks–something that was a real problem in the fast-changing food industry, where customer tastes are always changing and new products must be developed constantly. At the same time, the SWOT analysis identified an enormous strength: Campbell enjoyed huge economies of scale because of the enormous quantity of food products that it makes, and it also had a first-rate research and development division that had the capability to develop exciting new food products.

Using the information gained from this SWOT analysis, Conant and his managers decided that Campbell needed to use its product development skills to revitalize its core products and modify or reinvent them in ways that would appeal to increasingly health-conscious and busy consumers who did not want to take the time to prepare old-fashioned condensed soup. Moreover, it needed to expand its franchise in the health- and sports-, snack-, and luxury-food segments of the market. Another major need that managers saw was to find new ways to deliver Campbell's products to customers. To increase sales, Campbell's needed to tap into new food outlets, such as corporate cafeterias, college dining halls, and other mass eateries to expand consumers' access to its foods. Finally, Conant decided it was necessary to decentralize authority to managers at lower levels in the organization and give them the responsibility of bringing new kinds of soups, salsas, and chocolate products to the market. In this way he hoped to revitalize Campbell's slow-moving culture and speed the flow of improved and new products to the market.

Conant put his new plan into action, sales of soup started to rise, and he began to put more emphasis on sales of soup at outlets such as 7-11 and Subway and less on supermarket sales.[25] By 2004, analysts felt that he had made a significant difference in Campbell's performance but that there was still a lot to do as Campbell's operating margins were still shrinking. Carrying on the SWOT analysis, Conant decided Campbell should produce more products to meet the needs of the "low-carb diet," such as new kinds of low-carb bread and cookies. He also decided to shrink the company's operations to lower costs. His goal is to raise profit margins to the level of his major competitors Kraft and General Mills by 2007 using a new three-year plan based on this SWOT analysis.[26]

The Five Forces Model

A well-known model that helps managers isolate particular forces in the external environment that are potential threats is Michael Porter's five forces model. We discussed the first four in Chapter 5. Porter identified these five factors that are major threats because they affect how much profit organizations competing within the same industry can expect to make:

- *The level of rivalry among organizations in an industry.* The more that companies compete against one another for customers–for example, by lowering the prices of their products or by increasing advertising–the lower is the level of industry profits (low prices mean less profit).
- *The potential for entry into an industry.* The easier it is for companies to enter an industry–because, for example, barriers to entry, such as brand loyalty, are low–the more likely it is for industry prices and therefore industry profits to be low.
- *The power of suppliers.* If there are only a few suppliers of an important input, then suppliers can drive up the price of that input, and expensive inputs result in lower profits for the producer.
- *The power of customers.* If only a few large customers are available to buy an industry's output, they can bargain to drive down the price of that output. As a result, producers make lower profits.
- *The threat of substitute products.* Often, the output of one industry is a substitute for the output of another industry (plastic may be a substitute for steel in some applications, for example; similarly, bottled water is a substitute for cola). Companies that produce a product with a known substitute cannot demand high prices for their products, and this constraint keeps their profits low.

Porter argued that when managers analyze opportunities and threats they should pay particular attention to these five forces because they are the major threats that an organization will encounter. It is the job of managers at the corporate, business, and functional levels to formulate strategies to counter these threats so that an organization can respond to its task and general environments, perform at a high level, and generate high profits. At Campbell Conant performs such an analysis to identify the opportunities and threats stemming from the actions of food industry rivals.

Formulating Corporate-Level Strategies

Corporate-level strategy is a plan of action concerning which industries and countries an organization should invest its resources in to achieve its mission and goals. In developing a corporate-level strategy, managers ask: How should the growth and development of the company be managed in order to increase its ability to create value for its customers (and thus increase performance) over the long run? Managers of most organizations have the goal of growing their companies and actively seek out new opportunities to use the organization's resources to create more goods and services for customers. Examples of organizations growing rapidly are Google, chip maker AMD, Hyundai, and Toyota, whose managers pursue any feasible opportunity to use their companies' skills to provide customers with new products.

In addition, some managers must help their organizations respond to threats due to changing forces in the task or general environment. For example, customers may no longer be buying the kinds of goods and services a company is producing (bulky computer monitors or televisions), or other organizations may have entered the market and attracted away customers (this happened to Intel when AMD began to produce more powerful chips). Top managers aim to find the best strategies to help the organization respond to these changes and improve performance.

The principal corporate-level strategies that managers use to help a company grow, to keep it on top of its industry, and to help it retrench and reorganize to stop its decline are (1) concentration on a single business, (2) diversification, (3) international expansion, and (4) vertical integration. These four strategies are all based on one idea: An organization benefits from pursuing any one of them only when the strategy helps further increase the value of the organization's goods and services for customers. To increase the value of goods and services, a corporate-level strategy must help an organization, or one of its divisions, differentiate and add value to its products either by making them unique or special or by lowering the costs of value creation.

Concentration on a Single Business

Most organizations begin their growth and development with a corporate-level strategy aimed at concentrating resources in one business or industry in order to develop a strong competitive position within that industry. For example, McDonald's began as one restaurant in California, but its managers' long-term goal was to focus its resources in the fast-food business and use those resources to quickly expand across the United States.

Sometimes, concentration on a single business becomes an appropriate corporate-level strategy when managers see the need to reduce the size of their organizations to increase performance. Managers may decide to get out of certain industries, for example, when particular divisions lose their competitive advantage. Managers may sell off those divisions, lay off workers, and concentrate remaining organizational resources in another market or business to try to improve performance. This happened to electronics maker Hitachi when it was forced to get out of the CRT computer monitor business. Intense low-price competition existed in the computer monitor market because customers were increasingly switching from bulky CRT monitors to the newer, flat, LCD monitors. Hitachi announced it was closing three factories in Japan, Singapore, and Malaysia that produced CRT monitors and would use its resources to invest in the new LCD technology.[27] In contrast, when organizations are performing effectively, they often decide to enter new industries in which they can use their resources to create more value.

Diversification

diversification Expanding operations into a new business or industry and producing new goods or services.

Diversification is the strategy of expanding operations into a new business or industry and producing new goods or services.[28] Examples of diversification include PepsiCo's diversification into the snack-food business with the purchase of Frito Lay, tobacco giant Philip Morris's diversification into the brewing industry with the acquisition of Miller Beer, and General Electric's move into broadcasting with its acquisition of NBC. There are two main kinds of diversification: related and unrelated.

related diversification Entering a new business or industry to create a competitive advantage in one or more of an organization's existing divisions or businesses.

synergy Performance gains that result when individuals and departments coordinate their actions.

RELATED DIVERSIFICATION **Related diversification** is the strategy of entering a new business or industry to create a competitive advantage in one or more of an organization's existing divisions or businesses. Related diversification can add value to an organization's products if managers can find ways for its various divisions or business units to share their valuable skills or resources so that synergy is created.[29] **Synergy** is obtained when the value created by two divisions cooperating is greater than the value that would be created if the two divisions operated separately. For example, suppose two or more divisions within a diversified company can utilize the same manufacturing facilities, distribution channels, advertising campaigns, and so on. Each division that shares resources has to invest less in the shared functions than it would have to invest if it had full responsibility for the activity. In this way, related diversification can be a major source of cost savings.[30] Similarly, if one division's R&D skills can be used to improve another division's products, the second division's products may receive a competitive advantage.

Procter & Gamble's disposable diaper and paper towel businesses offer one of the best examples of the successful production of synergies. These businesses share the costs of procuring inputs such as paper and developing new technology to reduce manufacturing costs. In addition, a joint sales force sells both products to supermarkets, and both products are shipped by means of the same distribution system. This resource sharing has enabled both divisions to reduce their costs, and as a result, they can charge lower prices than their competitors and thus attract more customers.[31]

In pursuing related diversification, managers often seek to find new businesses where they can use the existing skills and resources in their departments to create synergies, add value to the new business, and hence improve the competitive position of the company. Alternatively, managers may acquire a company in a new industry because they believe that some of the skills and resources of the acquired company might improve the efficiency of one or more of their existing divisions. If successful, such skill transfers can help an organization to lower its costs or better differentiate its products because they create synergies between divisions.

unrelated diversification Entering a new industry or buying a company in a new industry that is not related in any way to an organization's current businesses or industries.

UNRELATED DIVERSIFICATION Managers pursue **unrelated diversification** when they enter new industries or buy companies in new industries that are not related in any way to their current businesses or industries. One main reason for pursuing unrelated diversification is that, sometimes, managers can buy a poorly performing company, transfer their management skills to that company, turn around its business, and increase its performance, all of which creates value.

Another reason for pursuing unrelated diversification is that purchasing businesses in different industries lets managers engage in *portfolio strategy,* which is apportioning financial resources among divisions to increase financial returns or spread risks among different businesses, much as individual investors do with their own portfolios. For example, managers may transfer funds from a rich division (a "cash cow") to a new and promising division (a "star") and, by appropriately allocating money between divisions, create value. Though used as a popular explanation in the 1980s for unrelated diversification, portfolio strategy ran into increasing criticism in the 1990s.[32]

Indeed, more and more companies and their managers have abandoned the strategy of unrelated diversification because there is evidence that too much diversification can cause managers to lose control of their organization's core business. Management experts suggest that although unrelated diversification might initially create value for a company, managers sometimes use portfolio strategy to expand the scope of their organization's businesses too much. When this happens, it becomes difficult for top managers to be knowledgeable about all of the organization's diverse businesses. Managers do not have the time to process all of the information required to adequately assess the strategy and performance of each division objectively, and organizational performance often suffers.

This problem began to occur at General Electric in the 1970s. As former CEO Reg Jones commented: "I tried to review each business unit plan in great detail. This effort took untold hours and placed a tremendous burden on the corporate executive office. After awhile I began to realize that no matter how hard we would work, we could not achieve the necessary in-depth understanding of the 40-odd business unit plans."[33] Unable to handle so much information, top managers are overwhelmed and eventually make important resource allocation decisions on the basis of only a superficial analysis of the competitive position of each division. This usually results in value being lost rather than created.[34]

Thus, although unrelated diversification can create value for a company, research evidence suggests that many diversification efforts have reduced value rather than created it.[35] As a consequence, during the 1990s there was a trend among many diversified companies to divest many of their unrelated divisions. Managers sold off divisions and concentrated organizational resources on their core business, focusing more on related diversification.[36] In the 1990s, for example, Sears divested all of the stock brokerage, insurance, and real-estate businesses it had acquired during the 1980s and concentrated on strengthening its core retailing activities to survive in its fight with Wal-Mart and Target.

International Expansion

As if planning the appropriate level of diversification was not a difficult enough decision, corporate-level managers also must decide on the appropriate way to compete internationally. A basic question confronts the managers of any organization that competes in more than one national market: To what extent should the organization customize features of its products and marketing campaign to different national conditions?[37]

global strategy Selling the same standardized product and using the same basic marketing approach in each national market.

multidomestic strategy Customizing products and marketing strategies to specific national conditions.

If managers decide that their organization should sell the same standardized product in each national market in which it competes, and use the same basic marketing approach, they adopt a **global strategy.**[38] Such companies undertake very little, if any, customization to suit the specific needs of customers in different countries. But if managers decide to customize products and marketing strategies to specific national conditions, they adopt a **multidomestic strategy.** Matsushita, with its Panasonic brand, has traditionally pursued a global strategy, selling the same basic TVs and VCRs in every market in which it does business and often using the same basic marketing approach. Unilever, the European food and household products company, has pursued a multidomestic strategy. Thus, to appeal to German customers, Unilever's German division sells a different range of food products and uses a different marketing approach than its North American division.

A study in contrasts. Matsushita, with its Panasonic brand (shown on the top), has largely pursued a global strategy, selling the same basic TVs and VCRs in every market and using a similar marketing message. Unilever, on the other hand, has pursued a multidomestic strategy, tailoring its product line and marketing approach to specific locations. On the bottom, the CEO of Hindustan Lever, Ltd., Keki Dadiseth, holds a box of Surf detergent.

Global and multidomestic strategies both have advantages and disadvantages. The major advantage of a global strategy is the significant cost savings associated with not having to customize products and marketing approaches to different national conditions. For example, Rolex watches, Ralph Lauren or Tommy Hilfiger clothing, Channel or Armani accessories or perfume, Dell computers, Chinese-made plastic toys and buckets, and U.S.-grown rice and wheat are all products that can be sold using the same marketing across many countries by simply changing the language. Thus, companies can save a significant amount of money. The major disadvantage of pursuing a global strategy is that, by ignoring national differences, managers may leave themselves vulnerable to local competitors that do differentiate their products to suit local tastes. This occurred in the British consumer electronics industry. Amstrad, a British computer and electronics company, got its start by recognizing and responding to local consumer needs. Amstrad captured a major share of the British audio market by ignoring the standardized inexpensive music centers marketed by companies pursuing a global strategy, such as Sony and Matsushita. Instead, Amstrad's product was encased in teak rather than metal and featured a control panel tailor-made to appeal to British consumers' preferences. To remain competitive in this market, Matsushita had to place more emphasis on local customization of its Panasonic and JVC brands.

The advantages and disadvantages of a multidomestic strategy are the opposite of those of a global strategy. The major advantage of a multidomestic strategy is that by customizing product offerings and marketing approaches to local conditions, managers may be able to gain market share or charge higher prices for their products. The major disadvantage is that customization raises production costs and puts the multidomestic company at a price disadvantage because it often has to charge prices higher than the prices charged by competitors pursuing a global strategy. Obviously, the choice between these two strategies calls for trade-offs.

Managers at Gillette, the well-known razor blade maker, created a strategy that combines the best features of both international strategies. Gillette has been a global company from the beginning, as its managers quickly saw the advantages of selling its razor blades abroad. By 2004, 65 percent of Gillette's revenues came from global sales, and this percentage is expected to increase.[39] Gillette's strategy over the years has been pretty constant: Find a new foreign country with a growing market for razor blades, form a strategic alliance with a local razor blade company and take a majority stake in it, invest in a large marketing campaign, and then build a modern factory to make razor blades and other products for the local market. For example, when Gillette entered Russia after the breakup of the Soviet Union, it saw a huge opportunity to increase sales. It formed a joint venture with a local company called Leninets Concern, which made a razor known as the Sputnik, and then with this base began to import its own brands into Russia. When sales growth rose sharply, Gillette decided to offer more products in the market and built a new plant in St. Petersburg.[40]

Today, Gillette operates 50 manufacturing facilities in more than 20 countries.[41] It establishes its factories in countries where labor and other costs are low and then distributes and markets its products to countries in that region of the world. In this sense it pursues a global strategy. However, all of Gillette's research and development and design take place in the United States. As it develops new kinds of razors, it equips its foreign factories to manufacture them when it decides that local customers are ready to trade up to the new product. So, for example, Gillette's latest razor may be introduced in a foreign country years later than in the United States. Thus, Gillette is customizing its product offering to the needs of different countries and also pursues a multidomestic strategy. By pursuing this international strategy, Gillette achieves low costs and still differentiates and customizes its product range to suit the needs of each country or world region. This strategy has proved very effective for Gillette, whose global sales and profits continue to increase.

CHOOSING A WAY TO EXPAND INTERNATIONALLY As we have discussed, a more competitive global environment has proved to be both an opportunity and a threat for organizations and managers. The opportunity is that organizations that expand globally are able to open new markets, reach more customers, and gain access to new sources of raw materials and to low-cost suppliers of inputs. The threat is that organizations that expand globally are likely to encounter new competitors in the foreign countries they enter and must respond to new political, economic, and cultural conditions.

Before setting up foreign operations, managers of companies such as Amazon.com, Lands' End, GE, Toys 'R' Us, and Boeing needed to analyze

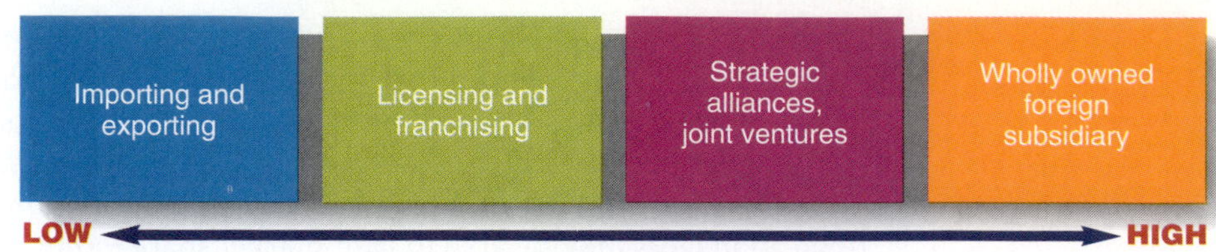

Figure 8.6
Four Ways of Expanding Internationally

the forces in the environment of a particular country (such as Korea or Brazil) in order to choose the right method to expand and respond to those forces in the most appropriate way. In general, four basic ways to operate in the global environment are importing and exporting, licensing and franchising, strategic alliances, and wholly owned foreign subsidiaries, Gillette's preferred approach. We briefly discuss each one, moving from the lowest level of foreign involvement and investment required of a global organization and its managers, and the least amount of risk, to the high end of the spectrum (see Figure 8.6).[42]

IMPORTING AND EXPORTING The least complex global operations are exporting and importing. A company engaged in **exporting** makes products at home and sells them abroad. An organization might sell its own products abroad or allow a local organization in the foreign country to distribute its products. Few risks are associated with exporting because a company does not have to invest in developing manufacturing facilities abroad. It can further reduce its investment abroad if it allows a local company to distribute its products.

exporting Making products at home and selling them abroad.

A company engaged in **importing** sells at home products that are made abroad (products it makes itself or buys from other companies). For example, most of the products that Pier 1 Imports, The Bombay Company, and The Limited sell to their customers are made abroad. In many cases the appeal of a product–Irish glass, French wine, Italian furniture, or Indian silk–is that it is made abroad. The Internet has made it much easier for companies to inform potential foreign buyers about their products; detailed product specifications and features are available online, and informed buyers can communicate easily with prospective sellers. The way in which Levi Strauss was forced to change its international approach from exporting to importing illustrates how the growth of low-cost manufacturing abroad has changed competition in many industries.

importing Selling at home products that are made abroad.

Managing Globally

Levi Strauss's Big Problems

Levi Strauss, the well-known jeans maker, was once the global leader in the apparel industry. Its jeans commanded a premium price as customers the world over perceived the value or status of wearing Levi jeans was worth paying extra for. Indeed, in Europe and Asia, Levi jeans were often sold at double or triple their U.S. price. No more. Levi is now fighting to lower its costs to be able to survive in the fast-changing jeans industry.

Levi's problems arose because of changes in the international strategies of other jeans makers and apparel companies. Early in the 1990s, other jeans makers such as VF Corp (which makes Wrangler jeans), Calvin Klein, and Polo outsourced the production of jeans to countries abroad where labor costs were lowest. With their lower costs, these companies then began to charge lower prices for their products and customers began to switch to buying their jeans.

Jean manufacturers have lowered costs by outsourcing production to countries abroad.

Then, in a significant move, apparel companies such as Wal-Mart, JCPenney, Sears, and Dillard's began to wonder why they should pay Levi a premium price for selling its jeans when they could sell jeans under their own labels at a lower price and still make more profit than if they sold Levi's jeans. So they contracted with low-cost foreign producers to make jeans under their own in-house labels. The result was that sales of Levi jeans plummeted as many customers began to buy jeans on the basis of their price.

Levi, because it still produced most of its jeans in the United States and exported them abroad, was caught unprepared and found it could no longer compete. It lost billions of dollars in the 1990s as sales plummeted; to survive, it was forced to change from exporting its jeans to importing its jeans from abroad–it outsourced all production to manufacturers abroad. Since 1997 it has closed all 35 of its U.S. manufacturing facilities and laid off over 30,000 employees.

Once it outsourced production abroad, Levi was able to reduce its prices to be competitive. Indeed, its prices fell so low that Wal-Mart began to sell Levi jeans in its stores. However, low prices mean low profits, and Levi's problems have continued into the 2000s as it struggles to find a way to compete successfully in a global market dominated by ruthless low-cost/price competition.

licensing Allowing a foreign organization to take charge of manufacturing and distributing a product in its country or world region in return for a negotiated fee.

franchising Selling to a foreign organization the rights to use a brand name and operating know-how in return for a lump-sum payment and a share of the profits.

LICENSING AND FRANCHISING In **licensing,** a company (the licenser) allows a foreign organization (the licensee) to take charge of both manufacturing and distributing one or more of its products in the licensee's country or world region in return for a negotiated fee. Chemical maker Du Pont might license a local factory in India to produce nylon or Teflon. The advantage of licensing is that the licenser does not have to bear the development costs associated with opening up in a foreign country; the licensee bears the costs. The risks associated with this strategy are that the company granting the license has to give its foreign partner access to its technological know-how and so risks losing control over its secrets.

Whereas licensing is pursued primarily by manufacturing companies, franchising is pursued primarily by service organizations. In **franchising,** a company (the franchiser) sells to a foreign organization (the franchisee) the rights to use its brand name and operating know-how in return for a lump-sum payment and share of the franchiser's profits. Hilton Hotels might sell a franchise to a local company in Chile to operate hotels under the Hilton name in return for a franchise payment. The advantage of franchising is that the franchiser does not have to bear the development costs of overseas expansion and avoids the many problems associated with setting up foreign operations. The downside is that the organization that grants the franchise may lose control over the way in which the franchisee operates and product quality may fall. In this way, franchisers, such as Hilton, Avis, and McDonald's, risk losing their good names. American customers who buy McDonald's hamburgers in Korea may reasonably expect those burgers to be as good as the ones they get at home. If they are not, McDonald's reputation will suffer over time. Once again, the Internet facilitates communication between partners and allows them to better meet each other's expectations.

strategic alliance An agreement in which managers pool or share their organization's resources and know-how with a foreign company, and the two organizations share the rewards and risks of starting a new venture.

STRATEGIC ALLIANCES One way to overcome the loss-of-control problems associated with exporting, licensing, and franchising is to expand globally by means of a strategic alliance. In a **strategic alliance,** managers pool or share their organization's resources and know-how with those of a foreign company, and the two organizations share the rewards or risks of starting a new venture in a foreign country. Sharing resources allows a U.S. company, for example, to take advantage of the high-quality skills of foreign manufacturers and the specialized knowledge of foreign managers about the needs of local customers and to reduce the risks involved in a venture. At the same time, the terms of the alliance give the U.S. company more control over how the good or service is produced or sold in the foreign country than it would have as a franchiser or licenser.

joint venture A strategic alliance among two or more companies that agree to jointly establish and share the ownership of a new business.

A strategic alliance can take the form of a written contract between two or more companies to exchange resources, or it can result in the creation of a new organization. A **joint venture** is a strategic alliance among two or more companies that agree to jointly establish and share the ownership of a new business.[43] An organization's level of involvement abroad increases in a joint venture because the alliance normally involves a capital investment in production facilities abroad in order to produce goods or services outside the home country. Risk, however, is reduced. The Internet and global teleconferencing provide the increased communication and coordination necessary for partners to work together on a global basis. In 2001, for example, Coca-Cola and Nestlé announced that they would form a joint venture and cooperate in marketing their teas, coffees, and health-oriented beverages to more than 50 countries in the world.[44] Similarly, BP Amoco and Italy's ENI announced that they would form a joint venture to build a $2.5 billion gas-liquefaction plant in Egypt.[45]

wholly owned foreign subsidiary Production operations established in a foreign country independent of any local direct involvement.

WHOLLY OWNED FOREIGN SUBSIDIARIES When managers decide to establish a **wholly owned foreign subsidiary,** they invest in establishing production operations in a foreign country independent of any local direct involvement. Many Japanese car component companies, for example, have established their own operations in the United States to supply U.S.-based Japanese carmakers such as Toyota and Honda with high-quality components.

Operating alone, without any direct involvement from foreign companies, an organization receives all of the rewards and bears all of the risks associated with operating abroad.[46] This method of international expansion is much more expensive than the others because it requires a higher level of foreign investment and presents managers with many more threats. However, investment in a foreign subsidiary or division offers significant advantages: It gives an organization high potential returns because the organization does not have to share its profits with a foreign organization, and it reduces the level of risk because the organization's managers have full control over all aspects of their foreign subsidiary's operations. Moreover, this type of investment allows managers to protect their technology and know-how from foreign organizations. Large, well-known companies like Du Pont, General Motors, Arthur Andersen, and Gillette, which have plenty of resources, make extensive use of wholly owned subsidiaries. No matter what means they choose to expand globally, however, companies have to be careful to design and select the right kind of information systems and Web sites to allow customers to buy their products.

Vertical Integration

When an organization is doing well in its business, managers often see new opportunities to create value by either producing their own inputs or distributing their own outputs. Managers at E. & J. Gallo Winery, for example, realized that they could lower Gallo's costs if the company produced its own wine bottles rather than buying them from a glass company. As a result, Gallo established a new division to produce glass bottles.

vertical integration A strategy that allows an organization to create value by producing its own inputs or distributing and selling its own outputs.

Vertical integration is the corporate-level strategy through which an organization becomes involved in producing its own inputs (*backward* vertical integration) or distributing and selling its own outputs (*forward* vertical integration).[47] A steel company that supplies its iron ore needs from company-owned iron ore mines is engaging in backward vertical integration. A personal computer company that sells its computers through company-owned distribution outlets, as Tandy did through its Radio Shack stores, is engaging in forward vertical integration.

Figure 8.7 illustrates the four main stages in a typical raw-material-to-consumer value chain; value is added at each stage. Typically, the primary operations of an organization take place in one of these stages. For a company based in the assembly stage, backward integration would involve establishing a new division in intermediate manufacturing or raw-material production, and forward integration would involve establishing a new division to distribute its products to wholesalers or to sell directly to customers. A division at one stage receives the product produced by the division in the previous stage, transforms it in some way–adding value–and then transfers the output at a higher price to the division at the next stage in the chain.

As an example of how the value chain works, consider the cola segment of the soft-drink industry. Raw-material suppliers include sugar companies and G. D. Searle, manufacturer of the artificial sweetener NutraSweet, which is used in diet colas. These companies sell their products to companies that make concentrate–such as Coca-Cola and PepsiCo, which mix these inputs with others to produce the cola concentrate that they market. In the process, they add value to these inputs. The concentrate producers then sell the concentrate to bottlers,

Figure 8.7 Stages in a Vertical Value Chain

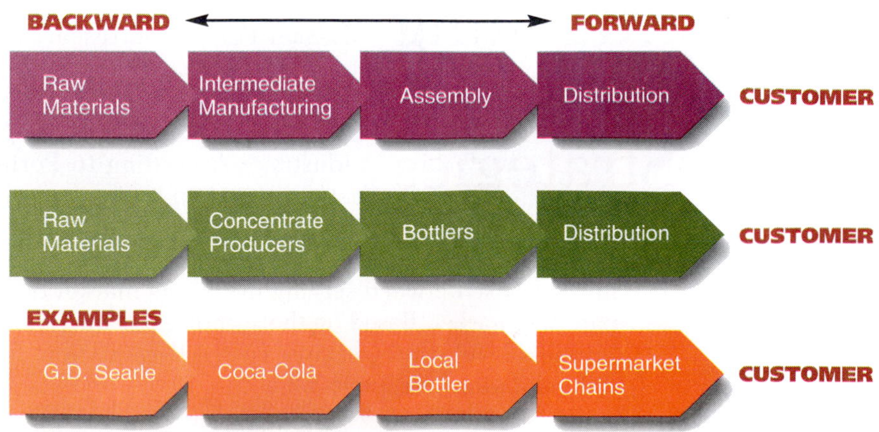

who add carbonated water to the concentrate and package the resulting drink—again adding value to the concentrate. Next, the bottlers sell the packaged product to various distributors, including retail stores such as Costco and Wal-Mart and fast-food chains such as McDonald's. These distributors add value by making the product accessible to customers. Thus, value is added by companies at each stage in the raw-material-to-consumer chain.

A major reason why managers pursue vertical integration is that it allows them either to add value to their products by making them special or unique or to lower the costs of value creation. For example, Coca-Cola and PepsiCo, in a case of forward vertical integration to build brand loyalty and enhance the differentiated appeal of their colas, decided to buy up their major bottlers to increase control over marketing and promotion efforts, which had been handled by the bottlers.[48] An example of using forward vertical integration to lower costs is Matsushita's decision to open company-owned stores to sell its Panasonic and JVC products and thus keep the profit that otherwise would be earned by independent retailers.[49]

Although vertical integration can help an organization to grow rapidly, it can be a problem when forces in the environment counter the strategies of the organization and make it necessary for managers to reorganize or retrench. Vertical integration can reduce an organization's flexibility to respond to changing environmental conditions. For example, IBM used to produce most of its own components for mainframe computers. While this made sense in the 1970s, it became a major handicap for the company in the fast-changing computer industry of the 1990s. The rise of organizationwide networks of personal computers meant slumping demand for mainframes. As demand fell, IBM found itself with an excess-capacity problem, not only in its mainframe assembly operations but also in component operations. Closing down this capacity cost IBM over $5 billion.[50]

When considering vertical integration as a strategy to add value, managers must be careful because sometimes vertical integration actually reduces an organization's ability to create value when the environment changes. This is why so many companies now outsource the production of component parts to other companies. IBM, however, has found a new opportunity for forward vertical integration in the 1990s.[51] It decided to provide IT consulting services to mainframe users and to advise them on how to install and manage any software packages they chose on their mainframes. Providing such IT services was so profitable for IBM that by 2000 it had recovered its market position.

Formulating Business-Level Strategies

Michael Porter, the researcher who developed the five forces model discussed earlier, also formulated a theory of how managers can select a business-level strategy, a plan to gain a competitive advantage in a particular market or industry.[52] According to Porter, managers must choose between the two basic ways of increasing the value of an organization's products: differentiating the product to add value or lowering the costs of value creation. Porter also argues that managers must choose between serving the whole market or serving just one segment or part of a market. Based on those choices, managers choose to pursue one of four business-level strategies: low cost, differentiation, focused low cost, or focused differentiation (see Table 8.2).

Table 8.2
Porter's Business-Level Strategies

	Number of Market Segments Served	
Strategy	**Many**	**Few**
Low cost	✓	
Focused low cost		✓
Differentiation	✓	
Focused differentiation		✓

Low-Cost Strategy

low-cost strategy Driving the organization's costs down below the costs of its rivals.

With a **low-cost strategy,** managers try to gain a competitive advantage by focusing the energy of all the organization's departments or functions on driving the organization's costs down below the costs of its rivals. This strategy, for example, would require that manufacturing managers search for new ways to reduce production costs, R&D managers focus on developing new products that can be manufactured more cheaply, and marketing managers find ways to lower the costs of attracting customers. According to Porter, organizations pursuing a low-cost strategy can sell a product for less than their rivals sell it and yet still make a profit because of their lower costs. Thus, organizations that pursue a low-cost strategy hope to enjoy a competitive advantage based on their low prices. For example, BIC pursues a low-cost strategy; it offers customers razor blades priced lower than Gillette's and ball-point pens less expensive than those offered by Cross or Waterford.

Differentiation Strategy

differentiation strategy Distinguishing an organization's products from the products of competitors in dimensions such as product design, quality, or after-sales service.

With a **differentiation strategy,** managers try to gain a competitive advantage by focusing all the energies of the organization's departments or functions on distinguishing the organization's products from those of competitors on one or more important dimensions, such as product design, quality, or after-sales service and support. Often, the process of making products unique and different is expensive. This strategy, for example, often requires that managers increase spending on product design or R&D to differentiate the product, and costs rise as a result. Organizations that successfully pursue a differentiation strategy may be able to charge a *premium price* for their products, a price usually much higher than the price charged by a low-cost organization. The premium price allows organizations pursuing a differentiation strategy to recoup their higher costs. Coca-Cola, PepsiCo, and Procter & Gamble are some of the many well-known companies that pursue a strategy of differentiation. They spend enormous amounts of money on advertising to differentiate, and create a unique image for, their products. However, just because companies can differentiate their products does not mean that there cannot be intense competition between them, as the following Managing Globally suggests.

Managing Globally

Strategy in the World Package Delivery Business

In 1971, Federal Express (FedEx) turned the package delivery world upside down when it began to offer overnight package delivery by air. Its founder, Fred Smith, had seen the opportunity for next-day delivery because both the U.S. Postal Service and United Parcel Service (UPS) were, at that time, taking several days to deliver packages. Smith was convinced there was pent-up demand for overnight delivery, and he was also convinced that customers would be willing to pay a high premium price to get such a unique new service, at least $15 a package at that time.[53] Smith was right; customers were willing to pay high prices for fast reliable delivery. By discovering and tapping into an unmet customer need, he redefined the package delivery industry.

Several companies imitated FedEx's new strategy and introduced their own air overnight service. None, however, could match FedEx's state-of-the-art information system that allowed continuous tracking of all packages in transit. Several of its competitors went out of business. A few, like Airborne Express, managed to survive by focusing or *specializing* on serving the needs of *one* particular group of customers–corporate customers–and by offering lower prices than FedEx.

The well-known road delivery package company UPS initiated an overnight air delivery service of its own in 1998.[54] UPS managers realized that the future of package delivery lay both on the road and in the air because different customer groups, with different needs, were emerging. It began to aggressively imitate FedEx's state-of-the-art operating and information systems, especially its tracking system. Slowly and surely UPS increased the number of overnight packages that it was delivering. In 1999, UPS announced two major innovations. First, it introduced a new tracking and shipping information system that matched, and even exceeded, the sophistication of the FedEx tracking system because it could work with *any* IT system used by corporate customers. (By contrast, customers had to install and use FedEx's proprietary IT, an approach that caused more work and cost for them.) Second, UPS integrated its overnight air service into its nationwide delivery service and created a seamless interface between these two different aspects of its business. This has given it a differentiation advantage over FedEx because UPS can deliver short-range and mid-distance packages, those being shipped within about 500 miles, more quickly than FedEx, as well as match the speed and reliability of FedEx's long-range operations.

FedEx's purchase of Kinko's will allow it to reach more customers by making each Kinko's store a base for its operations.

Competition between FedEx and UPS became intense in the early 2000s. Then, in 2003, both companies received a shock when the largest global package delivery company, DHL, announced that it would purchase Airborne Express and would thus become a direct competitor of FedEx and UPS. Soon, when DHL began a marketing campaign to emphasize the extent of its global reach and the speed of its operations, all three companies started to fight for customers and find new ways of differentiating their products. In 2003 FedEx announced that it would purchase Kinko's Copies and make each Kinko's store a base for its delivery operations. In doing so, it was following UPS's approach; UPS had purchased a chain of packaging stores and turned them into UPS stores. The fight is ongoing and which company will turn out to be the global leader is still unclear.

"Stuck in the Middle"

According to Porter's theory, managers cannot simultaneously pursue both a low-cost strategy and a differentiation strategy. Porter identified a simple correlation: Differentiation raises costs and thus necessitates premium pricing to recoup those high costs. For example, if BIC suddenly began to advertise heavily to try to build a strong global brand image for its products, BIC's costs would rise. BIC then could no longer make a profit simply by pricing its blades or pens lower than Gillette or Cross. According to Porter, managers must choose between a low-cost strategy and a differentiation strategy. He refers to managers and organizations that have not made this choice as being "stuck in the middle."

According to Porter, organizations stuck in the middle tend to have lower levels of performance than do those that pursue a low-cost or a differentiation strategy. To avoid being stuck in the middle, top managers must instruct departmental managers to take actions that will result in either low cost or differentiation.

However, exceptions to this rule can be found. In many organizations managers have been able to drive costs below those of rivals and simultaneously differentiate their products from those offered by rivals.[55] For example, Toyota's production system is reportedly the most efficient in the world. This efficiency gives Toyota a low-cost strategy vis-à-vis its rivals in the global car industry. At the same time, Toyota has differentiated its cars from those of rivals on the basis of superior design and quality. This superiority allows the company to charge a premium price for many of its popular models.[56] Thus, Toyota seems to be simultaneously pursuing both a low-cost and a differentiated business-level strategy. This example suggests that although Porter's ideas may be valid in most cases, very well managed companies such as Toyota, McDonald's, and Dell Computer may have both low costs and differentiated products.

Focused Low-Cost and Focused Differentiation Strategies

Both the differentiation strategy and the low-cost strategy are aimed at serving many or most segments of a particular market, such as for cars or computers. Porter identified two other business-level strategies that aim to serve the needs of customers in only one or a few market segments.[57] Managers pursuing a **focused low-cost strategy** serve one or a few segments of the overall market and aim to make their organization the lowest-cost company serving that segment. For example, Cott Corporation is the world's leading supplier of *retailer* brand-name carbonated soft drinks. With production facilities in Canada, the United States, and the United Kingdom, Cott produces, packages, and distributes a wide

focused low-cost strategy Serving only one segment of the overall market and being the lowest-cost organization serving that segment.

selection of retailer-brand beverages for grocery, mass-merchandise, drugstore, and convenience store chains. For example, all Wal-Mart soda sold under the Sam's brand name is made by Cott. However, note that while Cott is the world's leading supplier of *retailer-brand-name* sodas, it is focusing on a low-cost strategy. It makes no attempt to compete with Coke and Pepsi, which, as noted earlier, pursue a differentiation strategy and whose brand-name sodas dominate the global soda market.

focused differentiation strategy Serving only one segment of the overall market and trying to be the most differentiated organization serving that segment.

By contrast, managers pursuing a **focused differentiation strategy** serve just one or a few segments of the market and aim to make their organization the most differentiated company serving that segment. BMW, for example, pursues a focused strategy, producing cars exclusively for higher-income customers. By contrast, Toyota pursues a differentiation strategy and produces cars that appeal to consumers in almost all segments of the car market, from basic transportation (Toyota Tercel), through the middle of the market (Toyota Camry), to the high-income end of the market (Lexus).

As these examples suggest, companies pursuing either of these focused strategies have chosen to *specialize* in some way by directing their efforts at a particular kind of customer (such as serving the needs of babies or affluent customers) or even the needs of customers in a specific geographic region (customers on the East or West Coast).

Zara, a Spanish manufacturer of fashionable clothing, provides an excellent example of how a company can pursue both a low-cost and a differentiated focused strategy at the same time by using new information technologies. Well-known fashion houses like Channel, Dior, and Armani can charge thousands of dollars for the fashionable collections of suits and dresses that they introduce twice yearly in the fall and in the spring. Only the very rich can afford such differentiated and expensive clothing, and this has opened up a gap in the fashion market for companies that can supply fashionable clothes at lower prices. Essentially, these companies have the capabilities to pursue a focused differentiation and cost-leadership strategy.

While many clothing companies, such as the United State's The Gap, Sweden's Hennes & Mauritz, and England's Jaeger and Laura Ashley, have attempted to supply fashionable clothes at lower prices, none has succeeded as well as Spanish clothes maker Zara, whose sales have soared in recent years.[58] Zara has managed to position itself as the low-price/cost leader in the fashion segment of the clothing market because of the way it uses information technology. It has created an information system that allows it to manage its design and manufacturing process in a way that minimizes the inventory it has to carry–the major cost borne by a clothing retailer. However, its IT also gives instantaneous feedback on which clothes are selling well and in which countries, and this gives it a competitive advantage from differentiation. Specifically, Zara can manufacture more of a particular kind of dress or suit to meet high customer demand, decide which clothing should be sold in its rapidly expanding network of global stores, and constantly change the mix of clothes it offers customers to keep up with fashion. Moreover, it can do this at relatively small output levels, something which is also a part of a specialized, focused strategy.

Zara's IT also allows it to manage the interface between its design and manufacturing operations more efficiently. Zara only takes five weeks to design a new collection and then a week to make it. Other fashion houses, by contrast, can take six or more months to design the collection and then three more before it is available in stores.[59] This short time to market gives Zara great flexibility and allows the company to respond quickly to the rapidly changing fashion market in which fashions can change several times a year. Because of the quick manufacturing-to-sales cycle and just-in-time fashion, Zara offers its clothes collections at relatively low prices and still makes profits that are the envy of the fashion clothing industry.[60]

Formulating Functional-Level Strategies

functional-level strategy A plan that indicates how a function intends to achieve its goals.

Zara has developed many kinds of strengths in functions such as clothing design and IT that have given it a competitive advantage. **Functional-level strategy** is a plan of action to improve the ability of an organization's functions to create value. It is concerned with the actions that managers of individual functions (such as manufacturing or marketing) can take to add value to an organization's goods and services and thereby increase the value customers receive. The price that customers are prepared to pay for a product indicates how much they value an organization's products. The more customers value a product, the more they are willing to pay for it.

There are two ways in which functions can add value to an organization's products:

1. Functional managers can lower the costs of creating value so that an organization can attract customers by keeping its prices lower than its competitors' prices.
2. Functional managers can add value to a product by finding ways to differentiate it from the products of other companies.

If customers see more value in one organization's products than in the products of its competitors, they may be willing to pay premium prices. Thus, there must be a fit between functional- and business-level strategies if an organization is to achieve its mission and goal of maximizing the amount of value it gives customers. The better the fit between functional- and business-level strategies, the greater will be the organization's competitive advantage–its ability to attract customers and the revenue they provide.

Each organizational function has an important role to play in the process of lowering costs or adding value to a product (see Table 8.3, page 290). Manufacturing can find new ways to lower production costs or to build superior quality into the product to add value. Marketing, sales, and after-sales service and support can add value by, for example, building brand loyalty (as Coca-Cola and PepsiCo have done in the soft-drink industry) and finding more effective ways to attract customers. Human resource management can lower the costs of creating value by recruiting and training a highly productive workforce. The R&D function can lower the costs of creating value by developing more efficient production processes. Similarly, R&D can add value by developing new and improved products that customers value over established product offerings.

Creating value at the functional level requires the adoption of many state-of-the-art management techniques and practices that are discussed at length in the following chapter. We will just note here that it is the responsibility of managers at the functional level to identify these techniques and develop a functional-level plan that contains the strategies necessary to develop them. The important issue to remember is that all of these techniques can help an organization achieve a competitive advantage by lowering the costs of creating value or by adding value above and beyond that offered by rivals.

Table 8.3
How Functions Can Lower the Costs and Create Value or Add Value to Create a Competitive Advantage

Value-Creating Function	Ways to Lower the Cost of Creating Value (Low-Cost Advantage)	Ways to Add Value (Differentiation Advantage)
Sales and marketing Materials management Research and development Manufacturing Human resources management	• Find new customers • Find low-cost advertising methods • Use just-in-time inventory system/computerized warehousing • Develop long-term relationships with suppliers and customers • Improve efficiency of machinery and equipment • Design products that can be made more cheaply • Develop skills in low-cost manufacturing • Reduce turnover and absenteeism • Raise employee skills	• Promote brand-name awareness and loyalty • Tailor products to suit customers' needs • Develop long-term relationships with suppliers to provide high-quality inputs • Reduce shipping time to customers • Create new products • Improve existing products • Increase product quality and reliability • Hire highly skilled employees • Develop innovative training programs

Planning and Implementing Strategy

After identifying appropriate strategies to attain an organization's mission and goals, managers confront the challenge of putting those strategies into action. Strategy implementation is a five-step process:

1. Allocating responsibility for implementation to the appropriate individuals or groups.
2. Drafting detailed action plans that specify how a strategy is to be implemented.
3. Establishing a timetable for implementation that includes precise, measurable goals linked to the attainment of the action plan.
4. Allocating appropriate resources to the responsible individuals or groups.
5. Holding specific individuals or groups responsible for the attainment of corporate, divisional, and functional goals.

The planning process goes beyond the mere identification of strategies; it also includes actions taken to ensure that the organization actually puts its strategies into action. It should be noted that the plan for implementing a strategy might require radical redesign of the structure of the organization, the development of new control systems, and the adoption of a program for changing the culture of the organization. These are all issues that we address in the next three chapters.

Summary and Review

PLANNING Planning is a three-step process: (1) determining an organization's mission and goals; (2) formulating strategy; (3) implementing strategy. Managers use planning to identify and select appropriate goals and courses of action for an organization and to decide how to allocate the resources they need to attain those goals and carry out those actions. A good plan builds commitment for the organization's goals, gives the organization a sense of direction and purpose, coordinates the different functions and divisions of the organization, and controls managers by making them accountable for specific goals. In large organizations planning takes place at three levels: corporate, business or divisional, and functional or departmental. Although planning is typically the responsibility of a well-defined group of managers, the subordinates of those managers should be given every opportunity to have input into the process and to shape the outcome. Long-term plans have a time horizon of five years or more; intermediate-term plans, between one and five years; and short-term plans, one year or less.

DETERMINING MISSION AND GOALS AND FORMULATING STRATEGY Determining the organization's mission requires that managers define the business of the organization and establish major goals. Strategy formulation requires that managers perform a SWOT analysis and then choose appropriate strategies at the corporate, business, and functional levels. At the corporate level, organizations use strategies such as concentration on a single business, diversification, international expansion, and vertical integration to help increase the value of the goods and services provided to customers. At the business level, managers are responsible for developing a successful low-cost or differentiation strategy, either for the whole market or for a particular segment of it. At the functional level, departmental managers strive to develop and use their skills to help the organization either to add value to its products by differentiating them or to lower the costs of value creation.

IMPLEMENTING STRATEGY Strategy implementation requires that managers allocate responsibilities to appropriate individuals or groups, draft detailed action plans that specify how a strategy is to be implemented, establish a timetable for implementation that includes precise, measurable goals linked to the attainment of the action plan, allocate appropriate resources to the responsible individuals or groups, and hold individuals or groups accountable for the attainment of goals.

Management in Action

Topics for Discussion and Action

Discussion

1. Describe the three steps of planning. Explain how they are related.
2. How can scenario planning help managers predict the future?
3. What is the role of divisional and functional managers in the formulation of strategy?
4. Why is it important for functional managers to have a clear grasp of the organization's mission when developing strategies within their departments?
5. What is the relationship among corporate-, business-, and functional-level strategies, and how do they create value for an organization?

Action

6. Ask a manager about the kinds of planning exercises he or she regularly uses. What are the purposes of these exercises, and what are their advantages or disadvantages?
7. Ask a manager to identify the corporate-, business-, and functional-level strategies used by his or her organization.

Building Management Skills

How to Analyze a Company's Strategy

Pick a well-known business organization that has received recent press coverage and for which you can get the annual reports or 10K filings from your school library for a number of years. For this organization, do the following:

1. From the annual reports or 10K filings identify the main strategies pursued by the company over a 10-year period.
2. Try to identify why the company pursued these strategies. What reason was given in the annual reports, press reports, and so on?
3. Document whether and when any major changes in the strategy of the organization occurred. If changes did occur, try to identify the reason for them.
4. If changes in strategy occurred, try to determine the extent to which they were the result of long-term plans and the extent to which they were responses to unforeseen changes in the company's task environment.
5. What is the main industry that the company competes in?
6. What business-level strategy does the company seem to be pursuing in this industry?
7. What is the company's reputation with regard to productivity, quality, innovation, and responsiveness to customers in this industry? If the company has attained an advantage in any of these areas, how has it done so?
8. What is the current corporate-level strategy of the company? What is the company's stated reason for pursuing this strategy?
9. Has the company expanded internationally? If it has, identify its largest international market. How did the company enter this market? Did its mode of entry change over time?

Managing Ethically

A few years ago, IBM announced that it had fired the three top managers of its Argentine division because of their involvement in a scheme to secure a $250 million contract for IBM to provide and service the computers of one of Argentina's largest state-owned banks. The three executives paid $14 million of the contract money to a third company, CCR, which paid nearly $6 million to phantom companies. This $6 million was then used to bribe the bank executives who agreed to give IBM the contract.

These bribes are not necessarily illegal under Argentine law. Moreover, the three managers argued that all companies have to pay bribes to get new business contracts and they were not doing anything that managers in other companies were not.

Questions

1. Either by yourself or in a group decide if this business practice of paying bribes is ethical or unethical.
2. Should IBM allow its foreign divisions to pay bribes if all other companies are doing so?
3. If bribery is common in a particular country, what effect would this likely have on the nation's economy and culture?

Small Group Breakout Exercise

Low Cost or Differentiation?

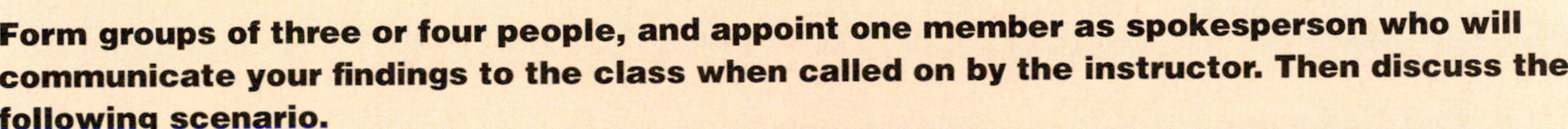

Form groups of three or four people, and appoint one member as spokesperson who will communicate your findings to the class when called on by the instructor. Then discuss the following scenario.

You are a team of managers of a major national clothing chain, and you have been charged with finding a way to restore your organization's competitive advantage. Recently, your organization has been experiencing increasing competition from two sources. First, discount stores such as Wal-Mart and Target have been undercutting your prices because they buy their clothes from low-cost foreign manufacturers while you buy most of yours from high-quality domestic suppliers. Discount stores have been attracting your customers who buy at the low end of the price range. Second, small boutiques opening in malls provide high-price designer clothing and are attracting your customers at the high end of the market. Your company has become stuck in the middle, and you have to decide what to do: Should you start to buy abroad so that you can lower your prices and begin to pursue a low-cost strategy? Should you focus on the high end of the market and become more of a differentiator? Or should you try to do both and pursue both a low-cost strategy and a differentiation strategy?

1. Using scenario planning, analyze the pros and cons of each alternative.
2. Think about the various clothing retailers in your local malls and city, and analyze the choices they have made about how to compete with one another along the low-cost and differentiation dimensions.

Exploring the World Wide Web

Go to the corporate Web site of Google (www.google.com/corporate/execs.html), click on "corporate info," and explore this site; in particular, click on "Google's history" and "The 10 Things" that guide Google's corporate philosophy.

1. How would you describe Google's mission and goals?
2. What is Google's business-level strategy?
3. What is Google's corporate-level strategy?

Be the Manager

A group of investors in your city is considering opening a new upscale supermarket to compete with the major supermarket chains that are currently dominating the city's marketplace. They have called you in to help them determine what kind of upscale supermarket they should open. In other words, how can they best develop a competitive advantage against existing supermarket chains?

Questions

1. List the supermarket chains in your city, and identify their strengths and weaknesses.
2. What business-level strategies are these supermarkets currently pursuing?
3. What kind of supermarket would do best against the competition? What kind of business-level strategy should it pursue?

Build Your Management Skills DVD

- **Test Your Knowledge:** (1) Elements of the Planning Process, (2) SWOT Analysis, (3) Porter's Five Forces, and (4) Levels of Strategy
- **Self-Assessment:** Assessing How Personality Type Impacts Your Goal-Setting Skills

BusinessWeek Case in the News

Volkswagen Slips Into Reverse

It has been a rough ride for Bernd Pischetsrieder since the former BMW boss took over as chief executive at Volkswagen in April 2002. VW's share price has fallen nearly 50 percent since then, wiping out $11 billion in market capitalization as profits plummeted at the $150 billion company.

On July 23, Pischetsrieder delivered more bad news—a 36 percent net profit drop in the first half of 2004. Profits for all of 2003 were already down by more than half, and just to take even more air out of VW's tires, the boss issued a grim earnings warning for this year. In three years—just half a model life cycle in the auto biz—the world's fourth-largest carmaker has gone from Europe's showcase turnaround to major-league laggard.

What's wrong? Volkswagen's vaunted brand premium—the implicit guarantee of quality and innovation that long allowed it to charge as much as 8 percent more than the competition for mass-market cars—is eroding fast. French, Asian, and even U.S. rivals are improving quality, bolstering manufacturing efficiency, and besting VW at design. Case in point: The Golf compact lost out in 2003 to the Peugeot 206 as Europe's best-selling car for the second year in a row. The all-new, richly priced Golf is running neck-and-neck with its aging French rival this year. To counter slow sales of its Golf in Europe, VW was forced in January to offer a $1,500 air-conditioning system for free and hefty dealer rebates on used-car trade-ins. In the United States, meanwhile, VW has slapped a $3,000 rebate on its aging Passat and joined the 0 percent financing game. U.S. losses are expected to reach $1.4 billion this year, due to dropping sales and the weak dollar's impact on reported earnings.

Another nasty surprise is in China, which until recently accounted for up to 24 percent of VW's operating profit. In late May, General Motors Corp., keen to dethrone VW as China's market leader, cut prices by 11 percent. VW matched the move. GM's sales doubled in the first half of 2004, while VW's fell 4.2 percent. VW commanded half the mainland market in 1999; now it controls just over a quarter. Pischetsrieder now expects China sales to grow only 5 percent to 7 percent in 2004, down from over 30 percent in recent years. "Our prime objective is profitability, not maintaining market share," he said in a July 23 conference call with financial analysts and journalists.

What's the way out? Pischetsrieder has launched a cost-savings program called ForMotion aimed at trimming $2.6 billion over two years, on top of the company's existing effort to squeeze costs by $1.1 billion a year. The plan seeks to cut $970 million in purchasing costs, $600 million in reduced staffing, and $360 million in restructured sales activities. VW is also beefing up its lucrative auto-finance business by buying a leading Dutch car-leasing company.

More models are coming, too: A souped-up Golf is due later this year, and Passat and Jetta remakes debut in 2004. In China, Pischetsrieder is investing $6 billion over the next four years and aims to double VW's production capacity, to 1.6 million cars, by 2008. VW is also introducing fresher models to the Chinese market—the Touareg sport utility, the Phaeton luxury sedan, the Audi A6, and a car that will be expressly designed for China. Pischetsrieder is shifting decision-making from VW's Wolfsburg headquarters to Beijing and sending experienced managers.

Pischetsrieder also has a winner in Audi. VW's $28 billion-in-revenue premium brand. Strong sales of Audi's luxury A8, the new A6 midsize sedan, and the hot A3 compact helped drive a 10 percent increase in operating profit, to $666 million, in the first half of 2004. Audi will introduce the rugged Pike's Peak SUV in 2005.

Cost cuts, new models, new focus, a strong luxury brand: sounds good. So why aren't investors impressed? Analysts who once expected 2004 to be a comeback year now say earnings will remain anemic through 2006. "VW is a huge ship. You can't turn it for miles and miles," says George C. Peterson, president of AutoPacific Inc. in Tustin, Calif.

One problem is that achieving big efficiencies is like shooting at a moving target. Pischetsrieder's cuts will help, but analysts say the effort pales in comparison with the thorough streamlining already achieved at Renault, Peugeot, and Chrysler. Besides, "VW has never faced up to its fundamental cost problem. It has never faced up to the unions," says John Wormald, a partner at London-based consultant Autopolis.

While rivals retooled, VW dallied. Labor costs at VW's factories are 17.4 percent of revenues, versus a European average of 15 percent, according to a July 27 report by Dresdner Kleinwort Wasserstein. Since closing a plant in Germany is politically impossible, analysts say, Pischetsrieder needs to accelerate cost-cutting dramatically and boost sales while improving plant flexibility. "The group is far from being on a sound recovery path," says Bruno Lapierre, an Exane BNP Paribas analyst, in a July 23 report.

VW has also blundered by neglecting to develop a stable of minivans and SUVs, which make up over 54 percent of industry sales in the United States. So far, VW's only offering is the Touareg SUV. "In the United States, it's playing with one hand behind its back. It has no lineup to match Honda and Toyota," says Peterson. "How did that escape them?"

Slow-Moving Managers

Pischetsrieder, who has a consensus-driven management style, is making little headway against a bureaucracy that is resistant to change. Insiders say VW's chronically weak management and poor execution were aggravated by the nine-year tenure of former CEO Ferdinand K. Piëch, a brilliant but autocratic engineer. "Of the top 100 managers, 50 are not used to making their own decisions or thinking on their own. They wait for the phone to ring to get their orders. They are used to being told what to do," says an auto-industry expert who is close to the company.

Pischetsrieder has sought to set up more democratic decision-making structures, but many say the pace of change is glacial. "What Pischetsrieder wants to do is right—to transform the organization, processes, and behavior," says one consultant. "The question is whether there is enough time to survive the tough period ahead." Looks like it's time for a radical shift of gears.

Questions

1. What is the source of Volkswagen's problems?
2. What strategies is it adopting to solve these problems?

Source: Gail Edmundson and Dexter Roberts, "Volkswagen Slips into Reverse." Reprinted from the August 9, 2004, issue of *BusinessWeek* by special permission.

BusinessWeek

Case in the News

Imagine Sony on Steroids

It has been a long wait for Sony Corp. For the past two years, the Japanese electronics giant has been gearing up for the second installment of its *Spider-Man* franchise, the web-slinging superstar that grossed a cool $403 million at the box office when Tobey Maguire last leapt into theaters in his red leotard. Since then, though, Sony has been a decidedly low-swinging outfit. Sinking sales of its TVs, personal digital devices, and video recorders zapped earnings last year, which fell by 23.4 percent, to $851 million, for the fiscal year ended on March 31. Film sales, meanwhile, fell 40 percent, to $320 million, off its *Spider-Man*-charged year, and music revenues struggled in the face of piracy and dwindling market share. So any signs of a comeback are welcome at Sony these days, whether they shoot webs or not.

The leading man in the Sony revival story is Sir Howard Stringer, a rumpled 62-year-old Welsh-born executive who has his own mission: to turn Sony's perennially underperforming entertainment unit into an engine for growth, not just an afterthought for a company built on electronic gizmos. And in recent months, Sir Howard has been moving faster than Spider-Man through Times Square.

Stringer has placed his biggest bet—$5 billion—in a bid to buy Kirk Kerkorian's Metro-Goldwyn-Mayer Inc. studio. That would give Sony Hollywood's largest collection of older movies just as new technologies for offering flicks on demand, over the Internet, and on DVD are taking off. That follows a November 2003, deal he engineered to merge his struggling music company with rival Bertelsmann's BMG unit. If approved by European and U.S. regulators, as expected this year, the merger will give the combined company 25 percent of the market while slicing an estimated $250 million from overhead. "For a while some of us weren't sure what Howard did at Sony," jokes former Viacom President Frank Biondi. "Now we see that he's remaking the entire operation."

And just in time. Stringer, Sony's vice chairman, is under pressure from Sony CEO Nobuyuki Idei to cut costs by 10 percent, part of an overall corporate mandate to reduce overhead companywide. At the same time, headquarters expects Stringer to help finally make good on the long-held—but rarely accomplished—goal of using Sony's movies, TV shows, and music to fuel sales of new consumer-electronic formats. Sony executives would not comment for this story.

For now, Stringer has focused heavily on cost-cutting. Last year, he forced out spendthrift music chief Thomas D. Mottola and installed former NBC President Andrew Lack, a deputy from Stringer's days as head of CBS. Lack slashed more than 1,000 jobs, cutting $100 million. At Sony's film studio, Stringer ordered more than 500 layoffs and has told film executives to rein in profit-participation that was among the richest in the industry. To add muscle, he brought in Michael Lynton, a turnaround expert who shrank costs at Time Warner Inc.'s international AOL operation. Lynton has been ordered to find more places to cut as he streamlines the often chaotic movie making process.

So far, so good But it's always easier to cut than create. While Sony has been profitable in 9 of 11 quarters, Stringer wants to stabilize earnings by grabbing MGM, which has a more than 4,000-film library that generates $450 million in cash flow from sales of DVDs and to cable TV. But MGM is still a long shot, in part because he had to jury-rig a financing scheme to reduce the parent company's involvement, bringing in two private equity firms and bidding mostly with debt. MGM now says it is looking at alternatives, which could lead to rich new bids from NBC or Time Warner, both of which are itching to get their hands on the studio.

Another Format Fight

If it does win MGM, Sony intends to combine those films with the 3,500 it currently owns to help push a next-generation DVD technology, called Blu-Ray, that offers films in high-definition. Sony needs the added muscle of a large collection of films to win over Hollywood, which is holding back, waiting for a competing high-definition DVD pushed by Sony's nemesis Toshiba, with help from Warner Bros. and possibly Microsoft. To promote its own format, Sony intends to start shipping versions of its movies on DVD and Blu-Ray in 2005, according to industry insiders. Sony "knows that getting a library is key to the Next Thing—in this case video-on-demand or the Internet," says DVD pioneer and industry consultant Warren Lieberfarb.

In the meantime, Sony is rolling out entertainment on the Internet through Movielink, an online service it pioneered that is now being operated by five major studios. As for the music business, Sony is hustling to catch up with the likes of Apple Computer Inc.'s iTunes. Last spring, it launched a new online music service called Connect, which has deals with McDonald's Corp. and United Airlines Inc. to offer coupons for songs. It's all part of Stringer's attempt to push the Japanese giant into a fast-consolidating entertainment world before it's too late.

Questions

1. What is Stringer's new business-level strategy for Sony and what steps has he taken to pursue it?
2. What kind of corporate-level strategy is he pursuing to help him increase Sony's performance?

Source: Ronald Grover and Tom Lowry, "Imagine Sony on Steroids." Reprinted from the July 12, 2004, issue of *BusinessWeek* by special permission.

CHAPTER

9 Value-Chain Management: Functional Strategies to Increase Quality, Efficiency, and Responsiveness to Customers

Learning Objectives

After studying this chapter, you should be able to:

- Explain the role of value-chain management in achieving superior quality, efficiency, and responsiveness to customers.
- Describe what customers want, and explain why it is so important for managers to be responsive to their needs.
- Explain why achieving superior quality is so important.
- Describe the challenges facing managers and organizations that seek to implement total quality management.
- Explain why achieving superior efficiency is so important.
- Differentiate among facilities layout, flexible manufacturing, just-in-time inventory, and process reengineering.

A Manager's Challenge

Bricks, Clicks, or Bricks-and-Clicks Supermarkets

How can managers increase operating performance?

The potential uses of information technology and the Internet for improving responsiveness to customers became clear to companies in many industries in the late 1990s. One of these industries was the food delivery or supermarket industry. Entrepreneurs decided that developing an online ordering system that allowed customers to use the Internet to order their food online and creating an operating system to deliver the food to their homes had enormous potential. For example, virtual grocer Webvan raised more than $1 billion to develop both the information system and the physical infrastructure of warehouses and hot and cold delivery trucks that it needed to deliver food to customers. Other competitors like GroceryWorks.com and Homegrocer.com made similar kinds of investments. These online stores did attract customers, and by 2000 they had more than $1 billion in sales. Bricks-and-mortar (B&M) supermarkets like Kroger Company, Albertson's, and Safeway watched with some trepidation as the online rivals developed and managed their operations. Should they respond with their own online stores? What else should they do?

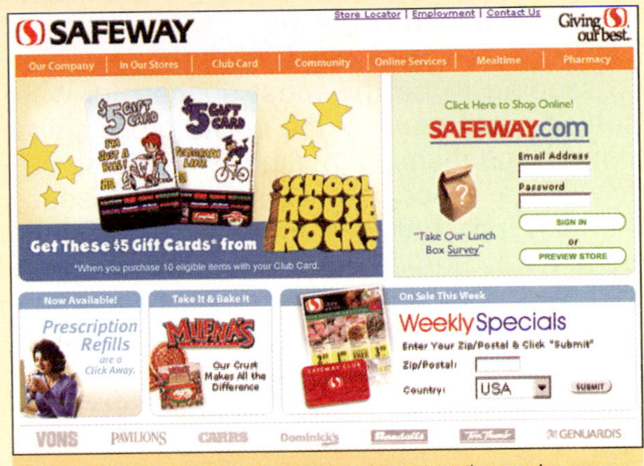

When customers order groceries from safeway.com, those orders are passed on to the B&M Safeway store for processing.

One of the first responses by B&M supermarkets was to take steps to make their customers' shopping experience much more enjoyable. First, they improved their operations by building large, new, attractive stores that contained a wide variety of produce. Second, they increasingly incorporated IT into their operations to improve customer satisfaction with their stores. For example, Kroger experimented with a wide variety of self-serving technology kiosks. Kiosks are physical units within the store, such as self-checkout units, check cashing units, bill payment units, and payment terminals, that perform specific services for customers. These kiosks improved operations because they helped stores eliminate lengthy checkout lines and helped the company focus more on customer service. Together, these moves have helped B&M supermarkets improve responsiveness to customers and increase the quality of their produce and service. They have also helped reduce operating costs because customers perform their own services, including of course selecting their own produce and delivering it to their homes.

The question of which operating system was going to be the most successful was settled when many of the online grocers like Webvan announced that they were going out of business because of mounting losses. Why? First, unlike their well-established B&M rivals, the new e-grocers did not possess the experience and ability to master the complex inventory management, sourcing, transportation, distribution, warehousing, and logistics necessary to operate successfully in this market. Second, e-grocers had totally underestimated the problems and costs of operating the production and physical delivery service necessary to get products to customers. The average cost of home delivery for Webvan and other grocers was around $30, a cost they could not pass on to the customers they were trying to attract. In the future e-grocers hoped to attract only well-heeled customers who could afford to pay the high delivery costs—a very small market segment. The virtual-grocery operating model was not working out.

After the collapse of Webvan, the other virtual grocers took a hard look at their operating systems. How could they provide high-quality, responsive customer service at a cost low enough to survive, especially when the large supermarket chains had major cost advantages because of their huge purchasing power, market coverage, and ability to obtain economies of scale? Some e-grocers decided to form alliances with B&M supermarkets. For example, in several cities safeway.com now lets its customers order at its online store but then passes the orders onto the B&M Safeway stores for processing.[1] Safeway's trucks then deliver the orders; this avoids all the costs of sourcing and warehousing. Other Web grocers have decided to focus only on one market and develop an operating system to service the needs of customers inside just one city market. For example, vons.com serves the needs of well-heeled customers in Southern California.[2]

Overview

Webvan and other virtual grocers used IT and the Internet to develop an operating system that may have been very responsive to customers but that was also very costly and inefficient compared to the systems used by the B&M supermarket chains. They also failed to develop functional strategies that could have helped their operating systems work more efficiently. The B&M supermarkets, on the other hand, made innovations in their materials management, sales, and information systems that allowed them to achieve superior quality, efficiency, and responsiveness to customers. Possessing these sources of competitive advantage, they retain control of the $175-billion-a-year grocery market.

In this chapter we focus on value-chain management and discuss the functional (or operational) strategies that managers can use to increase the performance of a company's operating system–specifically, to improve the quality of a company's goods and services, the efficiency with which they are produced, and the company's responsiveness to its customers. By the end of this chapter, you will understand the vital role value-chain management plays in building competitive advantage and creating a high-performing organization.

Value-Chain Management and Competitive Advantage

Value-chain management is the development of a set of functional-level strategies that increase the performance of the operating system a company uses to transform inputs into finished goods and services. An **operating system** is composed of the various different functional activities (like marketing, materials management, or production) an organization uses to acquire inputs, convert inputs into outputs, and dispose of the outputs (goods or services). Functional managers are responsible for managing an organization's operating system; they are the ones who decide what kind of functional strategies each function should pursue to build competitive advantage. Specifically, their job is to manage the value chain to determine where operating improvements might be made to increase quality, efficiency, and responsiveness to customers–and so give an organization a competitive advantage.

value-chain management The development of a set of functional-level strategies that increase the performance of the operating system a company uses to transform inputs into finished goods and services.

operating system The different functional activities an organization combines and uses to acquire inputs, convert inputs into outputs, and dispose of the outputs.

value chain The idea that a company is a chain of functional activities that transform inputs into an output of goods or services that customers value.

The Value Chain

The term **value chain** refers to the idea that a company is a chain of functional activities that transform inputs into an output of goods or services that customers value. The process of transforming inputs into outputs is composed of a number of functional operating activities, or an operating system, beginning with the need to acquire inputs, to design and control conversion processes, and to distribute and sell goods and services. Each activity adds value to the product and hence increases the price a company can charge for its products, as we discussed in the last chapter. In the value chain illustrated in Figure 9.1 (page 302) several important functional activities are represented.

The *production function* is responsible for the creation of a good or service. For physical products, when we talk about production, we generally mean manufacturing. For services such as banking or retailing, production typically takes place when the service is actually delivered to the customer (for example, when a bank originates a loan for a customer, it is engaged in "production" of the loan). By performing its activities efficiently, the production function of a company helps to lower its cost structure. For example, the efficient production operations of Honda and Toyota are helping those automobile companies achieve higher profitability relative to competitors such as General Motors. The production function of a company can also perform its activities in a way that is consistent with high product quality, which leads to differentiation (and higher value) and to lower costs.

There are several ways in which the *marketing and sales functions* of a company can help to create value. Through brand positioning and advertising, the marketing function can increase the value that customers perceive to be contained in a company's product. Insofar as these help to create a favorable impression of the company's product in the minds of customers, they increase value. For example, in the 1980s the French company Perrier persuaded U.S. customers that slightly carbonated bottled water was worth $1.50 per liter bottle, rather than the 25 cents it cost to purchase a gallon of spring water from the local supermarket. Perrier's marketing function essentially developed marketing strategies that increased the perception of value that customers ascribed to the product. In the 1990s, major U.S. companies such as Coca-Cola and PepsiCo rushed to bring out their own bottled-water labels to capitalize on customers' growing appetite for bottled water.

Figure 9.1
Functional Activities and the Value Chain

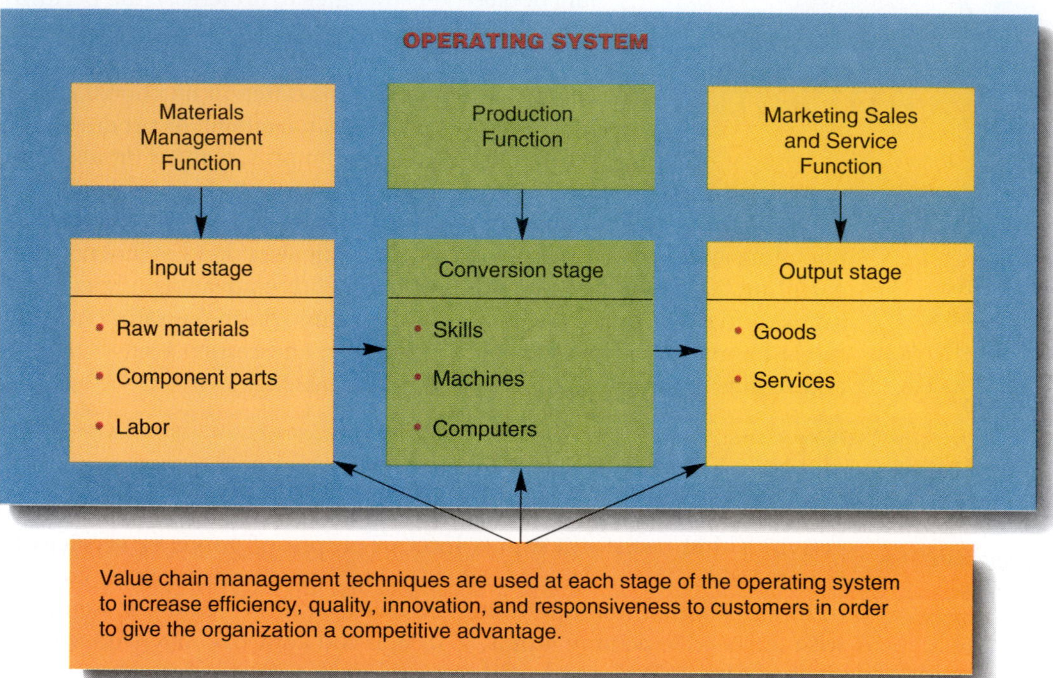

The role of the *service function* is to provide after-sales service and support. This function can create a perception of superior value in the minds of customers by solving customer problems and supporting customers after they have purchased the product. For example, FedEx can get its customers' parcels to any point in the world within 24 hours, thereby lowering the cost of their own value-creation activities.

The *materials management function* controls the movement of physical materials through the value chain, from procurement through production and into distribution. The efficiency with which this is carried out can significantly lower cost and thus create more value. Wal-Mart, the U.S. retailing giant, has the most efficient materials management function in the retail industry. By tightly controlling the flow of goods from its suppliers through its stores and into the hands of customers, Wal-Mart has eliminated the need to hold large inventories of goods. Lower inventories mean lower costs, and hence greater value creation.

Finally, the *information systems function* controls the electronic systems for managing inventory, tracking sales, pricing products, selling products, dealing with customer service inquires, and so on. Information systems, when coupled with the communications features of the Internet, are holding out the promise of being able to alter the efficiency and effectiveness with which a company manages its other value-creation activities. For example, in the opening case we saw how Kroger uses many new kinds of IT systems, such as self-checkout stations, to increase efficiency. However, we also saw that IT has efficiency-enhancing advantages only if *all* the other functions have developed the appropriate functional strategies. Because online grocers failed to understand the high costs associated with delivering groceries to customers, their value chains collapsed.

Functional Strategies and Competitive Advantage

In managing the value chain to create a high-performing operating system, functional managers need to attend to the four major goals discussed in Chapter 1:[3]

1. *To attain superior efficiency.* Efficiency is a measure of the amount of inputs required to produce a given amount of outputs. The fewer the inputs required to produce a given output, the higher is the efficiency and the lower the cost of outputs. For example, in 1990 it took the average Japanese auto company 16.8 employee-hours to build a car, while the average American car company took 25.1 employee-hours. Japanese companies at that time were more efficient and had lower costs than their American rivals.[4] By 2004, U.S. companies adopted more efficient manufacturing methods and narrowed the gap significantly; matching Japanese quality levels, however, has been more difficult.
2. *To attain superior quality.* Quality here means producing goods and services that are reliable–they do the job they were designed for and do it well.[5] Providing high-quality products creates a brand-name reputation for an organization's products. In turn, this enhanced reputation allows the organization to charge a higher price. In the automobile industry, for example, not only does Toyota have an efficiency-based cost advantage over many American and European competitors, but the higher quality of Toyota's products has also enabled the company to earn more money because customers are willing to pay a premium price for its cars.
3. *To attain superior speed, flexibility, and innovation.* Anything new or better about the way an organization operates or the goods and services it produces is the result of innovation. Innovation leads to advances in the kinds of products, production processes, management systems, organizational structures, and strategies that an organization develops. Successful innovation gives an

Assembly line workers for Japanese auto giant Toyota put tires onto Toyota's vehicle "Wish" at the company's Tsutsumi plant in Toyota, central Japan. Toyota is widely credited with pioneering a number of critical innovations in the way cars are built that have helped it achieve superior productivity and quality—the basis of Toyota's competitive advantage.

organization something unique that its rivals lack. This uniqueness may enhance value added and thereby allow the organization to differentiate itself from its rivals and attract customers who will pay a premium price for its product. For example, Toyota is widely credited with pioneering a number of critical innovations in the way cars are built, and these innovations have helped Toyota achieve superior productivity and quality–the basis of Toyota's competitive advantage.

4. *To attain superior responsiveness to customers.* An organization that is responsive to customers tries to satisfy their needs and give them exactly what they want. An organization that treats customers better than its rivals treats them provides a valuable service for which customers may be willing to pay a higher price.

In managing the value chain to add value, or lower the costs of creating value, functional managers need to find ways to attain superior quality, efficiency, innovation, and responsiveness to customers. Functional managers are responsible for ensuring that an organization has sufficient supplies of high-quality, low-cost inputs, and they are responsible for designing an operating system that creates high-quality, low-cost products that customers are willing to buy. Notice, however, that achieving superior efficiency, quality, and innovation is part of attaining superior responsiveness to customers. Customers want value for their money, and an organization that develops functional strategies that lead to a high-performing operating system creates new high-quality, low-cost products that best deliver this value to customers. For this reason, we begin by discussing how functional managers can design the operating system to increase responsiveness to customers. (The vital issue of how to foster and speed innovation is discussed separately in Chapter 19.)

Improving Responsiveness to Customers

Organizations produce outputs–goods or services–that are consumed by customers. All organizations, profit seeking or not for profit, have customers. Without customers, most organizations would cease to exist. Because customers are vital to the survival of most organizations, managers must correctly identify customers and pursue strategies that respond to their needs. This is why the marketing function plays such an important part in the value chain. Management writers recommend that marketing managers focus on defining their company's business in terms of the customer needs they are satisfying, and not simply the type of products they make or provide.[6] The credo of pharmaceutical company Johnson & Johnson, for example, begins, "We believe our first responsibility is to the doctors, nurses and patients, to mothers and fathers and all others who use our products and services."[7] Through the credo Johnson & Johnson's managers emphasize their commitment to exemplary customer service.

In contrast, in the early 2000s, Lucent Technologies decided that, given its expertise in transistor technology, it would focus on producing transistor-based Internet routers that could handle vast quantities of information. When it became clear that customers were choosing optical Internet routers because these routers could transfer information extremely quickly, Lucent lost a large part of its business. By 2004, Lucent had radically altered its strategies to focus on a narrow range of high-speed networking devices that allow Internet service providers to offer their business customers high-speed, secure Net access.[8]

What Do Customers Want?

Given that satisfying customer demands is central to the survival of an organization, an important question is, What do customers want? Specifying exactly what they want is not possible because their wants vary from industry to industry. However, it is possible to identify some universal product attributes that most customers in most industries want. Generally, other things being equal, most customers prefer:

1. A lower price to a higher price.
2. High-quality products to low-quality products.
3. Quick service to slow service. (They will always prefer good after-sales service and support to poor after-sales support.)
4. Products with many features to products with few features. (They will prefer a personal computer with a CD-ROM drive, lots of memory, and a powerful microprocessor to one without these features.)
5. Products that are, as far as possible, customized or tailored to their unique needs.

Of course, the problem is that other things are not equal. For example, providing high-quality, quick service and after-sales service and support, products with many features, and products that are customized raises operating costs and thus the price that must be charged to cover these costs, as Webvan and other online grocers discovered.[9] So customers' demands for these attributes typically conflict with their demands for low prices. Accordingly, customers must make a trade-off between price and preferred attributes, and so must managers. This price/attribute trade-off is illustrated in Figure 9.2.

Desired attributes of a product–such as high quality, service, speed, after-sales support, features, and customization–are plotted on the horizontal axis; price is plotted on the vertical axis. The solid line shows the price-attribute relationship–that is, the combination of price and attributes an organization can offer and still make a profit. As the figure illustrates, the higher the price the customer is willing to pay for a product, the more desired attributes the customer is able to get. Or, in other words, the more desired attributes that an organization builds into its products, the higher is the price that the organization has to charge to cover its costs. At price P_1 managers can offer a product with A_1 attributes. If managers

Figure 9.2
The Price-Attribute Relationship

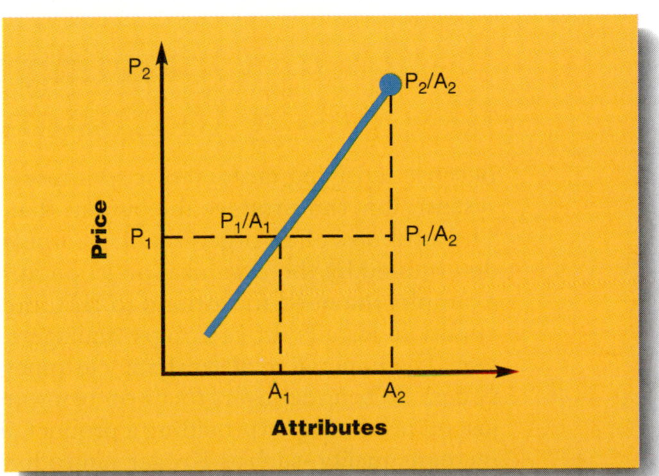

Figure 9.3
Kroger's Price-Attribute Relationship in 1991 and 2001

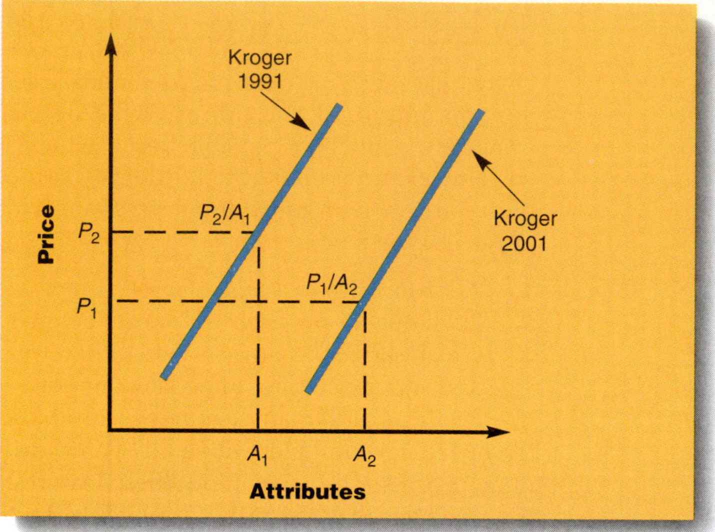

offer a product with A_2 attributes at price P_1, they will lose money because the price is too low to cover costs. A product with A_2 attributes needs a price of P_2 to be profitable for the organization. Thus, the nature of the organization's operating system limits how responsive managers can be to customers.

Given the limits imposed on managers by their existing operating system, what do the managers of a customer-responsive organization try to do? They try to develop functional strategies to push or shift the price-attribute curve to the right (toward the vertical dotted line in Figure 9.2) by developing new or improved operating systems that are able to deliver either more desired product attributes for the same price or the same product attributes for a lower price.[10]

Figure 9.3 shows the price-attribute curves for the Kroger supermarket chain in the 1990s, before its customer-oriented IT kiosks were put in place, and in the 2000s, when the IT and new store design was up and running. By accommodating customer demands for a greater variety of foods, increased quality, and quicker customer service, the new operating system allowed Kroger to offer more product attributes at a similar or even lower price to customers. Kroger's shift from a traditional to a modern, IT-oriented store operation thus increased its responsiveness to customers and did so without imposing higher costs.

Designing Operating Systems Responsive to Customers

Because satisfying customers is so important, managers try to design operating systems that can produce the outputs that have the attributes customers desire. The attributes of an organization's outputs–their quality, cost, and features–are determined by the organization's operating system.[11] As discussed earlier, for example, the need to respond to customer demands for competitively priced, quality foodstuffs drove Kroger managers to choose a new store operation system. The imperative of satisfying customer needs shaped Kroger's "production" system. When managers focus on being responsive to their customers, and not just on producing or providing a product, they see new ways to reduce costs and increase quality–such as Kroger's introduction of kiosks.

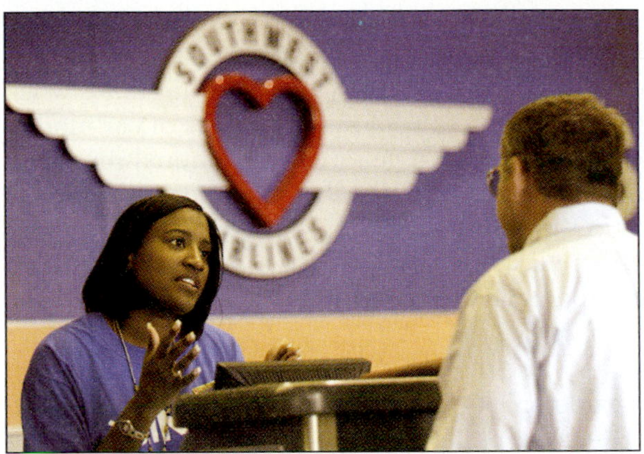

A Southwest ticket agent assists a customer. Southwest's operating system is geared toward satisfying customer demands for low-priced, reliable, and convenient air travel, making it one of the most consistently successful airlines in recent years. To help keep flights on schedule, Southwest's workforce has been cross-trained to perform multiple tasks. For example, the person who checks tickets might also help with baggage loading.

Since the ability of an organization to satisfy the demands of its customers derives from its operating system, managers need to devote considerable attention to value-chain management. Managers' desire to attract customers by shifting the price-attribute line to the right explains their adoption of many new functional strategies to build competitive advantage into their operating systems. These include total quality management, flexible manufacturing systems, just-in-time inventory, and, of course, new information systems and technologies that speed the sale and delivery of products to customers.

As an example of the link between responsiveness to customers and an organization's operating system, consider the success of Southwest Airlines. One of the most consistently successful airlines in the United States, Southwest Airlines has been expanding rapidly in the 2000s.[12] One reason for Southwest's success is that its managers created an operating system uniquely tailored to satisfy the demands of its customers: for low-priced, reliable (on-time), and convenient air travel. Southwest commands high customer loyalty precisely because its operating system delivers products, such as flights from Houston to Dallas, that have all the desired attributes: reliability, convenience, and low price.

Southwest's low-cost operating system focuses not only on improving the maintenance of aircraft but also on the company's ticket reservation system, route structure, flight frequency, baggage-handling system, and in-flight services. Each of these elements of Southwest's operating system is geared toward satisfying customer demands for low-priced, reliable, and convenient air travel. For example, Southwest offers a no-frills approach to in-flight customer service. No meals are served onboard, and there are no first-class seats. Southwest does not subscribe to the big reservation computers used by travel agents because the booking fees are too costly. Also, the airline flies only one aircraft, the fuel-efficient Boeing 737, which keeps training and maintenance costs down. All this translates into low prices for customers.

Southwest's reliability derives from the fact that it has the quickest aircraft turnaround time in the industry. A Southwest ground crew needs only 15 minutes to turn around an incoming aircraft and prepare it for departure. This speedy operation helps to keep flights on time. Southwest has such quick turnaround because it has a flexible workforce that has been cross-trained to perform multiple tasks. Thus, the person who checks tickets might also help with baggage loading if time is short.

Southwest's convenience comes from its scheduling multiple flights every day between its popular locations, such as Dallas and Houston, and its use of airports that are close to downtown (Hobby at Houston and Love Field at Dallas) instead of more distant major airports.[13] In sum, Southwest's excellent value-chain management has given it a competitive advantage in the airline industry.

Although managers must seek to improve their responsiveness to customers by improving their organizations' operating systems, they should *not* offer a level of responsiveness to customers that is more than that operating system can profitably sustain. The company that customizes every product to the unique demands of individual customers is likely to see its cost structure become so high that unit costs exceed unit revenues. This of course is what happened to Webvan and other online grocers. It also happened to Toyota in the 1990s when Toyota managers' drive to provide customers with many choices of car models and specifications increased costs faster than it generated additional revenues. At one point, Toyota factories were producing literally thousands of variations of Toyota's basic models, such as the Camry and Corolla. Managers at Toyota concluded that the costs of extreme customization were exceeding the benefits and cut back on the number of models and specifications of its cars.[14]

Improving Quality

As noted earlier, high-quality products are reliable, dependable, and satisfying; they do the job they were designed for and meet customer requirements.[15] Quality is a concept that can be applied to the products of both manufacturing and service organizations–goods such as a Toyota car or a Kroger steak or services such as Southwest Airlines flight service or customer service in a Citibank branch. Why do managers seek to control and improve the quality of their organizations' products?[16] There are two reasons (see Figure 9.4).

First, customers usually prefer a higher-quality product to a lower-quality product. So an organization able to provide, *for the same price,* a product of higher quality than a competitor's product is serving its customers better–it is being more responsive to its customers. Often, providing high-quality products creates a brand-name reputation for an organization's products. In turn, this enhanced reputation may allow the organization to charge more for its products than its competitors are able to charge, and thus it makes even greater profits. In 2004 Lexus was ranked number one, as it has been for the last decade, on the J. D. Power list of the 10 most reliable car manufacturers, and Toyota was close behind.[17] The high quality of Toyota/Lexus vehicles has enabled the company to charge higher prices for its cars than the prices charged by rival automakers.

The second reason for trying to boost product quality is that higher product quality can increase efficiency and thereby lower operating costs and boost profits. Achieving high product quality lowers operating costs because of the effect of quality on employee productivity: Higher product quality means less employee time is wasted in making defective products that must be discarded or in providing substandard services, and thus less time has to be spent fixing mistakes. This translates into higher employee productivity, which means lower costs.

Figure 9.4
The Impact of Increased Quality on Organizational Performance

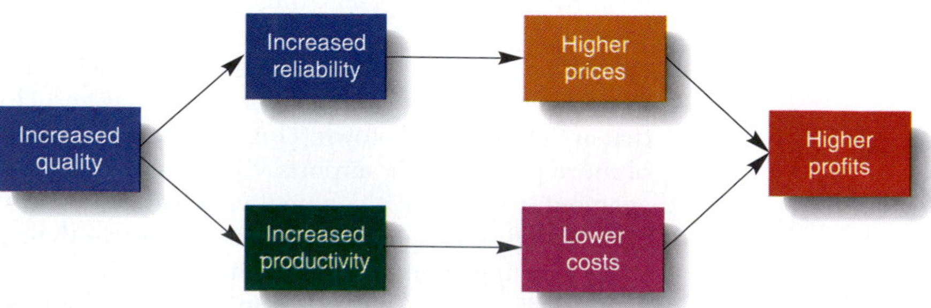

Total Quality Management

total quality management A management technique that focuses on improving the quality of an organization's products and services.

At the forefront of the drive to improve product quality is a technique known as total quality management.[18] **Total quality management (TQM)** focuses on improving the quality of an organization's products and services and stresses that all of an organization's value-chain activities should be directed toward this goal. Conceived as an organizationwide management program, TQM requires the cooperation of managers in every function of an organization if it is to succeed. The TQM concept was developed by a number of American consultants, including the late W. Edwards Deming, Joseph Juran, and A. V. Feigenbaum.[19]

What actions should managers take to implement a successful TQM program? The following 10 steps are necessary to make a TQM control system work.

1. *Build organizational commitment to quality.* TQM will do little to improve the performance of an organization unless all employees embrace it, and this often requires a change in an organization's culture.[20] At Citibank, discussed in detail in the next "Management Insight," the process of changing culture began at the top. First, a group of top managers, including the CEO, received training in TQM from consultants from Motorola. Each member of the top-management group was then given the responsibility of training a group at the next level in the hierarchy, and so on down through the organization until all 100,000 employees had received basic TQM training.
2. *Focus on the customer.* TQM practitioners see a focus on the customer as the starting point.[21] According to TQM philosophy, the *customer,* not managers in quality control or engineering, defines what quality is. The challenge is fourfold: (1) to identify what customers want from the good or service that the company provides; (2) to identify what the company actually provides to customers; (3) to identify the gap that exists between what customers want and what they actually get (the *quality gap*); and (4) to formulate a plan for closing the quality gap. The efforts of Citibank managers to increase responsiveness to customers illustrate this aspect of TQM well.

Management Insight

Citibank Uses TQM to Increase Customer Loyalty

Citibank is one of the leading global financial institutions and has established a goal of becoming *the* premier institution in the 21st century. To achieve this lofty goal, Citibank has started to use TQM to increase its responsiveness to customers, recognizing that, ultimately, its customer base and customer loyalty determine the bank's future success.

As the first step in its TQM effort, Citibank identified the factors that dissatisfy its customers. When analyzing the complaints, it found that most concerned the time it took to complete a customer's request, such as responding to an account problem or getting a loan. So Citibank's managers began to examine how they handled each kind of customer request. For each distinct request, they formed a cross-functional team that broke down a specific request into the steps between people and departments that were needed to complete the request. In analyzing them, teams found that often many steps in the process were unnecessary and could be replaced by using the right information systems. They also found that very often delays occurred because employees simply did not know how to handle a request. They were not being given the right kind of training, and when they couldn't handle a request, they simply put it aside until a supervisor could deal with it.

Citibank's second step to increase its responsiveness was to implement an organizationwide TQM program. Managers and supervisors were charged with reducing the complexity of the work process and finding the most effective way to process each particular request, such as a request for a loan. Managers were also charged with training employees to answer each specific request. The results were remarkable. For example, in the loan department the TQM program reduced the number of handoffs necessary to process a request by 75 percent. The department's average response time dropped from several hours to 30 minutes. By 2000, more than 92,000 employees worldwide had been trained in the new TQM processes, and Citibank could easily measure TQM's effectiveness by the increased speed with which it was handling an increased volume of customer requests.

3. *Find ways to measure quality.* Another crucial element of any TQM program is the creation of a measuring system that managers can consistently use to evaluate quality. Devising appropriate measures is relatively easy in manufacturing companies, where quality can be measured by criteria such as defects per million parts. It is more difficult in service companies, where outputs are less tangible. However, with a little creativity, suitable quality measures can be devised as they were by managers at Citibank. Similarly, at L.L.Bean, the mail-order retailer, managers use the percentage of orders that are correctly filled as one of their quality measures. The common theme running through these examples is that managers must identify what quality means from a *customer's* perspective and devise some measure that captures this.

4. *Set goals and create incentives.* Once a measure has been devised, managers' next step is to set a challenging quality goal and to create incentives for reaching that goal. At Citibank, the CEO set an initial goal of reducing customer complaints by 50 percent. One way of creating incentives to attain a goal is to link rewards, such as bonus pay and promotional opportunities, to the goal.

5. *Solicit input from employees.* Employees can be a major source of information about the causes of poor quality. Therefore, it is important for managers to establish a framework for soliciting employee suggestions about improvements that can be made. **Quality circles**–groups of employees who meet regularly to discuss ways to increase quality–are often created to achieve this goal. Companies also create self-managed teams to further quality improvement efforts. Whatever the means chosen to solicit input from lower-level employees, managers must be open to receiving, and acting on, bad news and criticism from employees.

quality circles Groups of employees who meet regularly to discuss ways to increase quality.

6. *Identify defects and trace them to their source.* A major source of product defects is the operating system. TQM preaches the need for managers to identify defects in the work process, trace those defects back to their source, find out why they occurred, and make corrections so that they do not occur again. To identify defects, Deming advocated the use of statistical procedures to spot variations in the quality of goods or services; however, IT makes the measurement of quality much easier.

inventory The stock of raw materials, inputs, and component parts that an organization has on hand at a particular time.

7. *Introduce just-in-time inventory systems.* **Inventory** is the stock of raw materials, inputs, and component parts that an organization has on hand at a particular

just-in-time (JIT) inventory system A system in which parts or supplies arrive at an organization when they are needed, not before.

time. Just-in-time inventory systems play a major role in the process of identifying and finding the source of defects in inputs. When the materials management function designs a **just-in-time (JIT) inventory system,** parts or supplies arrive at the organization when they are needed, not before. With a JIT inventory system component parts travel from suppliers to the assembly line in a small-wheeled container known as a *kanban*. Assembly-line workers empty the kanbans and then the empty container is sent back to the supplier as the signal to produce another small batch of component parts, and so the process repeats itself. This system can be contrasted with a *just-in-case* view of inventory, which leads an organization to stockpile excess inputs in a warehouse just in case it needs them to meet sudden upturns in demand.

Also, under a JIT inventory system, defective parts enter an organization's operating system immediately; they are not warehoused for months before use. This means that defective inputs can be quickly spotted. Materials managers can then trace the problem to the supply source and fix it before more defective parts are produced.

8. *Work closely with suppliers*. A major cause of poor-quality finished goods is poor-quality component parts. To decrease product defects, materials managers must work closely with suppliers to improve the quality of the parts they supply. Managers at Xerox worked closely with suppliers to get them to adopt TQM programs, and the result was a huge reduction in the defect rate of component parts. Managers also need to work closely with suppliers to get them to adopt a JIT inventory system, also required for high quality.

To implement JIT systems with suppliers, and to get suppliers to set up their own TQM programs, two steps are necessary. First, managers must reduce the number of suppliers with which their organizations do business. Second, managers need to develop cooperative long-term relationships with remaining suppliers. Over the years, managers at Dell Computer have reduced the number of suppliers they need to a minimum, which greatly streamlines their interactions with suppliers and leads to increased quality and lower-cost inputs.

9. *Design for ease of production*. The more steps required to assemble a product or provide a service, the more opportunities there are for making a mistake. It follows that designing products that have fewer parts or finding ways to simplify providing a service should be linked to fewer defects or customer complaints. For example, Dell continually redesigns the way it assembles its computers to reduce the number of assembly steps required and to search for new ways to reduce the number of components that have to be linked together. The consequence of these redesign efforts has been a fall in assembly costs and marked improvement in product quality that has led to Dell's becoming the number-one global PC maker. Dell also has strived to improve its procedures for helping customers who experience problems with their new PCs to solve them.

10. *Break down barriers between functions*. Successful implementation of TQM requires substantial cooperation between the different functions of an organization. Materials managers have to cooperate with manufacturing managers to find high-quality inputs that reduce manufacturing costs; marketing managers have to cooperate with manufacturing so that customer problems identified by marketing can be acted on; information systems have to cooperate with all of the other functions of the company to devise suitable IT training programs; and so on.

In essence, to increase quality, all functional managers need to cooperate to develop strategic plans that state goals exactly and spell out how they will be achieved. Managers should embrace the philosophy that mistakes, defects, and poor-quality materials are not acceptable and should be eliminated. Functional managers should spend more time working with employees and providing them with the tools they need to do the job. Managers should create an environment in which employees will not be afraid to report problems or recommend improvements. Output goals and targets need to include not only numbers or quotas but also some notion of quality to promote the production of defect-free output. Functional managers also need to train employees in new skills to keep pace with changes in the workplace. Finally, achieving better quality requires that managers develop organizational values and norms centered on improving quality.

Improving Efficiency

The third goal of value-chain management is to increase the efficiency of an organization's operating system. The fewer the inputs required to produce a given output, the higher will be the efficiency of the operating system. Managers can measure efficiency at the organization level in two ways. The measure known as *total factor productivity* looks at how well an organization utilizes all of its resources–such as labor, capital, materials, or energy–to produce its outputs. It is expressed in the following equation:

$$\text{Total factor productivity} = \frac{\text{outputs}}{\text{all inputs}}$$

The problem with total factor productivity is that each input is typically measured in different units: Labor's contribution to producing an output is measured by hours worked; the contribution of materials is measured by the amount consumed (for example, tons of iron ore required to make a ton of steel); the contribution of energy is measured by the units of energy consumed (for example, kilowatt-hours); and so on. To compute total factor productivity, managers must convert all the inputs to a common unit, such as dollars, before they can work the equation.

Although sometimes a useful measure of efficiency overall, total factor productivity obscures the exact contribution of an individual input–such as labor–to the production of a given output. Consequently, most organizations focus on specific measures of efficiency, known as *partial productivity,* which measures the efficiency of an individual unit. For example, the efficiency of labor inputs is expressed as

$$\text{Labor productivity} = \frac{\text{outputs}}{\text{direct labor}}$$

Labor productivity is most commonly used to draw efficiency comparisons between different organizations. For example, one study found that in 1994 it took the average Japanese automobile components supplier half as many labor-hours as the average British company to produce a part such as a car seat or exhaust system.[22] Thus, the study concluded, Japanese companies use labor more efficiently than British companies. In the last decade car companies throughout the world have been striving to catch up with the Japanese and many, such as GM and Ford, have closed the efficiency gap enormously.

The management of efficiency is an extremely important issue in most organizations, because increased efficiency lowers production costs, thereby allowing the organization to make a greater profit or to attract more customers by lowering its price. For example, in 1990 the price of the average personal computer sold in the United States was $3,000; by 1995 the price was about $1,800; and in 2004 it was about $500. This decrease occurred despite the fact that the power and capabilities of the average personal computer increased dramatically during this time period (microprocessors became more powerful, memory increased, modems were built in, and multimedia capability was added).

Why was the decrease in price possible? As discussed above, PC makers such as Dell focused on quality and used TQM to boost their efficiency by improving the quality of their components and making PCs easier to assemble. This allowed them to lower their costs and prices and still make a profit.[23] While TQM is an important step in the drive to raise efficiency, several other factors are also important, as discussed below.

Facilities Layout, Flexible Manufacturing, and Efficiency

Another factor that influences efficiency is the way managers decide to lay out or design an organization's physical work facilities. This is important for two reasons. First, the way in which machines and workers are organized or grouped together into workstations affects the efficiency of the operating system. Second, a major determinant of efficiency is the cost associated with setting up the equipment needed to make a particular product. **Facilities layout** is the process of designing the machine-worker interface to increase operating system efficiency. **Flexible manufacturing** is the set of techniques, usually IT-based, that attempt to reduce the costs associated with an operating system. For example, this might be the way computers are made on a production line or the way patients are routed through a hospital.

facilities layout The process of designing the machine-worker interface to increase operating system efficiency.

flexible manufacturing The set of techniques that attempt to reduce the costs associated with an operating system.

FACILITIES LAYOUT The way in which machines, robots, and people are grouped together affects how productive they can be. Figure 9.5 (page 314) shows three basic ways of arranging workstations: product layout, process layout, and fixed-position layout.

In a *product layout,* machines are organized so that each operation needed to manufacture a product or process a patient is performed at workstations arranged in a fixed sequence. In manufacturing, workers are stationary in this arrangement, and a moving conveyor belt takes the product being worked on to the next workstation so that it is progressively assembled. *Mass production* is the familiar name for this layout; car assembly lines are probably the best-known example. It used to be that product layout was efficient only when products were created in large quantities; however, the introduction of modular assembly lines controlled by computers is making it efficient to make products in small batches.

In a *process layout,* workstations are not organized in a fixed sequence. Rather, each workstation is relatively self-contained, and a product goes to whichever workstation is needed to perform the next operation to complete the product. Process layout is often suited to manufacturing settings that produce a variety of custom-made products, each tailored to the needs of a different kind of customer. For example, a custom furniture manufacturer might use a process layout so that different teams of workers can produce different styles of chairs or tables made from different kinds of woods and finishes. Such a layout also describes how a patient might go through a hospital from emergency room, to X-ray room, to operating theater, and so on. A process layout provides the flexibility

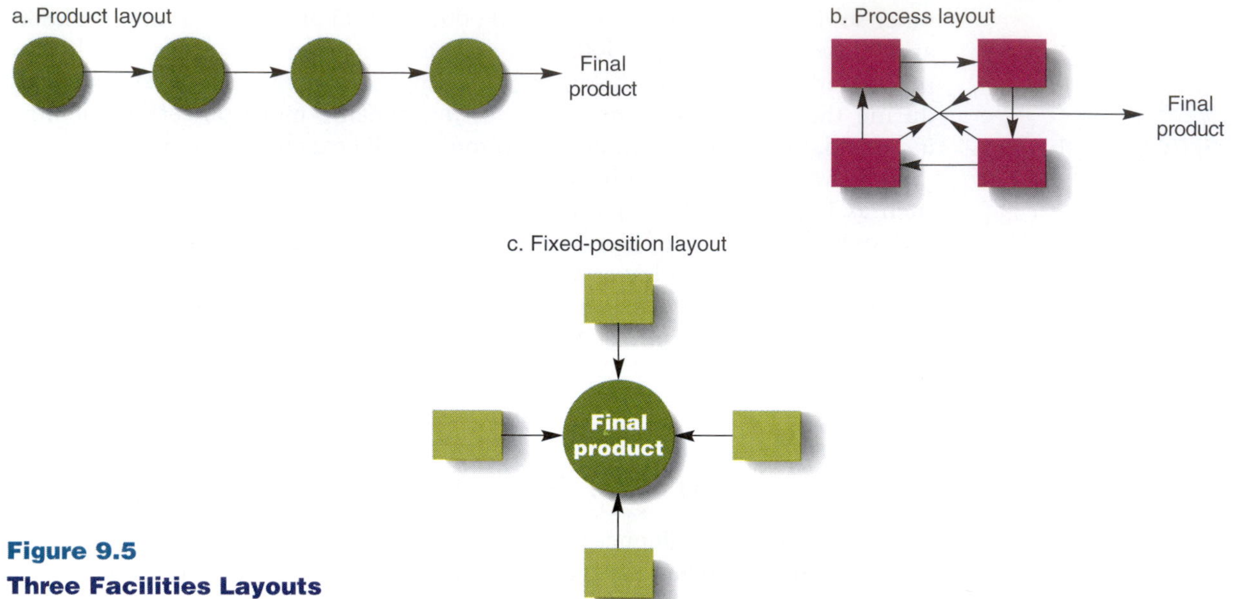

Figure 9.5
Three Facilities Layouts

needed to *change* a product, whether it is a PC or a patient. Such flexibility, however, often reduces efficiency because it is expensive.

In a *fixed-position layout,* the product stays in a fixed position. Its component parts are produced in remote workstations and brought to the production area for final assembly. Increasingly, self-managed teams are using fixed-position layouts. Different teams assemble each component part and then send the parts to the final assembly team, which makes the final product. A fixed-position layout is commonly used for products such as jet airlines, mainframe computers, and gas turbines–products that are complex and difficult to assemble or so large that moving them from one workstation to another would be difficult. The effects of moving from one facilities layout to another can be dramatic, as the following "Manager as a Person" suggests.

Manager as a Person

Paddy Hopkirk Improves Facilities Layout

Paddy Hopkirk established his car accessories business in Bedfordshire, England, shortly after he had shot to car-racing fame by winning the Monte Carlo Rally. Sales of Hopkirk's accessories, such as bicycle racks and axle stands, were always brisk, but Hopkirk was the first to admit that his operating system left a lot to be desired, so he invited consultants to help reorganize his operating system.

After analyzing his factory's operating system, the consultants realized that the source of the problem was the facilities layout Hopkirk had established. Over time, as sales grew, Hopkirk simply added new workstations to the operating system as they were needed. The result was a process layout in which the product being assembled moved in the irregular sequences shown in the "Before Change" half of Figure 9.6. The consultants suggested that to save time and effort, the workstations should be reorganized into the sequential product layout shown in the "After Change" illustration.

Figure 9.6
Changing a Facilities Layout

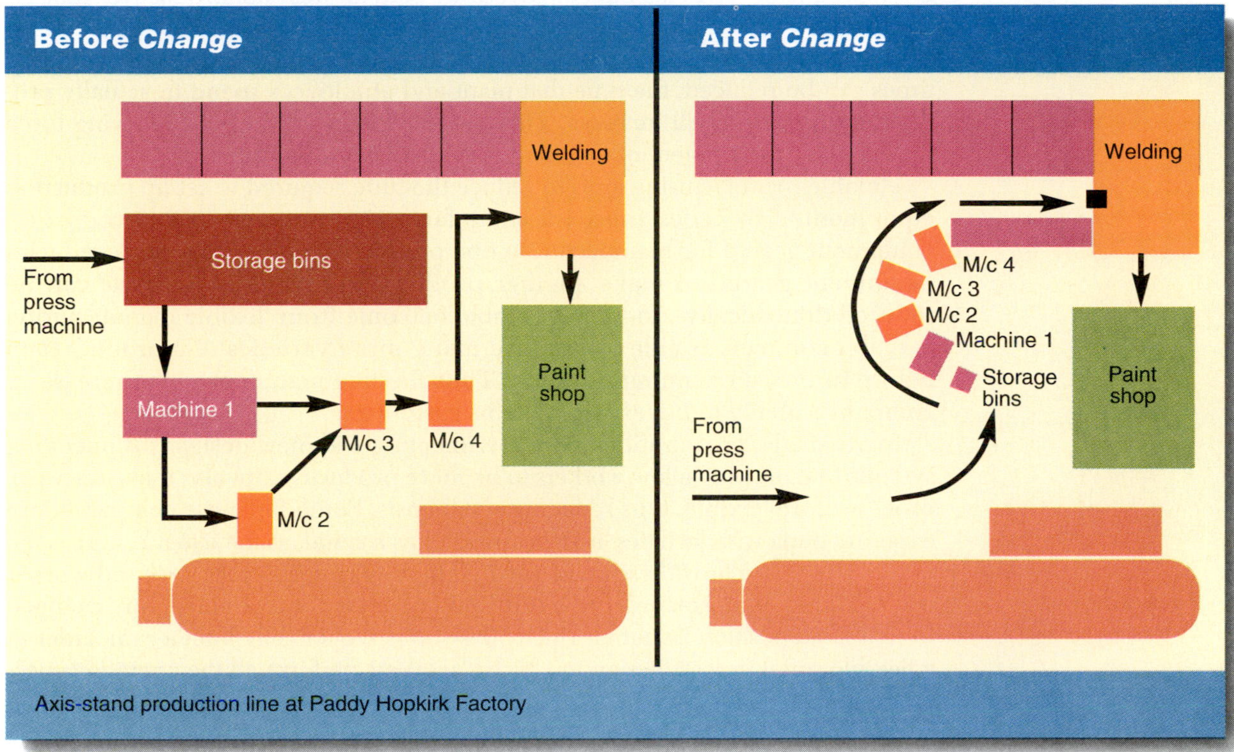

Source: "The Application of Kaizen to Facilities Layout," *Financial Times* of January 4, 1994, p. 12. Reprinted by permission of Financial Times Syndication, London.

Once this change was made, the results were dramatic. One morning the factory was an untidy sprawl of workstations surrounded by piles of crates holding semifinished components. Two days later, when the 170-person workforce came back to work, the machines had been brought together into tightly grouped workstations arranged in the fixed sequence shown in the illustration. The piles of components had disappeared, and the newly cleared floor space was neatly marked with color-coded lines mapping out the new flow of materials between workstations.

In the first full day of production, efficiency increased by as much as 30 percent. The space needed for some operations had been cut in half, and work-in-progress had been cut considerably. Moreover, the improved layout allowed for some jobs to be combined, freeing operators for deployment elsewhere in the factory. An amazed Hopkirk exclaimed, "I was expecting a change but nothing as dramatic as this . . . it is fantastic."[24]

FLEXIBLE MANUFACTURING In a manufacturing company, a major source of costs is the costs associated with setting up the equipment needed to make a particular product. One of these costs is the cost of production that is forgone because nothing is produced while the equipment is being set up. For example, components manufacturers often need as much as half a day to set up automated production equipment when switching from production of one component part (such as a washer ring for the steering column of a car) to another (such as a washer ring for the steering column of a truck). During this half-day, a manufacturing plant is not producing anything, but employees are paid for this "nonproductive" time.

It follows that if setup times for complex production equipment can be reduced, so can setup costs, and efficiency will rise. In other words, if setup times can be reduced, the time that plant and employees spend in actually producing something will increase. This simple insight has been the driving force behind the development of flexible manufacturing techniques.

Flexible manufacturing aims to reduce the time required to set up production equipment.[25] By redesigning the manufacturing process so that production equipment geared for manufacturing one product can be quickly replaced with equipment geared to make another product, setup times and costs can be reduced dramatically. Another favorable outcome from flexible manufacturing is that a company is able to produce many more varieties of a product than before in the same amount of time. Thus flexible manufacturing increases a company's ability to be responsive to its customers.

Increasingly, organizations are experimenting with new designs for operating systems that not only allow workers to be more productive but also make the work process more flexible, thus reducing setup costs. Some Japanese companies are experimenting with facilities layouts arranged as a spiral, as the letter Y, and as the number 6, to see how these various configurations affect setup costs and worker productivity. At a camcorder plant in Kohda, Japan, for example, Sony changed from a fixed-position layout in which 50 workers sequentially built a camcorder to a flexible spiral process design in which 4 workers perform all the operations necessary to produce the camcorder. This new layout allows the most efficient workers to work at the highest pace, and it reduces setup costs because workers can easily switch from one model to another, increasing efficiency by 10 percent.[26]

An interesting example of a company that built a new factory to obtain the benefits from flexible manufacturing is Igus Inc., headquartered in Cologne, Germany. Igus makes over 28,000 polymer bearings and energy supply cable products used in applications the world over. In the 1990s, Igus's managers realized they needed to build a new factory that could handle the company's rapidly growing product line. The product line was changing constantly as new products were innovated and old ones became obsolete. At Igus new products are often introduced on a daily basis, so this need for flexibility is the company's prime requirement. Moreover, because many of its products are highly customized, the specific and changing needs of its customers drive new product development.

Igus's new factory was designed with the need for flexibility in mind. As big as three football fields, nothing in the factory is tied down or bolted to the floor. All the machines, computers, and equipment can be moved and repositioned to suit changing product requirements. Moreover, all Igus employees are trained to be flexible and can perform many of the production tasks necessary. For example, when one new product line proved popular with customers, its employees and production operations were relocated four times as it grew into larger spaces. Igus can change its operating system at a moment's notice and with minimal disruption, and since the company operates seven days a week, 24 hours a day, these changes are occurring constantly.

To facilitate these changes, workers are equipped with power scooters to move around the plant quickly and reconfigure operations. This also allows them to move quickly to wherever in the factory their skills are most needed. Employees are also equipped with mobile phones so that they are always on call.

Igus's decision to create a flexible factory of the future has paid off. In the last decade its global sales have tripled.

Just-in-Time Inventory and Efficiency

Although JIT systems, such as Toyota's kanban system, were originally developed as part of the effort to improve product quality, they have major implications for efficiency. Major cost savings can result from increasing inventory turnover and reducing inventory holding costs, such as warehousing and storage costs and the cost of capital tied up in inventory. Although companies that manufacture and assemble products can obviously use JIT to great advantage, so can service organizations. Wal-Mart, the biggest retailer in the United States, uses JIT systems to replenish the stock in its stores at least twice a week. Many Wal-Mart stores receive daily deliveries. Wal-Mart's main competitors, Kmart and Sears, typically replenish their stock every two weeks. Wal-Mart can maintain the same service levels as these competitors but at one-fourth the inventory holding cost, a major source of cost saving. Faster inventory turnover has helped Wal-Mart achieve an efficiency-based competitive advantage in the retailing industry.[27]

One drawback of JIT systems is that they leave an organization without a buffer stock of inventory.[28] Although buffer stocks of inventory can be expensive to store, they can help an organization when it is affected by shortages of inputs brought about by a disruption among suppliers (such as a labor dispute at a key supplier). Moreover, buffer stocks can help an organization respond quickly to increases in customer demand–that is, they can increase an organization's responsiveness to customers. Even a small company can benefit from a kanban, as the experience of United Electric suggests in the following "Management Insight."

Management Insight

United Electric's Kanban System

United Electric Controls, headquartered in Watertown, Massachusetts, is the market leader in the application of threshold detection and switching technology. At one time, the company simply warehoused its inputs and dispensed them as needed. Then it decided to reduce costs by storing these inputs at their point of use in the production system. However, this also caused problems because inventories of some inputs actually started to increase while other inputs were used up without anyone knowing which input caused a stoppage in production.

So managers decided to experiment with a supplier kanban system even though United Electric had fewer than 40 suppliers who were totally up to date with its input requirements. Managers decided to store a three-week supply of parts in a central storeroom, a supply large enough to avoid unexpected shortages.[29] They began by asking their casting supplier to deliver inputs in kanbans and bins. Once a week, this supplier checks up on the bins to determine how much stock needs to be delivered the following week. Other suppliers were then asked to participate in this system, and now more than 35 of its major suppliers operate some form of the kanban system.

By all measures of performance, the results of using the kanban system have been successful. Inventory holding costs have fallen sharply. Products are delivered to all customers on time. And even new products' design-to-production cycles have dropped by 50 percent because suppliers are now involved much earlier in the design process so that they can supply new inputs as needed.

Self-Managed Work Teams and Efficiency

Another efficiency-boosting technique is the use of self-managed work teams.[30] The typical team consists of 5 to 15 employees who produce an entire product instead of just parts of it.[31] Team members learn all team tasks and move from job to job. The result is a flexible workforce, because team members can fill in for absent co-workers. The members of each team also assume responsibility for scheduling work and vacations, ordering materials, and hiring new members–previously all responsibilities of first-line managers. Because people often respond well to being given greater autonomy and responsibility, the use of empowered self-managed teams can increase productivity and efficiency. Moreover, cost savings arise from eliminating supervisors and creating a flatter organizational hierarchy, which further increases efficiency.

The effect of introducing self-managed teams is often an increase in efficiency of 30 percent or more, sometimes much more. After the introduction of flexible manufacturing technology and self-managed teams, a GE plant in Salisbury, North Carolina, increased efficiency by 250 percent compared with other GE plants producing the same products.[32]

Process Reengineering and Efficiency

process reengineering The fundamental rethinking and radical redesign of business processes to achieve dramatic improvement in critical measures of performance such as cost, quality, service, and speed.

Think of the value chain as a collection of functional activities or business processes that take one or more kinds of inputs and transform them to create an output that is of value to the customer.[33] **Process reengineering** is the fundamental rethinking and radical redesign of business processes (and thus the value chain) to achieve dramatic improvements in critical measures of performance such as cost, quality, service, and speed.[34] Order fulfillment, for example, can be thought of as a business process: When a customer's order is received (the input), many different functional tasks must be performed as necessary to process the order, and then the ordered goods are delivered to the customer (the output). Process reengineering boosts efficiency when it reduces the number of order-fulfillment tasks that must be performed, or reduces the time they take, and so reduces operating costs.

For an example of process reengineering in practice, consider how Ford Motor Company used it. One day a manager from Ford was working in its Japanese partner Mazda and discovered quite by accident that Mazda had only five people in its accounts payable department. The Ford manager was shocked, since Ford's U.S. operation had 500 employees in accounts payable. He reported his discovery to Ford's U.S. managers, who decided to form a task force to figure out why the difference existed.

"IF YOU'LL JUST SIT TIGHT, I'LL DIVE BACK DOWN INTO THE PRODUCT SPECS, QUOTES AND SAMPLES TO FIND A CONTRACT FOR YOU TO SIGN."

Ford managers discovered that procurement began when the purchasing department sent a purchase order to a supplier and sent a copy of the purchase order to Ford's accounts payable department. When the supplier shipped the goods and they arrived at Ford, a clerk at the receiving dock completed a form describing the goods and sent the form to accounts payable. The supplier, meanwhile, sent accounts payable an invoice. Thus, accounts payable received three documents relating to these goods: a copy of the original purchase order, the receiving document, and the invoice. If the information in all three was in agreement (most of the time it was), a clerk in accounts payable issued payment. Occasionally, however, all three documents did not agree. And Ford discovered that accounts payable clerks spent most of their time straightening out the 1 percent of instances in which the purchase order, receiving document, and invoice contained conflicting information.[35]

Ford managers decided to reengineer the procurement process to simplify it. Now when a buyer in the purchasing department issues a purchase order to a supplier, that buyer also enters the order into an online database. As before, suppliers send goods to the receiving dock. When the goods arrive, the clerk at the receiving dock checks a computer terminal to see whether the received shipment matches the description on the purchase order. If it does, the clerk accepts the goods and pushes a button on the terminal keyboard that tells the database the goods have arrived. Receipt of the goods is recorded in the database, and a computer automatically issues and sends a check to the supplier. If the goods do not correspond to the description on the purchase order in the database, the clerk at the dock refuses the shipment and sends it back to the supplier.

Payment authorization, which used to be performed by accounts payable, is now accomplished at the receiving dock. The new process has come close to eliminating the need for an accounts payable department. In some parts of Ford, the size of the accounts payable department has been cut by 95 percent. By reducing the head count in accounts payable, the reengineering effort reduced the amount of time wasted on unproductive activities, thereby increasing the efficiency of the total organization.

Information Systems, the Internet, and Efficiency

With the rapid spread of computers, the explosive growth of the Internet and corporate intranets (internal corporate computer networks based on Internet standards), and the spread of high-bandwidth fiber optics and digital wireless technology, the information systems function is moving to center stage in the quest for operating efficiencies and a lower cost structure. The impact of information systems on productivity is wide-ranging and potentially affects all other activities of a company. For example, Cisco Systems has been able to realize significant cost savings by moving its ordering and customer service functions online. The company has just 300 service agents handling all of its customer accounts, compared to the 900 it would need if sales were not handled online. The difference represents an annual saving of $20 million a year. Moreover, without automated customer service functions, Cisco calculates that it would need at least 1,000 additional service engineers, which would cost around $75 million. Dell Computer also makes extensive use of the Internet to lower its cost structure and differentiate itself from rivals, as the following "Information Technology Byte" discusses.

Information Technology Byte

How to Make Use of the Internet

By 2004, more than 90 percent of Dell's computers were sold online.[36] According to Michael Dell,

> *As I saw it, the Internet offered a logical extension of the direct (selling) model, creating even stronger relationships with our customers. The Internet would augment conventional telephone, fax, and face-to-face encounters, and give our customers the information they wanted faster, cheaper, and more efficiently.*[37]

Dell's Web site allows customers to customize their orders to get the system that best suits their particular requirements. By allowing customers to configure their orders, Dell increases its customer responsiveness. Dell has also put much of its customer service function online, reducing the need for telephone calls to customer service representatives and saving costs in the process. Each week, some 200,000 people access Dell's troubleshooting tips online. Each of these visits to Dell's Web site saves the company a potential $15, which is the average cost of a technical support call. If just 10 percent of these online visitors were to call Dell by telephone instead, it would cost the company $15.6 million per year.

Dell uses the Internet to manage its value chain, feeding real-time information about order flow to its suppliers, which use this information to schedule their own production, providing components to Dell on a just-in-time basis. Dell's ultimate goal is to drive all inventories out of the supply chain apart from inventory in transit between suppliers and Dell, effectively replacing inventory with information. In that way, Dell can drive significant costs out of its system.

More generally, companies like Cisco and Dell are using Web-based information systems to reduce the costs of coordination between the company and its customers and between the company and its suppliers. By using Web-based programs to automate customer and supplier interactions, the number of people required to manage these interfaces can be substantially reduced, thereby reducing costs. This trend extends beyond high-tech companies. Banks and financial service companies are finding that they can substantially reduce costs by moving customer accounts and support functions online. Such a move reduces the need for customer service representatives, bank tellers, stockbrokers, insurance agents, and others. For example, it costs about $1 to execute a transaction at a bank, such as shifting money from one account to another; over the Internet the same transaction costs about $0.01.

In sum, managers at all levels have important roles to play in developing functional strategies to improve the way a company's value chain operates to boost efficiency. Top management's role is to encourage efficiency improvements by, for example, emphasizing the need for continuous improvement or reengineering. Top management also must ensure that managers from different functions work together to find ways to increase efficiency. However, while top managers might recognize the need for such actions, functional-level managers are in the best position to identify opportunities for making efficiency-enhancing improvements to an organization's operating system. They are the managers who are involved in an organization's operating system on a day-to-day basis. Improving efficiency, like quality, is an ongoing, never-ending process.

Value-Chain Management: Some Remaining Issues

Achieving improved quality, efficiency, and responsiveness to customers often requires a profound change in the way managers perform the four functions of management and in a company's operating system. The ways managers plan, lead, control, and organize work activities all change as a company searches for ways to increase its competitive advantage. For example, planning often involves managers at all levels, and customers are brought into the planning process. The use of self-managed teams and empowered workers changes the way managers lead and organize employees, and employees become responsible for controlling many more dimensions of their work activities.

Obtaining the information necessary to improve the value chain becomes an important and never-ending task for functional managers. It is their job to collect relevant information about the competitive environment, such as (1) the future intentions of competitors, (2) the identity of new customers for the organization's products, and (3) the identity of new suppliers of crucial or low-cost inputs. They also need to seek out new ways to use resources more efficiently to hold down costs or to get close to customers and learn what they want.

Two issues that arise from the constant need to improve a company's operating system are, first, the need to use boundary-spanning roles to obtain valuable functional information and, second, the need to consider the ethical implications of adopting advanced value-chain management techniques.

Boundary-Spanning Roles

The ability of functional managers to gain access to the information they need to improve value-chain management is critical. The history of business is littered with numerous once-great companies whose managers did not recognize, and adapt their value chains to respond to, significant changes taking place in the competitive environment. Examples include Digital Equipment, a former leading computer maker now defunct because its CEO believed that "personal computers are just toys," and Eastern Airlines and Pan-Am, which were unable to survive because of their high operating costs in a competitive airline industry. History is also marked by companies whose managers made the wrong value-chain choices because they misinterpreted the competitive environment. Examples include Motorola managers who invested more than $3 billion in the Iridium satellite project that was abandoned in 2000 and the managers of the thousands of dot-coms, like Webvan (discussed earlier), who failed to understand the competitive dynamics of the online marketplace and underestimated the problems associated with delivering online products and services reliably to customers.

boundary spanning Interacting with individuals and groups outside the organization to obtain valuable information from the environment.

Managers can learn to perceive, interpret, and appreciate better the competitive environments by practicing **boundary spanning**–interacting with individuals and groups outside the organization to obtain valuable information from the environment.[38] Managers who engage in boundary-spanning activities seek ways not only to respond to forces in the environment but also to *directly influence and manage* the perceptions of suppliers and customers in that environment to increase their organizations' access to resources.

To understand how boundary spanning works, see Figure 9.7 (page 322). A functional manager in a boundary-spanning role in organization X establishes a personal or virtual link with a manager in a boundary-spanning role in organization Y.

Figure 9.7
The Nature of Boundary-Spanning Roles

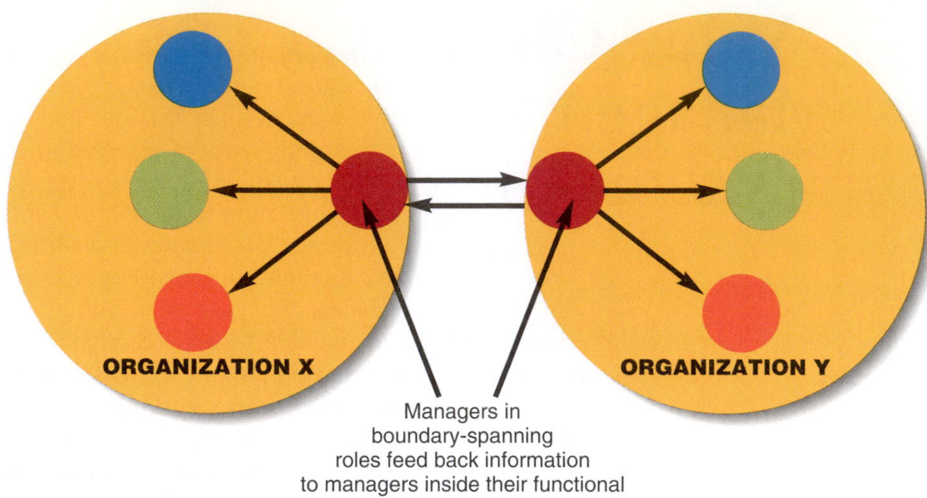
ORGANIZATION X
ORGANIZATION Y
Managers in boundary-spanning roles feed back information to managers inside their functional areas and organizations

The two managers communicate and share information that helps both of them understand the changing forces and conditions in the environment. These managers then share this information with other functional managers in their respective organizations so that all managers become better informed about events outside their own organization's boundaries. As a result, the managers in both organizations can make value-chain decisions that lead to a higher-performing operating system.

For an example of a manager performing a boundary-spanning role, consider the situation of a purchasing manager for Taco Bell. The purchasing manager is charged with finding the lowest-cost supplier of low-fat cheese and sour cream. To perform this task, the manager could write to major food companies and ask for price quotes. Or the manager could phone food company managers personally, develop an informal yet professional relationship with them, and, over time, learn from them which food companies are active in the low-fat food area and what they envision for the future. By developing such a relationship, the purchasing manager will be able to provide Taco Bell with valuable information that will allow Taco Bell's purchasing department to make well-informed choices. This flow of information from the environment may, in turn, allow marketing to develop more effective sales campaigns or product development to develop better-looking and better-tasting tacos. Note that personal communication is often necessary to supplement the information provided by IT.

What would happen if managers in *all* of an organization's functions performed boundary-spanning roles? The richness of the information available to managers throughout the organization probably would lead to an increase in the quality of managers' decision making and planning, enabling them to produce goods and services that customers prefer or to create advertising campaigns that attract new customers.

Searching for and collecting information to understand how changing trends and forces in the environment are affecting a company's operating system is an important boundary-spanning activity. Many organizations employ functional experts whose only job is to scan professional journals, trade association publications, and newspapers to identify changes in technology, government regulations, fashion trends, and so on, that will affect the way their organization operates. However, merely collecting information is not enough for the boundary-spanning manager. He or she must interpret what the information means and then practice **gatekeeping,** deciding what information to allow into the organization and what information to keep out. The nature of the information that the gatekeeper chooses to pass on to other managers will influence the decisions they make. Thus, accurate information processing is vital, and utilizing information technology can obviously help here.[39]

gatekeeping Deciding what information to allow into the organization and what information to keep out.

MANAGERS AS AGENTS OF CHANGE Note that although many of the outside forces affecting a company's value chain are independent of a particular organization (for example, basic advances in biotechnology or microprocessors), the actions managers of a particular organization take to change their company's operating system can have a significant effect on competition in their industry.[40] Many times, the choices functional managers make about which products to produce, and even about how to compete with other organizations, affect all companies in an industry. A good example of how the decisions of functional managers (or, in this case, of just one manager) can result in profound changes in the competitive environment is discussed in the following "Manager as a Person."

Manager as a Person

IBM's Bill Lowe Changes the Rules of the Game

In the mid-1980s IBM's Bill Lowe drafted a proposal for which repercussions were felt industrywide. In it he called for IBM to adopt an open-system architecture for its new PC—a departure from the company's normal practice of producing key components and software in-house so other companies could not buy them.

In 1980 Bill Lowe was a manager at IBM's entry systems division in Boca Raton, Florida. Lowe had watched the growth of the personal computer industry–dominated by Apple, Atari, and Radio Shack–with growing interest and apprehension. He believed that IBM, the dominant force in the mainframe computer industry, should also be a leading player in the fast-growing PC segment. Thus, in mid-1980, acting on his own initiative, he assembled a team of managers to draft a proposal describing how IBM could build a viable personal computer within a year.

Lowe's plan called for IBM to adopt an open-system architecture for the new personal computer. This meant that Lowe proposed a departure from the company's normal practice of producing key components and software in-house so that other companies could not buy them. He recommended that IBM buy components "off the shelf" from other producers. The key components that Lowe proposed to buy included Intel's 8088 microprocessor and a software operating system known as MS-DOS from Microsoft, then a little-known Seattle company. The advantage of this approach was that it would enable IBM to get a personal computer to the market quickly. The disadvantage was that it would allow other companies to produce IBM-compatible PCs by simply buying the same Intel microprocessor and MS-DOS operating system. Such a strategy represented a radical departure for IBM, which in the past had tried to stop imitation of its products by producing all key components in-house.[41]

Lowe's team submitted the plan to IBM's powerful corporate management committee, and in August 1980 received the authorization to go ahead. Just over a year later the first IBM PC was introduced into the marketplace. It was an overnight sensation and quickly grabbed the market lead from Apple. More important, however, Lowe's decision to go with an open-system architecture enabled a flood of imitators to enter the market.

Within two years, the imitators were producing PCs that were compatible with the IBM standard. The first of these imitators was Compaq Computer. Compaq was soon followed by a myriad of other companies, including current industry stars such as Dell and Gateway. The result was the creation of today's highly competitive PC industry, an industry that IBM is no longer a part of–it exited in 2000 after experiencing huge losses. Thus, Lowe's fateful decision to adopt open-system architecture forever changed competition in the personal computer industry.

Despite the performance-enhancing advantages of value-chain management, many reports have appeared in the popular press about widespread disillusionment with techniques such as TQM, JIT, flexible manufacturing, and reengineering. It is possible that many of the disillusioned organizations are those that failed to understand that implementing these value-chain techniques requires a marked shift in organizational culture–in the way managers think and act.[42] None of these techniques is a panacea that can be taken once, like a pill, to cure industrial ills. Making these techniques work within an organization can pose a significant challenge that calls for hard work and years of persistence by the sponsoring managers. Changing the way an organization works is a difficult and demanding task, as we discuss in detail in Chapter 11.

Ethical Implications

Managers also need to understand the ethical implications of the adoption of many of the value-chain management techniques discussed in this chapter. Although TQM, JIT, flexible manufacturing, and reengineering can all increase quality, efficiency, and responsiveness to customers, they may do so at great cost to employees. Employees may see the demands of their jobs increase as the result of TQM or, worse, may see themselves reengineered out of a job. For example, Toyota is the most efficient car manufacturer in the world, but some of its gains have been achieved at a significant cost to its employees, as discussed in the following "Ethics in Action."

Ethics in Action

The Human Cost of Improving Productivity

Hisashi Tomiki is the leader of a four-man self-managed team in a Toyota production plant, 200 miles south of Tokyo, Japan. Tomiki and his team work at a grueling pace to build cowls (steel chambers onto which windshields and steering columns are attached). Consider this description of Tomiki at work:

> *In two minutes Tomiki fits 24 metal pieces into designated slots on three welding machines; runs two large metal sheets through each of the machines, which weld on the parts; and fuses the two sheets together with two spot welds. There is little room for error. Once or twice an hour a mistake is made or a machine sticks, causing the next machine in line to stop. A yellow light flashes. Tomiki runs over. The squad must fix the part and work faster to catch up. A red button halts the production line if the problems are severe, but there is an unspoken rule against pushing it. Only once this day does Tomiki call in a special maintenance worker.*[43]

The experience of workers like Tomiki has become increasingly common–especially in the 2000s when the threat of outsourcing has led workers to accept management demands for a faster work pace. Workers are heard to complain that constant attempts to increase quality and reduce costs really means continuous speedup and added job stress from the increase in the pressure put on employees to perform. Although some pressure is good, beyond a certain point it can seriously harm employees. Moreover, consider the following quote from Jerry Miller, a former employee of US West, whose team of billing clerks reengineered themselves out of a job:

> *When we first formed our teams, the company came in talking teams and empowerment and promised that we wouldn't lose any jobs. It turns out all this was a big cover. The company had us all set up for reengineering. We showed them how to streamline the work, and now 9,000 people are gone. It was cut-your-own-throat. It makes you feel used.*[44]

Is it ethical to continually increase the demands placed on employees, regardless of the human cost in terms of job stress? It is obvious that the answer is no. Employee support is vital if the organization is to function effectively. What kinds of work pressures are legitimate, and what pressures are excessive? There is no clear answer to this question. Ultimately the issue comes down to the judgment of responsible managers seeking to act ethically.

Summary and Review

VALUE-CHAIN MANAGEMENT AND COMPETITIVE ADVANTAGE To achieve high performance, managers try to improve their responsiveness to customers, the quality of their products, and the efficiency of their organization. To achieve these goals, managers can use a number of value-chain management techniques to improve the way an organization's operating system operates.

IMPROVING RESPONSIVENESS TO CUSTOMERS To achieve high performance in a competitive environment, it is imperative that the operating system of an organization respond to customer demands. Managers try to design operating systems that produce outputs that have the attributes customers desire. One of the central tasks of value-chain management is to develop new and improved operating systems that enhance the ability of the organization to economically deliver more of the product attributes that customers desire for the same price. Techniques such as TQM, JIT, flexible manufacturing, and process reengineering are popular because they promise to do this. Managers should carefully analyze the links between responsiveness to customers and the operating system of an organization. The ability of an organization to satisfy the demands of its customers for lower prices, acceptable quality, better features, and so on, depends critically on the nature of the organization's operating system. As important as responsiveness to customers is, however, managers need to recognize that there are limits to how responsive an organization can be and still cover its costs.

IMPROVING QUALITY Managers seek to improve the quality of their organization's output because doing so enables them to better serve customers, to raise prices, and to lower production costs. Total quality management focuses on improving the quality of an organization's products and services and stresses that all of an organization's operations should be directed toward this goal. Putting TQM into practice requires having an organizationwide commitment to TQM, having a strong customer focus, finding ways to measure quality, setting quality improvement goals, soliciting input from employees about how to improve product quality, identifying defects and tracing them to their source, introducing just-in-time inventory systems, getting suppliers to adopt TQM practices, designing products for ease of manufacture, and breaking down barriers between functional departments.

IMPROVING EFFICIENCY Improving efficiency requires one or more of the following: the introduction of a TQM program, the adoption of flexible manufacturing technologies, the introduction of just-in-time inventory systems, the establishment of self-managed work teams, and the application of process reengineering. Top management is responsible for setting the context within which efficiency improvements can take place by, for example, emphasizing the need for continuous improvement. Functional-level managers bear prime responsibility for identifying and implementing efficiency-enhancing improvements in operating systems.

Management in Action

Topics for Discussion and Action

Discussion

1. What are the main challenges to be overcome in implementing a successful total quality management program?
2. Widespread dissatisfaction with the results of TQM programs has been reported in the popular press. Why do you think TQM programs frequently fail to deliver their promised benefits?
3. What is efficiency, and what are some of the techniques that managers can use to increase it?
4. Why is it important for managers to pay close attention to their organization's operating system if they wish to be responsive to their customers?
5. "Total customer service is the goal toward which most organizations should strive." To what degree is this statement correct?

Action

6. Ask a manager how quality, efficiency, and responsiveness to customers are defined and measured in his or her organization.
7. Go into a local store, restaurant, or supermarket and list the ways in which you think the organization is being responsive or unresponsive to the needs of its customers. How could this business's responsiveness to customers be improved?

Building Management Skills

Managing an Operating System

Choose an organization with which you are familiar—one that you have worked in or patronized or one that has received extensive coverage in the popular press. The organization should be involved in only one industry or business. Answer these questions about the organization:

1. What is the output of the organization?
2. Describe the operating system that the organization uses to produce this output.
3. What product attributes do customers of the organization desire?
4. Does its operating system allow the organization to deliver the desired product attributes?
5. Try to identify improvements that might be made to the organization's operating system to boost the organization's responsiveness to customers, quality, and efficiency.

Managing Ethically

Go back and review the "Ethics in Action" on the human costs of Toyota's production system. After implementing efficiency-improving techniques, many companies commonly lay off employees who are no longer needed. And, frequently, remaining employees must perform more tasks more quickly, a situation that can generate employee stress and other work-related problems.

Questions

1. Either by yourself or in a group think through the ethical implications of using some new functional strategy to improve organizational performance.
2. What criteria would you use to decide what kind of strategy is ethical to adopt and/or how far to push employees to raise the level of their performance?
3. How big a layoff, if any, is acceptable? If layoffs are acceptable, what could be done to reduce their harm to employees?

Small Group Breakout Exercise

How to Compete in the Sandwich Business

Form groups of three or four people, and appoint one member as the spokesperson who will communicate your findings to the whole class when called on by the instructor. Then discuss the following scenario.

You and your partners are thinking about opening a new kind of sandwich shop that will compete head-to-head with Subway and Thundercloud Subs. Because these chains have good brand-name recognition, it is vital that you find some source of competitive advantage for your new sandwich shop, and you are meeting to brainstorm ways of obtaining one.

1. Identify the product attributes that a typical sandwich shop customer wants the most.
2. In what ways do you think you will be able to improve on the operations and processes of existing sandwich shops and achieve a competitive advantage through better (a) product quality, (b) efficiency, or (c) responsiveness to customers?

Exploring the World Wide Web

Go to GM's Web site by typing the following address: (www.gm.com/automotive/gmpowertrain/news/press7.htm#). The page discusses TQM at GM's Livonia engine plant.

Read the press release; then go back to the principles of TQM discussed in this chapter. How has GM used TQM to attain superior quality and efficiency at its Livonia plant?

Be the Manager

How to Build Flat-Panel Displays

You are the top manager of a start-up company that will produce flat-screen displays for personal computer manufacturers like Dell and Compaq. The flat-screen-display market is highly competitive, so there is considerable pressure to reduce costs because prices fall rapidly due to competition. Also, personal computer makers are demanding ever-higher quality and better features to please customers. In addition, they demand that delivery of your product meets their production schedule needs. Functional managers want your advice on how to best meet these requirements, especially as they are in the process of recruiting new workers and building a production facility.

Questions

1. What kinds of techniques discussed in the chapter can help your functional managers to increase efficiency?
2. In what ways can they go about developing a program to increase quality?
3. What critical lessons do these managers need to learn about value-chain management?

Build Your Management Skills DVD

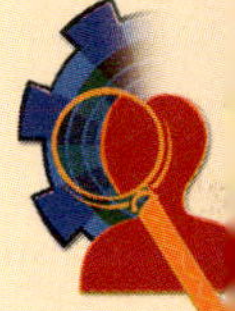

- **Test Your Knowledge:** (a) Project Planning and (b) Facilities Layout
- **Manager's Hot Seat:** Virtual Workplace: Out of Office Reply

BusinessWeek Case in the News

Big Brown's New Bag

For years, the bane of most Ford dealers was the auto maker's Rube Goldberg-like system of getting cars from factory to showroom. Cars could take as long as a month to arrive—that is, when they weren't lost along the way. And Ford Motor Co. was not always able to tell its dealers exactly what was coming, or even what was in inventory at the nearest rail yards. "We'd lose track of whole trainloads of cars," recalls Jerry Reynolds, owner of Prestige Ford in Garland, Texas. "It was crazy."

But three years ago, Ford handed its byzantine distribution network to an unlikely source for an overhaul: United Parcel Service Inc. In a joint venture with the carmaker, UPS engineers, with input from Reynolds and other dealers, redesigned Ford's entire North American delivery network, streamlining everything from the route cars take from the factory to how they're processed at regional sorting hubs. Ultimately, UPS deployed a tracking system similar to the one it uses to monitor 13.8 million packages daily—right down to slapping bar codes on the windshields of the 4 million cars rolling out of Ford's 19 North American plants each year and onto railcars.

The result: UPS has cut the time it takes autos to arrive at dealer lots by 40 percent, to 10 days on average. That saves Ford millions in working capital each year and makes it easy for its 6,500 dealers to track down the models most in demand. (General Motors Corp., by contrast, uses a proprietary online system for distribution; Chrysler Corp. contracts with Union Pacific Corp.) "It was the most amazing transformation I had ever seen," marvels Reynolds. "My last comment to UPS was: 'Can you get us spare parts like this?'"

Welcome to the new UPS. Ever since its humble beginnings in 1907 as a Seattle messenger service, the real story about UPS is how this traditionally insular and conservative enterprise has managed to reinvent itself time and again to keep growing. No matter how fearful the next step might have seemed, UPS took it. Back when the telephone became a household staple, founder James E. Casey remade his messenger service into a home delivery business for retailers. When Americans began buying cars and driving their purchases home, UPS reinvented itself again, fighting scores of legal battles so that its fleet could compete with the U.S. Postal Service.

Those moves have helped make UPS into the colossus it is today.

Last year, Big Brown earned $2.9 billion on $33.5 billion in revenues. And its stock, at about $74, has outperformed the market since the company went public in November 1999. Since then, UPS shares have generated total shareholder returns of 21 percent, compared with a negative 12 percent return for the Standard & Poor's 500-stock index.

Fast-Flowing Stream

To keep the momentum, UPS is undergoing its latest makeover. With its U.S. delivery business maturing, the company has been working feverishly to transform itself into a logistics expert. Last year, that end of the business accounted for $2.1 billion in revenues, or just 6 percent of the UPS total. But analysts believe logistics could provide a potentially huge new revenue stream—up to 20 percent of future growth by some estimates. Simply put, UPS wants to leverage decades of experience managing its own global delivery network to serve as the traffic manager for Corporate America's sprawling distribution networks—doing everything from scheduling the planes, trains, and ships on which goods move to owning and managing companies' distribution centers and warehouses. Just as important, says UPS, is that its strategy should also generate additional delivery business for its ubiquitous brown trucks and private air fleet. The pitch to customers: Let us manage the supply chain, while you focus on core marketing and product development. That way, says CEO Michael L. Eskew, 55, UPS can help companies "improve their cash flow, their customer service, and their productivity."

Consider its deal with Birkenstock Footprint Sandals Inc. UPS contracts with ocean carriers to get shoes made in Germany across the Atlantic to New Jersey ports, instead of routing them through the Panama Canal to the shoemaker's California warehouses. Each incoming shipment is whisked away to a UPS distribution hub and within hours, to retailers. By handing over its keys to UPS, Birkenstock has cut the time it takes to get shoes to stores by half, to just three weeks. "Our spring fashion merchandise shipped 100 percent on time—and it was the first time in history I've been able to say that," says Birkenstock's chief operating officer, Gene Kunde.

Questions

1. How can UPS help a company increase quality, efficiency, and responsiveness to customers?
2. What are UPS's core functional strengths?

Source: Dean Foust, "Big Brown's New Bag." Reprinted from the July 19, 2004, issue of *BusinessWeek* by special permission.

BusinessWeek Case in the News

Why 3M Feels Right at Home in China

American businesses have been tripping over themselves, and each other, to strengthen their hold on the Chinese market. But not 3M. The Minnesota manufacturer has already been there for two decades. With a sales office in Shanghai, 3M in 1984 became the first U.S. corporation to establish a wholly owned subsidiary in China. Its first products: sandpaper, electrical tape, and Scotch-Brite kitchen scrubbers.

Today, 3M is selling goods worth nearly $500 million annually in China, from industrial gear and components for consumer electronics to respiratory masks and the latest in Post-it Notes. Sales should hit $1 billion by 2007, predicts Kenneth Yu, managing director of 3M's operations in Greater China. Add in Taiwan and Hong Kong, and sales already approach $1 billion, which makes Greater China 3M's fastest-growing market. As for profits, with $1.37 billion in operating income last year, Asia already is 3M's No. 1 profit-making region, ahead of even the U.S. "Pretty eye-popping," says industry analyst Mark R. Gulley of Banc of America Securities.

Investing successfully overseas is nothing new to 3M. Although it began in the American heartland in 1902 as a sandpaper maker, 3M prides itself for going into international markets well ahead of the pack. The company started selling products outside the U.S. in 1929, and set up shop in Japan through a joint venture with NEC Corp. in 1953. Selling into more than 200 countries, 3M derived 58 percent of its 2003 revenues of $18.23 billion from foreign markets. Asia sales, at $4.33 billion in 2003, were two-and-a-half times sales in Latin America, Africa, and Canada combined, at $1.65 billion.

Of all its non-U.S. markets, though, China is clearly the most promising, say company executives and analysts. China's economy is growing at a rapid 9 percent clip, its factories fueling demand for lots of older industrial goods that have become slow sellers in the United States, such as abrasives and adhesives. Meanwhile, more and more of 3M's customers, from auto makers to consumer-electronics outfits, are flocking to China. And those customers are demanding that 3M relocate more of its operations there to stay in the supply chain. Also, China's labor costs are so low that it often makes more sense to make products there and export them, rather than produce the same goods in the United States or Europe for local consumption.

3M's own numbers confirm the company's geographic shift. Employment and capital spending are falling in the United States and Europe, while both are rising in Asia. 3M Chairman and Chief Executive W. James McNerney, Jr., concedes he has heard some grumbling about the new tilt. But he argues that he must build up operations in China to keep up with his competitors. "We follow the growth," McNerney says. "We're in a global marketplace, and being in China in an important way is important."

3M is doing more than just exploiting China's cheap labor. Although it has three manufacturing plants there, as well as 14 sales and service offices, its newest push is to expand its research and development laboratory in Shanghai. The facility now employs more than 100 people, and Jay V. Ihlenfeld, 3M's senior vice president for R&D, says he wants to triple that payroll as soon as he can. The aim is to customize products for the local market and work hand in hand with other manufacturers in China to come up with new export products.

Televisions and other consumer-electronics products figure prominently in 3M's expansion plans. 3M accounts for more than 75 percent of the world supply of the ultrathin optical films used to enhance the picture and brightness in flat-screen TVs, computer monitors, laptops, and cell phones, estimates analyst Gulley. 3M also has 75 percent of the market for lenses in rear-projection TVs, he says. As manufacturing of these products begins to migrate to China, 3M's sales should grow proportionately—and more R&D work will move to China as the company seeks to maintain its lead and fat margins. The lesson is clear: a pioneering spirit can pay off.

Questions

1. In what ways has GM's entry into China improved the way its value-chain operates?
2. How might its Chinese operations improve the performance of its U.S. car operations?

Source: Michael Arndt and Frederick Balfour, "Why 3M Feels Right at Home in China." Reprinted from the April 12, 2004, issue of *BusinessWeek* by special permission.

CHAPTER

10 Managing Organizational Structure

Learning Objectives

After studying this chapter, you should be able to:

- Identify the factors that influence managers' choice of an organizational structure.
- Explain how managers group tasks into jobs that are motivating and satisfying for employees.
- Describe the types of organizational structures managers can design, and explain why they choose one structure over another.
- Explain why there is a need to both centralize and decentralize authority.
- Explain why managers must coordinate and integrate among jobs, functions, and divisions as an organization grows.
- Explain why managers who seek new ways to increase efficiency and effectiveness are using strategic alliances and network structures.

A Manager's Challenge

Nokia, Dow, and the LEGO Company Revamp Their Global Structures to Raise Performance

How should managers organize to improve performance?

In 2004, suffering from its worst-ever annual losses, caused by a 25 percent decline in global sales, the LEGO company decided it needed to restructure its European operations.[1] Until 2004, the LEGO company had operated with three global subdivisions *inside* its European division—central, northern, and southern. Many problems had arisen with this structure: First, each subdivision was performing many of the same activities, so the duplication of activities was raising operating costs. Second, the subdivisions often did not cooperate and share information on new product developments or changes in customer needs. As a result, many opportunities were being lost, especially because this structure made it even more difficult to communicate with the LEGO company's other global divisions, such as its U.S. and Asian divisions.

Careful planning was needed in designing this LEGO structure.

The LEGO company's solution was to abolish these subdivisions and reunite them all into one European division under the control of its former top global marketer, Henrik Poulsen.[2] Poulsen reports to the LEGO company's CEO, just as do the heads of the LEGO company's other global divisions, and the company is hoping that this will lead to an increase in cooperation among its divisions around the world. The goal of the reorganization is to help the LEGO company's global divisions learn from one another and work together to develop toys that better suit the changing needs of customers throughout the world.

While the LEGO company is trying to solve its problem by combining its three European units into one, in 2004 U.S. giant Dow Chemicals decided that the best way to leverage the skills and resources of its global chemicals division was to split it into three different global product groups—the plastics, chemicals and intermediates, and performance chemicals groups.[3] Dow believes that when each group acts as a self-contained, unit this will make it easier for managers to focus on one range of chemical products that can then be delivered to customers around the world.[4] Note that, to raise performance, in Dow's case the issue was to create more product divisions, while the issue facing the LEGO company was to reduce the number of its market divisions.

Finally, Nokia, the Finnish company that is the world's leader in cellular phones, also made a change to its global structure in 2004. Nokia recognized that it had an important weakness in its product line, wireless business communications, by means of which, for example, a company can stay in touch with its workforce through some form of wireless communication such as laptops, Palm Pilots and other PDAs, or wireless phones that allow employees to share information and communicate with each other.

Since this part of the wireless market is rapidly growing, Nokia chairman Jornma Ollila decided to create a new global division to innovate wireless communication products and a new global product division, the Enterprise Solutions group. Moreover, to give the new divisions the autonomy to innovate products quickly, he set them up in New York and appointed a former HP manager, Mary McDowell, to develop an entry technology that will offer everything from server software to handsets and compete with giants like HP and IBM. Since the potential market in this area is expected to grow from $27 to $43 billion by 2007, Nokia hopes to obtain a significant share of this lucrative market to help boost its performance.[5]

Overview

As "A Manager's Challenge" suggests, the challenge facing managers in all three companies was to identify the best way to operate in new, more competitive industry environments. Managers in all three companies were forced to radically change the way they organized their employees and other resources to meet that challenge.

In Part 4 of this book, we examine how managers can organize and control human and other resources to create high-performing organizations. To organize and control (two of the four functions of management identified in Chapter 1), managers must design an organizational architecture that makes the best use of resources to produce the goods and services customers want. **Organizational architecture** is the combination of organizational structure, control systems, culture, and human resource management systems that together determine how efficiently and effectively organizational resources are used.

organizational architecture The organizational structure, control systems, culture, and human resource management systems that together determine how efficiently and effectively organizational resources are used.

By the end of this chapter, you will be familiar not only with various organizational structures but also with various factors that determine the organizational design choices that managers make. Then, in Chapters 11 and 12, we examine issues surrounding the design of an organization's control systems, culture, and human resource management systems.

Designing Organizational Structure

Organizing is the process by which managers establish the structure of working relationships among employees to allow them to achieve organizational goals efficiently and effectively. **Organizational structure** is the formal system of task and job reporting relationships that determines how employees use resources to achieve organizational

organizational structure A formal system of task and reporting relationships that coordinates and motivates organizational members so that they work together to achieve organizational goals.

organizational design The process by which managers make specific organizing choices that result in a particular kind of organizational structure.

goals.[6] **Organizational design** is the process by which managers make specific organizing choices about tasks and job relationships that result in the construction of a particular organizational structure.[7]

As noted in Chapter 2, according to *contingency theory,* managers design organizational structures to fit the factors or circumstances that are affecting the company the most and causing them the most uncertainty.[8] Thus, there is no one best way to design an organization: Design reflects each organization's specific situation, and researchers have argued that in some situations stable, mechanistic structures may be most appropriate while in others flexible, organic structures might be the most effective. Four factors are important determinants of the type of organizational structure or organizing method managers select: the nature of the organizational environment, the type of strategy the organization pursues, the technology (and particularly *information technology*) the organization uses, and the characteristics of the organization's human resources (see Figure 10.1).[9]

The Organizational Environment

In general, the more quickly the external environment is changing and the greater the uncertainty within it, the greater are the problems facing managers in trying to gain access to scarce resources. In this situation, to speed decision making and communication and make it easier to obtain resources, managers typically make organizing choices that bring flexibility to the organizational structure.[10] They are likely to decentralize authority and empower lower-level employees to make important operating decisions–a more organic structure. In contrast, if the external environment is stable, resources are readily available, and uncertainty is low, then less coordination and communication among people and functions is needed to obtain resources, and managers can make organizing choices that bring more stability or formality to the organizational structure. Managers in this situation prefer to make decisions within a clearly defined hierarchy of authority and use extensive rules and standard operating procedures to govern activities–a more mechanistic structure.

As we discussed in Chapter 6, change is rapid in today's marketplace, and increasing competition both at home and abroad is putting greater pressure on

Figure 10.1
Factors Affecting Organizational Structure

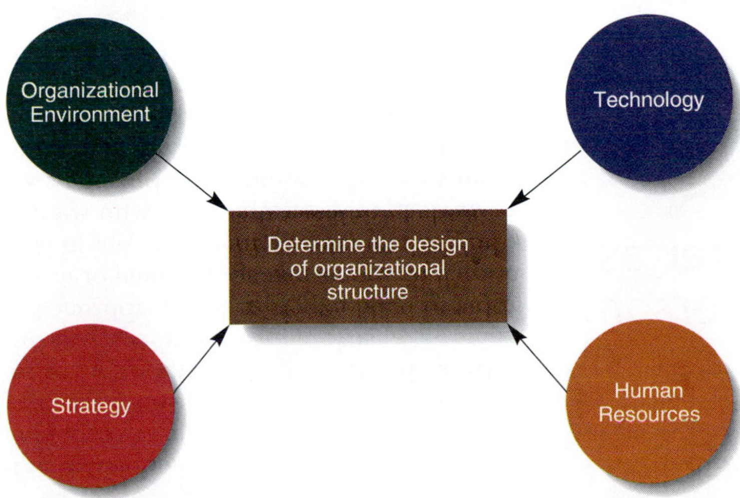

managers to attract customers and increase efficiency and effectiveness. Consequently, interest in finding ways to structure organizations–such as through empowerment and self-managed teams–to allow people and departments to behave flexibly has been increasing.

Strategy

As discussed in Chapter 8, once managers decide on a strategy, they must choose the right means of implementing it. Different strategies often call for the use of different organizational structures. For example, a differentiation strategy aimed at increasing the value customers perceive in an organization's goods and services usually succeeds best in a flexible structure; flexibility facilitates a differentiation strategy because managers can develop new or innovative products quickly–an activity that requires extensive cooperation among functions or departments. In contrast, a low-cost strategy that is aimed at driving down costs in all functions usually fares best in a more formal structure, which gives managers greater control over the expenditures and actions of the organization's various departments.[11]

In addition, at the corporate level, when managers decide to expand the scope of organizational activities by vertical integration or diversification, for example, they need to design a flexible structure to provide sufficient coordination among the different business divisions.[12] As discussed in Chapter 8, many companies have been divesting businesses because managers have been unable to create a competitive advantage to keep them up to speed in fast-changing industries. By moving to a more flexible structure, such as a product division structure, divisional managers gain more control over their different businesses. Finally, expanding internationally and operating in many different countries challenges managers to create organizational structures that allow organizations to be flexible on a global level.[13] As we discuss later, managers can group their departments or functions and divisions in several ways to allow them to effectively pursue an international strategy, as the story of eMachines and Gateway in the following "Manager as a Person" suggests.

Manager as a Person

Wayne Inouye Has to Restructure Gateway

In 2001, eMachines, a low-price computer maker whose machines sold for less than $800, was going bankrupt. The main problem? Low product quality because eMachines was organized in a way that led to inefficient manufacturing and ineffective service from its customer service reps, who seemed unable to help customers fix problems with their new computers. Wayne Inouye, a Japanese-American who was previously in charge of Best Buy's computer retailing division, was put in charge of restructuring the company to raise its performance if he could or to shut it down if he could not.

Inouye adopted a radical approach to restructuring eMachines. He decided to outsource the company's manufacturing and sales and customer service operations. Henceforth, eMachines computers would be assembled at low-cost global locations in countries like China or Malaysia, and software specialists in Bangalore, India, would handle its customer service operations. Furthermore, while eMachines used to sell most of its computers online or by advertising, Inouye decided that in the future it would sell its computers through retail partners such as Best Buy.

Gateway's board of directors was so impressed with Wayne Inouye's success in restructuring eMachines that it decided to acquire the company and hire Inouye as its new CEO.

After outsourcing all these activities, Inouye focused his company's efforts on marketing. Using an IT system that linked eMachines to its retailers, Inouye and his managers had real-time information on which computers were selling and why. With this information they then redesigned computers and sent the new computer specifications to their overseas manufacturers. In this way, the computers coming off the assembly line matched customers' current needs. The results of all these changes were astounding. By 2003 the company's sales exceeded $1 billion, and eMachines replaced Gateway to become the number-three global computer maker.

Gateway's board of directors closely monitored eMachines' performance. The success of Inouye's new strategy and structure led them to offer to buy eMachines if Inouye would become the CEO and take charge of merging its operations with Gateway. Inouye accepted. In 2004 he became the CEO of Gateway and restructured the company to raise its performance. His task was to design a new Gateway that would allow it to compete effectively against Dell, the market leader.[14]

Technology

Technology is the combination of skills, knowledge, tools, machines, computers, and equipment that are used in the design, production, and distribution of goods and services. As a rule, the more complicated the technology that an organization uses, the more difficult it is for managers and workers to impose strict control on technology or to regulate it efficiently. Thus, the more complicated the technology, the greater is the need for a flexible structure to enhance managers' ability to respond to unexpected situations and give them the freedom to work out new solutions to the problems they encounter. In contrast, the more routine the technology, the more appropriate is a formal structure, because tasks are simple and the steps needed to produce goods and services have been worked out in advance.

What makes a technology routine or complicated? One researcher who investigated this issue, Charles Perrow, argued that two factors determine how complicated or nonroutine technology is: task variety and task analyzability.[15] *Task variety* is the number of new or unexpected problems or situations that a person or function encounters in performing tasks or jobs. *Task analyzability* is the degree to which programmed solutions are available to people or functions to solve the problems they encounter. Nonroutine or complicated technologies are characterized by high task variety and low task analyzability; this means that many varied problems occur and that solving these problems requires significant nonprogrammed decision making. In contrast, routine technologies are characterized by low task variety and high task analyzability; this means that the problems encountered do not vary much and are easily resolved through programmed decision making.

Examples of nonroutine technology are found in the work of scientists in a research and development laboratory who develop new products or discover new drugs or are seen in the planning exercises an organization's top-management team uses to chart the organization's future strategy. Examples of routine technology include typical mass-production or assembly operations, where workers perform the same task repeatedly and where managers have already identified the programmed solutions necessary to perform a task efficiently. Similarly, in service organizations such as fast-food restaurants, the tasks that crew members perform in making and serving fast food are very routine.

The extent to which the process of actually producing or creating goods and services depends on people or machines is another factor that determines how nonroutine a technology is. The more the technology used to produce goods and services is based on the skills, knowledge, and abilities of people working together on an ongoing basis and not on automated machines that can be programmed in advance, the more complex the technology is. Joan Woodward, a professor who investigated the relationship between technology and organizational structure, differentiated among three kinds of technology on the basis of the relative contribution made by people or machines.[16]

small-batch technology Technology that is used to produce small quantities of customized, one-of-a-kind products and is based on the skills of people who work together in small groups.

Small-batch technology is used to produce small quantities of customized, one-of-a-kind products and is based on the skills of people who work together in small groups. Examples of goods and services produced by small-batch technology include custom-built cars, such as Ferraris and Rolls Royces, highly specialized metals and chemicals that are produced by the pound rather than by the ton, and the process of auditing in which a small team of auditors is sent to a company to evaluate and report on its accounts. Because small-batch goods or services are customized and unique, workers need to respond to each situation as required; thus, a structure that decentralizes authority to employees and allows them to respond flexibly is most appropriate with small-batch technology.

mass-production technology Technology that is based on the use of automated machines that are programmed to perform the same operations over and over.

Woodward's second kind of technology, **mass-production technology,** is based primarily on the use of automated machines that are programmed to perform the same operations time and time again. Mass production works most efficiently when each person performs a repetitive task. There is less need for flexibility, and a formal organizational structure is the preferred choice because it gives managers the most control over the production process. Mass production results in an output of large quantities of standardized products such as tin cans, Ford Tauruses, washing machines, and light bulbs, or even services such as a car wash or dry cleaning.

continuous-process technology Technology that is almost totally mechanized and is based on the use of automated machines working in sequence and controlled through computers from a central monitoring station.

The third kind of technology that Woodward identified, **continuous-process technology,** is almost totally mechanized. Products are produced by automated machines working in sequence and controlled through computers from a central monitoring station. Examples of continuous-process technology include large steel mills, oil refineries, nuclear power stations, and large-scale brewing operations. The role of workers in continuous-process technology is to watch for problems that may occur unexpectedly and cause dangerous or even deadly situations. The possibility of a machinery or computer breakdown, for example, is a major source of uncertainty associated with this technology. If an unexpected situation does occur, employees must be able to respond quickly and appropriately to prevent a disaster from resulting (such as an explosion in a chemical complex). The need for a flexible response makes a flexible organizational structure the preferred choice with this kind of technology.

INFORMATION TECHNOLOGY As we have seen in previous chapters, new information technologies are having profound effects on the way an organization operates. At the level of organizational structure, IT is changing methods of organizing. IT-enabled organizational structure allows for new kinds of tasks and job reporting relationships among electronically connected people that promote superior communication and coordination. For example, one type of IT-enabled organizational relationship is **knowledge management,** the sharing and integrating of expertise within and between functions and divisions through real-time, interconnected IT.[17] Some benefits from these arrangements include the development of synergies that may result in competitive advantage in the form of product or service differentiation–something Lego, Dow, and Nokia were seeking to achieve. Unlike the case with more rigid, bureaucratic organizing methods, new IT-enabled organizations can respond more quickly to changing environmental conditions such as increased global competition.

knowledge management The sharing and integrating of expertise within and between functions and divisions through real-time, interconnected IT.

The nature of an organization's technology is an important determinant of its structure. Today, many companies are trying to use IT in innovative ways to make their structures more flexible and to take advantage of the value-creating benefits of complex technology. Many of the ways in which IT affects organizing are discussed in this and later chapters.

Highly skilled employees, such as this nurse, have internalized strong professional values and norms of behavior through their education and training. Such employees usually desire freedom and autonomy and dislike close supervision. Flexible structures, characterized by decentralized authority and empowered employees, are well suited to the needs of highly skilled people.

Human Resources

A final important factor affecting an organization's choice of structure is the characteristics of the human resources it employs. In general, the more highly skilled an organization's workforce is and the more people are required to work together in groups or teams to perform their tasks, the more likely an organization is to use a flexible, decentralized structure. Highly skilled employees or employees who have internalized strong professional values and norms of behavior as part of their training usually desire freedom and autonomy and dislike close supervision. Accountants, for example, have learned the need to report company accounts honestly and impartially, and doctors and nurses have absorbed the obligation to give patients the best care possible.

Flexible structures, characterized by decentralized authority and empowered employees, are well suited to the needs of highly skilled people. Similarly, when people work in teams, they must be allowed to interact freely, which also is possible in a flexible organizational structure. Thus, when designing an organizational structure, managers must pay close attention to the workforce and to the work itself.

In summary, an organization's external environment, strategy, technology, and human resources are the factors to be considered by managers in seeking to design the best structure for an organization. The greater the level of uncertainty in the organization's environment, the more complex its strategy and technologies, and the more highly qualified and skilled its workforce, the more likely managers are to design a structure that is flexible and that can change quickly. The more stable the organization's environment, the less complex and more well understood its strategy or technology, and the less skilled its workforce, the more likely managers are to design an organizational structure that is formal and controlling.

How do managers design a structure to be either flexible or formal? The way an organization's structure works depends on the organizing choices managers make about four issues:

- How to group tasks into individual jobs.
- How to group jobs into functions and divisions.
- How to allocate authority in the organization among jobs, functions, and divisions.
- How to coordinate or integrate among jobs, functions, and divisions.

Grouping Tasks into Jobs: Job Design

job design The process by which managers decide how to divide tasks into specific jobs.

The first step in organizational design is **job design,** the process by which managers decide how to divide into specific jobs the tasks that have to be performed to provide customers with goods and services. Managers at McDonald's, for example, have decided how best to divide the tasks required to provide customers with fast, cheap food in each McDonald's restaurant. After experimenting with different job arrangements, McDonald's managers decided on a basic division of labor among chefs and food servers. Managers allocated all the tasks involved in actually cooking the food (putting oil in the fat fryers, opening packages of frozen french fries, putting beef patties on the grill, making salads, and so on) to the job of chef. They allocated all the tasks involved in giving the food to customers (such as greeting customers, taking orders, putting fries and burgers into bags, adding salt, pepper, and napkins, and taking money) to food servers. In addition, they created other jobs–the job of dealing with drive-in customers, the job of keeping the restaurant clean, and the job of overseeing employees and responding to unexpected events. The result of the job design process is a *division of labor* among employees, one that McDonald's managers have discovered through experience is most efficient.

Establishing an appropriate division of labor among employees is a critical part of the organizing process, one that is vital to increasing efficiency and effectiveness. At McDonald's, the tasks associated with chef and food server were split into different jobs because managers found that, for the kind of food McDonald's serves, this approach was most efficient. It is efficient because when each employee is given fewer tasks to perform (so that each job becomes more specialized), employees become more productive at performing the tasks that constitute each job.

At Subway sandwich shops, however, managers chose a different kind of job design. At Subway, there is no division of labor among the people who make the sandwiches, wrap the sandwiches, give them to customers, and take the money. The roles of chef and food server are combined into one. This different division of tasks and jobs is efficient for Subway and not for McDonald's because Subway serves a limited menu of mostly submarine-style sandwiches that are prepared to order. Subway's production system is far simpler than McDonald's, because McDonald's menu is much more varied and its chefs must cook many different kinds of foods.

Managers of every organization must analyze the range of tasks to be performed and then create jobs that best allow the organization to give customers

At Subway, the role of chef and server is combined into one, making the job "larger" than the jobs of McDonald's more specialized food servers. The idea behind job enlargement is that increasing the range of tasks performed by the worker will reduce boredom and fatigue. Would you prefer a "larger" job?

the goods and services they want. In deciding how to assign tasks to individual jobs, however, managers must be careful not to take **job simplification,** the process of reducing the number of tasks that each worker performs, too far.[18] Too much job simplification may reduce efficiency rather than increase it if workers find their simplified jobs boring and monotonous, become demotivated and unhappy, and, as a result, perform at a low level.

job simplification The process of reducing the number of tasks that each worker performs.

job enlargement Increasing the number of different tasks in a given job by changing the division of labor.

job enrichment Increasing the degree of responsibility a worker has over his or her job.

Job Enlargement and Job Enrichment

In an attempt to create a division of labor and design individual jobs to encourage workers to perform at a higher level and be more satisfied with their work, several researchers have proposed ways other than job simplification to group tasks into jobs: job enlargement and job enrichment.

Job enlargement is increasing the number of different tasks in a given job by changing the division of labor.[19] For example, because Subway food servers make the food as well as serve it, their jobs are "larger" than the jobs of McDonald's food servers. The idea behind job enlargement is that increasing the range of tasks performed by a worker will reduce boredom and fatigue and may increase motivation to perform at a high level–increasing both the quantity and the quality of goods and services provided.

Job enrichment is increasing the degree of responsibility a worker has over a job by, for example, (1) empowering workers to experiment to find new or better ways of doing the job, (2) encouraging workers to develop new skills, (3) allowing workers to decide how to do the work and giving them the responsibility for deciding how to respond to unexpected situations, and (4) allowing workers to monitor and measure their own performance.[20] The idea behind job enrichment is that increasing workers' responsibility increases their involvement in their jobs and thus increases their interest in the quality of the goods they make or the services they provide.

In general, managers who make design choices that increase job enrichment and job enlargement are likely to increase the degree to which people behave flexibly rather than rigidly or mechanically. Narrow, specialized jobs are likely to lead people to behave in predictable ways; workers who perform a variety of tasks and who are allowed and encouraged to discover new and better ways to perform their jobs are likely to act flexibly and creatively. Thus, managers who enlarge and enrich jobs create a flexible organizational structure, and those who simplify jobs create a more formal structure. If workers are grouped into self-managed work teams, the organization is likely to be flexible because team members provide support for each other and can learn from one another.

The Job Characteristics Model

J. R. Hackman and G. R. Oldham's job characteristics model is an influential model of job design that explains in detail how managers can make jobs more interesting and motivating.[21] Hackman and Oldham's model (see Figure 10.2)

Figure 10.2
The Job Characteristics Model

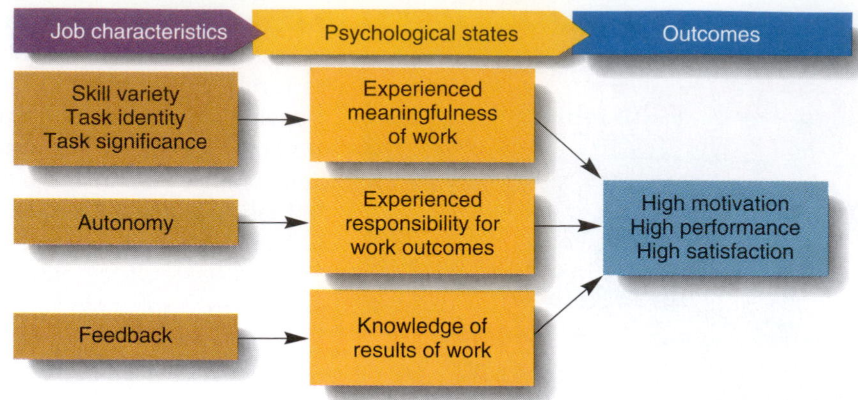

Source: Adapted from J. R. Hackman and G. R. Oldham, *Work Redesign* (Reading, MA: Addison-Wesley, 1980).

also describes the likely personal and organizational outcomes that will result from enriched and enlarged jobs.

According to Hackman and Oldham, every job has five characteristics that determine how motivating the job is. These characteristics determine how employees react to their work and lead to outcomes such as high performance and satisfaction and low absenteeism and turnover:

- *Skill variety*–the extent to which a job requires that an employee use a wide range of different skills, abilities, or knowledge. Example: The skill variety required by the job of a research scientist is higher than that called for by the job of a McDonald's food server.
- *Task identity*–the extent to which a job requires that a worker perform all the tasks necessary to complete the job from the beginning to the end of the production process. Example: A craftsworker who takes a piece of wood and transforms it into a custom-made piece of furniture such as a desk has higher task identity than does a worker who performs only one of the numerous operations required to assemble a television.
- *Task significance*–the degree to which a worker feels his or her job is meaningful because of its affect on people inside the organization such as coworkers or on people outside the organization such as customers. Example: A teacher who sees the effect of his or her efforts in a well-educated and well-adjusted student enjoys high task significance compared to a dishwasher who monotonously washes dishes as they come to the kitchen.
- *Autonomy*–the degree to which a job gives an employee the freedom and discretion needed to schedule different tasks and decide how to carry them out. Example: Salespeople who have to plan their schedules and decide how to allocate their time among different customers have relatively high autonomy compared to assembly-line workers whose actions are determined by the speed of the production line.
- *Feedback*–the extent to which actually doing a job provides a worker with clear and direct information about how well he or she has performed the job. Example: An air traffic controller whose mistakes may result in a midair collision receives immediate feedback on job performance; a person who compiles statistics for a business magazine often has little idea of when he or she makes a mistake or does a particularly good job.

Hackman and Oldham argue that these five job characteristics affect an employee's motivation because they affect three critical psychological states (see Figure 10.2). The more employees feel that their work is *meaningful* and that they are *responsible for work outcomes and responsible for knowing how those outcomes affect others,* the more motivating work becomes and the more likely employees are to be satisfied and to perform at a high level. Moreover, employees who have jobs that are highly motivating are called on to use their skills more and to perform more tasks, and they are given more responsibility for doing the job. All of the foregoing are characteristic of jobs and employees in flexible structures where authority is decentralized and where employees commonly work with others and must learn new skills to complete the range of tasks for which their group is responsible.

Grouping Jobs into Functions and Divisions

Once managers have decided which tasks to allocate to which jobs, they face the next organizing decision: how to group jobs together to best match the needs of the organization's environment, strategy, technology, and human resources. Most top-management teams decide to group jobs into departments and develop a functional structure to use organizational resources. As the organization grows, managers design a divisional structure or a more complex matrix or product team structure.

Choosing a structure and then designing it so that it works as intended is a significant challenge. As noted in Chapter 7, managers reap the rewards of a well-thought-out strategy only if they choose the right type of structure to implement and execute the strategy. The ability to make the right kinds of organizing choices is often what differentiates effective from ineffective managers.

Functional Structure

functional structure
An organizational structure composed of all the departments that an organization requires to produce its goods or services.

A *function* is a group of people, working together, who possess similar skills or use the same kind of knowledge, tools, or techniques to perform their jobs. Manufacturing, sales, and research and development are often organized into functional departments. A **functional structure** is an organizational structure composed of all the departments that an organization requires to produce its goods or services. Figure 10.3 (page 344) shows the functional structure that Pier 1 Imports, the home furnishings company, uses to supply its customers with a range of goods from around the world to satisfy their desires for new and innovative products.

Pier 1's main functions are finance and administration, merchandising (purchasing the goods), stores (managing the retail outlets), logistics (managing product distribution), marketing, human resources, and real estate. Each job inside a function exists because it helps the function perform the activities necessary for high organizational performance. Thus, within the logistics department are all the jobs necessary to efficiently distribute and transport products to stores, and inside the marketing department are all the jobs (such as promotion, photography, and visual communication) that are necessary to increase the appeal of Pier 1's products to customers.

There are several advantages to grouping jobs according to function. First, when people who perform similar jobs are grouped together, they can learn from observing one another and thus become more specialized and can perform at a higher level. The tasks associated with one job often are related to the tasks associated with another job, which encourages cooperation within a function. In Pier 1's

Figure 10.3
The Functional Structure of Pier 1 Imports

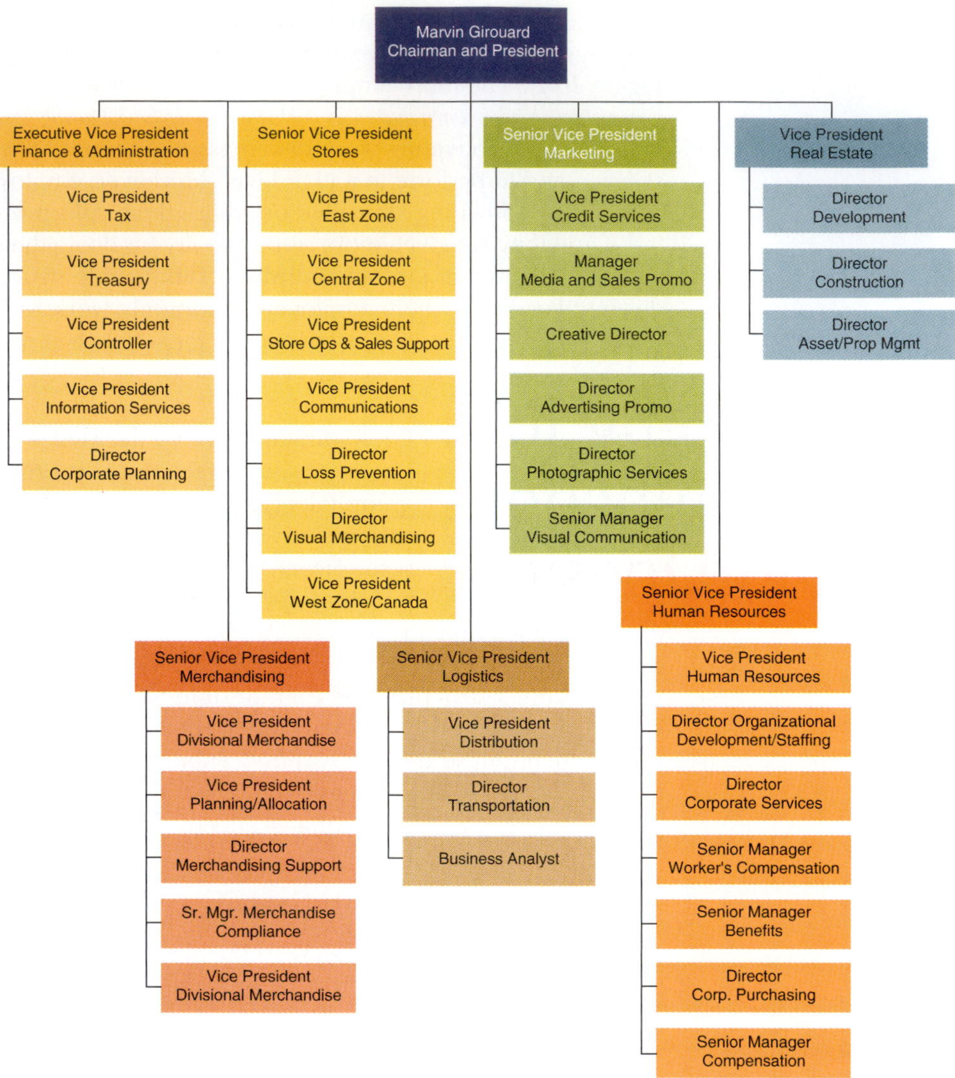

marketing department, for example, the person designing the photography program for an ad campaign works closely with the person responsible for designing store layouts and with visual communication experts. As a result, Pier 1 is able to develop a strong, focused marketing campaign to differentiate its products.

Second, when people who perform similar jobs are grouped together, it is easier for managers to monitor and evaluate their performance.[22] Imagine if marketing experts, purchasing experts, and real-estate experts were grouped together in one function and supervised by a manager from merchandising. Obviously, the merchandising manager would not have the expertise to evaluate all these different people appropriately. However a functional structure allows co-workers to evaluate how well other co-workers are performing their jobs, and if some co-workers are performing poorly, more experienced co-workers can help them develop new skills.

Finally, managers appreciate functional structure because it allows them to create the set of functions they need in order to scan and monitor the competitive environment and obtain information about the way it is changing.[23] With the right set of functions in place, managers are then in a good position to develop a strategy that allows the organization to respond to its changing situation. Employees in marketing can specialize in monitoring new marketing developments that will allow Pier 1 to better target its customers. For example, in 2004 Pier 1 announced that it was firing its current advertising agency and aggressively searching for a new one that could get the company closer to its customers.[24] Employees in merchandising can monitor all potential suppliers of home furnishings both at home and abroad to find the goods most likely to appeal to Pier 1's customers and manage Pier 1's global outsourcing supply chain.

As an organization grows, and particularly as its task environment and strategy change because it is beginning to produce a wider range of goods and services for different kinds of customers, several problems can make a functional structure less efficient and effective.[25] First, managers in different functions may find it more difficult to communicate and coordinate with one another when they are responsible for several different kinds of products, especially as the organization grows both domestically and internationally. Second, functional managers may become so preoccupied with supervising their own specific departments and achieving their departmental goals that they lose sight of organizational goals. If that happens, organizational effectiveness will suffer because managers will be viewing issues and problems facing the organization only from their own, relatively narrow, departmental perspectives.[26] Both of these problems can reduce efficiency and effectiveness.

Divisional Structures: Product, Market, and Geographic

As the problems associated with growth and diversification increase over time, managers must search for new ways to organize their activities to overcome the problems associated with a functional structure. Most managers of large organizations choose a **divisional structure** and create a series of business units to produce a specific kind of product for a specific kind of customer. Each *division* is a collection of functions or departments that work together to produce the product. The goal behind the change to a divisional structure is to create smaller, more manageable units within the organization. There are three forms of divisional structure (see Figure 10.4, page 346).[27] When managers organize divisions according to the *type of good or service* they provide, they adopt a product structure. When managers organize divisions according to the *area of the country or world* they operate in, they adopt a geographic structure. When managers organize divisions according to the *type of customer* they focus on, they adopt a market structure.

divisional structure An organizational structure composed of separate business units within which are the functions that work together to produce a specific product for a specific customer.

PRODUCT STRUCTURE Imagine the problems that managers at Pier 1 would encounter if they decided to diversify into producing and selling cars, fast food, and health insurance–in addition to home furnishings–and tried to use their existing set of functional managers to oversee the production of all four kinds of products. No manager would have the necessary skills or abilities to oversee those four products. No individual marketing manager, for example, could effectively market cars, fast food, health insurance, and home furnishings at the same time. To perform a functional activity successfully, managers must have experience in specific markets or industries. Consequently, if managers decide to diversify into new industries or to expand their range of products, they commonly design a product structure to organize their operations (see Figure 10.4a).

product structure An organizational structure in which each product line or business is handled by a self-contained division.

Using a **product structure,** managers place each distinct product line or business in its own self-contained division and give divisional managers the responsibility for devising an appropriate business-level strategy to allow the division to compete effectively in its industry or market.[28] Each division is self-contained because it has a complete set of all the functions–marketing, R&D, finance, and so on–that it needs to produce or provide goods or services efficiently and effectively. Functional managers report to divisional managers, and divisional managers report to top or corporate managers.

Grouping functions into divisions focused on particular products has several advantages for managers at all levels in the organization. First, a product structure allows functional managers to specialize in only one product area, so they are able to build expertise and fine-tune their skills in this particular area. Second, each division's managers can become experts in their industry; this expertise helps them choose and develop a business-level strategy to differentiate their products or lower their costs while meeting the needs of customers. Third, a product structure frees corporate managers from the need to supervise directly

Figure 10.4
Product, Market, and Geographic Structures

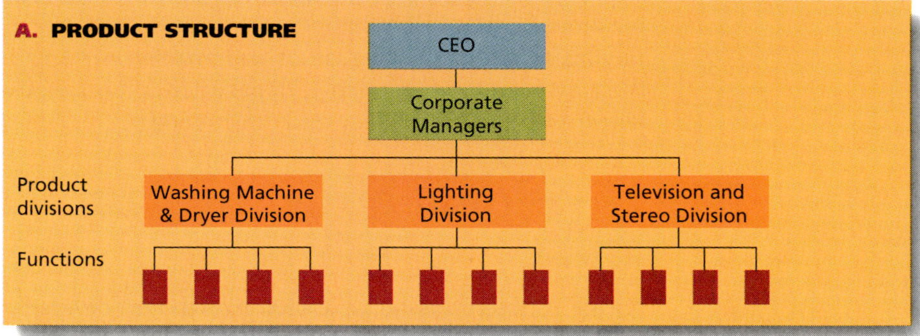

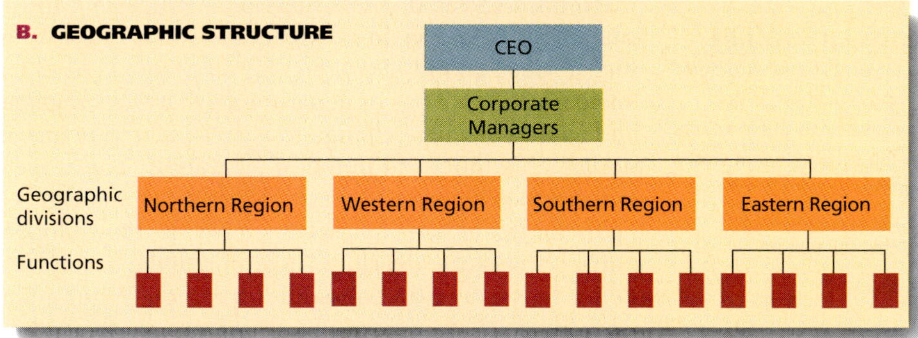

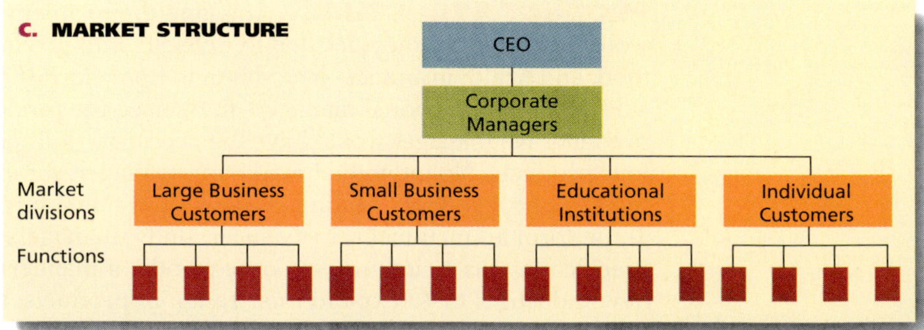

each division's day-to-day operations; this latitude allows corporate managers to create the best corporate-level strategy to maximize the organization's future growth and ability to create value. Corporate managers are likely to make fewer mistakes about which businesses to diversify into or how to best expand internationally, for example, because they are able to take an organizationwide view.[29] Corporate managers also are likely to evaluate better how well divisional managers are doing, and they can intervene and take corrective action as needed.

The extra layer of management, the divisional management layer, can improve the use of organizational resources. Moreover, a product structure puts divisional managers close to their customers and lets them respond quickly and appropriately to the changing task environment. Consider how Viacom, the huge media entertainment company, created a product structure.

Sumner Redstone, the billionaire chairman of Viacom, is continually making acquisitions that add to the range of entertainment products the company provides to its customers. Under Redstone, Viacom started in the cable and television business and expanded into several fields: entertainment, networks and broadcasting, video, music, theme parks, publishing, and television. In 2000, for example, Viacom acquired CBS television and BET.[30]

To manage Viacom's many different businesses effectively, Redstone decided to design a product structure (see Figure 10.5). He put each business in a separate division and gave managers in each division responsibility for making their business the number-one performer in its industry. Redstone recognized, however, that the different divisions could help each other and create synergies

Figure 10.5
Viacom's 2001 Product Structure

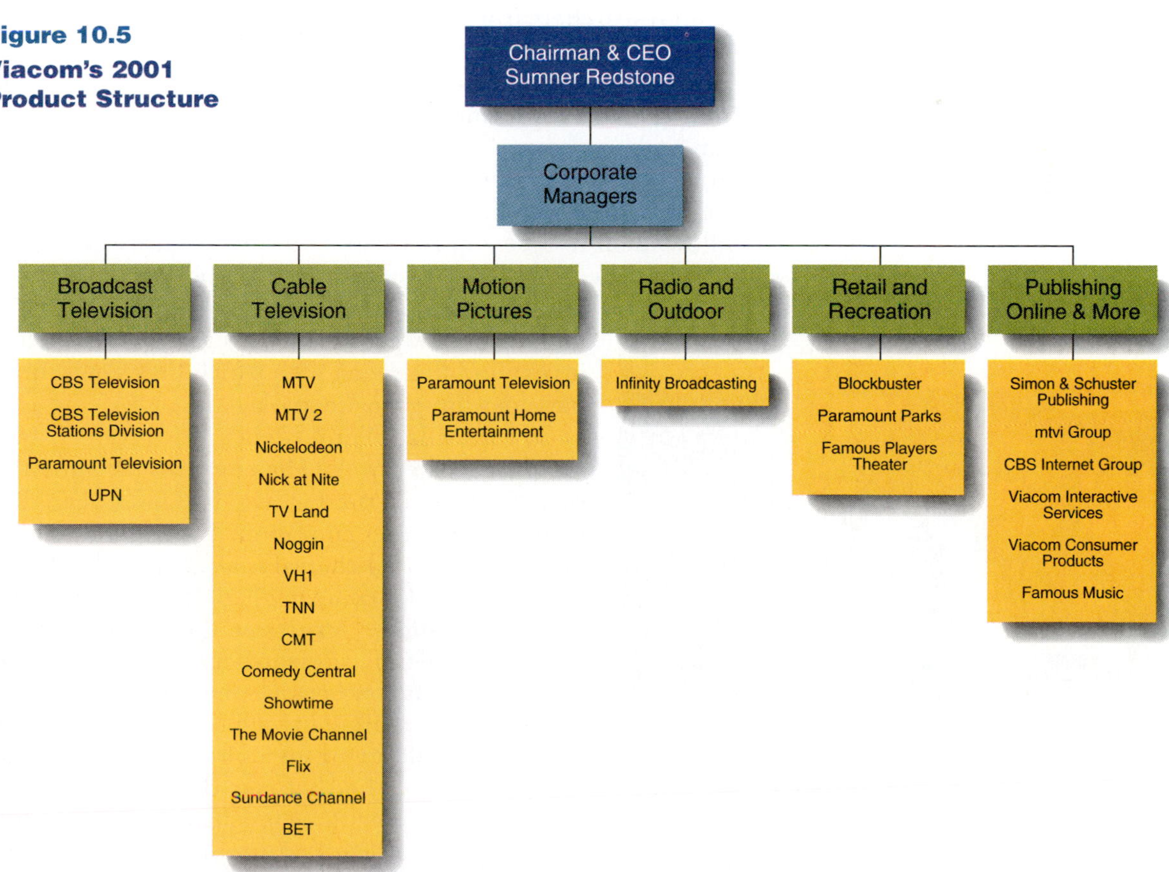

for Viacom by sharing their skills and resources. Blockbuster, for example, could launch a major advertising campaign to publicize the movies that Paramount makes and thus boost the visibility of both divisions' products, and Simon & Schuster could produce and publish specific books to tie in with the opening of a movie and thus boost ticket and book sales. To achieve these synergies, Redstone created a team of corporate managers who are responsible for working with the different divisional managers to identify new opportunities to create value. So far, this method of organizing has served Viacom well, and it has become one of the top-four media and entertainment companies.[31]

A pharmaceutical company that has recently adopted a new product structure to better organize its activities is profiled in the following "Management Insight."

Management Insight

GlaxoSmithKline's New Product Structure

The need to innovate new kinds of prescription drugs in order to boost performance is a continual battle for pharmaceutical companies. In the 2000s, many of these companies have been merging to try to increase their research productivity, and one of them, GlaxoSmithKline, was created from the merger between Glaxo Wellcome and SmithKline Beechum.[32] Prior to the merger, both companies experienced a steep decline in the number of new prescription drugs their scientists were able to invent. The problem facing the new company's top managers was how to best use and combine the talents of the scientists and researchers from both of the former companies to allow them to quickly innovate exciting new drugs.

Top managers realized that after the merger there would be enormous problems associated with coordinating the activities of the thousands of research scientists who were working on hundreds of different kinds of drug research programs. Understanding the problems associated with large size, the top managers decided to group the researchers into eight smaller product divisions to allow them to focus on particular clusters of diseases such as heart disease or viral infections. The members of each product division were told that they would be rewarded based on the number of new prescription drugs they were able to invent and the speed with which they could bring these new drugs to the market.

When Glaxo Wellcome and SmithKline Beechum merged, managers resolved the problem of how to coordinate the activities of thousands of research scientists by organizing them into product divisions focusing on clusters of diseases.

To date, GlaxoSmithKlein's new product structure has worked well. The company claimed that by 2004 research productivity had more than doubled since the reorganization. The number of new drugs moving into clinical trials had doubled from 10 to 20, and the company had 148 new drugs that were being tested.[33] Moreover, the company claims that the morale of its researchers has increased and turnover has fallen because the members of each division enjoy working together and collaborating to innovate lifesaving new drugs. The company expects to have the best new drug pipeline in its industry in the next three to four years.

geographic structure An organizational structure in which each region of a country or area of the world is served by a self-contained division.

GEOGRAPHIC STRUCTURE When organizations expand rapidly both at home and abroad, functional structures can create special problems because managers in one central location may find it increasingly difficult to deal with the different problems and issues that may arise in each region of a country or area of the world. In these cases, a **geographic structure,** in which divisions are broken down by geographic location, is often chosen (see Figure 10.4b). To achieve the corporate mission of providing next-day mail service, Fred Smith, CEO of Federal Express, chose a geographic structure and divided up operations by creating a division in each region. Large retailers like Macy's, Neiman Marcus, and Brooks Brothers also use a geographic structure. Since the needs of retail customers differ by region–for example, surfboards in California and down parkas in the Midwest–a geographic structure gives retail regional managers the flexibility they need to choose the range of products that best meets the needs of regional customers.

In adopting a *global geographic structure,* such as shown in Figure 10.6a, managers locate different divisions in each of the world regions where the organization operates. Managers are most likely to do this when they pursue a multidomestic strategy because customer needs vary widely by country or world region. For example, if products that appeal to U.S. customers do not sell in Europe, the Pacific Rim, or South America, then managers must customize the products to meet the needs of customers in those different world regions; a global geographic structure with global divisions will allow them to do this.

Figure 10.6
Global Geographic and Global Product Structures

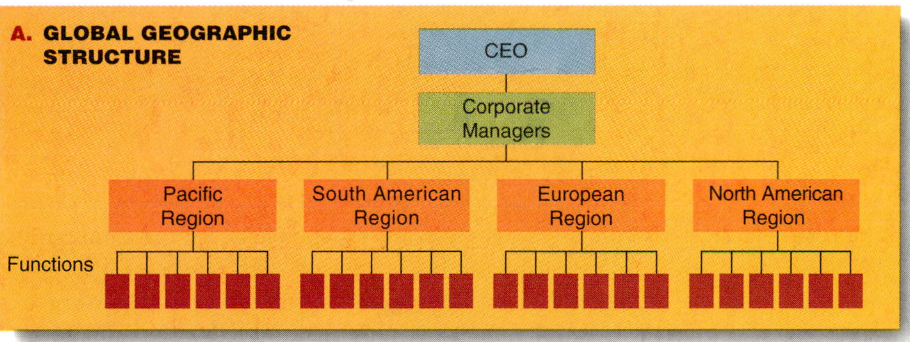

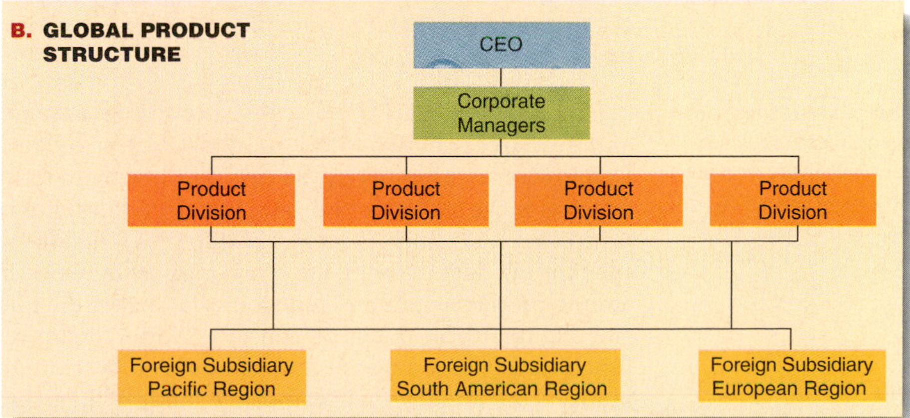

In contrast, to the degree that customers abroad are willing to buy the same kind of product, or slight variations thereof, managers are more likely to pursue a global strategy. In this case they are more likely to use a *global product structure.* In a global product structure, each product division, not the country and regional managers, takes responsibility for deciding where to manufacture its products and how to market them in foreign countries worldwide (see Figure 10.6b). Product division managers manage their own global value chains and decide where to establish foreign subsidiaries to distribute and sell their products to customers in foreign countries. As we noted at the beginning of this chapter, an organization's strategy is a major determinant of its structure both at home and abroad.

MARKET STRUCTURE Sometimes the pressing issue facing managers is to group functions according to the type of customer buying the product, in order to tailor the products the organization offers to each customer's unique demands. A computer company like Dell, for example, has several kinds of customers, including large businesses (which might demand networks of computers linked to a mainframe computer), small companies (which may need just a few PCs linked together), educational users in schools and universities (which might want thousands of independent PCs for their students), and individual users (who may want a high-quality multimedia PC so that they can play the latest video games).

market structure An organizational structure in which each kind of customer is served by a self-contained division; also called *customer structure.*

To satisfy the needs of diverse customers, a company might adopt a **market structure** (also called a *customer structure*), which groups divisions according to the particular kinds of customers they serve (see Figure 10.4c). A market structure allows managers to be responsive to the needs of their customers and allows them to act flexibly in making decisions in response to customers' changing needs.

Matrix and Product Team Designs

Moving to a product, market, or geographic divisional structure allows managers to respond more quickly and flexibly to the particular set of circumstances they confront. However, when the environment is dynamic and changing rapidly and uncertainty is high, even a divisional structure may not provide managers with enough flexibility to respond to the environment quickly. When customer needs or information technology are changing rapidly and the environment is very uncertain, managers must design the most flexible kind of organizational structure available: a matrix structure or a product team structure (see Figure 10.7).

matrix structure An organizational structure that simultaneously groups people and resources by function and by product.

MATRIX STRUCTURE In a **matrix structure,** managers group people and resources in two ways simultaneously: by function and by product.[34] Employees are grouped by *functions* to allow them to learn from one another and become more skilled and productive. In addition, employees are grouped into *product teams* in which members of different functions work together to develop a specific product. The result is a complex network of reporting relationships among product teams and functions that makes the matrix structure very flexible (see Figure 10.7a). Each person in a product team reports to two bosses: (1) a functional boss, who assigns individuals to a team and evaluates their performance from a functional perspective, and (2) the boss of the product team, who evaluates their performance on the team. Thus, team members are known as

Figure 10.7
Matrix and Product Team Structures

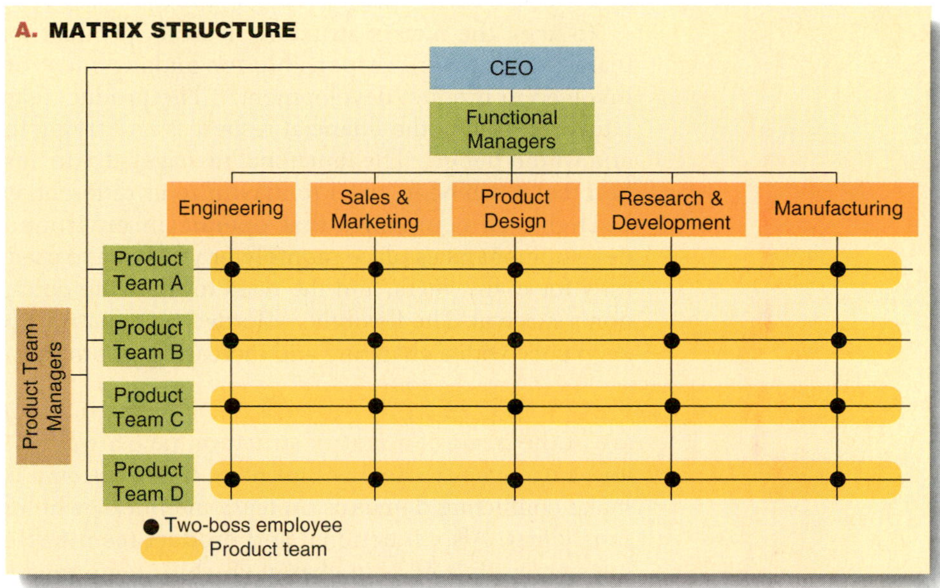

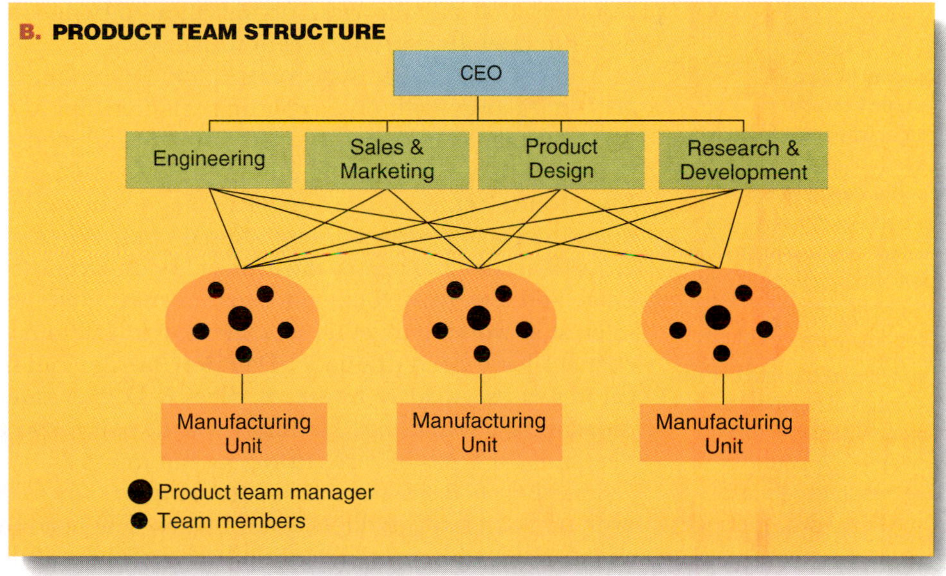

two-boss employees because they report to two managers. The functional employees assigned to product teams change over time as the specific skills that the team needs change. At the beginning of the product development process, for example, engineers and R&D specialists are assigned to a product team because their skills are needed to develop new products. When a provisional design has been established, marketing experts are assigned to the team to gauge how customers will respond to the new product. Manufacturing personnel join when it is time to find the most efficient way to produce the product. As their specific jobs are completed, team members leave and are reassigned to new teams. In this way the matrix structure makes the most use of human resources.

To keep the matrix structure flexible, product teams are empowered and team members are responsible for making most of the important decisions involved in product development.[35] The product team manager acts as a facilitator, controlling the financial resources and trying to keep the project on time and within budget. The functional managers try to ensure that the product is the best that it can be in order to maximize its differentiated appeal.

High-tech companies that operate in environments where new product development takes place monthly or yearly have used matrix structures successfully for many years, and the need to innovate quickly is vital to the organization's survival. The flexibility afforded by a matrix structure allows managers to keep pace with a changing and increasingly complex environment.[36]

PRODUCT TEAM STRUCTURE The dual reporting relationships that are at the heart of a matrix structure have always been difficult for managers and employees to deal with. Often, the functional boss and the product boss make conflicting demands on team members, who do not know which boss to satisfy first. Also, functional and product team bosses may come into conflict over precisely who is in charge of which team members and for how long. To avoid these problems, managers have devised a way of organizing people and resources that still allows an organization to be flexible but makes its structure easier to operate: a product team structure.

product team structure An organizational structure in which employees are permanently assigned to a cross-functional team and report only to the product team manager or to one of his or her direct subordinates.

cross-functional team A group of managers brought together from different departments to perform organizational tasks.

The **product team structure** differs from a matrix structure in two ways: (1) It does away with dual reporting relationships and two-boss managers, and (2) functional employees are permanently assigned to a cross-functional team that is empowered to bring a new or redesigned product to market. A **cross-functional team** is a group of managers brought together from different departments to perform organizational tasks. When managers are grouped into cross-departmental teams, the artificial boundaries between departments disappear, and a narrow focus on departmental goals is replaced with a general interest in working together to achieve organizational goals. The results of such changes have been dramatic: DaimlerChrysler can introduce a new model of car in two years, down from five; Black & Decker can innovate new products in months, not years; and Hallmark Cards can respond to changing customer demands for types of cards in weeks, not months.

Members of a cross-functional team report only to the product team manager or to one of his or her direct subordinates. The heads of the functions have only an informal, advisory relationship with members of the product teams–the role of functional managers is only to counsel and help team members, share knowledge among teams, and provide new technological developments that can help improve each team's performance (see Figure 10.7b).[37]

Increasingly, organizations are making empowered cross-functional teams an essential part of their organizational architecture to help them gain a competitive advantage in fast-changing organizational environments. For example, Newell Rubbermaid, the well-known maker of more than 5,000 household products, moved to a product team structure because its managers wanted to speed up the rate of product innovation. Managers created 20 cross-functional teams composed of five to seven people from marketing, manufacturing, R&D, finance, and other functions.[38] Each team focuses its energies on a particular product line, such as garden products, bathroom products, or kitchen products. These teams develop more than 365 new products a year. Another example of a company that now uses this structure is Lucent, profiled in the following "Management Insight."

Management Insight

How Three CEOs Worked to Reorganize Lucent

Lucent Technologies, which makes Internet routers and other communications equipment, was one of the high-flying high-tech companies of the 1990s. However, in 2001, Lucent's stock plunged to less than $7 a share from a high of more than $70 because of falling sales and mounting losses.[39] The reason? Its managers had backed the development of the wrong kind of router, one based on capacity rather than speed, and speed turned out to be what customers wanted. By contrast, Nortel Networks, one of Lucent's major competitors, had developed fast optical or light-based routers and now had 45 percent of the market compared to Lucent's 15 percent.

Among the many reasons for Lucent's poor decision making was the incredibly complex way it had been organized by its first CEO, Richard McGinn. To promote the speedy development of new products, McGinn had decided that Lucent should be set up as 11 different business divisions, each of which would focus on a particular product and market.[40] However, enormous communication and coordination problems arose, since managers in one division did not know what managers in the others were doing. Incompatible kinds of products were being developed, new technology was not being shared across divisions, and it was a nightmare trying to sell Lucent's range of products globally as the 11 business units were each handling their own global sales.

McGinn was forced to leave the company in October 2000. His successor, Henry Schacht, decided efficiency and effectiveness would increase if Lucent reorganized the 11 different divisions into just 5. This would make managers more accountable for their actions, and they would be better able to communicate inside each division. Schacht and his managers spent hundreds of millions of dollars to restructure the company and laid off over 15,000 employees.

By 2001, however, it was clear that Lucent could no longer afford the luxury of having even five divisions because of mounting losses and the need to reduce costs. In July and October, Schacht announced that Lucent would reorganize again both to reduce costs and to allow it to better focus its resources on speeding the new product development process. Another 20,000 employees were laid off (a total of almost one-half of Lucent's employees were laid off as a result of the restructuring). And Lucent announced that it was combining the five units into only two business divisions:[41] (1) the Integrated Network Solutions Division, which would handle all Lucent's "land-line" products such as routers, switching, and data software, and (2) the Mobility Solutions Division, which would handle the company's wireless products.

Managers hoped this new structure would perform more flexibly and allow Lucent to respond faster and more effectively to the rapidly changing information technology environment. They also hoped it would save billions of dollars and would be a much more efficient method of organizing. Finally, they hoped that with just two major divisions it would be far easier to coordinate and manage global sales, something vital if Lucent was to achieve a turnaround.

The reorganization failed, and Lucent's performance continued to deteriorate. Finally, in 2002 Lucent rehired one of its former top managers, Patricia Russo, who had left to join Kodak.[42] Russo recognized that Lucent's main problems were that each of its two product divisions lacked internal cohesion and that there was still bad communication with Lucent's Bell Labs, where most of its research and development took place. She decided to move to a product team structure to solve Lucent's problems. Now a centralized set of support functions, including Bell Labs and Lucent's marketing and supply chain management, works with each product division to speed product development. In addition, Russo insisted that each product division should break itself into cross-functional teams, each of which would focus on developing new products to compete in a fast-changing environment. As a result of this change, Lucent regained profitability by 2003 and its stock price increased, as investors felt that Russo had finally reinvented Lucent and found the right structure.

Hybrid Structure

hybrid structure The structure of a large organization that has many divisions and simultaneously uses many different organizational structures.

A large organization that has many divisions and simultaneously uses many different structures has a **hybrid structure.** Most large organizations use product division structures and create self-contained divisions; then each division's managers select the structure that best meets the needs of the particular environment, strategy, and so on. Thus, one product division may choose to operate with a functional structure, a second may choose a geographic structure, and a third may choose a product team structure because of the nature of the division's products or the desire to be more responsive to customers' needs. Target uses a hybrid structure based on grouping by customer and by geography.

As shown in Figure 10.8, Target operates its different store chains as four independent divisions in a market division structure. Its four market divisions are Mervyn's and Marshall Field's, which cater to the needs of affluent customers; Target Stores, which competes in the low-price segment; and target.direct, Target's Internet division, which manages online sales.

Beneath this organizational layer is another layer of structure because both Target Stores and Marshall Field's operate with a geographic structure that groups stores by region. Individual stores are under the direction of a regional

Figure 10.8
Target's Hybrid Structure

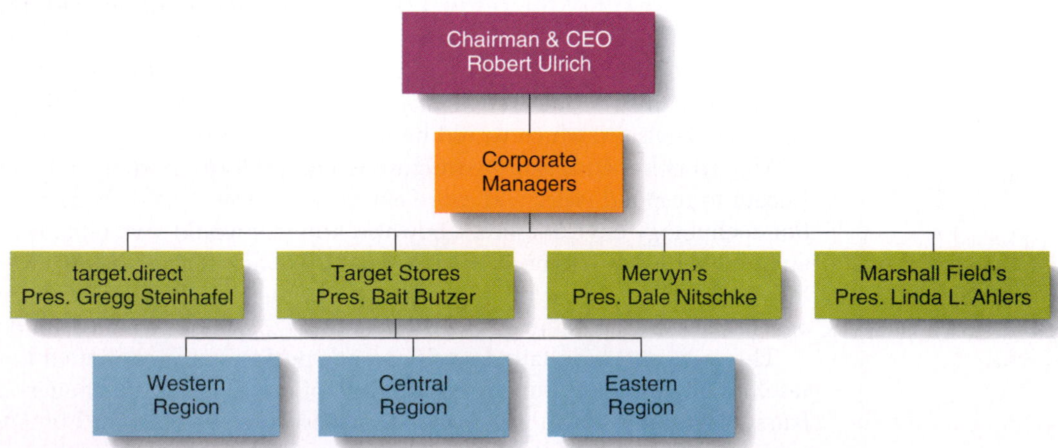

office, which is responsible for coordinating the market needs of the stores in its region and for responding to regional customer needs. The regional office feeds information back to divisional headquarters, where centralized merchandising functions make decisions for all Target or Marshall Field's stores.

Organizational structure may thus be likened to the layers of an onion. The outer layer provides the overarching organizational framework–most commonly a product or market division structure–and each inner layer is the structure that each division selects for itself in response to the contingencies it faces–such as a geographic or product team structure. The ability to break a large organization into smaller units or divisions makes it much easier for managers to change structure when the need arises–for example, when a change in technology or an increase in competition in the environment necessitates a change from a functional to a product team structure.

Coordinating Functions and Divisions

In organizing, managers have several tasks. The first is to group functions and divisions and create the organizational structures best suited to the contingencies they face. Their next task is to ensure that there is sufficient coordination or integration among functions and divisions so that organizational resources are used efficiently and effectively. Having discussed how managers divide organizational activities into jobs, functions, and divisions to increase efficiency and effectiveness, we now look at how they put the parts back together.

We look first at the way in which managers design the hierarchy of authority to coordinate functions and divisions so that they work together effectively. Then we focus on integration and examine the many different integrating mechanisms that managers can use to coordinate functions and divisions.

Allocating Authority

authority The power to hold people accountable for their actions and to make decisions concerning the use of organizational resources.

hierarchy of authority An organization's chain of command, specifying the relative authority of each manager.

span of control The number of subordinates who report directly to a manager.

As organizations grow and produce a wider range of goods and services, the size and number of their functions and divisions increase. To coordinate the activities of people, functions, and divisions and to allow them to work together effectively, managers must develop a clear hierarchy of authority.[43] **Authority** is the power vested in a manager to make decisions and use resources to achieve organizational goals by virtue of his or her position in an organization. The **hierarchy of authority** is an organization's chain of command–the relative authority that each manager has–extending from the CEO at the top, down through the middle managers and first-line managers, to the nonmanagerial employees who actually make goods or provide services. Every manager, at every level of the hierarchy, supervises one or more subordinates. The term **span of control** refers to the number of subordinates who report directly to a manager.

Figure 10.9 (page 356) shows a simplified picture of the hierarchy of authority and the span of control of managers in McDonald's in 2004. At the top of the hierarchy is Charlie Bell, CEO and chairman of McDonald's board of directors, who took control in 2004.[44] Bell is the manager who has ultimate responsibility for McDonald's performance, and he has the authority to decide how to use organizational resources to benefit McDonald's stakeholders.[45] Both Mike Roberts and Jim Skinner report directly to Bell. Roberts is the CEO of McDonald's domestic

Figure 10.9
The Hierarchy of Authority and Span of Control at McDonald's Corporation

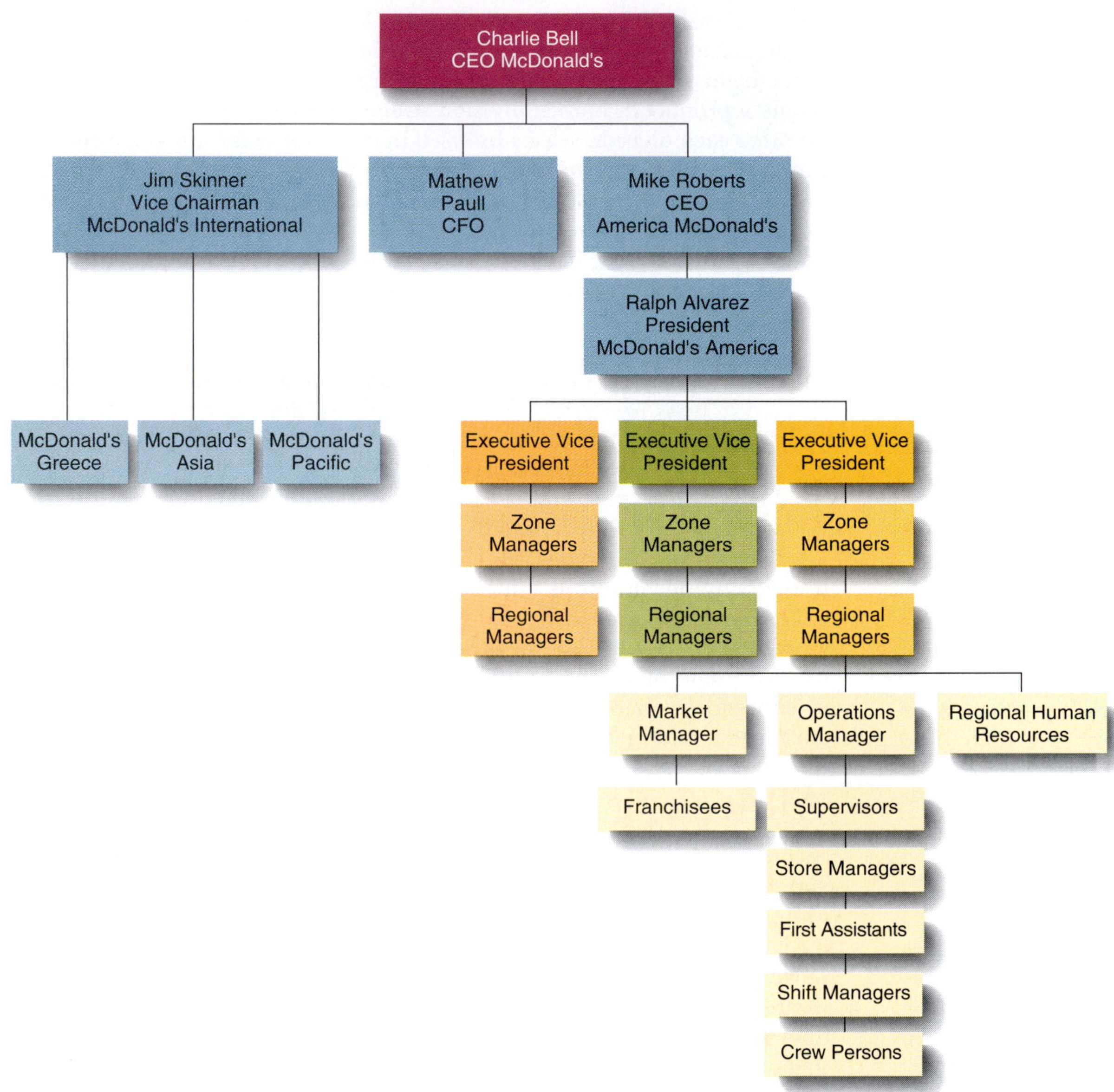

line manager Someone in the direct line or chain of command who has formal authority over people and resources lower down.

operations; Vice Chairman Skinner is the head of McDonald's overseas operations. They are next in the chain of command under Bell. Of special mention is Ralph Alvarez, who in July 2004 was appointed as president of domestic operations, reporting to Roberts. Also depicted is Chief Financial Officer Mathew Paull, who also reports directly to Bell; however, unlike the others, he is not a **line manager,** someone in the direct line or chain of command who has formal authority over people and resources. Rather, Paull is the **staff manager,** responsible for one of McDonald's specialist functions, finance.

staff manager A manager responsible for managing a specialist function, such as finance or marketing.

Managers at each level of the hierarchy confer on managers at the next level down the authority to make decisions about how to use organizational resources. Accepting this authority, those lower-level managers then become responsible for their decisions and are accountable for how well they make those decisions. Managers who make the right decisions are typically promoted, and organizations motivate managers with the prospects of promotion and increased responsibility within the chain of command.

Below Roberts are the other main levels or layers in the McDonald's USA chain of command–executive vice presidents, zone managers, regional managers, and supervisors. A hierarchy is also evident in each company-owned McDonald's restaurant. At the top is the store manager; at lower levels are the first assistant, shift managers, and crew personnel. McDonald's managers have decided that this hierarchy of authority best allows the company to pursue its business-level strategy of providing fast food at reasonable prices.

TALL AND FLAT ORGANIZATIONS As an organization grows in size (normally measured by the number of its managers and employees), its hierarchy of authority normally lengthens, making the organizational structure taller. A *tall* organization has many levels of authority relative to company size; a *flat* organization has fewer levels relative to company size (see Figure 10.10, page 358).[46] As a hierarchy becomes taller, problems that make the organization's structure less flexible and slow managers' response to changes in the organizational environment may result.

Communication problems may arise when an organization has many levels in the hierarchy. It can take a long time for the decisions and orders of upper-level managers to reach managers further down in the hierarchy, and it can take a long time for top managers to learn how well their decisions worked. Feeling out of touch, top managers may want to verify that lower-level managers are following orders and may require written confirmation from them. Middle managers, who know they will be held strictly accountable for their actions, start devoting more time to the process of making decisions to improve their chances of being right. They might even try to avoid responsibility by making top managers decide what actions to take.

Another communication problem that can result is the distortion of commands and orders being transmitted up and down the hierarchy, which causes managers at different levels to interpret what is happening differently. Distortion of orders and messages can be accidental, occurring because different managers interpret messages from their own narrow, functional perspectives. Or distortion can be intentional, occurring because managers low in the hierarchy decide to interpret information in a way that increases their own personal advantage.

Another problem with tall hierarchies is that they usually indicate that an organization is employing many managers, and managers are expensive. Managerial salaries, benefits, offices, and secretaries are a huge expense for organizations. Large companies such as IBM and General Motors pay their managers billions of dollars a year. In the early 2000s, hundreds of thousands of middle managers were laid off as dot-coms collapsed and high-tech companies such as Hewlett-Packard and Lucent attempted to reduce costs by restructuring and downsizing their workforces.

THE MINIMUM CHAIN OF COMMAND To ward off the problems that result when an organization becomes too tall and employs too many managers, top managers need to ascertain whether they are employing the right number of

Figure 10.10
Tall and Flat Organizations

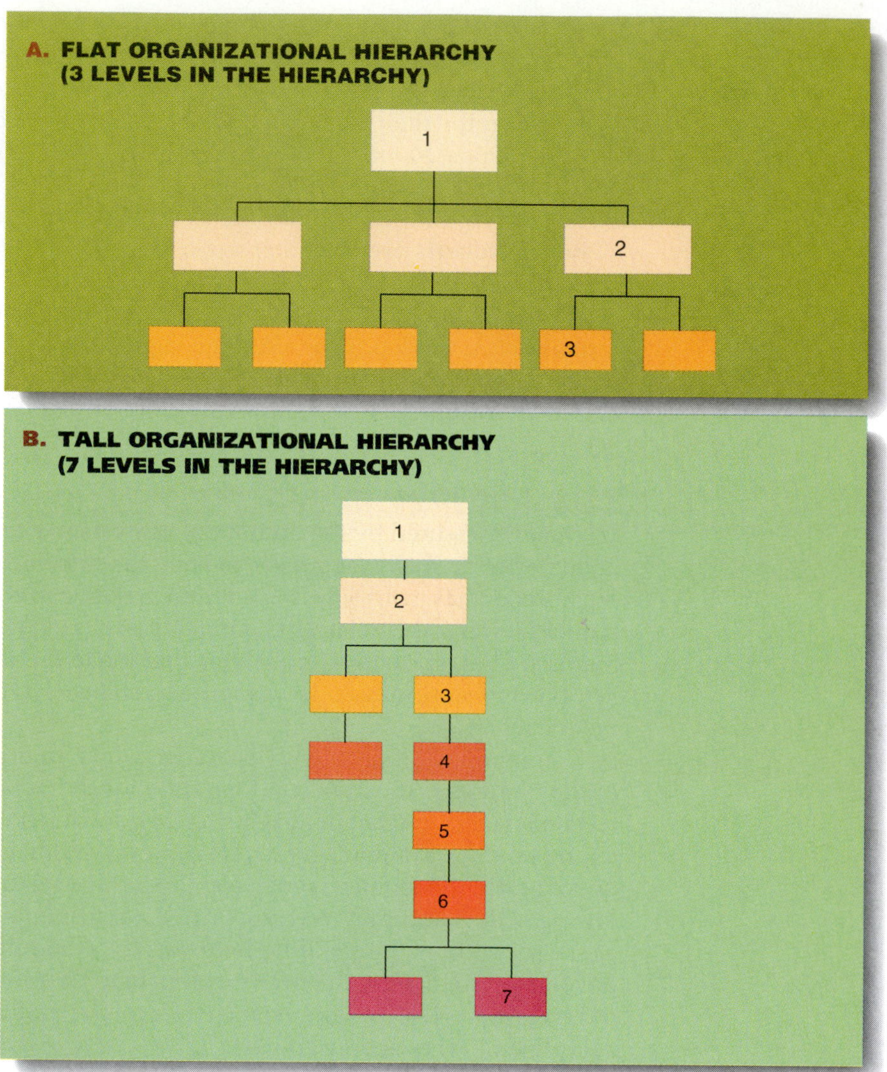

middle and first-line managers and whether they can redesign their organizational architecture to reduce the number of managers. Top managers might well follow a basic organizing principle–the principle of the minimum chain of command–which states that top managers should always construct a hierarchy with the fewest levels of authority necessary to efficiently and effectively use organizational resources.

Effective managers constantly scrutinize their hierarchies to see whether the number of levels can be reduced–for example, by eliminating one level and giving the responsibilities of managers at that level to managers above and empowering employees below. This practice has become increasingly common in the United States as companies that are battling low-cost foreign competitors search for new ways to reduce costs. One manager who is constantly trying to empower employees and keep the hierarchy flat is Colleen C. Barrett, the number-two executive of Southwest Airlines.[47] Barrett is the highest-ranking woman in the airline industry. At Southwest, she is well known for continually reaffirming Southwest's message that employees should feel free to go above and beyond their prescribed roles to provide better customer service. Her central message is that Southwest values and trusts its employees, who are empowered to take responsibility. Southwest employees are encouraged not to look to their superiors for guidance but, rather, to take responsibility to find ways to do the job better themselves. As a result, Southwest keeps the number of its middle managers to a minimum.

CENTRALIZATION AND DECENTRALIZATION OF AUTHORITY

Another way in which managers can keep the organizational hierarchy flat is by decentralizing authority to lower-level managers and nonmanagerial employees.[48] If managers at higher levels give lower-level employees the responsibility of making important decisions and only manage by exception, then the problems of slow and distorted communication noted previously are kept to a minimum. Moreover, fewer managers are needed because their role is not to make decisions but to act as coach and facilitator and to help other employees make the best decisions. In addition, when decision making is low in the organization and near the customer, employees are better able to recognize and respond to customer needs.

Decentralizing authority allows an organization and its employees to behave in a flexible way even as the organization grows and becomes taller. This is why managers are so interested in empowering employees, creating self-managed work teams, establishing cross-functional teams, and even moving to a product team structure. These design innovations help keep the organizational architecture flexible and responsive to complex task and general environments, complex technologies, and complex strategies.

Although more and more organizations are taking steps to decentralize authority, too much decentralization has certain disadvantages. If divisions, functions, or teams are given too much decision-making authority, they may begin to pursue their own goals at the expense of organizational goals. Managers in engineering design or R&D, for example, may become so focused on making the best possible product that they fail to realize that the best product may be so expensive that few people will be willing or able to buy it. Also, with too much decentralization, lack of communication among functions or among divisions may prevent possible synergies among them from ever materializing, and organizational performance suffers.

Top managers must seek the balance between centralization and decentralization of authority that best meets the four major contingencies an organization faces (see Figure 10.1). If managers are in a stable environment, are using well-understood technology, and are producing staple kinds of products (such as cereal, canned soup, books, or televisions), then there is no pressing need to decentralize authority, and managers at the top can maintain control of much of organizational decision making.[49] However, in uncertain, changing environments where high-tech companies are producing state-of-the-art products, top managers must empower employees and allow teams to make important strategic decisions so that the organization can keep up with the changes taking place. Electronic circuit board maker Plexus, profiled in the following "Managing Globally," provides a vivid example of the issues involved in decentralization.

Managing Globally

Plexus Uses Self-Managed Teams to Decentralize Authority

In the United States, over 2.3 million manufacturing jobs were lost to factories in low-cost countries abroad in 2003. While many large U.S. manufacturing companies have given up the battle, some companies like electronics maker Plexus Corp., based in Neenah, Wisconsin, have been able to find a way of organizing that has allowed them to survive and prosper in a low-cost manufacturing world. How have they done this? By decentralizing control to empowered work teams.

In the 1990s, Plexus saw the writing on the wall as more and more of its customers began to turn to manufacturers abroad to produce the electronic components that go into their products or even the whole product itself. The problem facing managers at Plexus was how to organize work activities to compete in a low-cost manufacturing world. U.S. companies cannot match the efficiency of foreign manufacturers in producing high volumes of a *single* product, such as millions of a particular circuit board used in a laptop computer. So Plexus's managers decided to focus their efforts on developing a manufacturing technology called "low-high" that could efficiently produce low volumes of *many* different kinds of products.

Plexus's managers worked as a team to design an organizational structure based on creating four "focused factories" in which control over production decisions is given to the workers, who perform all the operations involved in making a product. To allow authority to be decentralized, Plexus's managers cross-trained workers so that they can perform any particular operation in their "factory." With this approach, when work slows down at any point in the production of a particular product, a worker further along the production process can move back to help solve the problem that has arisen at the earlier stage.[50]

Employees who are closest to customers are better able to recognize and respond to customer needs. As organizations become taller, managers realize the need to empower employees at all levels to make decisions that will positively influence customer relationships. This is why managers are so interested in creating self-managed work teams, cross-functional teams, and even moving to a product structure.

Furthermore, managers organized workers into self-managed teams that are empowered to make all the decisions necessary to make a particular product in one of the four factories. Since each product is different, these teams have to quickly make the decisions necessary to assemble it if they are to do so in a cost-effective way–so decentralization is essential. The ability of these teams to make rapid decisions is vital on a production line, as time is money. Every minute a production line is not moving adds hundreds or thousands of dollars to production costs. So, to keep costs low, workers have to be able to decide how to react to unexpected contingencies and make nonprogrammed decisions.

Another important reason for decentralization is that when a changeover takes place from making one product to making another, nothing is being produced and thus it is vital that changeover time be kept to a minimum. At Plexus, managers, by allowing teams to experiment and by providing guidance, have reduced changeover time to as little as 30 minutes. The line is running and making products 80 percent of the time; it is stopped for only 20 percent.[51] This incredible flexibility, brought about by the way employees are organized, is the reason why Plexus is so efficient and can compete against low-cost manufacturers abroad.

Types of Integrating Mechanisms

integrating mechanisms Organizing tools that managers can use to increase communication and coordination among functions and divisions.

Much coordination takes place through the hierarchy of authority. In addition, managers can use various **integrating mechanisms** to increase communication and coordination among functions and divisions. The greater the complexity of an organization's structure, the greater is the need for coordination among people, functions, and divisions to make the organizational structure work efficiently and effectively.[52] Thus, when managers choose to adopt a divisional, matrix, or product team structure, they must use complex kinds of integrating mechanisms to achieve organizational goals. UPS and FedEx, for example, have complex geographic structures that need an enormous amount of coordination among regions to achieve the goal of next-day package delivery. They achieve this through the innovative use of integrating mechanisms such as computer-controlled tracking equipment and customer-liaison personnel to manage transactions quickly and efficiently.

Six integrating mechanisms are available to managers to increase communication and coordination.[53] These mechanisms–arranged on a continuum from simplest to most complex–are listed in Figure 10.11 with examples of the individuals

Figure 10.11
Types and Examples of Integrating Mechanisms

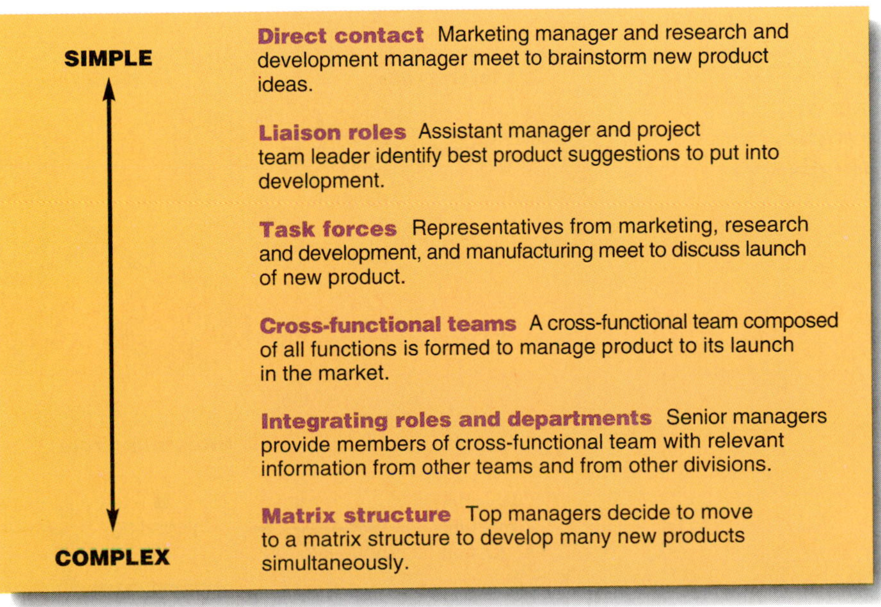
SIMPLE
COMPLEX
Direct contact Marketing manager and research and development manager meet to brainstorm new product ideas.
Liaison roles Assistant manager and project team leader identify best product suggestions to put into development.
Task forces Representatives from marketing, research and development, and manufacturing meet to discuss launch of new product.
Cross-functional teams A cross-functional team composed of all functions is formed to manage product to its launch in the market.
Integrating roles and departments Senior managers provide members of cross-functional team with relevant information from other teams and from other divisions.
Matrix structure Top managers decide to move to a matrix structure to develop many new products simultaneously.

or groups that might use them. In the remainder of this section we examine each one, moving from the simplest to the most complex.

DIRECT CONTACT Direct contact among managers creates a context within which managers from different functions or divisions can work together to solve mutual problems. However, several problems are associated with establishing contact among managers in different functions or divisions. Managers from different functions may have different views about what must be done to achieve organizational goals. But if the managers have equal authority (as functional managers typically do), the only manager who can tell them what to do is the CEO. If functional and divisional managers cannot reach agreement, no mechanism exists to resolve the conflict apart from the authority of the boss. The need to solve everyday conflicts, however, wastes top-management time and effort and slows decision making. In fact, one sign of a poorly performing organizational structure is the number of problems sent up the hierarchy for top managers to solve. To increase coordination among functions and divisions and to prevent these problems from emerging, top managers can incorporate more complex integrating mechanisms into their organizational architecture.

LIAISON ROLES Managers can increase coordination among functions and divisions by establishing liaison roles. When the volume of contacts between two functions increases, one way to improve coordination is to give one manager in each function or division the responsibility for coordinating with the other. These managers may meet daily, weekly, monthly, or as needed. Figure 10.12a depicts a liaison role; the small dot represents the person within a function who has responsibility for coordinating with the other function. The responsibility for coordination is part of the liaison's full-time job, and usually an informal relationship forms between the people involved, greatly easing strains between functions. Furthermore, liaison roles provide a way of transmitting information across an organization, which is important in large organizations whose employees may know no one outside their immediate function or division.

Figure 10.12
Forms of Integrating Mechanisms

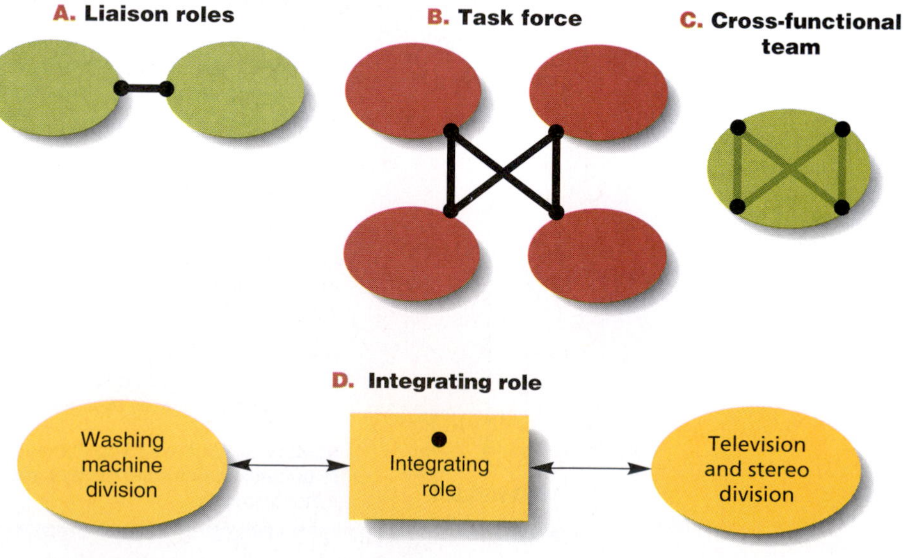

task force A committee of managers from various functions or divisions who meet to solve a specific, mutual problem; also called *ad hoc committee.*

TASK FORCES When more than two functions or divisions share many common problems, direct contact and liaison roles may not provide sufficient coordination. In these cases, a more complex integrating mechanism, a **task force,** may be appropriate (see Figure 10.12b). One manager from each relevant function or division is assigned to a task force that meets to solve a specific, mutual problem; members are responsible for reporting back to their departments on the issues addressed and the solutions recommended. Task forces are often called ad hoc committees because they are temporary; they may meet on a regular basis or only a few times. When the problem or issue is solved, the task force is no longer needed; members return to their normal roles in their departments or are assigned to other task forces. Typically, task force members also perform many of their normal duties while serving on the task force.

CROSS-FUNCTIONAL TEAMS In many cases, the issues addressed by a task force are recurring problems, such as the need to develop new products or find new kinds of customers. To address recurring problems effectively, managers are increasingly using permanent integrating mechanisms such as cross-functional teams (see Figure 10.12c). An example of a cross-functional team is a new product development committee that is responsible for the choice, design, manufacturing, and marketing of a new product. Such an activity obviously requires a great deal of integration among functions if new products are to be successfully introduced, and using a complex integrating mechanism such as a cross-functional team accomplishes this. Intel, for instance, emphasizes cross-functional teamwork. Its structure consists of over 90 cross-functional groups that meet regularly to set functional strategy in areas such as engineering and marketing and to develop business-level strategy.

The more complex an organization, the more important cross-functional teams become. Westinghouse, for example, has established a cross-functional team system to promote integration among divisions and improve organizational performance. As discussed previously, the product team structure is based on cross-functional teams to speed products to market. These teams assume responsibility for all aspects of product development.

INTEGRATING ROLES An *integrating role* is a role whose only function is to increase coordination and integration among functions or divisions to achieve performance gains from synergies (see Figure 10.12d). Usually, managers who perform integrating roles are experienced senior managers who can envisage how to use the resources of the functions or divisions to obtain new synergies. One study found that Du Pont, the giant chemical company, had created 160 integrating roles to provide coordination among the different divisions of the company and improve corporate performance.[54] Once again, the more complex an organization and the greater the number of its divisions, the more important integrating roles are.

MATRIX STRUCTURE When managers must be able to respond quickly to the task and general environments, they often use a matrix structure. The reason for choosing a matrix structure is clear. It contains many of the integrating mechanisms already discussed: The two-boss managers integrate between functions and product teams; the matrix is built on the basis of temporary teams or task forces; and each member of a team performs a liaison role. The matrix structure is flexible precisely because it is formed from complex integrating mechanisms.

In summary, to keep an organization responsive to changes in its task and general environments as the organization grows and becomes more complex, managers must increase coordination among functions and divisions by using complex integrating mechanisms. Managers must decide on the best way to organize their structures to create an organizational architecture that allows them to make the best use of organizational resources.

Strategic Alliances, B2B Network Structures, and IT

Recently, increasing globalization and the use of new IT have brought about two innovations in organizational architecture that are sweeping through U.S. and European companies: strategic alliances and business-to-business (B2B) network structures. A **strategic alliance** is a formal agreement that commits two or more companies to exchange or share their resources in order to produce and market a product.[55] Most commonly strategic alliances are formed because the companies share similar interests and believe they can benefit from cooperating. For example, Japanese car companies such as Toyota and Honda have formed many strategic alliances with particular suppliers of inputs such as car axles, gearboxes, and air-conditioning systems. Over time, these car companies work closely with their suppliers to improve the efficiency and effectiveness of the inputs so that the final product–the car produced–is of higher quality and very often can be produced at lower cost. Toyota and Honda have also established alliances with suppliers throughout the United States and Mexico because both companies now build several models of cars in these countries.

strategic alliance An agreement in which managers pool or share their organization's resources and know-how with a foreign company and the two organizations share the rewards and risks of starting a new venture.

Throughout the 1990s, the growing sophistication of IT with global intranets and teleconferencing has made it much easier to manage strategic alliances and allow managers to share information and cooperate. One outcome of this has been the growth of strategic alliances into a network structure. A **network structure** is a series of global strategic alliances that one or several organizations create with suppliers, manufacturers, and/or distributors to produce and market a product. Network structures allow an organization to manage its global value chain in order to find new ways to reduce costs and increase the quality of products–without incurring the high costs of operating a complex organizational structure (such as the costs of employing many managers). More and more U.S. and European companies are relying on global network structures to gain access to low-cost foreign sources of inputs, as discussed in Chapter 6. Shoemakers such as Nike and Adidas are two companies that have used this approach extensively.

network structure A series of strategic alliances that an organization creates with suppliers, manufacturers, and/or distributors to produce and market a product.

Nike is the largest and most profitable sports shoe manufacturer in the world. The key to Nike's success is the network structure that Nike founder and CEO Philip Knight created to allow his company to produce and market shoes. As noted in Chapter 8, the most successful companies today are trying to pursue simultaneously a low-cost and a differentiation strategy. Knight decided early that to do this at Nike he needed organizational architecture that would allow his company to focus on some functions, such as design, and leave others, such as manufacturing, to other organizations.

By far the largest function at Nike's Oregon headquarters is the design function, composed of talented designers who pioneered innovations in sports shoe design such as the air pump and Air Jordans that Nike introduced so successfully. Designers use computer-aided design (CAD) to design Nike shoes, and they electronically store all new product information, including manufacturing instructions. When the designers have finished their work, they electronically transmit all the blueprints for the new products to a network of Southeast Asian suppliers and manufacturers with which Nike has formed strategic alliances.[56] Instructions for the design of a new sole may be sent to a supplier in Taiwan; instructions for the leather uppers, to a supplier in Malaysia. The suppliers produce the shoe parts and send them for final assembly to a manufacturer in China with which Nike has established another strategic alliance. From China the shoes are shipped to distributors throughout the world. Ninety-nine percent of the 99 million pairs of shoes that Nike makes each year are made in Southeast Asia.

This network structure gives Nike two important advantages. First, Nike is able to respond to changes in sports shoe fashion very quickly. Using its global IT system, Nike literally can change the instructions it gives each of its suppliers overnight, so that within a few weeks its foreign manufacturers are producing new kinds of shoes.[57] Any alliance partners that fail to perform up to Nike's standards are replaced with new partners.

outsource To use outside suppliers and manufacturers to produce goods and services.

Second, Nike's costs are very low because wages in Southeast Asia are a fraction of what they are in the United States, and this difference gives Nike a low-cost advantage. Also, Nike's ability to **outsource** and use foreign manufacturers to produce all its shoes abroad allows Knight to keep the organization's U.S. structure flat and flexible. Nike is able to use a relatively inexpensive functional structure to organize its activities. However, sports shoe manufacturers' attempts to keep their costs low have led to many charges that Nike and others are supporting sweatshops that harm foreign workers, as the following "Ethics in Action" suggests.

Ethics in Action

Of Shoes and Sweatshops

As the production of all kinds of goods and services is being increasingly outsourced to poor regions and countries of the world, the behavior of companies that outsource production to subcontractors in these countries has come under increasing scrutiny. Nike, the giant sports shoe maker with sales of more than $9 billion a year, was one of the first to experience a backlash when critics revealed how workers in these countries were being treated. Indonesian workers were stitching together shoes in hot, noisy factories for only 80 cents a day or about $18 a month.[58] Workers in Vietnam and China fared better; they could earn $1.60 a day. In all cases, however, critics charged that at least $3 a day was needed to maintain an adequate living standard.

These facts generated an outcry in the United States, where Nike was roundly attacked for its labor practices; a backlash against sales of Nike products forced Phil Knight, Nike's billionaire owner, to reevaluate Nike's labor practices. Nike announced that henceforth all the factories producing its shoes and clothes would be independently monitored and inspected. After its competitor Reebok, which also had been criticized for similar labor practices, announced that it was raising wages in Indonesia by 20 percent, Nike raised them by 25 percent to $23 a month.[59] Small though this may seem, it was a huge increase to workers in these countries.

In Europe, another sportswear company, Adidas, had largely escaped such criticism. But in 1999 it was reported that in El Salvador, a Taiwan-based Adidas subcontractor was employing girls as young as 14 in its factories and making

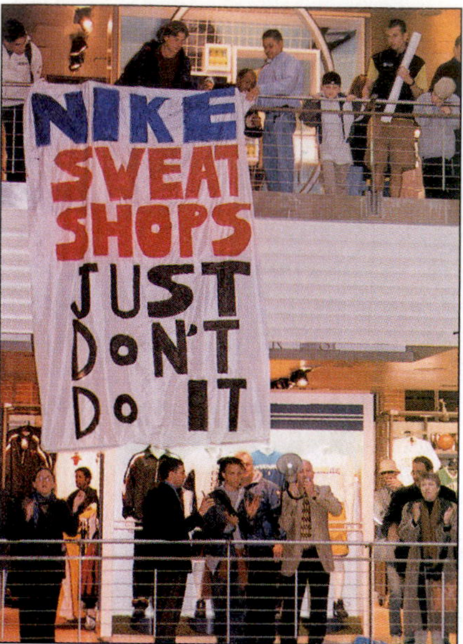

Members of United Students against Nike unfurl a banner at the Niketown store in New York accusing Nike of using sweatshop labor to produce its athletic apparel. Nike and other athletic apparel companies have since taken steps to ensure better working conditions for foreign workers.

them work for more than 70 hours a week. They were allowed to go to the restroom only twice a day, and if they stayed longer than three minutes, they lost a day's wages.[60] Adidas moved swiftly to avoid the public relations nightmare that Nike had experienced. Adidas announced that henceforth its subcontractors would be required to abide by more strict labor standards.

What happened in the sports shoe industry has happened throughout the clothing industry as well as other industries like electronics and toys in the 2000s. Companies such as Wal-Mart, Target, The Gap, Sony, and Mattel have all been forced to reevaluate the ethics of their labor practices and to promise to keep a constant watch on subcontractors in the future. A statement to this effect can be found on many of these companies' Web pages, for example, Nike's (www.nikebiz.com) and The Gap's (www.thegap.com), as mentioned in Chapter 4.

The ability of managers to develop a network structure to produce or provide the goods and services customers want, rather than create a complex organizational structure to do so, has led many researchers and consultants to popularize the idea of a **boundaryless organization.** Such an organization is composed of people linked by IT–computers, faxes, computer-aided design systems, and video teleconferencing–who may rarely, if ever, see one another face-to-face. People are utilized when their services are needed, much as in a matrix structure, but they are not formal members of an organization; they are functional experts who form an alliance with an organization, fulfill their contractual obligations, and then move on to the next project.

boundaryless organization An organization whose members are linked by computers, faxes, computer-aided design systems, and video teleconferencing and who rarely, if ever, see one another face-to-face.

knowledge management system A company-specific virtual information system that allows workers to share their knowledge and expertise and find others to help solve ongoing problems.

Large consulting companies, such as Arthur Andersen and McKinsey & Co., utilize their global consultants in this way. Consultants are connected by laptops to an organization's **knowledge management system,** its company-specific information system that systematizes the knowledge of its employees and provides them with access to other employees who have the expertise to solve the problems that they encounter as they perform their jobs.

The use of outsourcing and the development of network structures is increasing rapidly as organizations recognize the many opportunities they offer to reduce costs and increase organizational flexibility. U.S. companies spent $300 billion on global supply chain management in 2000. This push to lower costs has led to the development of electronic **business-to-business (B2B) networks** in which most or all of the companies in an industry (for example, carmakers) use the same software platform to link to each other and establish industry spec-

business to business (B2B) network A group of organizations that join together and use IT to link themselves to potential global suppliers to increase efficiency and effectiveness.

ifications and standards. Then, these companies jointly list the quantity and specifications of the inputs they require and invite bids from the thousands of potential suppliers around the world. Suppliers also use the same software platform, so electronic bidding, auctions, and transactions are possible between buyers and sellers around the world. The idea is that high-volume standardized transactions can help drive down costs at the industry level.

Today, with advances in IT, designing organizational architecture is becoming an increasingly complex management function. To maximize efficiency and effectiveness, managers must assess carefully the relative benefits of having their own organization perform a functional activity versus forming an alliance with another organization to perform the activity. It is still not clear how B2B networks and other forms of electronic alliances between companies will develop in the future.

Summary and Review

DESIGNING ORGANIZATIONAL STRUCTURE The four main determinants of organizational structure are the external environment, strategy, technology, and human resources. In general, the higher the level of uncertainty associated with these factors, the more appropriate is a flexible, adaptable structure as opposed to a formal, rigid one.

GROUPING TASKS INTO JOBS Job design is the process by which managers group tasks into jobs. To create more interesting jobs, and to get workers to act flexibly, managers can enlarge and enrich jobs. The job characteristics model provides a tool managers can use to measure how motivating or satisfying a particular job is.

GROUPING JOBS INTO FUNCTIONS AND DIVISIONS Managers can choose from many kinds of organizational structures to make the best use of organizational resources. Depending on the specific organizing problems they face, managers can choose from functional, product, geographic, market, matrix, product team, and hybrid structures.

COORDINATING FUNCTIONS AND DIVISIONS No matter which structure managers choose, they must decide how to distribute authority in the organization, how many levels to have in the hierarchy of authority, and what balance to strike between centralization and decentralization to keep the number of levels in the hierarchy to a minimum. As organizations grow, managers must increase integration and coordination among functions and divisions. Six integrating mechanisms are available to facilitate this: direct contact, liaison roles, task forces, cross-functional teams, integrating roles, and the matrix structure.

STRATEGIC ALLIANCES, B2B NETWORK STRUCTURES, AND IT To avoid many of the communication and coordination problems that emerge as organizations grow, managers are attempting to use IT to develop new ways of organizing. In a strategic alliance, managers enter into an agreement with another organization to provide inputs or to perform a functional activity. If managers enter into a series of these agreements, they create a network structure. A network structure, most commonly based on some shared form of IT, can be formed around one company, or a number of companies can join together to create an industry B2B network.

Management in Action

Topics for Discussion and Action

Discussion

1. Would a flexible or a more formal structure be appropriate for these organizations: (a) a large department store, (b) a Big Five accountancy firm, (c) a biotechnology company? Explain your reasoning.
2. Using the job characteristics model as a guide, discuss how a manager can enrich or enlarge subordinates' jobs.
3. How might a salesperson's job or a secretary's job be enlarged or enriched to make it more motivating?
4. When and under what conditions might managers change from a functional to (a) a product, (b) a geographic, or (c) a market structure?
5. How do matrix structure and product team structure differ? Why is product team structure more widely used?

Action

6. Compare the pros and cons of using a network structure to perform organizational activities and performing all activities in-house or within one organizational hierarchy.
7. What are the advantages and disadvantages of business-to-business networks?
8. Find a manager and identify the kind of organizational structure that his or her organization uses to coordinate its people and resources. Why is the organization using that structure? Do you think a different structure would be more appropriate? Which one?
9. With the same or another manager, discuss the distribution of authority in the organization. Does the manager think that decentralizing authority and empowering employees is appropriate?

Building Management Skills

Understanding Organizing

Think of an organization with which you are familiar, perhaps one you have worked in—such as a store, restaurant, office, church, or school. Then answer the following questions:

1. Which contingencies are most important in explaining how the organization is organized? Do you think it is organized in the best way?
2. Using the job characteristics model, how motivating do you think the job of a typical employee in this organization is?
3. Can you think of any ways in which a typical job could be enlarged or enriched?
4. What kind of organizational structure does the organization use? If it is part of a chain, what kind of structure does the entire organization use? What other structures discussed in the chapter might allow the organization to operate more effectively? For example, would the move to a product team structure lead to greater efficiency or effectiveness? Why or why not?
5. How many levels are there in the organization's hierarchy? Is authority centralized or decentralized? Describe the span of control of the top manager and of middle or first-line managers.
6. Is the distribution of authority appropriate for the organization and its activities? Would it be possible to flatten the hierarchy by decentralizing authority and empowering employees?

7. What are the principal integrating mechanisms used in the organization? Do they provide sufficient coordination among individuals and functions? How might they be improved?

8. Now that you have analyzed the way this organization is organized, what advice would you give its managers to help them improve the way it operates?

Managing Ethically

Suppose an organization is downsizing and laying off many of its middle managers. Some top managers charged with deciding who to terminate might decide to keep the subordinates they like, and who are obedient to them, rather than the ones who are difficult or the best performers. They might also decide to lay off the most highly paid subordinates even if they are high performers. Think of the ethical issues involved in designing a hierarchy, and discuss the following issues.

Questions

1. What ethical rules (see Chapter 4) should managers use to decide which employees to terminate when redesigning their hierarchy?
2. Some people argue that employees who have worked for an organization for many years have a claim on the organization at least as strong as that of its shareholders. What do you think of the ethics of this position—can employees claim to "own" their jobs if they have contributed significantly to its past success? How does a socially responsible organization behave in this situation?

Small Group Breakout Exercise

Bob's Appliances

Form groups of three or four people, and appoint one member as the spokesperson who will communicate your findings to the whole class when called on by the instructor. Then discuss the following scenario.

Bob's Appliances sells and services household appliances such as washing machines, dishwashers, ranges, and refrigerators. Over the years, the company has developed a good reputation for the quality of its customer service, and many local builders patronize the store. Recently, some new appliance retailers, including Circuit City and REX, have opened stores that also provide numerous appliances. In addition to appliances, however, to attract more customers these stores carry a complete range of consumer electronics products—televisions, stereos, and computers. Bob Lange, the owner of Bob's Appliances, has decided that if he is to stay in business, he must widen his product range and compete directly with the chains.

In 2002, he decided to build a 20,000-square-foot store and service center, and he is now hiring new employees to sell and service the new line of consumer electronics. Because of his company's increased size, Lange is not sure of the best way to organize the employees. Currently, he uses a functional structure; employees are divided into sales, purchasing and accounting, and repair. Bob is wondering whether selling and servicing consumer electronics is so different from selling and servicing appliances that he should move to a product structure (see figure) and create separate sets of functions for each of his two lines of business.[61]

You are a team of local consultants whom Bob has called in to advise him as he makes this crucial choice. Which structure do you recommend? Why?

FUNCTIONAL STRUCTURE

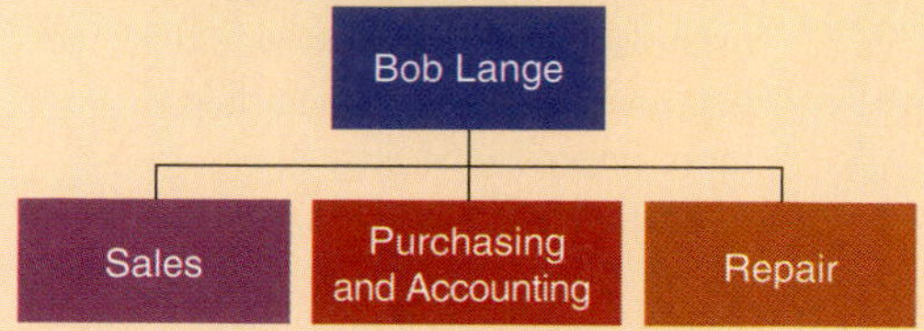

PRODUCT STRUCTURE

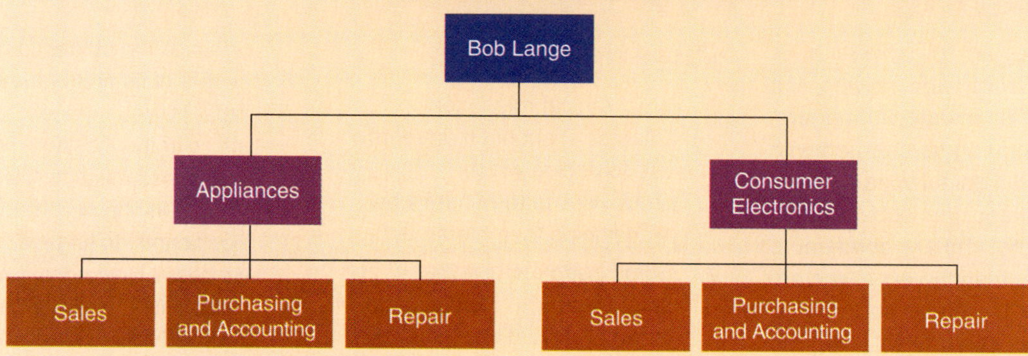

Exploring The World Wide Web

Go to the Web site of Kraft, the food services company (www.kraft.com). Click on "brands," and then click on "North America" and answer the following questions:

1. What kind of international structure do you think Kraft uses to manage its food operations?
2. Given the information on these pages, what kind of organizational structure do you think Kraft uses to manage its U.S. operations? Why do you think it uses this structure?
3. What do you think are the main challenges Kraft faces in managing its food business to improve performance?

Be the Manager

Speeding Up Web-Site Design

You have been hired by a Web-site design, production, and hosting company whose new animated Web-site designs are attracting a lot of attention and a lot of customers. Currently, employees are organized into different functions such as hardware, software design, graphic art, and Web-site hosting, as well as functions such as marketing and human resources. Each function takes its turn to work on a new project from initial customer request to final online Web-site hosting.

The problem the company is experiencing is that it typically takes one year from the initial idea stage to the time that the Web site is up and running; the company wants to shorten this time by half to protect and expand its market niche. In talking to other managers, you discover that they believe the company's current functional structure is the source of the problem—it is not allowing employees to develop Web sites fast enough to satisfy customers' demands. They want you to design a better one.

Questions

1. Discuss ways in which you can improve the way the current functional structure operates so that it speeds Web-site development.
2. Discuss the pros and cons of moving to a (a) multidivisional, (b) matrix, and (c) product team structure to reduce Web-site development time.
3. Which of these structures do you think is most appropriate and why?

Build Your Management Skills DVD

- **Test Your Knowledge:** (1) Mechanistic versus Organic Orgnizational Structures and (2) Allocating Authority
- **Self Assessment:** Identify Your Preferred Organizational Structure

BusinessWeek Case in the News

No Excuse Not To Succeed

Dressed in a cream-colored suit amid a sea of dark jackets, Antonio M. Perez looked more like an MC of a glitzy Vegas show than a corporate chieftain as he took the stage before a standing-room-only crowd of camera-shop owners and photo buffs in America's gambling mecca. And the chief operating officer of Eastman Kodak Co. displayed a showman's bravado when he declared: "Kodak holds a winning hand."

Certainly, some in the room figured Perez was bluffing. Kodak is desperately trying to reinvent itself for the Digital Age, and 58-year-old Perez, who oversaw Hewlett-Packard Co.'s rise to dominance in inkjet printers, was hired a year ago to lead the way. Kodak is in a race against time as its traditional film business disappears; Sales peaked at $14 billion in 1999 and have dropped to $13.3 billion in 2003. Today, Kodak finds itself in the awkward position of having to establish itself in a field dominated by others.

It's a painful irony for the company. For a century, Kodak enjoyed near-monopoly power—until Fuji Photo Film Co. came along. Kodak even came up with the first digital camera in 1975. But it is only now that the company is starting to capitalize on the technology.

Clear Vision

Perez has gotten off to a quick start at a company once known for its destructively slow decision-making. He has made clear what many at the Rochester (N.Y.) headquarters long denied—that Kodak's main business has to be digital imaging. In September, the company announced a sharper focus on digital businesses for its consumer, commercial, and health units that it predicts will increase the company's revenue 23 percent, to $16 billion, in 2006, and to $20 billion by 2010.

Perez helped figure out how to pay for the transition—mostly by reducing investment in film and laying off nearly a quarter of Kodak's 60,000 workforce. He has instilled a new discipline at the company that is speeding product development. And he is uncovering new uses for Kodak's 20,000 patents. "The intellectual property and know-how is unbelievable in the company," he says. "there is no excuse not to succeed."

But the toughest challenges still lie ahead. Perez has to get Kodak's engineers and marketers to work together to come up with products that will hold their own in areas where the company has little credibility. For example, after rummaging around Kodak's hallowed labs, Perez believes he has found a breakthrough technology that will change the inkjet printer business. And that is all he will say.

Sounds like wishful thinking to some. "It's not about patents. It's all about commercializing the technology," says Vyomesh Joshi, who worked under Perez at HP and now runs its imaging and printing group. "That's where they're going to have a hard time."

Perez, for all his showy enthusiasm, is well aware of the old attitude problems at Big Yellow. The biggest is a strange complacency—some call it arrogance—when it comes to selling what are widely acknowledged to be innovative products. "They tend to bring out one product and think, that's it—that they've now solved all the problems and the world will beat a path to their door," says Frank J. Romano, a professor of printing at Rochester Institute of Technology. The printer dock for the Kodak EasyShare digital camera is a case in point. Introduced last year, the dock finally made it easy for digital shutterbugs to print their photos without a computer. If, that is, they used a Kodak camera. Such proprietary standards are a no-no in the digital world. Although the dock topped $100 million in sales in its first year, it could have done much better. Now Kodak is looking for ways to make the dock work with other cameras.

Perez has helped change how Kodak operates to ensure the company doesn't make the same mistake again. He has sharpened the focus of an integrated product-delivery program that helps marketers and gearheads work more closely together. And Perez has sped the reorganization of each Kodak business unit into special product groups. These are teams dedicated to specific areas such as digital cameras, online services, or photo kiosks. By partly tying compensation to each group's performance, he expects better results.

Some employees and customers already note a faster pace. Kodak introduced six new digital cameras in February, double last year's number. And it raced to upgrade 3,300 photo-processing kiosks at CVS drugstores to wirelessly handle photos from camera phones. The old Kodak might have discouraged the change because it could cut into sales of disposable cameras.

Perez has found a company that for all its earlier conceit now sees the need for a change. That gives him a chance to turn Kodak into something it hasn't been for a while: a company whose best years are ahead of it.

Questions

1. What kinds of problems has Kodak been experiencing?
2. How has its COO been changing its organizational structure and design to respond to these problems?

Source: Faith Arner and Rachel Tiplady, "No Excuse Not to Succeed." Reprinted from the May 10, 2004, issue of *BusinessWeek* by special permission.

BusinessWeek Case in the News

How Xerox Got Up to Speed

Xerox Corp. thought it was doing a smart thing when it consolidated 36 administrative centers into 3 back in 1999. The copy king would be able to reap millions in cost savings. But the move came just as Xerox was also reorganizing its sales division. The simultaneous upheaval in two key units unleashed chaos across the company's billing system. Customers received invoices quoting prices they had never agreed to—or detailing equipment they had never ordered. Worse, the mistakes took months to sort out, prompting some longtime customers to defect. The so-called document company had failed miserably at its own documentation.

Five years later, Xerox can see the bright side of that fiasco. After struggling to fix the problem itself, it hired General Electric Capital to handle its billing. GE brought more than order to the process: It showed Xerox a whole new way to diagnose and fix its problems. If the company could omit steps from its design, manufacturing, and servicing processes, as well as fine-tune those that remained, it would be able to deliver better printers and copiers to customers far faster and at lower cost. "GE made progress with [our operations] much more quickly than we could," says Ursula M. Burns, president of Xerox Business Group Operations. Today, GE continues to handle Xerox's billing.

What did GE have that Xerox didn't? For one, years of experience in applying Six Sigma, the data-driven technique for eliminating defects in any business process. But GE had moved beyond Six Sigma to apply so-called lean manufacturing tools made famous by Toyota Motor Corp. in the 1980s. The combination—known as Lean Six Sigma—has taken root across corporate America in the past two years. Companies are using the techniques to analyze and improve tasks ranging from simple processes such as customer credit checks to complex product-design challenges. "Companies are starting to realize this is becoming a very competitive weapon," says Deborah Nightingale, engineering systems director of Massachusetts Institute of Technology's lean aerospace initiative.

Xerox kicked into high gear in late 2002 with training for top execs, including CEO Anne M. Mulcahy, who has spearheaded the effort. The company has since launched about 250 projects, both for itself and its customers. "We've gone at it with a vengeance," says Mulcahy. And the results are already rolling in: Xerox claims a $6 million return in 2003 on a $14 million investment in Lean Six Sigma. It expects an even bigger payoff this year.

One of the strengths of Lean Six Sigma is that it blankets the company. Previous quality initiatives may have addressed a particular factory operation or only a part of it. The point is not to automate complicated processes, but to "lean out" existing processes by removing unnecessary steps and then fix those that remain.

Sounds easy, but Mulcahy admits it can be a slog. Learning the dozens of analytical methods involved in Lean Six Sigma takes weeks of training. Figuring out what steps to trim or replace chews up time, too. But the hardest task is getting employees to accept that how they've always done things may not be the best way. "A lot of the work is soft, not hard," says Burns. But consultants say Xerox is succeeding because the CEO has made the program a priority. The head of the effort reports directly to Mulcahy, who herself is training to reach the yellow-belt level in the karate-like Lean Six Sigma regimen.

One of the "soft" challenges is tearing down walls to get different divisions to work together. This is never easy in a complex, big organization. Yet at Xerox, teams from supply, manufacturing, and research and development pulled it off to resolve a problem with a $500,000 printing press introduced last year. Customers quickly found that the fuser roll (which uses heat and pressure to bond toner to paper) was wearing out sooner than expected. The Xerox team used Lean Six Sigma tools to zero in on the cause in just one month. The oil on the roller was fouling up the works. "Not only had the chemical structure of the oil changed, but we didn't have enough of the oil that did work well," says John R. Laing, senior vice president for Xerox' supplies-delivery unit. The team worked with the oilmaker, which changed the chemistry, saving Xerox $2 million and keeping its customers happy.

Ultimately, Xerox's efforts are focused on getting new products to customers faster, which has meant taking steps out of the design process. Typically a high-end, $200,000 machine that can print 100 pages a minute takes three to five cycles of design, building, and testing before it reaches the customer. Taking just one of those cycles out of the process can shave up to a year off the time to market. For its new DocuTech print-on-demand machines launched in January, for example, Xerox used software to simulate an early design stage, saving the time and expense of building a prototype.

These days, Xerox has gotten so good at applying Lean Six Sigma that, like GE before, it's helping out its customers. In one case, the mail volume at a customer's document-management unit had grown out of control. Xerox moved in, streamlined the mailroom—with changes as simple as removing furniture—to use half the amount of space, and saved the company $180,000 in the process. From failing to fix its own operations to improving those of others is a big leap. Says Laing: "We've moved from being consciously incompetent to consciously competent." Now, Mulcahy is pushing Xerox to become unconsciously competent—the point where the tools are so ingrained that no one even thinks about them anymore.

Questions

1. What problems arose when Xerox first changed its organizational structure? Why did these problems arise?
2. How has the company been using 6 Sigma to solve its problems? How have these changes affected its organizational structure?

Source: Faith Arner and Adam Aston, "How Xerox Got Up to Speed." Reprinted from the May 3, 2004, issue of *BusinessWeek* by special permission.

CHAPTER 11 Organizational Control and Change

Learning Objectives

After studying this chapter, you should be able to:

- Define organizational control, and describe the four steps of the control process.
- Identify the main output controls, and discuss their advantages and disadvantages as means of coordinating and motivating employees.
- Identify the main behavior controls, and discuss their advantages and disadvantages as means of coordinating and motivating employees.
- Explain the role of clan control or organizational culture in creating an effective organizational architecture.
- Discuss the relationship between organizational control and change, and explain why managing change is a vital management task.

A Manager's Challenge

Bob Nardelli's New Controls Change Home Depot

How should managers control to improve performance?

Home Depot, based in Atlanta, Georgia, is the largest home-improvement retail chain in the United States. With sales of over $64 billion, it is one of the biggest Fortune 500 companies.[1] However, when Bob Nardelli became CEO of Home Depot in 2000, he entered a company whose sales and earnings were falling sharply. Nardelli's job was to change the way the company operated and turn around its performance.

After studying his new company, Nardelli was appalled to find that its previous top managers had paid little attention to the need to monitor and control Home Depot's store operations and to develop a centralized control system that provided detailed information on store performance. Home Depot operated with a decentralized, freewheeling culture in which each store manager treated his or her own store as a kind of personal fiefdom in which the manager had the right to control store activities as he or she saw fit.

In large part, this was because of the way Home Depot's two founders had told managers to operate—to grow their company quickly they instructed managers to do what they thought was best. While this may have been fine when the chain was growing rapidly, it was no longer acceptable at a time when it was experiencing intense competition from other chains such as Lowe's, which by 2000 was perceived as the leading home-improvement store in the nation. Nardelli's problem was how to change the company's culture and control systems—and change them quickly.

When Bob Nardelli became CEO of Home Depot in 2000, he was appalled to find previous top managers had paid little attention to controlling operations.

Fortunately, Nardelli knew exactly what to do. Before becoming Home Depot's CEO, he had been one of the most senior managers at GE. Nardelli had spent his career managing GE's lighting and power generation businesses, and he had been socialized into GE's culture, which was based on a highly cotrolled and structured management approach.[2] GE is renowned for controlling its operations through a sophisticated central information system that continually collects information about all aspects of its operations. Nardelli searched for ways to replicate GE's control system at Home Depot. By 2003, Nardelli had wrought enormous changes that totally transformed Home Depot's culture.

To improve the company's ability to monitor and control its materials management and purchasing activities, Nardelli shifted all merchandise buying to Atlanta. Previously eight different regional divisions had done their own purchasing for stores in their regions. He halved the size of the regional divisions and told them that henceforth they would be responsible not for purchasing but for improving customer sales and service, something that analysts pointed to as a major company weakness.[3] Now, Nardelli and his top-management team had a much firmer grasp of how inventory was flowing through Home Depot's stores, and they were in a better position to bargain for lower prices from suppliers.

Nardelli also devised a way to change the freewheeling values and norms that had previously controlled Home Depot's managers' behavior. He brought in a new top-management team, as well as scores of functional managers who had a military background and were thus used to a culture that emphasized the importance of following the hierarchy of authority and adhering to rules and procedures. He also started new leadership programs that taught store managers what kind of leadership approach they should adopt in their stores.

Finally, he created a whole series of new rules and procedures that managers at all levels should follow. They included new rules for managing the flow of inventory, for store displays, and for hiring, promoting, and evaluating employee performance. In following the new rules, managers at all levels now have to record and transmit data on all these issues to headquarters, using a sophisticated new IT system that Nardelli also created. So the links between the top and bottom of the company have been strengthened, and store managers have less autonomy as a result.

Nardelli's new methods for controlling Home Depot's operations have transformed the company. Many managers who did not like the new "top-down" corporate culture left the company; those who remained have bought into Nardelli's new centralized approach. They have done so because they can see its results: In 2003 Home Depot's sales increased by 11 percent, its earnings per share rose by a record 21 percent, and its stock price shot back up. Both employees and analysts recognize that Nardelli's revolutionary approach to controlling Home Depot has not only saved the company but also changed it forever.

Overview

As the experience of Home Depot suggests, the ways in which managers decide to control the behavior of their employees can have very different effects on the way employees behave. When managers make choices about how to influence and regulate their employees' behavior and performance, they establish the second foundation of organizational architecture, organizational control. And control is the essential ingredient that is needed to bring about and manage organizational change efficiently and effectively, as Bob Nardelli did at Home Depot.

As discussed in Chapter 10, the first task facing managers is to establish the structure of task and job reporting relationships that allows organizational members to use resources most efficiently and effectively. Structure alone, however, does not provide the incentive or motivation for people to behave in ways that help achieve organizational goals. The purpose of organizational control is to provide managers with a means of directing and motivating subordinates to work toward achieving organizational goals and to provide managers with specific feedback on how well an organization and its members are performing. Nardelli's new rules were intended to direct and motivate employee behavior; Home Depot's market share, profits, and customer satisfaction rating are measures that give it feedback on how well it is performing.

Organizational structure provides an organization with a skeleton, and control and culture give it the muscles, sinews, nerves, and sensations that allow managers to regulate and govern its activities. The managerial functions of organizing and controlling are inseparable, and effective managers must learn to make them work together in a harmonious way.

In this chapter, we look in detail at the nature of organizational control and describe the steps in the control process. We discuss three types of control available to managers to control and influence organizational members–output control, behavior control, and clan control (which operates through the values and norms of an organization's culture).[4] Finally, we discuss the important issue of organizational change, change that is possible only when managers have put in place a control system that allows them to alter the way people and groups behave. By the end of this chapter, you will appreciate the rich variety of control systems available to managers and understand why developing an appropriate control system is vital to increasing the performance of an organization and its members.

What is Organizational Control?

As noted in Chapter 1, *controlling* is the process whereby managers monitor and regulate how efficiently and effectively an organization and its members are performing the activities necessary to achieve organizational goals. As discussed in previous chapters, when planning and organizing, managers develop the organizational strategy and structure that they hope will allow the organization to use resources most effectively to create value for customers. In controlling, managers monitor and evaluate whether the organization's strategy and structure are working as intended, how they could be improved, and how they might be changed if they are not working.

Control, however, does not mean just reacting to events after they have occurred. It also means keeping an organization on track, anticipating events that might occur, and then changing the organization to respond to whatever opportunities or threats have been identified. Control is concerned with keeping employees motivated, focused on the important problems confronting the organization, and working together to make the changes that will help an organization perform more highly over time.

The Importance of Organizational Control

To understand the importance of organizational control, consider how it helps managers obtain superior efficiency, quality, responsiveness to customers, and innovation–the four building blocks of competitive advantage.

To determine how efficiently they are using their resources, managers must be able to accurately measure how many units of inputs (raw materials, human resources, and so on) are being used to produce a unit of output. Managers also must be able to measure how many units of outputs (goods and services) are being produced. A control system contains the measures or yardsticks that allow managers to assess how efficiently the organization is producing goods and services. Moreover, if managers experiment with changing the way the organization produces goods and services to find a more efficient way of producing them, these measures tell managers how successful they have been. For example, when managers at Ford decided to adopt a product team structure to design, engineer, and manufacture new car models, they used measures such as time taken to design a new car and cost savings per car produced to evaluate how well the new structure worked in comparison with the old structure. They found that the new one performed better. Without a control system in place, managers have no idea how well their organization is performing and how its performance can be improved–information that is becoming increasingly important in today's highly competitive environment.

Today, much of the competition among organizations revolves around increasing the quality of goods and services. In the car industry, for example, cars within each price range compete against one another in features, design, and reliability. Thus, whether a customer will buy a Ford Taurus, GM Cavalier, Chrysler Sebring, Toyota Camry, or Honda Accord depends significantly on the quality of each product. Organizational control is important in determining the quality of goods and services because it gives managers feedback on product quality. If the managers of carmakers consistently measure the number of customer complaints and the number of new cars returned for repairs, or if school principals measure how many students drop out of school or how achievement scores on nationally based tests vary over time, they have a good indication of how much quality they have built into their product–be it an educated student or a car that does not break down. Effective managers create a control system that consistently monitors the quality of goods and services so that they can make continuous improvements to quality–an approach to change that gives them a competitive advantage.

A Ford salesperson talks with a prospective car buyer. In the car industry, managers not only need to control the quality of their products but also the quality of their customer service. To improve its customer service, Ford implemented a control system that consists of regularly surveying customers about their experience with particular dealers. If a dealership receives too many complaints, Ford's managers investigate and propose solutions.

Managers can also help make their organizations more responsive to customers if they develop a control system that allows them to evaluate how well customer-contact employees are performing their jobs, as Home Depot now does. Monitoring employee behavior can help managers find ways to increase employees' performance levels, perhaps by revealing areas in which skill training can help employees or by finding new procedures that allow employees to perform their jobs better. When employees know that their behaviors are being monitored, they may also have more incentive to be helpful and consistent in how they act toward customers. To improve customer service, for example, Ford regularly surveys customers about their experiences with particular Ford dealers. If a dealership receives too many customer complaints, Ford's managers investigate the dealership to uncover the sources of the problems and suggest solutions; if necessary, they might even threaten to reduce the number of cars a dealership receives to force the dealer to improve the quality of its customer service.

Finally, controlling can raise the level of innovation in an organization. Successful innovation takes place when managers create an organizational setting in which employees feel empowered to be creative and in which authority is decentralized to employees so that they feel free to experiment and take risks. Deciding on the appropriate control systems to encourage risk taking is an important management challenge; organizational culture (discussed later in this chapter) becomes important in this regard. To encourage product teams at Ford to perform highly, top managers monitored the performance of each team separately–by examining how each team reduced costs or increased quality, for example–and used a bonus system related to performance to pay each team. The product team manager then evaluated each team member's individual performance, and the most innovative employees received promotions and rewards based on their superior performance.

Control Systems and IT

control systems Formal target-setting, monitoring, evaluation, and feedback systems that provide managers with information about how well the organization's strategy and structure are working.

Control systems are formal target-setting, monitoring, evaluation, and feedback systems that provide managers with information about whether the organization's strategy and structure are working efficiently and effectively.[5] Effective control systems alert managers when something is going wrong and give them time to respond to opportunities and threats. An effective control system has three characteristics: It is flexible enough to allow managers to respond as necessary to unexpected events; it provides accurate information and gives managers a true picture of organizational performance; and it provides managers with the information in a timely manner because making decisions on the basis of outdated information is a recipe for failure.

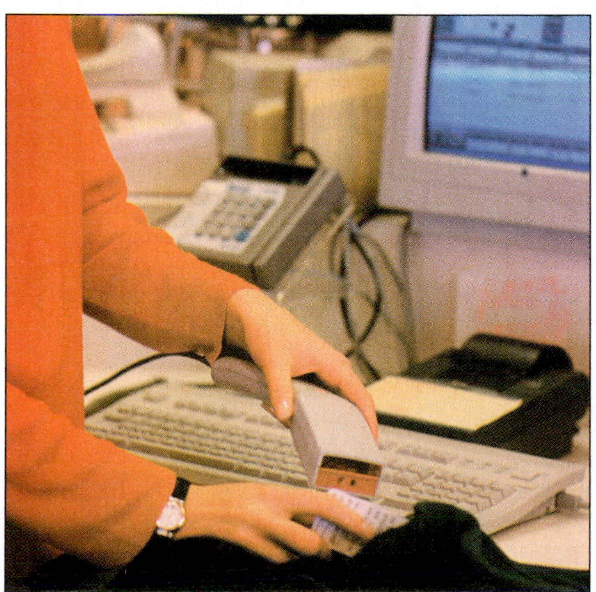

Scanning devices, such as the one shown here, are becoming common in all types of work processes, as more companies require real-time information about their products and customers.

New forms of IT have revolutionized control systems because they facilitate the flow of accurate and timely information up and down the organizational hierarchy and between functions and divisions. Today, employees at all levels of the organization routinely feed information into a company's information system or network and start the chain of events that affect decision making at some other part of the organization. This could be the department store clerk whose scanning of purchased clothing tells merchandise managers what kinds of clothing need to be reordered or the salesperson in the field who feeds into a wireless laptop information about customers' changing needs or problems.

Control and information systems are developed to measure performance at each stage in the process of transforming inputs into finished goods and services (see Figure 11.1, page 380). At the input stage, managers use **feedforward control** to anticipate problems before they arise so that problems do not occur later, during the conversion process.[6] For example, by giving stringent product specifications

Figure 11.1
Three Types of Control

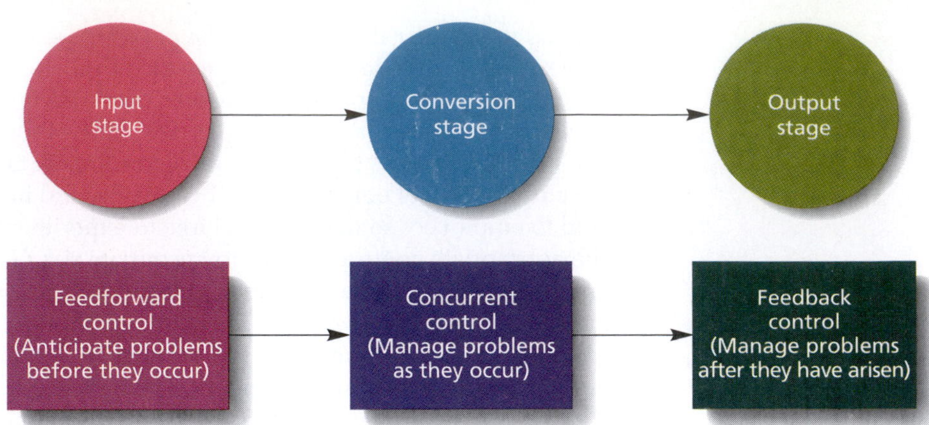

feedforward control Control that allows managers to anticipate problems before they arise.

to suppliers in advance (a form of performance target), an organization can control the quality of the inputs it receives from its suppliers and thus avoid potential problems during the conversion process. Also, IT can be used to keep in contact with suppliers and to monitor their progress. Similarly, by screening job applicants, often by viewing their résumés electronically, and using several interviews to select the most highly skilled people, managers can lessen the chance that they will hire people who lack the necessary skills or experience to perform effectively. In general, the development of management information systems promotes feedforward control that provides managers with timely information about changes in the task and general environments that may impact their organization later on. Effective managers always monitor trends and changes in the external environment to try to anticipate problems. (We discuss management information systems in detail in Chapter 18.)

concurrent control Control that gives managers immediate feedback on how efficiently inputs are being transformed into outputs so that managers can correct problems as they arise.

At the conversion stage, **concurrent control** gives managers immediate feedback on how efficiently inputs are being transformed into outputs so that managers can correct problems as they arise. Concurrent control through IT alerts managers to the need to react quickly to whatever is the source of the problem, be it a defective batch of inputs, a machine that is out of alignment, or a worker who lacks the skills necessary to perform a task efficiently. Concurrent control is at the heart of total quality management programs (discussed in Chapter 9), in which workers are expected to constantly monitor the quality of the goods or services they provide at every step of the production process and inform managers as soon as they discover problems. One of the strengths of Toyota's production system, for example, is that individual workers are given the authority to push a button to stop the assembly line whenever they discover a quality problem. When all problems have been corrected, the result is a finished product that is much more reliable.

feedback control Control that gives managers information about customers' reactions to goods and services so that corrective action can be taken if necessary.

At the output stage, managers use **feedback control** to provide information about customers' reactions to goods and services so that corrective action can be taken if necessary. For example, a feedback control system that monitors the number of customer returns alerts managers when defective products are being produced, and a management information system that measures increases or decreases in relative sales of different products alerts managers to changes in customer tastes so that they can increase or reduce the production of specific products.

The Control Process

The control process, whether at the input, conversion, or output stage, can be broken down into four steps: establishing standards of performance, and then measuring, comparing, and evaluating actual performance (see Figure 11.2).[7]

- Step 1: *Establish the standards of performance, goals, or targets against which performance is to be evaluated.*

At step 1 in the control process managers decide on the standards of performance, goals, or targets that they will use in the future to evaluate the performance of the entire organization or part of it (such as a division, a function, or an individual). The standards of performance that managers select measure efficiency, quality, responsiveness to customers, and innovation.[8] If managers decide to pursue a low-cost strategy, for example, then they need to measure efficiency at all levels in the organization.

At the corporate level, a standard of performance that measures efficiency is operating costs, the actual costs associated with producing goods and services, including all employee-related costs. Top managers might set a corporate goal of "reducing operating costs by 10 percent for the next three years" to increase efficiency. Corporate managers might then evaluate divisional managers for their ability to reduce operating costs within their respective divisions, and divisional managers might set cost-savings targets for functional managers. Thus, performance standards selected at one level affect those at the other levels, and ultimately the performance of individual managers is evaluated in terms of their ability to reduce costs. For example, in 2001 struggling Xerox Corp. named Anne Mulcahy as CEO and gave her the challenging task of turning around the company's fortunes. She was selected because of her 25-year reputation as a person who had been highly successful in reducing costs and increasing efficiency in Xerox's general markets division.[9] By 2004, Mulcahy had succeeded; Xerox began to make a profit again as it now could make the products customers wanted.

The number of standards of performance that an organization's managers use to evaluate efficiency, quality, and so on, can run into the thousands or hundreds of thousands. Managers at each level are responsible for selecting those standards that will best allow them to evaluate how well the part of the organization they are responsible for is performing.[10] Managers must be careful to choose the standards of performance that allow them to assess how well they

Figure 11.2
Four Steps in Organizational Control

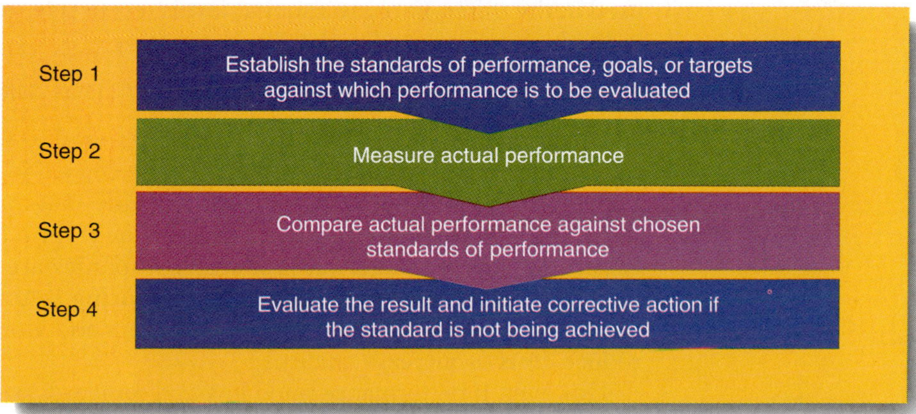
Step 1
Establish the standards of performance, goals, or targets against which performance is to be evaluated
Step 2
Measure actual performance
Step 3
Compare actual performance against chosen standards of performance
Step 4
Evaluate the result and initiate corrective action if the standard is not being achieved

are doing with all four of the building blocks of competitive advantage. If managers focus on just one (such as efficiency) and ignore others (such as determining what customers really want and innovating a new line of products to satisfy them), managers may end up hurting their organization's performance.

- Step 2: *Measure actual performance.*

Once managers have decided which standards or targets they will use to evaluate performance, the next step in the control process is to measure actual performance. In practice, managers can measure or evaluate two things: (1) the actual *outputs* that result from the behavior of their members and (2) the *behaviors* themselves (hence the terms *output control* and *behavior control* used below).[11]

Sometimes both outputs and behaviors can be easily measured. Measuring outputs and evaluating behavior is relatively easy in a fast-food restaurant, for example, because employees are performing routine tasks. Managers at Home Depot, in measuring the flow of inventory through stores, were using output control. Similarly, managers of a fast-food restaurant can quite easily measure outputs by counting how many customers their employees serve and how much money customers spend. Managers can easily observe each employee's behavior and quickly take action to solve any problems that may arise.

When an organization and its members perform complex, nonroutine activities that are intrinsically difficult to measure, it is much more difficult for managers to measure outputs or behavior.[12] It is very difficult, for example, for managers in charge of R&D departments at Merck or Microsoft to measure performance or to evaluate the performance of individual members because it can take 5 or 10 years to determine whether the new products that scientists are developing are going to be profitable. Moreover, it is impossible for a manager to measure how creative a research scientist is by watching his or her actions.

In general, the more nonroutine or complex organizational activities are, the harder it is for managers to measure outputs or behaviors.[13] Outputs, however, are usually easier to measure than behaviors because they are more tangible and objective. Therefore, the first kind of performance measures that managers tend to use are those that measure outputs. Then managers develop performance measures or standards that allow them to evaluate behaviors to determine whether employees at all levels are working toward organizational goals. Some simple behavior measures are (1) do employees come to work on time, and (2) do employees consistently follow the established rules for greeting and serving customers? Each type of output and behavior control and the way it is used at the different organizational levels–corporate, divisional, functional, and individual–is discussed in detail subsequently.

- Step 3: *Compare actual performance against chosen standards of performance.*

During step 3, managers evaluate whether–and to what extent–performance deviates from the standards of performance chosen in step 1. If performance is higher than expected, managers might decide that they set performance standards too low and may raise them for the next time period to challenge their subordinates.[14] Managers at Japanese companies are well known for the way they try to raise performance in manufacturing settings by constantly raising performance standards to motivate managers and workers to find new ways to reduce costs or increase quality.

However, if performance is too low and standards were not reached, or if standards were set so high that employees could not achieve them, managers must decide whether to take corrective action.[15] It is easy to take corrective action when the reasons for poor performance can be identified–for instance, high labor costs. To reduce costs, managers can search for low-cost foreign sources of supply, invest more in technology, or implement cross-functional teams. More often, however, the reasons for poor performance are hard to identify. Changes in the environment, such as the emergence of a new global competitor, a recession, or an increase in interest rates, might be the source of the problem. Within an organization, perhaps the R&D function underestimated the problems it would encounter in developing a new product or the extra costs of doing unforeseen research. If managers are to take any form of corrective action, step 4 is necessary.

- Step 4: *Evaluate the result and initiate corrective action (that is, make changes) if the standard is not being achieved.*

The final step in the control process is to evaluate the results and bring about change as appropriate. Whether performance standards have been met or not, managers can learn a great deal during this step. If managers decide that the level of performance is unacceptable, they must try to change the way work activities are performed to solve the problem. Sometimes, performance problems occur because the work standard was too high–for example, a sales target was too optimistic and impossible to achieve. In this case, adopting more realistic standards can reduce the gap between actual performance and desired performance.

However, if managers determine that something in the situation is causing the problem, then to raise performance they will need to change the way resources are being utilized.[16] Perhaps the latest technology is not being used; perhaps workers lack the advanced training needed to perform at a higher level; perhaps the organization needs to buy its inputs or assemble its products abroad to compete against low-cost rivals; perhaps it needs to restructure itself or reengineer its work processes to increase efficiency.

The simplest example of a control system is the thermostat in a home. By setting the thermostat, you establish the standard of performance with which actual temperature is to be compared. The thermostat contains a sensing or monitoring device, which measures the actual temperature against the desired temperature. Whenever there is a difference between them, the furnace or air-conditioning unit is activated to bring the temperature back to the standard. In other words, corrective action is initiated. This is a simple control system, for it is entirely self-contained and the target (temperature) is easy to measure.

Establishing targets and designing measurement systems is much more difficult for managers because the high level of uncertainty in the organizational environment causes managers to rarely know what might happen. Thus, it is vital for managers to design control systems to alert them to problems so that they can be dealt with before they become threatening. Another issue is that managers are not just concerned about bringing the organization's performance up to some predetermined standard; they want to push that standard forward, to encourage employees at all levels to find new ways to raise performance.

In the following sections, we consider the three most important types of control that managers use to coordinate and motivate employees to ensure they pursue superior efficiency, quality, innovation, and responsiveness to customers: output control, behavior control, and organizational culture or clan control (see Figure 11.3, page 384). Managers use all three to govern and regulate organizational activities, no matter what specific organizational structure is in place.

Figure 11.3
Three Organizational Control Systems

Type of control	Mechanisms of control
Output control	Financial measures of performance Organizational goals Operating budgets
Behavior control	Direct supervision Management by objectives Rules and standard operating procedures
Organizational culture/clan control	Values Norms Socialization

Output Control

All managers develop a system of output control for their organizations. First, they choose the goals or output performance standards or targets that they think will best measure efficiency, quality, innovation, and responsiveness to customers. Then they measure to see whether the performance goals and standards are being achieved at the corporate, divisional or functional, and individual levels of the organization. The three main mechanisms that managers use to assess output or performance are financial measures, organizational goals, and operating budgets.

Financial Measures of Performance

Top managers are most concerned with overall organizational performance and use various financial measures to evaluate performance. The most common are profit ratios, liquidity ratios, leverage ratios, and activity ratios. They are discussed below and summarized in Table 11.1.[17]

- *Profit ratios* measure how efficiently managers are using the organization's resources to generate profits. *Return on investment (ROI),* an organization's net income before taxes divided by its total assets, is the most commonly used financial performance measure because it allows managers of one organization to compare performance with that of other organizations. ROI allows managers to assess an organization's competitive advantage. *Gross profit margin* is the difference between the amount of revenue generated by a product and the resources used to produce the product. This measure provides managers with information about how efficiently an organization is utilizing its resources and about how attractive customers find the product. It also provides managers with a way to assess how well an organization is building a competitive advantage.
- *Liquidity ratios* measure how well managers have protected organizational resources to be able to meet short-term obligations. The *current ratio* (current assets divided by current liabilities) tells managers whether they have the resources available to meet the claims of short-term creditors. The *quick ratio* tells whether they can pay these claims without selling inventory.
- *Leverage ratios* such as the *debt-to-assets ratio* and the *times-covered ratio* measure the degree to which managers use debt (borrow money) or equity (issue

Table 11.1
Four Measures of Financial Performance

Profit Ratios			
Return on investment	=	$\frac{\text{net profit before taxes}}{\text{total assets}}$	Measures how well managers are using the organization's resources to generate profits.
Gross profit margin	=	$\frac{\text{sales revenues} - \text{cost of goods sold}}{\text{sales revenues}}$	The difference between the amount of revenue generated from the product and the resources used to produce the product.
Liquidity Ratios			
Current ratio	=	$\frac{\text{current assets}}{\text{current liabilities}}$	Do managers have resources available to meet claims of short-term creditors?
Quick ratio	=	$\frac{\text{current assets} - \text{inventory}}{\text{current liabilities}}$	Can managers pay off claims of short-term creditors without selling inventory?
Leverage Ratios			
Debt-to-assets ratio	=	$\frac{\text{total debt}}{\text{total assets}}$	To what extent have managers used borrowed funds to finance investments?
Times-covered ratio	=	$\frac{\text{profit before interest and taxes}}{\text{total interest charges}}$	Measures how far profits can decline before managers cannot meet interest changes. If ratio declines to less than 1, the organization is technically insolvent.
Activity Ratios			
Inventory turnover	=	$\frac{\text{cost of goods sold}}{\text{inventory}}$	Measures how efficiently managers are turning inventory over so that excess inventory is not carried.
Days sales outstanding	=	$\frac{\text{current accounts receivable}}{\text{sales for period divided by days in period}}$	Measures how efficiently managers are collecting revenues from customers to pay expenses.

new shares) to finance ongoing operations. An organization is highly leveraged if it uses more debt than equity, and debt can be very risky when profits fail to cover the interest on the debt.

- *Activity ratios* provide measures of how well managers are creating value from organizational assets. *Inventory turnover* measures how efficiently managers are turning inventory over so that excess inventory is not carried. *Days sales outstanding* provides information on how efficiently managers are collecting revenue from customers to pay expenses.

The objectivity of financial measures of performance is the reason why so many managers use them to assess the efficiency and effectiveness of their organizations. When an organization fails to meet performance standards such as

ROI, revenue, or stock price targets, managers know that they must take corrective action. Thus, financial controls tell managers when a corporate reorganization might be necessary, when they should sell off divisions and exit from businesses, or when they should rethink their corporate-level strategies.[18]

Although financial information is an important output control, financial information by itself does not provide managers with all the information they need about the four building blocks of competitive advantage. Financial results inform managers about the results of decisions they have already made; they do not tell managers how to find new opportunities to build competitive advantage in the future. To encourage a future-oriented approach, top managers must establish organizational goals that encourage middle and first-line managers to achieve superior efficiency, quality, innovation, and responsiveness to customers.

Organizational Goals

Once top managers consult with lower-level managers and set the organization's overall goals, they establish performance standards for the divisions and functions. These standards specify for divisional and functional managers the level at which their units must perform if the organization is to achieve its overall goals.[19] Each division is given a set of specific goals to achieve (see Figure 11.4). We saw in Chapter 8, for example, that former General Electric CEO Jack Welch and his successor Jeffrey Immelt have declared that the goal of each division is to be first or second in its industry in profit. Divisional managers then develop a business-level strategy (based on achieving superior efficiency or innovation) that they hope will allow them to achieve that goal.[20] In consultation with functional managers, they specify the functional goals that the managers of different functions need to achieve to allow the division to achieve its goals. For example, sales managers might be evaluated for their ability to increase sales; materials management managers, for their ability to increase the quality of inputs or lower their costs; R&D managers, for the number of products they innovate or the number of patents they receive. In turn, functional managers establish goals that first-line managers and nonmanagerial employees need to achieve to allow the function to achieve its goals.

Output control is used at every level of the organization, and it is vital that the goals set at each level harmonize with the goals set at other levels so that managers and other employees throughout the organization work together to attain the corporate goals that top managers have set.[21] It is also important that goals be set appropriately so that managers are motivated to accomplish them. If goals

Figure 11.4 Organizationwide Goal Setting

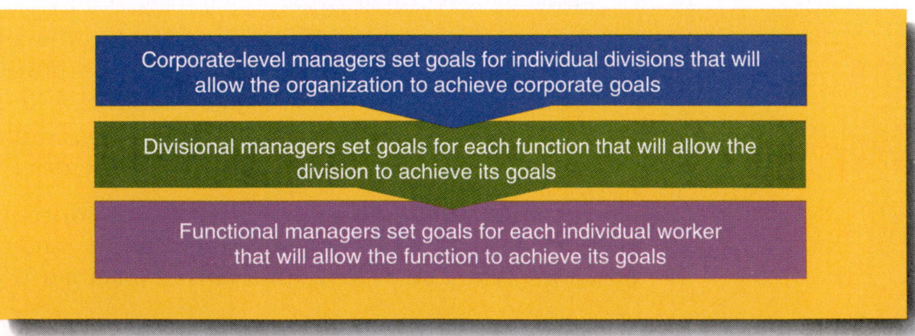

are set at an impossibly high level, managers might work only half-heartedly to achieve them because they are certain they will fail. In contrast, if goals are set so low that they are too easy to achieve, managers will not be motivated to use all their resources as efficiently and effectively as possible. Research suggests that the best goals are *specific, difficult goals*–goals that challenge and stretch managers' ability but are not out of reach and do not require an impossibly high expenditure of managerial time and energy. Such goals are often called *stretch goals*.

Deciding what is a specific, difficult goal and what is a goal that is too difficult or too easy is a skill that managers must develop. Based on their own judgment and work experience, managers at all levels must assess how difficult a certain task is, and they must assess the ability of a particular subordinate manager to achieve the goal. If they do so successfully, challenging, interrelated goals–goals that reinforce one another and focus on achieving overall corporate objectives–will energize the organization.

Operating Budgets

operating budget A budget that states how managers intend to use organizational resources to achieve organizational goals.

Once managers at each level have been given a goal or target to achieve, the next step in developing an output control system is to establish operating budgets that regulate how managers and workers attain their goals. An **operating budget** is a blueprint that states how managers intend to use organizational resources to achieve organizational goals efficiently. Typically, managers at one level allocate to subordinate managers a specific amount of resources to use to produce goods and services. Once they have been given a budget, these lower-level managers must decide how to allocate money for different organizational activities. They are then evaluated for their ability to stay within the budget and to make the best use of available resources. For example, managers at GE's washing machine division might have a budget of $50 million to spend on developing and selling a new line of washing machines. They must decide how much money to allocate to the various functions such as R&D, engineering, and sales so that the division generates the most customer revenue and makes the biggest profit.

Large organizations often treat each division as a singular or stand-alone responsibility center. Corporate managers then evaluate each division's contribution to corporate performance. Managers of a division may be given a fixed budget for resources and be evaluated on the amount of goods or services they can produce using those resources (this is a *cost* or *expense* budget approach). Or managers may be asked to maximize the revenues from the sales of goods and services produced (a *revenue* budget approach). Or managers may be evaluated on the difference between the revenues generated by the sales of goods and services and the budgeted cost of making those goods and services (a *profit* budget approach). Japanese companies' use of operating budgets and challenging goals to increase efficiency is instructive in this context.

In summary, three components–objective financial measures, challenging goals and performance standards, and appropriate operating budgets–are the essence of effective output control. Most organizations develop sophisticated output control systems to allow managers at all levels to keep accurate account of the organization so that they can move quickly to take corrective action as needed.[22] Output control is an essential part of management. The way in which Wal-Mart is using output control to expand internationally is discussed in the following "Managing Globally."

Managing Globally

Wal-Mart Uses Output Control to Expand Internationally

Retailing giant Wal-Mart has been aggressively expanding internationally in recent years to raise its performance. After moving into Mexico and Europe in the last decade, it began to contemplate entering the Japanese market. An opportunity arose in 2004 when Japan's third-largest supermarket chain, Daiei, which had been losing money for years and was heavily in debt, was put up for sale. Why was a supermarket chain in one of the world's most lucrative markets struggling?

Unlike efficient Japanese carmakers, which employ state-of-the-art IT-based output control systems to collect the detailed information needed to increase their efficiency, Japan's retailers had lagged behind in adopting the new systems. A major reason for this was historical. Until the 1990s, Japan's Large Scale Retail Store Law allowed small Japanese retailers to block the opening of large, efficient new stores in their neighborhoods for 10 years or more. Although the Japanese government weakened the law so that local storeowners could delay a store opening for only 18 months, there was no history of low-cost competition in the Japanese retail market. So retailers, such as supermarket chains, had never been forced to develop output controls to become more efficient.

A second reason for Daiei's problems revolved around Japan's system of distributing Japanese products. Traditionally, Japanese manufacturers sold their products only by means of wholesalers with which they had developed long-term business relationships. Because the wholesalers added their own price markup and controlled distribution, this made it much more difficult for supermarkets to compete on price and lowered competition. Less competition reduced the incentive for Japanese retailers to invest in materials management output control systems to increase their efficiency.

In contrast, Wal-Mart's focus on developing sophisticated output controls to monitor all aspects of its purchasing and sales activities made it the most efficient U.S. discount retailer in the 1990s. In fact, its skills in materials management allowed it to enter the U.S. supermarket industry and become a major competitor there. So, in 2004, to further its global expansion, Wal-Mart was contemplating the purchase of Daiei. Its managers believed that if Wal-Mart transplanted its proprietary IT-based output control systems into Daiei's operations, it could increase Daiei's efficiency by so much that the supermarket chain would become a highly profitable business. Wal-Mart's other plans for Daiei, should it purchase the company, include purchasing lower-priced goods from abroad in order to pursue a low-cost strategy. Thus, Wal-Mart's global control system, which allows it to identify and purchase products efficiently from manufacturers throughout the world, will help increase Daiei's efficiency.

A customer samples a meatball skewer and chats with the owner of a small grocery store in Tokyo. The mom-and-pop shops of Japan's old-style downtown shopping arcades are on shaky ground, facing competition from cheaper mega-outlets of the modern economic world.

If the purchase goes through, in the next decade Wal-Mart may become one of the strongest competitors in the Japanese retail market and, as it has done in the United States, force its competitors to adopt state-of-the-art output control systems. The question in the summer of 2004 was whether a Japanese company, seeing the threat posed by Wal-Mart, would offer a higher price for Daiei to prevent Wal-Mart's entering Japan.

Problems with Output Control

When designing an output control system, managers must be careful to avoid some pitfalls. For example, they must be sure that the output standards they create motivate managers at all levels and do not cause managers to behave in inappropriate ways to achieve organizational goals.

Suppose top managers give divisional managers the goal of doubling profits over a three-year period. This goal seems challenging and reachable when it is jointly agreed upon, and in the first two years profits go up by 70 percent. In the third year, however, an economic recession hits and sales plummet. Divisional managers think it is increasingly unlikely that they will meet their profit goal. Failure will mean losing the substantial monetary bonus tied to achieving the goal. How might managers behave to try to preserve their bonuses?

One course of action they might take is to find ways to reduce costs, since profit can be increased either by raising revenues or reducing costs. Thus, divisional managers might cut back on expensive research and development activities, delay maintenance on machinery, reduce marketing expenditures, and lay off middle managers and workers to reduce costs so that at the end of the year they will make their target of doubling profits and receive their bonuses. This tactic might help them achieve a short-run goal–doubling profits–but such actions could hurt long-term profitability or ROI (because a cutback in R&D can reduce the rate of product innovation, a cutback in marketing will lead to the loss of customers, and so on).

Problems of this sort occurred at Gillette when its new chairman, James M. Kilts, announced that the poorly performing company would not be experiencing a turnaround anytime in the near future. He attributed a large part of Gillette's problems to the overly ambitious sales and profit goals that his predecessor had set for managers of its divisions (razors and toiletries, Braun appliances, and Duracell batteries). To achieve these ambitious sales targets, divisional managers had slashed advertising budgets and loaded up on inventory hoping to sell it quickly and generate large revenues. However, this had backfired when customer demand dropped and a recession occurred.

Kilts saw that Gillette's managers had not been focusing on the right way to reduce costs. Because managers' salaries and bonuses were based on their ability to meet the ambitious goals that had been set for them, they had acted with a short-term mind-set. Managers had not been thinking about the long-term goal of trying to find the best balance between keeping costs under control, keeping customers happy, and keeping the pipeline of new products full.

Kilts announced that henceforth Gillette would no longer provide specific and unrealistic sales and earning targets that created a "circle of doom" and led managers to behave in just the ways that would prevent them from achieving company goals–by reducing advertising to reduce costs, for example. Kilts decided that Gillette would set long-term goals based on carefully drawn marketing plans that targeted products customers wanted and would lead to long-term sales growth. Also, Gillette would carefully examine its product line to focus its resources on products that offered the most payoff and to weed out poorly performing products that did not contribute much to the bottom line. The changes that Kilts made worked; in 2004 Gillette announced record sales and profits.[23]

As Gillette's experience suggests, long-run effectiveness is what managers should be most concerned about. Thus, managers must consider carefully how flexible they should be when using output control. If conditions change (as they will because of uncertainty in the task and general environments), it is probably better for top managers to communicate to managers lower in the hierarchy that they are aware of the changes taking place and are willing to revise and lower goals and standards. Indeed, many organizations schedule yearly revisions of their five-year plan and goals and use scenario planning to avoid the problems Gillette experienced.

The message is clear: Although output control is a useful tool for keeping managers and employees at all levels motivated and the organization on track, it is only a guide to appropriate action. Managers must be sensitive to how they use output control and must constantly monitor its effects at all levels in the organization. At Home Depot, output control was not being used appropriately; Nardelli rushed to create a sophisticated new information system that could collect the data he needed to measure its performance.

Behavior Control

Organizational structure by itself does not provide any mechanism that motivates managers and nonmanagerial employees to behave in ways that make the structure work or even improve the way it works–hence the need for control. Put another way, managers can develop an elegant organizational structure with highly appropriate task and reporting relationships, but it will work as designed only if managers also establish control systems that allow them to motivate and shape employee behavior.[24] Output control is one method of motivating employees; behavior control is another method. This section examines three mechanisms of behavior control that managers can use to keep subordinates on track and make organizational structures work as they are designed to work: direct supervision, management by objectives, and rules and standard operating procedures (see Figure 11.3).

Direct Supervision

The most immediate and potent form of behavior control is direct supervision by managers who actively monitor and observe the behavior of their subordinates, teach subordinates the behaviors that are appropriate and inappropriate, and intervene to take corrective action as needed. Moreover, when managers personally supervise subordinates, they lead by example and in this way can help subordinates develop and increase their own skill levels. (Leadership is the subject of Chapter 13.) Thus, control through personal supervision can be a very effective way of motivating employees and promoting behaviors that

increase efficiency and effectiveness.[25] In selecting new managers with a military background, Nardelli was using this form of control.

Nevertheless, certain problems are associated with direct supervision. First, it is very expensive because a manager can personally manage only a small number of subordinates effectively. Therefore, if direct supervision is the main kind of control being used in an organization, a lot of managers will be needed and costs will increase. For this reason, output control is usually preferred to behavior control; indeed, output control tends to be the first type of control that managers at all levels use to evaluate performance.

Second, direct supervision can demotivate subordinates if they feel that they are under such close scrutiny that they are not free to make their own decisions. Moreover, subordinates may start to pass the buck and avoid responsibility if they feel that their manager is waiting in the wings ready to reprimand anyone who makes the slightest error.

Third, as noted previously, for many jobs direct supervision is simply not feasible. The more complex a job is, the more difficult it is for a manager to evaluate how well a subordinate is performing. The performance of divisional and functional managers, for example, can be evaluated only over relatively long time periods (this is why an output control system is developed), so it makes little sense for top managers to continually monitor their performance.

Management by Objectives

management by objectives (MBO) A goal-setting process in which a manager and each of his or her subordinates negotiate specific goals and objectives for the subordinate to achieve and then periodically evaluate the extent to which the subordinate is achieving those goals.

To provide a framework within which to evaluate subordinates' behavior and, in particular, to allow managers to monitor progress toward achieving goals, many organizations implement some version of management by objectives. **Management by objectives (MBO)** is a system of evaluating subordinates for their ability to achieve specific organizational goals or performance standards and to meet operating budgets.[26] Most organizations make some use of management by objectives because it is pointless to establish goals and then fail to evaluate whether or not they are being achieved. Management by objectives involves three specific steps:

- Step 1: *Specific goals and objectives are established at each level of the organization.*

Management by objective starts when top managers establish overall organizational objectives, such as specific financial performance targets. Then objective setting cascades down throughout the organization as managers at the divisional and functional levels set their objectives to achieve corporate objectives.[27] Finally, first-level managers and workers jointly set objectives that will contribute to achieving functional goals.

- Step 2: *Managers and their subordinates together determine the subordinates' goals.*

An important characteristic of management by objectives is its participatory nature. Managers at every level sit down with each of the subordinate managers who report directly to them, and together they determine appropriate and feasible goals for the subordinate and bargain over the budget that the subordinate will need to achieve his or her goals. The participation of subordinates in the objective-setting process is a way of strengthening their commitment to achieving their goals and meeting their budgets.[28] Another reason why it is so important for subordinates (both individuals and teams) to participate in goal setting is that doing so enables them to tell managers what they think they can realistically achieve.[29]

- Step 3: *Managers and their subordinates periodically review the subordinates' progress toward meeting goals.*

Once specific objectives have been agreed on for managers at each level, managers are accountable for meeting those objectives. Periodically, they sit down with their subordinates to evaluate their progress. Normally, salary raises and promotions are linked to the goal-setting process, and managers who achieve their goals receive greater rewards than those who fall short. (The issue of how to design reward systems to motivate managers and other organizational employees is discussed in Chapter 13.)

In the companies that have decentralized responsibility for the production of goods and services to empowered teams and cross-functional teams, management by objectives works somewhat differently. Managers ask each team to develop a set of goals and performance targets that the team hopes to achieve–goals that are consistent with organizational objectives. Managers then negotiate with each team to establish its final goals and the budget the team will need to achieve them. The reward system is linked to team performance, not to the performance of any one team member.

Cypress Semiconductor offers an interesting example of how IT can be used to manage the MBO process quickly and effectively. In the fast-moving semiconductor business a premium is placed on organizational adaptability. At Cypress, CEO T. J. Rodgers was facing a problem. How could he control his growing, 1,500-employee organization without developing a bureaucratic management hierarchy? Rodgers believed that a tall hierarchy hinders the ability of an organization to adapt to changing conditions. He was committed to maintaining a flat and decentralized organizational structure with a minimum of management layers. At the same time, he needed to control his employees to ensure that they perform in a manner consistent with the goals of the company.[30] How could he achieve this without resorting to direct supervision and the management hierarchy that it implies?

To solve this problem, Rodgers implemented an online information system through which he can manage what every employee and team is doing in his fast-moving and decentralized organization. Each employee maintains a list of 10 to 15 goals, such as "Meet with marketing for new product launch" or "Make sure to check with customer X." Noted next to each goal are when it was agreed upon, when it is due to be finished, and whether it has been finished. All of this information is stored on a central computer. Rodgers claims that he can review the goals of all employees in about four hours and that he does so each week.[31] How is this possible? He manages by exception and looks only for employees who are falling behind. He then calls them, not to scold but to ask whether there is anything he can do to help them get the job done. It takes only about half an hour each week for employees to review and update their lists. This system allows Rodgers to exercise control over his organization without resorting to the expensive layers of a management hierarchy and direct supervision.

Bureaucratic Control

bureaucratic control Control of behavior by means of a comprehensive system of rules and standard operating procedures.

When direct supervision is too expensive and management by objectives is inappropriate, managers might turn to another mechanism to shape and motivate employee behavior: bureaucratic control. **Bureaucratic control** is control by means of a comprehensive system of rules and standard operating procedures (SOPs) that shapes and regulates the behavior of divisions, functions, and individuals. In Chapter 2, we discussed Weber's theory of bureaucracy and noted that all organizations use bureaucratic rules and procedures but some use them more than others.[32] The opening case describes the important role played by rules at Home Depot.

Rules and SOPs guide behavior and specify what employees are to do when they confront a problem that needs a solution. It is the responsibility of a manager to develop rules that allow employees to perform their activities efficiently and effectively. When employees follow the rules that managers have developed, their behavior is standardized–actions are performed the same way time and time again–and the outcomes of their work are predictable. And, to the degree that managers can make employees' behavior predictable, there is no need to monitor the outputs of behavior because standardized behavior leads to standardized outputs.

Suppose a worker at Toyota comes up with a way to attach exhaust pipes that reduces the number of steps in the assembly process and increases efficiency. Always on the lookout for ways to standardize procedures, managers make this idea the basis of a new rule that says, "From now on, the procedure for attaching the exhaust pipe to the car is as follows." If all workers followed the rule to the letter, every car would come off the assembly line with its exhaust pipe attached in the new way and there would be no need to check exhaust pipes at the end of the line. In practice, mistakes and lapses of attention do happen, so output control is used at the end of the line, and each car's exhaust system is given a routine inspection. However, the number of quality problems with the exhaust system is minimized because the rule (bureaucratic control) is being followed.

Service organizations such as retail stores, fast-food restaurants, and home-improvement stores attempt to standardize the behavior of employees by instructing them on the correct way to greet customers or the appropriate way to serve and bag food. Employees are trained to follow the rules that have proved to be most effective in a particular situation, and the better trained the employees are, the more standardized is their behavior and the more trust managers can have that outputs (such as food quality) will be consistent. An interesting example of how creating the wrong rules can reduce performance is discussed in the following "Management Insight."

Management Insight

How to Kill Customer Satisfaction

In the early 2000s, Gateway, the PC maker, saw its customer satisfaction rating plummet from third to fifth in consumer satisfaction with PC makers. This drop caused Gateway's managers considerable anxiety because they used this measure of customer satisfaction as an important indicator of their company's ongoing performance. Such a drop is very serious to a computer maker because the volume of its online sales depends on how easy it is for customers to put their mail-order computer together when it reaches their homes and how easy it is for them to get advice and good service when they encounter a software or hardware problem. Customer satisfaction ratings also directly affect a company's profits, and as Gateway's computer shipments slipped, the company began to lose money.

Why did customer satisfaction plummet? Mike Ritter, director of Gateway consumer marketing, discovered that the source of customer dissatisfaction was a series of new rules and policies the company had instituted for its customer service reps to follow because of its desire to reduce the increasing costs of after-sales service. As Gateway's product line had broadened and many different software and hardware options were made available to customers, the complexity of its customer service procedures had increased. Employees had to have a great deal more information at their disposal to solve customer problems. These problems were often made more serious when customers installed additional software on their computers, which then caused problems with the software already installed on the Gateway machine. As everyone who has installed new software knows, it can take considerable time to iron out the problems and get the new installation to work. Gateway was spending millions of dollars in employee time to solve these problems and desired to reduce this cost.

Ritter discovered that of the 15 rules and procedures the company had instituted for its customer service reps to follow, two rules in particular were the source of customer dissatisfaction. The first rule concerned the issue of customer-installed software. Gateway had told its service reps to inform customers that if they installed any other software on their machines, this would invalidate Gateway's warranty. This infuriated customers, who asked, Why shouldn't they install other necessary software? The second rule was one that rewarded customer support reps on the basis of how quickly they handled customer calls, meaning that the more calls they handled in an hour or day the higher their bonuses.

The joint effect of these two rules was that customer reps were now motivated to minimize the length of a service call and, in particular, were unwilling to help solve customer problems that resulted from installation of "outlawed software" since doing so took a lot of time. Obviously customers resented this treatment; the result was the big decline in customer satisfaction.

Once Gateway's managers realized the source of the problem, they abolished the 15 rules immediately. Within one month customer satisfaction jumped by over 10 percent. As Gateway's managers discovered, to prevent unexpected problems, it is necessary to carefully choose and evaluate the rules and policies used to control employees' behavior.

In contrast to the situation at Gateway, Dave Lilly, an ex-nuclear submarine commander, chose the *right* rules for siteROCK, a Web hosting company. SiteROCK's business is hosting and managing other companies' Web sites to keep them up and running and error free. A customer's site that goes down or runs haywire is the major enemy. To maximize the performance of his employees and to increase their ability to respond to unexpected online events, Lilly decided that they needed a comprehensive set of rules and standard operating procedures to cover all the major known problems.[33] Lilly insisted that every problem-solving procedure should be written down. SiteROCK's employees developed over 30 thick binders that list all the processes and checklists they need to follow when an unexpected event happens to solve a specific problem.

Moreover, again drawing from his military experience, Lilly instituted a "two-man rule": Whenever the unexpected happens, each employee must immediately tell a co-worker and the two together should attempt to solve the problem. The goal is simple: Use the rules to achieve a quick resolution of a complex issue. If the existing rules don't work, then employees must experiment, and when they find a solution, the solution is turned into a new rule to be included in the procedures book to aid the future decision making of all employees in the organization. Nardelli developed a similar system for Home Depot employees to follow.

Problems with Bureaucratic Control

Like all organizations, siteROCK makes extensive use of bureaucratic control because rules and SOPs effectively control routine organizational activities. With a bureaucratic control system in place, managers can manage by exception and intervene and take corrective action only when necessary. However, managers need to be aware of a number of problems associated with bureaucratic control, because such problems can reduce organizational effectiveness.[34]

First, establishing rules is always easier than discarding them. Organizations tend to become overly bureaucratic over time as managers do everything according to the rule book. If the amount of red tape becomes too great, decision making slows and managers react slowly to changing conditions. This sluggishness can imperil an organization's survival if agile new competitors emerge. Once a siteROCK employee has found a better rule, the old one is discarded.

Second, because rules constrain and standardize behavior and lead people to behave in predictable ways, there is a danger that people become so used to automatically following rules that they stop thinking for themselves. Thus, too much standardization can actually reduce the level of learning taking place in an organization and get the organization off track if managers and workers focus on the wrong issues. An organization thrives when its members are constantly thinking of new ways to increase efficiency, quality, and customer responsiveness. By definition, new ideas do not come from blindly following standardized procedures. Similarly, the pursuit of innovation implies a commitment by managers to discover new ways of doing things; innovation, however, is incompatible with the use of extensive bureaucratic control.

Managers must therefore be sensitive about the way they use bureaucratic control. It is most useful when organizational activities are routine and well understood and when employees are making programmed decisions–for example, in mass-production settings such as Ford or in routine service settings such as stores like Target or Midas Muffler. Bureaucratic control is much less useful in situations where nonprogrammed decisions have to be made and managers have to react quickly to changes in the organizational environment.

To use output control and behavior control, managers must be able to identify the outcomes they want to achieve and the behaviors they want employees to perform to achieve those outcomes. For many of the most important and significant organizational activities, however, output control and behavior control are inappropriate for several reasons:

- A manager cannot evaluate the performance of workers such as doctors, research scientists, or engineers by observing their behavior on a day-to-day basis.
- Rules and SOPs are of little use in telling a doctor how to respond to an emergency situation or a scientist how to discover something new.
- Output controls such as the amount of time a surgeon takes for each operation or the costs of making a discovery are very crude measures of the quality of performance.

How can managers attempt to control and regulate the behavior of their subordinates when personal supervision is of little use, when rules cannot be developed to tell employees what to do, and when outputs and goals cannot be measured at all or can be measured usefully only over long periods? One source of control increasingly being used by organizations is a strong organizational culture.

Organizational Culture and Clan Control

Organizational culture is another important control system that regulates and governs employee attitudes and behavior. As we discussed in Chapter 3, **organizational culture** is the shared set of beliefs, expectations, values, norms, and work routines that influences how members of an organization relate to one another and work together to achieve organizational goals. **Clan control** is the control exerted on individuals and groups in an organization by shared values, norms, standards of behavior, and expectations. Organizational culture is not an externally imposed system of constraints, such as direct supervision or rules and procedures. Rather, employees internalize organizational values and norms and then let these values and norms guide their decisions and actions. Just as people in society at large generally behave in accordance with socially acceptable values and norms–such as the norm that people should line up at the checkout counters in supermarkets–so are individuals in an organizational setting mindful of the force of organizational values and norms.

organizational culture The set of values, norms, standards of behavior, and common expectations that controls the ways in which individuals and groups in an organization interact with one another and work to achieve organizational goals.

clan control The control exerted on individuals and groups in an organization by shared values, norms, standards of behavior, and expectations.

Organizational culture is an important source of control for two reasons. First, it makes control possible in situations where managers cannot use output or behavior control. Second, and more important, when a strong and cohesive set of organizational values and norms is in place, employees focus on thinking about what is best for the organization in the long run–all their decisions and actions become oriented toward helping the organization perform well. For example, a teacher spends personal time after school coaching and counseling students; an R&D scientist works 80 hours a week, evenings, and weekends to help speed up a late project; a salesclerk at a department store runs after a customer who left a credit card at the cash register. An interesting example of a company that has built a strong culture based on close attention to developing the right set of output and behavior controls is UPS, profiled in the following "Manager as a Person."

Manager as a Person

James Casey Creates a Culture for UPS

United Parcel Service (UPS) controls more than three-fourths of the ground and air parcel service in the United States, delivering over 10 million packages a day in its fleet of 150,000 trucks.[35] It is also the most profitable company in its industry. UPS employs over 250,000 people, and since its founding as a bicycle-messenger service in 1907 by James E. Casey, UPS has developed a culture that has been a model for competitors such as FedEx and the U.S. Postal Service.

From the beginning, Casey made efficiency and economy the company's driving values and loyalty, humility, discipline, dependability, and intense effort the key norms and standards UPS employees should adopt. UPS has always gone to extraordinary lengths to develop and maintain these values and norms in its workforce.

First, its operating systems from the top of the company down to its trucking operations are the subject of intense scrutiny by the company's 3,000 industrial engineers. These engineers are constantly on the lookout for ways to measure outputs and behaviors to improve efficiency. They time every part of an employee's job. Truck drivers, for example, are instructed in extraordinary detail on how to perform their tasks: They must step from their truck with their right foot first, fold their money face-up, carry packages under their left arm, walk at a pace of 3 feet per second, and slip the key ring holding their truck keys over their third finger.[36] Employees are not allowed to have beards, must be carefully groomed, and are instructed in how to deal with customers. Drivers who perform below average receive visits from training supervisors who accompany them on their delivery routes and instruct them on how to raise their performance level. Not surprisingly, as a result of this intensive training and close behavior control, UPS employees internalize the company's strong norms about the appropriate ways to behave to help the organization achieve its values of economy and efficiency.

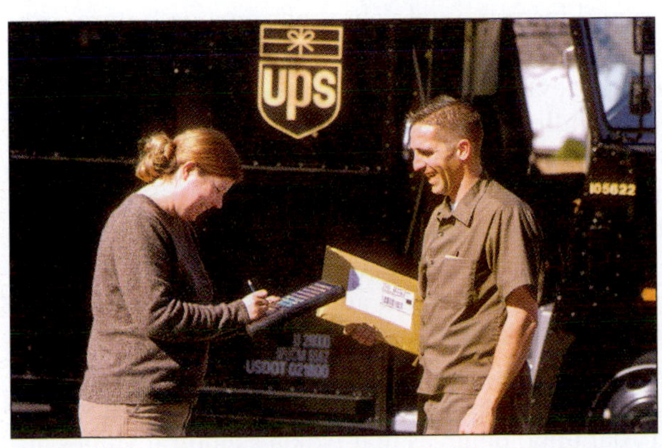

UPS drivers must follow strict guidelines regarding appearance, job performance, and customer interactions.

Its search to find the best set of output controls leads UPS to constantly develop and introduce the latest in IT into the company's operations, particularly its materials management operations. In fact, today UPS offers a consulting service to other companies in the area of global supply chain management. Its goal is to teach other companies how to pursue its values of efficiency and economy, values that the company has been pursuing for the last hundred years as a result of the values of its founder.

Adaptive Cultures Versus Inert Cultures

Many researchers and managers believe that employees of some organizations go out of their way to help the organization because it has a strong and cohesive organizational culture–an *adaptive culture* that controls employee attitudes and behaviors. Adaptive cultures, such as that at UPS, are cultures whose values and norms help an organization to build momentum and to grow and change as needed to achieve its goals and be effective. By contrast, *inert cultures* are those that lead to values and norms that fail to motivate or inspire employees; they lead to stagnation and often failure over time. What leads to an adaptive or inert culture?

Researchers have found that organizations with strong adaptive cultures, like 3M, UPS, Microsoft, and IBM, invest in their employees. They demonstrate their commitment to their members by, for example, emphasizing the long-term nature of the employment relationship and trying to avoid layoffs. These companies develop long-term career paths for their employees and invest heavily in training and development to increase employees' value to the organization. In these ways, terminal and instrumental values pertaining to the worth of human resources encourage the development of supportive work attitudes and behaviors.

In adaptive cultures employees often receive rewards linked directly to their performance and to the performance of the company as a whole. Sometimes, employee stock ownership plans (ESOPs) are developed in which workers as a group are allowed to buy a significant percentage of their company's stock. Workers who are owners of the company have additional incentive to develop skills that allow them to perform highly and search actively for ways to improve quality, efficiency, and performance. At Dell, for example, employees are able to buy Dell stock at a steep (15 percent) discount; this allows them to build a sizable stake in the company over time.

Some organizations, however, develop cultures with values that do not include protecting and increasing the worth of their human resources as a major goal. Their employment practices are based on short-term employment according to the needs of the organization and on minimal investment in employees who perform simple, routine tasks. Moreover, employees are not often rewarded based on their performance and thus have little incentive to improve their skills or otherwise invest in the organization to help it to achieve goals. If a company has an inert culture, poor working relationships frequently develop between the organization and its employees, and instrumental values of noncooperation, laziness, and loafing and work norms of output restriction are common.

Moreover, an adaptive culture develops an emphasis on entrepreneurship and respect for the employee and allows the use of organizational structures, such as the cross-functional team structure, that empower employees to make decisions and motivate them to succeed. By contrast, in an inert culture, employees are content to be told what to do and have little incentive or motivation to perform beyond minimum work requirements. As you might expect, the emphasis is on close supervision and hierarchical authority, which result in a culture that makes it difficult to adapt to a changing environment.

Nokia, the world's largest wireless phone maker, headquartered in Finland, is a good example of a company in which managers strived to create an adaptive culture.[37] Nokia's president, Matti Alahuhta, believes that Nokia's cultural values are based on the Finnish character: Finns are down-to-earth, rational, straightforward people. They are also very friendly and democratic people who do not believe in a rigid hierarchy based either on a person's authority or on social class. Nokia's

An aerial view of the cafeteria at Nokia's headquarters in Espoo, Finland. The open architecture of the building reflects the company's culture, which is based on informal and personal relationships and norms of cooperation and teamwork.

culture reflects these values because innovation and decision making are pushed right down to the bottom line, to teams of employees who take up the challenge of developing the ever-smaller and more sophisticated phones for which the company is known. Bureaucracy is kept to a minimum at Nokia; its adaptive culture is based on informal and personal relationships and norms of cooperation and teamwork.

To help strengthen its culture, Nokia has built a futuristic open-plan steel and glass building just outside Helsinki. Here, in an open environment, its research and development people can work together to innovate new kinds of wireless phones. More than one out of every three of Nokia's 60,000 employees work in research; what keeps these people together and focused is Nokia's company mission to produce phones that are better, cheaper, smaller, and easier to use than competitor's phones.[38] This is the "Nokia Way," a system of cultural values and norms that can't be written down but is always present in the values that cement people together and in the language and stories that its members use to orient themselves to the company.

Another company with an adaptive culture is Merck & Co., one of the largest producers of prescription drugs in the world. Much of Merck's success can be attributed to its ability to attract the very best research scientists, who come because its adaptive culture nurtures scientists and emphasizes values and norms of innovation. Scientists are given great freedom to pursue intriguing ideas even if the commercial payoff is questionable. Moreover, researchers are inspired to think of their work as a quest to alleviate human disease and suffering worldwide, and Merck has a reputation as an ethical company whose values put people above profits.

Although the experience of Nokia and Merck suggests that organizational culture can give rise to managerial actions that ultimately benefit the organization, this is not always the case. The cultures of some organizations become dysfunctional, encouraging managerial actions that harm the organization and discouraging actions that might lead to an improvement in performance.[39] For example, Sunflower Electric Power Corporation, a generation and transmission cooperative, almost went bankrupt in the early 2000s. A state committee of inquiry that was set up to find the source of the problem put the blame on Sunflower's CEO. The committee decided that he had created an abusive culture based on fear and blame that encouraged managers to fight over and protect their turf–an inert culture. Managers were afraid to rock the boat or make suggestions since they could not predict what would happen to them.

The CEO was fired and a new CEO, Chris Hauck, was appointed to change the cooperative's culture. He found it very hard to do so as his senior managers were so used to the old values and norms. One top manager, for example, engaged so frequently in the practice of berating one supervisor that the man became physically sick.[40] Hauck fired this and other managers as a signal that such behavior would no longer be tolerated. With the help of consultants, he went about the slow process of changing values and norms to emphasize cooperation, teamwork, and respect for others. Clearly, managers can influence the way their organizational culture develops over time, often in a short period of time, as Bob Nardelli has done at Home Depot.[41]

Organizational Change

As we have discussed above, many problems can arise if an organization's control systems are not designed correctly. One of these problems is that an organization cannot change or adapt in response to a changing environment unless it has effective control over its activities. Companies can lose this control over time, as happened to Home Depot and Gateway, or they can change in ways that make them more effective, as happened to UPS and Wal-Mart.

Interestingly enough, there is a fundamental tension or need to balance two opposing forces in the control process that influences the way organizations change. As just noted, organizations and their managers need to be able to control their activities and make their operations routine and predictable. At the same time, however, organizations have to be responsive to the need to change, and managers and employees have to "think on their feet" and realize when they need to depart from routines to be responsive to unpredictable events. In other words, even though adopting the right set of output and behavior controls is essential for improving efficiency, because the environment is dynamic and uncertain employees also need to feel that they have the autonomy to depart from routines as necessary to increase effectiveness. (See Figure 11.5.)

It is for this reason that many researchers believe that the highest-performing organizations are those that are constantly changing–and thus become experienced at doing so–in their search to become more efficient and effective. And companies like UPS, and more recently Home Depot, are constantly changing the mix of their activities to move forward even as they are seeking to make their existing operations more efficient. For example, UPS entered the air express parcel market, bought a chain of mailbox stores, and began offering a

Figure 11.5
Organizational Control and Change

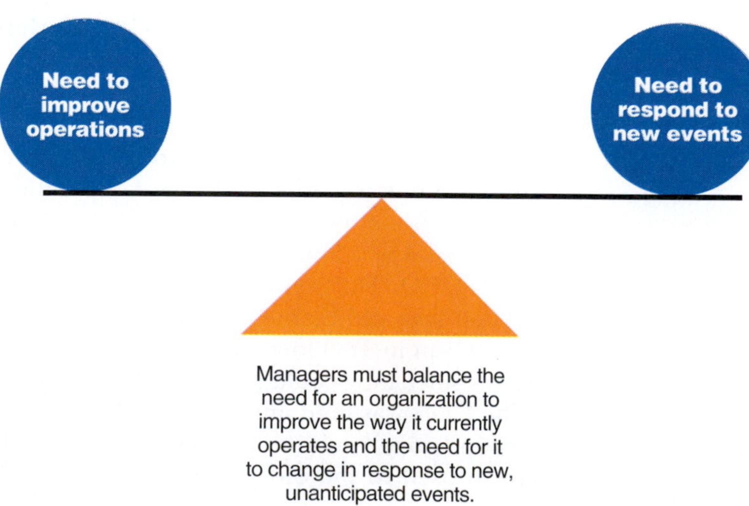
Need to improve operations
Need to respond to new events
Managers must balance the need for an organization to improve the way it currently operates and the need for it to change in response to new, unanticipated events.

Figure 11.6
Four Steps in the Organizational Change Process

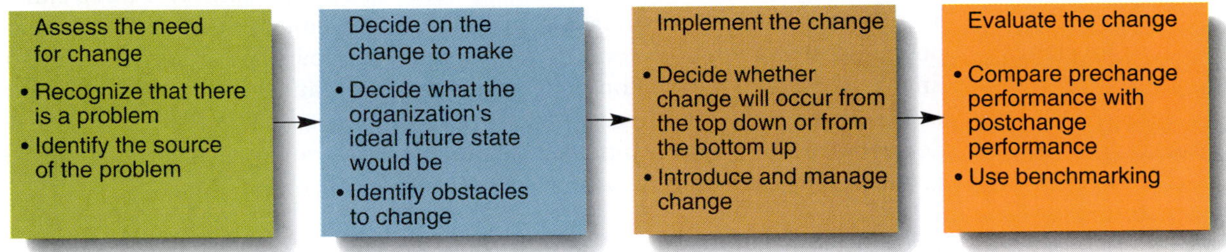
Assess the need for change
• Recognize that there is a problem
• Identify the source of the problem
Decide on the change to make
• Decide what the organization's ideal future state would be
• Identify obstacles to change
Implement the change
• Decide whether change will occur from the top down or from the bottom up
• Introduce and manage change
Evaluate the change
• Compare prechange performance with postchange performance
• Use benchmarking

consulting service. At the same time, it has been increasing the efficiency of its ground transport network.

The need to constantly search for ways to improve efficiency and effectiveness makes it vital that managers develop the skills necessary to manage change effectively. Several experts have proposed a model that managers can follow to implement change successfully.[42] **Organization change** is the movement of an organization away from its present state and toward some desired future state to increase its efficiency and effectiveness. Figure 11.6 outlines the steps that managers must take to manage change effectively. In the rest of this section we examine each one.

organization change The movement of an organization away from its present state and toward some desired future state to increase its efficiency and effectiveness.

Assessing the Need for Change

Organizational change can affect practically all aspects of organizational functioning, including organizational structure, culture, strategies, control systems, and groups and teams, as well as the human resource management system and critical organizational processes such as communication, motivation, and leadership. Organizational change can bring alterations in the ways managers carry out the critical tasks of planning, organizing, leading, and controlling and the ways they perform their managerial roles.

Deciding how to change an organization is a complex matter because change disrupts the status quo and poses a threat, prompting employees to resist attempts to alter work relationships and procedures. *Organizational learning,* the process through which managers try to increase organizational members' abilities to understand and appropriately respond to changing conditions, can be an important impetus for change and can help all members of an organization, including managers, effectively make decisions about needed changes.

Assessing the need for change calls for two important activities: recognizing that there is a problem and identifying its source. Sometimes the need for change is obvious, such as when an organization's performance is suffering. Often, however, managers have trouble determining that something is going wrong because problems develop gradually; organizational performance may slip for a number of years before a problem becomes obvious. Thus, during the first step in the change process, managers need to recognize that there is a problem that requires change.

Often the problems that managers detect have produced a gap between desired performance and actual performance. To detect such a gap, managers need to look at performance measures–such as falling market share or profits, rising costs, or employees' failure to meet their established goals or stay within budgets–which indicate whether change is needed. These measures are provided by organizational control systems, discussed earlier in the chapter.

To discover the source of the problem, managers need to look both inside and outside the organization. Outside the organization, they must examine how changes in environmental forces may be creating opportunities and threats that are affecting internal work relationships. Perhaps the emergence of low-cost competitors abroad has led to conflict among different departments that are trying to find new ways to gain a competitive advantage. Managers also need to look within the organization to see whether its structure is causing problems between departments. Perhaps a company does not have integrating mechanisms in place to allow different departments to respond to low-cost competition.

Deciding on the Change to Make

Once managers have identified the source of the problem, they must decide what they think the organization's ideal future state would be. In other words, they must decide where they would like their organization to be in the future—what kinds of goods and services it should be making, what its business-level strategy should be, how the organizational structure should be changed, and so on. During this step, managers also must engage in planning how they are going to attain the organization's ideal future state.

This step in the change process also includes identifying obstacles or sources of resistance to change. Managers must analyze the factors that may prevent the company from reaching its ideal future state. Obstacles to change are found at the corporate, divisional, departmental, and individual levels of the organization.

Corporate-level changes in an organization's strategy or structure, even seemingly trivial changes, may significantly affect how divisional and departmental managers behave. Suppose that to compete with low-cost foreign competitors, top managers decide to increase the resources spent on state-of-the-art machinery and reduce the resources spent on marketing or R&D. The power of manufacturing managers would increase, and the power of marketing and R&D managers would fall. This decision would alter the balance of power among departments and might lead to increased conflict as departments start fighting to retain their status in the organization. An organization's present strategy and structure are powerful obstacles to change.

Whether a company's culture is adaptive or inert facilitates or obstructs change. Organizations with entrepreneurial, flexible cultures, such as high-tech companies, are much easier to change than are organizations with more rigid cultures, such as those sometimes found in large, bureaucratic organizations like the military or General Motors.

The same obstacles to change exist at the divisional and departmental levels as well. Division managers may differ in their attitudes toward the changes that top managers propose and, if their interests and power seem threatened, will resist those changes. Managers at all levels usually fight to protect their power and control over resources. Given that departments have different goals and time horizons, they may also react differently to the changes that other managers propose. When top managers are trying to reduce costs, for example, sales managers may resist attempts to cut back on sales expenditures if they believe that problems stem from manufacturing managers' inefficiencies.

At the individual level, too, people are often resistant to change because change brings uncertainty and uncertainty brings stress. For example, individuals may resist the introduction of a new technology because they are uncertain about their abilities to learn it and effectively use it.

These obstacles make organizational change a slow process. Managers must recognize the potential obstacles to change and take them into consideration. Some obstacles can be overcome by improving communication so that all organizational members are aware of the need for change and of the nature of the changes being made. Empowering employees and inviting them to participate in the planning for change also can help overcome resistance and allay employees' fears. In addition, managers can sometimes overcome resistance by emphasizing group or shared goals such as increased organizational efficiency and effectiveness. In Home Depot's case, the company's declining performance made many of its managers who had previously resisted change realize that the change was ultimately in everyone's best interests because it would increase organizational performance. However, many of its store managers did leave the company because they didn't like its new culture and operating system. The larger and more complex an organization is, the more complex is the change process.

Implementing the Change

top-down change A fast, revolutionary approach to change in which top managers identify what needs to be changed and then move quickly to implement the changes throughout the organization.

bottom-up change A gradual or evolutionary approach to change in which managers at all levels work together to develop a detailed plan for change.

Generally, managers implement–that is, introduce and manage–change from the top down or from the bottom up.[43] **Top-down change** is implemented quickly: Top managers identify the need for change, decide what to do, and then move quickly to implement the changes throughout the organization. For example, top managers may decide to restructure and downsize the organization and then give divisional and departmental managers specific goals to achieve. With top-down change, the emphasis is on making the changes quickly and dealing with problems as they arise; it is revolutionary in nature, such as the change that took place at Home Depot.

Bottom-up change is typically more gradual or evolutionary. Top managers consult with middle and first-line managers about the need for change. Then, over time, managers at all levels work to develop a detailed plan for change. A major advantage of bottom-up change is that it can co-opt resistance to change from employees. Because the emphasis in bottom-up change is on participation and on keeping people informed about what is going on, uncertainty and resistance are minimized. Home Depot's new CEO did not have the luxury of adopting an evolutionary approach; he had to take swift action to turn around the company.

Evaluating the Change

benchmarking The process of comparing one company's performance on specific dimensions with the performance of other, high-performing organizations.

The last step in the change process is to evaluate how successful the change effort has been in improving organizational performance.[44] Using measures such as changes in market share, in profits, or in the ability of managers to meet their goals, managers compare how well an organization is performing after the change with how well it was performing before. Managers also can use **benchmarking,** comparing their performance on specific dimensions with the performance of high-performing organizations to decide how successful a change effort has been. For example, when Xerox was doing poorly in the 1980s, it benchmarked the efficiency of its distribution operations against that of L.L.Bean, the efficiency of its central computer operations against that of John Deere, and the efficiency of its marketing abilities against that of Procter & Gamble. Those three companies are renowned for their skills in these different areas, and by studying how they performed, Xerox was able to dramatically increase its own performance. Benchmarking is a key tool in total quality management, an important change program discussed in Chapter 9.

In summary, organizational control and change are closely linked because organizations operate in environments that are constantly changing and so managers must be alert to the need to change their strategies and structures. High-performing organizations are those whose managers are attuned to the need to continually modify the way they operate and which adopt techniques like empowered work groups and teams, benchmarking, and global outsourcing to remain competitive in a global world.

Summary and Review

WHAT IS ORGANIZATIONAL CONTROL? Controlling is the process whereby managers monitor and regulate how efficiently and effectively an organization and its members are performing the activities necessary to achieve organizational goals. Controlling is a four-step process: (1) establishing performance standards, (2) measuring actual performance, (3) comparing actual performance against performance standards, and (4) evaluating the results and initiating corrective action if needed.

OUTPUT CONTROL To monitor output or performance, managers choose goals or performance standards that they think will best measure efficiency, quality, innovation, and responsiveness to customers at the corporate, divisional, departmental or functional, and individual levels. The main mechanisms that managers use to monitor output are financial measures of performance, organizational goals, and operating budgets.

BEHAVIOR CONTROL In an attempt to shape behavior and induce employees to work toward achieving organizational goals, managers utilize direct supervision, management by objectives, and bureaucratic control by means of rules and standard operating procedures.

ORGANIZATIONAL CULTURE AND CLAN CONTROL Organizational culture is the set of values, norms, standards of behavior, and common expectations that control the ways individuals and groups in an organization interact with one another and work to achieve organizational goals. Clan control is the control exerted on individuals and groups by shared values, norms, standards of behavior, and expectations. Organizational culture is transmitted to employees through the values of the founder, the process of socialization, organizational ceremonies and rites, and stories and language. The way managers perform their management functions influences the kind of culture that develops in an organization.

ORGANIZATIONAL CONTROL AND CHANGE There is a need to balance two opposing forces in the control process that influences the way organizations change. On the one hand, managers need to be able to control organizational activities and make their operations routine and predictable. On the other hand, organizations have to be responsive to the need to change, and managers must understand when they need to depart from routines to be responsive to unpredictable events. The four steps in managing change are (1) assessing the need for change, (2) deciding on the changes to make, (3) implementing change, and (4) evaluating the results of change.

Management in Action

Topics for Discussion and Action

Discussion

1. What is the relationship between organizing and controlling?
2. How do output control and behavior control differ?
3. Why is it important for managers to involve subordinates in the control process?
4. What is organizational culture, and how does it affect the way employees behave?
5. What kind of controls would you expect to find most used in (a) a hospital, (b) the Navy, (c) a city police force. Why?

Action

6. Ask a manager to list the main performance measures that he or she uses to evaluate how well the organization is achieving its goals.
7. Ask the same or a different manager to list the main forms of output control and behavior control that he or she uses to monitor and evaluate employee behavior.
8. Interview some employees of an organization, and ask them about the organization's values, norms, socialization practices, ceremonies and rites, and special language and stories. Referring to this information, describe the organization's culture.

Building Management Skills

Understanding Controlling

For this exercise you will analyze the control systems used by a real organization such as a department store, restaurant, hospital, police department, or small business. It can be the organization that you investigated in Chapter 10 or a different one. Your objective is to uncover all the different ways in which managers monitor and evaluate the performance of the organization and employees.

1. At what levels does control take place in this organization?
2. Which output performance standards (such as financial measures and organizational goals) do managers use most often to evaluate performance at each level?
3. Does the organization have a management-by-objectives system in place? If it does, describe it. If it does not, speculate about why not.
4. How important is behavior control in this organization? For example, how much of managers' time is spent directly supervising employees? How formalized is the organization? Do employees receive a book of rules to instruct them about how to perform their jobs?
5. What kind of culture does the organization have? What are the values and norms? What effect does the organizational culture have on the way employees behave or treat customers?
6. Based on this analysis, do you think there is a fit between the organization's control systems and its culture? What is the nature of this fit? How could it be improved?

Managing Ethically

Some managers and organizations go to great lengths to monitor their employees' behavior, and they keep extensive records about employees' behavior and performance. Some organizations also seem to possess norms and values that cause their employees to behave in certain ways.

Questions

1. Either by yourself or in a group, think about the ethical implications of organizations' monitoring and collecting information about their employees. What kind of information is it ethical to collect or unethical to collect? Why? Should managers and organizations inform subordinates they are collecting such information?
2. Similarly, some organizations' cultures, like those of Arthur Andersen, the accounting firm, and of Enron, seemed to have developed norms and values that caused their members to behave in unethical ways. When and why does a strong norm that encourages high performance become one that can cause people to act unethically? How can organizations keep their values and norms from becoming "too strong"?

Small Group Breakout Exercise

How Best to Control the Sales Force?

Form groups of three or four people, and appoint one member as the spokesperson who will communicate your findings to the whole class when called on by the instructor. Then discuss the following scenario.

You are the regional sales managers of an organization that supplies high-quality windows and doors to building supply centers nationwide. Over the last three years, the rate of sales growth has slackened. There is increasing evidence that, to make their jobs easier, salespeople are primarily servicing large customer accounts and ignoring small accounts. In addition, the salespeople are not dealing promptly with customer questions and complaints, and this inattention has resulted in a drop in after-sales service. You have talked about these problems, and you are meeting to design a control system to increase both the amount of sales and the quality of customer service.

1. Design a control system that you think will best motivate salespeople to achieve these goals.
2. What relative importance do you put on (a) output control, (b) behavior control, and (c) organizational culture in this design.

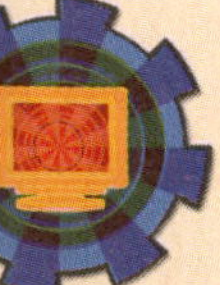

Exploring the World Wide Web

Go to the Web site of UBS, an investment bank (www.ubs.com). Click on "careers" and then click on "our culture" and read the statement about the bank's values and norms.

1. How would you expect UBS's values and norms to affect its employees' behavior?
2. How does UBS design its organizational structure to shape its culture?

Be the Manager

You have been asked by your company's CEO to find a way to improve the performance of its teams of Web-design and Web-hosting specialists and programmers. Each team works on a different aspect of Web-site production, and while each is responsible for the quality of its own performance, its performance also depends on how well the other teams perform. Your task is to create a control system that will help to increase the performance of each team separately and facilitate cooperation among the teams. This is necessary because the various projects are interlinked and affect one another just as the different parts of a car must fit together. Since competition in the Web-site production market is intense, it is imperative that each Web site be up and running as quickly as possible and incorporate all the latest advances in Web-site software technology.

Questions

1. What kind of output controls will best facilitate positive interactions both within the teams and among the teams?
2. What kind of behavior controls will best facilitate positive interactions both within the teams and among the teams?
3. How would you go about helping managers develop a culture to promote high team performance?

Build Your Management Skills DVD

- **Test Your Knowledge:** Categories of Managerial Control
- **Self Assessment:** Assessing Your Flexibility
- **Manager's Hot Seat:** Change: More Pain than Gain

BusinessWeek Case in the News

The "Constant Challenge" at eBay

Online auction site eBay just finished its annual member conference, eBay Live!, on June 26, bringing together more than 10,000 of its sellers and buyers in New Orleans. It's a chance for the most fanatic of eBay's 45 million active members to trade ideas, take classes in how to sell better, and lobby the online marketplace's staff for changes.

Part love fest and part bitch session, the show is an annual highlight for eBay Chief Executive Margaret C. Whitman, who takes the opportunity to mingle with the masses. As she gazed down on the show floor, Whitman shared her thoughts with *BusinessWeek* Silicon Valley Bureau Chief Robert D. Hof about how she copes with the contentious hordes on eBay and why, despite rumors that she might leave the company before long, she's happy with her job. Edited excerpts of their conversation follow:

Q: Is it difficult to manage sellers, many of whom seem to have little business experience?

A: Actually, most of these sellers know more about eBay than most [eBay] employees. They use it every single day. They're the experts. Folks have basically quit their day jobs to sell full-time on eBay. They do eBay before their kids come home from school. The businesses that have been built on this platform are remarkable.

Q: Some veteran sellers are fed up with eBay's constant tinkering with the site. How are you responding?

A: The community right now has seen a lot of change. We probably need to slow down that pace of change just a tad. It's hard for folks to adapt to so much change. That said, the underlying technology is changing, and the competitive landscape provides some new challenges. We want to make sure we strike the right balance between keeping pace with what's new and what's important in online commerce, and at the same time empower the people who are making their living on eBay.

Q: In particular, some sellers are very unhappy about how

eBay recently changed the organization of several product categories, which made it tougher for buyers to browse and thus hurt sales in some categories. Did their complaints hit home?

A: Absolutely. We think books and apparel went really well, helping buyers search for specific products more easily. Music was pretty good, too. As we ventured into pottery and glass, I think we may have moved too fast. There are still a lot of consumers in pottery and glass who like to browse, and that was disrupted somewhat by the category changes. We're going to slow down [those types of changes] until we determine the exact business impact on our sellers.

Q: How do you balance the competing demands of buyers and sellers?

A: It's an art, not a science. We've gotten pretty experienced at it now. We can anticipate the reaction because we ask both buyers and sellers. Then it comes back to: What's the right thing for the marketplace? Sometimes we come down on the side of the sellers, sometimes we come down on the side of the buyers. We really think hard about it.

We rarely make a big change without running a beta, where we run a new site in parallel with the existing one. We never used to do that, because we didn't have the technical capability. We do now.

Q: On eBay's own discussion boards, sellers aren't shy about pointing out what they view as problems. How do you sift through those complaints to determine what's really important?

A: The scale of this user base is so large that part of [managing it] is being able to parse what one ought to do based on the feedback. We have community development teams who know each discussion-board poster.

We think most of our sellers are very happy. But they're like the silent majority. We do extensive surveys of the community. For example, we surveyed 50,000 people on the changes to My eBay [a customized page for buyers and sellers]. About 80 percent liked it. If we get 80 percent approval, we're good to go.

Q: eBay's international business is growing much faster than in the United States. How does that change the nature of the company?

A: It used to be that the United States was largely the innovation engine. Now, it is the United States and Germany. And Germany has a very significant say in how this platform develops. So I think that as more countries get to that scale, we will include them even more in product-development strategy.

Q: Has the proliferation of eBay around the world changed how people buy and sell?

A: I hear all the time that Germans trade on the Italy site. They may not speak much Italian, but the site is laid out the same way, so they kind of know how to do it. And it's the same with French [going to] to the Italian site, and Germans to the U.K. one. In the long run, the way the site works consistently across geographies is going to be really important to global trade.

Q: The rumor on the floor of eBay Live! Is that you might leave eBay before long, possibly for Walt Disney (DIS), where CEO Michael Eisner has been under fire.

A: [Laughs] As far as I know, there isn't a vacancy at Disney. People speculate a lot. But I have to tell you, I have one of the best jobs in Corporate America. It's this unique blend of commerce and community. The community of users is endlessly interesting and endlessly surprising. That's what I love the most.

Questions

1. In what ways does eBay design its IT to control its relationships with buyers and sellers?
2. How does e-bay make sure that changes to its control systems over time improve interactions between buyers and sellers?

Source: Robert Hof, "The Constant Challenge at eBay." Reprinted from the June 30, 2004, issue of *BusinessWeek* by special permission. Copyright © 2004 by the McGraw-Hill Companies, Inc.

BusinessWeek Case in the News

Vital Signs at Humana

When Michael B. McCallister took over at Humana Inc. four years ago, the Louisville-based health insurer was on the critical list. Its commercial business was bleeding red ink, and it faced the potential loss of government contracts that constituted a third of its revenues. In the ultimate irony, the health insurer was suffering from a problem all too familiar to its customers: soaring employee health-care costs. After years of double-digit increases, McCallister was facing an expected 19.2 percent surge in his company's health costs in 2001.

That's when the 52-year-old former hospital administrator began his radical surgery. He quickly exited the 15 states where Humana's commercial group was weakest and moved to secure its grip on lucrative government contracts. And to rein in his own spiraling health-care costs, McCallister restructured Humana's health plan to coax 4,800 headquarters workers to manage their own health-care spending before the company's coverage kicked in. In doing so, McCallister hoped to sensitize his own employees to the true costs of medical care—and force them to be more discriminating in their use of high-cost specialists, emergency rooms, and procedures like CAT scans. He recalls: "I told my employees, 'I'm not going to be your father anymore. I'm going to set the table for you to make your own health decisions.'"

McCallister's triage paid off. Bolstered by a subsequent increase in Medicare reimbursements, he reversed the $382.4 million loss Humana suffered the year before he became CEO with a healthy $228 million profit in 2003.

But despite a strong first quarter this year—in which profits rose 117 percent—some investors clearly are betting that McCallister can't sustain his turnaround much longer. That's why McCallister is embarking on his boldest gambit to date: persuading his corporate clients to adopt the same "consumer-driven" health policies Humana successfully deployed three years ago. The move may represent McCallister's best shot at ensuring Humana's independence at a time when larger rivals like Anthem and UnitedHealth Group are gobbling up regional players like Humana. Even if he's successful, those giants may still target Humana—which has one-eighth the member base of UnitedHealth—for takeover, analysts say.

The theory behind the new medical plans is that the only way to break the spiral of ever-rising health-care costs is to give employees a direct incentive to reduce their expenses. Says McCallister: "We've tried everything else—legislative restrictions, turning doctors into risk-takers—but the one thing we haven't done is turn to the actual users of health care and power them up." Under the plans, workers get a basic level of annual medical coverage—say, $500 per family member. When those funds are exhausted, workers are subjected to a deductible, perhaps $3,000 per family. That sounds steep, but it's offset by the fact that employees are no longer paying monthly premiums for their coverage. Once the deductible is met, the employer generally provides full coverage of additional expenses for the year.

Critics worry that to save money, consumers may stint on care—creating bigger health problems, and bigger bills, down the road. McCallister dismisses such concerns, arguing that the biggest savings come from some simple shifts in consumer behavior—from costly specialists to primary-care physicians, and from branded drugs to cheaper generics. Humana does its part, offering Internet-based tools to help members compare health plans and monitor their expenses.

For all of McCallister's proselytizing, companies have been slow to embrace the new policies. Of the 3 million members in Humana's commercial accounts, just 225,000 have enrolled in SmartSuite. "There's a lot of inertia," McCallister admits. "But we're going through exactly what HMOs went through when they were introduced in the 1980s." McCallister has to hope that his customers see the light. Otherwise, Humana will remain vulnerable to getting swept aside in the rapidly evolving health-care industry.

Questions

1. How did CEO McAllister change Humana's control system to change the behavior of its employees?
2. How did he then try to change the behavior of his customers?

Source: Dean Foust, "Vital Signs at Humana." Reprinted from the July 12, 2004, issue of *BusinessWeek* by special permission.

CHAPTER

12 Human Resource Management

Learning Objectives

After studying this chapter, you should be able to:

- Explain why strategic human resource management can help an organization gain a competitive advantage.
- Describe the steps managers take to recruit and select organizational members.
- Discuss the training and development options that ensure organizational members can effectively perform their jobs.
- Explain why performance appraisal and feedback is such a crucial activity and list the choices managers must make in designing effective performance appraisal and feedback procedures.
- Explain the issues managers face in determining levels of pay and benefits.

A Manager's Challenge

Democracy in Action at Semco

How can managers provide employees with freedom and flexibility at work while ensuring their companies' survival and profitability?

Ricardo Semler was 21 years old (and one of the youngest graduates from the Harvard Business School MBA program) when he took his father's place as head of the family business, Semco, based in Sao Paolo, Brazil, in 1984.[1] His father, Antonio, had founded Semco in 1954 as a machine shop; the company went on to become a manufacturer of marine pumps for the shipbuilding industry, with $4 million a year in revenues when Ricardo Semler took over. Today, Semco's revenues are over $200 million a year from a diverse set of businesses ranging from industrial machinery, cooling towers, and facility management to environmental consulting and Web-based HRM outsourcing and inventory management services. Semco prides itself on being a premier provider of goods and services in its markets, provides goods and services only in markets that are complex and thus difficult for competitors to enter, and therefore has loyal customers who are willing to pay the higher prices it charges. In addition to growing over 30 percent a year and generating its own cash to support this growth (Semco is a private company), Semco is very profitable.[2]

Ricardo Semler believes in treating employees like adults.

Semler is the first to admit that Semco's phenomenal success is due to its human resources—its employees. In fact, Semler so firmly believes in Semco's employees that he and other top managers at Semco are reluctant to tell employees what to do. Semco has no rules, regulations, or organizational charts; hierarchy is eschewed; and workplace democracy rules the day. Employees have levels of freedom and autonomy unheard of in other companies, and flexibility and trust are built into every aspect of human resource management at Semco.[3]

Semler believes in employees' willingness and desire to be productive and efficient, make significant contributions to Semco, and ensure its continued profitability (which also benefits the employees in terms of their own compensation). Thus, employees have maximum freedom and determine issues ranging from where and when they work to how they are paid.[4] This approach flies in the face of contemporary management thought, yet Semco's ongoing success has made it a living case study in the business community. Semler himself has become a best-selling author of business books, such as *Maverick* and *The Seven-Day Weekend,* and is a Visiting Scholar at the Harvard Business School and the author of widely read *Harvard Business Review* articles.[5]

Human resource practices at Semco revolve around maximizing the contributions employees make to the company, and this begins by hiring individuals who want, can, and will contribute. Semco strives to ensure that all selection decisions are made based on relevant and complete information. Job candidates are first interviewed by the company as a group; the candidates meet many employees, receive a tour of the company, and interact with potential coworkers. This gives Semco a chance to size up candidates in ways more likely to reveal their true natures, and it gives the candidates a chance to learn about Semco. Once finalists are identified from the pool, multiple Semco employees interview them five or six more times to choose the best person(s) to be hired. The result is that both Semco and new hires make very informed decisions and are mutually committed to making the relation a success.[6]

Once hired, entry-level employees participate in the Lost in Space program, in which they rotate through different positions and units of their own choosing for about a year.[7] In this way, the new hires learn about their options and can decide where their interests lie, and the units they work in learn about the new hires. At the end of the year, the new employees may be offered a job in one of the units in which they worked, or they may seek a position elsewhere in Semco. Seasoned Semco employees are also encouraged to rotate positions and work in different parts of the company to keep themselves fresh, energized, and motivated and to give them the opportunity to contribute in new ways as their interests change.[8]

Employees at Semco are free to choose when and where they work.[9] Semler realizes that employees have lives outside the workplace and gives them the freedom to manage their work and free time; he does not expect them to work excessive hours either. What is expected of all employees and all units at Semco is performance.[10]

Performance is appraised at Semco in terms of results. Every six months, all business units are required to demonstrate that their continued operation is producing value for Semco and its customers. If a unit cannot do so, the unit will be disbanded. Similarly, all employees and managers must demonstrate that they are making valuable contributions and deserve to be "rehired." For example, each manager's performance is anonymously appraised by all of the employees who report to him or her, and the appraisals are made publicly available in Semco. As Semler puts it,

> We treat our employees like adults. If they screw up, they take the blame. And since they have to be rehired every six months, they know their jobs are always at risk. Ultimately, all we care about is performance. An employee who spends two days a week at the beach but still produces real value for customers and coworkers is a better employee than one who works ten-hour days but creates little value."[11]

Employees also can choose how they are paid from a combination of 11 different compensation options, ranging from fixed salaries, bonuses, and profit sharing to royalties on sales, royalties on profits, and meeting annual self-set goals. Flexibility in compensation promotes risk taking and innovation, according to Semler, and maximizes returns to employees in the form of their pay and to the company in terms of revenues and profitability.[12]

Flexibility, autonomy, the ability to change jobs often, and control of working hours and even compensation are some of the ways by which Semler strives to ensure that employees are involved in their work because they *want* to be; turnover at Semco is less than 1 percent annually.[13] And with human resource practices geared toward maximizing contributions and performance, Semco is well poised to continue to provide value to its customers.

Overview

Managers are responsible for acquiring, developing, protecting, and utilizing the resources that an organization needs to be efficient and effective. One of the most important resources in all organizations is human resources–the people involved in the production and distribution of goods and services. Human resources include all members of an organization, ranging from top managers to entry-level employees. Effective managers like Ricardo Semler in "A Manager's Challenge" realize how valuable human resources are and take active steps to make sure that their organizations build and fully utilize their human resources to gain a competitive advantage.

This chapter examines how managers can tailor their human resource management system to their organization's strategy and structure. We discuss in particular the major components of human resource management: recruitment and selection, training and development, performance appraisal, pay and benefits, and labor relations. By the end of this chapter, you will understand the central role human resource management plays in creating a high-performing organization.

Strategic Human Resource Management

human resource management Activities that managers engage in to attract and retain employees and to ensure that they perform at a high level and contribute to the accomplishment of organizational goals.

strategic human resource management The process by which managers design the components of a human resource management system to be consistent with each other, with other elements of organizational architecture, and with the organization's strategy and goals.

Organizational architecture (see Part 4) is the combination of organizational structure, control systems, culture, and a human resource management system that managers develop to use resources efficiently and effectively. **Human resource management (HRM)** includes all the activities managers engage in to attract and retain employees and to ensure that they perform at a high level and contribute to the accomplishment of organizational goals. These activities make up an organization's human resource management system, which has five major components: recruitment and selection, training and development, performance appraisal and feedback, pay and benefits, and labor relations (see Figure 12.1, page 414).

Strategic human resource management is the process by which managers design the components of an HRM system to be consistent with each other, with other elements of organizational architecture, and with the organization's strategy and goals.[14] The objective of strategic HRM is the development of an HRM system that enhances an organization's efficiency, quality, innovation, and responsiveness to customers–the four building blocks of competitive advantage. At Semco in "A Manager's Challenge," HRM practices ensure that employees make meaningful contributions, are innovative, are efficient, and provide value to customers.

As part of strategic human resource management, some managers have adopted "Six Sigma" quality improvement plans. These plans ensure that an organization's products and services are as free of error or defects as possible through a variety of human resource–related initiatives. Jack Welch, former CEO of General Electric Company, has indicated that these initiatives have

Figure 12.1
Components of a Human Resource Management System

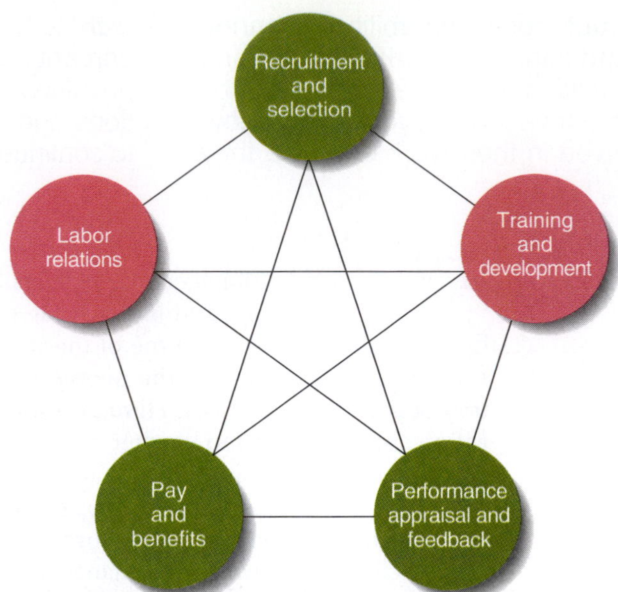

Each component of an HRM system influences the others, and all five must fit together

saved his company millions of dollars, and other companies, such as Whirlpool and Motorola, also have implemented Six Sigma initiatives. In order for such initiatives to be effective, however, top managers have to be committed to Six Sigma, employees must be motivated, and there must be demand for the products or services of the organization in the first place. David Fitzpatrick, head of Deloitte Consulting's Lean Enterprise Practice, estimates that most Six Sigma plans are not effective because the conditions for effective Six Sigma are not in place. For example, if top managers are not committed to the quality initiative, they may not devote the necessary time and resources to make it work and may lose interest in it prematurely.[15]

Effective strategic human resource management can not only help organizations be responsive to customers but also help corporate customers develop their own strategies and effectively utilize their own human resources, as indicated in the following "Information Technology Byte."

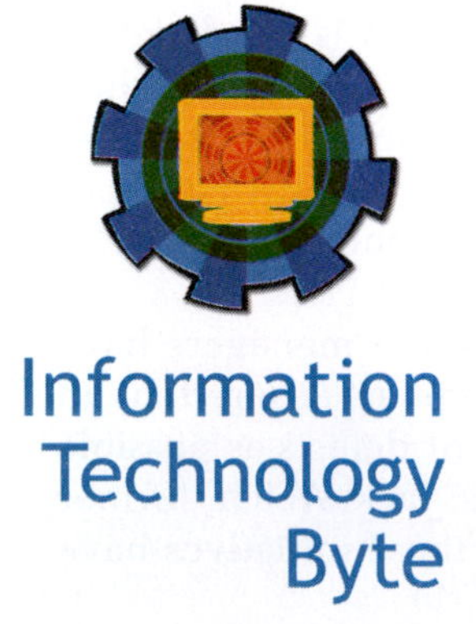

Information Technology Byte

IBM Researchers Help Corporate Customers Achieve Their Goals

IT giant IBM is shifting its focus from making mainframe computers to providing customers with complex technological services.[16] As part of this strategic change in focus, IBM is putting its scientists, mathematicians, and researchers in close contact with major corporate customers so that these specialists can learn firsthand the major challenges customers face in their technology needs. Learning about customers' businesses and challenges enables the IBM specialists to develop solutions, based on their expertise, that customers might not be aware of or even think possible. Once customers realize that they will have IBM's best and brightest not only working on their current problems and challenges but also considering how they can take advan-

In order to beat the competition, IBM concluded that J.P. Morgan Chase should act like a single bank, so that in any customer interaction, an employee would be able to pull all relevant information about that customer instantly.

tage of future developments, it is easier to convince them to choose IBM for their technology needs.[17]

For example, IBM mathematician Howard Sacher spent over a year meeting with top managers in charge of technology at J.P. Morgan Chase, learning about the current state of banking and future challenges and exploring how IBM could develop technological solutions to put Chase ahead of its competition in terms of responsiveness to customers.[18] Sacher determined that Chase should act like a single bank with its customers so that any Chase employee interacting with a customer at any branch would be able to pull up all relevant information about that customer instantly. Developing the technology to make the "one-bank" mentality a reality is actually a complicated problem due to Chase's multitude of services, ways of interacting with customers, recordkeeping procedures, and so forth.[19] Moreover, the technology needs to be in step with future developments and new technologies that banks will be unfolding to provide better service in the future. Sacher's efforts paid off when Chase awarded IBM a $5 billion contract to develop and manage its technological infrastructure.[20]

Similarly, IBM researcher Baruch Schieber, who has a PhD in computer science, met with top managers at Boston Coach (a car and limousine service company).[21] Boston Coach wanted to install wireless technology in its dispatch centers and cars to improve scheduling. With 900 drivers, Boston Coach's key challenge is to optimize scheduling while guaranteeing on-time service. After spending time in Boston Coach's dispatch center and learning all he could about the challenges of scheduling, Schieber was able to do much more with the wireless technology than managers at Boston Coach ever dreamed was possible. Schieber developed a computerized dispatch system that was able to take multiple factors into account and update and optimize drivers' schedules and routes throughout the day as conditions changed, enabling them to increase their volume of rides while still guaranteeing on-time service. Researchers like Sacher and Schieber find it very motivating to be able to solve real problems with their scientific expertise, and interacting with customers gives them ideas for their own research into new technologies and products.[22]

Overview of the Components of HRM

Managers use *recruitment and selection,* the first component of an HRM system, to attract and hire new employees who have the abilities, skills, and experiences that will help an organization achieve its goals. Microsoft Corporation, for example, has the goal of remaining the premier computer software company in the world. To achieve this goal, Bill Gates realizes the importance of hiring only the best software designers. When Microsoft hires new software designers, hundreds of highly qualified candidates with excellent recommendations are interviewed and rigorously tested; only the very best are hired. This careful attention to selection has contributed to Microsoft's competitive advantage. Microsoft has little trouble recruiting top programmers because candidates know they will be at the forefront of the industry if they work for Microsoft, utilizing the latest technology and working with the best people.[23]

After recruiting and selecting employees, managers use the second component, *training and development,* to ensure that organizational members develop the skills and abilities that will enable them to perform their jobs effectively in the present and the future. Training and development is an ongoing process; changes in technology and the environment, as well as in an organization's goals and strategies, often require that organizational members learn new techniques and ways of working. At Microsoft Corporation, newly hired program designers receive on-the-job training by joining small teams that include experienced employees who serve as mentors or advisers. New recruits learn firsthand from team members how to go about developing computer systems that are responsive to customers' programming needs.[24]

The third component, *performance appraisal and feedback,* serves two different purposes in HRM. First, performance appraisal can provide managers with the information they need to make good human resources decisions–decisions about how to train, motivate, and reward organizational members.[25] Thus, the performance appraisal and feedback component is a kind of *control system* that can be used with management by objectives (discussed in Chapter 10). Second, feedback from performance appraisal serves a developmental purpose for members of an organization. When managers regularly evaluate their subordinates' performance, they can provide employees with valuable information about their strengths and weaknesses and the areas in which they need to concentrate.

On the basis of performance appraisals, managers distribute *pay* to employees, part of the fourth component of an HRM system. By rewarding high-performing organizational members with pay raises, bonuses, and the like, managers increase the likelihood that an organization's most valued human resources are motivated to continue their high levels of contribution to the organization. Moreover, by linking pay to performance, high-performing employees are more likely to stay with the organization, and managers are more likely to fill positions that become open with highly talented individuals. *Benefits* such as health insurance are important outcomes that employees receive by virtue of their membership in an organization.

Last, but not least, *labor relations* encompass the steps that managers take to develop and maintain good working relationships with the labor unions that may represent their employees' interests. For example, an organization's labor relations component can help managers establish safe working conditions and fair labor practices in their offices and plants.

Managers must ensure that all five of these components fit together and complement their company's structure and control systems.[26] For example, if managers decide to decentralize authority and empower employees, they need to invest in training and development to ensure that lower-level employees have the knowledge and expertise they need to make the decisions that top managers would make in a more centralized structure.

Each of the five components of HRM influences the others (see Figure 12.1).[27] The kinds of people that the organization attracts and hires through recruitment and selection, for example, determine (1) the kinds of training and development that are necessary, (2) the way performance is appraised, and (3) the appropriate levels of pay and benefits. Managers at Microsoft ensure that their organization has highly qualified program designers by (1) recruiting and selecting the best candidates, (2) providing new hires with the guidance of experienced team members so that they learn how to be responsive to customers' needs when designing programs and systems, (3) appraising program designers' performance in terms of their individual contributions and their team's performance, and (4) basing programmers' pay on individual and team performance.

The Legal Environment of HRM

In the rest of this chapter we focus in detail on the choices managers must make in strategically managing human resources to attain organizational goals and gain a competitive advantage. Effectively managing human resources is a complex undertaking for managers, and we provide an overview of some of the major issues they face. Before we do, however, we need to look at how the legal environment affects human resource management.

equal employment opportunity The equal right of all citizens to the opportunity to obtain employment regardless of their gender, age, race, country of origin, religion, or disabilities.

The local, state, and national laws and regulations that managers and organizations must abide by add to the complexity of HRM. For example, the U.S. government's commitment to **equal employment opportunity (EEO)** has resulted in the creation and enforcement of a number of laws that managers must abide by. The goal of EEO is to ensure that all citizens have an equal opportunity to obtain employment regardless of their gender, race, country of origin, religion, age, or disabilities. Table 12.1 (page 418) summarizes some of the major EEO laws affecting HRM. Other laws, such as the Occupational Safety and Health Act of 1970, require that managers ensure that employees are protected from workplace hazards and safety standards are met.

In Chapter 4, we explained how effectively managing diversity is an ethical and business imperative and discussed the many issues surrounding diversity. EEO laws and their enforcement make the effective management of diversity a legal imperative as well. The Equal Employment Opportunity Commission (EEOC) is the division of the Department of Justice that enforces most of the EEO laws and handles discrimination complaints. In addition, the EEOC issues guidelines for managers to follow to ensure that they are abiding by EEO laws. For example, the Uniform Guidelines on Employee Selection Procedures issued by the EEOC (in conjunction with the Departments of Labor and Justice and the Civil Service Commission) provide managers with guidance on how to ensure that the recruitment and selection component of human resource management complies with Title VII of the Civil Rights Act (which prohibits discrimination based on gender, race, color, religion, and national origin).[28]

Contemporary challenges that managers face related to the legal environment include how to eliminate sexual harassment (see Chapter 4 for an in-depth discussion of sexual harassment), how to make accommodations for employees with disabilities, how to deal with employees who have substance abuse problems, and how to manage HIV-positive employees and employees with AIDS.[29] HIV-positive employees are infected with the virus that causes AIDS but may show no AIDS symptoms and may not develop AIDS in the near future. Often, such employees are able to perform their jobs effectively, and managers must take steps to ensure that they are allowed to do so and are not discriminated against in the workplace.[30] Employees with AIDS may or may not be able to perform their jobs effectively, and, once again, managers need to ensure that they are not unfairly discriminated against.[31] Many organizations have instituted

Table 12.1
Major Equal Employment Opportunity Laws Affecting HRM

Year	Law	Description
1963	Equal Pay Act	Requires that men and women be paid equally if they are performing equal work
1964	Title VII of the Civil Rights Act	Prohibits discrimination in employment decisions on the basis of race, religion, sex, color, or national origin; covers a wide range of employment decisions, including hiring, firing, pay, promotion, and working conditions
1967	Age Discrimination in Employment Act	Prohibits discrimination against workers over the age of 40 and restricts mandatory retirement
1978	Pregnancy Discrimination Act	Prohibits discrimination against women in employment decisions on the basis of pregnancy, childbirth, and related medical decisions
1990	Americans with Disabilities Act	Prohibits discrimination against individuals with disabilities in employment decisions and requires that employers make accommodations for such workers to enable them to perform their jobs
1991	Civil Rights Act	Prohibits discrimination (as does Title VII) and allows for the awarding of punitive and compensatory damages, in addition to back pay, in cases of intentional discrimination
1993	Family and Medical Leave Act	Requires that employers provide 12 weeks of unpaid leave for medical and family reasons including paternity and illness of a family member

AIDS awareness training programs to educate organizational members about HIV and AIDS, dispel unfounded myths about how HIV is spread, and ensure that individuals infected with the HIV virus are treated fairly and are able to be productive as long as they can be while not putting others at risk.[32]

Recruitment and Selection

Recruitment includes all the activities managers engage in to develop a pool of qualified candidates for open positions.[33] **Selection** is the process by which managers determine the relative qualifications of job applicants and their potential for performing well in a particular job. Prior to actually recruiting and selecting employees, managers need to engage in two important activities: human resource planning and job analysis (Figure 12.2).

Figure 12.2
The Recruitment and Selection System

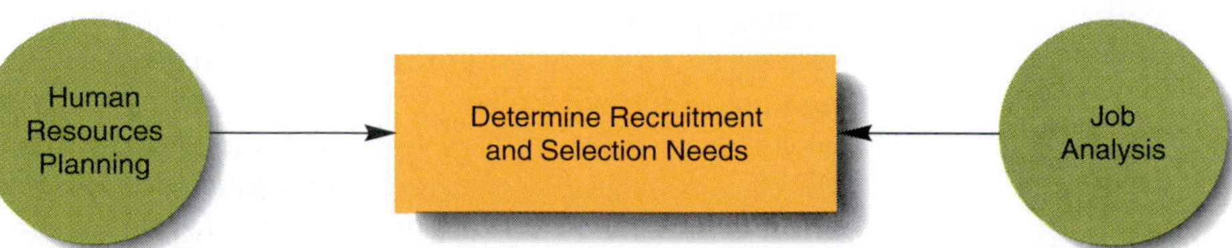

Human Resource Planning

recruitment Activities that managers engage in to develop a pool of qualified candidates for open positions.

selection The process that managers use to determine the relative qualifications of job applicants and their potential for performing well in a particular job.

human resource planning Activities that managers engage in to forecast their current and future needs for human resources.

outsource To use outside suppliers and manufacturers to produce goods and services.

Human resource planning includes all the activities managers engage in to forecast their current and future human resource needs. Current human resources are the employees an organization needs today to provide high-quality goods and services to customers. Future human resource needs are the employees the organization will need at some later date to achieve its longer-term goals.

As part of human resource planning, managers must make both demand forecasts and supply forecasts. *Demand forecasts* estimate the qualifications and numbers of employees an organization will need given its goals and strategies. *Supply forecasts* estimate the availability and qualifications of current employees now and in the future, as well as the supply of qualified workers in the external labor market.

As a result of their human resource planning, managers sometimes decide to **outsource** to fill some of their human resource needs. Instead of recruiting and selecting employees to produce goods and services, managers contract with people who are not members of their organization to produce goods and services. Managers in publishing companies, for example, frequently contract with freelance editors to copyedit new books that they intend to publish. Kelly Services is an organization that provides temporary typing, clerical, and secretarial workers to managers who want to use outsourcing to fill some of their human resource requirements in these areas.

Two reasons why human resource planning sometimes leads managers to outsource are flexibility and cost. First, outsourcing can give managers increased flexibility, especially when accurately forecasting human resource needs is difficult, human resource needs fluctuate over time, or finding skilled workers in a particular area is difficult. Second, outsourcing can sometimes allow managers to make use of human resources at a lower *cost*. When work is outsourced, costs can be lower for a number of reasons: The organization does not have to provide benefits to workers; managers are able to contract for work only when the work is needed; and managers do not have to invest in training. Outsourcing can be used for functional activities such as after-sales service on appliances and equipment, legal work, and the management of information systems. Roy Richie, general counsel for the Chrysler Corporation, uses temporary attorneys to write contracts and fill some of his department's human resource needs. As he says, "The math works. . . . Savings can be tremendous."[34]

Outsourcing does have its disadvantages, however. When work is outsourced, managers may lose some control over the quality of goods and services. Also, individuals performing outsourced work may have less knowledge of organizational practices, procedures, and goals and less commitment to an organization than regular employees. In addition, unions resist outsourcing because it has the potential to eliminate some of their members. To gain some of the flexibility and cost savings of outsourcing and avoid some of outsourcing's disadvantages, a number of organizations, such as Microsoft and IBM, rely on a pool of temporary employees to, for example, debug programs.

A major trend reflecting the increasing globalization of business is the outsourcing of office work, computer programming, and technical jobs from the United States and countries in western Europe, with high labor costs, to countries like India and China, with low labor costs.[35] For example, computer programmers in India and China earn a fraction of what their U.S. counterparts earn. In 2003, India alone provided over $9 billion worth of software and technological outsourcing services to companies in North America, western Europe,

Latin America, Asia and the Pacific Rim, and Japan; North American companies accounted for the majority of outsourcing to India.[36]

As companies gain experience in outsourcing software and technological services, managers are learning what kinds of work can be effectively outsourced and what work should probably not be outsourced. In India, for example, the workforce is highly trained and motivated, and cities like Bangalore are bustling with high-tech jobs and companies like Infosys Technologies, providing software services to companies abroad. Managers who have outsourcing experience have found that outsourcing works best for tasks that can be rule-based, do not require closeness/familiarity with customers and/or the customs and culture of the country in which the company is based, and do not require creativity.[37] When the work requires the recognition and solution of problems rather than the application of preexisting algorithms, creativity in developing solutions, and independent thinking and judgment without the guidance of standard operating procedures, performance might suffer from outsourcing. Essentially, the more complex and uncertain the work and the more it depends on being close to customers and the company itself, the less advantageous outsourcing tends to be.[38] As indicated in the following "Managing Globally," these trade-offs between gaining the cost advantages of outsourcing and being responsive to customers, providing effective services, and developing innovative products have led some managers to cease outsourcing certain kinds of tasks that might be better performed by an organization's own employees.[39]

Managing Globally

When Outsourcing Doesn't Make Sense

Hermant Kurande, one of the founders of Storability Software in Southborough, Massachusetts, and head of technology at the firm, started outsourcing three years ago. He outsourced software programming work to India, where labor costs were about 25 percent of what they would have been if the work were performed in-house. Storability tried different approaches to effectively utilizing low-cost Indian labor for its programming tasks, but after experiencing a number of problems, it decided to hire more programmers and now does most of its programming in the United States. While Kurande was born and educated in India and received his master's degree from the Indian Institute of Technology in Bombay, he found that the "depth of knowledge in the area we want to build software is not good enough among Indian programmers."[40]

Dey Ittycheria, also born in India and CEO of Bladelogic, which develops network management software in Waltham, Massachusetts, has faced similar challenges in his efforts to outsource programming to India. Bladelogic, whose customers include General Electric and Sprint, started outsourcing in 2001, soon after the company was founded. Even though the labor costs in India were 35 percent of what they would have been in the United States, Ittycheria found that it actually cost more to outsource work to India when he took into account productivity; as a result, most of Bladelogic's programming work is now done by its own employees in the United States.[41] Ittycheria and Kurande are not alone in their disenchantment with outsourcing programming. According to Nariman Bahravish, an economist with the consulting and forecasting firm Global Insight, "Only certain kinds of tasks can be outsourced–what can be set down as a set of rules . . . that which requires more creativity is more difficult to manage at a distance."[42]

Nonetheless, there are many kinds of tasks that can be effectively outsourced, and the cost savings for these tasks can be considerable. And some managers believe that many programming tasks can be effectively outsourced as well, even those requiring creativity. For example, according to Bassab Pradham, vice president for worldwide sales at Infosys Technologies, based in Bangalore, India, Infosys effectively provided over $700 million worth of data entry, programming, and technical support services to major North American companies like Cisco Systems, Visa International, and Boeing in 2003. However, Pradham does concede that "whenever the pace of innovation is very rapid . . . the work should be done closer to the client."[43] All in all, estimates from researchers studying workplace trends, such as the Cato Institute in Washington, DC, project that companies in the United States will continue to increase their utilization of outsourcing to lower costs in the next decade.[44] Clearly, though, managers need to carefully determine which tasks can be effectively outsourced and which can be better performed closer to home.[45]

Job Analysis

job analysis Identifying the tasks, duties, and responsibilities that make up a job and the knowledge, skills, and abilities needed to perform the job.

Job analysis is a second important activity that managers need to undertake prior to recruitment and selection.[46] **Job analysis** is the process of identifying (1) the tasks, duties, and responsibilities that make up a job (the *job description*), and (2) the knowledge, skills, and abilities needed to perform the job (the *job specifications*).[47] For each job in an organization, a job analysis needs to be done.

A job analysis can be done in a number of ways, including observing current employees as they perform the job or interviewing them. Often, managers rely on questionnaires compiled by jobholders and their managers. The questionnaires ask about the skills and abilities needed to perform the job, job tasks and the amount of time spent on them, responsibilities, supervisory activities, equipment used, reports prepared, and decisions made.[48] The Position Analysis Questionnaire (PAQ) is a comprehensive standardized questionnaire that many managers rely on to conduct job analyses.[49] It focuses on behaviors jobholders perform, working conditions, and job characteristics and can be used for a variety of jobs.[50] The PAQ contains 194 items organized into six divisions: (1) information input (where and how the jobholder acquires information to perform the job), (2) mental processes (reasoning, decision making, planning, and information processing activities that are part of the job), (3) work output (physical activities performed on the job and machines and devices used), (4) relationships with others (interactions with other people that are necessary to perform the job), (5) job context (the physical and social environment of the job), and (6) other job characteristics (such as work pace).[51] A trend, in some organizations, is toward more flexible jobs in which tasks and responsibilities change and cannot be clearly specified in advance. For these kinds of jobs, job analysis focuses more on determining the skills and knowledge workers need to be effective and less on specific duties.

After managers have completed human resource planning and job analyses for all jobs in an organization, they will know their human resource needs and the jobs they need to fill. They will also know the knowledge, skills, and abilities that potential employees need to perform those jobs. At this point, recruitment and selection can begin.

Employment Web sites like www.monster.com are becoming an increasingly popular external recruitment tool. One advantage of such Web sites is that they can reach out to a broader applicant pool and can even be used to fill global positions.

External and Internal Recruitment

As noted earlier, recruitment is what managers do to develop a pool of qualified candidates for open positions.[52] They traditionally have used two main types of recruiting: external and internal, which is now supplemented by recruiting over the Internet.

EXTERNAL RECRUITING When managers recruit externally to fill open positions, they look outside the organization for people who have not worked for the organization previously. There are multiple means through which managers can recruit externally–advertisements in newspapers and magazines, open houses for students and career counselors at high schools and colleges or on-site at the organization, career fairs at colleges, and recruitment meetings with groups in the local community.

Many large organizations send teams of interviewers to college campuses to recruit new employees. External recruitment can also take place through informal networks, as occurs when current employees inform friends about open positions in their companies or recommend people they know to fill vacant spots. Some organizations use employment agencies for external recruitment, and some external recruitment takes place simply through walk-ins–job hunters coming to an organization and inquiring about employment possibilities.

With all the downsizings and corporate layoffs that have taken place in recent years, you might think that external recruiting would be a relatively easy task for managers. However, it often is not, because even though many people may be looking for jobs, many of the jobs that are opening up require skills and abilities that these job hunters do not have. Managers needing to fill vacant positions and job hunters seeking employment opportunities are increasingly relying on the Web to make connections with each other through employment Web sites such as Monster.com[53] and Jobline International, Europe's largest electronic recruiting site, with operations in 12 countries.[54] Major corporations such as Coca-Cola, Cisco, Ernst & Young, Canon, and Telia have relied on Jobline to fill global positions.[55]

External recruiting has both advantages and disadvantages for managers. Advantages include having access to a potentially large applicant pool; being able to attract people who have the skills, knowledge, and abilities that an organization needs to achieve its goals; and being able to bring in newcomers who may have a fresh approach to problems and be up to date on the latest technology. These advantages have to be weighed against the disadvantages, including the relatively high costs of external recruitment. Employees recruited externally also lack knowledge about the inner workings of the organization and may need to receive more training than those recruited internally. Finally, when employees are recruited externally, there is always uncertainty concerning whether they will actually be good performers.

lateral move A job change that entails no major changes in responsibility or authority levels.

INTERNAL RECRUITING When recruiting is internal, managers turn to existing employees to fill open positions. Employees recruited internally are either seeking **lateral moves** (job changes that entail no major changes in responsibility or authority levels) or promotions. Internal recruiting has several advantages. First, internal applicants are already familiar with the organization (including its goals, structure, culture, rules, and norms). Second, managers already know candidates; they have considerable information about their skills and abilities and actual behavior on the job. Third, internal recruiting can help boost levels of employee motivation and morale, both for the employee who gets the job and for other workers. Those who are not seeking a promotion or who may not be ready for one can see that promotion is a possibility for the future; or a lateral move can alleviate boredom once a job has been fully mastered and can also be a useful way to learn new skills. Finally, internal recruiting is normally less time-consuming and expensive than external recruiting.

Given the advantages of internal recruiting, why do managers rely on external recruiting as much as they do? The answer is because of the disadvantages of internal recruiting–among them, a limited pool of candidates and a tendency among those candidates to be set in the organization's ways. Often, the organization simply does not have suitable internal candidates. Sometimes, even when suitable internal applicants are available, managers may rely on external recruiting to find the very best candidate or to help bring new ideas and approaches into their organization. When organizations are in trouble and performing poorly, external recruiting is often relied on to bring in managerial talent with a fresh approach. For example, when IBM's performance was suffering in the 1990s and the board of directors was looking for a new CEO, rather than consider any of IBM's existing top managers for this position, the board recruited Lou Gerstner, an outsider who had no previous experience in the computer industry.

HONESTY IN RECRUITING At times, when trying to recruit the most qualified applicants, managers may be tempted to paint overly rosy pictures of both the open positions and the organization as a whole. They may worry that if they are totally honest about advantages and disadvantages, they either will not be able to fill positions or will have fewer or less qualified applicants. A manager trying to fill a secretarial position, for example, may emphasize the high level of pay and benefits the job offers and fail to mention the fact that the position is usually a dead-end job offering few opportunities for promotion.

Research suggests that painting an overly rosy picture of a job and the organization is not a wise recruiting strategy. Recruitment is more likely to be effective when managers provide potential applicants with an honest assessment of both the advantages and the disadvantages of the job and organization. Such an assessment is called a **realistic job preview (RJP).**[56] RJPs can reduce the number of new hires who quit when their jobs and organizations fail to meet their unrealistic expectations, and they help applicants decide for themselves whether the job is right for them.

realistic job preview An honest assessment of the advantages and disadvantages of a job and organization.

Take the earlier example of the manager trying to recruit a secretary. The manager who paints a rosy picture of the job might have an easy time filling it but might end up with a secretary who expects to be promoted quickly to an administrative assistant position. After a few weeks on the job, the secretary may realize that a promotion is highly unlikely no matter how good his or her performance, become dissatisfied, and look for and accept another job. The manager then has to recruit, select, and train another new secretary. The manager could have avoided this waste of valuable organizational resources by using a realistic job preview. The RJP would have increased the likelihood of hiring a secretary who was comfortable with few promotional opportunities and subsequently would have been satisfied to remain on the job.

The Selection Process

Once managers develop a pool of applicants for open positions through the recruitment process, they need to find out whether each applicant is qualified for the position and likely to be a good performer. If more than one applicant meets these two conditions, managers must further determine which applicants are likely to be better performers than others. They have several selection tools to help them sort out the relative qualifications of job applicants and appraise their potential for being good performers in a particular job. These tools include background information, interviews, paper-and-pencil tests, physical ability tests, performance tests, and references (see Figure 12.3).[57]

BACKGROUND INFORMATION To aid in the selection process, managers obtain background information from job applications and from résumés. Such information might include the highest levels of education obtained, college majors and minors, type of college or university attended, years and type of work experience, and mastery of foreign languages. Background information can be helpful both to screen out applicants who are lacking key qualifications (such as a college degree) and to determine which qualified applicants are more promising than others. For example, applicants with a BS may be acceptable, but those who also have an MBA are preferable.

INTERVIEWS Virtually all organizations use interviews during the selection process. Interviews may be structured or unstructured. In *a structured interview,* managers ask each applicant the same standard questions (e.g., "What are your unique qualifications for this position?" and "What characteristics of a job are most important for you?"). Particularly informative questions may be those that prompt an interviewee to demonstrate skills and abilities needed for the job by answering the question. Sometimes called *situational interview questions,* these often present interviewees with a scenario that they would likely encounter on

Figure 12.3
Selection Tools

the job and ask them to indicate how they would handle it.[58] For example, applicants for a sales job may be asked to indicate how they would respond to a customer who complains about waiting too long for service, a customer who is indecisive, and a customer whose order is lost.

An *unstructured interview* proceeds more like an ordinary conversation. The interviewer feels free to ask probing questions to discover what the applicant is like and does not ask a fixed set of questions determined in advance. In general, structured interviews are superior to unstructured interviews because they are more likely to yield information that will help identify qualified candidates and are less subjective. Also, evaluations based on structured interviews may be less influenced by the interviewer's biases than evaluations based on unstructured interviews.

Even when structured interviews are used, however, the potential exists for the interviewer's biases to influence his or her judgment. Recall from Chapter 4 how the similar-to-me effect can cause people to perceive others who are similar to themselves more positively than those who are different and how stereotypes can result in inaccurate perceptions. Interviewers must be trained to avoid these biases and sources of inaccurate perceptions as much as possible. Many of the approaches to increasing diversity awareness and diversity skills described in Chapter 4 are used to train interviewers to avoid the effects of biases and stereotypes. In addition, using multiple interviewers can be advantageous as their individual biases and idiosyncrasies may cancel one another out.[59]

When conducting interviews, managers cannot ask questions that are irrelevant to the job in question; otherwise, their organizations run the risk of costly lawsuits. It is inappropriate and illegal, for example, to inquire about an interviewee's spouse or to ask questions about whether an interviewee plans to have children. Because questions such as these are irrelevant to job performance, they are discriminatory and violate EEO laws (see Table 12.1). Thus, interviewers need to be instructed in EEO laws and informed about questions that may violate those laws.

Managers can use interviews at various stages in the selection process. Some use interviews as initial screening devices; others use them as a final hurdle that applicants must jump. Regardless of when they are used, managers typically use other selection tools in conjunction with interviews because of the potential for bias and for inaccurate assessments of interviewees. Even though training and using structured rather than unstructured interviews can eliminate the effects of some biases, interviewers can still come to erroneous conclusions about interviewees' qualifications. Interviewees, for example, who make a bad initial impression or are overly nervous in the first minute or two of an interview tend to be judged more harshly than other, less nervous candidates, even if the rest of the interview goes well.

PAPER-AND-PENCIL TESTS The two main kinds of paper-and-pencil tests used for selection purposes are ability tests and personality tests. *Ability tests* assess the extent to which applicants possess the skills necessary for job performance, such as verbal comprehension or numerical skills. Autoworkers hired by General Motors, Chrysler, and Ford, for example, are typically tested for their ability to read and to do mathematics.[60]

Personality tests measure personality traits and characteristics relevant to job performance. Some retail organizations, for example, give job applicants honesty tests to determine how trustworthy they are. The use of personality tests (including honesty tests) for hiring purposes is controversial. Some critics maintain that honesty tests do not really measure honesty (that is, they are not valid) and can be faked by job applicants. Before using any paper-and-pencil tests for selection purposes, managers must have sound evidence that the tests are actually good predictors of performance on the job in question. Managers who use tests without such evidence may be subject to costly discrimination lawsuits.

PHYSICAL ABILITY TESTS For jobs requiring physical abilities, such as firefighting, garbage collecting, and package delivery, managers use physical ability tests that measure physical strength and stamina as selection tools. Autoworkers are typically tested for mechanical dexterity because this physical ability is an important skill for high job performance in many auto plants.[61]

PERFORMANCE TESTS *Performance tests* measure job applicants' performance on actual job tasks. Applicants for secretarial positions, for example, typically are required to complete a keyboarding test that measures how quickly and accurately they type. Applicants for middle- and top-management positions are sometimes given short-term projects to complete–projects that mirror the kinds of situations that arise in the job being filled–to assess their knowledge and problem-solving capabilities.[62]

Assessment centers, first used by AT&T, take performance tests one step further. In a typical assessment center, about 10 to 15 candidates for managerial positions participate in a variety of activities over a few days. During this time they are assessed for the skills an effective manager needs–problem-solving skills, organization skills, communication skills, and conflict resolution skills. Some of the activities are performed individually; others are performed in groups. Throughout the process, current managers observe the candidates' behavior and measure performance. Summary evaluations are then used as a selection tool.

REFERENCES Applicants for many jobs are required to provide references from former employers or other knowledgeable sources (such as a college instructor or adviser) who know the applicants' skills, abilities, and other personal characteristics. These individuals are asked to provide candid information about the applicant. References are often used at the end of the selection process to confirm a decision to hire. Yet the fact that many former employers are reluctant to provide negative information in references sometimes makes it difficult to interpret what a reference is really saying about an applicant.

In fact, several recent lawsuits filed by applicants who felt that they were unfairly denigrated or had their privacy invaded by unfavorable references from former employers have caused managers to be increasingly wary of providing any negative information in a reference, even if it is accurate. For jobs in which the jobholder is responsible for the safety and lives of other people, however, failing to provide accurate negative information in a reference does not just mean that the wrong person might get hired; it may also mean that other people's lives will be at stake.

THE IMPORTANCE OF RELIABILITY AND VALIDITY Whatever selection tools a manager uses, these tools need to be both reliable and valid. **Reliability** is the degree to which a tool or test measures the same thing each time it is administered. Scores on a selection test should be very similar if the same person is assessed with the same tool on two different days; if there is quite a bit of variability, the tool is unreliable. For interviews, determining reliability is more

reliability The degree to which a tool or test measures the same thing each time it is used.

complex because the dynamic is personal interpretation. That is why the reliability of interviews can be increased if two or more different qualified interviewers interview the same candidate. If the interviews are reliable, the interviewers should come to similar conclusions about the interviewee's qualifications.

validity The degree to which a tool or test measures what it purports to measure.

Validity is the degree to which a tool measures what it purports to measure–for selection tools, it is the degree to which the test predicts performance on the tasks or job in question. Does a physical ability test used to select firefighters, for example, actually predict on-the-job performance? Do assessment center ratings actually predict managerial performance? Do keyboarding tests predict secretarial performance? These are all questions of validity. Honesty tests, for example, are controversial because it is not clear that they validly predict honesty in such jobs as retailing and banking.

Managers have an ethical and legal obligation to use reliable and valid selection tools. Yet reliability and validity are matters of degree rather than all-or-nothing characteristics. Thus, managers should strive to use selection tools in such a way that they can achieve the greatest degree of reliability and validity. For ability tests of a particular skill, managers should keep up to date on the latest advances in the development of valid paper-and-pencil tests and use the test with the highest reliability and validity ratings possible for their purposes. Regarding interviews, managers can improve reliability by having more than one person interview job candidates.

Training and Development

Training and development help to ensure that organizational members have the knowledge and skills needed to perform jobs effectively, take on new responsibilities, and adapt to changing conditions. **Training** primarily focuses on teaching organizational members how to perform their current jobs and helping them acquire the knowledge and skills they need to be effective performers. **Development** focuses on building the knowledge and skills of organizational members so that they are prepared to take on new responsibilities and challenges. Training tends to be used more frequently at lower levels of an organization; development tends to be used more frequently with professionals and managers.

training Teaching organizational members how to perform their current jobs and helping them acquire the knowledge and skills they need to be effective performers.

development Building the knowledge and skills of organizational members so that they will be prepared to take on new responsibilities and challenges.

needs assessment An assessment of which employees need training or development and what type of skills or knowledge they need to acquire.

Before creating training and development programs, managers should perform a **needs assessment** to determine which employees need training or development and what type of skills or knowledge they need to acquire (see Figure 12.4, page 428).[63]

Types of Training

There are two types of training: classroom instruction and on-the-job training.

CLASSROOM INSTRUCTION Through classroom instruction, employees acquire knowledge and skills in a classroom setting. This instruction may take place within the organization or outside it, such as courses at local colleges and universities. Many organizations actually establish their own formal instructional divisions–some are even called "colleges"–to provide needed classroom instruction.

At Ethan Allen Interiors Inc., for example, employees from stores around the country attend Ethan Allen College at company headquarters in Danbury, Connecticut. During classes, employees acquire in-depth knowledge about the

Figure 12.4
Training and Development

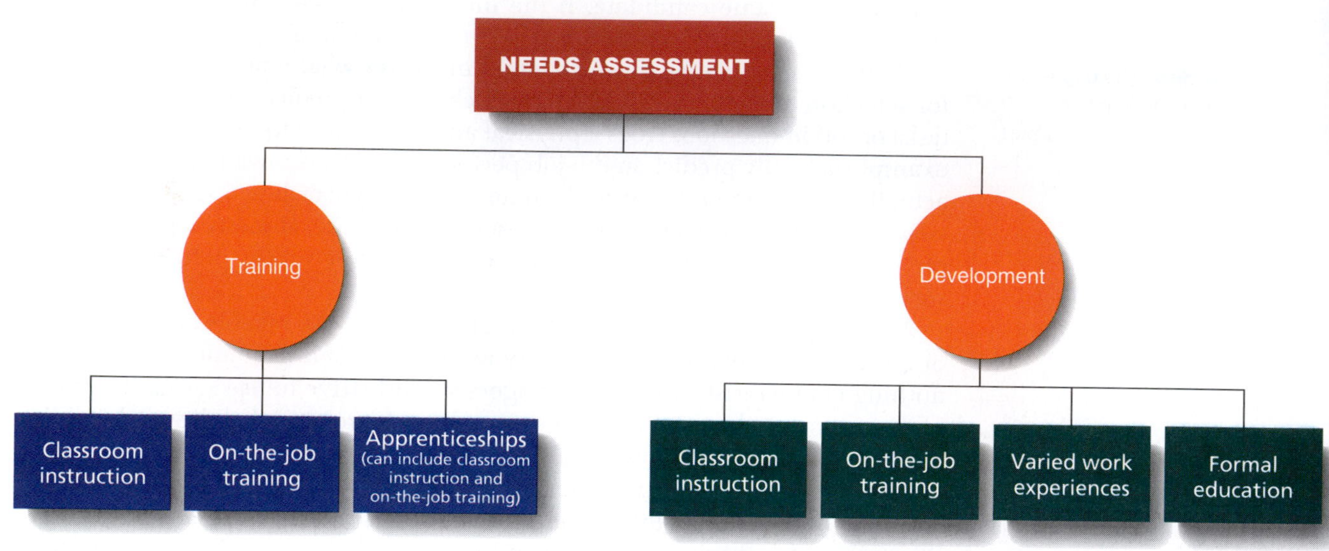

company's products and learn how to listen to customers and accurately assess their needs. In addition, the college provides instruction on such diverse topics as floor plans and window treatments. Training at Ethan Allen is an ongoing process. Veteran employees attend two- or three-day sessions at the college to brush up on their skills and keep abreast of the latest developments. M. Farooq Kathwari, chairman and CEO of Ethan Allen, believes that the classroom instruction that employees receive at Ethan Allen College has contributed significantly to his company's competitive advantage.[64]

Classroom instruction frequently includes the use of videos and role playing in addition to traditional written materials, lectures, and group discussions. *Videos* can be used to demonstrate appropriate and inappropriate job behaviors. For example, by watching an experienced salesperson effectively deal with a loud and angry customer in a video clip, inexperienced salespeople can develop skills in handling similar situations. During *role playing,* trainees either directly participate in or watch others perform actual job activities in a simulated setting. At McDonald's Hamburger University, for example, role playing helps franchisees acquire the knowledge and skills they need to manage their restaurants.

Of the various types of training available, simulations are often used for training people to perform complicated jobs, such as that of air traffic controller. Such jobs, in which errors carry a very high cost, require an extensive amount of learning.

Simulations also can be part of classroom instruction, particularly for complicated jobs that require an extensive amount of learning and in which errors carry a high cost. In a simulation, key aspects of the work situation and job tasks are duplicated as closely as possible in an artificial setting. For example, air traffic controllers are trained by simulations because of the complicated nature of the work, the extensive amount of learning involved, and the very high costs of air traffic control errors.

on-the-job training Training that takes place in the work setting as employees perform their job tasks.

ON-THE-JOB TRAINING In **on-the-job training,** learning occurs in the work setting as employees perform their job tasks. On-the-job training can be provided by co-workers or supervisors or can occur simply as jobholders gain experience and knowledge from doing the work, as is the case at Semco in "A Manager's Challenge." Newly hired waiters and waitresses in chains such as Red Lobster or The Olive Garden often receive on-the-job training from experienced employees. The supervisor of a new bus driver for a campus bus system may ride the bus for a week to ensure that the driver has learned the routes and follows safety procedures. Chefs learn to create new and innovative dishes by experimenting with different combinations of ingredients and cooking techniques. For all on-the-job training, employees learn by doing.

Managers often use on-the-job training on a continuing basis to ensure that their subordinates keep up to date with changes in goals, technology, products, or customer needs and desires. For example, sales representatives at Mary Kay Cosmetics Inc. receive ongoing training so that they are not only knowledgeable about new cosmetic products and currently popular colors but also reminded of Mary Kay's guiding principles. Mary Kay's expansion into Russia has been very successful, in part because of the ongoing training that Mary Kay's Russian salespeople receive.[65]

Types of Development

Although both classroom instruction and on-the-job training can be used for development purposes as well as training, development often includes additional activities such as varied work experiences and formal education.

VARIED WORK EXPERIENCES Top managers need to develop an understanding of, and expertise in, a variety of functions, products and services, and markets. To develop executives who will have this expertise, managers frequently make sure that employees with high potential have a wide variety of different job experiences, some in line positions and some in staff positions. Varied work experiences broaden employees' horizons and help them think more about the big picture. For example, one- to three-year stints overseas are being used increasingly to provide managers with international work experiences. With organizations becoming more global, managers need to develop an understanding of the different values, beliefs, cultures, regions, and ways of doing business in different countries.

Having a mentor (recall from Chapter 3 that a *mentor* is an experienced member of an organization who provides advice and guidance to a less experienced member, called a *protégé,*) can help managers seek out work experiences and assignments that will contribute to their development and gain the most they can from varied work experiences.[66] While some mentors and protégés hook up informally, organizations have found that formal mentorship programs can be valuable ways to contribute to the development of managers and all employees, as indicated in the following "Focus on Diversity."

Focus on Diversity

Development Through Mentoring

Lynn Tyson, vice president for investor relations at Dell, never had a mentor help her navigate her rise to the top and says that "most of the time I was shaking in my shoes." Realizing the benefits of mentors for protégé development, and for the ability of organizations to retain valued members, Tyson worked to develop a formal mentoring program at Dell. Tyson currently mentors 40 protégés and derives tremendous satisfaction from knowing that she has "the ability to make a difference in somebody's career."[67]

Formal mentoring programs ensure that mentoring takes place in an organization, structure the process, and make sure that diverse organizational members have equal access to mentors. Participants receive training, efforts are focused on matching up mentors and protégés so that meaningful developmental relationships ensue, and organizations can track reactions and assess the potential benefits of mentoring. Formal mentoring programs can also ensure that diverse members of an organization receive the benefits of mentoring. A recent study conducted by David A. Thomas, a professor at the Harvard Business School, found that members of racial minority groups at three large corporations who were very successful in their careers had the benefit of mentors. Clearly, all members of an organization can benefit from mentors; formal mentorship programs help organizations make this valuable development tool available to all employees.[68]

When diverse members of an organization lack mentors, their progress in the organization and advancement to high-level positions can be hampered. Ida Abott, a lawyer and consultant on work-related issues, recently presented a paper to the Minority Corporate Counsel Association in which she concluded, "The lack of adequate mentoring has held women and minority lawyers back from achieving professional success and has led to high rates of career dissatisfaction and attrition."[69]

Mentoring can benefit all kinds of employees in all kinds of work.[70] John Washko, a manager at the Four Seasons hotel chain, benefited from the mentoring he received from Stan Bromley on interpersonal relations and how to deal with employees; mentor Bromley, in turn, found that participating in the Four Seasons mentoring program helped him develop his own management style.[71] More generally, development is an ongoing process for all managers, and mentors often find that mentoring contributes to their own personal development.

FORMAL EDUCATION Many large corporations reimburse employees for tuition expenses they incur while taking college courses and obtaining advanced degrees. This is not just benevolence on the part of the employer or even a simple reward given to the employee; it is an effective way to develop employees who are able to take on new responsibilities and more challenging positions. For similar reasons, corporations spend thousands of dollars sending managers to executive development programs such as executive MBA programs. In these programs, experts teach managers the latest in business and management techniques and practices.

To save time and travel costs, managers are increasingly relying on *long-distance learning* to formally educate and develop employees. Using videoconferencing technologies, business schools such as the Harvard Business School, the University of Michigan, and Babson College are teaching courses on video screens in corporate conference rooms. Business schools are also customizing courses and degrees to fit the development needs of employees in a particular company. The University of Michigan uses long-distance learning, for example, to provide instruction for customized MBA degrees for employees of the Daewoo Corporation in Korea and Cathay Pacific Airways Ltd. in Hong Kong. In conjunction with Westcott Communications Inc., eight business schools have formed a new venture, Executive Education Network, to create and operate satellite classrooms in major corporations; almost 100 companies have already signed on, including Eastman Kodak Company, Walt Disney Company, and Texas Instruments.[72]

Transfer of Training and Development

Whenever training and development take place off the job or in a classroom setting, it is vital for managers to promote the transfer of the knowledge and skills acquired *to the actual work situation*. Trainees should be encouraged and expected to use their newfound expertise on the job.

Performance Appraisal and Feedback

The recruitment/selection and training/development components of a human resource management system ensure that employees have the knowledge and skills needed to be effective now and in the future. Performance appraisal and feedback complement recruitment, selection, training, and development. **Performance appraisal** is the evaluation of employees' job performance and contributions to the organization. **Performance feedback** is the process through which managers share performance appraisal information with their subordinates, give subordinates an opportunity to reflect on their own performance, and develop, with subordinates, plans for the future. Before performance feedback, performance appraisal must take place. Performance appraisal could take place without providing performance feedback, but wise managers are careful to provide feedback because it can contribute to employee motivation and performance.

performance appraisal The evaluation of employees' job performance and contributions to their organization.

performance feedback The process through which managers share performance appraisal information with subordinates, give subordinates an opportunity to reflect on their own performance, and develop, with subordinates, plans for the future.

Performance appraisal and feedback contribute to the effective management of human resources in several ways. Performance appraisal gives managers important information on which to base human resource decisions.[73] Decisions about pay raises, bonuses, promotions, and job moves all hinge on the accurate appraisal of performance. Performance appraisal can also help managers determine which workers are candidates for training and development and in what areas. Performance feedback encourages high levels of employee motivation and performance. It lets good performers know that their efforts are valued and appreciated. It also lets poor performers know that their lackluster performance needs improvement. Performance feedback can provide both good and poor performers with insight on their strengths and weaknesses and ways in which they can improve their performance in the future.

Types of Performance Appraisal

Performance appraisal focuses on the evaluation of traits, behaviors, and results.[74]

TRAIT APPRAISALS When trait appraisals are used, managers assess subordinates on personal characteristics that are relevant to job performance, such as skills, abilities, or personality. A factory worker, for example, may be evaluated based on her ability to use computerized equipment and perform numerical calculations. A social worker may be appraised based on his empathy and communication skills.

Three disadvantages of trait appraisals often lead managers to rely on other appraisal methods. First, possessing a certain personal characteristic does not ensure that the personal characteristic will actually be used on the job and result in high performance. For example, a factory worker may possess superior computer and numerical skills but be a poor performer due to low motivation. The second disadvantage of trait appraisals is linked to the first. Because traits do not always show a direct association with performance, workers and courts of law may view them as unfair and potentially discriminatory. The third disadvantage of trait appraisals is that they often do not enable managers to provide employees with feedback that they can use to improve performance. Because trait appraisals focus on relatively enduring human characteristics that change only over the long term, employees can do little to change their behavior in response to performance feedback from a trait appraisal. Telling a social worker that he lacks empathy provides him with little guidance about how to improve his interactions with clients, for example. These disadvantages suggest that managers should use trait appraisals only when they can demonstrate that the assessed traits are accurate and important indicators of job performance.

BEHAVIOR APPRAISALS Through behavior appraisals, managers assess how workers perform their jobs–the actual actions and behaviors that workers exhibit on the job. Whereas trait appraisals assess what workers are *like,* behavior appraisals assess what workers *do*. For example, with a behavior appraisal, a manager might evaluate a social worker on the extent to which he looks clients in the eye when talking with them, expresses sympathy when they are upset, and refers them to community counseling and support groups geared toward the specific problem they are encountering. Behavior appraisals are especially useful when *how* workers perform their jobs is important. In educational organizations such as high schools, for example, the number of classes and students taught is important, but also important is how they are taught or the methods teachers use to ensure that learning takes place.

Behavior appraisals have the advantage of providing employees with clear information about what they are doing right and wrong and how they can improve their performance. And because behaviors are much easier for employees to change than traits, performance feedback from behavior appraisals is more likely to lead to performance improvements.

RESULT APPRAISALS For some jobs, *how* people perform the job is not as important as *what* they accomplish or the results they obtain. With result appraisals, managers appraise performance by the results or the actual outcomes of work behaviors, as is the case at Semco in "A Manager's Challenge." Take the case of two new-car salespersons. One salesperson strives to develop personal relationships with her customers. She spends hours talking to them and frequently calls them up to see how their decision-making process is going. The other salesperson has a much more hands-off approach. He is very knowledgeable, answers customers' questions, and then waits for them to come to him. Both salespersons sell, on average, the same number of cars, and the customers of both are satisfied with the service they receive, according to postcards that the dealership mails to customers asking for an assessment of their satisfaction. The manager of the dealership appropriately uses result appraisals (sales and customer satisfaction) to evaluate the salespeople's performance because it does not matter which behavior salespeople use to sell cars as long as they sell the desired number and satisfy customers. If one salesperson sells too few cars, however, the manager can give that person performance feedback about his or her low sales.

objective appraisal An appraisal that is based on facts and is likely to be numerical.

subjective appraisal An appraisal that is based on perceptions of traits, behaviors, or results.

OBJECTIVE AND SUBJECTIVE APPRAISALS Whether managers appraise performance in terms of traits, behaviors, or results, the information they assess is either objective or subjective. **Objective appraisals** are based on facts and are likely to be numerical–the number of cars sold, the number of meals prepared, the number of times late, the number of audits completed. Managers often use objective appraisals when results are being appraised because results tend to be easier to quantify than traits or behaviors. When *how* workers perform their jobs is important, however, subjective behavior appraisals are more appropriate than result appraisals.

Subjective appraisals are based on managers' perceptions of traits, behaviors, or results. Because subjective appraisals rest on managers' perceptions, there is always the chance that they are inaccurate. (We discuss managerial perception in more detail in the next chapter.) This is why both researchers and managers have spent considerable time and effort on determining the best way to develop reliable and valid subjective measures of performance.

Some of the more popular subjective measures such as the graphic rating scale, the behaviorally anchored rating scale (BARS), and the behavior observation scale (BOS) are illustrated in Figure 12.5, page 434.[75] When graphic rating scales are used, performance is assessed along a continuum with specified intervals. With a BARS, performance is assessed along a scale with clearly defined scale points containing examples of specific behaviors. A BOS assesses performance by how often specific behaviors are performed. Many managers may use both objective and subjective appraisals. For example, a salesperson may be appraised both on the dollar value of sales (objective) and the quality of customer service (subjective).

In addition to subjective appraisals, some organizations employ *forced rankings* whereby supervisors must rank their subordinates and assign them to different categories according to their performance (which is subjectively appraised). For example, middle managers at Ford Motor Company are ranked by their supervisors in a forced distribution from A to C, with 10 percent of them receiving A's, 80 percent receiving B's, and 10 percent receiving C's.[76] The first year an employee receives a C, he or she does not receive a bonus, and after two years of C performance, a demotion or even firing is possible. Employees tend to not like these systems, as they believe they are unfair; managers at Ford have filed a class-action lawsuit because they feel Ford's ranking system is unfair.[77] Relying on relative performance through ranking systems can force managers to rate some of their subordinates as unsatisfactory even if this might not be true and can also result in an employee's performance being downgraded not because of any change he or she has made but because co-workers have improved their performance. In other organizations that use ranking systems, employees tend to voice similar concerns. For example, forced-ranking systems can result in a zero-sum, competitive environment that can discourage cooperation and teamwork.[78]

Figure 12.5
Subjective Measures of Performance

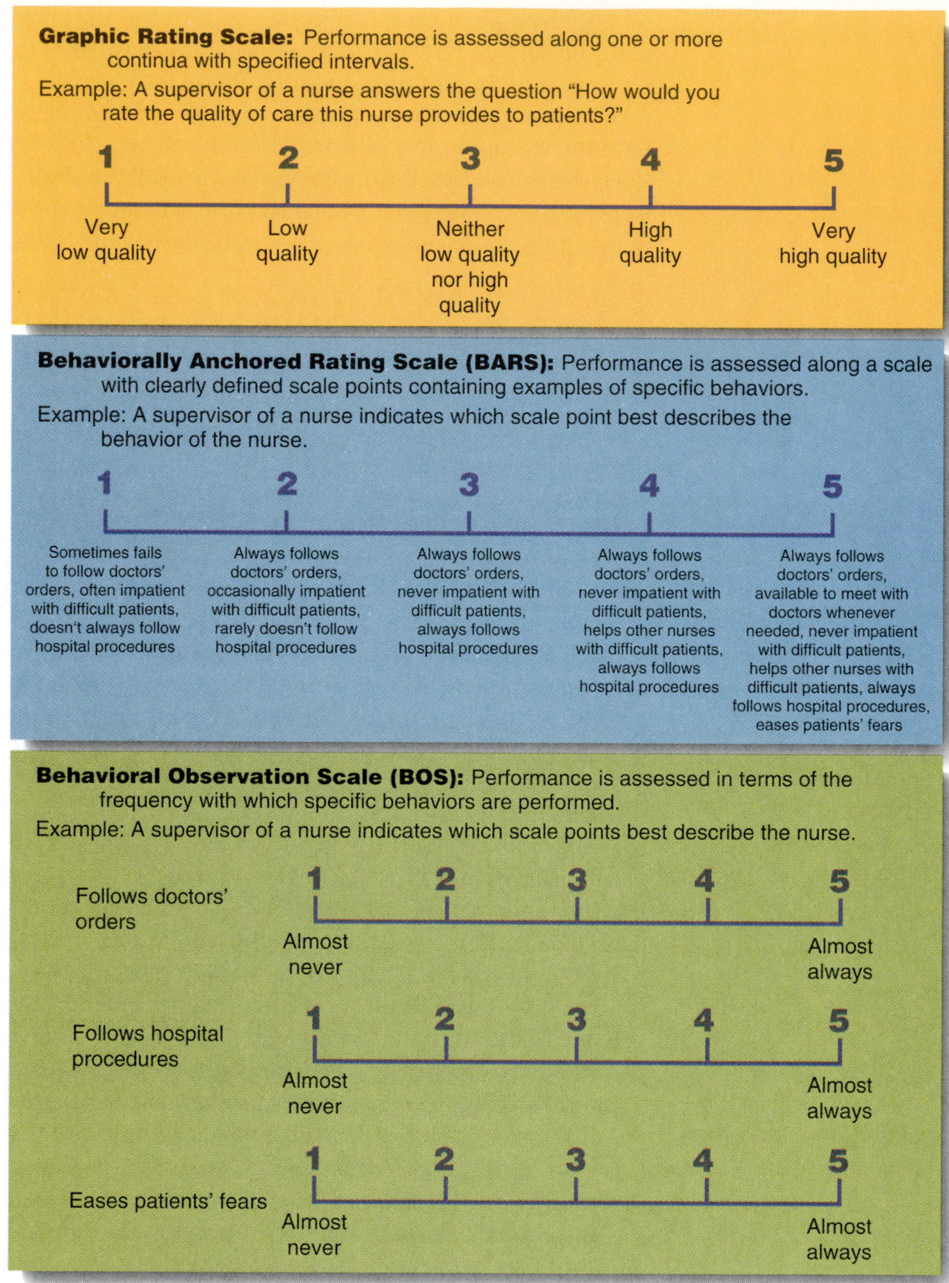

Graphic Rating Scale: Performance is assessed along one or more continua with specified intervals.
Example: A supervisor of a nurse answers the question "How would you rate the quality of care this nurse provides to patients?"
1 2 3 4 5
Very low quality
Low quality
Neither low quality nor high quality
High quality
Very high quality
Behaviorally Anchored Rating Scale (BARS): Performance is assessed along a scale with clearly defined scale points containing examples of specific behaviors.
Example: A supervisor of a nurse indicates which scale point best describes the behavior of the nurse.
1 2 3 4 5
Sometimes fails to follow doctors' orders, often impatient with difficult patients, doesn't always follow hospital procedures
Always follows doctors' orders, occasionally impatient with difficult patients, rarely doesn't follow hospital procedures
Always follows doctors' orders, never impatient with difficult patients, always follows hospital procedures
Always follows doctors' orders, never impatient with difficult patients, helps other nurses with difficult patients, always follows hospital procedures
Always follows doctors' orders, available to meet with doctors whenever needed, never impatient with difficult patients, helps other nurses with difficult patients, always follows hospital procedures, eases patients' fears
Behavioral Observation Scale (BOS): Performance is assessed in terms of the frequency with which specific behaviors are performed.
Example: A supervisor of a nurse indicates which scale points best describe the nurse.
Follows doctors' orders
1 2 3 4 5
Almost never
Almost always
Follows hospital procedures
1 2 3 4 5
Almost never
Almost always
Eases patients' fears
1 2 3 4 5
Almost never
Almost always

Who Appraises Performance?

We have been assuming that managers or the supervisors of employees evaluate performance. This is a pretty fair assumption, for supervisors are the most common appraisers of performance; indeed, each year 70 million U.S. citizens have their job performance appraised by their managers or supervisors.[79] Performance appraisal is an important part of most managers' job duties. Managers are responsible for not only motivating their subordinates to perform at a high level but also making many decisions hinging on performance appraisals, such as pay raises or promotions. Appraisals by managers can be usefully augmented by appraisals from other sources (see Figure 12.6).

SELF, PEERS, SUBORDINATES, AND CLIENTS When self-appraisals are used, managers supplement their evaluations with an employee's assessment of his or her own performance. Peer appraisals are provided by an employee's co-workers. Especially when subordinates work in groups or teams, feedback from peer appraisals can motivate team members while providing managers with important information for decision making. A growing number of companies are having subordinates appraise their managers' performance and leadership as well. And sometimes customers or clients provide assessments of employee performance in terms of responsiveness to customers and quality of service. Although appraisals from each of these sources can be useful, managers need to be aware of potential issues that may arise when they are used. Subordinates sometimes may be inclined to inflate self-appraisals, especially if organizations are downsizing and they are worried about their job security. Managers who are appraised by their subordinates may fail to take needed but unpopular actions out of fear that their subordinates will appraise them negatively.

360-DEGREE PERFORMANCE APPRAISALS To improve motivation and performance, some organizations include 360-degree appraisals and feedback in their performance appraisal systems, especially for managers. In a **360-degree appraisal,** a variety of people, beginning with the manager and including peers or co-workers, subordinates, superiors, and sometimes even customers or clients appraise a manager's performance. The manager receives feedback based on evaluations from these multiple sources.

360-degree appraisal
A performance appraisal by peers, subordinates, superiors, and sometimes clients who are in a position to evaluate a manager's performance.

The growing number of companies using 360-degree appraisals and feedback include AT&T Corp., Allied Signal Inc., Eastman Chemical Co., and Baxter International Inc.[80] For 360-degree appraisals and feedback to be effective, there has to be trust throughout an organization. More generally, trust is a critical

Figure 12.6
Who Appraises Performance?

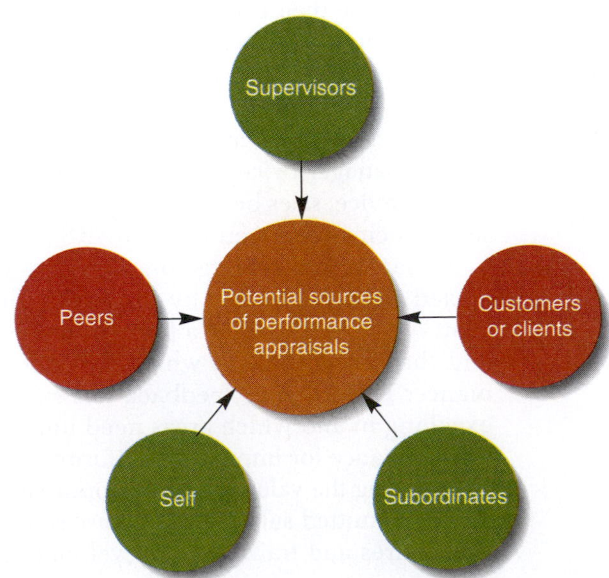

ingredient in any performance appraisal and feedback procedure. In addition, research suggests that 360-degree appraisals should focus on behaviors rather than traits or results and that managers need to carefully select appropriate raters. Moreover, appraisals tend to be more honest when made anonymously, as is the case at Semco in "A Manager's Challenge," and when raters have been trained in how to use 360-degree appraisal forms.[81] Additionally, managers need to think carefully about the extent to which 360-degree appraisals are appropriate for certain jobs and be willing to modify any system they implement when they become aware of unintended problems the appraisal system is responsible for.[82]

Even when 360-degree appraisals are used, it is sometimes difficult to design an effective process by which subordinates' feedback can be communicated to their managers. Advances in information technology provide organizations with a potential solution to this problem. For example, ImproveNow.com has online questionnaires that subordinates can fill out to evaluate the performance of their managers and provide the managers with feedback. Each subordinate of a particular manager completes the questionnaire independently, all responses are tabulated, and the manager is given specific feedback on behaviors in a variety of areas, such as rewarding good performance, looking out for subordinates' best interest and being supportive, and having a vision for the future.[83]

For example, Sonia Russomanno, a manager at Alliance Funding, a New Jersey mortgage lending organization, received feedback from her nine subordinates online from Improve.Now. She received an overall grade of B and specific feedback on a variety of dimensions. This experience drove home to Russomanno the importance of getting honest feedback from her subordinates and listening to it to improve her performance as a manager. She has changed how she rewards her subordinates as a result and plans on using this service in the future to see how she is doing.[84]

Effective Performance Feedback

For the performance appraisal and feedback component of a human resource management system to encourage and motivate high performance, managers must provide their subordinates with performance feedback. To generate useful information to feed back to their subordinates, managers can use both formal and informal appraisals. **Formal appraisals** are conducted at set times during the year and are based on performance dimensions and measures that have been specified in advance. A salesperson, for example, may be evaluated by his or her manager twice a year on the performance dimensions of sales and customer service, sales being objectively measured from sales reports and customer service being measured with a BARS (see Figure 12.5).

formal appraisal An appraisal conducted at a set time during the year and based on performance dimensions and measures that were specified in advance.

Managers in most large organizations use formal performance appraisals on a fixed schedule dictated by company policy, such as every six months or every year. An integral part of a formal appraisal is a meeting between the manager and the subordinate in which the subordinate is given feedback on performance. Performance feedback lets subordinates know which areas they are excelling in and which areas need improvement; it also should provide them with guidance for improving performance.

Realizing the value of formal appraisals, managers in many large corporations have committed substantial resources to updating their performance appraisal procedures and training low-level managers in how to use them and provide accurate feedback to employees. Top managers at the pharmaceutical company Hoffmann-La Roche Inc., for example, recently spent $1.5 million updating and improving their performance appraisal procedures. Alan Rubino, vice president of human resources for Hoffmann-La Roche, believes that this was money well spent because "people need to know exactly where they stand and what's required of them." Before Hoffmann-La Roche's new system was implemented, managers attended a three-day training and development session to improve their performance appraisal skills. The new procedures call for every manager and subordinate to develop a performance plan for subordinates for the coming year–a plan that is linked to the company's strategy and goals and approved by the manager's own superiors. Formal performance appraisals are conducted every six months, during which actual performance is compared to planned performance.[85]

informal appraisal An unscheduled appraisal of ongoing progress and areas for improvement.

Formal performance appraisals supply both managers and subordinates with valuable information; but subordinates often want feedback on a more frequent basis, and managers often want to motivate subordinates as the need arises. For these reasons many companies, including Hoffman-La Roche, supplement formal performance appraisal with frequent **informal appraisals,** for which managers and their subordinates meet as the need arises to discuss ongoing progress and areas for improvement. Moreover, when job duties, assignments, or goals change, informal appraisals can provide workers with timely feedback concerning how they are handling their new responsibilities.

Managers often dislike providing performance feedback, especially when the feedback is negative, but doing so is an important managerial activity.[86] Here are some guidelines for giving effective performance feedback that contributes to employee motivation and performance:

- *Be specific and focus on behaviors or outcomes that are correctable and within a worker's ability to improve.* Example: Telling a salesperson that he is too shy when interacting with customers is likely to do nothing more than lower his self-confidence and prompt the salesperson to become defensive. A more effective approach would be to give the salesperson feedback about specific behaviors to engage in–greeting customers as soon as they enter the department, asking customers whether they need help, and volunteering to help customers find items if they seem to be having trouble.
- *Approach performance appraisal as an exercise in problem solving and solution finding, not criticizing.* Example: Rather than criticizing a financial analyst for turning in reports late, the manager helps the analyst determine why the reports are late and identify ways to better manage her time.
- *Express confidence in a subordinate's ability to improve.* Example: Instead of being skeptical, a first-level manager tells a subordinate that he is confident that the subordinate can increase quality levels.
- *Provide performance feedback both formally and informally.* Example: The staff of a preschool receives feedback from formal performance appraisals twice a year. The director of the school also provides frequent informal feedback such as complimenting staff members on creative ideas for special projects, noticing when they do a particularly good job handling a difficult child, and pointing out when they provide inadequate supervision.
- *Praise instances of high performance and areas of a job in which a worker excels.* Example: Rather than focusing on just the negative, a manager discusses the areas her subordinate excels in as well as the areas in need of improvement.

- *Avoid personal criticisms and treat subordinates with respect.* Example: An engineering manager acknowledges her subordinates' expertise and treats them as professionals. Even when the manager points out performance problems to subordinates, she refrains from criticizing them personally.
- *Agree to a timetable for performance improvements.* Example: A first-level manager and his subordinate decide to meet again in one month to determine if quality levels have improved.

In following these guidelines, managers need to remember why they are giving performance feedback: to encourage high levels of motivation and performance. Moreover, the information that managers gather through performance appraisal and feedback helps them determine how to distribute pay raises and bonuses.

Pay and Benefits

Pay includes employees' base salaries, pay raises, and bonuses and is determined by a number of factors such as characteristics of the organization and the job and levels of performance. Employee *benefits* are based on membership in an organization (and not necessarily on the particular job held) and include sick days, vacation days, and medical and life insurance. In Chapter 13, we discuss the ways in which pay can motivate organizational members to perform at a high level, as well as the different kinds of pay plans managers can use to help an organization achieve its goals and gain a competitive advantage. As you will learn, it is important for pay to be linked to behaviors or results that contribute to organizational effectiveness, as is true at Semco in "A Manager's Challenge." Next, we focus on establishing an organization's pay level and pay structure.

Pay Level

pay level The relative position of an organization's pay incentives in comparison with those of other organizations in the same industry employing similar kinds of workers.

Pay level is a broad comparative concept that refers to how an organization's pay incentives compare, in general, to those of other organizations in the same industry employing similar kinds of workers. Managers must decide if they want to offer relatively high wages, average wages, or relatively low wages. High wages help ensure that an organization is going to be able to recruit, select, and retain high performers, but high wages also raise costs. Low wages give an organization a cost advantage but may undermine the organization's ability to select and recruit high performers and to motivate current employees to perform at a high level. Either of these situations may lead to inferior quality or inadequate customer service.

In determining pay levels, managers should take into account their organization's strategy. A high pay level may prohibit managers from effectively pursuing a low-cost strategy. But a high pay level may be well worth the added costs in an organization whose competitive advantage lies in superior quality and excellent customer service. As one might expect, hotel and motel chains with a low-cost strategy, such as Days Inn and Hampton Inns, have lower pay levels than chains striving to provide high-quality rooms and services, such as Four Seasons and Hyatt Regency.

Pay Structure

pay structure The arrangement of jobs into categories reflecting their relative importance to the organization and its goals, level of skill required, and other characteristics.

After deciding on a pay level, managers have to establish a pay structure for the different jobs in the organization. A **pay structure** clusters jobs into categories reflecting their relative importance to the organization and its goals, levels of skill required, and other characteristics managers consider to be important. Pay ranges are established for each job category. Individual jobholders' pay within job categories is then determined by factors such as performance, seniority, and skill levels.

There are some interesting global differences in pay structures. Large corporations based in the United States tend to pay their CEOs and top managers higher salaries than do their European or Japanese counterparts. There also is a much greater pay differential between employees at the bottom of the corporate hierarchy and those higher up the hierarchy in U.S. companies than in European or Japanese companies.[87]

Concerns have been raised over whether it is equitable or fair for CEOs of large companies in the United States to be making hundreds of thousands or millions of dollars in years when their companies are restructuring and laying off a large portion of their workforces.[88] Robert Allen, for example, the CEO of AT&T, came under intense scrutiny in 1996 because he was earning $5 million a year when AT&T announced plans to lay off thousands of employees. As indicated in the following "Ethics in Action," hefty pay packages for current top managers, and those leaving top-management posts, are alive and well in corporate America.

Ethics in Action

Is CEO Pay over the Top?

CEOs in the United States continue to earn phenomenal amounts of money despite public outcry and disgruntled shareholders. According to *BusinessWeek* magazine, for the three-year period from 2001 to 2003, the 25 highest-paid U.S. CEOs earned an average of $32.7 million a year, which is over 900 times larger than the salary of the typical U.S. worker.[89] Is a pay structure with such a huge pay differential between those at the very top and average employees ethical? Shareholders and the public are increasingly asking this very question and are asking large corporations to rethink their pay structures.[90] As a result of increasing scrutiny, pay levels of top managers are much more likely to be linked to the performance of their companies and their meeting of predetermined targets than they were before.[91]

Even more mind-boggling are the severance packages some CEOs and top managers receive when they leave their organizations. Steven Heyer was president and chief operating officer for Coca-Cola for three years; upon departing the company in June 2004, he received a $24 million severance package.[92]

Departing Coca-Cola CEO Douglas Daft received over $30 million in a severance package in 2004 even though the company's performance was far less than stellar during his leadership. Douglas Ivestor, CEO of Coca-Cola prior to Daft, continues to receive $675,000 per year from a consulting contract with the company, even though he received over $100 million in his severance package.[93]

Coca-Cola is not alone in paying phenomenal severance pay to departing top managers. For example, when Richard H. Brown left Electronic Data Systems Corp. as CEO in 2003 amid poor financial performance, he received a severance package of over $45 million. Leo Mullins, who retired from his position as CEO of Delta Airlines, received over $15 million in severance compensation.[94]

Why do companies pay departing executives so excessively? Some say offering such "golden parachutes" is necessary to recruit top talent. For some companies, generous departing payouts help ensure that confidential company information stays confidential and that ex-CEOs do not damage the reputations of the company with negative statements to the press.[95] In any case, in an era in which many workers are struggling to find and keep jobs and make ends meet, more and more people are questioning whether it is ethical for some top managers to be making so much money. Granted, some very highly paid CEOs have done wonders for their companies and created real value.[96] But what about those poorly performing CEOs who are pushed from their jobs with millions in severance pay to break their fall?

Benefits

Organizations are legally required to provide certain benefits to their employees, including workers' compensation, Social Security, and unemployment insurance. Workers' compensation provides employees with financial assistance if they become unable to work due to a work-related injury or illness. Social Security provides financial assistance to retirees and disabled former employees. Unemployment insurance provides financial assistance to workers who lose their jobs due to no fault of their own. The legal system in the United States views these three benefits as ethical requirements for organizations and thus mandates that they be provided.

Other benefits such as health insurance, dental insurance, vacation time, pension plans, life insurance, flexible working hours, company-provided day care, and employee assistance and wellness programs are provided at the option of employers. Benefits enabling workers to simultaneously balance the demands of their jobs and of their lives away from the office or factory are of growing importance for many workers who have competing demands on their all-too-scarce time and energy, as is the case at Semco in "A Manager's Challenge."

In some organizations, top managers determine which benefits might best suit the employees and organization and offer the same benefit package to all employees. Other organizations, realizing that employees' needs and desires might differ, offer **cafeteria-style benefit plans** that let employees themselves choose the benefits they want. Cafeteria-style benefit plans sometimes assist managers in dealing with employees who feel unfairly treated because they are

cafeteria benefit plan A plan from which employees can choose the benefits that they want.

unable to take advantage of certain benefits available to other employees who, for example, have children. Some organizations have success with cafeteria-style benefit plans; others find them difficult to manage.

More and more managers are viewing benefits as a means of attracting and retaining valued employees and helping these employees stay healthy, as indicated in the following "Focus on Diversity."

Focus on Diversity

Keeping Employees Happy and Healthy with Benefits

As health care costs are escalating and overstretched employees are finding it hard to take time out to exercise and take care of their health, more companies are providing benefits and incentives to promote employee wellness. AstraZeneca International offers its employees on-site counseling with a nutritionist and pays employees $125 for voluntarily taking a health risk assessment that covers wellness-related factors such as weight and nutrition.[97] Dole Food Company rewards employees with points toward gift certificates for participating in wellness activities provided on-site, such as yoga classes.[98]

For new working parents, leaving an infant with a caregiver for 8 or 10 hours a day can be traumatic. To ease the trauma and allow new parents to bond with their babies, Health Newsletter Direct, based in Evanston, Illinois, allows employees to bring their babies to work.[99] Since the program was first instituted, 14 parents have taken advantage of it. Mark Tatara, the first father to bring his baby to work, says this of the program: "The closeness with my child means more to me than I ever could have imagined . . . and my co-workers were excited about him being here."[100]

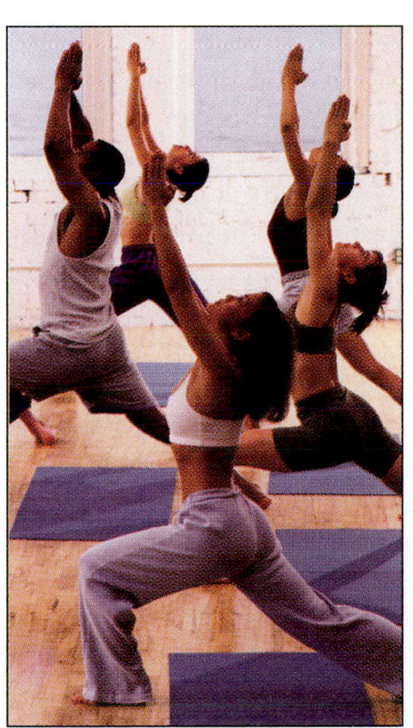

More and more companies are promoting employee wellness by providing incentives such points toward gift certificates for participating in yoga classes.

Same-sex domestic-partner benefits are also being used to attract and retain valued employees. Gay and lesbian workers are more and more reluctant to work for companies that do not provide them with the same kinds of benefits for their partners as those provided for partners of the opposite sex.[101] Kevin Ryan, CEO of DoubleClick, a budding high-tech company in New York that hired 80 new employees in the first two and a half months of 2004 due to its rapid growth trajectory, indicates that it is a business necessity for his workplace to welcome gay and lesbian employees.[102] His key concern is hiring the best, highly skilled people; once hired, all employees are welcome and afforded the same benefits regardless of their sexual orientation.[103]

Labor Relations

labor relations The activities that managers engage in to ensure that they have effective working relationships with the labor unions that represent their employees' interests.

Labor relations are the activities that managers engage in to ensure that they have effective working relationships with the labor unions that represent their employees' interests. Although the U.S. government has responded to the potential for unethical organizations and unfair treatment of workers by creating and enforcing laws regulating employment (including the EEO laws listed in Table 12.1), some workers believe that a union will ensure that their interests are fairly represented in their organizations.

Before we describe unions in more detail, let's take a look at some examples of important employment legislation. In 1938 the government passed the Fair Labor Standards Act, which prohibited child labor and made provisions for minimum wages, overtime pay, and maximum working hours to protect workers' rights. In 1963 the Equal Pay Act mandated that men and women performing equal work (work requiring the same levels of skill, responsibility, and effort performed in the same kind of working conditions) receive equal pay (see Table 12.1). In 1970 the Occupational Safety and Health Act mandated procedures for managers to follow to ensure workplace safety. These are just a few of the U.S. government's efforts to protect workers' rights. State legislatures also have been active in promoting safe, ethical, and fair workplaces.

Unions

Unions exist to represent workers' interests in organizations. Given that managers have more power than rank-and-file workers and that organizations have multiple stakeholders, there is always the potential that managers might take steps that benefit one set of stakeholders such as shareholders while hurting another such as employees. For example, managers may decide to speed up a production line to lower costs and increase production in the hopes of increasing returns to shareholders. Speeding up the line, however, could hurt employees forced to work at a rapid pace and may increase the risk of injuries. Also, employees receive no additional pay for the extra work they are performing. Unions would represent workers' interests in a scenario such as this one.

Congress acknowledged the role that unions could play in ensuring safe and fair workplaces when it passed the National Labor Relations Act of 1935. This act made it legal for workers to organize into unions to protect their rights and interests and declared certain unfair or unethical organizational practices to be illegal. The National Labor Relations Act also established the National Labor Relations Board (NLRB) to oversee union activity. Currently, the NLRB conducts certification elections, which are held among the employees of an organization to determine whether they want a union to represent their interests. The NLRB also makes judgments concerning unfair labor practices and specifies practices that managers must refrain from.

Employees might vote to have a union represent them for any number of specific reasons.[104] They may think that their wages and working conditions are in need of improvement. They may believe that managers are not treating them with respect. They may think that their working hours are unfair or that they need more job security or a safer work environment. Or they may be dissatisfied with management and find it difficult to communicate their concerns to their bosses. Regardless of the specific reason, one overriding reason is power: A united group inevitably wields more power than an individual, and this type of power may be especially helpful to employees in some organizations.

Although these would seem to be potent forces for unionization, some workers are reluctant to join unions. Sometimes this reluctance is due to the perception that union leaders are corrupt. Some workers may simply believe that belonging to a union might not do them much good or may actually cause more harm than good while costing them money in membership dues. Employees also might not want to be forced into doing something they do not want to, such as striking because the union thinks it is in their best interest. Moreover, although unions can be a positive force in organizations, sometimes they also can be a negative force, impairing organizational effectiveness. For example, when union leaders resist needed changes in an organization or are corrupt, organizational performance can suffer.

The percentage of U.S. workers represented by unions today is smaller than it was in the 1950s, an era when unions were especially strong.[105] The American Federation of Labor–Congress of Industrial Organizations (AFL-CIO) includes 64 voluntary member unions representing 13 million workers.[106] Union influence in manufacturing and heavy industries has been on the decline, presumably because their workers no longer see the need to be represented by unions. Recently unions have made inroads in other segments of the workforce, however, particularly the low-wage end. Garbage collectors in New Jersey, poultry plant workers in North Carolina, and janitors in Baltimore are among the growing numbers of low-paid workers who are currently finding union membership attractive. North Carolina poultry workers voted in a union in part because they thought it was unfair that they had to buy their own gloves and hairnets used on the job and had to ask their supervisors' permission to go to the restroom.[107] Union membership and leadership, traditionally dominated by white men, is also becoming increasingly diverse. For example, Linda Chavez-Thompson is the executive vice president of the AFL-CIO and the first woman and Hispanic to hold a top-management position in the federation.[108]

Labor officials in Washington, DC, also are becoming increasingly diverse. Elaine L. Chao, the 24th U.S. secretary of labor, is the first Asian-American woman to hold an appointment in a U.S. president's cabinet. Chao, who has extensive management experience as a former CEO of the United Way of America and also as a former director of the Peace Corps, is committed to equal opportunity in the workplace, the well-being of workers and their families, and increased flexibility in the workplace.[109]

Collective Bargaining

collective bargaining Negotiations between labor unions and managers to resolve conflicts and disputes about issues such as working hours, wages, benefits, working conditions, and job security.

Collective bargaining is negotiation between labor unions and managers to resolve conflicts and disputes and important issues such as working hours, wages, working conditions, and job security. Before sitting down with management to negotiate, union members sometimes go on strike to drive home their concerns to managers. Once an agreement that union members support has been reached (sometimes with the help of a neutral third party called a *mediator*), union leaders and managers sign a contract spelling out the terms of the collective bargaining agreement. We discuss conflict and negotiation in depth in Chapter 16, but some brief observations are in order here because collective bargaining is an ongoing consideration in labor relations.

The signing of a contract, for example, does not bring the collective bargaining process to a halt. Disagreement and conflicts can arise over the interpretation of the contract. In such cases, a neutral third party called an *arbitrator* is usually called in to resolve the conflict. An important component of a collective bargaining agreement is a *grievance procedure* through which workers who believe they are not being fairly treated are allowed to voice their concerns and have their interests represented by the union. Workers who think that they were unjustly fired in violation of a union contract, for example, may file a grievance, have the union represent them, and get their jobs back if an arbitrator agrees with them.

Union members sometimes go on strike when managers make decisions that the members think will hurt them and are not in their best interests. This is precisely what happened in 1996 when General Motors' North American assembly plants employing 177,000 workers were idled for 18 days. The strike originated in GM's Dayton, Ohio, brake assembly plants due to management's decision to buy some parts from other companies rather than make them in GM's own plants.[110] The United Auto Workers Union called a strike because outsourcing threatens union members' jobs. The agreement that the union and management, bargaining collectively, reached allowed the outsourcing to continue but contained provisions for the creation of hundreds of new jobs as well as for improvements in working conditions.[111]

Summary and Review

STRATEGIC HUMAN RESOURCE MANAGEMENT Human resource management (HRM) includes all the activities that managers engage in to ensure that their organizations are able to attract, retain, and effectively utilize human resources. Strategic HRM is the process by which managers design the components of a human resource management system to be consistent with each other, with other elements of organizational architecture, and with the organization's strategies and goals.

RECRUITMENT AND SELECTION Before recruiting and selecting employees, managers must engage in human resource planning and job analysis. Human resource planning includes all the activities managers engage in to forecast their current and future needs for human resources. Job analysis is the process of identifying (1) the tasks, duties, and responsibilities that make up a job and (2) the knowledge, skills, and abilities needed to perform the job. Recruitment includes all the activities that managers engage in to develop a pool of qualified applicants for open positions. Selection is the process by which managers determine the relative qualifications of job applicants and their potential for performing well in a particular job.

TRAINING AND DEVELOPMENT Training focuses on teaching organizational members how to perform effectively in their current jobs. Development focuses on broadening organizational members' knowledge and skills so that they will be prepared to take on new responsibilities and challenges.

PERFORMANCE APPRAISAL AND FEEDBACK Performance appraisal is the evaluation of employees' job performance and contributions to the organization. Performance feedback is the process through which managers share performance appraisal information with their subordinates, give them an opportunity to reflect on their own performance, and develop with them plans for the future. Performance appraisal provides managers with useful information for decision-making purposes. Performance feedback can encourage high levels of motivation and performance.

PAY AND BENEFITS Pay level is the relative position of an organization's pay incentives in comparison with those of other organizations in the same industry employing similar workers. A pay structure clusters jobs into categories according to their relative importance to the organization and its goals, the levels of skills required, and other characteristics. Pay ranges are then established for each job category. Organizations are legally required to provide certain benefits to their employees; other benefits are provided at the discretion of employers.

LABOR RELATIONS Labor relations include all the activities managers engage in to ensure that they have effective working relationships with the labor unions that may represent their employees' interests. The National Labor Relations Board oversees union activity. Collective bargaining is the process through which labor unions and managers resolve conflicts and disputes and negotiate agreements.

Management in Action

Topics for Discussion and Action

Discussion

1. Discuss why it is important for human resource management systems to be in sync with an organization's strategy and goals and with each other.
2. Discuss why training and development are ongoing activities for all organizations.
3. Describe the type of development activities you think middle managers are most in need of.
4. Evaluate the pros and cons of 360-degree performance appraisals and feedback. Would you like your performance to be appraised in this manner? Why or why not?
5. Discuss why two restaurants in the same community might have different pay levels.
6. Explain why union membership is becoming more diverse.

Action

7. Interview a manager in a local organization to determine how that organization recruits and selects employees.

Building Management Skills

Analyzing Human Resource Systems

Think about your current job or a job that you have had in the past. If you have never had a job, then interview a friend or family member who is currently working. Answer the following questions about the job you have chosen:

1. How are people recruited and selected for this job? Are the recruitment and selection procedures that the organization uses effective or ineffective? Why?
2. What training and development do people who hold this job receive? Is it appropriate? Why or why not?
3. How is performance of this job appraised? Does performance feedback contribute to motivation and high performance on this job?
4. What levels of pay and benefits are provided on this job? Are these levels of pay and benefits appropriate? Why or why not?

Managing Ethically

Some managers do not want to become overly friendly with their subordinates because they are afraid that if they do so, their objectivity when conducting performance appraisals and making decisions about pay raises and promotions will be impaired. Some subordinates resent it when they see one or more of their co-workers being very friendly with the boss; they are concerned about the potential for favoritism. Their reasoning runs something like this: If two subordinates are equally qualified for a promotion and one is a good friend of the boss and the other is a mere acquaintance, who is more likely to receive the promotion?

Questions

1. Either individually or in a group, think about the ethical implications of managers' becoming friendly with their subordinates.
2. Do you think that managers should feel free to socialize and become good friends with their subordinates outside the workplace if they so desire? Why or why not?

Small Group Breakout Exercise

Building a Human Resource Management System

Form groups of three or four people, and appoint one group member as the spokesperson who will communicate your findings to the whole class when called upon by the instructor. Then discuss the following scenario.

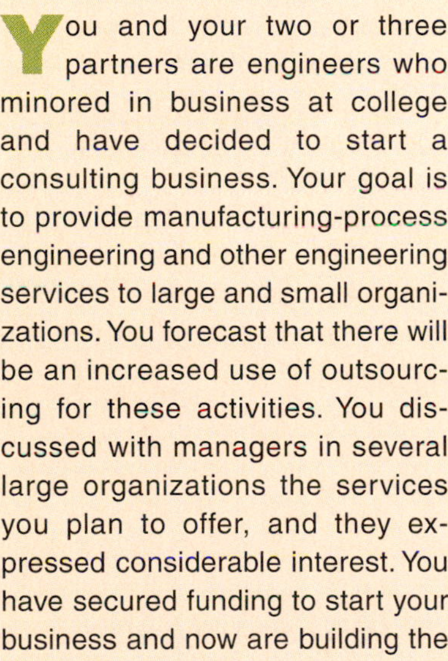

You and your two or three partners are engineers who minored in business at college and have decided to start a consulting business. Your goal is to provide manufacturing-process engineering and other engineering services to large and small organizations. You forecast that there will be an increased use of outsourcing for these activities. You discussed with managers in several large organizations the services you plan to offer, and they expressed considerable interest. You have secured funding to start your business and now are building the HRM system. Your human resource planning suggests that you need to hire between five and eight experienced engineers with good communication skills, two clerical/secretarial workers, and two MBAs who between them have financial, accounting, and human resource skills. You are striving to develop your human resources in a way that will enable your new business to prosper.

1. Describe the steps you will take to recruit and select (a) the engineers, (b) the clerical/secretarial workers, and (c) the MBAs.
2. Describe the training and development the engineers, the clerical/secretarial workers, and the MBAs will receive.
3. Describe how you will appraise the performance of each group of employees and how you will provide feedback.
4. Describe the pay level and pay structure of your consulting firm.

Exploring the World Wide Web

Go to www.net-temps.com, a Web site geared toward temporary employment. Imagine that you have to take a year off from college and are seeking a one-year position. Guided by your own interests, use this Web site to learn about your options and possible employment opportunities. What are the potential advantages of online job searching and recruiting? What are the potential disadvantages? Would you ever rely on a Web site like this to help you find a position? Why or why not?

Be the Manager

You are Walter Michaels and have just received some disturbing feedback. You are the director of human resources for Maxi Vision Inc., a medium-size window and glass-door manufacturer. You recently initiated a 360-degree performance appraisal system for all middle and upper managers at Maxi Vision, including yourself but excluding the most senior executives and the top-management team.

You were eagerly awaiting the feedback you would receive from the managers who report to you; you had recently implemented several important initiatives that affected them and their subordinates, including a complete overhaul of the organization's performance appraisal system. While the managers who report to you were evaluated based on 360-degree appraisals, their own subordinates were evaluated using a 20-question BARS scale you recently created that focuses on behaviors. Conducted annually, appraisals are an important input into pay raise and bonus decisions.

You were so convinced that the new performance appraisal procedures were highly effective that you hoped your own subordinates would mention them in their feedback to you. And boy did they! You were amazed to learn that the managers and their subordinates thought the new BARS scales were unfair, inappropriate, and a waste of time. In fact, the managers' feedback to you was that their own performance was suffering, based on the 360-degree appraisals they received, because their subordinates hated the new appraisal system and partially blamed their bosses, who were part of management. Some managers even admitted giving all their subordinates approximately the same scores on the scales so that their pay raises and bonuses would not be affected by their performance appraisals.

You couldn't believe your eyes when you read these comments. You had spent so much time developing what you thought was the ideal rating scale for this group of employees. Evidently, for some unknown reason, they were being very closed-minded and wouldn't give it a chance. Your own supervisor was aware of these complaints and said that it was a top priority for you to fix "this mess" (with the implication that you were responsible for creating it). What are you going to do?

Additional Activities on the Build Your Management Skills DVD

- **Test Your Knowledge:** (1) Stages of the Strategic HRM Process, (2) Training Methods, (3) Appraisal Methods, (4) Potential Errors in the Rating Process, (5) Recruitment Sources, and (6) Reliability and Validity
- **Self-Assessment:** What Is Your Communication Style Under Stress
- **Manager's Hot Seat:** Diversity in Hiring: Candidate Conundrum

BusinessWeek

Case in the News

How to Groom the Next Boss

Of all the challenges confronting managers and directors, few are as difficult or as critical as finding and training a chief executive-in-waiting. At Coca-Cola, Xerox, and Procter & Gamble, CEO successions have been marked by long searches, poor choices, or fumbled transitions. But a company with a well-prepared No. 2 can quell uncertainty, even in the worst emergencies. When McDonald's Corp. CEO James Cantalupo died of a heart attack on April 19, the board named Chief Operating Officer Charles H. Bell to his post within hours.

Kenneth W. Freeman, CEO of Quest Diagnostics Inc., was determined not to leave his company in the lurch. He started grooming his handpicked successor five years ago. When he transfers management of the $4.7 billion medical-testing company to Surya N. Mohapatra at the May 4 annual meeting, it will be the culmination of a meticulous succession process that experts say is a case study in how to choose a future CEO and prepare him for the job. Marc S. Effron, global practice leader for consultants Hewitt Associates Inc., says the careful succession planning at the Teterboro (N.J.)-based company will pay off with a new CEO who can hit the ground running. "It's incredibly unusual," says Effron of Freeman's efforts. "They're going to see the benefits."

Freeman's search for a successor started in 1999. He was on the brink of an acquisition spree that would triple Quest's revenues in five years. But he knew the buying binge couldn't last and that Quest's next CEO would need a science background to exploit advances in medicine and technology to generate internal growth. To identify candidates, he put 200 executives from Quest and a recently acquired rival through an *Apprentice*-like challenge: daylong case assignments that allowed him to see their leadership skills in action. "This was his legacy," says Audrey B. Smith, a consultant with Development Dimensions International who worked with Freeman. "He felt huge pressure to make the right decision."

Of all the executives, one stood out: his new chief operating officer. Mohapatra came to Quest in February 1999, from Picker International, a maker of medical imaging systems. He had extensive experience in cardiovascular disease and information technology—areas that would be crucial to Quest's future. What's more, he was CEO material. Says Freeman: "Here was a guy who was incredibly smart, who could balance a whole bunch of priorities at the same time, who could be incredibly focused, and who did not know the meaning of failure."

Four months after Mohapatra's arrival, Freeman named him president, giving him a clear—but by no means guaranteed—shot at the top job. The two men could not be more different. Mohapatra, a scientist with several patents to his name, grew up in India. Freeman, a New Yorker, had a long finance career at Corning Inc. When Corning Clinical Laboratories was spun off as Quest in 1996, Freeman became CEO, a position he says he had no intention of occupying for more than 10 years.

A skilled integrator of acquisitions and a Six Sigma devotee, Freeman believes that when a business outgrows its leader, as Quest has, the CEO should relinquish power. "Being a CEO is not a birthright," he says. "It's a privilege."

So almost immediately Freeman began the process of grooming Mohapatra. Experts say his willingness to give Mohapatra the spotlight reveals a remarkable maturity. "Part of the challenge in becoming successful is you become a little too caught up in your own abilities," says Effron. "If a CEO can look at himself as a caretaker of a firm, it's easier for him to hand it over to someone else." Even though Mohapatra, at 54, is a year older than Freeman, he has come to view his CEO as a mentor. Freeman says the two have built an incredible trust. "We constantly work to make sure the egos stay out of the picture."

Stage Fright

Front-runner or not, it quickly became clear that if Mohapatra was to be CEO he would need basic leadership skills. During his first week, one of the most glaring deficiencies, poor public speaking skills, became apparent. At a "town meeting" with employees in Baltimore, Mohapatra told the crowd of 800 that he was glad to be there—then clammed up. Freeman decided the best way to coax Mohapatra out of his shell was trial by fire. In the months that followed, he had Mohapatra make unscripted comments to employees, meet with shareholders, and field questions from analysts on conference calls. He is now a more polished, confident speaker.

As a scientist, Mohapatra had come to Quest with habits that Freeman felt could undermine him as a CEO. A deep thinker, he took weeks to make decisions that should only take days. And he was far more "hands-on" than he needed to be, sometimes reopening interviews for jobs that his subordinates were ready to fill. Freeman challenged Mohapatra to make faster decisions and give his executive team more authority. Every Sunday afternoon for five years, the two engaged in lengthy telephone conversations during which Freeman would analyze Mohapatra's evolving management style and suggest further improvements. It was, Freeman now concedes, "pure browbeating." Perhaps, but it worked. "Am I more ready now than I was four years ago? Absolutely," says Mohapatra.

Fine-tuning Mohapatra's management skills was only part of the challenge. Making him an active board participant was equally important. When he arrived, Mohapatra deferred to Freeman in board debates, contributing little. Freeman forced him to be more assertive—at first surreptitiously, by leaving the room during discussions, and later by asking him to conduct formal board presentations. Even after joining the board in 2002, Mohapatra continued to strike some directors as aloof. By changing the seating chart, Freeman was able to increase Mohapatra's face time with other directors. "You want someone to be able to speak their mind and participate," says Gail R. Wilensky, an independent director. "It helped."

When his long incubation ends, Mohapatra's success will be far from assured. Maintaining double-digit growth won't be easy as takeover targets become scarce. That's the way it is in business; the future is never assured. But Freeman has done about as much to increase the odds as a CEO can.

Questions

1. In what ways did Mohapatra receive valuable development from Freeman at Quest Diagnostics?
2. Why did Freeman seek out and develop someone to replace him as CEO?
3. Why is it so unusual for CEOs to take the steps that Freeman did to find someone to fill their position when they leave it?
4. What lessons can be learned from Freeman about the development of all managers, at low and high levels?

Source: L. Lavelle, "How to Groom the Next Boss." Reprinted from the May 10, 2004, issue of *BusinessWeek* by special permission.

BusinessWeek Case in the News

Software: Will Outsourcing Hurt America's Supremacy?

Stephen Haberman was one of a handful of folks in all of Chase County, Nebraska, who knew how to program a computer. In the spring of 1999, at the height of the Internet boom, the 17-year-old whiz wanted to strut his stuff outside of his windswept patch of prairie. He was too young for a nationwide programming competition sponsored by Microsoft Corp., so an older friend registered for him. Haberman wowed the judges with a flashy Web page design and finished second in the country. Emboldened, Stephen came up with a radical idea: Maybe he would skip college altogether and mine a quick fortune in dot-com gold. His mother, Cindy, put the kibosh on his plan. She steered him to a full scholarship at the University of Nebraska at Omaha.

Half a world away, in the western Indian city of Nagpur, a 19-year-old named Deepa Paranjpe was having an argument with her father. Sure, computer science was heating up, he told her. Western companies were frantically hiring Indians to scour millions of software programs and eradicate the much-feared millennium bug. But this craze would pass. The former railroad employee urged his daughter to pursue traditional engineering, a much safer course. Deepa had always respected her father's opinions. When he demanded perfection at school, she delivered nothing less. But she turned a deaf ear to his career advice and plunged into software. After all, this was the industry poised to change the world.

As Stephen and Deepa emerge this summer from graduate school—one in Pittsburgh, the other in Bombay—they'll find that their decisions of a half-decade ago placed their dreams on a collision course. The Internet links that were being pieced together at the turn of the century now provide broadband connections between multinational companies and brainy programmers the world over. For Deepa and tens of thousands of other Indian students, the globalization of technology offers the promise of power and riches in a blossoming local tech industry. But for Stephen and his classmates in the United States, the sudden need to compete with workers across the world ushers in an era of uncertainty. Will good jobs be waiting for them when they graduate? "I might have been better served getting an MBA," Stephen says.

U.S. software programmers' career prospects, once dazzling, are now in doubt. Just look at global giants, from IBM and Electronic Data Systems to Lehman Brothers and Merrill Lynch. They're rushing to hire tech workers offshore while liquidating thousands of jobs in America. In the past three years, offshore programming jobs have nearly tripled, from 27,000 to an estimated 80,000, according to Forrester Research Inc. And Gartner Inc. figures that by yearend, 1 of every 10 jobs in U.S. tech companies will move to emerging markets. In other words, recruiters who look at Stephen will also consider someone like Deepa—who's willing to do the same job for one-fifth the pay. U.S. software developers "are competing with everyone else in the world who has a PC," says Robert R. Bishop, chief executive of computer maker Silicon Graphics Inc.

For many of America's 3 million software programmers, it's paradise lost. Just a few years back, they held the keys to the Information Age. Their profession not only lavished many with stock options and six-figure salaries but also gave them the means to start companies that could change the world—the next Microsoft, Netscape, or Google. Now, these veterans of Silicon Valley and Boston's Route 128 exchange heart-rending job-loss stories on Web sites such as yourjobisgoingtoindia.com. Suddenly, the programmers share the fate of millions of industrial workers, in textiles, autos, and steel, whose jobs have marched to Mexico and China.

"Leap of Faith"

This exodus throws the future of America's tech economy into question. For decades, the U.S. has been the world's technology leader—thanks in large part to its dominance of software, now a $200 billion-a-year U.S. industry. Sure, foreigners have made their share of the machines. But the U.S. has held on to control of much of the innovative brainwork and reaped rich dividends, from Microsoft to the entrepreneurial hotbed of Silicon Valley. The question now is whether the U.S. can continue to lead the industry as programming spreads around the globe from India to Bulgaria. Politicians are jumping on the issue in the election season. And it will probably rage on for years, affecting everything from global trade to elementary-school math and science curriculums.

Countering the doomsayers, optimists from San Jose, California, to Bangalore see the offshore wave as a godsend, the latest productivity miracle of the Internet. Companies that manage it well—no easy task—can build virtual workforces spread around the world, not only soaking up low-cost talent but also tapping the biggest brains on earth to collaborate on complex projects. Marc Andreessen, Netscape Communications Corp.'s co-founder and now chairman of Opsware Inc., a Sunnyvale (Calif.) startup, sees this reshuffling of brainpower leading to bold new applications and sparking growth in other industries, from bioengineering to energy. This could mean a wealth of good new jobs, even more than U.S. companies could fill. "It requires a leap of faith," Andreessen admits. But "in 500 years of Western history, there has always been something new. Always always always always always.

This time, though, there's no guarantee that the next earth-shaking innovations will pop up in America. Deepa, for example, has high-speed Internet, a world-class university, and a venture-capital industry that's starting to take shape in Bombay. What's more, her home country is luring back entrepreneurs and technologists who lived in Silicon Valley during the bubble years. Many came home to India after the crash and now are sowing the seeds of California's startup culture throughout the subcontinent. What's to stop Deepa from mixing the same magic that Andreessen conjured a decade ago when he co-founded Netscape? It's clear that in a networked world, U.S. leadership in innovation will find itself under siege.

The fallout from this painful process could be toxic. One danger is that high-tech horror stories—the pink slips and falling wages—will scare the coming generation of American math whizzes away from software careers, starving the tech economy of brainpower. While the number of students in computer-science programs is holding steady—for now—the elite schools have seen applications fall by as much as 30 percent in two years. If that trend continues, the United States will be relying more than ever on foreign-born graduates for software innovation. And as more foreigners decide to start careers and companies back in their home countries, the United States could find itself lacking a vital resource. Microsoft CEO Steven A. Ballmer says the shortfall of U.S. tech students worries him more than any other issue. "The U.S. is No. 3 now in the world and falling behind quickly No. 1 [India] and No. 2 [China] in terms of computer-science graduates," he said in late 2003 at a forum in New York. . . .

While the departure of programming jobs is a major concern, it's not a national crisis yet. Unemployment in the industry is 7 percent. So far, the less-creative software jobs are the ones being moved offshore: bug-fixing, updating antiquated code, and routine programming tasks that require many hands. And some software companies are demonstrating that they can compete against lower-cost rivals with improved programming methods, more automation, and innovative business models.

For the rest of the decade, the United States will probably maintain a strong hold on its software leadership, even as competition grows. The vast U.S. economy remains the richest market for software and the best laboratory for new ideas. The country's universities are packed with global all-stars. And the U.S. capital markets remain second to none. But time is running short for Americans to address this looming challenge. John Parkinson, chief technologist at Cap Gemini Ernst & Young, estimates that U.S. companies, students, and universities have five years to come up with responses to global shifts. "Scenarios start to look wild and wacky after 2010," he says. And within a decade, "the new consumer base in India and China will be moving the world."

People Skills

To thrive in that wacky world, programmers like Stephen must undergo the career equivalent of an extreme makeover. Traditionally, the profession has attracted brainy introverts who are content to code away in isolation. With so much of that work going overseas, though, the most successful American programmers will be those who master people skills. The industry is hungry for liaisons between customers and basic programmers and for managers who can run teams of programmers scattered around the world. While pay for basic application development has plummeted 17.5 percent in the past two years, according to Foote Partners, a consultant in New Canaan, Conn., U.S. project managers have seen their pay rise an average of 14.3 percent since 2002.

Finding those high-status jobs won't be easy. Last summer, 34-year-old Hal Reed was so hungry for a programming job that he answered an ad in the *Boston Globe* for contract work at cMarkets, a Cambridge (Mass.) startup. The pay was $45,000—barely more than an outsourcing company charges for Indian labor. But he took it. Fortunately for him, he was able to convince his new boss quickly that he was much more than a programmer. He could lead a team. Within weeks, his boss nearly doubled Reed's pay and made him the chief software architect. "He had great strategic thinking skills," says Jon Carson, cMarkets' chief executive. "You can't outsource that."

To prepare students for the hot jobs, universities may need to revamp their computer-science programs. Carnegie Mellon University, where Stephen now studies, has already begun that process. His one-year master's program focuses on giving students the skills needed to manage teams and to play the role of software architect. Such workers are the visionaries who design massive projects or products that hundreds or even thousands of programmers flesh out.

The key players in the drama, including these two master's students, Stephen and Deepa, don't have the luxury to wait and see how it turns out. Their time is now. Deepa graduates in May from the Bombay campus of the Indian Institute of Technology, a top university nestled between two lakes. Stephen emerges three months later from the Pittsburgh campus of CMU.

The options they're eyeing illustrate the unfolding map of an industry in full mutation. A software career is no refuge for the faint of heart. Deepa, for example, could suffer if the U.S. government moves to block offshore development or if rocky experiences in foreign lands spark an industry backlash. And Stephen, if he misplays his hand, could find himself competing with lowballing Filipinos or Uruguayans.

For now, their stories reflect the moods in their two countries—one with lots to lose, the other with a world to win. Deepa is brimming with optimism about the future, convinced that her opportunities are limited by nothing more than her imagination. She is thinking not only about the next job but about the startup that she'll found after that. Stephen, by contrast, is cautious. Even at 22, he's attuned to the risks of a global market for software talent. While confident he'll make a good living, he's plotting out a career that sacrifices opportunities for a measure of safety. Self-protection, an afterthought five years ago, is a pillar of his strategy.

Multicultural Edge

Diversity is another advantage the U.S. has over India. Take a stroll with Deepa through the leafy ITT campus, and practically everyone is Indian. Stephen's scene at CMU, by contrast, feels like the U.N. Classmates joke in Asian and European languages, and a strong smell of microwaved curry floats in the air. This atmosphere extends to American tech companies. With their diverse workforces, American companies can field teams that speak Mandarin, Hindi, French, Russian—you name it. As global software projects take shape, with development ceaselessly following the path of daylight around the globe, multicultural teams have a big edge. Who better than U.S.-based workers to stitch together these projects and manage them? "These people can act as bridges to the global economy," says Amar Gupta, a technology professor at Massachusetts Institute of Technology's Sloan School of Management.

The question is whether the technology industry can respond quickly enough to a revolution that's racing ahead on Internet time. Stephen's former boss, Brookins, frets that the pace could overwhelm the coming generation of U.S. programmers, including his former Nebraska star. "He's a genius. He's the future of the country. [But] if the question is whether there's going to be a happy ending for Stephen, there's a big question mark there," Brookins says. Stephen is betting that quality and customer service will offset the cost advantage of having computer programmers 10 time zones away. He still sees software in the United States as a path to wealth—"though I won't really know until I get out there," he says.

While Stephen is busy mounting his defenses, Deepa is setting out on the hard climb to build Silicon India. Much like their two countries, the leader is looking cautiously over his shoulder while the challenger is chugging single-mindedly ahead. No matter which way they may zig or zag, both of them are prepared to encounter rough competition from every corner of the globe. There's no such thing as a safe distance in software anymore.

Questions

1. What challenges do software programmers in the United States face?
2. What challenges do software programmers in India face?
3. How has globalization changed high-tech fields like programming?
4. Why are people skills important for software programmers?

Source: S. Baker and M. Kripalani, "Software: Will Outsourcing Hurt America's Supremacy?" Reprinted from the March 1, 2004, issue of *BusinessWeek* by special permission.

CHAPTER

13 Motivation and Performance

Learning Objectives

After studying this chapter, you should be able to:

- Explain what motivation is and why managers need to be concerned about it.
- Describe from the perspectives of expectancy theory and equity theory what managers should do to have a highly motivated workforce.
- Explain how goals and needs motivate people and what kinds of goals are especially likely to result in high performance.
- Identify the motivation lessons that managers can learn from operant conditioning theory and social learning theory.
- Explain why and how managers can use pay as a major motivation tool.

A Manager's Challenge

Consistently Ranking as a Best Company to Work For: Tindell and Boone Inspire and Motivate at the Container Store

How can managers motivate employees in an industry known for high levels of turnover and low levels of motivation? Kip Tindell and Garrett Boone founded the Container Store in Dallas, Texas, in 1978 and currently serve as CEO and chairman, respectively. When they opened their first store, they were out on the floor trying to sell customers their storage and organization products that would economize on space and time and make purchasers' lives a little less complicated. The Container Store has grown to include 30 stores in eleven states; although the original store in Dallas had only 1,600 square feet, the stores today average around 25,000 square feet.[1] The phenomenal growth in the size of the stores has been matched by a 20 to 25 percent growth in annual sales.[2] Surprising enough, Tindell and Boone can still be found on the shop floor tidying shelves and helping customers carry out their purchases.[3] And that, perhaps, is an important clue to the secret of their success. The Container Store has been consistently ranked among *Fortune* magazine's "100 Best Companies to Work For" for five years running.[4] In 2004, the Container Store was third on this list (in 2000 and 2001, it was first; in 2002 and 2003, second).[5]

An employee at The Container Store provides customer assistance with a smile.

Early on, Tindell and Boone recognized that people are the Container Store's most valuable asset and that after hiring great people, one of the most important managerial tasks is motivating them. One would think that motivating employees might be especially challenging in the retail industry, which has an average annual turnover rate for full-time salespeople of more than 70 percent and an annual turnover rate for store managers of over 30 percent. The Container Store's comparable figures are fractions of these industry statistics, a testament to Tindell and Boone's ability to motivate.[6] As part of the *Fortune* survey, employees were anonymously polled about their trust in management, management's commitment to employees, how they felt about their jobs and working at the Container Store, and their day-to-day work life.[7] According to survey's findings, morale at the Container Store is "exuberant."[8]

How do Tindell and Boone do it? Essentially, by being clear about what is important at the Container Store, enabling employees to be high performers, rewarding employees in multiple ways, creating a fair and stimulating work environment, and treating employees like the highly capable individuals that they are.[9] Maintaining customer service and a motivated, enthusiastic workforce that is treated well are top priorities at the Container Store, as are honesty, openness, and trust.

While the majority of full-time salespeople have college degrees, they nonetheless receive more than 200 hours of training during their first year on the job (compared to an industry average under 10 hours).[10] This focus on training continues throughout employees' careers with the Container Store, consistent with Tindell and Boone's emphasis on customer service and employee motivation. Training focuses on the characteristics and advantages of each product, how to sell and provide superior customer service, and how to creatively meet customers' container and storage needs. Thus, employees feel confident that they can help customers—even those with very unusual container needs—and provide truly excellent service.[11]

Tindell and Boone also recognize the importance of rewarding employees for a job well done. For example, starting salaries for salespeople are around $40,000 and merit pay increases for superior sales performance are about 8 percent per year. To encourage high individual performance as well as teamwork and cooperation, both individual and team-based rewards are utilized at the Container Store. Some high-performing salespeople earn more than their store managers, which suits the store managers fine as long as equitable procedures are used and rewards are distributed fairly.[12]

Professional development is a valued outcome employees obtain from working at the Container Store. Employees are respected and are given the autonomy to best meet customers' needs however they see fit. Given all the training they receive (over 150 hours per year), employees are confident that they can do this. As Garrett Boone puts it, "Everybody we hire, we hire as a leader. Anybody in our store can take an action that you might think of typically being a manager's action."[13] Thus, employees really have the opportunity to learn and develop on the job, a situation that is somewhat of a rarity in retail sales.

Additionally, employees are treated with respect and have access to what is often privileged information in other companies, such as the amount of annual store sales. Employees also have flexible work options and flexible benefits; medical, dental, and 401k retirement plans; job security; a casual dress code; and access to a variety of wellness programs ranging from yoga classes and chair massages to a personalized, Web-based nutrition and exercise planner.[14] Equally important is the opportunity to work with other highly motivated individuals in an environment that exudes enthusiasm and excitement. Not only are the Container Store's employees motivated, but they also look forward to coming to work and feel as if their co-workers and managers are part of their family. Employees feel pride in what they do—helping customers organize their lives, save space and time, and have a better sense of well-being. Hence, they not only personally benefit from high performance but also feel good about the products they sell and the help they give customers.[15] Tindell and Boone evidently have never lost sight of the importance of motivation for both organizations and their members.

Overview

Even with the best strategy in place and an appropriate organizational architecture, an organization will be effective only if its members are motivated to perform at a high level. Tindell and Boone clearly realize this. One reason why leading is such an important managerial activity is that it entails ensuring that each member of an organization is motivated to perform highly and help the organization achieve its goals. When managers are effective, the outcome of the leading process is a highly motivated workforce. A key challenge for managers of organizations both large and small is to encourage employees to perform at a high level.

In this chapter we describe what motivation is, where it comes from, and why managers need to promote high levels of it for an organization to be effective and achieve its goals. We examine important theories of motivation: expectancy theory, need theories, equity theory, goal-setting theory, and learning theories. Each provides managers with important insights about how to motivate organizational members. The theories are complementary in that each focuses on a somewhat different aspect of motivation. Considering all of the theories together helps managers gain a rich understanding of the many issues and problems involved in encouraging high levels of motivation throughout an organization. Last, we consider the use of pay as a motivation tool. By the end of this chapter, you will understand what it takes to have a highly motivated workforce.

The Nature of Motivation

motivation Psychological forces that determine the direction of a person's behavior in an organization, a person's level of effort, and a person's level of persistence.

Motivation may be defined as psychological forces that determine the direction of a person's behavior in an organization, a person's level of effort, and a person's level of persistence in the face of obstacles.[16] The *direction of a person's behavior* refers to the many possible behaviors that a person could engage in. For example, employees at the Container Store know that they should do whatever is required to meet a customer's container needs and don't have to ask permission to do something out of the ordinary.[17] *Effort* refers to how hard people work. Employees at the Container Store exert high levels of effort to provide superior customer service. *Persistence* refers to whether, when faced with roadblocks and obstacles, people keep trying or give up. For example, when Hayden Tidwell, a salesperson at the Container Store in Dallas, couldn't find a box in the store that would hold a customer's painting, rather than giving up and telling the customer he was sorry, he persisted and made a custom-size box with cardboard and tape.[18]

Motivation is central to management because it explains *why* people behave the way they do in organizations[19]–why employees at the Container Store provide such excellent customer service and enjoy doing so. Motivation also explains why a waiter is polite or rude and why a kindergarten teacher really tries to get children to enjoy learning or just goes through the motions. It explains why some managers truly put their organizations' best interests first whereas others are more concerned with maximizing their salaries and why–more generally–some workers put forth twice as much effort as others.

intrinsically motivated behavior Behavior that is performed for its own sake.

Motivation can come from *intrinsic* or *extrinsic* sources. **Intrinsically motivated behavior** is behavior that is performed for its own sake; the source of motivation is actually performing the behavior, and motivation comes from doing the work itself. Many managers are intrinsically motivated; they derive a sense of accomplishment and achievement from helping the organization to achieve its goals and gain competitive advantages. Jobs that are interesting and challenging or high on the five characteristics described by the job characteristics model (see Chapter 9) are more likely to lead to intrinsic motivation than are jobs that are boring or do not make use of a person's skills and abilities. An elementary school teacher who really enjoys teaching children, a computer programmer who loves solving programming problems, and a commercial photographer who relishes taking creative photographs are all intrinsically motivated. For these individuals, motivation comes from performing their jobs whether it be teaching children, finding bugs in computer programs, or taking pictures.

extrinsically motivated behavior Behavior that is performed to acquire material or social rewards or to avoid punishment.

Extrinsically motivated behavior is behavior that is performed to acquire material or social rewards or to avoid punishment; the source of motivation is the consequences of the behavior, not the behavior itself. A car salesperson who is motivated by receiving a commission on all cars sold, a lawyer who is motivated by the high salary and status that go along with the job, and a factory worker who is motivated by the opportunity to earn a secure income are all extrinsically motivated. Their motivation comes from the consequences they receive as a result of their work behaviors.

People can be intrinsically motivated, extrinsically motivated, or both intrinsically and extrinsically motivated.[20] A top manager who derives a sense of accomplishment and achievement from managing a large corporation and strives to reach year-end targets to obtain a hefty bonus is both intrinsically and extrinsically motivated. Similarly, a nurse who enjoys helping and taking care of patients and is motivated by having a secure job with good benefits is both intrinsically and extrinsically motivated. At the Container Store, employees are both extrinsically motivated because they receive relatively high salaries and generous benefits and intrinsically motivated because they genuinely enjoy and get a sense of satisfaction out of doing their work and serving customers and look forward to coming to work each day. Whether workers are intrinsically motivated, extrinsically motivated, or both depends on a wide variety of factors: (1) workers' own personal characteristics (such as their personalities, abilities, values, attitudes, and needs), (2) the nature of their jobs (such as whether they have been enriched or where they are on the five core characteristics of the job characteristics model), and (3) the nature of the organization (such as its structure, its culture, its control systems, its human resource management system, and the ways in which rewards such as pay are distributed to employees).

outcome Anything a person gets from a job or organization.

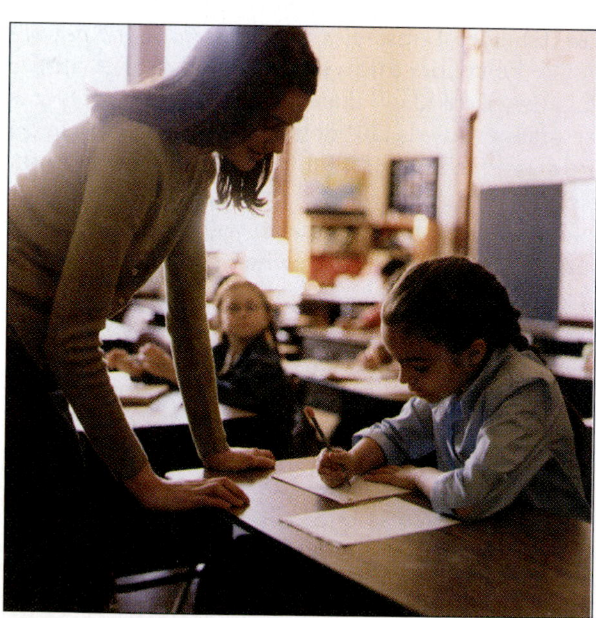

Jobs that are challenging are more likely to lead to intrinsic motivation because they make use of a person's skills and abilities. For example, when this elementary school teacher uses her teaching skills to explain a difficult concept, she is being intrinsically motivated by her work.

Regardless of whether people are intrinsically or extrinsically motivated, they join and are motivated to work in organizations to obtain certain outcomes. An **outcome** is anything a person gets from a job or organization. Some outcomes, such as autonomy, responsibility, a feeling of accomplishment, and the pleasure of doing interesting or enjoyable work,

Figure 13.1
The Motivation Equation

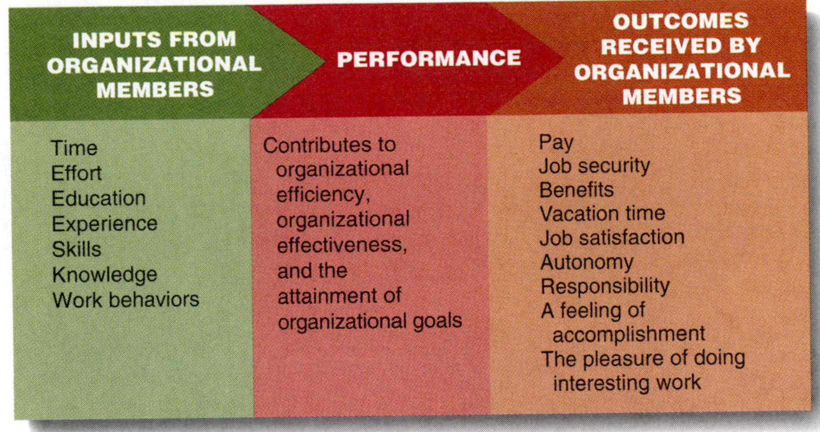

result in intrinsically motivated behavior. Other outcomes, such as pay, job security, benefits, and vacation time, result in extrinsically motivated behavior.

input Anything a person contributes to his or her job or organization.

Organizations hire people to obtain important inputs. An **input** is anything a person contributes to the job or organization, such as time, effort, education, experience, skills, knowledge, and actual work behaviors. Inputs such as these are necessary for an organization to achieve its goals. Managers strive to motivate members of an organization to contribute inputs–through their behavior, effort, and persistence–that help the organization achieve its goals. How do managers do this? They ensure that members of an organization obtain the outcomes they desire when they make valuable contributions to the organization. Managers use outcomes to motivate people to contribute their inputs to the organization. Giving people outcomes when they contribute inputs and perform well aligns the interests of employees with the goals of the organization as a whole because when employees do what is good for the organization, they personally benefit.

This alignment between employees and organizational goals as a whole can be described by the motivation equation depicted in Figure 13.1. Managers seek to ensure that people are motivated to contribute important inputs to the organization, that these inputs are put to good use or focused in the direction of high performance, and that high performance results in workers' obtaining the outcomes they desire.

expectancy theory The theory that motivation will be high when workers believe that high levels of effort lead to high performance and high performance leads to the attainment of desired outcomes.

Each of the theories of motivation discussed in this chapter focuses on one or more aspects of this equation. Each theory focuses on a different set of issues that managers need to address to have a highly motivated workforce. Together, the theories provide a comprehensive set of guidelines for managers to follow to promote high levels of employee motivation. Effective managers, such as Tindell and Boone in "A Manager's Challenge," tend to follow many of these guidelines, whereas ineffective managers often fail to follow them and seem to have trouble motivating organizational members.

Expectancy theory, formulated by Victor H. Vroom in the 1960s, posits that motivation is high when workers believe that high levels of effort lead to high performance and high performance leads to the attainment of desired outcomes.

Figure 13.2
Expectancy, Instrumentality, and Valence

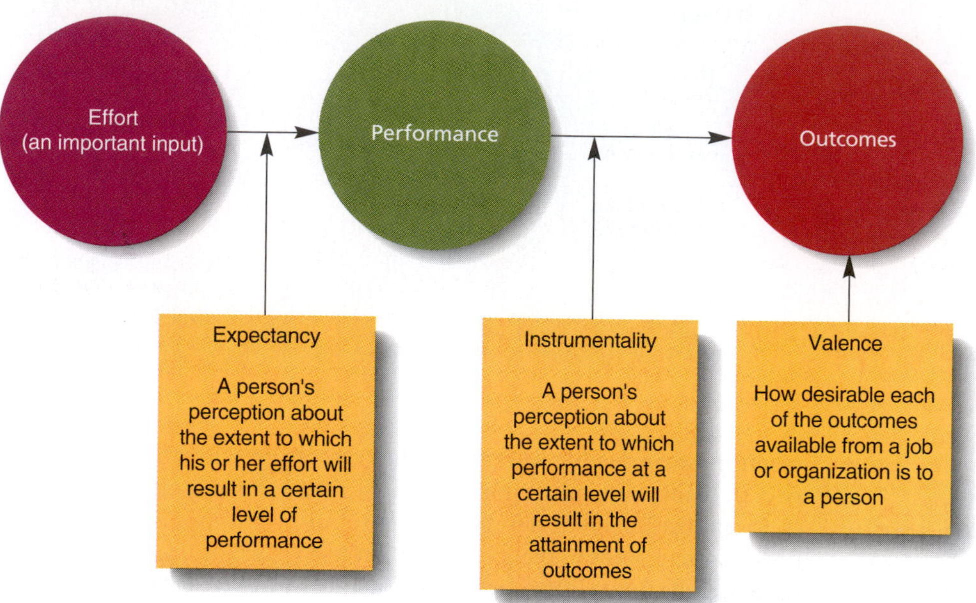

Expectancy theory is one of the most popular theories of work motivation because it focuses on all three parts of the motivation equation: inputs, performance, and outcomes. Expectancy theory identifies three major factors that determine a person's motivation: expectancy, instrumentality, and valence (see Figure 13.2).[21]

Expectancy

expectancy In expectancy theory, a perception about the extent to which effort results in a certain level of performance.

Expectancy is a person's perception about the extent to which effort (an input) results in a certain level of performance. A person's level of expectancy determines whether he or she believes that a high level of effort results in a high level of performance. People are motivated to put forth a lot of effort on their jobs only if they think that their effort will pay off in high performance–that is, if they have high expectancy. Think about how motivated you would be to study for a test if you thought that no matter how hard you tried, you would get a D. Think about how motivated a marketing manager would be who thought that no matter how hard he or she worked, there was no way to increase sales of an unpopular product. In these cases, expectancy is low, so overall motivation is also low.

Members of an organization are motivated to put forth a high level of effort only if they think that doing so leads to high performance.[22] In other words, in order for people's motivation to be high, expectancy must be high. Thus, in attempting to influence motivation, managers need to make sure that their subordinates believe that if they do try hard, they can actually succeed. One way managers can boost expectancies is through expressing confidence in their subordinates' capabilities. Garrett Boone in "A Manager's Challenge" expressed confidence in his subordinates when he stated, "Everybody we hire, we hire as a leader. Anybody in our store can take an action that you might think of typically being a manager's action."[23]

In addition to expressing confidence in subordinates, another way for managers to boost subordinates' expectancy levels and motivation is by providing training so that people have all the expertise needed for high performance, as indicated in the following "Information Technology Byte."

Information Technology Byte

Boosting Expectancy at Best Buy

The Best Buy chain of 629 stores selling electronics, computers, music and movies, and gadgets of all sorts is at an interesting crossroads.[24] With revenues for fiscal 2004 being over $24 billion, Best Buy has had another year of double-digit growth in revenues.[25] Best Buy currently has the biggest share of the consumer electronics market in the United States; its key competitors in this market include Wal-Mart, Circuit City, Dell, Target, and RadioShack.[26] However, Wal-Mart is increasing its presence in this market by increasing space in its stores for electronics, and Dell is direct-selling all kinds of electronics ranging from flat-panel TVs to MP3 players.[27]

Best Buy is betting its future on its salespeople and their ability to sell customers complete solutions to integrate all their home electronics, ranging from TVs and game players to computers, cameras, and camcorders, into a single system. Given advances in information technology, the advantages of convergence across home electronics are considerable but also complex for many customers.[28] By boosting salespeople's expectancies for being able to sell customers integrated systems, Best Buy hopes to retain its dominant position and distinguish itself from its competitors.

Selling home wireless and integrated systems to customers is complex. Best Buy boosts salespeople's expectancies by providing them with extensive training in on-site meetings and online. Electronic learning terminals in each department not only help salespeople learn how different systems work and can be sold as an integrated package but also enable them to keep up to date with the latest advances in technology and products. Salespeople also receive extensive training in how to determine customers' needs. As CEO Brad Anderson puts it, "You need to really understand why a customer is in the store and have a detailed knowledge about what products are available to meet that customer's needs. . . . And you need to have fun."[29] Experienced salespeople and managers observe their less experienced co-workers interacting with customers and, once the customer encounter is finished, discuss how it went, what the co-worker did that was effective, and how the co-worker might improve his or her interactions with future customers. When a salesperson successfully completes a significant sale, the store celebrates. Training to boost expectancy is such an integral part of selling at Best Buy that an important criteria for hiring is the extent to which a prospective employee will be "teachable."[30] All in all, the high expectancies salespeople at Best Buy have for selling integrated systems and solutions to customers may help Best Buy stay ahead of competitors like Wal-Mart, known for low prices but unlikely to be able to match Best Buy in terms of responsiveness to customers.[31]

Best Buy employees go through extensive training to help them with the complex task of selling home wireless and integrated systems.

Instrumentality

instrumentality In expectancy theory, a perception about the extent to which performance results in the attainment of outcomes.

Expectancy captures a person's perceptions about the relationship between effort and performance. **Instrumentality,** the second major concept in expectancy theory, is a person's perception about the extent to which performance at a certain level results in the attainment of outcomes (see Figure 13.2). According to expectancy theory, employees are motivated to perform at a high level only if they think that high performance will lead to (or is *instrumental* for attaining) outcomes such as pay, job security, interesting job assignments, bonuses, or a feeling of accomplishment. In other words, instrumentalities must be high for motivation to be high–people must perceive that because of their high performance they will receive outcomes.[32]

Managers promote high levels of instrumentality when they clearly link performance to desired outcomes. In addition, managers must clearly communicate this linkage to subordinates. By making sure that outcomes available in an organization are distributed to organizational members on the basis of their performance, managers promote high instrumentality and motivation. When outcomes are linked to performance in this way, high performers receive more outcomes than low performers. In "A Manager's Challenge," Boone and Tindell raise levels of instrumentality and motivation for Container Store employees by linking pay raises to performance.

Another example of high instrumentality contributing to high motivation can be found in the Cambodian immigrants who own, manage, and work in more than 80 percent of the doughnut shops in California.[33] These immigrants see high performance as leading to many important outcomes such as income, a comfortable existence, family security, and the autonomy provided by working in a small business. Their high instrumentality contributes to their high motivation to succeed.

Valence

valence In expectancy theory, how desirable each of the outcomes available from a job or organization is to a person.

Although all members of an organization must have high expectancies and instrumentalities, expectancy theory acknowledges that people differ in their preferences for outcomes. For many people, pay is the most important outcome of working. For others, a feeling of accomplishment or enjoying one's work is more important than pay. The term **valence** refers to how desirable each of the outcomes available from a job or organization is to a person. To motivate organizational members, managers need to determine which outcomes have high valence for them–are highly desired–and make sure that those outcomes are provided when members perform at a high level. From "A Manager's Challenge," it appears that not only pay but also autonomy, a stimulating work environment, enthusiastic co-workers, and generous benefits are highly valent outcomes for many employees at the Container Store.

Bringing It All Together

According to expectancy theory, high motivation results from high levels of expectancy, instrumentality, and valence (see Figure 13.3). If any one of these factors is low, motivation is likely to be low. No matter how tightly desired outcomes are linked to performance, if a person thinks it is practically impossible to perform at a high level, then motivation to perform at a high level is exceed-

Figure 13.3
Expectancy Theory

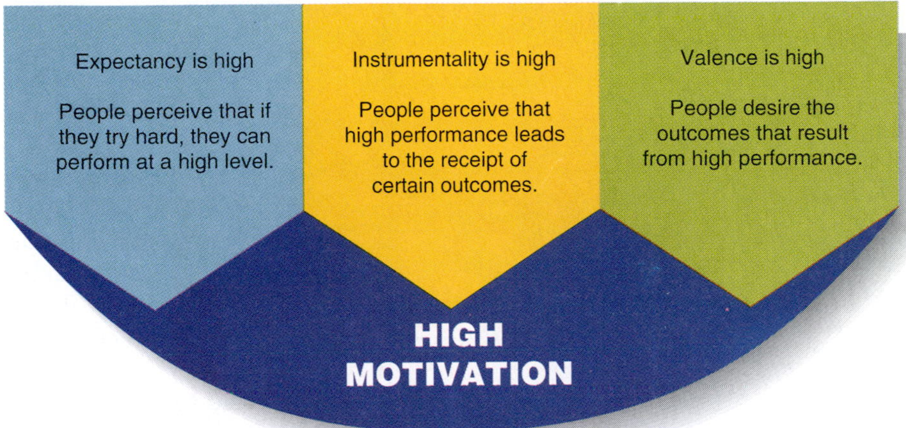
Expectancy is high
People perceive that if they try hard, they can perform at a high level.
Instrumentality is high
People perceive that high performance leads to the receipt of certain outcomes.
Valence is high
People desire the outcomes that result from high performance.
HIGH MOTIVATION

ingly low. Similarly, if a person does not think that outcomes are linked to high performance, or if a person does not desire the outcomes that are linked to high performance, then motivation to perform at a high level is low.

A key challenge for managers is encouraging high levels of motivation when trying to expand into new markets, especially markets in which an organization might have previously failed. As indicated in the following "Focus on Diversity," maintaining high levels of expectancy, instrumentality, and valence and learning from past failures are essential.

Focus on Diversity

Nike's Efforts to Appeal to Diverse Customers

Nike had some failures in the 1980s and 1990s trying to make inroads into new markets. Bowling shoes that left bowlers sliding down bowling alleys on the heels of bowling balls, a commercial for women's apparel that turned women off rather than on to Nike, and a golf shoe that was so uncomfortable employees nicknamed it "air-blister" were among Nike's missteps in trying to appeal to diverse customers in new markets.[34] Fast-forward to 2004, and Nike is once again trying to win over diverse customers in new markets. But this time around, managers have learned from their mistakes and are taking a new approach.[35]

A key element of Nike's new approach is motivating employees to develop products in nontraditional markets (for Nike) in ways that will lead to high expectancy and instrumentality as well as to products that diverse customers will want to buy. Nike is a huge brand, embraced both by athletes playing team sports and consumers young and old looking for athletic apparel and gear.[36] However, many a skateboarder would loathe having the Nike *swoosh* adorning her or his shoes or clothes. Skateboarders have their own subculture and brands;[37] as a poster in a Skatework's store in Redmond, California reads, "Don't do it!"[38]

How can employees be motivated to enter this challenging market and woo diverse customers who pride themselves on being hip and unconventional?

Nike Skate, an autonomous unit of Nike, which is taking aim at the skateboarding market, will have to win over a skateboarding culture whose motto is "Don't do it!"

Essentially, by working in a small "company," knowing the skateboarding subculture, and taking the time to develop products that they are confident will appeal to skateboarders. Nike Skate, headed by vice president Sandy Bodecker, a ski-racing coach, is an autonomous unit that began with 11 skateboarding employees. They took their time to develop products that would appeal to skateboarders, such as URL, E-Cue, Dunk SB, and Air Angus shoes.[39] And they also took pains to win over owners of skate shops who were initially reluctant to carry Nike merchandise out of fear that they would ultimately lose some of their customers when discount stores started selling the same Nike merchandise at lower prices. Offering skate shops exclusive rights to stock Nike's skate products helped to quell such fears.[40]

Nike Skate employees are immersed in the skateboarding culture, listening to music and paging through skateboarding magazines on the job. Managing the new product development process in this manner has helped managers and employees alike have high expectancy that they will be able to develop products that appeal to skateboarders, these products will be instrumental for the growth and revenues of the unit, and the products will appeal to customers. The skateboarding industry takes in about $1.4 billion in revenues annually. While Nike Skate's current revenues of about $25 million are just a fraction of the industry total, employees and managers alike are confident that their current approach to winning skateboarding customers will pay off and make Nike popular in this diverse segment of the sporting world.[41]

Need Theories

need A requirement or necessity for survival and well-being.

need theories Theories of motivation that focus on what needs people are trying to satisfy at work and what outcomes will satisfy those needs.

A **need** is a requirement or necessity for survival and well-being. The basic premise of **need theories** is that people are motivated to obtain outcomes at work that will satisfy their needs. Need theory complements expectancy theory by exploring in depth which outcomes motivate people to perform at a high level. Need theories suggest that to motivate a person to contribute valuable inputs to a job and perform at a high level, a manager must determine what needs the person is trying to satisfy at work and ensure that the person receives outcomes that help to satisfy those needs when the person performs at a high level and helps the organization achieve its goals.

There are several need theories. Here we discuss Abraham Maslow's hierarchy of needs, Clayton Alderfer's ERG theory, Frederick Herzberg's motivator-hygiene theory, and David McClelland's needs for achievement, affiliation, and power. These theories describe needs that people try to satisfy at work. In doing so, they provide managers with insights about what outcomes motivate members of an organization to perform at a high level and contribute inputs to help the organization achieve its goals.

Maslow's Hierarchy of Needs

Maslow's hierarchy of needs An arrangement of five basic needs that, according to Maslow, motivate behavior. Maslow proposed that the lowest level of unmet needs is the prime motivator and that only one level of needs is motivational at a time.

Psychologist Abraham Maslow proposed that all people seek to satisfy five basic kinds of needs: physiological needs, safety needs, belongingness needs, esteem needs, and self-actualization needs (see Table 13.1).[42] He suggested that these needs constitute a **hierarchy of needs,** with the most basic or compelling needs–physiological and safety needs–at the bottom. Maslow argued that these lowest-level needs must be met before a person strives to satisfy needs higher up in the hierarchy, such as self-esteem needs. Once a need is satisfied, Maslow proposed, it ceases to operate as a source of motivation. The lowest level of unmet needs in the hierarchy is the prime motivator of behavior; if and when this level is satisfied, needs at the next-highest level in the hierarchy motivate behavior.

Although this theory identifies needs that are likely to be important sources of motivation for many people, research does not support Maslow's contention that there is a need hierarchy or his notion that only one level of needs is motivational at a time.[43] Nevertheless, a key conclusion can be drawn from Maslow's theory: People try to satisfy different needs at work. To have a motivated workforce, managers must determine which needs employees are trying to satisfy in organizations and then make sure that individuals receive outcomes that satisfy their needs when they perform at a high level and contribute to

Table 13.1
Maslow's Hierarchy of Needs

	Needs	Description	Examples of How Managers Can Help People Satisfy These Needs at Work
Highest-level needs ↑	**Self-actualization needs**	The needs to realize one's full potential as a human being	By giving people the opportunity to use their skills and abilities to the fullest extent possible
	Esteem needs	The needs to feel good about oneself and one's capabilities, to be respected by others, and to receive recognition and appreciation	By granting promotions and recognizing accomplishments
	Belongingness needs	Needs for social interaction, friendship, affection, and love	By promoting good interpersonal relations and organizing social functions such as company picnics and holiday parties
	Safety needs	Needs for security, stability, and a safe environment	By providing job security, adequate medical benefits, and safe working conditions
↓ Lowest-level needs (most basic or compelling)	**Physiological needs**	Basic needs for things such as food, water, and shelter that must be met in order for a person to survive	By providing a level of pay that enables a person to buy food and clothing and have adequate housing

The lowest level of unsatisfied needs motivates behavior; once this level of needs is satisfied, a person tries to satisfy the needs at the next level.

organizational effectiveness. By doing this, managers align the interests of individual members with the interests of the organization as a whole. By doing what is good for the organization (that is, performing at a high level), employees receive outcomes that satisfy their needs.

In our increasingly global economy, managers must realize that citizens of different countries might differ in the needs they seek to satisfy through work.[44] Some research suggests, for example, that people in Greece and Japan are especially motivated by safety needs and that people in Sweden, Norway, and Denmark are motivated by belongingness needs.[45] In less developed countries with low standards of living, physiological and safety needs are likely to be the prime motivators of behavior. As countries become wealthier and have higher standards of living, needs related to personal growth and accomplishment (such as esteem and self-actualization) become important as motivators of behavior.

Alderfer's ERG Theory

Alderfer's ERG theory The theory that three universal needs—existence, relatedness, and growth—constitute a hierarchy of needs and motivate behavior. Alderfer proposed that needs at more than one level can be motivational at the same time.

Clayton Alderfer's **ERG theory** collapses the five categories of needs in Maslow's hierarchy into three universal categories–existence, relatedness, and growth–also arranged in a hierarchy (see Table 13.2). Alderfer agrees with Maslow that as lower-level needs become satisfied, a person seeks to satisfy higher-level needs. Unlike Maslow, however, Alderfer believes that a person can be motivated by needs at more than one level at the same time. A cashier in a supermarket, for example, may be motivated both by existence needs and by relatedness needs. The existence needs motivate the cashier to come to work regularly and not make mistakes so that his job will be secure and he will be

Table 13.2
Alderfer's ERG Theory

	Needs	Description	Examples of How Managers Can Help People Satisfy These Needs at Work
Highest-level needs ↑	**Growth needs**	The needs for self-development and creative and productive work	By allowing people to continually improve their skills and abilities and engage in meaningful work
	Relatedness needs	The needs to have good interpersonal relations, to share thoughts and feelings, and to have open two-way communication	By promoting good interpersonal relations and by providing accurate feedback
↓ **Lowest-level needs**	**Existence needs**	Basic needs for food, water, clothing, shelter, and a secure and safe environment	By promoting enough pay to provide for the basic necessities of life and safe working conditions

As lower-level needs are satisfied, a person is motivated to satisfy higher-level needs. When a person is unable to satisfy higher-level needs (or is frustrated), motivation to satisfy lower-level needs increases.

able to pay his rent and buy food. The relatedness needs motivate the cashier to become friends with some of the other cashiers and have a good relationship with the store manager. Alderfer also suggests that when people experience *need frustration* or are unable to satisfy needs at a certain level, they will focus all the more on satisfying the needs at the next-lowest level in the hierarchy.[46]

As with Maslow's theory, research does not support some of the specific ideas outlined in ERG theory, such as the existence of the three-level need hierarchy that Alderfer proposed.[47] However, for managers, the important message from ERG theory is the same as that from Maslow's theory: Determine what needs your subordinates are trying to satisfy at work, and make sure that they receive outcomes that satisfy these needs when they perform at a high level to help the organization achieve its goals.

Herzberg's Motivator-Hygiene Theory

Herzberg's motivator-hygiene theory A need theory that distinguishes between motivator needs (related to the nature of the work itself) and hygiene needs (related to the physical and psychological context in which the work is performed) and proposes that motivator needs must be met for motivation and job satisfaction to be high.

Adopting an approach different from Maslow's and Alderfer's, Frederick Herzberg focuses on two factors: (1) outcomes that can lead to high levels of motivation and job satisfaction and (2) outcomes that can prevent people from being dissatisfied. According to Herzberg's **motivator-hygiene theory,** people have two sets of needs or requirements: motivator needs and hygiene needs.[48] Motivator needs are related to the nature of the work itself and how challenging it is. Outcomes, such as interesting work, autonomy, responsibility, being able to grow and develop on the job, and a sense of accomplishment and achievement, help to satisfy motivator needs. To have a highly motivated and satisfied workforce, Herzberg suggested, managers should take steps to ensure that employees' motivator needs are being met.

Hygiene needs are related to the physical and psychological context in which the work is performed. Hygiene needs are satisfied by outcomes such as pleasant and comfortable working conditions, pay, job security, good relationships with co-workers, and effective supervision. According to Herzberg, when hygiene needs are not met, workers are dissatisfied, and when hygiene needs are met, workers are not dissatisfied. Satisfying hygiene needs, however, does not result in high levels of motivation or even high levels of job satisfaction. For motivation and job satisfaction to be high, motivator needs must be met.

Many research studies have tested Herzberg's propositions, and, by and large, the theory fails to receive support.[49] Nevertheless, Herzberg's formulations have contributed to our understanding of motivation in at least two ways. First, Herzberg helped to focus researchers' and managers' attention on the important distinction between intrinsic motivation (related to motivator needs) and extrinsic motivation (related to hygiene needs), covered earlier in the chapter. Second, his theory prompted researchers and managers to study how jobs could be designed or redesigned so that they are intrinsically motivating.

McClelland's Needs for Achievement, Affiliation, and Power

need for achievement The extent to which an individual has a strong desire to perform challenging tasks well and to meet personal standards for excellence.

Psychologist David McClelland has extensively researched the needs for achievement, affiliation, and power.[50] The **need for achievement** is the extent to which an individual has a strong desire to perform challenging tasks well and to meet

need for affiliation The extent to which an individual is concerned about establishing and maintaining good interpersonal relations, being liked, and having the people around him or her get along with each other.

need for power The extent to which an individual desires to control or influence others.

personal standards for excellence. People with a high need for achievement often set clear goals for themselves and like to receive performance feedback. The **need for affiliation** is the extent to which an individual is concerned about establishing and maintaining good interpersonal relations, being liked, and having the people around him or her get along with each other. The **need for power** is the extent to which an individual desires to control or influence others.[51]

While each of these needs is present in each of us to some degree, their importance in the workplace depends upon the position one occupies. For example, research suggests that high needs for achievement and for power are assets for first-line and middle managers and that a high need for power is especially important for upper managers.[52] One study found that U.S. presidents with a relatively high need for power tended to be especially effective during their terms of office.[53] A high need for affiliation may not always be desirable in managers and other leaders because it might lead them to try too hard to be liked by others (including subordinates) rather than doing all they can to ensure that performance is as high as it can and should be. Although most research on these needs has been done in the United States, some studies suggest that the findings may be applicable to people in other countries as well, such as India and New Zealand.[54]

Other Needs

Clearly more needs motivate workers than the needs described by the above four theories. For example, more and more workers are feeling the need for work-life balance and time to take care of their loved ones while simultaneously being highly motivated at work. Interestingly enough, recent research suggests that being exposed to nature (even just being able to see some trees from your office window) has many salutary effects and a lack of such exposure can actually impair well-being and performance.[55] Thus, having some time during the day when one can at least see nature may be another important need.

Managers of successful companies often strive to ensure that as many of their valued employees' needs as possible are satisfied in the workplace. This is illustrated by the following "Information Technology Byte" on the SAS Institute.

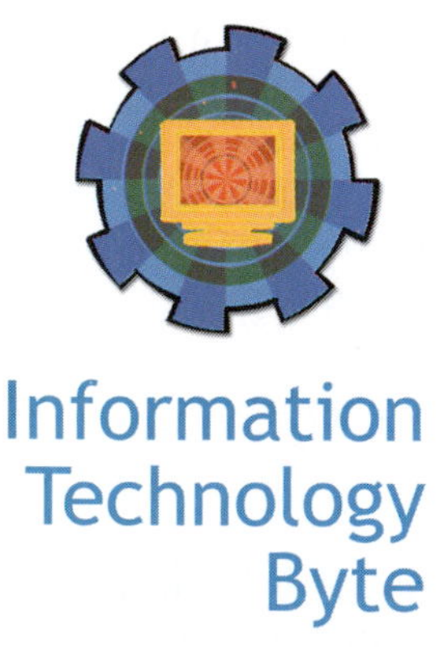

Information Technology Byte

High Motivation Rules at the SAS Institute

Close behind the Container Store in *Fortune* magazine's list of the 100 best companies to work for is the SAS Institute, which ranked eighth in 2004.[56] The SAS Institute is the world's largest privately owned software company, with over 8,000 employees worldwide and approximately $1.1 billion in sales.[57] Every indicator suggests that SAS employees are highly motivated and perform well while also working 35-hour weeks. How do managers at SAS do it? In large part, by ensuring that employees are highly motivated and the variety of needs they bring to the workplace are satisfied by doing a good job at SAS.[58]

Satisfying the need for intrinsically motivating work has also been a key priority at SAS. Managers strive to make sure that each employee is motivated by the work he or she performs, and employees are encouraged to change jobs to prevent becoming bored with their work (even if the job changes require that SAS provide additional training). Moreover, in contrast to the approach at

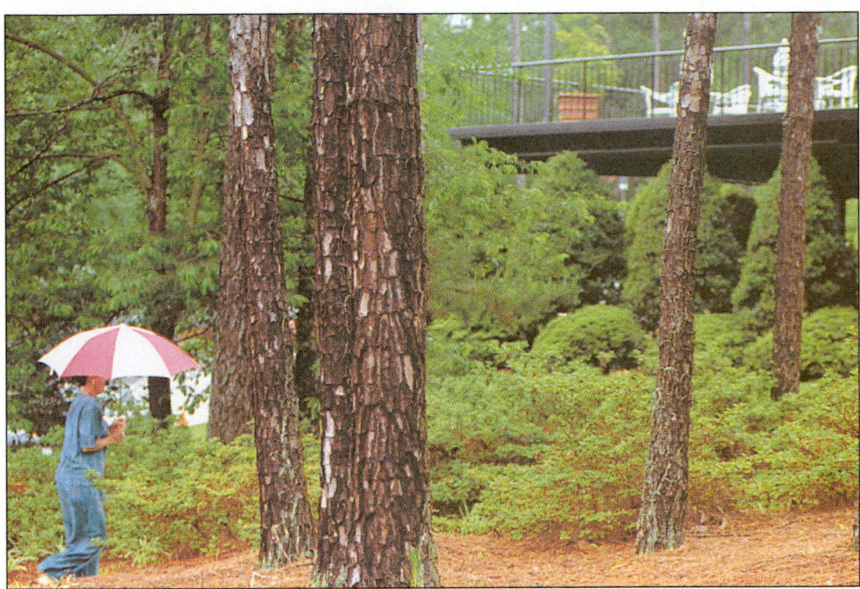

An SAS Institute employee makes her way to the dining hall on the 200-acre SAS campus located in Cary, N.C. SAS Institute is known as one of the best companies to work for in the country, offering jogging paths, a gymnasium, and a Montessori preschool on the campus.

some of the company's competitors, all new product development work at SAS is performed in-house, so employees have the opportunity to experience the excitement of developing a new product and seeing it succeed.[59]

The SAS Institute satisfies employees' needs for economic security by paying them fairly and providing them with secure jobs. Employees have their own offices, and the work environment is rich in pleasant vistas, whether they be artwork on the walls or views of the rolling hills of Cary, North Carolina, at company headquarters. Managers at SAS realize that needs for work-life balance are a top priority for many of their employees and seek to satisfy these needs in a variety of ways, including 35-hour workweeks, on-site day care and medical care, unlimited sick days, and high chairs in the company cafeteria so that employees can dine with their kids. Moreover, employees and their families are encouraged to use the 200 acres that surround company headquarters for family walks and picnics.[60]

While John Sall and chief executive James Goodnight, cofounders and co-owners of SAS, are considering an initial public offering (IPO) of SAS stock, Goodnight (who owns two-thirds of the company) has indicated that he will maintain control of SAS.[61] Thus, employees will most likely continue to be treated the way Goodnight would like to be treated himself, an enduring value at SAS since its founding in 1977.[62]

Equity Theory

Equity theory is a theory of motivation that concentrates on people's perceptions of the fairness of their work *outcomes* relative to, or in proportion to, their work *inputs*. Equity theory complements expectancy and need theories by focusing on how people perceive the relationship between the outcomes they receive from their jobs and organizations and

equity theory A theory of motivation that focuses on people's perceptions of the fairness of their work outcomes relative to their work inputs.

the inputs they contribute. Equity theory was formulated in the 1960s by J. Stacy Adams, who stressed that what is important in determining motivation is the *relative* rather than the *absolute* levels of outcomes a person receives and inputs a person contributes. Specifically, motivation is influenced by the comparison of one's own outcome-input ratio with the outcome-input ratio of a referent.[63] The *referent* could be another person or a group of people who are perceived to be similar to oneself; the referent also could be oneself in a previous job or one's expectations about what outcome-input ratios should be. In a comparison of one's own outcome-input ratio to a referent's outcome-input ratio, one's *perceptions* of outcomes and inputs (not any objective indicator of them) are key.

Equity

equity The justice, impartiality, and fairness to which all organizational members are entitled.

Equity exists when a person perceives his or her own outcome-input ratio to be equal to a referent's outcome-input ratio. Under conditions of equity (see Table 13.3), if a referent receives more outcomes than you receive, the referent contributes proportionally more inputs to the organization, so his or her outcome-input ratio still equals your outcome-input ratio. Maria Sanchez and Claudia King, for example, both work in a shoe store in a large mall. Sanchez is paid more per hour than King but also contributes more inputs, including being responsible for some of the store's bookkeeping, closing the store, and periodically depositing cash in the bank. When King compares her outcome-input ratio to Sanchez's (her referent's), she perceives the ratios to be equitable because Sanchez's higher level of pay (an outcome) is proportional to her higher level of inputs (bookkeeping, closing the store, and going to the bank).

Similarly, under conditions of equity, if you receive more outcomes than a referent, then your inputs are perceived to be proportionally higher. Continuing with our example, when Sanchez compares her outcome-input ratio to King's (her referent's) outcome-input ratio, she perceives them to be equitable because her higher level of pay is proportional to her higher level of inputs.

When equity exists, people are motivated to continue contributing their current levels of inputs to their organizations to receive their current levels of outcomes. If people wish to increase their outcomes under conditions of equity, they are motivated to increase their inputs.

inequity Lack of fairness.

underpayment inequity The inequity that exists when a person perceives that his or her own outcome-input ratio is less than the ratio of a referent.

overpayment inequity The inequity that exists when a person perceives that his or her own outcome-input ratio is greater than the ratio of a referent.

Inequity

Inequity, lack of fairness, exists when a person's outcome-input ratio is not perceived to be equal to a referent's. Inequity creates pressure or tension inside people and motivates them to restore equity by bringing the two ratios back into balance.

There are two types of inequity: underpayment inequity and overpayment inequity (see Table 13.3). **Underpayment inequity** exists when a person's own outcome-input ratio is perceived to be *less* than that of a referent. In comparing yourself to a referent, you think that you are *not* receiving the outcomes you should be, given your inputs. **Overpayment inequity** exists when a person perceives that his or her own outcome-input ratio is *greater* than that of a referent. In comparing yourself to a referent, you think that you are receiving *more* outcomes than you should be, given your inputs.

Table 13.3
Equity Theory

Condition	Person		Referent	Example
Equity	$\frac{\text{Outcomes}}{\text{Inputs}}$	=	$\frac{\text{Outcomes}}{\text{Inputs}}$	An engineer perceives that he contributes more inputs (time and effort) and receives proportionally more outcomes (a higher salary and choice job assignments) than his referent.
Underpayment inequity	$\frac{\text{Outcomes}}{\text{Inputs}}$	< (less than)	$\frac{\text{Outcomes}}{\text{Inputs}}$	An engineer perceives that he contributes more inputs but receives the same outcomes as his referent.
Overpayment inequity	$\frac{\text{Outcomes}}{\text{Inputs}}$	> (greater than)	$\frac{\text{Outcomes}}{\text{Inputs}}$	An engineer perceives that he contributes the same inputs but receives more outcomes than his referent.

Ways to Restore Equity

According to equity theory, both underpayment inequity and overpayment inequity create tension that motivates most people to restore equity by bringing the ratios back into balance.[64] When people experience *underpayment* inequity, they may be motivated to lower their inputs by reducing their working hours, putting forth less effort on the job, or being absent or they may be motivated to increase their outcomes by asking for a raise or a promotion. Susan Richie, a financial analyst at a large corporation, noticed that she was working longer hours and getting more work accomplished than a co-worker who had the same position, yet they both received the exact same pay and other outcomes. To restore equity, Richie decided to stop coming in early and staying late. Alternatively, she could have tried to restore equity by trying to increase her outcomes, say, by asking her boss for a raise.

When people experience underpayment inequity and other means of equity restoration fail, they can change their perceptions of their own or the referents' inputs or outcomes. For example, they may realize that their referent is really working on more difficult projects than they are or that they really take more time off from work than their referent does. Alternatively, if people who feel that they are underpaid have other employment options, they may leave the organization. As an example, John Steinberg, an assistant principal in a high school, experienced underpayment inequity when he realized that all of the other assistant principals of high schools in his school district had received promotions to the position of principal even though they had been in their jobs for a shorter time than he had been. Steinberg's performance had always been appraised as being high, so after his repeated requests for a promotion went unheeded, he found a job as a principal in a different school district.

When people experience *overpayment* inequity, they may try to restore equity by changing their perceptions of their own or their referents' inputs or outcomes. Equity can be restored when people realize that they are contributing more inputs than they originally thought. Equity also can be restored by perceiving the referent's inputs to be lower or the referent's outcomes to be higher than one originally thought. When equity is restored in this way, actual inputs and outcomes are unchanged and the person being overpaid takes no real action. What is changed is how people think about or view their or the referent's inputs and outcomes. For instance, Mary McMann experienced overpayment inequity when she realized that she was being paid $2 an hour more than a co-worker who had the same job as she did in a record store and who contributed the same amount of inputs. McMann restored equity by changing her perceptions of her inputs. She realized that she worked harder than her co-worker and solved more problems that came up in the store.

Experiencing either overpayment or underpayment inequity, you might decide that your referent is not appropriate because, for example, the referent is too different from yourself. Choosing a more appropriate referent may bring the ratios back into balance. Angela Martinez, a middle manager in the engineering department of a chemical company, experienced overpayment inequity when she realized that she was being paid quite a bit more than her friend who was a middle manager in the marketing department of the same company. After thinking about the discrepancy for a while, Martinez decided that engineering and marketing were so different that she should not be comparing her job to her friend's job even though they were both middle managers. Martinez restored equity by changing her referent; she picked a fellow middle manager in the engineering department as a new referent.

Motivation is highest when as many people as possible in an organization perceive that they are being equitably treated–their outcomes and inputs are in balance. Top contributors and performers are motivated to continue contributing a high level of inputs because they are receiving the outcomes they deserve. Mediocre contributors and performers realize that if they want to increase their outcomes, they have to increase their inputs. Managers of effective organizations, like Tindell and Boone at the Container Store, realize the importance of equity for motivation and performance and continually strive to ensure that employees believe they are being equitably treated.

Whether or not this employee receives pay for overtime depends on her status as an exempt or nonexempt employee.

The dot-com boom, subsequent bust, and a recession, along with increased global competition, have resulted in some workers' putting in longer and longer working hours (i.e., increasing their inputs) without any kind of increase in their outcomes. For those whose referents are not experiencing a similar change, perceptions of inequity are likely. According to Jill Andresky Fraser, author of *White Collar Sweatshop,* over 25 million U.S. workers work more than 49 hours per week in the office, almost 11 million work more than 60 hours per week in the office, and many also put in additional work hours at home. Moreover, advances in information technology, such as email and cell phones, have resulted in work intruding on home time, vacation time, and even special occasions.[65]

Goal-Setting Theory

goal-setting theory A theory that focuses on identifying the types of goals that are most effective in producing high levels of motivation and performance and explaining why goals have these effects.

Goal-setting theory focuses on motivating workers to contribute their inputs to their jobs and organizations; in this way it is similar to expectancy theory and equity theory. But goal-setting theory takes this focus a step further by considering as well how managers can ensure that organizational members focus their inputs in the direction of high performance and the achievement of organizational goals.

Ed Locke and Gary Latham, the leading researchers on goal-setting theory, suggest that the goals that organizational members strive to attain are prime determinants of their motivation and subsequent performance. A *goal* is what a person is trying to accomplish through his or her efforts and behaviors.[66] Just as you may have a goal to get a good grade in this course, so do members of an organization have goals that they strive to meet. For example, salespeople at Neiman Marcus strive to meet sales goals, while top managers pursue market share and profitability goals.

Goal-setting theory suggests that to stimulate high motivation and performance, goals must be *specific* and *difficult*.[67] Specific goals are often quantitative–a salesperson's goal to sell $200 worth of merchandise per day, a scientist's goal to finish a project in one year, a CEO's goal to reduce debt by 40 percent and increase revenues by 20 percent, a restaurant manager's goal to serve 150 customers per evening. In contrast to specific goals, vague goals such as "doing your best" or "selling as much as you can" do not have much motivational impact.

Difficult goals are hard but not impossible to attain. In contrast to difficult goals, easy goals are those that practically everyone can attain, and moderate goals are goals that about one-half of the people can attain. Both easy and moderate goals have less motivational power than difficult goals.

Regardless of whether specific, difficult goals are set by managers, workers, or teams of managers and workers, they lead to high levels of motivation and performance. When managers set goals for their subordinates, their subordinates must accept the goals or agree to work toward them; also, they should be committed to them or really want to attain them. Some managers find having subordinates participate in the actual setting of goals boosts their acceptance of and commitment to the goals. In addition, organizational members need to receive *feedback* about how they are doing; feedback can often be provided by the performance appraisal and feedback component of an organization's human resource management system (see Chapter 12). More generally, goals and feedback are integral components of performance management systems in organizations such as management by objectives (see Chapter 11).

Specific, difficult goals affect motivation in two ways. First, they motivate people to contribute more inputs to their jobs. Specific, difficult goals cause people to put forth high levels of effort, for example. Just as you would study harder if you were trying to get an A in a course instead of a C, so too will a salesperson work harder to reach a $200 sales goal instead of a $100 goal. Specific, difficult goals also cause people to be more persistent than easy, moderate, or vague goals when they run into difficulties. Salespeople who are told to sell as much as possible might stop trying on a slow day, whereas having a specific, difficult goal to reach causes them to keep trying.

A second way in which specific, difficult goals affect motivation is by helping people focus their inputs in the right direction. These goals let people know what they should be focusing their attention on, be it increasing the quality of customer service or sales or lowering new product development times. The fact that the goals are specific and difficult also frequently causes people to develop *action plans* for reaching them.[68] Action plans can include the strategies to attain the goals and timetables or schedules for the completion of different activities crucial to goal attainment. Like the goals themselves, action plans also help ensure that efforts are focused in the right direction and that people do not get sidetracked along the way.

When top managers take over troubled companies, it is often important for them to set specific, difficult goals for themselves and their employees in order to focus and direct their own efforts and the efforts of the company, as indicated in the following "Focus on Diversity."

Focus on Diversity

Dick Parsons Gets Time Warner Back on Track

When Richard "Dick" Parsons took over as CEO of the troubled AOL Time Warner (now called Time Warner), he was on the receiving end of numerous complaints from disgruntled shareholders. The stockholders were dissatisfied with the performance of the company, the quality of customer service at AOL, and even the company's new headquarters, which was under construction at New York City's Columbus Circle.[69] Parsons diplomatically responded to these complaints in his first meeting with shareholders.[70]

Parsons is leading a successful turnaround of Time Warner and his effectiveness as CEO, and now also as chairman of the board,[71] is at least partially attributable to the specific, difficult goals he sets for himself and to his practice of holding employees accountable for achieving their goals. Parsons identified key goals that he needed to pursue: Reduce debt levels, increase performance, shore up AOL, and motivate employees to want to achieve their goals. From day 1, his focus was on goals that could be accomplished in the near term (say, 6 to 12 months) rather than the lofty kinds of goals that had gotten the company into trouble.[72] And he worked to stay committed to these goals until they were accomplished. Prior to his assuming the top job, Time Warner was becoming known for "shifting gears every 30 days," according to Don Logan, who Parsons appointed as chairman of media and communication.[73]

So far Time Warner's performance under the leadership of CEO Dick Parson has earned the thumbs up sign from some tough critics.

In less than two years, Parsons has met many of his goals, and employees at Time Warner are meeting their goals. The stock price has risen considerably, and the company's debt has been reduced by $10 billion. Performance of divisions such as cable TV and Hollywood studios is up, and cooperation has replaced the power struggles and infighting that used to take place among top managers and feed down to employees.[74] And employee morale and motivation have improved as goals are being met and company performance is being enhanced. As Parsons indicates, "People have a sense we're making progress."[75]

In 2004, Parsons was named as one of the most powerful African-American executives by *Fortune* magazine.[76] It was Parsons' careful approach to setting Time Warner back on track with specific and difficult goals that has led the company to once again be making inroads in offering new technologies such as Internet protocol telephony.[77] Parsons also realizes the importance of intrinsic motivation. As he told the 2004 graduating class at New York University in his commencement address, "When you love what you do, work becomes something to be enjoyed rather than endured . . . seek to serve some good greater than your own."[78]

Although specific, difficult goals have been found to increase motivation and performance in a wide variety of jobs and organizations both in the United States and abroad, recent research suggests that they may detract from performance under certain conditions. When people are performing complicated and very challenging tasks that require a considerable amount of learning, specific, difficult goals may actually impair performance.[79] All of a person's attention needs to be focused on learning complicated and difficult tasks. Striving to reach a specific, difficult goal may detract from performance on complex tasks because some of a person's attention is directed away from learning about the task and toward trying to figure out how to achieve the goal. Once a person has learned the task and it no longer seems complicated or difficult, then the assignment of specific, difficult goals is likely to have its usual effects. Additionally, for work that is very creative and uncertain, specific, difficult goals may be detrimental.

Learning Theories

The basic premise of **learning theories** as applied to organizations is that managers can increase employee motivation and performance by the ways they link the outcomes that employees receive to the performance of desired behaviors in an organization and the attainment of goals. Thus, learning theory focuses on the linkage between performance and outcomes in the motivation equation (see Figure 13.1).

learning theories Theories that focus on increasing employee motivation and performance by linking the outcomes that employees receive to the performance of desired behaviors and the attainment of goals.

learning A relatively permanent change in knowledge or behavior that results from practice or experience.

Learning can be defined as a relatively permanent change in a person's knowledge or behavior that results from practice or experience.[80] Learning takes place in organizations when people learn to perform certain behaviors to receive certain outcomes. For example, a person learns to perform at a higher level than in the past or to come to work earlier because he or she is motivated to obtain the outcomes that result from these behaviors, such as a pay raise or praise from a supervisor. In "A Manager's Challenge," the Container Store's emphasis on training ensures that new hires learn how to provide excellent customer service and all employees continue their learning throughout their careers with the Container Store.

Of the different learning theories, operant conditioning theory and social learning theory provide the most guidance to managers in their efforts to have a highly motivated workforce.

Operant Conditioning Theory

operant conditioning theory The theory that people learn to perform behaviors that lead to desired consequences and learn not to perform behaviors that lead to undesired consequences.

According to **operant conditioning theory,** developed by psychologist B. F. Skinner, people learn to perform behaviors that lead to desired consequences and learn not to perform behaviors that lead to undesired consequences.[81] Translated into motivation terms, Skinner's theory means that people will be motivated to perform at a high level and attain their work goals to the extent that high performance and goal attainment allow them to obtain outcomes they desire. Similarly, people avoid performing behaviors that lead to outcomes they do not desire. By linking the performance of *specific behaviors* to the attainment of *specific outcomes,* managers can motivate organizational members to perform in ways that help an organization achieve its goals.

Operant conditioning theory provides four tools that managers can use to motivate high performance and prevent workers from engaging in absenteeism and other behaviors that detract from organizational effectiveness. These tools are positive reinforcement, negative reinforcement, extinction, and punishment.[82]

positive reinforcement Giving people outcomes they desire when they perform organizationally functional behaviors.

POSITIVE REINFORCEMENT **Positive reinforcement** gives people outcomes they desire when they perform organizationally functional behaviors. These desired outcomes, called *positive reinforcers,* include any outcomes that a person desires, such as pay, praise, or a promotion. Organizationally functional behaviors are behaviors that contribute to organizational effectiveness; they can include producing high-quality goods and services, providing high-quality customer service, and meeting deadlines. By linking positive reinforcers to the performance of functional behaviors, managers motivate people to perform the desired behaviors.

negative reinforcement Eliminating or removing undesired outcomes when people perform organizationally functional behaviors.

NEGATIVE REINFORCEMENT **Negative reinforcement** also can encourage members of an organization to perform desired or organizationally functional behaviors. Managers using negative reinforcement actually eliminate or remove undesired outcomes once the functional behavior is performed. These undesired outcomes, called *negative reinforcers,* can range from a manager's constant nagging or criticism to unpleasant assignments to the ever-present threat of losing one's job. When negative reinforcement is used, people are motivated to perform behaviors because they want to stop receiving or avoid undesired outcomes. Managers who try to encourage salespeople to sell more by threatening them with being fired are using negative reinforcement. In this case, the negative reinforcer is the threat of job loss, which is removed once the functional behavior is performed.

Whenever possible, managers should try to use positive reinforcement. Negative reinforcement can create a very unpleasant work environment and even a negative culture in an organization. No one likes to be nagged, threatened, or exposed to other kinds of negative outcomes. The use of negative reinforcement sometimes causes subordinates to resent managers and try to get back at them.

IDENTIFYING THE RIGHT BEHAVIORS FOR REINFORCEMENT Even managers who use positive reinforcement (and refrain from using negative reinforcement) can get into trouble if they are not careful to identify the right behaviors to reinforce–behaviors that are truly functional for the organization. Doing this is not always as straightforward as it might seem. First, it is crucial for managers to choose behaviors over which subordinates have control; in other words, subordinates must have the freedom and opportunity to perform the behaviors that are being reinforced. Second, it is crucial that these behaviors contribute to organizational effectiveness.

EXTINCTION Sometimes members of an organization are motivated to perform behaviors that actually detract from organizational effectiveness. According to operant conditioning theory, all behavior is controlled or determined by its consequences; one way for managers to curtail the performance of dysfunctional behaviors is to eliminate whatever is reinforcing the behaviors. This process is called **extinction.**

extinction Curtailing the performance of dysfunctional behaviors by eliminating whatever is reinforcing them.

Suppose a manager has a subordinate who frequently stops by his office to chat–sometimes about work-related matters but at other times about various topics ranging from politics to last night's football game. The manager and the subordinate share certain interests and views, so these conversations can get quite involved, and both seem to enjoy them. The manager, however, realizes that these frequent and sometimes lengthy conversations are actually causing him to stay at work later in the evenings to make up for the time he loses during the day. The manager also realizes that he is actually reinforcing his subordinate's behavior by acting interested in the topics the subordinate brings up and responding at length to them. To extinguish this behavior, the manager stops acting interested in these non-work-related conversations and keeps his responses polite and friendly but brief. No longer being reinforced with a pleasurable conversation, the subordinate eventually ceases to be motivated to interrupt the manager during working hours to discuss non-work-related issues.

PUNISHMENT Sometimes managers cannot rely on extinction to eliminate dysfunctional behaviors because they do not have control over whatever is reinforcing the behavior or because they cannot afford the time needed for extinction to work. When employees are performing dangerous behaviors or behaviors that are illegal or unethical, the behavior needs to be eliminated immediately. Sexual harassment, for example, is an organizationally dysfunctional behavior that cannot be tolerated. In such cases managers often rely on **punishment,** administering an undesired or negative consequence to subordinates when they perform the dysfunctional behavior. Punishments used by organizations range from verbal reprimands to pay cuts, temporary suspensions, demotions, and firings. Punishment, however, can have some unintended side effects–resentment, loss of self-respect, a desire for retaliation–and should be used only when necessary.

punishment Administering an undesired or negative consequence when dysfunctional behavior occurs.

To avoid the unintended side effects of punishment, managers should keep in mind these guidelines:

- Downplay the emotional element involved in punishment. Make it clear that you are punishing a person's performance of a dysfunctional behavior, not the person himself or herself.
- Try to punish dysfunctional behaviors as soon after they occur as possible, and make sure the negative consequence is a source of punishment for the individuals involved. Be certain that organizational members know exactly why they are being punished.
- Try to avoid punishing someone in front of others, for this can hurt a person's self-respect and lower esteem in the eyes of co-workers as well as make co-workers feel uncomfortable.[83] Even so, making organizational members aware that an individual who has committed a serious infraction has been punished can sometimes be effective in preventing future infractions and teaching all members of the organization that certain behaviors are unacceptable. For example, when organizational members are informed that a manager who has

sexually harassed subordinates has been punished, they learn or are reminded of the fact that sexual harassment is not tolerated in the organization.

Managers and students alike often confuse negative reinforcement and punishment. To avoid such confusion, keep in mind the two major differences between them. First, negative reinforcement is used to promote the performance of functional behaviors in organizations; punishment is used to stop the performance of dysfunctional behaviors. Second, negative reinforcement entails the *removal* of a negative consequence when functional behaviors are performed; punishment entails the *administration* of negative consequences when dysfunctional behaviors are performed.

organizational behavior modification (OB MOD) The systematic application of operant conditioning techniques to promote the performance of organizationally functional behaviors and discourage the performance of dysfunctional behaviors.

ORGANIZATIONAL BEHAVIOR MODIFICATION When managers systematically apply operant conditioning techniques to promote the performance of organizationally functional behaviors and discourage the performance of dysfunctional behaviors, they are engaging in **organizational behavior modification (OB MOD).**[84] OB MOD has been successfully used to improve productivity, efficiency, attendance, punctuality, safe work practices, customer service, and other important behaviors in a wide variety of organizations such as banks, department stores, factories, hospitals, and construction sites.[85] The five basic steps in OB MOD are described in Figure 13.4.

OB MOD works best for behaviors that are specific, objective, and countable, such as attendance and punctuality, making sales, or putting telephones together, all of which lend themselves to careful scrutiny and control. OB MOD may be questioned because of its lack of relevance to certain work behaviors (for example, the many work behaviors that are not specific, objective, and countable). Some people also have questioned it on ethical grounds. Critics of OB MOD suggest that it is overly controlling and robs workers of their dignity, individuality, freedom of choice, and even creativity. Supporters counter that OB MOD is a highly effective means of promoting organizational efficiency. There is some merit to both sides of this argument. What is clear, however, is that when used appropriately, OB MOD provides managers with a technique to motivate the performance of at least some organizationally functional behaviors.[86]

Social Learning Theory

social learning theory A theory that takes into account how learning and motivation are influenced by people's thoughts and beliefs and their observations of other people's behavior.

vicarious learning Learning that occurs when the learner becomes motivated to perform a behavior by watching another person perform it and be reinforced for doing so; also called *observational learning.*

Social learning theory proposes that motivation results not only from direct experience of rewards and punishments but also from a person's thoughts and beliefs. Social learning theory extends operant conditioning's contribution to managers' understanding of motivation by explaining (1) how people can be motivated by observing other people perform a behavior and be reinforced for doing so (*vicarious learning*), (2) how people can be motivated to control their behavior themselves (*self-reinforcement*), and (3) how people's beliefs about their ability to successfully perform a behavior affect motivation (*self-efficacy*).[87] We look briefly at each of these motivators.

VICARIOUS LEARNING **Vicarious learning,** often called *observational learning,* occurs when a person (the learner) becomes motivated to perform a behavior by watching another person (the model) perform the behavior and be positively reinforced for doing so. Vicarious learning is a powerful source of motivation on many jobs in which people learn to perform functional behaviors by watching others. Salespeople learn how to be helpful to customers, medical school

Figure 13.4
Five Steps in OB MOD

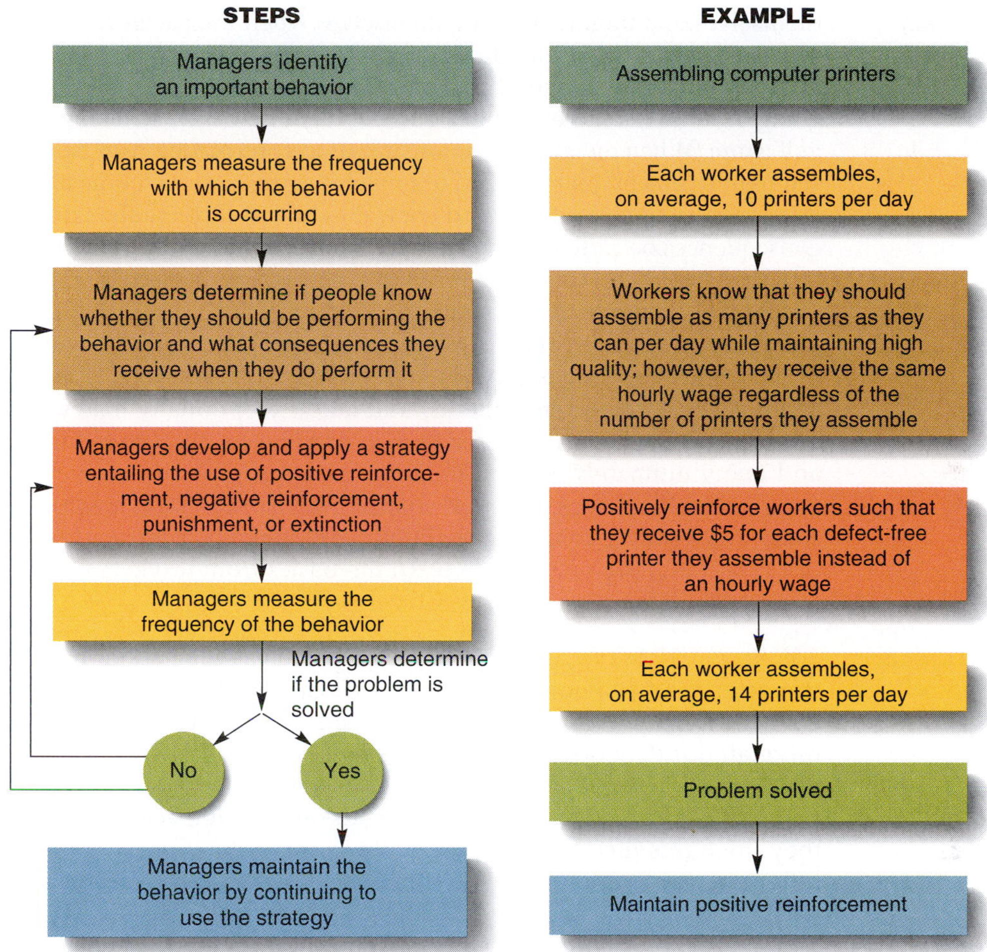

Source: Adapted from *Organizational Behavior Modification and Beyond* by F. Luthans and R. Kreitner (Scott, Foresman, 1985). With permission of the authors.

students learn how to treat patients, law clerks learn how to practice law, and nonmanagers learn how to be managers, in part, by observing experienced members of an organization perform these behaviors properly and be reinforced for them. In general, people are more likely to be motivated to imitate the behavior of models who are highly competent, are (to some extent) experts in the behavior, have high status, receive attractive reinforcers, and are friendly or approachable.[88]

To promote vicarious learning, managers should strive to have the learner meet the following conditions:

- The learner observes the model performing the behavior.
- The learner accurately perceives the model's behavior.
- The learner remembers the behavior.
- The learner has the skills and abilities needed to perform the behavior.
- The learner sees or knows that the model is positively reinforced for the behavior.[89]

self-reinforcer Any desired or attractive outcome or reward that a person gives to himself or herself for good performance.

SELF-REINFORCEMENT Although managers are often the providers of reinforcement in organizations, sometimes people motivate themselves through self-reinforcement. People can control their own behavior by setting goals for themselves and then reinforcing themselves when they achieve the goals.[90] **Self-reinforcers** are any desired or attractive outcomes or rewards that people can give to themselves for good performance, such as a feeling of accomplishment, going to a movie, having dinner out, buying a new CD, or taking time out for a golf game. When members of an organization control their own behavior through self-reinforcement, managers do not need to spend as much time as they ordinarily would trying to motivate and control behavior through the administration of consequences because subordinates are controlling and motivating themselves. In fact, this self-control is often referred to as the *self-management of behavior.*

Chinese students at the prestigious Jiaotong University in Shanghai exemplify how strong motivation through self-control can be. These students, many of whom are aspiring engineers, live in spartan conditions (a barely lit small room is home for seven students) and take exceptionally heavy course loads. They spend their spare time reading up on subjects not covered in their classes, and many ultimately hope to obtain engineering jobs overseas with high-tech companies. Illustrating high self-control, 22-year-old Yan Kangrong spends his spare time reading computer textbooks and designing software for local companies. As Kangrong puts it, "We learn the basics from teachers. . . . But we need to expand on this knowledge by ourselves."[91]

self-efficacy A person's belief about his or her ability to perform a behavior successfully.

SELF-EFFICACY **Self-efficacy** is a person's belief about his or her ability to perform a behavior successfully. Even with all the most attractive consequences or reinforcers hinging on high performance, people are not going to be motivated if they do not think that they can actually perform at a high level. Similarly, when people control their own behavior, they are likely to set for themselves difficult goals that will lead to outstanding accomplishments only if they think that they have the capability to reach those goals. Thus, self-efficacy influences motivation both when managers provide reinforcement and when workers themselves provide it.[92] The greater the self-efficacy, the greater is the motivation and performance. In "A Manager's Challenge," Tindell and Boone boost self-efficacy when they express confidence in their employees and view them all as leaders. Such verbal persuasion, as well as a person's own past performance and accomplishments and the accomplishments of other people, plays a role in determining a person's self-efficacy.

Pay and Motivation

In Chapter 12, we discussed how managers establish a pay level and structure for an organization as a whole. Here we focus on how, once a pay level and structure are in place, managers can use pay to motivate employees to perform at a high level and attain their work goals. Pay is used to motivate entry-level workers, first-line and middle managers, and even top managers such as CEOs. Pay can be used to motivate people to perform behaviors that help an organization achieve its goals, and it can be used to motivate people to join and remain with an organization.

Each of the theories described in this chapter alludes to the importance of pay and suggests that pay should be based on performance:

- *Expectancy theory.* Instrumentality, the association between performance and outcomes such as pay, must be high for motivation to be high. In addition, pay is an outcome that has high valence for many people.
- *Need theories.* People should be able to satisfy their needs by performing at a high level; pay can be used to satisfy several different kinds of needs.
- *Equity theory.* Outcomes such as pay should be distributed in proportion to inputs (including performance levels).
- *Goal-setting theory.* Outcomes such as pay should be linked to the attainment of goals.
- *Learning theories.* The distribution of outcomes such as pay should be contingent on the performance of organizationally functional behaviors.

As these theories suggest, to promote high motivation, managers should base the distribution of pay to organizational members on performance levels so that high performers receive more pay than low performers (other things being equal).[93] At General Mills, for example, the pay of all employees, ranging from mailroom clerks to senior managers, is based, at least in part, on performance.[94] A compensation plan basing pay on performance is often called a **merit pay plan.** Once managers have decided to use a merit pay plan, they face two important choices: whether to base pay on individual, group, or organizational performance or to use salary increases or bonuses.

merit pay plan A compensation plan that bases pay on performance.

Basing Merit Pay on Individual, Group, or Organizational Performance

Managers can base merit pay on individual, group, or organizational performance. When individual performance (such as the dollar value of merchandise a salesperson sells, the number of loudspeakers a factory worker assembles, and a lawyer's billable hours) can be accurately determined, individual motivation is likely to be highest when pay is based on individual performance.[95] When members of an organization work closely together and individual performance cannot be accurately determined (as in a team of computer programmers developing a single software package), pay cannot be based on individual performance, and a group- or organization-based plan must be used. When the attainment of organizational goals hinges on members' working closely together and cooperating with each other (as in a small construction company that builds custom homes), group- or organization-based plans may be more appropriate than individual-based plans.[96]

It is possible to combine elements of an individual-based plan with a group- or organization-based plan to motivate each individual to perform highly and, at the same time, motivate all individuals to work well together, cooperate with one another, and help one another as needed. Lincoln Electric, a very successful company and a leading manufacturer of welding machines, uses a combination individual- and organization-based plan.[97] Pay is based on individual performance. In addition, each year the size of a bonus fund depends on organizational performance. Money from the bonus fund is distributed to people on the basis of their contributions to the organization, attendance, levels of cooperation, and other indications of performance. Employees of Lincoln Electric are motivated to cooperate and help one another because when the firm as a whole performs well, everybody benefits by having a larger bonus fund. Employees also are motivated to contribute their inputs to the organization because their contributions determine their share of the bonus fund.

Salary Increase or Bonus?

Managers can distribute merit pay to people in the form of a salary increase or a bonus on top of regular salaries. Although the dollar amount of a salary increase or bonus might be identical, bonuses tend to have more motivational impact for at least three reasons. First, salary levels are typically based on performance levels, cost-of-living increases, and so forth, from the day people start working in an organization, which means that the absolute level of the salary is based largely on factors unrelated to *current* performance. A 5 percent merit increase in salary, for example, may seem relatively small in comparison to one's total salary. Second, a current salary increase may be affected by other factors in addition to performance, such as cost-of-living increases or across-the-board market adjustments. Third, because organizations rarely reduce salaries, salary levels tend to vary less than performance levels do. Related to this point is the fact that bonuses give managers more flexibility in distributing outcomes. If an organization is doing well, bonuses can be relatively high to reward employees for their contributions. However, unlike salary increases, bonus levels can be reduced when an organization's performance lags. All in all, bonus plans have more motivational impact than salary increases because the amount of the bonus can be directly and exclusively based on performance.[98]

Consistent with the lessons from motivation theories, bonuses can be linked directly to performance and vary from year to year and employee to employee, as at Gradient Corporation, a Cambridge, Massachusetts, environmental consulting firm.[99] Another organization that successfully uses bonuses is Nucor Corporation. Steelworkers at Nucor tend to be much more productive than steelworkers in other companies–probably because they can receive bonuses tied to performance and quality that are from 130 to 150 percent of their regular or base pay.[100]

employee stock option A financial instrument that entitles the bearer to buy shares of an organization's stock at a certain price during a certain period of time or under certain conditions.

In addition to receiving pay raises and bonuses, high-level managers and executives are sometimes granted employee stock options. **Employee stock options** are financial instruments that entitle the bearer to buy shares of an organization's stock at a certain price during a certain period of time or under certain conditions.[101] For example, in addition to salaries stock options are sometimes used to attract high-level managers. The exercise price is the stock price at which the bearer can buy the stock, and the vesting conditions specify when the bearer can actually buy the stock at the exercise price. The option's exercise price is generally set equal to the market price of the stock on the date it is granted, and the vesting conditions might specify that the manager has to have worked at the organization for 12 months or perhaps met some performance target (increase in profits) before being able to exercise the option. In high-technology firms and start-ups, options are sometimes used in a similar fashion for employees at various levels in the organization.[102]

From a motivation standpoint, stock options are used not so much to reward past individual performance but, rather, to motivate employees to work in the future for the good of the company as a whole. This is true because stock options issued at current stock prices have value in the future only if an organization does well and its stock price appreciates; thus, giving employees stock options should encourage them to help the organization improve its performance over time.[103] At high-technology start-ups and dot-coms, stock options have often motivated potential employees to leave promising jobs in larger companies and work for the start-ups. In the late 1990s and early 2000s, many dot-commers were devastated to learn not only that their stock options were worthless, because their companies went out of business or were doing poorly, but also that they were unemployed.

Examples of Merit Pay Plans

Managers can choose among several merit pay plans, depending on the work that employees perform and other considerations. Using *piece-rate pay,* an individual-based merit plan, managers base employees' pay on the number of units each employee produces, whether televisions, computer components, or welded auto parts. Managers at Lincoln Electric use piece-rate pay to determine individual pay levels. Advances in information technology are currently simplifying the administration of piece-rate pay in a variety of industries. For example, farmers have typically allocated piece-rate pay to farmworkers through a laborious, time-consuming process. Now, they can rely on metal buttons the size of a dime that farmworkers clip to their shirts or put in their pockets. Made by Dallas Semiconductor Corporation, these buttons are customized for use in farming by Agricultural Data Systems, based in Laguna Niguel, California.[104] Each button contains a semiconductor linked to payroll computers by a wandlike probe in the field.[105] The wand relays the number of boxes of fruit or vegetables that each worker picks as well as the type and quality of the produce picked, the location it was picked in, and the time and the date. The buttons are activated by touching them with the probe; hence, they are called Touch Memory Buttons. Managers generally find that the buttons save time, improve accuracy, and provide valuable information about their crops and yields.[106]

Using *commission pay,* another individual-based merit pay plan, managers base pay on a percentage of sales. Managers at the successful real-estate company Re/Max International Inc. use commission pay for their agents, who are paid a percentage of their sales. Some department stores, such as Neiman Marcus, use commission pay for their salespeople.

Examples of organizational-based merit pay plans include the Scanlon plan and profit sharing. The *Scanlon plan* (developed by Joseph Scanlon, a union leader in a steel and tin plant in the 1920s) focuses on reducing expenses or cutting costs; members of an organization are motivated to come up with and implement cost-cutting strategies because a percentage of the cost savings achieved during a specified time is distributed to the employees.[107] Under *profit sharing,* employees receive a share of an organization's profits. Approximately 16 percent of the employees in medium or large firms receive profit sharing, and about 25 percent of small firms give their employees a share of the profits.[108] Regardless of the specific kind of plan that is used, managers should always strive to link pay to the performance of behaviors that help an organization achieve its goals.

Japanese managers in large corporations have long shunned merit pay plans in favor of plans that reward seniority. However, more and more Japanese companies are adopting merit-based pay due to its motivational benefits, such as SiteDesign,[109] Tokio Marine and Fire Insurance, and Hissho Iwai, a trading organization.[110]

Summary and Review

THE NATURE OF MOTIVATION Motivation encompasses the psychological forces within a person that determine the direction of the person's behavior in an organization, the person's level of effort, and the person's level of persistence in the face of obstacles. Managers strive to motivate people to contribute their inputs to an organization, to focus these inputs in the direction of high performance, and to ensure that people receive the outcomes they desire when they perform at a high level.

EXPECTANCY THEORY According to expectancy theory, managers can promote high levels of motivation in their organizations by taking steps to ensure that expectancy is high (people think that if they try, they can perform at a high level), instrumentality is high (people think that if they perform at a high level, they will receive certain outcomes), and valence is high (people desire these outcomes).

NEED THEORIES Need theories suggest that to motivate their workforces, managers should determine what needs people are trying to satisfy in organizations and then ensure that people receive outcomes that satisfy these needs when they perform at a high level and contribute to organizational effectiveness.

EQUITY THEORY According to equity theory, managers can promote high levels of motivation by ensuring that people perceive that there is equity in the organization or that outcomes are distributed in proportion to inputs. Equity exists when a person perceives that his or her own outcome-input ratio equals the outcome-input ratio of a referent. Inequity motivates people to try to restore equity.

GOAL-SETTING THEORY Goal-setting theory suggests that managers can promote high motivation and performance by ensuring that people are striving to achieve specific, difficult goals. It is important for people to accept the goals, be committed to them, and receive feedback about how they are doing.

LEARNING THEORIES Operant conditioning theory suggests that managers can motivate people to perform highly by using positive reinforcement or negative reinforcement (positive reinforcement being the preferred strategy). Managers can motivate people to avoid performing dysfunctional behaviors by using extinction or punishment. Social learning theory suggests that people can also be motivated by observing how others perform behaviors and receive rewards, by engaging in self-reinforcement, and by having high levels of self-efficacy.

PAY AND MOTIVATION Each of the motivation theories discussed in this chapter alludes to the importance of pay and suggests that pay should be based on performance. Merit pay plans can be individual-, group-, or organization-based and can entail the use of salary increases or bonuses.

Management in Action

Topics for Discussion and Action

Discussion

1. Discuss why two people with similar abilities may have very different expectancies for performing at a high level.
2. Describe why some people have low instrumentalities even when their managers distribute outcomes based on performance.
3. Analyze how professors try to promote equity to motivate students.
4. Describe three techniques or procedures that managers can use to determine whether a goal is difficult.
5. Discuss why managers should always try to use positive reinforcement instead of negative reinforcement.

Action

6. Interview three people who have the same kind of job (such as salesperson, waiter/waitress, or teacher), and determine what kinds of needs they are trying to satisfy at work.
7. Interview a manager in an organization in your community to determine the extent to which the manager takes advantage of vicarious learning to promote high motivation among subordinates.

Building Management Skills

Diagnosing Motivation

Think about the ideal job that you would like to obtain upon graduation. Describe this job, the kind of manager you would like to report to, and the kind of organization you would be working in. Then answer the following questions:

1. What would be your levels of expectancy and instrumentality on this job? Which outcomes would have high valence for you on this job? What steps would your manager take to influence your levels of expectancy, instrumentality, and valence?
2. Whom would you choose as a referent on this job? What steps would your manager take to make you feel that you were being equitably treated? What would you do if, after a year on the job, you experienced underpayment inequity?
3. What goals would you strive to achieve on this job? Why? What role would your manager play in determining your goals?
4. What needs would you strive to satisfy on this job? Why? What role would your manager play in helping you satisfy these needs?
5. What behaviors would your manager positively reinforce on this job? Why? What positive reinforcers would your manager use?
6. Would there be any vicarious learning on this job? Why or why not?
7. To what extent would you be motivated by self-control on this job? Why?
8. What would be your level of self-efficacy on this job? Why would your self-efficacy be at this level? Should your manager take steps to boost your self-efficacy? If not, why not? If so, what would these steps be?

Managing Ethically

Sometimes pay is so contingent upon performance that it creates stress for employees. Imagine a salesperson who knows that if sales targets are not met, she or he will not be able to make a house mortgage payment or pay the rent.

Questions

1. Either individually or in a group, think about the ethical implications of closely linking pay to performance.
2. Under what conditions might contingent pay be most stressful, and what steps can managers take to try to help their subordinates perform effectively and not experience excessive amounts of stress?

Small Group Breakout Exercise

Increasing Motivation

Form groups of three or four people, and appoint one member as the spokesperson who will communicate your findings to the whole class when called on by the instructor. Then discuss the following scenario.

You and your partners own a chain of 15 dry-cleaning stores in a medium-size town. All of you are concerned about a problem in customer service that has surfaced recently. When any one of you spends the day, or even part of the day, in a particular store, clerks seem to provide excellent customer service, spotters are making sure all stains are removed from garments, and pressers are doing a good job of pressing difficult items such as silk blouses. Yet during those same visits customers complain to you about such things as stains not being removed and items being poorly pressed in some of their previous orders; indeed, several customers have brought garments in to be redone. Customers also sometimes comment on having waited too long for service on previous visits. You and your partners are meeting today to address this problem.

1. Discuss the extent to which you believe that you have a motivation problem in your stores.
2. Given what you have learned in this chapter, design a plan to increase the motivation of clerks to provide prompt service to customers even when they are not being watched by a partner.
3. Design a plan to increase the motivation of spotters to remove as many stains as possible even when they are not being watched by a partner.
4. Design a plan to increase the motivation of pressers to do a top-notch job on all clothes they press, no matter how difficult.

Exploring the World Wide Web

If you had the chance to choose which well-known corporation you would like to work for, which would it be? Now go to the Web site of that company and find out as much as you can about how it motivates employees. Also, using Google and other search engines, try to find articles in the news about this company. Based upon what you have learned, would this company still be your top choice? Why or why not?

Be the Manager

You supervise a team of marketing analysts who work on different snack products in a large food products company. The marketing analysts have recently received undergraduate degrees in business or liberal arts and have been on the job between one and three years. Their responsibilities include analyzing the market for their respective products, including competitors; tracking current marketing initiatives; and planning future marketing campaigns. They also need to prepare quarterly sales and expense reports for their products and estimated budgets for the next three quarters; to prepare these reports, they need to obtain data from financial and accounting analysts assigned to their products.

When they first started on the job, you took each marketing analyst through the reporting cycle, explaining what needs to be done, and how to accomplish it and emphasizing the need for timely reports. While preparing the reports can be tedious, you think the task is pretty straightforward and easily accomplished if the analysts plan ahead and allocate sufficient time for it. When reporting time approaches, you remind the analysts through emails and emphasize the need for accurate and timely reports in team meetings.

You believe that this element of the analysts' jobs couldn't be more straightforward. However, at the end of each quarter, the majority of the analysts turn their reports in a day or two late, and, worse yet, your own supervisor (whom the reports are eventually turned in to) has indicated that information is often missing and sometimes the reports contain errors. Once you started getting flak from your supervisor about this problem, you decided you better fix things, and quick. You met with the marketing analysts, explained the problem, told them to turn the reports in to you a day or two early so that you could look them over, and more generally emphasized that they really needed to get their act together. Unfortunately, things have not improved much, and you are spending more and more of your own time doing the reports. What are you going to do?

Additional Activities on the Build Your Management Skills DVD

- **Test Your Knowledge:** (1) Maslow's Hierarchy of Needs, (2) Reinforcement Theory, and (3) Reinforcing Performance
- **Self Assessment:** Assessing How Personality Type Affects Goal-Setting

BusinessWeek Case in the News

Coverup at Boeing?

More than a decade ago, Boeing Co. quietly began investigating an explosive internal issue: whether female employees were paid less than men. Several sophisticated salary studies concluded that the answer was yes. One 1998 report said "men are more likely to be hired into the high paying positions." A statistical analysis completed the same year noted that the pay gap for entry-level managers was $3,741.04.

Although she knew nothing of these sensitive analyses, Carol Jensen would not have found them surprising. The 64-year-old technical drafter had long complained that women were underpaid. "We were treated with little respect," recalls the mother of nine, who started working at Boeing in 1967 and was laid off in 2000. "The men believed that the only work for women at Boeing was behind a desk as a secretary."

In 2000, 38 women filed a class action in Seattle against the company for pay discrimination. The potential cost to Boeing exceeded $100 million. All of those salary studies Boeing had done through the years, of course, would have been dynamite evidence for the aggrieved women. But when their lawyers made routine pretrial requests for any statistical data the company might have compiled on gender pay differentials, the aerospace giant said it had no obligation to turn the studies over. Why? Because they had allegedly been prepared at the direction of Boeing's lawyers and were therefore protected by attorney-client privilege. That's a legal doctrine that shields confidential communications between executives and their attorneys from public disclosure. It's intended to allow managers to be candid with their legal counselors.

Behind the scenes, meanwhile, Boeing employees removed payroll-planning documents about pay discrimination from the company's files. In an e-mail dated August 27, 2001, compensation manager Paul A. Wells advised colleagues to get rid of drafts of these types of documents on the Salary Administration server because "that which is retained can potentially be subpoenaed and . . . those with access [to] the files can be called on to testify about the content." Wells declined to comment.

Systematic Campaign

It's a classic scenario—the type of confrontation that has served as dramatic fodder for countless movies: A big, powerful company bullies small, weak individuals. *Erin Brockovich, A Civil Action,* and many other legal thrillers tell this tale from the point of view of the victims. But *BusinessWeek* has obtained a rare view of the other side of the story: what takes place at the company. The federal judge overseeing the class action, Marsha J. Pechman, agreed to unseal more than 12,000 pages of internal Boeing documents on February 11 after *BusinessWeek* attorneys argued that they should be disclosed. This hidden corporate history raises questions as to whether the company and its lawyers engaged in a systematic campaign to hid evidence and take advantage of attorney-client privilege.

Having witnessed Boeing's intransigence for more than four years, highlighted by a ferocious battle to avoid disclosure of its salary studies, Judge Pechman dropped an even bigger bombshell on the company on May 11. Citing "an evolving awareness, as more facts come to light, of how Boeing had inappropriately tried to shield [the documents] from discovery," she ordered Boeing to hand over the series of salary analyses it had fought hardest to withhold—ones that left little room for doubting the company's knowledge of its pay disparities. That was only one of several rebukes Boeing received from the judge, as well as from a special master assigned to referee discovery disputes, during the course of the lawsuit. Though many questions remain about the company's conduct during the case, and a complete picture of the role played by Boeing's various managers and lawyers is still unavailable. Judge Pechman's rulings suggest that the company went beyond standard aggressive legal defense tactics.

Now that Boeing was faced with the prospect of telling jurors why its own internal documents seemingly contradicted its legal theory, the company suddenly became accommodating. Two days before the case was scheduled to go to trial, on May 17, Boeing made a settlement offer. While the two teams hammer out the details of the deal, which neither side will discuss, the case has been postponed. . . .

Spokesman Kenneth B. Mercer says Boeing is committed to honest business practices and equal opportunity. Because settlement talks in the Beck lawsuit aren't complete, he refuses to discuss the underlying facts of the case, the conduct of the company's attorneys, or any of the individual documents obtained by *BusinessWeek*—beyond saying Boeing thinks its hiring and promotion practices are fair. Mercer adds that the statistical studies Judge Pechman forced the company to turn over were intended to help eliminate pay disparities and that they "can't capture all of the critical factors that go into pay or promotion decisions."

Boeing's Mercer also noted that federal judge's have tossed out three similar gender-discrimination class actions filed against Boeing in Southern California, Kansas, and Missouri. A fourth suit, in Oklahoma, has been granted class-action status. The company says its high batting average against female pay-discrimination suits is proof that its compensation practices were legal. But plaintiffs' attorneys claim Boeing won mainly because it successfully suppressed the evidence that ultimately entered the Beck case.

Record Output of Jets

Troubling headlines are a comparatively new problem for Boeing. A company dominated by engineers, it traditionally focused on innovation and design. Executives believed that profits would naturally follow. During the Pentagon overbilling scandals of the late 1980s, Boeing was the least tarnished of the major contractors. But the culture started changing after its merger with the more aggressive McDonnell Douglas in 1997. That deal, along with tougher competition for government dollars in the Clinton years, shifted Boeing's emphasis to the bottom line.

Women first entered Boeing's workforce in large numbers during World War II—and they enabled the company to roll out record fleets of B-17 bombers. But when the war ended, Boeing's male-dominated culture returned in full force. When Carol Jensen joined in 1967, she was one of the first females to draw technical blueprints. "Men were getting the plum designing assignments," recalls

Jensen. "It was out-and-out discrimination, and a woman couldn't do anything about it."

Despite the anger of Jensen and others, female pay didn't become a serious concern at Boeing until 1996, when the labor Dept.'s Office of Federal Contract Compliance Program (OFCCP) ran a routine investigation of Boeing's mammoth Philadelphia plant. Under government contracting rules, the OFCCP has the right to audit whether federal contractors are complying with anti-discrimination laws. The agency does this by using a statistical method known as "median analysis." In broad terms, it compares the relationship between the median pay of male and female employees and their median job experience.

After informing Boeing that the OFCCP had discovered "a prima facie case of systemic discrimination concerning compensation of females and minorities" in Philadelphia, the agency audited nine other plants nationwide. The stakes for Boeing, the country's No. 2 federal contractor, were huge. With defense and space representing nearly half of its revenues and growing, the loss of federal contracts would be devastating.

Recognizing the seriousness of the inquiry, Boeing wasted no time launching a counterattack. It hired Jon A. Geier, a partner in the Washington (D.C.) office of Paul, Hastings, Janofsky & Walker LLP. One of his top priorities, he said in a declaration submitted in the Beck case, was developing a "legally defensible" statistical analysis of Boeing's pay practices to counter the one OFCCP used to evaluate pay discrimination. But there was one big problem: The findings of Geier's own Diversity Salary Analysis project, or DSA, also found pay disparities. Its 1997 report determined that females "are paid less." The next year's report noted that "gender differences in starting salaries generally continue and often increase as a result of salary planning decisions." Geier did not respond to requests for comment. . . .

"There Was a Lot More"

Despite Boeing's "extensive efforts," in the words of one in-house lawyer, not to forfeit the attorney-client privilege, the company did do a few things to jeopardize its eligibility for that legal protection. Its attorneys, for instance, gave DSA documents to managers outside their tightly guarded legal team. These execs used the information not just to fight the OFCCP inquiry but also to make broader salary decisions.

The OFCCP settled with Boeing for $4.5 million in November 1999. Boeing did not admit liability. On December 1, relieved human-resource execs and attorneys gathered to discuss their victory over the federal government, according to a meeting transcription obtained by *BusinessWeek*. Boeing's former director for employee relations, Marcella Fleming, declared that the company got off easy. "We thought that there was a lot more potential financial liability out there," Fleming told her colleagues. "And so, what we're paying for this deal in the long run is a lot less than we think we could have potentially paid." Fleming declined to comment for this story.

Boeing officials had little time to dwell on their triumph. On February 25, 2000, Seattle attorney Michael D. Helgren filed the Beck v. Boeing class action after some female employees told him their stories. The company enlisted the help of its chief outside law firm, Seattle-based Perkins Cole LLP. . . .

Almost immediately, the company resumed the aggressive strategies that had worked so well in the OFCCP investigation. After being deposed by attorney Helgren in September 2000, Boeing compensation manager Jeffrey K. Janders told colleagues in a memo that he wanted the Salary Planning Team to "delete the concept of target salaries"—the hypothetical pay increases Boeing executives believed would be necessary to create salary parity—"to prevent an audit trail where a substantial difference exists between target and planned salaries." Because Janders could not be reached for comment, *BusinessWeek* does not know the full context of the e-mail.

Helgren did not find out about these maneuvers until years later, but from the start he suspected that the company was not turning over all of the salary infromation it had. After Boeing's Hannah claimed that many of the pay-related documents his rival wanted were covered by attorney-client privilege, Helgren requested a so-called privilege log—a list containing a brief description of every document the company was withholding. A common tool in U.S. courts, these logs are intended to give plaintiffs' attorneys an idea of what material the defendant is holding back and why it is privileged without revealing any sensitive secrets. . . .

Suspecting that many of these documents did not deserve attorney-client privilege, Helgren asked for a judicial review of those covered by the privilege log. Judge Pechman assigned retired state court judge George Finkle the job of managing pretrial discovery disputes. After studying a 1,400-page sample of Boeing's DSA documents, Finkle rejected the claim that the studies were protected simply because attorneys were involved in producing them. The documents "served business purposes extending well beyond providing assistance in . . . anticipation of litigation," Finkle ruled on October 25, 2000. "Legal departments are not citadels in which public business or technical information may be placed to defeat discovery and thereby ensure confidentiality."

That should have been the end of Helgren's quest. Still, Boeing dragged its feet. The documents Judge Finkle ordered Boeing to give to plaintiffs' attorneys came slowly and in small batches. It wasn't until early 2004 that Boeing attorneys handed over some damning internal statistical salary studies that execs had not even previously acknowledged. For Helgren, these late-released documents proved Boeing not only knew about the pay discrimination but refused to take serious steps to eliminate it. "These pay disparities were caused by their own practices," Helgren says. "None of this was by chance. And they continued for years and years to avoid the problem."

Suddenly Amenable

In a last-ditch effort to prevent a jury from seeing these potential smoking guns, Boeing attorneys appealed Finkle's discovery order. They claimed that disclosing these documents would "materially and unfairly" bias the case. On March 11, Pechman denied Boeing's appeal. It was a huge boost for Helgren, who started gearing up for the trial, scheduled to begin on May 17. But on May 13, he got an unexpected call. A third party representing Boeing phoned to say the company was willing to talk settlement. Negotiations proceeded almost continuously until the next day at noon, when the two sides reached a tentative settlement.

While she is happy about the potential deal, plaintiff Jensen is reserving judgment about the company. Among her nine children are six adult daughters, and she currently "wouldn't let any of them work at Boeing." The pay gap there may disappear one day. But one thing Boeing will never be able to erase is its long history of underpaying women.

Questions

1. What inequities did women and minorities at Boeing experience?
2. What were the consequences of these inequities?
3. When managers became aware of the inequities, what did they do? Why didn't they do more?
4. What are the broader implications of the discrimination suits for Boeing and its future?

Source: S. Holmes and M. France, "Coverup at Boeing?" Reprinted from the June 28, 2004, issue of *BusinessWeek* by special permission. Copyright © 2004 by the McGraw-Hill Companies, Inc.

BusinessWeek Case in the News

A New Pay Scheme for Wal-Mart Workers

Is low pay at Wal-Mart Stores Inc. driving down wages and benefits nationwide? That's what critics contend—one reason pay scales at the nation's largest private employer have become part of the national political debate. Now, *BusinessWeek* has learned, the retail behemoth is preparing to introduce significant changes in its pay system in coming weeks. And that should ensure the debate gets even livelier.

According to some Wal-Mart workers, as well as union organizers and a lawyer who have talked to Wal-Mart workers in different parts of the country, big adjustments are coming. The changes they describe could mean raises for newer workers but penalties for higher-paid veterans. They could also limit the discretion of front-line managers to make decisions about pay rates and merit raises, a move that could help Wal-Mart battle charges of sexual discrimination. "Obviously they [Wal-Mart] have a bad reputation in terms of pay for the rank and file, and they need to improve that," says retail analyst Robert F. Buchanan at A.G. Edwards & Sons Inc.

Wal-Mart refuses to discuss or even acknowledge the new pay plan, which workers say they've been told will show up in paychecks starting in June. In explaining the change, Kathleen MacDonald, a 14-year Wal-Mart veteran at a supercenter in Aiken, S.C., says her bosses alluded to the bad publicity over Wal-Mart's pay and negative comments from politicians. Some managers have also told workers that the changes were a response to the massive sex-discrimination case filed three years ago against Wal-Mart, says Joseph M. Sellers, a lawyer for the plaintiffs in that suit. Workers have reported raises ranging from 8¢ an hour to $3 an hour under the new plan, he adds.

According to MacDonald and others, the new plan—whose details remain sketchy—divides workers into seven classes, at least in the supercenters. Starting wages would be clearly defined, as would progress from class to class. While Wal-Mart's pay system has some similar features now, those familiar with it say it has been loosely followed, with managers having wide discretion.

Under the plan, workers have been told, no one's pay would be reduced. But labor activists are fretting all the same. United Food & Commercial Workers organizer Stan Fortune says the new system, described to him by numerous workers, would includ a pay cap for each class—a possible disadvantage for longtime associates, as Wal-Mart calls its 1.2 million U.S. workers. And merit raises would be limited to about 5 percent of store employees.

What's more, workers say, annual raises would be set at a flat rate; not a percentage of salary. That would be another blow to veterans. Those with a "standard" annual evaluation would get 40¢ more an hour. Those "above standard" would get 55¢. Wal-Mart says its current full-time hourly workers average $9.64 an hour in its discount stores and supercenters. The old system usually gave even higher-paid workers at least a 4 percent raise. "If you're making double digits, this hurts you," says sales clerk MacDonald, who now earns $11.03 an hour. She doesn't yet know how she will fare.

Expecting the Worst

Nor is it clear how the changes will affect Wal-Mart's overall labor costs. Not surprisingly, union organizers expect the worst. "In the long term, it will cost [Wal-Mart] less" by driving up the turnover of senior workers, predicts Fortune, a former Wal-Mart store co-manager who left in 2001. He says Wal-Mart experimented with a similar plan at some of its Sam's Club warehouse stores last summer.

Despite grumblings from senior workers over the plan, Wal-Mart may be hoping to use it as "shark repellent against the unions," says analyst Buchanan. Indeed, Jon M. Lehman, another UFCW organizer and former Wal-Mart store manager, says some workers were told that their new pay plan was "just like a union contract" so there was no point in pursuing unionization. The UFCW has so far failed to organize a single U.S. store.

Faced with intense criticism, Wal-Mart seems to be shaking up its pay structure. But like nearly everything this giant does, that's sure to spark new firestorms.

Questions

1. What are the pros and cons of Wal-Mart's new pay scheme from a motivational perspective?
2. What are the potential motivational implications of limiting merit raises to 5 percent of store employees?
3. What are the potential motivational effects of annual raises being determined on a flat rate rather than as a percentage of current salary?
4. Why do you think Wal-Mart might be seeking to curb the ability of front-line managers to determine raises and pay rates? What effects might this have?

Source: W. Zellner, "A New Pay Scheme for Wal-Mart Workers." Reprinted from the June 14, 2004, issue of *BusinessWeek* by special permission.

CHAPTER

14 Leadership

Learning Objectives

After studying this chapter, you should be able to:

- Explain what leadership is, when leaders are effective and ineffective, and the sources of power that enable managers to be effective leaders.
- Identify the traits that show the strongest relationship to leadership, the behaviors leaders engage in, and the limitations of the trait and behavior models of leadership.
- Explain how contingency models of leadership enhance our understanding of effective leadership and management in organizations.
- Describe what transformational leadership is and explain how managers can engage in it.
- Characterize the relationship between gender and leadership.

A Manager's Challenge

Steve Ballmer Reinvents Microsoft

How can a manager remake a 55,000-strong company to simultaneously promote efficiency and innovation? When Steve Ballmer became CEO of Microsoft in 2000, he faced a daunting task that became even more daunting a few months into his tenure when the dot-com bust hit the IT world. With over 55,000 employees, Microsoft had grown into a huge corporation. Yet, under Bill Gates's leadership since its founding as a two-person start-up, Microsoft had been run and managed in a very centralized fashion from its earliest days through the 1990s.[1] When Ballmer took over as CEO, he realized that Microsoft needed to become more efficient, employees and managers needed to be empowered to make decisions, and internal structures and processes needed to be put in place to promote efficiency, timely decision making, and innovation. And employee morale needed a boost.[2] Microsoft needed a new vision—a vision for a new era in which stock options lost much of their value, competition was fierce, and Microsoft was a huge corporation that needed a new kind of leadership.

Microsoft CEO Steve Ballmer, right, laughs as he chats with colleagues. Ballmer's enthusiasm is his trademark.

Ballmer has been described as "the quintessential, larger-than-life, rah-rah leader, and the perfect foil for his geeky and erudite best buddy, Bill Gates."[3] His extraverted nature has led to many an antic at employee gatherings, such as a monkey dance, and his excitement is infectious. Above all else, Ballmer really cares about Microsoft and its future, and dynamism, passion, and enthusiasm are his trademarks.[4]

Ballmer has other important qualities that make him ideally suited to transform Microsoft. He is disciplined, process-oriented, and analytical, and he is driven to find ways t measure and maximize performance, innovation, and customer responsiveness and make sure that all employees receive important feedback, including that from customers. Importantly, Ballmer realizes that instituting processes to transform Microsoft and promote innovation and employee motivation is a complex and delicate task that must allow for both autonomy and empowerment and enable different units to coordinate their efforts to achieve synergies. One of the reasons decision making was so centralized under Gates's leadership was the overarching need for integration across units.[5] Gates feared that giving unit managers autonomy would result in a lack of coordination across units, coordination that is essential for developing integrated technologies to achieve Microsoft's vision of "seamless computing."[6]

By 2004, Ballmer had led sweeping changes at Microsoft. Microsoft has been divided into seven operating divisions, with division managers not only empowered to make decisions that would formerly be made by the CEO but also accountable for the financial performance of their divisions. Integration across divisions is achieved by a matrix kind of organization called *integrated innovation.* Software developers in each of the divisions know and keep in close contact with developers in other divisions, and a process called *software engineering strategy* lays out how responsibility for implementing a creative idea is distributed among members of a development team from different divisions. An online performance appraisal system for employees is in place (in the past, there was no formal performance appraisal process); stock options have been replaced with grants of restricted stock; and employees were able to cash in some of their underwater options through an arrangement with J.P. Morgan Chase, which led to over $345 million being distributed to employees with otherwise worthless options.[7]

Ballmer and Gates (now chairman of the board and chief software architect) share the same vision for Microsoft: to dramatically boost the perceived value of the company's technology by developing seamlessly integrated software that connects all kinds of electronics, PCs, communication devices, and the Internet through one system.[8] Getting employees psyched and motivated to rally around this vision has been a top priority for Ballmer. Working at Microsoft had always been more of a quest than a job in the old days. When the dot-com bubble burst, IT hit on hard times, and the economy declined, morale at Microsoft suffered and some valued employees left the company. Ballmer has infused empowered employees and managers with a new sense of purpose and has instituted processes to ensure that they know what needs to be done and receive the information and feedback to make it happen. Ballmer's new mission for Microsoft is "to enable people and businesses throughout the world to realize their full potential" (which replaces the former mission, penned in 1978, of "a computer on every desk and in every home").[9] Corporate goals include integration with customers and safe, reliable computing; values include honesty, integrity, respect, and open communication.[10]

Time will tell whether Ballmer's efforts will pay off in terms of transforming Microsoft into something more than just another large company hampered by its size and falling short of achieving new heights. In July 2004, with a flat share price and modest growth in revenues, Ballmer announced that he would try to reduce costs by $1 billion (at the time, Microsoft expenses were $300,000 per employee).[11] And he also reaffirmed Microsoft's commitment to innovating for its customers (current annual R&D expenditures are over $4 billion).[12] As a leader who walks the walk, Ballmer was recently on his hands and knees plugging in monitors in a conference room in the headquarters of General Motors, trying to fix a screen resolution problem for automobile design engineers. As GM's chief information officer, Ralph Szygenda, indicates, "This shows me Steve Ballmer cares."[13]

Overview

Steve Ballmer exemplifies the many facets of effective leadership. In Chapter 1 we explained that one of the four primary tasks of managers is leading. Thus, it should come as no surprise that leadership is a key ingredient in effective management. When leaders are effective, their subordinates or followers are highly motivated, committed, and high-performing. When leaders are ineffective, chances are good that their subordinates do not perform up to their capabilities, are demotivated, and may be dissatisfied as well. CEO Ballmer is a leader at the very top of an organization, but leadership is an important ingredient for managerial success at all levels of organizations: top management, middle management, and first-line management. Moreover, leadership is a key ingredient for managerial success for organizations large and small.

In this chapter we describe what leadership is and examine the major leadership models that shed light on the factors that contribute to a manager's being an effective leader. We look at trait and behavior models, which focus on what leaders are like and what they do, and contingency models–Fiedler's contingency model, path-goal theory, and the leader substitutes model–each of which takes into account the complexity surrounding leadership and the role of the situation in leader effectiveness. We also describe how managers can use transformational leadership to dramatically affect their organizations. By the end of this chapter, you will have a good appreciation of the many factors and issues that managers face in their quest to be effective leaders.

The Nature of Leadership

leadership The process by which an individual exerts influence over other people and inspires, motivates, and directs their activities to help achieve group or organizational goals.

leader An individual who is able to exert influence over other people to help achieve group or organizational goals.

Leadership is the process by which a person exerts influence over other people and inspires, motivates, and directs their activities to help achieve group or organizational goals.[14] The person who exerts such influence is a **leader.** When leaders are effective, the influence they exert over others helps a group or organization achieve its performance goals. When leaders are ineffective, their influence does not contribute to, and often detracts from, goal attainment. As "A Manager's Challenge" makes clear, Steve Ballmer is taking multiple steps to inspire and motivate Microsoft employees and direct them to achieve Microsoft's goals.

Beyond facilitating the attainment of performance goals, effective leadership increases an organization's ability to meet all the contemporary challenges discussed throughout this book, including the need to obtain a competitive advantage, the need to foster ethical behavior, and the need to manage a diverse workforce fairly and equitably. Leaders who exert influence over organizational members to help meet these goals increase their organizations' chances of success.

In considering the nature of leadership, we first look at leadership styles and how they affect managerial tasks and at the influence of culture on leadership styles. We then focus on the key to leadership, power, which can come from a variety of sources. Finally, we consider the contemporary dynamic of empowerment and how it relates to effective leadership.

Personal Leadership Style and Managerial Tasks

A manager's *personal leadership style*–that is, the specific ways in which a manager chooses to influence other people–shapes the way that manager approaches planning, organizing, and controlling (the other principal tasks of managing). Consider Steve Ballmer's personal leadership style in "A Manager's Challenge": He is dynamic, passionate, and enthusiastic. Yet he is also disciplined, analytical, and driven to boost Microsoft's performance and promote innovation. He trusts and respects his employees and empowers them to make decisions, but he also looks out for their well-being by, for example, arranging for them to cash in on underwater stock options. He has a vision for the future and is making needed changes to make that vision a reality while transforming Microsoft to effectively and efficiently function as a large, innovative company that really cares about its customers.[15]

Managers at all levels and in all kinds of organizations have their own personal leadership styles that determine not only how they lead their subordinates but also how they perform the other management tasks. Michael Kraus, owner and manager of a dry-cleaning store in the northeastern United States, for example, takes a hands-on approach to leadership. He has the sole authority for determining work schedules and job assignments for the 15 employees in his store (an organizing task), makes all important decisions by himself (a planning task), and closely monitors his employees' performance and rewards top performers with pay increases (a control task). Kraus's personal leadership style is effective in his organization. His employees are generally motivated, perform highly, and are satisfied, and his store is highly profitable.

Developing an effective personal leadership style often is a challenge for managers at all levels in an organization. This challenge is often exacerbated when times are tough, due, for example, to an economic downturn or a decline in customer demand. The dot-com bust and the slowing economy in the early 2000s provided many leaders with just such a challenge.

While leading is one of the four principal tasks of managing, a distinction is often made between managers and leaders. When this distinction is made, managers are thought of as those organizational members who establish and implement procedures and processes to ensure smooth functioning and who are accountable for goal accomplishment.[16] Leaders look to the future, chart the course for the organization, and attract, retain, motivate, inspire, and develop relationships with employees based on trust and mutual respect.[17] Leaders provide meaning and purpose, seek innovation rather than stability, and impassion employees to work together to achieve the leaders' vision.[18]

Keith Chong hangs up a freshly pressed shirt at his dry-cleaning business in Glendale, California. As owner and manager of a dry-cleaning business, Chong takes a hands-on approach to leadership.

The personal leadership style of founders often has an enduring effect on organizations, as indicated in the following "Ethics in Action."

Ethics in Action

John Mackey's Personal Leadership Style

John Mackey cofounded the Whole Foods Market in 1980 with two former partners in a 10,000-square-foot location in Austin, Texas, and is the company's current CEO and president. Today, with 150 stores and 29,500 employees, Whole Foods is moving toward being included in the Fortune 500 list of the biggest companies in America (in terms of size, Whole Foods is 508 on the list).[19] Whole Foods started out to promote healthy eating, and in its early days, the stores were dominated by nuts, grains, and fresh produce. The stores today stock all sorts of food products as long as they are healthy; Whole Food does not carry food containing trans fats, artificial colors or flavors, or chemical preservatives or made from animals that are not treated humanely.[20]

Mackey is casual and informal but also opinionated, blunt, and direct.[21] He combines good business sense and an eye for the bottom line with spirituality and ethical values. Whole Foods markets tend to have profit margins and prices that are higher than those of typical grocery stores; Mackey is a firm believer in the merits of capitalism and making money. On the spiritual side, he has indicated that "love is the only reality. Everything else is merely a dream or illusion."[22]

Mackey's opinionated and direct nature carries over into the ethical values he promotes at Whole Foods. While acknowledging that Whole Foods has multiple stakeholders, he maintains that the interests of customers and employees come before the interest of shareholders and that the local community and the natural environment are important stakeholders for Whole Foods. While Mackey is against labor unions, he is employee-focused and strives to treat employees well and make sure they are satisfied with their jobs (employees are called "team members").[23] Mackey does not believe in huge pay differentials between top managers and rank-and-file team members; at Whole Foods, no salary can be set higher than 14 times that of the average team member, and 94 percent of the stock options that Whole Foods gives to its team members are granted to nonexecutives. Five percent of Whole Foods' profits each year are donated to charity, and Whole Foods pays its team members for performing community service.[24]

Whole Foods co-founder John Mackey maintains that the interests of customers and employees, such as those pictured here, come before the interest of shareholders.

Whole Foods' mission, the company's Declaration of Interdependence, was formulated in 1985 by Mackey and around 60 team members during a series of weekend retreats and was revised once in the 1980s and twice in the 1990s.[25] The declaration emphasizes interdependence among multiple stakeholders–including customers, team members, shareholders, communities, the natural environment, and business partners–in helping Whole Foods live up to its motto of "Whole

Foods, Whole People, Whole Planet."[26] Prominent themes in the declaration are high quality; customer satisfaction; frequent, open, and honest communication; team-member happiness and fulfillment; the embracing of diversity; community involvement; and active support of environmental sustainability. The Declaration of Interdependence, or parts of it, not only is espoused by team members but is visible in Whole Foods stores on posters and in free pamphlets. Even so, Whole Foods acknowledges that things might not always be just as they should be at the company and that working and living by the declaration's principles is a work in progress.[27] What is never in question is Mackey's passion to pursue what he believes in.

Leadership Styles Across Cultures

Some evidence suggests that leadership styles vary not only among individuals but also among countries or cultures. Some research indicates that European managers tend to be more humanistic or people-oriented than both Japanese and American managers. The collectivistic culture in Japan places prime emphasis on the group rather than the individual, so the importance of individuals' own personalities, needs, and desires is minimized. Organizations in the United States tend to be very profit-oriented and thus tend to downplay the importance of individual employees' needs and desires. Many countries in Europe have a more individualistic perspective than Japan and a more humanistic perspective than the United States, and this may result in some European managers' being more people-oriented than their Japanese or American counterparts. European managers, for example, tend to be reluctant to lay off employees, and when a layoff is absolutely necessary, they take careful steps to make it as painless as possible.[28]

Another cross-cultural difference occurs in time horizons. Managers in any one country often differ in their time horizons, but there are also cultural differences. For example, U.S. organizations tend to have a short-run profit orientation, and thus U.S. managers' personal leadership styles emphasize short-run performance. Japanese organizations tend to have a long-run growth orientation, so Japanese managers' personal leadership styles emphasize long-run performance. Justus Mische, a personnel manager at the European organization Hoechst, suggests that "Europe, at least the big international firms in Europe, have a philosophy between the Japanese, long term, and the United States, short term."[29] Research on these and other global aspects of leadership is in its infancy; as it continues, more cultural differences in managers' personal leadership styles may be discovered.

Power: The Key to Leadership

No matter what one's leadership style, a key component of effective leadership is found in the *power* the leader has to affect other people's behavior and get them to act in certain ways.[30] There are several types of power: legitimate, reward, coercive, expert, and referent power (see Figure 14.1).[31] Effective leaders take steps to ensure that they have sufficient levels of each type and that they use the power they have in beneficial ways.

Figure 14.1
Sources of Managerial Power

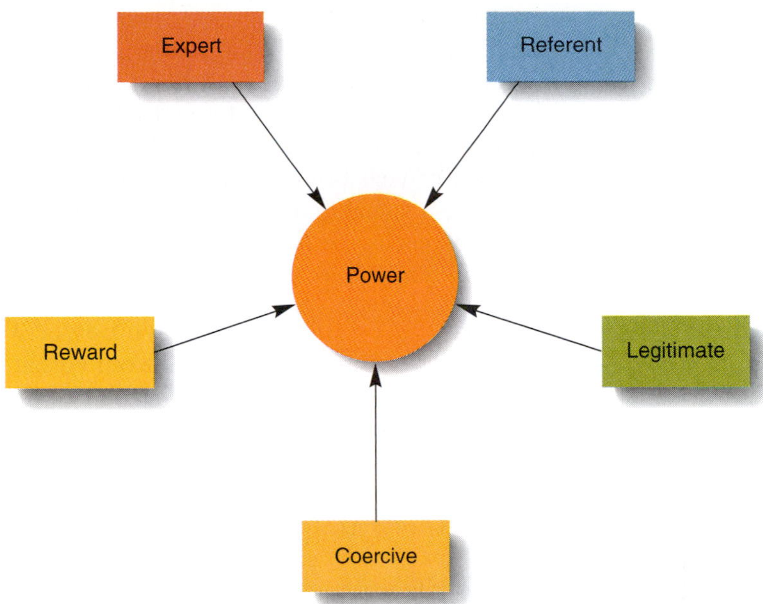

legitimate power The authority that a manager has by virtue of his or her position in an organization's hierarchy.

LEGITIMATE POWER **Legitimate power** is the authority a manager has by virtue of his or her position in an organization's hierarchy. Personal leadership style often influences how a manager exercises legitimate power. Take the case of Carol Loray, who is a first-line manager in a greeting card company and leads a group of 15 artists and designers. Loray has the legitimate power to hire new employees, assign projects to the artists and designers, monitor their work, and appraise their performance. She uses this power effectively. She always makes sure that her project assignments match the interests of her subordinates as much as possible so that they will enjoy their work. She monitors their work to make sure they are on track but does not engage in close supervision, which can hamper creativity. She makes sure her performance appraisals are developmental, providing concrete advice for areas where improvements could be made. Recently, Loray negotiated with her manager to increase her legitimate power so that now she can initiate and develop proposals for new card lines.

reward power The ability of a manager to give or withhold tangible and intangible rewards.

REWARD POWER **Reward power** is the ability of a manager to give or withhold tangible rewards (pay raises, bonuses, choice job assignments) and intangible rewards (verbal praise, a pat on the back, respect). As you learned in Chapter 13, members of an organization are motivated to perform at a high level by a variety of rewards. Being able to give or withhold rewards based on performance is a major source of power that allows managers to have a highly motivated workforce. Managers of salespeople in retail organizations like Neiman Marcus and Dillard's Department Stores, in car dealerships like DaimlerChrysler and Ford, and in travel agencies like Liberty Travel and the Travel Company often use their reward power to motivate their subordinates. Subordinates in organizations such as these often receive commissions on whatever they sell and rewards for the quality of their customer service, which motivate them to do the best they can.

Effective managers use their reward power in such a way that subordinates feel that their rewards signal that they are doing a good job and their efforts are appreciated. Ineffective managers use rewards in a more controlling manner (wielding the "stick' instead of offering the "carrot") that signals to subordinates that the manager has the upper hand. Managers also can take steps to increase their reward power. Carol Loray had the legitimate power to appraise her subordinates' performance, but she lacked the reward power to distribute raises and end-of-year bonuses until she discussed with her own manager why this would be a valuable motivational tool for her to use. Loray now receives a pool of money each year for salary increases and bonuses and has the reward power to distribute them as she sees fit.

coercive power The ability of a manager to punish others.

COERCIVE POWER **Coercive power** is the ability of a manager to punish others. Punishment can range from verbal reprimands to reductions in pay or working hours to actual dismissal. In the previous chapter, we discussed how punishment can have negative side effects such as resentment and retaliation and should be used only when necessary (for example, to curtail a dangerous behavior). Managers who rely heavily on coercive power tend to be ineffective as leaders and sometimes even get fired themselves. William J. Fife is one example; he was fired from his position as CEO of Giddings and Lewis Inc., a manufacturer of factory equipment, because of his overreliance on coercive power. In meetings, Fife often verbally criticized, attacked, and embarrassed top managers. Realizing how destructive Fife's use of punishment was for them and the company, these managers complained to the board of directors, who, after a careful consideration of the issues, asked Fife to resign.[32]

Excessive use of coercive power seldom produces high performance and is questionable ethically. Sometimes it amounts to a form of mental abuse, robbing workers of their dignity and causing excessive levels of stress. Overuse of coercive power can even result in dangerous working conditions. Better results and, importantly, an ethical workplace that respects employee dignity can be obtained by using reward power.

expert power Power that is based on the special knowledge, skills, and expertise that a leader possesses.

EXPERT POWER **Expert power** is based on the special knowledge, skills, and expertise that a leader possesses. The nature of expert power varies, depending on the leader's level in the hierarchy. First-level and middle managers often have technical expertise relevant to the tasks that their subordinates perform. Their expert power gives them considerable influence over subordinates. Carol Loray has expert power: She is an artist herself and has drawn and designed some of her company's top-selling greeting cards.

Some top managers derive expert power from their technical expertise. Craig Barret, CEO of Intel, has a PhD in materials science from Stanford University and is very knowledgeable about the ins and outs of Intel's business-producing semiconductors and microprocessors.[33] Similarly, Bill Gates, chairman of Microsoft, and CEO Steve Ballmer have expertise in software design; and Tachi Yamada, executive director and chairman of research and development at GlaxoSmithKline (profiled in "A Manager's Challenge" in Chapter 7), has an MD and was an active researcher and chairman of the Internal Medicine Department of the University of Michigan Medical School. Many top-level managers, however, lack technical expertise and derive their expert power from their abilities as decision makers, planners, and strategists. Jack Welch, the former, well-known leader and CEO of General Electric, summed it up this way: "The basic thing that we at the top of the company know is that we don't know the business. What we have, I hope, is the ability to allocate resources, people, and dollars."[34]

Effective leaders take steps to ensure that they have an adequate amount of expert power to perform their leadership roles. They may obtain additional training or education in their fields, make sure they keep up to date with the latest developments and changes in technology, stay abreast of changes in their fields through involvement in professional associations, and read widely to be aware of momentous changes in the organization's task and general environments. Expert power tends to be best used in a guiding or coaching manner rather than in an arrogant, high-handed manner.

referent power Power that comes from subordinates' and co-workers' respect, admiration, and loyalty.

REFERENT POWER **Referent power** is more informal than the other kinds of power. Referent power is a function of the personal characteristics of a leader; it is the power that comes from subordinates' and co-workers' respect, admiration, and loyalty. Leaders who are likable and whom subordinates wish to use as a role model are especially likely to possess referent power. Rochelle Lazarus, a top manager at the advertising agency Ogilvy & Mather, won IBM's worldwide advertising account in part because of her referent power.[35]

In addition to being a valuable asset for top managers like Lazarus, referent power can help first-line and middle managers be effective leaders as well. Sally Carruthers, for example, is the first-level manager of a group of secretaries in the finance department of a large state university. Carruthers's secretaries are known to be among the best in the university. Much of their willingness to go above and beyond the call of duty has been attributed to Carruthers's warm and caring nature, which makes each of them feel important and valued. Managers can take steps to increase their referent power, such as taking time to get to know their subordinates and showing interest in and concern for them.

Empowerment: An Ingredient in Modern Management

empowerment Expanding employees' tasks and responsibilities.

More and more managers today are incorporating into their personal leadership styles an aspect that at first glance seems to be the opposite of being a leader. In Chapter 1, we described how **empowerment**–the process of giving employees at all levels in the organization the authority to make decisions, be responsible for their outcomes, improve quality, and cut costs–is becoming increasingly popular in organizations. When leaders empower their subordinates, the subordinates typically take over some of the responsibilities and authority that used to reside with the leader or manager, such as the right to reject parts that do not meet quality standards, the right to check one's own work, and the right to schedule work activities. Empowered subordinates are given the power to make some of the decisions that their leaders or supervisors used to make.

Empowerment might seem to be the opposite of effective leadership because managers are allowing subordinates to take a more active role in leading themselves. In actuality, however, empowerment can contribute to effective leadership for several reasons:

- Empowerment increases a manager's ability to get things done because the manager has the support and help of subordinates who may have special knowledge of work tasks.

- Empowerment often increases workers' involvement, motivation, and commitment, and this helps ensure that they are working toward organizational goals.
- Empowerment gives managers more time to concentrate on their pressing concerns because they spend less time on day-to-day supervisory activities.

Effective managers like Steve Ballmer realize the benefits of empowerment. The personal leadership style of managers who empower subordinates often entails developing subordinates' ability to make good decisions as well as being their guide, coach, and source of inspiration. Empowerment is a popular trend in the United States at companies as diverse as United Parcel Service (a package delivery company) and Coram Healthcare Corporation (a provider of medical equipment and services). Empowerment is also taking off around the world.[36] For instance, companies in South Korea (such as Samsung, Hyundai, and Daewoo), in which decision making typically was centralized with the founding families, are now empowering managers at lower levels to make decisions.[37]

Trait and Behavior Models of Leadership

Leading is such an important process in all organizations–nonprofit organizations, government agencies, and schools, as well as for-profit corporations–that it has been researched for decades. Early approaches to leadership, called the *trait model* and the *behavior model,* sought to determine what effective leaders are like as people and what they do that makes them so effective.

The Trait Model

The trait model of leadership focused on identifying the personal characteristics that cause effective leadership. Researchers thought effective leaders must have certain personal qualities that set them apart from ineffective leaders and from people who never become leaders. Decades of research (beginning in the 1930s) and hundreds of studies indicate that certain personal characteristics do appear to be associated with effective leadership. (See Table 14.1 for a list of these.)[38] Notice that although this model is called the "trait" model, some of the personal characteristics that it identifies are not personality traits per se but, rather, are concerned with a leader's skills, abilities, knowledge, and expertise. As "A Manager's Challenge" shows, Steve Ballmer certainly appears to possess many of these characteristics (such as intelligence, knowledge and expertise, self-confidence, high energy, and integrity and honesty). Leaders who do not possess these traits may be ineffective.

Traits alone are not the key to understanding leader effectiveness, however. Some effective leaders do not possess all of these traits, and some leaders who do possess them are not effective in their leadership roles. This lack of a consistent relationship between leader traits and leader effectiveness led researchers to shift their attention away from traits and to search for new explanations for effective leadership. Rather than focusing on what leaders are like (the traits they possess), researchers began looking at what effective leaders actually do–in other words, at the behaviors that allow effective leaders to influence their subordinates to achieve group and organizational goals.

Table 14.1
Traits and Personal Characteristics Related to Effective Leadership

Trait	Description
Intelligence	Helps managers understand complex issues and solve problems
Knowledge and expertise	Helps managers make good decisions and discover ways to increase efficiency and effectiveness
Dominance	Helps managers influence their subordinates to achieve organizational goals
Self-confidence	Contributes to managers' effectively influencing subordinates and persisting when faced with obstacles or difficulties
High energy	Helps managers deal with the many demands they face
Tolerance for stress	Helps managers deal with uncertainty and make difficult decisions
Integrity and honesty	Helps managers behave ethically and earn their subordinates' trust and confidence
Maturity	Helps managers avoid acting selfishly, control their feelings, and admit when they have made a mistake

The Behavior Model

After extensive study in the 1940s and 1950s, researchers at Ohio State University identified two basic kinds of leader behaviors that many leaders in the United States, Germany, and other countries engaged in to influence their subordinates: consideration and initiating structure.[39]

consideration Behavior indicating that a manager trusts, respects, and cares about subordinates.

CONSIDERATION Leaders engage in **consideration** when they show their subordinates that they trust, respect, and care about them. Managers who truly look out for the well-being of their subordinates and do what they can to help subordinates feel good and enjoy their work perform consideration behaviors. In "A Manager's Challenge," Steve Ballmer engaged in consideration when he arranged for employees to receive cash for their underwater stock options.

initiating structure Behavior that managers engage in to ensure that work gets done, subordinates perform their jobs acceptably, and the organization is efficient and effective.

INITIATING STRUCTURE Leaders engage in **initiating structure** when they take steps to make sure that work gets done, subordinates perform their jobs acceptably, and the organization is efficient and effective. Assigning tasks to individuals or work groups, letting subordinates know what is expected of them, deciding how work should be done, making schedules, encouraging adherence to rules and regulations, and motivating subordinates to do a good job are all examples of initiating structure.[40] Michael Teckel, the manager of an upscale store selling imported men's and women's shoes in a midwestern city, engages in initiating structure when he establishes weekly work, lunch, and break schedules to ensure that the store has enough salespeople on the floor. Teckle also initiates structure when he discusses the latest shoe designs with his subordinates so that they are knowledgeable with customers, when he encourages adherence to the store's refund and exchange policies, and when he encourages his staff to provide high-quality customer service and to avoid a hard-sell approach. In "A Manager's Challenge," Steve Ballmer engaged in initiating structure when he divided Microsoft into divisions, instituted a formal performance appraisal system, and revamped the compensation system.

Initiating structure and consideration are independent leader behaviors. Leaders can be high on both, low on both, or high on one and low on the other. As indicated in the following "Managing Globally," many effective leaders like Fujio Cho of Toyota engage in both of these behaviors.

Managing Globally

Toyota Is on a Roll

Toyota president Fujio Cho is driven by speed and flexibility; cost-efficient and flexible production lines that can switch between multiple car models to meet changes in customer demand are his mantra. Toyota is close to becoming the third-largest automobile manufacturer in the United States (DaimlerChrysler currently has the number-three spot), has sales of over $140 billion, and has better profit margins than General Motors, Ford, and DaimlerChrysler.[41] Cho is leading a major transformation of Toyota to develop a global, flexible manufacturing system for making cars at record speed, with minimal defects, and in a cost-effective manner. And Toyota has $30 billion in cash and securities to weather any unforeseen problems. As Cho puts it, "This is a company that does not fear failure."[42] By all counts, Cho is effectively leading Toyota on a path to dominate the global car industry.[43]

Cho emphasizes consideration in his modest, cheerful approach to being on top of every problem and issue that Toyota faces. He is down to earth and genial. When he led the opening of Toyota's biggest factory in Georgetown, Kentucky, he often worked alongside employees on the factory floor and expressed appreciation for the work that they were doing. He also became involved in the local community and was a speaker at Rotary Club meetings. His concern for people shows through in the smile that often graces his face and in his affable manner of dealing with employees and letting them know he respects and cares about them.[44]

Cho has been engaging in initiating structure as he leads Toyota toward the goal of having 15 percent of total global automobile sales by 2010. For example, he spearheaded a program with suppliers to dramatically reduce the number of steps in making car parts and cars and has reduced Toyota's costs (without layoffs or plant shutdowns) by over $2.5 billion. The flexible, global manufacturing system he is developing will enable Toyota factories around the world to both customize cars for their local markets and make cars for other markets where customer demand exceeds supply, all in a speedy, cost-efficient manner. Cho instituted Toyota's Construction of Cost Competitiveness for the 21st Century (CCC21) program with the goal of reducing prices of components for

Toyota President Fujio Cho has set aggressive goals for the company (initiating structure), while also showing employees that he respects and cares about them (consideration).

new car models by 30 percent. *Kaizen,* Toyota's renowned system of continuous improvement, is being taken to another level by Cho, who is striving to make each and every Toyota plant capable of producing high-quality vehicles at low costs.[45] All in all, Cho's consideration and initiating structure are helping transform Toyota into a carmaker to be reckoned with.

Leadership researchers have identified leader behaviors similar to consideration and initiating structure. Researchers at the University of Michigan, for example, identified two categories of leadership behaviors, *employee-centered behaviors* and *job-oriented behaviors,* that correspond roughly to consideration and initiating structure, respectively.[46] Models of leadership popular with consultants also tend to zero in on these two kinds of behaviors. For example, Robert Blake and Jane Mouton's Managerial Grid focuses on *concern for people* (similar to consideration) and *concern for production* (similar to initiating structure). Blake and Mouton advise that effective leadership often requires both a high level of concern for people and a high level of concern for production.[47] As another example, Paul Hersey and Kenneth Blanchard's model focuses on *supportive behaviors* (similar to consideration) and *task-oriented behaviors* (similar to initiating structure). According to Hersey and Blanchard, leaders need to consider the nature of their subordinates when trying to determine the extent to which they should perform these two behaviors.[48]

You might expect that effective leaders and managers would perform both kinds of behaviors, but research has found that this is not necessarily the case. The relationship between performance of consideration and initiating-structure behaviors and leader effectiveness is not clear-cut. Some leaders are effective even when they do not perform consideration or initiating-structure behaviors, and some leaders are ineffective even when they do perform both kinds of behaviors. Like the trait model of leadership, the behavior model alone cannot explain leader effectiveness. Realizing this, researchers began building more complicated models of leadership, models focused not only on the leader and what he or she does but also on the situation or context in which leadership occurs.

Contingency Models of Leadership

Simply possessing certain traits or performing certain behaviors does not ensure that a manager will be an effective leader in all situations calling for leadership. Some managers who seem to possess the "right" traits and perform the "right" behaviors turn out to be ineffective leaders. Managers lead in a wide variety of situations and organizations and have various kinds of subordinates performing diverse tasks in a multiplicity of environmental contexts. Given the wide variety of situations in which leadership occurs, what makes a manager an effective leader in one situation (such as certain traits or certain behaviors) is not necessarily what that manager needs to be equally effective in a different situation. An effective army general might not be an effective university president; an effective manager of a restaurant might not be an effective manager of a clothing store; an effective coach of a football team might not be an effective manager of a fitness center; and an effective first-line manager in a manufacturing company might not be an effective middle manager. The traits or behaviors that may contribute to a manager's being an effective leader in one situation might actually result in the same manager being an ineffective leader in another situation.

Contingency models of leadership take into account the situation or context within which leadership occurs. According to contingency models, whether or not a manager is an effective leader is the result of the interplay between what the manager is like, what he or she does, and the situation in which leadership takes place. Contingency models propose that whether a leader who possesses certain traits or performs certain behaviors is effective depends on, or is contingent on, the situation or context. In this section, we discuss three prominent contingency models developed to shed light on what makes managers effective leaders: Fred Fiedler's contingency model, Robert House's path-goal theory, and the leader substitutes model. As you will see, these leadership models are complementary; each focuses on a somewhat different aspect of effective leadership in organizations.

Fiedler's Contingency Model

Fred E. Fiedler was among the first leadership researchers to acknowledge that effective leadership is contingent on, or depends on, the characteristics of the leader *and* of the situation. Fiedler's contingency model helps explain why a manager may be an effective leader in one situation and ineffective in another; it also suggests which kinds of managers are likely to be most effective in which situations.[49]

LEADER STYLE As with the trait approach, Fiedler hypothesized that personal characteristics can influence leader effectiveness. He used the term *leader style* to refer to a manager's characteristic approach to leadership and identified two basic leader styles: relationship-oriented and task-oriented. All managers can be described as having one style or the other.

relationship-oriented leaders Leaders whose primary concern is to develop good relationships with their subordinates and to be liked by them.

Relationship-oriented leaders are primarily concerned with developing good relationships with their subordinates and being liked by them. Relationship-oriented managers focus on having high-quality interpersonal relationships with subordinates. This does not mean, however, that the job does not get done when relationship-oriented leaders are at the helm. But it does mean that the quality of interpersonal relationships with subordinates is a prime concern for relationship-oriented leaders. Lawrence Fish, for example, is the chairman of Citizens Financial Group Inc. of Providence, Rhode Island, which has tripled its assets in the last three years. As the top manager who helped to engineer this rapid growth, Fish has never lost sight of the importance of good relationships and personally writes a thank-you note to at least one of his subordinates each day.[50]

task-oriented leaders Leaders whose primary concern is to ensure that subordinates perform at a high level.

Task-oriented leaders are primarily concerned with ensuring that subordinates perform at a high level. Task-oriented managers focus on task accomplishment and making sure the job gets done. Some task-oriented leaders, like the top managers of the family-owned C. R. England Refrigerated Trucking Company based in Salt Lake City, Utah, go so far as to closely measure and evaluate performance on a weekly basis to ensure subordinates are performing as well as they can.[51]

In his research, Fiedler measured leader style by asking leaders to rate the coworker with whom they have had the most difficulty working (called the *least-*

preferred co-worker or *LPC*) on a number of dimensions, such as whether the person is boring or interesting, gloomy or cheerful, enthusiastic or unenthusiastic, cooperative or uncooperative. Relationship-oriented leaders tend to describe the LPC in relatively positive terms; their concern for good relationships leads them to think about others in positive terms. Task-oriented leaders tend to describe the LPC in negative terms; their concern for task accomplishment causes them to think badly about others who make getting the job done difficult. Thus, relationship-oriented and task-oriented leaders are sometimes referred to as high-LPC and low-LPC leaders, respectively.

SITUATIONAL CHARACTERISTICS According to Fiedler, leadership style is an enduring characteristic; managers cannot change their style, nor can they adopt different styles in different kinds of situations. With this in mind, Fiedler identified three situational characteristics that are important determinants of how favorable a situation is for leading: leader-member relations, task structure, and position power. When a situation is favorable for leading, it is relatively easy for a manager to influence subordinates so that they perform at a high level and contribute to organizational efficiency and effectiveness. In a situation unfavorable for leading, it is much more difficult for a manager to exert influence.

leader-member relations The extent to which followers like, trust, and are loyal to their leader; a determinant of how favorable a situation is for leading.

LEADER-MEMBER RELATIONS The first situational characteristic that Fiedler described, **leader-member relations,** is the extent to which followers like, trust, and are loyal to their leader. Situations are more favorable for leading when leader-member relations are good.

task structure The extent to which the work to be performed is clear-cut so that a leader's subordinates know what needs to be accomplished and how to go about doing it; a determinant of how favorable a situation is for leading.

TASK STRUCTURE The second situational characteristic that Fiedler described, **task structure,** is the extent to which the work to be performed is clear-cut so that a leader's subordinates know what needs to be accomplished and how to go about doing it. When task structure is high, the situation is favorable for leading. When task structure is low, goals may be vague, subordinates may be unsure of what they should be doing or how they should do it, and the situation is unfavorable for leading.

Task structure was low for Geraldine Laybourne when she was a top manager at Nickelodeon, the children's television network. It was never precisely clear what would appeal to her young viewers, whose tastes can change dramatically, or how to motivate her subordinates to come up with creative and novel ideas.[52] In contrast, Herman Mashaba, founder and owner of Black Like Me, a hair care products company based in South Africa, seems to have relatively high task structure in his leadership situation. His company's goals are to produce and sell inexpensive hair care products to native Africans, and managers accomplish these goals by using simple yet appealing packaging and distributing the products through neighborhood beauty salons.[53]

position power The amount of legitimate, reward, and coercive power that a leader has by virtue of his or her position in an organization; a determinant of how favorable a situation is for leading.

POSITION POWER The third situational characteristic that Fiedler described, **position power,** is the amount of legitimate, reward, and coercive power a leader has by virtue of his or her position in an organization. Leadership situations are more favorable for leading when position power is strong.

COMBINING LEADER STYLE AND THE SITUATION By taking all possible combinations of good and poor leader-member relations, high and low task structure, and strong and weak position power, Fiedler identified eight leadership situations, which vary in their favorability for leading (see Figure 14.2).

Figure 14.2
Fiedler's Contingency Theory of Leadership

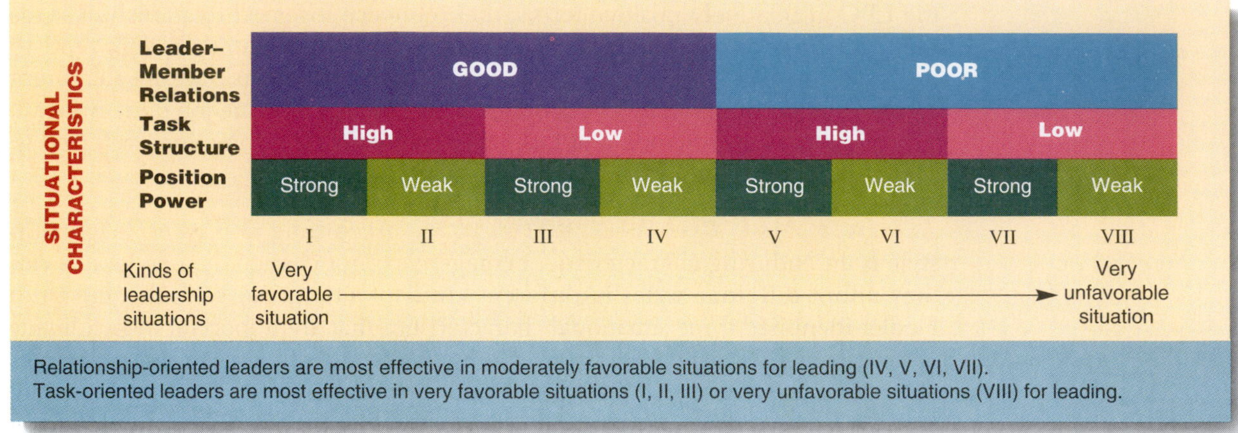

After extensive research, he determined that relationship-oriented leaders are most effective in moderately favorable situations (situations IV, V, VI, and VII in Figure 14.2) and task-oriented leaders are most effective in very favorable (situations I, II, and III) or very unfavorable situations (situation VIII).

PUTTING THE CONTINGENCY MODEL INTO PRACTICE Recall that, according to Fiedler, leader style is an enduring characteristic that managers cannot change. This suggests that to be effective, either managers need to be placed in leadership situations that fit their style or situations need to be changed to suit the managers. Situations can be changed, for example, by giving a manager more position power or taking steps to increase task structure, such as by clarifying goals.

Take the case of Mark Compton, a relationship-oriented leader employed by a small construction company, who was in a very unfavorable situation and having a rough time leading his construction crew. His subordinates did not trust him to look out for their well-being (poor leader-member relations); the construction jobs he supervised tended to be novel and complex (low task structure); and he had no control over the rewards and disciplinary actions his subordinates received (weak position power). Recognizing the need to improve matters, Compton's supervisor gave him the power to reward crew members with bonuses and overtime work as he saw fit and to discipline crew members for poor-quality work and unsafe on-the-job behavior. As his leadership situation improved to moderately favorable, so too did Compton's effectiveness as a leader and the performance of his crew.

Research studies tend to support some aspects of Fiedler's model but also suggest that, like most theories, it needs some modifications.[54] Some researchers have questioned what the LPC scale really measures. Others find fault with the model's premise that leaders cannot alter their styles. That is, it is likely that at least some leaders can diagnose the situation they are in and, when their style is inappropriate for the situation, modify their style so that it is more in line with what the leadership situation calls for.

House's Path-Goal Theory

path-goal theory A contingency model of leadership proposing that leaders can motivate subordinates by identifying their desired outcomes, rewarding them for high performance and the attainment of work goals with these desired outcomes, and clarifying for them the paths leading to the attainment of work goals.

In what he called **path-goal theory,** leadership researcher Robert House focused on what leaders can do to motivate their subordinates to achieve group and organizational goals.[55] The premise of path-goal theory is that effective leaders motivate subordinates to achieve goals by (1) clearly identifying the outcomes that subordinates are trying to obtain from the workplace, (2) rewarding subordinates with these outcomes for high performance and the attainment of work goals, and (3) clarifying for subordinates the *paths* leading to the attainment of work *goals*. Path-goal theory is a contingency model because it proposes that the steps managers should take to motivate subordinates depend on both the nature of the subordinates and the type of work they do.

Based on the expectancy theory of motivation (see Chapter 13), path-goal theory provides managers with three guidelines to follow to be effective leaders.

1. *Find out what outcomes your subordinates are trying to obtain from their jobs and the organization.* These outcomes can range from satisfactory pay and job security to reasonable working hours and interesting and challenging job assignments. After identifying these outcomes, the manager should have the *reward power* needed to distribute or withhold the outcomes. Mark Crane, for example, is the vice principal of a large elementary school. Crane determined that the teachers he leads are trying to obtain the following outcomes from their jobs: pay raises, autonomy in the classroom, and the choice of which grades they teach. Crane had reward power for the latter two outcomes, but the school's principal determined how the pool of money for raises was to be distributed each year. Because Crane was the first-line manager who led the teachers and was most familiar with their performance, he asked the principal (his boss) to give him some say in determining pay raises. Realizing that this made a lot of sense, his principal gave Crane full power to distribute raises and requested only that Crane review his decisions with him prior to informing the teachers about them.

2. *Reward subordinates for high performance and goal attainment with the outcomes they desire.* The teachers and administrators at Crane's school considered several dimensions of teacher performance to be critical to achieving their goal of providing high-quality education: excellent in-class instruction, special programs to enhance student interest and learning (such as science and computer projects), and availability for meetings with parents to discuss their children's progress and special needs. Crane distributed pay raises to the teachers based on the extent to which they performed highly on each of these dimensions. The top-performing teachers were given first choice of grade assignments and also had practically complete autonomy in their classrooms.

3. *Clarify the paths to goal attainment for subordinates, remove any obstacles to high performance, and express confidence in subordinates' capabilities.* This does not mean that a manager needs to tell subordinates what to do. Rather, it means that a manager needs to make sure that subordinates are clear about what they should be trying to accomplish and have the capabilities, resources, and confidence levels needed to be successful. Crane made sure that all the teachers understood the importance of the three targeted goals and asked them whether, to reach them, they needed any special resources or supplies for their classes. Crane also gave additional coaching and guidance to teachers who seemed to be struggling. For example, Patrick Conolly, in his first year of teaching after graduate school, was unsure about how to use special projects in a third-grade class and how to react to parents who were critical. Conolly's actual teaching was excellent, but he even felt insecure about how he was doing on this dimension. To help build Conolly's confidence, Crane told Conolly that he truly thought he could be one of the school's top teachers (which was true). He gave Conolly some ideas about special projects that worked particularly well with the third grade, such as a writing project. Crane also role-played teacher-parent interactions with Conolly. Conolly played the role of a particularly dissatisfied or troubled parent, while Crane played the role of a teacher trying to solve the underlying problem while making the parent feel that his or her child's needs were being met. Crane's efforts to clarify the paths to goal attainment for Conolly paid off: Within two years the local PTS voted Conolly teacher of the year.

Path-goal theory identifies four kinds of leadership behaviors that motivate subordinates:

- *Directive behaviors* are similar to initiating structure and include setting goals, assigning tasks, showing subordinates how to complete tasks, and taking concrete steps to improve performance.
- *Supportive behaviors* are similar to consideration and include expressing concern for subordinates and looking out for their best interests.
- *Participative behaviors* give subordinates a say in matters and decisions that affect them.
- *Achievement-oriented behaviors* motivate subordinates to perform at the highest level possible by, for example, setting very challenging goals, expecting that they be met, and believing in subordinates' capabilities.

Which of these behaviors should managers use to lead effectively? The answer to this question depends, or is contingent on, the nature of the subordinates and the kind of work they do.

Directive behaviors may be beneficial when subordinates are having difficulty completing assigned tasks, but they might be detrimental when subordinates are independent thinkers who work best when left alone. *Supportive* behaviors are often advisable when subordinates are experiencing high levels of stress. *Participative* behaviors can be particularly effective when subordinates' support of a decision is required. *Achievement-oriented* behaviors may increase motivation levels of highly capable subordinates who are bored from having too few challenges, but they might backfire if used with subordinates who are already pushed to their limit.

Effective managers seem to have a knack for determining what kinds of leader behaviors are likely to work in different situations and result in increased effectiveness, as indicated in the following "Management Insight."

Supporting Creativity

What do playing in an orchestra and designing high-status automobiles have in common? Both activities require creativity from artistic individuals. Effectively leading workers who are engaged in creative activities can be a challenge. For example, too much initiating structure can inhibit their creativity. Roger Nierenberg, conductor of the Stamford, Connecticut, Symphony Orchestra has long recognized this, and rather than being overly controlling with musicians, he emphasizes supportive behaviors. Nierenberg utilizes positive feedback to support his musicians, never blames them when things go wrong, and provides direction in an encouraging manner.[56]

A positive, encouraging style of leadership often gets the best results from creative employees—whether they're musicians or automobile designers.

Nierenberg's positive, encouraging style of leading and conducting also can be applied in more traditional work environments. For example, in his leadership classes for managers at major corporations, such as Lucent Technologies and Georgia-Pacific, he coaches the managers on how to commit to a course of action and direct their subordinates to attain it in a supportive, uncritical manner.[57]

This approach to leading creative workers is applied in other countries as well. For example, Chris Bangle, who heads BMW's global design efforts in Munich, Germany, takes great pains to shield creative designers of BMW interiors and exteriors from critical comments or negative feedback from others in the organization, such as market analysts and engineers. Rather than receiving critiques, designers need, above all else, support from leadership and the freedom to explore different designs, as well as encouraging direction to reach closure in a reasonably timely fashion.[58] Bangle sees this kind of encouraging and supportive leadership as key to BMW's competitive advantage in designing cars like "moving works of art that express the driver's love of quality."[59]

The Leader Substitutes Model

leadership substitute A characteristic of a subordinate or characteristic of a situation or context that acts in place of the influence of a leader and makes leadership unnecessary.

The leader substitutes model suggests that leadership is sometimes unnecessary because substitutes for leadership are present. A **leadership substitute** is something that acts in place of the influence of a leader and makes leadership unnecessary. This model suggests that under certain conditions managers do not have to play a leadership role–that members of an organization sometimes can perform highly without a manager exerting influence over them.[60] The leader substitutes model is a contingency model because it suggests that in some situations leadership is unnecessary.

Take the case of David Cotsonas, who teaches English at a foreign-language school in Cyprus, an island in the Mediterranean Sea. Cotsonas is fluent in Greek, English, and French, is an excellent teacher, and is highly motivated. Many of his students are businesspeople who have some rudimentary English skills and wish to increase their fluency to be able to conduct more of their business in English. He enjoys not only teaching them English but also learning about the work they do, and he often keeps in touch with his students after they finish his classes. Cotsonas meets with the director of the school twice a year to discuss semiannual class schedules and enrollments.

With practically no influence from a leader, Cotsonas is a highly motivated top performer at the school. In his situation, leadership is unnecessary because substitutes for leadership are present. Cotsonas's teaching expertise, his motivation, and his enjoyment of his work all are substitutes for the influence of a leader–in this case, the school's director. If the school's director were to try to exert influence over the way Cotsonas goes about performing his job, Cotsonas would probably resent this infringement on his autonomy, and it is unlikely that his performance would improve because he is already one of the school's best teachers.

As in Cotsonas's case, *characteristics of subordinates*–such as their skills, abilities, experience, knowledge, and motivation–can be substitutes for leadership.[61] *Characteristics of the situation or context*–such as the extent to which the work is interesting and enjoyable–also can be substitutes. When work is interesting and enjoyable, as it is for Cotsonas, jobholders do not need to be coaxed into performing because performing is rewarding in its own right. Similarly, when managers *empower* their subordinates or use *self-managed work teams* (discussed in detail in Chapter 15), the need for leadership influence from a manager is decreased because team members manage themselves.

Substitutes for leadership can increase organizational efficiency and effectiveness because they free up some of managers' valuable time and allow managers to focus their efforts on discovering new ways to improve organizational effectiveness. The director of the language school, for example, was able to spend much of his time making arrangements to open a second school in Rhodes, an island in the Aegean Sea, because of the presence of leadership substitutes, not only in the case of Cotsonas but for most of the other teachers at the school as well.

Bringing It All Together

Effective leadership in organizations occurs when managers take steps to lead in a way that is appropriate for the situation or context in which leadership occurs and for the subordinates who are being led. The three contingency models of leadership discussed above help managers hone in on the necessary ingredients for effective leadership. They are complementary in that each one looks at the leadership question from a different angle. Fiedler's contingency model explores how a manager's leadership style needs to be matched to that person's leadership situation for maximum effectiveness. House's path-goal theory focuses on how managers should motivate subordinates and describes the specific kinds of behaviors that managers can engage in to have a highly motivated workforce. The leadership substitutes model alerts managers to the fact that sometimes they do not need to exert influence over subordinates and thus can free up their time for other important activities. Table 14.2 recaps these three contingency models of leadership.

Transformational Leadership

Time and time again, throughout business history, certain leaders seem to literally transform their organizations, making sweeping changes to revitalize and renew operations. For example, in the 1990s, the chief executive of the German electronics company Siemens, Heinrich von Pierer, dramatically transformed his company. When von Pierer took over in 1992, Siemens had a rigid hierarchy in place, was suffering from increased global competition, and was saddled with a conservative, perfectionist culture that stifled creativity and innovation and slowed decision making. Von Pierer's changes at Siemens have been nothing short of revolutionary.[62] At the new Siemens, subordinates critique their managers, who receive training in how to be more democratic and participative

Table 14.2
Contingency Models of Leadership

Model	Focus	Key Contingencies
Fiedler's Contingency Model	Describes two leader styles, relationship-oriented and task-oriented, and the kinds of situations in which each kind of leader will be most effective	Whether or not a relationship-oriented or a task-oriented leader is effective is contingent on the situation
House's Path-Goal Theory	Describes how effective leaders motivate their followers	The behaviors that managers should engage in to be effective leaders are contingent on the nature of the subordinates and the work they do
Leader Substitutes Model	Describes when leadership is unnecessary	Whether or not leadership is necessary for subordinates to perform highly is contingent on characteristics of the subordinates and the situation

and spur creativity. Employees are no longer afraid to speak their minds, and the quest for innovation is a driving force throughout the company.

Von Pierer is literally transforming Siemens and its thousands of employees into being more innovative and taking the steps needed to gain a competitive advantage. When managers have such dramatic effects on their subordinates and on an organization as a whole, they are engaging in transformational leadership. **Transformational leadership** occurs when managers change (or transform) their subordinates in the following three important ways.[63]

transformational leadership Leadership that makes subordinates aware of the importance of their jobs and performance to the organization and aware of their own needs for personal growth and that motivates subordinates to work for the good of the organization.

1. *Transformational managers make subordinates aware of how important their jobs are for the organization and how necessary it is for them to perform those jobs as best they can so that the organization can attain its goals.* Von Pierer sent the message throughout Siemens not only that innovating, cost cutting, and increasing customer service and satisfaction were everyone's responsibilities but also that improvements could be and needed to be made in these areas. For example, when von Pierer realized that managers in charge of microprocessor sales were not aware of the importance of their jobs and of performing them in a top-notch fashion, he had managers from Siemens's top microprocessor customers give the Siemens's microprocessor managers feedback about their poor service and unreliable delivery schedules. The microprocessor managers quickly realized how important it was for them to take steps to improve customer service.

2. *Transformational managers make their subordinates aware of the subordinates' own needs for personal growth, development, and accomplishment.* Von Pierer has made Siemens's employees aware of their own needs in this regard through numerous workshops and training sessions, through empowering employees throughout the company, through the development of fast-track career programs, and through increased reliance on self-managed work teams.[64]

3. *Transformational managers motivate their subordinates to work for the good of the organization as a whole, not just for their own personal gain or benefit.* Von Pierer's message to Siemens's employees has been clear: Dramatic changes in the way they perform their jobs are crucial for the future viability and success of Siemens. As von Pierer puts it, "We have to keep asking ourselves: Are we flexible enough? Are we changing enough?"[65] One way von Pierer has tried to get all employees thinking in these terms is by inserting in the company magazine distributed to all employees self-addressed postcards urging them to send in their ideas for making improvements to him directly.

When managers transform their subordinates in these three ways, subordinates trust the manager, are highly motivated, and help the organization achieve its goals. As a result of von Pierer's transformational leadership, for example, a team of Siemens's engineers working in blue jeans in a rented house developed a tool control system in one-third the time and at one-third the cost of other similar systems developed at Siemens.[66] How do managers like von Pierer transform subordinates and produce dramatic effects in their organizations? There are at least three ways in which managers and other transformational leaders can influence their followers: by being a charismatic leader, by intellectually stimulating subordinates, and by engaging in developmental consideration (see Table 14.3).

Being a Charismatic Leader

charismatic leader An enthusiastic, self-confident leader who is able to clearly communicate his or her vision of how good things could be.

Transformational managers are **charismatic leaders.** They have a vision of how good things could be in their work groups and organizations that is in contrast with the status quo. Their vision usually entails dramatic improvements in group and organizational performance as a result of changes in the organization's structure, culture, strategy, decision making, and other critical processes and factors. This vision paves the way for gaining a competitive advantage. From "A Manager's Challenge" it is clear that part of Steve Ballmer's vision for Microsoft is boosting the perceived value of the company's technology through seamlessly integrated software, developing innovative software to meet the needs of corporate customers and consumers, and having an empowered workforce that effectively and efficiently develops creative integrative software that sets new standards.

Table 14.3
Transformational Leadership

Transformational Managers
- Are charismatic
- Intellectually stimulate subordinates
- Engage in developmental consideration

Subordinates of Transformational Managers
- Have increased awareness of the importance of their jobs and high performance
- Are aware of their own needs for growth, development, and accomplishment
- Work for the good of the organization and not just their own personal benefit

Charismatic leaders are excited and enthusiastic about their vision and clearly communicate it to their subordinates, as does Steve Ballmer. The excitement, enthusiasm, and self-confidence of a charismatic leader contribute to the leader's being able to inspire followers to enthusiastically support his or her vision.[67] People often think of charismatic leaders or managers as being "larger than life"; Steve Ballmer is often described this way. The essence of charisma, however, is having a vision and enthusiastically communicating it to others. Thus, managers who appear to be quiet and earnest can also be charismatic.

Stimulating Subordinates Intellectually

intellectual stimulation Behavior a leader engages in to make followers be aware of problems and view these problems in new ways, consistent with the leader's vision.

Transformational managers openly share information with their subordinates so that they are aware of problems and the need for change. The manager causes subordinates to view problems in their groups and throughout the organization from a different perspective, consistent with the manager's vision. Whereas in the past subordinates might not have been aware of some problems, may have viewed problems as a "management issue" beyond their concern, or may have viewed problems as insurmountable, the transformational manager's **intellectual stimulation** leads subordinates to view problems as challenges that they can and will meet and conquer. The manager engages and empowers subordinates to take personal responsibility for helping solve problems.[68]

Engaging in Developmental Consideration

developmental consideration Behavior a leader engages in to support and encourage followers and help them develop and grow on the job.

When managers engage in **developmental consideration,** they not only perform the consideration behaviors described earlier, such as demonstrating true concern for the well-being of subordinates, but go one step further. The manager goes out of his or her way to support and encourage subordinates, giving them opportunities to enhance their skills and capabilities and to grow and excel on the job.[69] Heinrich von Pierer engages in developmental consideration in numerous ways, such as providing counseling sessions with a psychologist for managers who are having a hard time adapting to the changes at Siemens and sponsoring hiking trips to stimulate employees to think and work in new ways.[70]

All organizations, no matter how large or small, successful or unsuccessful, can benefit when their managers engage in transformational leadership. Moreover, while the benefits of transformational leadership are often most apparent when an organization is in trouble, transformational leadership can be an enduring approach to leadership, leading to long-run organizational effectiveness.

The Distinction Between Transformational and Transactional Leadership

transactional leadership Leadership that motivates subordinates by rewarding them for high performance and reprimanding them for low performance.

Transformational leadership is often contrasted with transactional leadership. In **transactional leadership,** managers use their reward and coercive powers to encourage high performance. When managers reward high performers, reprimand or otherwise punish low performers, and motivate subordinates by reinforcing desired behaviors and extinguishing or punishing undesired ones, they are engaging in transactional leadership.[71] Managers who effectively influence their subordinates to achieve goals yet do not seem to be making the kind of dramatic changes that are part of transformational leadership are engaging in transactional leadership.

Many transformational leaders engage in transactional leadership. They reward subordinates for a job well done and notice and respond to substandard performance. But they also have their eyes on the bigger picture of how much better things could be in their organizations, how much more their subordinates are capable of achieving, and how important it is to treat their subordinates with respect and to help them reach their full potential.

Research has found that when leaders engage in transformational leadership, their subordinates tend to have higher levels of job satisfaction and performance.[72] Additionally, subordinates of transformational leaders may be more likely to trust their leaders and their organizations and feel that they are being fairly treated, and this, in turn, may positively influence their work motivation (see Chapter 13).[73]

Gender and Leadership

The increasing number of women entering the ranks of management, as well as the problems some women face in their efforts to be hired as managers or promoted into management positions, has prompted researchers to explore the relationship between gender and leadership. Although there are relatively more women in management positions today than there were 10 years ago, there are still relatively few women in top management and, in some organizations, even in middle management.

When women do advance to top-management positions, special attention often is focused on them and the fact that they are women. For example, women CEOs of large companies are still very rare; those who make it to the very top post, such as Meg Whitman of eBay, Carly Fiorina of Hewlett-Packard, and Andrea Jung of Avon, are very salient. As business writer Linda Tischler puts it, "In a workplace where women CEOs of major companies are so scarce . . . they can be identified, like rock stars, by first name only–Carly and Andrea and Oprah and Meg."[74] While women have certainly made inroads into leadership positions in organizations, they continue to be very underrepresented in top leadership posts (see Chapter 5). For example, it is estimated that the percentage of women in top leadership/partner positions in law firms is less than 16 percent. Less than 7 percent of the top-earning medical doctors are women, and of the corporate officers of the Fortune 500 largest U.S. companies, less than 16 percent are women.[75]

A widespread stereotype of women is that they are nurturing, supportive, and concerned with interpersonal relations. Men are stereotypically viewed as being directive and focused on task accomplishment. Such stereotypes suggest that women tend to be more relationship-oriented as managers and engage in more consideration behaviors, whereas men are more task-oriented and engage in more initiating-structure behaviors. Does the behavior of actual male and female managers bear out these stereotypes? Do women managers lead in different ways than men? Are male or female managers more effective as leaders?

Research suggests that male and female managers who have leadership positions in organizations behave in similar ways.[76] Women do not engage in more consideration than men, and men do not engage in more initiating structure than women. Research does suggest, however, that leadership style may vary

eBay CEO Meg Whitman holds up an eBay promotional truck in her office in San Jose, California. The handful of women CEOs, such as Whitman, tend to be very salient due to their scarcity. So scarce, in fact, they're often known by their first names—Carly, Andrea, Oprah, Meg.

between women and men. Women tend to be somewhat more participative as leaders than are men, involving subordinates in decision making and seeking their input.[77] Male managers tend to be less participative than are female managers, making more decisions on their own and wanting to do things their own way. Moreover, research suggests that men tend to be harsher when they punish their subordinates than do women.[78]

There are at least two reasons why female managers may be more participative as leaders than are male managers.[79] First, subordinates may try to resist the influence of female managers more than they do the influence of male managers. Some subordinates may never have reported to a woman before; some may incorrectly see a management role as being more appropriate for a man than for a woman; and some may just resist being led by a woman. To overcome this resistance and encourage subordinates' trust and respect, women managers may adopt a participative approach.

A second reason why female managers may be more participative is that they sometimes have better interpersonal skills than male managers.[80] A participative approach to leadership requires high levels of interaction and involvement between a manager and his or her subordinates, sensitivity to subordinates' feelings, and the ability to make decisions that may be unpopular with subordinates but necessary for goal attainment. Good interpersonal skills may help female managers have the effective interactions with their subordinates that are crucial to a participative approach.[81] To the extent that male managers have more difficulty managing interpersonal relationships, they may shy away from the high levels of interaction with subordinates necessary for true participation.

The key finding from research on leader behaviors, however, is that male and female managers do *not* differ significantly in their propensities to perform different leader behaviors. Even though they may be more participative, female managers do not engage in more consideration or less initiating structure than male managers.

Perhaps a question even more important than whether male and female managers differ in the leadership behaviors they perform is whether they differ in effectiveness. Consistent with the findings for leader behaviors, research suggests that across different kinds of organizational settings, male and female managers tend to be *equally effective* as leaders.[82] Thus, there is no logical basis for stereotypes favoring male managers and leaders or for the existence of the "glass ceiling" (an invisible barrier that seems to prevent women from advancing as far as they should in some organizations). Because women and men are equally effective as leaders, the increasing number of women in the workforce should result in a larger pool of highly qualified candidates for management positions in organizations, ultimately enhancing organizational effectiveness.[83]

An important factor for women's advancement to top leadership positions is obtaining a variety of work experiences.[84] Varied work experiences have proved very beneficial for Kathleen Ligocki, CEO and president of Tower Automotive, Inc., as profiled in the following "Focus on Diversity."

Focus on Diversity

Kathleen Ligocki Leads Tower Automotive

Kathleen Ligocki occupies perhaps one of the highest leadership positions held by a woman in the automotive industry. As CEO and a director of Tower Automotive, Ligocki leads an automobile components and assemblies firm that supplies car parts to every major automaker, has approximately 2.8 billion in sales, and operates in 13 countries in addition to the United States, ranging from Mexico, Germany, and Japan to Poland, Slovakia, Brazil, and India.[85]

With a BA in Chinese history and Renaissance art from Indiana University, Ligocki had no plans for a career in the automotive industry.[86] Upon receiving her undergraduate degree, she took a job as a foreman in a General Motors (GM) factory to earn money for graduate school. Much to her surprise, she realized she loved her work and went on to a number of different positions at GM and later at the Ford Motor Company; along the way, she also earned a master's degree from the Wharton Business School.[87] Ligocki's positions at Ford included director of strategies, CEO of Ford Mexico, and, most recently, vice president of Ford's Customer Service Division.[88]

Bill Ford was so impressed with Ligocki's leadership capabilities that he remarked just weeks before she accepted the Tower top post that she might someday be the one to lead Ford. In fact, when she discussed potentially leaving Ford to become CEO of Tower with Ford top managers, they tried to convince her to stay but also appreciated the kind of opportunity she would have at Tower. As Ligocki put it, "They encouraged me to stay, but they also understood–maybe Bill better than anybody–that this was an opportunity to run a publicly traded company. . . . Tower . . . was a company I thought had great strategic strengths. . . . But it needed operational work, which was a lot of what I had done at GM and Ford. So I felt I could offer something to the company."[89]

Tower Automotive CEO Kathleen Ligocki draws on her prior experience in various positions at Ford in transforming her company.

Varied work experiences in both line and administrative positions have paid off for Ligocki in terms of having a very motivating and rewarding career and being especially well suited for her current leadership position. In less than a few years in her current position, which she assumed in August 2003, she has already begun to transform Tower, diversifying both its corporate customers and the countries it operates in. Under Ligocki's leadership, Tower projects that its annual revenues in 2006 will be over \$3.3 billion.[90]

Emotional Intelligence and Leadership

Do the moods and emotions leaders experience on the job influence their behavior and effectiveness as leaders? Preliminary research suggests that this is likely to be the case. For example, one study found that when store managers experienced positive moods at work, salespeople in their stores provided high-quality customer service and were less likely to quit.[91]

Moreover, a leader's level of emotional intelligence (see Chapter 3) may play a particularly important role in leadership effectiveness.[92] For example, emotional intelligence may help leaders develop a vision for their organizations, motivate their subordinates to commit to this vision, and energize them to enthusiastically work to achieve this vision. Moreover, emotional intelligence may enable leaders to develop a significant identity for their organization and instill high levels of trust and cooperation throughout the organization while maintaining the flexibility needed to respond to changing conditions.[93]

Emotional intelligence also plays a crucial role in how leaders relate to and deal with their followers, particularly when it comes to encouraging followers to be creative.[94] Creativity in organizations is an emotion-laden process, as it often entails challenging the status quo, being willing to take risks and accept and learn from failures, and doing much hard work to bring creative ideas to fruition in terms of new products, services, or procedures and processes when uncertainty is bound to be high.[95] Leaders who are high on emotional intelligence are more likely to understand all the emotions surrounding creative endeavors, to be able to awaken and support the creative pursuits of their followers, and to provide the kind of support that enables creativity to flourish in organizations.[96]

Summary and Review

THE NATURE OF LEADERSHIP Leadership is the process by which a person exerts influence over other people and inspires, motivates, and directs their activities to help achieve group or organizational goals. Leaders are able to influence others because they possess power. The five types of power available to managers are legitimate power, reward power, coercive power, expert power, and referent power. Many managers are using empowerment as a tool to increase their effectiveness as leaders.

TRAIT AND BEHAVIOR MODELS OF LEADERSHIP The trait model of leadership describes personal characteristics or traits that contribute to effective leadership. However, some managers who possess these traits are not effective leaders, and some managers who do not possess all the traits are nevertheless effective leaders. The behavior model of leadership describes two kinds of behavior that most leaders engage in: consideration and initiating structure.

CONTINGENCY MODELS OF LEADERSHIP Contingency models take into account the complexity surrounding leadership and the role of the situation in determining whether a manager is an effective or ineffective leader. Fiedler's contingency model explains why managers may be effective leaders in one situation and ineffective in another. According to Fiedler's model, relationship-oriented leaders are most effective in situations that are moderately favorable for leading, and task-oriented leaders are most effective in situations that are very favorable or very unfavorable for leading. House's path-goal theory describes how effective managers motivate their subordinates by determining what outcomes their subordinates want, rewarding subordinates with these outcomes when they achieve their goals and perform at a high level, and clarifying the paths to goal attainment. Managers can engage in four different kinds of behaviors to motivate subordinates: directive behaviors, supportive behaviors, participative behaviors, or achievement-oriented behaviors. The leader substitutes model suggests that sometimes managers do not have to play a leadership role because their subordinates perform highly without the manager having to exert influence over them.

TRANSFORMATIONAL LEADERSHIP Transformational leadership occurs when managers have dramatic effects on their subordinates and on the organization as a whole and inspire and energize subordinates to solve problems and improve performance. These effects include making subordinates aware of the importance of their own jobs and high performance, making subordinates aware of their own needs for personal growth, development, and accomplishment, and motivating subordinates to work for the good of the organization and not just their own personal gain. Managers can engage in transformational leadership by being charismatic leaders, by intellectually stimulating subordinates, and by engaging in developmental consideration. Transformational managers also often engage in transactional leadership by using their reward and coercive powers to encourage high performance.

GENDER AND LEADERSHIP Female and male managers do not differ in the leadership behaviors that they perform, contrary to stereotypes suggesting that women are more relationship-oriented and men more task-oriented. Female managers sometimes are more participative than male managers, however. Research has found that women and men are equally effective as managers and leaders.

EMOTIONAL INTELLIGENCE AND LEADERSHIP The moods and emotions leaders experience on the job, and their ability to effectively manage these feelings, can influence their effectiveness as leaders. Moreover, emotional intelligence has the potential to contribute to leadership effectiveness in multiple ways, including encouraging and supporting creativity among followers.

Management in Action

Topics for Discussion and Action

Discussion

1. Describe the steps managers can take to increase their power and ability to be effective leaders.
2. Think of specific situations in which it might be especially important for a manager to engage in consideration and in initiating structure.
3. For your current job or for a future job you expect to hold, describe what your supervisor could do to strongly motivate you to be a top performer.
4. Discuss why managers might want to change the behaviors they engage in, given their situation, their subordinates, and the nature of the work being done. Do you think managers are able to readily change their leadership behaviors? Why or why not?
5. Discuss why substitutes for leadership can contribute to organizational effectiveness.
6. Describe what transformational leadership is and explain how managers can engage in it.
7. Discuss why some people still think that men make better managers than women even though research indicates that men and women are equally effective as managers and leaders.
8. Imagine that you are working in an organization in an entry-level position after graduation and have come up with what you think is a great idea for improving a critical process in the organization that relates to your job. In what ways might your supervisor encourage you to actually implement your idea? How might your supervisor discourage you from even sharing your idea with others?

Action

9. Interview a manager to find out how the three situational characteristics that Fiedler identified are affecting his or her ability to provide leadership.
10. Find a company that has dramatically turned around its fortunes and improved its performance. Determine whether a transformational manager was behind the turnaround and, if one was, what this manager did.

Building Management Skills

Analyzing Failures of Leadership

Think about a situation you are familiar with in which a leader was very ineffective. Then answer the following questions:

1. What sources of power did this leader have? Did the leader have enough power to influence his or her followers?
2. What kinds of behaviors did this leader engage in? Were they appropriate for the situation? Why or why not?
3. From what you know, do you think this leader was a task-oriented leader or a relationship-oriented leader? How favorable was this leader's situation for leading?
4. What steps did this leader take to motivate his or her followers? Were these steps appropriate or inappropriate? Why?
5. What signs, if any, did this leader show of being a transformational leader?

Managing Ethically

Managers who verbally criticize their subordinates, put them down in front of their co-workers, or use the threat of job loss to influence behavior are exercising coercive power. Some employees subject to coercive power believe that using it is unethical.

Questions

1. Either alone or in a group, think about the ethical implications of the use of coercive power.
2. To what extent do managers and organizations have an ethical obligation to put limits on the amount of coercive power that is exercised?

Small Group Breakout Exercise

Improving Leadership Effectiveness

Form groups of three to five people, and appoint one member as the spokesperson who will communicate your findings and conclusions to the whole class when called on by the instructor. Then discuss the following scenario.

You are a team of human resource consultants who have been hired by Carla Caruso, an entrepreneur who has started her own interior decorating business. A highly competent and creative interior decorator, Caruso established a working relationship with most of the major home builders in her community. At first, she worked on her own as an independent contractor. Then because of a dramatic increase in the number of new homes being built, she became swamped with requests for her services and decided to start her own company.

She hired a secretary-bookkeeper and four interior decorators, all of whom are highly competent. Caruso still does decorating jobs herself and has adopted a hands-off approach to leading the four decorators who report to her because she feels that interior design is a very personal, creative endeavor. Rather than pay the decorators on some kind of commission basis (such as a percentage of their customers' total billings), she pays them a premium salary, higher than average, so that they are motivated to do what's best for a customer's needs and not what will result in higher billings and commissions.

Caruso thought everything was going smoothly until customer complaints started coming in. The complaints ranged from the decorators' being hard to get hold of, promising unrealistic delivery times, and being late for or failing to keep appointments to their being impatient and rude when customers had trouble making up their minds. Caruso knows that her decorators are very competent and is concerned that she is not effectively leading and managing them. She wonders, in particular, if her hands-off approach is to blame and if she should change the manner in which she rewards or pays her decorators. She has asked for your advice.

1. Analyze the sources of power that Caruso has available to her to influence the decorators. What advice can you give her to either increase her power base or use her existing power more effectively?
2. Given what you have learned in this chapter (for example, from the behavior model and path-goal theory), does Caruso seem to be performing appropriate leader behaviors in this situation? What advice can you give her about the kinds of behaviors she should perform?
3. What steps would you advise Caruso to take to increase the decorators' motivation to deliver high-quality customer service?
4. Would you advise Caruso to try to engage in transformational leadership in this situation? If not, why not? If so, what steps would you advise her to take?

Exploring the World Wide Web

Go to the Web site of the Center for Creative Leadership (www.ccl.org). Spend some time browsing through the site to learn more about this organization, which specializes in leadership. Then click on "Coaching" and read about the different coaching programs and options the center provides. How do you think leaders might benefit from coaching? What kinds of leaders/managers may find coaching especially beneficial? Do you think coaching services such as those provided by the Center for Creative Leadership can help leaders become more effective? Why or why not?

Be the Manager

You are the CEO of a medium-size company that makes window coverings such as Hunter Douglas blinds and Douettes. Your company has a real cost advantage in terms of being able to make custom window coverings at costs that are relatively low in the industry. However, the performance of your company has been lackluster. In order to make needed changes and improve performance, you met with the eight other top managers in your company and charged them with identifying problems and missed opportunities in each of their areas and coming up with an action plan to address the problems and take advantage of opportunities.

Once you gave the managers the okay, they were charged with implementing their action plans in a timely fashion and monitoring the effects of their initiatives on a monthly basis for the next 8 to 12 months.

You approved each of the manager's action plans, and a year later most of the managers were reporting that their initiatives had been successful in addressing the problems and opportunities they had identified a year ago. However, overall company performance continues to be lackluster and shows no signs of improvement. You are confused and starting to question your leadership capabilities and approach to change. What are you going to do to improve the performance and effectiveness of your company?

Build Your Management Skills DVD

- **Test Your Knowledge:**
  (1) Sources of Power,
  (2) Path-Goal Theory, and
  (3) Fiedler's Contingency Model of Leadership
- **Self-Assessment:**
  (1) Assessing Your Leader-Member Exchange and
  (2) Do You Have What It Takes to Be a Leader?

BusinessWeek Case in the News

Coach's Driver Picks Up the Pace

Lew Frankfort runs a $1.3 billion company, Coach Inc., that is the nation's largest maker and retailer of handbags and one of the fastest-growing luxury brands in the world. He lives in a 100-year-old house in a fashionable New Jersey suburb and has a weekend place in the Hamptons. He just bought a $160,000 Aston Martin. And he doesn't mind letting you know that he's afraid of losing it all.

Without much prompting, Frankfort, 58, will recount a recurring dream that reflects his working-class childhood in the Bronx: In it, his home sits on a tree-covered hill on the edge of a rundown portion of his old haunts. "With one misstep, I would slide and my house would slide right back into the Bronx," he says.

That's the Lew Frankfort whose vulnerability endears him to the employees at Coach's mod loft headquarters on West 34th Street in Manhattan. Hardly a day goes by that he doesn't express his worry that Coach will lose its way, its edge, its status. "He's scared of failure, and he will tell you that," says his son, Sam, a 25-year-old associate at Bear, Stearns & Co. in New York.

As is often the case with successful executives, that fear is a foil to a supersize ambition. Frankfort, who has been chief executive of Coach since 1996, is trying to overturn the glamorous old order, where names like Louis Vuitton, Hermès, Prada, and Gucci have long ruled the $13 billion worldwide market for high-end leather goods and accessories. That's less unlikely than it sounds: Not since Tiffany & Co. helped define extravagance in the 1960s has an American luxury brand had as much cachet globally. Yet Frankfort wants supremacy—he wants to supplant Vuitton, the largest of them all. And, for now, that does seem a bit of a stretch. The French company's sales surged in the U.S. last year as it boosted advertising.

More Color, More Style

Still, a decade ago, Frankfort's notion would have seemed downright ludicrous. Coach sold sturdy leather bags that had all the panache of a lawyer's briefcase. In the 1990s, when Gucci Group, Vuitton, and Prada all revitalized themselves, Frankfort knew he had to radically update Coach's look, which had gone largely unchanged for years. In 1996 he hired Reed Krakoff, a hip young designer for Tommy Hilfiger Corp. "I told Lew that Reed would become the Tom Ford of Coach," Hilfiger recalls, referring to the star designer who turned Gucci into the darling of the fashionistas.

Krakoff, now 40, enlivened the brand by adding more color, more femininity—in short, more style. He developed bags using fabric, which of course is cheaper than leather, and helped boost profit margins. He also brightened up Coach's 242 stores and completely rethought its advertising. Sitting on a Coach suede chair in a conference room, Frankfort tells a portfolio manager why there is so much pink in this season's collections: "People still see Coach as a very serious brand, even though they find it feminine and fashionable." He and Krakoff like to call Coach a "quintessentially American brand"—one that is accessible, with prices about half those at Vuitton, but not too accessible.

At the same time, Frankfort has done something even more unusual for a luxury brand: He relies on a rigorous management and financial system. Frankfort is, at heart, a by-the-numbers executive, one who reserves his greatest praise for those who are "numerate." When the company's 30 top executives enter their offices in the morning, they are greeted with a voice mail providing sales figures from the day before. If managers don't know their numbers, Frankfort punishes them with even more exacting questions. "You need to make the numbers dance to stay invited to the party," says Michael Tucci, president of North American stores.

Frankfort says he picks apart numbers because they ground his decisions and "debunk myths." Coach also interviews 10,000 consumers a year about their shopping habits and tests new items at pilot stores. That's how Frankfort discovered that women would pay $328 for an everyday bag called the Hamptons Flap Satchel. The conventional wisdom was that most would resist spending more than $298. But since the satchel was first tested in 2002, it has become one of the company's best-selling items. It's the Procter & Gamble Co. approach to fashion. Or, as American designer Joseph Abboud puts it: "Lew has created a wonderful platform so Reed can express his creativity." . . .

It's not just Frankfort's reliance on numbers that sets him apart from some of his peers. Frankfort, who tends to wear Ralph Lauren made-to-measure suits, grew up without paying the least bit of attention to the fashion world. The son of a New York City policeman and a stay-at-home mom, he had such a bad speech impediment that he couldn't make himself understood until he was 4. After graduating from Hunter College and Columbia University's business school, he went to an investment bank. But soon he decided he wanted more meaningful work and joined the administration of Mayor John V. Lindsay. Over the next nine years, he rose to become a commissioner overseeing the city's day-care and Headstart programs.

Frankfort returned to the private sector when he was passed over for a promotion under Mayor Edward I. Koch, who recalls Frankfort as a "very good numbers guy." A friend suggested that Frankfort meet with Coach founder Miles Cahn, who hired him to head business development in 1979. Frankfort knew little about women's purses, but that didn't matter. Cahn wanted an outsider who could look at the business with fresh eyes. Frankfort opened Coach's first stores and developed its catalog business. When Cahn sold Coach to Sara Lee six years later, Frankfort became president; in 1996, he was named CEO.

Since then, Frankfort has led the company with the thoroughness of a good city bureaucrat and the passion of an entrepreneur. Even today, he e-mails his family when the stock reaches a new milestone. At weekly meetings, he and his executives review and adjust projections for each business division, all the way down to prices of individual items. The smallest numbers may jump out at him, such as the price of certain key chains to be sold this fall. They are set at $28 to $38, far less than most things Coach sells, and Frankfort wonders if such an item is too pedestrian. "It doesn't add to the aura of Coach," he says, suggesting that the group reconsider including them in the collection.

To remain focused on offering "affordable luxury," Frankfort says he won't be making any distracting acquisitions. He contends that Coach should be able to double sales again in four to five years on its own. But any brand is only one weak collection away from trouble—all the market research in the world can't always save you from that. And if Krakoff's success earns him a better offer somewhere else, he would be hard to replace. "One of Coach's biggest risks is that it could become a victim of its own success," says Lehman Brothers Inc. analyst Robert S. Drbul.

That, of course, would be Frankfort's worst nightmare. But despite—or perhaps because of—his fears of being on the edge, Coach doesn't look as if it's slipping yet.

Questions

1. How would you characterize Lew Frankfort's personal leadership style?
2. What traits does Frankfort appear to be high on?
3. What behaviors does Frankfort engage in?
4. Do you think Frankfort is a transformational leader? Why or why not?

Source: R. Berner, "Coach's Driver Picks Up the Pace." Reprinted from the March 29, 2004, issue of *BusinessWeek* by special permission.

BusinessWeek Case in the News

Reinventing Motorola

It takes Motorola Inc. employees about 30 seconds after they meet Edward J. Zander to realize how different their new boss is from their last one. Where Zander's predecessor, Christopher B. Galvin, was reserved, polite, and genteel, Zander is a brash Brooklynite, incessantly pumping hands and flashing his trademark mile-wide smile.

But in March, three months after taking over the chief executive post, Zander showed he also was going to be much more demanding. He gathered his top 20 execs in the company's downtown Chicago offices, some 30 miles from the Schaumburg, Ill., headquarters, for a two-day brainstorming session on how to improve Motorola's lackluster execution. His message: Employees will be held accountable for customer satisfaction, product quality, and even collaboration among business units. "If you don't cooperate and work together, I will kill you," he said. Today, Zander laughs: "That's surviving-and-growing-up-in-Brooklyn talk. It was my way of saying, "We're gong to fix this thing."

Zander is about as affable as CEOs come, but he's deadly serious about restoring Motorola to the top of the communications world. The tech veteran, who spent 15 years at computer giant Sun Microsystems Inc. and eventually became its president, is trying to reinvent Motorola as a nimble, unified technology company. His most dramatic effort to date is a plan to dismantle Motorola's debilitating bureaucracy and end a culture of internecine rivalries so intense that Motorola's own employees have referred to its business units as "warring tribes." And he's not leaving it to chance: He has made cooperation a key factor in determining raises and bonuses. "It's a damn different place," says Patrick J. Canavan, a 24-year veteran and Motorola's director for global governance. "Everyone is looking out for everyone else."

The changes are just beginning. *BusinessWeek* has learned that Zander has been exploring a major reorganization, and the first steps of the restructuring may be unveiled at an investor conference in Chicago on July 27. By October, Zander hopes to abandon Motorola's stovepipe divisions, which are focused on products like mobile phones and broadband gear, and reorganize operations around customer markets—one for the digital home, for example, and another for corporate buyers.

The reorganization will help Zander deliver on several new initiatives. Perhaps the most important is what the chief executive calls "seamless mobility." The idea is that Motorola should make it easy for consumers to transport any digital information—music, video, e-mail, phone calls—from the house to the car to the workplace. Mastering that technology would do more than boost cellphone sales. It also could make Motorola a key player in the digital home, helping it sell flat-panel TVs and broadband modems, home wireless networks, and gateways to manage digital content. Separately, *BusinessWeek* has learned that Motorola is planning a major push to sell more services to corporations. While Motorola sells communications gear to corporate customers now, Zander sees an important growth opportunity in managing networks for those companies. "We have to get more focused on that," said Zander in an interview with *BusinessWeek*. . . .

Honing a Concept

. . . Zander is planning to trim costs in coming months by shedding employees, according to insiders and analysts. He's also plotting management changes that will bring in more handpicked people to help execute his plans. On July 20, Motorola said the head of its mobile-phone division, Tom Lynch, would leave the company at the end of the summer. Zander declined to discuss any details of cost-cutting or executive changes.

But investors that want Zander to jettison poorly performing businesses may be disappointed. The CEO proceeded with the spin-off of Motorola's semiconductor unit that had been put in motion before he arrived—the deal took place on July 16, despite upheaval in the chips market. Still, insiders say he's impressed with the remaining portfolio of businesses, including the $4.4 billion wireless infrastructure business that some analysts have suggested that Motorola dump. . . .

"You're Sandbagging"

The Motorola vision starts with users sitting at home watching, say, the New York Yankees battling the Chicago White Sox. To leave home, they pause the video transfer it to their phone, walk into the garage and transfer the video to the car as they drive away. The car would switch to audio so as not to distract the driver and then switch back to video if the driver stops at a traffic light. Motorola has the technology portfolio to pursue the entire scenario. Besides phones and cable set-top boxes, it has a $2.3 billion automotive-electronics business that develops technologies for cars to communicate with outside networks.

The key will be beating rivals to market with innovative solutions. That's why Zander's top priority has been improving execution. The main driver is a new incentive plan. In the past, workers were compensated based on the revenue, profit, and cash generated in their particular sector. If one sector did well, its employees pulled in huge bonuses. A unit that didn't perform got little or nothing.

Zander has been relentless in trying to get the most out of his staff. A new bonus plan bases 25 percent on three key areas: customer satisfaction, product reliability, and the cost of poor quality. When the heads of each business unit first laid out their targets, Zander's no-nonsense roots showed; "You're sandbagging," he barked. Before long, the targets were more difficult, "We're driving for improvement year over year," says Michael J. Fenger, a vet Zander picked to improve corporate quality.

If Zander can maintain Motorola's momentum, the years ahead look promising. It's gaining share on the world's mobile-phone leader, Nokia, and the elements of Zander's master plan have yet to take root. "It's a big ship," Zander concedes—so it will take time to change direction. But it takes no time at all to see that Zander is committed to the challenge.

Questions

1. In what ways does Edward Zander differ from his predecessor, Christopher Galvin?
2. How is Edward Zander empowering Motorola employees?
3. What is Zander's vision for Motorola?
4. Do you think Zander will be able to successfully transform Motorola? Why or why not?

Source: R. O. Crockett, "Reinventing Motorola." Reprinted from the August 2, 2004, issue of *BusinessWeek* by special permission.

CHAPTER

15 Effective Groups and Teams

Learning Objectives

After studying this chapter, you should be able to:

- Explain why groups and teams are key contributors to organizational effectiveness.
- Identify the different types of groups and teams that help managers and organizations achieve their goals.
- Explain how different elements of group dynamics influence the functioning and effectiveness of groups and teams.
- Explain why it is important for groups and teams to have a balance of conformity and deviance and a moderate level of cohesiveness.
- Describe how managers can motivate group members to achieve organizational goals and reduce social loafing in groups and teams.

A Manager's Challenge

Teams Excel at Louis Vuitton and Nucor Corporation

How can managers use teams in different kinds of organizations and work environments to gain a competitive advantage? Groups and teams are relied on in all kinds of organizations, from those specializing in heavy industrial manufacturing to those in high-tech fields ranging from computer software development to biotechnology. Relying on groups and teams to accomplish work tasks is one thing; managing groups and teams in ways that enable them to truly excel and help an organization gain and maintain a competitive advantage is another, much more challenging endeavor. Managers at Louis Vuitton, the most profitable luxury brand in the world, and managers at Nucor Corporation, the largest producer of steel and biggest recycler in the United States, have succeeded in effectively using teams to produce luxury accessories and steel, respectively. Teams at both companies not only are effective but truly excel and have helped to make the companies leaders in their respective industries.[1]

At Louis Vuitton, a dedicated 20–30 person team works only on one product at a time; one such team might produce about 120 handbags like this one in a day.

Louis Vuitton, with $3.8 billion in revenues in 2003 and an operating margin of 45 percent, is the largest and most profitable producer of high-end luxury accessories.[2] Impeccable quality and high standards are a must for Louis Vuitton; when customers purchase a handbag such as the Boulogne Multicolor, which appeared in stores for the first time in March 2004 with a $1,500 price tag, they expect only the best. Teams at Louis Vuitton are so effective at making handbags and other accessories that not only are customers never disappointed but Vuitton's profit margins are much higher than those of its competitors such as Prada and Gucci.[3]

Teams with between 20 and 30 members make Vuitton handbags and accessories. The teams work on only one particular product at a time; a team with 24 members might produce about 120 handbags per day. Team members are empowered to take ownership for the goods they produce, are encouraged to suggest improvements, and are kept up to date on key facts such as products' selling prices and popularity. As Thierry Nogues, a team leader at a Vuitton factory in Ducey, France, puts it, "Our goal is to make everyone as multiskilled and autonomous as possible."[4]

In the case of the Boulogne Multicolor, a team found out that some of the studs on the handbag were interfering with the smooth operation of the zipper. The team's discovery led to a small design change that completely eliminated the problem.[5] By being involved in all aspects of the goods they produce, and having the skills and autonomy to ensure that all goods produced live up to the Vuitton brand name, employees take pride in their work and are highly motivated.

Headquartered in Charlotte, North Carolina, Nucor has operations in 14 states manufacturing all kinds of steel products ranging from steel joists, bars, and beams to steel decks and metal building systems.[6] Nucor has over 9,900 employees and over $6.2 billion in annual sales.[7]

Production workers at Nucor are organized into teams ranging in size from 8 to 40 members based on the kind of work the team is responsible for, such as rolling steel or operating a furnace. Team members have considerable autonomy to make decisions and creatively respond to problems and opportunities, and there are relatively few layers in the corporate hierarchy supporting the empowerment of teams.[8] Teams develop their own informal rules for behavior and make their own decisions. As long as team members follow organizational rules and policies (e.g., for safety) and meet quality standards, they are free to govern themselves. Managers act as coaches or advisers rather than supervisors, helping teams out when they need some additional outside assistance.[9]

To ensure that production teams are motivated to help Nucor achieve its goals, team members are eligible for weekly bonuses based on the team's performance. Essentially, these production workers receive base pay that does not vary and are eligible to receive weekly bonus pay that can average from 80 to 150 percent of their regular pay.[10] The bonus rate is predetermined by the work a team performs and the capabilities of the machinery they use. Given the immediacy of the bonus and its potential magnitude, team members are highly motivated to perform at a high level, develop informal rules that support high performance, and strive to help Nucor reach its goals. Moreover, because all members of a team receive the same amount of weekly bonus money, they are motivated to do their best for the team, cooperate, and help one another out.[11]

Crafting a luxury handbag and making steel joists couldn't be more different from each other in certain ways. Yet the highly effective teams at Louis Vuitton and Nucor share certain fundamental qualities. These teams really do take ownership of their work and are highly motivated to perform effectively. Team members have the skills and knowledge they need to be effective, they are empowered to make decisions about their work, and they know that their teams are making vital contributions to their organizations.[12]

Overview

Louis Vuitton and Nucor are not alone in using groups and teams to produce goods and services that best meet customers' needs. Managers in large companies such as Du Pont, Microsoft, and Ford and in small companies such as Web Industries, Perdue Farms, and Risk International Services are all relying on teams to help them gain a competitive advantage.[13] In this chapter we look in detail at how groups and teams can contribute to organizational effectiveness and the types of groups and teams used in organizations. We discuss how different elements of group dynamics influence the functioning and effectiveness of groups, and we describe how managers can motivate group members to achieve organizational goals and reduce social loafing in groups and teams. By the end of this chapter, you will appreciate why the effective management of groups and teams is a key ingredient for organizational performance and a source of competitive advantage.

Groups, Teams, and Organizational Effectiveness

A **group** may be defined as two or more people who interact with each other to accomplish certain goals or meet certain needs.[14] A **team** is a group whose members work *intensely* with one another to achieve a specific common goal or objective. As these definitions imply, all teams are groups but not all groups are teams. The two characteristics that distinguish teams from groups are the *intensity* with which team members work together and the presence of a *specific, overriding team goal or objective.*

group Two or more people who interact with each other to accomplish certain goals or meet certain needs.

team A group whose members work intensely with one another to achieve a specific common goal or objective.

As described in "A Manager's Challenge," members of production teams in Louis Vuitton and in Nucor work intensely together to achieve their goals, whether they are crafting high-quality handbags or making steel beams. In contrast, the accountants who work in a small CPA firm are a group: They may interact with one another to achieve goals such as keeping up to date on the latest changes in accounting rules and regulations, maintaining a smoothly functioning office, satisfying clients, and attracting new clients. But they are not a team because they do not work intensely with one another. Each accountant concentrates on serving the needs of his or her own clients.

Because all teams are also groups, whenever we use the term *group* in this chapter, we are referring to both groups *and* teams. As you might imagine, because members of teams work intensely together, teams can sometimes be difficult to form and it may take time for members to learn how to effectively work together. Groups and teams can help an organization gain a competitive advantage because they can (1) enhance its performance, (2) increase its responsiveness to customers, (3) increase innovation, and (4) increase employees' motivation and satisfaction (see Figure 15.1). In this section, we look at each of these contributions in turn.

Groups and Teams as Performance Enhancers

synergy Performance gains that result when individuals and departments coordinate their actions.

One of the main advantages of using groups is the opportunity to obtain a type of **synergy:** People working in a group are able to produce more or higher-quality outputs than would have been produced if each person had worked separately and all their individual efforts were later combined. The essence of synergy is captured in the saying "The whole is more than the sum of its parts." Factors that can contribute to synergy in groups include the ability of group members to bounce ideas off one another, to correct one another's mistakes, to solve problems immediately as they arise, to bring a diverse knowledge base to bear on a problem or goal, and to accomplish work that is too vast or all-encompassing for

Figure 15.1
Groups' and Teams' Contributions to Organizational Effectiveness

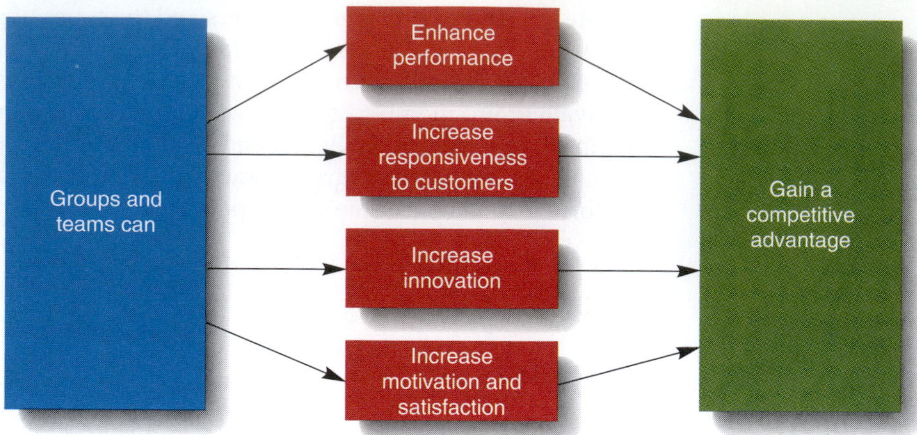

any one individual to achieve on his or her own. At Louis Vuitton and Nucor in "A Manager's Challenge," the kinds of work the production teams are responsible for could not be performed by an individual acting alone; it is only through the combined efforts of team members that luxury accessories and steel products can be produced efficiently and effectively.

To take advantage of the potential for synergy in groups, managers need to make sure that groups are composed of members who have complementary skills and knowledge relevant to the group's work. For example, at Hallmark Cards, synergies are created by bringing together all the different functions needed to create and produce a greeting card in a cross-functional team (a team composed of members from different departments or functions; see Chapter 10). For instance, artists, writers, designers, and marketing experts work together as members of a team to develop new cards.[15]

At Hallmark, the skills and expertise of the artists complement the contributions of the writers and vice versa. Managers also need to give groups enough autonomy so that the groups, rather than the manager, are solving problems and determining how to achieve goals and objectives, as is true in the cross-functional teams at Hallmark and the production teams in Louis Vuitton and Nucor in "A Manager's Challenge." To promote synergy, managers need to empower their subordinates and be coaches, guides, and resources for groups while refraining from playing a more directive or supervisory role, as is true at Louis Vuitton and Nucor. The potential for synergy in groups may be the reason why more and more managers are incorporating empowerment into their personal leadership styles (see Chapter 14).

When tasks are complex and involve highly sophisticated and rapidly changing technologies, achieving synergies in teams often hinges on having the appropriate mix of backgrounds and areas of expertise represented on the team. In large organizations with operations in many states and countries, it is often difficult for managers to determine which employees might have the expertise needed on a particular team or for a certain project. As profiled in the following "Information Technology Byte," new software applications can help managers identify employees with the expertise needed to achieve real synergies.

Information Technology Byte

Identifying Expertise to Achieve Synergies

Lockheed Martin Corporation has over 130,000 employees working in 939 different locations in over 450 cities in the United States and around the world.[16] These vast human resources provide Lockheed Martin with a tremendous amount of expertise to draw on to solve vexing problems and better meet customers' needs. However, it is a real challenge for managers to identify who in the company might actually have the expertise needed for a particular project or team.

Enter ActiveNet, a software application provided by Tacit Knowledge Systems Inc. ActiveNet scans documents in a company's computer systems, ranging from emails and instant messages to Word and PowerPoint documents, to identify areas of expertise based on what people write and the content of documents they produce;[17] the software creates searchable employee profiles based on this content.[18] For example, a Lockheed team of researchers in California was concerned about the potential for condensation to accumulate in missile canisters. Given all the work Lockheed does with missiles, it was likely that someone in the company had worked on this problem before. Through ActiveNet, the team was able to identify a researcher working in another California facility who had expertise in this area.[19]

Northrop Grumman has over 10,000 employees and faces similar challenges in identifying expertise needed to achieve synergies.[20] For example, when Werner Hinz, a Grumman engineer, was preparing a bid for the Pentagon to develop a new, unmanned airplane that could travel faster than the speed of sound, he needed someone with expertise in hypersonics on his team. Hinz couldn't think of any employees he knew with this expertise, so he used ActiveNet by typing in key phrases. ActiveNet provided Hinz with the name of an employee he had actually met and who worked in the same building as Hinz but whom Hinz did not know much about; after speaking to the employee on the phone, Hinz knew he had found the hypersonics expert he needed on his team to prepare the bid. (Hinz's team eventually was awarded a Pentagon contract of $1.5 million to design the new plane.)[21]

While an ActiveNet license is not inexpensive–it costs about $170 for each employee profile–it can help managers identify expertise needed for synergies in teams by allowing them to search employee profiles. ActiveNet also has privacy protections in place. For example, employees determine who can access which parts of their profiles, and the system does not keep copies of documents after they have been scanned for relevant content. And once ActiveNet identifies an individual in a content domain with regard to a particular query, that individual is contacted first, before his or her name is passed on to the person seeking expertise, to see if he or she wants to make contact with the person making the query, provide information anonymously, or ignore the query. After September 11, 2001, the CIA began using ActiveNet in its counterterrorist efforts.[22] To the extent that ActiveNet can help managers like Hinz find employees with needed expertise, it may help them achieve synergies in teams.

Groups, Teams, and Responsiveness to Customers

Being responsive to customers is not always easy. In manufacturing organizations, for example, customers' needs and desires for new and improved products have to be balanced against engineering constraints, production costs and feasibilities, government safety regulations, and marketing challenges. In service organizations such as health maintenance organizations (HMOs), being responsive to patients' needs and desires for prompt, high-quality medical care and treatment has to be balanced against meeting physicians' needs and desires and keeping health care costs under control. Being responsive to customers often requires the wide variety of skills and expertise found in different departments and at different levels in an organization's hierarchy. Sometimes, for example, employees at lower levels in an organization's hierarchy, such as sales representatives for a computer company, are closest to its customers and the most attuned to their needs. However, lower-level employees like salespeople often lack the technical expertise needed to come up with new product ideas; such expertise is found in the research and development department. Bringing salespeople, research and development experts, and members of other departments together in a group or cross-functional team can enhance responsiveness to customers. Consequently, when managers form a team, they need to make sure that the diversity of expertise and knowledge needed to be responsive to customers exists within the team; this is why cross-functional teams are so popular.

In a cross-functional team, the expertise and knowledge in different organizational departments are brought together in the skills and knowledge of the team members. Managers of high-performing organizations are careful to determine which types of expertise and knowledge are required for teams to be responsive to customers, and they use this information in forming teams.

Teams and Innovation

Innovation, the creative development of new products, new technologies, new services, or even new organizational structures, is a topic we discuss in detail in Chapter 18. Often, an individual working alone does not possess the extensive and diverse set of skills, knowledge, and expertise required for successful innovation. Managers can better encourage innovation by creating teams of diverse individuals who together have the knowledge relevant to a particular type of innovation rather than by relying on individuals working alone.

Using teams to innovate has other advantages as well. First, team members can often uncover one another's errors or false assumptions; an individual acting alone would not be able to do this. Second, team members can critique one another's approaches when need be and build off one another's strengths while compensating for weaknesses, one of the advantages of devil's advocacy and dialectical inquiry, discussed in Chapter 7.

To further promote innovation, managers are well advised to empower teams and make their members fully responsible and accountable for the innovation process. The manager's role is to provide guidance, assistance, coaching, and the resources team members need and *not* to closely direct or supervise their activities. To speed innovation, managers also need to form teams in which each member brings some unique resource to the team, such as engineering prowess, knowledge of production, marketing expertise, or financial savvy. Successful innovation sometimes requires that managers form teams with members from different countries and cultures.

Amazon uses teams to spur innovation, and many of the unique features on its Web site that enable it to be responsive to customers and meet their needs have been developed by teams, as indicated in the following "Information Technology Byte."

Information Technology Byte

Pizza Teams at Amazon

Jeff Bezos, founder and CEO of Amazon, is a firm believer in the power of teams to spur innovation. At Amazon, teams have considerable autonomy to develop their ideas and experiment without interference from managers or other groups. And teams are kept deliberately small. According to Bezos, no team should need more than two pizzas to feed its members. If more than two pizzas are needed to nourish a team, the team is too large. Thus, teams at Amazon typically have no more than about five to seven members.[23]

"Pizza teams" have come up with unique and popular innovations that individuals working alone might never have thought of. A team developed the "Gold Box" icon that customers can click on to receive special offers that expire within an hour of opening the treasure chest. Another team developed "Bottom of the Page Deals"–very low priced offers for everyday goods such as batteries and power bars.[24] And "Search Inside the Book," a massive undertaking that allows customers to search and read content from over 100,000 books, had its origins in a team.[25]

While Bezos gives teams autonomy to develop and run with their ideas, he also believes in the careful analysis and testing of ideas. A great advocate of the power of facts, data, and analysis, Bezos feels that whenever an idea can be tested through analysis, analysis should rule the day. When an undertaking is just too large or too uncertain or when data are lacking and hard to come by, Bezos and other experienced top managers make the final call.[26] But in order to make such judgment calls about implementing new ideas (either by data analysis or expert judgment), what really is needed are truly creative ideas. To date, teams have played a very important role in generating ideas that have helped Amazon be responsive to its customers, have a widely known Internet brand name, ride out the dot-com bust, and be the highly successful and innovative company it is today.[27]

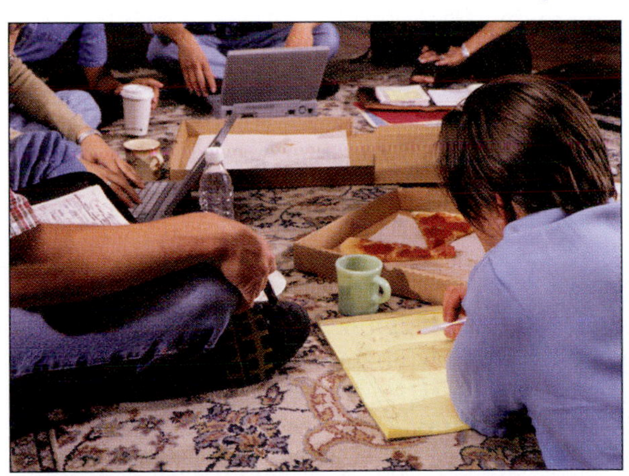

At Amazon, teams adhere to the two-pizza rule; that is, no team should need more than two pizzas to feed its members.

Groups and Teams as Motivators

Managers often decide to form groups and teams to accomplish organizational goals and then find that using groups and teams brings additional benefits. Members of groups, and especially members of teams (because of the higher intensity of interaction in teams), are likely to be more satisfied than they would have been if they were working on their own. The experience of working alongside other highly charged and motivated people can be very stimulating. In addition, working on a team can be very motivating: Team members more readily see how their efforts and expertise directly contribute to the achievement of team and organizational goals, and they feel personally responsible for the outcomes or results of their work. This has been the case at Louis Vuitton, Nucor, and Hallmark Cards.

The increased motivation and satisfaction that can accompany the use of teams can also lead to other outcomes, such as lower turnover. This has been Frank B. Day's experience as founder and CEO of Rock Bottom Restaurants Inc. To provide high-quality customer service, Day has organized the restaurants' employees into wait staff teams, whose members work together to refill beers, take orders, bring hot chicken enchiladas to the tables, or clear off the tables. Team members share the burden of undesirable activities and unpopular shift times, and customers no longer have to wait until a particular waitress or waiter is available. Motivation and satisfaction levels in Rock Bottom restaurants seem to be higher than in other restaurants, and turnover is about one-half of that experienced in other U.S. restaurant chains.[28]

Working in a group or team can also satisfy organizational members' needs for engaging in social interaction and feeling connected to other people. For workers who perform highly stressful jobs, such as hospital emergency and operating room staff, group membership can be an important source of social support and motivation. Family members or friends may not be able to fully understand or appreciate some sources of work stress that these group members experience firsthand. Moreover, group members may cope better with work stressors when they are able to share them with other members of their group. In addition, groups often devise techniques to relieve stress, such as the telling of jokes among hospital operating room staff.

Why do managers in all kinds of organizations rely so heavily on groups and teams? Effectively managed groups and teams can help managers in their quest for high performance, responsiveness to customers, and employee motivation. Before explaining how managers can effectively manage groups, however, we will describe the types of groups that are formed in organizations.

Types of Groups and Teams

To achieve their goals of high performance, responsiveness to customers, innovation, and employee motivation, managers can form various types of groups and teams (see Figure 15.2). **Formal groups** are those managers establish to achieve organizational goals. The formal work groups are *cross-functional* teams composed of members from different departments, such as those at Hallmark Cards, and *cross-cultural* teams composed of members from different cultures or countries, such as the teams at global carmakers. As you will see, some of the groups discussed in this section also can be considered to be cross-functional (if they are composed of members from different departments) or cross-cultural (if they are composed of members from different countries or cultures).

formal group A group that managers establish to achieve organizational goals.

Sometimes organizational members, managers or nonmanagers, form groups because they feel that groups will help them achieve their own goals or meet their own needs (for example, the need for social interaction). Groups formed in

Figure 15.2
Types of Groups and Teams in Organizations

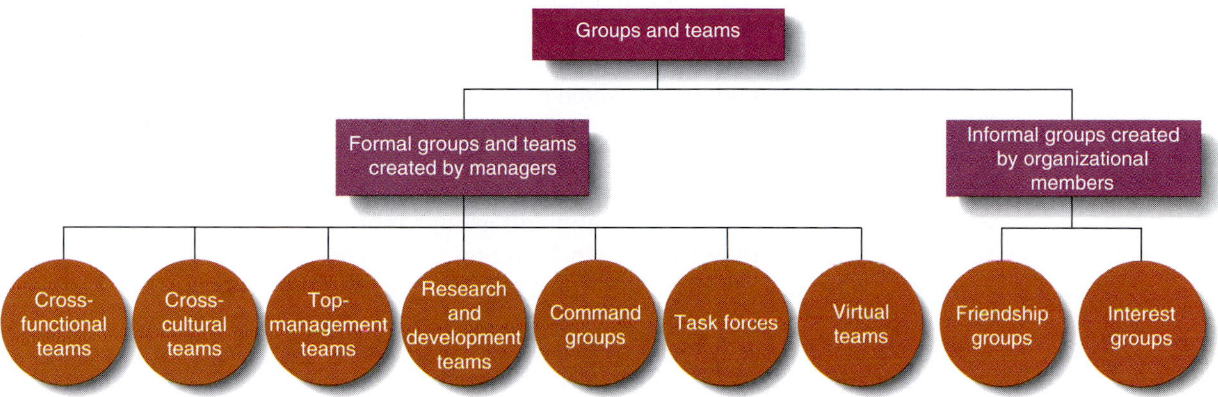

informal group A group that managers or nonmanagerial employees form to help achieve their own goals or meet their own needs.

this way are **informal groups.** Four nurses who work in a hospital and have lunch together twice a week constitute an informal group.

The Top-Management Team

top-management team A group composed of the CEO, the president, and the heads of the most important departments.

A central concern of the CEO and president of a company is to form a **top-management team** to help the organization achieve its mission and goals. Top-management teams are responsible for developing the strategies that result in an organization's competitive advantage; most have between five and seven members. In forming their top-management teams, CEOs are well advised to stress diversity–diversity in expertise, skills, knowledge, and experience. Thus, many top-management teams are also cross-functional teams: They are composed of members from different departments, such as finance, marketing, production, and engineering. Diversity helps ensure that the top-management team will have all the background and resources it needs to make good decisions. Diversity also helps guard against *groupthink,* faulty group decision making that results when group members strive for agreement at the expense of an accurate assessment of the situation (see Chapter 6).

Research and Development Teams

research and development team A team whose members have the expertise and experience needed to develop new products.

Managers in pharmaceuticals, computers, electronics, electronic imaging and other high-tech industries often create **research and development teams** to develop new products. Eric Fossum, for example, a researcher and manager with NASA's Jet Propulsion Laboratory at the California Institute of Technology, formed and heads a three-member R&D team that is developing a camera so small that its basic operational parts can fit on a single computer chip.[29] Managers select R&D team members on the basis of their expertise and experience in a certain area. Sometimes R&D teams are cross-functional teams with members from departments such as engineering, marketing, and production in addition to members from the research and development department.

Command Groups

command group A group composed of subordinates who report to the same supervisor; also called *department* or *unit.*

Subordinates who report to the same supervisor compose a **command group.** When top managers design an organization's structure and establish reporting relationships and a chain of command, they are essentially creating command groups. Command groups, often called *departments* or *units,* perform a significant amount of the work in many organizations. In order to have command groups that help an organization gain a competitive advantage, managers not only need to motivate group members to perform at a high level but also need to be effective leaders. Examples of command groups include the salespeople in a large department store in New York who report to the same supervisor, the employees of a small swimming pool sales and maintenance company in Florida who report to a general manager, the telephone operators at the MetLife insurance company who report to the same supervisor, and workers on an automobile assembly line in the Ford Motor Company who report to the same first-line manager.

Task Forces

task force A committee of managers or nonmanagerial employees from various departments or divisions who meet to solve a specific, mutual problem; also called *ad hoc committee.*

Managers form **task forces** to accomplish specific goals or solve problems in a certain time period; task forces are sometimes called *ad hoc committees.* For example, Michael Rider, owner and top manager of a chain of six gyms and fitness centers in the Midwest, created a task force composed of the general managers of each of the six gyms to determine whether the fitness centers should institute a separate fee schedule for customers who wanted to use the centers only for aerobics classes (and not use other facilities such as weights, steps, tracks, and swimming pools). The task force was given three months to prepare a report summarizing the pros and cons of the proposed change in fee schedules. Once the task force completed its report and reached the conclusion that the change in fee structure probably would reduce revenues rather than increase them and thus should not be implemented, it was disbanded. As in Rider's case, task forces can be a valuable tool for busy managers who do not have the time to personally explore an important issue in depth.

Sometimes managers need to form task forces whose work, so to speak, is never done. The task force may be addressing a long-term or enduring problem or issue facing an organization, such as how to most usefully contribute to the local community or how to make sure that the organization provides opportunities for potential employees with disabilities. Task forces that are relatively permanent are often referred to as *standing committees.* Membership in standing committees changes over time. Members may have, for example, a two- or three-year term on the committee, and memberships expire at varying times so that there are always some members with experience on the committee. Managers often form and maintain standing committees to make sure that important issues continue to be addressed.

Self-Managed Work Teams

self-managed work team A group of employees who supervise their own activities and monitor the quality of the goods and services they provide.

Self-managed work teams are teams in which team members are empowered and have the responsibility and autonomy to complete identifiable pieces of work. On a day-to-day basis, team members decide what the team will do, how it will do it, and which team members will perform which specific tasks.[30] Managers provide self-managed work teams with their overall goals (such as assembling defect-free computer keyboards) but let team members decide how to meet those goals. Managers usually form self-managed work teams to improve quality, increase motivation and satisfaction, and lower costs. Often, by creating self-managed work teams, they combine tasks that individuals working separately used to perform, so the team is responsible for the whole set of tasks that yields an identifiable output or end product.

In response to increasing competition, Johnson Wax, maker of well-known household products including Pledge furniture polish, Glade air freshener, and Windex window cleaner, formed self-managed work teams to find ways to cut costs. Traditionally, Johnson Wax used assembly-line production, in which workers were not encouraged or required to do much real thinking on the job, let alone determine how to cut costs. Things could not be more different at Johnson Wax now. Consider, for example, the nine-member self-managed work team that is responsible for molding plastic containers. Team members choose their own leader, train new members, have their own budget to manage, and are responsible for figuring out how to cut costs of molding plastic containers. Kim Litrenta, a 17-year veteran of Johnson's Waxdale, Wisconsin, plant sums up the effects of the change from assembly-line production to self-managed work teams this way: "In the past you'd have no idea how much things cost because you weren't involved in decisions. Now it's amazing how many different ways people try to save money."[31]

Managers can take a number of steps to ensure that self-managed work teams are effective and help an organization gain a competitive advantage:[32]

- Give teams enough responsibility and autonomy to be truly self-managing. Refrain from telling team members what to do or solving problems for them even if you (as a manager) know what should be done.
- Make sure that a team's work is sufficiently complex so that it entails a number of different steps or procedures that must be performed and results in some kind of finished end product.
- Carefully select members of self-managed work teams. Team members should have the diversity of skills needed to complete the team's work, have the ability to work with others, and want to be part of a team.
- As a manager, realize that your role vis-à-vis self-managed work teams calls for guidance, coaching, and supporting, not supervising. You are a resource for teams to turn to when needed.
- Analyze what type of training team members need and provide it. Working in a self-managed work team often requires that employees have more extensive technical and interpersonal skills.

Managers in a wide variety of organizations have found that self-managed work teams help the organization achieve its goals, as is true at Louis Vuitton and Nucor in "A Manager's Challenge."[33] However, self-managed work teams can run into trouble. Members are often reluctant to discipline one another by withholding bonuses from members who are not performing up to par or by firing members.[34] Buster Jarrell, a manager who oversees self-managed work teams in AES Corporation's Houston plant, has found that although self-managed work teams are highly effective, they have a very difficult time firing team members who are performing poorly.[35]

The Dallas office of the New York Life Insurance Co. recently experimented with having members of self-managed teams evaluate one another's performance and determine pay levels. Team members did not feel comfortable assuming this role, however, and managers ended up evaluating performance and determining pay levels.[36] One reason for team members' discomfort may be the close personal relationships they sometimes develop with one another. In addition, members of self-managed work teams may actually take longer to accomplish tasks, such as when team members have difficulties coordinating their efforts.

Virtual Teams

virtual team A team whose members rarely or never meet face-to-face but, rather, interact by using various forms of information technology such as email, computer networks, telephone, fax, and videoconferences.

Virtual teams are teams whose members rarely or never meet face-to-face but, rather, interact by using various forms of information technology such as email, computer networks, telephone, fax, and videoconferences. As organizations become increasingly global, with operations in far-flung regions of the world, and as the need for specialized knowledge increases due to advances in technology, managers can create virtual teams to solve problems or explore opportunities without being limited by the fact that team members need to be working in the same geographic location.[37]

Take the case of an organization that has manufacturing facilities in Australia, Canada, the United States, and Mexico and is encountering a quality problem in a complex manufacturing process. Each of its manufacturing facilities has a quality control team headed by a quality control manager. The vice president for production does not try to solve the problem by forming and leading a team at one of the four manufacturing facilities; instead, she forms and leads a virtual team composed of the quality control managers of the four plants and the plants' general managers. When these team members communicate via email and videoconferencing, a wide array of knowledge and experience is brought to bear to solve the problem.

The principal advantage of virtual teams is that they enable managers to disregard geographic distances and form teams whose members have the knowledge, expertise, and experience to tackle a particular problem or take advantage of a specific opportunity.[38] Virtual teams also can include members who are not actually employees of the organization itself; a virtual team might include members of a company that is used for outsourcing. More and more companies, including Compaq-Hewlett-Packard, Price-WaterhouseCoopers, Lotus Development, Kodak, Whirlpool, and VeriFone, are either using or exploring the use of virtual teams.[39]

There are two forms of information technologies that members of virtual teams rely on, synchronous technologies and asynchronous technologies.[40] *Synchronous technologies* enable virtual team members to communicate and interact with one another in real time simultaneously and include videoconferencing, teleconferencing, and electronic meetings. *Asynchronous technologies* delay communication and include email, electronic bulletin boards, and Internet Web sites. Many virtual teams use both kinds of technology depending on what projects they are working on.

Increasing globalization is likely to result in more organizations relying on virtual teams to a greater extent.[41] One of the major challenges members of virtual teams face is building a sense of camaraderie and trust among team members who rarely, if ever, meet face-to-face. To address this challenge, some organizations schedule recreational activities, such as ski trips, so that virtual team members can get together. Other organizations make sure that virtual team members have a chance to meet in person soon after the team is formed and then schedule periodic face-to-face meetings to promote trust, understanding, and cooperation in the teams.[42] The need for such meetings is underscored by research that suggests that while some virtual teams can be as effective as teams that meet face-to-face, virtual team members might be less satisfied with teamwork efforts and have fewer feelings of camaraderie or cohesion. (Group cohesiveness is discussed in more detail later in the chapter.)[43]

Research also suggests that it is important for managers to keep track of virtual teams and intervene when necessary by, for example, encouraging members of teams who do not communicate often enough to monitor their team's progress and make sure that team members actually have the time, and are recognized for, their virtual teamwork.[44] Additionally, when virtual teams are experiencing downtime or rough spots, managers might try to schedule face-to-face team time to bring team members together and help them focus on their goals.[45]

Friendship Groups

friendship group An informal group composed of employees who enjoy one another's company and socialize with one another.

The groups described so far are formal groups created by managers. **Friendship groups** are informal groups composed of employees who enjoy one another's company and socialize with one another. Members of friendship groups may have lunch together, take breaks together, or meet after work for meals, sports, or other activities. Friendship groups help satisfy employees' needs for interpersonal interaction, can provide needed social support in times of stress, and can contribute to people's feeling good at work and being satisfied with their jobs. Managers themselves often form friendship groups. The informal relationships that managers build in friendship groups can often help them solve work-related problems because members of these groups typically discuss work-related matters and offer advice.

Friendship groups like the one pictured here can be beneficial to an organization. They help satisfy employees' needs for interpersonal interaction, provide social support in times of stress, and can increase job satisfaction. Since group members often discuss work-related problems, they may even end up generating solutions that can be used on the job.

Interest Groups

interest group An informal group composed of employees seeking to achieve a common goal related to their membership in an organization.

Employees form informal **interest groups** when they seek to achieve a common goal related to their membership in an organization. Employees may form interest groups, for example, to encourage managers to consider instituting flexible working hours, providing on-site child care, improving working conditions, or more proactively supporting environmental protection. Interest groups can provide managers with valuable insights into the issues and concerns that are foremost in employees' minds. They also can signal the need for change.

Group Dynamics

The ways in which groups function and, ultimately, their effectiveness hinge on group characteristics and processes known collectively as *group dynamics*. In this section, we discuss five key elements of group dynamics: group size, tasks, and roles; group leadership; group development; group norms; and group cohesiveness.

Group Size, Tasks, and Roles

Managers need to take group size, group tasks, and group roles into account as they create and maintain high-performing groups and teams.

GROUP SIZE The number of members in a group can be an important determinant of members' motivation and commitment and group performance. There are several advantages to keeping a group relatively small–between two and nine members. Compared with members of large groups, members of small groups tend to (1) interact more with each other and find it easier to coordinate their efforts, (2) be more motivated, satisfied, and committed, (3) find it easier to share information, and (4) be better able to see the importance of their personal contributions for group success. A disadvantage of small rather than large groups is that members of small groups have fewer resources available to accomplish their goals.

division of labor Splitting the work to be performed into particular tasks and assigning tasks to individual workers.

Large groups–with 10 or more members–also offer some advantages. They have more resources at their disposal to achieve group goals than small groups do. These resources include the knowledge, experience, skills, and abilities of group members as well as their actual time and effort. Large groups also enable managers to obtain the advantages stemming from the **division of labor**–splitting the work to be performed into particular tasks and assigning tasks to individual workers. Workers who specialize in particular tasks are likely to become skilled at performing those tasks and contribute significantly to high group performance.

The disadvantages of large groups include the problems of communication and coordination and the lower levels of motivation, satisfaction, and commitment that members of large groups sometimes experience. It is clearly more difficult to share information with, and coordinate the activities of, 16 people rather than 8 people. Moreover, members of large groups might not think that their efforts are really needed and sometimes might not even feel a part of the group.

In deciding on the appropriate size for any group, managers attempt to gain the advantages of small-group size and, at the same time, form groups with sufficient resources to accomplish their goals and have a well-developed division of labor, as is true at Louis Vuitton and Nucor in "A Manager's Challenge." As a general rule of thumb, groups should have no more members than necessary to achieve a division of labor and provide the resources needed to achieve group goals. In R&D teams, for example, group size is too large when (1) members spend more time communicating what they know to others than applying what they know to solve problems and create new products, (2) individual productivity decreases, and (3) group performance suffers.[46]

task interdependence The degree to which the work performed by one member of a group influences the work performed by other members.

GROUP TASKS The appropriate size of a high-performing group is affected by the kind of tasks the group is to perform. An important characteristic of group tasks that affects performance is **task interdependence,** the degree to which the work performed by one member of a group influences the work performed by other members.[47] As task interdependence increases, group members need to interact more frequently and intensely with one another, and their efforts have to be more closely coordinated if they are to perform at a high level. Management expert James D. Thompson identified three types of task interdependence: pooled, sequential, and reciprocal (see Figure 15.3).[48]

pooled task interdependence The task interdependence that exists when group members make separate and independent contributions to group performance.

POOLED TASK INTERDEPENDENCE **Pooled task interdependence** exists when group members make separate and independent contributions to group performance; overall group performance is the sum of the performance of the individual members (see Figure 15.3a). Examples of groups that have pooled task interdependence include a group of teachers in an elementary school, a group of salespeople in a department store, a group of secretaries in an office, and a group of custodians in an office building. In these examples, group performance, whether it be the number of children who are taught and the quality of their education, the dollar value of sales, the amount of secretarial work completed, or the number of offices cleaned, is determined by summing the individual contributions of group members.

For groups with pooled interdependence, managers should determine the appropriate group size primarily from the amount of work to be accomplished. Large groups can be effective because group members work independently and do not have to interact frequently with one another. Motivation in groups with pooled interdependence will be highest when managers reward group members based on individual performance.

sequential task interdependence The task interdependence that exists when group members must perform specific tasks in a predetermined order.

SEQUENTIAL TASK INTERDEPENDENCE **Sequential task interdependence** exists when group members must perform specific tasks in a predetermined order; certain tasks have to be performed before others, and what one worker does affects the work of others (see Figure 15.3b). Assembly lines and mass-production processes are characterized by sequential task interdependence.

When group members are sequentially interdependent, group size is usually dictated by the needs of the production process–for example, the number of steps needed in an assembly line to efficiently produce a CD player. With sequential interdependence, it is difficult to identify individual performance because one group member's performance depends on how well others perform their tasks. A slow worker at the start of an assembly line, for example, causes all workers further down to work slowly. Thus, managers are often

Figure 15.3
Types of Task Interdependence

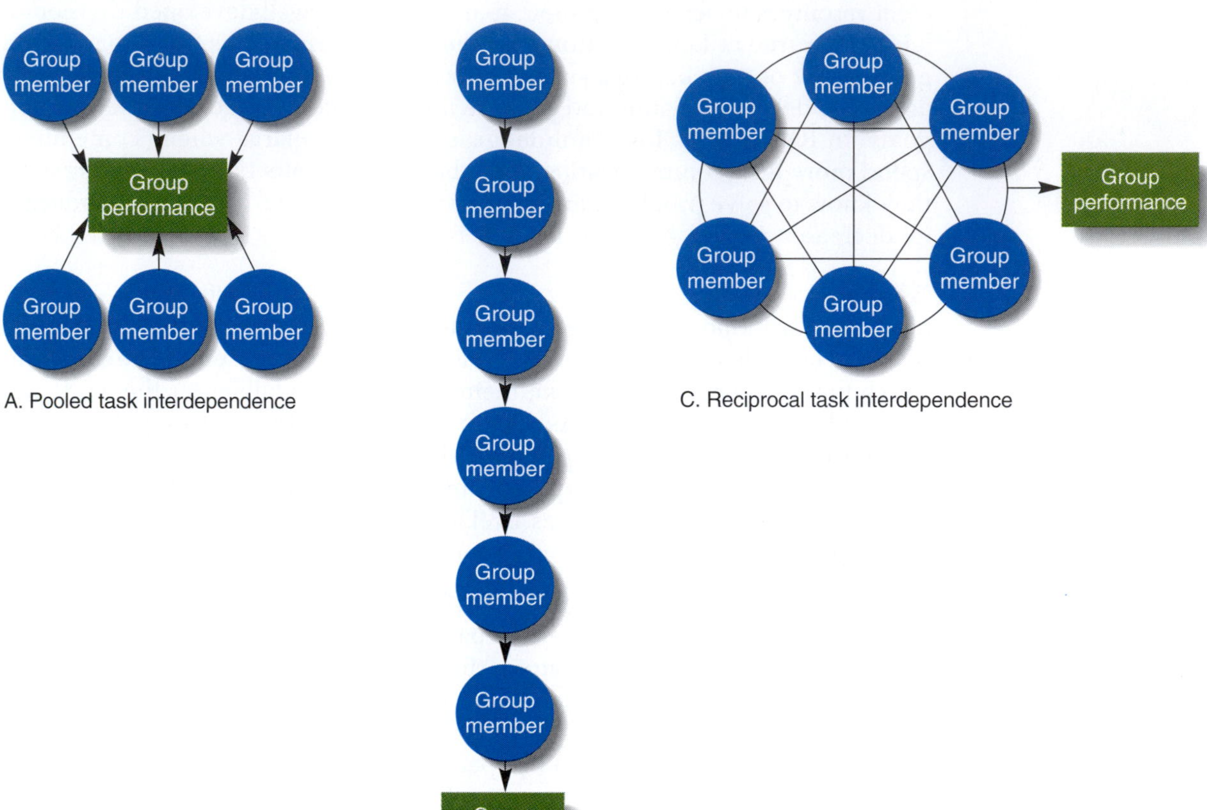

advised to reward group members for group performance. Group members will be motivated to perform highly because if the group performs well, each member will benefit. In addition, group members may put pressure on poor performers to improve so that group performance and rewards do not suffer.

reciprocal task interdependence The task interdependence that exists when the work performed by each group member is fully dependent on the work performed by other group members.

RECIPROCAL TASK INTERDEPENDENCE **Reciprocal task interdependence** exists when the work performed by each group member is fully dependent on the work performed by other group members; group members have to share information, intensely interact with one another, and coordinate their efforts in order for the group to achieve its goals (see Figure 15.3c). In general, reciprocal task interdependence characterizes the operation of teams, rather than other kinds of groups. The task interdependence of R&D teams, top-management teams, and many self-managed work teams is reciprocal.

When group members are reciprocally interdependent, managers are advised to keep group size relatively small because of the necessity of coordinating team members' activities. Communication difficulties can arise in teams with reciprocally interdependent tasks because team members need to interact frequently with one another and be available when needed. As group size increases, communication difficulties increase and can impair team performance.

When a group's members are reciprocally interdependent, managers also are advised to reward group members on the basis of group performance. Individual levels of performance are often difficult for managers to identify, and group-based rewards help ensure that group members will be motivated to perform at a high level and make valuable contributions to the group. Of course, if a manager can identify instances of individual performance in such groups, they too can be rewarded to maintain high levels of motivation. Microsoft and many other companies reward group members for their individual performance as well as for the performance of their group.

group role A set of behaviors and tasks that a member of a group is expected to perform because of his or her position in the group.

GROUP ROLES A **group role** is a set of behaviors and tasks that a member of a group is expected to perform because of his or her position in the group. Members of cross-functional teams, for example, are expected to perform roles relevant to their special areas of expertise. In our earlier example of cross-functional teams at Hallmark Cards, it is the role of writers on the teams to create verses for new cards, the role of artists to draw illustrations, and the role of designers to put verse and artwork together in an attractive and appealing card design. The roles of members of top-management teams are shaped primarily by their areas of expertise–production, marketing, finance, research and development–but members of top-management teams also typically draw on their broad-based expertise as planners and strategists.

In forming groups and teams, managers need to clearly communicate to group members the expectations for their roles in the group, what is required of them, and how the different roles in the group fit together to accomplish group goals. Managers also need to realize that group roles often change and evolve as a group's tasks and goals change and as group members gain experience and knowledge. Thus, to get the performance gains that come from experience or "learning by doing," managers should encourage group members to take the initiative to assume additional responsibilities as they see fit and modify their assigned roles. This process, called **role making,** can enhance individual and group performance.

role making Taking the initiative to modify an assigned role by assuming additional responsibilities.

In self-managed work teams and some other groups, group members themselves are responsible for creating and assigning roles. Many self-managed work teams also pick their own team leaders. When group members create their own roles, managers should be available to group members in an advisory capacity, helping them effectively settle conflicts and disagreements. At Johnsonville Foods, for example, the position titles of first-line managers have been changed to "advisory coach" to reflect the managers' new role vis-à-vis the self-managed work teams they oversee.[49]

Group Leadership

All groups and teams need leadership. Indeed, as we discussed in detail in Chapter 14, effective leadership is a key ingredient for high-performing groups, teams, and organizations. Sometimes managers assume the leadership role in groups and teams, as is the case in many command groups and top-management teams. Or a manager may appoint a member of a group who is not a manager to be group leader or chairperson, as is the case in a task force or standing committee. In other cases, group or team members may choose their own leaders, or a leader may emerge naturally as group members work together to achieve group goals. When managers empower members of self-managed work teams, they often let group members choose their own leaders. Some self-managed work teams find it effective to rotate the leadership role among their members. Whether leaders of groups and teams are managers or not, and whether they are appointed by managers or emerge naturally in a group, they play an important role in ensuring that groups and teams perform up to their potential.

Group Development over Time

As many managers overseeing self-managed teams have learned, it sometimes takes a self-managed work team two or three years to perform up to its true capabilities.[50] As their experience suggests, what a group is capable of achieving depends in part on its stage of development. Knowing that it takes considerable time for self-managed work teams to get up and running has helped managers have realistic expectations for new teams and know that they need to provide new team members with considerable training and guidance.

Although every group's development over time is somewhat unique, researchers have identified five stages of group development that many groups seem to pass through (see Figure 15.4).[51] In the first stage, *forming,* members try to get to know one another and reach a common understanding of what the group is trying to accomplish and how group members should behave. During this stage, managers should strive to make each member feel that he or she is a valued part of the group.

In the second stage, *storming,* group members experience conflict and disagreements because some members do not wish to submit to the demands of other group members. Disputes may arise over who should lead the group. Self-managed work teams can be particularly vulnerable during the storming stage. Managers need to keep an eye on groups at this stage to make sure that conflict does not get out of hand.

During the third stage, *norming,* close ties between group members develop, and feelings of friendship and camaraderie emerge. Group members arrive at a consensus about what goals they should be seeking to achieve and how group members should behave toward one another.

In the fourth stage, *performing,* the real work of the group gets accomplished. Depending on the type of group in question, managers need to take different steps at this stage to help ensure that groups are effective. Managers of command groups need to make sure that group members are motivated and that they are effectively leading group members. Managers overseeing self-managed work teams have to empower team members and make sure that teams are given enough responsibility and autonomy at the performing stage.

The last stage, *adjourning,* applies only to groups that eventually are disbanded, such as task forces. During adjourning a group is dispersed. Sometimes,

Figure 15.4
Five Stages of Group Development

adjourning takes place when a group completes a finished product, such as when a task force evaluating the pros and cons of providing on-site child care produces a report supporting its recommendation.

Managers should have a flexible approach to group development and should keep attuned to the different needs and requirements of groups at the various stages.[52] Above all else, and regardless of the stage of development, managers need to think of themselves as *resources* for groups. Thus, managers always should be striving to find ways to help groups and teams function more effectively.

Group Norms

group norms Shared guidelines or rules for behavior that most group members follow.

All groups, whether top-management teams, self-managed work teams, or command groups, need to control their members' behaviors to ensure that the group performs highly and meets its goals. Assigning roles to each group member is one way to control behavior in groups. Another important way in which groups influence members' behavior is through the development and enforcement of group norms.[53] **Group norms** are shared guidelines or rules for behavior that most group members follow. Groups develop norms concerning a wide variety of behaviors, including working hours, the sharing of information among group members, how certain group tasks should be performed, and even how members of a group should dress. At Nucor in "A Manager's Challenge," recall how production teams develop their own norms to ensure high performance and the attainment of the weekly bonus.

Managers should encourage members of a group to develop norms that contribute to group performance and the attainment of group goals. For example, group norms that dictate that each member of a cross-functional team should always be available for the rest of the team when his or her input is needed, return phone calls as soon as possible, inform other team members of travel plans, and give team members a phone number at which he or she can be reached when traveling on business help to ensure that the team is efficient, performs highly, and achieves its goals. A norm in a command group of secretaries that dictates that secretaries who happen to have a light workload in any given week should help out secretaries with heavier workloads helps to ensure that the group completes all assignments in a timely and efficient manner. And a norm in a top-management team that dictates that team members should always consult with one another before making major decisions helps to ensure that good decisions are made with a minimum of errors.

CONFORMITY AND DEVIANCE Group members conform to norms for three reasons: (1) They want to obtain rewards and avoid punishments. (2) They want to imitate group members whom they like and admire. (3) They have internalized the norm and believe it is the right and proper way to behave.[54] Consider the case of Robert King, who conformed to his department's norm of attending a fund-raiser for a community food bank. King's conformity could be due to (1) his desire to be a member of the group in good standing and to have friendly relationships with other group members (rewards), (2) his copying the behavior of other members of the department whom he respects and who always attend the fund-raiser (imitating other group members), or (3) his belief in the merits of supporting the activities of the food bank (believing that is the right and proper way to behave).

Failure to conform, or deviance, occurs when a member of a group violates a group norm. Deviance signals that a group is not controlling one of its member's behaviors. Groups generally respond to members who behave defiantly in one of three ways:[55]

1. The group might try to get the member to change his or her deviant ways and conform to the norm. Group members might try to convince the member of the need to conform, or they might ignore or even punish the deviant. For example, in a Jacksonville Foods plant Liz Senkbiel, a member of a self-managed work team responsible for weighing sausages, failed to conform to a group norm dictating that group members should periodically clean up an untidy room used to interview prospective employees. Because Senkbiel refused to take part in the team's cleanup efforts, team members reduced her monthly bonus by about $225 for a two-month period.[56] Senkbiel clearly learned the costs of deviant behavior in her team.
2. The group might expel the member.
3. The group might change the norm to be consistent with the member's behavior.

That last alternative suggests that some deviant behavior can be functional for groups. Deviance is functional for a group when it causes group members to evaluate norms that may be dysfunctional but are taken for granted by the group. Often, group members do not think about why they behave in a certain way or why they follow certain norms. Deviance can cause group members to reflect on their norms and change them when appropriate.

Take the case of a group of receptionists in a beauty salon who followed the norm that all appointments would be handwritten in an appointment book and at the end of each day the receptionist on duty would enter the appointments into the salon's computer system, which printed out the hairdressers' daily schedules. One day, a receptionist decided to enter appointments directly into the computer system at the time they were being made, bypassing the appointment book. This deviant behavior caused the other receptionists to think about why they were using the appointment book in the first place, since all appointments could be entered into the computer directly. After consulting with the owner of the salon, the group changed its norm. Now appointments are entered directly into the computer, which saves time and cuts down on scheduling errors.

ENCOURAGING A BALANCE OF CONFORMITY AND DEVIANCE

To effectively help an organization gain a competitive advantage, groups and teams need to have the right balance of conformity and deviance (see Figure 15.5). A group needs a certain level of conformity to ensure that it can control members' behavior and channel it in the direction of high performance and group goal accomplishment. A group also needs a certain level of deviance to ensure that dysfunctional norms are discarded and replaced with functional ones. Balancing conformity and deviance is a pressing concern for all groups, whether they are top-management teams, R&D teams, command groups, or self-managed work teams.

The extent of conformity and reactions to deviance within groups are determined by group members themselves. The three bases for conformity described above are powerful forces that more often than not result in group members' conforming to norms. Sometimes these forces are so strong that deviance rarely occurs in groups, and when it does, it is stamped out.

Figure 15.5
Balancing Conformity and Deviance in Groups

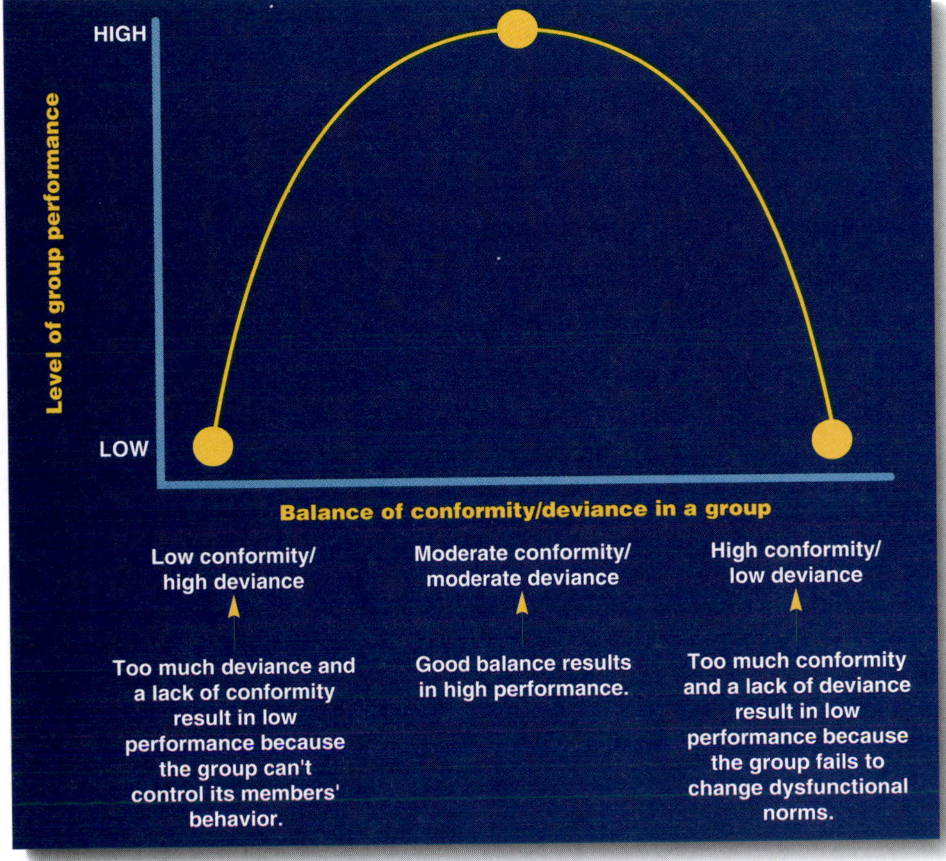

Managers can take several steps to ensure that there is enough tolerance of deviance in groups so that group members are willing to deviate from dysfunctional norms and, when deviance occurs in their group, reflect on the appropriateness of the violated norm and change the norm if necessary. First, managers can be role models for the groups and teams they oversee. When managers encourage and accept employees' suggestions for changes in procedures, do not rigidly insist that tasks be accomplished in a certain way, and admit when a norm that they once supported is no longer functional, they signal to group members that conformity should not come at the expense of needed changes and improvements. Second, managers should let employees know that there are always ways to improve group processes and performance levels and thus opportunities to replace existing norms with norms that will better enable a group to achieve its goals and perform at a high level. Third, managers should encourage members of groups and teams to periodically assess the appropriateness of their existing norms.

Managers in the innovative design firm Ideo, based in Palo Alto, California (Ideo's culture is described in Chapter 3) have excelled at ensuring that design teams have the right mix of conformity and deviance, resulting in Ideo's designing products in fields ranging from medicine to space travel to computing and personal hygiene, as indicated in the following "Focus on Diversity."

Focus on Diversity

Diversity of Thought and Respect for Ideas Reign at Ideo

Ideo designed many products we now take for granted. Ideo designed the first Apple mouse, the Palm handheld organizer, stand-up toothpaste containers, flexible shelving for offices, self-sealing drink bottles for sports, blood analyzers, and even equipment used in space travel.[57] Managers and designers at Ideo pride themselves on being experts at the process of innovation in general, rather than in any particular domain. Of course, the company has technical design experts, such as mechanical and electrical engineers, who work on products requiring specialized knowledge, but on the same teams with the engineers might be an anthropologist, a biologist, and a social scientist.[58]

Essentially, a guiding principle at Ideo is that innovation comes in many shapes and sizes and it is only through diversity in thought that people can recognize opportunities for innovation. To promote such diversity in thought, new product development at Ideo is a team effort.[59] Moreover, both conformity and deviance are encouraged on Ideo teams.

Deviance, thinking differently, and not conforming to expected ways of doing things and mind-sets are encouraged at Ideo. In fact, innovative ideas often flow when designers try to see things as they really are and are not blinded by thoughts of what is appropriate, what is possible, or how things should be. Often, constraints on new product design are created by designers themselves conforming to a certain mind-set about the nature of a product or what a product can or should do and look like. Ideo designers are encouraged to actively break down these constraints in their design teams.[60]

Managers at Ideo realize the need for a certain amount of conformity so that members of design teams can work effectively together and achieve their goals. Thus, conformity to a few very central norms is emphasized in Ideo teams. These norms include understanding what the team is working on (e.g., the product, market, or client need), observing real people in their natural environments, visualizing how new products might work and be used, evaluating and refining product prototypes, encouraging wild ideas, and never rejecting an idea simply because it sounds too crazy.[61] As long as these norms are followed, diversity of thought and even deviance serve to promote innovation at Ideo. In fact, another norm at Ideo is to study "rule breakers"–people who don't follow instructions for products, for example, or who try to put products to different uses–as these individuals might help designers identify problems with existing products and unmet consumer needs.[62] All in all, Ideo's focus on encouraging both deviance and conformity in design teams has benefited all of us as we use Ideo-designed products that seem so familiar we take them for granted. We forget these products weren't in existence until a design team at Ideo was called on by a client to develop a new product or improve an existing one.[63]

Group Cohesiveness

group cohesiveness The degree to which members are attracted to or loyal to their group.

Another important element of group dynamics that affects group performance and effectiveness is **group cohesiveness,** the degree to which members are attracted to or loyal to their group or team.[64] When group cohesiveness is high, individuals strongly value their group membership, find the group very appealing, and have strong desires to remain a part of the group. When group cohesiveness is low, group members do not find their group particularly appealing and have little desire to retain their group membership. Research suggests that managers should strive to have a moderate level of cohesiveness in the groups and teams they manage because that is most likely to contribute to an organization's competitive advantage.

CONSEQUENCES OF GROUP COHESIVENESS There are three major consequences of group cohesiveness: level of participation within a group, level of conformity to group norms, and emphasis on group goal accomplishment (see Figure 15.6).[65]

LEVEL OF PARTICIPATION WITHIN A GROUP As group cohesiveness increases, the extent of group members' participation within the group increases. Participation contributes to group effectiveness because group members are actively involved in the group, ensure that group tasks get accomplished, readily share information with each other, and have frequent and open communication (the important topic of communication is covered in depth in Chapter 16).

A moderate level of group cohesiveness helps to ensure that group members actively participate in the group and communicate effectively with one another. The reason why managers may not want to encourage high levels of cohesiveness is illustrated by the example of two cross-functional teams responsible for developing new toys. Members of the highly cohesive Team Alpha often have lengthy meetings that usually start with non-work-related conversations and jokes, meet more often than most of the other cross-functional teams in the company, and spend a good portion of their time communicating the ins and outs of their department's contribution to toy development to other team members. Members of the moderately cohesive Team Beta generally have efficient meetings in which ideas are communicated and discussed as needed, do not meet more often than necessary, and share the ins and outs of their expertise with one another to the extent needed for the development process. Teams Alpha and Beta have both developed some top-selling toys. However, it generally takes Team Alpha 30 percent longer to do so than Team Beta. This is why too much cohesiveness can be too much of a good thing.

Figure 15.6
Sources and Consequences of Group Cohesiveness

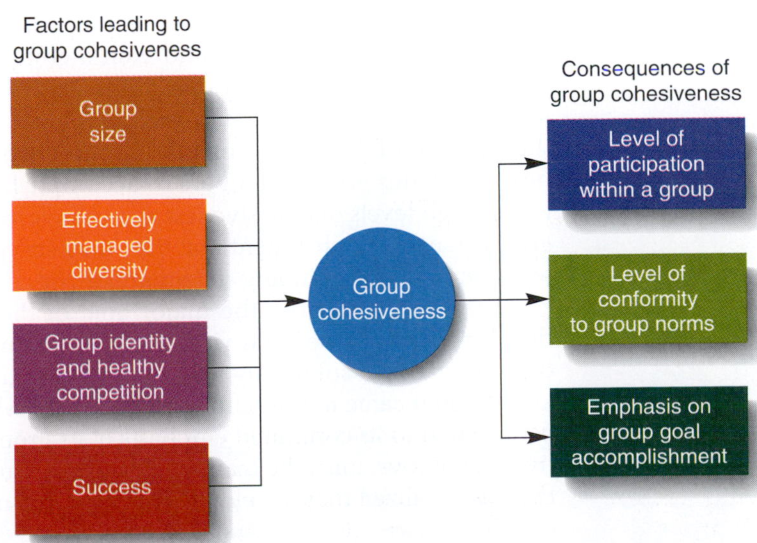

LEVEL OF CONFORMITY TO GROUP NORMS Increasing levels of group cohesiveness result in increasing levels of conformity to group norms, and when cohesiveness becomes high, there may be so little deviance in groups that group members conform to norms even when they are dysfunctional. In contrast, low cohesiveness can result in too much deviance and undermine the ability of a group to control its members' behaviors to get things done.

Teams Alpha and Beta in the toy company both had the same norm for toy development. It dictated that members of each team would discuss potential ideas for new toys, decide on a line of toys to pursue, and then have the team member from R&D design a prototype. Recently, a new animated movie featuring a family of rabbits produced by a small film company was an unexpected hit, and major toy companies were scrambling to reach licensing agreements to produce toy lines featuring the rabbits. The top-management team in the toy company assigned Teams Alpha and Beta to develop the new toy lines and to do so quickly to beat the competition.

Members of Team Alpha followed their usual toy development norm even though the marketing expert on the team believed that the process could have been streamlined to save time. The marketing expert on Team Beta urged the team to deviate from its toy development norm. She suggested that the team not have R&D develop prototypes but, instead, modify top-selling toys the company already made to feature rabbits and then reach a licensing agreement with the film company based on the high sales potential (given the company's prior success). Once the licensing agreement was signed, the company could take the time needed to develop innovative and unique rabbit toys with more input from R&D.

As a result of the willingness of the marketing expert on Team Beta to deviate from the norm for toy development, the toy company obtained an exclusive licensing agreement with the film company and had its first rabbit toys on the shelves of stores in a record three months. Groups need a balance of conformity and deviance, so a moderate level of cohesiveness often yields the best outcome, as it did in the case of Team Beta.

EMPHASIS ON GROUP GOAL ACCOMPLISHMENT As group cohesiveness increases, the emphasis placed on group goal accomplishment also increases within a group. A very strong emphasis on group goal accomplishment, however, does not always lead to organizational effectiveness. For an organization to be effective and gain a competitive advantage, the different groups and teams in the organization must cooperate with one another and be motivated to achieve *organizational goals,* even if doing so sometimes comes at the expense of the achievement of group goals. A moderate level of cohesiveness motivates group members to accomplish both group and organizational goals. High levels of cohesiveness can cause group members to be so focused on group goal accomplishment that they may strive to achieve group goals no matter what–even when doing so jeopardizes organizational performance.

At the toy company, the major goal of the cross-functional teams was to develop new toy lines that were truly innovative, utilized the latest in technology, and were in some way fundamentally distinct from other toys on the market. When it came to the rabbit project, Team Alpha's high level of cohesiveness contributed to its continued emphasis of its group goal of developing an innovative line of toys; thus, the team stuck with its usual design process. Team Beta, in contrast, realized that developing the new line of toys quickly was an important organizational goal that should take precedence over the group's goal of developing pathbreaking new toys, at least in the short run. Team Beta's moderate level of cohesiveness contributed to team members' doing what was best for the toy company in this case.

FACTORS LEADING TO GROUP COHESIVENESS Four factors contribute to the level of group cohesiveness (see Figure 15.6).[66] By influencing these *determinants of group cohesiveness,* managers can raise or lower the level of cohesiveness to promote moderate levels of cohesiveness in groups and teams.

GROUP SIZE As we mentioned earlier, members of small groups tend to be more motivated and committed than members of large groups. Thus, to promote cohesiveness in groups, when feasible, managers should form groups that are small to medium in size (about 2 to 15 members). If a group is low in cohesiveness and large in size, managers might want to consider the feasibility of dividing the group in two and assigning different tasks and goals to the two newly formed groups.

EFFECTIVELY MANAGED DIVERSITY In general, people tend to like and get along with others who are similar to themselves. It is easier to communicate with someone, for example, who shares your values, has a similar background, and has had similar experiences. However, as discussed in Chapter 4, diversity in groups, teams, and organizations can help an organization gain a competitive advantage. Diverse groups often come up with more innovative and creative ideas. One reason why cross-functional teams are so popular in organizations like Hallmark Cards is that the diversity in expertise represented in the teams results in higher levels of team performance.

In forming groups and teams, managers need to make sure that the diversity in knowledge, experience, expertise, and other characteristics necessary for group goal accomplishment is represented in the new groups. Managers then have to make sure that this diversity in group membership is effectively managed so that groups will be cohesive (see Chapter 5).

Employees at the Internet company Google, known as Googlers, play an informal game of street hockey in the company's parking lot two times a week. Friendly competition like this helps build group cohesiveness.

GROUP IDENTITY AND HEALTHY COMPETITION When group cohesiveness is low, managers can often increase it by encouraging groups to develop their own identities or personalities and to engage in healthy competition. This is precisely what managers at Eaton Corporation, based in Lincoln, Illinois, did. Eaton's employees manufacture products such as engine valves, gears, truck axles, and circuit breakers. Managers at Eaton created self-managed work teams to cut costs and improve performance. They realized, however, that the teams would have to be cohesive to ensure that they would strive to achieve their goals. Managers promoted group identity by having the teams give themselves names such as "The Hoods," "The Worms," and "Scrap Attack" (a team striving to reduce costly scrap-metal waste by 50 percent). Healthy competition among groups is promoted by displaying measures of each team's performance and the extent to which teams have met their goals on a large TV screen in the cafeteria and by rewarding team members for team performance.[67]

If groups are too cohesive, managers can try to decrease cohesiveness by promoting organizational (rather than group) identity and making the organization as a whole the focus of the group's efforts. Organizational identity can be promoted by making group members feel that they are valued members of the organization as a whole and by stressing cooperation across groups to promote the achievement of organizational goals. Excessive levels of cohesiveness also can be reduced by reducing or eliminating competition among groups and rewarding cooperation.

SUCCESS When it comes to promoting group cohesiveness, there is more than a grain of truth to the saying "Nothing succeeds like success." As groups become more successful, they become increasingly attractive to their members, and their cohesiveness tends to increase. When cohesiveness is low, managers can increase cohesiveness by making sure that a group can achieve some noticeable and visible successes.

Take the case of a group of salespeople in the housewares department of a medium-size department store. The housewares department was recently moved to a corner of the store's basement. Its remote location resulted in low sales because of infrequent customer traffic in that part of the store. The salespeople, who were generally evaluated favorably by their supervisors and were valued members of the store, tried various initiatives to boost sales, but to no avail. As a result of this lack of success and the poor performance of their department, their cohesiveness started to plummet. To increase and preserve the cohesiveness of the group, the store manager implemented a group-based incentive across the store. In any month, members of the group with the best attendance and punctuality records would have their names and pictures posted on a bulletin board in the cafeteria and would each receive a $50 gift certificate. The housewares group frequently had the best records, and their success on this dimension helped to build and maintain their cohesiveness. Moreover, this initiative boosted attendance and discouraged lateness throughout the store. As another example, teams at Nucor in "A Manager's Challenge" are likely to become cohesive when they consistently perform at a high level and team members are rewarded for team performance with a weekly bonus. And the cohesiveness of teams at Louis Vuitton is enhanced by their success at producing high-quality accessories.

Teams at Southwest Airlines are known for their cohesiveness. In fact, the organization as a whole is known for its cohesive, fun-loving culture, as profiled in the following "Management Insight."

Management Insight

Cohesiveness and Success at Southwest Airlines

Southwest Airlines' culture exudes cohesiveness. From hiring people who are fun, friendly, and caring to celebrating and throwing parties on each and every special occasion, Southwest's people-oriented culture emphasizes love, having a good time, excellent customer service, and an esprit de corps second to none.[68] At Southwest's headquarters in Dallas, the walls are covered with photos of employees, their pets, and their families. As Colleen Barrett, Southwest's president and chief operating officer, puts it, "This is an open scrapbook. We aren't uptight. . . . We are having a *party!* . . . We really do everything with passion. We scream at each other and we hug each other."[69]

Southwest Airlines employees Steve Hubbell (left), Rachel Hubbell (center), and Amy Weaver (right) participate in a welcoming ceremony at Philadelphia International Airport in May 2004, for the start of service in this new location. Teamwork has been a cornerstone of Southwest's success.

Teams at Southwest are known for their cohesiveness and esprit de corps as well. Take the case of the marketing team that Benjean Riedman leads as a Southwest district marketing manager in Seattle.[70] Team members work well together, help one another out, and are driven to market and sell Southwest in the Pacific Northwest. The team also gives to the local communities they serve through charitable activities and volunteer work. Riedman, for example, is on the grant and auction committees for the Ronald McDonald House in Seattle. Team members count on one another, and as Riedman puts it, "They are more than coworkers, they are family."[71]

Southwest Airlines' continuing success in an industry and environment in which other major airlines are floundering reinforces cohesiveness at the team and organizational levels. Southwest's earnings in 2003, at $442 million, were greater than the earnings of all other U.S. airlines put together.[72] After the tragic terrorist attacks on September 11, 2001, when other airlines were forced to lay off employees and still lost money, Southwest continued to earn a profit without having to lay off employees.[73] While Southwest's zany culture emphasizes playfulness, keeping costs low and providing excellent customer service are serious business at Southwest. From no assigned seats, meals, or entertainment on flights (except for that provided by witty flight attendants) to flying only Boeing 737s, Southwest's commitment to low costs is always on the front burner.[74] As all airlines have found their costs rising, due in part to rising fuel costs, Southwest has found new ways to cut costs. For example, Southwest recently closed three of its reservation centers to cut costs as more and more travelers are purchasing tickets online and is increasing its use of self-service check-in at airports.[75] Steps such as these will help to ensure Southwest's continued success; and success helps maintain cohesiveness at Southwest. As Southwest's legendary founder and chairman, Herb Kelleher, puts it, "We run this company to prepare ourselves for the bad times, which always come in business."[76]

Managing Groups and Teams for High Performance

Now that you have a good understanding of why groups and teams are so important for organizations, the types of groups that managers create, and group dynamics, we consider some additional steps that managers can take to make sure groups and teams perform highly and contribute to organizational effectiveness. Managers striving to have top-performing groups and teams need to (1) motivate group members to work toward the achievement of organizational goals, (2) reduce social loafing, and (3) help groups to manage conflict effectively.

Motivating Group Members to Achieve Organizational Goals

When work is difficult, tedious, or requires a high level of commitment and energy, managers cannot assume that group members will always be motivated to work toward the achievement of organizational goals. Consider the case of a group of house painters who paint the interiors and exteriors of new homes for a construction company and are paid on an hourly basis. Why should they strive to complete painting jobs quickly and efficiently if doing so will just make them feel more tired at the end of the day and they will not receive any tangible benefits? It makes more sense for the painters to adopt a more relaxed approach, to take frequent breaks, and to work at a leisurely pace. This relaxed approach, however, impairs the construction company's ability to gain a competitive advantage because it raises costs and increases the time needed to complete a new home.

Managers can motivate members of groups and teams to achieve organizational goals and create a competitive advantage by making sure that the members themselves benefit when the group or team performs highly, as is true at Nucor in "A Manager's Challenge." If members of a self-managed work team know that they will receive a weekly bonus based on team performance, they will be highly motivated to perform at a high level.

Managers often rely on some combination of individual and group-based incentives to motivate members of groups and teams to work toward the achievement of organizational goals and a competitive advantage, as is the case at Nucor in "A Manager's Challenge." When individual performance within a group can be assessed, pay is often determined by individual performance or by both individual and group performance. When individual performance within a group cannot be accurately assessed, then group performance should be the key determinant of pay levels. Approximately 75 percent of companies that use self-managed work teams base team members' pay in part on team performance.[77] A major challenge for managers is to develop a fair pay system that will lead to both high individual motivation and high group or team performance.

Other benefits that managers can make available to high-performance group members–in addition to monetary rewards–include extra resources such as equipment and computer software, awards and other forms of recognition, and choice of future work assignments. For example, members of self-managed work teams that develop new software at companies like Microsoft often value working on interesting and important projects; members of teams that have performed highly are rewarded by being assigned to interesting and important new projects.

At Ideo (profiled earlier in "Focus on Diversity"), managers motivate team members by making them feel important. As Tom Kelley, Ideo's general manager, puts it, "When people feel special, they'll perform beyond your wildest dreams."[78] To make Ideo team members feel special, Ideo managers plan unique and fun year-end parties, give teams the opportunity to take time off if they feel they need or want to, encourage teams to take field trips, and see pranks as a way to incorporate fun into the workplace.[79]

Reducing Social Loafing in Groups

We have been focusing on the steps that managers can take to encourage high levels of performance in groups. Managers, however, need to be aware of an

social loafing The tendency of individuals to put forth less effort when they work in groups than when they work alone.

important downside to group and team work: the potential for social loafing, which reduces group performance. **Social loafing** is the tendency of individuals to put forth less effort when they work in groups than when they work alone.[80] Have you ever worked on a group project in which one or two group members never seemed to be pulling their weight? Have you ever worked in a student club or committee in which some members always seemed to be missing meetings and never volunteered for activities? Have you ever had a job in which one or two of your co-workers seemed to be slacking off because they knew that you or other members of your work group would make up for their low levels of effort? If you have, you have witnessed social loafing in action.

Social loafing can occur in all kinds of groups and teams and in all kinds of organizations. It can result in lower group performance and may even prevent a group from attaining its goals. Fortunately, there are steps managers can take to reduce social loafing and sometimes completely eliminate it; we will look at three (see Figure 15.7).

1. *Make individual contributions to a group identifiable.* Some people may engage in social loafing when they work in groups because they think that they can hide in the crowd–that no one will notice if they put forth less effort than they should. Other people may think that if they put forth high levels of effort and make substantial contributions to the group, their contributions will not be noticed and they will receive no rewards for their work–so why bother.[81]

One way in which managers can effectively eliminate social loafing is by making individual contributions to a group identifiable so that group members perceive that low and high levels of effort will be noticed and individual contributions evaluated.[82] Managers can accomplish this by assigning specific tasks to group members and holding them accountable for their completion. Take the case of a group of eight employees responsible for reshelving returned books in a large public library in New York. The head librarian was concerned that there was always a backlog of seven or eight carts of books to be reshelved, even though the employees never seemed to be particularly busy and some even found time to sit down in the current-periodicals section to read newspapers and magazines. The librarian decided to try to eliminate the apparent social loafing by assigning each employee sole responsibility for reshelving a particular section of the library. Because the library's front-desk employees sorted the

Figure 15.7
Three Ways to Reduce Social Loafing

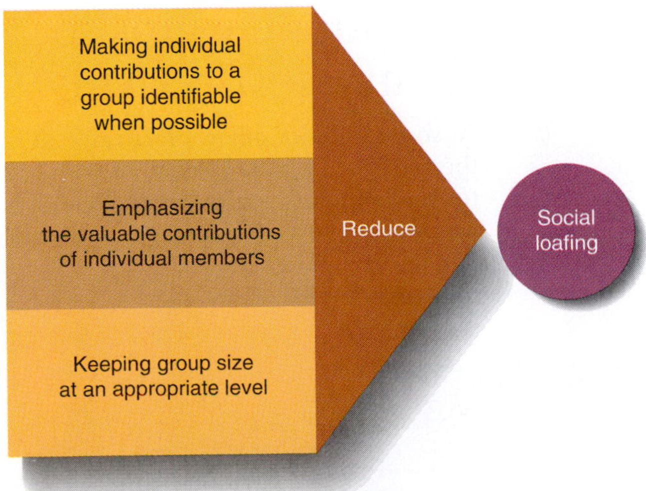
Making individual contributions to a group identifiable when possible
Emphasizing the valuable contributions of individual members
Keeping group size at an appropriate level
Reduce
Social loafing

books by section on the carts as they were returned, holding the shelvers responsible for particular sections was easily accomplished. Once the shelvers knew that the librarian could identify their effort or lack of effort, there were rarely any backlogs of books to be reshelved.

Sometimes the members of a group can cooperate to eliminate social loafing by making individual contributions identifiable. For example, members of a self-managed work team in a small security company who assemble control boxes for home alarm systems start each day by deciding who will perform which tasks that day and how much work each member and the group as a whole should strive to accomplish. Each team member knows that, at the end of the day, the other team members will know exactly how much he or she has accomplished. With this system in place, social loafing never occurs in the team. Remember, however, that in some teams, individual contributions cannot be made identifiable, as in teams whose members are reciprocally interdependent.

2. *Emphasize the valuable contributions of individual members.* Another reason why social loafing may occur is that people sometimes think that their efforts are unnecessary or unimportant when they work in a group. They feel the group will accomplish its goals and perform at an acceptable level whether or not they personally perform at a high level. To counteract this belief, when managers form groups, they should assign individuals to groups on the basis of the valuable contributions that *each* person can make to the group as a whole. Clearly communicating to group members why each person's contributions are valuable to the group is an effective means by which managers and group members themselves can reduce or eliminate social loafing.[83] This is most clearly illustrated in cross-functional teams where each member's valuable contribution to the team derives from a personal area of expertise. By emphasizing why each member's skills are important, managers can reduce social loafing in such teams.

3. *Keep group size at an appropriate level.* Group size is related to the causes of social loafing we just described. As size increases, identifying individual contributions becomes increasingly difficult and members are increasingly likely to think that their individual contributions are not very important. To overcome this, managers should form groups with no more members than are needed to accomplish group goals and perform highly.[84]

Helping Groups to Manage Conflict Effectively

At some point or other, practically all groups experience conflict either within the group (*intragroup* conflict) or with other groups (*intergroup* conflict). In Chapter 16 we discuss conflict in depth and explore ways to manage it effectively. As you will learn there, managers can take several steps to help groups manage conflict and disagreements.

Summary and Review

GROUPS, TEAMS, AND ORGANIZATIONAL EFFECTIVENESS A group is two or more people who interact with each other to accomplish certain goals or meet certain needs. A team is a group whose members work intensely with one another to achieve a specific common goal or objective. Groups and teams can contribute to organizational effectiveness by enhancing performance, increasing responsiveness to customers, increasing innovation, and being a source of motivation for their members.

TYPES OF GROUPS AND TEAMS Formal groups are groups that managers establish to achieve organizational goals; they include cross-functional teams, cross-cultural teams, top-management teams, research and development teams, command groups, task forces, self-managed work teams, and virtual teams. Informal groups are groups that employees form because they believe that the groups will help them achieve their own goals or meet their needs; they include friendship groups and interest groups.

GROUP DYNAMICS Key elements of group dynamics are group size, tasks, and roles; group leadership; group development; group norms; and group cohesiveness. The advantages and disadvantages of large and small groups suggest that managers should form groups with no more members than are needed to provide the group with the human resources it needs to achieve its goals and use a division of labor. The type of task interdependence that characterizes a group's work gives managers a clue about the appropriate size of the group. A group role is a set of behaviors and tasks that a member of a group is expected to perform because of his or her position in the group. All groups and teams need leadership.

Five stages of development that many groups pass through are forming, storming, norming, performing, and adjourning. Group norms are shared rules for behavior that most group members follow. To be effective, groups need a balance of conformity and deviance. Conformity allows a group to control its members' behavior to achieve group goals; deviance provides the impetus for needed change.

Group cohesiveness is the attractiveness of a group or team to its members. As group cohesiveness increases, so, too, does the level of participation and communication within a group, the level of conformity to group norms, and the emphasis on group goal accomplishment. Managers should strive to achieve a moderate level of group cohesiveness in the groups and teams they manage.

MANAGING GROUPS AND TEAMS FOR HIGH PERFORMANCE To make sure that groups and teams perform highly, managers need to motivate group members to work toward the achievement of organizational goals, reduce social loafing, and help groups to effectively manage conflict. Managers can motivate members of groups and teams to work toward the achievement of organizational goals by making sure that members personally benefit when the group or team performs highly.

Management in Action

Topics for Discussion and Action

Discussion

1. Why do all organizations need to rely on groups and teams to achieve their goals and gain a competitive advantage?
2. What kinds of employees would prefer to work in a virtual team? What kinds of employees would prefer to work in a team that meets face-to-face?
3. Think about a group that you are a member of, and describe that group's current stage of development. Does the development of this group seem to be following the forming, storming, norming, performing, and adjourning stages described in the chapter?
4. Think about a group of employees who work in a McDonald's restaurant. What type of task interdependence characterizes this group? What potential problems in the group should the restaurant manager be aware of and take steps to avoid?
5. Discuss the reasons why too much conformity can hurt groups and their organizations.
6. Why do some groups have very low levels of cohesiveness?
7. Imagine that you are the manager of a hotel. What steps will you take to reduce social loafing by members of the cleaning staff who are responsible for keeping all common areas and guest rooms spotless?

Action

8. Interview one or more managers in an organization in your local community to identify the types of groups and teams that the organization uses to achieve its goals. What challenges do these groups and teams face?

Building Management Skills

Diagnosing Group Failures

Think about the last dissatisfying or discouraging experience you had as a member of a group or team. Perhaps the group did not accomplish its goals, perhaps group members could agree about nothing, or perhaps there was too much social loafing. Now answer the following questions:

1. What type of group was this?
2. Were group members motivated to achieve group goals? Why or why not?
3. How large was the group, what type of task interdependence existed in the group, and what group roles did members play?
4. What were the group's norms? How much conformity and deviance existed in the group?
5. How cohesive was the group? Why do you think the group's cohesiveness was at this level? What consequences did this level of group cohesiveness have for the group and its members?
6. Was social loafing a problem in this group? Why or why not?
7. What could the group's leader or manager have done differently to increase group effectiveness?
8. What could group members have done differently to increase group effectiveness?

Managing Ethically

Some self-managed teams encounter a vexing problem: One or more members engage in social loafing, and other members are reluctant to try to rectify the situation. Social loafing can be especially troubling if team members' pay is based on team performance and social loafing reduces the team's performance and thus the pay of all members (even the highest performers). Even if managers are aware of the problem, they may be reluctant to take action because the team is supposedly self-managing.

Questions

1. Either individually or in a group, think about the ethical implications of social loafing in a self-managed team.
2. Do managers have an ethical obligation to step in when they are aware of social loafing in a self-managed team? Why or why not? Do other team members have an obligation to try to curtail the social loafing? Why or why not?

Small Group Breakout Exercise

Creating a Cross-Functional Team

Form groups of three or four people, and appoint one member as the spokesperson who will communicate your findings to the whole class when called on by the instructor. Then discuss the following scenario.

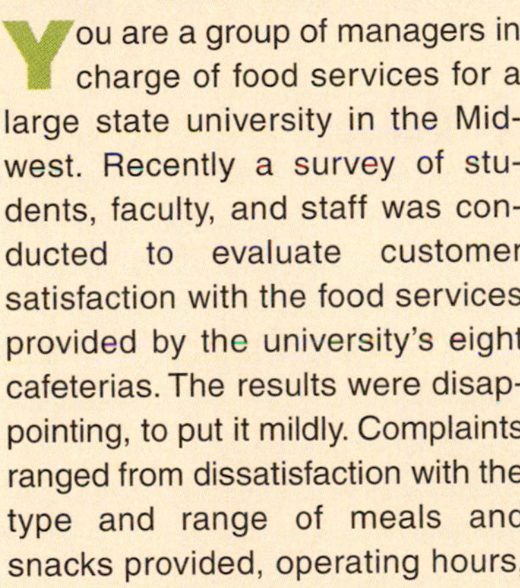

You are a group of managers in charge of food services for a large state university in the Midwest. Recently a survey of students, faculty, and staff was conducted to evaluate customer satisfaction with the food services provided by the university's eight cafeterias. The results were disappointing, to put it mildly. Complaints ranged from dissatisfaction with the type and range of meals and snacks provided, operating hours, and food temperature to frustration about unresponsiveness to current concerns about low-carbohydrate diets and the needs of vegetarians. You have decided to form a cross-functional team that will further evaluate reactions to the food services and will develop a proposal for changes to be made to increase customer satisfaction.

1. Indicate who should be on this important cross-functional team and explain why.
2. Describe the goals the team should be striving to achieve.
3. Describe the different roles that will need to be performed in this team.
4. Describe the steps you will take to help ensure that the team has a good balance between conformity and deviance and has a moderate level of cohesiveness.

Exploring the World Wide Web

Many consultants and organizations provide team-building services to organizations. While some managers and teams have found these services to be helpful, others have found them to be a waste of time and money—another consulting fad that provides no real performance benefits. Search online for team-building services, and look at the Web sites of a few consultants/companies in depth. Based on what you have read, what might be some of the advantages and disadvantages of team-building services? For what kinds of problems/issues might these services be beneficial, and when might they have little benefit or perhaps even do more harm than good?

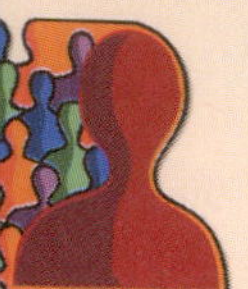

Be the Manager

You were recently hired in a boundary-spanning role for the global unit of an educational and professional publishing company. The company is headquartered in New York (where you work) and has divisions in multiple countries. Each division is responsible for translating, manufacturing, marketing, and selling a set of books in its country. Part of your responsibilities is interfacing with managers in each of the divisions in your region (Central and South America), overseeing their budgeting and financial reporting to headquarters, and leading a virtual team consisting of the top managers in charge of each of the divisions in your region. The virtual team's mission is to promote global learning, explore new potential opportunities and markets, and address ongoing problems. You communicate directly with division managers via telephone and email, as well as written reports, memos, and faxes. When virtual team meetings are convened, videoconferencing is often used.

After your first few virtual team meetings, you noticed that the managers seemed to be reticent about speaking up. Interestingly enough, when each manager communicates with you individually, primarily in telephone conversations, she or he tends to be very forthcoming and frank and you feel you have a good rapport with each of them. However, getting the managers to communicate with one another as a virtual team has been a real challenge. At the last meeting, you tried to prompt some of the managers to raise issues relevant to the agenda that you knew was on their minds from your individual conversations with them. Surprisingly, the managers skillfully avoided informing their teammates about the heart of the issues in question. You are confused and troubled. While you feel your other responsibilities are going well, you know that your virtual team is not operating like a team at all, and no matter what you try, discussions in virtual team meetings are forced and generally unproductive. What are you going to do to address this problem?

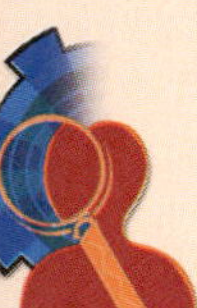

Additional Activities on the Build Your Management Skills DVD

- **Self-Assessment:** Team Roles Preference Scale
- **Manager's Hot Seat:** Working in Teams: Cross-Functional Dysfunction

BusinessWeek Case in the News

This Volvo Is Not a Guy Thing

Burning rubber, roaring engines. Grease and gas. Cars are a guy thing, right? The industry sure seems to think so. Auto ads tend to emphasize big, fast models, usually driven by a man—with a woman at his side, if at all—over user-friendly touches such as ergonomic seats. It's no surprise the crowd that designs, develops, builds, and sells autos remains a boys' club.

Yet on the other side of the sales desk, women sway a disproportionate share of car sales. According to industry studies, women purchase about two-thirds of vehicles and influence 80 percent of all sales. It's this gender gap that Volvo is trying to bridge with a concept car unveiled at the Geneva Auto Show on March 2. Shaped by all-female focus groups drawn from Volvo's workforce, the two-door hatchback was created by an all-woman management team. Dubbed Your Concept Car, or YCC, the resulting show car cost some $3 million to design and build and is packed with thoughtful design twists that attracted a big, spirited crowd in Geneva. "We found that by meeting women's expectations, we exceeded those of most men," said Hans-Olov Olsson, president and CEO of Volvo Cars, a unit of Ford Motor Co.

There's no guarantee the YCC will ever make it to a showroom. The auto industry uses concept cars as test beds for designs and technical innovations, and to gauge the public's reactions. Packed as it is with the latest gizmos, the YCC would be expensive: Volvo estimates a road version would cost about $65,000 and compete with luxury coupés built by the likes of Audi and Mercedes.

More James Bond than Soccer Mom, the YCC may just create enough buzz to hit the roads. Its gull-wing doors—which resemble the line of a bird's extended wings—are there as much for convenience and accessibility as for design chic. A button on the key fob stirs the YCC to life, raising the whole chassis a few inches to meet the driver, just as the upper door lifts hydraulically and the sill—the lower part of the door—slides under the car. The oversize opening makes stepping in and out a breeze, says Maria Widell Christiansen, the YCC's design manager. And because they're motor-driven, "the driver doesn't even need to touch the car to get in," she adds.

This hands-off approach is deliberate and consistent. Rather than a dirty, tough-to-unscrew gas cap, the YCC borrows a technology from race cars: When the gas button is pressed in the cockpit, a ball valve on the outside of the car rotates, exposing an opening for the fuel pump. Ditto for windshield-wiper fluid. Body panels are low-maintenance, too. Clad in a non-stick paint, they repel dirt.

Smart Parking

Much of the advanced technology in the YCC is hidden from view. Women in Volvo's focus group weren't willing to give up power but wanted cleaner, more efficient performance. Hence the 215-horsepower, five-cylinder, near-zero-emissions gas engine, which shuts off when not in motion and then fires up instantly with the help of an electric motor. This delivers a 10 percent boost in mileage, says Olson. There's also a nifty parallel-parking aid. When the car is aligned in front of an empty spot, sensors can confirm that, yes, it's big enough. Then, while the driver controls the gas and brake, the system self-steers the car into the spot.

In the cockpit, the design team focused on ergonomics and styling. "Access for women, in particular, can be difficult," says Jennifer Stockburger, an automotive-test engineer at *Consumer Reports,* who has been testing vehicle ergonomics into her ninth month of pregnancy. For small women, especially, "reaching out to shut a heavy door, or adjusting pedals, can be tough."

To tailor the cockpit to drivers, the YCC team developed and applied for a patent on the Ergovision system. At a dealership, the driver's body is laser-scanned in a booth. Volvo then calculates optimal positions for the seat belt, pedals, headrest, steering wheel, and seat, all of which is saved in the key fob. Each driver is "automatically custom-fitted" when they get in the car, says Camilla Palmertz, YCC's project manager.

Whether or not the YCC is eventually built, some of its design innovations are likely to show up in future Volvo models, says Olsson. The concept car will make its U.S. debut on April 7 at the New York International Auto Show. And no doubt plenty of gearhead guys will be there to admire its feminine wiles.

Questions

1. Why do men design most cars even though women are very influential in terms of actual car sales?
2. Why did Volvo rely on focus groups and a management team that were all composed of women to design the Volvo YCC?
3. Designed by women, does the YCC appeal to men? Why or why not?
4. What lessons can other automakers learn from Volvo's experience with the design of the YCC?

Source: A. Aston and G. Edmondson, "This Volvo Is Not a Guy Thing." Reprinted from the March 15, 2004, issue of *BusinessWeek* by special permission.

BusinessWeek Case in the News

Google: Why the World's Hottest Tech Company Will Struggle to Keep Its Edge

The spring sun shines brightly on the so-called Googleplex, the five-building campus of the hottest Internet search engine on earth. At lunchtime, hundreds of engineers at Google Inc. chow on free fare prepared by the former chef of the Grateful Dead. Kicking back? It's more like a fuel stop. They eat, paying little heed to co-founder Larry Page as he swoops by on skates. And as evening sets in, those same brainiacs, wedged three to six per office, huddle in quiet conference or patter away at their computers in unblinking concentration. Whether in sneakers or on skates, the Google crowd emits cerebral intensity and a near-palpable sense of urgency.

You'd think they would be celebrating. All around the world, Web-surfing humanity has found its way to Google's bare-bones Web site and picked up the simple formula, pecking out a few words and hitting enter. Google has blazed a new path of learning and turned its search engine into the keys to knowledge. . . .

Battle for the Heart

But Google's payday arrives just as the search phenom faces a withering battery of tests. The company's spectacular success has lured brawny competitors such as Microsoft and Yahoo! Inc. into the arena. . . .

And the battle is raging at Google's ramparts. Yahoo is leading the assault. In February, the portal giant fired up a new search engine that analysts say nearly matches Google's performance. More worrisome, Yahoo CEO Terry S. Semel is driving Yahoo to the next frontier, customized search. Instead of today's one-size-fits-all searches, he wants to offer queries tailored for an individual's tastes, interests, even location. . . .

Even if Google sidesteps that threat, it faces another, perhaps more daunting one. Microsoft is working to leverage every bit of its Windows monopoly in the effort to win the search market. Ballmer and Chairman William H. Gates III are working to embed search capabilities into nearly every aspect of future versions of the operating system. . . .

Google's trials would strain even a battle-hardened outfit geared for war. But the company still operates under freewheeling management, a vestige of its peaceful prosperity as a private company. Under a ruling triumvirate, no one exec has clear control. CEO Eric E. Schmidt, 48, was hired three years ago to provide experienced leadership. But his role, as he describes it, sounds more like a chief operating officer's than a CEO's. He says he handles "the day-to-day stuff," making sure the right people are talking and reaching out to partners. Decisions emerge from three-way negotiations between Schmidt and co-founders Page and Sergey Brin. It's the founders who chart Google's path, wielding veto power on strategy and technology moves. Engineers, meanwhile, work in the same culture of controlled chaos that built the startup. All are free to pursue pet projects. The result is an engineer's dream—but hell for planners. Some investors find the approach unsettling. "They do not sound even remotely like a fiercely competitive world-class company, [but] rather kids playing in a sandbox," says one Google investor, who plans on selling shortly after the IPO.

Breaking Point

The kids will have to grow up fast. Their giant rivals are not only knocking off Google's search engine, they're also plugging it in to just about everything they offer, from e-mail to job boards. This is an attempt to outflank Google and turn search into a ubiquitous feature, a commodity. To defend its market, Google must come up with a better model, one that establishes its search engine as a central platform for computing. This pushes Google to extend from its slender specialized base and venture into many of the same broad services the giants offer. To keep the big powers from feasting on its specialty, Google must stretch and become a sprawling power of its own. . . .

With such intense competitive pressure, Google's management could be stretched to the breaking point. Considering how rarely co-CEOs have been able to share an executive suite effectively, experts think it's only a matter of time before the power-sharing setup at Google dissolves. "If multiple people are making decisions, decisions don't get made," says David Yoffie, professor at Harvard Business School. "At Google, there are tens or hundreds of projects going on simultaneously. Ultimately one person has to make a decision."

Schmidt responds that Google's consensus-management structure, while maddening at times, is effective. It combines Page and Brin's technology expertise and his own operations experience. "We try to run as a group, because partnerships make better decisions," says Schmidt, adding, "It's very, very lonely if you're the only person with a very hard decision to make." He takes exception to the idea that he acts like a COO. Rather, he compares Google to Yahoo and auction titan eBay, where the founders shaped the strategic vision, though they didn't have the chief executive title. "I've tried very hard to have this be a founder-driven company," he says. "It's what most other high-tech companies have done."

Schmidt's supporters say that the CEO's style may send an inaccurate signal about his power in the company. "Eric likes to be self-deprecating," says Bill Campbell, chairman of Intuit who has served as a management adviser to Google for 2 1/2 years. "He's not the COO. He's the CEO of the company and does a good job of it."

Google execs also maintain that the company's freewheeling engineering culture is not a liability but an asset. To offset Microsoft and Yahoo's crushing advantage in size, scope, and customers, they say, the far smaller Google requires breakthrough innovations. The company, which receives about 1,000 résumés a day, has hired hundreds of engineers and scores of top-ranked PhDs in recent years. By giving them free rein to pursue new ideas, Google expects to come up with services, from e-mail to community networks, that set its larger competitors back on their heels. "What we really talk about is how we can attract and develop this creative culture," says Schmidt. "Innovation comes from invention, which you cannot schedule." . . .

Lightning-Fast

Google execs are betting their technological expertise will help them make up the difference. Page, 31, is the son of a computer science professor and a database consultant, while the Russian-born Brin, 30, is the son of a math professor and a scientist at NASA. The duo hatched a breakthrough search algorithm at a time when virtually everyone else considered Internet search a developer's cul de sac. The next job, just as important, was to make their service lightning-fast. The Google team pulled this off by stitching together some 10,000 servers and building, in effect, their own supercomputer. This jerry-rigged approach gave Google a sizable lead on the competition in both software and hardware. The pattern was set: While well-organized foes would bring revenues from the tried-and-true, Google's unbridled engineers would blaze new trails.

Page and Brin's radical management philosophy is derived from their experiences in the labs of Stanford University's computer science program. Google's managers rarely tell engineers what projects to tackle. Instead, execs keep a "Top 100" priorities list (which today numbers more than 240 items), and engineers gravitate to issues that interest them, forming fluid working groups that can last weeks or months. Engineers are urged to spend about one day a week working on their own personal research projects, no matter how offbeat, in hopes of sparking the Next Big Thing. "We're encouraging creativity and tolerating chaos," says Wayne Rosing, Google's vice president for engineering. "We turn that dial all the way over to loud."

Google coddles even its engineers' zaniest ideas. In one project, techies were grappling with the problem of displaying information from the Internet on cell-phone screens, recalls a former Google employee. They went as far as pondering a laser that would scan the user's retina, creating the appearance of a larger screen. Ideas such as these are often included on the Top 100 list. An "S" next to the project stands for "skunkworks" and protects it from premature reviews and criticism.

To foster a culture of creativity, the company's campus is a veritable theme park for propellar heads. Engineers unwind by playing roller hockey in the downstairs garage or racing remote-control blimps through the offices. Segway scooters, which retail at $4,000, are parked around campus, offering a novel way to navigate between buildings. Perks are lavish, from two flat-screen monitors on each computer to $800 digital toilets, equipped with remote controls to adjust seat temperature and water pressure.

Brin and Page have been searching for the right mix of freedom and discipline for years. Back in 2000, the co-founders first hunkered down with Schmidt, then CEO of corporate software maker Novell Inc. Schmidt, a veteran of the software industry with the bruises to show for it, was taking a thrashing at the hands of Microsoft. Earlier, he had weathered similar ordeals as a top exec at Sun Microsystems Inc. He was not considered a remarkable visionary, but that was one field where Page and Brin didn't need help. What they looked for was a grown-up manager, someone to turn Google into a real business, much the way Tim Koogle had taken over from Yahoo's young founders five years earlier.

The conversation naturally turned to technology. Almost immediately, Schmidt found himself in an argument that dragged on for most of the 90-minute meeting. Page and Brin were curt and headstrong, but Schmidt was impressed by their intelligence and passion. He left the meeting intrigued. Schmidt watched the company grow, and the next year he took over, first as chairman and four months later as CEO.

"It's Just Brutal"

Google finally had its grown-up. Page, who had been CEO, stepped down to president for products. Brin, formerly chairman, shifted to president for technology. Yet Schmidt, in his three-year tenure, has left the management structure intact. And the two founders aren't shy about flexing their muscle. "We've actually had a number of initiatives—I'd rather not go into specifics—where somebody, usually Larry or Sergey, says, 'Look, this thing's just not good enough.' And it's just brutal," Schmidt concedes.

To their credit, Page and Brin have made a string of inspired strategic moves that would make even the boldest tycoon blush with envy. They steadfastly refused to clutter the home page with splashy ads or links to other Web sites, maintaining a zippy, minimalist design that has scarcely changed to this day. They scorned the marketing mania of the Internet boom, killing a multimillion-dollar advertising plan in 1999 and relying instead on word-of-mouth to build their hip and innovative brand. They built a business out of selling paid ads alongside search results, which turned Google into a money machine. Most important, they provided fast and reliable results, propelling Google from handling less than 1 percent of Web searches in 2000 to over 50 percent today. . . .

Questions

1. What are the advantages of Google's being led by a three-person top-management team (i.e., cofounders Larry Page and Sergey Brin and CEO Eric Schmidt)?
2. What are the potential disadvantages of this approach?
3. Why does Google let engineers form fluid working groups as they pursue projects that intrigue them?
4. Does Google and its top-management team need a more disciplined approach to innovation and management? Why or why not?

Source: B. Elgin, J. Greene, and S. Hamm, "Google: Why the World's Hottest Tech Company Will Struggle to Keep Its Edge." Reprinted from the May 3, 2004, issue of *BusinessWeek* by special permission.

CHAPTER

16 Communication

Learning Objectives

After studying this chapter, you should be able to:

- Explain why effective communication helps an organization gain a competitive advantage.
- Describe the communication process and explain the role of perception in communication.
- Define information richness, and describe the information richness of communication media available to managers.
- Describe the communication networks that exist in groups and teams.
- Explain how advances in technology have given managers new options for managing communication.
- Describe important communication skills that managers need as senders and as receivers of messages.

A Manager's Challenge

Electronic vs. Face-to-Face Communication: Lessons from Jong-Yong Yun

How can managers achieve a good balance between face-to-face and electronic communication?

Advances in information technology have changed the way managers and all organizational members communicate with one another. Email has become such a ubiquitous part of organizational life that some managers and employees are loathe to be out of touch even when on the road, on vacation, or after working hours when not near their PCs or laptops—hence, the popularity of the Blackberry, which allows users to send and receive email anywhere on a device the size of a cell phone.

Business people stop at a cyber cafè to check their email. At what point does connectivity start to interfere with productivity?

Of course, these technological advances are supposed to help organizational members work smarter and better and improve communication. Have they lived up to their promise? Some managers think not and fear that email has taken on a life of its own, hindering rather than enhancing communication and productivity. Take the case of Vickie Farrell, vice president of Teradata, a unit of NCR Corporation.[1] Farrell believes that the ever-present stream of email messages, and the expectations on the part of senders that they will be responded to quickly, interferes with productivity, creativity, and innovation. It is hard to think, never mind engage in forward-looking thinking and develop truly creative ideas, when being bombarded with a constant stream of email messages and responding to them. Managers and many employees could spend most of their days sending and receiving emails without getting any other work done—especially the kind of work that requires all of one's attention to deal with a vexing problem, think long term, and develop creative solutions. As Farrell puts it, "The messages keep coming and coming. . . . Now it has gotten to the point where you can spend your entire day doing nothing but answering e-mail. It's intrusive and disruptive."[2] Farrell deliberately sets time aside during the day when she will not look at or answer emails so that she can focus on her "real" work.[3]

Jong-Yong Yun, the celebrated CEO and vice chairman of Samsung Electronics, is one manager who seems to have a good handle on communication. Leading a company that is at the forefront of information technology,[4] Yun knows how powerful and efficient electronic communication can be. At the same time, as a leader, he knows that email, videoconferences, and other forms of electronic communication cannot replace face-to-face contact when managers are dealing with real issues in today's dynamic workplace.[5] Since becoming CEO in 1996, Yun has literally transformed Samsung into the most profitable global consumer electronics company and biggest manufacturer of DRAM chips in the world.[6] Prior to Yun's leadership, Samsung was a complacent bureaucracy, pursuing growth and not too concerned about profits.[7] Yun believes that the heart of any business is in the field and that no matter how convenient electronic communication can be (which he, of course, takes advantage of), it is no replacement for face-to-face communication. Thus, Yun devotes a lot of his time to communicating with employees on-site and face-to-face—both in Korea (where Samsung is based) and in other countries—so that he can personally witness ongoing operations and talk to employees at all levels about the challenges they face and opportunities for improvements. Yun explains,

> *This gives me the opportunity to freely discuss matters with the person directly involved, from the top management to the junior staff of that work site. While many people believe that developments in digital technology have brought convenience. . . . I still believe that no innovation can replace the valuable information that is gathered through direct discussions.*[8]

Yun visits plants, sales offices, and even retailers to learn what is going on in the field, listens to employees regardless of their rank or position in the company, and frequently asks questions of those closest to operations to learn firsthand of problems and opportunities.[9] Of course, he also takes advantage of information technology (but not as a replacement for face-to-face contact). Thus, he instituted an electronic hotline whereby any employee can send him suggestions or complaints with confidentiality guaranteed. For example, employees in one R&D unit in a factory complained that they were having trouble getting an air conditioner that was needed to keep important equipment at the proper temperature; the air conditioner was in place the day after the complaint was received.[10]

Yun has propelled Samsung into being a global force with annual profits of $5 billion on sales of over $54 billion.[11] Thus, it is not surprising that Yun has received numerous accolades in the business press, such as being ranked the fifth most powerful person in business in Asia by *Fortune* magazine in 2004 and one of the best managers of 2003 by *BusinessWeek* magazine.[12] And while Yun excels as a leader and manager in numerous ways, clearly, his commitment to good communication has contributed to his ongoing success at Samsung.[13]

Overview

Even with all the advances in information technology that are available to managers, face-to-face communication continues to play a very important role in organizations, as Yun realizes in "A Manager's Challenge." While Yun certainly takes advantage of IT to receive and respond quickly to employee concerns, he also recognizes the importance of communicating with employees in person at their work sites. Ironically, the proliferation of email has its downside as well; managers like Vickie Farrell are deliberately scheduling time-outs from email to take control of their workdays and engage in strategic thinking.[14] The experiences of Farrell, Yun, and other managers and employees underscore the fact that IT is a tool to improve human communication, not a substitute for human communication. Hence, managers must never lose sight of the fact that people are at the center stage of effective communication. Ineffective communication is detrimental for managers, employees, and organizations; it can lead to poor performance, strained interpersonal relations, poor-quality service, and dissatisfied customers. For an organization to be effective and gain a competitive advantage, managers at all levels need to be good communicators.

In this chapter, we describe the nature of communication and the communication process and explain why all managers and their subordinates need to be effective communicators. We describe the communication media available to managers and the factors they need to consider in selecting a communication medium for each message they send. We consider the communication networks that organizational members rely on, and we explore how advances in information technology have expanded managers' range of communication options. We describe the communication skills that help managers be effective senders and receivers of messages. By the end of this chapter, you will have a good appreciation of the nature of communication and the steps that managers can take to ensure that they are effective communicators.

Communication and Management

Communication is the sharing of information between two or more individuals or groups to reach a common understanding.[15] "A Manager's Challenge" highlights some important aspects of this definition. First and foremost, no matter how electronically based, communication is a human endeavor and involves individuals and groups. Second, communication does not take place unless a common understanding is reached. Thus, when you call a business to speak to a person in customer service or billing and are bounced back and forth between endless automated messages and menu options and eventually hang up in frustration, communication has not taken place.

communication The sharing of information between two or more individuals or groups to reach a common understanding.

The Importance of Good Communication

In Chapter 1, we described how an organization can gain a competitive advantage when managers strive to increase efficiency, quality, responsiveness to customers, and innovation. Good communication is essential for attaining each of these four goals and thus is a necessity for gaining a competitive advantage.

Managers can *increase efficiency* by updating the production process to take advantage of new and more efficient technologies and by training workers to operate the new technologies and expand their skills. Good communication is necessary for managers to learn about new technologies, implement them in their organizations, and train workers in how to use them. Similarly, *improving quality* hinges on effective communication. Managers need to communicate to all members of an organization the meaning and importance of high quality and the routes to attaining it. Subordinates need to communicate quality problems and suggestions for increasing quality to their superiors, and members of self-managed work teams need to share their ideas on improving quality with one another.

Good communication can also help to increase responsiveness to customers. When the organizational members who are closest to customers, such as department store salespeople and bank tellers, are empowered to communicate customers' needs and desires to managers, managers are better able to respond to these needs. Managers, in turn, must communicate with other organizational members to determine how best to respond to changing customer preferences.

Innovation, which often takes place in cross-functional teams, also requires effective communication. Members of a cross-functional team developing a new kind of compact disc player, for example, must effectively communicate with one another to develop a disc player that customers will want, that will be of high quality, and that can be produced efficiently. Members of the team also must communicate with managers to secure the resources they need for developing the disc player and to keep managers informed of progress on the project. Innovation in organizations is increasingly taking place on a global level, making effective communication all the more important, as illustrated in the following "Managing Globally."

Managing Globally

Global Innovation Hinges on Global Communication

GE Healthcare Technologies, headquartered in Waukesha, Wisconsin, makes CT scanners.[16] In order to make the best scanners that meet the needs of doctors and patients around the world with next-generation technology, new product development and manufacture is truly a global endeavor at GE. Take the case of the new LightSpeed VCT scanner (*VCT* stands for "volume controlled tomography"), which debuted in 2004 with a price tag of $2 million and is among the quickest and highest-resolution scanners available in the world.[17] The LightSpeed can perform a full-body scan in under 10 seconds and yields a three-dimensional picture of patients' hearts within five heartbeats.[18]

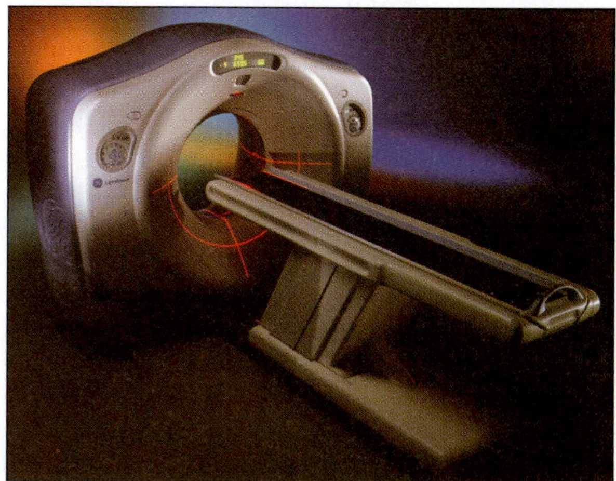

The team responsible for GE's LightSpeed VCT scanner, which can perform a full-body scan in less than 10 seconds, was made up of individuals from at least six different countries.

The LightSpeed was developed through true global collaboration. GE managers not only spoke with doctors (including cardiologists and radiologists) around the world to find out what their needs were and what kinds of tests they would perform with the LightSpeed but also gathered information about differences among patients in various countries. Engineers in Hino (Japan), Buc (France), and Waukesha developed the electronics for the LightSpeed. Other parts, such as the automated table that patients lie on, are made in Beijing (China) and Hino. Software for the LightSpeed was written in Haifa (Israel), Bangalore (India), Buc, and Waukesha.[19]

Effective global communication was a challenge and a necessity to successfully develop the LightSpeed. As Brian Duchinsky, GE's general manager for global CT, puts it, "If we sat around in this cornfield west of Milwaukee, we wouldn't come up with the same breadth of good ideas. But yet, getting six countries on the phone to make a decision can be a pain."[20]

GE managers facilitated effective communication in a number of ways–participating in daily conference calls, making sure that teams in different countries depended on one another, developing an internal Web site devoted to the LightSpeed, encouraging teams to ask one another for help, and holding face-to-face meetings in different locations. While much communication took place electronically, such as through conference calls, face-to-face meetings were also important. As Bob Armstrong, GE's general manager for engineering, indicates, "You need to get your people together in one place if you want them to really appreciate how good everyone is, and how good you are as a team."[21]

Effective communication is necessary for managers and all members of an organization to increase efficiency, quality, responsiveness to customers, and innovation and thus gain a competitive advantage for the organization. Managers therefore must have a good understanding of the communication process if they are to perform effectively.

The Communication Process

The communication process consists of two phases. In the *transmission phase,* information is shared between two or more individuals or groups. In the *feedback phase,* a common understanding is ensured. In both phases, a number of distinct stages must occur for communication to take place (see Figure 16.1).[22]

sender The person or group wishing to share information.

message The information that a sender wants to share.

Starting the transmission phase, the **sender,** the person or group wishing to share information with some other person or group, decides on the **message,** what information to communicate. Then the sender translates the message into symbols or language, a process called **encoding;** often messages are encoded into words. **Noise** is a general term that refers to anything that hampers any stage of the communication process.

Figure 16.1
The Communication Process

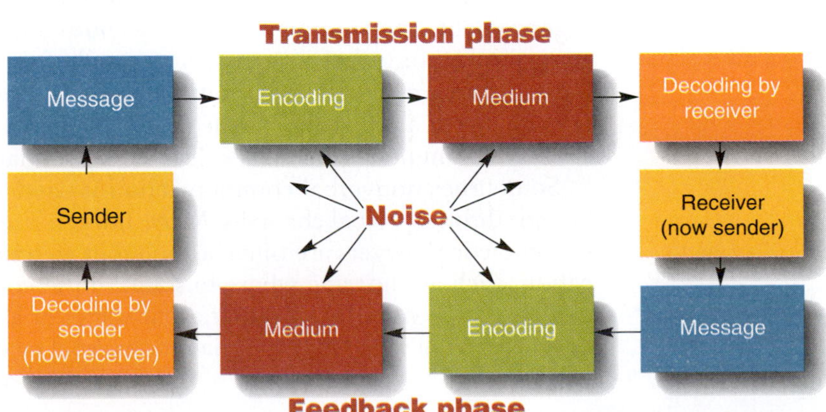

encoding Translating a message into understandable symbols or language.

noise Anything that hampers any stage of the communication process.

receiver The person or group for which a message is intended.

medium The pathway through which an encoded message is transmitted to a receiver.

decoding Interpreting and trying to make sense of a message.

Once encoded, a message is transmitted through a medium to the **receiver,** the person or group for which the message is intended. A **medium** is simply the pathway, such as a phone call, a letter, a memo, or face-to-face communication in a meeting, through which an encoded message is transmitted to a receiver. At the next stage, the receiver interprets and tries to make sense of the message, a process called **decoding.** This is a critical point in communication.

The feedback phase is initiated by the receiver (who becomes a sender). The receiver decides what message to send to the original sender (who becomes a receiver), encodes it, and transmits it through a chosen medium (see Figure 16.1). The message might contain a confirmation that the original message was received and understood or a restatement of the original message to make sure that it has been correctly interpreted, or it might include a request for more information. The original sender decodes the message and makes sure that a common understanding has been reached. If the original sender determines that a common understanding has not been reached, sender and receiver cycle through the whole process as many times as needed to reach a common understanding. Feedback eliminates misunderstandings, ensures that messages are correctly interpreted, and enables senders and receivers to reach a common understanding.

verbal communication The encoding of messages into words, either written or spoken.

nonverbal communication The encoding of messages by means of facial expressions, body language, and styles of dress.

The encoding of messages into words, written or spoken, is **verbal communication.** We can also encode messages without using written or spoken language. **Nonverbal communication** shares information by means of facial expressions (smiling, raising an eyebrow, frowning, dropping one's jaw), body language (posture, gestures, nods and shrugs), and even style of dress (casual, formal, conservative, trendy). For example, as they walk around GM plants, top managers in General Motors wear slacks and sport jackets rather than suits to communicate or signal that GM's old bureaucracy has been dismantled and that the company is decentralized and more informal than it used to be.[23] The trend toward increasing empowerment of the workforce has led some managers to dress informally to communicate that all employees of an organization are team members, working together to create value for customers.

Nonverbal communication can be used to back up or reinforce verbal communication. Just as a warm and genuine smile can back up words of appreciation for a job well done, a concerned facial expression can back up words of sympathy for a personal problem. In such cases, the congruence between the verbal and the nonverbal communication helps to ensure that a common understanding is reached.

Sometimes when members of an organization decide not to express a message verbally, they inadvertently do so nonverbally. People tend to have less control over nonverbal communication, and often a verbal message that is withheld gets expressed through body language or facial expressions. A manager who agrees to a proposal that she or he actually is not in favor of may unintentionally communicate her or his disfavor by grimacing.

Sometimes nonverbal communication is used to send messages that cannot be sent through verbal channels. Many lawyers are well aware of this communication tactic. Lawyers are often schooled in techniques of nonverbal communication, such as choosing where to stand in the courtroom for maximum effect and using eye contact during different stages of a trial. Lawyers sometimes get into trouble for using inappropriate nonverbal communication in an attempt to influence juries. In a Louisiana court, prosecuting attorney Thomas Pirtle was admonished and fined $2,500 by Judge Yada Magee for shaking his head in an expression of doubt, waving his arms indicating disfavor, and chuckling when the attorneys for the defense were stating their case.[24]

The Role of Perception in Communication

Perception plays a central role in communication and affects both transmission and feedback. In Chapter 5, we defined *perception* as the process through which people select, organize, and interpret sensory input to give meaning and order to the world around them. We mentioned that perception is inherently subjective and is influenced by people's personalities, values, attitudes, and moods as well as by their experience and knowledge. When senders and receivers communicate with each other, they are doing so based on their own subjective perceptions. The encoding and decoding of messages and even the choice of a medium hinge on the perceptions of senders and receivers.

In addition, perceptual biases can hamper effective communication. Recall from Chapter 5 that *biases* are systematic tendencies to use information about others in ways that result in inaccurate perceptions. In Chapter 5, we described a number of biases that can result in the unfair treatment of diverse members of an organization. The same biases also can lead to ineffective communication. For example, *stereotypes*–simplified and often inaccurate beliefs about the characteristics of particular groups of people–can interfere with the encoding and decoding of messages.

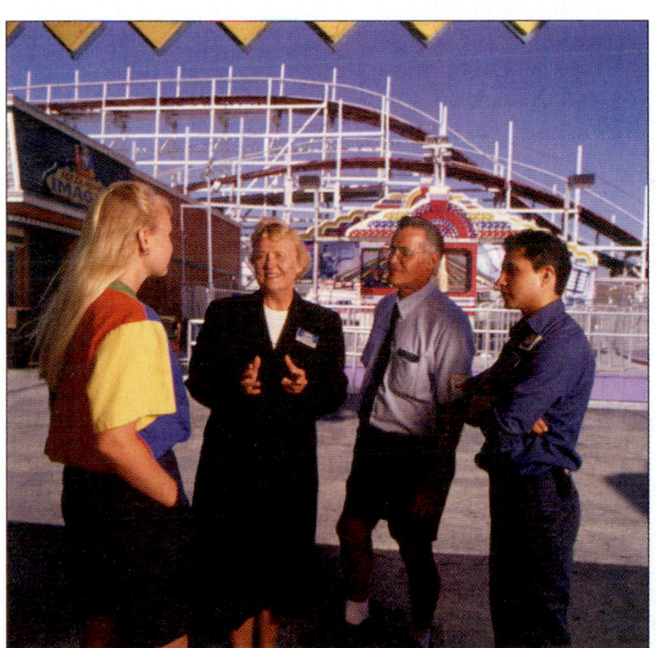

A group of amusement park employees representing several generations engage in an impromptu meeting. Since stereotypes can interfere with communication, to make sure the message gets through, effective managers perceive other people based on their actual behaviors, knowledge, skills, and abilities.

Suppose a manager stereotypes older workers as being fearful of change. When this manager encodes a message to an older worker about an upcoming change in the organization, she may downplay the extent of the change so as not to make the older worker feel stressed. The older worker, however, fears change no more than his younger colleagues fear it and thus decodes the message to mean that only a minor change is going to be made. The older worker fails to adequately prepare for the change, and his performance subsequently suffers because of his lack of preparation for the change. Clearly, the ineffective communication was due to the manager's inaccurate assumptions about older workers. Instead of relying on stereotypes, effective managers strive to perceive other people accurately by focusing on their actual behaviors, knowledge, skills, and abilities. Accurate perceptions, in turn, contribute to effective communication.

The Dangers of Ineffective Communication

Because managers must communicate with others to perform their various roles and tasks, managers spend most of their time communicating, whether in meetings, in telephone conversations, through email, or in face-to-face interactions. Indeed, some experts estimate that managers spend approximately 85 percent of their time engaged in some form of communication.[25]

Effective communication is so important that managers cannot just be concerned that they themselves are effective communicators; they also have to help their subordinates be effective communicators. When all members of an organization are able to communicate effectively with one another and with people outside the organization, the organization is much more likely to perform highly and gain a competitive advantage.

When managers and other members of an organization are ineffective communicators, organizational performance suffers and any competitive advantage the organization might have is likely to be lost. Moreover, poor communication sometimes can be downright dangerous and even lead to tragic and unnecessary loss of human life. For example, researchers from Harvard University recently studied the causes of mistakes, such as a patient receiving the wrong medication, in two large hospitals in the Boston area. They discovered that some mistakes in hospitals occur because of communication problems–physicians' not having the information they need to correctly order medications for their patients or nurses' not having the information they need to correctly administer medications. The researchers concluded that some of the responsibility for these mistakes lies with hospital management, which has not taken active steps to improve communication.[26]

Communication problems in the cockpit of airplanes and between flying crews and air traffic controllers are unfortunately all too common, sometimes with deadly consequences. In the late 1970s, two jets collided in Tenerife (one of the Canary Islands) because of miscommunication between a pilot and the control tower, and 600 people were killed. The tower radioed to the pilot, "Clipper 1736 report clear of runway." The pilot mistakenly interpreted this message to mean that he was cleared for takeoff.[27] Unfortunately, errors like this one are not a thing of the past. A safety group at NASA tracked more than 6,000 unsafe flying incidents and found that communication difficulties caused approximately 529 of them.[28] And NASA has its own communication difficulties.[29] In 2004, NASA released a report detailing communication problems at the International Space Station jointly managed and staffed by NASA and the Russian space agency; the problems included inadequate record keeping, missing information, and failure to keep data current.[30]

Information Richness and Communication Media

To be effective communicators, managers (and other members of an organization) need to select an appropriate communication medium for *each* message they send. Should a change in procedures be communicated to subordinates in a memo sent through email? Should a congratulatory message about a major accomplishment be communicated in a letter, in a phone call, or over lunch? Should a layoff announcement be made in a memo or at a plant meeting?

Should the members of a purchasing team travel to Europe to cement a major agreement with a new supplier, or should they do so through faxes? Managers deal with these questions day in and day out.

There is no one best communication medium for managers to rely on. In choosing a communication medium for any message, managers need to consider three factors. The first and most important is the level of information richness that is needed. **Information richness** is the amount of information a communication medium can carry and the extent to which the medium enables the sender and receiver to reach a common understanding.[31] The communication media that managers use vary in their information richness (see Figure 16.2).[32] Media high in information richness are able to carry an extensive amount of information and generally enable receivers and senders to come to a common understanding.

information richness The amount of information that a communication medium can carry and the extent to which the medium enables the sender and receiver to reach a common understanding.

The second factor that managers need to take into account in selecting a communication medium is the *time* needed for communication, because managers' and other organizational members' time is valuable. Managers at United Parcel Service, for example, dramatically reduced the amount of time they spent on communicating by using videoconferences instead of face-to-face communication, which required that managers travel overseas.[33]

The third factor that affects the choice of a communication medium is the *need for a paper or electronic trail* or some kind of written documentation that a message was sent and received. A manager may wish to document in writing, for example, that a subordinate was given a formal warning about excessive lateness.

In the remainder of this section we examine four types of communication media that vary along these three dimensions (information richness, time, and paper or electronic trail).[34]

Face-to-Face Communication

Face-to-face communication is the medium that is highest in information richness. When managers communicate face-to-face, they not only can take advantage of verbal communication but also can interpret each other's nonverbal signals such as facial expressions and body language. A look of concern or

Figure 16.2
The Information Richness of Communication Media

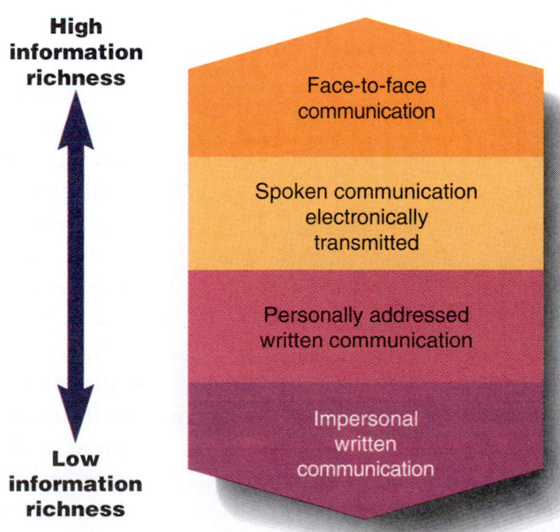

puzzlement can sometimes say more than a thousand words, and managers can respond to such nonverbal signals on the spot. Face-to-face communication also enables managers to receive instant feedback. Points of confusion, ambiguity, or misunderstanding can be resolved, and managers can cycle through the communication process as many times as needed to reach a common understanding.

management by wandering around A face-to-face communication technique in which a manager walks around a work area and talks informally with employees about issues and concerns.

Management by wandering around is a face-to-face communication technique that is effective for many managers at all levels in an organization.[35] Rather than scheduling formal meetings with subordinates, managers walk around work areas and talk informally with employees about issues and concerns that both employees and managers may have. These informal conversations provide managers and subordinates with important information and at the same time foster the development of positive relationships. William Hewlett and David Packard, founders and former top managers of Hewlett-Packard, found management by wandering around to be a highly effective way of communicating with their employees.

Because face-to-face communication is highest in information richness, you might think that it should always be the medium of choice for managers. This is not the case, however, because of the amount of time it takes and the lack of a paper or electronic trail resulting from it. For messages that are important, personal, or likely to be misunderstood, it is often well worth managers' time to use face-to-face communication and, if need be, supplement it with some form of written communication documenting the message.

Advances in information technology are providing managers with new communication media that are close substitutes for face-to-face communication. Many organizations, such as American Greetings Corp. and Hewlett-Packard, are using *videoconferences* to capture some of the advantages of face-to-face communication (such as access to facial expressions) while saving time and money because managers in different locations do not have to travel to meet with one another. During a videoconference, managers in two or more locations communicate with each other over large TV or video screens; they not only hear each other but also see each other throughout the meeting.

In addition to saving travel costs, videoconferences sometimes have other advantages. Managers at American Greetings have found that decisions get made more quickly when videoconferences are used, because more managers can be involved in the decision-making process and therefore fewer managers have to be consulted outside the meeting itself. Managers at Hewlett-Packard have found that videoconferences have shortened new product development time by 30 percent for similar reasons. Videoconferences also seem to lead to more efficient meetings. Some managers have found that their meetings are 20 to 30 percent shorter when videoconferences are used instead of face-to-face meetings.[36]

Video conferencing allows for face-to-face communication between two or more people. It also saves on travel costs and the time involved flying to other locations.

Taking videoconferences one step further, IBM and TelePort Corporation have joined forces to build virtual dining rooms in which top managers can actually have "power meals" with other managers in another location. Managers in one location are seated around a large, round table bisected by a huge video screen on which they are able to see (life-size) their dining partners in another location sitting around the same kind of table having the same kind of meal. Even though managers may be hundreds or thousands of miles apart, they can eat together as they discuss pressing concerns. The cameras enabling the transmission of the video images are hidden in flower arrangements so as not to unnerve the diners.[37]

Spoken Communication Electronically Transmitted

After face-to-face communication, spoken communication electronically transmitted over phone lines is second highest in information richness (see Figure 16.2). Although managers communicating over the telephone do not have access to body language and facial expressions, they do have access to the tone of voice in which a message is delivered, the parts of the message the sender emphasizes, and the general manner in which the message is spoken, in addition to the actual words themselves. Thus, telephone conversations have the capacity to convey extensive amounts of information. Managers also can ensure that mutual understanding is reached because they can get quick feedback over the phone and answer questions.

Voice mail systems and answering machines also allow managers to send and receive verbal electronic messages over telephone lines. Voice mail systems are companywide systems that enable senders to record messages for members of an organization who are away from their desks and allow receivers to access their messages even when hundreds of miles away from the office. Such systems are obviously a necessity when managers are frequently out of the office, and managers on the road are well advised to periodically check their voice mail.

Personally Addressed Written Communication

Lower than electronically transmitted verbal communication in information richness is personally addressed written communication (see Figure 16.2). One of the advantages of face-to-face communication and verbal communication electronically transmitted is that they both tend to demand attention, which helps ensure that receivers pay attention. Personally addressed written communication such as memos and letters also have this advantage. Because they are addressed to a particular person, the chances are good that the person will actually pay attention to (and read) them. Moreover, the sender can write the message in a way that the receiver is most likely to understand. Like voice mail, written communication does not enable a receiver to have his or her questions answered immediately, but when messages are clearly written and feedback is provided, common understandings can still be reached.

Even if managers use face-to-face communication, sending a follow-up in writing is often necessary for messages that are important or complicated and need to be referred to later on. This is precisely what Karen Stracker, a hospital administrator, did when she needed to tell one of her subordinates about an important change in the way the hospital would be handling denials of insurance benefits. Stracker met with the subordinate and described the changes face-to-face. Once she was sure that the subordinate understood them, she handed her a sheet of instructions to follow, which essentially summarized the information they had discussed.

Email also fits into this category of communication media because senders and receivers are communicating through personally addressed written words. The words, however, are appearing on their personal computer screens rather than on pieces of paper. Email is so widespread in the business world that some managers such as Vickie Farrell in "A Manager's Challenge" are finding that they have to deliberately take time out from checking their email to get their work done, think about pressing concerns, and come up with new and innovative ideas.[38] Email etiquette is a growing concern for managers whose in-boxes are overloaded with ever more messages. Certain etiquette norms are obvious– don't send jokes or witty passages, and don't flag messages as important just to get someone's attention or make sure they are read. Other etiquette norms may be more subtle. For example, to save time, Andrew Giangola, a manager at Simon & Schuster, a book publisher, used to type all his email messages in capital letters. He was surprised when a receiver of one of his messages responded, "Why are you screaming at me?" Messages in capital letters are often perceived as being shouted or screamed, and thus Giangola's routine use of capital letters was bad email etiquette. Here are some other guidelines from polite emailers: Always punctuate messages; do not ramble on or say more than you need to; do not act as though you do not understand something when in fact you do understand it; and pay attention to spelling and format. To avoid embarrassments like Giangola's, managers at Simon & Schuster created a task force that developed guidelines for email etiquette.[39]

The growing popularity of email has also enabled many workers and managers to become *telecommuters,* people who are employed by organizations and work out of offices in their own homes. There are approximately 44 million telecommuters in the United States.[40] Many telecommuters indicate that the flexibility of working at home enables them to be more productive and, at the same time, be closer to their families and not waste time traveling to and from the office.[41] In a recent study conducted by Georgetown University, 75 percent of the telecommuters surveyed said their productivity increased and 83 percent said their home life improved once they started telecommuting.[42]

Unfortunately, the widespread use of email has been accompanied by growing abuse of email. There have been cases of employees sexually harassing coworkers through email, sending pornographic content via email, and sending messages that disparage certain employees or groups.[43]

Managers need to develop a clear policy specifying what company email can and should be used for and what is out of bounds. Managers also should clearly communicate this policy to all members of the organization, as well as inform them of the procedures that will be used when email abuse is suspected and the consequences that will result when email abuse is confirmed.

According to the American Management Association, while the majority of organizations have a written policy about email usage, most do not have written guidelines for instant messaging.[44] *Instant messaging* allows people who are online and linked through a buddy or contact list to send instant messages back and forth through a small window on their computer screens without having to go through the steps of sending and receiving emails.[45]

What about surfing the Internet on company time? According to a study conducted by Websense, approximately half of the employees surveyed indicated that they surfed the Web at work, averaging about two hours per week.[46] Most visited news and travel sites, but about 22 percent of the male respondents and 12 percent of the female respondents indicated that they visited pornographic Web sites.[47] Of all those surveyed, 56 percent said that they sent personal emails at work. The majority of those surveyed felt that sending personal emails and surfing the Web had no effect on their performance, and 27 percent thought that doing so improved their productivity.[48] Other statistics suggest that while overall there is more Intenet usage at home than at work, individuals who use the Internet at work spend more time on it and visit more sites than do those who use it at home.[49] As indicated in the following "Ethics in Action," personal emails and Internet surfing at work present managers with some challenging ethical dilemmas.

Ethics in Action

Monitoring Email and Internet Usage

A growing number of companies provide managers and organizations with tools to track the Web sites their employees visit and the emails they send. For example, Stellar Internet Monitoring LLC, based in Naples, Florida, sells software that managers can access anywhere to find out exactly how much time employees have spent at specific Web sites.[50] Currently, a little over half of the large corporations in the United States monitor their employees' email; the percentage is higher among high-technology organizations. Only about half of the organizations that monitor email let their employees know about the monitoring.[51]

Monitoring employees raises concerns about privacy. Most employees would not like to think that their bosses were listening to their phone conversations; similarly, monitoring emails and tracking Internet usage seems like an invasion of privacy to some.[52] Given the increasingly long working hours many employees are clocking in, should personal emails and Internet usage be closely scrutinized? Clearly, when illegal and unethical email usage is suspected, such as sexually harassing co-workers or divulging confidential company information to third parties, monitoring may be called for. But should it be a normal part of organizational life, even when there are no indications of a real problem?

Essentially, this dilemma revolves around issues of trust. Procter & Gamble does not monitor individuals unless there appears to be a need to do so. P&G has 98,000 employees working in 80 countries, and the different countries have different laws and different internal organizational rules and norms.[53] Rather than monitoring individuals to see if they are abiding by the particular standards at the location where they work, P&G monitors electronic communication at its work sites in the aggregate to spot patterns. As Sandy Hughes, head of P&G's Global Privacy Council, puts it, "At some level, you have to trust your employees are going to be doing the right things."[54] Interestingly enough, research suggests that people are less likely to lie in email than they are in phone calls or face-to-face conversations.[55]

Impersonal Written Communication

Impersonal written communication is lowest in information richness but is well suited for messages that need to reach a large number of receivers. Because such messages are not addressed to particular receivers, feedback is unlikely, so managers must make sure that messages sent by this medium are written clearly in language that all receivers will understand.

Managers often find company newsletters useful vehicles for reaching large numbers of employees. Many managers give their newsletters catchy names to spark employee interest and also to inject a bit of humor into the workplace. Managers at the pork-sausage maker Bob Evans Farms Inc. called their newsletter "The Squealer" for many years but recently changed the title to "The Homesteader" to reflect the company's broadened line of products. Managers at American Greetings Corp., at Yokohama Tire Corp., and at Eastman Kodak call their newsletters "Expressions," "TreadLines," and "Kodakery," respectively. Managers at Quaker State Corp. held a contest to rename their newsletter. Among the 1,000 names submitted were "The Big Q Review," "The Pipeline," and "Q.S. Oil Press"; the winner was "On Q."[56]

Managers can use impersonal written communication for various messages, including announcements of rules, regulations, policies, newsworthy information, changes in procedures, and the arrival of new organizational members. Impersonal written communication also can convey instructions about how to use machinery or how to process work orders or customer requests. For these kinds of messages, the paper or electronic trail left by this communication medium can be invaluable for employees.

information overload The potential for important information to be ignored or overlooked while tangential information receives attention.

communication networks The pathways along which information flows in groups and teams and throughout the organization.

Just as with personal written communication, impersonal written communication can be delivered and retrieved electronically, and this is increasingly the case in companies large and small. Unfortunately, the ease with which electronic messages can be spread has led to their proliferation. Many managers' and workers' electronic in-boxes are so backlogged that often they do not have time to read all the electronic work-related information available to them. The problem with such **information overload** is the potential for important information to be ignored or overlooked (even that which is personally addressed) while tangential information receives attention. Moreover, information overload can result in thousands of hours and millions of dollars in lost productivity. In "A Manager's Challenge," Vickie Farrell has gotten so overloaded with email that she cannot read or respond to it all; she has told her co-workers to call her when sending an important message so that she will be sure to read and respond to it on a timely basis.[57]

Communication Networks

Although various communication media are utilized, communication in organizations tends to flow in certain patterns. The pathways along which information flows in groups and teams and throughout an organization are called **communication networks.** The type of communication network that exists in a group depends on the nature of the group's tasks and the extent to which group members need to communicate with one another in order to achieve group goals.

Communication Networks in Groups and Teams

As you learned in Chapter 14, groups and teams, whether they are cross-functional teams, top-management teams, command groups, self-managed work teams, or task forces, are the building blocks of organizations. Four kinds of communication networks can develop in groups and teams: the wheel, the chain, the circle, and the all-channel network (see Figure 16.3).

WHEEL NETWORK In a wheel network, information flows to and from one central member of the group. Other group members do not need to communicate with one another to perform highly, so the group can accomplish its goals by directing all communication to and from the central member. Wheel networks are often found in command groups with pooled task interdependence. Picture a group of taxi cab drivers who report to the same dispatcher, who is also their supervisor. Each driver needs to communicate with the dispatcher, but the drivers do not need to communicate with one another. In groups such as this, the wheel network results in efficient communication, saving time without compromising performance. Although found in groups, wheel networks are not found in teams because they do not allow for the intense interactions characteristic of teamwork.

Figure 16.3 Communication Networks in Groups and Teams

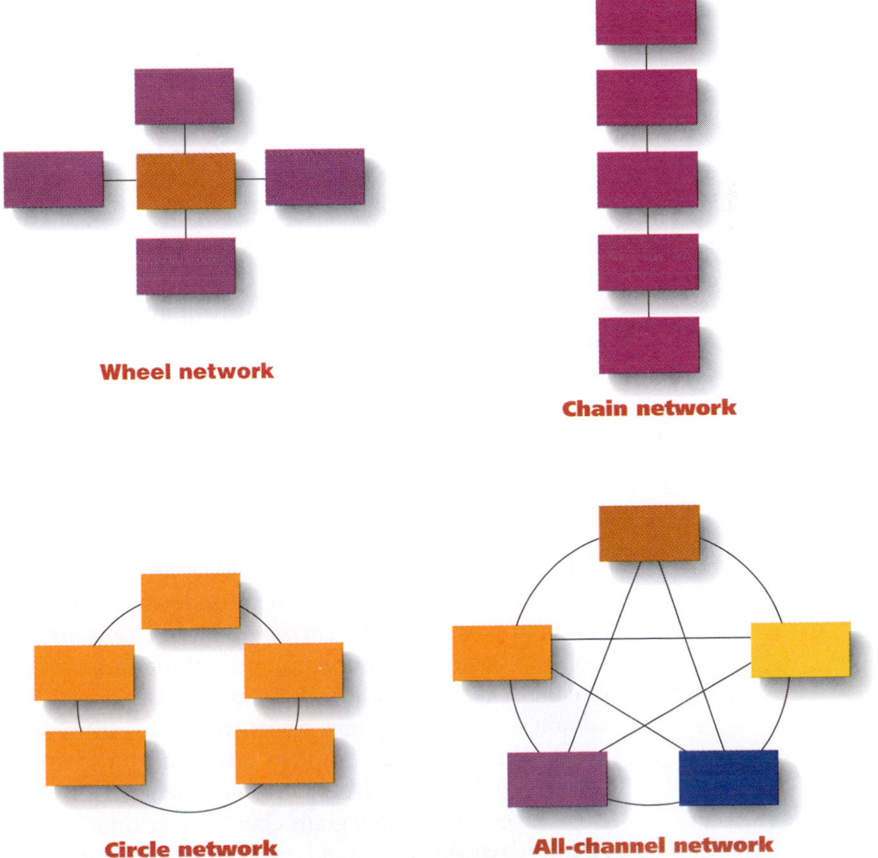

CHAIN NETWORK In a chain network, members communicate with one another in a predetermined sequence. Chain networks are found in groups with sequential task interdependence, such as in assembly-line groups. When group work has to be performed in a predetermined order, the chain network is often found because group members need to communicate with those whose work directly precedes and follows their own. Like wheel networks, chain networks tend not to exist in teams because of the limited amount of interaction among group members.

CIRCLE NETWORK In a circle network, group members communicate with others who are similar to them in experiences, beliefs, areas of expertise, background, office location, or even where they sit when the group meets. Members of task forces and standing committees, for example, tend to communicate with others who have similar experiences or backgrounds. People also tend to communicate with people whose offices are next to their own. Like wheel and chain networks, circle networks are most often found in groups that are not teams.

ALL-CHANNEL NETWORK An all-channel network is found in teams. It is characterized by high levels of communication: Every team member communicates with every other team member. Top-management teams, cross-functional teams, and self-managed work teams frequently have all-channel networks. The reciprocal task interdependence often found in such teams requires that information flows in all directions. Computer software specially designed for use by work groups can help maintain effective communication in teams with all-channel networks because it provides team members with an efficient way to share information with one another.

Organizational Communication Networks

An organization chart may seem to be a good summary of an organization's communication network, but often it is not. An organization chart summarizes the *formal* reporting relationships in an organization and the formal pathways along which communication takes place. Often, however, communication is *informal* and flows around issues, goals, projects, and ideas instead of moving up and down the organizational hierarchy in an orderly fashion. Thus, an organization's communication network includes not only the formal communication pathways summarized in an organization chart but also informal communication pathways along which a great deal of communication takes place (see Figure 16.4)

Communication can and should occur across departments and groups as well as within them and up and down and sideways in the corporate hierarchy. Communication up and down the corporate hierarchy is often called *vertical* communication. Communication among employees at the same level in the hierarchy, or sideways, is called *horizontal* communication. Managers obviously cannot determine in advance what an organization's communication network will be, nor should they try to. Instead, to accomplish goals and perform at a high level, organizational members should be free to communicate with whomever they need to contact. Because organizational goals change over time, so too do organizational communication networks. Informal communication networks can contribute to an organiza-

Figure 16.4
Formal and Informal Communication Networks in an Organization

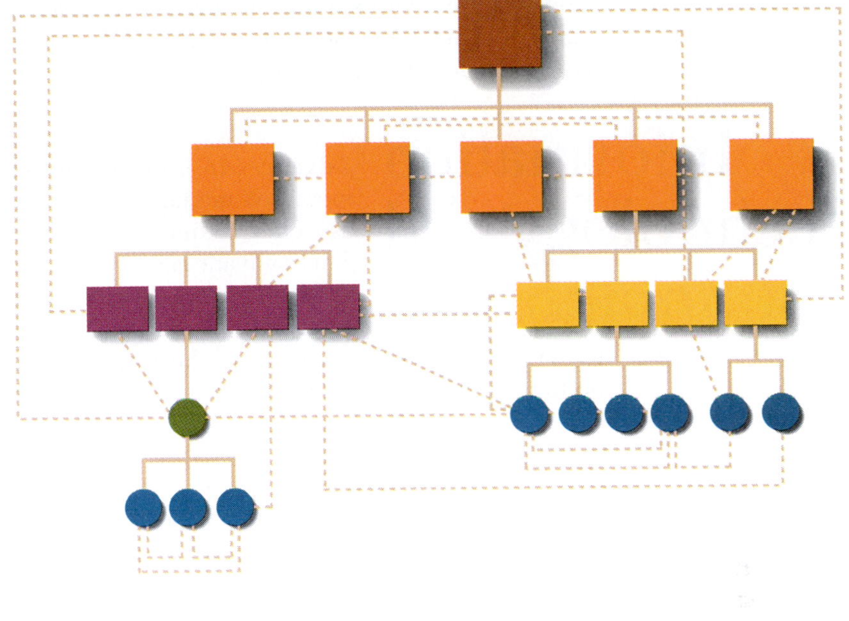

tion's competitive advantage because they help ensure that organizational members have the information they need when they need it to accomplish their goals.

grapevine An informal communication network along which unofficial information flows.

The **grapevine** is an informal organizational communication network along which unofficial information flows quickly, if not always accurately.[58] People in an organization who seem to know everything about everyone are prominent in the grapevine. Information spread over the grapevine can be on issues of either a business nature (an impending takeover) or a personal nature (the CEO's separation from his wife).

External Networks

In addition to participating in networks within an organization, managers, professional employees, and those with work-related ties outside their employing organization often are part of external networks whose members span a variety of companies. For example, scientists working in universities and in corporations often communicate in networks formed around common underlying interests in a particular topic or subfield. As another example, physicians working throughout the country belong to specialty professional associations that help them keep up to date on the latest advances in their fields. For some managers and professionals, participation in such interest-oriented networks is just as important, or even more important, than participation in internal company networks. Networks of contacts who are working in the same discipline or field or who have similar expertise and knowledge can be very helpful, for example, when an individual wants to change jobs or even find a job after a layoff. Unfortunately, as a result of discrimination and stereotypes, some of these networks are off-limits to certain individuals due to gender or race. For example, the term *old boys' network* alludes to the fact that networks of contacts for job leads, government contracts, or venture capital funding have often been dominated by men and less welcoming of women.[59]

Information Technology and Communication

Advances in information technology have dramatically increased managers' abilities to communicate with others as well as to quickly access information to make decisions. Three advances that are having major impacts on managerial communication are the Internet, intranets, and groupware. However, as profiled in "A Manager's Challenge," managers must not lose sight of the fact that communication is essentially a human endeavor, no matter how much it may be facilitated by IT.

The Internet

Internet A global system of computer networks.

The **Internet** is a global system of computer networks that is easy to join and is used by employees of organizations around the world to communicate inside and outside their companies. Over 160 million people in the United States alone use the Internet, and the use of broadband connections (in place of dial-up service) is dramatically increasing.[60] Table 16.1 lists the 15 countries with the most Internet users.[61]

On the Internet, the World Wide Web is the "business district" with multimedia capabilities. Companies' home pages on the Web are like offices that potential customers can visit. In attractive graphic displays on home pages, managers communicate information about the goods and services they offer, why customers should want to purchase them, how to purchase them, and where to purchase them. By surfing the Web and visiting competitors' home pages, managers can see what their competitors are doing.[62] Each day, hundreds of new companies add themselves to the growing number of organizations on the World Wide Web.[63] According to a recent study, the six "Web-savviest" nations (taking into account usage of broadband connections) in descending order are Denmark, Great Britain, Sweden, Norway, Finland, and the United States.[64]

By all counts, use of the Internet for communication is burgeoning. Nevertheless, some managers and organizations do not conduct business over the Internet. Ironically, the very reason why the Internet was created and why it is so popular–it allows millions of senders and receivers of messages to share vast amounts of information with one another–has hampered its use for certain business transactions because of a lack of security. Just as managers do not want to freely distribute information about their accounts to the public, customers do not want to disclose their credit card numbers via the Internet. Experts suggest, however, that the Internet can be made reasonably secure so that accounts, credit cards, business documents, and even monetary transactions are relatively safe.

Gene Spafford, a professor who is working on Purdue University's computer-security research project called COAST, suggests that although perfect security can never be obtained with any form of communication, good security on the Internet is certainly possible.[65] In addition, when considering security on the Internet, managers need to compare it to the security of alternative communication media. Scott McNealy, chairman and CEO of Sun Microsystems, says that his email is much more secure and harder for unwanted intruders to access than is his regular mail, which is just dropped into an unlocked box.[66]

Table 16.1
Top 15 Countries in Internet Usage

Country	Internet Users
United States	160,700,000
Japan	64,800,000
China	54,500,000
Germany	30,350,000
United Kingdom	27,150,000
South Korea	26,900,000
Italy	20,850,000
Canada	17,830,000
France	16,650,000
India	16,580,000
Brazil	15,840,000
Russia	13,500,000
Australia	10,450,000
Spain	10,390,000
Taiwan	9,510,000

Source: Computer Industry Almanac, Inc.; obtained from "Top 15 Countries in Internet Usage, 2002," www.infoplease.com.

Intranets

intranet A companywide system of computer networks.

Growing numbers of managers are finding that the technology on which the World Wide Web and the Internet are based has enabled them to improve communication within their own companies. These managers are using the technology that allows information sharing over the Internet to share information within their own companies through company networks called **intranets.** Intranets are being used not just in high-tech companies such as Sun Microsystems and Digital Equipment but also in companies such as Chevron, Goodyear, Levi Strauss, Pfizer, Chrysler, Motorola, and Ford.[67]

Intranets allow employees to have many kinds of information at their fingertips (or keyboards). Directories, phone books, manuals, inventory figures, product specifications, information about customers, biographies of top managers and the board of directors, global sales figures, minutes from meetings, annual reports, delivery schedules, and up-to-the minute revenue, cost, and profit figures are just a few examples of the information that can be shared through intranets. Intranets can be accessed with different kinds of computers so that all members of an organization can be linked together. Intranets are protected from unwanted intrusions, by hackers or by competitors, by means of firewall security systems that ask users to provide passwords and other pieces of identification before they are allowed to access the intranet.[68]

The advantage of intranets lies in their versatility as a communication medium. They can be used for a number of different purposes by people who may have little expertise in computer software and programming. While some managers complain that the Internet is too crowded and the World Wide Web too glitzy, informed managers are realizing that using the Internet's technology to create their own computer network may be one of the Internet's biggest contributions to organizational effectiveness.

Groupware and Collaboration Software

groupware Computer software that enables members of groups and teams to share information with one another.

Groupware is computer software that enables members of groups and teams to share information with one another to improve their communication and performance. In some organizations, such as the Bank of Montreal, managers have had success in introducing groupware into the organization; in other organizations, such as the advertising agency Young & Rubicam, managers have encountered considerable resistance to groupware.[69] Even in companies where the introduction of groupware has been successful, some employees resist using it. Some clerical and secretarial workers at the Bank of Montreal, for example, were dismayed to find that their neat and accurate files were being consolidated into computer files that would be accessible to many of their co-workers.

Managers are most likely to be able to successfully use groupware in their organizations as a communication medium when certain conditions are met:[70]

1. The work is group- or team-based, and members are rewarded, at least in part, for group performance.
2. Groupware has the full support of top management.
3. The culture of the organization stresses flexibility and knowledge sharing, and the organization does not have a rigid hierarchy of authority.
4. Groupware is being used for a specific purpose and is viewed as a tool that enables group or team members to work more effectively together, not as a personal source of power or advantage.
5. Employees receive adequate training in the use of computers and groupware.[71]

Employees are likely to resist using groupware and managers are likely to have a difficult time implementing it when people are working primarily on their own and are rewarded for their own individual performances.[72] Under these circumstances, information is often viewed as a source of power, and people are reluctant to share information with others by means of groupware.

Take the case of three salespeople who sell insurance policies in the same geographic area; each is paid based on the number of policies he or she sells and on his or her retention of customers. Their supervisor invested in groupware and encouraged them to use it to share information about their sales, sales tactics, customers, insurance providers, and claim histories. The supervisor told the salespeople that having all this information at their fingertips would allow them to be more efficient as well as sell more policies and provide better service to customers.

Even though they received extensive training in how to use the groupware, the salespeople never got around to using it. Why? They all were afraid that giving away their secrets to their co-workers might reduce their own commissions. In this situation, the salespeople were essentially competing with one another and thus had no incentive to share information. Under such circumstances, a groupware system may not be a wise choice of communication medium. Conversely, had the salespeople been working as a team and had they received bonuses based on team performance, groupware might have been an effective communication medium.

For an organization to gain a competitive advantage, managers need to keep up to date on advances in information technology such as groupware. But managers should not adopt these or other advances without first considering carefully how the advance in question might improve communication and performance in their particular groups, teams, or whole organization. Moreover, as highlighted in "A Manager's Challenge," managers need to keep in mind that all of these advances in IT are tools for people to use to facilitate effective communication; they are not replacements for face-to-face communication.

Collaboration software is groupware that aims to promote collaborative, highly interdependent interactions among members of a team and provide the team with an electronic meeting site for communication.[73] For work that is truly team-based, entails a number of highly interdependent yet distinct components, and involves team members with distinct areas of expertise who need to closely coordinate their efforts, collaboration software can be a powerful communication tool, as profiled in the following "Information Technology Byte."

Information Technology Byte

Collaboration Software Facilitates Communication in Teams

Collaboration software provides members of a team with an online work site where they can post, share, and save data, reports, sketches, and other documents; keep calendars; have team-based online conferences; and send and receive messages. The software can also keep and update progress reports, survey team members about different issues, forward documents to managers, and let users know which of their team members are also online and at the site.[74] Having an integrated online work area can help to organize and centralize the work of a team, help to ensure that information is readily available as needed, and also help team members to make sure that important information is not overlooked. Collaboration software can be much more efficient than email or instant messaging for managing ongoing team collaboration and interaction that is not face-to-face. Moreover, when a team does meet face-to-face, all documents the team might need in the course of the meeting are just a click away.[75]

The New York–based public relations company Ketchum Inc. uses collaboration software for some of its projects. For example, Ketchum is managing public relations, marketing, and advertising for a new charitable program that Fireman's Fund Insurance Co. has undertaken. By using the eRoom software provided by Documentum (a part of EMC Corporation), Ketchum employees working on the project at six different locations, employee representatives from Fireman's, and a graphics company that is designing a Web site for the program can share plans, documents, graphic designs, and calendars at an online work site.[76] Members of the Ketchum-Fireman team get email alerts when something has been modified or added to the site. As Ketchum's chief information officer Andy Roach puts it, "The fact that everyone has access to the same document means Ketchum isn't going to waste time on the logistics and can focus on the creative side."[77]

Another company taking advantage of collaboration software is Honeywell International Inc. Managers at Honeywell decided to use the SharePoint collaboration software provided by Microsoft, in part because it can be integrated with other Microsoft software such as Outlook. So, for example, if a team using SharePoint makes a change to the team's calendar, that change will be automatically made in team members' Outlook calendars.[78] Clearly, collaboration software has the potential to enhance communication efficiency and effectiveness in teams.

Communication Skills for Managers

Some of the barriers to effective communication in organizations have their origins in senders. When messages are unclear, incomplete, or difficult to understand, when they are sent over an inappropriate medium, or when no provision for feedback is made, communication suffers. Other communication barriers have their origins in receivers. When receivers pay no attention to or do not listen to messages or when they make no effort to understand the meaning of a message, communication is likely to be ineffective. Sometimes advanced information technology such as automated phone systems can hamper effective communication to the extent that the human element is missing.

To overcome these barriers and effectively communicate with others, managers (as well as other organizational members) must possess or develop certain communication skills. Some of these skills are particularly important when managers *send* messages; others are critical when managers receive messages. These skills help ensure that managers will be able to share information, will have the information they need to make good decisions and take action, and will be able to reach a common understanding with others.

Communication Skills for Managers as Senders

Organizational effectiveness depends on the ability of managers (as well as other organizational members) to effectively send messages to people both inside and outside the organization. Table 16.2 summarizes seven communication skills that help ensure that when managers send messages, they are properly understood and the transmission phase of the communication process is effective. Let's see what each skill entails.

SEND CLEAR AND COMPLETE MESSAGES Managers need to learn how to send a message that is clear and complete. A message is clear when it is easy for the receiver to understand and interpret, and it is complete when it contains all the information that the sender and receiver need to reach a common understanding. In striving to send messages that are both clear and complete, managers must learn to anticipate how receivers will interpret messages and must adjust messages to eliminate sources of misunderstanding or confusion.

ENCODE MESSAGES IN SYMBOLS THE RECEIVER UNDERSTANDS Managers need to appreciate that when they encode messages, they should use symbols or language that the receiver understands. When sending messages in English to receivers whose native language is not English, for example, it is important to use commonplace vocabulary and to avoid using clichés that, when translated, may make little sense and sometimes are either comical or insulting.

jargon Specialized language that members of an occupation, group, or organization develop to facilitate communication among themselves.

Jargon, specialized language that members of an occupation, group, or organization develop to facilitate communication among themselves, should never be used when communicating with people outside the occupation, group, or organization. For example, truck drivers refer to senior-citizen drivers as "double-knits," compact cars as "rollerskates," highway dividing lines as "paints,"

Table 16.2
Seven Communication Skills for Managers as Senders of Messages

- Send messages that are clear and complete.
- Encode messages in symbols that the receiver understands.
- Select a medium that is appropriate for the message.
- Select a medium that the receiver monitors.
- Avoid filtering and information distortion.
- Ensure that a feedback mechanism is built into messages.
- Provide accurate information to ensure that misleading rumors are not spread.

double or triple freight trailers as "pups," and orange barrels around road construction areas as "Schneider eggs." Using this jargon among themselves results in effective communication because they know precisely what is being referred to. But if a truck driver used this language to send a message to a receiver who did not drive trucks (such as "That rollerskate can't stay off the paint"), the receiver would have no idea what the message meant.[79]

SELECT A MEDIUM APPROPRIATE FOR THE MESSAGE As you have learned, when relying on verbal communication, managers can choose from a variety of communication media, including face-to-face communication in person, written letters, memos, newsletters, phone conversations, email, voice mail, faxes, and videoconferences. When choosing among these media, managers need to take into account the level of information richness required, time constraints, and the need for a paper or electronic trail. A primary concern in choosing an appropriate medium is the nature of the message. Is it personal, important, nonroutine, and likely to be misunderstood and in need of further clarification? If it is, face-to-face communication is likely to be in order.

SELECT A MEDIUM THE RECEIVER MONITORS Another factor that managers need to take into account when selecting a communication medium is whether the medium is one that the receiver monitors. Managers differ in the communication media they pay attention to. Many managers simply select the communication medium that they themselves use the most and are most comfortable with, but doing this can often lead to ineffective communication. Managers who dislike telephone conversations and too many face-to-face interactions may prefer to use email, send many email messages per day, and check their own email every few hours. Managers who prefer to communicate with people in person or over the phone may have email addresses but rarely use email and forget to check for email messages. No matter how much a manager likes email, sending email to someone who does not check his or her email is futile. Learning which managers like things in writing and which prefer face-to-face interactions and then using the appropriate medium enhances the chance that receivers will actually receive and pay attention to messages.

A related consideration is whether receivers have disabilities that hamper their ability to decode certain messages. A blind receiver, for example, cannot read a written message. Managers should ensure that employees with disabilities have resources available to communicate effectively with others. For example, deaf employees can effectively communicate over the telephone by using text-typewriters that have a screen and a keyboard on which senders can type messages. The message travels along the phone lines to special operators called communication assistants, who translate the typed message into a text that the receiver can listen to. The receiver's spoken replies are translated into typewritten text by the communication assistants and appear on the sender's screen. The communication assistants relay messages back and forth to each sender and receiver.[80] Additionally, use of fax and email instead of phone conversations can aid deaf employees.

filtering Withholding part of a message because of the mistaken belief that the receiver does not need or will not want the information.

AVOID FILTERING AND INFORMATION DISTORTION **Filtering** occurs when senders withhold part of a message because they (mistakenly) think that the receiver does not need the information or will not want to receive it. Filtering can occur at all levels in an organization and in both vertical and horizontal communication. Rank-and-file workers may filter messages they send to first-line managers, first-line managers may filter messages to middle managers, and middle managers may filter messages to top managers. Such filtering is most likely to take place when messages contain bad news or problems that subordinates are afraid they will be blamed for. Managers need to hear bad news and be aware of problems as soon as they occur so that they can take swift steps to rectify the problem and limit the damage it may have caused.

Some filtering takes place because of internal competition in organizations or because organizational members fear that their power and influence will be diminished if others have access to some of their specialized knowledge. As indicated in the following "Managing Globally" reducing filtering and improving communication are often key ingredients to the successful turnaround of a troubled organization.

Managing Globally

Haruo Kawahara Transforms Kenwood and Improves Communication

When Haruo Kawahara became CEO of Japanese Kenwood Corp., things couldn't seem worse. Kenwood makes consumer electronics such as car audio and home audio systems, navigation systems, and wireless radio. Kenwood had close to $1 billion in debt and had been in the red for three consecutive years when Kawahara came on board.[81] As CEO, Kawahara proceeded to quickly make tough decisions (including reforms in financial, business, cost, and management areas) to restructure Kenwood and help the company earn a $35.9 million profit in fiscal 2003.[82] Thus far, Kawahara's transformation of Kenwood has been praised in the business world.[83] As Prem Samtani, an analyst at hedge fund Sofear Global Research Ltd., indicates of restructuring

Part of CEO Haruo Kawahara's approach to reorganization at Japanese Kenwood Corporation has been to encourage a more open communication style.

in Japan, "In Japan it has been extremely difficult to implement. . . . Kawahara is an impressive leader."[84]

Interestingly enough, working at General Electric and United Technologies in the late 1960s (Kawahara went on to spend 41 years at Toshiba in Japan) made Kawahara realize the power of good communication. According to Kawahara, while Japanese employees excel at many things (such as product redesign, efficient manufacturing, and continuous improvement) and are good communicators within their teams and work units, communication and transfer of knowledge and information throughout Japanese organizations is often lacking.[85]

In Kawahara's experience, outside some Japanese employees' teams or work units, much filtering of information takes place; secrecy rather than openness is the norm.[86] Thus, complex projects that require collaboration across multiple units often run into trouble. This is partly due to the Japanese culture's tendency to use oral communication rather than documentation as in the United States. Kawahara is changing this mindset at Kenwood and, by all counts, succeeding.[87]

information distortion Changes in the meaning of a message as the message passes through a series of senders and receivers.

Information distortion occurs when the meaning of a message changes as the message passes through a series of senders and receivers. Some information distortion is accidental–due to faulty encoding and decoding or to a lack of feedback. Other information distortion is deliberate. Senders may alter a message to make themselves or their groups look good and to receive special treatment.

Managers themselves should avoid filtering and distorting information. But how can they eliminate these barriers to effective communication throughout their organization? They need to establish trust throughout the organization. Subordinates who trust their managers believe that they will not be blamed for things beyond their control and will be treated fairly. Managers who trust their subordinates provide them with clear and complete information and do not hold things back.

INCLUDE A FEEDBACK MECHANISM IN MESSAGES Because feedback is essential for effective communication, managers should build a feedback mechanism into the messages they send. They either should include a request for feedback or indicate when and how they will follow up on the message to make sure that it was received and understood. When managers write letters and memos or send faxes, they can request that the receiver respond with comments and suggestions in a letter, memo, or fax; schedule a meeting to discuss the issue; or follow up with a phone call. By building feedback mechanisms such as these into their messages, managers ensure that they get heard and are understood.

rumors Unofficial pieces of information of interest to organizational members but with no identifiable source.

PROVIDE ACCURATE INFORMATION **Rumors** are unofficial pieces of information of interest to organizational members but with no identifiable source. Rumors spread quickly once they are started, and usually they concern topics that organizational members think are important, interesting, or amusing. Rumors, however, can be misleading and can cause harm to individual employees and their organizations when they are false, malicious, or unfounded. Managers can halt the spread of misleading rumors by providing organizational members with accurate information on matters that concern them.

Table 16.3
Three Communication Skills for Managers as Receivers of Messages

- Pay attention.
- Be a good listener.
- Be empathetic.

Communication Skills for Managers as Receivers

Managers receive as many messages as they send. Thus, managers must possess or develop communication skills that allow them to be effective receivers of messages. Table 16.3 summarizes three of these important skills, which we examine here in greater detail.

PAY ATTENTION Because of their multiple roles and tasks, managers often are overloaded and forced to think about several things at once. Pulled in many different directions, they sometimes do not pay sufficient attention to the messages they receive. To be effective, however, managers should always pay attention to messages they receive, no matter how busy they are. When discussing a project with a subordinate, an effective manager focuses on the project and not on an upcoming meeting with his or her own boss. Similarly, when managers are reading written communications, they should focus their attention on understanding what they are reading; they should not be sidetracked into thinking about other issues.

BE A GOOD LISTENER Managers (and all other members of an organization) can do several things to be good listeners. First, managers should refrain from interrupting senders in the middle of a message so that senders do not lose their train of thought and managers do not jump to erroneous conclusions based on incomplete information. Second, managers should maintain good eye contact with senders so that senders feel their listeners are paying attention; doing this also helps managers focus on what they are hearing. Third, after receiving a message, managers should ask questions to clarify points of ambiguity or confusion. Fourth, managers should paraphrase, or restate in their own words, points senders make that are important, complex, or open to alternative interpretations; this is the feedback component so critical to successful communication.

Managers, like most people, often like to hear themselves talk rather than listen to others. Part of being a good communicator, however, is being a good listener, an essential communication skill for managers as receivers of messages transmitted face-to-face and over the telephone.

BE EMPATHETIC Receivers are empathetic when they try to understand how the sender feels and try to interpret a message from the sender's perspective, rather than viewing the message from only their own point of view. Marcia Mazulo, the chief psychologist in a public school system in the Northwest, recently learned this lesson after interacting with Karen Sanchez, a new psychologist on her staff. Sanchez was distraught after meeting with the parent of a child she had been working with extensively. The parent was difficult to talk to and argumentative and was not supportive of her own child. Sanchez told Mazulo how upset she was, and Mazulo responded by reminding Sanchez that she was a professional and that dealing with such a situation was part of her job. This feedback upset Sanchez further and caused her to storm out of the room.

In hindsight, Mazulo realized that her response had been inappropriate. She had failed to empathize with Sanchez, who had spent so much time with the child and was deeply concerned about the child's well-being. Rather than dismissing Sanchez's concerns, Mazulo realized, she should have tried to understand how Sanchez felt and given her some support and advice for dealing positively with the situation.

Understanding Linguistic Styles

Consider the following scenarios:

- A manager from New York is having a conversation with a manager from Iowa City. The Iowa City manager never seems to get a chance to talk. He keeps waiting for a pause to signal his turn to talk, but the New York manager never pauses long enough. The New York manager wonders why the Iowa City manager does not say much. He feels uncomfortable when he pauses and the Iowa City manager says nothing, so he starts talking again.
- Elizabeth compliments Bob on his presentation to upper management and asks Bob what he thought of her presentation. Bob launches into a lengthy critique of Elizabeth's presentation and describes how he would have handled it differently. This is hardly the response Elizabeth expected.
- Catherine shares with comembers of a self-managed work team a new way to cut costs. Michael, another team member, thinks her idea is a good one and encourages the rest of the team to support it. Catherine is quietly pleased by Michael's support. The group implements "Michael's" suggestion, and it is written up as such in the company newsletter.
- Robert was recently promoted and transferred from his company's Oklahoma office to its headquarters in New Jersey. Robert is perplexed because he never seems to get a chance to talk in management meetings; someone else always seems to get the floor. Robert's new boss wonders whether Robert's new responsibilities are too much for him, although Robert's supervisor in Oklahoma rated him highly and said he is a real "go-getter." Robert is timid in management meetings and rarely says a word.

linguistic style A person's characteristic way of speaking.

What do these scenarios have in common? Essentially, they all describe situations in which a misunderstanding of linguistic styles leads to a breakdown in communication. The scenarios are based on the research of linguist Deborah Tannen, who describes **linguistic style** as a person's characteristic way of speaking. Elements of linguistic style include tone of voice, speed, volume, use of pauses, directness or indirectness, choice of words, credit taking, and use of questions, jokes, and other manners of speech.[88] When people's linguistic styles differ and these differences are not understood, ineffective communication is likely.

The first and last scenarios illustrate regional differences in linguistic style.[89] The Iowa City manager and Robert from Oklahoma expect the pauses that signal turn taking in conversations to be longer than the pauses made by their colleagues in New York and New Jersey. This difference causes communication problems. The Iowan and transplanted Oklahoman think that their eastern colleagues never let them get a word in edgewise, and the easterners cannot figure out why their colleagues from the Midwest and South do not get more actively involved in conversations.

Differences in linguistic style can be a particularly insidious source of communication problems because linguistic style is often taken for granted. People rarely think about their own linguistic styles and often are unaware of how linguistic styles can differ. In the example above, Robert never realized that when dealing with his New Jersey colleagues, he could and should jump into conversations more quickly than he used to do in Oklahoma, and his boss never realized that Robert felt that he was not being given a chance to speak in meetings.

The aspect of linguistic style just described, length of pauses, differs by region in the United States. Much more dramatic differences in linguistic style occur cross-culturally.

CROSS-CULTURAL DIFFERENCES Managers from Japan tend to be more formal in their conversations and more deferential toward upper-level managers and people with high status than are managers from the United States. Japanese managers do not mind extensive pauses in conversations when they are thinking things through or when they think that further conversation might be detrimental. In contrast, U.S. managers (even managers from regions of the United States where pauses tend to be long) find very lengthy pauses disconcerting and feel obligated to talk to fill the silence.[90]

Another cross-cultural difference in linguistic style concerns the appropriate physical distance separating speakers and listeners in business-oriented conversations.[91] The distance between speakers and listeners is greater in the United States, for example, than it is in Brazil or Saudi Arabia. Citizens of different countries also vary in how direct or indirect they are in conversations and the extent to which they take individual credit for accomplishments. Japanese culture, with its collectivist or group orientation, tends to encourage linguistic styles in which group rather than individual accomplishments are emphasized. The opposite tends to be true in the United States.

These and other cross-cultural differences in linguistic style can and often do lead to misunderstandings. For example, when a team of American managers presented a proposal for a joint venture to Japanese managers, the Japanese managers were silent as they thought about the implications of what they had just heard. The American managers took this silence as a sign that the Japanese managers wanted more information, so they went into more detail about the proposal. When they finished, the Japanese were silent again, not only frustrating the Americans but also making them wonder whether the Japanese were at all interested in the project. The American managers suggested that if the Japanese already had decided that they did not want to pursue the project, there was no reason for the meeting to continue. The Japanese were truly bewildered. They were trying to carefully think out the proposal, yet the Americans thought they were not interested!

Cross-cultural differences in communication styles can be dramatic. For example, the distance between speakers is greater in the United States than it is in Brazil, such as with these business people in Sao Paolo. Researching such differences before trying to negotiate with those from other cultures can help avoid misunderstandings.

Communication misunderstandings and problems like this can be overcome if managers make themselves familiar with cross-cultural differences in linguistic styles. If the American managers and the Japanese managers had realized that periods of silence are viewed differently in Japan and in the United States, their different linguistic styles might have been less troublesome barriers to communication. Before managers communicate with people from abroad, they should try to find out as much as they can about the aspects of linguistic style that are specific to the country or culture in question. Expatriate managers who have lived in the country in question for an extended period of time can be good sources of information about linguistic styles because they are likely to have experienced firsthand some of the differences that citizens of a country are not aware of. Finding out as much as possible about cultural differences also can help managers learn about differences in linguistic styles because the two are often closely linked.

GENDER DIFFERENCES Referring again to the four scenarios that open this section, you may be wondering why Bob launched into a lengthy critique of Elizabeth's presentation after she paid him a routine compliment on his presentation, or you may be wondering why Michael got the credit for Catherine's idea in the self-managed work team. Research conducted by Tannen and other linguists has found that the linguistic styles of men and women differ in practically every culture or language.[92] Men and women take their own linguistic styles for granted and thus do not realize when they are talking with someone of a different gender that differences in their styles may lead to ineffective communication.

In the United States, women tend to downplay differences between people, are not overly concerned about receiving credit for their own accomplishments, and want to make everyone feel more or less on an equal footing so that even poor performers or low-status individuals feel valued. Men, in contrast, tend to emphasize their own superiority and are not reluctant to acknowledge differences in status. These differences in linguistic style led Elizabeth to routinely compliment Bob on his presentation even though she thought that he had not done a particularly good job. She asked him how her presentation was so that he could reciprocate and give her a routine compliment, putting them on an equal footing. Bob took Elizabeth's compliment and question about her own presentation as an opportunity to confirm his superiority, never realizing that all she was expecting was a routine compliment. Similarly, Michael's enthusiastic support for Catherine's cost-cutting idea and her apparent surrender of ownership of the idea after she described it led team members to assume incorrectly that the idea was Michael's.[93]

Do some women try to prove that they are better than everyone else, and are some men unconcerned about taking credit for ideas and accomplishments? Of course. The gender differences in linguistic style that Tannen and other linguists have uncovered are general tendencies evident in *many* women and men, not in *all* women and men.

Where do gender differences in linguistic style come from? Tannen suggests that they begin developing in early childhood. Girls and boys tend to play with children of their own gender, and the ways in which girls and boys play are quite different. Girls play in small groups, engage in a lot of close conversation, emphasize how similar they are to one another, and view boastfulness negatively. Boys play in large groups, emphasize status differences, expect leaders to emerge who boss others around, and give one another challenges to try to meet. These differences in styles of play and interaction result in differences in linguistic styles when boys and girls grow up and communicate as adults. The ways in which men communicate emphasize status differences and play up relative strengths; the ways in which women communicate emphasize similarities and downplay individual strengths.[94]

Interestingly, gender differences are also turning up in the ways that women and men use email and electronic forms of communication. For example, Susan Herring, a researcher at Indiana University, has found that in public electronic forums such as message boards and chat rooms, men tend to make stronger assertions, be more sarcastic, and be more likely to use insults and profanity than women, while women are more likely to be supportive, agreeable, and polite.[95] David Silver, a researcher at the University of Washington, has found that women are more expressive electronic communicators and encourage others to express their thoughts and feelings, while men are briefer and more to the point.[96] Interestingly enough, some men are finding email to be a welcome way to express their feelings to people they care about. For example, real estate broker Mike Murname finds it easier to communicate with, and express his love for, his grown children via email.[97]

MANAGING DIFFERENCES IN LINGUISTIC STYLES Managers should not expect to change people's linguistic styles and should not try to. To be effective, managers need to understand differences in linguistic styles. Knowing, for example, that some women are reluctant to speak up in meetings not because they have nothing to contribute but because of their linguistic style should lead managers to ensure that these women have a chance to talk. And a manager who knows that certain people are reluctant to take credit for ideas can be extra careful to give credit where it is deserved. As Tannen points out, "Talk is the lifeblood of managerial work, and understanding that different people have different ways of saying what they mean will make it possible to take advantage of the talents of people with a broad range of linguistic styles."[98]

Summary and Review

COMMUNICATION AND MANAGEMENT Communication is the sharing of information between two or more individuals or groups to reach a common understanding. Good communication is necessary for an organization to gain a competitive advantage. Communication occurs in a cyclical process that entails two phases, transmission and feedback.

INFORMATION RICHNESS AND COMMUNICATION MEDIA Information richness is the amount of information a communication medium can carry and the extent to which the medium enables the sender and receiver to reach a common understanding. Four categories of communication media, in descending order of information richness, are face-to-face communication (includes videoconferences), spoken communication electronically transmitted (includes voice mail), personally addressed written communication (includes email), and impersonal written communication.

COMMUNICATION NETWORKS Communication networks are the pathways along which information flows in an organization. Four communication networks found in groups and teams are the wheel, the chain, the circle, and the all-channel network. An organization chart summarizes formal pathways of communication, but communication in organizations is often informal, as is true of communication through the grapevine.

INFORMATION TECHNOLOGY AND COMMUNICATION The Internet is a global system of computer networks that managers around the world use to communicate within and outside their companies. The World Wide Web is the multimedia business district on the Internet. Intranets are internal communication networks that managers can create to improve communication, performance, and customer service. Intranets use the same technology that the Internet and World Wide Web are based on. Groupware is computer software that enables members of groups and teams to share information with one another to improve their communication and performance.

COMMUNICATION SKILLS FOR MANAGERS There are various barriers to effective communication in organizations. To overcome these barriers and effectively communicate with others, managers must possess or develop certain communication skills. As senders of messages, managers should send messages that are clear and complete, encode messages in symbols the receiver understands, choose a medium appropriate for the message and monitored by the receiver, avoid filtering and information distortion, include a feedback mechanism in the message, and provide accurate information to ensure that misleading rumors are not spread. Communication skills for managers as receivers of messages include paying attention, being a good listener, and being empathetic. Understanding linguistic styles is also an essential communication skill for managers. Linguistic styles can vary by geographic region, gender, and country or culture. When these differences are not understood, ineffective communication can occur.

Management in Action

Topics for Discussion and Action

Discussion

1. Which medium (or media) do you think would be appropriate for each of the following kinds of messages that a subordinate could receive from his or her boss: (a) a raise, (b) not receiving a promotion, (c) an error in a report prepared by the subordinate, (d) additional job responsibilities, and (e) the schedule for company holidays for the upcoming year? Explain your choices.
2. Discuss the pros and cons of using the Internet and World Wide Web for communication within and between organizations.
3. Why do some organizational members resist using groupware?
4. Why do some managers find it difficult to be good listeners?
5. Explain why subordinates might filter and distort information about problems and performance shortfalls when communicating with their bosses. What steps can managers take to eliminate filtering and information distortion?
6. Explain why differences in linguistic style, when not understood by senders and receivers of messages, can lead to ineffective communication.

Action

7. Interview a manager in an organization in your community to determine with whom he or she communicates on a typical day, what communication media he or she uses, and which typical communication problems the manager experiences.

Building Management Skills

Diagnosing Ineffective Communication

Think about the last time you experienced very ineffective communication with another person—someone you work with, a classmate, a friend, a member of your family. Describe the incident. Then answer the following questions:

1. Why was your communication ineffective in this incident?
2. What stages of the communication process were particularly problematic and why?
3. Describe any filtering or information distortion that occurred.
4. Do you think differences in linguistic styles adversely affected the communication that took place? Why or why not?
5. How could you have handled this situation differently so that communication would have been effective?

Managing Ethically

Many employees use their company's Internet connections and email systems to visit Web sites and send personal emails and instant messages.

Questions

1. Either individually or in a group, explore the ethics of using an organization's Internet connection and email system for personal purposes at work and while away from the office. Should employees have some rights to use this resource? When does their behavior become unethical?
2. Some companies keep track of the way their employees use the company's Internet connection and email system. Is it ethical for managers to read employees' personal emails or to record Web sites that employees visit? Why or why not?

Small Group Breakout Exercise

Reducing Resistance to Advances in Information Technology

Form groups of three or four people, and appoint one member as the spokesperson who will communicate your findings to the whole class when called on by the instructor. Then discuss the following scenario.

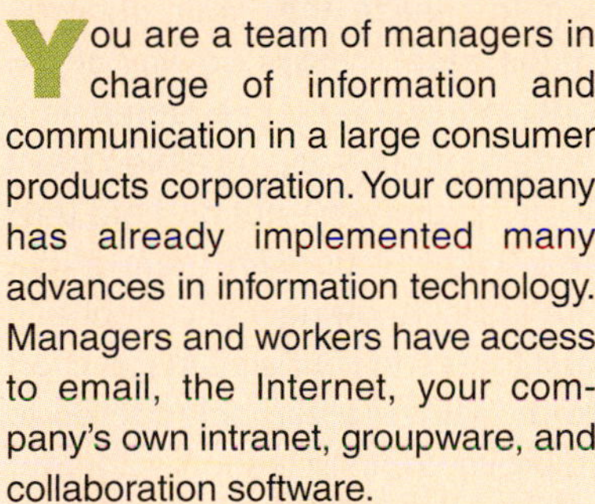

You are a team of managers in charge of information and communication in a large consumer products corporation. Your company has already implemented many advances in information technology. Managers and workers have access to email, the Internet, your company's own intranet, groupware, and collaboration software.

Many employees use the technology, but the resistance of some is causing communication problems. A case in point is the use of groupware and collaboration software. Many teams in your organization have access to groupware and are encouraged to use it. While some teams welcome this communication tool and actually have made suggestions for improvements, others are highly resistant to sharing documents on their teams' online workspaces.

Although you do not want to force people to use the technology, you want them to at least try it and give it a chance. You are meeting today to develop strategies for reducing resistance to the new technologies.

1. One resistant group of employees is made up of top managers. Some of them seem computer-phobic and are highly resistant to sharing information online, even with sophisticated security precautions in place. What steps will you take to get these managers to have more confidence in electronic communication?
2. A second group of resistant employees consists of middle managers. Some middle managers resist using your company's intranet. Although these managers do not resist the technology per se and do use electronic communication for multiple purposes, including communication, they seem to distrust the intranet as a viable way to communicate and get things done. What steps will you take to get these managers to take advantage of the intranet?
3. A third group of resistant employees is made up of members of groups and teams who do not want to use the groupware that has been provided to them. You think that the groupware could improve their communication and performance, but they seem to think otherwise. What steps will you take to get these members of groups and teams to start using groupware?

Exploring the World Wide Web

Atos Origin is a global information technology company that provides IT services to major corporations to improve, facilitate, integrate, and manage operations, information, and communication across multiple locations. Based in France and the Netherlands, Atos Origin provided much of the IT for the 2004 Olympic Games in Athens, Greece.[99] Visit Atos Origin's Web site at www.atosorigin.com, and read about this company and the services it provides to improve communication. Then read the case studies on the Web site. How can companies like Atos Origin help managers improve communication effectiveness in their organizations? What kinds of organizations and groups are most likely to benefit from services provided by Atos Origin? Why is it beneficial for some organizations to contract with firms like Atos Origin for their IT and communication needs rather than meet these needs internally with their own employees?

Be the Manager

You supervise support staff for an Internet merchandising organization that sells furniture over the Internet. You always thought that you needed to expand your staff, and just when you were about to approach your boss with such a request, business slowed. Thus, your plan to try to add new employees to your staff is on hold.

However, you have noticed a troubling pattern of communication with your staff. Ordinarily, when you want one of your staff members to work on a task, you email that subordinate the pertinent information. For the last few months, your email requests have gone unheeded, and your subordinates seem to respond to your requests only after you visit them in person and give them a specific deadline. Each time, they apologize for not getting to the task sooner but say that they are so overloaded with requests that they sometimes even stop answering their phones. Unless someone asks for something more than once, your staff seems to feel the request is not that urgent and can be put on hold. You think this state of affairs is dysfunctional and could lead to serious problems down the road. Also, you are starting to realize that your subordinates seem to have no way of prioritizing tasks—hence, some very important projects you asked them to complete were put on hold until you followed up with them about the tasks. Knowing you cannot add employees to your staff in the short term, what are you going to do to improve communication with your overloaded staff?

Additional Activities on the Build Your Management Skills DVD

- **Self-Assessment:** (1) Active Listening Skills Inventory and (2) What is Your Communication Style Under Stress
- **Test Your Knowledge:** (1) Choosing the Best Communication Medium and (2) Barriers to Effective Communications
- **Manager's Hot Seat:** (1) Listening Skills: Yeah, Whatever and (2) Privacy: Burned by the Firewall?

BusinessWeek **Case in the News**

Blogging with the Boss's Blessing

Log on to Sara Ford's Web log, and you'll get a cinema verité look into her daily world. You'll learn about her addiction to TV shows starring Richard Dean Anderson (aka MacGyver), her geek penchant for jokes with punchlines like "F1 F1!," and why she adores Gore-Tex. But most important, you'll learn that 26-year-old Sara Ford is a software design engineer at Microsoft Corp., blogging away from her fluorescent-lit office in Redmond, Wash. Her most prominent posts are ones about the product she's working on, its latest bugs, and inside dope for users such as the "hide underline letters checkbox issue." There's also her day-in-the-life workplace diary, complete with a glossary decoding Microsoft arcana and strategies for nabbing extra espresso coupons. Customers post replies. Ideas are swapped. Bonds are formed. And Bill Gates is happy.

Until recently, the thought of employees blabbing freely to the masses about their work on company time—without the suits from PR hovering over them to stay "on message"—would have created panic in the executive suite. But in the past year, employee blogs have begun to multiply across Corporate America—and a growing number of companies approve. It started mostly as a techie thing when engineers and product developers at places such as Macromedia, Sun Microsystems, and Dell began posting first-draft free-for-alls of their own volition as a way of communicating with customers, each other, and the outside world. Though employees represent just a fraction of the 2.7 million bloggers today, experts predict they will grow robustly as consumers demand information in a more unvarnished way.

Increasingly, execs see employee blogs as a way to transform a transaction with a faceless behemoth into a personal relationship with an employee. Blogs are also hyper efficient at driving product innovation. And they create loyal audiences. Once people get hooked, they keep coming back for more. "This is nothing less than revolutionary," says Dave Winer, a fellow at Harvard Law School's Berkman Center for Internet & Society.

It's revolutionary because companies have usually been more concerned with controlling their message than conversing with customers. Blogging changes that by establishing "a connection through real human beings speaking like real human beings, which is something companies have forgotten how to do," says David Weinberger, the Boston-based co-author of *The Cluetrain Manifesto*.

Microsoft has been one of the biggest evangelists. A year ago, it had about 100 corporate bloggers. Today there are 800. They post pictures of company refrigerators—there's one that has all Coke and one that has all Pepsi—and spout off on everything from the death of Boots the cat to renaming Longhorn, Microsoft's long-anticipated new operating system, "Longwait." Indeed, Chairman William H. Gates III is so certain that corporate blogging is the next gold rush in communications that he's practically handing out the pails and shovels by enabling any employee to create a blog within two seconds. Microsoft doesn't train employees in the fine art of blogs, but employees hold meetings to talk about them. The blogs carry disclaimers, but other than that, "our outspoken policy on blogging is: Don't be stupid," says product manager Adam Sohn.

Going Further

Other companies, such as publisher Ziff-Davis, started the process by setting up internal blogs that proved enormously helpful to teams by cutting down on e-mail. They also let employees learn what was appropriate when blogging to the outside. Nike is going further. This month the company launched a blog of its own—"The Art of Speed"—and hired hip gossip blogger extraordinaire, Gawker Media, to produce it. Nike says Gawker has the following it wants to reach.

Given blogging's ability to give nobodies such awesome powers—*The New York Post* headlined the way political bloggers did in former Senate Majority Leader Trent Lott as "The Internet's First Scalp"—you'd think the idea of workers firing off would strike companies as akin to putting dynamite in the playpen. This is, after all, a medium once referred to as the electronic Jerry Springer.

Indeed, blogs can be dangerous, representing a new legal netherworld. Microsoft's most famous blogger, Robert "Scobleizer" Scoble once got into big trouble in a previous job for talking up a rival's products. Therein lies the rub: The most truthful they are, the more valuable blogs are to customers. It's likely only a matter of time before some workplace pundit spills a trade secret, unwittingly leaks a clandestine launch date, or takes a swipe at a CEO that turns into slander.

For now, though, many are running the risk. In an era of fragmental media, with companies struggling to get their message out any which way, blogs are becoming a kind of undercover megaphone. One way to think of them is as the latest guerrilla marketing tool, a new kind of brand bait.

They'll likely backfire, though, if employers attempt to exert control. "Companies inevitably will try to co-opt blogs," says Dan Gillmore, author of *We, the Media,* a book about blogging due out next month.

Until then, happy reading.

Questions

1. What are the potential advantages of blogging at work by employees in high-tech companies?
2. What are the potential disadvantages?
3. For what other kinds of companies might blogging be potentially advantageous?
4. Are there organizations in which blogging should be prohibited? Why or why not?

Source: M. Conlin and A. Park, "Blogging with the Boss's Blessing." Reprinted from the June 28, 2004, issue of *BusinessWeek* by special permission. Copyright © 2004 by the McGraw-Hill Companies, Inc.

BusinessWeek Case in the News

Fortress India?

A line of neatly dressed workers files into the Golden Millennium, a shimmering glass-and-steel building in central Bangalore. One by one, they swipe ID cards through a reader, then empty their pockets and bags and stuff cell phones, PDAs, and even pens and notebooks into lockers as a dour security guard watches. Staffers ending their shifts, meanwhile, are busy shredding notes of conversations with customers. At the reception desk, visitors sign a daunting four-page form promising not to divulge anything they see inside—and even then are only allowed to peer into the workspace through thick windows.

A top-secret military contractor? Hardly. This is one of four call centers run by ICICI Onesource, which employs 4,000 young Indians to process credit-card bills and make telemarketing calls for big U.S. and European banks, insurers, and retailers. And ICICI isn't the only outsourcing company worried about security. Call center operators such as Mphasis BFL, Wipro Spectramind, and 24/7 Customer, as well as back-office subsidiaries of companies such as General Electric, are quickly adding state-of-the-art systems to monitor phone conversations, guard data, and watch workers' every move.

Why the extreme caution? After rushing to shift telemarketing and back-office work to India in recent years to tap low wages, U.S. and European companies are under growing pressure from regulators and legislators to guarantee the privacy of their customers' financial and health-care data. India's $3.6 billion business-process services industry is eager to defuse the issue. When the backlash against offshore outsourcing erupted last year, opponents first focused on curbing government contracts and temporary U.S. work visas for foreign tech workers. Now security and privacy fears have become the hot excuses "for new barriers to trade in services and information technology," says Jerry Rao, chairman of the National Association of Service & Software Cos. (Nasscom), India's IT trade group.

Pending Legislation

Today 186 bills that aim to limit offshore outsourcing are pending in the U.S. Congress and 40 state legislatures. Dozens of those involve restrictions on transmission of data. For example, the SAFE ID Act, sponsored by Senator Hillary Clinton (D-N.Y.), and a similar House bill by Representative Edward J. Markey (D-Mass.), would require businesses to notify U.S. consumers before sending personal information overseas—and would bar companies from denying service or charging a higher price if customers balk. Although no such bills have been enacted so far, "next year I think all of this legislation will be back and spike up again as a huge issue," especially if the U.S. recovery stalls, says R. Bruce Josten, a U.S. Chamber of Commerce executive vice-president who helped industry fight the legislation.

Identity theft and credit-card fraud are huge problems globally. There's little evidence, though, to suggest consumer data are at any greater risk in India than in the U.S. Sure, India's privacy laws aren't as stringent as in the West. But most highly sensitive data belonging to U.S. or European companies are stored on their own servers at home, with access from India tightly controlled. If an American is defrauded, the U.S. company that farmed out the work is legally responsible.

Indian call centers, meanwhile, sign their contracts in the U.S. and can thus be sued there by their corporate customers. What's more, there is only one known case of fraud. Last year a programmer for India's Geometric Software Solutions Co. tried to sell a U.S. client's intellectual property. He was arrested and is awaiting trial in India.

Still, given the charged emotions over outsourcing, India's IT industry knows even a few incidents will generate devastating publicity. So call centers like Mphasis BFL Ltd., which employs 6,000 workers performing sensitive tasks such as processing personal tax returns and credit-card statements for U.S. clients, are leaving little to chance. If the U.S. company prefers, consumers' names, Social Security numbers, and credit-card numbers can be masked. Computer terminals at Mphasis lack hard drives, e-mail, CD-ROM drives, or other ways to store, copy, or forward data. Indian accountants only view data from U.S. servers for specific tasks. Video cameras watch over the sea of cubicles. Every phone conversation is recorded and can be monitored on a system installed by Melville (N.Y.)-based Verint Systems Inc. And since data theft is often committed by disgruntled former employees, Mphasis can lock a staffer out and cut access to PCs and phones three minutes after a resignation. A year ago that process took three days. "Fears about identity theft can be aggravated when people learn their data are in a foreign country," says Mphasis Vice-Chairman Jeroen Tas. "So we feel it is better to address these concerns up front.

Such precautions don't come cheap. It costs about $1,000 per worker to install the Verint system that records, stores, and analyzes voice conversations. Yet Verint has signed up 100 local and multinational centers in India. "There has been a big push in the past year or so as the competition focuses more on quality," says Mariann McDonagh, Verint's vice-president for global marketing. Indian centers also pay up to $300 per worker for background checks, a big expense given their explosive growth, and high attrition rates. It's also cumbersome. Due to India's lack of online databases, verifying education and work experience can take weeks.

But while security practices in India now match or surpass those at most U.S. call centers, the legal system still needs work. Indian law on computer hacking inside companies is fuzzy, and privacy enforcement is weak. India's IT industry is addressing those vulnerabilities, Nasscom is working with the government to bring India's data-privacy laws more in line with the U.S. And it intends to have the security practices of all its 860 members audited by international accounting firms. Nasscom has helped Bombay's police department set up a cybercrime unit, training officers to investigate data theft. Similar units are planned in nine other cities. India's goal, says Nasscom Vice-President Sunil Mehta, is "to have the best data-security provisions and be a trusted sourcing destination."

Given the ingenuity of today's cyberscammers, some embarrassing incident seems inevitable. But India's IT-services industry is determined to show that the world's financial and health secrets are as safe in Bangalore as they are anywhere.

Questions

1. What security and privacy concerns does outsourcing back-office work and telemarketing to India pose?
2. Do the same kinds of concerns apply to back-office work and telemarketing performed in countries like the United States? Why or why not?
3. How do the precautions taken in India to protect security and privacy compare to those in the United States?
4. What are the costs of these precautions, and do they have any unintended potential negative consequences?

Source: P. Engardio, J. Puliyenthuruthel, and M. Kripalani, "Fortress India?" Reprinted from the August 16, 2004, issue of *BusinessWeek* by special permission.

CHAPTER

17 Managing Organizational Conflict, Politics, and Negotiation

Learning Objectives

After studying this chapter, you should be able to:

- Explain why conflict arises, and identify the types and sources of conflict in organizations.
- Describe conflict management strategies that managers can use to resolve conflict effectively.
- Understand the nature of negotiation and why integrative bargaining is more effective than distributive negotiation.
- Describe ways in which managers can promote integrative bargaining in organizations.
- Explain why managers need to be attuned to organizational politics and describe the political strategies that managers can use to become politically skilled.

A Manager's Challenge

Bridging Cultures and Mind-sets at Toyota

How can managers effectively bridge cultures and mind-sets to capitalize on their organizations' strengths while being responsive to customers in different markets?

Jim Press, chief operating officer and executive vice president of Toyota Motor Sales USA, is a master at effectively managing conflict and using power to help Toyota achieve record levels of revenues and profits from its North American operations. For fiscal 2003, Toyota USA's revenues were $46 billion (revenues at this level would place a company in the number 25 spot of the Fortune 500 list of largest companies); its combined profits for April, May, and June of 2004 were $2.6 billion, 29 percent higher than profits for the same period a year earlier.[1]

Toyota USA Vice President Jim Press uses his keen understanding of both the U.S. auto market and Toyota's culture and approach to reach win-win solutions.

While Toyota's engineering and manufacturing expertise is world-renowned, success in the U.S. market hinges on being responsive to the desires of U.S. customers. Press is highly influential within Toyota, and thus within the U.S. auto industry as a whole, given Toyota's strong presence, because of his deep understanding of this market and his ability to effectively manage conflict, bridge cultures and mind-sets, and keep Toyota in tune with, and responsive to, U.S. customers while capitalizing on the company's own strengths in engineering and manufacturing.[2]

Toyota's culture, values, and norms could result in a certain lack of responsiveness to customers in major markets outside Japan, such as the United States. Japanese engineers and managers in Toyota tend to be risk-averse and not eager to introduce new models without having a deep understanding and experience base to fall back on. Their risk aversion can also lead to strong apprehensions and fears about things going wrong.[3]

Toyota's engineering and manufacturing ethos stresses efficiency, high quality, lean production, and continuous improvement. Not enamored of the bigger engines and brawny horsepower that appeal to U.S. customers, Toyota has typically concentrated on fuel-efficient, smaller engines.[4] Efficient utilization of space, avoidance of unnecessary features, and precise engineering and manufacturing have been priorities at Toyota. When it comes to engineering and manufacturing, Toyota stands out as a perfectionist among its rivals in the auto industry, and thus it has the highest profit margins.[5]

Jim Press is extremely powerful within Toyota precisely because he is so ingrained in the U.S. auto market and because he is intimately familiar with Toyota's culture and approach. Press has always loved cars: At age 13, he was tinkering with old cars as a hobby and washing cars in his uncle's car dealership; he has worked in the auto industry ever since, graduating from Kansas State University in 1967.[6]

More so than most top managers, Press seems to really understand what U.S. car buyers want and what will appeal to them. Gauging the ever-changing tastes and needs of car buyers is a never-ending pursuit for Press, so he is very close to Toyota's dealerships, as dealers are closest to customers. Press regularly visits dealerships and talks with all kinds of employees, ranging from salespeople and mechanics to receptionists, to keep on top of this dynamic market. As he puts it, "The strength of this company is its relationship with customers, and dealers are our lifeblood. . . . They see problems, issues, change. If we do something wrong, they get bruised."[7]

Press's closeness to the U.S. car buyer, an intimate familiarity with Toyota's culture and decision-making style gleaned from working at Toyota for the past 34 years, and an uncanny ability to effectively manage conflict and exercise his own power within the company have proved to be a win-win situation for Press and Toyota. Press spends two weeks out of every month in Japan working with Japanese managers and engineers to help them appreciate the psyche of U.S. car buyers and collaboratively develop new products that are responsive to the U.S. market and embody Toyota's excellence in engineering and manufacturing. Dr. Schoichiro Toyoda, the honorary chairman of Toyota, suggests that Press, one of 44 managing officers (and one of 5 non-Japanese managing officers) of Toyota is a "force for change."[8]

For an American to be a "force for change" in a Japanese company and effectively manage conflicting opinions and perspectives to reach win-win solutions is a real managerial challenge. Press's soft-spoken, patient, yet determined, demeanor, in combination with an organizational culture that emphasizes listening,[9] will likely lead Toyota USA to new heights in the U.S. auto industry.[10]

Overview

Successful leaders such as Jim Press in "A Manager's Challenge" are able to effectively use their power to influence others and to manage conflict to achieve win-win solutions. In Chapter 14 we described how managers, as leaders, exert influence over other people to achieve group and organizational goals and how managers' sources of power enable them to exert such influence. In this chapter we describe why managers need to develop the skills necessary to manage organizational conflict, politics, and negotiation if they are going to be effective and achieve their goals, as does Jim Press.

We describe conflict and the strategies that managers can use to resolve it effectively. We discuss one major conflict resolution technique, negotiation, in detail, outlining the steps managers can take to be good negotiators. Lastly, we discuss the nature of organizational politics, and the political strategies that managers can use to maintain and expand their power and use it effectively. By the end of this chapter, you will appreciate why managers must develop the skills necessary to manage these important organizational processes if they are to be effective and achieve organizational goals.

Organizational Conflict

organizational conflict The discord that arises when the goals, interests, or values of different individuals or groups are incompatible and those individuals or groups block or thwart one another's attempts to achieve their objectives.

Organizational conflict is the discord that arises when the goals, interests, or values of different individuals or groups are incompatible and those individuals or groups block or thwart one another's attempts to achieve their objectives.[11] Conflict is an inevitable part of organizational life because the goals of different stakeholders such as managers and workers are often incompatible. Organizational conflict also can exist between departments and divisions that compete for resources or even between managers who may be competing for promotion to the next level in the organizational hierarchy.

It is important for managers to develop the skills necessary to manage conflict effectively. In addition, the level of conflict present in an organization has important implications for organizational performance. Figure 17.1 illustrates the relationship between organizational conflict and performance. At point A, there is little or no conflict and organizational performance suffers. Lack of conflict in an organization often signals that managers emphasize conformity at the expense of new ideas, are resistant to change, and strive for agreement rather than effective decision making. As the level of conflict increases from point A to point B, organizational effectiveness is likely to increase. When an organization has an optimum level of conflict (point B), managers are likely to be open to, and encourage, a variety of perspectives, look for ways to improve organizational functioning and effectiveness, and view debates and disagreements as a necessary ingredient for effective decision making. As the level of conflict increases from point B to point C, conflict escalates to the point where organizational performance suffers. When an organization has a dysfunctionally high level of conflict, managers are likely to waste organizational resources to achieve their own ends, to be more concerned about winning political battles than about doing what will lead to a competitive advantage for their organization, and to try to get even with their opponents rather than make good decisions.

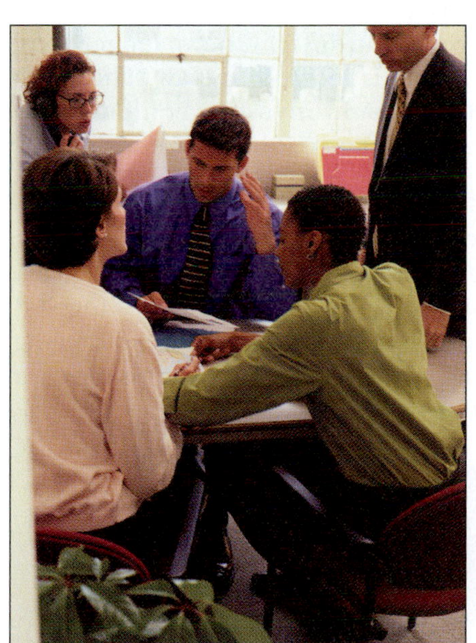
The signs of mounting tension in this picture are unmistakable. Since some degree of conflict is inevitable and desirable, conflict is a force that needs to be managed rather than eliminated.

Conflict is a force that needs to be managed rather than eliminated.[12] Managers should never try to eliminate all conflict but, rather, should try to keep conflict at a moderate and functional level to promote change efforts that benefit the organization. To manage conflict, managers must understand the types and sources of conflict and be familiar with certain strategies that can be effective in dealing with it.

Types of Conflict

There are several types of conflict in organizations: interpersonal, intragroup, intergroup, and interorganizational (see Figure 17.2).[13] Understanding how these types differ can help managers to deal with conflict.

Figure 17.1
The Effect of Conflict on Organizational Performance

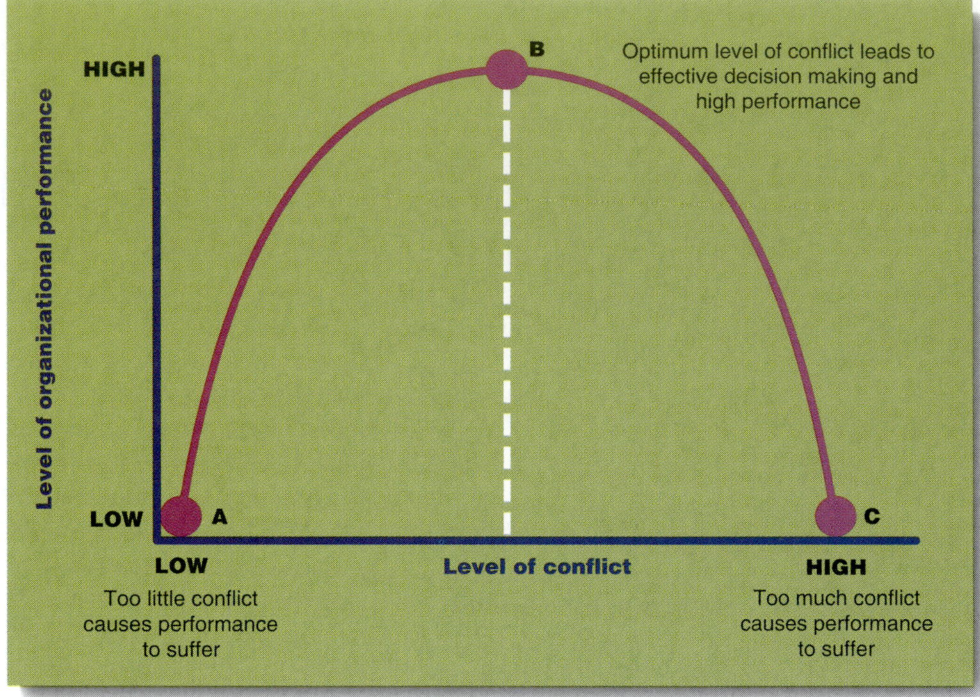

INTERPERSONAL CONFLICT Interpersonal conflict is conflict between individual members of an organization, occurring because of differences in their goals or values. Two managers may experience interpersonal conflict when their values concerning protection of the environment differ. One manager may argue that the organization should do only what is required by law. The other manager may counter that the organization should invest in equipment to reduce emissions even though the organization's current level of emissions is below the legal limit.

INTRAGROUP CONFLICT Intragroup conflict is conflict that arises within a group, team, or department. When members of the marketing department in a clothing company disagree about how they should spend budgeted advertising dollars for a new line of men's designer jeans, they are experiencing intragroup conflict. Some of the members want to spend all the money on

Figure 17.2
Types of Conflict in Organizations

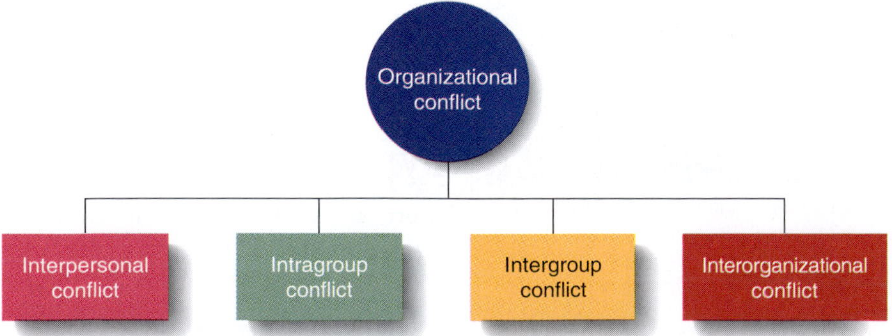

advertisements in magazines. Others want to devote half of the money to billboards and ads in city buses and subways.

INTERGROUP CONFLICT Intergroup conflict is conflict that occurs between groups, teams, or departments. R&D departments, for example, sometimes experience intergroup conflict with production departments. Members of the R&D department may develop a new product that they think production can make inexpensively by using existing manufacturing capabilities. Members of the production department, however, may disagree and believe that the costs of making the product will be much higher. Managers of departments usually play a key role in managing intergroup conflicts such as this.

INTERORGANIZATIONAL CONFLICT Interorganizational conflict is conflict that arises across organizations. Sometimes interorganizational conflict arises when managers in one organization feel that another organization is not behaving ethically and is threatening the well-being of certain stakeholder groups.

Sources of Conflict

Conflict in organizations springs from a variety of sources. The ones that we examine here are different goals and time horizons, overlapping authority, task interdependencies, different evaluation or reward systems, scarce resources, and status inconsistencies (see Figure 17.3).[14]

DIFFERENT GOALS AND TIME HORIZONS Recall from Chapter 10 that an important managerial activity is organizing people and tasks into departments and divisions to accomplish an organization's goals. Almost inevitably, this grouping results in the creation of departments and divisions that have different goals and time horizons, and the result can be conflict. Production and production managers, for example, usually concentrate on efficiency and cost cutting; they have a relatively short time horizon and focus on producing quality goods or services in a timely and efficient manner. In contrast, marketing

Figure 17.3
Sources of Conflict in Organizations

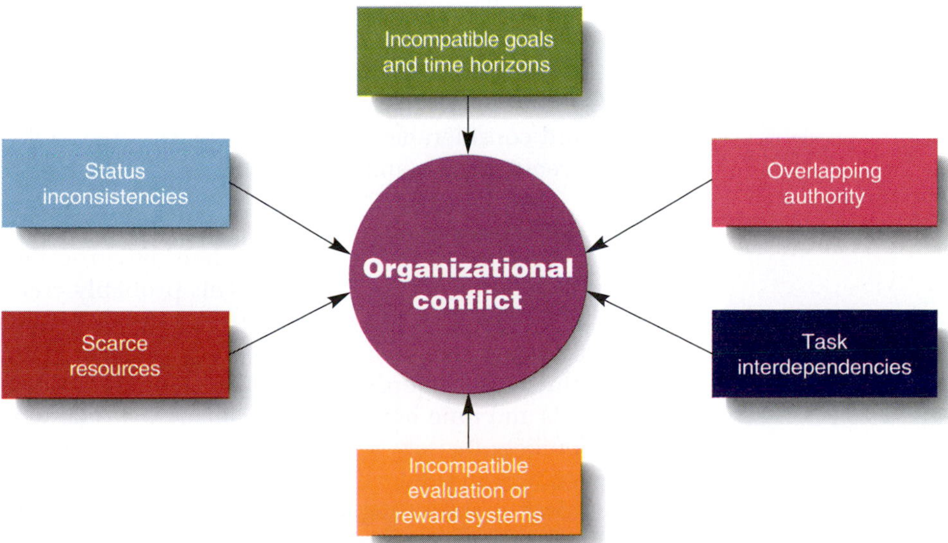

and marketing managers focus on sales and responsiveness to customers. Their time horizon is longer than that of production because they are trying to be responsive not only to customers' needs today but also to their changing needs in the future to build long-term customer loyalty. These fundamental differences between marketing and production are often breeding grounds for conflict.

Suppose production is behind schedule in its plan to produce a specialized product for a key customer. The marketing manager believes that the delay will reduce sales of the product and therefore insists that the product be delivered on time even if saving the production schedule means increasing costs by paying production workers overtime. The production manager says that she will happily schedule overtime if marketing will pay for it. Both managers' positions are reasonable from the perspective of their own departments and conflict is likely.

In "A Manager's Challenge," Jim Press's goal of being responsive to U.S. customers is sometimes different from the goal of Toyota's Japanese product designers and engineers, efficiently utilizing space and conserving fuel. These conflicting goals are illustrated by Toyota's experience in the minivan market. In the late 1980s, Toyota focused on creating an ideal minivan with precise engineering. The 1991 Previa embodied Toyota's engineering expertise and efficient use of space; the engine of the Previa was situated between the front and rear seats. While Toyota's engineers were delighted, its U.S. customers were not–they found the Previa was not spacious enough and was difficult to move around in due to the bump in the floor between the rows of seats where the engine was.[15] Press knew that U.S. customers preferred larger, roomier minivans with many cup holders, and he convinced the Japanese product designers to give the U.S. market what it wanted. The result was the 1998 Sienna minivan, which, while roomier than the Previa, was still not big enough for U.S. tastes. With the 2004 Sienna, Press and Toyota succeeded in giving U.S. customers the space and features they want in a minivan; the model has sold remarkably well.[16]

OVERLAPPING AUTHORITY When two or more managers, departments, or functions claim authority for the same activities or tasks, conflict is likely.[17] This is precisely what happened when heirs of the Forman liquor distribution company, based in Washington, DC, inherited the company from their parents. One of the heirs, Barry Forman, wanted to control the company and was reluctant to share power with the other heirs. Several of the heirs felt that they had authority over certain tasks crucial to Forman's success (such as maintaining good relationships with the top managers of liquor companies). What emerged was a battle of wills and considerable conflict, which escalated to the point of being dysfunctional, requiring the family to hire a consulting firm to help resolve it.[18]

TASK INTERDEPENDENCIES Have you ever been assigned a group project for one of your classes and had one group member who consistently failed to get things done on time? This probably created some conflict in your group because other group members were dependent on the late member's contributions to complete the project. Whenever individuals, groups, teams, or departments are interdependent, the potential for conflict exists.[19] With differing goals and time horizons, the managers of marketing and production come into conflict precisely because the departments are interdependent. Marketing is dependent on production for the goods it markets and sells, and production is dependent on marketing for creating demand for the things it makes.

DIFFERENT EVALUATION OR REWARD SYSTEMS The way in which interdependent groups, teams, or departments are evaluated and rewarded can be another source of conflict.[20] Production managers, for example, are evaluated and rewarded for their success in staying within budget or lowering costs while maintaining quality. So they are reluctant to take any steps that will increase costs, such as paying workers high overtime rates to finish a late order for an important customer. Marketing managers, in contrast, are evaluated and rewarded for their success in generating sales and satisfying customers. So they often think that overtime pay is a small price to pay for responsiveness to customers. Thus, conflict between production and marketing is rarely unexpected.

SCARCE RESOURCES Management is the process of acquiring, developing, protecting, and utilizing the resources that allow an organization to be efficient and effective (see Chapter 1). When resources are scarce, management is all the more difficult and conflict is likely.[21] When resources are scarce, for example, divisional managers may be in conflict over who has access to financial capital, and organizational members at all levels may be in conflict over who gets raises and promotions.

STATUS INCONSISTENCIES The fact that some individuals, groups, teams, or departments within an organization are more highly regarded than others in the organization can also create conflict. In some restaurants, for example, the chefs have relatively higher status than the people who wait on tables. Nevertheless, the chefs receive customers' orders from the wait staff and the wait staff can return to the chefs food that their customers or they think is not acceptable. This status inconsistency–high-status chefs taking orders from low-status wait staff–can be the source of considerable conflict between chefs and the wait staff. For this reason some restaurants require that the wait staff put orders on a spindle, thereby reducing the amount of direct order giving from the wait staff to the chefs.[22]

Conflict Management Strategies

If an organization is to achieve its goals, managers must be able to resolve conflicts in a functional manner. *Functional conflict resolution* means that the conflict is settled by compromise or by collaboration between the parties in conflict (later in the chapter we discuss other, typically less functional ways in which conflicts are sometimes resolved).[23] *Compromise* is possible when each party is concerned about not only its own goal accomplishment but also the goal accomplishment of the other party and is willing to engage in a give-and-take exchange and make concessions until a reasonable resolution of the conflict is reached. *Collaboration* is a way of handling conflict in which the parties to a conflict try to satisfy their goals without making any concessions and, instead, come up with a way to resolve their differences that leaves them both better off.[24] Jim Press and his Japanese counterparts in Toyota manage conflict through collaboration; by frequently meeting, listening to each other, and patiently working through their differences, they are able to design and manufacture cars that appeal to U.S. customers and embody the engineering and manufacturing strengths of Toyota.

In addition to compromise and collaboration, there are three other ways in which conflicts are sometimes handled: accommodation, avoidance, and competition.[25] When *accommodation* takes place, one party to the conflict simply gives in to the demands of the other party. Accommodation typically takes place when one party has more power than the other and is able to pursue its goal attainment at the expense of the weaker party. From an organizational perspective, accommodation is often ineffective, as the two parties are not cooperating with each other, they are unlikely to want to cooperate in the future, and the weaker party who gives in or accommodates the more powerful party might look for ways to get back at the stronger party in the future.

When conflicts are handled by *avoidance,* the two parties to a conflict try to ignore the problem and do nothing to resolve the disagreement. Avoidance is often ineffective since the real source of the disagreement has not been addressed, conflict is likely to continue, and communication and cooperation are hindered.

Competition occurs when each party to a conflict tries to maximize its own gain and has little interest in understanding the other party's position and arriving at a solution that will allow both parties to achieve their goals. Competition can actually escalate levels of conflict as each party tries to outmaneuver the other. As a way of handling conflict, competition is ineffective for the organization since the two sides to a conflict are more concerned about "winning" the battle than cooperating to arrive at a solution that is best for the organization and acceptable to both sides. Handling conflicts through accommodation, avoidance, or competition is ineffective from an organizational point of view because the two parties to a conflict do not cooperate with each other and work toward a mutually acceptable solution to their differences.

When the parties to a conflict are willing to cooperate with each other and through compromise or collaboration devise a solution that each finds acceptable, an organization is more likely to achieve its goals.[26] Conflict management strategies that managers can use to ensure that conflicts are resolved in a functional manner focus on individuals and on the organization as a whole. Following, we describe four strategies that focus on individuals: increasing awareness of the sources of conflict, increasing diversity awareness and skills, practicing job rotation or temporary assignments, and using permanent transfers or dismissals when necessary. We also describe two strategies that focus on the organization as a whole: changing an organization's structure or culture and directly altering the source of conflict.

STRATEGIES FOCUSED ON INDIVIDUALS

INCREASING AWARENESS OF THE SOURCES OF CONFLICT Sometimes conflict arises because of communication problems and interpersonal misunderstandings. For example, differences in linguistic styles (see Chapter 16) may lead some men in work teams to talk more, and take more credit for ideas, than women in those teams. These communication differences can result in conflict when the men incorrectly assume that the women are uninterested or less capable because they participate less and the women incorrectly assume that the men are being bossy and are not interested in their ideas because they seem to do all the talking. By increasing people's awareness of this source of conflict, managers can help to resolve conflict functionally. Once men and women realize that the source of their conflict is differences in linguistic styles, they can take steps to interact with each other more effectively. The men can give the women more of a chance to provide input, and the women can be more proactive in providing this input.

Sometimes personalities clash in an organization. In these situations, too, managers can help resolve conflicts functionally by increasing organizational members' awareness of the source of their difficulties. For example, some people who are not inclined to take risks may come into conflict with those who are prone to taking risks. The non-risk-takers might complain that those who welcome risk propose outlandish ideas without justification, while the risk-takers might complain that their innovative ideas are always getting shot down. When both types of people are made aware that their conflicts are due to fundamental differences in their ways of approaching problems, they will likely be better able to cooperate in coming up with innovative ideas that entail only moderate levels of risk.

INCREASING DIVERSITY AWARENESS AND SKILLS Interpersonal conflicts also can arise because of diversity. Older workers may feel uncomfortable or resentful about reporting to a younger supervisor, a Hispanic may feel singled out in a group of white workers, or a female top manager may feel that members of her predominantly male top-management team band together whenever one of them disagrees with one of her proposals. Whether these feelings are justified, they are likely to cause recurring conflicts. Many of the techniques we described in Chapter 5 for increasing diversity awareness and skills can help managers effectively manage diversity and resolve conflicts that have their origins in differences between organizational members.

Today one would hope that cases of overt discrimination would be on the decline (see Chapter 5). Disturbingly, recent cases of discrimination suggest that it remains a significant challenge for managers to overcome, as indicated in the following "Focus on Diversity."

Focus on Diversity

Sexual Discrimination at Merrill Lynch

In April 2004, a panel of arbitrators concluded that Merrill Lynch & Company, the largest U.S. brokerage house, discriminated against women who were stockbrokers at the firm. The arbitrators ruled that "Merrill's failure to train, counsel or discipline employees who engaged in sexual harassment constitutes discrimination with malice or reckless indifference to the federally protected rights of female employees."[27]

E. Hydie Sumner, a former broker at a San Antonio, Texas, Merrill Lynch office, filed the suit claiming that her boss harassed her, as well as other female and minority employees. When she made complaints to Merrill Lynch about the harassment, her boss circulated a magazine article entitled "Stop Complaining" that indicated that too much complaining can result in losing your job. The arbitration panel awarded Sumner $2.2 million in punitive damages, back pay, and lost earnings.[28]

Unfortunately, the Merrill case is not an isolated instance. In July 2004, another brokerage firm, Morgan Stanley, settled a lawsuit brought by the Equal Employment Opportunity Commission for $54 million. Allison Schieffelein, a former bond trader at Morgan Stanley, was the lead plaintiff in the case, which alleged discrimination and harassment against women at the firm. Schieffelein was awarded $12 million as part of the settlement, a $40 million fund was set up for distribution among other women included in the case, and $2 million was set aside for diversity programs at the firm.[29]

While the Merrill Lynch and Morgan Stanley suits were based on treatment of women in the 1990s, new cases of alleged discrimination against women and minorities continue to make headlines to this day. For example, in August 2004, Shirley Ellis filed a national class-action lawsuit against Costco Wholesale Corporation, claiming that women were discriminated against when promotion decisions were made for managerial positions.[30] While the outcome of this case is yet to be seen, it is clear that eradicating discrimination and harassment is a pressing concern for managers (see Chapter 5).

PRACTICING JOB ROTATION OR TEMPORARY ASSIGNMENTS Sometimes conflicts arise because individual organizational members simply do not have a good understanding of the work activities and demands that others in an organization face. A financial analyst, for example, may be required to submit monthly reports to a member of the accounting department. These reports have a low priority for the analyst, and he typically turns them in a couple of days late. On the due date, the accountant always calls up the financial analyst, and conflict ensues as the accountant describes in detail why she must have the reports on time and the financial analyst describes everything else he needs to do. In situations such as this, job rotation or temporary assignments, which expand organizational members' knowledge base and appreciation of other departments, can be a useful way of resolving the conflict. If the financial analyst spends some time working in the accounting department, he may appreciate better the need for timely reports. Similarly, a temporary assignment in the finance department may help the accountant realize the demands a financial analyst faces and the need to streamline unnecessary aspects of reporting.

USING PERMANENT TRANSFERS OR DISMISSALS WHEN NECESSARY Sometimes when other conflict resolution strategies do not work, managers may need to take more drastic steps, including permanent transfers or dismissals.

Suppose two first-line managers who work in the same department are always at each other's throats; frequent bitter conflicts arise between them even though they both seem to get along well with the other employees. No matter what their supervisor does to increase their understanding of each other, these conflicts keep occurring. In this case, the supervisor may want to transfer one or both managers so that they do not have to interact as frequently.

When dysfunctionally high levels of conflict occur among top managers who cannot resolve their differences and understand each other, it may be necessary for one of them to leave the company. This is how Gerald Levin managed dysfunctionally high levels of conflict among top managers when he was chairman of Time Warner (later Levin was CEO of AOL Time Warner). Robert Daly and Terry Semel, one of the most respected management teams in Hollywood and top managers in the Warner Brothers film company, had been in conflict with Michael Fuchs, a long-time veteran of Time Warner and head of the music division, for two years. As Semel described it, the company "was running like a dysfunctional family, and it needed one management team to run it."[31] Levin realized that Time Warner's future success rested on resolving this conflict, that it was unlikely that Fuchs would ever be able to work effectively with Daly and Semel, and that he risked losing Daly and Semel to another company if he did not resolve the conflict. Faced with that scenario, Levin asked Fuchs to resign.[32]

STRATEGIES FOCUSED ON THE WHOLE ORGANIZATION

CHANGING AN ORGANIZATION'S STRUCTURE OR CULTURE Conflict can signal the need for changes in an organization's structure or culture. Sometimes, managers can effectively resolve conflict by changing the organizational structure they use to group people and tasks.[33] As an organization grows, for example, the *functional structure* (composed of departments such as marketing, finance, and production) that was effective when the organization was small may cease to be effective, and a shift to a *product structure* might effectively resolve conflicts (see Chapter 10).

Managers also can effectively resolve conflicts by increasing levels of integration in an organization. Recall from Chapter 15 that Hallmark Cards increased integration by using cross-functional teams to produce new cards. The use of cross-functional teams speeded new card development and helped to resolve conflicts between different departments. Now, when a writer and an artist have a conflict over the appropriateness of the artist's illustrations, they do not pass criticisms back and forth from one department to another, because they are on the same team and can directly resolve the issue on the spot.

Sometimes managers may need to take steps to change an organization's culture to resolve conflict (see Chapter 3). Norms and values in an organizational culture might inadvertently promote dysfunctionally high levels of conflict that are difficult to resolve. For instance, norms that stress respect for formal authority may create conflict that is difficult to resolve when an organization creates self-managed work teams and managers' roles and the structure of authority in the organization change. Values stressing individual competition may make it difficult to resolve conflicts when organizational members need to put others' interests ahead of their own. In circumstances such as these, taking steps to change norms and values can be an effective conflict resolution strategy.

negotiation A method of conflict resolution in which the two parties in conflict consider various alternative ways to allocate resources to each other in order to come up with a solution acceptable to them both.

third-party negotiator An impartial individual with expertise in handling conflicts and negotiations who helps parties in conflict reach an acceptable solution.

ALTERING THE SOURCE OF CONFLICT When conflict is due to overlapping authority, different evaluation or reward systems, and status inconsistencies, managers can sometimes effectively resolve the conflict by directly altering the source of the conflict–the overlapping authority, the evaluation or reward system, or the status inconsistency. For example, managers can clarify the chain of command and reassign tasks and responsibilities to resolve conflicts due to overlapping authority.

Negotiation

A particularly important conflict resolution technique for managers and other organizational members to use in situations where the parties to a conflict have approximately equal levels of power is negotiation. During **negotiation,** the parties to a conflict try to come up with a solution acceptable to themselves by considering various alternative ways to allocate resources to each other.[34] Sometimes the two sides involved in a conflict negotiate directly with each other. Other times, a **third-party negotiator** is relied on. Third-party negotiators are impartial individuals who are not directly involved in the conflict and have special expertise in handling conflicts and negotiations;[35] they are relied on to help the two negotiating parties reach an acceptable resolution of their conflict.[36] When a third-party negotiator acts as a **mediator,** his or her role in the negotiation process is to facilitate an effective negotiation between the two parties; mediators do not force either party to make concessions nor can they force an agreement to resolve a conflict. **Arbitrators,** on the other hand, are third-party negotiators who can impose what they believe is a fair solution to a dispute that both parties are obligated to abide by.[37]

mediator A third-party negotiator who facilitates negotiations but has no authority to impose a solution.

arbitrator A third-party negotiator who can impose what he or she thinks is a fair solution to a conflict that both parties are obligated to abide by.

Distributive Negotiation and Integrative Bargaining

distributive negotiation Adversarial negotiation in which the parties in conflict compete to win the most resources while conceding as little as possible.

integrative bargaining Cooperative negotiation in which the parties in conflict work together to achieve a resolution that is good for them both.

There are two major types of negotiation–distributive negotiation and integrative bargaining.[38] In **distributive negotiation,** the two parties perceive that they have a "fixed pie" of resources that they need to divide.[39] They take a competitive, adversarial stance. Each party realizes that he or she must concede something but is out to get the lion's share of the resources.[40] The parties see no need to interact with each other in the future and do not care if their interpersonal relationship is damaged or destroyed by their competitive negotiation.[41] In distributive negotiations, conflicts are handled by competition.

In **integrative bargaining,** the parties perceive that they might be able to increase the resource pie by trying to come up with a creative solution to the conflict. They do not view the conflict competitively, as a win-or-lose situation; instead, they view it cooperatively, as a win-win situation in which both parties can gain. Trust, information sharing, and the desire of both parties to achieve a good resolution of the conflict characterize integrative bargaining.[42] In integrative bargaining, conflicts are handled through collaboration and/or compromise.

Consider how Adrian Hofbeck and Joseph Steinberg, partners in a successful German restaurant in the Midwest, resolved their recent conflict. Hofbeck and Steinberg founded the restaurant 15 years ago, share management responsibilities, and share equally in the restaurant's profits. Hofbeck recently decided that he wanted to retire and sell the restaurant, but retirement was the last thing Steinberg had in mind; he wanted to continue to own and manage the restaurant. Distributive negotiation was out of the question, for Hofbeck and Steinberg were close friends and valued their friendship; neither wanted to do something that would hurt the other or their continuing relationship. So they opted for integrative bargaining, which they thought would help them resolve their conflict so that both could achieve their goals and maintain their friendship.

Strategies to Encourage Integrative Bargaining

There are five strategies that managers in all kinds of organizations can rely on to facilitate integrative bargaining and avoid distributive negotiation: emphasizing superordinate goals; focusing on the problem, not the people; focusing on interests, not demands; creating new options for joint gain; and focusing on what is fair (see Table 17.1).[43] Hofbeck and Steinberg used each of these strategies to resolve their conflict.

Table 17.1
Negotiation Strategies for Integrative Bargaining

- Emphasize superordinate goals.
- Focus on the problem, not the people.
- Focus on interests, not demands.
- Create new options for joint gain.
- Focus on what is fair.

EMPHASIZING SUPERORDINATE GOALS *Superordinate goals* are goals that both parties agree to regardless of the source of their conflict. Increasing organizational effectiveness, increasing responsiveness to customers, and gaining a competitive advantage are just a few of the many superordinate goals that members of an organization can emphasize during integrative bargaining. Superordinate goals help parties in conflict to keep in mind the big picture and the fact that they are working together for a larger purpose or goal despite their disagreements. Hofbeck and Steinberg emphasized three superordinate goals during their bargaining: ensuring that the restaurant continued to survive and prosper, allowing Hofbeck to retire, and allowing Steinberg to remain an owner and manager as long as he wished.

As indicated in the following "Management Insight," a focus on superordinate goals has helped promote integrative bargaining between The Chrysler Group and the United Autoworkers Union (UAW).

Management Insight

Superordinate Goals at Chrysler

Tom LaSorda, chief operating officer of The Chrysler Group (the American division of the German DaimlerChrysler AG), is the first child of union leaders to rise to a top-management position in any of the three largest U.S. auto companies.[44] LaSorda's parents were both active in labor unions, and his father, Frank LaSorda, was president of the Windsor, Ontario, local unit of the UAW from 1977 to 1982. Frank LaSorda was on a 12-member committee that negotiated with the loan guarantee board during Chrysler's bankruptcy bailout in the 1980s and made many concessions on the part of the union to keep Chrysler going. As Frank puts it, "Tom wouldn't have that job, he wouldn't have any corporation to lead, if it weren't for the hard decisions. . . . We made three concessions in 13 months, and each was worse than the last."[45]

The loan guarantee board, Chrysler management, and the UAW were able to reach those historic agreements due to their superordinate goal of rescuing Chrsyler. Today, relations between the UAW and U.S. automakers, including Chrysler, are considered better than they have ever been, as both sides have the superordinate goal of surviving and thriving in the face of intense global competition from powerhouses such as Toyota (see "A Manager's Challenge").[46]

UAW President Ron Gettelfinger, second from left, shakes hands with Dieter Zetsche, president of DaimlerChrysler AG's Chrysler Group, as UAW vice president Nate Gooden, left, shakes hands with Wolfgang Bernhard, Chrysler Group COO, during contract negotiations in Auburn Hills, Michigan, in July 2003.

Take the case of a recent and historic agreement made between The Chrysler Group, the UAW, and three auto suppliers.[47] The agreement involves a major investment in Chrysler's Toledo, Ohio, production facility that currently makes the Jeep Liberty and Wrangler SUVs.[48] Three suppliers, Durr Industries, Kuka Group, and Hyundai Mobis, will build part of the Jeep Wrangler with their own employees in their own plants on the site, allowing Chrysler to spend less money on investing in plants and more on product development.[49] Suppliers, Tom LaSorda and other top managers at Chrysler, and the UAW see the agreement and overall $2.1 billion investment in the Toledo site as a way to help Chrysler remain competitive. This superordinate goal has allowed all parties to put aside their differences and work together.[50] As Lloyd Mahaffey, the regional director of the UAW for Toledo, puts it, "This project keeps approximately 3,800 jobs right here in Toledo, it enables us to implement new ways to become competitive in a rapidly changing time for our industry."[51]

FOCUSING ON THE PROBLEM, NOT THE PEOPLE People who are in conflict may not be able to resist the temptation to focus on the other party's shortcomings and weaknesses, thereby personalizing the conflict. Instead of attacking the problem, the parties to the conflict attack each other. This approach is inconsistent with integrative bargaining and can easily lead both parties into a distributive negotiation mode. All parties to a conflict need to keep focused on the problem or on the source of the conflict and avoid the temptation to discredit one another.

Given their strong friendship, this was not much of an issue for Hofbeck and Steinberg, but they still had to be on their guard to avoid personalizing the conflict. Steinberg recalls that when they were having a hard time coming up with a solution, he started thinking that Hofbeck, a healthy 57-year-old, was lazy to want to retire so young: "If only he wasn't so lazy, we would never be in the mess we're in right now." Steinberg never mentioned these thoughts to Hofbeck (who later admitted that sometimes he was annoyed with Steinberg for being such a workaholic), because he realized that doing so would hurt their chances for reaching an integrative solution.

FOCUSING ON INTERESTS, NOT DEMANDS Demands are *what* a person wants; interests are *why* the person wants them. When two people are in conflict, it is unlikely that the demands of both can be met. Their underlying interests, however, can be met, and meeting them is what integrative bargaining is all about.

Hofbeck's demand was that they sell the restaurant and split the proceeds. Steinberg's demand was that they keep the restaurant and maintain the status quo. Obviously, both demands could not be met, but perhaps their interests could be. Hofbeck wanted to be able to retire, invest his share of the money from the restaurant, and live off the returns on the investment. Steinberg wanted to continue managing, owning, and deriving income from the restaurant.

CREATING NEW OPTIONS FOR JOINT GAIN Once two parties to a conflict focus on their interests, they are on the road to achieving creative solutions to the conflict that will benefit them both. This win-win scenario means that rather than having a fixed set of alternatives from which to choose, the two parties can come up with new alternatives that might even expand the resource pie.

Hofbeck and Steinberg came up with three such alternatives. First, even though Steinberg did not have the capital, he could buy out Hofbeck's share of the restaurant. Hofbeck would provide the financing for the purchase, and in return Steinberg would pay him a reasonable return on his investment (the same kind of return he could have obtained had he taken his money out of the restaurant and invested it). Second, the partners could seek to sell Hofbeck's share in the restaurant to a third party under the stipulation that Steinberg would continue to manage the restaurant and receive income for his services. Third, the partners could continue to jointly own the restaurant. Steinberg would manage it and receive a proportionally greater share of its profits than Hofbeck, who would be an absentee owner not involved in day-to-day operations but would still receive a return on his investment in the restaurant.

FOCUSING ON WHAT IS FAIR Focusing on what is fair is consistent with the principle of distributive justice, which emphasizes the fair distribution of outcomes based on the meaningful contributions that people make to organizations (see Chapter 5). It is likely that two parties in conflict will disagree on certain points and prefer different alternatives that each party believes may better serve his or her own interests or maximize his or her own outcomes. Emphasizing fairness and distributive justice will help the two parties come to a mutual agreement about what the best solution is to the problem.

Steinberg and Hofbeck agreed that Hofbeck should be able to cut his ties with the restaurant if he chose to do so. They thus decided to pursue the second alternative described above and seek a suitable buyer for Hofbeck's share. They were successful in finding an investor who was willing to buy out Hofbeck's share and let Steinberg continue managing the restaurant. And they remained good friends.

When managers pursue these five strategies and encourage other organizational members to do so, they are more likely to be able to effectively resolve their conflicts through integrative bargaining. In addition, throughout the negotiation process, managers and other organizational members need to be aware of, and on their guard against, the biases that can lead to faulty decision making (see Chapter 7).[52]

As indicated in the following "Information Technology Byte," when negotiations involve complex and multiple parameters, or negotiators lack the time to engage in the negotiation process themselves, negotiation software can sometimes be beneficial.

Information Technology Byte

Computerized Negotiations

Some negotiations, especially those taking place between members of different organizations and involving multiple parameters, can be very time-consuming. For negotiations that overstretched employees simply do not have the time to deal with, negotiation software can be a blessing.[53]

For example, physicians and insurance companies are often in the position of negotiating payment schedules; physicians want prompter payments for their services, while insurance companies prefer lengthier payment schedules. Using software provided by SplitTheDifference, the physicians and insurance companies can come to a mutually acceptable agreement.[54] Based on information from both parties, the software presents proposals to physicians (e.g., prompter payments for a discount on fees paid), who can accept the proposal or reject it and come back with a counteroffer. The negotiation proceeds until a deal has been struck; if after three rounds, no deal has been struck, both parties revert to the terms of the initial contract/claim between the physician and the insurance company.[55]

Other companies are developing software to deal with more complex kinds of negotiations. For example, the Project A team at Fujitsu Laboratories of America is developing software that can tabulate millions of different scenarios involving negotiations where the two parties might initially have far more points of divergence than of agreement.[56] Computers can process information and find solutions more quickly than humans, so by using information on people's preferences, computers can come up with a vast array of potential solutions that can be cycled through. For example, the Project A team is working on software that can facilitate negotiations between a purchasing agent and a supplier by taking into account both parties' preferences and relative priorities for factors such as delivery times, quantities, reliability, quality, shipping costs and methods, size, color, and whatever else might be relevant for the negotiation at hand to come up with a solution that both parties find acceptable. Dave Marvit, who heads the Project A Team, puts it this way, "Good negotiators know you can do better if you add more business terms to the discussions. . . . Not just price, but time and others. The computers can handle more parameters so more value can be squeezed out of the transaction. It's the opposite of a zero-sum game."[57]

Organizational Politics

organizational politics Activities that managers engage in to increase their power and to use power effectively to achieve their goals and overcome resistance or opposition.

political strategies Tactics that managers use to increase their power and to use power effectively to influence and gain the support of other people while overcoming resistance or opposition.

Managers must develop the skills necessary to manage organizational conflict in order for an organization to be effective. Suppose, however, that top managers are in conflict over the best strategy for an organization to pursue or the best structure to adopt to utilize organizational resources efficiently. In such situations, resolving conflict is often difficult, and the parties to the conflict resort to organizational politics and political strategies to try to resolve the conflict in their favor.

Organizational politics are the activities that managers (and other members of an organization) engage in to increase their power and to use power effectively to achieve their goals and overcome resistance or opposition.[58] Managers often engage in organizational politics to resolve conflicts in their favor.

Political strategies are the specific tactics that managers (and other members of an organization) use to increase their power and to use power effectively to influence and gain the support of other people while overcoming resistance or opposition. Political strategies are especially important when managers are planning and implementing major changes in an organization: Managers need not only to gain support for their change initiatives and influence organizational members to behave in new ways but also to overcome often strong opposition from people who feel threatened by the change and prefer the status quo. By increasing their power, managers are better able to make needed changes. In addition to increasing their power, managers also must make sure that they use their power in a way that actually enables them to influence others.

"I don't mean to keep popping in on you, sir, but I just naturally gravitate toward power."

The Importance of Organizational Politics

The term *politics* has a negative connotation for many people. Some may think that managers who are political have risen to the top not because of their own merit and capabilities but because of whom they know. Or people may think that political managers are self-interested and wield power to benefit themselves, not their organization. There is a grain of truth to this negative connotation. Some managers do appear to misuse their power for personal benefit at the expense of their organization's effectiveness.

Nevertheless, organizational politics are often a positive force. Managers striving to make needed changes often encounter resistance from individuals and groups who feel threatened and wish to preserve the status quo. Effective managers engage in politics to gain support for and implement needed changes. Similarly, managers often face resistance from other managers who disagree with their goals for a group or for the organization and with what they are trying to accomplish. Engaging in organizational politics can help managers overcome this resistance and achieve their goals.

Indeed, managers cannot afford to ignore organizational politics. Everyone engages in politics to a degree–other managers, co-workers, and subordinates, as well as people outside an organization, such as suppliers. Those who try to ignore politics might as well bury their heads in the sand because in all likelihood they will be unable to gain support for their initiatives and goals.

Political Strategies for Gaining and Maintaining Power

Managers who use political strategies to increase and maintain their power are better able to influence others to work toward the achievement of group and organizational goals. (Recall from Chapter 14 that legitimate, reward, coercive, expert, and referent powers help managers influence others as leaders.) By controlling uncertainty, making themselves irreplaceable, being in a central position, generating resources, and building alliances, managers can increase their power (see Figure 17.4).[59] We next look at each of these strategies.

CONTROLLING UNCERTAINTY Uncertainty is a threat for individuals, groups, and whole organizations and can interfere with effective performance and goal attainment. For example, uncertainty about job security is threatening for many workers and may cause top performers (who have the best chance of finding another job) to quit and take a more secure position with another organization. When an R&D department faces uncertainty about customer preferences, its members may waste valuable resources on developing a product, such as smokeless cigarettes, that customers do not want. When top managers face uncertainty about global demand, they may fail to export products to countries that want them and thus may lose a source of competitive advantage.

Managers who are able to control and reduce uncertainty for other managers, teams, departments, and the organization as a whole are likely to see their power increase.[60] Managers of labor unions gain power when they can eliminate uncertainty over job security for workers. Marketing and sales managers gain power when they can eliminate uncertainty for other departments such as R&D by accurately forecasting customers' changing preferences. Top managers gain power when they are knowledgeable about global demand for an organization's products. Managers who are able to control uncertainty are likely to be in demand and be sought after by other organizations.

MAKING ONESELF IRREPLACEABLE Managers gain power when they have valuable knowledge and expertise that allow them to perform activities that no one else can handle. This is the essence of being irreplaceable.[61] The

Figure 17.4
Political Strategies for Increasing Power

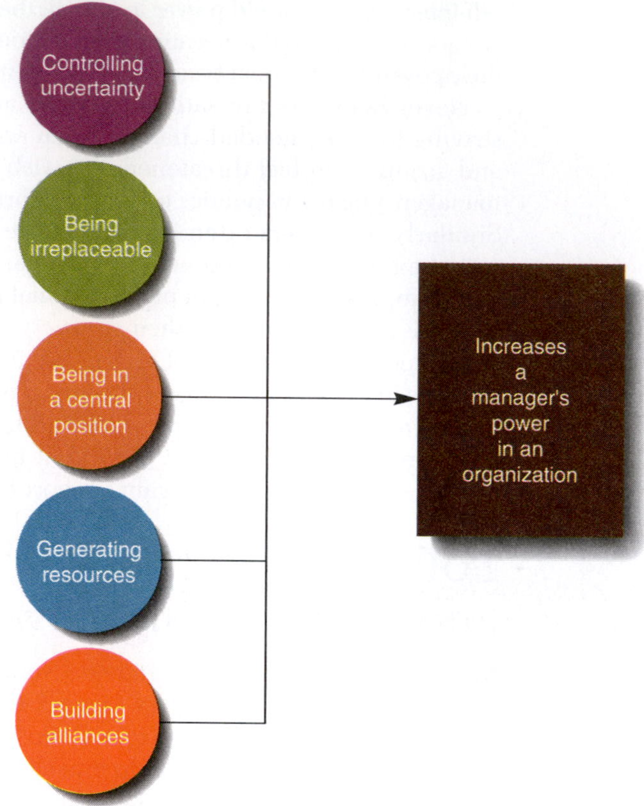

more central these activities are to organizational effectiveness, the more power managers gain from being irreplaceable. In "A Manager's Challenge," Jim Press gains power from being irreplaceable. The combination of in-depth knowledge of Toyota and its culture; an understanding of the pulse of the U.S. auto market; and his soft-spoken, patient, and determined manner of collaboratively working through conflicts for win-win solutions is hard to find in other top managers.[62]

BEING IN A CENTRAL POSITION Managers in central positions are responsible for activities that are directly connected to an organization's goals and sources of competitive advantage and often are located in key positions in important communication networks in an organization.[63] Managers in central positions have control over crucial organizational activities and initiatives and have access to important information. Other organizational members are dependent on them for their knowledge, expertise, advice, and support, and the success of the organization as a whole is seen as riding on these managers. These consequences of being in a central position are likely to increase managers' power.

Managers who are outstanding performers, have a wide knowledge base, and have made important and visible contributions to their organizations are likely to be offered central positions that will increase their power, as is true of Jim Press in "A Manager's Challenge."

GENERATING RESOURCES Organizations need three kinds of resources to be effective: (1) input resources such as raw materials, skilled workers, and financial capital; (2) technical resources such as machinery and computers; and (3) knowledge resources such as marketing or engineering expertise. To the extent that a manager is able to generate one or more of these kinds of resources for an organization, that manager's power is likely to increase.[64] In universities, for example, professors who win large grants to fund their research, from associations such as the National Science Foundation and the Army Research Institute, gain power because of the financial resources they are generating for their departments and the university as a whole.

Andrew C. Sigler, chairman of the board of the paper producer Champion International Corporation, gained so much power from generating resources that he remained at the top of a Fortune 500 company for 20 years despite Champion's poor returns to shareholders. A sudden rise in paper prices turned Champion's fortunes around, but insiders attribute at least part of Sigler's staying power at the top to his close relationships with major investors such as billionaires Warren Buffett and Laurence Tisch; these ties enabled him to generate capital for Champion.[65]

BUILDING ALLIANCES When managers build alliances, they develop mutually beneficial relationships with people both inside and outside the organization. The two parties to an alliance support one another because doing so is in their best interests, and both parties benefit from the alliance. Alliances provide managers with power because they provide the managers with support for their initiatives. Partners to alliances provide support because they know that the managers will reciprocate when their partners need support. Alliances can help managers achieve their goals and implement needed changes in organizations because they increase managers' levels of power.

Many powerful top managers focus on building alliances not only inside their organizations but also with individuals, groups, and organizations in the task and general environments on which their organizations are dependent for resources. These individuals, groups, and organizations enter into alliances with managers because doing so is in their best interests and they know that they can count on the managers' support when they need it. When managers build alliances, they need to be on their guard to ensure that everything is aboveboard, ethical, and legal.

Political Strategies for Exercising Power

Politically skilled managers not only have a good understanding of, and ability to use, the five strategies to increase their power; they also have a good appreciation of strategies for exercising their power. These strategies generally focus on how managers can use their power *unobtrusively*."[66] When managers exercise power unobtrusively, other members of an organization may not be aware that the managers are using their power to influence them. They may think that they support these managers for a variety of reasons: because they believe it is the rational or logical thing to do, because they believe that doing so is in their own best interests, or because they believe that the position or decision that the managers are advocating is legitimate or appropriate.

The unobtrusive use of power may sound devious, but managers typically use this strategy to bring about change and achieve organizational goals. Political strategies for exercising power to gain the support and concurrence of others include relying on objective information, bringing in an outside expert, controlling the agenda, and making everyone a winner (see Figure 17.5).[67]

Figure 17.5
Political Strategies for Exercising Power

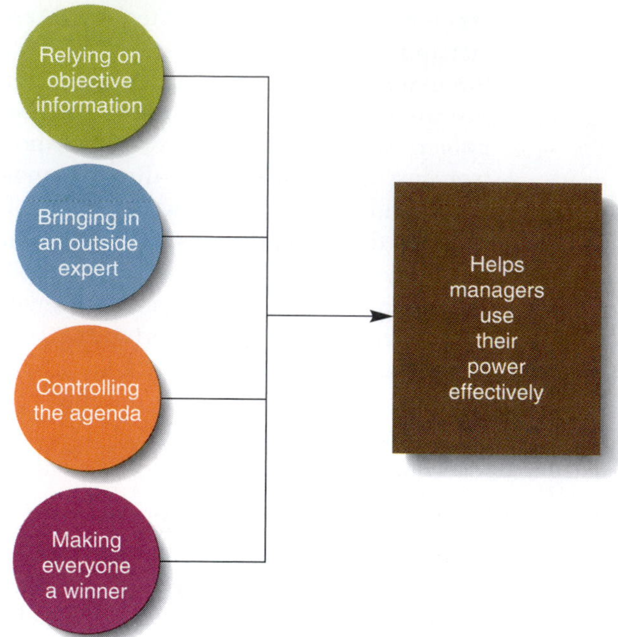

RELYING ON OBJECTIVE INFORMATION Managers require the support of others to achieve their goals, implement changes, and overcome opposition. One way for a manager to gain this support and overcome opposition is to rely on objective information that supports the manager's initiatives. Reliance on objective information leads others to support the manager because of the facts; objective information causes others to believe that what the manager is proposing is the proper course of action. By relying on objective information, politically skilled managers unobtrusively exercise their power to influence others.

Take the case of Mary Callahan, vice president of Better Built Cabinets, a small cabinet company in the Southeast. Callahan is extremely influential in the company; practically every new initiative that she proposes to the president and owner of the company is implemented. Why is Callahan able to use her power in the company so effectively? Whenever she has an idea for a new initiative that she thinks the company might pursue, she and her subordinates begin by collecting objective information supporting the initiative. Recently, Callahan decided that Better Built should develop a line of high-priced European-style kitchen cabinets. Before presenting her proposal to Better Built's president, she compiled objective information showing that (1) there was strong unmet demand for these kinds of cabinets, (2) Better Built could manufacture them in its existing production facilities, and (3) the new line had the potential to increase Better Built's sales by 20 percent while not detracting from sales of the company's other cabinets. Presented with this information, the president agreed to Callahan's proposal. Moreover, the president and other members of Better Built whose cooperation was needed to implement the proposal supported it because they thought it would help Better Built gain a competitive advantage. Using objective information to support her position enabled Callahan to unobtrusively exercise her power and influence others to support her proposal.

BRINGING IN AN OUTSIDE EXPERT Bringing in an outside expert to support a proposal or decision can, at times, provide managers with some of the same benefits that the use of objective information does. It lends credibility to a manager's initiatives and causes others to believe that what the manager is proposing is the appropriate or rational thing to do. Suppose Callahan had hired a consultant to evaluate whether her idea was a good one. The consultant reports back to the president that the new European-style cabinets are likely to fulfill Callahan's promises and increase Better Built's sales and profits. As with objective information, this information provided by an objective expert can lend a sense of legitimacy to Callahan's proposal and allow her to unobtrusively exercise power to influence others.

Although you might think that consultants and other outside experts are neutral or objective, they sometimes are hired by managers who want them to support a certain position or decision in an organization. For instance, when managers are facing strong opposition from others who fear that a decision will harm their or their departments' interests, the managers may bring in an outside expert. They hope this expert will be perceived as a neutral observer to lend credibility and "objectivity" to their point of view. The support of an outside expert may cause others to believe that a decision is indeed the right one. Of course, sometimes consultants and other outside experts actually are brought into organizations to be objective and provide managers with guidance on the appropriate course of action to take.

CONTROLLING THE AGENDA Managers also can exercise power unobtrusively by controlling the agenda–influencing which alternatives are considered or even whether a decision is made.[68] When managers influence the alternatives that are considered, they can make sure that each considered alternative is acceptable to them and that undesirable alternatives are not in the feasible set. In a hiring context, for example, managers can exert their power unobtrusively by ensuring that job candidates whom they do not find acceptable do not make their way onto the list of finalists for an open position. They do this by making sure that these candidates' drawbacks or deficiencies are communicated to everyone involved in making the hiring decision. When three finalists for an open position are discussed and evaluated in a hiring meeting, a manager may seem to exert little power or influence and just go along with what the rest of the group wants. However, the manager may have exerted power in the hiring process unobtrusively, by controlling which candidates made it to the final stage.

Sometimes managers can prevent a decision from being made. A manager in charge of a community relations committee, for example, may not favor a proposal for the organization to become more involved in local youth groups such as the Boy Scouts and the Girl Scouts. The manager can exert influence in this situation by not including the proposal on the agenda for the committee's next meeting. Alternatively, the manager could place the proposal at the end of the agenda for the meeting and feel confident that the committee will run out of time and not get to the last items on the agenda because that is what always happens. Either not including the proposal or putting it at the end of the agenda enables the manager to unobtrusively exercise power. Committee members do not perceive this manager as trying to influence them to turn down the proposal. Rather, the manager has made the proposal into a nonissue that is not even considered.

MAKING EVERYONE A WINNER Often, politically skilled managers are able to exercise their power unobtrusively because they make sure that everyone whose support they need benefits personally from providing that support. By making everyone a winner, a manager is able to influence other organizational members because these members see supporting the manager as being in their best interest.

When top managers turn around troubled companies, while some organizational members and parts of the organization are bound to suffer due to restructurings that often entail painful layoffs, the power of the turnaround CEO often accelerates as it becomes clear that the future of the company is on surer footing and the organization and its stakeholders are winners as a result of the change effort, as indicated in the following "Manager as a Person."

Manager as a Person

Ghosn Remakes Nissan

As CEO, Carlos Ghosn has made sweeping changes at Nissan Motor Corp., changes that transformed the company and dramatically improved its fortunes. When Ghosn became CEO of Nissan in 1999, things couldn't have been worse. Nissan was hemorrhaging money, and its plants were operating at only 51 percent of their total capacity.[69] Ghosn acted boldly and decisively to turn the tides at Nissan, closing five manufacturing facilities, cutting the size of Nissan's labor force by 23,000, and moving more of Nissan's manufacturing from Japan to the United States.[70]

Why the shift in production from Japan to the United States? Essentially, the Japanese market for cars is weak, the U.S. market is relatively stronger, currency problems are avoided, and it simply makes more sense to make cars in the markets in which they are sold.[71] Hence, this shift is not surprising from an economic perspective, but it is surprising from a cultural perspective, given Japan's emphasis on job security for employees.

Nissan Motor Co. President Carlos Ghosn, left, is applauded by employees as he arrives at a dealer in Fukuoka, southwestern Japan. Ghosn, who was sent in by French automaker Renault SA to fix the struggling Nissan, is now more than just an executive—he's a star.

In 2000, Nissan lost $6.2 billion; as Ghosn puts it, "We were a collapsing company."[72] In the fiscal year that ended in March 2004, Nissan earned a record $7.29 billion in operating profits.[73] When Ghosn first took over, prospects for Nissan were so dismal that his decisive steps were supported not only because of his legitimate power as CEO but also because Nissan's stakeholders realized that change was needed for anyone to remain a winner. In addition to returning Nissan to profitability, Ghosn accelerated its growth trajectory,[74] introducing 13 new models in the U.S. market.[75] While Nissan, like all major corporations, faces challenges–such as quality concerns regarding cars produced at one of its newer plants in Canton, Mississippi[76]–Ghosn, since becoming CEO, has clearly strived and succeeded at making multiple Nissan stakeholders winners, thereby enhancing his own power and influence within the company.[77]

Summary and Review

ORGANIZATIONAL CONFLICT Organizational conflict is the discord that arises when the goals, interests, or values of different individuals or groups are incompatible and those individuals or groups block or thwart each other's attempts to achieve their objectives. Four types of conflict arising in organizations are interpersonal conflict, intragroup conflict, intergroup conflict, and interorganizational conflict. Sources of conflict in organizations include different goals and time horizons, overlapping authority, task interdependencies, different evaluation or reward systems, scarce resources, and status inconsistencies. Conflict management strategies focused on individuals include increasing awareness of the sources of conflict, increasing diversity awareness and skills, practicing job rotation or temporary assignments, and using permanent transfers or dismissals when necessary. Strategies focused on the whole organization include changing an organization's structure or culture and altering the source of conflict.

NEGOTIATION Negotiation is a conflict resolution technique used when parties to a conflict have approximately equal levels of power and try to come up with an acceptable way to allocate resources to each other. In distributive negotiation, the parties perceive that there is a fixed level of resources for them to allocate, and they compete to receive as much as possible at the expense of the other party, not caring about their relationship in the future. In integrative bargaining, both parties perceive that they may be able to increase the resource pie by coming up with a creative solution to the conflict, trusting each other, and cooperating with each other to achieve a win-win resolution. Five strategies that managers can use to facilitate integrative bargaining are to emphasize superordinate goals; focus on the problem, not the people; focus on interests, not demands; create new options for joint gain; and focus on what is fair.

ORGANIZATIONAL POLITICS Organizational politics are the activities that managers (and other members of an organization) engage in to increase their power and to use power effectively to achieve their goals and overcome resistance or opposition. Effective managers realize that politics can be a positive force that enables them to make needed changes in an organization. Five important political strategies for gaining and maintaining power are controlling uncertainty, making oneself irreplaceable, being in a central position, generating resources, and building alliances. Political strategies for effectively exercising power focus on how to use power unobtrusively and include relying on objective information, bringing in an outside expert, controlling the agenda, and making everyone a winner.

Management in Action

Topics for Discussion and Action

Discussion

1. Discuss why too little conflict in an organization can be just as detrimental as too much conflict.
2. Why are compromise and collaboration more effective ways of handling conflict than accommodation, avoidance, and competition?
3. Why should managers promote integrative bargaining rather than distributive negotiation?
4. How can managers promote integrative bargaining?
5. Why do organizational politics affect practically every organization?
6. Why do effective managers need good political skills?
7. What steps can managers take to ensure that organizational politics are a positive force leading to a competitive advantage, not a negative force leading to personal advantage at the expense of organizational goal attainment?
8. Think of a member of an organization whom you know and who is particularly powerful. What political strategies does this person use to increase his or her power?
9. Why is it best to use power unobtrusively? How are people likely to react to power that is exercised obtrusively?

Action

10. Interview a manager in a local organization to determine the kinds of conflicts that occur in his or her organization and the strategies that are used to manage them.

Building Management Skills

Effective and Ineffective Conflict Resolution

Think about two recent conflicts that you had with other people, one conflict that you felt was effectively resolved (C1) and one that you felt was ineffectively resolved (C2). The other people involved could be co-workers, students, family members, friends, or members of an organization that you are a member of. Answer the following questions:

1. Briefly describe C1 and C2. What type of conflict was involved in each of these incidents?
2. What was the source of the conflict in C1 and in C2?
3. What conflict management strategies were used in C1 and in C2?
4. What could you have done differently to more effectively manage conflict in C2?
5. How was conflict resolved in C1 and in C2?

Managing Ethically

One political strategy managers can engage in is controlling the agenda by subtly influencing which alternatives are considered or even whether a decision is up for discussion. Some employees believe that this can be unethical and prevent important issues from being raised and points of view from being expressed.

Questions

1. Either individually or in a group, think about the ethical implications of controlling the agenda as a political strategy.
2. What steps can managers and organizations take to ensure that this strategy does not result in important issues and differing points of view being suppressed in an organization?

Small Group Breakout Exercise

Negotiating a Solution

Form groups of three or four people. One member of your group will play the role of Jane Rister, one member will play the role of Michael Schwartz, and one or two members will be observer(s) and spokesperson(s) for your group.

Jane Rister and Michael Schwartz are assistant managers in a large department store. They report directly to the store manager. Today they are meeting to discuss some important problems they need to solve but about which they disagree.

The first problem hinges on the fact that either Rister or Schwartz needs to be on duty whenever the store is open. For the last six months, Rister has taken most of the least desirable hours (nights and weekends). They are planning their schedules for the next six months. Rister thought Schwartz would take more of the undesirable times, but Schwartz has informed Rister that his wife has just gotten a nursing job which requires that she work weekends, so he needs to stay home weekends to take care of their infant daughter.

The second problem concerns a department manager who has had a hard time retaining salespeople in his department. The turnover rate in his department is twice that in the other store departments. Rister thinks the manager is ineffective and wants to fire him. Schwartz thinks the high turnover is just a fluke and the manager is effective.

The last problem concerns Rister's and Schwartz's vacation schedules. Both managers want to take off the week of July 4, but one of them needs to be in the store whenever it is open.

1. The group members playing Rister and Schwartz assume their roles and negotiate a solution to these three problems.
2. Observers take notes on how Rister and Schwartz negotiate solutions to their problems.
3. Observers determine the extent to which Rister and Schwartz use distributive negotiation or integrative bargaining to resolve their conflicts.
4. When called on by the instructor, observers communicate to the rest of the class how Rister and Schwartz resolved their conflicts, whether they used distributive negotiation or integrative bargaining, and their actual solutions.

Exploring the World Wide Web

Think of a major conflict in the business world that you have read about in the newspaper in the past few weeks. Then search on the Web for magazine and newspaper articles presenting differing viewpoints and perspectives on the conflict. Based on what you have read, how are the parties to this conflict handling it? Is their approach functional or dysfunctional and why?

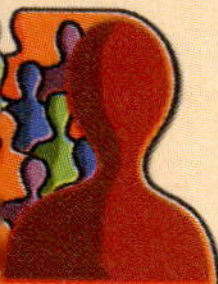

Be the Manager

You are a middle manager in a large corporation and lately feel that you are being caught between a rock and a hard place. Times are tough; your unit has experienced layoffs; your surviving subordinates are overworked and demoralized; and you feel that you have no meaningful rewards, such as the chance for a pay raise, bonus, or promotion, to motivate them with. Your boss keeps increasing the demands on your unit as well as the unit's responsibilities. Moreover, you believe that you and your subordinates are being unfairly blamed for certain problems beyond your control. You believe that you have the expertise and skills to perform your job effectively and also that your subordinates are capable and effective in their jobs. Yet you feel that you are on shaky ground and powerless given the current state of affairs. What are you going to do?

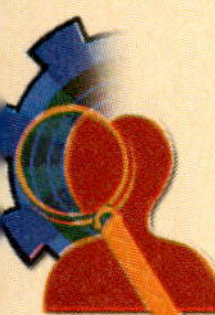

Additional Activities on the Build Your Management Skills DVD

- **Test Your Knowledge:** Styles of Handling Conflict
- **Self-Assessment:** (1) Assessing Your Perspective Taking and (2) What Is Your Primary Conflict-Handling Style?
- **Manager's Hot Seat:** Negotiation: Thawing the Salary Freeze

BusinessWeek Case in the News

Things Aren't Going Better at Coke

When it comes to turning around a troubled company, timing is often everything. And hopes were running high when E. Neville Isdell took the helm of beleaguered Coca-Cola Co. in early June. After six years of mostly disappointing profits, Coke had just recorded a surprising surge in first-quarter earnings. With a new guy in the driver's seat and some promising new products on the way, Coke's dark days looked like they might be winding down.

No such luck. Just two months into his new job, Isdell's honeymoon is over. He's facing a host of problems, from sluggish growth in once-lucrative international markets such as Germany and Mexico to tepid consumer reception of new products like the much-ballyhooed C2 cola. But what seems also to have spooked investors are reports of simmering tensions between Coke and its increasingly powerful independent bottlers. What it all comes down to is syrup—how much of the stuff the bottlers will buy, and what price they're willing to pay. For years, the bottlers were at the mercy of Coke headquarters, as the cola giant pushed through huge increases on the price it charged for the prized concentrate. Now, the bottlers, newly empowered through a string of acquisitions, are fighting back.

Nothing would be more unsettling than a showdown between Coke and its largest bottler, Coca-Cola Enterprises Inc. (CCE)—a mega-bottler that now controls about 80 percent of the U.S. market as well as parts of Europe. CCE's strategy has been to raise sharply the price it charges grocers and other retailers. That's boosting its profit margins—but at the expense of Coke. Higher retail prices mean consumers buy less of its soda, so bottlers don't need to buy as much syrup from headquarters. For the second quarter, Coke's volume sales rose a mere 1 percent, well below its 5 percent target. That's Coke's lowest quarterly increase in volume sales since the 1970s, says Emanuel Goldman, an independent beverage analyst in Hillsborough, Calif. And it helps explain why Coke's operating income, after subtracting currency gains, rose just 7 percent in the second quarter, about half what some analysts expected.

Investors are fretting. Coke's shares have fallen more than 10 percent in the two weeks since the earnings news, leaving them near their low for the year. Says Nancy Crouse, a senior vice-president at Delaware Investments, a Philadelphia money manager that holds 3 million Coke shares: "I don't have as much confidence as I did three or four months ago of their ability to drive the profitability of the business."

More price hikes from CCE and other bottlers are expected, which could cut even further into concentrate sales. One reason for the continued hikes: the prospect of sharp increases in the cost of key commodities like resin and aluminum. The likelihood of a further bump up in price "will put CCE and Coke in direct conflict . . . at a time when tension is already running high between the two," notes Morgan Stanley analyst William Pecoriello.

Officials from Coke have long maintained that relations with CCE are fine, though they declined to comment for this story. CCE, in a conference call with analysts, assured investors that they have no issues with Coke. Still, the problems between Coke and some of its bottlers could force Isdell to make some radical moves—including buying back some of its bottlers. That, of course, would be the ultimate irony. It was way back in 1986 that Coke spun off its domestic bottling operations into the entity now known as CCE.

That move was a cornerstone of then-Chairman Roberto C. Goizueta's efforts to turbocharge Coke's returns by removing billions in bottling debt from its balance sheet. Selling syrup is also a much more lucrative business than bottling. The move worked brilliantly for years, and Goizueta was hailed as a genius. But, as they say, what goes around comes around. Now, the bottlers are all too willing to flex their muscle. Although Coke still owns 39 percent of CCE shares, that has fallen steadily over the years. With Coke no longer calling the shots, Isdell is finding that there's no quick or easy way to get the fizz back into Coke.

Questions

1. What are the sources of conflict between Coca-Cola and its bottlers?
2. How did these conflicts arise?
3. How are the conflicts currently being handled?
4. What should CEO Isdell do now to effectively manage this conflict?

Source: D. Foust, "Things Aren't Going Better at Coke." Reprinted from the August 16, 2004, issue of *BusinessWeek* by special permission.

BusinessWeek Case in the News

Fiat's Last Chance

Ferrari Chief Executive Luca Cordero di Montezemolo has earned a hero's status in Italy for reviving the once-ailing auto icon and acing four Formula One championships in a row. He proved that Italy can rebuild a high-tech contender and come from behind just when all seems lost. Now the 56-year-old manager has to do a command performance for Ferrari's $58 billion parent. On May 30, three days after the death of former Chairman Umberto Agnelli, Montezemolo was named chairman of troubled Fiat, Italy's largest industrial group.

Montezemolo's top priority is clinching a turnaround at the ailing, $24 billion Fiat Auto, which nearly pushed the group into bankruptcy in 2002. Over the past five years, Fiat Auto racked up $9.3 billion in net losses—and the bleeding hasn't stopped. Several new models finally seem to be reversing a dire decline in sales. But to secure a solid recovery, the Turin-based auto maker needs to keep hot models coming, boost factory flexibility, and overhaul sales and marketing debilitated by years of underinvestment and mismanagement.

Montezemolo, a skilled marketer with a deep appreciation for cutting-edge technology and production, might well be the steady hand that could help steer Fiat back to health. At Ferrari, Montezemolo restored lost brand luster in part through ingenious marketing, including persuading the Museum of Modern Art in New York to do a splashy retrospective on Ferrari's design over the decades—a high-gloss exhibition that other major museums in Berlin and Tokyo have since restaged. Fiat, too, has a tarnished brand that needs refurbishing.

But fixing Fiat is not all Montezemolo has on his agenda. On May 27 he became president of the Italian employers' association, Confindustria—where Job One is reversing Italy's alarming industrial decline. The country's exports are eroding, investment is stymied, and promised economic reforms are stalled—Fiat's woes writ large. The double role thrusts Montezemolo squarely into the void left by the March 2002 death of late Fiat Chairman Giovanni Agnelli, who once ran Confindustria and who for a generation personified Italy Inc.

For Montezemolo, who is known for his ability to coax opposing parties toward a common goal, the rescue of Fiat would be an object lesson in how Italy can reinvent itself. A turnaround plan launched at Fiat 12 months ago has helped trim losses, while the sale of some $8.5 billion in group assets, including insurer Toro Assicurazioni, injected urgently needed capital for a new generation of cars. Vehicle sales at Fiat Auto are up 13 percent in the last six months—and demand for Fiat's newly launched Panda supermini and Idea subcompact minivan is outstripping supply. "The new products are wonderful. Fiat can finally join the race," says Christoph Stürmer, senior market researcher Global Insight in Frankfurt.

Problem-Plagued

But the 105-year-old auto maker remains plagued by inflexible production lines that can only produce one model. To boot, intransigent labor unions have blocked plant closures, making it harder for Fiat to return to profitability. Its five factories in Italy plus those in Brazil and Poland can produce some 2.5 million cars a year, but last year the company made only 1.8 million. Unable to trim its production overhead sharply, Fiat will need a strong rebound in sales to survive. "Fiat's on its last chance," says Jochen Gehrke, auto analyst at Kepler Equities in Frankfurt. "If they produce flops, the game is over." In the first quarter, Fiat Group halved its losses to $192 million. But analysts note a worrying rise in net debt to $5.4 billion and forecast that the group will run a negative free cash flow of $1 billion to $1.5 billion in 2004.

While Fiat last year raised $2.2 billion in a rights issue, its financial credibility will be on the line as early as June 2005, when a $3.6 billion convertible bond comes due. That's when a group of eight Italian banks has the option of turning the bonds into a controlling 24 percent equity stake. Bankers and analysts say it is unlikely Fiat will be able to repay the bond.

Even sooner, in January 2005, Fiat's put option with General Motors Corp. could trigger a crisis of confidence. The two are negotiating to eliminate the option, which allows Fiat Group to sell its share in its auto maker to GM. The Detroit company insists the put is no longer valid, but Fiat wants to be paid for the value it represents. Yet if Fiat fails to reach an agreement with GM by yearend and continues to post heavy losses, the put will be worthless, analysts say. "That's the moment of truth," says Albrecht Denninghoff, auto analyst at Hypo-und Vereinsbank in Munich, noting that such an assessment would kill investors' appetites for another capital increase.

Adding to Fiat's woes, CEO Giuseppe Morchio resigned on May 30 following the appointment of Montezemolo. Morchio wanted the combined position of chairman and CEO. Fiat's board named board member Sergio Marchionne, 52, the CEO of Swiss testing and inspection company SGS, as successor on June 2. Despite Marchionne's strong turnaround credentials, many worry about the discontinuity plaguing Fiat's top management, which has seen five CEOs in three years.

Industry Boss

Those close to the company say Montezemolo will work closely with his team. The problem is, Montezemolo may have taken on more than any manager could handle by agreeing to help oversee Fiat's recovery and turn around Italian industry at the same time. To be sure, the long-time friend of the Agnellis—he grew up playing with the Turin dynasty's children—has the complete trust of the family, including John P. Elkann, 28, the grandson of Gianni Agnelli, who was recently named vice-chairman of Fiat. Montezemolo also has able execs in Marchionne and Herbert Demel, the former Audi executive and first outsider brought in to run Fiat Auto. But Fiat's condition is fragile, and one more wrong turn might be its last.

Meanwhile, an industry boss, Montezemolo will seek to defuse tensions between Silvio Berlusconi's center-right government, which has failed to deliver on economic reforms, and the unions, which have blocked them. Montezemolo will now sit in the hot seat on explosive issues such as pension reform, tax cuts, and labor market reform. Also on the front burner: A vital overhaul of education, research and development, and innovation policy. "I don't ever tire of saying: It's innovation, innovation, innovation," Montezemolo said during an inaugural speech as industry chief on May 27. Exactly. If only Fiat—and Italy—had heard those words sooner.

Questions

1. What sources of power does Montezemolo possess?
2. How might he expand and maintain his power in the top job at Fiat?
3. Is conflict being effectively handled at Fiat?
4. What steps should Montezemolo take to effectively manage conflict at Fiat and turn around Fiat's fortunes?

Source: G. Edmondson, "Fiat's Last Chance." Reprinted from the June 14, 2004, issue of *BusinessWeek* by special permission.

CHAPTER

18 Utilizing Advanced Information Technology

Learning Objectives

After studying this chapter, you should be able to:

- Differentiate between data and information and list the attributes of useful information.
- Describe three reasons why managers must have access to information to perform their tasks and roles effectively.
- Describe the computer hardware and software innovations that have created the IT revolution.
- Differentiate among seven different kinds of management information systems.
- Explain how advances in IT can give an organization a competitive advantage.

A Manager's Challenge

IBM's "Business-on-Demand" IT

How can managers create competitive advantage through IT?

In the poor economic conditions of the early 2000s, the stock prices of most companies that make and sell information technology (IT) plunged as their main customers—other business companies—slashed their IT budgets. Searching for ways to lower costs, the problem facing a company seeking to purchase new IT was deciding which components of computer hardware and software would result in the greatest gains in profitability. Convincing a company to spend millions or billions of dollars to buy new kinds of software and hardware is a daunting task facing the sales force of a company that sells IT today.

One of the company's facing this challenge is IBM, which makes, sells, and services a vast array of computer hardware and software. To maintain its leading position in the highly competitive IT industry, Sam Palmisano, who became IBM's CEO in 2002, announced a bold new business model for IBM called *Business on Demand.* Over the long run, he claims, companies that adopt IBM's new IT will generate millions or billions of dollars in savings in operating costs.

IBM's Business on Demand software allows computing power to move between computers both inside and between companies. Industry specific "expert systems" can even help managers solve problems by making better business decisions and controlling a company's operations.

To promote its new business model, IBM told its customers to think of information and computing power as being a fluid, like water, contained in the hundreds or thousands of computers that are the "reservoirs" or "lakes" of a large company's IT system. This water flows between computers in a company's computer network through the fiber-optic cables that connect them. Thus, computing power, like water, can potentially be moved between computers both inside a company and between companies, as long as all the computers are linked seamlessly together. *Seamless* means that computer hardware or software does not create information "logjams," which disrupt the flow of information and computing power.

To allow the potential computing power of all a company's computers to be shared, IBM's software engineers developed new e-business software that enabled the computers to work seamlessly together. Among its other capabilities, this software allows computer operators to monitor hundreds of different computers at the same time and shift work from one machine to another to distribute a company's computing power to wherever it is most needed. This has several cost-saving advantages. First, companies can run their computers at a much higher level, close to capacity, thereby greatly improving IT productivity and reducing operating costs. Second, to ensure that its customers never experience a "drought," IBM uses its own vast computer capacity as a kind of bank or reservoir that customers can tap into whenever their own systems become overloaded. For example, using IBM's e-business software, companies can shift any excess work to IBM's computers rather than investing tens of millions of dollars in extra computers—a huge cost saving. Third, when a company's computers are seamlessly networked together, they can function as a "supercomputer," a computer with immense information processing power, which can easily cost upward of $50 million just to purchase and tens of millions more to maintain.

IBM decided to implement its new e-business IT in its own company to show customers the cost-saving potential of its new products. Previously, IBM allowed its many different product divisions to choose whatever software they liked to manage their own purchasing and supply chain activities. In 2003, Palmisano appointed star manager Linda Stanford to overhaul IBM's whole supply chain, which amounts to $44 billion in yearly purchases. She is responsible for developing software to link them all into a single e-business system. IBM expects this will result in a 5 percent productivity gain each year for the next 5 to 10 years—which translates into savings of $2 billion a year. IBM is telling its customers that they can expect to see similar savings if they purchase its software.

IBM's new e-business system also has many other performance-enhancing benefits. Its thousands of consultants are experts in particular industries, such as the car, financial services, or retail industries. They have a deep understanding of the particular problems facing companies in those industries and how to solve them. Palmisano asked IBM's consultants to work closely with its software engineers to find ways to incorporate their knowledge into advanced software that can be implanted into a customer's IT system.

IBM has developed 17 industry-specific "expert systems," which consist of problem-solving software managers can use to make better business decisions and control a company's operations. One expert system is being developed for the pharmaceutical industry. Using this new software, a pharmaceutical company's interlinked computers will be able to function as a supercomputer and simulate and model the potential success of new drugs under development. Currently, only 5 to 10 percent of new drugs make it to the market. IBM believes that its new IT could raise that rate to over 50 percent, which would lead to billions of dollars in cost savings.[1]

Overview

As the experience of IBM suggests, there are enormous opportunities for managers to find new ways to use advanced information technology (IT) to increase the flow of knowledge and speed communication and decision making in an organization. Thus, the adoption of new IT can help give an organization a competitive advantage and lead to high performance.

In this chapter we begin by looking at the relationship between information and the manager's job and then examine the ongoing IT revolution. Then we discuss several types of specific management information systems, each of which is based on a different sort of IT, which can help managers perform their jobs more efficiently and effectively. Next, we examine the impact that rapidly evolving IT is having on managers' jobs and on an organization's competitive advantage. By the end of this chapter, you will understand the profound ways in which new developments in IT, and the way managers utilize IT, are shaping managers' functions and roles.

Information and the Manager's Job

Managers cannot plan, organize, lead, and control effectively unless they have access to information. Information is the source of the knowledge and intelligence that they need to make the right decisions. Information, however, is not the same as data.[2] **Data** is raw, unsummarized, and unanalyzed facts such as volume of sales, level of costs, or number of customers. **Information** is data that are organized in a meaningful fashion, such as in a graph showing the change in sales volume or costs over time. Data alone do not tell managers anything; information, in contrast, can communicate a great deal of useful knowledge to the person who receives it–such as a manager who sees sales falling or costs rising. The distinction between data and information is important because one of the purposes of IT is to help managers transform data into information in order to make better managerial decisions.

data Raw, unsummarized, and unanalyzed facts.

information Data that are organized in a meaningful fashion.

To further clarify the difference between data and information, consider the case of a manager in a supermarket who must decide how much shelf space to allocate to two breakfast cereal brands for children: Dentist's Delight and Sugar Supreme. Most supermarkets use checkout scanners to record individual sales and store the data on a computer. Accessing this computer, the manager might find that Dentist's Delight sells 50 boxes per day and Sugar Supreme sells 25 boxes per day. These raw data, however, are of little help in assisting the manager to decide about how to allocate shelf space. The manager also needs to know how much shelf space each cereal currently occupies and how much profit each cereal generates for the supermarket.

Suppose the manager discovers that Dentist's Delight occupies 10 feet of shelf space and Sugar Supreme occupies 4 feet and that Dentist's Delight generates 20 cents of profit a box while Sugar Supreme generates 40 cents of profit a box. By putting these three bits of data together (number of boxes sold, amount of shelf space, and profit per box), the manager gets some useful information on which to base a decision: Dentist's Delight generates $1 of profit per foot of shelf space per day [(50 boxes × $.20)/10 feet], and Sugar Supreme generates $2.50 of profit per foot of shelf space per day [(25 boxes × $.40)/4 feet]. Armed with this information, the manager might decide to allocate less shelf space to Dentist's Delight and more to Sugar Supreme.

Attributes of Useful Information

Four factors determine the usefulness of information to a manager: quality, timeliness, completeness, and relevance (see Figure 18.1).

QUALITY Accuracy and reliability determine the quality of information.[3] The greater the accuracy and reliability, the higher is the quality of information. For IT to work well, the information that it provides must be of high quality. If managers conclude that the quality of information provided by the IT they use

Figure 18.1
Factors Affecting the Usefulness of Information

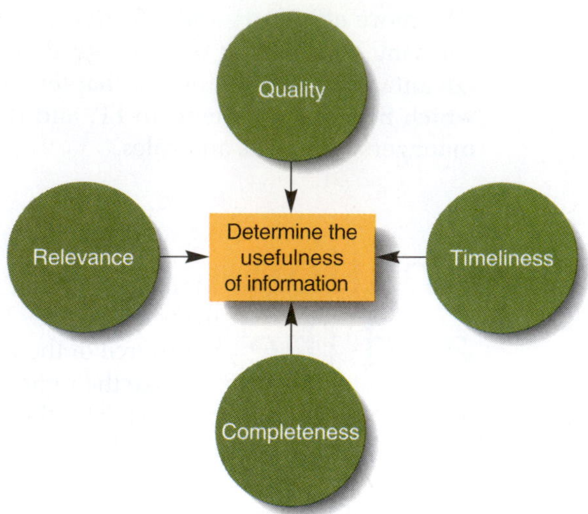

is low, they are likely to lose confidence in it and stop using it. Alternatively, if managers base decisions on low-quality information, poor and even disastrous decision making can result. For example, the partial meltdown of the nuclear reactor at Three Mile Island in Pennsylvania during the 1970s was the result of poor information caused by an IT malfunction. While their computer screens indicated to engineers controlling the reactor that there was enough water in the reactor core to cool the nuclear pile, this was in fact not the case. The consequences included the partial meltdown of the reactor and the release of radioactive gas into the atmosphere.

TIMELINESS Information that is timely is available when it is needed for managerial action, not after the decision has been made. In today's rapidly changing world, the need for timely information often means that information must be available on a real-time basis.[4] **Real-time information** is information that reflects current conditions. In an industry that experiences rapid changes, real-time information may need to be updated frequently.

real-time information Frequently updated information that reflects current conditions.

Airlines use real-time information on the number of flight bookings and competitors' prices to adjust their prices on an hour-to-hour basis to maximize their revenues. Thus, for example, the fare for flights from New York to Seattle might change from one hour to the next as fares are reduced to fill empty seats and raised when most seats have been sold. Airlines use real-time information on reservations to adjust fares at the last possible moment to fill planes and maximize revenues. U.S. airlines make more than 80,000 fare changes each day.[5] Obviously, the managers who make such pricing decisions need real-time information about the current state of demand in the marketplace.

COMPLETENESS Information that is complete gives managers all the information they need to exercise control, achieve coordination, or make an effective decision. Recall from Chapter 7, however, that managers rarely have access to complete information. Instead, because of uncertainty, ambiguity, and bounded rationality, they have to make do with incomplete information.[6] One of the functions of information systems is to increase the completeness of the information that managers have at their disposal.

RELEVANCE Information that is relevant is useful and suits a manager's particular needs and circumstances. Irrelevant information is useless and may actually hurt the performance of a busy manager who has to spend valuable time determining whether information is relevant. Given the massive amounts of information that managers are now exposed to and humans' limited information-processing capabilities, the people who design information systems need to make sure that managers receive only relevant information.

Today, software agents are increasingly being used by managers to scan and sort incoming email and prioritize it. A *software agent* is a software program that can be used to perform simple tasks such as scanning incoming information for relevance, taking some of the burden away from managers. Moreover, by recording and analyzing a manager's own efforts to prioritize incoming information, the software agent can mimic the manager's preferences and thus perform such tasks more effectively. For example, the software agent can automatically reprogram itself to place incoming email from the manager's boss at the top of the pile.[7]

What Is Information Technology?

information technology The set of methods or techniques for acquiring, organizing, storing, manipulating, and transmitting information.

management information system (MIS) A specific form of IT that managers utilize to generate the specific, detailed information they need to perform their roles effectively.

Information technology is the set of methods or techniques for acquiring, organizing, storing, manipulating, and transmitting information.[8] A **management information system (MIS)** is a specific form of IT that managers select and utilize to generate the specific, detailed information they need to perform their roles effectively. Management information systems have existed for as long as there have been organizations–a long time indeed. Before the computer age, most systems were paper-based: Clerks recorded important information on documents (often in duplicate or triplicate) in the form of words and numbers; sent a copy of the document to superiors, customers, or suppliers, as the case might be; and stored other copies in files for future reference.

Rapid advances in the power of IT–specifically, through the development of more and more sophisticated computer hardware and software–are having a fundamental impact on managers, their organizations, and their suppliers and customers, as suggested by the developments at IBM in "A Manager's Challenge."[9] So important are these advances in IT that organizations that have not adopted new IT, or have done so ineffectively, have become uncompetitive compared with those that have adopted it.[10] In the 2000s, the increasing productivity and efficiency of business has been attributed to advancing IT.

Managers need information for three reasons: to make effective decisions, to control the activities of the organization, and to coordinate the activities of the organization. Following we examine these uses of information in detail.

Information and Decisions

Much of management (planning, organizing, leading, and controlling) is about making decisions. For example, the marketing manager must decide what price to charge for a product, what distribution channels to use, and what promotional messages to emphasize. The manufacturing manager must decide how much of a product to make and how to make it. The purchasing manager must decide from whom to purchase inputs and what inventory of inputs to hold. The human relations manager must decide how much employees should be paid, how they should be trained, and what benefits they should be given. The engineering manager must make decisions about new product design. Top managers must decide how to allocate scarce financial resources among competing projects, how best to structure and control the organization, and what business-level strategy the organization should be pursuing. And, regardless of their functional orientation, all managers have to make decisions about matters such as what performance evaluation to give to a subordinate.

Decision making cannot be effective in an information vacuum. To make effective decisions, managers need information, both from inside the organization and from external stakeholders. When deciding how to price a product, for example, marketing managers need information about how consumers will react to different prices. They need information about unit costs because they do not want to set the price below the cost of production. And they need information about competitive strategy, since pricing strategy should be consistent with an organization's competitive strategy. Some of this information will come from outside the organization (for example, from consumer surveys) and some from inside the organization (information about unit production costs comes from manufacturing). As this example suggests, managers' ability to make effective decisions rests on their ability to acquire and process information.

Information and Control

As discussed in Chapter 11, *controlling* is the process whereby managers regulate how efficiently and effectively an organization and its members are performing the activities necessary to achieve organizational goals.[11] Managers achieve control over organizational activities by taking four steps (see Figure 11.2): (1) They establish measurable standards of performance or goals. (2) They measure actual performance. (3) They compare actual performance against established goals. (4) They evaluate the result and take corrective action if necessary.[12] The package delivery company DHL, for example, has a delivery goal: to deliver 95 percent of the packages it picks up by noon the next day.[13] Throughout the United States, DHL has thousands of ground stations (branch offices that coordinate the pickup and delivery of packages in a particular area) that are responsible for the physical pickup and delivery of packages. DHL managers monitor the delivery performance of these stations on a regular basis; if they find that the 95 percent goal is not being attained, they determine why and take corrective action if necessary.[14]

To achieve control over any organizational activity, managers must have information. To control a ground station, a manager at DHL needs to know how many of that station's packages are being delivered by noon. To get this information, the manager needs to make sure that IT is in place. Packages to be shipped by DHL are scanned with a handheld scanner by the DHL driver who first picks them up. The pickup information is sent by a wireless link to a central computer at DHL's headquarters. The packages are scanned again by the truck driver when they are delivered. The delivery information is also transmitted to DHL's central computer. By accessing the central computer, a manager can quickly find out not only what percentage of packages are delivered by noon of the day after they were picked up but also how this information breaks down on a station-by-station basis.[15]

Management information systems are used to control a variety of operations within organizations. In accounting, for example, information systems can be used to monitor expenditures and compare them against budgets.[16] To track expenditures against budgets, managers need information on current expenditures, broken down by relevant organizational units. Accounting information systems are designed to provide managers with such information. An example of IT used to monitor and control the daily activities of employees is the online MBO information system used by T. J. Rodgers at Cypress Semiconductor, discussed in Chapter 11. Rodgers implemented IT that allows him to review the goals of all his employees in about four hours.[17] At first glance, it might seem that advances in IT would have a limited impact on the business of an office furniture maker; however, this assumption would be incorrect, as the following "Management Insight" suggests.

Management Insight

Herman Miller's Office of the Future

In recent years, managers at Herman Miller have been finding countless ways to use IT and the Internet to give their company a competitive advantage over rival office furniture makers (OFMs) such as Steelcase and Hon.[18] From the beginning, like managers at the other OFMs, Miller's managers saw the potential of the Internet for selling Miller office furniture to potential business customers. The other companies' Web sites were online advertisements for their products, services, capabilities, and other relevant marketing and historical information. However, very quickly, managers realized the true potential of email both inside a company on its intranet and between companies over the Internet. In Herman Miller's case, the expanding use of the Internet followed a definite pattern.

First, Miller's managers developed IT that linked all the company's dealers and salespeople to its manufacturing hub so that sales orders could be coordinated with the custom design department and with manufacturing, enabling customers to receive pricing and scheduling information promptly. Then, with this customer delivery system in place, Miller developed IT to link its manufacturing operations with its network of suppliers so that its input supply chain would be coordinated with its customer needs.

Miller's managers noticed that the company's competitors moved quickly to imitate its IT, so they began to search for new ways to take advantage of the opportunities it offered. When they realized that IT could transform the office furniture business itself, they began to define Herman Miller as a "digital" enterprise. Infused with e-business, the company saw its mission as not just to improve efficiency by reducing costs but also to change the way the customer experienced "Herman Miller" and increase value for the customer. Miller's managers accomplished this in several different ways.

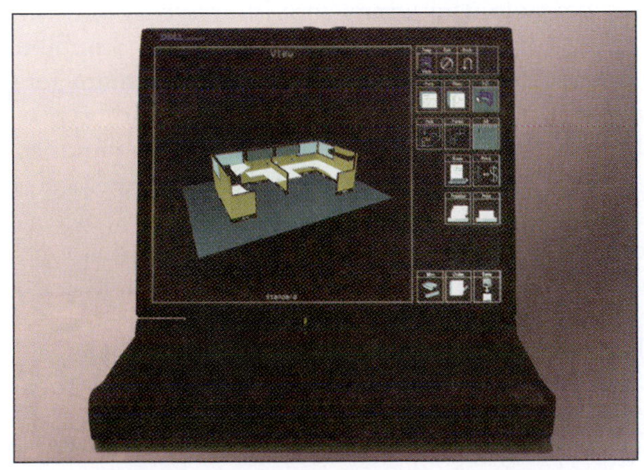

Hermann Miller's 2-Axis program allows customers to experiment with and customize the office furniture designs that Hermann Miller's designers create. The result is a finished design that is best adapted to each customer's unique needs.

One of their main Web initiatives was the establishment of an e-learning tool, Uknowit.com, which became Herman Miller's online university. Via the Web thousands of Miller's employees and dealers are currently enrolled in Uknowit.com, where they choose from 85 courses covering technology, products and services, product applications, consultative/selling skills, and industry competitive knowledge. The benefits to Miller, its dealers, and its customers from this IT initiative are improved speed to market and better ability to respond to competitors' tactics. That is, salespeople and dealers now have the information and tools they need to better compete for and keep customers. In the office furniture industry the average ramp-up time for a new sales associate is typically 24 to 36 months due to the complexity of the products and sales cycle/process. Utilizing e-learning has cut this in half.

Moreover, the office furniture business offers highly customized solutions to its customers. A main source of competitive advantage is the ability to give customers exactly what they want and at the right price. Traditionally, the contract furniture industry had a hard time meeting deadlines for customized furniture solutions, and delivery to customers was often late. As a result of Miller's new information systems, its salespeople are giving design and manufacturing more accurate and timely information, which has reduced the incidence of sales and specification errors during the selling process. Also, with the new systems time to market has been reduced, and Miller is committed to being able to offer customers highly customized furniture in 10 business days or less.

Of course, all these IT initiatives have been costly to Herman Miller. Thousands of hours of management time have been spent developing the information systems and providing content, such as information on competitors for the company's online classes. Herman Miller's managers are looking at the long term; they believe they have created a real source of competitive advantage for their company that will sustain it in the years ahead.

Information and Coordination

Coordinating department and divisional activities to achieve organizational goals is another basic task of management. As an extreme example of the size of the coordination task that managers face, consider the coordination effort involved in building Boeing's most recent commercial jet aircraft, the 777.[19] The 777 is composed of 3 million individual parts and thousands of major components. Managers at Boeing have to coordinate the production and delivery of all of these parts so that every part arrives at Boeing's Everett, Washington, facility exactly when it is needed (for example, the wings should arrive before the engines). Boeing managers jokingly refer to this task as "coordinating 3 million parts in flying formation." To achieve this high level of coordination, managers need information about which supplier is producing what, when it is to be produced, and when it is to be delivered. Managers also need this information so that they are able to track the delivery performance of suppliers against expectations and receive advance warning of any likely problems. To meet these needs, managers at Boeing established a computer-based information system that links Boeing to all its suppliers and can track the flow of 3 million component parts through the production process–an immense task.

As we noted in previous chapters, the coordination problems that managers face in managing their global supply chains to take advantage of national differences in the costs of production are increasing. To deal with global coordination problems, managers have been adopting sophisticated IT that helps them coordinate the flow of materials, semifinished goods, and finished products throughout the world. Consider, for example, how Bose Corporation, which manufactures some of the world's best-known high-fidelity speakers, manages its global supply chain.

Bose purchases almost all of the electronic and nonelectronic components for its speakers from independent suppliers. About 50 percent of its purchases are from foreign suppliers, the majority of which are in the Far East. The challenge for managers is to coordinate this globally dispersed supply chain to minimize Bose's inventory and transportation costs. Minimizing these costs requires that component parts arrive at Bose's assembly plant just in time to enter the production process and not before. Bose also has to remain responsive to customer demands. This requirement means that the company has to respond quickly to increases in demand for certain kinds of speakers, such as outdoor speakers in the summer. Failure to respond quickly can cause the loss of a big order to competitors. Since Bose does not want to hold extensive inventories at its Massachusetts plant, the need to remain responsive to customer demands requires that Bose's suppliers be able to respond rapidly to increased demand for component parts.

The responsibility for coordinating the supply chain to simultaneously minimize inventory and transportation costs and respond quickly to customer demands belongs to Bose's logistics managers. They contracted with W. N. Procter, a Boston-based supply chain manager, to develop logistics IT that gives Bose the real-time information it needs to track parts as they move through the global supply chain. The IT is known as ProcterLink. When a shipment leaves a supplier, it is logged into ProcterLink.[20] From that point on, Bose can track the supplies as they move across the globe toward Massachusetts. This system allows Bose to fine-tune its production scheduling so that supplies enter the production process exactly when they are needed.

How well this system works was illustrated when one Japanese customer unexpectedly doubled its order for Bose speakers. Bose had to gear up its manufacturing in a hurry, but many of its components were stretched out across long distances. By using ProcterLink, Bose was able to locate the needed parts in its supply chain. It then broke them out of the normal delivery chain and moved them by air freight to get them to the assembly line in time for the accelerated schedule. As a result, Bose was able to meet the request of its customer.

The IT Revolution

Advances in IT have allowed managers to develop computer-based management information systems that provide timely, complete, relevant, and high-quality information. As we have discussed, IT allows companies like IBM, Herman Miller, and Bose to improve their responsiveness to customers, minimize costs, and thus improve their competitive position. To better understand the current revolution in IT, in this section we examine several key aspects of advanced IT.

The Tumbling Price of Information

The IT revolution began with the development of the first computers–the hardware of IT–in the 1950s. The language of computers is a *digital* language of zeros and ones. Words, numbers, images, and sound can all be expressed in zeros and ones. Each letter in the alphabet has its own unique code of zeros and ones, as does each number, each color, and each sound. For example, the digital code for the number 20 is 10100. In the language of computers it takes a lot of zeros and ones to express even a simple sentence, to say nothing of complex color graphics or moving video images. Nevertheless, modern computers can read, process, and store millions of instructions per second (an *instruction* is a line of software code) and thus vast amounts of zeros and ones. It is this awesome power that forms the foundation of the current IT revolution.

The "brains" of modern computers are microprocessors (Intel's Pentium and Itanium chips are microprocessors). Between 1991 and 2001, the relative cost of computer processing fell so dramatically that Gordon Moore, a computer guru, noted, "If the auto industry advanced as rapidly as the semiconductor industry, a Rolls Royce would get a half a million miles per gallon, and it would be cheaper to throw it away than to park it."[21] As the costs of acquiring, organizing, storing, and transmitting information have tumbled, computers have become almost as common as wireless phones and microwaves.[22] In addition, advances in microprocessor technology have led to dramatic reductions in the cost of communication between computers, which also have contributed to the falling price of information and information systems.

Wireless Communications

Another trend of considerable significance for modern IT has been the rapid growth of wireless communication technologies, particularly digital communications. Wireless service was first offered in the United States in 1983. Initially, growth was slow, but since 1990 wireless service has spread rapidly. In 1984 there were 100,000 cellular subscribers in the United States;[23] in 1994 there were 16 million; and by 2001 this figure had mushroomed to 110 million.[24] Nokia, the world's largest maker of mobile phones, said that it expects the number of global users to rise 33 percent by 2007, to 2 billion up from 1.5 billion in 2004.[25]

Wireless communication is significant for the IT revolution because it facilitates the linking together of computers, which greatly increases their power and adaptability. It is already possible to purchase a battery-operated laptop computer that has a wireless modem built in to facilitate communication with a "home" computer. An engineer or salesperson working in the field can send information to, and receive information from, the home office by using the wireless capabilities built into computers. Because a computer no longer has to be plugged in to a hard-wired telephone line, accessing a company's centralized computer system is much easier than it used to be.

A "mobile messenger" holds a laptop computer featuring the new wireless computer connection at a McDonald's restaurant in New York City. In 2003, McDonald's launched a major wireless Internet rollout in New York City and in three major U.S. markets.

Computer Networks

The tumbling price of computing power and information and the use of wireless communication channels have facilitated **networking,** the exchange of information through a group or network of interlinked computers. The most common arrangement now emerging is a four-tier network consisting of personal digital assistants (PDAs), clients, servers, and a mainframe (see Figure 18.2). At the outer nodes of a typical four-tier system are the *PDAs,* such as wireless smart phones and electronic organizers like the Palm Pilot, which allow users to email

Figure 18.2
A Typical Four-Tier Information System

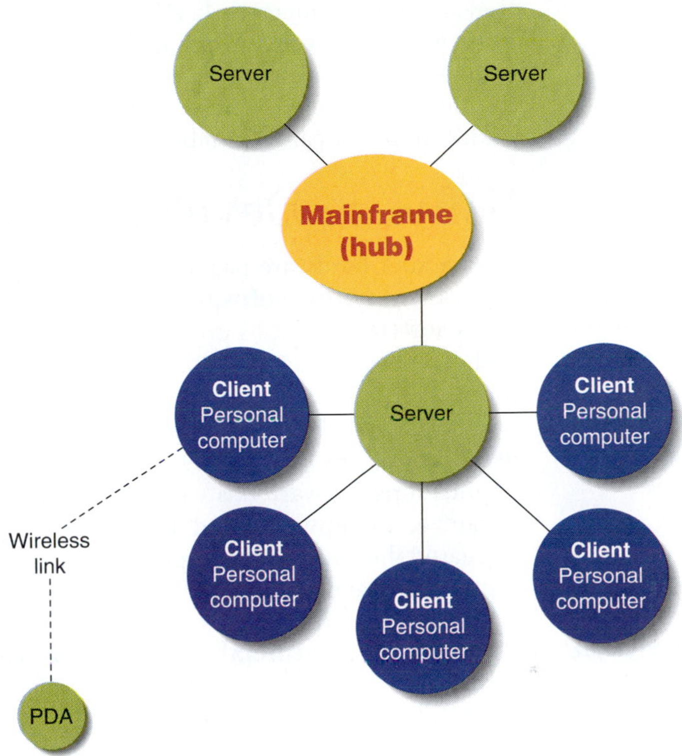

networking The exchange of information through a group or network of interlinked computers.

co-workers and which provide access to files on their PCs and on the company's intranet. Next in the network are the personal computers (PCs) that sit on the desks of individual users. These personal computers, referred to as clients, are linked to a local server, a high-powered midrange computer that "serves" the client personal computers. Servers often store power-hungry software programs that can be run more effectively on the server than on an individual's personal computer. Servers may also manage several printers that can be used by hundreds of clients, store data files, and handle email communications between clients. The client computers linked directly to a server constitute a *local area network (LAN)*. Within any organization there may be several LANs–for example, one in every division and function.

At the hub of a four-tier system are mainframe computers. *Mainframes* are large and powerful computers that can be used to store and process vast amounts of information. The mainframe can also be used to handle electronic communications between personal computers situated in different LANs. In addition, the mainframe may be connected to mainframes in other organizations and, through them, to LANs in other organizations. Increasingly, the Internet, a worldwide network of interlinked computers, is used as the conduit for connecting the computer systems of different organizations, but IBM can also perform this service, as "A Manager's Challenge" suggests.

A manager with a PDA or PC hooked into a four-tier system can access data and software stored in the local server, in the mainframe, or through the Internet in computers based in another organization. A manager can therefore communicate electronically with other individuals hooked into the system, whether they are in the manager's LAN, in another LAN within the manager's organization, or in another organization altogether. Moreover, with wireless communication an individual with the necessary IT can hook into the system from any location–at home, on a boat, on the beach, in the air–anywhere a wireless communication link can be established.

Software Developments

operating system software Software that tells computer hardware how to run.

applications software Software designed for a specific task or use.

If computer hardware has been developing rapidly, so has computer software. **Operating system software** tells the computer hardware how to run. **Applications software,** such as programs for word processing, spreadsheets, graphics, and database management, is software developed for a specific task or use. The increase in the power of computer hardware has allowed software developers to write increasingly powerful programs that are, at the same time, increasingly user-friendly. By harnessing the rapidly growing power of microprocessors, applications software has vastly increased the ability of managers to acquire, organize, manipulate, and transmit information. In doing so, it also has increased the ability of managers to coordinate and control the activities of their organization and to make decisions, as discussed earlier.

artificial intelligence Behavior performed by a machine that, if performed by a human being, would be called "intelligent."

Artificial intelligence is another interesting and potentially fruitful software development. **Artificial intelligence** has been defined as behavior by a machine that, if performed by a human being, would be called "intelligent."[26] Artificial intelligence has already made it possible to write programs that can solve problems and perform simple tasks. For example, software programs variously called *software agents, softbots,* or *knowbots* can be used to perform simple managerial tasks such as sorting through reams of data or incoming email messages to look for important data and messages. The interesting feature of these programs is that from "watching" a manager sort through such data they can "learn" what his or her preferences are. Having done this, they then can take over some of this work from the manager, freeing more time to work on other tasks. Most of these programs are still in the development stage, but they may be commonplace within a decade.[27]

"Well, being single and a robot, I'm able to put in a lot of overtime."

Another software development that is starting to have an impact on the manager's job is speech recognition software. Currently speech recognition software must be "trained" to recognize and understand each individual's voice, and it requires that the speaker pause after each word. The increasing power of microprocessors, however, has enabled the development of faster speech recognition programs that can handle more variables and much greater complexity. Now a manager driving down the road can communicate with a PC through a wireless link and give that computer complex voice instructions.[28]

Types of Management Information Systems

Six more types of management information systems are particularly helpful in providing managers with the information they need to make decisions and to coordinate and control organizational resources: transaction-processing systems, operations information systems, decision support systems, expert systems, enterprise resource planning systems, and e-commerce systems (see Figure 18.3). These systems are arranged along a continuum according to the sophistication of the IT they are based on–IT that determines their ability to provide managers with the information they need to make nonprogrammed decisions. (Recall from Chapter 7 that nonprogrammed decision making occurs in response to unusual, unpredictable opportunities and threats.) We examine each of these systems after focusing on the management information system that preceded them all: the organizational hierarchy.

The Organizational Hierarchy: The Traditional Information System

Traditionally, managers have used the organizational hierarchy as the main system for gathering the information necessary to make decisions and coordinate and control activities (see Chapter 10 for a detailed discussion of organizational structure and hierarchy). According to business historian Alfred Chandler, the use of the hierarchy as an information network was perfected by railroad companies in the United States during the 1850s.[29] At that time, the railroads were the largest industrial organizations in the United States. By virtue of their size and geographic spread, they faced unique problems of coordination and control. In the 1850s, railroad companies started to solve these problems by designing hierarchical management structures that provided senior managers with the information they needed to achieve coordination and control and to make decisions about the running of the railroads.

Daniel McCallum, superintendent of the Erie Railroad in the 1850s, realized that the lines of authority and responsibility defining the Erie's management hierarchy also represented channels of communication along which information traveled. McCallum established what was perhaps the first modern management

Figure 18.3
Six Computer-Based Management Information Systems

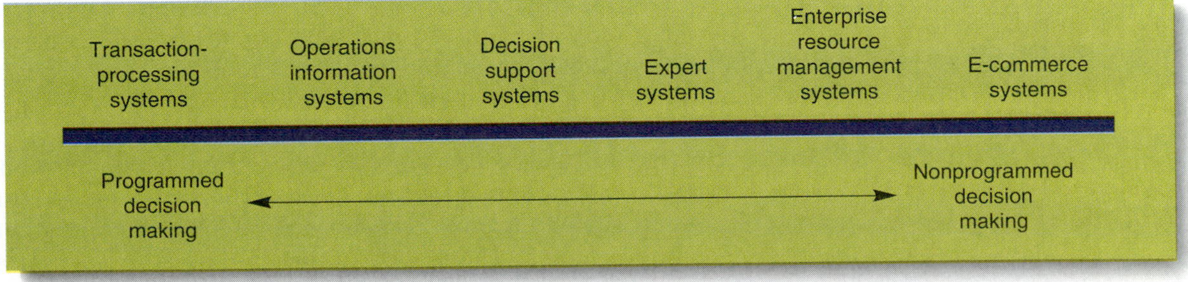

information system. Regular daily and monthly reports were sent up the management chain so that top managers could make decisions about, for example, controlling costs and setting freight rates. Decisions were then relayed back down the hierarchy so they could be carried out. Imitating the railroads, most other organizations used their hierarchies as systems for collecting and channeling information. This practice began to change only when computer-based IT became more reasonably priced in the 1960s.

Although hierarchy is a useful information system, it has several drawbacks. First, when an organization has many layers of managers, it takes a long time for information and requests to travel up the hierarchy and for decisions and answers to travel back down. This slow pace can reduce the *timeliness* and usefulness of the information and prevent an organization from responding quickly to changing market conditions.[30] Second, information can be distorted as it moves from one layer of management to another, and information distortion reduces the *quality* of information.[31] Third, because managers have only a limited span of control, as an organization grows larger, its hierarchy lengthens and this tall structure can make the hierarchy a very expensive information system. The popular idea that companies with tall management hierarchies are bureaucratic and unresponsive to the needs of their customers arises from the inability of tall hierarchies to effectively process data and provide managers with timely, complete, relevant, and high-quality information. Until modern IT came along, however, the management hierarchy was the best information system available.

Transaction-Processing Systems

transaction-processing system A management information system designed to handle large volumes of routine, recurring transactions.

A **transaction-processing system** is an MIS designed to handle large volumes of routine, recurring transactions (see Figure 18.3). Transaction-processing systems began to appear in the early 1960s with the advent of commercially available mainframe computers. They were the first type of computer-based IT adopted by many organizations, and today they are commonplace. Bank managers use a transaction-processing system to record deposits into, and payments out of, bank accounts. Supermarket managers use a transaction-processing system to record the sale of items and to track inventory levels. More generally, most managers in large organizations use a transaction-processing system to handle tasks such as payroll preparation and payment, customer billing, and payment of suppliers.

Operations Information Systems

operations information system A management information system that gathers, organizes, and summarizes comprehensive data in a form that managers can use in their nonroutine coordinating, controlling, and decision-making tasks.

Many types of MIS followed hard on the heels of transaction-processing systems in the 1960s as companies like IBM advanced IT. An **operations information system** is an MIS that gathers comprehensive data, organizes them, and summarizes them in a form that is of value to managers. Whereas a transaction-processing system processes *routine* transactions, an operations information system provides managers with information that they can use in their *nonroutine* coordinating, controlling, and decision-making tasks. Most operations information systems are coupled with a transaction-processing system. An operations information system typically accesses data gathered by a transaction-processing system, processes those data into useful information, and organizes that information into a form accessible to managers. Managers often use an operations information system to get sales, inventory, accounting, and other performance-related information. For example, the information that T. J. Rodgers at Cypress

Semiconductors gets on individual employee goals and performance is provided by an operations information system.

DHL uses an operations information system to track the performance of its 500 or so ground stations. Each ground station is evaluated according to four criteria: delivery (the goal is to deliver 95 percent of all packages by noon the day after they are picked up), productivity (measured by the number of packages shipped per employee-hour), controllable cost, and station profitability. Each ground station also has specific delivery, efficiency, cost, and profitability targets that it must attain. Every month DHL's operations information system is used to gather information on these four criteria and summarize it for top managers, who are then able to compare the performance of each station against its previously established targets. The system quickly alerts senior managers to underperforming ground stations, so they can intervene selectively to help solve any problems that may have given rise to the poor performance.[32]

Decision Support Systems

decision support system An interactive computer-based management information system that managers can use to make nonroutine decisions.

A **decision support system** provides computer-built models that help managers make better nonprogrammed decisions.[33] Recall from Chapter 7 that *nonprogrammed decisions* are decisions that are relatively unusual or novel, such as decisions to invest in new productive capacity, develop a new product, launch a new promotional campaign, enter a new market, or expand internationally. Although an operations information system organizes important information for managers, a decision support system gives managers a model-building capability and so provides them with the ability to manipulate information in a variety of ways. Managers might use a decision support system to help them decide whether to cut prices for a product. The decision support system might contain models of how customers and competitors would respond to a price cut. Managers could run these models and use the results as an aid to decision making.

The stress on the word *aid* is important, for in the final analysis a decision support system is not meant to make decisions for managers. Rather, its function is to provide managers with valuable information that they can use to improve the quality of their decisions. A good example of a sophisticated decision support system, developed by Judy Lewent, chief financial officer of the U.S. pharmaceutical company Merck, is given in the following "Manager as a Person."

Manager as a Person

How Judy Lewent Became One of the Most Powerful Women in Corporate America

With annual sales of over $40 billion, Merck is one of the world's largest developers and marketers of advanced pharmaceuticals.[34] In 2003, the company spent more than $3 billion on R&D to develop new drugs–an expensive and difficult process that is fraught with risks. Most new drug ideas fail to make it through the development process. It takes an average of $300 million and 10 years to bring a new drug to market, and 7 out of 10 new drugs fail to make a profit for the developing company.

Given the costs, risks, and uncertainties involved in the new drug development process, Judy Lewent, the former director of capital analysis at Merck,

Judy Lewent, Chief Financial Officer of Merck, consults with managers of Sweden's Astra Pharmaceuticals, as they work out the details of their global venture

decided to develop a decision support system that could help managers make more effective R&D investment decisions. Her aim was to give Merck's top managers the information they needed to evaluate proposed R&D projects on a case-by-case basis. The system that Lewent and her staff developed is referred to in Merck as the "Research Planning Model."[35] At the heart of this decision support system is a sophisticated model. The input variables to the model include data on R&D spending, manufacturing costs, selling costs, and demand conditions. The relationships among the input variables are modeled by means of several equations that factor in the probability of a drug's making it through the development process and to market. The outputs of this modeling process are the revenues, cash flows, and profits that a project might generate.

The Merck model does not use a single value for an input variable, nor does it compute a single value for each output. Rather, a range is specified for each input variable (such as high, medium, and low R&D spending). The computer repeatedly samples at random from the range of values for each input variable and produces a probability distribution of values for each output. So, for example, instead of stating categorically that a proposed R&D project will yield a profit of $500 million, the decision support system produces a probability distribution. It might state that although $500 million is the most likely profit, there is a 25 percent chance that the profit will be less than $300 million and a 25 percent chance that it will be greater than $700 million.

Merck now uses Lewent's decision support system to evaluate all proposed R&D investment decisions. In addition, Lewent has developed other decision support system models that Merck's managers can use to help them decide, for example, whether to enter into joint ventures with other companies or how best to hedge foreign exchange risk. As for Lewent, her reward was promotion to the position of chief financial officer of Merck, and she became one of the most powerful women in corporate America.

Most decision support systems are geared toward aiding middle managers in the decision-making process. For example, a loan manager at a bank might use a decision support system to evaluate the credit risk involved in lending money to a particular client. Very rarely does a top manager use a decision support system. One reason for this may be that most electronic management information systems are not yet sophisticated enough to handle effectively the ambiguous types of problems facing top managers. To improve this situation, information systems professionals have been developing a variant of the decision support system: an executive support system.

executive support system A sophisticated version of a decision support system that is designed to meet the needs of top managers.

An **executive support system** is a sophisticated version of a decision support system that is designed to meet the needs of top managers. Lewent's Research Planning Model is actually an executive support system. One of the defining characteristics of executive support systems is user-friendliness. Many of them include simple pull-down menus to take a manager through a decision analysis problem. Moreover, they may contain stunning graphics and other visual features to encourage top managers to use them.[36] Increasingly, executive support systems are being used to link top managers so that they can function as a team; this type of executive support system is called a **group decision support system.**

group decision support system An executive support system that links top managers so that they can function as a team.

Expert Systems and Artificial Intelligence

expert system A management information system that employs human knowledge, embedded in a computer, to solve problems that ordinarily require human expertise.

Expert systems are the most advanced management information systems available. An **expert system** is a system that employs human knowledge, embedded in computer software, to solve problems that ordinarily require human expertise.[37] Expert systems are a variant of artificial intelligence.[38] Mimicking human expertise (and intelligence) requires IT that can at a minimum (1) recognize, formulate, and solve a problem; (2) explain the solution; and (3) learn from experience.

Recent developments in artificial intelligence that go by names such as "fuzzy logic" and "neural networks" have resulted in computer programs that, in a primitive way, try to mimic human thought processes. Although artificial intelligence is still at a fairly early stage of development, an increasing number of business applications are beginning to emerge in the form of expert systems. General Electric, for example, has developed an expert system to help troubleshoot problems in the diesel locomotive engines it manufactures. The expert system was originally based on knowledge collected from David Smith, GE's former top locomotive troubleshooter. A novice engineer or technician can use the system to uncover a fault by spending only a few minutes at a computer terminal. The system also can explain to the user the logic of its advice, thereby serving as a teacher as well as a problem solver. The system is based on a flexible, humanlike thought process, and it can be updated to incorporate new knowledge as it becomes available. GE has installed the system in every railroad repair shop that it serves, thus eliminating delays and boosting maintenance productivity.[39]

Enterprise Resource Planning Systems

To achieve high performance, it is not sufficient just to develop an MIS inside each of a company's functions or divisions to provide better information and knowledge. It is also vital that managers in the different functions and divisions have access to information about the activities of managers in *other* functions and divisions. The greater the flow of information and knowledge among functions and divisions, the more learning can take place, and this builds a company's stock of knowledge and expertise. This knowledge and expertise is the source of its competitive advantage and profitability.

enterprise resource planning (ERP) systems Multimodule application software packages that coordinate the functional activities necessary to move products from the product design stage to the final customer stage.

In the last 25 years, a revolution has taken place in IT as software companies have worked to develop enterprise resource planning systems, which essentially incorporate most aspects of the MISs just discussed, as well as much more. **Enterprise resource planning (ERP) systems** are multimodule application software packages that allow a company to link and coordinate the entire set of functional activities and operations necessary to move products from the initial product design stage to the final customer stage. Essentially, ERP systems (1) help each individual function improve its functional-level skills and (2) improve integration among all functions so that they work together to build a competitive advantage for the company. Today, choosing and designing an ERP system to improve the way a company operates is the biggest challenge facing the IT function inside a company. To understand why almost every large global company has installed an ERP system in the last few decades, it is necessary to return to the concept of the value chain, introduced in Chapter 8.

Recall that a company's *value chain* is composed of the sequence of functional activities that are necessary to make and sell a product. The value-chain idea focuses attention on the fact that each function, in sequence, performs its activities to add or contribute value to a product. Once one function has made its contribution, it then hands the product over to the next function, which makes its own contribution, and so on down the line.

The primary activity of marketing, for example, is to uncover new or changing customer needs or new groups of customers and then decide what kinds of products should be developed to appeal to those customers. It then shares or "hands off" its information to product development, where engineers and scientists work to develop and design the new products. In turn, manufacturing and materials management then work to find ways to produce the new products as efficiently as possible. Then, sales is responsible for finding the best way to convince customers to buy these products.

The value chain is useful in demonstrating the sequence of activities necessary to bring products to the market successfully. In an IT context, however, it suggests the enormous amount of information and communication that needs to take place to link and coordinate the activities of all the various functions. Installing an ERP system for a large company can cost tens of millions of dollars. The following "Management Insight" discusses the ERP system designed and sold by the German IT company, SAP.

Management Insight

SAP's ERP System

SAP is the world's leading supplier of ERP software; it introduced the world's first ERP system in 1973. So great was the demand for its software that it had to train thousands of consultants from companies like IBM, HP, Accenture, and Cap Gemini to install and customize its software to meet the needs of companies in different industries throughout the world.

The popularity of SAP's ERP is that it manages all the stages of a company's value chain, both individually and as a collection. SAP's software has modules specifically devoted to each of a company's core functional activities. Each module contains a set of "best practices," or the optimum way to perform specific activities, that SAP's IT experts have found results in the biggest increases in efficiency, quality, innovation, and responsiveness to customers. SAP's ERP is therefore "*the* expert system of expert systems." SAP claims that when a company reconfigures its IT system to make SAP's software work, it can achieve productivity gains of 30 to 50 percent, which amounts to many billions of dollars of savings for large companies.[40]

For each function in the value chain, SAP has a software module that it installs on a function's LAN. Each function then inputs its data into that module in the way specified by SAP. For example, the sales function inputs all the information about customer needs required by SAP's sales module, and the materials management function inputs information about the product specifications it requires from suppliers into SAP's materials management module. These modules give functional managers real-time feedback on the status of their particular functional activities. Essentially, each SAP module functions as an expert system that can reason through the information functional managers put into it. It then provides them with recommendations as to how they can improve functional operations. However, the magic of ERP does not stop there.

SAP's ERP software also connects across functions. Managers in all functions have access to the other functions' expert systems, and SAP's software is designed to alert managers when their functional activities will be affected by changes taking place in another function. Thus, SAP's ERP allows managers across the organization to better coordinate their activities, and this can be a major source of competitive advantage. Moreover, SAP software on corporate mainframe computers takes the information from all the different functional and divisional expert systems and creates a companywide ERP system that provides top managers with an overview of the operations of the whole company. In essence, SAP's ERP creates a sophisticated top-level expert system that can reason through the huge volume of information being provided by the company's functions. It can then recognize and diagnose common problems and issues in that information and develop and recommend organizationwide solutions for those problems and issues. Top managers armed with this information can then use it to improve the fit between their strategies and the changing environment.

As an example of how an ERP system works, let's examine how SAP's software allows managers to better coordinate their activities to speed product development. Suppose marketing has discovered some new unmet customer need, suggested what kind of product needs to be developed, and forecasted that the demand for the product will be 40,000 units a year. With SAP's IT, engineers in product development use their expert system to work out how to design the new product in a way that builds in quality at the lowest possible cost. Manufacturing managers, watching product development's progress, are working *simultaneously* to find the best way to make the product, and thus use their expert system to find out how to keep operating costs at a minimum.

Remember, SAP's IT gives all the other functions access to this information; they can tap into what is going on between marketing and manufacturing in real time. So materials management managers watching manufacturing make its plans can simultaneously plan how to order supplies of inputs or components from global suppliers or how and when to ship the final product to customers to keep costs at a minimum. At the same time, HRM is tied into the ERP system and uses its expert system to forecast the type and cost of the labor that will be required to carry out the activities in the other functions–for example, the number of manufacturing employees who will be required to make the product or the number of salespeople who will be needed to sell the product to achieve the 40,000 sales forecast.

How does this build competitive advantage and profitability? First, it speeds up the product development process; companies can bring products to market much more quickly, thereby generating higher sales revenues. Second, SAP's IT focuses on how to drive down operating costs while keeping quality high. Third, SAP's IT is oriented toward the final customer; its customer relationship management (CRM) module watches how customers respond to the new product and then feeds back this information quickly to the other functions.

To see what this means in practice, let's jump ahead three months and suppose that the CRM component of SAP's ERP software reports that actual sales are 20 percent below target. Further, the software has reasoned that the problem is due to the fact that the product lacks one crucial feature that customers want. The product is a smart phone, for example, and customers must have a built-in digital camera. Sales decides this issue deserves major priority and alerts managers in all the other functions about the problem. Now managers can begin to make decisions about how to manage this unexpected situation.

Engineers in product development, for example, use their expert system to work out how much it would cost, and how long it would take, to modify the product so that it includes the missing feature, the digital camera, that customers require. Managers in other functions watch the engineers' progress through the ERP system and can make suggestions for improvement. In the meantime, manufacturing managers know about the slow sales and have already cut back on production to avoid a buildup of the unsold product in the company's warehouse. They are also planning how to phase out this product and introduce the next version, with the digital camera, to keep costs as low as possible. Similarly, materials management managers are contacting digital-camera makers to find out how much such a camera will cost and when it can be supplied. In the meantime, marketing managers are researching how they came to miss this crucial product feature and are developing new sales forecasts to estimate demand for the modified product. They announce a revised sales forecast of 75,000 units of the modified product.

It takes the engineers one month to modify the product, but because SAP's IT has been providing information on the modified product to managers in manufacturing and materials management, the product hits the market only two months later. Within weeks, the sales function reports that early sales figures for the product have greatly exceeded even marketing's revised forecast. The company knows it has a winning product, and top managers give the go-ahead for manufacturing to build a second production line to double production of the product. All the other functions are expecting this decision; in fact, they have already been experimenting with their SAP modules to find out how long it will take them to respond to such a move. Each function provides the others with its latest information so that they can all adjust their functional activities accordingly.

All this quick and responsive action has been made possible because of the ERP system. Compare this situation to that of a company which relies only on a paper-based system, in which salespeople fill in paper sales reports. In such a company, it would take many times as long to find out about slow sales; it might take six months to a year for the company to find out that its sales projections were wrong. In the meantime, manufacturing, producing according to plan, will generate a huge stock of unsold products, which is a major source of operating costs. When the sales problem is finally uncovered, managers from the different functions will have to make frantic phone calls and hold face-to-face meetings to decide what to do. It might take another six months for the modified product to come into production, so more than one year of time, and huge potential profits, will have been lost.

In the ERP example, *efficiency* is promoted because a company has a better control of its manufacturing and materials management activities. *Quality* is increased because an increased flow of information between functions allows for a better-designed product. *Innovation* is speeded because a company can rapidly change its products to suit the changing needs of customers. Finally, *responsiveness to customers* improves because using its CRM software module, sales can better manage and react to customer's changing needs and provide better service and support to back up the sales of the product. ERP's ability to promote competitive advantage is the reason why managers in so many companies, large and small, are moving to find the best ERP "solution" for their particular companies.

E-Commerce Systems

e-commerce Trade that takes place between companies, and between companies and individual customers, using IT and the Internet.

business-to-business (B2B) commerce Trade that takes place between companies using IT and the Internet to link and coordinate the value chains of different companies.

B2B marketplace An Internet-based trading platform set up to connect buyers and sellers in an industry.

business-to-customer (B2C) commerce Trade that takes place between a company and individual customers using IT and the Internet.

E-commerce is trade that takes place between companies, and between companies and individual customers, using IT and the Internet. **Business-to-business (B2B) commerce** is trade that takes place *between* companies using IT and the Internet to link and coordinate the value chains of *different* companies. (See Figure 18.4.) The goal of B2B commerce is to increase the profitability of making and selling goods and services. B2B commerce increases profitability because it allows companies to reduce their operating costs or because it may improve product quality. A principal B2B software application is **B2B marketplaces,** Internet-based trading platforms that have been set up in many industries to connect buyers and sellers. To participate in a B2B marketplace, companies adopt a common software standard that allows them to search for and share information with one another. Then, companies can work together over time to find ways to reduce costs or improve quality.

Business-to-customer (B2C) commerce is trade that takes place *between* a company and individual customers using IT and the Internet. Using IT to connect directly to the customer means that companies can avoid having to use intermediaries, such as wholesalers and retailers, who capture a significant part of the profit being created in the value chain. The use of Web sites and online stores also allows companies to provide their customers with much more information about the value of their products. This often allows them to attract more customers and thus generate higher sales revenues. We discuss this important issue in depth in the chapters on marketing and sales.

In the last five years, computer software makers including Microsoft, Oracle, SAP, and IBM, have rushed to make their products work seamlessly with the

Figure 18.4 Types of E-Commerce

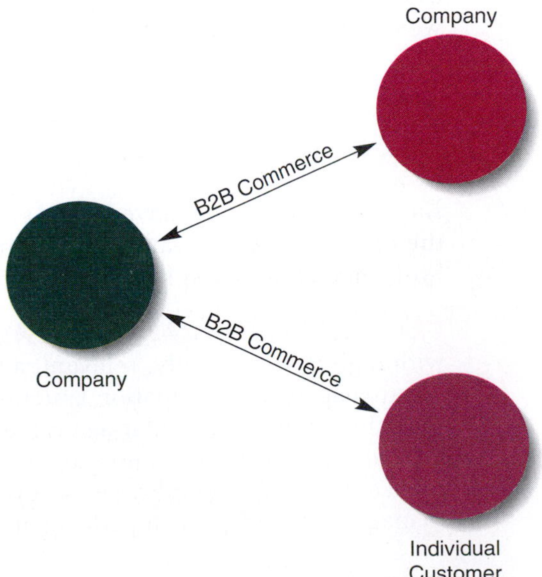

Internet to respond to global companies' growing demand for e-commerce software. Previously, their software had been configured to work only on a particular company's intranet. Now, they had to develop software that would network the computer systems of companies to their suppliers and customers.

Today, the challenge facing managers is to select the e-commerce software that allows the seamless exchange of information between companies anywhere in the world. The stakes are high; we saw in "A Manager's Challenge" how IBM's new thrust is toward on-demand software. SAP has also rushed to update its ERP modules to allow for transactions over the Internet. It calls its new B2B commerce software "mySAP," and today every one of its modules is Internet-compatible. Microsoft is promoting its .Net Internet software, which is compatible with all its other Windows software and is vigorously competing with IBM and SAP to raise its share of this growing software market.

In summary, by using computer-based MISs, managers have more control over a company's activities and operations and can work to improve its competitive advantage and profitability. Today, the IT function is becoming increasingly important because IT managers select which kind of hardware and software a company will use and also train employees to use it.

The Impact and Limitations of Information Systems and Technology

The advances in IT and management information systems described in this chapter are having important effects on managers and organizations. By improving the ability of managers to coordinate and control the activities of the organization and by helping managers make more effective decisions, modern IT has become a central component of any organization's structure. And evidence that IT can be a source of competitive advantage is growing; organizations that do not adopt leading-edge IT are likely to be at a competitive disadvantage. In this section we examine how the rapid advances in IT are affecting organizational structure and competitive advantage. We also examine problems associated with implementing management information systems effectively, as well as the limitations of MISs.

Information Systems and Organizational Structure

Rapid advances in IT have been associated with a "delayering" (flattening) of the organizational hierarchy and a move toward greater decentralization and horizontal information flows within organizations (see Figure 18.5).[41]

FLATTENING ORGANIZATIONS By electronically providing managers with high-quality, timely, relevant, and relatively complete information, modern management information systems have reduced the need for tall management hierarchies. Consider again the computer-based operations information system that T. J. Rodgers uses at Cypress Semiconductor to review the performance of his 1,500 employees. Ten years ago, Rodgers might have needed 100 managers to conduct such performance reviews; now he can do them himself in

Figure 18.5
How Computer-Based Information Systems Affect the Organizational Hierarchy

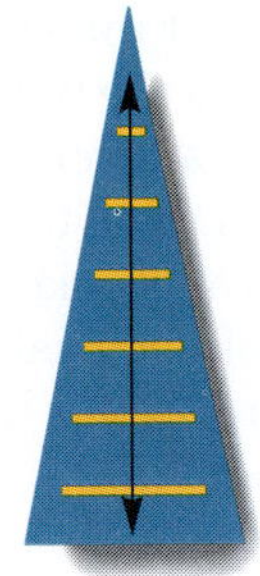

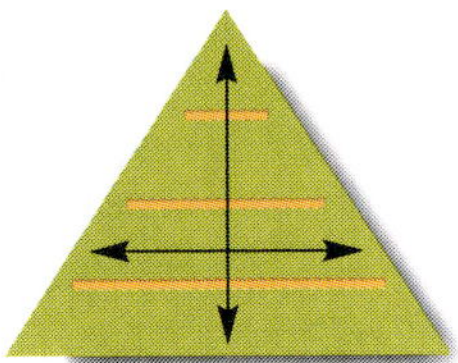

Before

Tall structure
primarily up-down
communication

After

Flat structure
both up-down
and lateral
communication

four hours a week. Modern information systems have reduced the need for a hierarchy to function as a means of controlling the activities of the organization. In addition, they have reduced the need for a management hierarchy to coordinate organizational activities.

HORIZONTAL INFORMATION FLOWS Fired by the growth of four-tier mainframe-server-client-PDA computing architecture (see Figure 18.2), expansion of organizationwide computer networks has been rapid in recent years. Email systems, the development of software programs for sharing documents electronically, and the development of intranets (see Chapter 15) have accelerated this trend. An important consequence has been the increase of horizontal information flows within organizations, something illustrated well by the experiences of Tel Co. and Soft Co.

Information Technology Byte

Information Flows at Tel Co. and Soft Co.

Despite being part of a high-tech company, managers at Tel Co. were slow to adopt an internal electronic mail system (email) to facilitate communication throughout the company. Soft Co., by contrast, is a software company in which managers virtually "live online" and most communication between them takes place by means of email. Commenting on how the two companies differ, a manager who moved from Tel Co. to Soft Co. said:

At Tel Co. I would take two boxes of memos and company reports home with me each weekend to read. Then I had to go through all this stuff, most of which was irrelevant to my job, to find those pieces of paper that mattered to me. It was very time-consuming, very unproductive. At Soft Co. there is no paper to take home; most communication takes place via the company's email system. I use a software agent to scan all my incoming email and prioritize it [a software agent is a computer program that can perform certain tasks–such as sorting through and prioritizing incoming email]. This saves a massive amount of time. The system alerts me instantly to email that is relevant to my job.[42]

This manager also noted that the use of an email system led to other communication differences between the two companies. At Tel Co. communication is primarily vertical; middle managers send information up the organizational hierarchy, and top managers send their responses back down. At Soft Co., however, communication between managers at different levels has become far less structured, and because of the email system there is much less emphasis on formal channels of communication. Email allows managers at any level to communicate easily with one another, so managers at Soft Co. communicate directly with whomever they need to contact to get the job done. Also, email has resulted in much more cross-functional, horizontal communication because it is so easy for managers in different functions to communicate.

The observations of this manager about communication flows at Tel Co. and Soft Co. were confirmed in a study undertaken by Alta Analytics, a management consulting company.[43] Figure 18.6 shows maps of the communication flows between managers based in different departments at Tel Co. and Soft Co. The boxes in these two maps are employees grouped by function. To make these maps, Alta asked employees to name every manager with whom they had communication in any form–phone, meeting, memo, email–in the past week. If two people agreed that they had three or more important contacts, the mapmakers drew a line between their boxes, indicating a significant link.

The differences between the two companies are immediately apparent. At Tel Co., the general manager communicated only with four senior functional managers, all of whom had a direct reporting relationship with him; there were hardly any links between the marketing and production departments; and a handful of functional managers accounted for most of the interfunctional communication. At Soft Co., there was a much richer flow of communication between managers in the different functions, as indicated by the number of lines connecting the different boxes. Clearly, boundaries between

Figure 18.6
Communication Flows at Tel Co. and Soft Co.

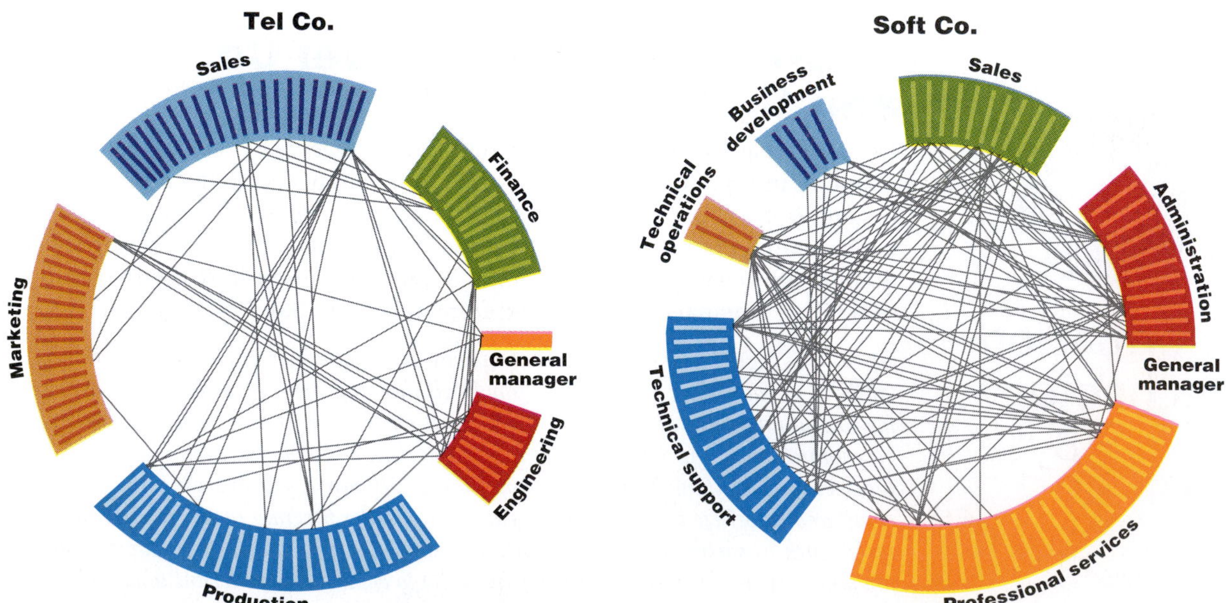

Source: T. A. Stewart, "Managing in a Wired Company," *Fortune,* July 11, 1994, 54. © 1994 Time, Inc. Reprinted with permission. NETMAP® is a registered trademark for the NETMAP Software Systems, Alta Analytics, Inc., Westerville, OH.

functions mean little at Soft Co., as do differences in rank. Almost everybody talks to everybody else because of Soft Co.'s email system. At Soft Co. the development of organizationwide computer networks has broken down the barriers that have traditionally separated functional departments and divisions and the result has been improved performance.

IT and Competitive Advantage

State-of-the-art IT can improve the competitiveness of an organization. Indeed, the search for competitive advantage is driving much of the rapid development and adoption of IT systems. By improving the decision-making capability of managers, for example, management information systems like executive support systems and decision support systems should help an organization enhance its competitive position. Similarly, by reducing the need for hierarchy, modern information systems can directly increase an organization's efficiency. One reason for an increase in efficiency is that the use of advanced information systems can reduce the number of employees required to perform organizational activities. At one time, for example, 13 layers of management separated Eastman Kodak's general manager of manufacturing and factory workers. With information systems, now the number of layers is four. Similarly, Intel found that by increasing the sophistication of its information systems, it could cut the number of hierarchical layers in the organization from 10 to 5.[44]

William Davidow and Michael Malone, coauthors of *The Virtual Corporation*, coined the term *virtual products* to describe the way information systems can improve an organization's responsiveness to customers. They argue that information systems and technology are allowing companies to customize their product offerings without incurring any extra cost penalty, and indeed in ways that may reduce costs.

In spite of the popularity of computerized management information systems, sometimes face-to-face communication is still the best way to sort through the "thick information," or information rich in meaning and significance. According to Mintzberg, such information must be dug out, on site, by people closely involved in the events they wish to influence.

Limitations of IT

For all of their usefulness, IT in general and management information systems in particular have some limitations. A serious potential problem is that in all of the enthusiasm for management information systems, electronic communication by means of a computer network, and the like, a vital *human* element of communication might be lost. Some kinds of information cannot be aggregated and summarized on an MIS report. Henry Mintzberg noted that *thick information* is often required to coordinate and control an enterprise and to make informed decisions; Mintzberg means information rich in meaning and significance, far beyond that which can be quantified and aggregated.[45] According to Mintzberg, such information must be dug out, on-site, by people closely involved in the events they wish to influence.

The importance of thick information is a strong argument in favor of using electronic communication to support face-to-face communication, not to replace it. For example, it would be wrong to make a judgment about an individual's performance merely by "reading the numbers" provided by an MIS. Instead, the numbers should be used to alert managers to individuals who may have a performance problem. The nature of this performance problem should then be explored in a face-to-face meeting, during which thick information can be gathered. As a top Boeing manager noted,

In our company, the use of e-mail and videoconferencing has not reduced the need to visit people at other sites; it has increased it. E-mail has facilitated the establishment of communications channels between people who previously would not communicate, which is good, but direct visits are still required to cement any working relationships that evolve out of these electronic meetings."[46]

At Soft Co., discussed earlier, managers were heard to complain that one drawback of their internal email system is that people spend a lot of time behind closed doors looking at computer screens and communicating electronically and very little time interacting directly with other managers.[47] When this is the case in an organization, management decisions may suffer because of a lack of thick information.

Another limitation of IT in organizations is that despite its many advantages there are still technological problems to be overcome.[48] One of these is the lack of consistent technological standards throughout the divisions or functions of an organization if a company uses different kinds of software systems, made by different IT companies, that impede communication and decision making. For example, different manufacturers of computer and communication equipment use different technical standards. For example, an IBM mainframe may be manufactured according to technical standards different from those of a Sun or Compaq server or an Apple personal computer. These different standards make it difficult to integrate various machines into a seamless computer network, and machines designed according to different standards may find it difficult to "talk" to one another. One reason for the growing popularity of SAP's ERP is that it solves these problems because it provides a common IT standard throughout a company.

Managers can take several steps to make it easier and quicker to implement an MIS. First, they have to develop a list of the organization's principal goals and then decide on the major types of information they need to collect to measure how well they are achieving those goals. Second, while making this analysis, managers should audit their current MISs to determine the degree to which the information they are currently collecting is accurate, reliable, timely, and relevant. Third, managers need to investigate what other sources of information might be available to measure and improve efficiency, quality, innovation, and responsiveness to customers. For example, are organizational members using state-of-the-art IT like wireless email, computer-assisted design, and four-tier designs? It is useful to benchmark competitors to determine what kinds of systems they are using.

Fourth, when this analysis is complete, managers need to build support for the introduction of an advanced MIS and convince employees that the system will help raise job and organizational performance. Fifth, managers should create formal training programs, with appropriate backup support, to help train employees to use the new information system and technology, making sure that the system is as user-friendly as possible. Sixth, managers should emphasize that the MIS is not a substitute for face-to-face communication and that employees at all levels should be involved in a continuing discussion about how best to take advantage of ongoing developments in IT to create a competitive advantage.

Summary and Review

INFORMATION AND THE MANAGER'S JOB Computer-based information systems are central to the operation of most organizations. By providing managers with high-quality, timely, relevant, and relatively complete information, properly implemented information systems can improve managers' ability to coordinate and control the operations of an organization and to make effective decisions. Moreover, information systems can help the organization to attain a competitive advantage through their beneficial impact on productivity, quality, innovation, and responsiveness to customers. Thus, modern information systems are an indispensable management tool.

THE IT REVOLUTION Over the last 30 years there have been rapid advances in the power, and rapid declines in the cost, of IT. Falling prices, wireless communication, computer networks, and software developments have all radically improved the power and efficacy of computer-based information systems.

TYPES OF MANAGEMENT INFORMATION SYSTEMS Traditionally managers used the organizational hierarchy as the main system for gathering the information they needed to coordinate and control the organization and to make effective decisions. Today, managers use six main types of computer-based information systems. Listed in ascending order of sophistication, they are transaction-processing systems, operations information systems, decision support systems, expert systems, enterprise resource planning systems, and e-commerce systems.

THE IMPACT AND LIMITATIONS OF INFORMATION SYSTEMS AND TECHNOLOGY Modern information systems and technology have changed organizational structure by making it flatter and by encouraging more cross-functional communication. In turn, this has helped organizations achieve a competitive advantage.

Management in Action

Topics for Discussion and Action

Discussion

1. To be useful, information must be of high quality, be timely, be relevant, and be as complete as possible. Why does a tall management hierarchy, when used as a management information system, have negative effects on these desirable attributes?
2. What is the relationship between IT and competitive advantage?
3. Because of the growth of high-powered low-cost wireless communications and IT such as videoconferencing, many managers soon may not need to come into the office to do their jobs. They will be able to work at home. What are the pros and cons of such an arrangement?
4. Many companies have reported that it is difficult to implement advanced management information systems such as ERP systems. Why do you think this is so? How might the roadblocks to implementation be removed?
5. How can IT help in the new product development process?
6. Why is face-to-face communication between managers still important in an organization?

Action

7. Ask a manager to describe the main kinds of IT that he or she uses on a routine basis at work.

Building Management Skills

Analyzing Management Information Systems

Pick an organization about which you have some direct knowledge. It may be an organization that you worked for in the past or are in contact with now (such as the college or school that you attend). For this organization, do the following:

1. Describe the management information systems that are used to coordinate and control organizational activities and to help make decisions.
2. Do you think that the organization's existing MISs provide managers with high-quality, timely, relevant, and relatively complete information? Why or why not?
3. How might advanced IT be used to improve the competitive position of this organization? In particular, try to identify the impact that a new MIS might have on the organization's efficiency, quality, innovation, and responsiveness to customers.

Managing Ethically

The use of management information systems, such as ERPs, often gives employees access to confidential information from all functions and levels of an organization. Employees have access to important information about the company's products that is of great value to competitors. As a result, many companies monitor employees use of the intranet and Internet to prevent an employee from acting unethically, for example, by selling this information to competitors. On the other hand, with access to this information employees might discover that their company has been engaging in unethical or even illegal practices.

Questions

1. Ethically speaking, how far should a company go to protect its proprietary information given that it needs to also protect the privacy of its employees? What steps can it take?
2. When is it ethical for employees to give information about a company's unethical/illegal practices to a third party such as a newspaper or government agency?

Small Group Breakout Exercise

Using New Management Information Systems

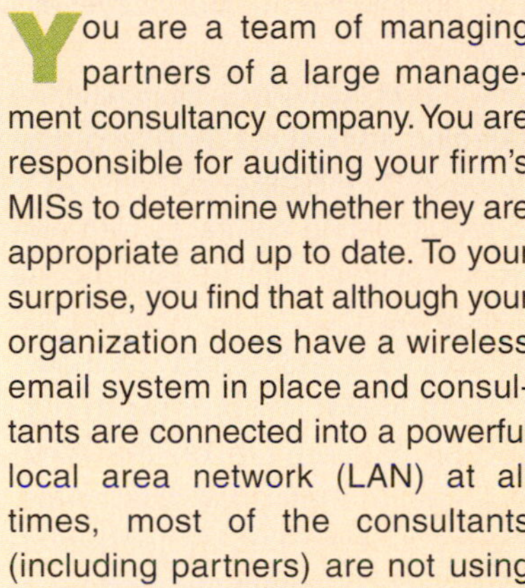

Form groups of three or four people, and appoint one member as the spokesperson who will communicate your findings to the whole class when called on by the instructor. Then discuss the following scenario.

You are a team of managing partners of a large management consultancy company. You are responsible for auditing your firm's MISs to determine whether they are appropriate and up to date. To your surprise, you find that although your organization does have a wireless email system in place and consultants are connected into a powerful local area network (LAN) at all times, most of the consultants (including partners) are not using this technology. It seems that most important decision making still takes place through the organizational hierarchy.

Given this situation, you are concerned that your organization is not exploiting the opportunities offered by new IT to obtain a competitive advantage. You have discussed this issue and are meeting to develop an action plan to get consultants to appreciate the need to learn and use the new IT.

1. What advantages can you tell consultants they will obtain when they use the new IT?
2. What problems do you think you may encounter in convincing consultants to use the new IT?
3. What kind of steps might you take to motivate consultants to learn to use the new technology?

Exploring the World Wide Web

Go to IBM's website (www.ibm.com), and under the "services" tab click "On Demand." Read about the latest developments in IBM's on-demand business and look at the case study on Sak's Fifth Avenue. Then answer the following questions:

1. What are the main ways in which IBM's on-demand IT can help companies?
2. In what ways did IBM's IT help Sak's improve its performance? (If the Sak's case study is no longer available, pick another.)

Be the Manager

You are one of the managers of a small specialty furniture maker of custom-made tables, chairs, and cabinets. You've been charged with finding ways to use IT and the Internet to identify new business opportunities that can improve your company's competitive advantage, for example, ways to reduce costs or attract customers.

Questions

1. What are the various forces in a specialty furniture maker's task environment that have the most effect on its performance.
2. What kinds of IT or MISs can be used to help the company better manage these forces?
3. In what ways can the Internet be used to help this organization improve its competitive position?

Additional Activities on the Build Your Management Skills DVD

- **Test Your Knowledge:** Technological Change
- **Manager's Hot Seat:** Privacy: Burned by the Firewall?

BusinessWeek Case in the News

America Online Gets Clicking

Last year, the revival that lifted the rest of the online industry left America Online Inc. in the dust. Even as a rebound in ads sent 2003 profits at rival Yahoo! Inc. spiking 123 percent, AOL's subscribers jumped ship in droves for low-cost dial-up competitors or broadband providers. Ad revenue sank 40 percent, to $787 million, and federal investigators continued to probe AOL's past ad deals for accounting irregularities. As operating earnings before depreciation and amortization fell 2 percent, to $1.5 billion, Wall Street started betting that Time Warner Inc. would ditch AOL the first chance it got.

But AOL's date with the dump has been postponed, if not canceled. On June 24, Time Warner paid $435 million in cash to buy Advertising.com Inc., a leading online-ad-placement company that should help boost AOL's ad revenue. "Our emphasis is on building up the AOL business," says Time Warner CEO Richard D. Parsons.

Chalk up one for AOL CEO Jonathan F. Miller. After struggling to regain focus after its rocky 2001 merger with Time Warner, AOL is finding its footing again with Miller's new strategy: providing a menu of online services ranging from full-blown broadband service to á là carte online music subscriptions to cheap, no-frills dial-up access. "We'd gotten behind in the market," he says. "We're putting in a business model appropriate to where the world is going."

Miller hasn't yet proven that the world will order from his menu, but a rebound in AOL's advertising and global businesses will buy him time. Combined with cost cuts, that should produce the double-digit profit growth this year that Time Warner expects, says Richard Greenfield, media analyst at Fulcrum Global Partners LLC. Still, the heart of Miller's strategy—persuading customers who have signed up with another broadband provider to also buy AOL's broadband services—is a gamble. "They haven't turned the battleship around yet," says David Card, online-media analyst at Jupiter Research.

In the new world, Miller is counting on profit gains, not revenue growth, to float AOL's boat. The company's old $23.90-a-month dial-up service made for fat revenues but slimmer profits, thanks to the cost of providing network connections. New, lower-priced broadband services will produce less revenue but higher margins since AOL won't have to pay network access fees. It expects earnings from ads, broadband and premium services, and global sales to rise 30 percent to 50 percent annually over the next few years.

Not Just Eyeballs

An ad revival is starting to help. For the first time since 2001, ad revenue should rise 11 percent in 2004, to $873 million, says Deutsche Bank (DB). Advertising.com should send them up even more. It specializes in a new results-driven approach: charging advertisers for the number of online transactions generated by ads, not just the number of eyeballs reached.

Meanwhile, Miller is stanching the bleeding from AOL's dwindling dial-up base. To preserve margins, AOL is renegotiating contracts with network providers such as MCI Inc. As dial-up members leave, AOL can cut network costs associated with them.

That leaves Miller freer to pursue his "superstore on the Web" strategy. To match low-cost rivals, there's a new $9.95-a-month dial-up Netscape Communications service. For members considering a move to broadband rivals, there's a $14.95-a-month AOL for Broadband service. How will he persuade consumers to buy AOL's package of content and services if they use someone else's pipe to get online? By offering bite-size premium services such as $8.95-a-month online music subscriptions. And AOL is offering free samples of content from Time Warner's video-on-demand and Road Runner broadband units. The plan shows signs of working. In the first quarter, 600,000 people signed up for the broadband services, for a total of 3.5 million.

AOL remains a long way from a sustained revival. But with healthier ad sales, slimmer costs, and a rosier global outlook, Miller—and Time Warner—can afford to throw the dice for now.

Questions

1. What are Miller's new strategies for AOL?
2. How is he changing AOL to achieve them?

Source: Catherine Yang, Tom Lowry, and Ben Elgin, "America Online Gets Clicking." Reprinted from the July 12, 2004, issue of *BusinessWeek* by special permission.

BusinessWeek Case in the News

Netflix: Moving into Slo-Mo?

For Netflix Inc., the online movie-rental service, its second-quarter earnings report was as ugly as *Ishtan's* debut. On July 15, the company reported net income that was lighter than Wall Street had expected. Worse, it said that marketing expenses were headed north because online advertising was getting pricier—this just months after Netflix assured investors those expenses wouldn't rise this year. In the next two trading days, the shares plunged 37 percent, to $20.17. [The marketing cost increase] was a risk that was out there and was denied by the company," says David A. Rocker, managing partner at Rocker Partners LP, which had a short position in the stock.

The biggest challenge is just arriving. Video-rental giant Blockbuster Inc. just unveiled a trial DVD-by-mail service that costs only $20 a month—a third less than analysts expected. If Blockbuster sticks with that figure, Netflix, which boosted its price from $20 to $22 in June, may have to roll back its increase. "That would have pretty broad implications," says analyst Jason Avilio of First Albany Capital Inc. CEO Reed Hastings vows to hold steady at $22, which Avilio estimates will mean net income of $70 million on $810 million in revenues next year. But the analyst ran estimates for the lower rate at *BusinessWeek's* request. The result: Profits would fall to $38 million in 2005.

One week of bad news is hardly the end of Netflix. It's still by far the leading online DVD-rental service, with 2.1 million subscribers and 80 percent customer growth. The company still predicts it will reach 5 million subscribers by 2006. Amid the bad news, Netflix actually raised its 2004 net income target, to between $12.6 million and $22.1 million. "We're completely on track," says Hastings.

That's not all bravado. Analysts estimate that Netflix has five times as many DVD-by-mail subscribers as Wal-Mart Stores Inc. and an even greater lead on Blockbuster. Netflix has proprietary software that uses factors such as customer's past rentals to help subscribers find movies they like. About half its customers rate movies. And its 24 distribution centers let it ship to 80 percent of American addresses overnight by U.S. mail, compared with two or three days for rivals. Says analyst Derek Brown of Pacific Growth Equities: "Competition isn't affecting the company's ability to grow."

Combine strong growth with weaker-than-expected financials, and chances rise that Netflix will be acquired. Possible buyers include online players such as Amazon.com, and telcos like Verizon Communications. Amazon sells DVDs and, like Netflix, gets a competitive edge from customer ratings. Verizon, which is battling cable-TV companies, could use Netflix to enter the video-on-demand business. Both companies declined comment.

If Netflix doesn't get scooped up, video-on-demand looms as a long-term threat. Cable companies say film buffs will soon have little reason to trek to the video store, or the mailbox. "You can order a movie from your sofa and not be premeditated about what you want," says David Pugliese, vice-president for marketing at Cox Communications Inc. Consultant PricewaterhouseCoopers figures 20 million U.S. households will use VOD in 2007, up from 6 million last year.

Netflix is scrambling to position itself for the competition ahead. Hastings says the company will begin delivering movies over the Net next year. Still, Netflix figures it has time before video-on-demand presents serious competition. "If Netflix isn't a major player when VOD arrives, we've screwed up," says Jay C. Hoag, a Netflix director. . . .

Questions

1. How have changes in Netflix's task environment been affecting the company?
2. How are its managers responding to these changes?

Source: Timothy J. Mullaney and Tom Lowry, "Netflix: Moving into Slo-Mo?" Reprinted from the August 2, 2004, issue of *BusinessWeek* by special permission.

CHAPTER

19 Promoting Innovation, Product Development, and Entrepreneurship

Learning Objectives

After studying this chapter, you should be able to:

- Explain managers' role in facilitating product development.
- Identify the factors that shorten the product life cycle and explain why reducing product development time increases the level of industry competition.
- Identify the goals of product development and explain the relationships among them.
- Explain the principles of product development and describe the way in which managers can encourage and promote innovation.
- Describe how managers can encourage and promote entrepreneurship to help create a learning organization.

A Manager's Challenge

How Google Encourages Innovation and Product Development

How do you build an innovative company? The history of Google, the Internet search engine company, began in 1995 when two Stanford graduate computer science students, Sergey Brin and Larry Page, decided to collaborate to develop a new kind of search engine technology. They understood the limitations of existing search engines, and by 1998 they had developed a superior engine that they felt was ready to go online. They raised $1 million from family, friends, and risk-taking "angel" investors to buy the hardware necessary to connect Google to the Internet.

Google co-founders Sergey Brin, left, and Larry Page at company headquarters in Mountain View, California, January 2004.

At first, Google answered 10,000 inquiries a day, but in a few months it was answering 500,000. By fall 1999, it was handling 3 million; by fall 2000, 60 million; and in spring 2001, 100 million per day. In the 2000s Google has become the leading search engine; it is one of the top-five most used Internet companies, and rivals like Yahoo and Microsoft are working hard to catch up and beat Google at its own game.

Google's explosive growth is largely due to the culture of entrepreneurship and innovation its founders cultivated from the start. Although by 2004 Google had grown to 1,900 employees worldwide, its founders claim that Google still maintains a small-company feel because its culture empowers its employees, who are called staffers or "Googlers," to create the best software possible. Brin and Page created Google's entrepreneurial culture in several ways.

From the beginning, lacking space and seeking to keep operating costs low, Google staffers worked in "high-density clusters." Three or four employees, each equipped with a high-powered Linux workstation, shared a desk, couch, and chairs that were large rubber balls, working together to improve the company's technology. Even when Google moved into more spacious surroundings at its "Googleplex" headquarters building, staffers continued to work in shared spaces. Google designed the building so that staffers are constantly meeting one another in its funky lobby; in its Google Café, where everyone eats together; in its state-of-the-art recreational facilities; and in its "snack rooms," equipped with bins packed with cereals, gummi bears, yogurt, carrots, and make-your-own cappuccino. Google also created many social gatherings of employees, such as a TGIF open meeting and a twice-weekly outdoor roller hockey game where staffers are encouraged to bring down the founders.[1]

All this attention to creating what might be the "grooviest" company headquarters in the world did not come about by chance. Brin and Page knew that Google's most important strength would be its ability to attract the best software engineers in the world and then motivate them to perform well. Common offices, lobbies, cafés, and so on, bring staffers into close contact with one another, develop collegiality, and encourage them to share their new ideas with their colleagues and to constantly improve Google's search engine technology and find new ways to expand the company. The freedom Google gives its staffers to pursue new ideas is a clear indication of its founders' desire to empower them to be innovative and to look off the beaten path for new ideas. Finally, recognizing that staffers who innovate important new software applications should be rewarded for their achievements, Google's founders give them stock in the company, effectively making staffers its owners as well.

Their focus on entrepreneurship did not blind Brin and Page to the need to build a viable competitive strategy so that Google could compete effectively in the cutthroat search engine market. They recognized, however, that they lacked business experience; they had never had to craft strategies to compete with giants like Microsoft and Yahoo. Moreover, they also had never been responsible for building a strong set of functions and designing organizational structure. So they set about recruiting a team of talented and experienced top managers to help them manage their company. In fact, they decided to give control of their company to Eric Schmidt, who came from Novell, where he had been in charge of strategic planning, management, and technology development.

Brin and Page's entrepreneurial ability, and their understanding that successful product development requires building a strong organizational architecture, has paid off. In August 2004, Google went public, and its shares, which were sold at $85 a share, were worth over $100 each by the end of the first day of trading. This made Brin and Page's stake in the company worth more that $2 billion each in 2004—clearly it can pay to be an entrepreneur.

Overview

Google prospers because of the entrepreneurial genius of its founders, their ability to create a culture that encourages staffers to be innovative, and their willingness to delegate authority for product development to managers and staffers. Managing innovation is an increasingly important aspect of a manager's job in an era of dramatic changes in advanced information technology. Promoting successful new product development is difficult and challenging, and some product development efforts are much more successful than others. Google is performing at a high level, while thousands of other dot-coms, including many search engine companies such as Magellan and Openfind, have gone out of business.

In this chapter we examine the actions managers can take to improve the ability of their organizations to be innovative by developing new goods and services, a main building block of competitive advantage. We discuss the relationship between technological change, product innovation, and competition. We examine the goals of product development efforts. We explain several principles for structuring an organization's product development effort to attain these goals, and we examine the nature of entrepreneurship and discuss steps managers can take to promote entrepreneurship inside organizations. By the end of this chapter, you will understand why, in today's rapidly changing environment, managers' ability to effectively manage innovation, product development, and entrepreneurship is often the key to an organization's success and even survival.

Innovation, Technological Change, and Competition

As discussed in Chapter 6, *technology* comprises the skills, know-how, experience, body of scientific knowledge, tools, machines, computers, and equipment used in the design, production, and distribution of goods and services. Technology is involved in all organizational activities, and its rapid change makes technological change a significant factor in almost every organizational innovation.[2]

The two main types of technological change are quantum and incremental. **Quantum technological change** is a fundamental shift in technology that results in the innovation of new kinds of goods and services. Two examples are the development of the Internet, which has revolutionized the computer industry, and the development of genetic engineering (biotechnology), which is promising to revolutionize the treatment of illness with the development of genetically engineered medicines. McDonald's development of the principles behind the provision of fast food also qualifies as a quantum technological change.

quantum technological change A fundamental shift in technology that results in the innovation of new kinds of goods and services.

Incremental technological change is change that refines existing technology and leads to gradual improvements or refinements in products over time. Since 1971, for example, Intel has made a series of incremental improvements to its original 4004 microprocessor, leading to the introduction of its 8008, 8086, 286, 386, and 486; its first Pentium chip in 1993; the Pentium 4 in 2000; the Itanium in 2001; and its latest, the Pentium 4 with HT technology in 2004.[3] Similarly, Google's staffers have made thousands of incremental improvements to the company's search engine itself, such as changes that have enhanced the Google directory and given the engine the ability to search via wireless devices. Staffers also led Google to thinking globally, and soon Google had 10 language versions of its engine up and running for users who search in their native tongues.

incremental technological change Change that refines existing technology and leads to gradual improvements or refinements in products over time.

Products that result from quantum technological changes are called **quantum product innovations** and are relatively rare. Managers in most organizations spend most of their time managing products that result from incremental technological changes; such products are called **incremental product innovations.** For example, every time Dell or HP puts a new, faster Intel chip into a PC, or Google improves its search engine's capability, the company is making incremental product innovations. Similarly, every time engineers in an automobile company redesign a car model, and every time McDonald's managers try to improve the flavor and texture of burgers and fries, they are engaged in product development efforts designed to lead to incremental product innovations. The fact that incremental change is less dramatic than quantum change does not imply that incremental product innovations are unimportant. In fact, as discussed below, it is often managers' ability to successfully manage incremental product development that results in success or failure in an industry.

quantum product innovations Products that result from quantum technological changes.

incremental product innovations Products that result from incremental technological changes.

The Effects of Technological Change

The consequences of quantum and incremental technological change are all around us. Microprocessors, personal computers, wireless smart phones, personal digital assistants, word-processing software, computer networks, digital cameras and camcorders, DVD players, genetically engineered medicines, fast food, online information services, superstores, and mass travel either did not exist a generation ago or were considered to be exotic and expensive products. Now these products are commonplace, and they are being improved all the time. Many of the organizations whose managers helped develop and exploit new technologies have reaped enormous gains. They include many of the most successful and rapidly growing organizations of our times, such as Dell Computer (personal computers), Microsoft (computer software), Intel (microprocessors), Nokia (microprocessors, wireless phones, and pagers), Sony (camcorders and DVDs), Matsushita (videocassette recorders), Amgen (biotechnology), McDonald's (fast food), Wal-Mart (superstores), and Carnival Cruises (cruise ships).

While some organizations have benefited from technological change, others have seen their markets threatened and their futures placed in doubt. Traditional telephone companies the world over have seen their market dominance threatened by new companies offering Internet, broadband, and wireless telephone technology. For example, AT&T and other long-distance companies have been suffering from increased competition because of advances in telecommunications. In 2004 AT&T announced that it would exit the unprofitable residential phone business to focus its resources on business customers, an area where profit margins are much greater.[4] The decline of once-dominant consumer electronics companies such as RCA can be directly linked to their failure to innovate products such as VCRs and compact disc players.

Technological change offers both an opportunity and a threat.[5] On the one hand, it helps create new product opportunities that managers and their organizations can exploit. On the other hand, new and improved products can harm or even destroy the demand for older, established products. Wal-Mart has put thousands of small stores out of business, and McDonald's has caused thousands of small diners to close, in part because both organizations have been so innovative in their production systems that they can give customers lower-priced products. Thousands of small, specialized bookstores have closed in the United States in the last five years as a result of advances in IT that made online bookselling possible. Similarly, the development of the microprocessor by Intel has helped create a host of new product opportunities for entrepreneurs, who have created thousands of companies that provide innovative computer software and hardware. At the same time, microprocessors have destroyed demand for older products and ruined organizations whose managers did not see the changes in time and act on them. Managers of typewriter companies, for example, might have noticed that the new technology would compete directly with their products and moved to acquire or merge with new computer companies. Most did not, however, and once-famous companies like Smith Corona are out of business. The nature of entrepreneurship is discussed in detail later in this chapter.

Product Life Cycles and Product Development

When technology is changing, organizational survival requires that managers quickly adopt and apply new technologies to innovate products. Managers who do not do so soon find that they have no market for their products–and destroy their organizations. The rate of technological change in an industry–and particularly the length of the product life cycle–determines how important it is for managers to innovate.

product life cycle
Changes in demand for a product that occur from its introduction through its growth and maturity to its decline.

The **product life cycle** reflects the changes in demand for a product that occur over time.[6] Demand for most successful products passes through four stages: the embryonic stage, growth, maturity, and decline (see Figure 19.1). In the *embryonic stage* a product has yet to gain widespread acceptance; customers are unsure what the product has to offer, and demand for it is minimal. If a product does become accepted by customers (and many do not), demand takes off and the product enters its growth stage. In the *growth stage* many consumers are entering the market and buying the product for the first time; demand increases rapidly. This is the stage that personal digital assistants, such as smart phones, are currently in.

The growth stage ends and the *mature stage* begins when market demand peaks because most customers have already bought the product (there are relatively few first-time buyers left). At this stage demand is typically replacement demand. In the car market, for example, people who already have a car and are either trading up or replacing an old model buy most cars. Products such as wireless phones, PCs for home use, and online information services are also currently in this stage. The *decline stage* follows the mature stage if and when demand for a product falls. Falling demand often occurs because a product has become technologically

Figure 19.1
A Product Life Cycle

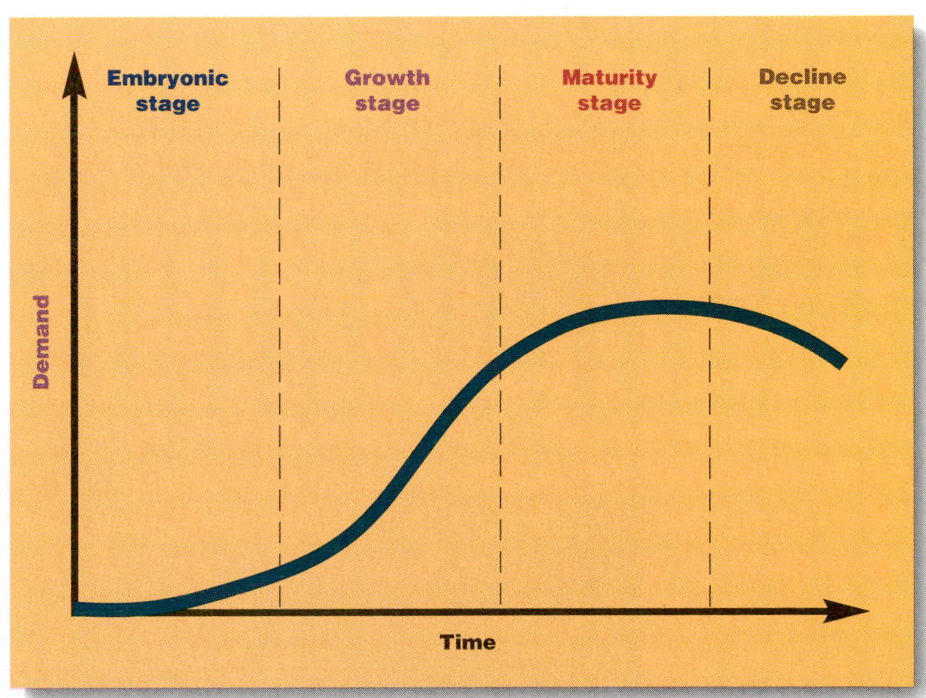

obsolescent and been superseded by a more advanced product. For example, demand for every generation of VCR, CD, or DVD falls as the products are superseded by newer, technically advanced models with more features. In 2004, leading electronic companies such as Sony and Philips announced that they had adopted a new standard for DVD players known as the "blue laser" standard because it uses a blue, rather than red, laser beam; the new technology means that DVDs will be able to hold six times as much content as they did in 2004.

THE RATE OF TECHNOLOGICAL CHANGE One of the main determinants of the length of a product's life cycle is the rate of technological change.[7] Figure 19.2 illustrates the relationship between the rate of technological change and the length of product life cycles. In some industries–such as personal computers, semiconductors, and disk drives–technological change is rapid and product life cycles are very short. For example, technological change is so rapid in the computer disk-drive industry that a disk-drive model becomes technologically obsolete about 12 months after introduction. The same is true in the personal computer industry, where product life cycles have shrunk from three years during the late 1980s to a few months today.

In other industries the product life cycle is somewhat longer. In the car industry, for example, the average product life cycle is about five years. Even so, the life cycle of a car is relatively short because fairly rapid technological change is producing a continual stream of incremental innovations in car design, such as the introduction of door and overhead airbags, advanced electronic microcontrollers, plastic body parts, and more fuel-efficient engines, as in Toyota's Prius, which is powered by gas and an electric motor. In contrast, in many basic industries where the pace of technological change is slower, product life cycles tend to be much longer. In steel or electricity, for example, change in product technology is very limited, and products such as steel girders and electric cable can remain in the mature stage indefinitely.

Figure 19.2
The Relationship Between Technological Change and Length of the Product Life Cycle

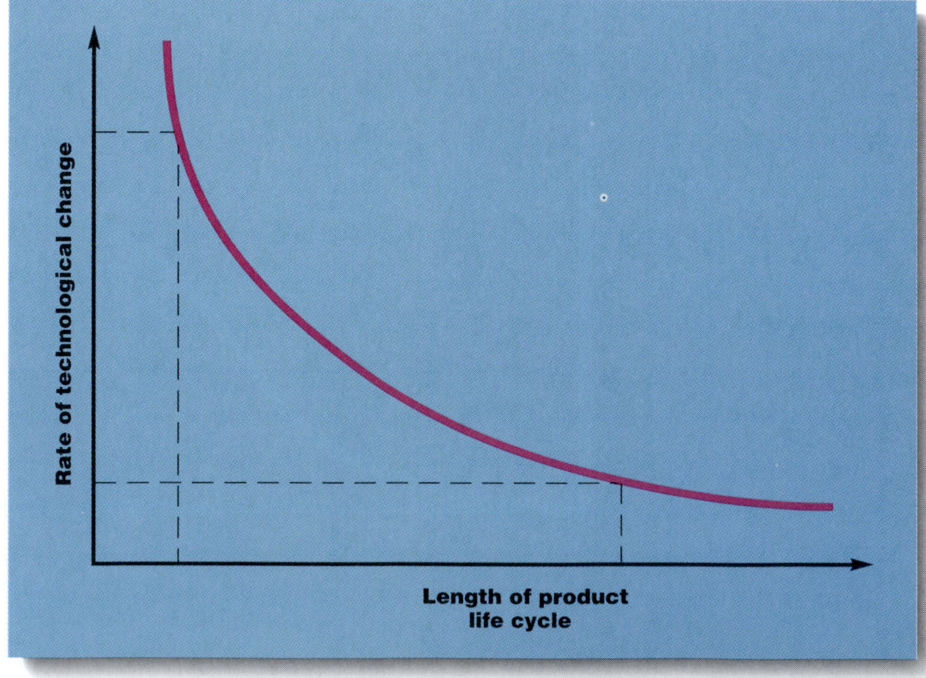

THE ROLE OF FADS AND FASHIONS Fads and fashion are important determinants of the length of product life cycles.[8] A five-year-old car design is likely to be technologically outmoded and to look out of date and thus lose its attractiveness to customers. Similarly, in the restaurant business, the demand for certain kinds of food changes rapidly. The Cajun or Southwest cuisine popular one year may be history the next as Caribbean fare becomes the food of choice. Fashion considerations are even more important in the high-fashion end of the clothing industry, where last season's clothing line is usually out of date by the next season and product life cycles may last no more than three months. Thus, fads and fashions are another reason why product life cycles may be short.

MANAGERIAL IMPLICATIONS Whether short product life cycles are caused by rapid technological change, changing fads and fashions, or some combination of the two, the message for managers is clear: The shorter the length of a product's life cycle, the more important it is to innovate products quickly and continuously. In industries where product life cycles are very short, managers must continually develop new products; otherwise, their organizations may go out of business. The PC company that cannot develop a new and improved product line every three to six months will soon find itself in trouble. The fashion house that fails to develop a new line of clothing for every season cannot succeed, nor can the small restaurant, club, or bar that is not alert to current fads and fashions. Car companies have a little more time, but even here it is vital that managers continually develop new and improved models every five years or so.

Increasingly, there is evidence that in a wide range of industries product life cycles are becoming more compressed as managers focus their organizations' resources on innovation to increase responsiveness to customers. To attract new customers, managers are trying to outdo each other by being the first to market with a product that incorporates a new technology or that plays to a new fashion trend.[9] In the automobile industry a typical five-year product life cycle is being reduced to three years as companies are increasingly competing with one another to attract new customers and encourage existing customers to upgrade and buy their newest products.[10] The way in which shrinking product life cycles for microprocessors have affected competition is considered in the following "Management Insight."

Management Insight

Shrinking Product Life Cycles Hurt Intel and Help AMD

Intel's microprocessors are the brains of 85 percent of the personal computers sold worldwide. Intel's dominance in this business can be traced back to IBM's 1980 decision to use Intel's 8086 microprocessor in its first PC. Since then Intel has produced a series of ever-more-powerful microprocessors, including the 286, the 386, the 486, and the Pentium chips.

In 1965, Gordon Moore, one of Intel's founders, made a famous observation, now called "Moore's law," in which he predicted that the number of transistors per integrated circuit would double every 18 months. Moore's law still holds true today thanks to the technology of companies like Intel, as indicated in Figure 19.3, which shows how the power of Intel's chips has continued to increase.[11]

Figure 19.3
Moore's Law: Intel's Evolving Microprocessors

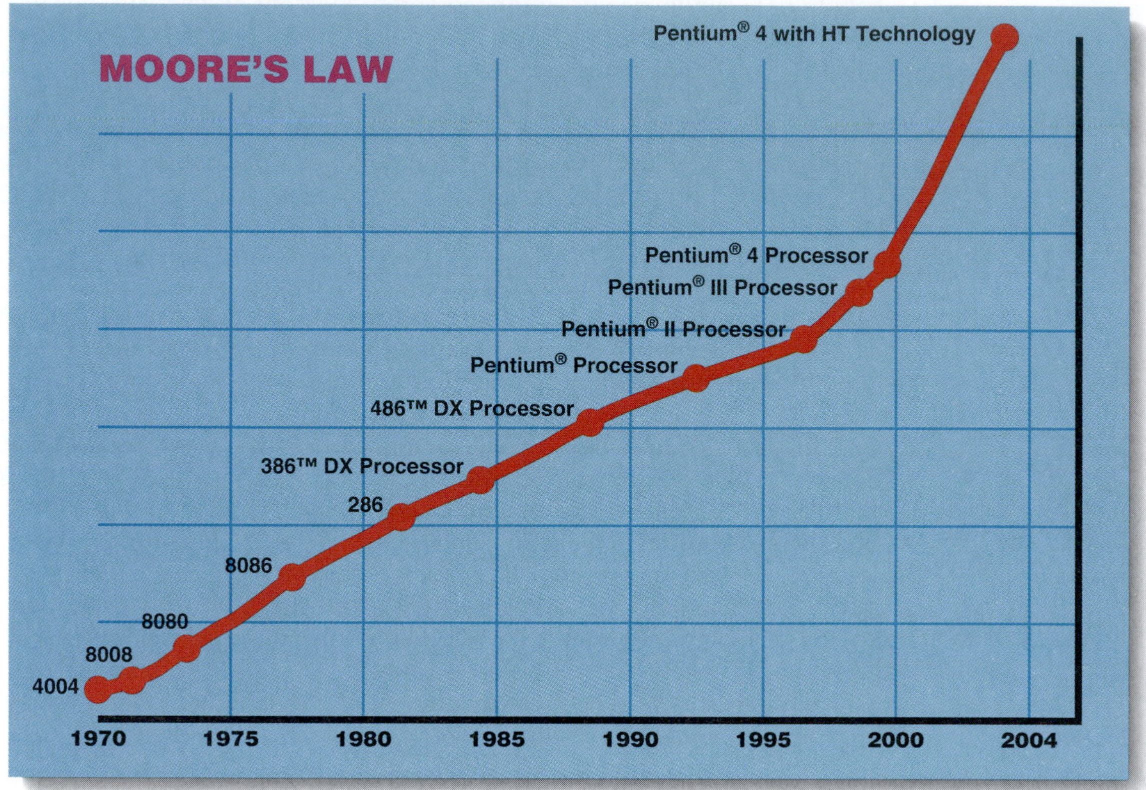

Source: www.intel.com/research/silicon/mooreslaw.htm. Reprinted by permission of Intel Corporation, copyright © Intel Corporation 2004.

Intel has not had things all its own way, however. In the 1990s, several companies began making clones of Intel chips that can manipulate computer software in the same way as an Intel chip. Once a clone is introduced, chip prices fall, and so do Intel's profit margins. One of these companies, AMD, has been having increasing success.

In the past, the source of Intel's competitive advantage over companies like AMD was that these companies couldn't start to design a clone of Intel's next microprocessor until they actually obtained it. So, for each new microprocessor, Intel normally had months or even years of lead time before AMD could develop a clone. The time it takes AMD to clone an Intel microprocessor has been shrinking, however. It took AMD five years to come up with a compatible processor after Intel released its 386 chip in 1985. Matching Intel's next generation, the 486, took three years. Intel began volume production of the Pentium in early 1993. AMD introduced its clone, the P5, just two years later. To stay ahead of the competition, Intel responded by increasing the speed of its own product development process–effectively shrinking the length of its own product life cycles. Intel released its successor to the Pentium, the Pentium Pro, in 1995–developing it in half the time it had taken to replace the 486 with the Pentium–to keep the pressure on its rivals.

The unthinkable happened in 2000 when AMD announced that it was introducing a new chip, the Athlon, that was faster than Intel's then-fastest Pentium, the Pentium 4. AMD had the lead for several months. However, in August 2001

Intel announced that it had broken the key 2-gigahertz milestone, effectively doubling the speed of its computer processors in only 18 months, once again confirming Moore's law.[12] Since then, Intel has further upgraded its Pentium 4 by adding "HT" technology; however, by 2004 it had become clear that AMD had gained an important competitive advantage over Intel because Intel had made a major product development error when designing its Pentium chips.

Intel believed that computer speed was what customers wanted, so it designed its Pentium chip to be very fast; however, fast chips are power-hungry and produce a lot of heat. In fact, by 2003 what customers wanted was a chip that could handle the needs of multimedia computers, which demanded better video and sound quality. The new Pentium 4 produced too much heat to use in advanced multimedia PCs, as well as in notebook PCs and other wireless devices. The Pentium chip was not designed with this market in mind at all, and Intel was forced to scramble to design new chips that could be used in these applications. This process is extremely complicated, and by 2004 Intel had fallen behind on its promise to provide a low-heat chip and announced that the chip would be delayed until 2005.[13] AMD, in the meantime, had no such problem and by 2004 had grabbed 50 percent of the PC chip market. Moore's law seems to be in jeopardy because the way customers use PCs is changing and speed is no longer the most important quality of a leading microprocessor

Product Development

In this section we examine the steps that managers can take to promote innovation and encourage product development. *Product development* is the process or procedure that managers use to bring new or improved kinds of goods and services to the market. First, we discuss the goals of product development; second, we describe some principles for guiding and speeding the product development process; and third, we discuss some problems associated with managing product development successfully.

Goals of Product Development

When managers and organizations face the choice of innovating products or going out of business, what product development goals should they pursue? Most researchers and consultants recommend that managers aim to reduce development time, maximize a product's fit with customer needs, maximize product quality, and maximize manufacturability–the efficiency and ease of production (see Figure 19.4).[14]

REDUCING DEVELOPMENT TIME Product development time begins with the initial conception of a product and ends with its introduction into the market. Reducing product development time has become a key competitive priority of managers because doing so offers three important advantages.[15] First, the management team that reduces development time may be the first to market a product that incorporates new, state-of-the-art features.[16] Those managers will be able to charge a high price for the product and earn high profits. Moreover, the earlier that managers are able to bring a new product to the market, relative to competitors, the longer is the period in which they will be able to charge high prices and obtain high profits.

Figure 19.4
Four Goals of New Product Development

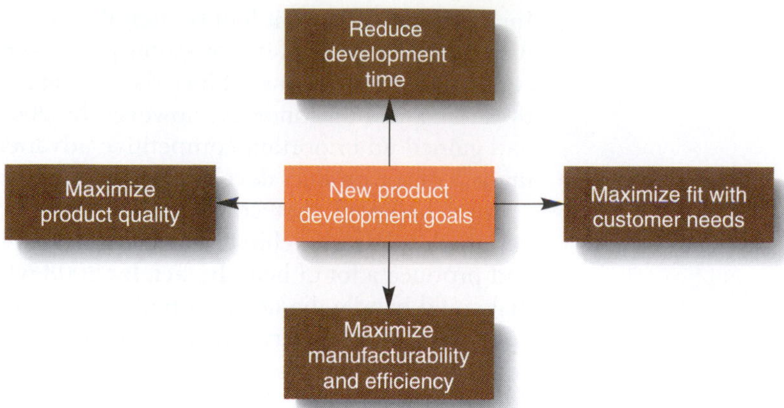

This advantage is the reason why Intel's managers make such huge efforts to reduce the time required to develop a new microprocessor. It is also why disk-drive manufacturers like Quantum Corporation put so much emphasis on shortening development time. Quantum's managers know that if they can get a new model disk drive to market before competitors such as Seagate Technologies, they can charge a higher price until competitors introduce their new models. In contrast, managers slow to introduce new products will have to charge lower prices to attract customers.

A second advantage of reducing product development time is that managers who can shorten the time can upgrade their products relatively quickly and incorporate state-of-the-art technology as soon as it becomes available. Managers with more advanced products are better able to serve customer needs, build brand loyalty, and stay one step ahead of slower competitors.

A third advantage of reducing development time is that managers find it easier to experiment with new products and replace them with a superior product if they fail to meet customer needs. For example, Toyota's first minivan was a disaster. Recognizing this, Toyota's engineers were able to redesign the minivan within 18 months–instead of the three to five years typical at other car companies. The result was the Previa, one of the most successful minivans ever made.

MAXIMIZING THE FIT WITH CUSTOMER NEEDS Many new products fail when they reach the marketplace because they were not designed with customer needs in mind.[17] Some, like Intel's Pentium chip, may succeed at first but fail when customers need change. Surveys of companies have found that the most common reason why new products flop when they get to the marketplace is that managers did not understand or care about the needs of their customers.[18] It follows that maximizing the fit between a product's attributes and customers' needs is one of the main elements of successful product development.

Strange as it may seem, one reason why many managers fail to investigate whether a new technology can actually satisfy a customer need is that managers are dazzled by the technology itself. Take Steve Jobs, one of the two cofounders of Apple Computer. After Jobs left Apple in 1985, he started a company called NeXT to manufacture high-powered personal computers. Captivated by the most advanced technology, Jobs made sure that the NeXT machines incorporated innovative features such as optical disk drives and hi-fidelity sound. However, the NeXT system failed to gain market share because customers simply did not want many of these features. The optical disk drives turned customers off because they made it difficult to switch work from a personal computer using a regular disk drive to a NeXT machine. Moreover, the microprocessor for the NeXT machine could not run Microsoft's popular software. NeXT failed because Jobs was so dazzled by leading-edge technology that he lost sight of customer needs.[19]

In 2003, Jobs was once again Apple's CEO (see Chapter 1), and he stunned analysts when he announced that Apple was entering the music business–opening an online music download store and introducing the new Apple iPod music player. This time Jobs did discover what customers wanted, and the iPod became a runaway success and has rejuvenated the company.

Management Insight

You Must Give Customers What They Want

While Apple's iPod is still a hot seller, many other products today are also being designed with customer needs at the forefront. This is especially true in the multifunction-device market, where customers, especially young, college-age customers, are seeking to get the best value for their money by buying the device that offers them the most functions in a small package. One of these is the "Sidekick," offered by T-Mobile, which combines a phone, e-mail, Web browsing, instant messaging, a digital camera, personal information management functions, *and* games. Manufactured by Danger Inc., it is growing in popularity because, at a price of $250, it offers value for money.[20]

Tony Hawk arrives at the T-Mobile Sidekick II Party at The Grove in Los Angeles, August 2004. Competition in the multifunctional device market is intense.

Other products proving popular are Web video cameras that offer animated video instant messaging beyond the still kind and handheld computers, such as PalmOne's Zire72, which doubles as a video camera and also plays MP3 files.[21] Nevetheless, customers are willing to abandon multifunctional devices if the price is right. Averatec Inc.'s C3500 convertible notebook, whose display swivels back on itself for longhand writing, is popular because it starts at around $1,300; such a device was over $2,000 just a year earlier.

Companies like Sony, Panasonic, and Nokia, which have been slow to recognize how much customers like multifunctional devices, have been hurt badly by companies like Apple and Danger. Competition is intense in this industry as companies race to develop the incremental innovations that can make the difference between commercial success and failure. For example, users can type or handwrite their notes on tablet personal computers.

MAXIMIZING PRODUCT QUALITY If managers introduce into the marketplace new products that have not been properly engineered and that suffer from substandard quality, their company's efforts to attract customers are doomed.[22] Poor quality is often the result of managers' rushing a product to market in an attempt to reduce development time. Although development time is important, so is product quality. Meeting development time goals with a poor-quality product can be self-defeating.

MAXIMIZING MANUFACTURABILITY AND EFFICIENCY The production process used to manufacture a product can either shorten or lengthen the development time and result in either low or high manufacturing costs–thereby affecting efficiency.[23] Consider what happens when product engineers design a product but fail to keep manufacturing requirements in mind. After examining specifications for the product, the manufacturing managers tell the product engineers that the product cannot be manufactured efficiently and cost-effectively because of the way it is designed. The engineers then must redesign the product, thereby lengthening its development time.

Poor design may raise manufacturing costs because, for example, the product has numerous components and is costly to assemble. Consultants recommend that ensuring that products can be made as efficiently as possible should be a key goal of managers' product development efforts.[24]

Principles of Product Development

How can managers increase their organizations' ability to innovate new goods and services and so increase competitive advantage? Here, we examine several ways in which managers can organize and control the product development process to reduce development time, maximize the product's fit with customer needs, maximize quality, and maximize both manufacturability and efficiency.

The steps that Monte Peterson, former CEO of Thermos, took to develop a new barbecue grill show how good product development should proceed. Peterson had no doubt about how to increase Thermos's sales of barbecue grills: Promote new product development and create new and improved models. Peterson assembled a cross-functional product development team of six middle managers from marketing, engineering, manufacturing, and finance. He told them to develop a new barbecue grill and to do so in 18 months. To ensure that these managers were not spread too thin, he assigned them to this product development team only. Peterson also arranged for leadership of the team to rotate. Initially, to focus on what customers wanted, the marketing manager would take the lead; then, when technical developments became the main consideration, leadership would switch to engineering; and so on.

Team members christened the group the "Lifestyle team." To find out what people really wanted in a grill, the marketing manager and nine subordinates spent a month on the road visiting customers. While in the field, the Lifestyle team set up focus groups, visited people's homes, and even videotaped barbecues. What team members found surprised them. The stereotype of Dad with apron and chef's hat slaving over a smoky barbecue grill was wrong. More women were barbecuing, and many cooks were tired of messy charcoal. Many homeowners were spending big money building decks, and they did not like rusty grills that spoiled the appearance of their decks. Moreover, environmental and safety issues were also increasing in importance. In California charcoal starter fluid is considered a pollutant and is banned; in New Jersey the use of charcoal and gas grills on the balconies of condos and apartments has been prohibited to avoid fires.

When the marketing group discussed their findings, they decided that Thermos had to produce a new kind of product. What they needed was a barbecue grill that looked like a handsome piece of furniture, required no pollutants such as charcoal starter fluid, and made the food taste good. The grill also had to be safe enough to be used by apartment and condo dwellers–which meant it had to be electric.

Within one year the basic attributes of the product were defined, and leadership of the team moved to engineering. The product engineers had been working on electric grill technology for about six months–ever since marketing had alerted them that an electric grill was a likely possibility. The critical task for engineering was to design a grill that gave food the cookout taste that conventional electric grills could not provide because they did not get hot enough. To raise the cooking temperature, Thermos's engineers drew on its vacuum technology and designed a domed vacuum top that trapped heat inside the grill. They also built electric heat rods directly into the surface of the grill. These, along with the vacuum top, made the grill hot enough to sear meat and give it brown barbecue lines and a barbecue taste.[25]

Manufacturing had been active from the early days of the development process, making sure that any proposed design could be produced economically. Because manufacturing was involved from the beginning, the team avoided some costly mistakes. At one critical team meeting the engineers said they wanted tapered legs on the grill. Manufacturing explained that tapered legs would have to be custom-made–and would raise manufacturing costs–and persuaded the team to go with straight legs.

When the new grill was introduced on schedule, it was an immediate success and became a best-seller. The study of many product development successes, such as that of Thermos's Lifestyle team, suggests four principles that managers can follow to increase the likelihood of success for their product development efforts.[26]

PRINCIPLE 1: ESTABLISH A STAGE-GATE DEVELOPMENT FUNNEL

One of the most common mistakes that managers make in product development is trying to fund too many new projects at any one time.[27] This approach spreads limited financial, technical, and human resources too thinly over too many different projects. As a consequence, no single project is given the resources that are required to make it succeed.

Given this potential problem, managers need to develop a structured process for evaluating product development proposals and deciding which to support and which to reject. A common solution is to establish a **stage-gate development funnel,** a planning model that forces managers to make choices among competing projects so that organizational resources are not spread thinly over too many projects.[28] The funnel gives managers control over product development and allows them to intervene and take corrective action quickly and appropriately (see Figure 19.5).

stage-gate development funnel
A planning model that forces managers to make choices among competing projects so that organizational resources are not spread thinly over too many projects.

At stage 1, the development funnel has a wide mouth, so top managers initially can encourage employees to come up with as many new product ideas as possible. Managers can create incentives for employees to come up with ideas. Many organizations run "bright-idea programs" that reward employees whose ideas eventually make it through the development process. Other organizations allow research scientists to devote a certain amount of work time to their own projects. Top managers at Hewlett-Packard and 3M, for example, have a 15 percent rule: They expect a research scientist to spend 15 percent of the workweek working on a project of his or her own choosing. Ideas may be submitted by individuals or by groups. Brainstorming (see Chapter 7) is a technique that managers frequently use to encourage new ideas.

New product ideas are written up as brief proposals. The proposals are submitted to a cross-functional team of managers, who evaluate each proposal at gate 1. The cross-functional team considers a proposal's fit with the organization's strategy and its technical feasibility. Proposals that are consistent with the strategy of the organization and are judged technically feasible pass through

Figure 19.5
A Stage-Gate Development Funnel

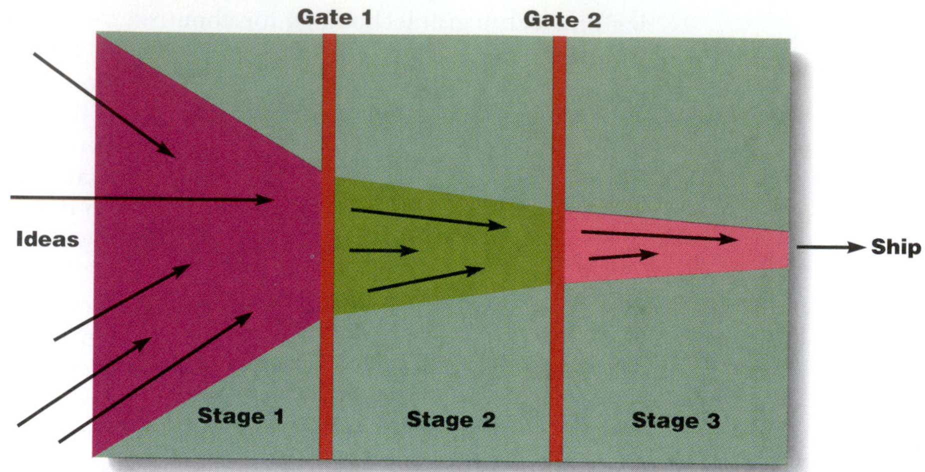

gate 1 and into stage 2. Other proposals are turned down (although the door is often left open for reconsidering a proposal at a later date).

product development plan A plan that specifies all of the relevant information that managers need in order to decide whether to proceed with a full-blown product development effort.

The primary goal in stage 2 is to draft a detailed product development plan. The **product development plan** specifies all of the relevant information that managers need to make a decision about whether to go ahead with a full-blown product development effort. The product development plan should include strategic and financial objectives, an analysis of the product's market potential, a list of desired product features, a list of technological requirements, a list of financial and human resource requirements, a detailed development budget, and a time line that contains specific milestones (for example, dates for prototype completion and final launch).

A cross-functional team of managers normally drafts this plan. Good planning requires a good strategic analysis (see Chapter 8), and team members must be prepared to spend considerable time in the field with customers, trying to understand their needs. Drafting a product development plan generally takes about three months. Once completed, the plan is reviewed by a senior management committee at gate 2 (see Figure 19.5). These managers focus on the details of the plan to see whether the proposal is attractive (given its market potential) and viable (given the technological, financial, and human resources that would be needed to develop the product). Senior managers making this review keep in mind all other product development efforts currently being undertaken by the organization. One goal at this point is to ensure that limited organizational resources are used to their maximum effect.

contract book A written agreement that details product development factors such as responsibilities, resource commitments, budgets, time lines, and development milestones.

At gate 2 projects are rejected, sent back for revision, or allowed to pass through to stage 3, the development phase. Product development starts with the formation of a cross-functional team that is given primary responsibility for developing the product. In some companies, at the beginning of stage 3 top managers and cross-functional team members sign a **contract book,** a written agreement that details factors such as responsibilities, resource commitments, budgets, time lines, and development milestones.[29] Signing the contract book is viewed as the symbolic launch of a product development effort. The contract book is also a document against which actual development progress can be measured. At Motorola, for example, team members and top management negotiate a contract and sign a contract book at the launch of a development effort, thereby signaling their commitment to the objectives contained in the contract.[30]

The stage 3 development effort can last anywhere from 6 months to 10 years, depending on the industry and type of product. Some electronics products have development cycles of 6 months, but it takes from 3 to 5 years to develop a new car, about 5 years to develop a new jet aircraft, and as long as 10 years to develop a new medical drug.

PRINCIPLE 2: ESTABLISH CROSS-FUNCTIONAL TEAMS A smooth-running cross-functional team seems to be a critical component of successful product development, as suggested by the experience of Thermos.[31] Marketing, engineering, and manufacturing personnel were **core members** of a successful product development team–the people who have primary responsibility for the product development effort. Other people besides core members work on the project as and when the need arises, but the core members (generally from three to six individuals) stay with the project from inception to completion of the development effort (see Figure 19.6).

core members The members of a team who bear primary responsibility for the success of a project and who stay with a project from inception to completion.

The reason for using a cross-functional team is to ensure a high level of coordination and communication among managers in different functions, which increases group cohesiveness and performance, as we saw in Chapter 14. Input from both marketing and manufacturing members of Thermos's Lifestyle team determined the characteristics of the barbecue that the engineers on the team ended up designing.

If a cross-functional team is to succeed, it must have the right kind of leadership and it must be managed in an effective manner.[32] To be successful, a product development team needs a team leader who can rise above a functional background and take a cross-functional view.[33] In addition to having effective leadership, successful cross-functional product development teams have several other key characteristics.[34] Often, core members of successful teams are located close to one another in the same office space to foster a sense of shared mission and commitment to a development program. Successful teams develop a clear

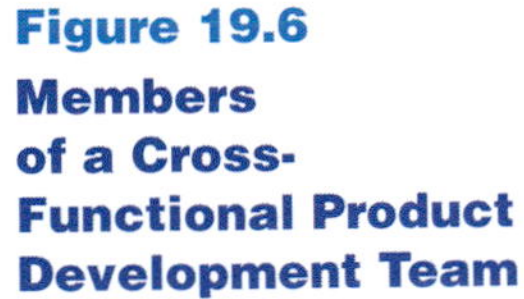

Figure 19.6 Members of a Cross-Functional Product Development Team

sense of their objectives and how they will be achieved, the purpose again being to create a sense of shared mission. A clear, explicit statement of objectives allows the team to measure its actual performance against its plan.

PRINCIPLE 3: USE CONCURRENT ENGINEERING Traditional product development is a sequential process consisting of five steps: opportunity identification, concept development, product design, process design, and commercial production (see Figure 19.7a). Opportunity development occurs at stage 1 of the stage-gate funnel (see Figure 19.6), commercial production occurs at stage 3, and the other three steps occur at stage 2. The problem with sequential product development is that long product development times, poor product quality, and high manufacturing costs are likely if there is no direct communication among the manufacturing managers who develop the concept and the engineering or R&D managers who design the product. In many organizations engineers in R&D design a product and then "throw it over the wall" to manufacturing. The result can be a design that is too costly to manufacture. If solving this problem requires redesign, manufacturing sends the product back to the design engineers, thereby lengthening development time.

Cross-functional teams can help solve this problem, and it is also helpful to alter the process so that it is partly parallel rather than sequential. In partly parallel product development, one step begins before the prior step is finished, and managers from one function are familiar with what is going on in other functions (see Figure 19.7b). The goal is to facilitate **concurrent engineering,** the simultaneous design of the product and of the process for manufacturing the product.[35] Recall that in the interests of reducing manufacturing costs, manufacturing members of the Lifestyle team at Thermos persuaded their colleagues in engineering to design an electric grill with straight legs. That is an example of concurrent engineering. The usual outcome of concurrent engi-

concurrent engineering The simultaneous design of the product and of the process for manufacturing the product.

Figure 19.7 Sequential and Partly Parallel Development Processes

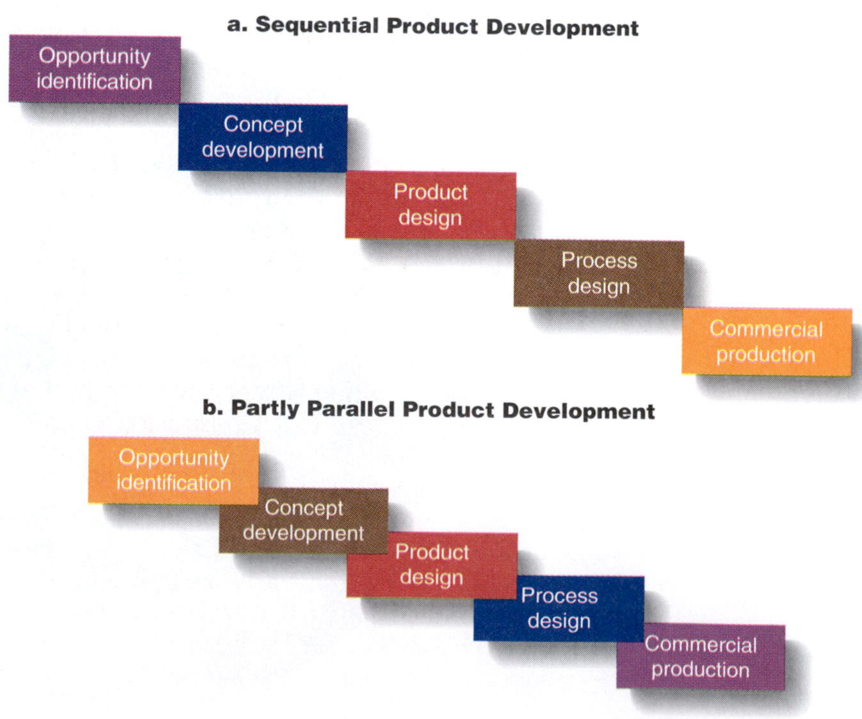

neering is a product that is easy to manufacture. Concurrent engineering thus helps to reduce manufacturing costs and to increase product quality. The other benefit of a partly parallel process is that it reduces development time, for two reasons. The whole development process is compressed, and concurrent engineering reduces the probability that costly and time-consuming product redesigns will be needed.

PRINCIPLE 4: INVOLVE BOTH CUSTOMERS AND SUPPLIERS

Many new products fail when they reach the marketplace because they were designed with scant attention to customer needs. Successful product development requires inputs from more than just an organization's members; also needed are inputs from customers and suppliers.[36] At Thermos, team members spent a month on the road visiting customers to identify their needs. The revolutionary electric barbecue grill was a direct result of this process. In other cases, companies have found it worthwhile to include customer representatives as peripheral members of their product development team. Boeing's approach to designing its most recent commercial jet aircraft, the 400-seat 777, provides an example of the value of including customers in the design process.

To build a plane designed with customer needs in mind, Boeing invited eight U.S. and foreign airlines to help its engineers design the aircraft. For almost a year, technical representatives from these airlines took up residence in Boeing's Everett facility and met with the engineering staff assigned to the 777 project. This was a dramatic shift for Boeing, which in the past had been very secretive about its design work.

Input from the eight carriers clearly determined the shape of the 777. They wanted a fuselage that was wider than rival McDonnell-Douglas and Airbus models so that they could pack another 30 or so seats onto the aircraft. The result is an aircraft that is 5 inches wider than the McDonnell-Douglas MD-11 and 25 inches wider than the Airbus A-330. They wanted a plane in which the galleys and lavatories could be relocated almost anywhere within the plane within hours. Boeing therefore designed a plane whose interior can be completely changed in three or four hours, configured with one, two, or three classes to fit whatever a carrier's market of the moment demands. And they wanted better overhead bins for carry-on baggage, so Boeing designed new overhead bins to meet their requirements.[37]

Besides consulting customers, Boeing also brought 18 of its major suppliers into the 777 program and told them exactly what it wanted from them. Suppliers consulted with Boeing's project engineers. As a result, many potential production problems were solved ahead of time, thereby reducing the need for costly design changes late in the development process.

Including suppliers in the product development process is clearly another important factor in successful product development. When suppliers are responsible for major components of a product (such as the tail section of the 777), it is important to extend the principle of concurrent engineering to embrace them so that they, too, can manufacture quality components in a timely, cost-effective way.

Many of the information technologies discussed in Chapter 18 are becoming an increasingly important part of concurrent engineering. The way in which Boeing used computer-aided design (CAD) to design the 777, the first airliner to be designed entirely by computer, provides a graphic illustration of the advantages of CAD. Each of the thousands of components of the 777 was first engineered and tested in virtual space by means of three-dimensional CAD technology to make sure that everything fit together. If parts did not fit, they were redesigned on the computer until they did. Only then were real parts and subassemblies manufactured. By using CAD, Boeing dramatically reduced the need for expensive mockups and design changes and shortened development time.[38] The use of CAD technology in product development has exploded in recent years as design engineers employed by carmakers, furniture makers, and architects have found that CAD allows them to cut down on design time and improve the accuracy of their engineering drawings.[39]

In sum, managers need to recognize that successful product development cuts across roles and functions and requires a high level of integration. They should recognize the importance of common values and norms in promoting the high levels of cooperation and cohesiveness necessary to build a culture for innovation. They also should be careful to reward successful innovators and make heroes of the employees and teams that develop successful new products. Finally, managers should fully utilize the four principles of product development to guide the process.

Problems with Product Development

Given today's rapid rate of technological change and its impact on the length of product life cycles, successful product development has become a major source of competitive advantage in many industries. To survive and compete successfully, managers must look for ways to reduce development time, achieve a close fit between new product attributes and customer demands, and maximize the quality and ease of production of new products. The four principles for effective product development described above indicate some of the actions that managers are taking to increase the effectiveness of product development efforts.

These principles, however, have not been universally adopted. The track record for product development is actually quite poor. Several studies have concluded that most product development projects either are terminated before completion or result in the production of new products that flop when they reach the marketplace.[40]

Although many managers know the theory underlying successful product development, making that theory work within an organization can be very difficult. Revolutionizing product development requires a break with traditional ways of thinking and managing. The establishment of cross-functional teams can help top managers redirect power and responsibility away from functional managers and toward the leaders and core members of product development teams. Not surprisingly, functional managers often resent such challenges to their authority and resist attempts to limit their power and influence within the organization. However, by assessing the need for change, deciding on the change to make, implementing the change, and evaluating the change (see Figure 11.7), top managers will be well positioned to overcome resistance and move the organization toward its desired future state.

entrepreneur An individual who notices opportunities and takes responsibility for mobilizing the resources necessary to produce new and improved goods and services.

Entrepreneurship

At the heart of innovation and product development are **entrepreneurs,** individuals who notice opportunities and take responsibility for mobilizing the resources necessary to produce new and improved goods and services. Entrepreneurs start new business ventures

Valerie Bottorff, right, Alison McDaniel, center, and Christina Spencer stand outside the Alison's Relocations, Inc., office in Anchorage, Alaska, in August 2004. Alison McDaniel began operating Alison's Relocations, Inc., in 1997 out of her apartment. Today McDaniel manages the growing moving business with the help of her family. McDaniel is one of thousands of female entrepreneurs in Alaska, contributing more than a billion dollars in revenue to the state's economy each year, according to Sam Dickey of the Small Business Administration's Alaska office.

and do all of the planning, organizing, leading, and controlling necessary to meet organizational goals. Most commonly entrepreneurs assume all the risk and receive all the returns associated with the new business venture. These people are the Bill Gateses or Liz Claibornes of the world, who make vast fortunes when their businesses succeed. Or they are among the millions of people who start new business ventures only to lose their money when they fail. Despite the fact that an estimated 80 percent of small businesses fail in the first three to five years, by some estimates 38 percent of men and 50 percent of women in today's workforce want to start their own companies.[41]

Some managers, scientists, and researchers employed by existing companies engage in entrepreneurial activity. They are involved in the innovation and product development process described in this chapter. To distinguish these individuals from entrepreneurs who found their own businesses, employees of existing organizations who notice opportunities for either quantum or incremental product improvements and are responsible for managing the product development process are known as **intrapreneurs.** In general, then, **entrepreneurship** is the mobilization of resources to take advantage of an opportunity to provide customers with new or improved goods and services.

There is an interesting relationship between entrepreneurs and intrapreneurs. Many intrapreneurs become dissatisfied when their superiors decide neither to support nor to fund new product ideas and development efforts that the intrapreneurs think will succeed. What do intrapreneurs who feel that they are getting nowhere do? Very often they decide to leave their employers and start their own organizations to take advantage of their new product ideas. In other words, intrapreneurs become entrepreneurs and found companies that may compete with the companies they left.

intrapreneur A manager, scientist, or researcher who works inside an existing organization and notices opportunities for product improvements and is responsible for managing the product development process.

entrepreneurship The mobilization of resources to take advantage of an opportunity to provide customers with new or improved goods and services.

Frustrated intrapreneurs who became entrepreneurs have started many of the world's most successful organizations. William Hewlett and David Packard left Fairchild Semiconductor, an early industry leader, when managers of that company would not support their ideas; their company soon outperformed Fairchild. Compaq Computer was founded by Rod Canion and some of his colleagues, who left Texas Instruments (TI) when managers there would not support Canion's idea that TI should develop its own personal computer. To prevent the departure of talented people, organizations need to take steps to promote internal entrepreneurship. In the remainder of this section we consider issues involved in promoting successful entrepreneurship in both new and existing organizations.

Entrepreneurship and New Ventures

The fact that a significant number of entrepreneurs were frustrated intrapreneurs provides a clue about the personal characteristics of people who are likely to start a new venture and bear all the uncertainty and risk associated with being an entrepreneur.

CHARACTERISTICS OF ENTREPRENEURS Entrepreneurs are likely to be high on the personality trait of *openness to experience,* meaning that they are predisposed to be original, to be open to a wide range of stimuli, to be daring, and to take risks. Entrepreneurs also are likely to have an *internal locus of control* and believe that they are responsible for what happens to them and that their own actions determine important outcomes such as the success or failure of a new business. People with an external locus of control, in contrast, would be very unlikely to leave a secure job in an organization and assume the risk associated with a new venture.

Entrepreneurs are likely to have a high level of *self-esteem* and feel competent and capable of handling most situations–including the stress and uncertainty surrounding a plunge into a risky new venture. Entrepreneurs are also likely to have a high *need for achievement* and have a strong desire to perform challenging tasks and meet high personal standards of excellence. A good example of an entrepreneur with these personal characteristics is the potter, George Ohr, discussed in Chapter 7, whose vases are pictured throughout this book. The way he persevered over the years to produce pots and vases no one would buy, yet kept his confidence in his abilities, shows the faith entrepreneurs must have in themselves. Although Ohr was not successful, a good example of an entrepreneur with these qualities who founded a new company and has led it successfully since then is Omar Maden, profiled in the following "Manager as a Person."

Manager as a Person

Omar Maden Creates a New Company

In 1962, fifteen-year old Omar Maden fled Cuba alone and penniless and was resettled with foster parents in Portland, Oregon. Five years later he was drafted into the U.S. Army during the Vietnam war, and the former Afro-Cuban found himself working on command and control communication technology for artillery and missiles. At the end of the war, Maden's superior officers encouraged him to remain in the Army because of his considerable technical skills. Maden became an Army information technology expert, and rose through the ranks to become a major. He was transferred to the Pentagon, where he was responsible for implementing some key logistics communication technologies.[42]

After retiring from the Army in the mid-1980s, Maden decided he could use his IT skills to become an independent consultant. Using a home equity loan and his personal savings, he started Maden Technologies. Soon his previous employer, the Army, began to call on his services. Maden's big break came when he was hired to oversee deployment of the Army's logistics center for the Desert Storm campaign during the first war with Iraq. He and his team of highly trained IT analysts fashioned a field communication system that offered Desert Storm's commanders instantaneous performance feedback, which put them in total control of all mobile military resources. Maden's systems excelled, and his success in managing this venture led to more contracts. Within 10 years Maden Technologies had become one of the Pentagon's largest research and development contractors.

Since 1995, Maden has organized his IT analysts into teams to develop the different communication products that the Army needed. For example, one team converted the military's internal email system into a battlefield tool that allows everyone to communicate with everyone else. Another team developed a smart card that has embedded in it a soldier's complete personal, medical, and military record. The cards were issued to 4 million Army personnel in 2002.

Omar Maden has successfully guided his company through the transition from fulfilling government contracts to selling its high-tech expertise to the private sector.

Realizing that his company's technological innovations and skills could be used more widely, in the 2000s Maden has been trying to reposition his company as a technology service provider to industry. His employees have been pushing him to do this because they have received large stock options for their major contributions and are anxious to see their company succeed on a national level. Moreover, using his military experience, Maden has been careful to assign authority for each project to the members of the team responsible for developing each product to encourage innovation and entrepreneurial behavior. Team members are given wide authority to make decisions, and each team works closely with its customers–Army officers–so that they can be sure they are designing a product that matches the Army's current and future needs.[43]

To further these ambitious goals, Maden has been buying and taking over many small companies that have technological skills complementary to his company. For example, he bought Reply Networks, which facilitates delivery of bulk email. He also bought Enlighten for its cross-platform software for managing corporate networks. With this software one team of a company's managers can work across the Windows, Sun, or Linux operating systems simultaneously–an enterprise management solution not previously possible. This software would revolutionize the way company networks are managed and is a potential blockbuster business.[44] Clearly, entrepreneurship and innovation go hand in hand at Maden Technologies.

ENTREPRENEURSHIP AND MANAGEMENT Given that entrepreneurs are predisposed to activities that are somewhat adventurous and risky, in what ways can people become involved in entrepreneurial ventures? One way is to start a business from scratch. Taking advantage of computer-based information systems, many people are starting solo ventures and going it alone. The total number of small-office and home-office workers is more than 40 million, and each year more than a million new solo entrepreneurs join the ranks of the more than 29 million self-employed.

When people who go it alone succeed, they frequently need to hire other people to help them run the business. Michael Dell, for example, began his computer business as a college student and within weeks had hired several people to help him to assemble computers from the component parts he bought from suppliers. From his solo venture grew Dell Computer, the largest computer manufacturing company in the world today.

Some entrepreneurs who found a new business often have difficulty managing the organization as it grows; entrepreneurship is *not* the same as management. Management encompasses all the decisions involved in planning, organizing, leading, and controlling resources. Entrepreneurship is noticing an opportunity to satisfy a customer need and then mobilizing resources to make a product that satisfies that need. When an entrepreneur has produced something that customers want, entrepreneurship gives way to management, as the pressing need becomes providing the product both efficiently and effectively.

Frequently, a founding entrepreneur lacks the skills, patience, and experience to engage in the difficult and challenging work of management. Some entrepreneurs find it very hard to delegate authority because they are afraid to risk their company by letting others manage it. As a result, they become overloaded, and the quality of their decision making declines. Other entrepreneurs lack the detailed knowledge necessary to establish state-of-the-art information systems and technology or to create the operations management procedures that are vital to increase the efficiency of their organizations' production systems. Thus, to succeed, it is necessary to do more than create a new product; an entrepreneur must hire managers who can create an operating system that will let a new venture survive and prosper. This is what Google, profiled in "A Manager's Challenge," did when it hired CEO Eric Schmidt.

DEVELOPING A PLAN FOR A NEW BUSINESS One crucial factor that can help promote the success of a new venture is a clear business plan. The purpose of a business plan is to guide the development of the new business, just as the stage-gate development funnel guides the product development effort. The steps in the development of a business plan are listed in Table 19.1.

Planning for a new business begins when an entrepreneur notices an opportunity to develop a new or improved good or service for the whole market or for a specific market niche. For example, an entrepreneur might notice an opportunity in the fast-food market to provide customers with healthy fast food such as rotisserie chicken served with fresh vegetables. This is what the founders of the Boston Market restaurant chain did.

The next step is to test the feasibility of the new product idea. The entrepreneur conducts as thorough a strategic planning exercise as possible, using the SWOT analysis technique discussed in Chapter 8. First, the entrepreneur analyzes opportunities and threats. For example, a potential threat might be that KFC will decide to imitate the idea and offer its customers rotisserie chicken (KFC actually did this after Boston Market identified the new market niche). The entrepreneur should conduct a thorough analysis of the external environment (see Chapter 6) to test the potential of a new product idea and must be willing to abandon an idea if it seems likely that the threats and risks may overwhelm the

Table 19.1
Developing a Business Plan

1. Notice a Product Opportunity, and Develop a Basic Business Idea
   - Goods/services
   - Customers/markets
2. Conduct a Strategic (SWOT) Analysis
   - Identify opportunities
   - Identify threats
   - Identify strengths
   - Identify weaknesses
3. Decide Whether the Business Opportunity Is Feasible
4. Prepare a Detailed Business Plan
   - Statement of mission, goals, and financial objectives
   - Statement of strategic objectives
   - List of necessary resources
   - Organizational time line of events

opportunities and returns. Entrepreneurship is always a very risky process, and many entrepreneurs become so committed to their new ideas that they ignore or discount the potential threats and forge ahead–only to lose their shirts.

If the environmental analysis suggests that the product idea is feasible, the next step is to examine the strengths and weaknesses of the idea. At this stage the main strength is the resources possessed by the entrepreneur. Does the entrepreneur have access to an adequate source of funds? Does the entrepreneur have any experience in the fast-food industry, such as having managed a restaurant? To identify weaknesses, the entrepreneur needs to assess how many and what kinds of resources will be necessary to establish a viable new venture–such as a chain of chicken restaurants. Analysis might reveal that the new product idea will not generate an adequate return on investment. Or it might reveal that the entrepreneur needs to find partners to help provide the resources necessary to open a chain on a scale sufficient to generate a high-enough return on investment.

After conducting a thorough SWOT analysis, if the entrepreneur decides that the new product idea is feasible, the hard work begins–developing the actual business plan that will be used to attract investors or funds from banks. Included in the business plan should be the same basic elements as in the product development plan: (1) a statement of the organization's mission, goals, and financial objectives; (2) a statement of the organization's strategic objectives, including an analysis of the product's market potential, based on the SWOT analysis that has already been conducted; (3) a list of all the functional and organizational resources that will be required to successfully implement the new product idea, including a list of technological, financial, and human resource requirements; and (4) a time line that contains specific milestones for the entrepreneur and others to use to measure the progress of the venture, such as target dates for the final design and the opening of the first restaurant.

Many entrepreneurs do not have the luxury of having a team of cross-functional managers to help develop a detailed business plan. This is obviously true of solo ventures. One reason why franchising has become so popular in the United States is that an entrepreneur can purchase and draw on the business plan and experience of an already existing company, thereby reducing the risks associated with opening a new business. Entrepreneurs today can purchase the right to open a Subway Sandwich Shop. The founders of that chain, however, had to develop the business plan that made the franchise possible.

In sum, entrepreneurs have a number of significant challenges to confront and conquer if they are to be successful. It is not uncommon for an entrepreneur to fail repeatedly before finding a venture that proves successful. It also is not uncommon for an entrepreneur who establishes a successful new company to sell it in order to move on to new ventures that promise new risks and returns. An example of such an entrepreneur is Wayne Huizenga, who bought many small waste disposal companies to create the giant WMX waste disposal company, which he eventually sold. A few years later Huizenga took control of Blockbuster Video and, by opening and buying other video store chains, turned Blockbuster Video into the biggest video chain in the United States, only to sell it to Viacom.

Intrapreneurship and Organizational Learning

The intensity of competition today, particularly from agile, small companies, has made it increasingly important for large, established organizations to promote and encourage intrapreneurship to raise the level of innovation and organizational learning. A learning organization (see Chapter 7) encourages all employees to identify opportunities and solve problems, thus enabling the organization to continuously experiment, improve, and increase its ability to provide customers with new and improved goods and services. The higher the level of intrapreneurship is, the higher will be the levels of learning and innovation. How can organizations promote organizational learning and intrapreneurship?

product champion A manager who takes "ownership" of a project and provides the leadership and vision that take a product from the idea stage to the final customer.

PRODUCT CHAMPIONS One way to promote intrapreneurship is to encourage individuals to assume the role of **product champion,** a manager who takes "ownership" of a project and provides the leadership and vision that take a product from the idea stage to the final customer. 3M, a company well known for its attempts to promote intrapreneurship, encourages all its managers to become product champions and identify new product ideas. A product champion becomes responsible for developing a business plan for the product. Armed with this business plan, the champion appears before 3M's product development committee, a team of senior 3M managers who probe the strengths and weaknesses of the plan to decide whether it should be funded. If the plan is accepted, the product champion assumes responsibility for product development. The following "Management Insight" describes how Don Frey worked with Lee Iacocca to develop the Ford Mustang in the early 1960s and illustrates the importance of the product champion role.

Management Insight

How to Champion a Product at Ford

Don Frey, an engineer in Ford Motor Company's research laboratories, was always assigned to projects that seemed new and interesting. However, he never got to talk to Ford's customers and never got involved in operational decision making about what to offer the customer and how much new developments would cost. As a result, for many years, he and other R&D engineers worked on products that never got to market because the work of the engineers was not linked to the needs of the customers. Frustrated by the lack of payoff from his work, Frey began to question the utility of a corporate research laboratory that was so far removed from operations and the market.

In 1957, he moved from the research laboratory to head Ford's passenger-car design department so that he could be closer to market operations. In this new position, Frey was much closer to the customer and directed the energies of his department to producing innovations that customers wanted and were willing to pay for. Frey soon concluded that in the automobile business the best R&D was incremental; year by year innovations to better meet customer demands for safety, luxury, or utility should be the goal of product development. He also saw how important it was to use customer complaints as a guide for investing resources to get the most benefit.

Equipped with this new perspective on innovation, Frey was made a member of Ford's top planning committee in 1961. Quickly Frey and his staff saw the possibility of developing a new car for the emerging "sporty car segment" of the car market. Frey began to champion the development of a new car to meet this need. Ford, however, had just lost a fortune developing the ill-fated Edsel and was reluctant to invest in a brand new car. Frey could not get top management to support his idea.

Frey decided to go ahead, however. Because there was no corporate support for Frey's ideas, all of the early engineering and styling of what became

Ford introduced the first Mustang in April 1964. Its sporty look and peppy performance have always given it strong appeal to youthful car buyers.

the Mustang was carried out with bootleg funds–that is, funds earmarked for one project but used for something else. By 1962, Frey and his team had produced the first working prototype of the Mustang and believed they had a winner. Top management in general and Henry Ford II in particular were not impressed and offered no support, still fearing the new car might turn out to be another Edsel. Luckily for the Mustang team, Lee Iacocca became vice president and general manager of Ford in 1962, and he bought into the Mustang concept. Believing that the Mustang would be a huge success, Iacocca risked his reputation to convince top management to back the idea. In fall 1962, after much pressure, funds to produce the car were allocated.

With Frey as product champion, the Mustang raced from approval to market in only 18 months. When the Mustang was introduced in 1964, it was an instant success, and over 400,000 Mustangs were sold. Frey went on to champion other innovations in Ford vehicles, such as disc brakes and radial tires. Reflecting on his experiences as a product champion, he offered some "coaching tips" for future product champions: Innovation can start anywhere, even from small beginnings, and product champions must be prepared to use all the skill they have to pull people and resources together and to resist top managers and financial experts who use numbers to kill new ideas.[45] As Frey's experiences suggest, innovation is a risky business, and product champions have to go out on a limb to take on the disbelievers.

SKUNKWORKS AND NEW VENTURE DIVISIONS The idea behind the product champion role is that employees who feel ownership for a project are inclined to act like outside entrepreneurs and go to great lengths to make the project succeed. Using skunkworks and new venture divisions can also strengthen this feeling of ownership. A **skunkworks** is a group of intrapreneurs who are deliberately separated from the normal operation of an organization–for example, from the normal chain of command–to encourage them to devote all their attention to developing new products. The idea is that if these people are isolated, they will become so intensely involved in a project that development time will be relatively brief and the quality of the final product will be enhanced. The term *skunkworks* was coined at the Lockheed Corporation, which formed a team of design engineers to develop special aircraft such as the U2 spy plane. The secrecy with which this unit functioned and speculation about its goals led others to refer to it as "the skunkworks."

skunkworks A group of intrapreneurs who are deliberately separated from the normal operation of an organization to encourage them to devote all their attention to developing new products.

Large organizations can become tall, inflexible, and bureaucratic, and these conditions are not ideal for encouraging learning and experimentation. Recognizing this problem, many organizations create new venture divisions, separate from the parent organization and free from close scrutiny, to take charge of product development. A **new venture division** is an autonomous division that is given all the resources it needs to develop and market a new product. In essence, a new venture division functions in the same way that a new venture would; the division's managers become intrapreneurs in charge of product

new venture division An autonomous division that is given all the resources it needs to develop and market a new product.

development. The hope is that this new setting will encourage a high level of organizational learning and entrepreneurship.

REWARDS FOR INNOVATION To encourage managers to bear the uncertainty and risk associated with the hard work of entrepreneurship, it is necessary to link performance to rewards. Increasingly, companies are rewarding intrapreneurs on the basis of the outcome of the product development process. Intrapreneurs are granted large bonuses if their projects succeed, or they are granted stock options that can make them millionaires if the product sells well. Both Microsoft and Cisco Systems, for example, have made hundreds of their employees multimillionaires as a result of the stock options they were granted as part of their reward package. In addition to receiving money, successful intrapreneurs can expect to receive promotion to the ranks of top management. Most of 3M's top managers, for example, reached the executive suite because they had a track record of successful entrepreneurship. Organizations must reward intrapreneurs equitably if they wish to prevent them from leaving and becoming outside entrepreneurs who might form a new venture that competes directly against them. Nevertheless, intrapreneurs frequently do so.

Summary and Review

INNOVATION, TECHNOLOGICAL CHANGE, AND COMPETITION The high level of technological change in today's world creates new opportunities for managers to market new products but can destroy the market for older products. Rapid technological change and changing fads and fashions can shorten product life cycles. The shorter a product life cycle is, the greater is the importance of product development as a competitive weapon.

PRODUCT DEVELOPMENT Successful product development requires that managers pursue four goals: reducing development time, maximizing the product's fit with customer needs, maximizing its quality, and maximizing its manufacturability. To meet these goals, managers should follow four principles of product development: (1) Establish a structured stage-gate development funnel for evaluating and controlling different product development efforts; (2) establish cross-functional teams composed of individuals from different functional departments, and give each team a leader who can rise above his or her functional background; (3) use concurrent engineering, the simultaneous design of the product and of the process for manufacturing the product, to reduce development time and increase manufacturability and product quality; (4) involve both customers and suppliers in the development process.

ENTREPRENEURSHIP Entrepreneurship is the mobilization of resources to take advantage of an opportunity to provide customers with new or improved goods and services. Entrepreneurs find new ventures of their own. Intrapreneurs work inside organizations and manage the product development process. Organizations need to encourage intrapreneurship because it leads to organizational learning and innovation.

Management in Action

Topics for Discussion and Action

Discussion

1. Identify two industries where product life cycles are short and product development is an important competitive imperative. Identify two industries where product life cycles are long. What factors make the length of the product life cycle different in these industries?
2. When product life cycles are long, is product development not an important consideration for a company? Explain your answer.
3. The microprocessor that Intel developed can be classified as a quantum product innovation. Identify two other quantum product innovations, and explore their implications for product development.
4. What do you think are the greatest impediments to successful product development within an organization?
5. Why is it so important for managers to shorten the duration of product development? What steps can management take to reduce development time? What risks are associated with compressing development time?
6. What are the four principles of successful product development? How do they affect one another?

Action

7. Ask a manager to describe an example of incremental product improvement in which he or she was involved. What was it? What were the problems surrounding it? Did it succeed?

Building Management Skills

Promoting Successful Product Development

Pick a well-known company that is operating in an industry characterized by technological change (such as Apple Computer in the personal computer industry, Amgen in biotechnology, America Online in information services, Microsoft in computer software). Then answer the following questions:

1. What is the source of technological change in the company's task and general environments?
2. What is the average length of the product life cycle in the company's industry?
3. Approximately how many new products has the company introduced over the last five years?
4. How successful have the company's product development efforts been?
5. What accounts for the company's product successes? What accounts for its failures?
6. From what you have been able to find out, do you think there is potential for improving the company's product development efforts? If so, how?

Managing Ethically

Google employees who find ways to improve the performance of Google's search engine and innovate new online services receive stock in the company. So do managers, such as its CEO, whose skills and experience have improved its performance and made Google a highly profitable company. While Google is very generous with its stock, which has made many of its employees millionaires, many other companies provide little or no reward to employees for their innovation and entrepreneurship. Thus, for example, a researcher who comes up with an idea for a new product that makes the company hundreds of millions a year might receive only a $50,000 bonus or a promotion that results in a 10 percent salary increase.

Questions

1. From an ethical perspective, do you think employees should have the right to profit from their own inventions? If so, how much of the proceeds from the invention should an employee receive?
2. If an employee develops an idea for a new product while working for a company, is it ethical for him or her to leave this company and then develop the product alone or sell it to another company?

Small Group Breakout Exercise

Keeping Up with Your Customers

Form groups of three or four people, and appoint one member as the spokesperson who will communicate your findings to the whole class when called on by the instructor. Then discuss the following scenario.

You are the top managers in charge of a chain of stores selling high-quality, high-priced men's and women's clothing. Store sales are flat, and you are increasingly concerned that the clothing your stores offer to customers is failing to satisfy changing customer needs. You think that the purchasing managers are failing to spot changing fads and fashions in time, and you believe that store management is not doing enough to communicate to the purchasing managers what customers are demanding. You want to revitalize your organization's product development process, and this, in the case of your stores, means stocking the products that customers want.

1. Clearly state how and why each of the four goals of product development (development time, customer needs, quality, and manufacturability) is relevant to your organization.
2. Develop a program, based on the four principles of product development, that you intend to implement in your stores to achieve these goals. For example, how will you encourage input from employees and customers, and who will be responsible for managing the program?

Exploring the World Wide Web

Go to the Web site of Wind River Systems, a software company, at www.windriver.com. Under the services tab, click "industry insight," and then download the case study "Best Industry Management Practices." After reviewing the case study, answer the following questions.

1. Which of the steps of good product development discussed in the chapter does Wind River use?
2. What other kinds of best practices does it use to speed product development?

Be the Manager

You have been called in to advise a team of entrepreneurs who have invented a new kind of soft drink flavored with South American herbs and spices. The drink has been tested in a small market and has received an enthusiastic response from tasters. The entrepreneurs wish to know how to best develop a business plan that will give them the most chance of establishing a competitive advantage.

Questions

1. Analyze the task environment of the soft-drink industry to decide which forces are most likely to impact the new company.
2. Given this analysis what are the various means/strategies by which the company should produce, bottle, and distribute its new soft drink to customers to maximize its competitive advantage?
3. Which strategy do you think will be most effective for the company in the long run?

Additional Activities on the Build Your Management Skills DVD

- **Test Your Knowledge:** Characteristics of Successful Entrepreneurs

BusinessWeek Case in the News

Toshiba: Time to Reboot

Not long ago, Toshiba Corp.'s strengths in advanced technology—from microsize hard drives to long-lived batteries—earned it the top spot in the global notebook PC market. While desktop makers were trapped in margin-crunching price wars, Toshiba raked in cash on its sleek alternatives. By 2000, one out of every seven notebooks sold in the world was a Toshiba.

Toshiba's technical lead hasn't lasted, though. Worse, notebooks have become almost as commoditized as desktop PCs. Today, the company has fallen to No. 3 in notebooks as rivals Dell Inc. and Hewlett-Packard Co. have beefed up their laptop businesses and outsourced manufacturing to Taiwan and China. For the year ended March 31, Toshiba's $253 million profit, on sales of $49 billion, was dragged down by the PC arm's $193 million loss. "We were proud of our quality, so it was difficult for us [to change]," says President Tadashi Okamura. "That was our mistake."

Okamura aims to correct the error. His plan: Focus on higher-margin products such as advanced memory chips and consumer electronics, while shifting most PC production to cheaper locales. And this time around, Toshiba will cooperate more energetically with partners—sometimes even rivals—to develop new products.

The success of Okamura's plan will depend largely on fixing the PC business. His goal is to outsource at least half of Toshiba's PC production to Taiwanese manufacturers, up from about 30 percent today. Most of the rest of Toshiba's computers will be made at its factory in Hangzhou, China, while output at Japanese plants will be cut by 75 percent, to 20,000 computers a month—just 4 percent of Toshiba's total. While rivals "are concentrating on commodity products," Okamura also hopes to restore Toshiba's premium reputation via features such as TV tuners, longer-lasting batteries, and higher quality audio.

Okamura's reorganization push has reshaped Toshiba's chip division. He shuttered low-margin PC-memory plants while expanding output of higher-margin flash chips used in digital cameras. Last year, Toshiba's chip unit had operating profits of $1 billion, up 85 percent from 2002. Toshiba chip fabs were also early entrants to China, where the company already runs a research and development center. More recently, Toshiba has taken small stakes in Shanghai's Semiconductor Manufacturing International Corp. and TCL Corp., one of China's top producers of TVs and cell phones. Company execs say these alliances should help fuel 15 percent annual sales growth in China and boost chip sales there from $1.3 billion today to $5.3 billion by 2010.

Collaboration is critical. Toshiba's consumer-electronics group developed a new flat-panel TV technology with Canon, for instance. The semiconductor unit is working with IBM and Sony Corp. on new "cell" chips for games and other gear. With NEC, Toshiba is developing new generation DVD players that can hold the massive amounts of data needed for high-definition television. Once consumers see HDTV, "standard DVD won't satisfy them," says Hisashi Yamada, a top Toshiba engineer working on the player.

Skeptics wonder whether Okamura's plan can cure what ails Toshiba. In PCs, for example, Dell and HP continue to wage a price war. Some experts argue that Toshiba should spin off its chip business so the unit can more easily raise the funds to build new factories without being weighed down by the troubled PC group.

Consumer electronics is only getting tougher, too. European rivals Thomson Corp. and Alcatel have signed their own deals with TCL, which could limit the scope of Toshiba's China ambitions. The TV business, meanwhile could get even more competitive with the likes of Dell and Gateway jumping into the fray. "Every major consumer-electronics company is positioning TV as its major product," says Ikuo Matsuhashi, a Goldman Sachs analyst in Tokyo.

The naysayers make a persuasive case. Still, Toshiba execs are confident this round of restructuring will suffice, and that the chip and PC businesses will perform better under the same roof. Okamura's offshoring plan marks "a very big change in direction," says Yoshiharu Izumi, an analyst at J.P. Morgan in Tokyo. That's what Okamura likes to hear. And he's determined to prove he can save the tech powerhouse he runs without tearing it apart.

Questions

1. What are the causes of Toshiba's poor performance?
2. What steps are managers taking to turn around the company? How would you describe their new strategies?

Source: Bruce Einhorn, "Toshiba: Time to Reboot." Reprinted from the June 21, 2004, issue of *BusinessWeek* by special permission.

BusinessWeek Case in the News

Inventing to Order

Few companies would willingly gamble billions on a long shot. Yet when it comes to research and development, many do. Every year companies in the Standard & Poor's 500 stock index pour more than $100 billion into R&D. Sometimes it results in the kind of groundbreaking science that gave us lasers and AIDS drugs. More often it results in dead ends or intriguing innovations that nobody wants.

At Dow Chemical Co., scientists seeking a better batting average are using an approach that has been catching on in recent years, but with a twist. Before it heads for the lab, Dow solicits a wish list of products or technical characteristics from customers. If Dow can make what they want—and enough companies agree to buy it—Dow scientists will return to the lab and invent to order. The idea is similar to efforts at open-market innovation attempted elsewhere, but is designed to build in guaranteed demand.

Dow's latest innovation, a stretch fiber called XLA, shows the potential of the "reverse innovation" approach. By taking the market's pulse first, Dow discovered what its rivals so far had not: that apparel makers wanted a "soft stretch" fiber with a natural feel. That insight allowed scientists to return to the lab and develop a fiber that met their needs. While it's too early to tell if XLA will succeed, the signs are encouraging: Three apparel makers have rolled out shirts with XLA in recent months, and Dow will begin mass production in the fall. Dow thinks XLA could generate $300 million in sales in 10 years.

It won't be any cakewalk. Already, XLA has a tough rival in Lycra T400, a stretch fiber launched by DuPont Co. a few months before XLA. Koch Industries, which purchased T400 in April, is ramping up capacity. Compared with XLA, T400 has more stretch, less shrinkage, and better wrinkle resistance. Still, Dow thinks XLA's superior texture can help it crack markets that have been off-limits to spandex, including men's dress shirts. Says Jean Aukerman, global brand manager for XLA: "We're trying to expand stretch into new segments."

When Dow began looking into fibers in 1998, it turned to ISIS International Inc., a Monroe (Conn.)

consultant that over the past decade has helped Dow plastics launch five products. To start, ISIS gathered execs from more than two dozen companies that use fibers, promising to give them first crack at any new product that emerged from the process. ISIS CEO Richard A. Siegel got them to describe the characteristics they wanted that were unavailable. Says Siegel: "We're asking the market, 'What do you need?' and telling the client 'Here's what you need to invent.'"

With that insight, Siegel pinpointed six opportunities that could yield $1 billion a year in new business. Of special interest: the apparel market's desire for a new fiber with soft stretch, cottony feel, and resistance to heat and chemicals. For Dow, this was a revelation. Until then, Kurt W. Swogger, Dow plastics' vice-president for R&D, and his team believed the big money was in a spandex-type fiber that could undercut rivals on price. That critical insight—that the market wanted an alternative to spandex, not a low-cost imitator—helped Dow avoid a huge error.

In months, Dow scientists had a prototype they thought met the market needs. Over the next three years, it was tested by 14 yarn, fabric, and apparel producers and was fine-tuned by Dow. By September 2002, Dow was ready to launch XLA and began working with spinners and weavers to create fabrics using the fiber. Earlier this year shirts with XLA by Calvin Klein, Perry Ellis, and Tommy Hilfiger showed up in U.S. department stores, where shirtmakers say they're getting an enthusiastic reception. And Dow has invested $30 million in a plant in Tarragona, Spain, where it plans to start production in a few months.

Questions

1. Why does Dow involve customers in the planning process?
2. What effects does this have on its strategy and culture?

Source: Louis Lavelle, "Inventing to Order." Reprinted from the July 5, 2004, issue of *BusinessWeek* by special permission.

Chapter 1 Video Case: The Legacy of GE's Jack Welch

As General Electric's chairman, Jack Welch was one of the world's most powerful corporate leaders. He was also viewed as one of America's toughest executives and an icon to be admired. The now-retired Welch, his famous management style, and his accomplishments have been the subjects of books and university business classes.

Under Welch, from 1981 to 2001, GE became the world's most valuable company, with a market value of $406 billion. Welch spurred that dramatic growth by performing management functions his own way. He chose not to follow the traditional strategy of sticking with what a company knows but instead, accumulated diverse businesses. Originally a manufacturer of household appliances, lighting, and jet engines, GE bought NBC as well as companies offering medical products, financial services, and car leasing.

Welch restructured GE before restructuring became common among large corporations. Although his company was profitable, Welch sold some of GE's subsidiaries and reduced the payroll. Some 118,000 jobs—about one in four—were slashed. The deep cuts earned Welch the nickname "Neutron Jack," a moniker he is said to have detested. Welch endured the criticism and continued his practice of identifying, keeping, and rewarding high-performing employees at General Electric.

Welch is known for dismantling GE's large bureaucracy and opening up corporate communication. Some have said that Welch listened as much as he talked and that he always spoke in a straightforward manner. He excelled at personal interaction and motivation and as the top executive was highly visible in his company. Welch visited and taught at GE's famous Management Development Institute in Crotonville, New York. His leadership style centered on having strong employees and managers at all levels and empowering them to make decisions and engage in what he called "boundaryless thinking."[1]

Some people who worked with Welch have described the former chairman's interaction as more aggressive than egalitarian or cooperative. Others have said that Welch's often-used motivational technique was the fear factor: perform or hit the road. Welch determined in the early 1980s that to be at the top, GE could not fill management positions with deadwood—people who felt comfortable, secure, and protected from competition in their jobs within the depths of a large corporation. Welch thought it was better for individuals performing at the lowest levels to move on in other directions when they are young. During his tenure at GE, Welch selected the best people he could find and then trained and promoted them. Many who learned from him took their leadership skills to other large firms. Some of Welch's "lieutenants" head some of the world's major corporations, such as Home Depot, TRW, 3M, and others.

Widely publicized and lauded, Welch's leadership techniques also surface in noncorporate environments. The head of the Junior League of London, a nonprofit organization of volunteers offering social services, has employed Welch-style principles to motivate her group's 400 members.

Of course, Jack Welch's years at GE included not only stunning corporate accomplishments but also setbacks and controversies. A proposed merger with Honeywell was rejected by European Union regulators. The Environmental Protection Agency under the Bush administration ordered GE, at a cost of $500 million, to clean up 40 miles of Hudson River bottom polluted by PCBs before the substances were banned. After Welch's exit from GE in September 2001, critics attacked his substantial benefit package, including an arrangement that provided more than $2 million a year for an array of perks such as air transportation and personal services. Welch promptly agreed to give back $2 million.

Questions

1. In what ways did Jack Welch perform the leadership function effectively?
2. Identify the type of skills—conceptual, human, or technical—that was most likely Jack Welch's strong suit when he was GE's top executive. Explain.
3. Would you like to work for a leader like Jack Welch? What would be the advantages? What would be the disadvantages?

Chapter 2 Video Case: The Evolution of Management

Since its emergence more than a century ago, after the industrial revolution, the field of management thought has expanded and changed to reflect societal, political, and economic influences. Characterized by four approaches—classical, behavioral, systems, and contingency—management thought has continuously impacted the workplace.

The industrial revolution saw sweeping changes—factories, large labor forces, dependence on machinery, and mass production of goods. By the late 1800s, U.S. business efficiency was not keeping pace with advances in assembly-line technology. Owners and managers grappled with new issues: workers' fear of losing jobs to machines and fear of the machines themselves; lack of experience in operating large factories; and the need for new authority structures. These issues were addressed by the two-pronged classical approach, consisting of scientific management and administrative management.

Scientific management was spurred by the work of Frederick Taylor, a major influence on management thought in the early 1900s. In the Philadelphia steel mills, Taylor witnessed "soldiering," whereby employees deliberately slowed production so that management would not know the speed at which the work could be done. Taylor concluded that management's failure to pay attention to workers caused the productivity problems, and he defined management's role in four points, based on standardization. The manager, said Taylor, is to (1) determine the single best way to perform a given task, (2) scientifically select and teach each worker, (3) cooperate with workers and give incentives to make sure tasks are performed the one best way, and (4) divide work and responsibility between management and workers.

In contrast to scientific management, administrative management's focus is on organizing the work of a whole organization rather than concentrating on individual workers. This branch of the classical approach holds that the management function can be applied to any organization regardless of size or type.

The classical approach assumes that work is a rational activity that people engage in to make money; thus, their behavior on the job is predictable and easily comprehended—an assumption that is not always the case. In the 1920s and 1930s, the behavioral approach took management in a different direction. A famous behavioral study headed by Elton Mayo took place over nine years at Western Electric's Hawthorne Plant in Chicago. Researchers who experimented with working conditions, such as changes in light levels, hours worked, rest periods, and incentives, found that such conditions had no direct effect on productivity but that good social relationships at work did.

In the 1950s, the systems approach brought a view of the organization as a set of interrelated parts—inputs, the transformation process, outputs, and feedback—that should be managed as one entity to reach a common objective. Integrating earlier theories, W. Edwards Deming championed "total quality," which calls for continuous improvements and statistical process control to increase quality.

The systems approach led to the contingency approach, which recognized the need to consider an organization's external environment and to adapt. This approach calls for managers to identify important factors in specific situations, look at how factors are intertwined, and determine causes and effects of management decisions.

Questions

1. Among his contributions to management thought, Frederick Taylor outlined the roles of a manager. Are these roles still relevant today? Explain.
2. What change in the direction of management theory and practice did the Hawthorne studies prompt?
3. Compare scientific management, as developed by Frederick Taylor, and management science theory, as espoused by W. Edwards Deming.

Chapter 3 Video Case: A Tale of Two Women

Common threads run through the careers of Sylvia Rhone of Elektra Records and Carly Fiorina of Hewlett-Packard. Both rose from clerical jobs to top positions at major companies in competitive industries. Both have degrees from respected universities, and both are known for their interpersonal skills and willingness to take risks.

At Elektra Records, artists such as Tracy Chapman, Natalie Cole, Metallica, or Vitamin C are generally the ones in the spotlight. Another kind of spotlight shines on chairperson and CEO Sylvia Rhone, a black woman at the top in an industry run almost exclusively by white men. Referring to the attention as a magnifying glass, Rhone is well aware that her accomplishments or lack thereof can influence opportunities given to other women, especially black women.

Rhone, who grew up in New York's Harlem, started her career as a secretary for Buddha Records. After working in marketing and promotion at ABC and Atlantic Records, she became president and CEO of EastWest Records and then facilitated its merger with Elektra, a subsidiary of Time Warner/Turner. As Elektra's head, Rhone deals with very different constituencies in different settings—the artists in the studio and the executives in the boardroom. She has a degree from the University of Pennsylvania's Wharton School of Business. "I know how to manage a company financially and combine it with solid relationships with creative people," Rhone has said. "It's those two worlds that I fuse together."[1]

Rhone admits to having no musical ability but a strong love for music. Elektra artist Lars Ulrich, Metallica's drummer, praises Rhone's "great set of ears," rare in most of the industry's business managers. She also has an instinct for spotting new cultural trends and stars—crucial in the high-stakes, $14 billion music industry.

To explain her rise to the top at Elektra, Rhone credits her instinct and her proclivity to take chances. Her business, she says, is about having the guts to make risky decisions and live with them. In Rhone's tenure as Elektra's CEO, the company's market share tripled and several of its artists have gone gold—each selling at least half a million CDs.

In the face of her professional achievements, Rhone says her personal life provides her greatest rewards. She is very close to her 20-something daughter and is happy that her parents, who sacrificed to give her the best possible education, are proud of her.

Hewlett-Packard CEO Carly Fiorina started her career after earning a liberal arts degree from Stanford University and spending a few weeks in law school. In her first job at HP, she typed shipping forms. Fiorina got into sales at AT&T, worked her way up through the ranks there, and then oversaw the spin-off of Lucent Technologies from AT&T.[2] In 1999, she was named the top executive at HP, the world's second-largest computer firm and thirteenth-largest U.S. company.

The first woman CEO of a company included in the Dow Jones Industrial Average, Fiorina has graced the covers of major magazines and was named by *Forbes* as one of the most powerful women in business. She would prefer to talk about her industry rather than her gender. Even after enduring harassment, labeling, and doubt in her ability, Fiorina says she was not held back because of being a woman. She always believed in herself, knew what she wanted, and worked hard.

Fiorina's greatest challenge has been to energize a large, older computer company in a highly competitive, rapidly changing high-tech industry. Increasing the challenge is HP's immense size, especially after it merged with Compaq Computer Corporation, and its numerous product offerings, which include servers, storage systems, software, personal and handheld computers, printers, and digital cameras. Fiorina believes that her company's strategy of "high-tech, low-cost, and best total customer experience" will help HP win out over rivals.[3]

Questions

1. Which of the "Big Five" personality traits do you think Sylvia Rhone and Carly Fiorina share?
2. Describe the locus of control of Rhone and Fiorina.
3. As revealed by the videos, what are some terminal and instrumental values held by Rhone? By Fiorina? How might their childhoods and early adulthoods have influenced their values?

Chapter 4 Video Case: Enron

In August 2001, Enron vice president Sherron Watkins wrote an anonymous letter to her boss, Kenneth Lay, chairman of energy and telecommunications at the giant company. The memo warned that the company might "implode in a wave of accounting scandals." After meeting with Watkins, Lay called for Enron's attorneys at Vinson & Elkins to look into questionable partnership deals. In mid-October 2001, Enron announced a $618 third-quarter loss and a write-off of $1.2 billion.[1] In December 2001, Enron—America's seventh-largest company in 2000—filed for chapter 11 bankruptcy. Investment companies and individual investors lost billions; Enron employees lost jobs and retirement savings.

When a congressional subcommittee began looking into Enron's collapse in January 2002, it released Watkins's letter. Watkins subsequently testified that former CEO Jeffrey Skilling, who had left Enron in August 2001, misled Lay about Enron's finances and that Skilling knew chief financial officer Andy Fastow had improperly profited from questionable partnerships set up to hide Enron's debt. At the hearings Skilling, who had sold $66 million of his Enron stock during the previous three years while encouraging employees to continue buying company stock to fund their retirement, denied knowledge of any improprieties. Referring to the fact that Enron employees lost all their retirement investment, Skilling said it was "very tough."

The Justice Department and the Securities and Exchange Commission began lengthy criminal proceedings against Enron. Suits charged that Enron executives had committed fraud, inflating the value of the company's stock through false and misleading statements and the omission of material information. In 2004 a shocked public heard recordings of Enron traders' conversations that included cursing and derisive laughter about plans to cheat the public. By September 2004, some 30 individuals had been charged in various Justice Department and SEC cases.[2] Among them were Skilling and Lay, who each pleaded not guilty. Lay, who over five years had received around $325 million in salary, bonuses, stock option gains, and stock sales, claimed he did not know what Fastow was doing.[3] Several Enron executives, including Fastow, pleaded guilty to criminal conduct and became government witnesses in hopes of receiving reduced prison sentences.

The Enron demise also brought down Arthur Andersen, the 89-year-old, Chicago-based accounting firm that had been paid over $1 million a week by Enron. With a team working inside the Enron building, Andersen had performed the traditional accounting function of auditing Enron's financial statements but also served as Enron's internal auditor to help the company manage risk, a situation that critics have called a conflict of interest. At Enron's collapse, David Duncan, the Andersen auditor who had certified Enron's false financial reports, ordered massive record shredding and computer deleting. To limit damage, Andersen placed all blame on Duncan, fired him, and apologized in full-page newspaper ads for "errors in judgment . . . by Andersen personnel." Such actions could not prevent legal action against Andersen. In the Enron hearings, documents from Enron's law firm Vinson & Elkins showed that Andersen auditors knew of Enron's questionable financial practices. Andersen was charged with obstructing the Security and Exchange Commission's investigation of Enron. Duncan himself pleaded guilty to obstruction of justice and became a key prosecution witness.[4] In June 2002 Andersen was convicted; and in August 2002 the state of Texas revoked the firm's operating license, and a federal judge fined the company $500,000 and sentenced it to five years' probation.[5]

Andersen—once an accounting giant with 85,000 employees and thousands of clients—did not survive. Several banking and securities firms that had deals with Enron suffered consequences in the form of fines, shareholder lawsuits, and criminal indictments of individuals. Meanwhile, Enron continued to sell assets as part of a reorganization plan to emerge from bankruptcy.

Sherron Watkins, who along with two other women executives was praised as a whistle-blower, was named Person of the Year in 2002 by *Time*. She resigned from Enron, wrote a book about her experiences, and began speaking to groups. Says Watkins, "I tell college students to be certain that ethics are at the top. Don't stay with a company that isn't ethical because something like an Enron could happen to you."[6]

Questions

1. Which groups of stakeholders were harmed when Enron collapsed? Explain how each group was affected.
2. Which approach to social responsibility do you think Enron demonstrated? Which approach did Arthur Andersen demonstrate? Justify your choice for each company.
3. How does reputation affect the success of a service organization such as Arthur Andersen?

Chapter 5 Video Case: Affirmative Action Allowed in College Admissions

Equal opportunity has been part of the American legal landscape for decades. Laws such as Title VII of the Civil Rights Act of 1964 and the Equal Employment Act of 1972 prohibit discrimination on the basis of gender, race, national origin, religion, creed, or disability. In enforcing such laws, the Equal Employment Opportunity Commission (EEOC) first encouraged employers and other organizations to follow guidelines. Then the EEOC started asking employers to prepare affirmative action programs, specific plans to increase opportunities for members of groups traditionally underrepresented in the workforce. Through affirmative action, businesses and government organizations, including schools and universities, have taken a proactive stance in recruiting women, racial and ethnic minorities, and handicapped individuals.

On June 23, 2003, the U.S. Supreme Court ruled on affirmative action in two cases involving college admissions. The two lawsuits had been brought in 1996 and 1997 by white students who were denied admission to the undergraduate and law schools of the University of Michigan,[1] which practiced affirmative action. In one case, the Court voted 6-3 to end the university's system of automatically giving black and Hispanic applicants a fixed number of points in the admissions process. The Court said that the practice made race a decisive factor rather than just one of many in determining who was admitted.[2]

In the second ruling, the Court said a student's race could be used in admission decisions as long as the process was "individualized, not inflexible or mechanical." For huge schools like Michigan, that will mean hiring more admissions officers to read applications individually. An NAACP Legal Defense Fund representative admitted that the right process will require time and money expenditures by colleges and universities. One critic pointed out the challenge of devising an individualized process to consider tens of thousands of applications.

The Supreme Court said that the goal of achieving diversity justified using race in admissions. In casting the deciding vote in the 5-4 decision, Judge Sandra Day O'Connor said that campus diversity better prepares students for a diverse society. She cited business groups that supported affirmative action programs as beneficial in a global society and military leaders who wanted to ensure a racially diverse body of officers. In its opinion the Court said that a school's affirmative action program should not be permanent and that after another 25 years racial preferences may no longer be necessary.

Clarence Thomas, the only African-American Supreme Court justice, rejected both of the University of Michigan's affirmative action programs. He said that "blacks can achieve in every avenue of American life without the meddling of university administrators." President Bush expressed support for the overall goal of diversity but condemned any use of quotas in trying to achieve diversity.

Many university administrators applauded the Supreme Court's ruling. Schools such as the University of Texas, which had dropped affirmative action programs because of federal court rulings, considered bringing them back to boost the number of black students. Affirmative action programs have both supporters and detractors on college campuses. For students admitted to colleges without an affirmative action program in place, it can be a point of pride that they were accepted on merit alone. Other students believe that affirmative action serves the purpose of making sure minority students get the consideration they deserve.

Many large companies, including General Motors Corp., had filed briefs supporting the University of Michigan. After spending years developing voluntary affirmative action plans, they worried that a decision could go beyond Michigan and suggest that employers roll back their programs. A group of military officers also filed briefs; military academies strongly support affirmative action as a way to increase the numbers of black and Hispanic officers in the armed services, where 40 percent of enlisted personnel are minorities while 91 percent of officers are white.[3]

The American public seems undecided about whether affirmative action provides the best means of ensuring diversity. Polls show that Americans are overwhelmingly opposed to giving minorities preferences in jobs, promotions, or university admissions but also overwhelmingly in favor of diversity.[4]

Questions

1. What are the reasons for considering a person's race for employment or college admissions?
2. Why do some people believe it is not fair to consider race in college admissions or employment decisions?
3. Are affirmative action programs the only way for businesses, schools, and other organizations to achieve diversity? Are such programs the best way?

Chapter 6 Video Case: McDonald's Supersize

Sitting on his couch one Thanksgiving, filmmaker Morgan Spurlock came up with the idea of making *Supersize Me,* a documentary of Spurlock's month-long experience of eating only at McDonald's. The idea was inspired by two women who sued McDonald's for their obesity and weight problems. When McDonald's responded by saying its food is healthy and nutritious and cannot be linked to the plaintiffs' obesity, Spurlock felt compelled to act. Although a fast-food fan himself—he continued to eat fast food after making the film—he thought McDonald's stepped over the line by saying its food is good for you.

For 30 straight days Spurlock visited the Golden Arches to eat three meals each day. From his first breakfast of an Egg McMuffin, he proceeded to eat every item on the menu—several times during the month. He ate *only* McDonald's food and had to "supersize" an item if offered. During this trial, Spurlock claimed, he gained about 25 pounds, saw his cholesterol count shoot up alarmingly, and generally felt terrible, with headaches and stomachaches.

McDonald's spokesman Walter Riker called the film a gimmick to make money and said it distorts the quality and variety available at McDonald's. Nevertheless, the fast-food franchise dropped its supersize items. The firm claimed the decision was a matter of menu simplification, but industry insiders believed it was the result of public shame and the likelihood of a legal attack much like that against the tobacco industry.[1] Spurlock's response was that he ate everything at McDonald's during the month, and he believes his film probably had an impact on the company's decision to eliminate supersizing. Spurlock also states that the unscientific poll he took while eating at McDonald's showed that only about 1 in 10 customers ordered a salad. He observed customers buying burgers, fries, and shakes—the food that tastes good, as he put it. Eliminating giant portions from the menu is a step in the right direction, but not a solution.

While Spurlock's documentary focuses on McDonald's, he hopes it will bring attention to the American diet and childhood obesity. He selected McDonald's because it is a global icon with 30,000 restaurants in more than 100 countries on six continents.[2] Of course, McDonald's is not solely responsible for the fast-food culture that permeates U.S. society and has made its way into the school lunch programs. Sloppy Joes, with makings from the federal government, are served to schoolchildren because they are inexpensive, and pizzas and sodas are contracted from corporations—all while schools cut back on physical education classes. Many kids are getting overweight and sick at younger ages, with the attendant social and health care costs.[3] Spurlock acknowledges that McDonald's accepted its corporate responsibility by eliminating supersize items. He hopes that after people see his film, they will take personal responsibility when they go to a fast-food restaurant and order smaller amounts or healthier items.

The problem Spurlock hopes his documentary will call attention to—obesity—is becoming a global epidemic. According to the World Health Organization (WHO), there are over 300 million obese adults worldwide, with 115 million of them living in developing countries.[4] Childhood obesity is also growing rapidly; 25 percent of American children, 16 percent of Russian children, and 7 percent of Chinese children ages 6 to 18 are overweight or obese.[5] Obesity has been linked to numerous health problems including heart disease, stroke, various cancers, depression, and arthritis. While the causes of this worldwide epidemic are many—lifestyle, genetics, and television—the food industry finds itself at the center of the controversy, in particular the fast-food industry, which some claim has perfected marketing techniques such as supersizing that are designed to get people to eat more food.[6] To deal with the growing epidemic of diet-related diseases, WHO is developing a global strategy that includes diet and exercise guidelines intended to help national governments combat obesity.[7] WHO recognizes that food and beverage firms must be part of the solution and welcomes their involvement. At McDonald's, the New Tastes menu of healthier foods recently introduced in the United Kingdom is a step in the right direction.

Questions

1. What did Morgan Spurlock hope to accomplish with his film *Supersize Me*? Why did he select McDonald's rather than one of the many other fast food chains?
2. Do you think the film had any influence on the decision McDonald's made to drop supersize items from its menu? What forces in the environment explain the eating habits of McDonald's customers and the trend toward obesity?
3. Do McDonald's and other fast-food chains bear any responsibility for global obesity? What can they do to reduce it? What role can WHO play in solving this global epidemic?

Chapter 7 Video Case: *Columbia* Space Shuttle Disaster and the Future of NASA

Early on February 1, 2003, television viewers watched in disbelief and sadness as the space shuttle *Columbia,* returning from its mission, seemed simply to break apart. Later in a scathing report, investigators of the *Columbia* space shuttle disaster said that management practices at NASA were as much to blame for the accident that killed seven astronauts as was the foam that broke away from the fuel tank and hit the left wing during blast-off. The report basically concludes that NASA knew of problems with the foam insulation over a long period of time but never invested the time or energy needed to resolve the problem. Former astronaut and NBC analyst Sally Ride agrees with the findings. She notes that foam has been falling off the external tanks since the first shuttle launch and that it has fallen off on nearly every flight. Ride believes the foam problem was an accident waiting to happen, which of course did. NASA had recognized the foam as a serious problem and tried to fix it, but, unfortunately, for some reason the foam didn't get as much attention as the many other problems NASA faced during the past decade.

Columbia is a sad reminder of the *Challenger* disaster 17 years earlier. In the case of *Challenger,* engineers suspected problems with O-rings but didn't fix them. It appears that NASA didn't learn from its mistakes with *Challenger,* and, more importantly, that a deeper problem exists: Safety concerns are not given top priority. According to Ride, while NASA officials do not suppress dissenting views, they do not encourage them. She notes that managers had the view that foam couldn't really cause a problem and they weren't looking to hear engineers tell them they were wrong. Echoes of *Challenger?* Ride thinks so. The further the investigation into *Columbia* progressed, the more echoes were heard. The lessons learned in the years after 1986 seem to have been lost.

To ensure the vitality of the space program, NASA must change its culture. The can-do spirit must change to one of safety first; let's make sure we've done everything possible to guarantee safety. Changing the culture will take strong leadership and personal investment at all levels within NASA. Budgets and schedules can no longer be emphasized at the cost of safety. Processes must be put in place to make sure that anyone aware of a safety problem comes forward and is heard effectively up through the chain of management.

Safety is not the only issue putting pressure on the space program; NASA is also being scrutinized over its mission. For years NASA has been facing questions such as, What are we doing in space, and what is the payoff? Since the *Challenger* explosion, the goal has been to conduct scientific experiments and to construct the International Space Station, where people can live and work for months. But some experts say the science is just not that good. According to Professor Robert Park, none of the science from either the space shuttle or the space station has had a significant impact. While it may in fact be good research, Park thinks it simply is not very important. For instance, the shuttle and space station fly the same orbit John Glenn achieved in 1963; much of what could be learned has already been learned.

Because of questions about its mission, NASA lives with constant budget pressure, which can threaten safety. The age of equipment is a concern, especially with the pressure applied to it. The idea that NASA has passed along useful products such as Teflon and Tang has also been questioned. According to Park, most of the products were developed independently; manufacturers found it good business to say their offerings had been developed in the space program.

With concerns over safety, budgets, and even its mission, what does the future hold for the space program? Only one thing is certain: The U.S. space program is in desperate need of a vision, one that was absent long before the *Columbia* disaster.

Questions

1. What seems to be the major problem facing NASA? What types of errors were made by managers? Was overconfidence a problem?
2. What must NASA accomplish to ensure the vitality of the space program? Do you think groupthink accounts for some of NASA's problems?
3. How could the steps in the decision-making process assist NASA in overcoming some of its problems?

Chapter 8 Video Case: JetBlue Airways

The day before JetBlue Airways made its first flight, founder and CEO David Neeleman gave an interview aboard a plane at New York's Kennedy International Airport. A smiling Neeleman exuded confidence and optimism as he explained what consumers could expect from the new low-cost national airline: A320 planes, the most technologically advanced in the world; friendly service; leather seats; larger overhead bins for more storage; and in each seat back, satellite television featuring 24 channels. Industry newcomer JetBlue faced many challenges, however. Even history was against the upstart company; no airline founded since 1996 had survived; only a few founded in the last 25 years were still in business.

Even with the odds against him, Neeleman thought he had a plan to succeed. First, he brought experience. JetBlue is the third airline Neeleman has been involved with—he once worked for low-fare pioneer Southwest Airlines—so he understood the pitfalls in this business. Additionally, the airline started out with a significant amount of capital, about $130 million, which enabled JetBlue to purchase new planes at the outset and order 82 more. Third, Neeleman's plan called for JetBlue to avoid some competition from the major airlines by flying in and out of airports that were not used or were underserved by major carriers. JetBlue's premier flights were out of Kennedy Airport to two cities, Buffalo and Fort Lauderdale. Neeleman's ambitious plan was to add one new city and one new plane about every month.

JetBlue's pricing was perhaps the linchpin of its strategy. For advanced-purchase seats, fares were set as low as $79 from New York to Florida. With the most expensive fare set at $159, JetBlue placed itself as a low-price carrier, but with premier service. One of Neeleman's aims was to overcome the perception that low fares mean poor-quality service. To "bring humanity back to air travel," as he put it, JetBlue would hire the best people and train them well.

JetBlue's entry into the market escalated the already intense competition in the airline industry. Within its first four years of operation, the airline was serving 25 cities, just as Neeleman had planned.[1] By 2004, revenues were approaching $1 billion.[2] During this time the major airlines' revenues fell 10 percent, and they are not expected to ever fully rebound.[3] With the majors (American, Delta, Continental, Northwest, United, and US Airways) struggling with high costs and dissatisfied customers, low-cost airlines like JetBlue and Southwest have been demonstrating how to make passengers happy while showing a profit. The difference has come down to costs. Southwest's operating costs per flight have been roughly half of those at major airlines, and JetBlue's costs at 6.4 cents a mile have been even lower than Southwest's 7.4 cents.[4] When the economy was in high gear several years ago, the major airlines had a huge run-up in union wages. The low-fare airlines generally pay employees less and get more work from them. Because discount airlines also fly more direct flights, they don't have to wait for connections and can turn planes around faster; planes make money when they are in the air. Finally, JetBlue and other low-fare carriers can select the markets where they see the largest opportunities. As new companies, they don't have large national and international networks established.

Growth can bring problems, and all has not been perfect at JetBlue. Stock prices reached a peak in October 2003 at $47 a share and fell to $23 in 2004.[5] Some industry analysts say the airline expanded too fast, adding new routes and planes faster than demand. Also, JetBlue faces competition from other new low-fare airlines, such as AirTran, ATA, and Spirit, as well as those backed by the majors, such as Sony and Ted, started by Delta and United, respectively. Managing expansion has been the downfall of many firms in numerous industries. Southwest Airlines took 27 years to grow to 280 planes.[6] David Neeleman has remained optimistic, seeing many new markets and plenty of opportunities for low-fare airlines and planning routes out of La Guardia, New York's other main airport.

Questions

1. What is the role of the CEO, such as David Neeleman, in developing plans and strategies? What traits are needed to be successful in this role?
2. What was Neeleman's plan for entering the airline market? Which factors were in his favor, and which were against him?
3. Why do growth companies like JetBlue often struggle with expansion? How could planning assist managers in overcoming the risks associated with rapid growth and expansion?

Chapter 9 Video Case: Starbucks: Building Relationships with Coffee Growers

As the world's largest supplier of premium-based coffee, Starbucks goes to great lengths to satisfy its customers. Since the company started in 1971, it has grown to nearly 6,000 outlets in 30 countries, with sales in excess of $3.5 billion. A key to Starbucks' success is the relationship the firm has established with coffee growers.

Starbucks depends on the coffee bean for its success. Coffee is grown in 70 tropical nations, and quality varies tremendously from region to region. Starbucks buys a special grade of coffee—one grown at high altitudes—that is very dense. This density or compaction of flavors creates specialty coffee. The specialty-coffee industry has grown tremendously but still accounts for only 10 percent of worldwide coffee purchases.

During the past five years, the supply of coffee produced has exceeded demand. As a result, the price has fallen below the break-even point for most producers, and small producers find that they can't survive in this environment. Starbucks realizes it needs quality growers so that quality coffee will be available in years to come.

To ensure a steady supply of specialty-coffee beans, Starbucks invests heavily in its relationships with suppliers. Starbucks buys primarily from small farmers, teaching them how to produce specialty coffee. Starbucks also pays above market price for coffee, thereby enabling small farmers to stay in business. Prices are set for a year, so farmers lock in a profit.

To stabilize prices, Starbucks has begun to negotiate long-term contracts with growers. As a result, Starbucks is guaranteed a regular supply of products and growers are assured of future sales at predictable prices. Farmers can then invest in their business to ensure supply in the years ahead.

Starbucks has recently partnered with Ecologic Enterprise Ventures and Conservation International, two nonprofit organizations, to provide affordable credit to coffee farmers in Latin America. This works like a bridge loan to farmers who are ecologically friendly so that they can pay their pickers until the crop is harvested. As with the long-term contracts, this arrangement helps to ensure that growers will be around for years to come.

Starbucks has also begun to sell Fair Trade Coffee. To be certified by Fair Trade Labeling (FLO) Organizations International, coffee producers must belong to democratically run cooperatives or associations and must implement crop management and environmental protection plans. Price incentives are used to encourage producers to work toward organic production. In return, they are guaranteed a fair price, long-term relationships with importers, and credit. Starbucks offers Fair Trade Coffee in its retail stores, and the product is coffee of the day at least once a month.

Starbucks has also partnered with Conservation International to encourage environmentally friendly coffee-growing practices in a reserve in Mexico. Trees are no longer cut down to plant coffee trees. The result is a smooth, mellow coffee grown in shade, the very popular Shade Grown Mexico.

Questions

1. Why are relationships with growers critical to Starbucks' success in satisfying its customers?
2. What strategies are used by Starbucks to improve relationships with suppliers? How could these strategies lead to a competitive advantage?
3. Why is quality critical in the specialty-coffee industry? How do relationships with both suppliers and other organizations influence quality at Starbucks?

Chapter 10 Video Case: Now Who's Boss?

How can managers really find out what's involved in the jobs their employees do? Do the work themselves, of course. That's what Jonathan Tisch, chairman and CEO of Loews Hotels, did at his Miami Beach property. For days, he donned uniforms and worked in six entry-level jobs—bellman, breakfast cook, room-service waiter, front-desk clerk, pool attendant, and housekeeper. Tisch was watched not only by his employees but also by viewers who saw *Now Who's Boss?* when the segment was aired on the Learning Channel.

For the role reversal, employees worked alongside Tisch or kept a close eye as he checked in guests, cooked omelets, delivered drinks poolside, or made beds with hospital corners and military precision. The CEO put himself and his ego on the line; he is shown fumbling, sweating, and struggling through various tasks. Afterward, the usual jobholders were asked to critique his performance. Tisch says he wanted honest assessments, and he got them, including a grade of C for his turn as housekeeper.

Working at hotel service jobs was not a totally new experience for Tisch, who grew up in the hospitality business. His family owned a chain of hotels along the East Coast, from New York to Miami. As a child, Tisch helped out in hotel kitchens during family vacations. At 16, he held a paying job as desk clerk at one of his family's hotels.[1] It had been a long time, however, since the CEO had worked in a service job.

The experience opened Tisch's eyes to the difficulty of the work and the amount of training and experience required to do it well. As a desk clerk, he lacked the computer skills needed to quickly register guests; he saw firsthand the demands of welcoming tired or cranky arrivals. In Miami's summer heat, he felt the discomfort of polyester uniforms. He spent an exhausting three hours cleaning a room instead of the typical half hour. The housekeepers laughed when Tisch recounted his troubles and applauded when he expressed his respect for them and his appreciation for the demands of their job—the toughest one, the CEO found. Respect for employees and rapport with them are two big benefits he derived. "People say, 'If the CEO is willing to clean toilets and make beds, then he must care about us.'"[2]

The job switching required hard work and a significant amount of executive time—a half day per job—but Tisch saw tremendous value in it. "I thought I had all the answers," he says, "but looking at all these positions with the eye of a CEO, I learned a lot."[3] Tisch started a companywide "Now Who's Boss?" day. Every year the managers and senior staff of each hotel take a day to work in a service job. Employee roundtables often follow so that Loews personnel can share and evaluate experiences. The communication helps everyone recognize what's required in the day-to-day running of a hotel.

The hotel business has changed in the 35 years Tisch has been involved; it is now very technical and highly competitive. But he says the nature of the hospitality industry has stayed the same for hundreds of years: "When you are in the hotel business, you have to create partnerships with employees and guests."[4]

Questions

1. Describe how jobs would be designed at a hotel such as Loews.
2. Describe the organizational structure of a Loews hotel.
3. According to the job characteristics model, how would you rate the jobs performed by hotel employees?

Chapter 11 Video Case: BP: Building a Global Brand

British Petroleum (BP) was a midsize international company before 1998. Then, over four years, the company doubled in size and expanded into new markets. A merger with Amoco gave BP an important position in the American market. BP then acquired Arco, another American firm, to gain a coast-to-coast presence in the United States. Acquiring the lubricant brand Castrol, the German company Aral, and several other firms resulted in a strong presence in the European market. Growing from 55,000 employees to 117,000, BP emerged as one of the world's largest energy companies and faced the challenge of reinventing itself as a global corporation.

The merging of nine companies made BP a company with no common past, but its leaders recognized the need for a common future. BP undertook a major initiative to rebrand itself so that everyone in the organization could identify with the large new company. The objective was to create a sense of belonging through a new set of values with which all employees could align and relate in their everyday dealings with customers and other stakeholders.

To create the new brand, BP consulted employees from all of its component companies. Four core values were identified:

Performance—about meeting goals, including financial performance.

Innovation—about allowing your people to seek new solutions to new problems.

Progressive—relating to an attitude that constantly challenges the organization and recognizes diversity.

Green—representing the organization's responsibility to society and the environment (for example, searching for new types of fuels and engines).

BP looks at these four values as its corporate brand, what BP stands for, and how it operates. They influence the approach everyone at BP takes. These core values move beyond cultural differences and business environments throughout the world. Ways of doing business may differ, but the values remain the same. For instance, the operating guidelines BP has established in Columbia are stricter than those required by the local and national legislatures. BP applies its core values even if doing so means taking a more difficult route.

Employees were crucial to the successful implementation of the new brand. A major challenge was to unify, excite, and motivate the entire organization. To get employees to understand and commit to the core values, BP made the brand a major part of a training process that occurs throughout employees' careers. In "brand modules," employees discuss with team leaders the core values and what they actually mean in their daily lives. Once employees internalize the firm's values, delivery across various cultures comes naturally.

After the new brand was developed, it had to be communicated externally. BP faced the challenge of changing consumers' negative view of the oil industry. One strategy was to base marketing efforts on the core values to create a positive response in the minds of customers and to establish a new type of relationship with society. BP put one group in charge of worldwide communication to develop a consistent message to the public and at the same time be responsive to local needs.

Questions

1. Why was it important for BP to change its brand? What was the objective of the rebranding initiative?
2. What role did employees have in establishing the four core values? How does the set of values influence the behavior of BP employees?
3. What challenges did BP face in implementing the new brand? How did BP meet those challenges?

Chapter 12 Video Case: The SAS Institute

SAS originated in 1976 when several partners in North Carolina, supported by the U.S. Department of Agriculture, developed software to be used by the land grant universities to determine crop yield. When the universities didn't want the product, the partners decided to market it themselves and founded the SAS Institute in Raleigh, North Carolina. Today, SAS is the world's largest privately held software company, producing high-end analytic, data-mining, and data-warehousing software. With customers in more than 30 countries and more than 3.5 million users, SAS has worldwide revenue in excess of $1.3 billion.

At SAS, it all begins with people. As other firms in the industry have downsized, SAS has continued to hire. While the firm has had 93,000 applicants to fill 500 jobs, SAS realizes that a 10 million employee shortfall (according to the Bureau of Labor Statistics) will occur in the next five to seven years. Thus, creating an environment that attracts and retains the best people is critical. At SAS, the objective is to place the best person in every position and to maximize performance through a stimulating environment and incentives. Managers use every recruitment tool available to identify the most qualified candidates. According to Jeff Chambers, vice president of human resources, the challenge is not getting applicants but selecting the best and brightest. The human resource department screens applicants and then leaves the ultimate decision to the individual hiring manager. Usually the manager will make sure all team members interview applicants to be certain they have the needed skills and can work as part of a team.

Human resource management at SAS begins with planning. In a five-step process, managers (1) prepare an employee inventory, (2) prepare a job analysis, (3) assess future human resource demand, (4) assess future human resource supply, and (5) establish a strategic plan.

SAS focuses on quality rather than quantity, so managers spend a lot of time interviewing and evaluating prospects. Management believes that spending more time on the front end results in greater retention in the long run. At SAS, turnover is less than 5 percent, and average tenure is almost 12 years.

SAS promotes from within whenever possible, since providing opportunities to advance within the company helps retain people. Training and development occur through mentoring—junior staff working with senior staff—online training, internships, and apprenticeships. In-house classes covering everything from technical skills to human relations support the training. The SAS work-life program fosters personal growth, and programs like the lunchtime learning series help increase employee wellness and loyalty.

In addition to offering competitive salaries and bonuses, SAS provides a rich benefit plan to attract and keep valued employees. Benefits include health care, on-site recreation and fitness, and heavily subsidized on-site day care. In developing its benefit package, SAS takes great care to solicit employee needs. For example, SAS found an effective way to provide retirement health care. Other benefits such as telecommuting (working from home), job sharing, and flextime make SAS attractive to prospective employees.

Given the investment SAS makes in its people, performance appraisal is necessary to make sure the company receives a return on its investment. Performance appraisal at SAS aims to help employees see where they fit in the overall picture—what they do well, what they don't do so well, where they need to improve, how their jobs help meet department and division goals.

If SAS has a formula for success, it is creating a work environment in which employees are respected and treated well. This practice not only distinguishes SAS from competitors but also saves money; the firm estimates that low turnover saves $80 million to $100 million a year. SAS recognizes that people are an asset and that quality software can be produced only by quality people.

Questions

1. Why does SAS place so much emphasis on recruiting and retaining top employees? What are some of the benefits the company uses to attract and keep the best people?
2. How does training and development occur at SAS? What tools are used to support training efforts?
3. What is the goal of the performance appraisal system used at SAS?

Chapter 13 Video Case: Working for the Best: The Container Store

The Container Store management hopes that customers will immediately notice two things: great products and happy employees. A perennial among the top five on lists of best companies, The Container Store twice has been selected by *Fortune* magazine as the number-one company to work for in the United States. According to chairman and co-founder Garrett Boone, this recognition results directly from hiring great people—one of the six foundation principles that constitute the company's culture. The key is for employees to provide great customer service *when* it is needed, whether it be helping a customer organize a garage or closet or answering a simple question. Great service requires motivated employees who are empowered to exceed customer expectations.

How are employees at The Container Store motivated to provide great customer service? Managers have applied several theories of motivation to develop a culture in which jobs are interesting and employees are not afraid to take a chance. They are not afraid to fail. While Taylor and the scientific management proponents emphasized efficiency and proper programming, The Container Store takes a much more humanistic approach to motivating by recognizing a wide range of employee needs.

In the 1950s, psychologist Abraham Maslow theorized that people are motivated to satisfy current needs in the categories of physiological, safety, social, esteem, and self-actualization. The categories form a hierarchy, with the most basic needs, physiological and safety, at the bottom. The higher-level needs—social, esteem, and self-actualization—are at the top of the hierarchy. The Container Store plays a role in meeting all these employee needs. Wages, among the highest in the industry, help individuals satisfy physiological needs and motivate employees to perform at higher levels of productivity. The environment helps people feel emotionally secure by stressing such values as integrity, honesty, and open communication. Social needs are met by The Container Store's family atmosphere, where people feel they belong to a group. By recognizing employees both formally and informally when they do something extra special, the company helps employees meet the need for esteem. Finally, the highest-level need of self-actualization is met by encouraging employees to reach their highest potential. Many part-time employees become full-time employees; many of the managers began their careers as part-timers. The turnover at The Container Store provides some evidence that employees' needs are being met. The company averages about 15 to 20 percent in an industry where turnover is 90 to 100 percent annually.

The Container Store also seeks out managers who follow McGregor's (Chapter 2) Theory Y in their assumptions about employees. Theory Y assumes that workers are not lazy by nature and, when the opportunity arises, will do what is best for the organization. Following this belief fosters a relaxed atmosphere and empowered workers. Employees are expected to think for themselves and are given the authority to make decisions without checking with a manager first.

Pride in the work itself is also obvious at The Container Store. Employees are cross-trained so that they understand everyone else's job, a practice that makes jobs more interesting and prepares employees to make decisions should the need arise. In effect, employees operate much like a store manager, capable of making decisions that generate better customer service.

The Container Store also emphasizes coaching and learning. Managers work with employees on a daily and weekly basis to help them develop skills, work on weaknesses, and enhance strengths. Victor Vroom's expectancy theory states that the amount of effort employees put in depends on their expectations of the outcome. Similarly, equity theory deals with the question "If I do a good job, will it be worth it? What's fair?" When it comes to employee expectations and equity, the key point is that organizations communicate effectively. Kip Tendell, The Container Store's president and CEO, says that communication is the number-one factor when it comes to motivation. Open communication extends down to the team level, where peers are encouraged to share their knowledge with one another regardless of position.

Questions

1. Using Maslow's hierarchy of needs, explain how The Container Store satisfies the needs of its employees.
2. How are workers at The Container Store motivated?
3. Why don't managers at The Container Store use just one approach in motivating employees?

Chapter 14 Video Case: Martha Stewart and Celebrity CEOs

In the healthy business climate and stock market boom of the 1990s, CEOs gained attention as the value of their companies soared. Growing stock portfolios and tremendous media focus on corporate leaders led investors, employees, and the public to view many executives as celebrities and even gurus.

Companies also joined in the hero worship. CEOs became valued more for their charisma than their experience, says Rakesh Khurana of the Harvard Business School. Over 17 years he studied the selection process 850 firms used to find top executives, and he found a major change. CEOs traditionally have been promising executives that companies developed for years to take over the top job. In the 90s, however, boards often looked instead for a well-known executive outside their organization in the hopes that bringing on a personable, dynamic, and media-savvy CEO would spur investors and then stock prices.

To find a CEO who fit the bill, companies often use headhunters—and pay these middlemen well. For example, Gerry Roache, the headhunter who placed Michael Armstrong at AT&T, receives one-third of the executive's first year's pay, a cut that could sometimes be millions. Do the firms get their money's worth by bringing in a celebrity CEO rather than developing managers the old-fashioned way? Even executive recruiter Roache has commented, quite candidly, that "if management and directors worked harder at management development, we [headhunters] would be close to being out of business." Several companies—Kodak, Xerox, and AT&T among them—have found that having a celebrity CEO does not guarantee a better bottom line. Perhaps it's much better to have an executive who doesn't get publicity for his or her personality but who concentrates on the business. Under Marsh Carter, for example, Boston's State Street Bank experienced 700 percent growth in stock value in the 90s. Probably the ultimate celebrity CEO has been Martha Stewart, whose company, Martha Stewart Living Omnimedia, has been tied closely to its founder from the start. Few executives have received as much media exposure as Stewart, who starred in her television program and infused her magazine with her point of view. After her conviction in an insider-trading case brought by the Securities and Exchange Commission, Stewart resigned from her company's board of directors and stepped down as the chief creative officer. She assumed a new role as founding editorial director, in which she will give input on new products.

Stewart's resignation furthered the attempt to separate Martha Stewart the person from the brand bearing her ubiquitous name. The company changed the *Martha Stewart Living* magazine logo by shrinking her name to a smaller box and enlarging the typeface for *Living.* It also made plans for a new nationwide PBS program called *Everyday Foods,* which would use the staff Stewart had assembled but not her name. The firm also planned to drop its catalog business, although it would keep its direct-to-consumer floral business and its Web site.[1]

Many industry analysts thought the move to distance Stewart from her company was the right one, since the brand was badly damaged in the enormous publicity surrounding her case. The magazine suffered huge losses—40 percent—in advertising revenue. Yet others said that removing Stewart's name left the company with very little, because it had no "diva" to replace her.[2] Some said that despite being tarnished in public opinion, the Stewart name was still good among millions of women. Even after her trial and conviction, the mass-market brand she founded, Martha Stewart Everyday, continued to sell well in retail stores. One retailer commented that the brand has always sold well because the quality is consistent and also because Stewart and her company understand the tastes of "Middle America."[3] Kmart extended its agreement with Martha Stewart Omnimedia and will hold the rights to the brand through 2009.[4]

In spite of her legal troubles, Martha Stewart continued building her celebrity status as she wrote two books and conducted book signings. Facing a sentence of five months in jail and five months of home confinement, the irrepressible Stewart said publicly that after serving her jail time, she planned to reclaim her company.

Questions

1. How does the personal characteristic called charisma affect leadership?
2. What do you think are the sources of Martha Stewart's power?
3. Can a leader retain or reclaim power and effectiveness after going through a situation like Martha Stewart's?

Chapter 15 Video Case: Pike Place Fish

Pike Place Fish is located in Seattle's historic, open-air Pike Place Market. People come from many parts of the world to see the fish mongers throwing fish and having fun and to buy high-quality seafood and have it shipped home. From a humble beginning as a small fish stand, Pike Place Fish has gained a big reputation. The change began when a young employee said, "Let's be world famous," and the owner responded, "Why not?"

John Yokoyama worked at Pike Place Fish when the owner offered to sell him the business in 1965. Only 25, Yokoyama was reluctant to buy the struggling market, but after much thought he decided to give it a try. Yokoyama knew nothing about managing people, and his management style was that of a tyrant: You do what I tell you or else. Pike Place Fish did not do well, and Yokoyama was close to failing. That's when Jim Bergquist entered the scene.

A consultant whose wife worked at the fish market, Bergquist approached Yokoyama with a proposition: Give me three months and I'll improve your business, or else I'll quit. They agreed. Then, when they were trying to decide their strategy, the young worker made his wild suggestion. At first the partners regarded the notion of becoming world famous as a joke, but the idea began to grow on them. They adopted the idea and added the words *world famous* to the company's logo and had them printed on shipping boxes.

What does it mean to be world famous? That's what Yokoyama, Bergquist, and their crew had to figure out. They decided it means making a difference in the lives of customers and others with whom they come into contact. "For us it means going beyond just providing outstanding service to people," explains Yokoyama. "We're out to discover how we can make their day. We've made a commitment to have our customers leave with the experience of having been served. They experience being . . . appreciated whether they buy fish or not."[1]

Providing such an experience for customers requires total commitment. At Pike Place Fish, there are no jobs but, rather, positions available for those who make the team. You have to commit to the purpose—being world famous—or you won't even want to be on the team. New employees sometimes take three months to understand the distinction—*being* world famous rather than merely wanting to be or believing you are—and become productive team members.

A big change for John Yokoyama was sharing responsibility and power with workers. Yokoyama found that the best way to manage the type of team he needed was to stay out of employees' way and let them be creative and manage themselves. Inspirational management is the preferred style. Pike Place Fish creates a context for personal growth and development. For instance, someone who wants to master the art of filleting fish will be coached to reach that goal. Anyone can be a coach, and everyone is allowed to coach others. The intention is for the coach to empower the other person to achieve. When coaching is needed, everyone has the responsibility to step up and contribute.

Pike Place Fish has earned its fame without advertising, except on its Web site.[2] The company's success, the team says, is the result of its vision and commitment to making a difference for people.

Questions

1. What does it mean at Pike Place Fish to be world famous?
2. What role do teams play in Pike Place Fish's quest to be world famous? Why does it take new employees time, in some cases three months, to become productive team members?
3. How does Pike Place Fish create the context for workers to reach their maximum potential? What role do managers play in creating and nurturing this atmosphere?

Chapter 16 Video Case: A Clash of Styles at Midnight Visions

Situation

Pilar Grimault, senior account manager at Midnight Visions, a New York–based advertising agency, has called creative designer Miguel Valentino into her office. Miguel is young (26 years old), creative, energetic, and sometimes arrogant. Pilar is well liked by most, despite her strong style, but feared by some. While Miguel's work on the Jezebel account has been a creative success, the client complained because Miguel went over budget by a considerable amount. Pilar has called a meeting to discuss the situation with Miguel and make sure it doesn't happen again.

First Meeting

Miguel arrives at the meeting quite happy about the projects he's been working on. Pilar tries to discuss the Jezebel account, but Miguel appears to be disinterested; his cell phone rings, and his attention drifts. When Pilar finally brings up the budget, Miguel becomes defensive and upset. Pilar shares in the responsibility for going over budget and even seems apologetic. Pilar suggests that Miguel's assistant prepare a weekly update on the budgets for all his accounts, but Miguel balks at the idea. He thinks the product comes first, and as an artist, he can't spend his time on budgets. Pilar reiterates that the problem must be resolved or it will fall on her shoulders. Miguel says "Whatever," and leaves as the meeting ends.

Manager's View: Pilar thinks Miguel was distracted and was not concentrating. He needs to be more professional and focus on his work. Although he is an artist, he needs to accept constructive criticism and realize that budgets are important, even if he does a good job on the creative side.

Second Meeting

This meeting takes a more serious tone. Pilar tells Miguel he is being taken off the Jezebel account for the remainder of the campaign. At first, Miguel can't believe it; he is argumentative and blames Pilar for taking the account away. She explains that the client asked that he be taken off the account for reasons discussed during their first meeting. She reminds him that he didn't listen to her advice, and Miguel seems to finally understand. Pilar tells him that he must communicate better with her and his clients about the budget and the status of projects. Miguel asks what he specifically needs to do to communicate better. Pilar suggests he submit a budget report every Friday and they meet the following Tuesday to discuss the report. Miguel records everything and realizes as he leaves that he and Pilar can be a successful team.

Manager's View: Pilar thinks Miguel was more receptive during their second meeting. While he took the news hard, he was more serious, more professional, and more attentive. If the problem happens again, she won't be so easy on him. Pilar won't lose an account because of Miguel.

Questions

1. How do the two meetings between Pilar and Miguel illustrate the importance of good communication? How would you rate Pilar's communication skills as a sender? As a receiver?
2. Where did the communication process break down between Pilar and Miguel during their first meeting? Do you agree with Pilar's assessment of the first meeting?
3. How do you explain Miguel's apparent change in attitude during his second meeting with Pilar? Do you think Pilar has effectively communicated to Miguel that if the problem occurs again, his job is in jeopardy?

Chapter 17 Video Case: Trouble at Disney

In a letter dated November 30, 2003, Roy Disney resigned from the Walt Disney Company as chairman of the feature animation division and vice chairman of the board of directors. Roy, whose father Roy Disney and uncle Walt Disney founded the company, was the last family member active in the Disney empire. "It is my sincere belief that it is you who should be leaving and not me," chairman Michael Eisner told Roy Disney. "Accordingly, I once again call for your resignation or retirement."

In 1984, Roy Disney headed the restructuring team that installed Eisner in the job of chairman and CEO of the Disney company, which was under tremendous pressure at the time. Roy had resigned from the company's board to protest the direction it was going in. Eisner and Disney had a genial relationship for many years. Eisner was respectful to the man who had brought him into the company and to the Disney name.

Eisner's deference to Roy Disney and the firm's traditions were especially evident during successful years at the company; in tougher times the relationship soured. Some say Roy Disney's resignation was a preemptive strike because the board was going to vote him off. The previous year, in the interest of good corporate governance, the board had adopted a mandatory retirement age of 72 for board members, 75 if they were former CEOs. At 73, Roy Disney voted for the policy change, perhaps thinking a Disney family member would be given special consideration.

The problems facing Disney have remained the same for several years. ABC television, which Disney acquired in 1995, has trailed in prime-time ratings. ABC Family Channel, a cable channel Disney purchased, has also struggled. While Disney's film studio has had a few hits, most notably *Pirates of the Caribbean,* the company's theme park business has not recovered since 9/11.

To make matters worse, in January 2004, Pixar Animation Studios ended its partnership with the Walt Disney Company. Pixar had scored a string of five box office hits, starting with *Toy Story* in 1995 and including *Finding Nemo,* the highest-grossing animated film ever. The split came as a surprise to some, because the relationship had been so successful. According to media analyst Jordan Rohan, when something is going that well, you usually don't walk away from it. Pixar executives thought the creative content their studios provided was worth more than a 50 percent share of the profits. Pixar founder and chief executive Steve Jobs wanted to seek a deal that gives the company full ownership of its productions. Disney's own animated films have had mixed success in recent years.

The problems plaguing the Disney company did not force Eisner out, but they did give Roy Disney more ammunition to urge shareholders to vote against him. On March 4, 2004, more than 43 percent of the voting shareholders gave Eisner a vote of no confidence. At that, the board unanimously decided to separate the positions of chairman and chief executive officer; it allowed Eisner to keep his title of CEO but named George Mitchell the new chairman.[1] Six months later, in September 2004, Eisner announced that he would step down as Disney's CEO when his contract expired in 2006. Some analysts commented that Eisner, a strong-willed and combative leader with a tight hold on power within the company, may have intended to prevent more battles over his leadership and to try to rebuild his legacy, which was clouded by declining earnings, a falling stock price, and numerous controversies.[2]

Questions

1. What are the types and sources of conflict between Roy Disney and Michael Eisner? How has Eisner's power diminished in recent years?
2. What strategies could have been used to avoid Pixar's decision to end its relationship with the Disney Company?
3. In your opinion, does Disney need change? If so, how could the change process be managed?

Chapter 18 Video Case: Louisville Slugger (Hillerich & Bradsby)

What do Babe Ruth's 60th home run, Joe Di Maggio's 56-game hitting streak, Ted Williams' .406 season, and Hank Aaron's record-breaking 715th home run have in common? They all were accomplished with Louisville Slugger bats manufactured on the Ohio River at Hillerich & Bradsby (H&B).[1] Best known for its bats—its wooden bats claim 60 percent of the major league market—H&B, based in Louisville, Kentucky, also manufactures a variety of baseball, golf, and hockey equipment for amateur and professional athletes.

The company was founded in 1857 as J.F. Hillerich & Son to manufacture butter churns. It entered the baseball market when one of Hillerich's sons, Bud, promised a star player he could make a bat for him. H&B began producing aluminum bats in 1928 and today relies on the wooden and aluminum bat business for nearly three-quarters of its annual revenues.

The company remains family-run; John Hillerich IV, the fourth-generation CEO, took over the private company from his father. He feels the pressure heading a successful company that is over 120 years old, as competition in the industry has intensified like never before. The Louisville Slugger bat now competes with bats made by a host of other sources, ranging from carpenters to Amish craftspeople. To gain an advantage, H&B looked at its internal system in order to streamline operations. The company needed to address everything from order entry problems to production deficiencies to returns. The overview led to discussion of a new system to handle the flow of information.

H&B had a big decision to make: It could either reconfigure its information system or start over with a new system designed to streamline the information flow in support of the sales operation and supply change management, as well as accounting, finance, and marketing. Management realized it needed a new system to improve the company's dismal shipping record; about 40 percent of its orders were being shipped on time. The managers opted for the enterprise resource planning (ERP) system, designed to simplify all processes by storing all information in one common database and automatically updating the information in every stage of production.

Implementation of the new ERP system usually takes years, and the transition from the old system to the new one is difficult. Since the ERP system uses real-time information, the production department manufactures only the inventory that the sales department has requested, so the shipping department has the proper amount of inventory to send to customers. The benefits of ERP are bottom-line savings for the company and improved morale as frustration from repetitive tasks and missing information dissipates. H&B managers thought that the cost of implementing the new system was worth the potential savings. Communication between production and sales had been inefficient, as well as that with management. Getting an answer to one simple question could take a week.

The first step in streamlining production was to identify problems and devise the needs of the new ERP system. Then, the German company SAP was chosen to provide the software. With the SAP system, a common server holds all the company's information. Every personal computer (PC) is connected to the server. Once data are entered, they are stored in the server, where everyone can access the data from a PC.

During the 18-month configuration process, morale sagged as long-time employees struggled to change the way they worked. Some employees left during training classes, stress levels temporarily increased, and some production processes failed. H&B managers thought about halting the new system, but after struggling through implementation, the company began seeing benefits; it took five years to see quantifiable results. Now the company ships 85 percent of its orders on time and complete, compared to 40 percent before the SAP system. Top customers surveyed rate H&B in the 90 to 95 percent satisfaction category.

Questions

1. What role do information systems play at H&B? What were the trade-offs between reconfiguring the old information system and designing a new one?
2. Why was the transition to the new system difficult? What can managers do to make this type of transition go more smoothly?
3. What were some of the benefits of the new system?

Chapter 19 Video Case: Toying with Success: The McFarlane Companies

Todd McFarlane, president and CEO of the McFarlane Companies, is an entrepreneur who understands the importance of product development. Comics, sports, toys, and rock-and-roll have all benefited from his creativity. When Todd's dream to play major league baseball didn't happen, he fell back on another interest he developed as a teenager—drawing superheroes. He faced the same question faced by all entrepreneurs: Could he make money pursuing his dream? He sent his sketches to prospective employers, and after 300 rejection letters Todd got a job freelancing for Marvel Comics. Working many hours for low pay, Todd made a name for himself and by 1990 was the highest-paid comic book artist in the industry.

Frustrated over creative differences and his desire to own the rights to his characters, Todd quit, took six other artists with him, and started his own company. He went from artist to entrepreneur overnight. While industry experts predicted he would last less than a year, Todd didn't even think about the future. *Spawn,* his first comic, sold 107 million copies.

Entrepreneurship rewards individuals willing to take risks. In Todd's case, the need to control his destiny drove his aspirations. His path is similar to that taken by many: receiving training at a large company, and then leaving when he decided he could provide a better product on his own.

Today's dynamic business environment has a tremendous effect on the success or failure of entrepreneurs like Todd McFarlane. Economics plays a key role at the McFarlane Companies. Todd must protect the many intellectual properties the firm creates and licenses; laws are crucial to survival. The business uses technology to support and spark creativity in developing new products. The competitive environment drives quality at McFarlane, which produces high-quality products even if they cost more and thus gains an edge over competitors. The CEO uses the Web to interact with his key demographic, or, as he puts it, the "freaks" with long hair and cool tattoos. Spawn.com provides a place where fans can interact with each other and with the company. Finally, the global influence on business impacts all the other environments. Knowing he can't control the global environment, Todd focuses on managing what he can control.

Todd's purchase of Mark McGwire's 70th home-run ball for $3 million illustrates his willingness to take a risk and focus on what he controls. While many thought he was crazy, Todd saw an opportunity. He combined the ball with several other McGwire and Sosa balls to create the McFarlane Collection, which was displayed in every major league stadium and led to enormous publicity. A portion of the proceeds was donated to the Lou Gehrig Foundation. Most significant, Todd began a relationship with professional sports that led to his obtaining the exclusive rights to nearly every professional sports-team toy license.

Questions

1. What traits do entrepreneurs like Todd McFarlane possess that distinguish them from other individuals? What are the risks and rewards faced by entrepreneurs?
2. How does today's dynamic business environment influence the success or failure of the McFarlane Companies?
3. Why is the development of new products such as sports figures critical to the McFarlane Companies?

Glossary

ACCOMODATIVE APPROACH Companies and their managers behave legally and ethically and try to balance the interests of different stakeholders as the need arises.

ACHIEVEMENT ORIENTATION A worldview that values assertiveness, performance, success, and competition.

ADAPTIVE CULTURE A culture whose values and norms help an organization to build momentum, grow, and change as needed to achieve its goals.

ADMINISTRATIVE MANAGEMENT The study of how to create an organizational structure that leads to high efficiency and effectiveness.

ADMINISTRATIVE MODEL An approach to decision making that explains why decision making is inherently uncertain and risky and why managers usually make satisfactory rather than optimum decisions.

AGREEABLENESS The tendency to get along well with other people.

ALDERFER'S ERG THEORY The theory that three universal needs–existence, relatedness, and growth–constitute a hierarchy of needs and motivate behavior. Alderfer proposed that needs at more than one level can be motivational at the same time.

AMBIGUOUS INFORMATION Information that can be interpreted in multiple and often conflicting ways.

APPLICATIONS SOFTWARE Software designed for a specific task or use.

ARBITRATOR A third-party negotiator who can impose what he or she thinks is a fair solution to a conflict that both parties are obligated to abide by.

ARTIFICIAL INTELLIGENCE Behavior performed by a machine that, if performed by a human being, would be called "intelligent."

ATTITUDE A collection of feelings and beliefs.

ATTRACTION-SELECTION-ATTRITION FRAMEWORK (ASA) A model that explains how personality may influence organizational culture.

AUTHORITY The power to hold people accountable for their actions and to make decisions concerning the use of organizational resources.

BARRIERS TO ENTRY Factors that make it difficult and costly for an organization to enter a particular task environment or industry.

BEHAVIORAL MANAGEMENT The study of how managers should behave to motivate employees and encourage them to perform at high levels and be committed to the achievement of organizational goals.

BENCHMARKING Comparing performance on specific dimensions with the performance of other, high-performing organizations.

BIAS The systematic tendency to use information about others in ways that result in inaccurate perceptions.

BOTTOM-UP CHANGE A gradual or evolutionary approach to change in which managers at all levels work together to develop a plan for change.

BOUNDARY SPANNING Interacting with individuals and groups outside the organization to obtain valuable information from the environment.

BOUNDARYLESS ORGANIZATION An organization whose members are linked by computers, faxes, computer-aided design systems, and video teleconferencing and who rarely, if ever, see one another face-to-face.

BOUNDED RATIONALITY Cognitive limitations that constrain one's ability to interpret, process, and act on information.

BRAND LOYALTY Customers' preference for the products of organizations currently existing in the task environment.

BUREAUCRACY A formal system of organization and administration designed to ensure efficiency and effectiveness.

BUREAUCRATIC CONTROL Control of behavior by means of a comprehensive system of rules and standard operating procedures.

BUSINESS-TO-BUSINESS (B2B) COMMERCE Trade that takes place between companies using IT and the Internet to link and coordinate the value chains of different companies.

BUSINESS-TO-BUSINESS (B2B) NETWORK A group of organizations that join together and use IT to link themselves to potential global suppliers to increase efficiency and effectiveness.

BUSINESS-TO-CUSTOMER (B2C) COMMERCE Trade that takes place between a company and individual customers using IT and the Internet.

BUSINESS-LEVEL PLAN Divisional managers' decisions pertaining to divisions' long-term goals, overall strategy, and structure.

BUSINESS-LEVEL STRATEGY A plan that indicates how a division intends to compete against its rivals in an industry.

CAFETERIA BENEFIT PLAN A plan from which employees can choose the benefits that they want.

CENTRALIZATION The concentration of authority at the top of the managerial hierarchy.

CHARISMATIC LEADER An enthusiastic, self-confident leader able to clearly communicate his or her vision of how good things could be.

CLAN CONTROL The control exerted on individuals and groups in an organization by shared values, norms, standards of behavior, and expectations.

CLASSICAL DECISION-MAKING MODEL A prescriptive approach to decision making based on the assumption that the decision maker can identify and evaluate all possible alternatives and their consequences and rationally choose the most appropriate course of action.

CLOSED SYSTEM A system that is self-contained and thus not affected by changes occurring in its external environment.

COERCIVE POWER The ability of a manager to punish others.

COLLECTIVE BARGAINING Negotiations between labor unions and managers to resolve conflicts and disputes about issues such as working hours, wages, benefits, working conditions, and job security.

COLLECTIVISM A worldview that values subordination of the individual to the goals of the group and adherence to the principle that people should be judged by their contribution to the group.

COMMAND ECONOMY An economic system in which the government owns all businesses and specifies which and how many goods and services are produced and the prices at which they are sold.

COMMAND GROUP A group composed of subordinates who report to the same supervisor; also called *department* or *unit*.

COMMUNICATION The sharing of information between two or more individuals or groups to reach a common understanding.

COMMUNICATIONS NETWORKS The pathways along which information flows in groups and teams and throughout the organization.

COMPETENCIES The specific set of skills, abilities, and experiences that allows one manager to perform at a higher level than another manager in a particular setting.

COMPETITIVE ADVANTAGE The ability of one organization to outperform other organizations because it produces desired goods or services more efficiently and effectively than they do.

COMPETITORS Organizations that produce goods and services that are similar to a particular organization's goods and services.

CONCEPTUAL SKILLS The ability to analyze and diagnose a situation and to distinguish between cause and effect.

CONCURRENT CONTROL Control that gives managers immediate feedback on how efficiently inputs are being transformed into outputs so that managers can correct problems as they arise.

CONCURRENT ENGINEERING The simultaneous design of the product and of the process for manufacturing the product.

CONSCIENTIOUSNESS The tendency to be careful, scrupulous, and persevering.

CONSIDERATION Behavior indicating that a manager trusts, respects, and cares about subordinates.

CONTINGENCY THEORY The idea that the organizational structures and control systems managers choose depend on–are contingent on–characteristics of the external environment in which the organization operates.

CONTINUOUS-PROCESS TECHNOLOGY Technology that is almost totally mechanized and is based on the use of automated machines working in sequence and controlled through computers from a central monitoring station.

CONTRACT BOOK A written agreement that details product development factors such as responsibilities, resource commitments, budgets, time lines, and development milestones.

CONTROL SYSTEMS Formal target-setting, monitoring, evaluation, and feedback systems that provide managers with information about how well the organization's strategy and structure are working.

CONTROLLING Evaluating how well an organization is achieving its goals and taking action to maintain or improve performance; one of the four principal functions of management.

CORE MEMBERS The members of a team who bear primary responsibility for the success of a project and who stay with a project from inception to completion.

CORPORATE-LEVEL PLAN Top management's decisions pertaining to the organization's mission, overall strategy, and structure.

CORPORATE-LEVEL STRATEGY A plan that indicates in which industries and national markets an organization intends to compete.

CREATIVITY A decision maker's ability to discover original and novel ideas that lead to feasible alternative courses of action.

CROSS-FUNCTIONAL TEAM A group of managers brought together from different departments to perform organizational tasks.

CULTURE SHOCK The feelings of surprise and disorientation that people experience when they do not understand the values, folkways, and mores that guide behavior in a culture.

CUSTOMERS Individuals and groups that buy the goods and services that an organization produces.

DATA Raw, unsummarized, and unanalyzed facts.

DECISION MAKING The process by which managers respond to opportunities and threats by analyzing options and making determinations about specific organizational goals and courses of action.

DECISION SUPPORT SYSTEM An interactive computer-based management information system that managers can use to make nonroutine decisions.

DECODING Interpreting and trying to make sense of a message.

DEFENSIVE APPROACH Companies and their managers behave ethically to the degree that they stay within the law and abide strictly with legal requirements.

DELPHI TECHNIQUE A decision-making technique in which group members do not meet face-to-face but respond in writing to questions posed by the group leader.

DEMOGRAPHIC FORCES Outcomes of changes in, or changing attitudes toward, the characteristics of a population, such as age, gender, ethnic origin, race, sexual orientation, and social class.

DEPARTMENT A group of people who work together and possess similar skills or use the same knowledge, tools, or techniques to perform their jobs.

DEVELOPMENT Building the knowledge and skills of organizational members so that they will be prepared to take on new responsibilities and challenges.

DEVELOPMENTAL CONSIDERATION Behavior a leader engages in to support and encourage followers and help them develop and grow on the job.

DEVIL'S ADVOCACY Critical analysis of a preferred alternative, made in response to challenges raised by a group member who, playing the role of devil's advocate, defends unpopular or opposing alternatives for the sake of argument.

DIALECTICAL INQUIRY Critical analysis of two preferred alternatives in order to find an even better alternative for the organization to adopt.

DIFFERENTIATION STRATEGY Distinguishing an organization's products from the products of competitors in dimensions such as product design, quality, or after-sales service.

DISCIPLINE Obedience, energy, application, and other outward marks of respect for a superior's authority.

DISTRIBUTIVE JUSTICE A moral principle calling for the distribution of pay raises, promotions, and other organizational resources to be based on meaningful contributions that individuals have made and not on personal characteristics over which they have no control.

DISTRIBUTIVE NEGOTIATION Adversarial negotiation in which the parties in conflict compete to win the most resources while conceding as little as possible.

DISTRIBUTORS Organizations that help other organizations sell their goods or services to customers.

DIVERSIFICATION Expanding operations into a new business or industry and producing new goods or services.

DIVERSITY Differences among people in age, gender, race, ethnicity, religion, sexual orientation, socioeconomic background, and capabilities/disabilities.

DIVISION A business unit that has its own set of managers and functions or departments and competes in a distinct industry.

DIVISION OF LABOR Splitting the work to be performed into particular tasks and assigning tasks to individual workers.

DIVISIONAL MANAGERS Managers who control the various divisions of an organization.

DIVISIONAL STRUCTURE An organizational structure composed of separate business units within which are the functions that work together to produce a specific product for a specific customer.

E-COMMERCE Trade that takes place between companies, and between companies and individual customers, using IT and the Internet.

ECONOMIC FORCES Interest rates, inflation, unemployment, economic growth, and other factors that affect the general health and well-being of a nation or the regional economy of an organization.

ECONOMIES OF SCALE Cost advantages associated with large operations.

EFFECTIVENESS A measure of the appropriateness of the goals an organization is pursuing and of the degree to which the organization achieves those goals.

EFFICIENCY A measure of how well or how productively resources are used to achieve a goal.

EMOTIONAL INTELLIGENCE The ability to understand and manage one's own moods and emotions and the moods and emotions of other people.

EMOTIONS Intense, relatively short-lived feelings.

EMPLOYEE STOCK OPTION A financial instrument that entitles the bearer to buy shares of an organization's stock at a certain price during a certain period of time or under certain conditions.

EMPOWERMENT The expansion of employees' knowledge, tasks, and responsibilities.

ENCODING Translating a message into understandable symbols or language.

ENTERPRISE RESOURCE PLANNING (ERP) SYSTEMS Multimodule application software packages that coordinate the functional activities necessary to move products from the product design stage to the final customer stage.

ENTREPRENEUR An individual who notices opportunities and takes responsibility for mobilizing the resources necessary to produce new and improved goods and services.

ENTREPRENEURSHIP The mobilization of resources to take advantage of an opportunity to provide customers with new or improved goods and services.

ENTROPY The tendency of a closed system to lose its ability to control itself and thus to dissolve and disintegrate.

ENVIRONMENTAL CHANGE The degree to which forces in the task and general environments change and evolve over time.

EQUAL EMPLOYMENT OPPORTUNITY The equal right of all citizens to the opportunity to obtain employment regardless of their gender, age, race, country of origin, religion, or disabilities.

EQUITY The justice, impartiality, and fairness to which all organizational members are entitled.

EQUITY THEORY A theory of motivation that focuses on people's perceptions of the fairness of their work outcomes relative to their work inputs.

ESCALATING COMMITMENT A source of cognitive bias resulting from the tendency to commit additional resources to a project even if evidence shows that the project is failing.

ESPRIT DE CORPS Shared feelings of comradeship, enthusiasm, or devotion to a common cause among members of a group.

ETHICAL DECISION A decision that reasonable or typical stakeholders would find acceptable because it aids stakeholders, the organization, or society.

ETHICAL DILEMMA The quandry people find themselves in when they have to decide if they should act in a way that might help another person or group even though doing so might go against their own self-interest.

ETHICS The inner-guiding moral principles, values, and beliefs that people use to analyze or interpret a situation and then decide what is the right or appropriate way to behave.

ETHICS OMBUDSMAN A manager responsible for teaching ethical standards to all employees and monitoring their conformity to those standards.

EXECUTIVE SUPPORT SYSTEM A sophisticated version of a decision support system that is designed to meet the needs of top managers.

EXPATRIATE MANAGERS Managers who go abroad to work for a global organization.

EXPECTANCY In expectancy theory, a perception about the extent to which effort results in a certain level of performance.

EXPECTANCY THEORY The theory that motivation will be high when workers believe that high levels of effort lead to high performance and high performance leads to the attainment of desired outcomes.

EXPERT POWER Power that is based on the special knowledge, skills, and expertise that a leader possesses.

EXPERT SYSTEM A management information system that employs human knowledge, embedded in a computer, to solve problems that ordinarily require human expertise.

EXPORTING Making products at home and selling them abroad.

EXTERNAL LOCUS OF CONTROL The tendency to locate responsibility for one's fate in outside forces and to believe that one's own behavior has little impact on outcomes.

EXTINCTION Curtailing the performance of dysfunctional behaviors by eliminating whatever is reinforcing them.

EXTRAVERSION The tendency to experience positive emotions and moods and to feel good about oneself and the rest of the world.

EXTRINSICALLY MOTIVATED BEHAVIOR Behavior that is performed to acquire material or social rewards or to avoid punishment.

FACILITIES LAYOUT The process of designing the machine-worker interface to increase production system efficiency.

FEEDBACK CONTROL Control that gives managers information about customers' reactions to goods and services so that corrective action can be taken if necessary.

FEEDFORWARD CONTROL Control that allows managers to anticipate problems before they arise.

FILTERING Withholding part of a message out of the mistaken belief that the receiver does not need or will not want the information.

FIRST-LINE MANAGER A manager who is responsible for the daily supervision of nonmanagerial employees.

FLEXIBLE MANUFACTURING The set of techniques that attempt to reduce the costs associated with an operating system.

FOCUSED DIFFERENTIATION STRATEGY Serving only one segment of the overall market and trying to be the most differentiated organization serving that segment.

FOCUSED LOW-COST STRATEGY Serving only one segment of the overall market and being the lowest-cost organization serving that segment.

FOLKWAYS The routine social conventions of everyday life.

FORMAL APPRAISAL An appraisal conducted at a set time during the year and based on performance dimensions and measures that were specified in advance.

FORMAL GROUP A group that managers establish to achieve organizational goals.

FRANCHISING Selling to a foreign organization the rights to use a brand name and operating know-how in return for a lump-sum payment and a share of the profits.

FREE-MARKET ECONOMY An economic system in which private enterprise controls production and the interaction of supply and demand determines which and how many goods and services are produced and how much consumers pay for them.

FREE-TRADE DOCTRINE The idea that if each country specializes in the production of the goods and services that it can produce most efficiently, this will make the best use of global resources.

FRIENDSHIP GROUP An informal group composed of employees who enjoy each other's company and socialize with each other.

FUNCTION A unit or department in which people have the same skills or use the same resources to perform their jobs.

FUNCTIONAL-LEVEL PLAN Functional managers' decisions pertaining to the goals that they propose to pursue to help the division attain its business-level goals.

FUNCTIONAL-LEVEL STRATEGY A plan that indicates how a function intends to achieve its goals.

FUNCTIONAL MANAGERS Managers who supervise the various functions, such as manufacturing, accounting, and sales, within a division.

FUNCTIONAL STRUCTURE An organizational structure composed of all the departments that an organization requires to produce its goods or services.

GATEKEEPING Deciding what information to allow into the organization and what information to keep out.

GENDER SCHEMAS Preconceived beliefs or ideas about the nature of men and women, their traits, attitudes, behaviors, and preferences.

GENERAL ENVIRONMENT The wide-ranging economic, technological, sociocultural, demographic, political and legal, and global forces that affect an organization and its task environment.

GEOGRAPHIC STRUCTURE An organizational structure in which each region of a country or area of the world is served by a self-contained division.

GLASS CEILING A metaphor alluding to the invisible barriers that prevent minorities and women from being promoted to top corporate positions.

GLOBAL FORCES Outcomes of changes in international relationships; changes in nations' economic, political, and legal systems; and changes in technology, such as falling trade barriers, the growth of representative democracies, and reliable and instantaneous communication.

GLOBAL ORGANIZATIONS Organizations that operate and compete in more than one country.

GLOBAL OUTSOURCING The purchase of inputs from foreign suppliers, or the production of inputs abroad, to lower production costs and improve product quality or design.

GLOBAL STRATEGY Selling the same standardized product and using the same basic marketing approach in each national market.

GOAL-SETTING THEORY A theory that focuses on identifying the types of goals that are most effective in producing high levels of motivation and performance and explaining why goals have these effects.

GRAPEVINE An informal communication network along which unofficial information flows.

GROUP Two or more people who interact with each other to accomplish certain goals or meet certain needs.

GROUP COHESIVENESS The degree to which members are attracted or loyal to a group.

GROUP DECISION SUPPORT SYSTEM An executive support system that links top managers so that they can function as a team.

GROUP NORMS Shared guidelines or rules for behavior that most group members follow.

GROUP ROLE A set of behaviors and tasks that a member of a group is expected to perform because of his or her position in the group.

GROUPTHINK A pattern of faulty and biased decision making that occurs in groups whose members strive for agreement among themselves at the expense of accurately assessing information relevant to a decision.

GROUPWARE Computer software that enables members of groups and teams to share information with one another.

HAWTHORNE EFFECT The finding that a manager's behavior or leadership approach can affect workers' level of performance.

HERZBERG'S MOTIVATOR-HYGIENE THEORY A need theory that distinguishes between motivator needs (related to the nature of the work itself) and hygiene needs (related to the physical and psychological context in which the work is performed) and proposes that motivator needs must be met for motivation and job satisfaction to be high.

HEURISTICS Rules of thumb that simplify decision making.

HIERARCHY OF AUTHORITY An organization's chain of command, specifying the relative authority of each manager.

HOSTILE WORK ENVIRONMENT SEXUAL HARASSMENT Telling lewd jokes, displaying pornography, making sexually oriented remarks about someone's personal appearance, and other sex-related actions that make the work environment unpleasant.

HUMAN RELATIONS MOVEMENT A management approach that advocates the idea that supervisors should receive behavioral training to manage subordinates in ways that elicit their cooperation and increase their productivity.

HUMAN RESOURCE MANAGEMENT Activities that managers engage in to attract and retain employees and to ensure that they perform at a high level and contribute to the accomplishment of organizational goals.

HUMAN RESOURCE PLANNING Activities that managers engage in to forecast their current and future needs for human resources.

HUMAN SKILLS The ability to understand, alter, lead, and control the behavior of other individuals and groups.

HYBRID STRUCTURE The structure of a large organization that has many divisions and simultaneously uses many different organizational structures.

ILLUSION OF CONTROL A source of cognitive bias resulting from the tendency to overestimate one's own ability to control activities and events.

IMPORTING Selling at home products that are made abroad.

INCREMENTAL PRODUCT INNOVATIONS Products that result from incremental technological changes.

INCREMENTAL TECHNOLOGICAL CHANGE Change that refines existing technology and leads to gradual improvements or refinements in products over time.

INDIVIDUAL ETHICS Personal standards and values that determine how people view their responsibilities to others and how they should act in situations when their own self-interest is at stake.

INDIVIDUALISM A worldview that values individual freedom and self-expression and adherence to the principle that people should be judged by their individual achievements rather than by their social background.

INDUSTRY LIFE CYCLE The changes that take place in an industry as it goes through the stages of birth, growth, shakeout, maturity, and decline.

INEQUITY Lack of fairness.

INFORMAL APPRAISAL An unscheduled appraisal of ongoing progress and areas for improvement.

INFORMAL GROUP A group that managers or nonmanagerial employees form to help achieve their own goals or meet their own needs.

INFORMAL ORGANIZATION The system of behavioral rules and norms that emerge in a group.

INFORMATION Data that are organized in a meaningful fashion.

INFORMATION DISTORTION Changes in the meaning of a message as the message passes through a series of senders and receivers.

INFORMATION OVERLOAD The potential for important information to be ignored or overlooked while tangential information receives attention.

INFORMATION RICHNESS The amount of information that a communication medium can carry and the extent to which the medium enables the sender and receiver to reach a common understanding.

INFORMATION SYSTEM A system for acquiring, organizing, storing, manipulating, and transmitting information.

INFORMATION TECHNOLOGY The means by which information is acquired, organized, stored, manipulated, and transmitted.

INITIATING STRUCTURE Behavior that managers engage in to ensure that work gets done, subordinates perform their jobs acceptably, and the organization is efficient and effective.

INITIATIVE The ability to act on one's own, without direction from a superior.

INPUT Anything a person contributes to his or her job or organization.

INSTRUMENTAL VALUE A mode of conduct that an individual seeks to follow.

INSTRUMENTALITY In expectancy theory, a perception about the extent to which performance results in the attainment of outcomes.

INTEGRATING MECHANISMS Organizing tools that managers can use to increase communication and coordination among functions and divisions.

INTEGRATIVE BARGAINING Cooperative negotiation in which the parties in conflict work together to achieve a resolution that is good for them both.

INTELLECTUAL STIMULATION Behavior a leader engages in to make followers aware of problems and view these problems in new ways, consistent with the leader's vision.

INTEREST GROUP An informal group composed of employees seeking to achieve a common goal related to their membership in an organization.

INTERNAL LOCUS OF CONTROL The tendency to locate responsibility for one's fate within oneself.

INTERNET A global system of computer networks.

INTRANET A companywide system of computer networks.

INTRAPRENEUR A manager, scientist, or researcher who works inside an existing organization and notices opportunities for product improvements and is responsible for managing the product development process.

INTRINSICALLY MOTIVATED BEHAVIOR Behavior that is performed for its own sake.

INTUITION Feelings, beliefs, and hunches that come readily to mind, require little effort and information gathering, and result in on-the-spot decisions.

INVENTORY The stock of raw materials, inputs, and component parts that an organization has on hand at a particular time.

JARGON Specialized language that members of an occupation, group, or organization develop to facilitate communication among themselves.

JOB ANALYSIS Identifying the tasks, duties, and responsibilities that make up a job and the knowledge, skills, and abilities needed to perform the job.

JOB DESIGN The process by which managers decide how to divide tasks into specific jobs.

JOB ENLARGEMENT Increasing the number of different tasks in a given job by changing the division of labor.

JOB ENRICHMENT Increasing the degree of responsibility a worker has over his or her job.

JOB SATISFACTION The collection of feelings and beliefs that managers have about their current jobs.

JOB SIMPLIFICATION The process of reducing the number of tasks that each worker performs.

JOB SPECIALIZATION The process by which a division of labor occurs as different workers specialize in different tasks over time.

JOINT VENTURE A strategic alliance among two or more companies that agree to jointly establish and share the ownership of a new business.

JUSTICE RULE An ethical decision is a decision that distributes benefits and harms among people and groups in a fair, equitable, or impartial way.

JUST-IN-TIME (JIT) INVENTORY SYSTEM A system in which parts or supplies arrive at an organization when they are needed, not before.

KNOWLEDGE MANAGEMENT The sharing and integrating of expertise within and between functions and divisions through real-time, interconnected IT.

KNOWLEDGE MANAGEMENT SYSTEM A company-specific virtual information system that allows workers to share their knowledge and expertise and find others to help solve ongoing problems.

LABOR RELATIONS The activities that managers engage in to ensure that they have effective working relationships with the labor unions that represent their employees' interests.

LATERAL MOVE A job change that entails no major changes in responsibility or authority levels.

LEADER An individual who is able to exert influence over other people to help achieve group or organizational goals.

LEADER-MEMBER RELATIONS The extent to which followers like, trust, and are loyal to their leader; a determinant of how favorable a situation is for leading.

LEADERSHIP The process by which an individual exerts influence over other people and inspires, motivates, and directs their activities to help achieve group or organizational goals.

LEADERSHIP SUBSTITUTE Characteristics of subordinates or characteristics of a situation or context that act in place of the influence of a leader and make leadership unnecessary.

LEADING Articulating a clear vision and energizing and enabling organizational members so that they understand the part they play in achieving organizational goals; one of the four principal functions of management.

LEARNING A relatively permanent change in knowledge or behavior that results from practice or experience.

LEARNING ORGANIZATION An organization in which managers try to maximize the ability of individuals and groups to think and behave creatively and thus maximize the potential for organizational learning to take place.

LEARNING THEORIES Theories that focus on increasing employee motivation and performance by linking the outcomes that employees receive to the performance of desired behaviors and the attainment of goals.

LEGITIMATE POWER The authority that a manager has by virtue of his or her position in an organization's hierarchy.

LICENSING Allowing a foreign organization to take charge of manufacturing and distributing a product in its country or world region in return for a negotiated fee.

LINE MANAGER Someone in the direct line or chain of command who has formal authority over people and resources lower down.

LINE OF AUTHORITY The chain of command extending from the top to the bottom of an organization.

LINGUISTIC STYLE A person's characteristic way of speaking.

LONG-TERM ORIENTATION A worldview that values thrift and persistence in achieving goals.

LOW-COST STRATEGY Driving the organization's costs down below the costs of its rivals.

MANAGEMENT The planning, organizing, leading, and controlling of human and other resources to achieve organizational goals efficiently and effectively.

MANAGEMENT BY OBJECTIVES (MBO) A goal-setting process in which a manager and each of his or her subordinates negotiate specific goals and objectives for the subordinate to achieve and then periodically evaluate the extent to which the subordinate is achieving those goals.

MANAGEMENT INFORMATION SYSTEM (MIS) A specific form of IT that managers utilize to generate the specific, detailed information they need to perform their roles effectively.

MANAGEMENT BY WANDERING AROUND A face-to-face communication technique in which a manager walks around a work area and talks informally with employees about issues and concerns.

MANAGEMENT SCIENCE THEORY An approach to management that uses rigorous quantitative techniques to help managers make maximum use of organizational resources.

MANAGERIAL ROLE The set of specific tasks that a manager is expected to perform because of the position he or she holds in an organization.

MARKET STRUCTURE An organizational structure in which each kind of customer is served by a self-contained division; also called *customer structure.*

MASLOW'S HIERARCHY OF NEEDS An arrangement of five basic needs that, according to Maslow, motivate behavior. Maslow proposed that the lowest level of unmet needs is the prime motivator and that only one level of needs is motivational at a time.

MASS-PROUDCTION TECHNOLOGY Technology that is based on the use of automated machines that are programmed to perform the same operations over and over.

MATRIX STRUCTURE An organizational structure that simultaneously groups people and resources by function and by product.

MECHANISTIC STRUCTURE An organizational structure in which authority is centralized, tasks and rules are clearly specified, and employees are closely supervised.

MEDIATOR A third-party negotiator who facilitates negotiations but has no authority to impose a solution.

MEDIUM The pathway through which an encoded message is transmitted to a receiver.

MENTORING A process by which an experienced member of an organization (the mentor) provides advice and guidance to a less experienced member (the protégé) and helps the less experienced member learn how to advance in the organization and in his or her career.

MERIT PAY PLAN A compensation plan that bases pay on performance.

MESSAGE The information that a sender wants to share.

MIDDLE MANAGER A manager who supervises first-line managers and is responsible for finding the best way to use resources to achieve organizational goals.

MISSION STATEMENT A broad declaration of an organization's purpose that identifies the organization's products and customers and distinguishes the organization from its competitors.

MIXED ECONOMY An economic system in which some sectors of the economy are left to private ownership and free-market mechanisms and others are owned by the government and subject to government planning.

MOOD A feeling or state of mind.

MORAL RIGHTS RULE An ethical decision is one that best maintains and protects the fundamental or inalienable rights and privileges of the people affected by it.

MORES Norms that are considered to be central to the functioning of society and to social life.

MOTIVATION Psychological forces that determine the direction of a person's behavior in an organization, a person's level of effort, and a person's level of persistence.

MULTIDOMESTIC STRATEGY Customizing products and marketing strategies to specific national conditions.

NATIONAL CULTURE The set of values that a society considers important and the norms of behavior that are approved or sanctioned in that society.

NEED A requirement or necessity for survival and well-being.

NEED FOR ACHIEVEMENT The extent to which an individual has a strong desire to perform challenging tasks well and to meet personal standards for excellence.

NEED FOR AFFILIATION The extent to which an individual is concerned about establishing and maintaining good interpersonal relations, being liked, and having other people around them get along with one another.

NEED FOR POWER The extent to which an individual desires to control or influence others.

NEED THEORIES Theories of motivation that focus on what needs people are trying to satisfy at work and what outcomes will satisfy those needs.

NEEDS ASSESSMENT An assessment of which employees need training or development and what type of skills or knowledge they need to acquire.

NEGATIVE AFFECTIVITY The tendency to experience negative emotions and moods, to feel distressed, and to be critical of oneself and others.

NEGATIVE REINFORCEMENT Eliminating or removing undesired outcomes when people perform organizationally functional behaviors.

NEGOTIATION A method of conflict resolution in which the two parties in conflict consider various alternative ways to allocate resources to each other in order to come up with a solution acceptable to them both.

NETWORK STRUCTURE A series of strategic alliances that an organization creates with suppliers, manufacturers, and/or distributors to produce and market a product.

NETWORKING The exchange of information through a group or network of interlinked computers.

NEW VENTURE DIVISION An autonomous division that is given all the resources it needs to develop and market a new product.

NOISE Anything that hampers any stage of the communication process.

NOMINAL GROUP TECHNIQUE A decision-making technique in which group members write down ideas and solutions, read their suggestions to the whole group, and discuss and then rank the alternatives.

NONPROGRAMMED DECISION MAKING Nonroutine decision making that occurs in response to unusual, unpredictable opportunities and threats.

NONVERBAL COMMUNICATION The encoding of messages by means of facial expressions, body language, and styles of dress.

NORMS Unwritten, informal codes of conduct that prescribe how people should act in particular situations.

NURTURING ORIENTATION A worldview that values the quality of life, warm personal friendships, and services and care for the weak.

OBJECTIVE APPRAISAL An appraisal that is based on facts and is likely to be numerical.

OBSTRUCTIONIST APPROACH Companies and their managers choose *not* to behave in a socially responsible way and behave unethically and illegally.

OCCUPATIONAL ETHICS Standards that govern how members of a profession, trade, or craft should conduct themselves when performing work-related tasks.

ON-THE-JOB TRAINING Training that takes place in the work setting as employees perform their job tasks.

OPEN SYSTEM A system that takes in resources from its external environment and converts them into goods and services that are then sent back to that environment for purchase by customers.

OPENNESS TO EXPERIENCE The tendency to be original, have broad interests, be open to a wide range of stimuli, be daring, and take risks.

OPERANT CONDITIONING THEORY The theory that people learn to perform behaviors that lead to desired consequences and learn not to perform behaviors that lead to undesired consequences.

OPERATING BUDGET A budget that states how managers intend to use organizational resources to achieve organizational goals.

OPERATING SYSTEM SOFTWARE Software that tells computer hardware how to run.

OPERATION INFORMATION SYSTEM A management information system that gathers, organizes, and summarizes comprehensive data in a form that managers can use in their nonroutine coordinating, controlling, and decision-making tasks.

OPERATIONS MANAGEMENT The management of any aspect of the production system that transforms inputs into finished goods and services.

OPERATIONS MANAGER A manager who is responsible for managing an organization's production system and for determining where operating improvements might be made.

OPTIMUM DECISION The most appropriate decision in light of what managers believe to be the most desirable future consequences for their organization.

ORDER The methodical arrangement of positions to provide the organization with the greatest benefit and to provide employees with career opportunities.

ORGANIC STRUCTURE An organizational structure in which authority is decentralized to middle and first-line managers and tasks and roles are left ambiguous to encourage employees to cooperate and respond quickly to the unexpected.

ORGANIZATION CHANGE The movement of an organization away from its present state and toward some desired future state to increase its efficiency and effectiveness.

ORGANIZATIONAL ARCHITECTURE The organizational structure, control systems, culture, and human resource management systems that together determine how efficiently and effectively organizational resources are used.

ORGANIZATIONAL BEHAVIOR The study of the factors that have an impact on how individuals and groups respond to and act in organizations.

ORGANIZATIONAL BEHAVIOR MODIFICATION (OB MOD) The systematic application of operant conditioning techniques to promote the performance of organizationally functional behaviors and discourage the performance of dysfunctional behaviors.

ORGANIZATIONAL CITIZENSHIP BEHAVIORS (OCBs) Behaviors that are not required of organizational members but that contribute to and are necessary for organizational efficiency, effectiveness, and gaining a competitive advantage.

ORGANIZATIONAL COMMITMENT The collection of feelings and beliefs that managers have about their organization as a whole.

ORGANIZATIONAL CONFLICT The discord that arises when the goals, interests, or values of different individuals or groups are incompatible and those individuals or groups block or thwart one another's attempts to achieve their objectives.

ORGANIZATIONAL CULTURE The shared set of beliefs, expectations, values, norms, standards for behavior, and work solutions that influence the ways in which individuals, groups, and teams interact with one another and cooperate to achieve organizational goals.

ORGANIZATIONAL DESIGN The process by which managers make specific organizing choices that result in a particular kind of organizational structure.

ORGANIZATIONAL ENVIRONMENT The set of forces and conditions that operate beyond an organization's boundaries but affect a manager's ability to acquire and utilize resources.

ORGANIZATIONAL ETHICS The guiding practices and beliefs through which a particular company and its managers view their responsibility toward their stakeholders.

ORGANIZATIONAL LEARNING The process through which managers seek to improve employees' desire and ability to understand and manage the organization and its task environment.

ORGANIZATIONAL PERFORMANCE A measure of how efficiently and effectively a manager uses resources to satisfy customers and achieve organizational goals.

ORGANIZATIONAL POLITICS Activities that managers engage in to increase their power and to use power effectively to achieve their goals and overcome resistance or opposition.

ORGANIZATIONAL SOCIALIZATION The process by which newcomers learn an organization's values and norms and acquire the work behaviors necessary to perform jobs effectively.

ORGANIZATIONAL STAKEHNOLDERS Shareholders, employees, customers, suppliers, and others who have an interest, claim, or stake in an organization and in what it does.

ORGANIZATIONAL STRUCTURE A formal system of task and reporting relationships that coordinates and motivates organizational members so that they work together to achieve organizational goals.

ORGANIZING Structuring working relationships in a way that allows organizational members to work together to achieve organizational goals; one of the four principal functions of management.

OUTCOME Anything a person gets from a job or organization.

OUTSOURCE To use outside suppliers and manufacturers to produce goods and services.

OVERPAYMENT INEQUITY The inequity that exists when a person perceives that his or her own outcome-input ratio is greater than the ratio of a referent.

OVERT DISCRIMINATION Knowingly and willingly denying diverse individuals access to opportunities and outcomes in an organization.

PATH-GOAL THEORY A contingency model of leadership proposing that leaders can motivate subordinates by identifying their desired outcomes, rewarding them for high performance and the attainment of work goals with these desired outcomes, and clarifying for them the paths leading to the attainment of work goals.

PAY LEVEL The relative position of an organization's pay incentives in comparison with those of other organizations in the same industry employing similar kinds of workers.

PAY STRUCTURE The arrangement of jobs into categories reflecting their relative importance to the organization and its goals, level of skill required, and other characteristics.

PERCEPTION The process through which people select, organize, and interpret what they see, hear, touch, smell, and taste to give meaning and order to the world around them.

PERFORMANCE APPRAISAL The evaluation of employees' job performance and contributions to their organization.

PERFORMANCE FEEDBACK The process through which managers share performance appraisal information with subordinates, give subordinates an opportunity to reflect on their own performance, and develop, with subordinates, plans for the future.

PERSONALITY TRAITS Enduring tendencies to feel, think, and act in certain ways.

PLANNING Identifying and selecting appropriate goals and courses of action; one of the four principal functions of management.

POLITICAL AND LEGAL FORCES Outcomes of changes in laws and regulations, such as the deregulation of industries, the privatization of organizations, and the increased emphasis on environmental protection.

POLITICAL STRATEGIES Tactics that managers use to increase their power and to use power effectively to influence and gain the support of other people while overcoming resistance or opposition.

POOLED TASK INTERDEPENDENCE The task interdependence that exists when group members make separate and independent contributions to group performance.

POSITION POWER The amount of legitimate, reward, and coercive power that a leader has by virtue of his or her position in an organization; a determinant of how favorable a situation is for leading.

POSITIVE REINFORCEMENT Giving people outcomes they desire when they perform organizationally functional behaviors.

POTENTIAL COMPETITORS Organizations that presently are not in a task environment but could enter if they so choose.

POWER DISTANCE The degree to which societies accept the idea that inequalities in the power and well-being of their citizens are due to differences in individuals' physical and intellectual capabilities and heritage.

PRACTICAL RULE An ethical decision is one that a manager has no reluctance about communicating to people outside the company because the typical person in a society would think it is acceptable.

PRIOR HYPOTHESIS BIAS A cognitive bias resulting from the tendency to base decisions on strong prior beliefs even if evidence shows that those beliefs are wrong.

PROACTIVE APPROACH Companies and their managers actively embrace socially responsible behaviors going out of their way to learn about the needs of different stakeholder groups and utilizing organizational resources to promote the interests of all stakeholders.

PROCEDURAL JUSTICE A moral principle calling for the use of fair procedures to determine how to distribute outcomes to organizational members.

PROCESS REENGINEERING The fundamental rethinking and radical redesign of business processes to achieve dramatic improvement in critical measures of performance such as cost, quality, service, and speed.

PRODUCT CHAMPION A manager who takes "ownership" of a project and provides the leadership and vision that take a product from the idea stage to the final customer.

PRODUCT DEVELOPMENT PLAN A plan that specifies all of the relevant information that managers need in order to decide whether to proceed with a full-blown product development effort.

PRODUCT LIFE CYCLE Changes in demand for a product that occur from its introduction through its growth and maturity to its decline.

PRODUCT STRUCTURE An organizational structure in which each product line or business is handled by a self-contained division.

PRODUCT TEAM STRUCTURE An organizational structure in which employees are permanently assigned to a cross-functional team and report only to the product team manager or to one of his or her direct subordinates.

PRODUCTION BLOCKING A loss of productivity in brainstorming sessions due to the unstructured nature of brainstorming.

PRODUCTION SYSTEM The system that an organization uses to acquire inputs, convert the inputs into outputs, and dispose of the outputs.

PROFESSIONAL ETHICS Standards that govern how members of a profession are to make decisions when the way they should behave is not clear-cut.

PROGRAMMED DECISION MAKING Routine, virtually automatic decision making that follows established rules or guidelines.

PUNISHMENT Administering an undesired or negative consequence when dysfunctional behavior occurs.

QUALITY CIRCLES Groups of employees who meet regularly to discuss ways to increase quality.

QUANTUM PRODUCT INNOVATIONS Products that result from quantum technological changes.

QUANTUM TECHNOLOGICAL CHANGE A fundamental shift in technology that results in the innovation of new kinds of goods and services.

QUID PRO QUO SEXUAL HARASSMENT Asking for or forcing an employee to perform sexual favors in exchange for some reward or to avoid negative consequences.

REAL-TIME INFORMATION Frequently updated information that reflects current conditions.

REALISTIC JOB PREVIEW An honest assessment of the advantages and disadvantages of a job and organization.

REASONED JUDGMENT A decision that takes time and effort to make and results from careful information gathering, generation of alternatives, and evaluation of alternatives.

RECEIVER The person or group for which a message is intended.

RECIPROCAL TASK INTERDEPENDENCE The task interdependence that exists when the work performed by each group member is fully dependent on the work performed by other group members.

RECRUITMENT Activities that managers engage in to develop a pool of qualified candidates for open positions.

REFERENT POWER Power that comes from subordinates' and co-workers' respect, admiration, and loyalty.

RELATED DIVERSIFICATION Entering a new business or industry to create a competitive advantage in one or more of an organization's existing divisions or businesses.

RELATIONSHIP-ORIENTED LEADERS Leaders whose primary concern is to develop good relationships with their subordinates and to be liked by them.

RELIABILITY The degree to which a tool or test measures the same thing each time it is used.

REPRESENTATIVE DEMOCRACY A political system in which representatives elected by citizens and legally accountable to the electorate form a government whose function is to make decisions on behalf of the electorate.

REPRESENTATIVENESS BIAS A cognitive bias resulting from the tendency to generalize inappropriately from a small sample or from a single vivid event or episode.

REPUTATION The esteem or high repute that individuals or organizations gain when they behave ethically.

RESEARCH AND DEVELOPMENT TEAM A team whose members have the expertise and experience needed to develop new products.

RESTRUCTURING Downsizing an organization by eliminating the jobs of large numbers of top, middle, and first-line managers and nonmanagerial employees.

REWARD POWER The ability of a manager to give or withhold tangible and intangible rewards.

RISK The degree of probability that the possible outcomes of a particular course of action will occur.

ROLE The specific tasks that a person is expected to perform because of the position he or she holds in an organization.

ROLE MAKING Taking the initiative to modify an assigned role by assuming additional responsibilities.

RULES Formal written instructions that specify actions to be taken under different circumstances to achieve specific goals.

RUMORS Unofficial pieces of information of interest to organizational members but with no identifiable source.

SATISFICING Searching for and choosing an acceptable, or satisfactory, response to problems and opportunities, rather than trying to make the best decision.

SCENARIO PLANNING The generation of multiple forecasts of future conditions followed by an analysis of how to respond effectively to each of those conditions; also called *contingency planning*.

SCHEMA An abstract knowledge structure that is stored in memory and makes possible the interpretation and organization of information about a person, event, or situation.

SCIENTIFIC MANAGEMENT The systematic study of relationships between people and tasks for the purpose of redesigning the work process to increase efficiency.

SELECTION The process that managers use to determine the relative qualifications of job applicants and their potential for performing well in a particular job.

SELF-EFFICACY A person's belief about his or her ability to perform a behavior successfully.

SELF-ESTEEM The degree to which individuals feel good about themselves and their capabilities.

SELF-MANAGED WORK TEAM A group of employees who supervise their own activities and monitor the quality of the goods and services they provide.

SELF-REINFORCER Any desired or attractive outcome or reward that a person gives to himself or herself for good performance.

SENDER The person or group wishing to share information.

SEQUENTIAL TASK INTERDEPENDENCE The task interdependence that exists when group members must perform specific tasks in a predetermined order.

SHORT-TERM ORIENTATION A worldview that values personal stability or happiness and living for the present.

SKUNKWORKS A group of intrapreneurs who are deliberately separated from the normal operation of an organization to encourage them to devote all their attention to developing new products.

SMALL-BATCH TECHNOLOGY Technology that is used to produce small quantities of customized, one-of-a-kind products and is based on the skills of people who work together in small groups.

SOCIAL LEARNING THEORY A theory that takes into account how learning and motivation are influenced by people's thoughts and beliefs and their observations of other people's behavior.

SOCIAL LOAFING The tendency of individuals to put forth less effort when they work in groups than when they work alone.

SOCIAL RESPONSIBILITY The way a company's managers and employees view their duty or obligation to make decisions that protect, enhance, and promote the welfare and well-being of stakeholders and society as a whole.

SOCIAL STRUCTURE The arrangement of relationships between individuals and groups in a society.

SOCIETAL ETHICS Standards that govern how members of a society should deal with one another in matters involving issues such as fairness, justice, poverty, and the rights of the individual.

SOCIOCULTURAL FORCES Pressures emanating from the social structure of a country or society or from the national culture.

SPAN OF CONTROL The number of subordinates who report directly to a manager.

STAFF MANAGER A manager responsible for managing a specialist function such as finance or marketing.

STAGE-GATE DEVELOPMENT FUNNEL A planning model that forces managers to make choices among competing projects so that organizational resources are not spread thinly over too many projects.

STAKEHOLDERS The people and groups that supply a company with its productive resources and so have a claim on and stake in the company.

STANDARD OPERATING PROCEDURES Specific sets of written instructions about how to perform a certain aspect of a task.

STEREOTYPE Simplistic and often inaccurate beliefs about the typical characteristics of particular groups of people.

STRATEGIC ALLIANCE An agreement in which managers pool or share their organization's resources and know-how with a foreign company and the two organizations share the rewards and risks of starting a new venture.

STRATEGIC HUMAN RESOURCE MANAGEMENT The process by which managers design the components of a human resource management system to be consistent with one another, with other elements of organizational architecture, and with the organization's strategy and goals.

STRATEGY A cluster of decisions about what goals to pursue, what actions to take, and how to use resources to achieve goals.

STRATEGY FORMULATION Analysis of an organization's current situation followed by the development of strategies to accomplish its mission and achieve its goals.

SUBJECTIVE APPRAISAL An appraisal that is based on perceptions of traits, behaviors, or results.

SUPPLIERS Individuals and organizations that provide an organization with the input resources that it needs to produce goods and services.

SWOT ANALYSIS A planning exercise in which managers identify organizational strengths (S), weaknesses (W), environmental opportunities (O), and threats (T).

SYNERGY Performance gains that result when individuals and departments coordinate their actions.

SYSTEMATIC ERRORS Errors that people make over and over and that result in poor decision making.

TARIFF A tax that a government imposes on imported or, occasionally, exported goods.

TASK ENVIRONMENT The set of forces and conditions that originate with suppliers, distributors, customers, and competitors and affect an organization's ability to obtain inputs and dispose of its outputs because they influence managers on a daily basis.

TASK FORCE A committee of managers or nonmanagerial employees from various departments or divisions who meet to solve a specific, mutual problem; also called *ad hoc committee.*

TASK INTERDEPENDENCE The degree to which the work performed by one member of a group influences the work performed by other members.

TASK-ORIENTED LEADERS Leaders whose primary concern is to ensure that subordinates perform at a high level.

TASK STRUCTURE The extent to which the work to be performed is clear-cut so that a leader's subordinates know what needs to be accomplished and how to go about doing it; a determinant of how favorable a situation is for leading.

TEAM A group whose members work intensely with one another to achieve a specific, common goal or objective.

TECHNICAL SKILLS Job-specific knowledge and techniques required to perform an organizational role.

TECHNOLOGICAL FORCES Outcomes of changes in the technology that managers use to design, produce, or distribute goods and services.

TECHNOLOGY The combination of skills and equipment that managers use in the design, production, and distribution of goods and services.

TERMINAL VALUE A lifelong goal or objective that an individual seeks to achieve.

THEORY X A set of negative assumptions about workers that lead to the conclusion that a manager's task is to supervise workers closely and control their behavior.

THEORY Y A set of positive assumptions about workers that lead to the conclusion that a manager's task is to create a work setting that encourages commitment to organizational goals and provides opportunities for workers to be imaginative and to exercise initiative and self-direction.

360-DEGREE APPRAISAL A performance appraisal by peers, subordinates, superiors, and sometimes clients who are in a position to evaluate a manager's performance.

THIRD-PARTY NEGOTIATOR An impartial individual with expertise in handling conflicts and negotiations who helps parties in conflict reach an acceptable solution.

TIME HORIZON The intended duration of a plan.

TOP-DOWN CHANGE Change that is implemented quickly throughout an organization by upper-level managers.

TOP-MANAGEMENT TEAM A group composed of the CEO, COO, and heads of the most important departments.

TOP MANAGER A manager who establishes organizational goals, decides how departments should interact, and monitors the performance of middle managers.

TOTAL QUALITY MANAGEMENT A management technique that focuses on improving the quality of an organization's products and services.

TOTALITARIAN REGIME A political system in which a single party, individual, or group holds all political power and neither recognizes nor permits opposition.

TRAINING Teaching organizational members how to perform their current jobs and helping them acquire the knowledge and skills they need to be effective performers.

TRANSACTION-PROCESSING SYSTEM A management information system designed to handle large volumes of routine, recurring transactions.

TRANSACTIONAL LEADERSHIP Leadership that motivates subordinates by rewarding high performance and reprimanding them for low performance.

TRANSFORMATIONAL LEADERSHIP Leadership that makes subordinates aware of the importance of their jobs and performance to the organization and aware of their own needs for personal growth and that motivates subordinates to work for the good of the organization.

TRUST A person's confidence and faith in another person's goodwill.

UNCERTAINTY Unpredictability.

UNCERTAINTY AVOIDANCE The degree to which societies are willing to tolerate uncertainty and risk.

UNDERPAYMENT INEQUITY The inequity that exists when a person perceives that his or her own outcome-input ratio is less than the ratio of a referent.

UNETHICAL DECISION A decision that a manager would prefer to disguise or hide from other people because it enables a company or a particular individual to gain at the expense of society or other stakeholders.

UNITY OF COMMAND A reporting relationship in which an employee receives orders from, and reports to, only one superior.

UNITY OF DIRECTION The singleness of purpose that makes possible the creation of one plan of action to guide managers and workers as they use organizational resources.

UNRELATED DIVERSIFICATION Entering a new industry or buying a company in a new industry that is not related in any way to an organization's current businesses or industries.

UTILITARIAN RULE An ethical decision is a decision that produces the greatest good for the greatest number of people.

VALENCE In expectancy theory, how desirable each of the outcomes available from a job or organization is to a person.

VALIDITY The degree to which a tool or test measures what it purports to measure.

VALUE-CHAIN MANAGEMENT The development of a set of functional-level strategies that increase the performance of the operating system a company uses to transform inputs into finished goods and services.

VALUE SYSTEM The terminal and instrumental values that are guiding principles in an individual's life.

VALUES Ideas about what a society believes to be good, right, desirable, or beautiful.

VERBAL COMMUNICATION The encoding of messages into words, either written or spoken.

VERTICAL INTEGRATION A strategy that allows an organization to create value by producing its own inputs or distributing and selling its own outputs.

VICARIOUS LEARNING Learning that occurs when the learner becomes motivated to perform a behavior by watching another person perform it; also called *observational learning*.

VIRTUAL TEAM A team whose members rarely or never meet face-to-face but rather interact by using various forms of information technology such as email, computer networks, telephone, fax, and videoconferences.

WHOLLY OWNED FOREIGN SUBSIDIARY Production operation established in a foreign country independent of any local direct involvement.

Credits

Notes

Chapter 1

1. M. Moritz, *The Little Kingdom: The Private Story of Apple Computer* (New York: Morrow, 1984).

2. R. Cringely, *Accidental Empires* (New York: Harper Business, 1994); B. Dumaine, "America's Toughest Bosses," *Fortune,* October 18, 1993, 38–50.

3. www.apple.com, 2004.

4. Ibid.

5. G. R. Jones, *Organizational Theory, Design, and Change* (Upper Saddle River, NJ: Pearson, 2003).

6. J. P. Campbell, "On the Nature of Organizational Effectiveness," in P. S. Goodman, J. M. Pennings, et al., *New Perspectives on Organizational Effectiveness* (San Francisco: Jossey-Bass, 1977).

7. M. J. Provitera, "What Management Is: How It Works and Why It's Everyone's Business," *Academy of Management Executive* 17 (August 2003), 152–54.

8. J. McGuire and E. Matta, "CEO Stock Options: The Silent Dimension of Ownership," *Academy of Management Journal* 46 (April 2003), 255–66.

9. www.apple.com, press releases, 2000, 2001, 2003.

10. J. G. Combs and M. S. Skill, "Managerialist and Human Capital Explanations for Key Executive Pay Premium: A Contingency Perspective," *Academy of Management Journal* 46 (February 2003), 63–74.

11. H. Fayol, *General and Industrial Management* (New York: IEEE Press, 1984). Fayol actually identified five different managerial functions, but most scholars today believe these four capture the essence of Fayol's ideas.

12. P. F. Drucker, *Management Tasks, Responsibilities, and Practices* (New York: Harper & Row, 1974).

13. D. McGraw, "The Kid Bytes Back," *U.S. News & World Report,* December 12, 1994, 70–71.

14. www.apple.com, press release, 2003.

15. N. Byrnes, "Avon: The New Calling," *Business Week* (September 18, 2000): 136–48; C. Hawn, "Tag Team," *Forbes* (January 11, 1999): 184–86; J. Pellet, "Ding-Dong Avon Stalling," *Chief Executive* (June 2000): 26–31; P. Sellers, "Big, Hairy, Audacious Goals Don't Work–Just Ask P&G," *Fortune* (April 3, 2000): 39–44.

16. www.avon.com, 2004.

17. A Backover, "Lucent Names Kodak's Russo CEO," www.usatoday.com, 2002.

18. www.lucent.com, press release, 2003.

19. www.lucent.com, 2004.

20. G. McWilliams, "Lean Machine–How Dell Fine-Tunes Its PC Pricing to Gain Edge in a Slow Market," *The Wall Street Journal,* June 8, 2001, A1.

21. J. Kotter, *The General Managers* (New York: Free Press, 1992).

22. C. P. Hales, "What Do Managers Do? A Critical Review of the Evidence," *Journal of Management Studies,* January 1986: 88–115; A. I. Kraul, P. R. Pedigo, D. D. McKenna, and M. D. Dunnette, "The Role of the Manager: What's Really Important in Different Management Jobs," *Academy of Management Executive,* November 1989, 286–93.

23. A. K. Gupta, "Contingency Perspectives on Strategic Leadership," in D. C. Hambrick, ed., *The Executive Effect: Concepts and Methods for Studying Top Managers* (Greenwich, CT: JAI Press, 1988), 147–78.

24. D. G. Ancona, "Top Management Teams: Preparing for the Revolution," in J. S. Carroll, ed., *Applied Social Psychology and Organizational Settings* (Hillsdale, NJ: Erlbaum, 1990); D. C. Hambrick and P. A Mason, "Upper Echelons: The Organization as a Reflection of Its Top Managers," *Academy of Management Journal* 9 (1984), 193–206.

25. T. A. Mahony, T. H. Jerdee, and S. J. Carroll, "The Jobs of Management," *Industrial Relations* 4 (1965), 97–110; L. Gomez-Mejia, J. McCann, and R. C. Page, "The Structure of Managerial Behaviors and Rewards," *Industrial Relations* 24 (1985), 147–54.

26. W. R. Nord and M. J. Waller, "The Human Organization of Time: Temporal Realities and Experiences," *Academy of Management Review* 29 (January 2004), 137–140.

27. R. Stewart, "Middle Managers: Their Jobs and Behaviors," in J. W. Lorsch, ed., *Handbook of Organizational Behavior* (Englewood Cliffs, NJ: Prentice-Hall, 1987), 385–91.

28. K. Labich, "Making over Middle Managers," *Fortune,* May 8, 1989, 58–64.

29. B. Wysocki, "Some Companies Cut Costs Too Far, Suffer from Corporate Anorexia," *The Wall Street Journal,* July 5, 1995, A1.

30. V. U. Druskat and J. V. Wheeler, "Managing from the Boundary: The Effective Leadership of Self-Managing Work Teams," *Academy of Management Journal* 46 (August 2003), 435–58.

31. S. R. Parker, T. D. Wall, and P. R. Jackson, "That's Not My Job: Developing Flexible Work Orientations," *Academy of Management Journal* 40 (1997), 899–929.

32. B. Dumaine, "The New Non-Manager," *Fortune,* February 22, 1993, 80–84.

33. www.ciu.com, 2004.

34. www.crm.com, 2004.

35. H. Mintzberg, "The Manager's Job: Folklore and Fact," *Harvard Business Review,* July–August 1975, 56–62.

36. H. Mintzberg, *The Nature of Managerial Work* (New York: Harper & Row, 1973).

37. Ibid.

38. M. N. Ruderman, P. J. Ohlott, K. Panzer, and S. N. King, "Benefits of Multiple Roles for Managerial Women," *Academy of Management Journal* 45 (April 2002), 369–87.

39. N. Kelleher, "Short-Term Rentals Is All Booked Up," *Boston Herald,* January 17, 1995, 26.

40. R. H. Guest, "Of Time and the Foreman," *Personnel* 32 (1955), 478–86.

41. L. Hill, *Becoming a Manager: Mastery of a New Identity* (Boston: Harvard Business School Press, 1992).

42. Ibid.

43. R. L. Katz, "Skills of an Effective Administrator," *Harvard Business Review,* September–October 1974, 90–102.

44. Ibid.

45. P. Tharenou, "Going Up? Do Traits and Informal Social Processes Predict Advancing in Management," *Academy of Management Journal* 44 (October 2001), 1005–18.

46. C. J. Collins and K. D. Clark, "Strategic Human Resource Practices, Top Management Team Social Networks, and Firm Performance: The Role of Human Resource Practices in Creating Organizational Competitive Advantage," *Academy of Management Journal* 46 (December 2003), 740–52.

47. S. C. de Janasz, S. E. Sullivan, and V. Whiting, "Mentor Networks and Career Success: Lessons for Turbulent Times," *Academy of Management Executive,* 17 (November 2003), 78–92.

48. H. G. Baum, A. C. Joel, and E. A. Mannix, "Management Challenges in a New Time," *Academy of Management Journal* 45 (October 2002), 916–31.

49. A. Shama, "Management Under Fire: The Transformation of Management in the Soviet Union and Eastern Europe," *Academy of Management Executive* 10 (1993), 22–35.

50. K. Seiders and L. L. Berry, "Service Fairness: What It Is and Why It Matters," *Academy of Management Executive* 12 (1998), 8–20.

51. T. Donaldson, "Editor's Comments: Taking Ethics Seriously–A Mission Now More Possible," *Academy of Management Review* 28 (July 2003), 363–67.

52. C. Anderson, "Values-Based Management," *Academy of Management Executive* 11 (1997), 25–46.

53. W. H. Shaw and V. Barry, *Moral Issues in Business,* 6th ed. (Belmont, CA: Wadsworth, 1995); T. Donaldson, *Corporations and Morality* (Englewood Cliffs, NJ: Prentice-Hall, 1982).

54. www.lucent.com, press release, 2004.

55. www.fda.com, 2004.

56. www.consumerreports.com, 2003.

57. N. Vardi, "Poison Pills," forbes.com, April 19, 2004.

58. www.fda.org, press releases, 2004.

59. S. Jackson et al., *Diversity in the Workplace: Human Resource Initiatives* (New York: Guilford Press, 1992).

60. G. Robinson and C. S. Daus, "Building a Case for Diversity," *Academy of Management Executive* 3 (1997), 21–31; S. J. Bunderson and K. M. Sutcliffe, "Comparing Alternative Conceptualizations of Functional Diversity in Management Teams: Process and Performance Effects," *Academy of Management Journal* 45 (October 2002), 875–94.

61. D. Jamieson and J. O'Mara, *Managing Workforce 2000: Gaining a Diversity Advantage* (San Francisco: Jossey-Bass, 1991).

62. www.uboc.com, 2004.

63. Ibid.

64. J.Hickman, C. Tkaczyk, E. Florian, and J. Stemple, "The 50 Best Companies for Minorities to Work For," *Fortune,* July 7, 2003, 55–8.

65. A. R. Randel and K. S. Jaussi, "Functional Background Identity, Diversity, and Individual Performance in Cross-Functional Teams," *Academy of Management Journal* 46 (December 2003), 763–75.

66. "Union Bank of California Honored by U.S. Labor Department for Employment Practices," press release, September 11, 2000.

67. T. H. Cox and S. Blake, "Managing Cultural Diversity: Implications for Organizational Competitiveness," *Academy of Management Executive,* August 1991, 49–52.

68. D. R. Tobin, *The Knowledge Enabled Organization* (New York: AMACOM, 1998).

Chapter 2

1. H. Ford, "Progressive Manufacture," *Encyclopedia Britannica,* 13th ed. (New York: Encyclopedia Co., 1926).

2. R. Edwards, *Contested Terrain: The Transformation of the Workplace in the Twentieth Century* (New York: Basic Books, 1979).

3. A. Smith, *The Wealth of Nations* (London: Penguin, 1982).

4. Ibid., 110.

5. J. G. March and H. A. Simon, *Organizations* (New York: Wiley, 1958).

6. L. W. Fry, "The Maligned F. W. Taylor: A Reply to His Many Critics," *Academy of Management Review* 1 (1976), 124–29.

7. F. W. Taylor, *Shop Management* (New York: Harper, 1903); F. W. Taylor, *The Principles of Scientific Management* (New York: Harper, 1911).

8. J. A. Litterer, *The Emergence of Systematic Management as Shown by the Literature from 1870–1900* (New York: Garland, 1986).

9. H. R. Pollard, *Developments in Management Thought* (New York: Crane, 1974).

10. D. Wren, *The Evolution of Management Thought* (New York: Wiley, 1994), 134.

11. Edwards, *Contested Terrain.*

12. J. M. Staudenmaier, Jr., "Henry Ford's Big Flaw," *Invention and Technology* 10 (1994), 34–44.

13. H. Beynon, *Working for Ford* (London: Penguin, 1975).

14. Taylor, *Scientific Management.*

15. F. B. Gilbreth, *Primer of Scientific Management* (New York: Van Nostrand Reinhold, 1912).

16. F. B. Gilbreth, Jr., and E. G. Gilbreth, *Cheaper by the Dozen* (New York: Crowell, 1948).

17. D. Roy, "Efficiency and the Fix: Informal Intergroup Relations in a Piece Work Setting," *American Journal of Sociology* 60 (1954), 255–66.

18. M. Weber, *From Max Weber: Essays in Sociology,* ed. H. H. Gerth and C. W. Mills (New York: Oxford University Press, 1946); M. Weber, *Economy and Society,* ed. G. Roth and C. Wittich (Berkeley: University of California Press, 1978).

19. C. Perrow, *Complex Organizations,* 2d ed. (Glenview, IL: Scott, Foresman, 1979).

20. Weber, *From Max Weber,* 331.

21. See Perrow, *Complex Organizations,* chap. 1, for a detailed discussion of these issues.

22. H. Fayol, *General and Industrial Management* (New York: IEEE Press, 1984).

23. Ibid., 79.

24. T. J. Peters and R. H. Waterman, Jr., *In Search of Excellence: Lessons from America's Best-Run Companies* (New York: Harper & Row, 1982).

25. R. E. Eccles and N. Nohira, *Beyond the Hype: Rediscovering the Essence of Management* (Boston: Harvard Business School Press, 1992).

26. L. D. Parker, "Control in Organizational Life: The Contribution of Mary Parker Follett," *Academy of Management Review* 9 (1984), 736–45.

27. P. Graham, *M. P. Follett–Prophet of Management: A Celebration of Writings from the 1920s* (Boston: Harvard Business School Press, 1995).

28. M. P. Follett, *Creative Experience* (London: Longmans, 1924).

29. E. Mayo, *The Human Problems of Industrial Civilization* (New York: Macmillan, 1933); F. J. Roethlisberger and W. J. Dickson, *Management and the Worker* (Cambridge: Harvard University Press, 1947).

30. D. W. Organ, "Review of *Management and the Worker,* by F. J. Roethlisberger and W. J. Dickson," *Academy of Management Review* 13 (1986), 460–64.

31. D. Roy, "Banana Time: Job Satisfaction and Informal Interaction," *Human Organization* 18 (1960), 158–61.

32. For an analysis of the problems in determining cause from effect in the Hawthorne studies and in social settings in general, see A. Carey, "The Hawthorne Studies: A Radical Criticism," *American Sociological Review* 33 (1967), 403–16.

33. D. McGregor, *The Human Side of Enterprise* (New York: McGraw-Hill, 1960).

34. Ibid., 48.

35. Peters and Waterman, *In Search of Excellence.*

36. J. Pitta, "It Had to Be Done and We Did It," *Forbes,* April 26, 1993, 148–52.

37. www.hp.com, press release, June 2001.

38. www.hp.com, press releases, 2003–2004.

39. T. Dewett and G. R. Jones, "The Role of Information Technology in the Organization: A Review, Model, and Assessment," *Journal of Management,* 2001, 27, 313–46.

40. W. E. Deming, *Out of the Crisis* (Cambridge: MIT Press, 1986).

41. J. D. Thompson, *Organizations in Action* (New York: McGraw-Hill, 1967).

42. D. Katz and R. L. Kahn, *The Social Psychology of Organizations* (New York: Wiley, 1966); Thompson, *Organizations in Action.*

43. T. Burns and G. M. Stalker, *The Management of Innovation* (London: Tavistock, 1961); P. R. Lawrence and J. R. Lorsch, *Organization and Environment* (Boston: Graduate School of Business Administration, Harvard University, 1967).

44. Burns and Stalker, *The Management of Innovation.*

45. www.sony.com, 2001.

46. P. Abrahams, "Sony Celebrates the Results of Fine-Tuning," *Financial Times,* April 4, 2001, 5.

47. www.sony.com, 2001.

48. C. W. L. Hill and G. R. Jones, *Strategic Management: An Integrated Approach,* 3d ed. (Boston: Houghton Mifflin, 1995).

Chapter 3

1. "PAETEC Signs Exclusive Agreement with Los Angeles Area Hotel and Lodging Association," *PAETEC News Current Press Releases,* February 18, 2004.

2. "Partnership Pays Off for OSS Player," in Ray Le Maistre, International (ed.), *Boardwatch,* January 28, 2004 (www.boardwatch.com).

3. "Offerings The PAETEC Solutions Portfolio," www.paetec.com, March 8, 2004.

4. D. Dorsey, "Happiness Pays," *Inc. Magazine* February 2004, 89–94.

5. Ibid.

6. "Company Profile about PAETEC," www.paetec.com, March 8, 2004.

7. Dorsey, "Happiness Pays."

8. R News Staff, "Paetec Gives Bonuses," www.rnews.com, March 8, 2004.

9. Dorsey, "Happiness Pays."

10. Ibid.

11. Ibid.

12. Ibid.

13. Ibid.

14. "Company Profile About PAETEC."

15. C. Hymowitz and G. Stern, "At Procter & Gamble, Brands Face Pressure and So Do Executives," *The Wall Street Journal* May 10, 1993, A1, A8; Z. Schiller, "Ed Artzt's Elbow Grease Has P&G Shining," *BusinessWeek,* October 10, 1994, 84–86.

16. S. Carpenter, "Different Dispositions, Different Brains," *Monitor on Psychology,* February 2001, 66–68.

17. J. M. Digman, "Personality Structure: Emergence of the Five-Factor Model," *Annual Review of Psychology* 41 (1990), 417–40; R. R. McCrae and P. T. Costa, "Validation of the Five-Factor Model of Personality Across Instruments and Observers," *Journal of Personality and Social Psychology* 52 (1987), 81–90; R. R. McCrae and P. T. Costa, "Discriminant Validity of NEO-PIR Facet Scales," *Educational and Psychological Measurement* 52 (1992), 229–37.

18. Digman, "Personality Structure"; McCrae and Costa, "Validation of the Five-Factor Model"; McCrae and Costa, "Discriminat Validity"; R. P. Tett and D. D. Burnett, "A Personality Trait–Based Interactionist Model of Job Performance," *Journal of Applied Psychology* 88, no. 3 (2003), 500–17.

19. L. A. Witt and G. R. Ferris, "Social Skills as Moderator of Conscientiousness-Performance Relationship: Convergent Results Across Four Studies," *Journal of Applied Psychology* 88(5) (2003), 809–20; M. J. Simmering, J. A. Colquitte, R. A. Noe, and C. O. L. H. Porter, "Conscientiousness, Autonomy Fit, and Development: A Longitudinal Study," *Journal of Applied Psychology* 88, no. 5 (2003), 954–63.

20. M. R. Barrick and M. K. Mount, "The Big Five Personality Dimensions and Job Performance: A Meta-Analysis," *Personnel Psychology* 44 (1991), 1–26.

21. Digman, "Personality Structure"; McCrae and Costa, "Validation of the Five-Factor Model"; McCrae and Costa, "Discriminant Validity."

22. "Crain's New York Business, Breaking News/This Week's Issue," April 15, 2004, www.crainsny.com/news.cms?newsId=4472.

23. S. J. Palmisano, "Samuel J. Palmisano Chairman of the Board and Chief Executive Officer IBM Corporation," April 15, 2004, www.ibm.com/ibm/sjp.

24. S. Lohr, "Big Blues Big Bet: Less Tech, More Touch," *The New York Times,* January 25, 2004, 3(1).

25. Ibid.

26. Ibid.

27. Ibid.

28. J. B. Rotter, "Generalized Expectancies for Internal Versus External Control of Reinforcement," *Psychological Monographs* 80 (1966), 1–28; P. Spector, "Behaviors in Organizations as a Function of Employees' Locus of Control," *Psychological Bulletin* 91 (1982), 482–97.

29. "Hedge Fund Association: Who We Are," March 19, 2004, www.thehfa.org/.

30. R. D. Atlas, "Fund Inquiry Informant Discloses Her Identity," *The New York Times* December 9, 2003.

31. Ibid.

32. N. Harrington, "Acting with Courage," *Fast Company,* April 15, 2004 (www.fastcompany.com/fast50_04/winners/harrington.html).

33. Atlas, "Fund Inquiry Informant."

34. J. Brockner, *Self-Esteem at Work* (Lexington, MA: Lexington Books, 1988).

35. D. C. McClelland, *Human Motivation* (Glenview, IL: Scott, Foresman, 1985); D. C. McClelland, "How Motives, Skills, and Values Determine What People Do," *American Psychologist* 40 (1985), 812–25; D. C. McClelland, "Managing Motivation to Expand Human Freedom," *American Psychologist* 33 (1978), 201–10.

36. D. G. Winter, *The Power Motive* (New York: Free Press, 1973).

37. M. J. Stahl, "Achievement, Power, and Managerial Motivation: Selecting Managerial Talent with the Job Choice Exercise," *Personnel Psychology* 36 (1983), 775–89; D. C. McClelland and D. H. Burnham, "Power Is the Great Motivator," *Harvard Business Review* 54 (1976), 100–10.

38. R. J. House, W. D. Spangler, and J. Woycke, "Personality and Charisma in the U.S. Presidency: A Psychological Theory of Leader Effectiveness," *Administrative Science Quarterly* 36 (1991), 364–96.

39. G. H. Hines, "Achievement, Motivation, Occupations and Labor Turnover in New Zealand," *Journal of Applied Psychology* 58 (1973), 313–17; P. S. Hundal, "A Study of Entrepreneurial Motivation: Comparison of Fast- and Slow-Progressing Small Scale Industrial Entrepreneurs in Punjab, India," *Journal of Applied Psychology* 55 (1971), 317–23.

40. M. Rokeach, *The Nature of Human Values* (New York: Free Press, 1973).

41. Ibid.

42. Ibid.

43. "Putnam Whistle-Blower Cites Threats, Beating with Bricks," *Houston Chronicle,* January 28, 2004, 3D.

44. Ibid.

45. "Sen. Fitgerald to Chair Senate Hearing on Mutual Funds; Hearing to Focus on Hidden Fees and Misgoverance," www.senate.gov/~fitzgerald/currentnews/current1.htm, January 27,m 2004; A. Weinberg, "Putnam Employee Testifies Before Senate," www.forbes.com/business/2001/01/27/cx_aw_0127funds.html, January 27, 2004.

46. "Putnam Whistle-Blower Cites Threats."

47. A. P. Brief, *Attitudes In and Around Organizations* (Thousand Oaks, CA: Sage, 1998).

48. M. Irvine, "In Search of the Simple Life," *Houston Chronicle,* February 1, 2004, 8A; M. Irvine, "Simple Life Holds Appeal for Young Professionals," the.honoluluadvertiser.com/article/2004/Jan/26.bz/bz10a.html, January 26, 2004; "More Young People Pursuing Simpler Life," msnbc.msn.com/id/4062706, January 26, 2004.

49. Ibid.

50. Ibid.

51. Ibid.

52. D. W. Organ, *Organizational Citizenship Behavior: The Good Soldier Syndrome* (Lexington, MA: Lexington Books, 1988).

53. J. M. George and A. P. Brief, "Feeling Good–Doing Good: A Conceptual Analysis of the Mood at Work–Organizational Spontaneity Relationship," *Psychological Bulletin* 112 (1992), 310–29.

54. W. H. Mobley, "Intermediate Linkages in the Relationship Between Job Satisfaction and Employee Turnover," *Journal of Applied Psychology* 62 (1977), 237–40.

55. "Managers View Workplace Changes More Positively Than Employees," *The Wall Street Journal,* December 13, 1994, A1.

56. J. E. Mathieu and D. M. Zajac, "A Review and Meta-Analysis of the Antecedents, Correlates, and Consequences of Organizational Commitment," *Psychological Bulletin* 108(1990), 171–94.

57. E. Slate, "Tips for Negotiations in Germany and France." *HR Focus,* July 1994, 18.

58. D. Watson and A. Tellegen, "Toward a Consensual Structure of Mood," *Psychological Bulletin* 98 (1985), 219–35.

59. Ibid.

60. J. M. George, "The Role of Personality in Organizational Life: Issues and Evidence," *Journal of Management* 18 (1992), 185–213.

61. J. P. Forgas, "Affect in Social Judgments and Decisions: A Multi-Process Model," in M. Zanna, ed., *Advances in Experimental and Social Psychology* vol. 25 (San Diego, CA: Academic Press, 1992), 227–75; J. P. Forgas and J. M. George, "Affective Influences on Judgments and Behavior in Organizations: An Information Processing Perspective," *Organizational Behavior and Human Decision Processes* 86 (2001), 3–34; J. M. George, "Emotions and Leadership: The Role of Emotional Intelligence," *Human Relations* 53 (2000), 1027–55; W. N. Morris, *Mood: The Frame of Mind* (New York: Springer-Verlag, 1989).

62. George, "Emotions and Leadership."

63. J. M. George and K. Bettenhausen, "Understanding Prosocial Behavior, Sales Performance, and Turnover: A Group Level Analysis in a Service Context," *Journal of Applied Psychology* 75 (1990), 698–709.

64. George and Brief, "Feeling Good-Doing Good"; J. M. George and J. Zhou, "Understanding When Bad Moods Foster Creativity and Good Ones Don't: The Role of Context and Clarity of Feelings," paper presented at the Academy of Management Annual Meeting, 2001; A. M. Isen and R. A. Baron, "Positive Affect as a Factor in Organizational Behavior," in B. M. Staw and L. L. Cummings, eds., *Research in Organizational Behavior,* vol. 13 (Greenwich, CT: JAI Press, 1991), 1–53.

65. J. D. Greene, R. B. Sommerville, L. E. Nystrom, J. M. Darley, and J. D. Cohen, "An FMRI Investigation of

Emotional Engagement in Moral Judgment," *Science,* September 14, 2001, 2105–08; L. Neergaard, "Brain Scans Show Emotions Key to Resolving Ethical Dilemmas," *Houston Chronicle,* September 14, 2001, 13A.

66. L. Berton, "It's Audit Time! Send in the Clowns," *The Wall Street Journal,* January 18, 1995, B1, B6.

67. R. C. Sinclair, "Mood, Categorization Breadth, and Performance Appraisal: The Effects of Order of Information Acquisition and Affective State on Halo, Accuracy, Informational Retrieval, and Evaluations," *Organizational Behavior and Human Decision Processes* 42 (1988), 22–46.

68. D. Goleman, *Emotional Intelligence* (New York: Bantam Books, 1994); J. D. Mayer and P. Salovey, "The Intelligence of Emotional Intelligence," *Intelligence* 17 (1993), 433–42; J. D. Mayer and P. Salovey, "What Is Emotional Intelligence?" in P. Salovey and D. Sluyter, eds., *Emotional Development and Emotional Intelligence: Implications for Education* (New York: Basic Books, 1997); P. Salovey and J. D. Mayer, "Emotional Intelligence," *Imagination, Cognition, and Personality* 9 (1989–1990), 185–211.

69. S. Epstein, *Constructive Thinking* (Westport, CT: Praeger, 1998).

70. "Leading by Feel," *Inside the Mind of the Leader* (January 2004), 27–37.

71. P. C. Early and R. S. Peterson, "The Elusive Cultural Chameleon: Cultural Intelligence as a New Approach to Intercultural Training for the Global Manger," *Academy of Management Learning and Education* 3, no. 1 (2004), 100–15.

72. George, "Emotions and Leadership"; S. Begley, "The Boss Feels Your Pain," *Newsweek,* October 12, 1998, 74; D. Goleman, *Working With Emotional Intelligence* (New York: Bantam Books, 1998).

73. J. Bercovici, "Remembering Bernie Goldhirsh," www.medialifemagazine.com/news2003/jun03/jun30/4_thurs/news1thursday.html, April 15, 2004.

74. B. Burlingham, "Legacy: The Creative Spirit," *INC.,* September, 2003, 11–12.

75. Ibid.

76. Ibid.

77. Ibid.

78. Ibid.

79. "Bernard Goldhirsh, Magazine Founder and MIT Alumnus, Dies at 63," web.mit.edu/newsoffice/nr/2003/goldhirsh.html, July 1, 2003.

80. "Leading by Feel," *Inside the Mind of the Leader,* January, 2004, 27–37.

81. George, "Emotions and Leadership."

82. J. Zhou and J. M. George, "Awakening Employee Creativity: The Role of Leader Emotional Intelligence," *Leadership Quarterly* 14 (2003), 545–68.

83. A. Jung, "Leading by Feel: Seek Frank Feedback," *Inside the Mind of the Leader,* January 2004, 31.

84. H. M. Trice and J. M. Beyer, *The Cultures of Work Organizations* (Englewood Cliffs, NJ: Prentice-Hall, 1993).

85. B. Schneider and D. B. Smith, eds., *Personality and Organizations,* (Mahway, NJ: Lawrence Erlbaum, 2004, 347–69; J. E. Slaughter, M. J. Zickar, S. Highhouse, and D. C. Mohr, "Personality Trait Inferences About Organizations: Development of a Measure and Assessment of Construct Validity," *Journal of Applied Psychology* 89, no. 1 (2004), 85–103.

86. T. Kelley, *The Art of Innovation: Lessons in Creativity from IDEO, America's Leading Design Firm* (New York: Random House, 2001).

87. "Personality and Organizational Culture," B. Schneider and D. B. Smith.

88. B. Schneider, "The People Make the Place," *Personnel Psychology* 40 (1987), 437–53.

89. "Personality and Organizational Culture," B. Schneider and D. B. Smith.

90. Ibid.

91. B. Schneider, H. B. Goldstein, and D. B. Smith, "The ASA Framework: An Update," *Personnel Psychology* 48 (1995), 747–73; J. Schaubroeck, D. C. Ganster, and J. R. Jones, "Organizational and Occupational Influences in the Attraction-Selection-Attrition Process," *Journal of Applied Psychology* 83 (1998), 869–91.

92. Kelley, The Art of Innovation.

93. Ibid.

94. "Personality and Organizational Culture," B. Schneider and D. B. Smith.

95. Kelley, *The Art of Innovation.*

96. George, "Emotions and Leadership."

97. Kelley, *The Art of Innovation.*

98. Ibid.

99. D. C. Feldman, "The Development and Enforcement of Group Norms," *Academy of Management Review* 9 (1984), 47–53.

100. G. R. Jones, *Organizational Theory, Design, and Change* (Englewood Cliffs, NJ: Prentice-Hall, 2003).

101. H. Schein, "The Role of the Founder in Creating Organizational Culture," *Organizational Dynamics* 12 (1983), 13–28.

102. J. M. George, "Personality, Affect, and Behavior in Groups," *Journal of Applied Psychology* 75 (1990), 107–16.

103. J. Van Maanen, "Police Socialization: A Longitudinal Examination of Job Attitudes in an Urban Police Department," *Administrative Science Quarterly* 20 (1975), 207–28.

104. www.intercotwest.com/Disney; M. N. Martinez, "Disney Training Works Magic," *HRMagazine,* May 1992, 53–57.

105. P. L. Berger and T. Luckman, *The Social Construction of Reality* (Garden City, NY: Anchor Books, 1967).

106. H. M. Trice and J. M. Beyer, "Studying Organizational Culture Through Rites and Ceremonials," *Academy of Management Review* 9 (1984), 653–69.

107. Kelley, *The Art of Innovation.*

108. H. M. Trice and J. M. Beyer, *The Cultures of Work Organizations* (Englewood Cliffs, NJ: Prentice-Hall, 1993).

109. B. Ortega, "Wal-Mart's Meeting Is a Reason to Party," *The Wall Street Journal,* June 3, 1994, A1.

110. Trice and Beyer, "Studying Organizational Culture."

111. Kelley, *The Art of Innovation.*

112. S. McGee, "Garish Jackets Add to Clamor of Chicago Pits," *The Wall Street Journal,* July 31, 1995, C1.

113. K. E. Weick, *The Social Psychology of Organization* (Reading, MA: Addison-Wesley, 1979).

114. B. McLean and P. Elkind, *The Smartest Guys in the Room: The Amazing Rise and Scandalous Fall of Enron* (New York: Penguin Books, 2003); R. Smith and J. R. Emshwiller, *24 Days: How Two* Wall Street Journal *Reporters Uncovered the Lies That Destroyed Faith in Corporate America* (New York: HarperCollins, 2003); M. Swartz and S. Watkins, *Power Failure: The Inside Story of the Collapse of ENRON* (New York: Doubleday, 2003).

Chapter 4

1. www.yahoo.com, 2004.
2. www.napster.com, 2004.
3. C. W. L. Hill, "Napster," in C. W. L. Hill and G. R. Jones, *Strategic Management: An Integrated Approach* (Boston: Houghton Mifflin, 2004).
4. A. E. Tenbrunsel, "Misrepresentation and Expectations of Misrepresentation in an Ethical Dilemma: The Role of Incentives and Temptation," *Academy of Management Journal* 41 (June 1998), 330–40.
5. D. Kravets, "Supreme Court to Hear Case on Medical Pot," www.yahoo.com, June 29, 2004.
6. www. yahoo.com, 2003; www.mci.com, 2004.
7. J. Child, "The International Crisis of Confidence in Corporations," *Academy of Management Executive* 16 (August 2002), 145–48.
8. T. Donaldson, "Editor's Comments: Taking Ethics Seriously–A Mission Now More Possible," *Academy of Management Review* 28 (July 2003), 463–67.
9. R. E. Freeman, *Strategic Management: A Stakeholder Approach* (Marshfield, MA: Pitman, 1984).
10. J. A. Pearce, "The Company Mission as a Strategic Tool," *Sloan Management Review*, Spring 1982, 15–24.
11. C. I. Barnard, *The Functions of the Executive* (Cambridge, MA: Harvard University Press, 1948).
12. Freeman, *Strategic Management.*
13. "The Jobs Challenge," *The Economist*, July 14, 2001, 56.
14. P. S. Adler, "Corporate Scandals: It's Time for Reflection in Business Schools," *Academy of Management Executive* 16 (August 2002), 148–50.
15. T. L. Beauchamp and N. E. Bowie, eds., *Ethical Theory and Business* (Englewood Cliffs, NJ: Prentice-Hall, 1979); A. MacIntyre, *After Virtue* (South Bend, IN: University of Notre Dame Press, 1981).
16. R. E. Goodin, "How to Determine Who Should Get What," *Ethics*, July 1975, 310–21.
17. E. P. Kelly, "A Better Way to Think About Business" (book review), *Academy of Management Executive* 14 (May 2000), 127–129.
18. T. M. Jones, "Ethical Decision Making by Individuals in Organizations: An Issue Contingent Model," *Academy of Management Journal* 16 (1991), 366–95; G. F. Cavanaugh, D. J. Moberg, and M. Velasquez, "The Ethics of Organizational Politics," *Academy of Management Review* 6 (1981), 363–74.
19. L. K. Trevino, "Ethical Decision Making in Organizations: A Person-Situation Interactionist Model," *Academy of Management Review* 11 (1986), 601–17; W. H. Shaw and V. Barry, *Moral Issues in Business*, 6th ed. (Belmont, CA: Wadsworth, 1995).
20. T. M. Jones, "Instrumental Stakeholder Theory: A Synthesis of Ethics and Economics," *Academy of Management Review* 20 (1995), 404–37.
21. B. Victor and J. B. Cullen, "The Organizational Bases of Ethical Work Climates," *Administrative Science Quarterly* 33 (1988), 101–25.
22. D. Collins, "Organizational Harm, Legal Consequences and Stakeholder Retaliation," *Journal of Business Ethics* 8 (1988), 1–13.
23. R. C. Soloman, *Ethics and Excellence* (New York: Oxford University Press, 1992).
24. T. E. Becker, "Integrity in Organizations: Beyond Honesty and Conscientiousness," *Academy of Management Review* 23 (January 1998), 154–62.
25. S. W. Gellerman, "Why Good Managers Make Bad Decisions," in K. R. Andrews, ed., *Ethics in Practice: Managing the Moral Corporation* (Boston: Harvard Business School Press, 1989).
26. J. Dobson, "Corporate Reputation: A Free Market Solution to Unethical Behavior," *Business and Society* 28 (1989), 1–5.
27. M. S. Baucus and J. P. Near, "Can Illegal Corporate Behavior Be Predicted? An Event History Analysis," *Academy of Management Journal* 34 (1991), 9–36.
28. Trevino, "Ethical Decision Making in Organizations."
29. A. S. Waterman, "On the Uses of Psychological Theory and Research in the Process of Ethical Inquiry," *Psychological Bulletin* 103, no. 3 (1988), 283–98.
30. M. S. Frankel, "Professional Codes: Why, How, and with What Impact?" *Ethics* 8 (1989), 109–15.
31. J. Van Maanen and S. R. Barley, "Occupational Communities: Culture and Control in Organizations," in B. Staw and L. Cummings, eds., *Research in Organizational Behavior*, vol. 6 (Greenwich, CT: JAI Press, 1984), 287–365.
32. Jones, "Ethical Decision Making by Individuals in Organizations."
33. E. Gatewood and A. B. Carroll, "The Anatomy of Corporate Social Response," *Business Horizons*, September–October 1981, 9–16.
34. Ibid.
35. R. Johnson, "Ralston to Buy Beechnut, Gambling It Can Overcome Apple Juice Scandal," *The Wall Street Journal*, September 18, 1989, B11.
36. M. Friedman, "A Friedman Doctrine: The Social Responsibility of Business Is to Increase Its Profits," *New York Times Magazine*, September 13, 1970, 33.
37. Conlin, "Where Layoffs Are a Last Resort"; Southwest Airlines Fact Sheet, www.southwest.com, 2004.
38. G. R. Jones, *Organizational Theory: Text and Cases* (Englewood Cliffs, NJ: Prentice-Hall, 2003).
39. P. E. Murphy, "Creating Ethical Corporate Structure," *Sloan Management Review*, Winter 1989, 81–87.
40. C. Stavraka, "Strong Corporate Reputation at J&J Boosts Diversity Recruiting Efforts," DiversityInc.com, February 16, 2001.
41. "Our Credo," www.jj.com, 2004.
42. Ibid.
43. L. L. Nash, *Good Intentions Aside* (Boston: Harvard Business School Press, 1993).
44. Ibid.; L. L. Nash, "Johnson & Johnson's Credo," in *Corporate Ethics: A Prime Business Asset* (New York: Business Roundtable, February 1988).
45. Nash, *Good Intentions Aside.*
46. Stavraka, "Strong Corporate Reputation."
47. Nash, *Good Intentions Aside.*

Chapter 5

1. U.S. Department of Labor, Women's Bureau, "Nontraditional Occupations for Women in 2003," www.dol.gov/wb, April 28, 2004.
2. C. Hymowitz, "In the U.S., What Will It Take to Create Diverse Boardrooms?" *The Wall Street Journal*, July 8, 2003, B1.
3. Ibid.
4. Ibid.

5. Ibid.

6. M. Nusbaum, "Breaking into More Male Strongholds," *The New York Times,* November 15, 2003, C9.

7. Ibid.

8. L. M. Sixel, "Making Diversity Work a Full-Time Job for This Doctor," *Houston Chronicle,* April 16, 2004.

9. Ibid.

10. P. Tyre, "MS. Top Cop," *Newsweek,* April 12, 2004, 48–49.

11. Ibid.

12. D. McCracken, "Winning the Talent War for Women," *Harvard Business Review,* November–December 2000, 159–67.

13. W. B. Swann, Jr., J. T. Polzer, D. C. Seyle, and S. J. Ko, "Finding Value in Diversity: Verification of Personal and Social Self-Views in Diverse Groups," *Academy of Management Review* 29, no. 1 (2004), 9–27.

14. "Usual Weekly Earnings Summary," *News: Bureau of Labor Statistics,* April 16, 2004 (www.bls.gov/news.release/whyeng.nr0.htm); "Facts on Affirmative Action in Employment and Contracting," *Americans for a Fair Chance,* January, 28, 2004 (fairchance.civilrights.org/research_center/details.cfm?id=18076); "Household Data Annual Averages," www.bls.gov, April 28, 2004.

15. "Prejudice: Still on the Menu," *BusinessWeek,* April 3, 1995, 42.

16. "She's a Woman, Offer Her Less," *BusinessWeek,* May 7, 2001, 34.

17. "Glass Ceiling Is a Heavy Barrier for Minorities, Blocking Them from Top Jobs," *The Wall Street Journal,* March 14, 1995, A1.

18. "Catalyst Report Outlines Unique Challenges Faced By African-American Women in Business," Catalyst news release, February 18, 2004.

19. C. Gibson, "Nation's Median Age Highest Ever, but 65-and-Over Population's Growth Lags, Census 2000 Shows," *U.S. Census Bureau News,* May 30, 2001, (www.census.gov).

20. "Table 2: United States Population Projections by Age and Sex: 2000–2050," *U.S. Census Board, International Data Base,* Table 094, April 28, 2004 (www.census.gov/ipc/www.idbprint.html).

21. U.S. Equal Employment Opportunity Commission, "Federal Laws Prohibiting Job Discrimination Questions and Answers," www.eeoc.gov, June 20, 2001.

22. "Sex by Industry by Class of Worker for the Employed Civilian Population 16 Years and Over," *American FactFinder,* October 15, 2001 (factfinder.census.gov/). "2002 Catalyst Census of Women Corporate Officers and Top Earners in the Fortune 500," www.catalystwomen.org, August 17, 2004.

23. "Profile of Selected Economic Characteristics: 2000," *American FactFinder,* October 15, 2001 (factfinder.census.gov). "Usual Weekly Earnings Summary," www.bls.gov/news.release, August 17, 2004.

24. "2000 Catalyst Census of Women Corporate Officers and Top Earners of the Fortune 500," www.catalystwomen.org October 21, 2001; S. Wellington, M. Brumit Kropf, and P. R. Gerkovich, "What's Holding Women Back?" *Harvard Business Review,* June 2003, 18–19; D. Jones, "The Gender Factor," USAToday.com, December 30, 2003. "2002 Catalyst Census of Women Corporate Officers and Top Earners in the Fortune 500," www.catalystwomen.org, August 17, 2004.

25. T. Gutner, "Wanted: More Diverse Directors," *BusinessWeek,* April 30, 2001, 134. "2003 Catalyst Census of Women Board Directors," www.catalystwomen.org, August 17, 2004.

26. Ibid.

27. R. Sharpe, "As Leaders, Women Rule," *BusinessWeek,* November 20, 2000, 75–84.

28. Ibid.

29. "New Catalyst Study Reveals Financial Performance Is Higher for Companies with More Women at the Top," Catalyst news release, January 26, 2004.

30. B. Guzman, "The Hispanic Population," U.S. Census Bureau, May 2001; U.S. Census Bureau, "Profiles of General Demographic Characteristics," May 2001; U.S. Census Bureau, "Revisions to the Standards for the Classification of Federal Data on Race and Ethnicity," November 2, 2000, 1–19.

31. L. Chavez, "Just Another Ethnic Group," *The Wall Street Journal,* May 14, 2001, A22.

32. Bureau of Labor Statistics, "Civilian Labor Force 16 and Older by Sex, Age, Race, and Hispanic Origin, 1978, 1988, 1998, and Projected 2008," (stats.bls.gov/emp/), October 16, 2001.

33. U.S. Census Bureau, "Profile of General Demographic Characteristics: 2000," *Census 2000,* www.census.gov.

34. U.S. Census Bureau, "Census Bureau Projects Tripling of Hispanic and Asian Populations in 50 Years; Non-Hispanic Whites May Drop to Half of Total Populations," www.census.gov/Press-Release/www/releases/archives/population/001720.html, March 18, 2004; "Asians Projected to Lead Next Population Growth Surge," *Houston Chronicle,* May 1, 2004, 3A.

35. "Table 1: United States Population Projections by Race and Hispanic Origin: 2000–2050," www.census.gov/Press-Release, March 18, 2004.

36. "Census Bureau Projects Tripling"; "Asians Projected to Lead Next Population Growth Surge."

37. Associated Press, "Asian Population in U.S. in 2050," *Newsday.com–AP National News,* April 30, 2004, (www.newsday.com/news/nationworld/nation/wire/sns-ap-asians-glance,0,157).

38. "Table 1: United States Population Projections by Race and Hispanic Origin."

39. Ibid.

40. "Census Bureau Projects Tripling"; "Asians Projected to Lead Next Population Growth Surge."

41. "Reports Says Disparities Abound Between Blacks, Whites," *Houston Chronicle,* March 24, 2004, 7A.

42. Ibid.

43. J. Flint, "NBC to Hire More Minorities on TV Shows," *The Wall Street Journal,* January 6, 2000, B13.

44. J. Poniewozik, "What's Wrong with This Picture?" *Time,* June 1, 2001 (www.Time.com).

45. Ibid.

46. National Association of Realtors, "Real Estate Industry Adapting to Increasing Cultural Diversity," *PR Newswire,* May 16, 2001.

47. "Toyota Apologizes to African Americans over Controversial Ad," Kyodo News Service, Japan, May 23, 2001.

48. J. H. Coplan, "Putting a Little Faith in Diversity," *BusinessWeek,* December 21, 2000 (BusinessWeek Online).

49. Ibid.

50. Ibid.

51. J. N. Cleveland, J. Barnes-Farrell, and J. M. Ratz, "Accommodation in the Workplace," *Human Resource Management Review* 7 (1997), 77–108; A. Colella, "Coworker Distributive Fairness Judgments of the Workplace Accommodations of Employees with Disabilities," *Academy of Management Review* 26 (2001), 100–16.

52. Colella, "Coworker Distributive Fairness Judgments"; D. Stamps, "Just How Scary Is the ADA," *Training* 32 (1995), 93–101; M. S. West and R. L. Cardy, "Accommodating Claims of Disability: The Potential Impact of Abuses," *Human Resource Management Review* 7 (1997), 233–46.

53. G. Koretz, "How to Enable the Disabled," *BusinessWeek,* November 6, 2000 (BusinessWeek Archives).

54. Colella, "Coworker Distributive Fairness Judgments."

55. "Notre Dame Disability Awareness Week 2004 Events," www.nd.edu/~bbuddies/daw.html, April 30, 2004.

56. P. Hewitt, "UH Highlights Abilities, Issues of the Disabled," *Houston Chronicle,* October 22, 2001, 24A.

57. Ibid.

58. J. M. George, "AIDS/AIDS-Related Complex," in L. H. Peters, C. R. Greer, and S. A. Youngblood, eds., *The Blackwell Encyclopedic Dictionary of Human Resource Management* (Oxford, UK: Blackwell, 1997), 6–7.

59. George, "AIDS Awareness Training."

60. S. Armour, "Firms Juggle Stigma, Needs of More Workers with HIV," *USA Today,* September 7, 2000, B1.

61. Ibid.

62. Ibid.; S. Vaughn, "Career Challenge; Companies' Work Not Over in HIV and AIDS Education," *Los Angeles Times,* July 8, 2001.

63. R. Brownstein, "Honoring Work Is Key to Ending Poverty," *Detroit News,* October 2, 2001, 9; G. Koretz, "How Welfare to Work Worked," *BusinessWeek,* September 24, 2001 (BusinessWeek Archives).

64. "As Ex-Welfare Recipients Lose Jobs, Offer Safety Net," *The Atlanta Constitution,* October 10, 2001, A18.

65. "Profile of Selected Economic Characteristics: 2000," *American FactFinder,* (factfinder.census.gov/).

66. U.S. Census Bureau, "Poverty–How the Census Bureau Measures Poverty," *Census 2000,* September 25, 2001.

67. U.S. Census Bureau, "Poverty 2000," www.census.gov/, October 26, 2001.

68. I. Lelchuk, "Families Fear Hard Times Getting Worse/$30,000 in the Bay Area Won't Buy Necessities, Survey Says," *San Francisco Chronicle,* September 26, 2001, A13; S. R. Wheeler, "Activists: Welfare-to-Work Changes Needed," *Denver Post,* October 10, 2001, B6.

69. B. Carton, "Bedtime Stories: In 24-Hour Workplace, Day Care Is Moving to the Night Shift," *The Wall Street Journal,* July 6, 2001, A1, A4.

70. Ibid.

71. Ibid.

72. Ibid.

73. "Google View Question: Q: Homosexual Statistics," (answers.google.com/answers/threadview?id=271269), April 30, 2004.

74. J. Hempel, "Coming Out in Corporate America," *BusinessWeek,* December 15, 2003, 64–72.

75. Ibid.

76. J. Files, "Study Says Discharges Continue Under 'Don't Ask, Don't Tell,'" *The New York Times,* March 24, 2004, A14; J. Files, "Gay Ex-Officers Say 'Don't Ask Doesn't Work,'" *The New York Times,* December 10, 2003, A14.

77. Hempel, "Coming Out in Corporate America."

78. Ibid.

79. Ibid.

80. Ibid.

81. "For Women, Weight May Affect Pay," *Houston Chronicle,* March 4, 2004, 12A.

82. V. Valian, *Why So Slow? The Advancement of Women* (Cambridge, MA: MIT Press, 2000).

83. S. T. Fiske and S. E. Taylor, *Social Cognition,* 2d ed. (New York: McGraw-Hill, 1991); Valian, *Why So Slow?*

84. Valian, *Why So Slow?*

85. S. Rynes and B. Rosen, "A Field Survey of Factors Affecting the Adoption and Perceived Success of Diversity Training," *Personnel Psychology* 48 (1995), 247–70; Valian, *Why So Slow?*

86. V. Brown and F. L. Geis, "Turning Lead into Gold: Leadership by Men and Women and the Alchemy of Social Consensus," *Journal of Personality and Social Psychology* 46 (1984), 811–24; Valian, *Why So Slow?*

87. Valian, *Why So Slow?*

88. J. Cole and B. Singer, "A Theory of Limited Differences: Explaining the Productivity Puzzle in Science," in H. Zuckerman, J. R. Cole, and J. T. Bruer, eds., *The Outer Circle: Women in the Scientific Community* (New York: Norton, 1991), 277–310; M. F. Fox, "Sex, Salary, and Achievement: Reward-Dualism in Academia," *Sociology of Education* 54 (1981), 71–84; J. S. Long, "The Origins of Sex Differences in Science," *Social Forces* 68 (1990), 1297–1315; R. F. Martell, D. M. Lane, and C. Emrich, "Male-Female Differences: A Computer Simulation," *American Psychologist* 51 (1996), 157–58; Valian, *Why So Slow?*

89. Ibid.

90. R. Folger and M. A. Konovsky, "Effects of Procedural and Distributive Justice on Reactions to Pay Raise Decisions," *Academy of Management Journal* 32 (1989), 115–30; J. Greenberg, "Organizational Justice: Yesterday, Today, and Tomorrow," *Journal of Management* 16 (1990), 399–402; "O. Janssen, "How Fairness Perceptions Make Innovative Behavior Much or Less Stressful," *Journal of Organizational Behavior* 25 (2004), 201–15.

91. Catalyst, "The Glass Ceiling in 2000: Where Are Women Now?" www.catalystwomen.org, October 21, 2001; Bureau of Labor Statistics, 1999; Catalyst, "1999 Census of Women Corporate Officers and Top Earners"; "1999 Census of Women Board Directors of the Fortune 1000"; Catalyst, "The Glass Ceiling in 2000"; Catalyst, "Women of Color in Corporate Management: Opportunities and Barriers, 1999," www.catalystwomen.org, October 21, 2001.

92. "Household Data Annual Averages," www.bls.gov, April 28, 2004.

93. Ibid.

94. A. M. Jaffe, "At Texaco, the Diversity Skeleton Still Stalks the Halls," *The New York Times,* December 11, 1994, sec. 3, p. 5.

95. Greenberg, "Organizational Justice"; M. G. Ehrhart, "Leadership and Procedural Justice Climate as Antecedents of Unit-Level Organizational Citizenship Behavior," *Personnel Psychology* 57 (2004), 61–94; A.

Colella, R. L. Paetzold, and M. A. Belliveau, "Factors Affecting Coworkers' Procedural Justice Inferences of the Workplace Accommodations of Employees with Disabilities," *Personnel Psychology* 57 (2004), 1–23.

96. G. Robinson and K. Dechant, "Building a Case for Business Diversity," *Academy of Management Executive* (1997), 3, 32–47.

97. A. Patterson, "Target 'Micromarkets' Its Way to Success; No 2 Stores Are Alike," *The Wall Street Journal,* May 31, 1995, A1, A9.

98. L. Rodriguez, "Immigrant Group Wields Power in Native Tongue," *Houston Chronicle,* February 1, 2004, 5D.

99. J. Moreno, "From the Barrios to Big Business," *Houston Chronicle,* February 1, 2004, 1D.

100. Ibid.

101. Ibid.

102. M. Vann, "South by South First," *The Austin Chronicle,* March 10, 2000 (www.austinchronicle.com/issues/dispatch/2000-03-10/food_roundup12.html).

103. Moreno, "From the Barrios to Big Business."

104. "The Business Case for Diversity: Experts Tell What Counts, What Works," DiversityInc.com, October 23, 2001.

105. B. Hetzer, "Find a Niche–and Start Scratching," *BusinessWeek,* September 14, 1998 (BusinessWeek Archives).

106. K. Aaron, "Woman Laments Lack of Diversity on Boards of Major Companies," *The Times Union,* May 16, 2001 (www.timesunion.com).

107. "The Business Case for Diversity."

108. B. Frankel, "Measuring Diversity Is One Sure Way of Convincing CEOs of Its Value," DiversityInc.com, October 5, 2001.

109. A. Stevens, "Lawyers and Clients," *The Wall Street Journal,* June 19, 1995, B7.

110. B. McMenamin, "Diversity Hucksters," *Forbes,* May 22, 1995, 174–76.

111. J. Kahn, "Diversity Trumps the Downturn," *Fortune,* July 9, 2001, 114–16.

112. H. R. Schiffmann, *Sensation and Perception: An Integrated Approach* (New York: Wiley, 1990).

113. A. E. Serwer, "McDonald's Conquers the World," *Fortune,* October 17, 1994, 103–16.

114. S. T. Fiske and S. E. Taylor, *Social Cognition* (Reading, MA: Addison-Wesley, 1984).

115. J. S. Bruner, "Going Beyond the Information Given," in H. Gruber, G. Terrell, and M. Wertheimer, eds., *Contemporary Approaches to Cognition* (Cambridge, MA: Harvard University Press, 1957); Fiske and Taylor, *Social Cognition.*

116. Fiske and Taylor, *Social Cognition.*

117. V. Valian, *Why So Slow?*

118. D. Bakan, *The Duality of Human Existence* (Chicago: Rand McNally, 1966); J. T. Spence and R. L. Helmreich, *Masculinity and Femininity: Their Psychological Dimensions, Correlates, and Antecedents* (Austin: University of Texas Press, 1978); J. T. Spence and L. L. Sawin, "Images of Masculinity and Femininity: A Reconceptualization," in V. E. O'Leary, R. K. Unger, and B. B. Wallston, eds., *Women, Gender, and Social Psychology* (Hillsdale, NJ: Erlbaum, 1985), 35–66; Valian, *Why So Slow?*

119. Valian, *Why So Slow?*

120. Serwer, "McDonald's Conquers the World"; P. R. Sackett, C. M. Hardison, and M. J. Cullen, "On Interpreting Stereotype Threat as Accounting for African American–White Differences on Cognitive Tests," *American Psychologist* 59, no. 1 (January 2004), 7–13; C. M. Steele and J. A. Aronson, "Stereotype Threat Does Not Live by Steele and Aronson," *American Psychologist* 59, no. 1 (January 2004), 47–55; P. R. Sackett, C. M. Hardison, and M. J. Cullen, "On the Value of Correcting Mischaracterizations of Stereotype Threat Research," *American Psychologist* 59, no. 1 (January 2004), 47–49; D. M. Amodio, E. Harmon-Jones, P. G. Devine, J. J. Curtin, S. L. Hartley, and A. E. Covert, "Neural Signals for the Detection of Unintentional Race Bias," *Psychological Science* 15, no. 2 (2004), 88–93.

121. M. Loden and J. B. Rosener, *Workforce America! Managing Employee Diversity as a Vital Resource* (Burr Ridge, IL: Irwin, 1991).

122. E. D. Pulakos and K. N. Wexley, "The Relationship Among Perceptual Similarity, Sex, and Performance Ratings in Manager-Subordinate Dyads," *Academy of Management Journal* 26 (1983), 129–39.

123. Fiske and Taylor, *Social Cognition.*

124. "Court Expands Sex Discrimination Lawsuit Against Wal-Mart Stores," walmart.walmartclass.com/clients/walmart/press_release/2002-09-10-067168, press release, May 1, 2004.

125. "Suit Alleges Gender Bias at Wal-Mart," *Houston Chronicle,* June 20, 2001, 10C.

126. National Organization for Women, "Good News, Case Against Wal-Mart Gets a Green Light," www.now.org/issues/wfw/041904walmart.html, April 19, 2004; "Wal-Mart: Merchant of Shame," www.now.org.issues/wfw/wal-mart.html, May 1, 2004; W. Zellner, "Analyzing the 'Sins' of Wal-Mart," *BusinessWeek Online* April 15, 2004 (www.businessweek.com); "Wal-Mart Tops Most Admired List," *CNNMoney,* February 24, 2004, (money.cnn.com/2004/02/23/news/companies/fortune_best) National Organization for Women, "Wal-Mart: The Facts," www.now.org/issues/wfw/wm-facts.html, May 1, 2004.

127. Ibid.

128. "Suit Alleges Gender Bias at Wal-Mart."

129. M. Conlin and W. Zellner, "Is Wal-Mart Hostile to Women?" *BusinessWeek,* July 16, 2001 (BusinessWeek Archives).

130. "Court Expands Sex Discrimination Lawsuit," National Organization for Women, "Wal-Mart: Merchant of Shame"; Zellner, "Analyzing the 'Sins' of Wal-Mart"; "Wal-Mart Tops Most Admired List"; National Organization for Women, "Wal-Mart: The Facts."

131. J. Floyd, "Wal-Mart Accused of Bias," abcNews.com, June 19, 2001.

132. "Court Expands Sex Discrimination Lawsuit Against"; National Organization for Women, "Wal-Mart: Merchant of Shame"; Zellner, "Analyzing the 'Sins' of Wal-Mart"; "Wal-Mart Tops Most Admired List"; National Organization for Women, "Wal-Mart: The Facts."

133. Floyd, "Wal-Mart Accused of Bias."

134. Ibid.

135. A. G. Greenwald and M. Banaji, "Implicit Social Cognition: Attitudes, Self-Esteem, and Stereotypes," *Psychological Review* 102 (1995), 4–27.

136. A. Fisher, "Ask Annie: Five Ways to Promote Diversity in the Workplace," *Fortune,* April 23, 2004 (www.fortune.com/fortune/subs/print/0,15935,455997,

00.html); E. Bonabeau, "Don't Trust Your Gut," *Harvard Business Review,* May 2003, 116–123.

137. A. P. Carnevale and S. C. Stone, "Diversity: Beyond the Golden Rule," *Training & Development,* October 1994, 22–39.

138. Fisher, "Ask Annie."

139. B. A. Battaglia, "Skills for Managing Multicultural Teams," *Cultural Diversity at Work* 4 (1992); Carnevale and Stone, "Diversity: Beyond the Golden Rule."

140. Swann et al., "Finding Value in Diversity."

141. Valian, *Why So Slow?*

142. A. P. Brief, R. T. Buttram, R. M. Reizenstein, S. D. Pugh, J. D. Callahan, R. L. McCline, and J. B. Vaslow, "Beyond Good Intentions: The Next Steps Toward Racial Equality in the American Workplace," *Academy of Management Executive,* November 1997, 59–72.

143. Ibid.

144. Ibid.

145. Ibid.

146. T. Cole, "Linking Diversity to Executive Compensation," *Diversity Inc.,* August–September 2003, 58–62.

147. B. Mandell and S. Kohler-Gray, "Management Development That Values Diversity," *Personnel* March 1990, 41–47.

148. B. Filipczak, "25 Years of Diversity at UPS," *Training,* August 1992, 42–46.

149. D. A. Thomas, "Race Matters: The Truth About Mentoring Minorities," *Harvard Business Review,* April 2001, 99–107.

150. Ibid.

151. S. N. Mehta, "Why Mentoring Works," *Fortune,* July 9, 2000.

152. Ibid.; Thomas, "Race Matters."

153. "Chevron Settles Claims of 4 Women at Unit as Part of Sex Bias Suit," *The Wall Street Journal,* January 22, 1995, B12.

154. D. K. Berman, "TWA Settles Harassment Claims at JFK Airport for $2.6 Million," *The Wall Street Journal,* June 25, 2001, B6.

155. A. Lambert, "Insurers Help Clients Take Steps to Reduce Sexual Harassment," *Houston Business Journal,* March 19, 2004 (Houston.bizjournals.com/Houston/stories/2004/03/22/focus4.html).

156. T. Segal, "Getting Serious About Sexual Harassment," *Business Week,* November 9, 1992, 78–82.

157. U.S. Equal Employment Opportunity Commission, "Facts About Sexual Harassment," www.eeoc.gov/facts/fs-sex.html, May 1, 2004.

158. Carton, "Muscled Out? At Jenny Craig, Men Are Ones Who Claim Sex Discrimination," *The Wall Street Journal,* November 29, 1994, A1, A7.

159. R. L. Paetzold and A. M. O'Leary-Kelly, "Organizational Communication and the Legal Dimensions of Hostile Work Environment Sexual Harassment," in G. L. Kreps, ed., *Sexual Harassment: Communication Implications* (Cresskill, NJ: Hampton Press, 1993).

160. M. Galen, J. Weber, and A. Z. Cuneo, "Sexual Harassment: Out of the Shadows," *Fortune,* October 28, 1991, 30–31.

161. A. M. O'Leary-Kelly, R. L. Paetzold, and R. W. Griffin, "Sexual Harassment as Aggressive Action: A Framework for Understanding Sexual Harassment," paper presented at the annual meeting of the Academy of Management, Vancouver, August 1995.

162. B. S. Roberts and R. A. Mann, "Sexual Harassment in the Workplace: A Primer," http:www3.uakron.edu/lawrev/robert1.html, May 1, 2004.

163. "Former FedEx Driver Wins EEOC Lawsuit," *Houston Chronicle,* February 26, 2004, 9B.

164. Ibid.

165. A. R. Moses, "Multimillion Dollar Sex Harassment Suit Goes to State's High Court," www.legalpr.com/12-9-03Neil_Martin_AP.html May 2, 2004; "Appeals Court Upholds Sexual Harassment Verdict Against Automaker," www.fansoffieger.com/lgibler.htm, May 2, 2004; A. R. Moses, "State Top Court to Hear DCX Bias Appeal," *Detroit Free Press,* December 10, 2003 (www.freep.com); "Employers Eye Outcome of Sexual Harassment Appeal by Carmaker," *Global Diversity @ Work,* February 2004 (www.diversityatwork.com/new/feb04/Chrysler%20lawsuit.htm); Michigan Supreme Court, Office of Public Information, "Sexual Harassment, Reverse Discrimination Suits Among Cases to Be Heard by Michigan Supreme Court," December 9, 2003.

166. Moses, "Multimillion Dollar Sex Harassment Suit"; "Appeals court upholds sexual harassment verdict"; Moses, "State Top Court to hear DCX Bias Appeal"; "Employers Eye Outcome of Sexual Harassment Appeal"; Michigan Supreme Court: Office of Public Information, "Sexual Harassment, Reverse Discrimination Suits."

167. Ibid.

168. S. J. Bresler and R. Thacker, "Four-Point Plan Helps Solve Harassment Problems," *HR Magazine,* May 1993, 117–24.

169. "Du Pont's Solution," *Training,* March 1992, 29.

170. B. S. Roberts and R. A. Mann, "Sexual Harassment in the Workplace: A Primer," www3.uakron.edu/lawrev/robert1.html, May 1, 2004.

171. Ibid.

Chapter 6

1. www.nestle.com, 2004.

2. L. J. Bourgeois, "Strategy and Environment: A Conceptual Integration," *Academy of Management Review* 5 (1985), 25–39.

3. M. E. Porter, *Competitive Strategy* (New York: Free Press, 1980).

4. "Coca-Cola Versus Pepsi-Cola and the Soft Drink Industry," Harvard Business School Case 9-391-179.

5. A. K. Gupta and V. Govindarajan, "Cultivating a Global Mindset," *Academy of Management Executive* 16 (February 2002), 116–27.

6. "Boeing's Worldwide Supplier Network," *Seattle Post-Intelligence,* April 9, 1994, 13.

7. I. Metthee, "Playing a Large Part," *Seattle Post-Intelligence,* April 9, 1994, 13.

8. R. J. Trent and R. M. Monczke, "Pursuing Competitive Advantage Through Integrated Global Sourcing," *Academy of Management Executive* 16 (May 2002), 66–81.

9. R. B. Reich, *The Work of Nations* (New York: Knopf, 1991).

10. "Business: Link in the Global Chain," *The Economist,* June 2, 2001, 62–63.

11. M. E. Porter, *Competitive Advantage* (New York: Free Press, 1985).

12. www.walmart.com, 2004.

13. "The Tech Slump Doesn't Scare Michael Dell, *BusinessWeek,* April 16, 2001, 48.

14. T. Levitt, "The Globalization of Markets," *Harvard Business Review,* May–June 1983, 92–102.

15. T. Deveny et al., "McWorld?" *BusinessWeek,* October 13, 1986, 78–86.

16. www.walmart.com, 2004.

17. A. Chen and M. Hicks, "Going Global? Avoid Culture Clashes," *PC Week,* April 3, 2000, 65.

18. T. W. Malnight, "Emerging Structural Patterns Within Multinational Corporations: Toward Process-Based Structures," 44 (December 2001), 1187–1211.

19. M. Troy, "Global Group Ready for New Growth Phase," *DSN Retailing Today,* June 5, 2000, 11.

20. "Dell CEO Would Like 40 Percent PC Market Share," www.dailynews.yahoo.com, June 20, 2001.

21. www.dell.com, 2004.

22. For views on barriers to entry from an economics perspective, see Porter, *Competitive Strategy.* For the sociological perspective, see J. Pfeffer and G. R. Salancik, *The External Control of Organization: A Resource Dependence Perspective* (New York: Harper & Row, 1978).

23. Porter, *Competitive Strategy;* J. E. Bain, *Barriers to New Competition* (Cambridge, MA: Harvard University Press, 1956); R. J. Gilbert, "Mobility Barriers and the Value of Incumbency," in R. Schmalensee and R. D. Willig, eds., *Handbook of Industrial Organization,* vol. 1 (Amsterdam: North Holland, 1989).

24. www.amazon.com, press release, May 2001.

25. C. W. L. Hill, "The Computer Industry: The New Industry of Industries," in Hill and Jones, *Strategic Management: An Integrated Approach* (Boston: Houghton Mifflin, 2003).

26. J. Bhagwati, *Protectionism* (Cambridge, MA; MIT Press, 1988).

27. www.yahoo.com, July 18, 2004.

28. J. Schumpeter, *Capitalism, Socialism and Democracy* (London: Macmillan, 1950), 68. Also see R. R. Winter and S. G. Winter, *An Evolutionary Theory of Economic Change* (Cambridge, MA: Harvard University Press, 1982).

29. "The Coming Clash of Logic," *The Economist,* July 3, 1993, 21–23.

30. S. Sherman, "The New Computer Revolution," *Fortune,* June 14, 1993, 56–84.

31. N. Goodman, *An Introduction to Sociology* (New York: HarperCollins, 1991); C. Nakane, *Japanese Society* (Berkeley: University of California Press, 1970).

32. The Economist, *The Economist Book of Vital World Statistics* (New York: Random House, 1990).

33. For a detailed discussion of the importance of the structure of law as a factor explaining economic change and growth, see D. C. North, *Institutions, Institutional Change and Economic Performance* (Cambridge: Cambridge University Press, 1990).

34. www.delta.com, 2004; www.united.com, 2004.

35. www.ford.com, 2004.

36. www.gm.com, 2004; www.daimlerchrysler.com, 2004; www.renault.com, 2004.

37. J. Green, "Riding Together," *BusinessWeek,* February 26, 2001, 46–49.

38. www.nissanusa.com, 2004; www.mazdausa.com, 2004.

39. www.gm.com, 2004; L. Cohn, "GM Tries to Show Who's Boss," *BusinessWeek,* March 12, 2001, 54–56.

40. C. Tierney, A. Bowden, and I. M. Kunii, "Who Says It's Iffy Now," *BusinessWeek,* October 23, 2001, 64.

41. R. B. Reich, *The Work of Nations* (New York: Knopf, 1991).

42. J. Bhagwati, *Protectionism.*

43. www.cnn.com, 2004.

44. M. A. Carpenter and J. W. Fredrickson, "Top Management Teams, Global Strategic Posture, and the Moderating Role of Uncertainty," *Academy of Management Journal* 44 (June 2001), 533–46.

45. Bhagwati, *Protectionism.*

46. For a summary of these theories, see P. Krugman and M. Obstfeld, *International Economics: Theory and Policy* (New York: HarperCollins, 1991). Also see C. W. L. Hill, *International Business* (New York: McGraw-Hill, 1997), Chap. 4.

47. A. M. Rugman, "The Quest for Global Dominance," *Academy of Management Executive* 16 (August 2002), 157–60.

48. www.wto.org.com, 2004.

49. www.wto.org.com, 2001

50. C. A. Bartlett and S. Ghoshal, *Managing Across Borders* (Boston: Harvard Business School Press, 1989).

51. C. Arnst and G. Edmondson, "The Global Free-for-All," *BusinessWeek,* September 26, 1994, 118–26.

52. www.hp.com, 2004.

53. W. Konrads, "Why Leslie Wexner Shops Overseas," *BusinessWeek,* February 3, 1992, 30.

54. E. B. Tylor, *Primitive Culture* (London: Murray, 1971).

55. For details on the forces that shape culture, see Hill, *International Business,* Chap. 2.

56. G. Hofstede, B. Neuijen, D. D. Ohayv, and G. Sanders, "Measuring Organizational Cultures: A Qualitative and Quantitative Study Across Twenty Cases," *Administrative Science Quarterly* 35 (1990), 286–316.

57. M. H. Hoppe, "Introduction: Geert Hofstede's Culture's Consequences: International Differences in Work-Related Values," *Academy of Management Executive* 18 (February 2004), 73–75.

58. R. Bellah, *Habits of the Heart: Individualism and Commitment in American Life* (Berkeley: University of California Press, 1985).

59. R. Bellah, *The Tokugawa Religion* (New York: Free Press, 1957).

60. C. Nakane, *Japanese Society* (Berkeley: University of California Press, 1970).

61. Ibid.

62. G. Hofstede, "The Cultural Relativity of Organizational Practices and Theories," *Journal of International Business Studies,* Fall 1983, 75–89.

63. Hofstede et al., "Measuring Organizational Cultures."

64. J. Perlez, "GE Finds Tough Going in Hungary," *The New York Times,* July 25, 1994, C1, C3.

65. www.ge.com, 2004.

66. J. P. Fernandez and M. Barr, *The Diversity Advantage* (New York: Lexington Books, 1994).

Chapter 7

1. M. Arndt, "Pharmaceuticals: For Drugmakers, There's No Panacea," *Business Week Online,* January 12, 2004 (www.businessweek.com:/print/magazine/content/04_02/b3865615.htm?mz); M. Boyle, "AMGEN," *Fortune* April 9, 2004 (www.fortune.com/fortune/subs/print/0,15935,612314,00.html).

2. P. O'Connell, ed., "What's Next for Pharma?" *Business Week Online* January 5, 2004 (www.businessweek.com:/print/technology/content/jan2.../tc2004015_0769_tc074.htm?t).

3. K. Kelleher, "The Drug Pipeline Flows Again," *Business 2.0,* April 2004, 50–51.

4. Ibid.

5. "Tachi Yamada, M.D., www.forbes.com, Person Tearsheet, May 6, 2004. (www.forbes.com/FromMktGuideId PersonTearsheet.jhtml?passesMktGuided ID=47566).

6. Kelleher, "The Drug Pipeline Flows Again."

7. Ibid.

8. Ibid.

9. Ibid.

10. Ibid.

11. J. Simons, "Merck's Man in the Hot Seat," *Fortune,* February 23, 2004, 111–14.

12. "Tadataka Yamada (Aged 58) Executive Director, Chairman Research & Development Appointed to the Board on 1st January 2004," GlaxoSmithKline, May 6, 2004 (www.gsk.com/bios/bio_yamada.htm).

13. Simons, "Merck's Man in the Hot Seat."

14. Kelleher, "The Drug Pipeline Flows Again"; Simons, "Merck's Man in the Hot Seat."

15. G. P. Huber, *Managerial Decision Making* (Glenview, IL: Scott, Foresman, 1993).

16. Kelleher, "The Drug Pipeline Flows Again."

17. H. A. Simon, *The New Science of Management* (Englewood Cliffs, NJ: Prentice-Hall, 1977).

18. D. Kahneman, "Maps of Bounded Rationality: A Perspective on Intuitive Judgment and Choice," Prize Lecture, December 8, 2002; E. Jaffe, "What Was I thinking? Kahneman Explains How Intuition Leads Us Astray," *American Psychological Society* 17, no. 5 (May 2004), 23–26.

19. One should be careful not to generalize too much here, however; for as Peter Senge has shown, programmed decisions rely on the implicit assumption that the environment is in a steady state. If environmental conditions change, then sticking to a routine decision rule can produce disastrous results. See P. Senge, *The Fifth Discipline: The Art and Practice of the Learning Organization* (New York: Doubleday, 1990).

20. Kahneman, "Maps of Bounded Rationality"; Jaffe, "What Was I Thinking?"

21. Ibid.

22. J. Smutniak, "Freud, Finance and Folly: Human Intuition Is a Bad Guide to Handling Risk," *The Economist* 24 (January 2004), 5–6.

23. Kahneman, "Maps of Bounded Rationality"; Jaffe, "What Was I Thinking?"

24. Ibid.

25. J. Pfeffer, "Curbing the Urge to Merge," *Business 2.0,* July 2003, 58; Smutniak, "Freud, Finance and Folly."

26. Kahneman, "Maps of Bounded Rationality"; Jaffe, "What Was I Thinking?"

27. Pfeffer, "Curbing the Urge to Merge"; Smutniak, "Freud, Finance and Folly."

28. Pfeffer, "Curbing the Urge to Merge."

29. Ibid.

30. H. A. Simon, *Administrative Behavior* (New York: Macmillan, 1947), 79.

31. H. A. Simon, *Models of Man* (New York: Wiley, 1957).

32. K. J. Arrow, *Aspects of the Theory of Risk Bearing* (Helsinki: Yrjo Johnssonis Saatio, 1965).

33. Ibid.

34. N. Gull, "Plan B (and C and D and . . .)," *Inc.,* March 2004, 40.

35. Ibid.

36. Ibid.

37. B. Neill, "Nothing Sells a Printer Like the Promise of Good Service," *Business Journal of Portland,* January 5, 2004 (www.bizjournals.com/Portland/stories/2004/01/05/story4.html?t=printable); "Associated Business Systems Fact Sheet," www.associatedbusiness.com/news_detail.asp?id=6, May 11, 2004.

38. "Associated Business Sytems Ranks as One of America's Fastest Growing Private Companies," *Associated Business Systems News,* May 11, 2004 (www.associatedbusiness.com/news_detail.asp?id=7).

39. "A Company Built on Service," *Associated Business Systems News,* May 11, 2004 (www.associatedbusiness.com/news_detail.asp?id=5); "Associated Business Systems Acquires Rik Metcalf Business Machines Inc.," *Associated Business Systems News,* May 11, 2004 (www.associatedbusiness.com/news_detail.asp?id=8); Associated Business Systems, "About ABS," www.associatedbusiness.com/about_abs.asp, May 11, 2004 "Associated Business Systems Financial Fact Sheet," www.hoovers.com/associated-business-systems/–ID__106735–/free-co-fin-factsheet.xhtml, May 11, 2004; "Associated Business Systems Company Profile," *Yahoo! Finance,* May 11, 2004 (biz.yahoo.com.ic/106/106735.html).

40. "HP Expands into the $24 Billion Copier Market and Selects Only the Best to Launch Its New Product Line," *Associated Business Systems News,* November 24, 2003 (www.associatedbusiness.com/news_detail.asp?id=9); A. Ernshaw, "Portland Dealer Chosen for HP Copier Launch," *Business Journal of Portland,* November 28, 2003 (www.bizjournals.com/Portland/stories/2003/11/24/daily41.html?t=printable); "Associated Business Systems Core Brands," www.associatedbusiness.com/core_brands.asp., May 11, 2004.

41. Gull, "Plan B."

42. R. L. Daft and R. H. Lengel, "Organizational Information Requirements, Media Richness and Structural Design," *Management Science* 32 (1986), 554–71.

43. Simons, "Merck's Man in the Hot Seat."

44. R. Cyert and J. March, *Behavioral Theory of the Firm* (Englewood Cliffs, NJ: Prentice-Hall, 1963).

45. J. G. March and H. A. Simon, *Organizations* (New York: Wiley, 1958).

46. H. A. Simon, "Making Management Decisions: The Role of Intuition and Emotion," *Academy of Management Executive* 1 (1987), 57–64.

47. M. H. Bazerman, *Judgment in Managerial Decision Making* (New York: Wiley, 1986). Also see Simon, *Administrative Behavior.*

48. "Sun Microsystems–Investor Relations: Officers and Directors," www.sun.com/aboutsun/investor/

sun_facts/officers_directors.html, June 1, 2004; "How Sun Delivers Value to Customers," *Sun Microsytems–Investor Relations: Support & Training,* June 1, 2004 (www.sun.com/aboutsun/investor/sun_facts/core_strategies.html); "Sun at a Glance," *Sun Microsystems–Investor Relations: Sun Facts,* June 1, 2004 (www.sun.com/aboutsun/investor/sun_facts/index.html); "Plug in the System, and Everything Just Works," *Sun Microsystems–Investor Relations: Product Portfolio,* June 1, 2004 (www.sun.com/aboutsun/investor/sun_facts/portfolio/html).

49. N. J. Langowitz and S. C. Wheelright, "Sun Microsystems, Inc. (A)," Harvard Business School Case 686-133.

50. R. D. Hof, "How to Kick the Mainframe Habit," *BusinessWeek,* June 26, 1995, 102–04.

51. Bazerman, *Judgment in Managerial Decision Making;* Huber, *Managerial Decision Making;* J. E. Russo and P. J. Schoemaker, *Decision Traps* (New York: Simon & Schuster, 1989).

52. M. D. Cohen, J. G. March, and J. P. Olsen, "A Garbage Can Model of Organizational Choice," *Administrative Science Quarterly* 17 (1972), 1–25.

53. Ibid.

54. Bazerman, *Judgment in Managerial Decision Making.*

55. Senge, *The Fifth Discipline.*

56. E. de Bono, *Lateral Thinking* (London: Penguin, 1968); Senge, *The Fifth Discipline.*

57. Russo and Schoemaker, *Decision Traps.*

58. Bazerman, *Judgment in Managerial Decision Making.*

59. B. Berger, "NASA: One Year After *Columbia*–Bush's New Vision Changes Agency's Course Mid-stream," *Space News Business Report,* January 26, 2004 (www.space.com/spacenews/businessmonday_040126.html).

60. Ibid.

61. P. Reinert, "Study by NASA Executives Supports *Columbia* Panel," *Houston Chronicle,* February 11, 2004, 6A.

62. Ibid.

63. Ibid.

64. J. Glanz and J. Schwartz, "Dogged Engineer's Effort to Assess Shuttle Damage," *The New York Times,* September 26, 2003 A1.

65. M. L. Wald and J. Schwartz, "NASA Chief Promises a Shift in Attitude," *The New York Times,* August 28, 2003, A23.

66. Glanz and Schwartz, "Dogged Engineer's Effort."

67. Ibid.

68. M. Dunn, "Remaking NASA One Step at a Time," July 3, 2004 www.msnbc.msn.com/id/3158779, July 3, 2004.

69. Ibid.

70. M. Dunn, "NASA Lags in Shuttle Patch Development," www.sunherald.com/mld/sunherald/news/photos/8966629.htm?template=cont, June 19, 2004.

71. Ibid.

72. Dunn, "Remaking NASA One Step at a Time."

73. Russo and Schoemaker, *Decision Traps.*

74. D. Kahneman and A. Tversky, "Judgment Under Uncertainty: Heuristics and Biases," *Science* 185 (1974), 1124–31.

75. C. R. Schwenk, "Cognitive Simplification Processes in Strategic Decision Making," *Strategic Management Journal* 5 (1984), 111–28.

76. An interesting example of the illusion of control is Richard Roll's hubris hypothesis of takeovers. See R. Roll, "The Hubris Hypothesis of Corporate Takeovers," *Journal of Business* 59 (1986), 197–216.

77. B. M. Staw, "The Escalation of Commitment to a Course of Action," *Academy of Management Review* 6 (1981), 577–87.

78. M. J. Tang, "An Economic Perspective on Escalating Commitment," *Strategic Management Journal* 9 (1988), 79–92.

79. S. N. Mehta, "Lessons from the Lucent Debacle," *Fortune,* February 5, 2001, 143–48.

80. Russo and Schoemaker, *Decision Traps.*

81. Ibid.

82. M. Warner, "Under the Knife," *Business 2.0,* February 2004, 84–89.

83. "John D. Halamka, MD. Curriculum Vitae," informatics.caregroup.harvard.edu/people/jhalamka/, July 5, 2004.

84. Warner, "Under the Knife."

85. Ibid.

86. J. Halamka, "Business-Technologist Visions: Health-Care Prognosis," *Information Week,* July 5, 2004 (www.informationweek.com/shared/printableArticle.jhtml?articleID=6512215).

87. Warner, "Under the Knife."

88. Ibid.

89. I. L. Janis, *Groupthink: Psychological Studies of Policy Decisions and Disasters,* 2d ed. (Boston: Houghton Mifflin, 1982).

90. C. R. Schwenk, *The Essence of Strategic Decision Making* (Lexington, MA: Lexington Books, 1988).

91. See R. O. Mason, "A Dialectic Approach to Strategic Planning," *Management Science* 13 (1969), 403–14; R. A. Cosier and J. C. Aplin, "A Critical View of Dialectic Inquiry in Strategic Planning," *Strategic Management Journal* 1 (1980), 343–56; I. I. Mitroff and R. O. Mason, "Structuring III–Structured Policy Issues: Further Explorations in a Methodology for Messy Problems," *Strategic Management Journal* 1 (1980), 331–42.

92. Mason, "A Dialectic Approach to Strategic Planning."

93. D. M. Schweiger and P. A. Finger, "The Comparative Effectiveness of Dialectic Inquiry and Devil's Advocacy," *Strategic Management Journal* 5 (1984), 335–50.

94. Mary C. Gentile, *Differences That Work: Organizational Excellence Through Diversity* (Boston: Harvard Business School Press, 1994); F. Rice, "How to Make Diversity Pay," *Fortune,* August 8, 1994, 78–86.

95. B. Hedberg, "How Organizations Learn and Unlearn," in W. H. Starbuck and P. C. Nystrom, eds., *Handbook of Organizational Design,* vol. 1 (New York: Oxford University Press, 1981), 1–27.

96. Senge, *The Fifth Discipline.*

97. Ibid.

98. P. M. Senge, "The Leader's New Work: Building Learning Organizations," *Sloan Management Review,* Fall 1990, 7–23.

99. W. Zellner, K. A. Schmidt, M. Ihlwan, and H. Dawley, "How Well Does Wal-Mart Travel," *BusinessWeek,* September 3, 2001, 82–84.

100. B. Watson, "The Mad Potter of Biloxi," *Smithsonian,* February 2004, 88–94.

101. Ibid.

102. Ibid.

103. "Expect the Unexpected," *Economist Technology Quarterly,* September 6, 2003, 5.

104. C. Hymowitz, "The Best Innovations Are Those That Come from Smart Questions," *The Wall Street Journal,* April 13, 2004, B1.

105. Ibid.

106. Ibid.

107. Ibid.

108. R. W. Woodman, J. E. Sawyer, and R. W. Griffin, "Towards a Theory of Organizational Creativity," *Academy of Management Review* 18 (1993), 293–321.

109. T. J. Bouchard, Jr., J. Barsaloux, and G. Drauden, "Brainstorming Procedure, Group Size, and Sex as Determinants of Problem Solving Effectiveness of Individuals and Groups," *Journal of Applied Psychology* 59 (1974), 135–38.

110. M. Diehl and W. Stroebe, "Productivity Loss in Brainstorming Groups: Towards the Solution of a Riddle," *Journal of Personality and Social Psychology* 53 (1987), 497–509.

111. D. H. Gustafson, R. K. Shulka, A. Delbecq, and W. G. Walster, "A Comparative Study of Differences in Subjective Likelihood Estimates Made by Individuals, Interacting Groups, Delphi Groups, and Nominal Groups," *Organizational Behavior and Human Performance* 9 (1973), 280–91.

112. N. Dalkey, *The Delphi Method: An Experimental Study of Group Decision Making* (Santa Monica, CA: Rand Corp., 1989).

Chapter 8

1. www.cott.com, 2004.

2. A. Chandler, *Strategy and Structure: Chapters in the History of the American Enterprise* (Cambridge, MA: MIT Press, 1962).

3. Ibid.

4. F. J. Aguilar, "General Electric: Reg Jones and Jack Welch," in *General Managers in Action* (Oxford: Oxford University Press, 1992).

5. www.ge.com, 2001.

6. Aguilar, *General Managers in Action.*

7. Aguilar, "General Electric."

8. C. W. Hofer and D. Schendel, *Strategy Formulation: Analytical Concepts* (St. Paul, MN: West, 1978).

9. H. Fayol, *General and Industrial Management* (1884; New York: IEEE Press, 1984).

10. Ibid., 18.

11. A. P. De Geus, "Planning as Learning," *Harvard Business Review,* March–April 1988, 70–74.

12. P. Wack, "Scenarios: Shooting the Rapids," *Harvard Business Review,* November–December 1985, 139–50.

13. P. J. H. Schoemaker, "Multiple Scenario Development: Its Conceptual and Behavioral Foundation," *Strategic Management Journal* 14 (1993), 193–213.

14. R. Phelps, C. Chan, S. C. Kapsalis, "Does Scenario Planning Affect Firm Performance?" *Journal of Business Research,* March 2001, 223–32.

15. J. A. Pearce, "The Company Mission as a Strategic Tool," *Sloan Management Review,* Spring 1992, 15–24.

16. D. F. Abell, *Defining the Business: The Starting Point of Strategic Planning* (Englewood Cliffs, NJ: Prentice-Hall, 1980).

17. C. Palmeri, "Mattel: Up the Hill Minus Jill," *BusinessWeek,* April 9, 2001, 53–54.

18. www.mattel.com, 2001.

19. www.mattel.com, 2004.

20. G. Hamel and C. K. Prahalad, "Strategic Intent," *Harvard Business Review,* May–June 1989, 63–73.

21. J. Shinal, "Why Cisco's Comeback Plan Is a Long Shot," *BusinessWeek,* May 21, 2001, 42.

22. E. A. Locke, G. P. Latham, and M. Erez, "The Determinants of Goal Commitment," *Academy of Management Review* 13 (1988), 23–39.

23. www.cisco.com, 2004.

24. K. R. Andrews, *The Concept of Corporate Strategy* (Homewood, IL: Irwin, 1971).

25. G. Mulvihill, "Campbell Is Really Cooking," San Diego Tribune.com, August 5, 2004.

26. W. D. Crotty, "Campbell Soup Is Not So Hot," MotleyFool.com, May 24, 2004.

27. www.hitachi.com, 2001.

28. E. Penrose, *The Theory of the Growth of the Firm* (Oxford: Oxford University Press, 1959).

29. M. E. Porter, "From Competitive Advantage to Corporate Strategy," *Harvard Business Review* 65 (1987), 43–59.

30. D. J. Teece, "Economies of Scope and the Scope of the Enterprise," *Journal of Economic Behavior and Organization* 3 (1980), 223–47.

31. M. E. Porter, *Competitive Advantage: Creating and Sustaining Superior Performance* (New York: Free Press, 1985).

32. For a review of the evidence, see C. W. L. Hill and G. R. Jones, *Strategic Management: An Integrated Approach,* 5th ed. (Boston: Houghton Mifflin, 2003), chap. 10.

33. C. R. Christensen et al., *Business Policy Text and Cases* (Homewood, IL: Irwin, 1987), 778.

34. C. W. L. Hill, "Conglomerate Performance over the Economic Cycle," *Journal of Industrial Economics* 32 (1983), 197–213.

35. V. Ramanujam and P. Varadarajan, "Research on Corporate Diversification: A Synthesis," *Strategic Management Journal* 10 (1989), 523–51. Also see A. Shleifer and R. W. Vishny, "Takeovers in the 1960s and 1980s: Evidence and Implications," in R. P. Rumelt, D. E. Schendel, and D. J. Teece, *Fundamental Issues in Strategy* (Boston: Harvard Business School Press, 1994).

36. J. R. Williams, B. L. Paez, and L. Sanders, "Conglomerates Revisited," *Strategic Management Journal* 9 (1988), 403–14.

37. C. A. Bartlett and S. Ghoshal, *Managing Across Borders* (Boston: Harvard Business School Press, 1989).

38. C. K. Prahalad and Y. L. Doz, *The Multinational Mission* (New York: Free Press, 1987).

39. www.gillette.com, 2004.

40. "Gillette Co.'s New $40 Million Razor Blade Factory in St Petersburg Russia," *Boston Globe,* June 7, 2000, C6.

41. www.gillette.com, 2004.

42. R. E. Caves, *Multinational Enterprise and Economic Analysis* (Cambridge: Cambridge University Press, 1982).

43. B. Kogut, "Joint Ventures: Theoretical and Empirical Perspectives," *Strategic Management Journal* 9 (1988), 319–33.

44. "Venture with Nestle SA Is Slated for Expansion," *The Wall Street Journal,* April 15, 2001, B2.

45. B. Bahree, "BP Amoco, Italy's ENI Plan $2.5 Billion Gas Plant, *The Wall Street Journal,* March 6, 2001, A16.

46. N. Hood and S. Young, *The Economics of the Multinational Enterprise* (London: Longman, 1979).

47. M. K. Perry, "Vertical Integration: Determinants and Effects," in R. Schmalensee and R. D. Willig, *Handbook of Industrial Organization,* vol. 1 (New York: Elsevier Science, 1989).

48. T. Muris, D. Scheffman, and P. Spiller, "Strategy and Transaction Costs: The Organization of Distribution in the Carbonated Soft Drink Industry," *Journal of Economics and Management Strategy* 1 (1992), 77–97.

49. "Matsushita Electric Industrial (MEI) in 1987," Harvard Business School Case 388-144.

50. P. Ghemawat, *Commitment: The Dynamic of Strategy* (New York: Free Press, 1991).

51. www.ibm.com, 2001.

52. M. E. Porter, *Competitive Strategy* (New York: Free Press, 1980).

53. www.federalexpress.com, 2001.

54. www.ups.com, 2001.

55. C. W. L. Hill, "Differentiation Versus Low Cost or Differentiation and Low Cost: A Contingency Framework," *Academy of Management Review* 13 (1988), 401–12.

56. For details, see J. P. Womack, D. T. Jones, and D. Roos, *The Machine That Changed the World* (New York: Rawson Associates, 1990).

57. Porter, *Competitive Strategy.*

58. www.zara.com, 2001

59. C. Vitzthum, "Just-in-Time-Fashion," *The Wall Street Journal,* May 18, 2001, B1, B4.

60. www.zara.com, 2001.

Chapter 9

1. www.safeway.com, 2004.

2. Ibid.

3. Hill and Jones, *Strategic Management: An Integrated Approach.* Boston, Mass: Houghton-Mifflin Co., 2004.

4. Womack, Jones, and Roos, *The Machine That Changed the World.*

5. See D. Garvin, "What Does Product Quality Really Mean?" *Sloan Management Review* 26 (Fall 1984), 25–44; P. B. Crosby, *Quality Is Free* (New York: Mentor Books, 1980); A. Gabor, *The Man Who Discovered Quality* (New York: Times Books, 1990).

6. D. F. Abell, *Defining the Business: The Starting Point of Strategic Planning* (Englewood Cliffs, NJ: Prentice-Hall, 1980).

7. For details, see "Johnson & Johnson (A)," Harvard Business School Case 384-053.

8. www.lucent.com, 2004.

9. M. E. Porter, *Competitive Advantage* (New York: Free Press, 1985).

10. According to Richard D'Aveni, the process of pushing price-attribute curves to the right is a characteristic of the competitive process. See R. D'Aveni, *Hypercompetition* (New York: Free Press, 1994).

11. This is a central insight of the modern manufacturing literature. See R. H. Hayes and S. C. Wheelwright, "Link Manufacturing Process and Product Life Cycles," *Harvard Business Review,* January–February 1979, 127–36; R. H. Hayes and S. C. Wheelwright, "Competing Through Manufacturing," *Harvard Business Review* January–February 1985, 99–109.

12. www.southwest.com, 2004.

13. B. O'Brian, "Flying on the Cheap," *The Wall Street Journal,* October 26, 1992, A1; B. O'Reilly, "Where Service Flies Right," *Fortune,* August 24, 1992, 116–17; A. Salpukas, "Hurt in Expansion, Airlines Cut Back and May Sell Hubs," *The Wall Street Journal,* April 1, 1993, A1, C8.

14. K. Done, "Toyota Warns of Continuing Decline," *Financial Times,* November 23, 1993, 23.

15. The view of quality as reliability goes back to the work of Deming and Juran; see Gabor, *The Man Who Discovered Quality.*

16. See Garvin, "What Does Product Quality Really Mean?"; Crosby, *Quality Is Free;* Gabor, *The Man Who Discovered Quality.*

17. www.jdpa.com, 2004.

18. See J. W. Dean and D. E. Bowen, "Management Theory and Total Quality: Improving Research and Practice Through Theory Development," *Academy of Management Review* 19 (1994), 392–418.

19. For general background information, see J. C. Anderson, M. Rungtusanatham, and R. G. Schroeder, "A Theory of Quality Management Underlying the Deming Management Method," *Academy of Management Review* 19 (1994), 472–509; "How to Build Quality," *The Economist,* September 23, 1989, 91–92; Gabor, *The Man Who Discovered Quality;* Crosby, *Quality Is Free.*

20. Bowles, "Is American Management Really Committed to Quality?" *Management Review* (April 1992), 42–46.

21. Gabor, *The Man Who Discovered Quality.*

22. J. Griffiths, "Europe's Manufacturing Quality and Productivity Still Lag Far Behind Japan's," *Financial Times,* November 4, 1994, 11.

23. S. McCartney, "Compaq Borrows Wal-Mart's Idea to Boost Production," *The Wall Street Journal,* June 17, 1994, B4.

24. R. Gourlay, "Back to Basics on the Factory Floor," *Financial Times,* January 4, 1994, 12.

25. P. Nemetz and L. Fry, "Flexible Manufacturing Organizations: Implications for Strategy Formulation," *Academy of Management Review* 13 (1988), 627–38; N. Greenwood, *Implementing Flexible Manufacturing Systems* (New York: Halstead Press, 1986).

26. M. Williams, "Back to the Past," *The Wall Street Journal,* October 24, 1994, A1.

27. G. Stalk and T. M. Hout, *Competing Against Time* (New York: Free Press, 1990).

28. For an interesting discussion of some other drawbacks of JIT and other "Japanese" manufacturing techniques, see S. M. Young, "A Framework for Successful Adoption and Performance of Japanese Manufacturing Practices in the United States," *Academy of Management Review* 17 (1992), 677–701.

29. T. Stundza, "Massachusetts Switch Maker Switches to Kanban," *Purchasing,* November 16, 2000, 103.

30. B. Dumaine, "The Trouble with Teams," *Fortune,* September 5, 1994, 86–92.

31. See C. W. L. Hill, "Transaction Cost Economizing as a Source of National Competitive Advantage: The Case of Japan," *Organization Science,* 2, 1994; M. Aoki, *Information, Incentives, and Bargaining in the Japanese Economy* (Cambridge: Cambridge University Press, 1989).

32. J. Hoerr, "The Payoff from Teamwork," *BusinessWeek,* July 10, 1989, 56–62.

33. M. Hammer and J. Champy, *Re-engineering the Corporation* (New York: HarperBusiness, 1993), 35.

34. Ibid., 46.

35. Ibid.

36. www.dell.com, 2004.

37. Michael Dell, *Direct from Dell: Strategies That Revolutionized an Industry* (New York: HarperBusiness, 1999), 91.

38. J. S. Adams, "The Structure and Dynamics of Behavior in Boundary Spanning Roles," in M. D. Dunnette, ed., *The Handbook of Industrial and Organizational Psychology* (Chicago: Rand McNally, 1976).

39. For a discussion of sources of organizational inertia, see M. T. Hannah and J. Freeman, "Structural Inertia and Organizational Change," *American Sociological Review* 49 (1984), 149–64.

40. Not everyone agrees with this assessment. Some argue that organizations and individual managers have little impact on the environment. See Hannah and Freeman, "Structural Inertia and Organizational Change."

41. R. X. Cringeley, *Accidental Empires* (New York: HarperBusiness, 1993).

42. For example, see Houlder, "Two Steps Forward, One Step Back"; Kumar Naj, "Shifting Gears," *The Wall Street Journal,* May 7, 1993, A1; and D. Greising, "Quality: How to Make It Pay," *Business Week,* August 8, 1994, 54–59.

43. L. Helm and M. Edid, "Life on the Line: Two Auto Workers Who Are Worlds Apart," *Business Week,* September 30, 1994, 76–78.

44. Dumaine, "The Trouble with Teams."

Chapter 10

1. www.lego.com, 2004.

2. B. Carter, "Lego Centralizes European Activity to Combat Losses," *Marketing,* January 15, 2004, 1.

3. "Dow Revamps Its Corporate Structure," *Chemical Market Reporter,* December 15, 2003, 3.

4. www.dow.com, 2004.

5. A. Reinhardt, "Can Nokia Capture Mobile Workers?" *Business Week,* February 9, 2004, 80.

6. G. R. Jones, *Organizational Theory, Design and Change: Text and Cases* (Upper Saddle River: Prentice-Hall, 2003).

7. J. Child, *Organization: A Guide for Managers and Administrators* (New York: Harper & Row, 1977).

8. P. R. Lawrence and J. W. Lorsch, *Organization and Environment* (Boston: Graduate School of Business Administration, Harvard University, 1967).

9. R. Duncan, "What Is the Right Organizational Design?" *Organizational Dynamics,* Winter 1979, 59–80.

10. T. Burns and G. R. Stalker, *The Management of Innovation* (London: Tavistock, 1966).

11. D. Miller, "Strategy Making and Structure: Analysis and Implications for Performance," *Academy of Management Journal* 30 (1987), 7–32.

12. A. D. Chandler, *Strategy and Structure* (Cambridge, MA: MIT Press, 1962).

13. J. Stopford and L. Wells, *Managing the Multinational Enterprise* (London: Longman, 1972).

14. www.gateway.com, 2004.

15. C. Perrow, *Organizational Analysis: A Sociological View* (Belmont, CA: Wadsworth, 1970).

16. J. Woodward, *Management and Technology* (London: Her Majesty's Stationery Office, 1958).

17. Ibid.

18. F. W. Taylor, *The Principles of Scientific Management* (New York: Harper, 1911).

19. R. W. Griffin, *Task Design: An Integrative Approach* (Glenview, IL: Scott, Foresman, 1982).

20. Ibid.

21. J. R. Hackman and G. R. Oldham, *Work Redesign* (Reading, MA: Addison-Wesley, 1980).

22. J. R. Galbraith and R. K. Kazanjian, *Strategy Implementation: Structure, System, and Process,* 2d ed. (St. Paul, MN: West, 1986).

23. Lawrence and Lorsch, *Organization and Environment.*

24. www.pier1.com, 2001.

25. Jones, *Organizational Theory.*

26. Lawrence and Lorsch, *Organization and Environment.*

27. R. H. Hall, *Organizations: Structure and Process* (Englewood Cliffs, NJ: Prentice-Hall, 1972); R. Miles, *Macro Organizational Behavior* (Santa Monica, CA: Goodyear, 1980).

28. Chandler, *Strategy and Structure.*

29. G. R. Jones and C. W. L. Hill, "Transaction Cost Analysis of Strategy-Structure Choice," *Strategic Management Journal* 9 (1988), 159–72.

30. www.viacom.com, 2004.

31. Ibid.

32. www.gsk.com, 2004.

33. Ibid.

34. S. M. Davis and P. R. Lawrence, *Matrix* (Reading, MA: Addison-Wesley, 1977); J. R. Galbraith, "Matrix Organization Designs: How to Combine Functional and Project Forms," *Business Horizons* 14 (1971), 29–40.

35. L. R. Burns, "Matrix Management in Hospitals: Testing Theories of Matrix Structure and Development," *Administrative Science Quarterly* 34 (1989), 349–68.

36. C. W. L. Hill, *International Business* (Homewood, IL: Irwin, 2003).

37. Jones, *Organizational Theory.*

38. A. Farnham, "America's Most Admired Company," *Fortune,* February 7, 1994, 50–54.

39. www.lucent.com, 2001.

40. C. Arnst, R. O. Crockett, A. Reinhardt, and J. Shinai, "Lucent: Clean Break, Clean Slate," *Business Week,* November 6, 2000, 172–80.

41. www.lucent.com, 2001.

42. www.lucent.com, 2004.

43. P. Blau, "A Formal Theory of Differentiation in Organizations," *American Sociological Review* 35 (1970), 684–95.

44. S. Grey, "McDonald's CEO Announces Shifts of Top Executives," *The Wall Street Journal,* July 16, 2004, A11.

45. www.mcdonalds.com, 2004.

46. Child, *Organization.*

47. S. McCartney, "Airline Industry's Top-Ranked Woman Keeps Southwest's Small-Fry Spirit Alive," *The Wall Street Journal,* November 30, 1995, B1.

48. P. M. Blau and R. A. Schoenherr, *The Structure of Organizations* (New York: Basic Books, 1971)

49. Jones, *Organizational Theory.*

50. www.plexus.com, 2004.

51. W. M. Bulkeley, "Plexus Strategy: Smaller Runs of More Things," *The Wall Street Journal,* October 8, 2003, B1, B12.

52. Lawrence and Lorsch, *Organization and Environment,* 50–55.

53. J. R. Galbraith, *Designing Complex Organizations* (Reading, MA: Addison-Wesley, 1977), chap. 1; Galbraith and Kazanjian, *Strategy Implementation,* chap. 7.

54. Lawrence and Lorsch, *Organization and Environment,* 55.

55. B. Kogut, "Joint Ventures: Theoretical and Empirical Perspectives," *Strategic Management Journal* 9 (1988), 319–32.

56. G. S. Capowski, "Designing a Corporate Identity," *Management Review,* June 1993, 37–38.

57. J. Marcia, "Just Doing It," *Distribution,* January 1995, 36–40.

58. "Nike Battles Backlash from Overseas Sweatshops," *Marketing News,* November 9, 1998, 14.

59. J. Laabs, "Mike Gives Indonesian Workers a Raise," *Workforce,* December 1998, 15–16.

60. W. Echikson, "It's Europe's Turn to Sweat About Sweatshops," *BusinessWeek,* July 19, 1999, 96.

61. Copyright © 2001, Gareth R. Jones.

Chapter 11

1. www.homedepot.com, 2004.

2. C. Hymowitz, "Home Depot's CEO Led a Revolution, but Left Some Behind," *The Wall Street Journal,* March 16, 2004, B1.

3. "Home Depot Shifts Its Merchandise Buying," *The Wall Street Journal,* July 31, 2001, B12.

4. W. G. Ouchi, "Markets, Bureaucracies, and Clans," *Administrative Science Quarterly* 25 (1980), 129–41.

5. P. Lorange, M. Morton, and S. Ghoshal, *Strategic Control* (St. Paul, MN: West, 1986).

6. H. Koontz and R. W. Bradspies, "Managing Through Feedforward Control," *Business Horizons,* June 1972, 25–36.

7. E. E. Lawler III and J. G. Rhode, *Information and Control in Organizations* (Pacific Palisades, CA: Goodyear, 1976).

8. C. W. L. Hill and G. R. Jones, *Strategic Management: An Integrated Approach,* 6th ed. (Boston: Houghton Mifflin, 2003).

9. W. M. Bulkeley and J. S. Lublin, "Xerox Appoints Insider Mulcahy to Execute Turnaround as CEO," *The Wall Street Journal,* July 27, 2001, A2.

10. E. Flamholtz, "Organizational Control Systems as a Management Tool," *California Management Review,* Winter 1979, 50–58.

11. W. G. Ouchi, "The Transmission of Control Through Organizational Hierarchy," *Academy of Management Journal* 21 (1978), 173–92.

12. W. G. Ouchi, "The Relationship Between Organizational Structure and Organizational Control," *Administrative Science Quarterly* 22 (1977), 95–113.

13. Ouchi, "Markets, Bureaucracies, and Clans."

14. W. H. Newman, *Constructive Control* (Englewood Cliffs, NJ: Prentice-Hall, 1975).

15. J. D. Thompson, *Organizations in Action* (New York: McGraw-Hill, 1967).

16. R. N. Anthony, *The Management Control Function* (Boston: Harvard Business School Press, 1988).

17. Ouchi, "Markets, Bureaucracies, and Clans."

18. Hill and Jones, *Strategic Management.*

19. R. Simons, "Strategic Orientation and Top Management Attention to Control Systems," *Strategic Management Journal* 12 (1991), 49–62.

20. G. Schreyogg and H. Steinmann, "Strategic Control: A New Perspective," *Academy of Management Review* 12 (1987), 91–103.

21. B. Woolridge and S. W. Floyd, "The Strategy Process, Middle Management Involvement, and Organizational Performance," *Strategic Management Journal* 11 (1990), 231–41.

22. J. A. Alexander, "Adaptive Changes in Corporate Control Practices," *Academy of Management Journal* 34 (1991), 162–93.

23. www.gillette.com, 2004.

24. Hill and Jones, *Strategic Management.*

25. G. H. B. Ross, "Revolution in Management Control," *Management Accounting* 72 (1992), 23–27.

26. P. F. Drucker, *The Practice of Management* (New York: Harper & Row, 1954).

27. S. J. Carroll and H. L. Tosi, *Management by Objectives: Applications and Research* (New York: Macmillan, 1973).

28. R. Rodgers and J. E. Hunter, "Impact of Management by Objectives on Organizational Productivity," *Journal of Applied Psychology* 76 (1991), 322–26.

29. M. B. Gavin, S. G. Green, and G. T. Fairhurst, "Managerial Control Strategies for Poor Performance over Time and the Impact on Subordinate Reactions," *Organizational Behavior and Human Decision Processes* 63 (1995), 207–21.

30. www.cypress.com, 2001.

31. B. Dumaine, "The Bureaucracy Busters," *Fortune,* June 17, 1991, 46.

32. D. S. Pugh, D. J. Hickson, C. R. Hinings, and C. Turner, "Dimensions of Organizational Structure," *Administrative Science Quarterly* 13 (1968), 65–91.

33. B. Elgin, "Running the Tightest Ships on the Net," *BusinessWeek,* January 29, 2001, 125–26.

34. P. M. Blau, *The Dynamics of Bureaucracy* (Chicago: University of Chicago Press, 1955).

35. www.ups.com, 2004.

36. J. Van Maanen, "Police Socialization: A Longitudinal Examination of Job Attitudes in an Urban Police Department," *Administrative Science Quarterly* 20 (1975), 207–28.

37. www.nokia.com, 2001.

38. P. de Bendern, "Quirky Culture Paves Nokia's Road to Fortune," www.yahoo.com, 2000.

39. K. E. Weick, *The Social Psychology of Organization* (Reading, MA: Addison-Wesley, 1979).

40. J. W. Schulz, L. C. Hauck, and R. M. Hauck, "Using the Power of Corporate Culture to Achieve Results: A Case Study of Sunflower Electric Power Corporation," *Management Quarterly* 2 (2001), 2–19.

41. J. P. Kotter and J. L. Heskett, *Corporate Culture and Performance* (New York: Free Press, 1992).

42. L. Brown, "Research Action: Organizational Feedback, Understanding and Change," *Journal of Applied Behavioral Research* 8 (1972), 697–711; P. A. Clark, *Action Research and Organizational Change* (New York: Harper & Row, 1972); N. Margulies and A. P. Raia, eds., *Conceptual Foundations of Organizational Development* (New York: McGraw-Hill, 1978).

43. W. L. French and C. H. Bell, *Organizational Development* (Englewood Cliffs, NJ: Prentice-Hall, 1990).

44. W. L. French, "A Checklist for Organizing and Implementing an OD Effort," in W. L. French, C. H. Bell, and R. A. Zawacki, eds., *Organizational Development and Transformation* (Homewood, IL: Irwin, 1994), 484–95.

Chapter 12

1. "Who's in Charge Here? No One," *The Observer,* April 27, 2003 (observer.guardian.co.uk/business/story/0,6903,944138,00.html); "Ricardo Semler, CEO, Semco SA," Cnn.com, June 29, 2004 (cnn.worldnews.printthis.clickability.com/pt/cpt&title=cnn.com); D. Kirkpatrick, "The Future of Work: An 'Apprentice'-style Office?" *Fortune,* pril 14, 2004 (www.fortune.com/fortune/subs/print/0,15935,611068,00.html); A. Strutt and R. Van Der Beek, "Report from HR2004," www.mce.be/hr2004/reportd2.htm, July 2, 2004; R. Semler, "Seven-Day Weekend Returns Power to Employees," workopolis.com, May 26, 2004 (globeandmail.workopolis.com/servlet/content/qprinter/20040526/cabooks26).

2. Semler, *The Seven-Day Weekend: Changing the Way Work Works* (New York: Penguin, 2003).

3. Ibid.

4. Ibid.

5. R. Semler, "Managing Without Managers," *Harvard Business Review* 67, no. 5 (September–October 1989), 76–84; R. Semler, "Why My Former Employees Still Work for Me," *Harvard Business Review* 72, no. 1 (January–February 1994), 64–74; "Personal Histories: Leaders Remember the Moments and People That Shaped Them," *Harvard Business Review,* Reprint R0111B (December 2001).

6. A. Strutt, "Interview with Ricardo Semler," *Management Centre Europe,* April 2004 (www.mce.be/knowledge/392/35).

7. Semler, *The Seven-Day Weekend.*

8. Ibid.

9. "Extreme Flextime," *Inc.,* April 2004, 91.

10. Semler, *The Seven-Day Weekend.*

11. R. Semler, "How We Went Digital Without a Strategy," *Harvard Business Review* 78, no. 5 (September–October 2000), 51–56.

12. Ibid.

13. Semler, *The Seven-Day Weekend.*

14. J. E. Butler, G. R. Ferris, and N. K. Napier, *Strategy and Human Resource Management* (Cincinnati: Southwestern Publishing, 1991); P. M. Wright and G. C. McMahan, "Theoretical Perspectives for Strategic Human Resource Management," *Journal of Management* 18 (1992), 295–320.

15. L. Clifford, "Why You Can Safely Ignore Six Sigma," *Fortune,* January 22, 2001, 140.

16. S. J. Palmisano, "How the U.S. Can Keep Its Innovation Edge," *BusinessWeek,* November 17, 2003, 34.

17. F. Warner, "Brains for Sale," *Fast Company,* January 2004, 88–89.

18. Ibid.

19. Ibid.

20. Ibid.

21. Ibid.

22. Ibid.

23. J. B. Quinn, P. Anderson, and S. Finkelstein, "Managing Professional Intellect: Making the Most of the Best," *Harvard Business Review,* March–April 1996, 71–80.

24. Ibid.

25. C. D. Fisher, L. F. Schoenfeldt, and J. B. Shaw, *Human Resource Management* (Boston: Houghton Mifflin, 1990).

26. Wright and McMahan, "Theoretical Perspectives."

27. L. Baird and I. Meshoulam, "Managing Two Fits for Strategic Human Resource Management," *Academy of Management Review* 14, 116–28; J. Milliman, M. Von Glinow, and M. Nathan, "Organizational Life Cycles and Strategic International Human Resource Management in Multinational Companies: Implications for Congruence Theory," *Academy of Management Review* 16, (1991), 318–39; R. S. Schuler and S. E. Jackson, "Linking Competitive Strategies with Human Resource Management Practices," *Academy of Management Executive* 1 (1987), 207–19; P. M. Wright and S. A. Snell, "Toward an Integrative View of Strategic Human Resource Management," *Human Resource Management Review* 1 (1991), 203–25.

28. Equal Employment Opportunity Commission, "Uniform Guidelines on Employee Selection Procedures," *Federal Register* 43 (1978), 38290–315.

29. R. Stogdill II, R. Mitchell, K. Thurston, and C. Del Valle, "Why AIDS Policy Must Be a Special Policy," *BusinessWeek,* February 1, 1993, 53–54.

30. J. M. George, "AIDS/AIDS-Related Complex," in L. Peters, B. Greer, and S. Youngblood, eds., *The Blackwell Encyclopedic Dictionary of Human Resource Management* (Oxford, England: Blackwell Publishers, 1997).

31. Ibid.

32. J. M. George, "AIDS Awareness Training," in Peters et al., *The Blackwell Encyclopedic Dictionary;* Stogdill et al., "Why AIDS Policy Must Be a Special Policy."

33. S. L. Rynes, "Recruitment, Job Choice, and Post-Hire Consequences: A Call for New Research Directions," in M. D. Dunnette and L. M. Hough, eds., *Handbook of Industrial and Organizational Psychology,* vol. 2 (Palo Alto, CA: Consulting Psychologists Press, 1991), 399–444.

34. R. L. Sullivan, "Lawyers a la Carte," *Forbes,* September 11, 1995, 44.

35. D. Wessel, "The Future of Jobs: New Ones Arise; Wage Gap Widens," *The Wall Street Journal,* April 2, 2004, A1, A5; "Relocating the Back Office," *The Economist,* December 13, 2003, 67–69.

36. E. Porter, "Send Jobs to India? U.S. Companies Say It's Not Always Best," *The New York Times,* April 28, 2004, A1, A7.

37. Ibid.

38. Ibid.

39. Ibid.

40. Ibid.

41. Ibid.

42. Ibid.

43. Ibid.

44. "Relocating the Back Office."

45. Wessel, "The Future of Jobs."

46. R. J. Harvey, "Job Analysis," in Dunnette and Hough, *Handbook of Industrial and Organizational Psychology,* 71–163.

47. E. L. Levine, *Everything You Always Wanted to Know About Job Analysis: A Job Analysis Primer* (Tampa, FL: Mariner Publishing, 1983).

48. R. L. Mathis and J. H. Jackson, *Human Resource Management,* 7th ed. (Minneapolis: West, 1994).

49. E. J. McCormick, P. R. Jeannerette, and R. C. Mecham, *Position Analysis Questionnaire* (West Lafayette, IN: Occupational Research Center, Department of Psychological Sciences, Purdue University, 1969).

50. Fisher et al., *Human Resource Management;* Mathis and Jackson, *Human Resource Management;* R. A. Noe, J. R. Hollenbeck, B. Gerhart, and P. M. Wright, *Human Resource Management: Gaining a Competitive Advantage* (Burr Ridge, IL: Irwin, 1994).

51. Fisher et al., *Human Resource Management;* E. J. McCormick, *Job Analysis: Methods and Applications* (New York: American Management Association, 1979); E. J. McCormick and P. R. Jeannerette, "The Position Analysis Questionnaire" in S. Gael, ed., *The Job Analysis Handbook for Business, Industry, and Government* (New York: Wiley, 1988); Noe et al., *Human Resource Management.*

52. Rynes, "Recruitment, Job Choice, and Post-Hire Consequences."

53. R. Sharpe, "The Life of the Party? Can Jeff Taylor Keep the Good Times Rolling at Monster.com?," *Business Week,* June 4, 2001 (*Business Week* Archives).

54. www.monster.com, June 2001.

55. www.jobline.org/, June 2001; www.jobline.org, Jobline press releases, June 20, 2001, May 8, 2001.

56. S. L. Premack and J. P. Wanous, "A Meta-Analysis of Realistic Job Preview Experiments," *Journal of Applied Psychology,* 70 (1985), 706–19; J. P. Wanous, "Realistic Job Previews: Can a Procedure to Reduce Turnover also Influence the Relationship between Abilities and Performance?" *Personnel Psychology* 31 (1978), 249–58; J. P. Wanous, *Organizational Entry: Recruitment, Selection, and Socialization of Newcomers* (Reading, MA: Addison-Wesley, 1980).

57. R. M. Guion, "Personnel Assessment, Selection, and Placement," in Dunnette and Hough, *Handbook of Industrial and Organizational Psychology,* 327–97.

58. Noe, et al., *Human Resource Management;* J. A. Wheeler and J. A. Gier, "Reliability and Validity of the Situational Interview for a Sales Position," *Journal of Applied Psychology* 2 (1987), 484–87.

59. Noe, et al., *Human Resource Management.*

60. J. Flint, "Can You Tell Applesauce from Pickles?" *Forbes,* October 9, 1995, 106–08.

61. Ibid.

62. "Wanted: Middle Managers, Audition Required," *The Wall Street Journal,* December 28, 1995, A1.

63. I. L. Goldstein, "Training in Work Organizations," in Dunnette and Hough, *Handbook of Industrial and Organizational Psychology,* 507–619.

64. S. Overman, "Ethan Allen's Secret Weapon," *HRMagazine,* May 1994, 61.

65. N. Banerjee, "For Mary Kay Sales Reps in Russia, Hottest Shade Is the Color of Money," *The Wall Street Journal,* August 30, 1995, A8.

66. T. D. Allen, L. T. Eby, M. L. Poteet, E. Lentz, and L. Lima, "Career Benefits Associated with Mentoring for Protégés: A Meta-Analysis," *Journal of Applied Psychology* 89, no. 1, (2004), 127–36.

67. P. Garfinkel, "Putting a Formal Stamp on Mentoring," *The New York Times* January 18, 2004, BU10.

68. Ibid.

69. Ibid.

70. Allen, et al., "Career Benefits Associated with Mentoring"; L. Levin, "Lesson Learned: Know Your Limits. Get Outside Help Sooner Rather than Later," *Business Week Online,* July 5, 2004 (www.businessweek.com); "Family, Inc.," *Business Week Online,* November 10, 2003 (www.businessweek.com); J. Salamon, "A Year with a Mentor. Now Comes the Test," *The New York Times,* September 30, 2003, B1, B5.

71. Garfinkel, "Putting a Formal Stamp on Mentoring."

72. J. A. Byrne, "Virtual B-Schools," *Business Week,* October 23, 1995, 64–68.

73. Fisher et al., *Human Resource Management.*

74. Ibid.; G. P. Latham and K. N. Wexley, *Increasing Productivity Through Performance Appraisal* (Reading, MA: Addison-Wesley, 1982).

75. T. A. DeCotiis, "An Analysis of the External Validity and Applied Relevance of Three Rating Formats," *Organizational Behavior and Human Performance* 19 (1977), 247–66; Fisher, et al., *Human Resource Management.*

76. J. Muller, K. Kerwin, D. Welch, P. L. Moore, D. Brady, "Ford: It's Worse Than You Think," *Business Week,* June 25, 2001 (*Business Week* Archives).

77. Ibid.

78. L. M. Sixel, "Enron Rating Setup Irks Many Workers," *Houston Chronicle,* February 26, 2001, 1C.

79. J. S. Lublin, "It's Shape-Up Time for Performance Reviews," *The Wall Street Journal,* October 3, 1994, B1, B2.

80. J. S. Lublin, "Turning the Tables: Underlings Evaluate Bosses," *The Wall Street Journal,* October 4, 1994, B1, B14; S. Shellenbarger, "Reviews from Peers Instruct–and Sting," *The Wall Street Journal,* October 4, 1994, B1, B4.

81. C. Borman and D. W. Bracken, "360 Degree Appraisals," in C. L. Cooper and C. Argyris, eds., *The Concise Blackwell Encyclopedia of Management* (Oxford, England: Blackwell Publishers, 1998), 17; D. W. Bracken, "Straight Talk About Multi-Rater Feedback," *Training and Development* 48 (1994), 44–51; M. R. Edwards, W. C. Borman, and J. R. Sproul, "Solving the Double-Bind in Performance Appraisal: A Saga of Solves, Sloths, and Eagles," *Business Horizons,* 85 (1985), 59–68.

82. M. A. Peiperl, "Getting 360° Feedback Right," *Harvard Business Review,* January 2001, 142–47.

83. A. Harrington, "Workers of the World, Rate Your Boss!" *Fortune,* September 18, 2000, 340, 342, www.ImproveNow.com, June 2001.

84. Ibid.

85. Lublin, "It's Shape-Up Time for Performance Reviews."

86. S. E. Moss and J. I. Sanchez, "Are Your Employees Avoiding You? Managerial Strategies for Closing the Feedback Gap," *Academy of Management Executive* 18, no. 1 (2004), 32–46.

87. J. Flynn and F. Nayeri, "Continental Divide over Executive Pay," *Business Week,* July 3, 1995, 40–41.

88. J. A. Byrne, "How High Can CEO Pay Go?" *Business Week,* April 22, 1996, 100–06.

89. "Executive Pay," *Business Week,* April 19, 2004, 106–10.

90. Ibid.

91. L. Lavelle, "The Gravy Train May Be Drying Up," *Business Week,* April 5, 2004, 52–53.

92. C. Terhune, B. McKay, C. Mollenkamp, and J. S. Lublin, "Coke Tradition: CEOs Go Better with a Fat Send-Off," *The Wall Street Journal,* June 11, 2004, B1, B3.

93. Ibid.

94. Ibid.

95. Ibid.

96. "Executive Pay."

97. E. Tahmincioglu, "Paths to Better Health (On the Boss's Nickel)," *The New York Times,* May 23, 2004, BU7.

98. Ibid.

99. C. Kleiman, "Babe in Arms Benefit Pays Off in Loyalty," *Houston Chronicle,* January 26, 2004, 1D, 3D.

100. Ibid.

101. S. Shellenbarger, "Amid Gay Marriage Debate, Companies Offer More Benefits to Same-Sex Couples," *The Wall Street Journal,* March 18, 2004, D1.

102. Ibid.

103. Ibid.

104. S. Premack and J. E. Hunter, "Individual Unionization Decisions," *Psychological Bulletin* 103 (1988), 223–34.

105. M. B. Regan, "Shattering the AFL-CIO's Glass Ceiling," *BusinessWeek,* November 13, 1995, 46.

106. www.aflcio.org/, June 2001.

107. G. P. Zachary, "Some Unions Step Up Organizing Campaigns and Get New Members," *The Wall Street Journal,* September 1, 1995, A1, A2.

108. Regan, "Shattering the AFL-CIO's Glass Ceiling"; www.aflcio.org, June 2001; R. S. Dunham, "Big Labor: So Out It's 'Off the Radar Screen,'" *BusinessWeek,* March 26, 2001 (*BusinessWeek* Archives).

109. "The Honorable Elaine L. Chao United States Secretary of Labor," www.dol.gov/dol/_sec/public/aboutosec/chao.htm, June 25, 2001.

110. R. Blumenstein, "Ohio Strike That Is Crippling GM Plants Is Tied to Plan to Outsource Brake Work," *The Wall Street Journal,* March 12, 1996, A3–A4.

111. J. Hannah, "GM Workers Agree to End Strike," *Bryan-College Station Eagle,* March 23, 1996, A12.

Chapter 13

1. M. Duff, "Top-Shelf Employees Keep Container Store on Track," www.looksmart.com, www.findarticles.com, March 8, 2004; M. K. Ammenheuser, "The Container Store Helps People Think Inside the Box," www.icsc.org, May 2004.

2. "Learn About Us," www.containerstore.com, June 26, 2001.

3. Ibid.

4. J. Schlosser and J. Sung, "The 100 Best Companies to Work For," *Fortune,* January 8, 2001, 148–68.

5. "The Container Store," www.careerbuilder.com, July 13, 2004; "Tom Takes Re-imaginee to PBS," *Case Studies,* www.tompeters.com, March 15, 2004; "2004 Best Companies to Work For," www.fortune.com, July 12, 2004.

6. D. Roth, "My Job at the Container Store," *Fortune,* January 10, 2000 (www.fortune.com, June 26, 2001).

7. "Fortune 2004: 100 Best Companies to Work For," January 12, 2004; www.containerstore.com/careers/FortunePR_2004.jhtml?message=/repository/messages/fortuneCareer.jhtml.

8. R. Levering, M. Moskowitz, and S. Adams, "The 100 Best Companies to Work For," *Fortune* 149, no. 1, 2004, 56–78.

9. T. A. Stewart, "Just Think: No Permission Needed," *Fortune,* January 8, 2001 (Fortune.com, June 26, 2001).

10. "The Container Store Tops *Fortune's* 100 Best List for Second Year in a Row," www.containerstore.com, December 18, 2000.

11. "The Container Store Sells Products That Are Difficult to Sell," *San Gabriel Valley Tribune,* July 12, 2004 (docs.newsbank.com); D. De Marco, "Eager Workers Train at Washington D.C.'s Soon-to-Open Container Store," *Knight Ridder Tribune Business News,* February 27, 2004 (gateway.proquest.com).

12. Roth, "My Job at the Container Store."

13. Stewart, "Just Think: No Permission Needed."

14. R. Yu, "Some Texas Firms Start Wellness Programs to Encourage Healthier Workers," *Knight Ridder Tribune Business News,* July 7, 2004 (gateway.proquest.com); Levering et al., "The 100 Best Companies to Work For."

15. Roth, "My Job at the Container Store."

16. R. Kanfer, "Motivation Theory and Industrial and Organizational Psychology," in M. D. Dunnette and L. M. Hough, eds., *Handbook of Industrial and Organizational Psychology,* 2d ed., vol. 1 (Palo Alto, CA: Consulting Psychologists Press, 1990), 75–170.

17. Stewart, "Just Think: No Permission Needed."

18. Roth, "My Job at the Container Store."

19. G. Latham, "The Study of Work Motivation in the 20th Century," in L. Koppes, ed., *The History of Industrial and Organizational Psychology* (Hillsdale, NJ: Laurence Erlbaum, in press).

20. N. Nicholson, "How to Motivate Your Problem People," *Harvard Business Review,* January 2003, 57–65.

21. J. P. Campbell and R. D. Pritchard, "Motivation Theory in Industrial and Organizational Psychology," in M. D. Dunnette, ed., *Handbook of Industrial and Organizational Psychology* (Chicago: Rand McNally, 1976), 63–130; T. R. Mitchell, "Expectancy-Value Models in Organizational Psychology," in N. T. Feather, ed., *Expectations and Actions: Expectancy-Value Models in Psychology* (Hillsdale, NJ: Erlbaum, 1982), 293–312; V. H. Vroom, *Work and Motivation* (New York: Wiley, 1964).

22. N. Shope Griffin, "Personalize Your Management Development," *Harvard Business Review* 8, no. 10, 2003, 113–19.

23. Stewart, "Just Think: No Permission Needed."

24. M. Copeland, "Best Buy's Selling Machine," *Business 2.0,* July 2004, 91–102.

25. L. Heller, "Best Buy Still Turning on the Fun," *DSN Retailing Today* 43, no. 13, (July 5, 2004), 3.

26. Copeland, "Best Buy's Selling Machine"; S. Pounds, "Big-Box Retailers Cash in on South Florida Demand for Home Computer Repair," *Knight Ridder Tribune Business News,* July 5, 2004 (gateway.proquest.com); J. Bloom, "Best Buy Reaps the Rewards of Risking Marketing Failure," *Adveristing Age* 75, no. 25 (June 21, 2004), 16.

27. Copeland, "Best Buy's Selling Machine"; L. Heller, "Discount Turns Up the Volume: PC Comeback, Ipod Popularity Add Edge," *DSN Retailing Today* 43, no. 13 (July 5, 2004), 45.

28. Copeland, "Best Buy's Selling Machine."

29. Ibid.

30. Ibid.

31. Ibid.

32. T. J. Maurer, E. M. Weiss, and F. G. Barbeite, "A Model of Involvement in Work-Related Learning and Development Activity: The Effects of Individual, Situational, Motivational, and Age Variables," *Journal of Applied Psychology* 88, no. 4 (2003), 707–24.

33. J. Kaufman, "How Cambodians Came to Control California Doughnuts," *The Wall Street Journal,* February 22, 1995, A1, A8.

34. B. Stone, "Nike's Short Game," *Newsweek,* January 26, 2004, 40–41.

35. A. Holloway, "The Man Who Put the Boing in Nike," *CB Media Limited,* March 15, 2004 (LexisNexis).

36. D. Edwards, "Adultescents: The Over-40s Trying to Be Teens," *The Mirror,* February 3, 2004 (LexisNexis).

37. R. A. Martin, "The Rebirth of the New York Sneakerhead," *The New York Times,* July 11, 2004 (www.nytimes.com); R. J. Moody, "Nike Puts Faith in Savier," *American City Business Journal* 20, no. 52 (February 20, 2004), 1.

38. Stone, "Nike's Short Game."

39. Ibid.

40. Ibid.

41. Ibid.

42. A. H. Maslow, *Motivation and Personality* (New York: Harper & Row, 1954); Campbell and Pritchard, "Motivation Theory in Industrial and Organizational Psychology."

43. Kanfer, "Motivation Theory and Industrial and Organizational Psychology."

44. S. Ronen, "An Underlying Structure of Motivational Need Taxonomies: A Cross-Cultural Confirmation," in H. C. Triandis, M. D. Dunnette, and L. M. Hough, eds., *Handbook of Industrial and Organizational Psychology,* vol. 4 (Palo Alto, CA: Consulting Psychologists Press, 1994), 241–69.

45. N. J. Adler, *International Dimensions of Organizational Behavior,* 2d ed. (Boston: P.W.S.-Kent, 1991); G. Hofstede, "Motivation, Leadership and Organization: Do American Theories Apply Abroad?" *Organizational Dynamics,* Summer 1980, 42–63.

46. C. P. Alderfer, "An Empirical Test of a New Theory of Human Needs," *Organizational Behavior and Human Performance* 4 (1969), 142–75; C. P. Alderfer, *Existence, Relatedness, and Growth: Human Needs in Organizational Settings* (New York: Free Press, 1972); Campbell and Pritchard, "Motivation Theory in Industrial and Organizational Psychology."

47. Kanfer, "Motivation Theory and Industrial and Organizational Psychology."

48. F. Herzberg, *Work and the Nature of Man* (Cleveland: World, 1966).

49. N. King, "Clarification and Evaluation of the Two-Factor Theory of Job Satisfaction," *Psychological Bulletin* 74 (1970), 18–31; E. A. Locke, "The Nature and Causes of Job Satisfaction," in Dunnette, *Handbook of Industrial and Organizational Psychology,* 1297–1349.

50. D. C. McClelland, *Human Motivation* (Glenview, IL: Scott, Foresman, 1985); D. C. McClelland, "How Motives, Skills, and Values Determine What People Do," *American Psychologist* 40 (1985), 812–25; D. C. McClelland, "Managing Motivation to Expand Human Freedom," *American Psychologist* 33 (1978), 201–10.

51. D. G. Winter, *The Power Motive* (New York: Free Press, 1973).

52. M. J. Stahl, "Achievement, Power, and Managerial Motivation: Selecting Managerial Talent with the Job Choice Exercise," *Personnel Psychology* 36 (1983), 775–89; D. C. McClelland and D. H. Burnham, "Power Is the Great Motivator," *Harvard Business Review* 54 (1976), 100–10.

53. R. J. House, W. D. Spangler, and J. Woycke, "Personality and Charisma in the U.S. Presidency: A Psychological Theory of Leader Effectiveness," *Administrative Science Quarterly* 36 (1991), 364–96.

54. G. H. Hines, "Achievement, Motivation, Occupations, and Labor Turnover in New Zealand," *Journal of Applied Psychology* 58 (1973), 313–17; P. S. Hundal, "A Study of Entrepreneurial Motivation: Comparison of Fast- and Slow-Progressing Small Scale Industrial Entrepreneurs in Punjab, India," *Journal of Applied Psychology* 55 (1971), 317–23.

55. R. A. Clay, "Green Is Good for You," *Monitor on Psychology,* April 2001, 40–42.

56. Schlosser and Sung, "The 100 Best Companies to Work For"; Levering et al., "The 100 Best Companies to Work For."

57. E. P. Dalesio, "Quiet Giant Ready to Raise Its Profits," *Houston Chronicle,* May 6, 2001, 4D; Levering et al., "The 100 Best Companies to Work For."

58. J. Pfeffer, "SAS Institute: A Different Approach to Incentives and People Management Practices in the Software Industry," Harvard Business School Case HR-6, January, 1998; "Saluting the Global Awards Recipients of Arthur Andersen's Best Practices Awards 2000," www.fortune.com, September 6, 2000; N. Stein, "Winning the War to Keep Top Talent," September 6, 2000, www.fortune.com.

59. Ibid.

60. Ibid.

61. Dalesio, "Quiet Giant Ready."

62. Pfeffer, "SAS Institute"; "Saluting the Global Awards Recipients"; Stein, "Winning the War to Keep Top Talent."

63. J. S. Adams, "Toward an Understanding of Inequity," *Journal of Abnormal and Social Psychology* 67 (1963), 422–36.

64. Ibid.; J. Greenberg, "Approaching Equity and Avoiding Inequity in Groups and Organizations," in J. Greenberg and R. L. Cohen, eds., *Equity and Justice in Social Behavior* (New York: Academic Press, 1982), 389–435; J. Greenberg, "Equity and Workplace Status: A Field Experiment," *Journal of Applied Psychology* 73 (1988), 606–13; R. T. Mowday, "Equity Theory Predictions of Behavior in Organizations," in R. M. Steers and L. W. Porter, eds., *Motivation and Work Behavior* (New York: McGraw-Hill, 1987), 89–110.

65. A. Goldwasser, "Inhuman Resources," ecompany.com, March 2001, 154–55.

66. E. A. Locke and G. P. Latham, *A Theory of Goal Setting and Task Performance* (Englewood Cliffs, NJ: Prentice-Hall, 1990).

67. Ibid.; J. J. Donovan and D. J. Radosevich, "The Moderating Role of Goal Commitment on the Goal Difficulty–Performance Relationship: A Meta-Analytic Review and Critical Analysis," *Journal of Applied Psychology* 83 (1998), 308–15; M. E. Tubbs, "Goal Setting: A Meta-Analytic Examination of the Empirical Evidence," *Journal of Applied Psychology* 71 (1986), 474–83.

68. E. A. Locke, K. N. Shaw, L. M. Saari, and G. P. Latham, "Goal Setting and Task Performance: 1969–1980," *Psychological Bulletin* 90 (1981), 125–52.

69. J. L. Roberts, "Prime Time for Parsons," *Newsweek,* December 22, 2003, 40–44.

70. S. Mehta, "Parsons Takes on Helm," *Fortune,* May 16, 2002 (www.fortune.com).

71. R. D. Parsons, www.timewarner.com/senior_management/bio/Parsons Richa.adp, March 1, 2004.

72. M. Gunther and S. N. Mehta, "AOL Time Warner: What's on Dick Parsons' To-Do List," *Fortune,* April 28, 2002 (www.fortune.com).

73. Roberts, "Prime Time for Parsons."

74. Ibid.

75. Ibid.

76. "Most Powerful Black Executives: Richard Parsons," *Fortune,* July 14, 2004 (www.aoltimewarner.com).

77. Roberts, "Prime Time for Parsons."

78. "Richard Parsons: New York University Commencement," www.timewarner.com, May 13, 2004.

79. P. C. Earley, T. Connolly, and G. Ekegren, "Goals, Strategy Development, and Task Performance: Some Limits on the Efficacy of Goal Setting," *Journal of Applied Psychology* 74 (1989), 24–33; R. Kanfer and P. L. Ackerman, "Motivation and Cognitive Abilities: An Integrative/Aptitude-Treatment Interaction Approach to Skill Acquisition," *Journal of Applied Psychology* 74 (1989), 657–90.

80. W. C. Hamner, "Reinforcement Theory and Contingency Management in Organizational Settings," in H. Tosi and W. C. Hamner, eds., *Organizational Behavior and Management: A Contingency Approach* (Chicago: St. Clair Press, 1974).

81. B. F. Skinner, *Contingencies of Reinforcement* (New York: Appleton-Century-Crofts, 1969).

82. H. W. Weiss, "Learning Theory and Industrial and Organizational Psychology," in Dunnette and Hough, *Handbook of Industrial and Organizational Psychology,* 171–221.

83. Hamner, "Reinforcement Theory and Contingency Management."

84. F. Luthans and R. Kreitner, *Organizational Behavior Modification and Beyond* (Glenview, IL: Scott, Foresman, 1985); A. D. Stajkovic and F. Luthans, "A Meta-Analysis of the Effects of Organizational Behavior Modification on Task Performance, 1975–95," *Academy of Management Journal* 40 (1997), 1122–49.

85. A. D. Stajkovic and F. Luthans, "Behavioral Management and Task Performance in Organizations: Conceptual Background, Meta-Analysis, and Test of Alternative Models," *Personnel Psychology* 56 (2003), 155–194.

86. Ibid.; F. Luthans and A. D. Stajkovic, "Reinforce for Performance: The Need to Go Beyond Pay and Even Rewards," *Academy of Management Executive* 13, no. 2 (1999), 49–56; G. Billikopf Enciina and M. V. Norton, "Pay Method Affects Vineyard Pruner Performance," www.cnr.berkeley.edu/ucce50/ag-labor/7research/7calag05.htm.

87. A. Bandura, *Principles of Behavior Modification* (New York: Holt, Rinehart and Winston, 1969); A. Bandura, *Social Learning Theory* (Englewood Cliffs, NJ: Prentice-Hall, 1977); T. R. V. Davis and F. Luthans, "A Social Learning Approach to Organizational Behavior," *Academy of Management Review* 5 (1980), 281–90.

88. A. P. Goldstein and M. Sorcher, *Changing Supervisor Behaviors* (New York: Pergamon Press, 1974); Luthans and Kreitner, *Organizational Behavior Modification and Beyond.*

89. Bandura, *Social Learning Theory;* Davis and Luthans, "A Social Learning Approach to Organizational Behavior"; Luthans and Kreitner, *Organizational Behavior Modification and Beyond.*

90. A. Bandura, "Self-Reinforcement: Theoretical and Methodological Considerations," *Behaviorism* 4 (1976), 135–55.

91. P. Engardio, "A Hothouse of High-Tech Talent," *BusinessWeek/21st Century Capitalism* (1994), 126.

92. A. Bandura, "Self-Efficacy Mechanism in Human Agency," *American Psychologist* 37 (1982), 122–27; M. E. Gist and T. R. Mitchell, "Self-Efficacy: A Theoretical Analysis of Its Determinants and Malleability," *Academy of Management Review* 17 (1992), 183–211.

93. E. E. Lawler III, *Pay and Organization Development* (Reading, MA: Addison-Wesley, 1981).

94. The Risky New Bonuses," *Newsweek,* January 16, 1995, 42.

95. Lawler, *Pay and Organization Development.*

96. Ibid.

97. J. F. Lincoln, *Incentive Management* (Cleveland: Lincoln Electric Company, 1951); R. Zager, "Managing Guaranteed Employment," *Harvard Business Review* 56 (1978), 103–15.

98. Lawler, *Pay and Organization Development.*

99. M. Gendron, "Gradient Named 'Small Business of Year,'" *Boston Herald,* May 11, 1994, 35.

100. W. Zeller, R. D. Hof, R. Brandt, S. Baker, and D. Greising, "Go-Go Goliaths," *BusinessWeek,* February 13, 1995, 64–70.

101. "Stock Option," *Encarta World English Dictionary,* (www.dictionary.msn.com, June 28, 2001); personal interview with Professor Bala Dharan, Jones Graduate School of Business, Rice University, June 28, 2001.

102. Personal interview with Professor Bala Dharan.

103. Ibid.

104. A. J. Michels, "Dallas Semiconductor," *Fortune,* May 16, 1994, 81.

105. M. Betts, "Big Things Come in Small Buttons," *Computerworld,* August 3, 1992, 30.

106. M. Boslet, "Metal Buttons Toted by Crop Pickers Act as Mini Databases," *The Wall Street Journal,* June 1, 1994, B3.

107. C. D. Fisher, L. F. Schoenfeldt, and J. B. Shaw, *Human Resource Management* (Boston: Houghton Mifflin, 1990); B. E. Graham-Moore and T. L. Ross, *Productivity Gainsharing* (Englewood Cliffs, NJ: Prentice-Hall, 1983); A. J. Geare, "Productivity from Scanlon Type Plans," *Academy of Management Review* 1 (1976), 99–108.

108. J. Labate, "Deal Those Workers In," *Fortune,* April 19, 1993, 26.

109. K. Belson, "Japan's Net Generation," *BusinessWeek,* March 19, 2001, (*BusinessWeek* Archives, June 27, 2001).

110. K. Belson, "Taking a Hint from the Upstarts," *BusinessWeek,* March 19, 2001 (*BusinessWeek* Archives, June 27, 2001); "Going for the Gold," *BusinessWeek,* March 19, 2001 (*BusinessWeek* Archives, June 27, 2001); "What the Government Can Do to Promote a Flexible Workforce," *BusinessWeek,* March 19, 2001 (*BusinessWeek* Archives, June 27, 2001).

Chapter 14

1. B. Schlender, "Ballmer Unbound: How Do You Impose Order on a Giant, Runaway Mensa Meeting? Just Watch Microsoft's CEO," *Fortune,* January 26, 2004, 117–24.

2. Ibid.

3. Ibid.

4. "Steve Ballmer," AskMen.com, July 24, 2004.

5. Schlender, "Ballmer Unbound."

6. J. Evers, "Gates Pitches 'Seamless Computing' to Developers," *InfoWorld,* July 24, 2004 (www.infoworld.com); "Bill Gates Talks Seamless Computing, Security, and Linux," *InformationWeek,* December 1, 2003 (www.informationweek.com/story/showArticle.jhtml?articleID=16400867); B. Gates, "Seamless Computing: Hardware Advances for a New Generation of Software," Windows Hardware Engineering Conference (WinHEC) Washington State Convention and Trade Center, Seattle, May 4, 2004.

7. Schlender, "Ballmer Unbound."

8. Evers, "Gates Pitches 'Seamless Computing' to Developers"; "Bill Gates Talks Seamless Computing, Security, and Linux"; Gates, "Seamless Computing."

9. Schlender, "Ballmer Unbound."

10. Ibid.

11. S. Hamm, "Microsoft's Worst Enemy: Success," *BusinessWeek,* July 19, 2004, 33; "Microsoft CEO Seeks to Avoid 'Big Company Ills,'" *U.S. Business News,* July 7, 2004 (www.msnbc.msn.com/id/5386384).

12. Ibid.

13. S. Hamm and P. Burrows, "Why High Tech Has to Stay Humble," *BusinessWeek Online,* January 19, 2004 (www.businessweek.com).

14. G. Yukl, *Leadership in Organizations,* 2d ed. (New York: Academic Press, 1989); R. M. Stogdill, *Handbook of Leadership: A Survey of the Literature* (New York: Free Press, 1974).

15. Schlender, "Ballmer Unbound."

16. W. D. Spangler, R. J. House, and R. Palrecha, "Personality and Leadership," in B. Schneider and D. B. Smith, eds., *Personality and Organizations* (Mahwah, NJ: Lawrence Erlbaum, 2004), 251–290.

17. Ibid.; "Leaders vs. Managers: Leaders Master the Context of Their Mission, Managers Surrender to It," www.msue.msu.edu/msue/imp/modtd/visuals/tsld029.htm, July 28, 2004; "Leadership," Leadership Center at Washington State University; M. Maccoby, "Understanding the Difference Between Management and Leadership," *Research Technology Management* 43, no. 1 (January–February, 2000), 57–59 (www.maccoby.com/articles/UtDBMaL.html); P. Coutts, "Leadership vs. Management," www.telusplanet.net/public/pdcoutts/leadership/LdrVsMgnt.htm, October 1, 2000; S. Robbins, "The Difference Between Managing and Leading," www.Entrepreneur.com/article/0,4621,304743,00.html, November 18, 2002; W. Bennis, "The Leadership Advantage," *Leader to Leader* 12 (Spring 1999), (www.pfdf.org/leaderbooks/121/spring99/bennis/html).

18. Spangler et al., "Personality and Leadership"; "Leaders vs. Managers"; "Leadership"; Maccoby, "Understanding the Difference Between Management and Leadership"; Coutts, "Leadership vs. Management"; Robbins, "The Difference Between Managing and Leading"; Bennis, "The Leadership Advantage."

19. J. Gertner, "The Virtue in $6 Heirloom Tomatoes," *The New York Times,* June 6, 2004 (www.nytimes.com).

20. Ibid.; W. Zellner, "John Mackey's Empire: Peace, Love, and the Bottom Line," *BusinessWeek Online,* December 7, 1998 (www.businessweek.com/@@cUnEBIYQB3qr3QcA/archives/1998/b3607112.arc.htm); "Whole Foods Market Expands into U.K.," www.wholefoodsmarket.com/investor/freshwild.html, January 16, 2004; "Whole Foods Market Opens Largest Supermarket in Manhattan, a Naturally Sought After Destination," www.wholefoodsmarket.com/company/pr_02-05-04.html, July 12, 2004.

21. R. Rayasam, "His Nutritious 15 Minutes," *Houston Chronicle,* July 4, 2004, D5.

22. Gertner, "The Virtue in $6 Heirloom Tomatoes."

23. Rayasam, "His Nutritious 15 Minutes."

24. Gertner, "The Virtue in $6 Heirloom Tomatoes."

25. Ibid.

26. "Declaration of Independence," www.wholefoods.com/company/declaration.html, July 28, 2004.

27. Gertner, "The Virtue in $6 Heirloom Tomatoes"; Rayasam, "His Nutritious 15 Minutes"; "Declaration of Independence."

28. R. Calori and B. Dufour, "Management European Style," *Academy of Management Executive* 9, no. 3 (1995), 61–70.

29. Ibid.

30. H. Mintzberg, *Power in and Around Organizations* (Englewood Cliffs, NJ: Prentice-Hall, 1983); J. Pfeffer, *Power in Organizations* (Marshfield, MA: Pitman, 1981).

31. R. P. French, Jr., and B. Raven, "The Bases of Social Power," in D. Cartwright and A. F. Zander, eds., *Group Dynamics* (Evanston, IL: Row, Peterson, 1960), 607–23.

32. R. L. Rose, "After Turning Around Giddings and Lewis, Fife Is Turned Out Himself," *The Wall Street Journal,* June 22, 1993, A1.

33. A. Grove, "How Intel Makes Spending Pay Off," *Fortune,* February 22, 1993, 56–61; "Craig R. Barrett, Chief Executive Officer: Intel Corporation," *Intel,* July 28, 2004 (www.intel.com/pressroom/kits/bios/barrett/bio.htm).

34. M. Loeb, "Jack Welch Lets Fly on Budgets, Bonuses, and Buddy Boards," *Fortune,* May 29, 1995, 146.

35. M. Arndt, "Nardelli: Taking on a Fixer-Upper," *BusinessWeek* December 18, 2000 (*BusinessWeek* Archives); C. Hymowitz, "Home Depot's CEO Led a Revolution, but Left Some Behind," *The Wall Street Journal,* March 16, 2004, B1.

36. P. Sellers, "Exit the Builder, Enter the Repairman," *Fortune,* March 19, 2001, 87–88; "The Home Depot Reports Record First Quarter 2004 Earnings," ir.homedepot.com/ReleaseDetail.cfm?ReleaseID=135414, May 18, 2004.

37. Hymowitz, "Home Depot's CEO Led a Revolution."

38. Ibid.

39. Ibid.

40. "The Home Depot Reports Record First Quarter 2004 Earnings."

41. Ibid.

42. L. Bird, "Lazarus's IBM Coup Was All About Relationships," *The Wall Street Journal,* May 26, 1994, B1, B7.

43. T. M. Burton, "Visionary's Reward: Combine 'Simple Ideas' and Some Failures; Result: Sweet Revenge," *The Wall Street Journal,* February 3, 1995, A1, A5.

44. L. Nakarmi, "A Flying Leap Toward the 21st Century? Pressure from Competitors and Seoul May Transform the Chaebol," *BusinessWeek,* March 20, 1995, 78–80.

45. B. M. Bass, *Bass and Stogdill's Handbook of Leadership: Theory, Research, and Managerial Applications,* 3d ed. (New York: Free Press, 1990); R. J. House and M. L. Baetz, "Leadership: Some Empirical Generalizations and New Research Directions," in B. M. Staw and L. L. Cummings, eds., *Research in Organizational Behavior,* vol. 1 (Greenwich, CT: JAI Press, 1979), 341–423; S. A. Kirpatrick and E. A. Locke, "Leadership: Do Traits Matter?" *Academy of Management Executive* 5, no. 2 (1991). 48–60; Yukl, *Leadership in Organizations;* G. Yukl and D. D. Van Fleet, "Theory and Research on

Leadership in Organizations," in M. D. Dunnette and L. M. Hough, eds., *Handbook of Industrial and Organizational Psychology,* 2d ed., vol. 3 (Palo Alto, CA: Consulting Psychologists Press, 1992), 147–97.

46. E. A. Fleishman, "Performance Assessment Based on an Empirically Derived Task Taxonomy," *Human Factors* 9 (1967), 349–66; E. A. Fleishman, "The Description of Supervisory Behavior," *Personnel Psychology* 37 (1953), 1–6; A. W. Halpin and B. J. Winer, "A Factorial Study of the Leader Behavior Descriptions," in R. M. Stogdill and A. I. Coons, eds., *Leader Behavior: Its Description and Measurement* (Columbus Bureau of Business Research, Ohio State University, 1957); D. Tscheulin, "Leader Behavior Measurement in German Industry," *Journal of Applied Psychology* 56 (1971), 28–31.

47. E. A. Fleishman and E. F. Harris, "Patterns of Leadership Behavior Related to Employee Grievances and Turnover," *Personnel Psychology* 15 (1962), 43–56.

48. B. Bremner and C. Dawson, "Can Anything Stop Toyota?" *BusinessWeek,* November 17, 2003, 114–22.

49. Ibid.

50. "Toyota Announces Best-Ever June Sales: Sets Second-Quarter and First-Half Sales Records," www.toyota.com/about/news/corporate/2004/070/01-1-sales.html, August 2, 2004.

51. Bremner and Dawson, "Can Anything Stop Toyota?"

52. Ibid.; "Toyota's Alabama Plant Featured in Company's Latest Corporate Ad," www.toyota.com/about/news/corporate/2004/07/29-1-ads.html, August 2, 2004.

53. R. Likert, *New Patterns of Management* (New York: McGraw-Hill, 1961); N. C. Morse and E. Reimer, "The Experimental Change of a Major Organizational Variable," *Journal of Abnormal and Social Psychology* 52 (1956), 120–29.

54. R. R. Blake and J. S. Mouton, *The New Managerial Grid* (Houston: Gulf, 1978).

55. P. Hersey and K. Blanchard, *Management of Organizational Behavior: Utilizing Human Resources* (Englewood Cliffs, NJ: Prentice-Hall, 1982).

56. F. E. Fiedler, *A Theory of Leadership Effectiveness* (New York: McGraw-Hill, 1967); F. E. Fiedler, "The Contingency Model and the Dynamics of the Leadership Process," in L. Berkowitz, ed., *Advances in Experimental Social Psychology* (New York: Academic Press, 1978).

57. J. Rebello, "Radical Ways of Its CEO Are a Boon to Bank," *The Wall Street Journal,* March 20, 1995, B1, B3.

58. J. Fierman, "Winning Ideas from Maverick Managers," *Fortune,* 78 February 6, 1995, 66–80.

59. Ibid.

60. M. Schuman, "Free to Be," *Forbes,* May 8, 1995, 78–80.

61. House and Baetz, "Leadership"; L. H. Peters, D. D. Hartke, and J. T. Pohlmann, "Fiedler's Contingency Theory of Leadership: An Application of the Meta-Analysis Procedures of Schmidt and Hunter," *Psychological Bulletin* 97 (1985), 274–85; C. A. Schriesheim, B. J. Tepper, and L. A. Tetrault, "Least Preferred Co-Worker Score, Situational Control, and Leadership Effectiveness: A Meta-Analysis of Contingency Model Performance Predictions," *Journal of Applied Psychology* 79 (1994), 561–73.

62. M. G. Evans, "The Effects of Supervisory Behavior on the Path-Goal Relationship," *Organizational Behavior and Human Performance* 5 (1970), 277–98; R. J. House, "A Path-Goal Theory of Leader Effectiveness," *Administrative Science Quarterly* 16 (1971), 321–38; J. C. Wofford and L. Z. Liska, "Path-Goal Theories of Leadership: A Meta-Analysis," *Journal of Management* 19 (1993), 857–76.

63. J. Rosenfeld, "Lead Softly, but Carry a Big Baton," *Fast Company* (July 2001), 46–48.

64. Ibid.; "What Is the Music Paradigm?" www.themusicparadigm.com/what_is.asp, July 20, 2004; "Roger Nierenberg," www.goldstars.com/roger_nierenberg.htm, July 30, 2004.

65. C. Bangle, "The Ultimate Creativity Machine: How BMW Turns Art into Profit," *Harvard Business Review,* January, 2001, 47–55.

66. Ibid., 48; www.bmw.com, September 11, 2001.

67. S. Kerr and J. M. Jermier, "Substitutes for Leadership: Their Meaning and Measurement," *Organizational Behavior and Human Performance* 22 (1978), 375–403; P. M. Podsakoff, B. P. Niehoff, S. B. MacKenzie, and M. L. Williams, "Do Substitutes for Leadership Really Substitute for Leadership? An Empirical Examination of Kerr and Jermier's Situational Leadership Model," *Organizational Behavior and Human Decision Processes* 54 (1993), 1–44.

68. Kerr and Jermier, "Substitutes for Leadership"; Podsakoff et al., "Do Substitutes for Leadership Really Substitute for Leadership?"

69. K. Miller, "Siemens Shapes Up," *BusinessWeek,* May 1, 1995, 52–53.

70. B. M. Bass, *Leadership and Performance Beyond Expectations* (New York: Free Press, 1985); Bass, *Bass and Stogdill's Handbook of Leadership;* Yukl and Van Fleet, "Theory and Research on Leadership."

71. G. E. Schares, J. B. Levine, and P. Coy, "The New Generation at Siemens," *BusinessWeek,* March 9, 1992, 46–48.

72. Miller, "Siemens Shapes Up."

73. Ibid.

74. J. A. Conger and R. N. Kanungo, "Behavioral Dimensions of Charismatic Leadership," in J. A. Conger, R. N. Kanungo, and Associates, *Charismatic Leadership* (San Francisco: Jossey-Bass, 1988).

75. Bass, *Leadership and Performance Beyond Expectations;* Bass, *Bass and Stogdill's Handbook of Leadership;* Yukl and Van Fleet, "Theory and Research on Leadership."

76. Ibid.

77. Miller, "Siemens Shapes Up."

78. Bass, *Leadership and Performance Beyond Expectations.*

79. Bass, *Bass and Stogdill's Handbook of Leadership;* B. M. Bass and B. J. Avolio, "Transformational Leadership: A Response to Critiques," in M. M. Chemers and R. Ayman, eds., *Leadership Theory and Research: Perspectives and Directions* (San Diego: Academic Press, 1993), 49–80; B. M. Bass, B. J. Avolio, and L. Goodheim, "Biography and the Assessment of Transformational Leadership at the World Class Level," *Journal of Management* 13 (1987), 7–20; J. J. Hater and B. M. Bass, "Supervisors Evaluations and Subordinates' Perceptions of Transformational and Transactional Leadership," *Journal of Applied Psychology* 73, (1988), 695–702; R. Pillai, "Crisis and Emergence of

Charismatic Leadership in Groups: An Experimental Investigation," *Journal of Applied Psychology* 26 (1996), 543–62; J. Seltzer and B. M. Bass, "Transformational Leadership: Beyond Initiation and Consideration," *Journal of Management* 16 (1990), 693–703; D. A. Waldman, B. M. Bass, and W. O. Einstein, "Effort, Performance, Transformational Leadership in Industrial and Military Service," *Journal of Occupation Psychology* 60 (1987), 1–10.

80. R. Pillai, C. A. Schriesheim, and E. S. Williams, "Fairness Perceptions and Trust as Mediators of Transformational and Transactional Leadership: A Two-Sample Study," *Journal of Management* 25 (1999), 897–933.

81. L. Tischler, "Where Are the Women?" *Fast Company,* February, 2004, 52–60.

82. Ibid.

83. A. H. Eagly and B. T. Johnson, "Gender and Leadership Style: A Meta-Analysis," *Psychological Bulletin* 108 (1990), 233–56.

84. Ibid.

85. The Economist, "Workers Resent Scoldings from Female Bosses," *Houston Chronicle,* August 19, 2000, 1C.

86. Ibid.

87. Ibid.

88. Ibid.

89. A. H. Eagly, S. J. Karau, and M. G. Makhijani, "Gender and the Effectiveness of Leaders: A Meta-Analysis," *Psychological Bulletin* 117 (1995), 125–45.

90. Ibid.

91. Tischler, "Where Are the Women?"

92. J. Porretto, "Autos Attract a Winner," *Houston Chronicle,* July 17, 2004, D2.

93. K. Ligocki, "From Art History Student to CEO," *Women Working 2000 and Beyond,* July 30, 2004 (www.womenworking2000.com/feature/index/php?id=29).

94. "Biographical Sketch of Kathleen Ligocki," *Detroit Free Press,* July 3, 2004 (www.freep.com/news/statewire/sw100484_200407803.htm); "Biographical sketch of Kathleen Ligocki," *The Journal Gazette,* July 3, 2004, (www.fortwayne.com/mld/journalgazette/business/9074506.htm).

95. Porretto, "Autos Attract a Winner"; "Biographical Sketch of Kathleen Ligocki," *Detroit Free Press;* "Biographical Sketch of Kathleen Ligocki," *The Journal Gazette;* Ligocki, "From Art History Student to CEO."

96. Porretto, "Autos Attract a Winner."

97. Ibid.

98. J. M. George and K. Bettenhausen, "Understanding Prosocial Behavior, Sales Performance, and Turnover: A Group-Level Analysis in a Service Context," *Journal of Applied Psychology,* 75 (1990), 698–709.

99. J. M. George, "Emotions and Leadership: The Role of Emotional Intelligence," *Human Relations* 53 (2000), 1027–55.

100. Ibid.

101. J. Zhou and J. M. George, "Awakening Employee Creativity: The Role of Leader Emotional Intelligence," *The Leadership Quarterly* 14, no. 4–5 (August–October, 2003), 545–68.

102. Ibid.

103. Ibid.

Chapter 15

1. C. Matlack, R. Tiplady, D. Brady, R. Berner, and H. Tashiro, "The Vuitton Machine," *BusinessWeek,* March 22, 2004, 98–102; "America's Most Admired Companies," *Fortune.com,* August 18, 2004 (www.fortune.com/fortune/mostadmired/snapshot/0,15020,383,00.html); "Art Samberg's Ode to Steel," *Big Money Weekly,* June 29, 2004 (trading.sina/com/trading/rightside/bigmoney_weekly_040629.b5.shtml); "Nucor Reports Record Results for First Quarter of 2004," www.nucor.com/financials.asp?finpage=newsreleases, August 18, 2004; "Nucor Reports Results for First Half and Second Quarter of 2004," www.nucor.com/financials.asp?finpage=newsreleases; J. C. Cooper, "The Price of Efficiency," *BusinessWeek Online,* March 22, 2004, (www.businessweek.com/magazine/content/04_12/b3875603.htm).

2. C. Matlack et al., "The Vuitton Machine."

3. Ibid.

4. Ibid.

5. Ibid.

6. www.nucor.com, November 21, 2001.

7. "About Nucor," www.nucor.com/aboutus.htm, August 18, 2004.

8. M. Arndt, "Out of the Forge and into the Fire," *BusinessWeek,* June 18, 2001 (BusinessWeek Archives).

9 S. Baker, "The Minimill That Acts Like a Biggie," *BusinessWeek,* September 30, 1996, 101–04; S. Baker, "Nucor," *BusinessWeek,* February 13, 1995, 70; S. Overman, "No-Frills at Nucor," *HR Magazine,* July 1994, 56–60.

10. www.nucor.com, November 21, 2001.

11. Baker, "The Minimill That Acts Like a Biggie"; Baker, "Nucor"; Overman, "No-Frills at Nucor"; www.nucor.com.

12. Matlack et al., "The Vuitton Machine"; "About Nucor"; "America's Most Admired Companies"; "Art Samberg's Ode to Steel"; "Nucor Reports Record Results for First Quarter of 2004"; "Nucor Reports Results for First Half and Second Quarter of 2004."

13. W. R. Coradetti, "Teamwork Takes Time and a Lot of Energy," *HRMagazine,* June 1994, 74–77; D. Fenn, "Service Teams That Work," *Inc.,* August 1995, 99; "Team Selling Catches On, but Is Sales Really a Team Sport?" *The Wall Street Journal,* March 29, 1994, A1.

14. T. M. Mills, *The Sociology of Small Groups* (Englewood Cliffs, NJ: Prentice-Hall, 1967); M. E. Shaw, *Group Dynamics* (New York: McGraw-Hill, 1981).

15. R. S. Buday, "Reengineering One Firm's Product Development and Another's Service Delivery," *Planning Review,* March–April 1993, 14–19; J. M. Burcke, "Hallmark's Quest for Quality Is a Job Never Done," *Business Insurance,* April 26, 1993, 122; M. Hammer and J. Champy, *Reengineering the Corporation* (New York: HarperBusiness, 1993); T. A. Stewart, "The Search for the Organization of Tomorrow," *Fortune,* May 18, 1992, 92–98.

16. T. Claburn, "Lockheed Finds a Way to Connect Questions with Answers," *InformationWeek,* June 14, 2004 (www.informationweek.com/showArticle.jhtml?articleID=21700462).

17. "Lockheed Martin Licenses Tacit to Network Space Systems Employees," www.tacit.com/company/news/press/2004.05.24.html, May 24, 2004.

18. P. Kaihla, "The Matchmaker in the Machine," *Business 2.0,* February 2004, 52–55.

19. Claburn, "Lockheed Finds a Way."

20. Kaihla, "The Matchmaker in the Machine."

21. Ibid.

22. Ibid.

23. A. Deutschman, "Inside the Mind of Jeff Bezos," *Fast Company,* August 2004, 50–58.

24. Ibid.

25. Ibid.

26. Ibid.

27. "Online Extra: Jeff Bezos on Word-of-Mouth Power," *BusinessWeek Online,* August 2, 2004 (www.businessweek.com); R. D. Hof, "Reprogramming Amazon," *BusinessWeek Online,* December 22, 2003 (www.businessweek.com).

28. S. Dallas, "Rock Bottom Restaurants: Brewing Up Solid Profits," *BusinessWeek,* May 22, 1995, 74.

29. L. Armstrong and L. Holyoke, "NASA's Tiny Camera Has a Wide-Angle Future," *BusinessWeek,* March 6, 1995, 54–55.

30. J. A. Pearce II and E. C. Ravlin, "The Design and Activation of Self-Regulating Work Groups," *Human Relations* 11 (1987), 751–82.

31. R. Henkoff, "When to Take on the Giants," *Fortune,* May 30, 1994, 111, 114.

32. B. Dumaine, "Who Needs a Boss?" *Fortune,* May 7, 1990, 52–60; Pearce and Ravlin, "The Design and Activation of Self-Regulating Work Groups."

33. Dumaine, "Who Needs a Boss"; A. R. Montebello and V. R. Buzzotta, "Work Teams That Work," *Training and Development,* March 1993, 59–64.

34. T. D. Wall, N. J. Kemp, P. R. Jackson, and C. W. Clegg, "Outcomes of Autonomous Work Groups: A Long-Term Field Experiment," *Academy of Management Journal* 29 (1986): 280–304.

35. A. Markels, "A Power Producer Is Intent on Giving Power to Its People," *The Wall Street Journal,* July 3, 1995, A1, A12.

36. J. S. Lublin, "My Colleague, My Boss," *The Wall Street Journal,* April 12, 1995, R4, R12.

37. W. R. Pape, "Group Insurance," *Inc.* (Inc. Technology Supplement), June 17, 1997, 29–31; A. M. Townsend, S. M. DeMarie, and A. R. Hendrickson, "Are You Ready for Virtual Teams?" *HRMagazine,* September 1996, 122–26; A. M. Townsend, S. M. DeMarie, and A. M. Hendrickson, "Virtual Teams: Technology and the Workplace of the Future," *Academy of Management Executive* 12, no. 3 (1998) 17–29.

38. Townsend et al., "Virtual Teams."

39. Pape, "Group Insurance,"; Townsend et al., "Are You Ready for Virtual Teams?"

40. D. L. Duarte and N. T. Snyder, *Mastering Virtual Teams* (San Francisco: Jossey-Bass, 1999); K. A. Karl, "Book Reviews: *Mastering Virtual Teams,*" *Academy of Management Executive,* August 1999, 118–19.

41. B. Geber, "Virtual Teams," *Training* 32, no. 4 (August 1995), 36–40; T. Finholt and L. S. Sproull, "Electronic Groups at Work," *Organization Science* 1 (1990), 41–64.

42. Geber, "Virtual Teams."

43. E. J. Hill, B. C. Miller, S. P. Weiner, and J. Colihan, "Influences of the Virtual Office on Aspects of Work and Work/Life Balance," *Personnel Psychology* 31 (1998), 667–83; S. G. Strauss, "Technology, Group Process, and Group Outcomes: Testing the Connections in Computer-Mediated and Face-to-Face Groups," *Human-Computer Interaction* 12 (1997), 227–66; M. E. Warkentin, L. Sayeed, and R. Hightower, "Virtual Teams Versus Face-to-Face Teams: An Exploratory Study of a Web-Based Conference System," *Decision Sciences* 28, no. 4 (Fall 1997), 975–96.

44. S. A. Furst, M. Reeves, B. Rosen, and R. S. Blackburn, "Managing the Life Cycle of Virtual Teams," *Academy of Management Executive* 18, no. 2 (May 2004), 6–20.

45. Ibid.

46. A. Deutschman, "The Managing Wisdom of High-Tech Superstars," *Fortune,* October 17, 1994, 197–206.

47. J. D. Thompson, *Organizations in Action* (New York: McGraw-Hill, 1967).

48. Ibid.

49. Lublin, "My Colleague, My Boss."

50. R. G. LeFauve and A. C. Hax, "Managerial and Technological Innovations at Saturn Corporation," *MIT Management,* Spring 1992, 8–19.

51. B. W. Tuckman, "Developmental Sequences in Small Groups," *Psychological Bulletin* 63 (1965), 384–99; B. W. Tuckman and M. C. Jensen, "Stages of Small Group Development," *Group and Organizational Studies* 2 (1977), 419–27.

52. C. J. G. Gersick, "Time and Transition in Work Teams: Toward a New Model of Group Development," *Academy of Management Journal* 31 (1988), 9–41; C. J. G. Gersick, "Marking Time: Predictable Transitions in Task Groups," *Academy of Management Journal* 32 (1989), 274–309.

53. J. R. Hackman, "Group Influences on Individuals in Organizations," in M. D. Dunnette and L. M. Hough, eds., *Handbook of Industrial and Organizational Psychology,* 2d ed., vol. 3 (Palo Alto, CA: Consulting Psychologists Press, 1992), 199–267.

54. Ibid.

55. Ibid.

56. Lublin, "My Colleague, My Boss."

57. T. Kelley and J. Littman, *The Art of Innovation* (New York: Doubleday, 2001).

58. B. Nussbaum, "The Power of Design," *BusinessWeek,* May 17, 2004, 86–94.

59. Ibid.

60. Ibid.

61. Kelley and Littman, *The Art of Innovation.*

62. Ibid., www.ideo.com; "1999 Idea Winners," *BusinessWeek,* June 7, 1999 (BusinessWeek Archives).

63. Nussbaum, "The Power of Design."

64. L. Festinger, "Informal Social Communication," *Psychological Review* 57 (1950), 271–82; Shaw, *Group Dynamics.*

65. Hackman, "Group Influences on Individuals in Organizations"; Shaw, *Group Dynamics.*

66. D. Cartwright, "The Nature of Group Cohesiveness," in D. Cartwright and A. Zander, eds., *Group Dynamics,* 3d ed. (New York: Harper & Row, 1968); L. Festinger, S. Schacter, and K. Black, *Social Pressures in Informal Groups* (New York: Harper & Row, 1950); Shaw, *Group Dynamics.*

67. T. F. O'Boyle, "A Manufacturer Grows Efficient by Soliciting Ideas from Employees," *The Wall Street Journal,* June 5, 1992, A1, A5.

68. C. Barrett, "Customer Service Agent," *Colleen's Corner,* August 20, 2004 (www.southwest.com/about_swa/about_swa.html); "Southwest Celebrates

Its One Millionth Online Checkin Customer: Houston Resident Showered with Balloons, Confetti, and a Lot of Southwest LUV!" www.southwest.com, May 24, 2004.

69. A. Serwer, "The Hottest Thing in the Sky," *Fortune* 8 (March 2004), 86–103.

70. C. Flannigan, "February 2004 Star of the Month," www.southwest.com, August 8, 2004.

71. Ibid.

72. A. Serwer, "The Hottest Thing in the Sky."

73. Ibid.

74. M. Ardnt, "Flying Budget, but in Style," *BusinessWeek Online,* March 15, 2004 (www.businessweek.com?).

75. J. C. Cooper, "The Price of Efficiency," *BusinessWeek Online,* March 22, 2004 (www.businessweek.com).

76. Serwer, "The Hottest Thing in the Sky."

77. Lublin, "My Colleague, My Boss."

78. Kelley and Littman, "The Art of Innovation," p. 93.

79. Kelley and Littman, "The Art of Innovation."

80. P. C. Earley, "Social Loafing and Collectivism: A Comparison of the United States and the People's Republic of China," *Administrative Science Quarterly* 34 (1989), 565–81; J. M. George, "Extrinsic and Intrinsic Origins of Perceived Social Loafing in Organizations," *Academy of Management Journal* 35 (1992), 191–202; S. G. Harkins, B. Latane, and K. Williams, "Social Loafing: Allocating Effort or Taking It Easy," *Journal of Experimental Social Psychology* 16 (1980), 457–65; B. Latane, K. D. Williams, and S. Harkins, "Many Hands Make Light the Work: The Causes and Consequences of Social Loafing," *Journal of Personality and Social Psychology* 37 (1979), 822–32; J. A. Shepperd, "Productivity Loss in Performance Groups: A Motivation Analysis," *Psychological Bulletin* 113 (1993), 67–81.

81. George, "Extrinsic and Intrinsic Origins"; G. R. Jones, "Task Visibility, Free Riding, and Shirking: Explaining the Effect of Structure and Technology on Employee Behavior," *Academy of Management Review* 9 (1984), 684–95; K. Williams, S. Harkins, and B. Latane, "Identifiability as a Deterrent to Social Loafing: Two Cheering Experiments," *Journal of Personality and Social Psychology* 40 (1981), 303–11.

82. S. Harkins and J. Jackson, "The Role of Evaluation in Eliminating Social Loafing," *Personality and Social Psychology Bulletin* 11 (1985), 457–65; N. L. Kerr and S. E. Bruun, "Ringelman Revisited: Alternative Explanations for the Social Loafing Effect," *Personality and Social Psychology Bulletin* 7 (1981), 224–31; Williams et al., "Identifiability as a Deterrent to Social Loafing"; Harkins and Jackson, "The Role of Evaluation in Eliminating Social Loafing"; Kerr and Bruun, "Ringelman Revisited."

83. M. A. Brickner, S. G. Harkins, and T. M. Ostrom, "Effects of Personal Involvement: Thought-Provoking Implications for Social Loafing," *Journal of Personality and Social Psychology* 51 (1986), 763–69; S. G. Harkins and R. E. Petty, "The Effects of Task Difficulty and Task Uniqueness on Social Loafing," *Journal of Personality and Social Psychology* 43 (1982), 1214–29.

84. B. Latane, "Responsibility and Effort in Organizations," in P. S. Goodman, ed., *Designing Effective Work Groups* (San Franciso: Jossey-Bass, 1986); Latane, Williams, and Harkins, "Many Hands Make Light the Work"; I. D. Steiner, *Group Process and Productivity* (New York: Academic Press, 1972).

Chapter 16

1. C. Hymowitz, "Missing from Work: The Chance to Think, Even to Dream a Little," *The Wall Street Journal,* March 23, 2004, B1.

2. Ibid.

3. Ibid.

4. Y. J. Yong, "CEO Message," www.samsung.com, August 22, 2004; "Yun Jong Yong: Biography," www.hwwilson.com, August 22, 2004.

5. C. Chandler, "CEO Voices: Jong-Yong Yun," *Fortune,* July 26, 2004.

6. "2004 Most Powerful People in Business: Jong-Yong Yun," *Fortune,* August 22, 2004 (www.fortune.com/fortune/subs/mostpowerful/asia/snapshot/ 0,21105,5,00.html); "Overhauling Samsung," *BusinessWeek Online,* January 10, 2000 (www.businessweek.com:/2000/00_02/b3663060.htm?scriptFramed).

7. L. Kraar, "Asia's Businessman of the Year," *Fortune,* January 24, 2000 (www.fortune.com).

8. Chandler, "CEO Voices."

9. Kraar, "Asia's Businessman of the Year."

10. Ibid.

11. "2004 Most Powerful People in Business."

12. "Yun Jong Yong", *BusinessWeek Online,* January 12, 2004 (www.businessweek.com); "Yun Jong Yong"; "2004 Most Powerful People in Business"; Kraar, "Asia's Businessman of the Year."

13. Chandler, "CEO Voices."

14. Hymowitz, "Missing from Work."

15. C. A. O'Reilly and L. R. Pondy, "Organizational Communication," in S. Kerr, ed., *Organizational Behavior* (Columbus, OH: Grid, 1979).

16. "World's First Volume Computed Tomography (VCT) System, Developed by GE Healthcare, Scanning Patients at Froedtert," www.gehealthcare.com/company/pressroom/releases/pr_release_9722.html, June 18, 2004.

17. S. Kirsner, "Time [Zone] Travelers," *Fast Company,* August, 2004, 60–66.

18. "New CT Scanner by GE Healthcare Advances Imaging Technology," *Wisconsin Technology Network,* June 21, 2004 (www.wistechnology.com).

19. Kirsner, "Time [Zone] Travelers."

20. Ibid.

21. Ibid.

22. E. M. Rogers and R. Agarwala-Rogers, *Communication in Organizations* (New York: Free Press, 1976).

23. W. Nabers, "The New Corporate Uniforms," *Fortune,* November 13, 1995, 132–56.

24. R. B. Schmitt, "Judges Try Curbing Lawyers' Body-Language Antics," *The Wall Street Journal,* September 11, 1997, B1, B7.

25. D. A. Adams, P. A. Todd, and R. R. Nelson, "A Comparative Evaluation of the Impact of Electronic and Voice Mail on Organizational Communication," *Information & Management* 24 (1993), 9–21.

26. R. Winslow, "Hospitals' Weak Systems Hurt Patients, Study Says," *The Wall Street Journal,* July 5, 1995, B1, B6.

27. B. Newman, "Global Chatter," *The Wall Street Journal,* March 22, 1995, A1, A15.

28. "Miscommunications Plague Pilots and Air-Traffic Controllers," *The Wall Street Journal,* August 22, 1995, A1.

29. P. Reinert, "Miscommunication Seen as Threat to Space Station," *Houston Chronicle,* September 24, 2003, 6A.

30. W. E. Leary, "NASA Report Says Problems Plague Space Station Program," *The New York Times,* February 28, 2004, A12.

31. R. L. Daft, R. H. Lengel, and L. K. Trevino, "Message Equivocality, Media Selection, and Manager Performance: Implications for Information Systems," *MIS Quarterly* 11 (1987), 355–66; R. L. Daft and R. H. Lengel, "Information Richness: A New Approach to Managerial Behavior and Organization Design," in B. M. Staw and L. L. Cummings, eds., *Research in Organizational Behavior* (Greenwich, CT: JAI Press, 1984).

32. R. L. Daft, *Organization Theory and Design* (St. Paul, MN: West, 1992).

33. "Lights, Camera, Meeting: Teleconferencing Becomes a Time-Saving Tool," *The Wall Street Journal,* February 21, 1995, A1.

34. Daft, *Organization Theory and Design.*

35. T. J. Peters and R. H. Waterman, Jr., *In Search of Excellence* (New York: Harper & Row, 1982); T. Peters and N. Austin, *A Passion for Excellence: The Leadership Difference* (New York: Random House, 1985).

36. "Lights, Camera, Meeting."

37. B. Ziegler, "Virtual Power Lunches Will Make Passing the Salt an Impossibility," *The Wall Street Journal,* June 28, 1995, B1.

38. Hymowitz, "Missing from Work."

39. "E-Mail Etiquette Starts to Take Shape for Business Messaging," *The Wall Street Journal,* October 12, 1995, A1.

40. "Telecommuters Bring Home Work and Broadband," www.emarketer.com/Article.aspx?1002943, July 20, 2004.

41. E. Baig, "Taking Care of Business—Without Leaving the House," *Business Week,* April 17, 1995, 106–07.

42. "Life Is Good for Telecommuters, but Some Problems Persist," *The Wall Street Journal,* August 3, 1995, A1.

43. "E-Mail Abuse: Workers Discover High-Tech Ways to Cause Trouble in the Office," *The Wall Street Journal,* November 22, 1994, A1; "E-Mail Alert: Companies Lag in Devising Policies on How It Should Be Used," *The Wall Street Journal,* December 29, 1994, A1.

44. "2004 Workplace E-Mail and Instant Messaging Survey Summary," American Management Association and the ePolicy Institute's Nancy Flynn, www.amanet.org, 2004.

45. J. Tyson, "How Instant Messaging Works," computer.howstuffworks.com, August 23, 2004.

46. "Study: Workers Are Surfing on Company Time," www.medialifemagazine.com/news2004/may04/may03/3_wed/news8wednesday.html, May 5, 2004.

47. Ibid.

48. Ibid.

49. ClikZ Stats staff, "U.S. Web Usage and Traffic, July 2004," www.clickz.com/stats/big_picture/traffic_patterns/article.php/3395351, August 23, 2004.

50. L. Conley, "The Privacy Arms Race," *Fast Company,* July, 2004, 27–28.

51. Ibid.

52. Ibid.

53. "P & G Who We Are: Purpose, Values, and Principles," www.pg.com/company/who_we_are/ppv.jhtml, August 25, 2004; L. Conley, "Refusing to Gamble on Privacy," *Fast Company,* July 2004 (pf.fastcompany.com/magazine/84.essay_hughes.html).

54. Conley, "The Privacy Arms Race,"

55. J. O'Neil, "E-Mail Doesn't Lie (That Much)," *The New York Times,* March 2, 2004, D6.

56. "Employee-Newsletter Names Include the Good, the Bad, and the Boring," *The Wall Street Journal,* July 18, 1995, A1.

57. Hymowitz, "Missing from Work."

58. O. W. Baskin and C. E. Aronoff, *Interpersonal Communication in Organizations* (Santa Monica, CA: Goodyear, 1989).

59. T. Gutner, "Move Over, Bohemian Grove," *Business Week,* February 19, 2001, 102.

60. "We've All Got Mail," *Newsweek,* May 15, 2001, 73K; "Diversity Deficit," *Business Week Online,* May 14, 2001; "Dial-Up Users Converting to Broadband in Droves," www.emarketer.com/Article.aspx?1003009, August 23, 2004.

61. "Top 15 Countries in Internet Usage, 2002," www.infoplease.com/ipa/A0908185.html, August 25, 2004.

62. J. Sandberg, "Internet's Popularity in North America Appears to Be Soaring," *The Wall Street Journal,* October 30, 1995, B2.

63. "How to Research Companies," Oxford Knowledge Company, www.Oxford-Knowledge.co.uk, September 16, 2004.

64. "Survey: Denmark Is Web-Savviest Nation," *MSNBC.com,* April 19, 2004 (www.msnbc.msn.com/id/4779944/1/displaymode/1098/); L. Grinsven, "U.S. Drops on Lists of Internet Savvy," *Houston Chronicle,* April 20, 2004, 6B.

65. J. W. Verity and R. Hof, "Bullet-Proofing the Net," *Business Week,* November 13, 1995, 98–99.

66. Ibid.

67. M. J. Cronin, "Ford's Intranet Success," *Fortune,* March 30, 1998, 158; M. J. Cronin, "Intranets Reach the Factory Floor," *Fortune,* June 10, 1997; A. L. Sprout, "The Internet Inside Your Company," *Fortune,* November 27, 1995, 161–68; J. B. White, "Chrysler's Intranet: Promise vs. Reality," *The Wall Street Journal,* May 13, 1997, B1, B6.

68. Ibid.

69. G. Rifkin, "A Skeptic's Guide to Groupware," *Forbes ASAP,* 1995, 76–91.

70. Ibid.

71. Ibid.

72. "Groupware Requires a Group Effort," *Business Week,* June 26, 1995, 154.

73. M. Totty, "The Path to Better Teamwork," *The Wall Street Journal,* May 20, 2004, R4; "Collaborative Software," *Wikipedia,* August 25, 2004 (en.wikipedia.org/wiki/Collaborative_software); "Collaborative Groupware Software," www.svpal.org/~grantbow/groupware.html, August 25, 2004.

74. Totty, "The Path to Better Teamwork"; "Collaborative Software."

75. Ibid; "Collaborative Groupware Software."

76. Totty, "The Path to Better Teamwork"; "Collaborative Software."

77. Ibid.

78. Ibid.

79. "On the Road," *Newsweek,* June 6, 1994, 8.

80. A. Wakizaka, "Faxes, E-Mail, Help the Deaf Get Office Jobs," *The Wall Street Journal,* October 3, 1995, B1, B5.

81. I. M. Kunii, "Tuning into a Turnaround," *Business Week Online,* June 23, 2003 (www.businessweek.com).

82. Ibid.; D. Storey, "Kenwood Chief Touts Turnaround," *Mobile Radio Technology,* February 1, 2003 (iwce-mrt.com/ar/radio_kenwood_chief_touts/index.htm).

83. Storey, "Kenwood Chief Touts Turnaround."

84. I. M. Kunii, "Tuning into a Turnaround."

85. "The American Way," *The Economist,* April 3, 2004, 88–90.

86. Ibid.

87. Ibid.

88. D. Tannen, "The Power of Talk," *Harvard Business Review,* September–October 1995, 138–48; D. Tannen, *Talking from 9 to 5* (New York: Avon Books, 1995).

89. Tannen, "The Power of Talk"; Tannen, *Talking from 9 to 5.*

90. Ibid.

91. Ibid.

92. Tannen, "The Power of Talk."

93. Ibid.; Tannen, *Talking from 9 to 5.*

94. Ibid.

95. J. Cohen, "He Writes, She Writes," *Houston Chronicle,* July 7, 2001, C1–C2.

96. Ibid.

97. Ibid.

98. Tannen, "The Power of Talk," 148.

99. S. Kirsner, "Time [Zone] Travelers."

Chapter 17

1. A. Taylor, III, "Toyota's Secret Weapon," *Fortune,* August 23, 2004, 60–66.

2. Ibid.

3. Ibid.

4. M. Hanley, "Toyota Shows Imposing Full-Size Truck Concept, New Highlander Hybrid," *cars.com,* January 4, 2004 (www.cars.com); D. Welch, "Commentary: Detroit Is over a ($50) Barrel," *BusinessWeek Online,* September 13, 2004 (www.businessweek.com).

5. Taylor, "Toyota's Secret Weapon."

6. Ibid.

7. Ibid.

8. Ibid.

9. Ibid.

10. C. Dawson, "Buy a Toyota, Get a Mortgage," *BusinessWeek Online,* September 13, 2004 (www.businessweek.com).

11. J. A. Litterer, "Conflict in Organizations: A Reexamination," *Academy of Management Journal* 9 (1966), 178–86; S. M. Schmidt and T. A. Kochan, "Conflict: Towards Conceptual Clarity," *Administrative Science Quarterly* 13 (1972), 359–70; R. H. Miles, *Macro Organizational Behavior* (Santa Monica, CA: Goodyear, 1980).

12. S. P. Robbins, *Managing Organizational Conflict: A Nontraditional Approach* (Englewood Cliffs, NJ: Prentice-Hall, 1974); L. Coser, *The Functions of Social Conflict* (New York: Free Press, 1956).

13. L. L. Putnam and M. S. Poole, "Conflict and Negotiation," in F. M. Jablin, L. L. Putnam, K. H. Roberts, and L. W. Porter, eds., *Handbook of Organizational Communication: An Interdisciplinary Perspective* (Newbury Park, CA: Sage, 1987), 549–99.

14. L. R. Pondy, "Organizational Conflict: Concepts and Models," *Administrative Science Quarterly* 2 (1967), 296–320; R. E. Walton and J. M. Dutton, "The Management of Interdepartmental Conflict: A Model and Review," *Administrative Science Quarterly* 14 (1969): 62–73.

15. Taylor, "Toyota's Secret Weapon."

16. Ibid.

17. G. R. Jones and J. E. Butler, "Managing Internal Corporate Entrepreneurship: An Agency Theory Perspective," *Journal of Management* 18 (1992), 733–49.

18. T. Petzinger, Jr., "All Happy Businesses Are Alike, but Heirs Bring Unique Conflicts," *The Wall Street Journal,* November 17, 1995, B1.

19. J. A. Wall, Jr., "Conflict and Its Management," *Journal of Management* 21 (1995), 515–58.

20. Walton and Dutton, "The Management of Interdepartmental Conflict."

21. Pondy, "Organizational Conflict."

22. W. F. White, *Human Relations in the Restaurant Industry* (New York: McGraw-Hill, 1948).

23. R. L. Pinkley and G. B. Northcraft, "Conflict Frames of Reference: Implications for Dispute Processes and Outcomes," *Academy of Management Journal* 37 (February 1994), 193–206.

24. K. W. Thomas, "Conflict and Negotiation Processes in Organizations," in M. D. Dunnette and L. M. Hough, eds., *Handbook of Industrial and Organizational Psychology,* 2d ed., vol. 3 (Palo Alto, CA: Consulting Psychologists Press, 1992), 651–717.

25. Ibid.

26. Pinkley and Northcraft, "Conflict Frames of Reference."

27. P. McGeehan, "Panel Finds Bias Against Women in Merrill Lynch," *The New York Times,* April 21, 2004, A1, C2.

28. Ibid.

29. P. McGeehan, "The Women of Wall Street Get Their Day in Court," *The New York Times,* July 11, 2004, BU5; E. McClam, "Brokerage Pays to Settle Sex Bias Cases," *Houston Chronicle,* July 13, 2004, D1.

30. S. Greenhouse, "Woman Sues Costco, Claiming Sex Bias in Promotions," *The New York Times,* August 18, 2004, C3.

31. E. Shapiro, J. A. Trachtenberg, and L. Landro, "Time Warner Settles Feud by Pushing Out Music Division's Fuchs," *The Wall Street Journal,* November 17, 1995, A1, A6.

32. Ibid.

33. P. R. Lawrence, L. B. Barnes, and J. W. Lorsch, *Organizational Behavior and Administration* (Homewood, IL: Irwin, 1976).

34. R. J. Lewicki and J. R. Litterer, *Negotiation* (Homewood, IL: Irwin, 1985); G. B. Northcraft and M. A. Neale, *Organizational Behavior* (Fort Worth, TX: Dryden, 1994); J. Z. Rubin and B. R. Brown, *The Social Psychology of Bargaining and Negotiation* (New York: Academic Press, 1975).

35. C. Bendersky, "Organizational Dispute Resolution Systems: A Complementarities Model," *Academy of Management Review* 28 (October 2003), 643–57.

36. R. E. Walton, "Third Party Roles in Interdepartmental Conflicts," *Industrial Relations* 7 (1967), 29–43.

37. "Meaning of Arbitrator," *hyperdictionary,* September 4, 2004 (www.hyperdictionary.com); "Definitions of arbitrator on the Web," www.google.com, September 4, 2004.

38. L. Thompson and R. Hastie, "Social Perception in Negotiation," *Organizational Behavior and Human Decision Processes* 47 (1990), 98–123.

39. Thomas, "Conflict and Negotiation Processes in Organizations."

40. R. J. Lewicki, S. E. Weiss, and D. Lewin, "Models of Conflict, Negotiation and Third Party Intervention: A Review

and Synthesis," *Journal of Organizational Behavior* 13 (1992), 209–52.

41. Northcraft and Neale, *Organizational Behavior.*

42. Lewicki et al., "Models of Conflict, Negotiation and Third Party Intervention"; Northcraft and Neale, Organizational Behavior; D. G. Pruitt, "Integrative Agreements: Nature and Consequences," in M. H. Bazerman and R. J. Lewicki, eds., *Negotiating in Organizations* (Beverly Hills, CA: Sage, 1983).

43. R. Fischer and W. Ury, *Getting to Yes* (Boston: Houghton Mifflin, 1981); Northcraft and Neale, *Organizational Behavior.*

44. D. Hakim, "A Union Label, Inside Out," *Sunday Business,* July 4, 2004 (query.nytimes.com).

45. Ibid.

46. Ibid.

47. M. Phelan, "DCX, UAW, Suppliers OK Historic Teamwork," *Detroit Free Press,* September 4, 2004 (www.freep.com).

48. "Chrysler Group's CEO Tom LaSorda Says 'Fully Flexible Corporation' Is Key to Weathering Rapidly Changing Market Conditions," *Automotive.com,* August 4, 2004 (www.automotive.com); D. Howes, "Chrysler's LaSorda Faces His Biggest Challenge Yet," *The Detroit News Auto Insider,* February 17, 2004 (www.detnews.com/2004/insiders/0403/26/b01-66807.html); "Chrysler Group COO Tom LaSorda Frames 'Moment of Opportunity' for Young Leaders to Shape the Future of the Automotive Industry," *Eyewitness News,* August 17, 2004 (www.media.daimlerchrysler.com); "Supplier Co-location Concept," *PR Newswire,* August 3, 2004 (www.uaw-daimlerchryslerntc.org); D. Howes, "Chrysler Hits Higher Gear, LaSorda Says," *The Detroit News Auto Insider,* February 20, 2004 (www.detnews.com/2004/autosinsider/0402/230a01e-69983.htm).

49. Phelan, "DCX, UAW, Suppliers OK Historic Teamwork."

50. "Chrysler Group's CEO Tom LaSorda Says 'Fully Flexible Corporation' Is Key"; Howes, "Chrysler's LaSorda Faces His Biggest Challenge yet"; "Chrysler Group COO Tom LaSorda Frames 'Moment of Opportunity'"; "Supplier Co-location Concept"; Howes, "Chrysler Hits Higher Gear."

51. "Chrysler Group Toledo Project Highlights Supplier Co-location Concept," www.daimlerchrysler.com, August 3, 2004.

52. P. J. Carnevale and D. G. Pruitt, "Negotiation and Mediation," *Annual Review of Psychology* 43 (1992), 531–82.

53. K. Belson, "Digital Dealmakers Meet in the Middle," *The New York Times,* September 11, 2003, E1, E4.

54. "About Us," www.splitthedifference.com/aboutUs/, September 5, 2004.

55. Belson, "Digital Dealmakers Meet in the Middle."

56. Ibid.; "Fujitsu America, Inc.," www.fujitsu.com/us/about/OtherOps/FAI, September 5, 2004.

57. Belson, "Digital Dealmakers Meet in the Middle."

58. A. M. Pettigrew, *The Politics of Organizational Decision Making* (London: Tavistock, 1973); Miles, Macro Organizational Behavior.

59. D. J. Hickson, C. R. Hinings, C. A. Lee, R. E. Schneck, and D. J. Pennings, "A Strategic Contingencies Theory of Intraorganizational Power," *Administrative Science Quarterly* 16 (1971), 216–27; C. R. Hinings, D. J. Hickson, J. M. Pennings, and R. E. Schneck, "Structural Conditions of Interorganizational Power," *Administrative Science Quarterly* 19 (1974), 22–44; J. Pfeffer, *Power in Organizations* (Boston: Pitman, 1981).

60. Pfeffer, *Power in Organizations.*

61. Ibid.

62. Taylor, "Toyota's Secret Weapon."

63. M. Crozier, "Sources of Power of Lower Level Participants in Complex Organizations," *Administrative Science Quarterly* 7 (1962), 349–64; A. M. Pettigrew, "Information Control as a Power Resource," *Sociology* 6 (1972), 187–204.

64. Pfeffer, *Power in Organizations;* G. R. Salancik and J. Pfeffer, "The Bases and Uses of Power in Organizational Decision Making," *Administrative Science Quarterly* 19 (1974), 453–73; J. Pfeffer and G. R. Salancik, *The External Control of Organizations: A Resource Dependence View* (New York: Harper & Row, 1978).

65. J. S. Lublin, "Despite Poor Returns, Champion's Chairman Hangs On for 21 Years," *The Wall Street Journal,* October 31, 1995, A1, A5.

66. Pfeffer, *Power in Organizations.*

67. Ibid.

68. Ibid.

69. B. Bremner, "Japan: A Tale of Two Mergers," *BusinessWeek,* May 10, 2004, 42.

70. C. Dawson, "Nissan: Saying Sayonara," *BusinessWeek Online,* September 24, 2001; Bremner, "Japan: A Tale of Two Mergers."

71. Dawson, "Nissan: Saying Sayonara."

72. Bremner, "Japan: A Tale of Two Mergers."

73. "Nissan Reports Record Results for FY03," www.nissan-global.com, September 3, 2004.

74. "Nissan's Carlos Ghosn in Exclusive Interview on LBC," *AME Info,* August 14, 2004 (www.ameinfo.com/news/Detailed/43880.html).

75. D. Welch, "Nissan: The Squeaks Get Louder," *BusinessWeek Online,* May 17, 2004 (www.businessweek.com).

76. Ibid.

77. Bremner, "Japan: A Tale of Two Mergers."

Chapter 18

1. www.ibm.com, 2004.

2. N. B. Macintosh, *The Social Software of Accounting Information Systems* (New York: Wiley, 1995).

3. C. A. O'Reilly, "Variations in Decision Makers' Use of Information: The Impact of Quality and Accessibility," *Academy of Management Journal* 25 (1982), 756–71.

4. G. Stalk and T. H. Hout, *Competing Against Time* (New York: Free Press, 1990).

5. L. Uchitelle, "Airlines off Course," *San Francisco Chronicle,* September 15, 1991, 7.

6. R. Cyert and J. March, *Behavioral Theory of the Firm* (Englewood Cliffs, NJ: Prentice-Hall, 1963).

7. R. Brandt, "Agents and Artificial Life," *BusinessWeek: The Information Revolution,* special issue, 1994, 64–68.

8. E. Turban, *Decision Support and Expert Systems* (New York: Macmillan, 1988).

9. R. I. Benjamin and J. Blunt, "Critical IT Issues: The Next Ten Years," *Sloan Management Review,* Summer 1992, 7–19; W. H. Davidow and M. S. Malone, *The Virtual Corporation* (New York: HarperBusiness, 1992).

10. Davidow and Malone, *The Virtual Corporation;* M. E. Porter, *Competitive Advantage* (New York: Free Press, 1984).

11. S. M. Dornbusch and W. R. Scott, *Evaluation and the Exercise of Authority* (San Francisco: Jossey-Bass, 1975).

12. J. Child, *Organization: A Guide to Problems and Practice* (London: Harper and Row, 1984).

13. www.dhl.com, 2004.

14. Ibid.

15. Ibid.

16. Macintosh, *The Social Software of Accounting Information Systems.*

17. www.cypress.com, 2004.

18. www.hermanmiller.com, 2004

19. www.boeing.com, 2004.

20. P. Bradley, "Global Souring Takes Split-Second Timing," *Purchasing,* July 20, 1989, 52–58.

21. www.intel.com, 2001.

22. J. J. Donovan, *Business Re-engineering with IT* (Englewood Cliffs, NJ: Prentice-Hall, 1994); C. W. L. Hill, "The Computer Industry: The New Industry of Industries," in C. W. L. Hill and G. R. Jones, *Strategic Management: An Integrated Approach,* 3d ed. (Boston: Houghton Mifflin, 1995).

23. M. B. Gordon, "The Wireless Services Industry: True Competition Emerges," *The Red Herring,* September–October 1994, 60–62.

24. www.nwfusion.com, 2001.

25. www.nokia.com, 2004.

26. E. Rich, *Artificial Intelligence* (New York: McGraw-Hill, 1983).

27. Brandt, "Agents and Artificial Life."

28. www.ibm.com, 2004.

29. A. D. Chandler, *The Visible Hand* (Cambridge, MA: Harvard University Press, 1977).

30. C. W. L. Hill and J. F. Pickering, "Divisionalization, Decentralization, and Performance of Large United Kingdom Companies," *Journal of Management Studies* 23 (1986), 26–50.

31. O. E. Williamson, *Markets and Hierarchies: Analysis and Antitrust Implications* (New York: Free Press, 1975).

32. C. W. L. Hill, "Airborne Express." In C. W. L. Hill and G. R. Jones, *Strategic Management: An Integrated Approach* (Boston: Houghton-Mifflin, 2004).

33. Turban, *Decision Support and Expert Systems.*

34. www.merck.com, 2004

35. N. A. Nichols, "Scientific Management at Merck: An Interview with CFO Judy Lewent," *Harvard Business Review,* January–February 1994, 88–91.

36. Turban, *Decision Support and Expert Systems.*

37. Ibid., 346.

38. Rich, *Artificial Intelligence.*

39. P. P. Bonisson and H. E. Johnson, "Expert Systems for Diesel Electric Locomotive Repair," *Human Systems Management* 4 (1985), 1–25.

40. G. R. Jones, "SAP and the Enterprise Resource Planning Industry," in C. W. L. Hill and G. R. Jones, *Strategic Management: An Integrated Approach,* 6th ed. (Boston: Houghton Mifflin, 2003).

41. Davidow and Malone, *The Virtual Corporation.*

42. The companies are real, but their names are fictitious. Information was obtained from a personal interview with a senior manager who had experience with both companies' information systems.

43. T. A. Stewart, "Managing in a Wired Company," *Fortune,* July 11, 1994, 54.

44. Ibid., 168.

45. H. Mintzberg, *Mintzberg on Management: Inside Our Strange World of Organizations* (New York: Free Press, 1989).

46. From an interview conducted by C. W. L. Hill with a senior Boeing manager.

47. Stewart, "Managing in a Wired Company," 54.

48. See J. R. Meredith, "The Implementation of Computer Based Systems," *Journal of Operational Management,* October 1981; Turban, *Decision Support and Expert Systems;* R. J. Thierauf, *Effective Management and Evaluation of IT* (London: Quorum Books, 1994).

Chapter 19

1. www.google.com, 2004.

2. See R. D'Aveni, *Hyper-Competition* (New York: Free Press, 1994); P. Anderson and M. L. Tushman, "Technological Discontinuities and Dominant Design: A Cyclical Model of Technological Change," *Administrative Science Quarterly* 35 (1990), 604–33.

3. www.intel.com, 2004.

4. www.att.com, 2004.

5. J. A. Schumpeter, *Capitalism, Socialism and Democracy* (New York: Harper, 1942).

6. V. P. Buell, *Marketing Management* (New York: McGraw-Hill, 1985).

7. See M. M. J. Berry and J. H. Taggart, "Managing Technology and Innovation: A Review," *R & D Management* 24 (1994), 341–53; K. B. Clark and S. C. Wheelwright, *Managing New Product and Process Development* (New York: Free Press, 1993).

8. E. Abrahamson, "Managerial Fads and Fashions: The Diffusion and Rejection of Innovations," *Academy of Management Review* 16 (1991), 586–612.

9. See Berry and Taggart, "Managing Technology and Innovation"; M. Gort and J. Klepper, "Time Paths in the Diffusion of Product Innovations," *Economic Journal,* September 1982, 630–53. Looking at the history of 46 products, Gort and Klepper found that the length of time before other companies entered the markets created by a few inventive companies declined from an average of 14.4 years for products introduced before 1930 to 4.9 years for those introduced after 1949–implying that product life cycles were being compressed. Also see A. Griffin, "Metrics for Measuring Product Development Cycle Time," *Journal of Production and Innovation Management* 10 (1993), 112–25.

10. Clark and Wheelwright, *Managing New Product and Process Development.* Also see G. Stalk and T. M. Hout, *Competing Against Time* (New York: Free Press, 1990).

11. www.intel.com, 2001

12. "Intel Chip Hits 2 Gigahertz Milestone," yahoo.com, 2001.

13. C. Edwards, "This Is Not the Intel We All Know," *BusinessWeek Online,* August 6, 2004.

14. See Clark and Wheelwright, *Managing New Product and Process Development;* R. E. Gomory, "From the Ladder of Science to the Product Development Cycle," *Harvard Business Review,* November–December 1989,

99–105; Stalk and Hout, *Competing Against Time.*

15. See M. R. Millson, D. P. Raj, and D. Wilemon, "A Survey of Major Approaches for Accelerating New Product Development," *Journal of Product Innovation Management* 9 (1992), 53–69; Stalk and Hout, *Competing Against Time.*

16. In the language of strategic management, the company may be able to capture a first-mover advantage. See C. W. L. Hill, M. Heeley, and J. Sakson, "Strategies for Profiting from Technological Product Innovation," *Advances in Global High Technology Management* 3 (1993), 79–95.

17. See E. Mansfield, "How Economists See R&D," *Harvard Business Review,* November–December 1981, 98–106; B. Avishai and W. Taylor, "Customers Drive a Technology Driven Company," *Harvard Business Review,* November–December 1989, 107–14.

18. B. Dumaine, "Payoff from the New Management," *Fortune,* December 13, 1993, 103–10.

19. C. Power et al., "Flops: Too Many New Products Fail," *BusinessWeek,* August 16, 1993, 76–82.

20. www.danger.com, 2004.

21. www.palmone.com, 2004.

22. K. B. Clark and T. Fujimoto, "The Power of Product Integrity," *Harvard Business Review,* November–December 1990, 107–19.

23. Ibid.

24. K. B. Clark and T. Fujimoto, "Lead Time in Automobile Product Development: Explaining the Japanese Advantage," *Journal of Engineering and Technology Management* 6 (1989), 25–58.

25. B. Dumaine, "Payoff from the New Management."

26. C. W. L. Hill, "The Efficacy of the New Product Development Process," working paper, University of Washington, 1994.

27. Clark and Wheelwright, *Managing New Product and Process Development.*

28. Ibid.

29. G. K. Gill, "Motorola Inc.: Bandit Pager Project," Harvard Business School Case 690-043.

30. Ibid.

31. A. Griffin and J. R. Hauser, "Patterns of Communication Among Marketing, Engineering, and Manufacturing," *Management Science* 38 (1992), 360–73; R. K. Moenaert, W. E. Sounder, A. D. Meyer, and D. Deschoolmeester, "R&D-Marketing Integration Mechanisms, Communication Flows, and Innovation Success," *Journal of Production and Innovation Management* 11 (1994), 31–45.

32. See G. Barczak and D. Wileman, "Leadership Differences in New Product Development Teams," *Journal of Product Innovation Management* 6 (1989), 259–67; E. F. McDonough and G. Barczak, "Speeding Up New Product Development: The Effects of Leadership Style and Source of Technology," *Journal of Product Innovation Management* 8 (1991), 203–11; Clark and Fujimoto, "The Power of Product Integrity."

33. Clark and Wheelwright, *Managing New Product and Process Development.*

34. Clark and Fujimoto, "The Power of Product Integrity."

35. J. R. Heartly, *Concurrent Engineering* (Cambridge, MA: Productivity Press, 1992).

36. See B. Avishai and W. Taylor, "Customers Drive a Technology Driven Company"; W. E. Sounder, "Managing Relations Between R&D and Marketing in New Product Development Projects," *Journal of Product Innovation Management* 5 (1988), 6–19; B. J. Zinger and M. M. Madique, "A Model of New Product Development: An Empirical Test," *Management Science* 36 (1990), 867–83.

37. C. W. L. Hill, "The Boeing Corporation: Commercial Aircraft Operations," in C. W. L. Hill and G. R. Jones, *Strategic Management: An Integrated Approach,* 3d ed. (Boston: Houghton Mifflin, 1995).

38. Information from remarks made by Boeing Vice President Dean Cruze in a presentation to an MBA class at the University of Washington.

39. "The Mind's Eye," *The Economist,* survey of manufacturing technology, March 5, 1994, 11.

40. Mansfield, "How Economists See R&D."

41. T. Lonier, "Some Insights and Statistics on Working Solo," www.workingsolo.com.

42. N. Irwin, "Defying the Slump," *Washington Post,* May 7, 2001, 3.

43. G. R. Simpson, "Maden Technologies Gets Ready to Make Its Presence Felt, *The Wall Street Journal,* February 15, 2001, A2.

44. www.madentech.com, 2001.

45. D. Frey, "Learning the Ropes: My Life as a Product Champion," *Harvard Business Review,* September–October 1991, 46–56.

Chapter 1 Video Case

1. Russell H. Mouritsen, "Boundaryless Thinking," *The American Salesman* 49, no. 8 (August 2004), 12.

Chapter 3 Video Case

1. Bevolyn Williams-Harold, *Black Enterprise* 28, no. 1 (August 1997), 76.

2. "Business: Losing the HP Way," *The Economist,* August 21, 2004, 58.

3. Pui-Wing Tan, "H-P Posts 34% Increase in Profit; Sales of PCs, Printers Rise; Robust Revenue Forecast Is Given for Fiscal 2nd Half," *The Wall Street Journal,* eastern ed., May 19, 2004, A3.

Chapter 4 Video Case

1. Jodie Morse and Amanda Bower, "The Party Crasher," *Time,* December 30–January 6, 2003, 53.

2. John R. Emshwiller, "Enron Ex-Chief of Telecom Unit Pleads Guilty," *The Wall Street Journal,* eastern ed., September 1, 2004, B2.

3. Allan Sloan, "Lay's a Victim? Not a Chance," *Newsweek,* July 19, 2004, 50.

4. Cathy Booth Thomas, "Will Enron's Auditor Sing?" *Time,* May 20, 2002, 44.

5. Barbara Elmore, "Life After Andersen," *Baylor Business Review* 20, no. 1 (Spring 2003), 2.

6. Alice Haythornthwaite and Lesley Bolton, "Analysis: Enron Whistleblower–Power Point," Accountancy 133, no. 1325 (January 2004), 64.

Chapter 5 Video Case

1. June Kronholz, Robert Tomsho, and Charles Forelle, "High Court's Ruling on Race Could Affect Business Hiring," *The Wall Street Journal,* eastern ed., June 23, 2003, A1.

2. June Kronholz, Robert Tomsho, Daniel Golden, and Robert S. Greenberger, "Race Matters: Court Preserves Affirmative Action–Preferences in Admissions Survive, but Justices Condemn Point System–Win for Business and Military," *The Wall Street Journal,* eastern ed., June 24, 2003, A1.

3. Kronholz et al., "High Court's Ruling."

4. Ibid.

Chapter 6 Video Case

1. "Supersize Silliness," *The Wall Street Journal,* eastern ed., March 8, 2004, A16.

2. Morgan Spurlock and Brian Braiker, "Anything for Art?" *Newsweek,* February 9, 2004, 4.

3. Richard Schickel, "Pigging Out to Make a Point," *Time,* June 7, 2004, 67.

4. Katherine Stapp, "The Sugar Fix," *Multinational Monitor* 25, no.1–2 (January–February 2004), 7.

5. Hope Cristol, "Trends in Global Obesity," *The Futurist* 36, no. 3 (May–June 2002), 10.

6. Jonathan Lowell, "The Food Industry and Its Impact on Obesity: A Case Study," *British Food Journal* 106, no. 2–3 (2004), 238.

7. Camilla Palmer, Camilla, and Colin Grimshaw, "WHO Denounces McDonald's over 'Joint Initiatives,'" *Marketing,* April 3, 2003, 1.

Chapter 8 Video Case

1. Susan O'Neill, "Plane Bargains," *Kiplinger's Personal Finance,* July 2004, 114–115.

2. Sally B. Donnelly, "Friendlier Skies," *Time,* January 26, 2004, 39.

3. Rana Foroohar, "The Royal Treatment," *Newsweek,* May 17, 2004, E28.

4. "Jet Blue Skies," *Money,* April 2003, 56.

5. Jeremy Kahn, "Investors Head for the Exits at JetBlue," *Fortune,* February 23, 2004, 40.

6. Wendy Zellner, "Is JetBlue's Flight Plan Flawed?" *BusinessWeek,* February 16, 2004, 72.

Chapter 10 Video Case

1. Katrina Brooker, "Like Father, Like Son," *Fortune,* June 28, 2004, 114.

2. Maggie Rauch, "Field Day," *Incentive* 178, no. 5 (May 2004), 36.

3. Ibid., 38.

4. Scott Hume, "Jonathan Tisch," *Restaurants and Institutions,* April 1, 2004, 23.

Chapter 14 Video Case

1. Denise Lugo, "Martha: Will She Live On? Going Private, After Jail, May Be Better Solution than Dumping the Brand," *The Investment Dealer's Digest: IDD,* August 9, 2004, 1.

2. Ibid.

3. Mike Duff, "Note to Stewart Wannabes: Don't Count Martha Out," *DSN Retailing Today,* August 2, 2004, 6.

4. Ibid.

Chapter 15 Video Case

1. www.pikeplacefish.com/about/about.htm, 1.

2. Ibid., 2.

Chapter 17 Video Case

1. Mark Goldhaber, "Eisner No Longer Disney Chair," *The Business of Magic,* March 4, 2004 (www.mouseplanet.com/dan/bm040304mg.htm).

2. Bruce Orwall, "Disney's Eisner Will Quit in 2006 After Surviving Bruising Battles," *The Wall Street Journal,* September 10, 2004, 1 (online.wsj.com/article_print/0,,SB109477293633014269,00.html).

Chapter 18 Video Case

1. Monte Burke, "Carry a Big Stick," *Forbes,* April 14, 2003, 220.

Photo Credits

Chapter 1

P1-1, page 3, © Kim Kulish/CORBIS

P1-2, page 9, AP/Wide World Photos

P1-3, page 11, Courtesy of Lucent Technologies, Inc.

P1-4, page 17, © Brian Lee/CORBIS

P1-5, page 18, © Nathan Michaels/SuperStock

P1-6, page 22, © Mark Peterson/Redux Pictures

P1-7, page 30, © James Leynse/CORBIS

P1-8, page 31, © Bill Aron/PhotoEdit

Chapter 2

P2-1a, page 41, © Austrian Archives/CORBIS

P2-1b, page 41, © Chad Ehlers/International Stock

P2-2, page 45, © Bettmann/CORBIS

P2-3, page 47, © Bettmann/CORBIS

P2-4, page 49, 20th Century Fox/Courtesy The Kobal Collection

P2-5, page 57, Courtesy Regina A. Greenwood and Henley Management College

P2-6, page 58, © Fox Photos/Getty Images

P2-7, page 61, © Justin Sullivan/Getty Images

Chapter 3

P3-1, page 75, Courtesy of PAETEC Communications

P3-2, page 81, Courtesy of IBM Corporate Archives

P3-3, page 83, © Spencer Platt/Getty Images

P3-4, page 91, © PITCHAL FREDERIC/CORBIS SYGMA

P3-5, page 97, © Mark Richards/PhotoEdit

P3-6, page 100, Courtesy Texas A&M University

P3-7, page 101, © Mark Peterson/CORBIS

Chapter 4

P4-1, page 113, © Color Day Productions/Getty Images/The Image Bank

P4-2, page 117, The Granger Collection, New York

P4-3, page 121, © Vince Bucci/Getty Images

P4-4, page 124, © Bruce Burkhardt/CORBIS

P4-5, page 131, © Darren McCollester/Getty Images

P4-6, page 136, Courtesy of Ben & Jerry's Homemade, Inc.

Chapter 5

P5-1, page 147, AP/Wide World Photos

P5-2, page 153, © SCHWARZ SHAUL/CORBIS SYGMA

P5-3, page 155, Courtesy of The Centers for Disease Control and Prevention/Business Responds to AIDS

P5-4, page 164, Courtesy of Arandas Franchise, Inc.

P5-5, page 166, © TORU YAMANAKA/Getty Images

P5-6, page 172, © PhotoDisc Green/Getty Images

Chapter 6

P6-1, page 189, Courtesy of Nestlé SA

P6-2, page 195, AP/Wide World Photos

P6-3, page 200, AP/Wide World Photos

P6-4, page 202, © Widgetstudio/Getty Images

P6-5, page 203, © Chris Hondros/Getty Images

P6-6, page 210, AP/Wide World Photos

P6-7, page 214, AP/Wide World Photos

Chapter 7

P7-1, page 223, Courtesy of GlaxoSmithKline

P7-2, page 228, © Layne Kennedy/CORBIS

P7-3, page 231, AP/Wide World Photos

P7-4, page 238, Courtesy of NASA

P7-5, page 241, © Ted Goff, www.tedgoff.com

P7-6, page 243, © Ryan McVay/Getty Images

P7-7, page 248, © Ohr-O'Keefe Museum of Art

Chapter 8

P8-1, page 259, Courtesy of Cott Corporation

P8-2, page 269, AP/Wide World Photos

P8-3, page 273, AP/Wide World Photos

P8-3a, page 278, AP/Wide World Photos

P8-3b, page 278, © Pablo Bartholomew/Getty News/Liaison

P8-4, page 281, © Mark Richards/PhotoEdit

P8-5, page 286, AP/Wide World Photos

Chapter 9

P9-1, page 299, Safeway, Inc. www.safeway.com 2004

P9-2, page 303, © TOSHIFUMI KITAMURA/AFP/Getty Images

P9-3, page 307, AP/Wide World Photos

P9-4, page 318, © 2004 Ted Goff from cartoonbank.com. All Rights Reserved

P9-5, page 323, Courtesy of IBM Corporate Archives

Chapter 10

P10-1, page 333, AP/Wide World Photos

P10-2, page 337, Courtesy of Gateway, Inc.

P10-3, page 339, Don Tremain/PhotoDisc Green/Getty Images

P10-4, page 341, © Jeffery Allan Salter/CORBIS

P10-5, page 348, Kim Steele/Photodisc Green/Getty Images

P10-6, page 360, Jack Hollingsworth/Photodisc Red/Getty Images

P10-7, page 366, AP/Wide World Photos

Chapter 11

P11-1, page 375, © WILLIAM PHILPOTT/Reuters/CORBIS

P11-2, page 378, ©Willie Hill, Jr. / The Image Works

P11-3, page 379, © Tomas del Amo/ Index Stock

P11-4, page 388, AP/Wide World Photos

P11-5, page 391, © 2002 Scott Adams, Inc. All rights reserved. Licensed by United Features Syndicate.

P11-6, page 397, ©David Frazier/ The Image Works

P11-7, page 399AP/Wide World Photos

Chapter 12

P12-1, page 411, ©James Leynse/ CORBIS

P12-2, page 415, Keith Brofsky/ PhotoDisc/Getty Images

P12-5, page 428, Jack Hollingsworth/ Getty Images

P12-6, page 438, © 1996 Scott Adams, Inc. All rights reserved. Licensed by United Features Syndicate.

P12-7, page 441, Ryan McVay/ Getty Images

Chapter 13

P13-1, page 455, Courtesy The Container Store

P13-2, page 458, Ryan McVay/PhotoDisc/Getty Images

P13-3, page 461, AP/Wide World Photos

P13-4, page 464, © Syracuse Newspapers/ Suzanne Dunn/The Image Works

P13-5, page 469, AP/Wide World Photos

P13-6, page 472, © Bill Varie/CORBIS

P13-7, page 474, AP/Wide World Photos

Chapter 14

P14-1, page 493, AP/Wide World Photos

P14-2, page 496, AP/Wide World Photos

P14-3, page 497, © Geri Engberg/The Image Works

P14-5, page 504, © Fujifotos/The Image Works

P14-6, page 511, © Tony Freeman/ PhotoEdit

P14-7, page 517, AP/Wide World Photos

P14-8, page 518, AP/Wide World Photos

Chapter 15

P15-1, page 529, © Eric Ryan/Getty Images

P15-2, page 535, Ryan McVay/ Photodisc Blue/Getty Images

P15-4, page 541, © Photodisc/Getty Images

P15-5a, page 553, Courtesy of Google

P15-5b, page 555, © William Thomas Cain/Getty Images

Chapter 16

P16-1, page 567, © Cindy Charles/ PhotoEdit

P16-2, page 570, Courtesy of GE Healthcare

P16-3, page 573, © Cindy Charles/ PhotoEdit

P16-4, page 576, © Jon Feingersh/ CORBIS

P16-5, page 590, Courtesy of Kenwood Corporation

P16-6, page 594, © Larry Dale Gordon/ Getty Images/The Image Bank

Chapter 17

P17-1, page 605, © Bryan Mitchell/ Getty Images

P17-2, page 607, © Ryan McVay/ PhotoDisc/Getty Images

P17-3, page 617, AP/Wide World Photos

P17-4, page620, © The New Yorker Collection, 1988 Dana Fradon from cartoonbank.com. All Rights Reserved.

P17-5, page 626, AP/Wide World Photos

Chapter 18

P18-1, page 635, Lawrence Lawry/ Getty/RF

P18-2, page 641, Courtesy Herman Miller, Inc.

P18-3, page 644, © Stephen Chernin/ Getty Images

P18-4, page 646, © The New Yorker Collection, 1996 Ed Fisher from cartoonbank.com. All Rights Reserved.

P18-5, page 650, AP/Wide World Photos

P18-6, page 659, © Digital Vision/Getty Images

Chapter 19

P19-1, page 667, AP/Wide World Photos

P19-2, page 677, AP/Wide World Photos

P19-3, page 685, AP/Wide World Photos

P19-4, page 687, Courtesy of Maden Technologies

P19-5, page 691, AP/Wide World Photos

Index

Names

Subjects

Companies